WHAT'S A SERVING SIZE?

1 serving of fruit looks like:

FRUITS

1 medium peach or

1 mango

1 medium apple or 1 cup chopped apples or

1 8-inch banana

1 cup (8 fl. oz) 100% fruit juice compar with

1 serving of vegetables looks like:

VEGETABLES

2 cups lettuce or

1 cup cooked broccoli or

7 baby carrots

1 large bell pepper

1 serving of dairy looks like:

DAIRY

8 oz yogurt

1 cup (8 fl. oz) milk compar with

How Much Do I Eat?

When you're creating a healthful diet for yourself, or doing a diet assessment project, it's important to keep in mind not only the types of foods you eat, but also how much. However, it can be difficult to know what a particular number of cups, ounces, or ounce-equivalents looks like. Here is a visual tip sheet that will help you translate the food on your plate into common serving sizes. Tear it out and bring it with you to the dining hall, the café, or the kitchen table.

A "Hand-y" Way to Estimate Serving Size

The following photos show how to judge serving sizes with something you always have with you—your hand.

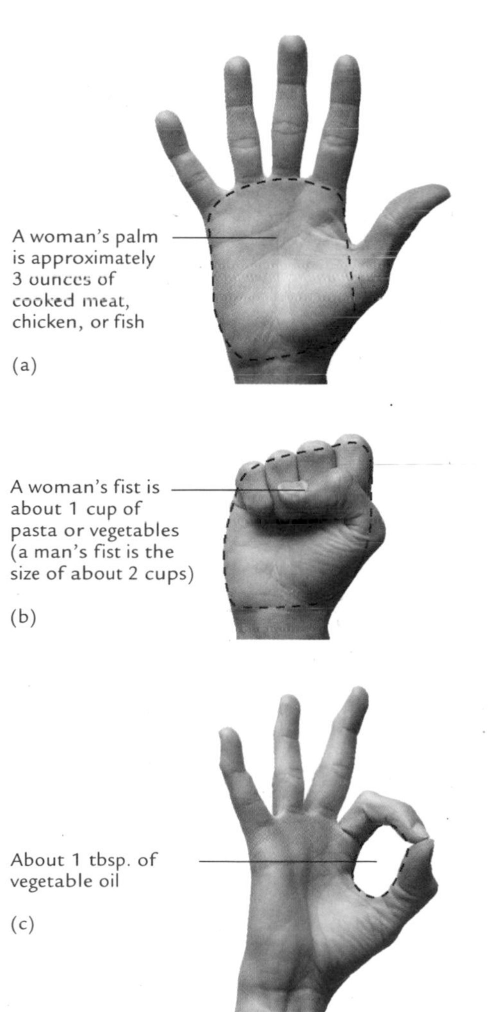

1 serving of grains looks like:

GRAINS

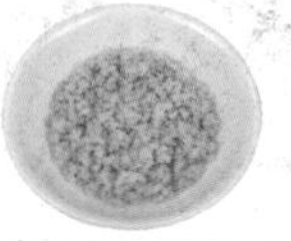
1/2 cup rice

or

1/2 cup pasta

or

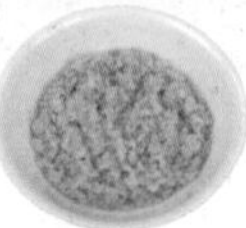
1/2 cup oatmeal

=

1/2 baseball

1 slice bread

1 cup cereal

1 piece cornbread

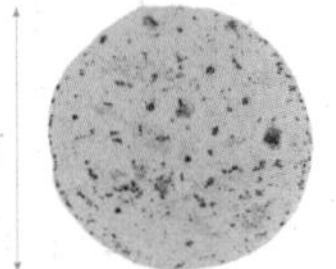
one 6-inch tortilla

one 3-inch (mini) bagel

1 serving of meat or beans looks like:

MEAT & BEANS

3 oz chicken

or

5 oz steak

or

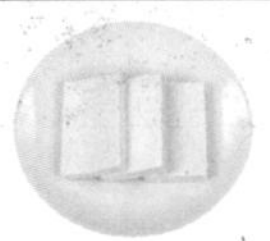
4 oz pork

or

6 oz tofu

=

mouse

3 oz fish

=

checkbook

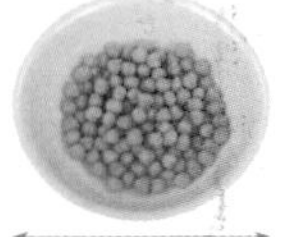
1/2 cup garbanzo beans

or

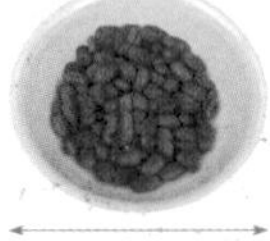
1/2 cup pinto beans

=

light bulb

1 oz peanuts

or

1 oz almonds

or

2 T. peanut butter

=

ping pong ball

1 serving of fats looks like:

FATS

1 t. butter

1 oz potato chips

1 T. salad dressing

2 T. cream cheese

or

2 T. olive oil

=

ping pong ball

ALCOHOL

One "drink" of alcohol is defined as the amount of a beverage that provides 1/2 fl. oz of alcohol, which normally equals 1-1/2 oz of distilled spirits, 5 oz of wine, or 12 oz of beer or wine cooler.

Dietary Reference Intakes: RDA, AI*

Life-Stage Group	Vitamins													
	Vitamin A (μg/d)[a]	Vitamin D (μg/d)[b]	Vitamin E (mg/d)[c]	Vitamin K (μg/d)	Thiamin (mg/d)	Riboflavin (mg/d)	Niacin (mg/d)[d]	Pantothenic Acid (mg/d)	Biotin (μg/d)	Vitamin B_6 (mg/d)	Folate (μg/d)[e]	Vitamin B_{12} (μg/d)	Vitamin C (mg/d)	Choline (mg/d)
Infants														
0–6 mo	400*	5*	4*	2.0*	0.2*	0.3*	2*	1.7*	5*	0.1*	65*	0.4*	40*	125*
7–12 mo	500*	5*	5*	2.5*	0.3*	0.4*	4*	1.8*	6*	0.3*	80*	0.5*	50*	150*
Children														
1–3 y	300	5*	6	30*	0.5	0.5	6	2*	8*	0.5	150	0.9	15	200*
4–8 y	400	5*	7	55*	0.6	0.6	8	3*	12*	0.6	200	1.2	25	250*
Males														
9–13 y	600	5*	11	60*	0.9	0.9	12	4*	20*	1.0	300	1.8	45	375*
14–18 y	900	5*	15	75*	1.2	1.3	16	5*	25*	1.3	400	2.4	75	550*
19–30 y	900	5*	15	120*	1.2	1.3	16	5*	30*	1.3	400	2.4	90	550*
31–50 y	900	5*	15	120*	1.2	1.3	16	5*	30*	1.3	400	2.4	90	550*
51–70 y	900	10*	15	120*	1.2	1.3	16	5*	30*	1.7	400	2.4	90	550*
>70 y	900	15*	15	120*	1.2	1.3	16	5*	30*	1.7	400	2.4	90	550*
Females														
9–13 y	600	5*	11	60*	0.9	0.9	12	4*	20*	1.0	300	1.8	45	375*
14–18 y	700	5*	15	75*	1.0	1.0	14	5*	25*	1.2	400	2.4	65	400*
19–30 y	700	5*	15	90*	1.1	1.1	14	5*	30*	1.3	400	2.4	75	425*
31–50 y	700	5*	15	90*	1.1	1.1	14	5*	30*	1.3	400	2.4	75	425*
51–70 y	700	10*	15	90*	1.1	1.1	14	5*	30*	1.5	400	2.4	75	425*
>70 y	700	15*	15	90*	1.1	1.1	14	5*	30*	1.5	400	2.4	75	425*
Pregnancy														
≤18 y	750	5*	15	75*	1.4	1.4	18	6*	30*	1.9	600	2.6	80	450*
19–30 y	770	5*	15	90*	1.4	1.4	18	6*	30*	1.9	600	2.6	85	450*
31–50 y	770	5*	15	90*	1.4	1.4	18	6*	30*	1.9	600	2.6	85	450*
Lactation														
≤18 y	1,200	5*	19	75*	1.4	1.4	17	7*	35*	2.0	500	2.8	115	550*
19–30 y	1,300	5*	19	90*	1.4	1.4	17	7*	35*	2.0	500	2.8	120	550*
31–50 y	1,300	5*	19	90*	1.4	1.4	17	7*	35*	2.0	500	2.8	120	550*

Data from: Reprinted with permission from the Dietary Reference Intakes series, National Academies Press. Copyright 1997, 1998, 2000, 2001, by the National Academy of Sciences. These reports may be accessed via www.nap.edu. Courtesy of the National Academies Press, Washington, DC.

Note: This table is adapted from the DRI reports; see www.nap.edu. It lists Recommended Dietary Allowances (RDAs), with Adequate Intakes (AIs) indicated by an asterisk (*). RDAs and AIs may both be used as goals for individual intake. RDAs are set to meet the needs of almost all (97 percent to 98 percent) individuals in a group. For healthy breast-fed infants, the AI is the mean intake. The AI for other life-stage and gender groups is believed to cover the needs of all individuals in the group, but lack of data prevent being able to specify with confidence the percentage of individuals covered by this intake.

[a] Given as retinal activity equivalents (RAE).

[b] Also known as calciferol. The DRI values are based on the absence of adequate exposure to sunlight.

[c] Also known as α-tocopherol.

[d] Given as niacin equivalents (NE), except for infants 0–6 months, which are expressed as preformed niacin.

[e] Given as dietary folate equivalents (DFE).

Dietary Reference Intakes: RDA, AI*

	Elements											
Life-Stage Group	**Calcium (mg/d)**	**Phosphorus (mg/d)**	**Magnesium (mg/d)**	**Iron (mg/d)**	**Zinc (mg/d)**	**Selenium (µg/d)**	**Iodine (µg/d)**	**Copper (µg/d)**	**Manganese (mg/d)**	**Fluoride (mg/d)**	**Chromium (µg/d)**	**Molybdenum (µg/d)**
Infants												
0–6 mo	210*	100*	30*	0.27*	2*	15*	110*	200*	0.003*	0.01*	0.2*	2*
7–12 mo	270*	275*	75*	11	3	20*	130*	220*	0.6*	0.5*	5.5*	3*
Children												
1–3 y	500*	460	80	7	3	20	90	340	1.2*	0.7*	11*	17
4–8 y	800*	500	130	10	5	30	90	440	1.5*	1*	15*	22
Males												
9–13 y	1,300*	1,250	240	8	8	40	120	700	1.9*	2*	25*	34
14–18 y	1,300*	1,250	410	11	11	55	150	890	2.2*	3*	35*	43
19–30 y	1,000*	700	400	8	11	55	150	900	2.3*	4*	35*	45
31–50 y	1,000*	700	420	8	11	55	150	900	2.3*	4*	35*	45
51–70 y	1,200*	700	420	8	11	55	150	900	2.3*	4*	30*	45
>70 y	1,200*	700	420	8	11	55	150	900	2.3*	4*	30*	45
Females												
9–13 y	1,300*	1,250	240	8	8	40	120	700	1.6*	2*	21*	34
14–18 y	1,300*	1,250	360	15	9	55	150	890	1.6*	3*	24*	43
19–30 y	1,000*	700	310	18	8	55	150	900	1.8*	3*	25*	45
31–50 y	1,000*	700	320	18	8	55	150	900	1.8*	3*	25*	45
51–70 y	1,200*	700	320	8	8	55	150	900	1.8*	3*	20*	45
>70 y	1,200*	700	320	8	8	55	150	900	1.8*	3*	20*	45
Pregnancy												
≤18 y	1,300*	1,250	400	27	12	60	220	1,000	2.0*	3*	29*	50
19–30 y	1,000*	700	350	27	11	60	220	1,000	2.0*	3*	30*	50
31–50 y	1,000*	700	360	27	11	60	220	1,000	2.0*	3*	30*	50
Lactation												
≤18 y	1,300*	1,250	360	10	13	70	290	1,300	2.6*	3*	44*	50
19–30 y	1,000*	700	310	9	12	70	290	1,300	2.6*	3*	45*	50
31–50 y	1,000*	700	320	9	12	70	290	1,300	2.6*	3*	45*	50

Data from: Reprinted with permission from the Dietary Reference Intakes series, National Academies Press. Copyright 1997, 1998, 2000, 2001, by the National Academy of Sciences. These reports may be accessed via www.nap.edu. Courtesy of the National Academies Press, Washington, DC.

Note: This table is adapted from the DRI reports; see www.nap.edu. It lists Recommended Dietary Allowances (RDAs), with Adequate Intakes (AIs) indicated by an asterisk (*). RDAs and AIs may both be used as goals for individual intake. RDAs are set to meet the needs of almost all (97 percent to 98 percent) individuals in a group. For healthy breast-fed infants, the AI is the mean intake. The AI for other life-stage and gender groups is believed to cover the needs of all individuals in the group, but lack of data prevent being able to specify with confidence the percentage of individuals covered by this intake.

The Do's and Don'ts of the DRIs

The Reference Values and Their Meaning	When Planning Your Diet
Estimated Average Requirement (EAR)	**Don't** use this amount.
Recommended Dietary Allowances (RDA)	**Do** aim for this amount!
Adequate Intake (AI)	**Do** aim for this amount if an RDA isn't available.
Tolerable Upper Intake Level (UL)	**Don't** exceed this amount on a daily basis.
Acceptable Macronutrient Distribution Range (AMDR)	**Do** follow these guidelines regarding the percentage of carbohydrates, protein, and fat in your diet.

Tolerable Upper Intake Levels (UL[a])

Vitamins

Life-Stage Group	Vitamin A (µg/d)[b]	Vitamin C (mg/d)	Vitamin D (µg/d)	Vitamin E (mg/d)[c,d]	Niacin (mg/d)[d]	Vitamin B_6 (mg/d)	Folate (µg/d)[d]	Choline (g/d)
Infants								
0–6 mo	600	ND[e]	25	ND	ND	ND	ND	ND
7–12 mo	600	ND	25	ND	ND	ND	ND	ND
Children								
1–3 y	600	400	50	200	10	30	300	1.0
4–8 y	900	650	50	300	15	40	400	1.0
Males, Females								
9–13 y	1,700	1,200	50	600	20	60	600	2.0
14–18 y	2,800	1,800	50	800	30	80	800	3.0
19–70 y	3,000	2,000	50	1,000	35	100	1,000	3.5
>70 y	3,000	2,000	50	1,000	35	100	1,000	3.5
Pregnancy								
≤18 y	2,800	1,800	50	800	30	80	800	3.0
19–50 y	3,000	2,000	50	1,000	35	100	1,000	3.5
Lactation								
≤18 y	2,800	1,800	50	800	30	80	800	3.0
19–50 y	3,000	2,000	50	1,000	35	100	1,000	3.5

Elements

Life-Stage Group	Boron (mg/d)	Calcium (g/d)	Copper (µg/d)	Fluoride (mg/d)	Iodine (µg/d)	Iron (mg/d)	Magnesium (mg/d)[f]	Manganese (mg/d)	Molybdenum (µg/d)	Nickel (mg/d)	Phosphorus (g/d)	Selenium (µg/d)	Vanadium (mg/d)[g]	Zinc (mg/d)
Infants														
0–6 mo	ND	ND	ND	0.7	ND	40	ND	ND	ND	ND	ND	45	ND	4
7–12 mo	ND	ND	ND	0.9	ND	40	ND	ND	ND	ND	ND	60	ND	5
Children														
1–3 y	3	2.5	1,000	1.3	200	40	65	2	300	0.2	3	90	ND	7
4–8 y	6	2.5	3,000	2.2	300	40	110	3	600	0.3	3	150	ND	12
Males, Females														
9–13 y	11	2.5	5,000	10	600	40	350	6	1,100	0.6	4	280	ND	23
14–18 y	17	2.5	8,000	10	900	45	350	9	1,700	1.0	4	400	ND	34
19–70 y	20	2.5	10,000	10	1,100	45	350	11	2,000	1.0	4	400	1.8	40
>70 y	20	2.5	10,000	10	1,100	45	350	11	2,000	1.0	3	400	1.8	40
Pregnancy														
≤18 y	17	2.5	8,000	10	900	45	350	9	1,700	1.0	3.5	400	ND	34
19–50 y	20	2.5	10,000	10	1,100	45	350	11	2000	1.0	3.5	400	ND	40
Lactation														
≤18 y	17	2.5	8,000	10	900	45	350	9	1,700	1.0	4	400	ND	34
19–50 y	20	2.5	10,000	10	1,100	45	350	11	2,000	1.0	4	400	ND	40

Data from: Adapted from the Dietary Reference Intakes series, National Academies Press. Copyright 1997, 1998, 2000, 2001, by the National Academy of Sciences. These reports may be accessed via www.nap.edu. Courtesy of the National Academies Press, Washington, DC.

[a] UL = The maximum level of daily nutrient intake that is likely to pose no risk of adverse effects. Unless otherwise specified, the UL represents total intake from food, water, and supplements. Due to lack of suitable data, ULs could not be established for vitamin K, thiamin, riboflavin, vitamin B_{12}, pantothenic acid, biotin, or carotenoids. In the absence of ULs, extra caution may be warranted in consuming levels above recommended intakes.

[b] As preformed vitamin A only.

[c] As α-tocopherol; applies to any form of supplemental α-tocopherol.

[d] The ULs for vitamin E, niacin, and folate apply to synthetic forms obtained from supplements, fortified foods, or a combination of the two.

[e] ND = Not determinable due to lack of data of adverse effects in this age group and concern with regard to lack of ability to handle excess amounts. Source of intake should be from food only to prevent high levels of intake.

[f] The ULs for magnesium represent intake from a pharmacological agent only and do not include intake from food and water.

[g] Although vanadium in food has not been shown to cause adverse effects in humans, there is no justification for adding vanadium to food, and vanadium supplements should be used with caution. The UL is based on adverse effects in laboratory animals, and this data could be used to set a UL for adults but not children and adolescents.

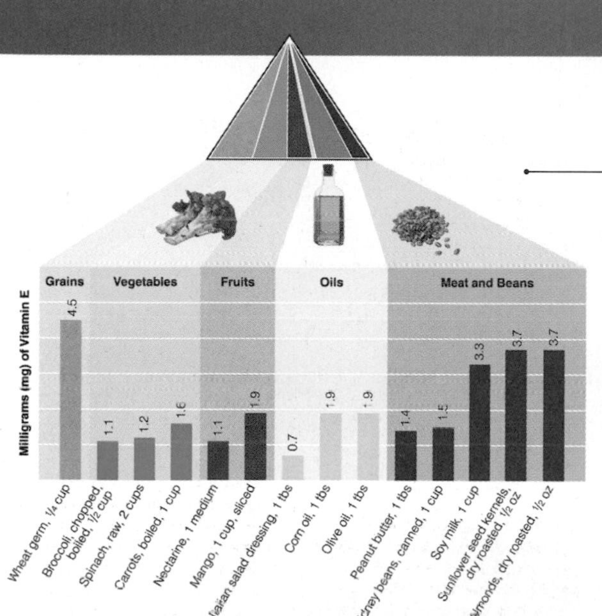

Nutrients-At-a-Glance

Food Source Diagrams found within each Visual Summary Table are tied to MyPyramid. Students can immediately see how the food sources relate to the food groups of the pyramid and determine the best food source for each nutrient.

lant effects of vitamin E.) People taking anticoagulant medication and vitamin E supplements should be monitored by their doctor to avoid a potentially serious situation in which their blood can't clot quickly enough to stop the bleeding from a wound.

While the upper level of 1,000 milligrams was set to keep you safe, it may actually be too high. A recent study showed that people at risk for heart disease who took 400 IU or more of vitamin E daily for at least one year had an overall higher risk of dying. One theory suggests that too much vitamin E may disrupt the balance of other antioxidants in the body, causing more harm than good.

Though rare, a chronic vitamin E deficiency can cause nerve problems, muscle weakness, and uncontrolled movement of body parts. Because vitamin E is an antioxidant and is found in the membranes of red blood cells, a deficiency can also increase the susceptibility of cell membranes to damage by free radicals.

Individuals who can't absorb fat properly may fall short of their vitamin E needs.

TABLE TIPS

Enjoying Your Es

Add fresh spinach and broccoli to your lunch salad.

Add a slice of avocado or use guacamole as a spread on sandwiches.

Spread peanut butter on apple slices for a sweet treat.

Top low-fat yogurt with wheat germ for a healthy snack.

Pack a handful of almonds in a zip-closed bag for a mid-afternoon snack.

Real-Life Applications

Table Tips provide easy-to-follow suggestions that students can use to easily incorporate key nutrients into their daily diets.

Terms to Know
alpha-tocopherol ■ anticoagulant ■ hemorrhage

HOW DO STUDENTS

think critically and practice better nutrition?

RATE YOURSELF

Do You Have a Whole-Grain-Friendly Diet?

On most days of the week:

1. I eat whole-grain cereals, like raisin bran, etc.	**True** ☐	**False** ☐
2. I eat whole-wheat breads and/or English muffins.	**True** ☐	**False** ☐
3. I eat brown rice instead of white rice.	**True** ☐	**False** ☐
4. I snack on popcorn, rather than chips and pretzels.	**True** ☐	**False** ☐
5. I consume whole-wheat pasta, rather than regular pasta.	**True** ☐	**False** ☐

Answers

If you answered "true" to three or more questions, you have a whole-grain-friendly diet! If not, read on!

How do students learn more about their health?

Rate Yourself

These self-assessments help students better determine their current nutritional habits and identify areas for improvement.

How do students know if what they read or hear about nutrition is accurate?

Chapter-opening Quizzes

Quizzes target myths and misperceptions about nutrition and health.

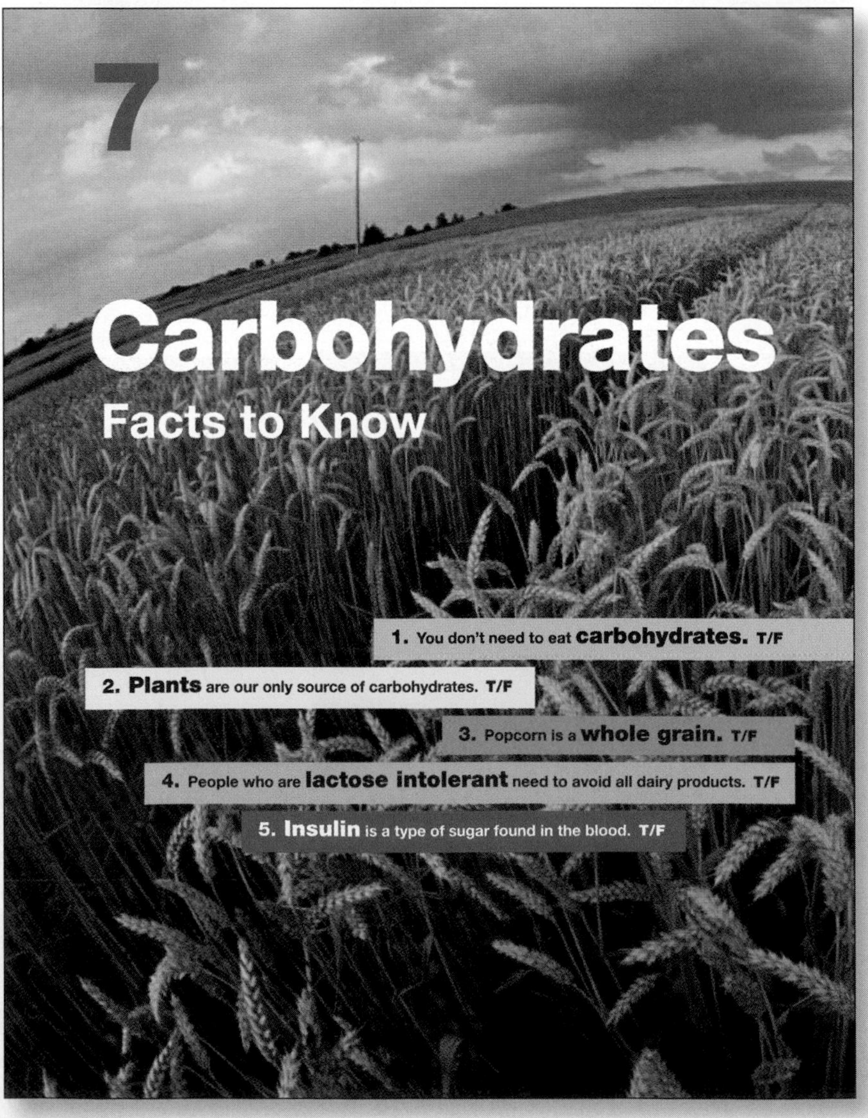

Table 8.1

Sugar Smacked!

Food Groups	Teaspoons of Added Sugar
Bread, Cereal, Rice, Pasta	
Bread, 1 slice	0
Cookies, 2 medium	🥄
Doughnut, 1 medium	🥄
Cake, frosted, 1/16 average	🥄🥄🥄🥄🥄
Pie, fruit, 2 crust, 1/6, 8" pie	🥄🥄🥄🥄🥄🥄
Fruit	
Fruit, canned in juice, ½ cup	0
Fruit, canned in heavy syrup, ½ cup	🥄🥄🥄🥄
Milk, Yogurt, and Cheese	
Milk, plain, 1 cup	0
Chocolate milk, 2% fat, 1 cup	🥄🥄🥄
Yogurt, low fat, plain, 8 oz	0
Yogurt, fruit, sweetened, 8 oz	🥄🥄🥄🥄🥄🥄🥄
Chocolate shake, 10 fl oz	🥄🥄🥄🥄🥄🥄🥄🥄🥄
Other	
Chocolate bar, 2 ounces	🥄🥄🥄🥄🥄🥄
Fruit drink, ade, 12 fl oz	🥄🥄🥄🥄🥄🥄🥄🥄🥄🥄🥄🥄

🥄 = 1 teaspoon of sugar

Data from USDA, *Dietary Guidelines for Americans,* (5th ed., 2000).

TABLE TIPS

Lowering Your Intake of Added Sugars

Mix chocolate milk with an equal amount of regular low-fat milk.

Mix equal amounts of sweetened cereal with an unsweetened variety for a breakfast cereal with half the added sugar.

Drink water rather than soda or sweetened beverages throughout the day.

Buy sweets, such as candy and cookies, in individual-serving-size pouches rather than large packages. The less you buy, the less you'll eat.

Mix an ounce of 100 percent fruit juice with 10 ounces of sparkling water for a no-sugar-added "fruit" drink.

◀ What can students do to eat better?

Table Tips

Tips provide easy-to-follow practical suggestions for readers to create healthier meals and snacks, and liven up menus.

How can students make fast, easy, and nutritious meals on their own? ▶

UCook and UDo

These hands-on features are highlighted at the end of each Concept, and appear on the Companion Website. **UCook** features delicious, easy-to-prepare recipes built around each Concept's content including per serving nutrition information. **UDo** provides strategies for making positive personal nutrition choices, emphasizing ease, variety, and appropriateness for a college community.

Check out these recipes and more

UCook

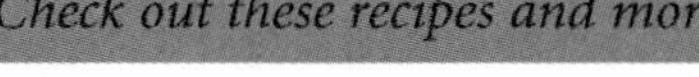

Strawberry Yogurt Shake

Sip a serving of fruit through a straw with this refreshing Strawberry Yogurt Shake, which can be whipped together in minutes using fresh or thawed frozen strawberries and any 100 percent juice.

UDo

Sweet on Sweets

Visit our website to see one student's typical daily diet—high in added sugars and low in fiber. Use Table 8.1 ("Sugar Smacked!") and Figure 8.5 ("Food Sources of Fiber") in this concept and see if you can come up with healthier choices to satisfy a sweet tooth and provide fiber.

WHERE CAN YOU FIND

www.mynutritionlab.com

MyNutritionLab is the online course management system that makes it easy for you to organize your class, personalize your students' educational experience, and push their learning to the next level. MyDietAnalysis 4.0 will be available as a single sign-on to MyNutritionLab. MyNutritionLab makes learning easy for students with its easy navigation on a chapter-by-chapter basis.

Hear It

This section contains 30 MP3s related to the chapter opening case studies.

See It

Students can access more than 15 videos to extend their learning on important nutrition topics.

Do It

Hands-on activities related to the text include the UCook recipes UDo healthy strategies, Rate Yourself self assessments, and Pop Quiz for each chapter.

Read It

This section also contains chapter objectives to direct student learning, plus the new eText. Pearson eText is easy for students to read. Users can create notes, highlight text in different colors, create book marks, zoom, click hyperlinked words and phrases to view definitions, and view in single-page or two-page view. Pearson eText also links students to associated media files, enabling them to view an animation as they read the text.

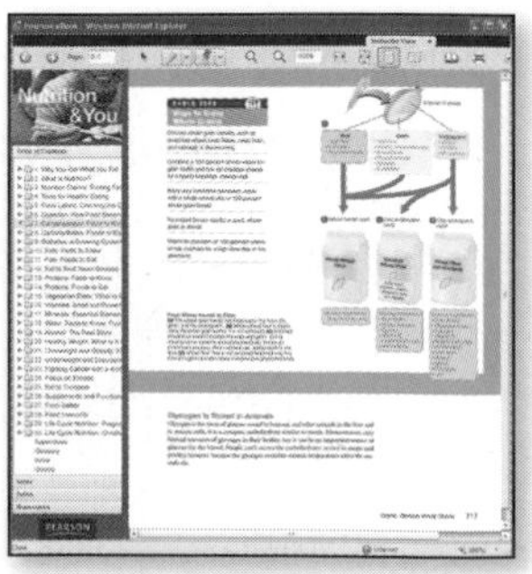

Review It

Contains quizzes for each chapter, along with access to flashcards that are available as downloads to a mobile phone.

HOW CAN STUDENTS access practical help and study tips?

Companion Website www.pearsonhighered.com/blake

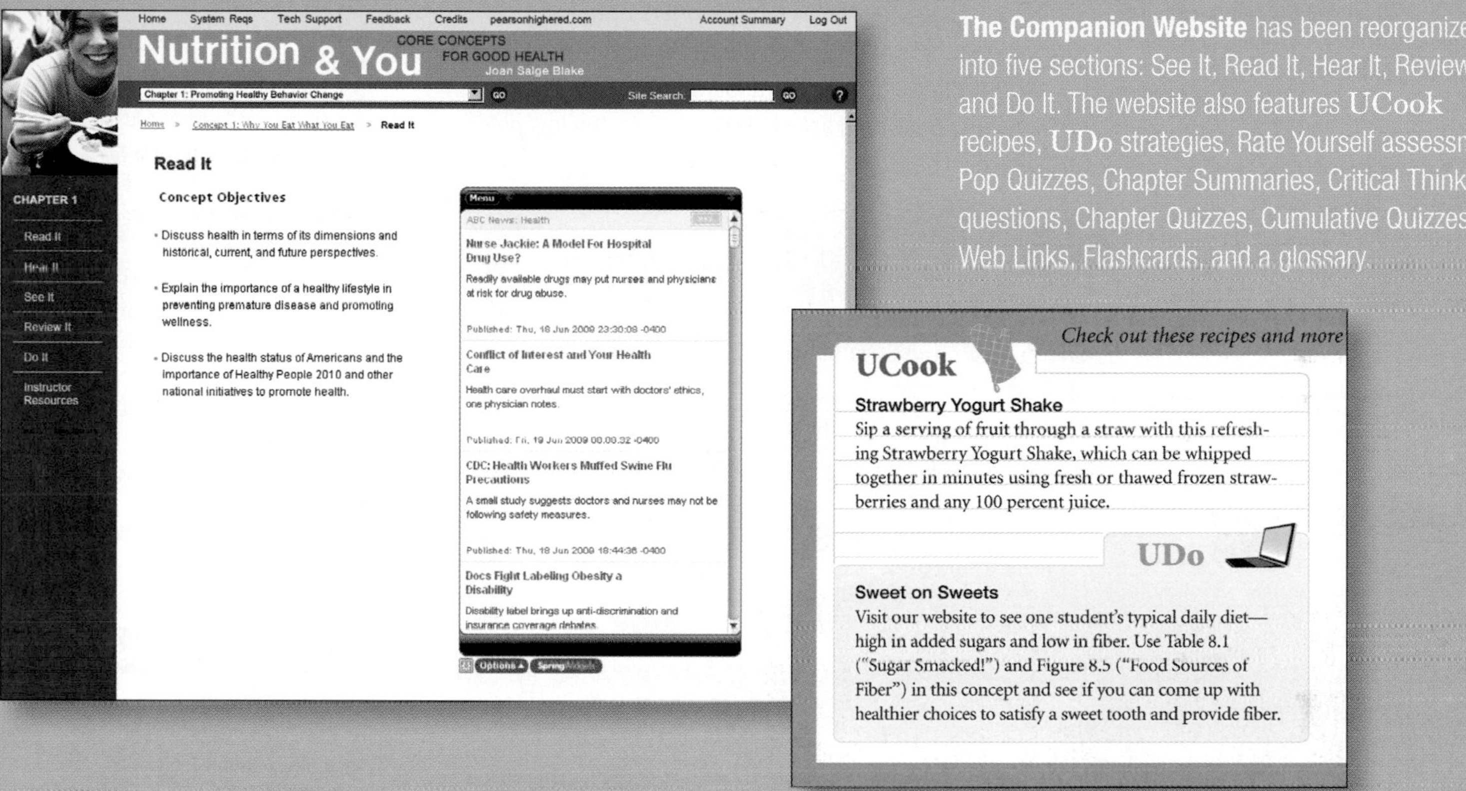

The Companion Website has been reorganized into five sections: See It, Read It, Hear It, Review It, and Do It. The website also features UCook recipes, UDo strategies, Rate Yourself assessments, Pop Quizzes, Chapter Summaries, Critical Thinking questions, Chapter Quizzes, Cumulative Quizzes, Web Links, Flashcards, and a glossary.

How can you motivate students to assess their own diets?

www.mydietanalysis.com

MyDietAnalysis was developed by the nutrition database experts at ESHA Research, Inc. and is tailored for use in college nutrition courses. It offers an accurate, reliable, and easy-to-use program for your students' diet analysis needs. MyDietAnalysis features a database of nearly 20,000 foods and multiple reports. Available on CD-ROM or online, the program allows students to track their diet and activity, and generate and submit reports electronically. MyDietAnalysis is also available as a single sign-on to MyNutritionLab.

NEW! Features of MyDietAnalysis 4.0

MyDietAnalysis 4.0 is coming for your spring semester classes! You will be able to track when your students have completed their diet analysis project, and your students' errors will be reduced. Ask your Pearson representative for more information!

- **Set up a roster of students and see when they have completed their projects,** all within MyDietAnalysis's easy-to-use interface.
- **View a class-wide nutritional average.** MyDietAnalysis will allow you to see a nutritional profile of your entire class, enabling you to base your lecture on your students' needs.
- **Video help covers the topic students struggle with most.** Students will also take a quiz after each video to ensure they understand how to set up and use the program.

ADDITIONAL teaching and learning resources

Instructor Resource DVD (IR-DVD)

The IR-DVD allows for "click and play" in the classroom—no downloading required, and also includes:

- PowerPoint lecture outlines with embedded links to animations and *ABC News* Lecture Launcher Videos
- Jeopardy-type quiz show
- Instructor Manual
- Test Bank Microsoft® Word files and Computerized TestGen® Test Bank
- Questions for Classroom Response Systems (CRS) in PowerPoint format, allowing you to import the questions into your own CRS

This valuable teaching resource offers everything you need to create lecture presentations and course materials, including JPEG and PowerPoint® files of all the art, tables, and selected photos from the text as well as videos.

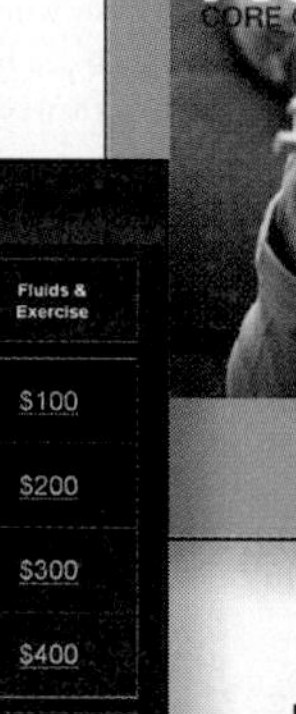

Chapter 11: Nutrition and Fitness

Physical Fitness	Energy Sources for Exercise	Nutrient Needs for Exercise	Fluids & Exercise
$100	$100	$100	$100
$200	$200	$200	$200
$300	$300	$300	$300
$400	$400	$400	$400

FINAL ROUND

What Happens to the Carbohydrates You Eat?

Digesting a meal of p... cherries (sucrose a...
- You digest carb... intestines.
- Saliva contains ...
  - Starts breakin... pasta into sma...

Play Video | abc NEWS

ABC News Video Clips

These 15 Video clips, created in partnership with *ABC News*, range from 5-10 minutes in length and can be used to stimulate classroom discussion. Digital versions of the videos are integrated into the PowerPoint lecture outline, and are available in a separate, full-screened version. Videos are available with closed-captioning.

Lecture Teaching Tips

Joan Salge Blake, author of ***Nutrition & You: Core Concepts for Good Health,*** presents eight brief demonstrations of successful lecture strategies for presenting concepts such as "The Hidden Fat in Your Sweets and Treats," "Sodium—What You Need Versus What You Consume," and "What Does 100 Calories Look Like?"

For Instructors

Instructor Manual
978-0-321-64233-2 • 0-321-64233-3

Printed Test Bank
978-0-321-64234-9 • 0-321-64234-1

Instructor Resource DVD
978-0-321-64273-8 | 0-321-64273-2
See left side of this page for a full description.

Great Ideas: Active Ways to Teach Nutrition
978-0-321-59646-8 • 0-321-59646-3

MyDietAnalysis 4.0 Premium Website
www.mydietanalysis.com

TestGen Computerized Test Bank
978-0-321-64235-6 • 0-321-64235-X

Course Management Options

WebCT
www.pearsonhighered.com/webct

Blackboard
www.pearsonhighered.com/blackboard

MyNutritionLab
MyNutritionLab™ with MyDietAnalysis
www.mynutritionlab.com

For Students

Companion Website
www.pearsonhighered.com/blake

Food Composition Table
978-0-321-66793-9 • 0-321-66793-X

MyDietAnalysis 3.0 Stand-alone CD-ROM
978-0-321-66769-4 • 0-321-66769-7

MyDietAnalysis 4.0 Student Access Kit
978-0-321-66814-1 • 0-321-66814-6

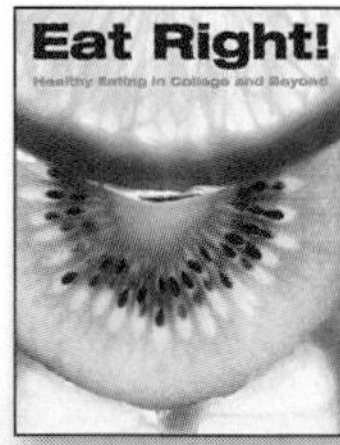

Eat Right! Healthy Eating in College and Beyond
by Janet Anderson, et al.
ISBN-13: 978-0-8053-8288-4
ISBN-10: 0-8053-8288-7

This handy, full-color 80 page booklet provides practical guidelines, tips, shopper's guides, and recipes so students can put healthy eating guidelines into action. Topics include: How to choose healthy foods in a cafeteria, dorm room, and fast food restaurant; eating on a budget; weight management tips; vegetarian alternatives; and guidelines on alcohol and health.

Nutrition & You

CORE CONCEPTS FOR GOOD HEALTH

Joan Salge Blake
MS, RD, LDN
Boston University

Benjamin Cummings
Boston Columbus Indianapolis New York San Francisco Upper Saddle River
Amsterdam Cape Town Dubai London Madrid Milan Munich Paris Montréal Toronto
Delhi Mexico City São Paulo Sydney Hong Kong Seoul Singapore Taipei Tokyo

Senior Acquisitions Editor: Sandra Lindelof
Project Editor: Susan Scharf
Development Manager: Barbara Yien
Development Editor: Laura Bonazzoli
Editorial Assistant: Brianna Paulson
Managing Editor: Deborah Cogan
Production Supervisors: Caroline Ayres, Dorothy Cox
Production Management: S4Carlisle Publishing Services
Compositor: S4Carlisle Publishing Services
Copyeditor: Deb Debord
Text and Cover Designer: Marilyn Perry
Illustrator: Precision Graphics
Photo Researcher: Roman Barnes
Manufacturing Buyer: Jeffrey Sargent
Senior Marketing Manager: Neena Bali
Market Development Manager: Brooke Suchomel
Text Printer: Courier Kendallville
Cover Printer: Lehigh Phoenix

Cover Photo Credit: Radius Images/Jupiter Images

ISBN 10: 0-321-60247-1; ISBN 13: 978-0-321-60247-3 (Student edition)
ISBN 10:0-321-64252-X; ISBN 13: 978-0-321-64252-3 (Professional copy)

Library of Congress Cataloging-in-Publication Data
Blake, Joan Salge.
Nutrition & you: core concepts for good health/Joan Salge Blake.
p. cm.
Includes bibliographical references and index.
ISBN 978-0-321-60247-3
1. Nutrition—Textbooks. I. Title. II. Title: Nutrition and you.
QP141.B63 2011
612.3—dc22 2009041910

1 2 3 4 5 6 7 8 9 10—CRK—13 12 11 10 09

Benjamin Cummings
is an imprint of

www.pearsonhighered.com

Brief Contents

Contents

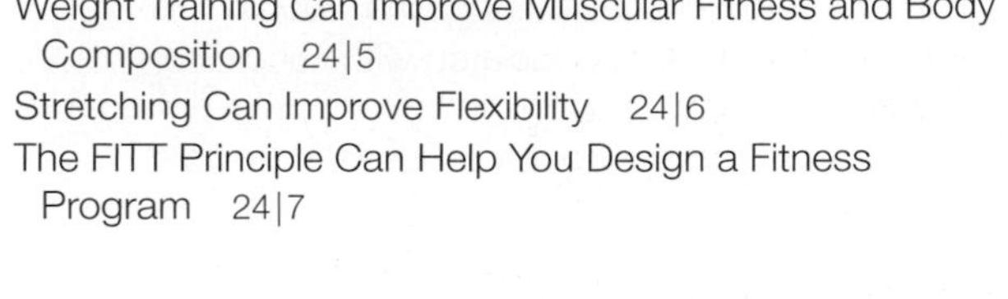

27 Food Safety

28 Food Insecurity

29 Life Cycle Nutrition: Pregnancy through Infancy

Features

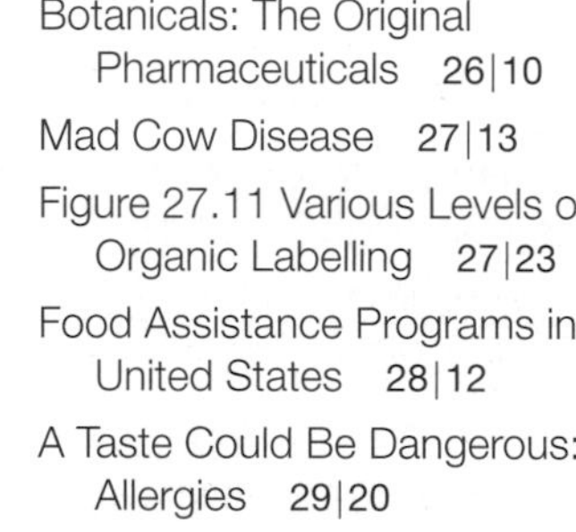

Feature Boxes

Rate Yourself

UCook/UDo

Table Tips

About the Author

Joan Salge Blake is a clinical Associate Professor and the Dietetics Internship Director at Boston University's College of Health and Rehabilitation Sciences (Sargent College). She received her MS from Boston University and is currently working towards her doctorate. She teaches both graduate and undergraduate nutrition courses. She has also been a guest lecturer at the Boston University Goldman School of Dental Medicine.

Joan is a member of the American Dietetic Association and the Massachusetts Dietetic Association (MDA) and has been a presenter and Presiding Officer at both the ADA annual meeting and MDA annual convention. She has been a recipient of the Outstanding Dietitian (2009), Outstanding Dietetic Educator (2007), and Young Dietitian of the Year awards. She also received the Whitney Powers Excellence in Teaching Award from Boston University. Joan is an ADA National Media Spokesperson and conducts over 100 media interviews annually. Her nutrition segments can be seen regularly on Fox25 television, Boston.

About the Author

Foreword

Joan Salge Blake's latest book, *Nutrition & You: Core Concepts for Good Health,* is a "consumer"oriented introductory text aimed at making reliable nutrition information available to students with little or no nutritional background. Written in an engaging and innovative way, it provides students with the information they need to make positive and healthful changes in their lives now and in the future.

Joan makes this essential information accessible by using an array of learning tools and strategies, including a focus on key concepts, clear and inviting graphics, and Visual Summary Tables for the macronutrients, vitamins, and minerals—all designed to make this foundational nutrition information relevant and easy to understand. She makes it all about the reader by personalizing the learning and helping students to appreciate what good nutrition can mean to them.

Joan knows what consumers and students need to know and how to make learning interesting and practical. She has been an educator for over 10 years, teaching both graduate and undergraduate nutrition courses. Her background as an American Dietetic Association National Spokesperson has also given her the experience to understand what consumers of nutrition information want and need in real-life terms, and how to deliver it.

Congratulations, Joan.

Jessie Pavlinac, MS, RD, CSR, LD
President, American Dietetic Association, 2009–2010

Why I Wrote *Nutrition & You: Core Concepts for Good Health*

Everything good they say about Salge Blake is true. I got in the best shape of my life because of this class and I eat so healthy now.

You'll probably finish this class with a whole new outlook on diet and exercise . . . and you'll probably be a lot healthier!

—excerpts from Boston University student comments (ratemyprofessor.com)

I wrote *Nutrition & You: Core Concepts for Good Health* for *you.* For years, I have taught an Introduction to Nutrition course—using my nonmajors-oriented textbook *Nutrition & You*—to a packed classroom of 200 students, at the unseemly hour of 8:00 a.m. The students keep coming year after year because I deliver accurate nutrition science and information in an easy-to-understand, entertaining format, and even more importantly, because I personalize the information for them, so that they can immediately apply it to their lives and lifestyles.

Oftentimes, months, even years after completing my class, students email me, brimming with pride that they are still successfully applying the diet and lifestyle strategies that they learned from the text and in the class. These past students had reached and maintained a healthy weight, lowered their cholesterol, and/or achieved a healthier blood pressure, all based on the personalized information they received. This feedback prompted me to write *Nutrition & You: Core Concepts for Good Health,* to provide a new group of students—those of you who probably have not encountered the content previously in another course or who may not take any further nutrition classes—with essential nutritional tools in a readable fashion, so that you can achieve lasting good health.

As a college student, you are exposed to a steady stream of nutrition and health information from the media, your family and friends, and the Internet. While it may seem that Google has all the answers to nutrition questions, I have frequently seen students fall victim to misinformation derived from a quick Internet search or a few slick websites. With that in mind, *Nutrition & You: Core Concepts for Good Health* was designed to be user-friendly but packed with the irreducible basics of sound nutrition information. In addition, the text goes beyond the latest nutrition science by also providing helpful advice and targeted strategies to help you easily incorporate what you learn into your busy life. The text is written to meet your nutritional concerns and answer your questions, so that you can make healthful (and delicious!) choices.

As you read *Nutrition & You: Core Concepts for Good Health,* I want you to feel as though I am speaking directly to *you.* For this reason, the text is written in a conversational tone, and it's designed to visually communicate the latest nutrition topics in an engaging, easy-to-follow way.

The information in this textbook is arranged in a deliberate "What," "Why," and "How" format. Each concept will tell you:

What the nutrition concept is;

Why it is important and the role it plays in your body; and, most importantly,

How to easily adjust your lifestyle based on what you have learned.

Feel free to follow me on Twitter at: http://twitter.com/joansalgeblake.

Happy reading and good health!

Text Overview and Organization

As nutrition information changes with ever-evolving research, and non-stop media coverage of health and nutrition issues, the need for reliable, well-grounded, essential information is greater than ever.

Nutrition & You: Core Concepts for Good Health addresses the instructor's need for foundational nutrition information targeted at students with limited or no background in the subject, presented in a lively and easy-to-adapt format that allows optimal flexibility in presenting the course material. Key aspects of the text's organization and features include the following:

Concepts Organization: Rather than using conventional, longer chapters that require a linear course organization, this text organizes 30 core topics into brief, independent, key "concepts" designed to work individually or in sync with one another. Each concept covers a fundamental nutrition topic, with page numbering, design, and features that allow instructors to select only those concepts they choose to cover within the scope of their course. When used as a whole text, the information unfolds in a logical progression.

Visual Summary Tables: These engaging table spreads, covering the macronutrients, vitamins, and minerals, have become a hallmark of the Blake texts. In this edition, they are geared specifically toward an introductory, general audience by providing key nutrient information that is appropriately detailed for a basic, introductory course. All the Visual Summary Tables cover the basics of *what* each nutrient is; its main *functions*; the reader's *daily needs*; its *food sources*; and the *consequences* of consuming either too much or too little of the nutrient.

Additional Pedagogic Features: In addition, the text includes an array of unique features and tools designed to bring this core nutrition information "home" to students and to provide them with myriad ways to use it everyday in their lives. These include:

- **UCook:** These easy-to-prepare, delicious recipes are built around each concept and are geared toward a student's lifestyle. The recipe names are listed at the end of each concept and can be found in their entirety on the companion website, including the key nutritional breakdown per serving.
- **UDo:** These practical tips and strategies for making positive personal nutrition choices emphasize ease, variety, and appropriateness for a college community. UDo activities are listed at the end of each concept and students follow links to the companion website for more information and follow-ups.
- **Table Tips:** These engaging margin features occur throughout the book and provide student-friendly practical suggestions for readers to create healthier meals and snacks and liven up their menus.
- **Rate Yourself:** This self-assessment feature provides students with questions and challenges to help them accurately assess their current nutritional habits and identify areas for improvement.
- **The Take-Home Message:** This summary feature revisits key content as it unfolds in each concept and crystallizes information into concise points that support content retention.
- **Top Five Points to Remember:** This useful reference feature boils down the primary aspects of each concept into a handy list at the end of each chapter.
- **Case Study:** Each concept begins with a specific case study highlighting diverse people with varying health, nutrition, and lifestyle issues that students can relate to, follow, and learn from.

- **Opening Quiz:** These chapter-opening quizzes target myths and misperceptions about nutrition and health.
- **Boxed Features:** Within each concept, these informative boxes highlight various significant, controversial, or unexpected aspects of the material to explore in greater detail.
- **Food Source diagrams:** Featured in many Visual Summary Tables, these engaging graphics are linked to MyPyramid, the USDA-based food reference tool, enabling students to easily identify many common food sources within the MyPyramid format.
- **Test Yourself:** This review of content organized as key questions and answers, along with a list of Web Resources, appears at the end of each concept.

Resources for Instructors

Instructor Manual

978-0-321-64233-2 / 0-321-64233-3

This practical resource includes detailed outlines summarizing each concept, suggested group discussion questions and activities, key terms, *ABC News* video discussion questions, sample syllabi, tips and activities for integrating MyDietAnalysis into lesson plans, and a selection of *Great Ideas in Teaching Nutrition* newsletters chock full of teacher-tested tips and information.

Instructor Resource DVD (IR-DVD) with Computerized Test Bank

978-0-321-64273-8 / 0-321-64273-2

This valuable teaching resource offers everything you need to create lecture presentations and course materials, including JPEG and PowerPoint® files of the art, tables, and selected photos from the text, as well as "stepped-out" art for selected figures from the text and supporting animations. The IR-DVD also includes:

- PowerPoint lecture outlines with embedded links to the animations and *ABC News* Lecture Launcher Videos
- A *Jeopardy*-type quiz show
- The *Lecture Teaching Tips* author video
- The *Instructor Manual*
- Test Bank Microsoft Word® files and Computerized Test Bank
- Questions for Classroom Response Systems (CRS) in PowerPoint format, allowing you to import the questions into your own CRS

Printed Test Bank

978-0-321-64234-9 / 0-321-64234-1

The test bank, available in both print and computerized formats, provides short answer, multiple-choice, true/false, matching, and essay questions for each concept within the text.

Great Ideas! Active Ways to Teach Nutrition

978-0-321-59646-8 / 0-321-59646-3

This updated, revised booklet compiles the best ideas from nutrition instructors across the country on innovative ways to teach nutrition topics with an emphasis on active learning. Broken into useful pedagogic areas, including targeted and general classroom activities, and an overview of active learning principles, this booklet provides tips and suggestions for classroom activities that can be used to teach almost any topic.

MyNutritionLab

www.mynutritionlab.com

Powered by CourseCompass™, MyNutritionLab includes everything you need to teach introductory nutrition in one convenient place, with content that can be customized for each course. Students and instructors can access *ABC News* video clips, animations, *eThemes of the Times*, study tools, myeBook, quizzes, gradebook, access to the Tutor Center, the Student Study Guide, and much more. MyDietAnalysis 3.0 is available via a single log-on to MyNutritionLab.

MyNutritionLab™ Instructor Access Kit

www.mynutritionlab.com

978-0-321-64276-9 / 0-321-64276-7

Provides Instructor access to MyNutritionLab™.

MyNutritionLab™ with MyDietAnalysis

978-0-321-64275-2 / 0-321-64275-9

www.mynutritionlab.com

Powered by CourseCompass™, MyNutritionLab includes everything you need to teach introductory nutrition in one convenient place, with content that can be customized for each course. Students and instructors can access *ABC News* video clips, animations, *eThemes of the Times*, study tools, an e-book, quizzes, gradebook, access to the Tutor Center, the Student Study Guide, and much more. MyDietAnalysis 3.0 is available as a single sign-on to MyNutritionLab.

MyNutritionLab™ with MyDietAnalysis Instructor Access Kit

978-0-321-64277-6 / 0-321-64277-5

Provides Instructor access to MyNutritionLab™ with MyDietAnalysis.

WebCT Premium

978-0-321-64282-0 / 0-321-64282-1

www.pearsonhighered.com/webct

This resource includes preloaded text-specific quizzes, animations, and more, along with course-management resources and a Tutor Center link.

Blackboard Premium

978-0-321-64280-6 / 0-321-64280-5

www.pearsonhighered.com/blackboard

This resource includes preloaded text-specific quizzes, animations, and more, along with course-management resources and a Tutor Center link.

Companion Website

www.pearsonhighered.com/blake

The companion website features a new Practical Nutrition Tips author video, in addition to interactive Get Real and Nutrition Sleuth activities, Careers in Nutrition interviews, chapter quizzes, Two Points of View analysis questions, eLearn links, web links, flashcards, and a glossary.

TestGen®

978-0-321-64235-6 / 0-321-64235-X

This supplement provides short answer, multiple-choice, true/false, matching, fill-in-the-blank, and essay questions for each chapter of the text in computerized format.

Resources for Students

Eat Right! Healthy Eating in College and Beyond

978-0-8053-8288-4 / 0-8053-8288-7

By Janet Anderson et al.

This handy, full-color 80-page booklet provides practical guidelines, tips, shoppers' guides, and recipes, so that students can put healthy eating information into practice. Topics include how to choose healthy foods in a cafeteria, dorm, and fast-food restaurants; eating on a budget; weight-management tips; vegetarian alternatives; and guidelines on alcohol and health.

MyNutritionLab™ Student Access Kit

978-0-321-64278-3 / 0-321-64278-3

MyNutritionLab with MyDietAnalysis Student Access Kit

978-0-321-64279-0 / 0-321-64279-1

WebCT Student Access Kit

978-0-321-64283-7 / 0-321-64283-X

Blackboard Student Access Kit

978-0-321-64281-3 / 0-321-64281-3

Companion Website

www.pearsonhighered.com/blake

The companion website features a new Practical Nutrition Tips author video, in addition to interactive Get Real and Nutrition Sleuth activities, Careers in Nutrition interviews, chapter quizzes, Two Points of View analysis questions, eLearn links, web links, flashcards, and a glossary.

Acknowledgments

It takes a huge team of creative and hard-working players to produce a dynamic textbook. *Nutrition & You: Core Concepts for Good Health* is no exception. I personally want to thank all of those who passionately shared their expertise and support to make this textbook better than I could have envisioned.

Beginning with the dynamic staff at Benjamin Cummings, I would like to thank Acquisitions Editor Sandy Lindelof, who believed in the need for this book and helped make my vision a reality. Thanks also to Barbara Yien, Development Manager, for her support in making the book a standout. Many, many thanks go to Laura Bonazzoli, my sharp-as-a-tack Development Editor, whose insight and devotion to the project greatly improved this text in so many ways.

It takes an organized manager to make sure the team runs on a schedule. Thank goodness for Susan Scharf, my Project Editor, who kept me on track, especially when the FedEx packages came as frequently as the daily newspaper, and who expertly guided the project from inception to completion. Thanks also to Susan Malloy and Marie Beaugureau for their support, and to our ever-sharp Editorial Assistant, Brianna Paulson, for her many contributions and expert assistance. I'm also grateful to Katie Seibel for her help in developing the excellent supplemental print materials that accompany this edition.

Creating a textbook is a major production, so many thanks go to Caroline Ayres and Dorothy Cox, Production Supervisors extraordinaire, and to Norine Strang, our Publishing Editor and Compositor, for her tireless attention and professionalism. Thanks also to Deborah Cogan, Senior Managing Editor for production, for her guidance and keen oversight, and to Jeff Sargent, our talented Manufacturing Buyer.

Visually, *Nutrition & You: Core Concepts for Good Health* comes alive with photos, illustrations, and numerous graphic features. Front and center, many thanks to Marilyn Perry for designing the eye-catching cover as well as the wonderful interior design of this textbook. Many of the vivid photos are due to the keen eyes of Roman Barnes, our Photo Researcher, with thanks to Alan Smithee, Senior Photo Manager, for his guidance and support. I am grateful to the folks at Precision Graphics for providing the precise illustrations needed to explain complex topics in an engaging, easy-to-grasp format. All good textbooks need a cracker-jack Media Producer, so I want to thank the talented Aimee Pavy. Thanks also to Mansour Bethoney for his wonderful collaboration with me on developing the new Practical Nutrition Tips video.

Marketing takes energy, passion, and a creative mind. That's exactly what Neena Bali, our tireless Senior Marketing Manager, and her energetic marketing team brought to this project in so many ways. Thanks also to Brooke Suchomel, Market Development Manager, for helping us review and guide the text to its audience. And my thanks also go to Lillian Carr and her talented creative team for their marketing expertise and talent.

An additional and heartfelt thank you goes to my research assistant, Susan Tripp, who went over and above the call of duty by helping me fill the pages of *Nutrition & You: Core Concepts for Good Health* with accurate facts and who helped develop some of our supplements.

Lastly, endless thanks to my family, **A**dam, **B**rendan, and **C**raig, for their love and support when I was working more than I should have been.

Joan Salge Blake

Joan Salge Blake

Contributors and Reviewers

Many thanks to the following contributors and reviewers for their valuable assistance:

Orville Bigelow
California State University, Los Angeles

Sarah Blake
Boston University

Carol Bradley
Stephen F. Austin State University

Sarah Butler
Boston University

Tammy Darke
Mt. San Antonio College

Johanna Donnenfield
Scottsdale Community College

Brenda Eissenstat
Pennsylvania State University

Michelle Futrell
College of Charleston

Karen Geismar
Texas A & M University

Eun-Jeong Ha
Kent State University

Erin Holt
University of Nebraska, Kearney

Peggy A. Johnston
University of Nebraska, Kearney

Lynn Parker Klees
Pennsylvania State University

Christina Ranelle
Texas Christian University

Doris Schomberg
Alamance Community College

Susan Tripp, R.D.

Sandra Weatherilt
Mt. San Antonio College

I am nothing without my ABCs.

Thanks.

1

Why You Eat What You Eat

1. **Nutrients** don't necessarily provide calories. **T/F**

2. **Phytochemicals** are harmful chemicals found in processed foods. **T/F**

3. You tend to **eat more** when you eat with others. **T/F**

4. **Advertising** is ineffective when it comes to influencing people's food choices. **T/F**

5. The **food choices** that are available to you overall are very similar to those that were available to your grandparents. **T/F**

It's the night before the big biology exam, and Elizabeth, a junior, is in high-stress mode in a down-to-the-wire cram session. She pours herself a tall glass of caffeinated cola, opens a family-size bag of rippled potato chips, and nervously plows through it. She snacks and studies through the night, stuffing as much information as possible into her head and too many chips into her stomach. After 3 jittery hours of sleep, she heads to her 8 a.m. exam feeling tired, groggy, and still uncomfortably stuffed from her chip-and-soda cram session.

Would you be surprised to learn that Elizabeth did not do very well on her exam? Do you, like Elizabeth, sometimes eat snacks or other foods because you're stressed, rather than hungry? What other factors do you think influence your food choices, and how can you make sound nutritional decisions?

Answers

1. True. Many people believe that all nutrients provide calories, but only three—carbohydrates, fats, and proteins—really do. Water, vitamins, and minerals are also classified as nutrients, and they don't provide calories. See page 3.
2. False. Phytochemicals are plant chemicals that—although they are not classified as nutrients—are thought to play a role in protecting your body against some chronic diseases. Turn to page 3 for details.
3. True. Eating dinner with others has been shown to increase the size of the meal by over 40%, and the more people present, the more you tend to eat. Check it out on page 4.
4. False. Companies spend an enormous amount of money on advertising to persuade you to purchase their food products and, whether you realize it or not, it often works. In fact, advertisers have been marketing their products to you since you were a child. To find out why, turn to pages 5 and 6.
5. False. Not by a long shot—as nutrition discoveries and sciences advance, so do the types of foods available to you. Turn to page 7 to uncover how food choices have changed over the generations.

From the minute you were born, you began performing three automatic behaviors: You slept, you ate, and you expelled your waste products. You didn't need to think about these actions, and you didn't have to decide to do them. You also didn't need to make choices about how much sleep to get, what to eat, or when to go to the bathroom. Life was so easy back then.

Now that you're older, these actions, particularly eating, are anything but automatic. You make many decisions every day about what to eat, and for reasons that you may not even be aware of. For instance, think about what you ate for breakfast this morning: Do you know *why* you chose those foods to start your day? Sometimes it's easy to identify things influencing your food choices, but those sources of information can conflict. For instance, yummy-looking meals and snacks you see on TV might be the very foods that news reports are advising you to avoid. In this concept, we'll help you recognize *why* you eat *what* you eat. You'll learn how improved knowledge about nutrition can help you make better food choices, and how a few small but important changes can have a positive impact on your health.

What Drives Our Food Choices?

What did you have for dinner last night? Where did you eat it? Who were you with? How did you feel?

Do you ever think about what drives your food choices? Or are you on autopilot as you stand in line at the sandwich shop and squint at yet another lit menu board? Do you adore some foods and eat them often, while avoiding others with a vengeance? Perhaps you have a grandmother who encourages you to eat more (and more!) of her traditional home cooking. You obviously need food to survive, but beyond your basic instinct to eat are many other factors that affect what goes into your stomach. Let's discuss some of them now.

We Need to Eat and Drink to Live

This isn't exactly what's meant by the phrase "You are what you eat," but it's close.

All creatures need fuel to function, and humans are no exception. We get our fuel from food in the form of chemical compounds that are collectively known as **nutrients.** These nutrients work together to provide energy, growth, and maintenance and to regulate numerous body processes. Three of the six classes of nutrients—carbohydrates, fats (part of the larger class of lipids), and proteins—provide energy in the form of **kilocalories.** Two other classes of nutrients, vitamins and minerals, help regulate many body processes, including your body's ability to break down food and convert it into energy, called **metabolism.** Some nutrients also play other supporting roles. The last class of nutrient, water, is found in all foods and beverages, and it is so vital to life that you couldn't live more than a few days without it. We will explore each of these nutrients in more depth in Concept 2, and in much more detail throughout this book.

Foods also provide nonnutritive compounds that help maintain and repair your body in order to keep it healthy. For instance, plant-based foods provide **phytochemicals,** plant chemicals that—although not classified as nutrients—are thought to play a role in protecting your body against some chronic diseases. In contrast, some other nonnutritive compounds in foods are less beneficial. For instance, alcohol can confer health benefits if consumed in very small amounts, but it's not a nutrient and in excessive amounts can pack on the pounds, harm your liver, and increase your risk of suffering a traumatic injury or an accidental death. So why do people drink alcohol? We'll answer that question and more in Concept 19.

The basic need to replenish our bodies with daily fuel drives us to eat, but what exactly are the factors that drive our food choices? Before reading on, Rate Yourself to discover the factors driving your choice of foods.

RATE YOURSELF

Do Outside Factors Influence Your Food Choices?

Rate yourself to see!

1. Whenever I meet friends, we get something to eat or drink, no matter the time of day.
   True ☐ **False** ☐
2. I sometimes find myself walking past a coffee shop, fast-food restaurant, or convenience store and am compelled to buy something to eat.
   True ☐ **False** ☐
3. When I am bored, stressed, or sad, I snack.
   True ☐ **False** ☐
4. I always eat or drink something when I am studying, even if I am not hungry.
   True ☐ **False** ☐
5. I always eat when I go out to a movie in a movie theatre.
   True ☐ **False** ☐

Answers:

If you answered "true" to most of these questions, then you are not alone. Many of our food choices are driven by influences that surround us every day! Read on to find out more.

Many Factors Influence Our Choice of Foods

You probably think your favorite foods taste delicious—that's why they're your favorites! You choose certain other foods because they're staples of your culture, or

nutrients Compounds found in foods that sustain your body processes. There are six classes of nutrients: carbohydrates, fats (lipids), proteins, vitamins, minerals, and water.

kilocalorie (kcal) A unit of measurement of energy in foods.

metabolism The numerous reactions that occur within the cells of the body, whereby the calories in foods are converted to energy.

phytochemicals Compounds found in plant foods that may play a role in fighting chronic diseases.

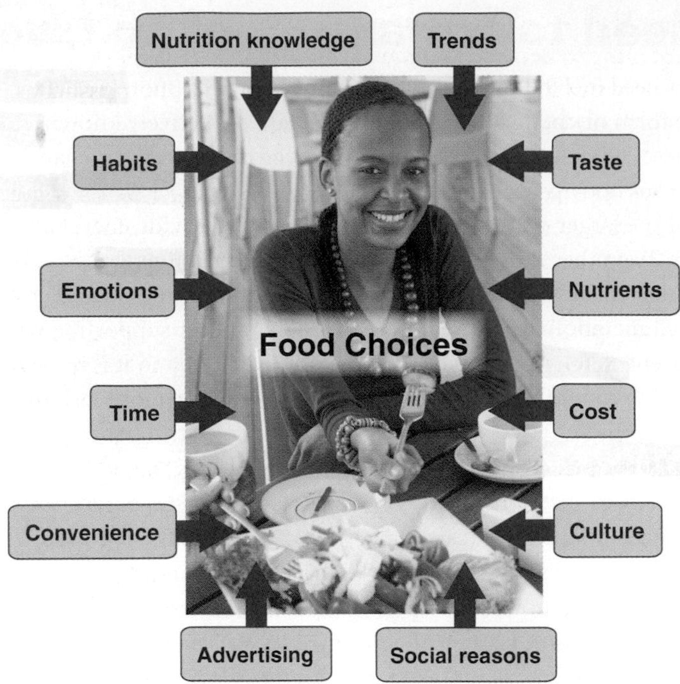

Figure 1.1 Factors Influencing Food Choices

they've become an important aspect of your social life. Some of your food selections are determined by trends, influenced by media messages, or reflect the amount of time or money you have available. Sometimes, you choose a food just because it's *there*! Let's explore each of these factors more closely (Figure 1.1).

Taste and Culture

Research confirms that, when it comes to making food choices, taste is the most important consideration.[1] This shouldn't be too much of a surprise, considering that there are at least 10,000 taste buds in your mouth, mainly on your tongue. Your taste buds tell you that chocolate cheesecake is sweet, fresh lemon juice is sour, and a pretzel is salty.

What you choose to put on your plate is often influenced by your culture. A student in Mexico might be feasting on a dinner with corn tortillas and tamales, as maize (corn) is a staple of Mexican cuisine. In India, meals commonly include lentils and other legumes with rice and vegetables, whereas many Native Americans enjoy stews of mutton (sheep), corn, and other vegetables. In Japan, fish, soy, and rice would be front and center on your plate.

A culture's cuisine is greatly influenced by the environment. That includes not only the climate and soil conditions but also the native plants and animals, as well as the distance people live from rivers, lakes, or the sea. People tend to consume foods that are accessible and eat very few foods that are scarce. For example, native Alaskans feast on fish because it is plentiful, but they eat little fresh produce, which is difficult to grow locally.

One in four Americans is of Hispanic, Native American, Asian, or African descent. Cultural food preferences often influence food choices.

Social Customs and Trends

Eating is an important way to bond with others. Every year, on the fourth Thursday in November, over 95 percent of Americans gather with family and friends to consume close to 700 million pounds of turkey as they celebrate Thanksgiving.[2] Some Americans never eat turkey on any other day of the year! Moreover, people are likely to eat more on Thanksgiving than on any other Thursday, and this is partly because of all the other people eating with them. Eating dinner with others has been shown to increase the size of the meal by over 40 percent and, the more people present, the more you'll eat.[3] For instance, chances are that you'll choose a dessert, even if you are not hungry, because everyone else is having one. Enjoying your meals in the campus cafeteria allows you to socialize with your classmates, who might influence what and how much you eat.

Food, friends, and football—a way of life.

For many people, activities such as watching a football game with fellow fans, or going to a movie with friends, involve particular foods. More pizzas are sold on Super Bowl Sunday than on any other day of the year.[4] Movie theatre owners bank on your buying popcorn, candy, and beverages at their concession stands before heading in to watch the film. Income from these snack items can account for up to half of a theatre's total profits. And if you're with a group of friends, you're even more likely to buy these snacks. Research shows that people purchase more movie concession snacks when socializing in a group.[5]

Your food choices are also affected by popular trends. For instance, home cooks in the 1950s bought bags of newfangled frozen vegetables in order to provide healthy meals in less time. A few decades later, vegetables went upscale and consumers bought them as part of ready-to-heat stir-fry mixes. Today, shoppers pay a premium price for convenient bags of fresh veggies, such as carrots, that have been pre-washed and peeled, sliced, or diced. Similarly, decades ago, the only way to enjoy iced tea was to brew it and chill it yourself. Now most markets provide dozens of choices in flavored and enhanced bottled teas, which are the beverage of choice for many college students. As food manufacturers pour more money into research and development, who knows what tomorrow's trendy food items will be?

Food Advertisements: Help or Hindrance?

With so much money being spent on the advertising of foods, it should be easy for the consumer to eat a healthy diet. So why are rates of obesity and chronic diseases, linked to nutrition, on the rise? Is the consumer pressured by food companies to buy more heavily advertised foods, such as sweetened beverages, cookies, candies, and snack items? Margo G. Wootan, director of nutrition policy at the Center for Science in the Public Interest (CSPI), believes that we are.

> "Company practices have a big effect on people's food preferences and choices. While some experts are still scratching their heads and wondering why obesity rates have been skyrocketing in adults and children, all you need to do is look around to see why: The current food environment does not support healthy choices. There are many powerful forces—and powerful companies—working against Americans' efforts to eat well and maintain a healthy weight. They include advertising and marketing, large portion sizes, eating out, food availability everywhere, too many sugary soft drinks, and junk food in schools."

Food advertising on television affects children's food choices, as well as what they ask their parents to purchase.

To back up her claim, Wootan cites studies on the effectiveness of food advertising in children demonstrating that food advertising gets children's attention and affects their food choices, their food purchases, and what they ask their parents to buy. For example, a well documented study by the National Academies' Institute of Medicine strongly concluded that marketing really works—it affects children's diets and health.

Wootan claims that marketing healthy foods can also work. As evidence, she points to sales of the citrus fruit Darling Clementines, which increased 25 percent after the Nickelodeon characters Dora the Explorer and SpongeBob SquarePants were displayed on the packaging. She advises: "Food manufacturers and restaurants also should develop new products and reformulate existing products to add more fruits and vegetables."

Advertising

Open a magazine or newspaper or switch on the television and you'll soon see an advertisement for food. Manufacturers spend over $10 billion annually on food advertising, with over $700 million each spent on the marketing of breakfast cereals, candy, and gum. Another $500 million is spent on advertising carbonated soft drinks.[6] In comparison, when was the last time you saw an advertisement for broccoli? Have you ever seen an ad for broccoli?

Food companies know the enormous influence that advertisements have on people's purchases and eating habits, especially those of children and adolescents. American children view up to 40,000 television commercials every year. An estimated $200 billion of household purchases are influenced by children under the age of 12. On Saturday morning, more than half of the between-cartoon ads that children watch are for foods. Of these, over 40 percent are for sweets and treats such as candy, soft drinks, chips, and sugary breakfast cereals.[7] Consider this the next time you see a child asking for sweet sugar puffs in the cereal aisle of your local supermarket.

By the time you graduate from high school, you have probably viewed over 350,000 **television advertisements.**

In contrast, commercials for fruits and vegetables are almost nonexistent, which is a shame because healthy foods can be marketed successfully. When the dairy industry noted a decline in milk consumption among Americans in 1994, it launched the *Got Milk?* ad campaign featuring celebrities wearing milk mustaches. This campaign strove to make drinking milk sexy, and it worked. Milk sales increased by nearly 1.5 billion pounds, which is the equivalent of about 45 pounds of milk being sold for each advertising dollar spent.[8]

Cost, Time, and Convenience

According to the United States Department of Agriculture, 11 percent of American households experience food insecurity; that is, the people living in these households are not able to meet their nutrient needs every day.[9] These people may be forced to base their food choices mainly on cost. You'll learn more about food insecurity in the United States and elsewhere in Concept 28.

When it comes to preparing food, time is often limited; because of this, the foods that people choose have changed over the years. Recent research shows that Americans, especially working women with families, now want to spend less than 15 minutes preparing a meal.[10] As a result, supermarkets have changed the kinds of foods they sell, as well as how the food is presented.

If chicken is on the menu tonight, you can go to the poultry section in the store and buy it uncooked, or you can go to the take-out section of the store and buy it hot off the rotisserie, precooked and stuffed with bread crumbs or grilled with teriyaki sauce. You can often also find cooked vegetables and a rice side dish to take home and reheat with the chicken.

Convenience also influences food choices because foods that are right in front of us are more likely to be eaten! Let's say you have a long walk back to your dorm building after your last class of the day. On the way, you pass a food stand selling slices of pizza. They look and smell great, you're hungry, and you buy one. Or consider coffee: Decades ago, the most convenient way to get a cup of coffee was to brew it yourself. Americans today are more likely to get their java from one of the 17,000 coffee shops, carts, and kiosks across the United States.[11] And pizza and coffee are just two examples of a broad trend: In the 1970s, Americans spent about 25 percent of their total household food budget on eating out. Compare that with almost 45 percent today.[12]

Cartoon characters are often used to advertise products to children.

Habits and Emotions Influence Not Only What You Eat but Also When You Eat

Many people start their day with a bowl of cereal and a glass of orange juice. In fact, ready-to-eat cereals are the number-one breakfast food choice among Americans, and citrus juice is the top juice choice for most people in the morning.[13] Why? For many, the only answer is habit.

Your daily routine and habits can dictate not only what you eat but also *when* you eat. When you get home from work or school, do you head straight for the refrigerator, whether or not you're hungry? Do you always snack when you watch television at night? Or when you're studying?

Emotions also influence your food choices. Do you remember Elizabeth, from the opening of this concept? Filled with anxiety the night before her big exam, she ate her way through a family-sized bag of potato chips. Does this sound familiar? When the going gets tough, the tough often eat. Many people use food as an emotional crutch during times of stress, sadness, or disappointment.

Happiness can also trigger eating. Many people celebrate their end-of-term good grades or a promotion at work with a special meal with friends or family. On vacation, you likely reward yourself with fun, relaxation, and, of course, good food. No matter your mood, food is often part of how you express your emotions.

The Take-Home Message **Food provides the nutrients your body needs to function, and the foods that you choose are influenced by many factors. Taste is the primary reason certain foods become your favorites. The availability of certain foods has made them a part of your culture and daily habits. Advertising, food trends, cost, limits on your time, convenience, habits, and emotions also influence your food choices.**

While brown rice is a healthy whole-grain addition to any meal, it takes close to an hour to cook. For time-strapped consumers, food manufacturers have developed instant brown rice that cooks in 10 minutes, as well as a precooked, microwavable variety that reheats in less than 2 minutes.

Your Food Choices Differ from Those of Past Generations

Times have changed and so have food choices. Your great-grandparents probably never went into a market looking for foods high in calcium, omega-3 fatty acids, or phytochemicals. But as nutrition research continues to discover links between what we eat and how we feel, this science is translated into dietary advice, and even into new food products and choices. Many of the foods available to you were not available to past generations. Think about it: Did your grandparents' parents drink yogurt smoothies or eat whole-wheat pasta? Such products reflect our contemporary understanding of the role nutrition plays in keeping us healthy, now and in the future.

Nutrition Science Has Begun to Significantly Influence Our Food Choices

Today we might say that "You are what you eat" summarizes our beliefs about the role nutrition plays in your health. But for people living in the early decades of the

Being overweight and eating high-fat diets contribute to several of the leading diseases among Americans.

twentieth century, the role of nutrition in health could be more appropriately summarized as "You are what you *don't* eat." That is, people were concerned about health problems created by nutrient *deficiencies*. For instance, for centuries a crippling and sometimes fatal bone disease called *rickets* afflicted infants and children worldwide. Then, through a variety of experiments in the first three decades of the twentieth century, scientists concluded that the miracle ingredient in cod liver oil that prevents rickets is vitamin D. Around that time, researchers discovered that a deficiency of a previously unknown vitamin, which they named thiamin, prompted the disease *beriberi*, which causes muscle wasting and nerve damage. A Nobel Prize in Medicine was even handed out for discovering the role vitamin B_{12} plays in treating a certain type of anemia. In other words, as the role of nutrient deficiencies in certain diseases came to be understood, our diet became our medicine.

As the century progressed, Uncle Sam put the new nutrition research into action. Laws were passed requiring the enrichment of refined grain products with several vitamins, including thiamin, and the mineral iron. The milkman began delivering milk that had been fortified with vitamin D. Salt was enriched with iodine. And the infamous RDA's (Recommended Dietary Allowances, now called Dietary Reference Intakes) were developed and became the gold standard for nutritional guidance.

Now fast forward to later in the century, when your parents were told that nutrient deficiencies were less of a problem and disease prevention was the name of the game. Beriberi sounded more like a rock group than a disease they had to worry about. Burgers morphed into Whopper-sized portions. Microwave ovens gave a new meaning to the words *convenience food*. Ben teamed up with Jerry.

A **cheeseburger** at a restaurant today is almost twice as big as it was 20 years ago!

Unfortunately, Americans were celebrating with diets too high in saturated fat and dietary cholesterol, a recipe tailor-made for America's number-one killer, heart disease. The numbers on the bathroom scale were going in one direction, *up*, and our blood pressure was following. Our bones were hungry for calcium and vitamin D, not to prevent childhood rickets but to ward off our grandparent's osteoporosis, a disease of weak, porous bones that break easily. A wealth of research was uncovering evidence that a healthful diet can be a powerful weapon against heart disease, certain cancers, a condition of high blood sugar called type 2 diabetes, strokes, and osteoporosis—the leading diseases among Americans.

So Uncle Sam stepped in again. This time, federal nutrition experts stacked the basic food groups recommendations into a pyramid shape to help us stack the odds of a healthy diet on our side. The contents of packaged foods became less of a mystery, thanks to new food labeling laws. The B vitamin folate was added to foods to fight certain birth defects. Olive oil and soy became savvy, and everyone in Hollywood wanted to wear milk mustaches. Fortunately, vitamin D–fortified milk tastes better than cod liver oil. Once again, our diet was our medicine.

Enter the twenty-first century and this class on nutrition. Hopefully, what you discover will influence your own food choices, because a more nourishing diet will empower you with increased control over your health. Throughout this text the message will be continually reinforced, that you are what you eat—which by the way, is true!

Turning Nutrition Knowledge into Action One Bite at a Time

As with any college course you take, you won't master the entire contents of a nutrition course on the first day or even in the first month of classes. Each class builds upon the next, so that by the end of the term you are empowered with knowledge that will affect your reasoning, judgment, and decision making about the foods you choose to eat.

As you learn more about the powerful role nutrition plays in your health, you can slowly make gradual adjustments in your food choices. While no one food choice or change will likely make a major impact on your health, many small adjustments in your diet can. Each concept in this book goes beyond providing accurate nutrition information by providing practical strategies and tips that will encourage you to eat your way to better health—one bite at a time.

The Take-Home Message **Nutrition knowledge has increased tremendously over the last century and has greatly influenced America's food choices. Concerns about nutrition and health have shifted from the prevention of deficiency diseases, such as rickets and beriberi, to the prevention of chronic diseases, such as heart disease and type 2 diabetes.**

Check out these recipes and more suggestions at **www.pearsonhighered.com/blake**

UCook

Fluffy Lemon Pie

Eating well doesn't mean you need to skimp on occasional delicious treats! Check out our website for this divine pie recipe – it will turn you into a believer!

UDo

Small Steps, Big Gains

In the life of a busy student, it may seem impossible to make dramatic changes in your lifestyle without feeling overwhelmed. The good news is that you don't need to make drastic changes to reap big health benefits. Taking small steps can produce BIG gains. Visit our website to learn how to begin.

The Top Five Points to Remember

1. There are six categories of nutrients: carbohydrates, lipids (fats), proteins, vitamins, minerals, and water. Your body needs a mixture of these nutrients in specific amounts to stay healthy.
2. In addition to nutrients, foods provide nonnutritive compounds, such as phytochemicals, substances in plant-based foods that may play a role in helping you fight chronic diseases.
3. Food choices are influenced by personal taste, culture, social life, advertising, accessibility, and time constraints. You eat out of habit, in response to your emotions, and, of course, because food is delicious.
4. Nutrition knowledge has increased tremendously over the last century and has greatly influenced America's food choices. Concerns about nutrition and health have shifted from the prevention of deficiency diseases, such as rickets and beriberi, to the prevention of chronic diseases, such as heart disease and type 2 diabetes.
5. Small changes to your diet, made over time, can have a positive impact on your long-term health.

Test Yourself

1. Which of the following are nutrients?
   a. phytochemicals
   b. carbohydrates
   c. kilocalories
   d. all of the above
2. Which of the following can influence your food choices?
   a. your ethnic background
   b. your busy schedule
   c. your emotions
   d. all of the above
3. A culture's cuisine is most greatly influenced by its
   a. wealth.
   b. environment.
   c. population density.
   d. level of education.

4. At the beginning of the twentieth century, Americans
   a. understood that vitamin D prevents a bone disease called rickets.
   b. understood that thiamin prevents a muscle and nerve disease called beriberi.
   c. understood that taking cod liver oil can prevent a bone disease called rickets.
   d. began fortifying foods with folic acid to prevent certain birth defects.
5. In changing your food choices to improve your health, the most sensible way to start is
   a. to make several minor adjustments to your diet gradually.
   b. to become a vegetarian.
   c. to eliminate all sweets from your diet.
   d. to eliminate all fats from your diet.

Answers

1. (b) Carbohydrates are one of six classes of nutrients. Phytochemicals are nonnutritive compounds found in plant foods and thought to assist in protecting us from chronic disease. Kilocalories are the units used for measuring the energy in foods.
2. (d) Your food choices are influenced by many factors, including your ethnic background, the limited time you may have to devote to food preparation, and your emotions.
3. (b) While any of the four factors listed can influence a culture's cuisine, the greatest influence is exerted by its environment.
4. (c) At the beginning of the twentieth century, Americans knew only that consuming cod liver oil somehow prevents rickets. They did not understand what precise nutrient is involved in preventing rickets, beriberi, or certain birth defects.
5. (a) The best way to begin improving your nutrition is to make several minor adjustments to your diet gradually. It's not necessary to become a vegetarian or to eliminate all sweets or fats from your diet. In fact, even if it were possible to consume a totally sugar- and/or fat-free diet, it wouldn't be healthy!

Web Resources

- For more on the history of the Food and Drug Administration (FDA), visit: www.fda.gov/oc/history/resourceguide/default.htm
- Visit the FDA's Centennial Events (1906 to 2006) in protecting and promoting public health at: www.fda.gov/centennial/default.htm
- For an overview of good nutrition, visit the Centers for Disease Control and Prevention's (CDC's) Nutrition for Everyone at: http://cdc.gov/nccdphp/dnpa/nutrition/nutrition_for_everyone/index.htm

2

What Is Nutrition?

1. Heart disease is the leading cause of **death** in the United States. **T/F**

2. **Nutritional genomics** studies how to manipulate plant and animal genes to produce better quality foods. **T/F**

3. Carbohydrates, vitamins, and fat all provide you with **energy.** **T/F**

4. **Water** is a nutrient. **T/F**

5. As long as you take a **vitamin pill,** you don't have to worry about eating healthy foods. **T/F**

David is a big guy with a big appetite. A typical day starts with a cheese omelet and toast for breakfast, a super-size fast-food meal for lunch, and extra helpings at dinner—not to mention between-meal candy bars, chips, and sodas. Throughout high school, he kept his weight under control playing basketball, but now that he's commuting to technical school and working in his dad's auto-parts store, he rarely even gets together with friends for a pick-up game. So it's not surprising that, since school started, he's gained over 10 pounds.

Over dinner one night, his mother expresses concern. A native Hawaiian, she's struggled with obesity ever since moving to the mainland as a teen, and she doesn't want to see David develop the same problems she's dealing with: high blood pressure, high blood sugar, and shortness of breath. "Why don't you stop by the recreation center before you start your homework tonight?" she suggests. "Maybe there's a league you can join for the winter."

"I don't have time for that stuff anymore," David answers. "But don't worry. I'm healthy, and I can control my weight. I just have to stop eating so much of your home cooking!"

Should David be concerned about his weight? What about his diet, lack of physical activity, or genetics? What role do these things play in promoting or reducing our health? In this concept, you'll find out why nutrition is so important to your health, and how it interacts with physical activity, genetics, and other factors to influence your risk for disease. We'll also describe the essential nutrients introduced in Concept 1 and discuss the best way for you to get a healthy level of nutrients every day.

Answers

1. True. Heart disease is the leading cause of death among Americans. The good news is that your diet can play an important role in preventing it. For more information, turn to page 4.
2. False. Nutritional genomics studies how the foods we eat influence the functioning of our genes. Turn to page 5 for details.
3. False. Carbohydrates and fat provide energy, but vitamins are not an energy source. They do play important roles in helping your body use both carbohydrates and fat. To find out more, turn to page 6.
4. True. Water is absolutely essential to survival. Check it out on page 7.
5. False. A supplement can augment a healthy diet, but it can't replace it. To find out why, turn to page 8.

What Is Nutrition and Why Is Good Nutrition So Important?

Whereas food is the source of the nutrients your body needs, **nutrition** is about more than just food. Nutrition is the science of how the nutrients and compounds in foods nourish you, help you function, and affect your health. In Concept 1, you learned that nutrition knowledge has an important influence on our food choices. So let's start increasing that nutrition knowledge by taking a closer look at the relationship between nutrition and health.

Health Is More Than the Absence of Disease

Would you describe yourself as healthy? If you're like many people, you would, even though you sometimes experience illnesses—a cold, a headache, an upset stomach—that make you feel bad. Health isn't the total absence of all disease. In fact, some people who live with a challenge such as blindness or paralysis would describe themselves as healthy because they are happy, free from pain, have energy and vitality, and are able to function well in society, accomplishing the daily tasks they set for themselves. So what does it mean to be healthy? According to the World Health Organization, "**Health** is a state of complete physical, mental and social well-being, and not merely the absence of disease or infirmity."[1] Sounds great, but how do we get there?

nutrition The science that studies how the nutrients and compounds in foods nourish and affect body functions and health.

health A state of complete physical, mental, and social well-being; not merely the absence of disease or infirmity.

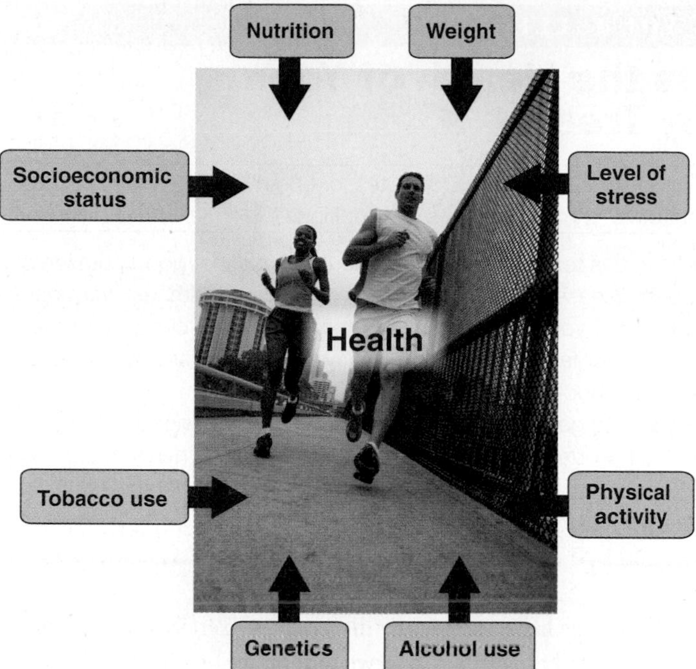

Figure 2.1 Factors Influencing Health
Although the major factors influencing any one person's health can vary, the factors shown above are among the most significant throughout a population.

Many factors are widely acknowledged to influence health (Figure 2.1), such as:

- Nutrition. You'll learn about the link between good nutrition and good health throughout this book.
- Level of physical activity. Regular physical activity contributes significantly to your health. We'll discuss this topic in depth in Concept 25.
- Weight. Both underweight and obesity increase your risk of disease, and both are associated with a decreased life expectancy.[2] More on this in Concept 20.
- Tobacco use. A history of smoking, chewing tobacco, or exposure to tobacco smoke increases your risk for chronic diseases, including heart disease, stroke, and cancer. We'll explore these links in Concepts 12, 17, and 24.
- Alcohol use. Both chronic alcohol abuse and binge drinking are risk factors for traumatic injury, accidental death, and chronic diseases, such as certain types of cancer and liver disease. For more information, see Concept 19.
- Level of stress. Chronic stress, especially job strain, is a major risk factor for ill health.[3]
- Socioeconomic status. Low income and social status can be a predictor of health problems, partly because of the chronic stress that financial problems can create, and the potential for people to use food, alcohol, and tobacco to cope with this stress.[4]
- Genetics. Your genetic inheritance—that is, the genes you inherited from your parents—influences the way your body uses food, your tendency to gain or lose weight, and the relationship between certain substances in foods and your overall health. We'll talk more about this shortly, but before reading on, Rate Yourself to find out the health of your family tree!

The prevalence of people who are food insecure—those who lack enough food to eat daily—has risen to 11 percent of Americans.

Now that you've learned about the main factors that influence your health, which do you think David, the student in our opening story, might want to consider?

RATE YOURSELF 

How Is the Health of Your Family Tree?

Is there a history of heart disease, diabetes, or obesity in your family?	**Yes** ☐	**No** ☐
What about other chronic diseases or conditions?	**Yes** ☐	**No** ☐

Before you read this textbook and learn about the role that good nutrition plays in preventing chronic diseases and maintaining overall good health, ask your parents and grandparents about your family's health history. If there are certain diseases or conditions that run in your family, you'll want to pay particular attention to these as you read about them in this book.

An easy way to gather information about your family's health history is by visiting My Family Health Portrait at: http://familyhistory.hhs.gov. When you enter in your family medical history, it provides a family tree report. Save a copy of this family health history for future reference.

How do you think his heart-unhealthy diet, lack of exercise, and recent weight gain, coupled with his family history of overweight, might be affecting his overall health?

Good Nutrition Contributes to Health

Why does good nutrition contribute to good health? First, your body needs adequate amounts of all the nutrients to function properly. A chronic lack of even one nutrient will impact your body's ability to function in the short term. For instance, a deficiency of iron can make you feel weak, tired, and short of breath and increases your susceptibility to infection. Chronic deficiencies, excesses, and imbalances of many nutrients can also affect your long-term health: As we just noted, both underweight and obesity decrease life expectancy.

Good nutrition plays a role in reducing the risk of four of the top 10 leading causes of death in the United States, including the top three—heart disease, cancer, and stroke—as well as diabetes (Table 2.1). Good nutrition also plays an important role in preventing other diseases and conditions that can reduce your quality of life. For instance, a healthy diet can help keep bones strong and reduce your risk of osteoporosis, a condition characterized by poor bone density and an increased risk of

Table 2.1

Leading Causes of Death in the United States

Disease/Cause of Death	Nutrition-Related	Other
1. **Heart Disease**	X	
2. **Cancer**	X	
3 **Stroke**	X	
4. Respiratory Diseases		X
5. Accidents		X
6. **Diabetes**	X	
7. Influenza/Pneumonia		X
8. Alzheimer's Disease		X
9. Kidney Disease		X
10. Blood Poisoning		X

Data from: Centers for Disease Control and Prevention, "Leading Causes of Death in the United States," 2006, www.cdc.gov/nchs/fastats/lcod.htm.

fracture. Eating right will also help you better manage your body weight, which in turn will reduce your risk of developing obesity, diabetes, and high blood pressure.

Nutritional Genomics Studies the Relationship between Diet and Genes

In the early years of the twenty-first century, nutrition research increasingly began to uncover links between what we eat and our personal health. One exciting area of new research is **nutritional genomics.** Genomics is the study of genes, their functions in your body, and how the environment may influence *gene expression*. Gene expression is the processing of genetic information to create a specific protein. Your genes determine your inherited, specific traits, such as the color of your hair or the relative thickness of the bones of your skeleton. Nutritional genomics was given a boost in 2000 by the completion of the **Human Genome Project,** which established the complete set and sequencing of **deoxyribonucleic acid (DNA)** in human cells. DNA is the substance of which genes are made. It contains the instructions that cells use to build proteins that compose and direct the activities of your body.

Nutritional genomics is concerned with how components in the foods you eat interact on a cellular level with the expression of your genes. Certain dietary components can influence different people's genes in different ways, creating specific responses in your body that are unlike those in another person. For example, one combination of a variety of dietary fats might lower your risk of heart disease because of your unique genetic makeup, whereas a different combination lowers the risk of heart disease in someone else. Nutritional genomics can help determine the recommended combination of types of fats for different people, based on an analysis of each person's genetic makeup.[5] As more becomes known about the application of nutritional genomics, you will have more control over how your diet affects your long-term health. We'll discuss nutritional genomics more in Concept 13.

The Take-Home Message Nutrition is the scientific study of how the nutrients and compounds in foods nourish your body. Good nutrition plays a role in reducing the risk of many chronic diseases and conditions. Other factors contributing to health are physical activity, weight, the use of tobacco and alcohol, stress level, socioeconomic status, and genetics. Long-term imbalances of many nutrients will affect your health. Nutritional genomics is the study of how specific dietary components affect the expression of your genes and your health.

What Are the Essential Nutrients and Why Do You Need Them?

As noted in Concept 1, you are a product of what you eat, what you *don't* eat, and what you may eat *too much* of. You want to eat the best combination of a variety of foods to meet your nutritional needs and to be healthy. To do that, you need to understand the roles of the essential nutrients in your body, and which foods to eat to

nutritional genomics The field of study that researches the relationship between nutrition and genomics (the study of genes and gene expression).

Human Genome Project The project sponsored by the United States government to determine the complete set and sequencing of DNA in the body's cells and identify all human genes.

deoxyribonucleic acid (DNA) Genetic material within cells that develops the synthesis of proteins in the body and directs bodily activities.

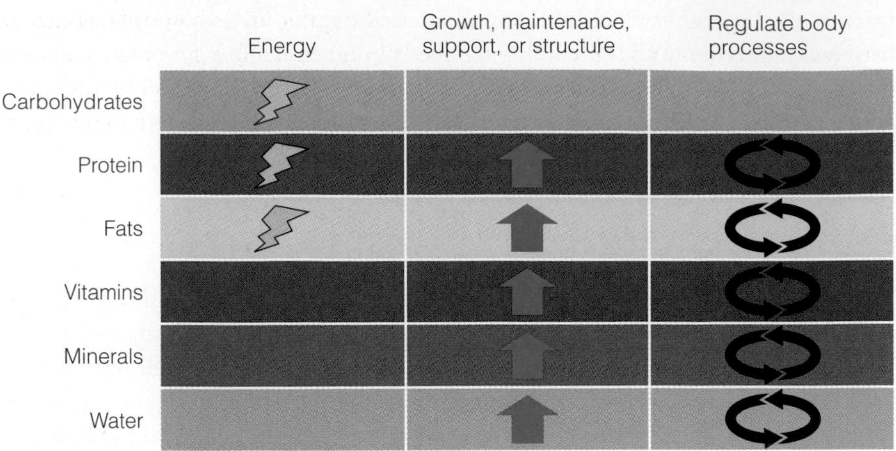

Figure 2.2 Nutrients and Their Functions
Nutrients work closely together to provide energy, structure, and support and to regulate body processes.

get them. The classes of nutrients we introduced in Concept 1—which include carbohydrates, lipids, proteins, vitamins, minerals, and water—are all *essential* because you must have them to function. (Alcohol, in contrast, is not an essential nutrient; although it provides energy in the form of kilocalories, your body does not need it to function.)

Carbohydrates, lipids (fats), and proteins are called **macronutrients,** because you need higher amounts of them in your diet. Vitamins and minerals, although equally important to your health, are considered **micronutrients** because you need them in smaller amounts. You need to consume the final nutrient, water, in generous amounts daily, to keep well hydrated.

Kilocalories (more commonly called *calories*, which is the term we will use throughout this book) from the macronutrients are used as energy during the process of metabolism, and many vitamins and minerals are essential to this process. Vitamins and minerals are also needed for growth and reproduction and to help repair and maintain your body (Figure 2.2), though they do not provide energy.

Although each nutrient is unique, they are all equally important, as they work together in numerous ways to keep you healthy. An imbalance of just one will affect your health. Let's take a closer look at the macro- and micronutrients, as well as water.

Carbohydrates, Fats, and Proteins Provide Energy

Carbohydrates, fats (lipids), and proteins are the energy-providing nutrients, because they contain calories. When we talk about energy, we mean that your body breaks down these nutrients and "burns" them to fuel your activities and internal functioning. The energy in food is measured in calories. One calorie equals the amount of energy needed to raise the temperature of 1 kilogram (a liter) of water 1 degree Celsius. Carbohydrates and protein provide 4 calories per gram, and fats provide 9 calories per gram. The number of calories in a given food can be determined by measuring the weight, in grams, of each of the three nutrients in one serving of the food.

Carbohydrates supply the simple sugar, called glucose, that your cells use as the major energy source to fuel your body. Most of your daily calories should come from carbohydrates. Fats are another major fuel source. They also help cushion your organs to prevent damage and act as insulation under your skin to help maintain your body temperature. Proteins can be used as energy, but they are better used

macronutrients The energy-containing essential nutrients that you need in higher amounts: carbohydrates, lipids (fats), and proteins.

micronutrients The essential nutrients you need in smaller amounts: vitamins and minerals.

to build and maintain your tissues, muscles, and organs. You also need protein to make most enzymes and some hormones, to help transport other nutrients, and to maintain a healthy immune system. A healthy diet should provide adequate amounts of carbohydrates and fats for energy, as well as enough protein to maintain and repair your body. You must consume a healthy combination of all three macronutrients, so that excesses, deficiencies, and imbalances don't occur, increasing your risk of chronic disease.

Vitamins and Minerals Are Essential for Metabolism

You need vitamins and minerals in order to use carbohydrates, fats, and proteins and to sustain various chemical reactions. A deficiency of vitamins and minerals can cause side effects, including fatigue, stunted growth, weak bones, and organ damage.

Many vitamins and minerals aid *enzymes,* which are substances that speed up reactions in your body. For example, many of the B vitamins help enzymes speed up digestion of carbohydrates and fats. Some minerals, such as calcium and phosphorus, assist reactions that help maintain and strengthen your teeth and bones. The role of carbohydrates, proteins, and fats in your body depends upon your consuming enough vitamins and minerals in your daily diet.

Vitamins are **organic** compounds; that is, they contain the substance carbon. Your body is able to make some vitamins, such as vitamin D, but most need to be acquired from food.

Minerals are **inorganic** substances; that is, they don't contain carbon. Minerals play a role in many body processes and are key to the structure of some tissues, such as bone. A deficiency of any of the minerals can cause disease symptoms. Anyone who has ever suffered from iron-deficiency anemia can tell you that falling short of your daily iron needs, as just one example, can cause fatigue and interfere with your ability to function.

Water Is Vital for Many Processes in Your Body

Staying hydrated is an important part of staying healthy, since water is vital to key body functions. As part of the fluid medium inside your cells, water helps chemical reactions take place. Water also bathes the outside of your cells, playing a key role in transporting vital nutrients and oxygen to, and removing waste products from, your cells. Water helps maintain your body temperature and acts as a lubricant for your joints, eyes, mouth, and intestinal tract. It surrounds your organs and cushions them from injury.

The Take-Home Message **Your body needs carbohydrates, fats (lipids), proteins, vitamins, minerals, and water to survive. These six classes of nutrients have numerous roles in your body, which you need in specific amounts for good health. Carbohydrates, fats, and proteins provide energy, while vitamins, minerals, and water are needed to use these energy-producing nutrients and to maintain good health. Water is part of the medium inside and outside your cells that carries nutrients to, and waste products from, your cells. Water also helps maintain your body temperature and acts as a lubricant and protective cushion for your organs.**

organic A characteristic of compounds that contain carbon.

inorganic A characteristic of compounds that do not contain carbon and are not formed by living things. Inorganic compounds include minerals, water, and salts.

How Should You Get These Important Nutrients?

There is no question that you need all six classes of nutrients to function properly. But is there an advantage to consuming them through food, rather than taking them as supplements? Is there more to a healthy diet than just meeting your basic nutrient needs? Let's look at these questions in more detail.

The Best Way to Meet Your Nutrient Needs Is with a Well-Balanced Diet

Many foods provide a variety of nutrients. For example, low-fat milk is high in carbohydrates and protein and provides a small amount of fat. It's also a good source of the vitamins A, D, and riboflavin, as well as the minerals potassium and calcium, and it is approximately 90 percent water by weight. While milk contains a substantial variety of all six classes of nutrients, any single food item doesn't need to provide all the nutrients to be good for you. Rather, a well-balanced diet from a variety of foods can provide you with all of these important nutrients over the course of a day (Figure 2.3).

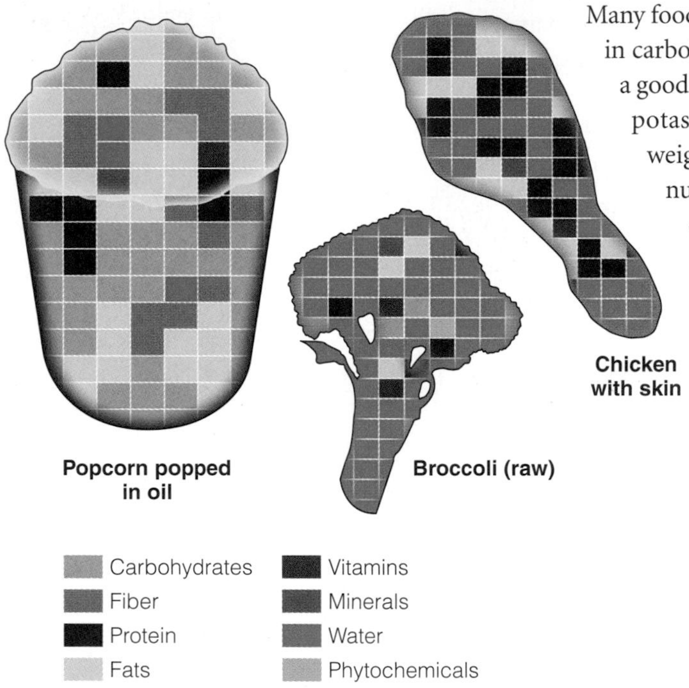

Popcorn popped in oil

Broccoli (raw)

Chicken with skin

Carbohydrates
Fiber
Protein
Fats
Vitamins
Minerals
Water
Phytochemicals

Figure 2.3 Nutrients in Foods
Foods provide more than calories. In addition to nutrients, such as carbohydrates, vitamins, and minerals, they contain beneficial nonnutritive compounds, such as phytochemicals.

A well-balanced diet also provides dietary compounds, such as phytochemicals and **fiber,** that have been shown to help fight many diseases. At least 900 different phytochemicals have been identified in plant-based foods and more are likely to be discovered. Don't assume, however, that these compounds can be extracted from the foods, put in a pill, and still produce the same positive effect on your health. The disease-fighting properties of phytochemicals most likely go beyond the compounds themselves, working with fiber, nutrients, or unknown substances in foods to provide a combined, positive effect on your health.

Fiber is the portion of plant foods that isn't digested in the small intestine. Some foods, such as whole grains, fruits, and vegetables, that are high in fiber are also phytochemical powerhouses. Studies have shown that diets rich in these foods fight disease.

Also, let's not forget some of the other obvious benefits of getting your nutrients from food. The delicious texture and aroma of foods coupled with the social pleasure of sharing meals are lost when you pop a pill to meet your nutrient needs. However, there are some individuals who *should* take a supplement if food alone can't meet their needs.

You Can Meet Some Nutrient Needs with a Supplement

Although many people can get all their nutrients through their diet, others have dietary restrictions or higher nutrient needs such that they would benefit from taking a supplement along with eating a healthy diet. For example, someone who is lactose intolerant (has difficulty digesting milk products) may have to meet his or her calcium needs with other sources, such as a calcium supplement. Pregnant women

fiber The portion of plant foods that isn't digested in the small intestine.

should take an iron supplement, because their increased need for this mineral is unlikely to be met through diet alone. As you can see, a well-balanced diet and dietary supplements aren't mutually exclusive. In some situations, they should be combined as the best nutritional strategy for good health.

Even with an abundance of foods and the availability of supplements for those who need them, the diets of Americans aren't as healthy as they could be. Let's find out why this is the case.

The Take-Home Message A well-balanced diet will likely meet all of your nutrient needs and will provide a variety of compounds that may help prevent chronic diseases. People who cannot meet their nutrient needs through food alone may benefit from taking a supplement.

The incidence of overweight and obesity among adults and children is rising in the United States.

How Does the Average American Diet Stack Up?

Most Americans are exceeding their needs for total calories, as well as for two nutrients, saturated fat and sodium. Too much saturated fat in the diet is associated with heart disease, and excessive dietary sodium plays a role in high blood pressure, increasing the risk of having a heart attack or a stroke. At the same time, Americans are failing to meet their needs for other nutrients that are important to health, such as vitamin E, calcium, and fiber.[6] As people take in more calories than they need and burn fewer calories because of sedentary lifestyles, they create a recipe for poor health.

Overweight and Obesity Are on the Rise?

Americans have been battling the bathroom scale for decades, and the scale is winning: Both **overweight** and **obesity** have become epidemic in the United States (Figure 2.4). Over 65 percent of American adults and 15 percent of children age 6 to 19 are overweight.[7] Along with the weight gain have come higher rates of type 2 diabetes, especially among children, and increased rates of heart disease, cancer, and stroke. Ironically, being overweight doesn't mean being well nourished. In fact, many of the poorest Americans are obese and malnourished. The box feature "Poor, Obese, and Malnourished: A Troubling Paradox" addresses this astonishing phenomenon.

The prevalence of **obesity** among Americans has more than doubled since the late 1970s.

Improving Americans' Diets Is One Goal of *Healthy People 2010*

Since 1979, the U.S. surgeon general has been issuing calls for a nationwide health improvement program. The current edition of this report is ***Healthy People 2010,*** which contains a set of health objectives for the nation to achieve by 2010. The next edition, *Healthy People 2020,* released in 2010, will continue to improve upon the nation's health by focusing on critical public health issues (check the Companion Website for the most up-to-date information).

overweight Carrying extra weight on your body in relation to your height. (See Concepts 20 and 21 for the clinically defined weight range.)

obesity Carrying an excessive amount of body fat above the level of being overweight. (See Concepts 20 and 21 for the clinically defined level.)

Healthy People 2010 A set of disease prevention and health promotion objectives for Americans to meet during the first decade of the new millennium.

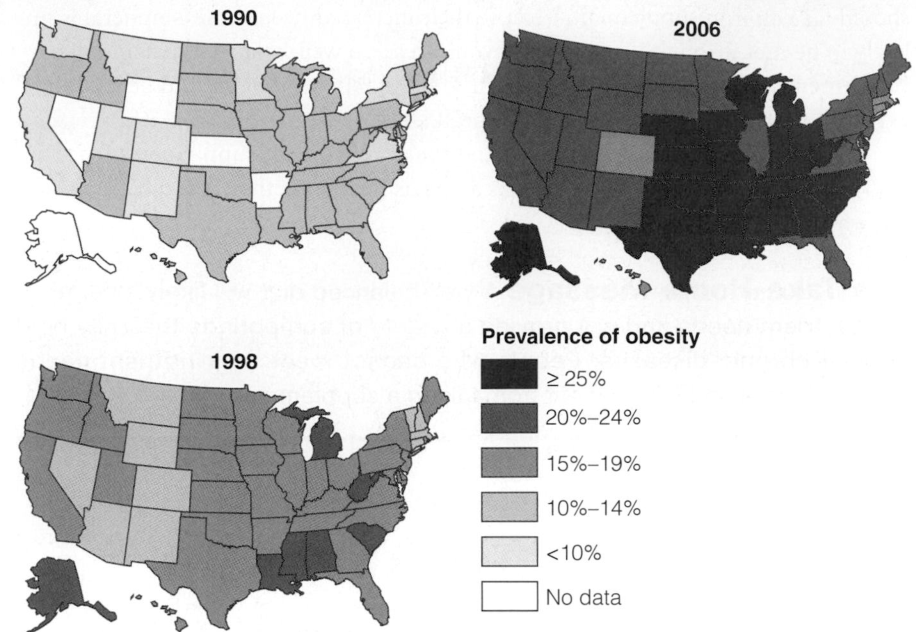

Figure 2.4 Obesity Trends among U.S. Adults
Over the last two decades, rates of obesity have risen significantly in the United States, as indicated by these maps.

Data from: Centers for Disease Control and Prevention, "Overweight and Obesity: Obesity Trends," 2006, available at www.cdc.gov/nccdphp/dnpa/obesity/trend/maps/index.htm.

Healthy People 2010 focuses on two broad goals: (1) to help all Americans increase their life expectancy and improve their quality of life and (2) to eliminate health disparities among different segments of the population. There are 28 areas of focus in *Healthy People 2010*, ranging from ensuring that Americans have adequate access to medical care to making improvements in their diets and physical activity. Objectives have been developed within each focus area.

For example, "Nutrition and Overweight" is one focus area; its goal is to promote good health and reduce the chronic diseases associated with poor diet and overweight. There are numerous objectives within this focus area that, if fulfilled, will help Americans improve their diets and reduce their weight. See Table 2.2 for the list of objectives in this focus area.

As you can see from Table 2.2, although the first objective is for 60 percent of Americans to reach a healthy weight by 2010, only 42 percent of Americans met this

Table 2.2

Healthy People 2010 Nutrition and Overweight Objectives

Objectives	Target for Americans (%)	Status of Americans (%)
Increase the proportion of adults who are at a healthy weight	60	42
Reduce the proportion of adults who are obese	15	23
Increase the proportion of persons age 2 years and older who consume at least two daily servings of fruit	75	28
Increase the proportion of persons age 2 years and older who consume at least three daily servings of vegetables, with at least one-third being dark green or deep yellow vegetables	50	3
Increase the proportion of persons age 2 years and older who consume at least six daily servings of grain products, with at least three being whole grains	50	7

Poor, Obese, and Malnourished: A Troubling Paradox

Food costs money, so people who are poor have less money to buy food. Therefore, people who are poor are less likely to be overweight or obese—right? Makes sense, but the conclusion is wrong. In survey after survey, rates of obesity turn out to be highest among people with the lowest incomes. The numbers are greater for women than for men, but for both genders Americans living near or below the poverty level have much higher rates of obesity than affluent Americans.[1] And despite their obesity, these lowest-income Americans are also malnourished. How can this be so?

In 1995, a pediatrician named William Dietz, now considered a leading expert on obesity, published an account of a 7-year-old patient: a girl weighing more than twice her ideal body weight and living in poverty. Dietz entitled his case study "Does Hunger Cause Obesity?" and proposed two possible scenarios where it might:[2]

Poverty doesn't rule out obesity, and obesity doesn't rule out malnutrition. They can, and do, co-exist.

- When a family lacks money, they choose foods that provide them with the greatest number of calories at the lowest cost. These foods tend to be high in fat and sugar and low in nutrients, such as vitamins, minerals, and fiber. Thus, although overfed, individuals on this kind of diet can be significantly malnourished.
- When a person experiences hunger, the body adapts by slowing energy expenditure and "hoarding" calories: In other words, episodes of food shortages might cause increased body fat.

More recently, Angie Tagtow, head of the Hunger and Environmental Nutrition group, identified another possible link among hunger, malnutrition, and obesity: the family's living environment.[3] Economics influences not only what a family can afford to buy but also where they can afford to live, and this affects their proximity to quality food stores and farmers' markets versus fast-food restaurants and convenience stores. Economics also affects access to transportation, social services, and nutrition education and assistance.

Adam Drewnowski, director of the Center for Public Health Nutrition of the University of Washington, adds one more factor: the greater palatability of low-cost foods. In other words, chips and cookies tend to satisfy our taste buds more than peppers and pears. He cites laboratory studies suggesting that we're more likely to overeat cheap junk foods, and contends that limited money for food may shift a poor family's purchases toward more palatable foods that fill them up with the maximum calories at the minimum cost.[4]

Drewnowski points out that a low-income family of four gets $104 a week in food assistance, which breaks down to $3.71 per person per day.[5] Think about it: If you had just $3.71 to buy a day's worth of food, how would you spend it? Would you be more concerned with getting the right balance of nutrients or purchasing high-volume, less nutritious foods that keep hunger at bay throughout the day?

objective in 2000, the start of *Healthy People 2010*.[8] Current research suggests that Americans' body weights are increasing rather than decreasing. When it comes to eating adequate amounts of fruits, vegetables, and whole grains, which are all beneficial to managing one's weight, Americans have plenty of room for improvement.

The Take-Home Message **Rates of overweight and obese Americans are increasing, yet many people are falling short of some nutrient needs. *Healthy People 2010* is a set of health objectives for Americans for the first decade of the new millennium. The goals of *Healthy People 2010* are to help Americans increase their life expectancy and improve their quality of life, as well as to eliminate health disparities among different segments of the population. "Nutrition and Overweight" is one focus area of *Healthy People 2010*.**

UCook

Very Veggie Egg Scramble Burrito

Remember David, from our opening story? His daily breakfast of a cheesy omelet is causing him to start his day with a heavy amount of heart-unhealthy cholesterol and saturated fat. If you love omelets but also love your heart, try this great breakfast burrito.

UDo

Eat Well—for Less!

Eating healthfully doesn't have to drain your wallet. To learn how, visit the link on the Companion Website.

The Top Five Points to Remember

1. There are six categories of nutrients: carbohydrates, lipids (fats), proteins, vitamins, minerals, and water. Your body needs a mixture of these nutrients in specific amounts to stay healthy. Carbohydrates, fats, and proteins provide the energy that your body needs. The majority of your daily calories should come from carbohydrates. You also need adequate amounts of fats and proteins. Most of the proteins you eat should be used to build and maintain your body tissues, muscles, and organs, rather than for energy.
2. Vitamins and minerals are important for metabolism and the proper use of carbohydrates, fats, and proteins. Many vitamins aid enzymes in your body. Water is an essential nutrient that is vital for many functions. It bathes the inside and outside of your cells, helps maintain your body temperature, and acts as a lubricant and protective cushion for your organs.
3. Health is a state of complete physical, mental, and social well-being. Nutrition plays an important role in promoting health and preventing many of the leading causes of death in the United States, including heart disease, cancer, stroke, and a certain type of diabetes.
4. Nutrition is a science, and new discoveries are continually made. Nutritional genomics is the integration of nutrition and genomics. Genomics is the study of genes, their functions in your body, and how the environment, including the foods and nutrients you eat, influences the expression of your genes and thus your health.
5. Eating a well-balanced diet is the best way to meet your nutrient and health needs. Vitamin and mineral supplements can help complete a healthy diet but should not replace foods.

Test Yourself

1. Nutrition is
   a. the study of genes, how they function in your body, and how the environment can influence your genes.
   b. the study of how your body functions.
   c. the scientific study of how nutrients and compounds in the foods you eat nourish and affect your body functions and health.
   d. the study of hormones and how they function in your body.
2. The majority of your daily calories should come from
   a. fats.
   b. carbohydrates.
   c. vitamins and minerals.
   d. water.
3. Which nutrients may help enzymes function in your body?
   a. carbohydrates
   b. vitamins
   c. minerals
   d. both b and c
4. Health is
   a. the absence of disease.
   b. the absence of infirmity.
   c. influenced by good nutrition and regular physical activity.
   d. both a and b.
5. The two broad goals of *Healthy People 2010* are
   a. to help Americans increase their life expectancy and improve their quality of life.
   b. to increase the hours Americans sleep each night.
   c. to eliminate health disparities among different segments of the population.
   d. both a and c.
   e. both a and b.

Answers

1. (c) Nutrition is about how nutrients affect your body and health. The study of genes is called genomics. Physiology is the study of how your body functions. The study of hormones and their function in your body is called endocrinology.
2. (b) The majority of your daily calories should come from carbohydrates. Vitamins, minerals, and water don't provide calories. Fats do contain calories, but fats shouldn't be the main source of energy in your diet.
3. (d) Certain vitamins and minerals may aid enzymes in your body. Carbohydrates don't aid enzymes; instead, these nutrients need enzymes to be properly metabolized.
4. (c) Both good nutrition and regular physical activity increase the likelihood that we will enjoy good health. Recall that the World Health Organization defines health as a state of complete physical, mental, and social well-being and not merely the absence of disease or infirmity.
5. (d) The two broad goals are increasing life expectancy and quality of life and reducing health disparities among groups of Americans. Increasing the amount of hours Americans sleep isn't a goal of *Healthy People 2010*.

Web Resources

- For more on the World Health Organization, visit: www.who.int/en
- For more on obesity in America, visit: www.obesityinamerica.org/geographic.html

3 Nutrition Claims

Sorting Fact from Fiction

1. The **scientific method** is the process scientists use to design experiments. **T/F**

2. Epidemiology is the study of **epidemics.** **T/F**

3. Nutrition **information** reported by national news organizations may not be reliable. **T/F**

4. You can get good nutrition advice from anyone who is called a **nutritionist.** **T/F**

5. Nutrition information found on the **Internet** is bogus. **T/F**

Jimmy, a star performer on his high school football team, is determined to make the team at college. To be competitive, he wants to gain muscle mass fast. He scans the Internet and finds lots of sites promoting supplements that can "add muscle quickly" and "guarantee" that their supplements work, with a money-back return policy. Encouraged, Jimmy charges almost $100 worth of supplements to his credit card and awaits his package. Do you think he made a good decision? Is the Internet a reliable source of information about nutrition, weight loss, or general health? What about magazine articles? And if the evening news is supposedly trustworthy, why is the information it reports often so contradictory?

Just ask anyone who is trying to lose weight, for example, about how hard it is to keep up with the latest diet advice. In the 1970s, carbohydrates were considered the biggest culprit in packing on the pounds, and we were told that a protein-rich, low-carbohydrate diet was the name of the weight loss game. A decade later, avoiding fat was considered the key to winning the battle of the bulge. By 2000, carbohydrates had been ousted yet again, with protein-rich diets back in vogue. But now protein-heavy diets seem to be fading, and high-carbohydrate diets are once again touted as the best way to fight weight gain. Are you frustrated yet?

Although dietary advice seems to change with the daily news (although it actually doesn't), this bombardment of nutrition news can be a positive thing. You live in an era when much is known, but more important information is continually uncovered about what you eat and how it affects your body. Like any science, nutrition is not stagnant. Discoveries will continue to be made about the role that diet and foods play in keeping you healthy. Nevertheless, you don't want to base nutrition decisions on information that isn't reliable, or that doesn't apply to you. In this concept, you'll find out how to identify trustworthy sources of nutrition information.

Answers

1. False. Conducting an experiment is one step in the scientific method, which is a process used to generate sound research findings. Check it out on pages 2 and 3.
2. False. Epidemiology is the study of populations; for example, the percentage of vegetarians in the United States. Turn to page 4 for details.
3. True. News organizations typically report on studies that have just been published. These may be the first studies done on a subject, and they can be overturned by later studies. Alternatively, the studies' results can be influenced by researcher bias, design errors, or other problems. To find out how to evaluate nutrition studies in the news, see page 6.
4. False. Anyone can call him- or herself a nutritionist. To find out whose advice you can trust, turn to pages 7 and 8.
5. Not necessarily! There are plenty of websites run by government agencies, universities, and health care organizations that provide accurate, reliable information about nutrition. See page 7 through 10.

consensus The collective opinion of a group of experts based on a body of information.

scientific method A process of experimental steps scientists use to generate sound research findings.

hypothesis An idea scientists generate as a tentative explanation for their observations prior to further study and testing.

What's the Real Deal When It Comes to Nutrition Research?

Even though popular wisdom and trends seem to change with the wind, scientific knowledge about nutrition doesn't change that frequently. While the media publicize results from studies deemed newsworthy, in reality it takes many, many affirming research studies before a **consensus** is reached about nutrition advice. News of the results of one study is just that: news. Headlines in newspapers, lead articles on websites, and the sound bites on television often report the results of a single, recent research study. In contrast, authoritative advice comes from recognized health organizations or committees, such as the American Heart Association or the Dietary Guidelines Committee, and reflects a consensus of expert opinions on the issue. The feature box "Evaluating Media Headlines with a Critical Eye" on page 6 discusses how to scrutinize information about current research findings and not get caught up in media hype.

Sound Nutrition Research Begins with the Scientific Method

Research studies that generate nutrition information are based on a process called the **scientific method.** Scientists are like detectives. They observe something in the natural world, ask questions, come up with an idea (called a **hypothesis**) that might offer an explanation for their observations, and then test their hypothesis with an experiment to see if their findings support it. There are many steps in the scientific method and many adjustments made along the way before scientists can be confident that they have gained enough information to support their hypothesis. In fact, the entire process can take years to complete.

Let's walk through a nutrition-related study in which scientists used the scientific method to study rickets. Recall from Concept 2 that rickets is a potentially severe and even fatal disease in children in which the bones throughout the body weaken. For instance, the spine and ribcage can become so distorted that breathing is impaired, and the leg bones can become so weakened that they are unable to hold up the child's body weight, and they curve outward ("bow legs"). In the nineteenth century, parents often relied on folk remedies to treat diseases; in the case of rickets, they used cod-liver oil because it seemed to prevent the disorder as well as cure it, although no one knew how.

The first step of the scientific method is to make an observation and ask questions. Originally, scientists were piqued by the cod-liver oil curing phenomenon. They asked themselves why cod-liver oil cures rickets (Figure 3.1). In the second step of the scientific method, a hypothesis is formulated. Because cod-liver oil is very rich in vitamin A, scientists initially thought that this vitamin must be the curative factor. To confirm this, scientists proceeded to the next step in the scientific method, conducting an experiment.

The scientists altered the cod-liver oil to destroy all of its vitamin A. The altered oil was given to rats that had been fed a diet that caused rickets. Surprisingly, the rats were still cured of

Nutrition-related research findings are often the lead stories in newspapers and magazines, as well as on websites.

If you Google the word *nutrition,* you will get a list of about 125 million hits in less than a second.
Eighty million American adults surf the Internet daily, looking for health information.

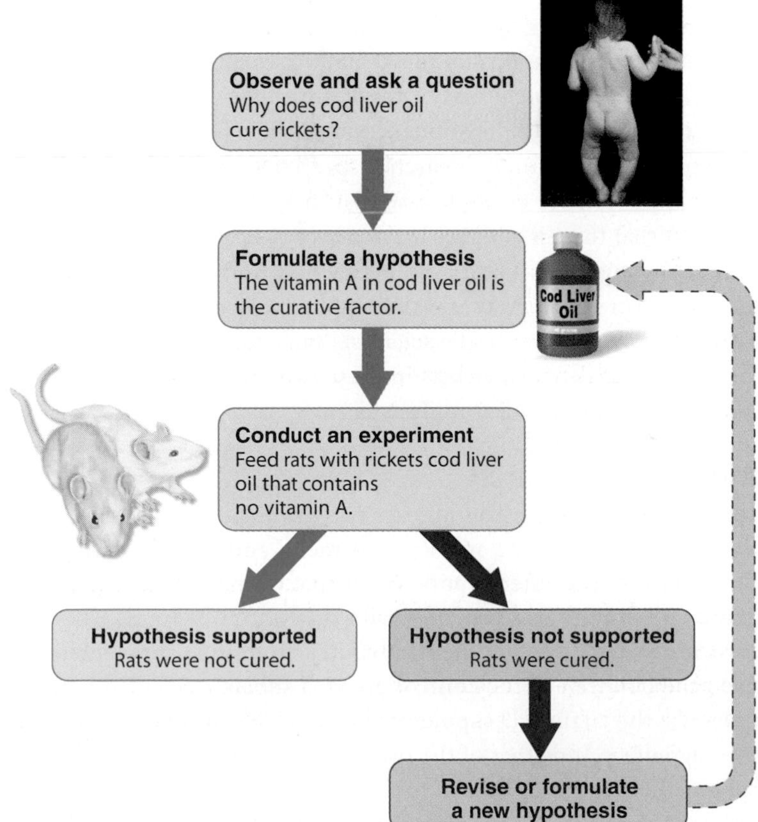

Figure 3.1 Steps of the Scientific Method
The scientific method is used to conduct credible research in nutrition and other scientific fields.

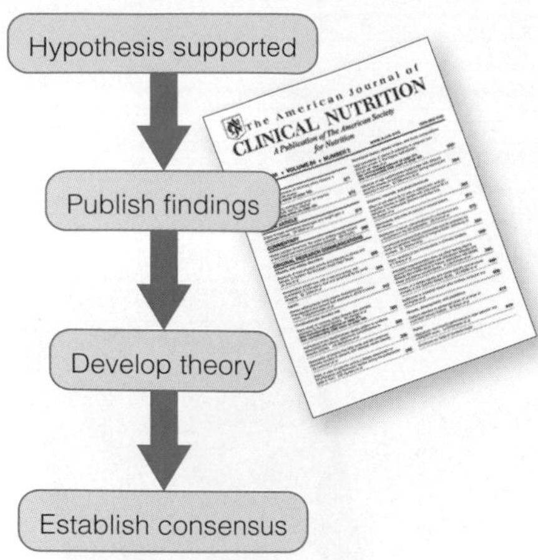

Figure 3.2 A Hypothesis Can Lead to Scientific Consensus
When a hypothesis is supported by research, the results are published in peer-reviewed journals. Once a hypothesis has been supported by several subsequent experiments, a theory can be developed and a consensus can be reached in the scientific community.

rickets. This disproved the scientists' original hypothesis that vitamin A was the curative factor. They then needed to modify their hypothesis, as it was obvious that there was something else in the cod-liver oil that cured rickets. They next hypothesized that it was the vitamin D that cured the rats and conducted another experiment to confirm this hypothesis, which it did.

The next step in the scientific method involves sharing these findings with the scientific community. What good would it be to make this fabulous discovery if other scientists couldn't find out about it? To do this, scientists summarize and submit their research findings to a **peer-reviewed journal** (Figure 3.2). Other scientists (peers) then look at the researchers' findings to make sure that they are sound. If they are, the research study is published in the journal. (If this relationship between vitamin D and rickets had been discovered today, it would probably be the lead story on CNN.)

As more and more studies were done that confirmed that vitamin D can prevent and cure rickets, a theory developed. We now know with great certainty that vitamin D can prevent rickets and that a deficiency of vitamin D will cause it. Because of this, there is a consensus among health professionals as to the importance of vitamin D in the diets of children.

Research Studies and Experiments Confirm Hypotheses

Scientists can use different types of experiments to test hypotheses. The rickets experiment just described is called a *laboratory experiment,* as it was done in the confines of a lab. In the fields of nutrition and health, laboratory experiments are often conducted using animals, such as rats. Research conducted with humans is usually observational or experimental.

Observational Research

Observational research involves looking at factors in two or more groups of subjects to see if there is a relationship to a certain disease or another health outcome. For example, researchers might study rates of breastfeeding in infants with and without rickets, to see if breastfeeding influences the incidence of the disease.

One type of observational research is *epidemiological research,* which looks at populations of people. For example, scientists may look at people who live in Norway and notice that there is a higher incidence of rickets among children there than in Australia. Through their observation, they may find a relationship between the lack of sun exposure in Norway and the high incidence of rickets there compared with sunny Australia. However, the scientists can't rule out the possibility that the difference in the incidence of rickets in these two populations may also be due to other factors in the subjects' diet or lifestyle.

Experimental Research

Experimental research involves at least two groups of subjects. One group, the *experimental group,* is given a specific treatment, and another group, the *control group,* isn't. For instance, after hypothesizing that vitamin D cures rickets, scientists would have randomly assigned children with rickets to two groups. They would have given the children in the experimental group a vitamin D supplement but would have given the children in the control group a substance, called a **placebo,** that looked just like the vitamin D supplement but contained only sugar or some other nonactive ingredient. If neither of the two groups of subjects knew which substance they received, then they were "blind" to the treatment. If the scientists who were giving the placebo and the vitamin D supplement also couldn't distinguish between the

peer-reviewed journal A research journal in which fellow scientists (peers) review studies to assess their accuracy and soundness before publication.

observational research Research that involves looking at factors in two or more groups of subjects to see if there is a relationship to certain outcomes.

experimental research Research involving at least two groups of subjects.

placebo In a research study, a substance or item with no therapeutic value, provided to members of a control group to test it against expectations.

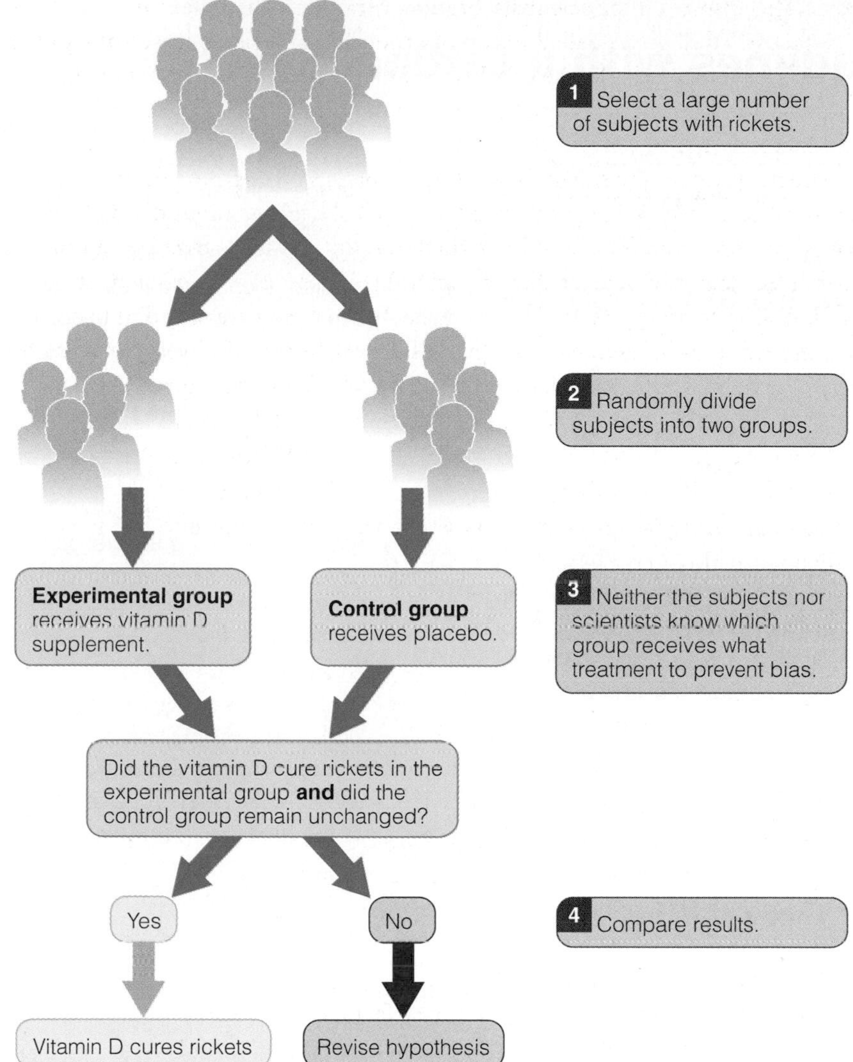

Figure 3.3 Controlled Scientific Experiments
Scientists use experimental research to test hypotheses.

two treatments and didn't know which group received which, this would be called a **double-blind, placebo-controlled study.**

The scientists would also have to make sure that all other significant factors were the same for both groups during the experiment. For example, since the scientists knew that sun exposure has a therapeutic effect on rickets, they couldn't let the children in the control group go outside in the sunshine while keeping the children in the experimental group inside. The exposure to sunshine would change the outcome of the experiment. Similarly, they'd have to ensure that the children were eating exactly the same diet for the duration of the study.

A double-blind, placebo-controlled study is considered the "gold standard" of research, because all of the factors that might influence the study results are kept the same for the groups of subjects, and neither the subjects nor the researchers are biased, as they don't know which group has received which treatment (Figure 3.3).

Although the results of many experiments fail to support the initial hypotheses, a great many discoveries are made. And with continuing research, one discovery builds upon another. Though it may seem frustrating when the findings of one research study dispute the results of another from just a few months before, even contradictory findings help advance scientific knowledge, in part because of the

double-blind, placebo-controlled study A study designed and conducted in such a way that neither the study participants nor the experimenters know to whom a treatment is given.

Evaluating Media Headlines with a Critical Eye

October 31, 2005

An Apple a Day for Health? Mars Recommends Two Bars of Chocolate

By Alexei Barrionuevo, *The New York Times*

After reading this headline, you may be tempted to toss out the apple and get yourself a couple of chocolate bars. However, you would be doing a disservice to your health if you didn't read below this tantalizing headline, which is designed to grab your attention but not necessarily tell you the whole story.

The media are routinely bombarded by press releases from medical journals, food companies, organizations, and universities about research being conducted and/or conferences being sponsored by those institutions. These releases are sent for one reason: to gain publicity. Reputable news organizations that report these findings will seek out independent experts in the field to weigh in on the research and, just as importantly, explain how these findings relate to the public. If you don't read beyond the headlines, you are probably missing important details of the story. Even worse, if you begin making dietary and lifestyle changes based on each news flash, you become a scientific guinea pig.

When a headline piques your interest, read the article with a critical eye, and ask yourself the following questions.

1. **Was the research finding published in a peer-reviewed journal?**
   You can be confident that studies published in a peer-reviewed journal have been thoroughly reviewed by experts in this area of research. In most cases, the study does not get published. If the research isn't published in a peer-reviewed journal, you have no way of knowing if the study was conducted in an appropriate manner and whether the findings are accurate. A study about the possible virtues of chocolate in fighting heart disease that is published in the *New England Journal of Medicine* has more credibility than a similar article published in a baking magazine.
2. **Was the study done using animals or humans?**
   Animals are animals and humans are humans. Experiments with animals are often used to study how a particular substance affects a health outcome. But if the study is conducted in rats, it doesn't necessarily mean that the substance will have the same effect if consumed by humans. This doesn't mean that animal studies are frivolous. They are important steppingstones to designing and conducting similar experiments involving humans.
3. **Do the study participants resemble me?**
   When you read or hear about studies involving humans, you always want to find out more information about the individuals who took part in the research. For example, were the people in the candy bar study college-aged subjects or older individuals with heart disease and high blood pressure? If older adults were studied, then would these findings be of any benefit to young adults who don't have high blood pressure or heart disease?
4. **Is this the first time I've heard about this?**
   A single study in a specific area of research is a lonely entity in the scientific world. Is this the first study regarding the designer chocolate bars? If the media article doesn't confirm that other studies have also supported these findings, this initial study may be the *only* study of its kind. Wait until you hear that these research findings are confirmed from a reputable health organization, such as the American Heart Association, before considering making any changes in your diet. These organizations will only change their advice based on a consensus of research findings.

In your lifetime, you are going to read thousands of newspaper and website headlines, as well as watch and listen to who-knows-how-many similar television and radio reports. Your critical thinking skills in evaluating the sources and information presented will be your best friend when it comes to deciding which blurbs to believe. These skills may also save you considerable money by helping you avoid nutrition gimmicks. When it comes to assessing nutrition information in the media, it's worth your time and effort to find out where it came from and why (or if) you should care.

Note: You can view the referenced article at www.nytimes.com.

questions they raise. Why did the first study show one result and a second study something different? In tackling such questions, scientists continue to advance our understanding of the world around us, and within us.

The Take-Home Message The scientific method is a process scientists use to generate data that test the validity of a hypothesis. Many research studies are conducted—typically over many years or even decades—before a consensus is reached about nutrition recommendations. A double-blind, placebo-controlled study is considered the "gold standard" of research because all of the factors that might influence the study results are kept the same for the groups of subjects, and neither the subjects nor the researchers know which group has received which treatment.

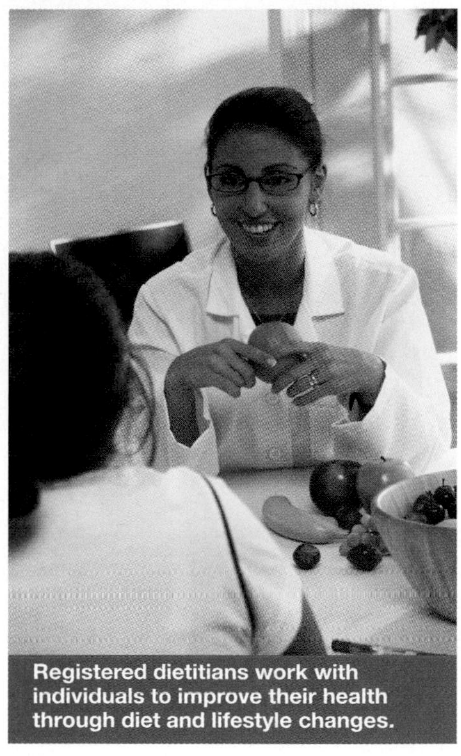

Registered dietitians work with individuals to improve their health through diet and lifestyle changes.

Where Can You Turn for Nutrition Advice?

Now that you've learned the characteristics of scientific research studies, you'll be better able to evaluate the reports you read in the press. But what about those times when you need specific advice—advice that applies just to you?

You Can Trust the Advice of Nutrition Experts

If you want legal advice, you seek the expertise of a lawyer. If you think you might need a knee operation, you consult an orthopedic surgeon. If you want nutrition advice, to whom should you turn? Of course, you want to speak with a credible expert who has training in the field of nutrition. So who are these people and where do you find them?

One option is to seek the expertise of a **registered dietitian (RD)**. An RD has completed at least a bachelor's degree at an accredited university or college in the United States that offers specific coursework in nutrition and has been approved by the American Dietetic Association (ADA). RDs have also completed an ADA-approved supervised practice, and passed a national exam administered by the ADA. They are qualified to provide *medical nutrition therapy*, in which they assess a patient's medical history and current health needs and develop a treatment plan, including nutrition counseling and dietary changes with the goal of improving the patient's health.

RDs work with their patients to make dietary changes that can help prevent or manage the symptoms of many diseases, such as heart disease, diabetes, digestive disorders, and obesity. Many physicians refer patients with such disorders to RDs for nutrition advice and guidance. RDs must participate in continuing professional education in order to remain current in the fast-changing world of nutrition, medicine, and health and to maintain their registration. RDs work in hospitals and other health care facilities, private practice, universities, and medical schools; with professional athletic teams or food companies; and in other nutrition-related businesses. Jimmy, whom you read about in the beginning of this concept, would have benefited from the sound advice of an RD, rather than relying on the Internet to help him with his nutrition needs.

Individuals with advanced degrees in nutrition can also provide credible nutrition information. People with a master of science in public health (MPH) degree,

registered dietitian (RD) A health professional who has completed at least a bachelor's degree in an accredited university or college in the United States, has completed a supervised practice, and has passed an exam administered by the American Dietetic Association (ADA).

which involves some nutrition courses, or a master of science (MS) degree in nutrition at an accredited university or college can also be sources of information.

Public health nutritionists typically have an undergraduate degree in nutrition, but unless they have completed a supervised practice, they are not eligible to take the ADA exam and cannot become an RD. Many of these individuals work in government agencies, organizing community outreach nutrition programs, such as programs for the elderly.

In order to protect the health of the public receiving nutrition information, over 40 states in the United States currently license nutrition professionals, who must meet specified educational and experience criteria to be considered experts in the field. A person who meets these qualifications is a **licensed dietitian (LD)** and, so, has the letters *LD* after his or her name. Because RDs have completed the rigorous standards set forth by the ADA, they automatically meet the criteria for LD, and many have both *RD* and *LD* after their names.

Be careful when taking nutrition advice from a trainer at a gym or a person who works at a local health food store. Whereas some of these people may have both training and experience in nutrition science, many do not, and thus are unlikely to be able to give you information based on solid scientific evidence. Anyone can call him- or herself a **nutritionist,** even people who have taken no accredited courses in nutrition.

You also need to beware of individuals who specialize in health **quackery.** Such scammers will try to entice you to buy their products by using personal testimonials and false claims that aren't backed up by sound science and research. Americans spend billions of dollars annually on fraudulent health products, an injustice that Stephen Barrett, MD, a nationally known author and consumer advocate, has been trying to fight for decades. His website, quackwatch.org, helps consumers identify quackery and make educated decisions about health-related information and products. Dr. Barrett's list of common deceptive statements made by health quacks is provided in the box feature "Quackwatchers."

You Can Get Accurate Nutrition Information on the Internet

Mark Twain once said, "Be careful about reading health books. You could die of a misprint." If he were alive today, he probably would have included websites that dole out health advice. Over 70 percent of American adult Internet users—or 117 million people—have surfed more than 3 million websites, looking for health and medical information.[1] Identifying quackery is important when you read about nutrition on the Internet. The Web is overflowing with nutrition information and *mis*information.

Don't assume that a slick website is a sound website. Although many websites, such as Shape Up America! (www.shapeup.org) and the Tufts Health & Nutrition Newsletter (www.healthletter.tufts.edu) provide credible, reliable, up-to-date nutrition information, anyone with computer skills can put up a slick website. The National Institutes of Health (NIH) has developed 10 questions that you should consider when viewing a nutrition- or health-related website.[2] (Some of these guidelines can also apply to other media information sources, such as popular magazines.) Jimmy would have benefited from reading the following list before making his online purchase:

1. **Who runs the site?**
   Credible websites are willing to show their credentials. For example, the National Center for Complementary and Alternative Medicine (www.nccam.nih.gov) provides information about its association with the NIH and its

public health nutritionist An individual who may have an undergraduate degree in nutrition but isn't a Registered Dietician(RD).

licensed dietitian (LD) An individual who has met specified educational and experience criteria that a state licensing board has deemed necessary to be considered an expert in the field of nutrition. A Registered Dietician(RD) meets all the qualifications to be an LD.

nutritionist A generic term with no recognized legal or professional meaning. Some people may call themselves nutritionists without having any credible training in nutrition.

quackery The promotion and selling of health products and services of questionable validity. A quack is a person who promotes these products and services in order to make money.

Quackwatchers

Consumers beware. The snake oil salesmen of yesteryear never left the building. They just left the oil behind and moved on to selling herbs, nutrition supplements, and other products, many on the Internet. Jimmy, the student you read about at the beginning of this concept, learned this quickly when his $100 bottle of placebos arrived at his doorstep. Savvy salespeople introduce health fears into your mind and then offer goods to address those newly created fears. They make unrealistic promises and guarantees. And though they often boast about a "money back guarantee," good luck trying to get it.

To avoid falling for one of their shady schemes, you should be leery of infomercials, magazine ads, and websites that try to convince you that:

- Most Americans are not adequately nourished.
- Everyone should take vitamin supplements.
- You need supplements or special drinks to relieve stress or give you energy.
- You can lose a lot of weight in a short amount of time.
- Their products can produce amazing results and cure whatever ails you.
- Your behavior is caused by your diet.
- Herbs are safe because they are natural.
- Sugar will poison you.
- A hair sample can identify nutrient deficiencies.
- Your MD or RD is a quack and you should not listen to them.
- There is no risk, as there is a money-back guarantee!

Data from: S. Barrett, Signs of a "Quacky" Web Site and Twenty-Five Ways to Spot Quacks and Vitamin Pushers. http://quackwatch.org.

extensive ongoing research and educational programs. If you have to spend more than a minute trying to find out who runs the website, you should click to another site.

2. **Who pays for the site?**
Running a website is expensive, and finding out who's paying for a particular site will tell you something about the reliability of its content. Websites sponsored by the government (with urls ending in .gov), a nonprofit organization (ending in .org), or an academic institution (.edu) are typically more reliable than many commercial websites (.com or .net). Some commercial websites, such as *Web*MD, carry articles that can be reliable if they are written by credible health professionals, but other websites may be promoting information to suit a company's own purposes.

   For example, if the funding source for the website is a vitamin and mineral supplement company, are all the articles geared toward supporting the use of supplements? Does the website have advertisers and do their products influence the website's content? You need to investigate the website's possible bias in favor of the products or services of the funding source.
3. **What is the purpose of the site?**
After you answer the first two questions, look for the "About This Site" link. This will help you understand the website's purpose. For example, at Nutrition.gov, the purpose is to "provide easy access to the best food and nutrition information across the federal government." This website doesn't exist to sell you anything but, rather, to help you find reliable information.

4. **Where does the information come from?**
   You should always know who wrote what you are reading. Is the author a qualified nutrition expert or did he or she interview qualified individuals? If the site obtained information from another source, is that source cited?
5. **What is the basis of the information?**
   Is the article's information based on medical facts and figures that have references? For example, any medical news items released on the American Heart Association website (www.americanheart.org) includes the medical journal from which the information came. In fact, the website often includes the opinions of experts regarding the news items.
6. **How is the information selected?**
   A physician who is a well-known medical expert for a major television network once commented that he spends most of his time not delivering medical advice but trying to stop the networks from publicizing health news that isn't credible. Always look to see if the website has an editorial board of medical and health experts and if qualified individuals review or write the content before it is released.
7. **How current is the information?**
   Once a website is on the Internet, it will stay there until someone removes it. Consequently, the health information you read may not be up-to-date. Always check to see when the content was written and, if it is over a year old, whether it has been updated.
8. **How does the site choose links to other sites?**
   Some medical sites don't link to other sites, as they don't have control over the other sites' credibility and content. Others do link, if they are confident that these sites meet their criteria. Some sites receive financial reimbursement from the links they post. Don't always assume that the link is credible.
9. **What information is collected about you and why?**
   Websites track the pages that you click on in order to analyze their more popular topics. Sometimes, they elicit personal information, such as your gender, age, and health concerns. After collecting data on your viewing selections and your personal information, they can sell this information to interested companies. These companies can create promotional materials about their goods and services targeted to your needs. Credible sites should tell you about their privacy policy and if they will or will not give this information to other sources. A website's privacy policy is often found in a link at the bottom of its screens.
10. **How does the site manage interactions with visitors?**
    You should always be able to easily find the contact information of the website's owners, should you have any concerns or questions. If the site has a chat room or an ongoing discussion group, you should know how it is moderated. Read the discussion group dialogue before you jump in.

The Take-Home Message **Sound nutrition advice is based on years of research using the scientific method. You should take nutrition advice only from a credible source, such as a registered dietitian or another valid nutrition expert. When obtaining nutrition information from the Internet, you need to peruse the site carefully to make sure that it is credible, it contains up-to-date information, and its content isn't influenced by those who fund and support the website.**

UCook

Stuffed Sweet Potatoes
These stuffed sweet potatoes are so sweet that leftovers can be eaten as a dessert or snack! You'll find the full recipe on our website.

UDo

Spotting a Bogus Weight-Loss Product
When a miraculous weight-loss product sounds a little too good to be true, it probably is! Learn more on how to identify quackery on our website, listed above.

The Top Five Points to Remember

1. Sound nutrition information is the result of numerous scientific studies based on the scientific method. The scientific method begins when a scientist makes an observation, asks a question, and formulates a hypothesis, a possible explanation for the observation. The next step is to conduct an experiment, the results of which will either support or fail to support the hypothesis. If the hypothesis is not supported, it can be revised or a new hypothesis formulated.
2. Research findings should be reviewed by and shared with the medical and scientific community. If further studies confirm the initial findings, eventually a consensus among scientists develops, and a theory is formulated. You should never change your diet or lifestyle based on the findings of just one or a few studies.
3. A double-blind, placebo-controlled study is an experiment in which not only the study participants but also the researchers do not know which group of subjects has received the treatment and which has received the placebo. It is considered the "gold standard" of research.
4. Nutritional advice should come from credible sources. Individuals who call themselves nutritionists may or may not have a credible nutrition education. Always assess the source of the nutrition information to make sure that it is from a credible source.
5. You can obtain accurate information about nutrition and health from Internet sources, but you should evaluate them carefully. Factors to consider are who runs and pays for the site, the purpose of the site, the source and basis of the information, how the information is selected, and how current the content is. Also consider whether the site links to other sites, collects information about you, enables you to contact the owners, and/or appropriately monitors chat groups.

Test Yourself

1. In scientific research, a consensus is
   a. an idea generated by scientists based on their observations.
   b. an opinion of a group of experts based on a collection of scientific information.
   c. a commonly agreed-upon set of facts about an observed phenomenon.
   d. a process used to generate data to support a theory.
2. The first step in the scientific method is to
   a. make observations and ask questions.
   b. form a hypothesis.
   c. do an experiment.
   d. develop a theory.
3. You decide to have your diet assessed and be counseled by a nutrition professional because you want to lose weight. Which of the following individuals would be the most credible source of information?
   a. an employee of your local health food store
   b. your personal trainer at the gym
   c. a registered dietitian
   d. a nutritionist
4. When exploring a website that provides nutrition and health information, which of the following should you look at to assess its content?
   a. who wrote it
   b. when it was written
   c. when it was last updated
   d. all of the above
5. Which of the following would be a reliable source of nutrition information?
   a. an article discussing toxins in commercial coffee beans that is written by an importer of organic coffees
   b. an article citing a recently published study on the effectiveness of coral calcium on a site run by a producer of coral calcium supplements
   c. an article about rickets written by a physician and published on his professional website, accompanied by an advertisement for vitamin D supplements
   d. none of the above

Answers

1. (b) A consensus is an opinion shared by a group of experts based on a collection of scientific information. It is not a process or a set of facts, nor is it merely an idea about something observed.
2. (a) The scientific method begins with scientists observing and asking questions. From this step, a hypothesis follows. The scientists then test their hypothesis using an experiment. After many experiments confirm their hypothesis, they develop a theory.
3. (c) Unless the salesperson and personal trainer are registered dietitians, they are not qualified to provide nutrition counseling. A nutritionist may not necessarily have any credible training in nutrition.
4. (d) When reading nutrition and health information on the Internet, it is very important to make sure the source is qualified to provide this information. Because you also need to assess if the information is current, you should find out when it was written and if it has been or needs to be updated.
5. (d) None of these sources is reliable because all present conflicts of interest; that is, the information in the articles is provided to promote the sale of products offered or advertised on the site.

Web Resources

Examples of reliable nutrition and health websites include:

- Agricultural Research Service: www.nal.usda.gov/fnic/foodcomp
- American Cancer Society: www.cancer.org
- American College of Sports Medicine: www.acsm.org
- American Diabetes Association: www.diabetes.org
- American Dietetic Association: www.eatright.org
- American Heart Association: www.amhrt.org
- American Institute for Cancer Research: www.aicr.org
- American Medical Association: www.ama.assn.org
- Centers for Disease Control and Prevention: www.cdc.gov
- Center for Science in the Public Interest: www.cspinet.org
- Food Allergy Network: www.foodallergy.org
- Food and Drug Administration: www.fda.gov
- Food and Nutrition Information Center: www.nal.usda.gov/fnic
- National Cholesterol Education Program: www.nhlbi.nih.gov/about/ncep
- National Institutes of Health: www.nih.gov
- National High Blood Pressure Program: www.nhlbi.nih.gov/hbp
- National Osteoporosis Foundation: www.nof.org
- Shape Up America!: www.shapeup.org
- Tufts University Health & Nutrition Newsletter: www.healthletter.tufts.edu
- U.S. Department of Agriculture: www.nutrition.gov
- Vegetarian Resource Group: www.vrg.org
- Weight Control Information Network: www.win.niddk.nih.gov/index.htm

4

1. **Overeating** can contribute to malnutrition. **T/F**

2. Most of your daily **energy intake** should come from protein. **T/F**

3. To be healthy, you should be **physically active** at least three times a week. **T/F**

4. Generally speaking, as your intake of **salt** goes up, so does your blood pressure. **T/F**

5. According to the U.S. Department of Agriculture, there are five basic **food groups.** **T/F**

Tools for Healthy Eating

Each day, Zoe walks the 15 minutes between the apartment she shares with her parents and younger sister and the university campus where she's studying to be a teacher. Money is tight, so she packs a lunch—usually peanut butter and jelly on whole-wheat bread, some carrot sticks, and a piece of fruit.

In addition, she tries to keep her lunches varied by eating a different fruit each day, and mixing it up with low-fat yogurts and a few unsalted nuts. In the evenings, she often practices stretching, and tries to get in a a longer run every few days.

Although she doesn't know it, Zoe is following several of the recommendations of the *Dietary Guidelines for Americans 2005*. What are the *Guidelines*, and how can following them help reduce your risk of developing a chronic disease? What other tools are available to help you design a healthy diet? Read on.

Answers

1. True. Overnutrition is a form of malnutrition. Check it out on page 3.
2. False. Carbohydrates should comprise the major percentage of your daily calories. Turn to page 4 for details.
3. False. You should be physically active for at least 30 minutes *daily*. To find out why, turn to page 6.
4. True. You should keep your salt intake below 1 teaspoon daily to help reduce your risk of high blood pressure. To learn more, turn to page 7.
5. True. The five basic food groups are grains, vegetables, fruit, milk, and meat and beans. Turn to page 13 to find out more about the food groups and how MyPyramid can help guide your food choices.

What Is Healthy Eating and What Tools Can Help?

Healthy eating is characterized by balance, variety, and moderation. As a student, you are probably familiar with these principles from other areas of your life. Think about how you balance your time among work, school, and your family and friends. You engage in a variety of activities to avoid being bored, and you enjoy each in moderation, since spending too much time on one activity (such as working) would reduce the amount of time you could spend on others (such as studying, socializing, or sleeping). An unbalanced life soon becomes unhealthy and unhappy. Likewise, your diet must be balanced, varied, and moderate in order to be healthy.

- A balanced diet includes healthy proportions of all nutrients. For instance, a student subsisting largely on bread, bagels, muffins, crackers, chips, and cookies might be eating too much carbohydrate and fat but too little protein, vitamins, and minerals.
- A varied diet includes many different foods. A student who habitually chooses the same foods for breakfast, lunch, and dinner is not likely to be consuming the wide range of phytochemicals, fiber, and other benefits that a more varied diet could provide.
- A moderate diet provides adequate amounts of nutrients and energy. Both crash diets and overconsumption are immoderate.

In short, you need to consume a variety of foods, some more moderately than others, and balance your food choices to meet your nutrient and health needs. Zoe, whom you read about in the opening of this concept, has a balanced and varied lunch that provides whole grains, protein-rich peanut butter, a vegetable, and a piece of fruit. If all of Zoe's other meals are this balanced and varied, she is likely eating a healthy diet.

A diet that lacks variety and is unbalanced can cause **undernutrition,** a state whereby you are not meeting your nutrient needs. If you were to consume only grains, such as bread and rice, and avoid other foods, such as milk products, fruits, vegetables, and meats, your body wouldn't get enough protein and other important nutrients. You would eventually become **malnourished.**

undernutrition A state of malnutrition in which a person's nutrient and/or calorie needs aren't met through the diet.

malnourished The long-term outcome of consuming a diet that doesn't meet nutrient needs.

In contrast, **overnutrition** occurs when a diet provides too much of a nutrient, such as iron, which can be toxic in high amounts, or too many calories, which can lead to obesity. As we saw in Concept 2, a person who is overnourished can also be malnourished. Some people who are obese consume a diet laden with less nutritious snack foods and sweets—foods that should be eaten in moderation. These foods often displace more nutrient-rich choices, leaving the person malnourished.

Fortunately, the United States government provides several tools that can help you avoid both under- and overnutrition including:

- The *Dietary Reference Intakes (DRIs)*, which provide recommendations regarding your nutrient needs
- The *Dietary Guidelines for Americans*, which provide broad dietary and lifestyle advice
- *MyPyramid*, which is a food guidance system that helps you implement the recommendations in the DRIs and the advice in the *Dietary Guidelines.* MyPyramid provides personalized food choices from among a variety of food groups to help you create a balanced diet.

Together, these tools can help you plan a varied, moderate, and balanced diet that meets your nutrient and health needs. Next, we'll take a look at each, beginning with the DRIs.

The Take-Home Message **A healthy diet is balanced, varied, and moderate. The United States government provides several tools to assist you in planning a healthy diet. These include the Dietary Reference Intakes, the *Dietary Guidelines for Americans*, and the MyPyramid food guidance system.**

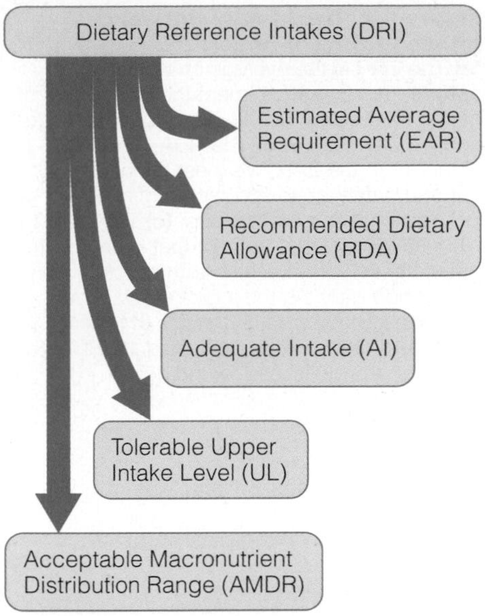

Figure 4.1 The Dietary Reference Intakes
When planning your diet, focus on the RDAs or AIs and the AMDR. Avoid consuming the UL of any nutrient.

What Are the Dietary Reference Intakes?

The **Dietary Reference Intakes (DRIs)** are issued by the Food and Nutrition Board of the National Academy of Sciences' Institute of Medicine. They specify the amounts of each nutrient that people need to consume in order to maintain good health, prevent nutrient deficiencies and chronic diseases, and avoid unhealthy excesses.[1] The Institute of Medicine periodically updates these recommendations so that they reflect the latest scientific research. Since they were first published in the 1940s, the DRIs have been updated 10 times.

Because nutrient needs change with age, and because needs are different for men and women, the recommendations for each nutrient differ according to a person's age and gender. In other words, a teenager may need more of a specific nutrient than a 55-year-old (and vice versa), and women need more of certain nutrients during pregnancy and lactation, so they all have different DRIs.

DRIs Encompass Five Reference Values

The DRIs comprise the five reference values identified in Figure 4.1. Each of these values is unique, serving a different need in planning a healthy diet. In planning your diet, you would use either the RDA or the AI. The AMDR provides an additional planning

overnutrition A state of excess nutrients and/or calories in the diet.

Dietary Reference Intakes (DRIs) A collection of five specific reference values for the essential nutrients needed to maintain good health, prevent chronic diseases, and avoid unhealthy excesses. The five reference values are: the estimated average requirement (EAR); the recommended dietary allowance (RDI); the adequate intake (AI); the tolerable upper intake level (UL); and the acceptable macronutrient distribution range (AMDR).

Figure 4.2 The Dietary Reference Intakes (DRIs) in Action
(a) The EAR is the average amount of a nutrient that is likely to meet the daily needs of half of the healthy individuals in a specific age and gender group. **(b)** The RDA, which is higher than the EAR, will meet the needs of approximately 97 to 98 percent of healthy individuals in a specific group. **(c)** The UL is the highest amount of a nutrient that is unlikely to pose any risk of adverse health effects even if consumed daily. As the intake of a nutrient increases above the UL, the risk of toxicity increases. Consuming more than the RDA but less than the UL is safe for individuals.

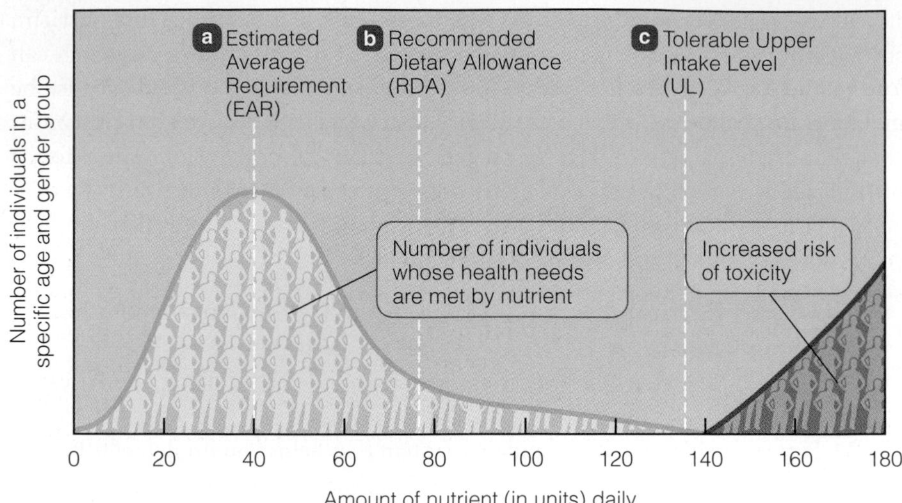

tool that can be used for diet planning. Let's define these values and look at how they're useful to you.

The *Estimated Average Requirement (EAR)* is the average amount of a nutrient that is known to meet the needs of 50 percent of the individuals in a similar age and gender group (Figure 4.2). The EAR is a starting point to determine the amount of a nutrient individuals should consume daily for good health.

Let's use Figure 4.2 to locate the EAR for Nutrient X. As you can see from the figure, the EAR for Nutrient X is about 40 units. This means that half of the people studied were able to meet their needs by consuming 40 units of this nutrient. However, the other half would need more than this amount to be healthy.

This is where the *Recommended Dietary Allowance (RDA)* comes in. The RDA is based on the EAR, but it is set higher; it represents the average amount of a nutrient that meets the needs of nearly all (97 to 98 percent) of the individuals in a similar group. The RDA for Nutrient X in Figure 4.2 is 75 units. At this intake, nearly all of the individuals in this group will meet their needs for this nutrient.

If there is insufficient scientific information to determine the EAR for a nutrient, the RDA can't be developed. When this happens, an *Adequate Intake (AI)* is determined instead. The AI is the next best scientific estimate of the amount of a nutrient that groups of similar individuals should consume to maintain good health.

Because consuming too much of some nutrients can be harmful, the *Tolerable Upper Intake Level (UL)* was developed. The UL is the highest amount of a nutrient that is unlikely to cause harm if the amount is consumed daily. The higher the consumption above the UL, the higher the risk of **toxicity**. You should not try to consume the UL of a nutrient. There isn't any known benefit from consuming a higher amount, and doing so may cause health problems.

The DRI also contain a range of intakes for the energy-containing nutrients: carbohydrates, proteins, and fats. This range is called the *Acceptable Macronutrient Distribution Range (AMDR)*, as follows:

- Carbohydrates should comprise 45 to 65 percent of your daily calories
- Fat should comprise 20 to 35 percent of your daily calories
- Proteins should comprise 10 to 35 percent of your daily calories

Consuming these nutrient types in these ranges will ensure that you meet your calorie and nutrient needs, as well as reduce your risk of developing chronic diseases, such as heart disease and obesity.

toxicity The level at which exposure to a substance becomes harmful.

How to Use the DRIs

You can use the DRIs to make healthy food choices and plan a quality diet. Your goal should be to meet the RDA or the AI of all the nutrients, but not exceed the UL. On the inside cover of your textbook, you will find the DRIs for all the nutrients you need daily, in addition to a table (The Do's and Don'ts of the DRIs) summarizing them.

Each concept in this textbook will further explain what each nutrient is, why it is important, how much you need to consume, and how to get enough, without consuming too much, in your diet. While the new DRIs were released to prevent undernutrition, the *Dietary Guidelines for Americans* were developed out of concern about overnutrition among Americans. We'll examine that next.

While the new DRIs were released to prevent undernutrition, the *Dietary Guidelines for Americans* were developed out of concern about overnutrtion among Americans. We'll examine that next.

The Take-Home Message **The Dietary Reference Intakes (DRIs) are a collection of five specific reference values that help you determine your daily nutrient needs to maintain good health, prevent chronic diseases, and avoid unhealthy excesses. The reference values include the EAR, RDA, AI, UL, and AMDR. Try to meet your RDA or AI and consume below the UL for each nutrient daily.**

TABLE TIPS

Tip Top Nutrition Tips

Use traffic light colors to help you vary your lunchtime veggie choices. Add tomato slices (red) to your sandwich and carrots (yellow/orange) to your tossed salad (green).

Pop a snack-pack size of light microwave popcorn for a portion-controlled whole-grain snack.

Say "so long" to the elevator and hoof it up the stairs to get some extra physical activity into your day.

To limit your sweets to a reasonable amount, read the nutrition label and stick to a single serving that is no more than about 100 calories. Note that many big bars and bags contain more than double this amount.

Plan your dinner using at least one food from each of the food groups. Add tomato-pepper salsa (fruits and vegetables) and a can of rinsed black beans (meat and beans) to your macaroni (grain) and cheese (dairy) for a nutritionally complete meal.

What Are the *Dietary Guidelines for Americans*?

The *Dietary Guidelines for Americans* were developed to inform Americans about the impact that diet and lifestyle choices can have on their health. As early as the 1970s, research had shown that Americans' overconsumption of foods rich in fat, cholesterol, and sodium was increasing their risk for chronic diseases.[2] In 1977, the U.S. government released the *Dietary Goals for Americans,* which were designed to improve Americans' diets and to reduce the incidence of overnutrition and its associated health problems.[3] In 1980, these were updated as the *Dietary Guidelines for Americans.* Since 1990, the U.S. Department of Agriculture (USDA) and the Department of Health and Human Services (DHHS) have been mandated by law to update the guidelines every five years.[4]

The ***Dietary Guidelines for Americans 2005*** reflect the most current recommendations for good health. They are designed to help you improve the quality of your diet and lower your risk for conditions such as high blood pressure, high blood cholesterol levels, and overweight, as well as chronic diseases, such as diabetes, heart disease, certain cancers, and osteoporosis. Following these guidelines could reduce American adults' risk of dying from these disorders by as much as 9 to 16 percent.[5] The feature box "The *Dietary Guidelines for Americans* at a Glance" provides an overview of the guidelines and will help you incorporate them into your life. The updated *Dietary Guidelines* 2010 will continue to provide health recommendations based on the latest science and can be accessed at www.DietaryGuidelines.gov.

Dietary Guidelines for Americans 2005 Guidelines published in 2005 that provide dietary and lifestyle advice to healthy individuals age 2 and older to help them maintain good health and prevent chronic diseases.

The Take-Home Message **The *Dietary Guidelines for Americans 2005* provide dietary and lifestyle advice to healthy individuals age 2 and older to help them maintain good health and prevent chronic diseases.**

The *Dietary Guidelines for Americans* at a Glance

The *Dietary Guidelines for Americans 2005* is divided into nine closely related, and often intertwined, categories that address various health concerns. The following is only a short overview of the vast amount of information in each category. Most concepts in this book elaborate on at least one of these guidelines and shows you how to easily make additional diet and lifestyle changes to improve your health. The complete guidelines and more information are available online at www.healthierus.gov/dietaryguidelines.

Adequate Nutrients within Calorie Needs

The Health Concern in a Nutshell: Many Americans are consuming more calories than they need yet are still falling short of receiving some important nutrients.

It's Recommended That You: Consume a variety of nutrient-dense foods and beverages within and among the basic food groups, but be careful not to exceed the number of calories you need daily to maintain a healthy weight.

Weight Management

The Health Concern in a Nutshell: Over 65 percent of Americans are overweight and, so, are at an increased risk of heart disease, cancer, stroke, and diabetes mellitus—some of the major causes of death in the United States.

It's Recommended That You: Maintain a balance between the number of calories that you consume daily and the amount you need to maintain a healthy weight. Daily physical activity will help, as it allows you to eat some additional calories while maintaining your weight. If you need to lose weight, take in fewer calories and increase your physical activity level.

Physical Activity

The Health Concern in a Nutshell: Even though being physically active reduces the risk of many chronic diseases, over half of American adults don't exercise enough to gain this protective effect. To make matters worse, 25 percent of Americans are considered "couch potatoes" because they don't move at all during their leisure time.

It's Recommended That You: Try to be physically active every day. You should spend at least 30 minutes a day in moderately intense physical activity, such as brisk walking, roller blading, or aerobic dancing. If you engage in more vigorous activities, such as jogging or a step aerobics class, you'll reap even more health benefits. If weight loss is your goal, increase your exercise to at least 60 minutes of a moderate-intensity activity throughout the day.

Food Groups to Encourage

The Health Concern in a Nutshell: Americans are falling short of the recommended amounts of whole grains, fat-free and low-fat milk products, whole fruits, and vegetables.

It's Recommended That You: Eat more from these food groups on a daily basis. Remember this phrase: "Give three two me, please." Have at least *three* servings of whole grains and *three* servings of fat-free or low-fat milk products daily. Enjoy at least

What Is the MyPyramid Food Guidance System?

food guidance systems Visual diagrams that provide a variety of food recommendations to help create a well-balanced diet.

With so many nutrient and dietary recommendations in the DRIs and the *Dietary Guidelines,* you may be wondering how to keep them straight and plan a diet that meets all of your nutritional needs. Luckily, there are several carefully designed **food guidance systems** to help you select the best foods for your diet. These illustrated systems depict healthy food choices from a variety of food groups and show you how to proportion your food choices. Many countries have developed food guidance systems based on their food supply, their cultural food preferences, and the nutritional needs of their population (see Figure 4.3 on page 8).[6]

two cups of a variety of fruit and at least *two* and a half cups of colorful vegetables throughout the day.

Fats

The Health Concern in a Nutshell: While some fat is essential, too much saturated and *trans* fat, as well as dietary cholesterol, is unhealthy for your heart.

It's Recommended that You: Keep your dietary fat to between 20 and 35 percent of your daily calories and get mostly heart-healthy, unsaturated fats, such as those found in vegetable oils, nuts, and fish. Consume less than 10 percent of your calories from saturated fat, found mainly in animal-based foods, by choosing only lean meats, skinless poultry, and low-fat dairy foods. Eat fewer commercially made baked goods that are made with *trans* fats. Consume less than 300 milligrams of dietary cholesterol daily.

Carbohydrates

The Health Concern in a Nutshell: Although carbohydrate-rich foods, such as whole grains, lean dairy foods, whole fruits, and vegetables, are excellent sources of nutrients, foods high in sugary carbohydrates tend to be high in calories and not as nutrient-rich. These less healthy carbohydrate sources may also displace more nutritious foods in your diet.

It's Recommended that You: Choose lean dairy products, whole grains, fruits, and vegetables more often than sugary soft drinks, candy, bakery items, and fruit drinks.

Sodium and Potassium

The Health Concern in a Nutshell: Most Americans will develop high blood pressure sometime in their life. A continually high blood pressure increases your risk of heart disease and stroke. Generally, as your intake of salt goes up, so does your blood pressure. Whereas potassium can help lower blood pressure, most individuals don't eat enough potassium-rich fruits and vegetables for this to be effective.

It's Recommended that You: Keep your sodium intake to less than 2,300 milligrams (approximately 1 teaspoon) of salt daily. Avoid salting your foods and choose processed foods made with less salt. Make sure that you consume plenty of fruits and vegetables daily.

Alcoholic Beverages

The Health Concern in a Nutshell: Though consuming alcohol in moderation may be heart-healthy for some individuals, it can be harmful to others, depending on their age, medical history, and lifestyle.

It's Recommended that You: Avoid alcohol if you are a woman of childbearing age who may become pregnant, a pregnant or lactating woman, under the age of 21, or taking medications that can interact with alcohol; if you have a specific medical condition for which doctors advise against alcohol consumption; if you are an alcoholic; or if you are driving or operating machinery—your judgment may be impaired by alcohol consumption.

Food Safety

The Health Concern in a Nutshell: Each year, over 70 million Americans suffer from foodborne illnesses, also known as food poisoning, from consuming foods contaminated with bacteria, parasites, and viruses.

It's Recommended that You: Properly clean, prepare, and store your foods.

Some researchers have also developed food guidance systems to help individuals reduce their risk of certain diseases. For example, the Dietary Approaches to Stop Hypertension (DASH) diet is based on an eating style that has been shown to lower a person's blood pressure significantly. High blood pressure is a risk factor for heart disease and stroke. The DASH diet will be discussed in Concept 17.

MyPyramid is the most recent food guidance system released by the USDA for Americans. Released in 2005, it depicts the recommendations in the *Dietary Guidelines for Americans 2005* (see Figure 4.4, page 9). Using information about yourself that you provide on the MyPyramid website, it recommends the number of servings you need to consume from each food group to meet the DRIs for your nutrient needs, based on your calorie needs. In essence, MyPyramid provides a personalized diet plan based on the latest nutrition and health recommendations.

MyPyramid A food guidance system that illustrates the recommendations in the *Dietary Guidelines for Americans 2005* and the Dietary Reference Intakes (DRIs) nutrient goals.

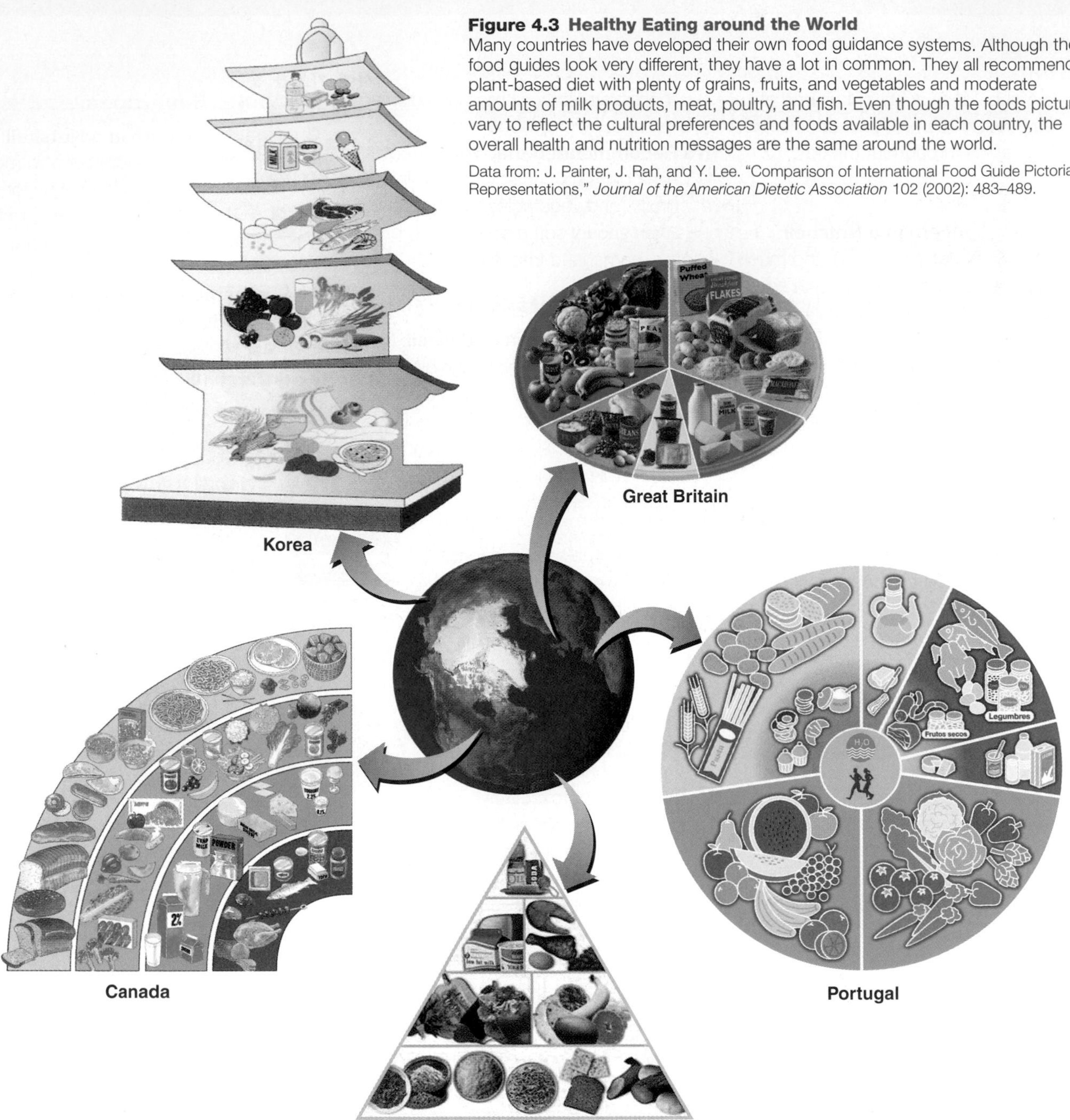

Figure 4.3 Healthy Eating around the World
Many countries have developed their own food guidance systems. Although these food guides look very different, they have a lot in common. They all recommend a plant-based diet with plenty of grains, fruits, and vegetables and moderate amounts of milk products, meat, poultry, and fish. Even though the foods pictured vary to reflect the cultural preferences and foods available in each country, the overall health and nutrition messages are the same around the world.

Data from: J. Painter, J. Rah, and Y. Lee. "Comparison of International Food Guide Pictorial Representations," *Journal of the American Dietetic Association* 102 (2002): 483–489.

MyPyramid Emphasizes Changes in Diet, Physical Activity, and Eating Behaviors

In addition to showing a variety of foods that can make up a healthy diet, MyPyramid illustrates the diet and lifestyle themes of physical activity, proportionality, moderation, variety, personalization, and gradual improvement. See Figure 4.4 for explanations about how each of these themes is shown in the MyPyramid diagram.

The figure climbing the pyramid reminds you to engage in physical activity. As you remember, the *Dietary Guidelines* recommend that you be physically active for at least 30 minutes daily. Being physically active helps you stay fit and reduces your risk

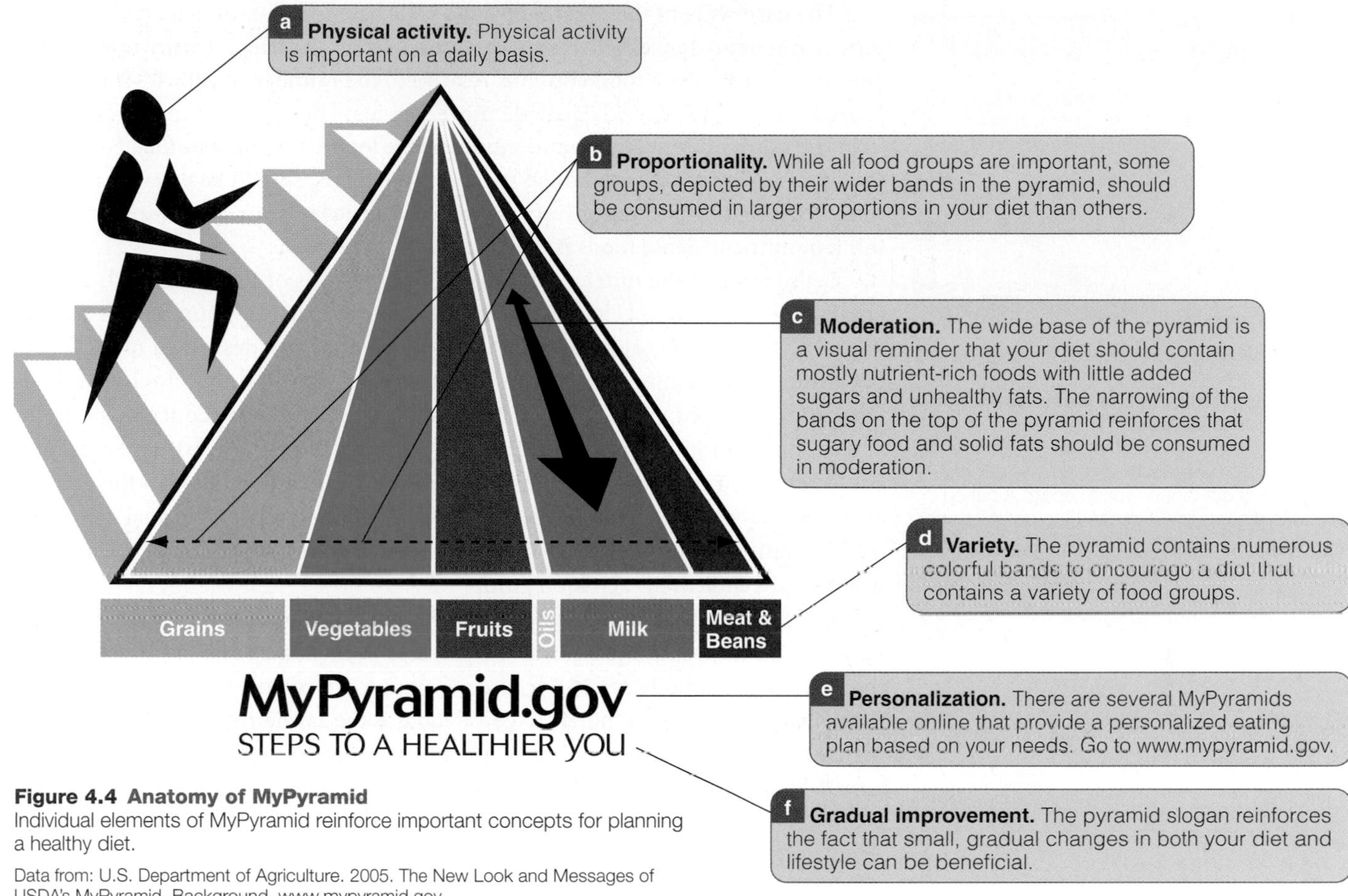

Figure 4.4 Anatomy of MyPyramid
Individual elements of MyPyramid reinforce important concepts for planning a healthy diet.

Data from: U.S. Department of Agriculture. 2005. The New Look and Messages of USDA's MyPyramid, Background. www.mypyramid.gov.

of chronic diseases. Also, the more physical activity you do, the more calories (food) you can eat without compromising your weight.

The widths of the color bands in MyPyramid reinforce **proportionality,** or how much of your total diet should be eaten from each of the five food groups. For instance, the wider bands of the grains, vegetables, fruits, and lean milk groups tell you that these should provide the bulk of your diet. The comparatively thinner bands of oils, and meat and beans group mean that these should be eaten in lesser amounts. Rate Yourself to see how well proportioned your diet is!

RATE YOURSELF ★★★★★

Does Your Diet Have Proportionality?

Answer "yes" or "no" to the following questions.

1. Are grains the main food choice at all your meals? **Yes** ☐ **No** ☐
2. Do you often forget to eat vegetables? **Yes** ☐ **No** ☐
3. Do you typically eat fewer than 3 pieces of fruit daily? **Yes** ☐ **No** ☐
4. Do you often have fewer than 3 cups of milk daily? **Yes** ☐ **No** ☐
5. Is the portion of meat, chicken, or fish the largest item on your dinner plate? **Yes** ☐ **No** ☐

Answer

If you answered "yes" to three or more of these questions, it is likely that your diet lacks proportionality.

proportionality The relationship of one entity to another. For example, grains, fruits, and vegetables should be consumed in a higher proportion to oils and meats in the diet.

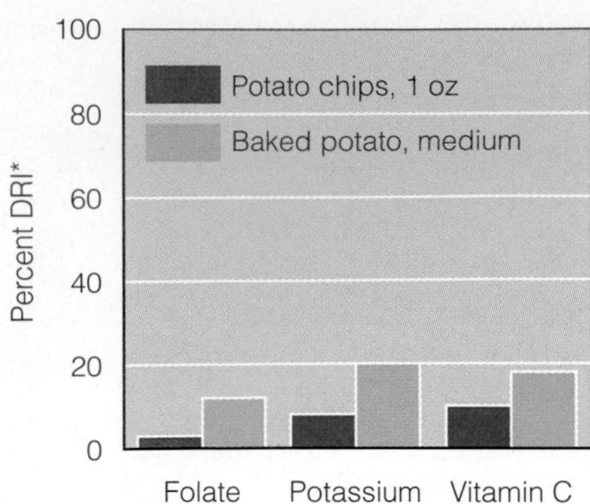

Figure 4.5 Which Is the Healthier Way to Enjoy Your Potatoes?
While 1 ounce of potato chips and one medium baked potato have similar amounts of calories, their nutrient content is worlds apart. A baked potato is more nutrient dense than potato chips.

Note: Based on the percentage of the DRI for 19- to 50-year-old males. All these percentages apply to females in the same age range except for vitamin C. Females have lower vitamin C needs than males, so a baked potato provides over 20 percent of the DRI for this vitamin for women.

The narrowing of the pyramid from a wide base to a thin tip tells you to choose mostly **nutrient-dense** foods from each food group. *Nutrient density* refers to the amount of nutrients a food contains relative to the number of calories it contains. More nutrient-dense foods provide more nutrients per calorie (and in each bite) than less nutrient-dense foods and should be the foundation of your diet. Foods near the tip of MyPyramid, with added sugar and solid fats, should be eaten in moderation, because they add fewer nutrient-dense calories to your diet. Another way to think of nutrient-dense foods is that they are nutrient-*rich*.

Let's compare the nutrient density of two versions of the same food: a baked potato and potato chips (Figure 4.5). Both are in the vegetable group, and have about the same number of calories, but the baked potato provides much more folate, potassium, and vitamin C than the deep-fried chips. If you routinely choose foods with a lot of added sugars and saturated fats, you'll need to reduce the amount and/or kinds of foods you eat elsewhere, to compensate for those extra calories. This could cause you to displace healthier foods in your diet. If you don't adjust for the extra calories you're consuming, but eat them in addition to your normal diet, you'll quickly gain weight. Figure 4.6 helps you identify some nutrient-dense and less healthy food choices in each food group.

Finally, the multicolored bands in MyPyramid tell you to eat a variety of foods. Eating foods from each food group will increase your chances of consuming all 40 of the nutrients your body needs. Because no single food or food group provides all the nutrients, a varied diet of nutrient-dense foods is the savviest strategy. Figure 4.7 on the next page provides tips on how to choose a variety of foods from each food group. Following MyPyramid and choosing nutrient-dense foods within each food group enable you to eat a diet that provides well over 100 percent of the DRIs for many of the nutrients you need daily.[7]

The interactive website component of MyPyramid is designed to help you plan a personalized diet based on your dietary and lifestyle needs. We will discuss this in more detail shortly.

Remember, "Rome wasn't built in a day." Adopting a healthier diet and lifestyle, and changing long-term eating habits, takes time. The slogan "Steps to a Healthier You" and the steps on the side of MyPyramid reinforce the need for gradual improvement.

nutrient-dense The amount of nutrients per calorie in a given food. High nutrient-dense foods provide more nutrients per calorie than lower nutrient-dense foods.

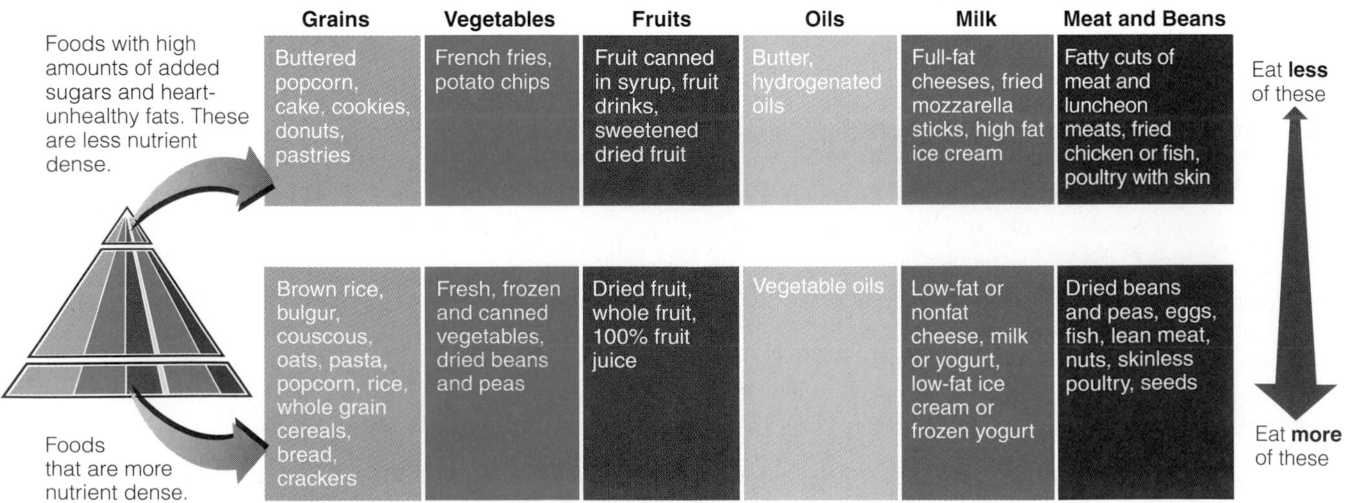

Figure 4.6 My Nutrient-Dense Pyramid
Nutrient-dense foods provide more nutrition per calorie. Choose nutrient-dense food more often to build a well-balanced diet.

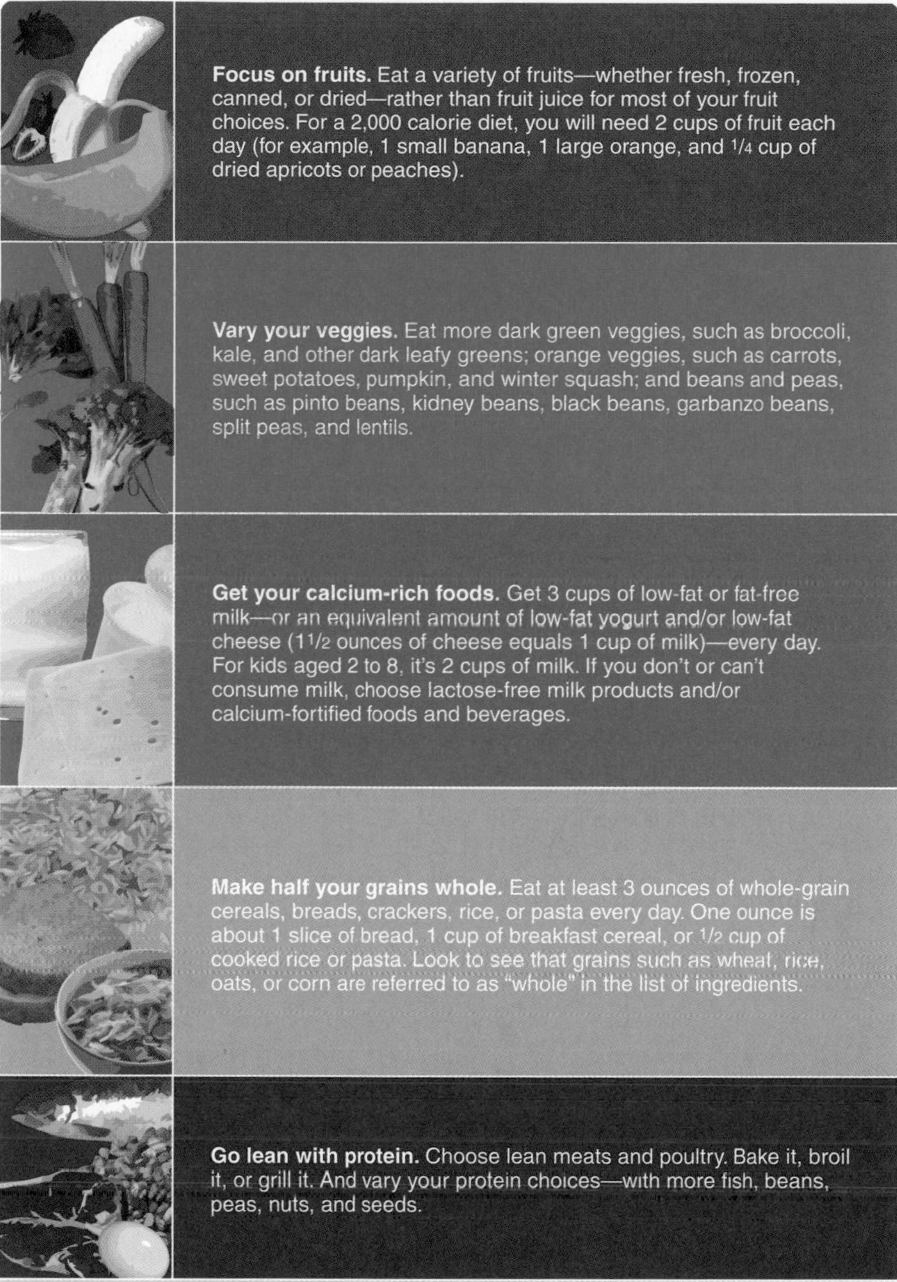

Figure 4.7 Mix Up Your Choices within Each Food Group

Data from: USDA Consumer Brochure. "Finding Your Way to a Healthier You." Based on the *Dietary Guidelines for Americans*.

Americans from 2 to 18 years of age spend an average of almost 5½ hours watching television and playing video games every day.

How to Use MyPyramid

You now know that you should eat a variety of nutrient-dense foods to be healthy, but you may be wondering how much from each food group *you,* personally, should be eating. The MyPyramid interactive website at www.mypyramid.gov will give you the exact numbers of servings to eat from each food group based on your daily calorie needs.

Your calorie needs are based on your age and gender (two factors beyond your control), as well as your activity level (a factor you can control). As you just read, the more active you are, the more calories you burn to fuel your activities, and the more calories you can (and need to) consume in foods.

Table 4.1
What Is Moderate and Vigorous Activity?

Do you know what exercise is moderate and what is vigorous? Check your assumptions.

Moderate Activities Expend 3½ to 7 Calories a Minute	Vigorous Activities Expend More Than 7 Calories a Minute
Walking briskly	Jogging or running
Bicycling 5 to 9 mph	Bicycling more than 10 mph
Shooting hoops	Playing competitive sports, such as basketball, soccer, or lacrosse
Using free weights	Rowing on a machine vigorously
Doing yoga	Doing karate, judo, or tae kwon do
Walking a dog	Jumping rope

Data adapted from: Centers for Disease Control and Prevention. General Physical Activities Defined by Level of Intensity. www.cdc.gov. Accessed March 2009.

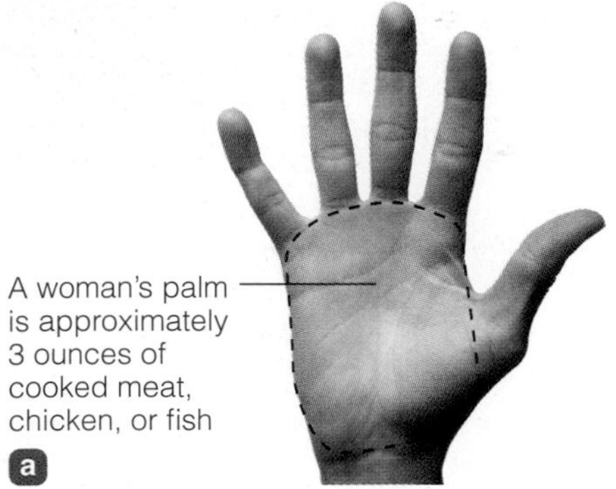

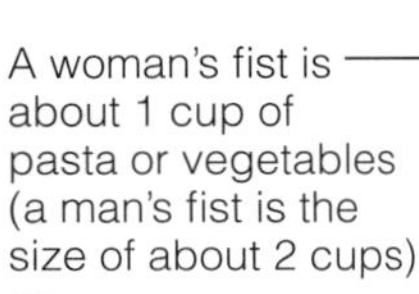
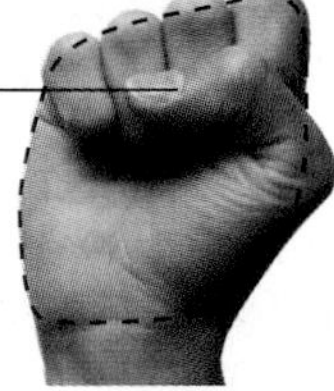

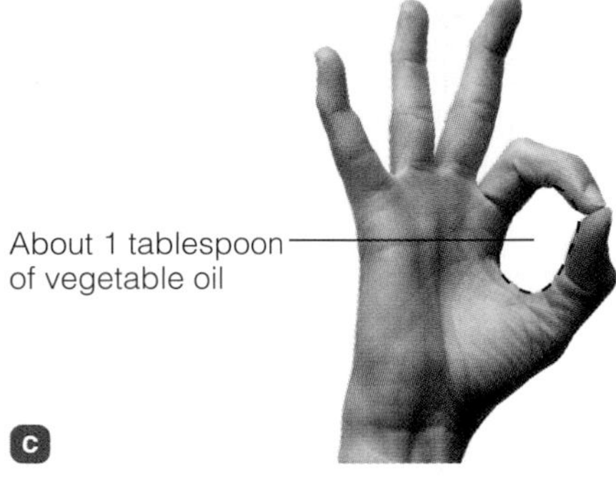

Figure 4.8 What's a Serving? Eat with Your Hands!
Your hands can guide you in estimating portion sizes.

At the website, you will enter your age, gender, and activity level. Based on this information, your daily calorie needs will be determined and your personalized eating plan, specifying the exact number of servings from each of the MyPyramid food groups, will be provided. With this information, you can plan your meals and snacks for the day. If you cannot go to the website, you can obtain similar information by using Tables 4.1 and 4.2. Let's use the tables to obtain your MyPyramid recommendations.

The first step in creating your personalized MyPyramid is to figure out how many calories you should be eating daily. To do this, you need to find out how active you are. Use Table 4.1 to see some examples of moderate and vigorous activity; based on these examples, do you think you are moderately or vigorously active? Next, look at Table 4.2 for the number of calories you need based on your activity level, age, and gender. When you know the number of calories you need daily, Table 4.3 will tell you how many servings from each food group you should consume to obtain those calories healthfully. This is the equivalent of *your* personalized MyPyramid.

Let's say that you are a moderately active female who needs 2,000 calories daily. To meet this level healthfully, you should consume:

- six servings from the grains group
- 2½ cups of dark green, orange, starchy, and other vegetables and some legumes
- 2 cups of fruits
- 3 cups of fat-free or low-fat milk and yogurt
- 5½ ounces of lean meat, poultry, and fish or the equivalent in meat alternatives, such as beans
- 3 tablespoons of vegetable oils over the course of the day

If you are having difficulty figuring out what 1 cup of vegetables, 3 ounces of meat, or 1 tablespoon of salad dressing looks like, use Figure 4.8. It provides an easy way to eyeball your serving sizes. Zoe, whom you met earlier, has a lunch that includes servings from the grain group (whole wheat bread), meat and beans group (peanut butter), vegetables (carrot sticks), and fruit (a piece of fruit). If she added a carton of yogurt or a glass of milk, she would have consumed foods from all the food groups!

If all of your food selections are low in fat and added sugar, the recommended number of food group servings listed above will provide a total of about 1,740 calories. This means that, after meeting your food group requirements, you have about 260 of your 2,000 calories left. This is your **discretionary calorie allowance** (see Figure 4.9). You can "spend" these calories on extra servings of foods such as grains, fruits, or vegetables, or occasionally on added fat or a dessert.

discretionary calorie allowance Calories left over in the diet once all nutrient needs have been met from the basic food groups.

Table 4.2

How Many Calories Do You Need Daily?

The number of calories you need daily is based on your age, gender, and activity level.[a]

Males				Females			
Age	Sedentary[a]	Moderately Active	Active	Age	Sedentary	Moderately Active	Active
16–18	2,400	2,800	3,200	**18**	1,800	2,000	2,400
19–20	2,600	2,800	3,000	**19–20**	2,000	2,200	2,400
21–25	2,400	2,800	3,000	**21–25**	2,000	2,200	2,400
26–30	2,400	2,600	3,000	**26–30**	1,800	2,000	2,400
31–35	2,400	2,600	3,000	**31–35**	1,800	2,000	2,200
36–40	2,400	2,600	2,800	**36–40**	1,800	2,000	2,200
41–45	2,200	2,600	2,800	**41–45**	1,800	2,000	2,200
46–50	2,200	2,400	2,800	**46–50**	1,800	2,000	2,200

[a]These calorie levels are based on the Institute of Medicine's Estimated Energy Requirements from *Dietary Reference Intakes: Macronutrients Report*, 2002. Sedentary: partaking in less than 30 minutes a day of moderate physical activity in addition to daily activities. Moderately active: partaking in at least 30 minutes and up to 60 minutes a day of moderate physical activity in addition to daily activities. Active: partaking in 60 or more minutes a day of moderate physical activity in addition to daily activities.

Data from: U.S. Department of Agriculture. MyPyramid food intake pattern calorie levels. www.mypyramid.gov. Accessed March 2009.

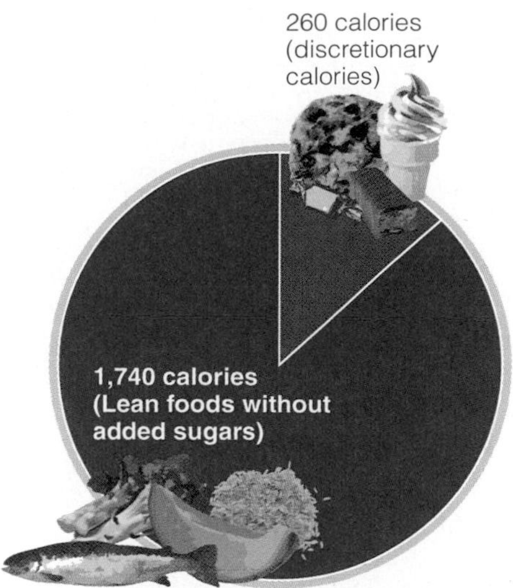

Figure 4.9 How Discretionary Calories Fit into a Balanced Diet
If you select mostly nutrient-dense, lean foods that don't contain added sugar, you may have leftover calories to "spend" on extra helpings or a sweet dessert.

Table 4.3

How Much Should You Eat from Each Food Group?

The following are suggested amounts to consume daily from each of the basic food groups and the oils based on your daily calorie needs. Remember that most of your choices should be fat-free or low fat and contain little added sugar.

Calorie Level	Grains (oz eq)	Vegetables (cups)	Fruits (cups)	Oil (tsp)	Milk (cups)	Meat and Beans (oz eq)
1,400	5	1.5	1.5	4	2	4
1,600	5	2	1.5	5	3	5
1,800	6	2.5	1.5	5	3	5
2,000	6	2.5	2	6	3	5.5
2,200	7	3	2	6	3	6
2,400	8	3	2	7	3	6.5
2,600	9	3.5	2	8	3	6.5
2,800	10	3.5	2.5	8	3	7
3,000	10	4	2.5	10	3	7
3,200	10	4	2.5	11	3	7

Grains: Includes all foods made with wheat, rice, oats, cornmeal, or barley, such as bread, pasta, oatmeal, breakfast cereals, tortillas, and grits. In general, one slice of bread, 1 cup of ready-to-eat cereal, or ½ cup of cooked rice, pasta, or cooked cereal is considered 1 ounce equivalent (oz eq) from the grains group. *At least half of all grains consumed should be whole grains, such as whole wheat bread, oats, or brown rice.*

Vegetables: Includes all fresh, frozen, canned, and dried vegetables and vegetable juices. In general, 1 cup of raw or cooked vegetables or vegetable juice, or 2 cups of raw leafy greens, is considered 1 cup from the vegetable group.

Fruits: Includes all fresh, frozen, canned, and dried fruits and fruit juices. In general, 1 cup of fruit, 100 percent fruit juice, or ½ cup of dried fruit is considered 1 cup from the fruit group.

Oils: Includes vegetable oils, such as canola, corn, olive, soybean, and sunflower oil; nuts; avocados; mayonnaise; salad dressings made with oils; and soft margarine.

Milk: Includes all fat-free and low-fat milk, yogurt, and cheese. In general, 1 cup of milk or yogurt, 1½ ounces of natural cheese, or 2 ounces of processed cheese is considered 1 cup from the milk group.

Meat and beans: In general, 1 ounce of lean meat, poultry, or fish; one egg, 1 tbs peanut butter, ¼ cup cooked dry beans, or ½ ounce nuts or seeds is considered 1 ounce equivalent (oz eq) from the meat and beans group.

Data from: U.S. Department of Agriculture, MyPyramid food intake pattern calorie levels. www.mypyramid.com. Accessed March 2009.

The calorie levels and distribution of food groups in MyPyramid are calculated using the leanest food choices with no added sugar. So if you pour whole milk (high in fat) over your sweetened cereal (added sugar) instead of using skim milk (fat-free) to drench your shredded wheat (no added sugar), the extra fat and sugar use up some of your discretionary calories. As you can see in Table 4.4, these discretionary calories can be used up quickly, depending on the foods you choose.

Let's now use these recommended amounts of servings from each food group and plan a 2,000-calorie menu. Figure 4.10 on page 15 shows how servings from the various food groups can create well-balanced meals and snacks throughout the day.

Although this menu is balanced and the foods are nutrient dense, it is unlikely that every day will be this ideal. The good news is that your nutrient needs are averaged over several days, or a week, of eating. If one day you eat insufficient servings of one food group or a specific nutrient, you can make up for it the next day. For example, let's say that you don't eat enough fruit one day but do eat an extra serving of grains. The next day you can adjust your diet by cutting back on your grain servings and adding an extra serving of fruit.

Table 4.4

Using Discretion with Discretionary Calories

As you can see, your discretionary calories can be used up quickly, depending on your food selections.

Choosing:	Over:	Will Cost You:
Whole milk (1 cup)	Fat-free milk (1 cup)	65 discretionary calories
Roasted chicken thigh with skin (3 oz)	Roasted chicken breast, skinless (3 oz)	70 discretionary calories
Glazed doughnut, yeast-type (3¾" diameter)	English muffin (one muffin)	165 discretionary calories
French fries (one medium order)	Baked potato (one medium)	299 discretionary calories
Regular soda (one can, 12 fl oz)	Diet soda (one can, 12 fl oz)	150 discretionary calories

Data from: U.S. Department of Agriculture. MyPyramid. How Do I Count the Discretionary Calories I Eat? www.mypyramid.gov. Accessed March 2009.

Table 4.5

A Combination of Good Food

Many of the foods you eat are probably mixed dishes that contain servings from multiple food groups. The following list should help you estimate the servings from each food group for some popular food items. Because the preparation process can vary greatly among recipes, these are only estimates.

Food and Sample Portion	Grains Group (oz eq)	Vegetable Group (cups)	Fruit Group (cups)	Milk Group (cups)	Meat and Beans Group (oz eq)	Estimated Total Calories
Cheese pizza, thin crust (one slice from medium pizza)	1	⅛	0	½	0	215
Macaroni and cheese (1 cup, made from packaged mix)	2	0	0	½	0	260
Bean and cheese burrito (one)	2½	⅛	0	1	2	445
Chicken fried rice (1 cup)	1½	¼	0	0	1	270
Large cheeseburger	2	0	0	⅓	3	500
Turkey sub sandwich (6" sub)	2	½	0	¼	2	320
Peanut butter and jelly sandwich (one)	2	0	0	0	2	375
Apple pie (one slice)	2	0	¼	0	0	280

Data from: U.S. Department of Agriculture, Mixed Dishes in MyPyramid. www.mypyramid.gov. Accessed March 2009.

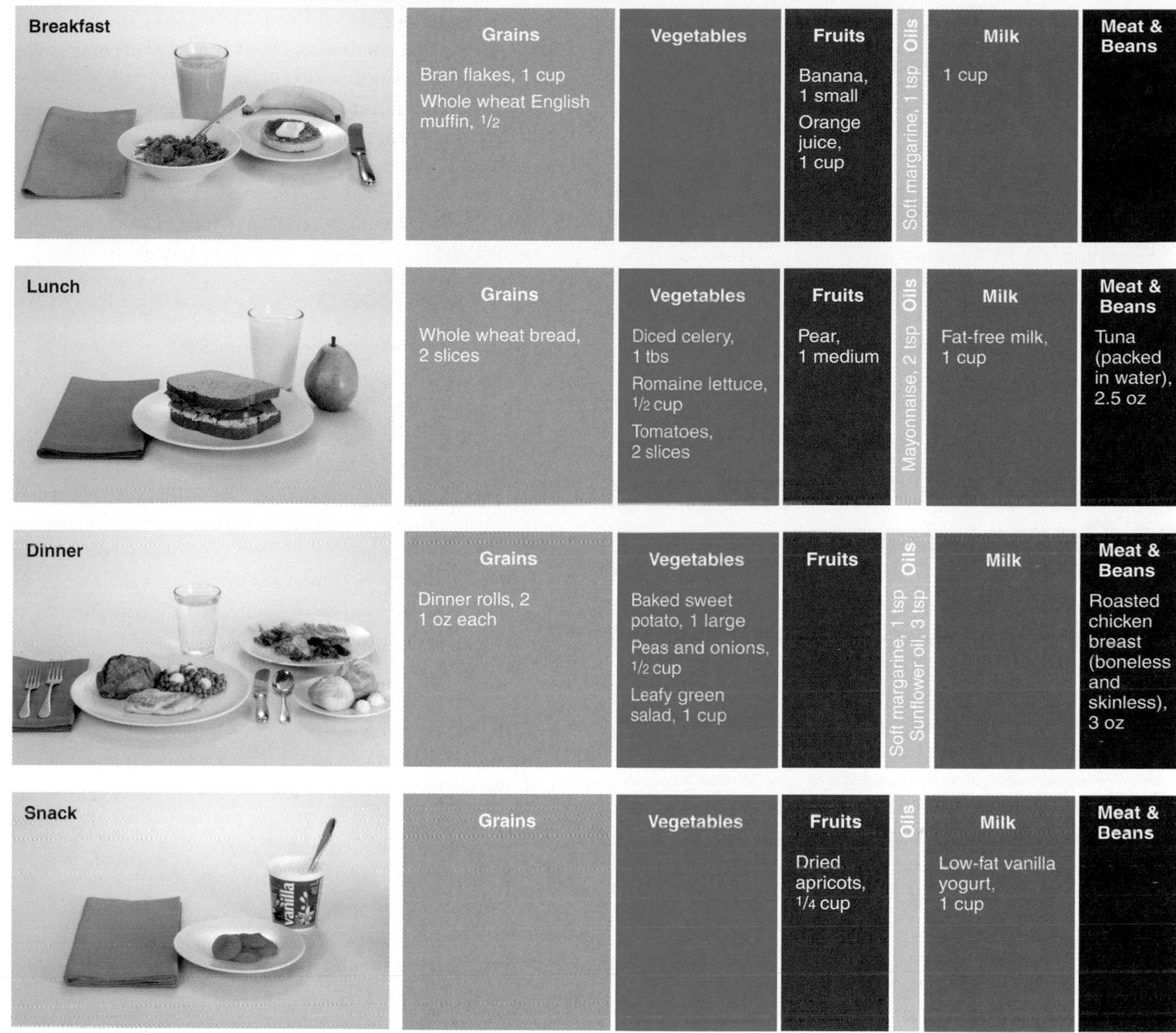

Figure 4.10 Using MyPyramid to Plan a Healthy Diet
A variety of foods from each food group creates a well-balanced diet.

If the foods at your meals are sometimes mixed dishes that contain a combination of foods, such as pizza, then they probably contribute servings from more than one food group. Table 4.5 provides examples of foods that contribute servings from multiple groups.

The Take-Home Message **MyPyramid is the latest food guidance system developed by the USDA. It is a personalized Internet-based educational tool that helps you choose a well-balanced diet from all the food groups to meet your nutrient needs. It emphasizes daily physical activity; a varied diet rich in fruits, vegetables, whole grains, and lean dairy products; and only a moderate amount of foods high in unhealthy fats, sugar, salt, and alcohol. MyPyramid encourages you to make gradual, small changes in your diet and lifestyle.**

UCook

Quick Brown Rice and Carrot Sauté

If your diet is falling short of whole grains from the grain group and veggies from the vegetable group, try this yummy Quick Brown Rice & Carrot Sauté.

UDo

Planning YOUR Pyramid

How does your daily diet measure up to MyPyramid recommendations? Visit our website and learn how to use the MyPyramid Tracker to evaluate your daily food choices.

The Top Five Points to Remember

1. The Dietary Reference Intakes (DRIs) are specific reference values, based on your age and gender, for the essential nutrients you need daily. The DRIs are designed to prevent nutrient deficiencies, maintain good health, prevent chronic diseases, and avoid unhealthy excesses. The DRIs consist of the Estimated Average Requirement, Recommended Dietary Allowance, Adequate Intake, Tolerable Upper Intake Level, and Acceptable Macronutrient Distribution Range.
2. The *Dietary Guidelines for Americans 2005* gives the current nutrition and physical activity recommendations for healthy Americans age 2 and older. These guidelines are designed to help individuals improve their diets to lower their risk of chronic diseases and conditions such as diabetes mellitus, heart disease, certain cancers, osteoporosis, obesity, high blood pressure, and high blood cholesterol levels.
3. Food guidance systems are carefully designed visual recommendations of food groups that provide a variety of food choices for creating a well-balanced diet. Many countries have developed food guidance systems based on their food supply, their cultural food preferences, and the specific nutritional needs of their citizens.
4. MyPyramid is the USDA's latest food guidance system. It visually represents many of the recommendations in the *Dietary Guidelines for Americans 2005* and helps you meet your daily DRIs for these nutrients. MyPyramid recommends the number of servings you should eat every day from each food group based on your calorie needs. There are five food groups: grains, vegetables, fruits, milk, and meat and beans. Oils are also shown on MyPyramid.
5. MyPyramid emphasizes daily physical activity, proportionality among the food groups, and variety within the food groups, as well as moderation when consuming foods with unhealthy fats and added sugar. It provides a personalized eating plan based on your needs and encourages gradual improvements in your diet and lifestyle choices to improve your health.

Test Yourself

1. The *Dietary Guidelines for Americans 2005* recommend that you
   a. consume adequate nutrients within your calorie needs and be physically active daily.
   b. stop smoking and walk daily.
   c. sleep 8 hours a night and jog every other day.
   d. consume adequate nutrients within your calorie needs and stop smoking.
2. The Estimated Average Intake (EAR) is
   a. the estimated amount of a nutrient that you should consume daily to be healthy.
   b. the amount of a nutrient that meets the average needs of 50 percent of individuals in a specific age and gender group.
   c. the maximum safe amount of a nutrient that you should consume daily.
   d. the healthy range of intake for carbohydrates, proteins, or fats designed to meet your nutrient needs and reduce your risk of chronic disease.
3. MyPyramid is a food guidance system that
   a. can help you implement the recommendations in the DRIs.
   b. can help you use the advice in the *Dietary Guidelines for Americans.*
   c. provides personalized food choices from among a variety of food groups to help you create a balanced diet.
   d. does all of the above.
4. Which of the following are the food groups in MyPyramid?
   a. grains, vegetables, milk, sweets, and meat and beans
   b. grains, fruits, alcohol, sweets, and meat and beans
   c. grains, vegetables, fruits, milk, and meat and beans
   d. grains, vegetables, sweets, alcohol, and meat and beans
5. Which of the following foods is most nutrient dense?
   a. an orange ice pop
   b. an orange
   c. orange-flavored punch
   d. orange sherbet

Answers

1. (a) The *Dietary Guidelines for Americans* recommend that you consume a balanced diet to meet your nutrient needs without overconsuming calories and that you be physically active daily. Though the *Dietary Guidelines* do not specifically address stopping smoking, this is a habit worth kicking. Walking or jogging daily is a wonderful way to be physically active. Sleeping 8 hours a night isn't mentioned in the *Dietary Guidelines* but is another terrific lifestyle habit.
2. (b) The EAR is the amount of a nutrient that would meet the needs of half of the individuals in a specific age and gender group. The EAR is used to obtain the Recommended Dietary Allowance, which is the amount of a nutrient that you should consume daily to maintain good health. The Tolerable Upper Intake Level is the maximum amount of a nutrient that you can consume on a regular basis that is unlikely to cause harm. The Acceptable Macronutrient Distribution Range identifies the healthy range of intake for carbohydrates, proteins, and fats.
3. (d) MyPyramid is a food guidance tool that helps you create a balanced diet, so that you can eat healthily. It is designed to help you meet the nutrient needs recommended in the DRIs and implement the advice in the *Dietary Guidelines for Americans.*
4. (c) Grains, vegetables, fruit, milk, and meat and beans are the five basic food groups in MyPyramid. Sweets and alcohol are not food groups and should be limited in the diet.
5. (b) While an orange ice pop and orange sherbet may be refreshing treats on a hot day, the orange is by far the most nutrient-dense food among the choices. The orange-flavored punch is a sugary drink with orange flavoring.

Web Resources

- For more tips and resources for MyPyramid, visit: www.MyPyramid.gov
- For current and upcoming dietary guidelines, see the United States Department of Agriculture website at: www.DietaryGuidelines.gov

5

Food Labels

Cracking the Code

1. All packaged foods must contain a **food label.** T/F

2. Food manufacturers decide what **information** to list on a food label. T/F

3. Food labels must **identify** the name and address of the manufacturer or distributor. T/F

4. A **health claim** on a label must state the beneficial component the food contains and the disease or condition it can improve. T/F

5. Foods with labels bearing claims about their role in health or body function are **better choices** than the same foods without these claims. T/F

Jessie, a 19-year-old biology major, has been told by her doctor to restrict her sodium intake to keep her borderline high blood pressure from becoming full-fledged high blood pressure (hypertension). Although Jessie tries to make sodium-conscious food choices, she also likes to microwave a mug of hot soup in her dorm room as a snack. If she read the label on her soup, she might be surprised to discover that her frequent soup snacks are delivering a lot more sodium than her regular meals.

Imagine walking down the supermarket aisle and finding all the foods on the shelves packaged in plain cardboard boxes and unmarked aluminum cans. How would you know if a plain box contained a pound of pasta or 100 dog biscuits, or if blank cans held chicken soup or crushed pineapple?

You rely on food labels more than you think so it's worth taking the time to learn how to read them. At first, deciphering food label information might seem confusing. But once you've cracked the code, you'll be able to confidently decide which foods to buy and which to leave on the shelf.

Answers

1. True. The FDA requires a food label on all packaged food items, and specific information must be included. To find out exactly what must be disclosed on the food label, check out page 2.
2. False. There are strict guidelines about the information that must be listed on a food label. See pages 2 and 3.
3. True. The Food and Drug Administration (FDA) requires that the name and address of the food manufacturer or distributor be identified on the food label. See pages 2 and 3 for more.
4. True. Turn to pages 9 and 10 to learn more about the types of health claims that food manufacturers may use.
5. Not necessarily. For example, milk provides calcium and vitamin D, which are essential for healthy bones. This fact remains true whether or not the milk carton proclaims it. Check it out on pages 9 through 12.

What Makes Food Labels So Important?

Food labels serve three important functions that make them helpful tools for anyone who wants to eat a healthy diet. First and foremost, they tell you what's inside the package. Second, they contain a Nutrition Facts panel, which identifies the calories and nutrients in a serving of the food. Third, they list Daily Values (DVs), which help you determine how those calories and nutrients will fit into your overall diet.

The Food Label Tells You What's in the Package

To help consumers make informed food choices, the Food and Drug Administration (FDA) regulates the labeling of all packaged foods in the United States.[1] The FDA mandates that every packaged food be labeled with:

- The name of the food
- The net weight (the weight of the food in the package, excluding the weight of the package or packing material)
- The name and address of the manufacturer or distributor
- A list of ingredients in descending order by weight, with the heaviest item listed first
- Nutrition information, including total calories, calories from fat, total fat, saturated fat, *trans* fats, cholesterol, sodium, total carbohydrate, dietary fiber, sugars, vitamin A, vitamin C, calcium, and iron
- Serving sizes that are uniform among similar products, which allows consumers easier comparison shopping
- An indication of how a serving of the food fits into an overall daily diet
- Uniform definitions for descriptive label terms, such as *light* and *fat-free*
- Health claims that are accurate and science-based, if made about the food or one of its components

Cereal box readers will read the information on the box as many as 12 times before they consume the last spoonful!

- The presence of any of eight common allergens that might be present in the food, including milk, eggs, fish, shellfish, tree nuts (cashews, walnuts, almonds, etc.), peanuts, wheat, and soybeans[2]

In addition, foods that have been manufactured with organically grown ingredients are allowed to display an organic seal if they meet certain criteria. We'll say more about organic foods in Concept 27.

Very few foods are exempt from carrying a Nutrition Facts panel on the label. Such foods include plain coffee and tea; some spices, flavorings, and other foods that don't provide a significant amount of nutrients; deli items, bakery foods, and other ready-to-eat foods that are prepared and sold in retail establishments; restaurant meals; and foods produced by small businesses (companies that have total annual sales of less than $500,000).[3]

Compare the two food labels in Figure 5.1. Notice that the amount and type of nutrition information on the 1925 box of cereal are vague and less informative than the more recent version, which meets the FDA's current labeling requirements.

Figure 5.1 Out with the Old and in with the New
(a) A cereal box from the 1920s carried vague nutrition information. **(b)** Today, manufacturers must adhere to strict labeling requirements mandated by the FDA.

a

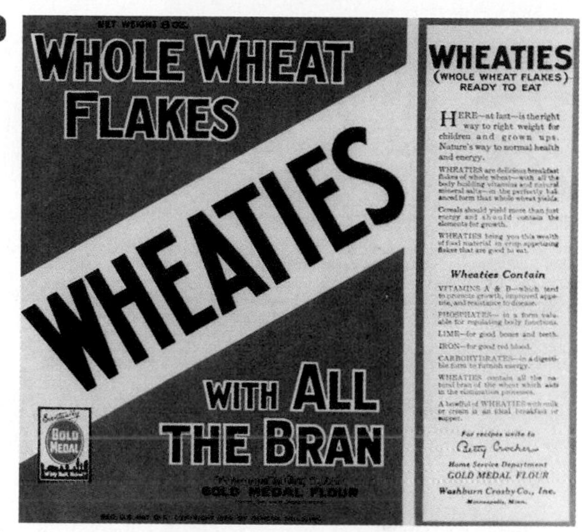

b

The **Nutrition Facts panel** lists standardized serving sizes, specific nutrients, and shows how a serving of the food fits into a healthy diet by stating its contribution to the percentage of the Daily Value for each nutrient. The old cereal box doesn't contain this information.

The **name** of the product must be displayed on the front label.

The **ingredients** must be listed in descending order by weight. This format is missing in the old box. Whole grain wheat is the predominant ingredient in the current cereal box.

The **net weight** of the food in the box must now be located at the bottom of the package.

The Nutrition Facts Panel Provides a Nutritional Snapshot of the Food

Suppose you're in the dairy aisle of a supermarket, trying to select a carton of milk. You want to watch your fat intake, so you have narrowed your choices to reduced-fat 2 percent milk or nonfat milk. How do they compare in terms of calories, fat, and other nutrients per serving? How do you decide which is more healthful? The answer is simple: Look at the labels. All the information that you need to make a smart choice is provided on one area of the label, the **Nutrition Facts panel.**

The Nutrition Facts panel provides a nutritional snapshot of the food inside a package. By law, the panel must list amounts of the following in one serving of the food:

- Calories and calories from fat
- Total fat, saturated fat, and *trans* fat
- Cholesterol
- Sodium
- Total carbohydrate, dietary fiber, and sugars
- Protein
- Vitamin A, vitamin C, calcium, and iron[4]

Nutrition Facts panel The area on a food label that provides a uniform listing of specific nutrients obtained in one serving of the food.

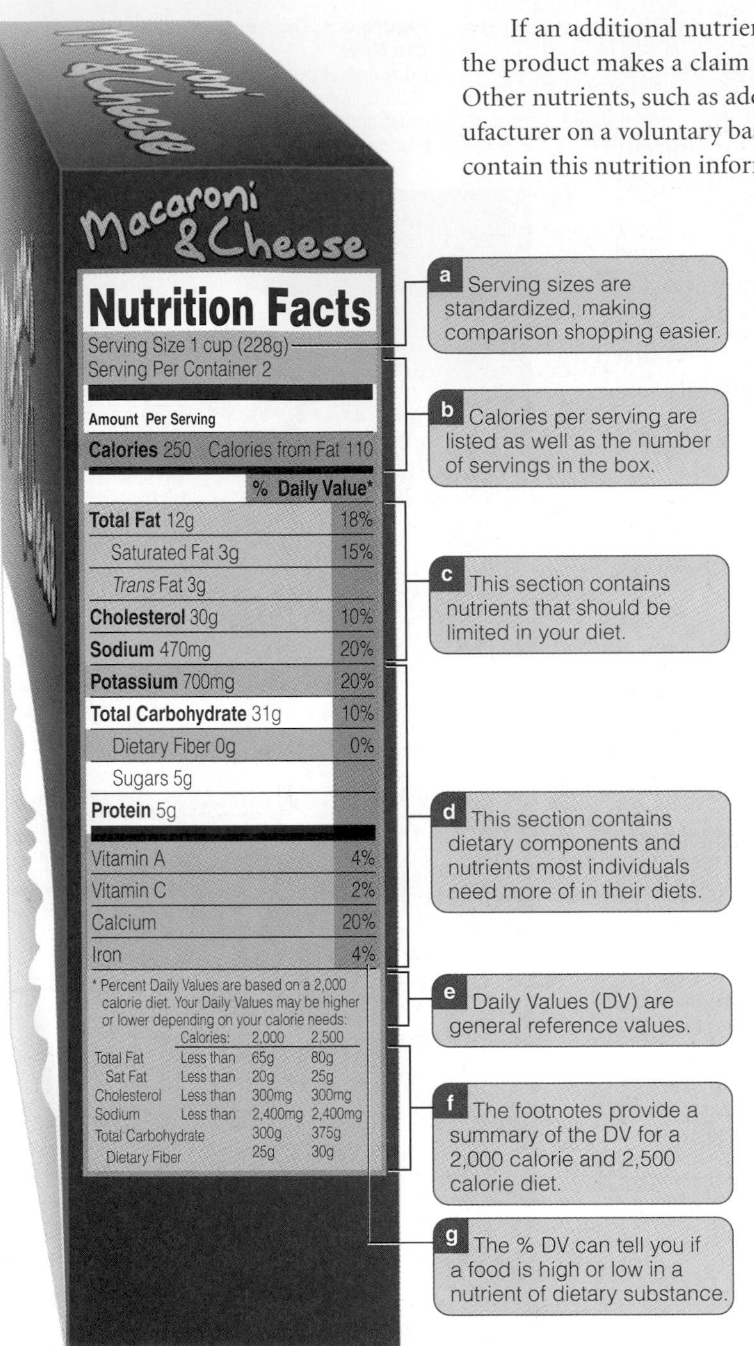

Figure 5.2 Understanding the Nutrition Facts Panel
Know how to read and understand the Nutrition Facts panel of a label.

Data from: Center for Food Safety and Applied Nutrition. "How to Understand and Use the Nutrition Facts Label." 2004.

If an additional nutrient, such as vitamin E or vitamin D, has been added, or if the product makes a claim about a nutrient, then that nutrient must also be listed. Other nutrients, such as additional vitamins and minerals, can be listed by the manufacturer on a voluntary basis. The majority of the packaged foods you purchase will contain this nutrition information.

Let's learn how to decipher the Nutrition Facts panel (Figure 5.2). At the top of the panel is the serving size. By law, the serving size must be listed both by weight in grams (less useful to you) and in common household measures, such as cups and ounces (more useful to you). Because serving sizes are standardized among similar food products, you can compare one brand of macaroni and cheese with a different brand to assess which one better meets your needs.

The rest of the information on the panel is based on the listed serving size (in this case, 1 cup) of the food. For example, if you ate two servings (2 cups) of this macaroni and cheese, which is the number of servings in the entire box, you would double the nutrient information on the label to calculate the calories, as well as the amount of fat and other nutrients. The servings per container are particularly useful for portion control.

Below the serving size are listed the calories per serving. The calories from fat give you an idea of what proportion of the food's calories comes from fat. In this box of macaroni and cheese, 110 out of a total of 250 calories—that is, nearly half—are from fat.

Next are the nutrients that you should limit or add to your diet. Americans typically eat too much fat, including saturated fat, *trans* fat, and cholesterol, and too much sodium. These are on the label to remind you to monitor your intake. In contrast, Americans tend to fall short in dietary fiber, vitamins A and C, and iron. These are on the label to remind you to make sure to choose foods rich in these substances. As you can see, the Nutrition Facts panel can be your best shopping guide to foods that are low in the nutrients you want to limit (such as saturated fat) and high in the nutrients that you want to eat in higher amounts (such as fiber).

Are you wondering what determines if a food contains a "high" or "low" amount of a specific nutrient? That's where the Daily Values come into play.

The Daily Values Help You See How Foods Fit into Your Diet

Unlike the DRIs, which are precise recommended amounts you should eat of each nutrient, the **Daily Values (DVs)** listed on the Nutrition Facts panel give you a ballpark idea of how the nutrients in the foods you buy fit into your overall diet. They are established reference levels of nutrients, based on a 2,000-calorie diet, that are used only on food labels.

Daily Values (DVs) Established reference levels of nutrients, based on a 2,000-calorie diet, that are used on food labels.

For example, if calcium is listed at 20 percent, a serving of that food provides 20 percent of most adults' daily requirement for calcium. If you are under 19 years of age or older than 50, your calcium needs are higher than the reference number used for the DV. Also, since the DVs on the food label are based on a 2,000-calorie diet, if you need more or fewer than 2,000 calories daily, some of your DV values may be higher or lower than those listed on the Nutrition Facts panel.

The DVs are based on older reference levels and are not as current as the DRIs. For example, whereas the DRIs recommend an upper level of dietary sodium of no more than 2,300 milligrams (daily), the DVs use less than 2,400 mg as the reference level.

There are no DVs listed on the label for *trans* fat (a type of unhealthy fat we'll discuss in Concept 10), sugars, and protein. This is because there isn't enough information available to set reference values for *trans* fat and sugars, and consuming adequate protein isn't a health problem for most Americans.

If a serving provides 20 percent or more of the DV, it is considered high in that nutrient. For example, a serving of macaroni and cheese is high in sodium (not a healthy attribute), but is also high in calcium (a healthy attribute). If you eat this entrée for lunch, you'll need to eat less sodium during the rest of the day. However, the good news is that a serving of this pasta meal also provides 20 percent of the DV for calcium.

If a nutrient provides 5 percent or less of the DV, it is considered low in that nutrient. A serving of macaroni and cheese doesn't provide much fiber, vitamin A, vitamin C, or iron. You will need to eat other foods to supply your diet with these nutrients on the days that you eat macaroni and cheese.

Finally, if the food package is large enough to accommodate it, a footnote may be included at the bottom of the label. This provides a summary of the total DVs for a 2,000-calorie diet, as well as for a 2,500-calorie diet. Think of this area as a little "cheat sheet" to help you when you are shopping, so that you don't have to memorize the values. As you can see from the footnote, you should try to keep your sodium intake under 2,400 milligrams daily. Since you know that macaroni and cheese is high in sodium, providing 20 percent of the DV, or 470 milligrams, of sodium, you should try to keep the sodium in your remaining food choices during the day to under 2,000 milligrams.

Now that you know how to read the Nutrition Facts panel, let's return to the milk question posed earlier and use what you've learned to compare the reduced-fat 2 percent and nonfat milk labels in Figure 5.3. Let's start at the top:

a. Both cartons have the same standardized 1-cup serving, which makes the comparison easy.

b. The reduced-fat milk has 50 percent more calories than the nonfat milk. Almost 40 percent of the calories in the reduced-fat milk are from fat.

c. Use the percent of the DV to assess whether the milk is considered high or low in a given nutrient. For instance, a serving of reduced-fat milk provides more than 5 percent of the DV

Figure 5.3 Using the Nutrition Facts Panel to Comparison Shop
The Nutrition Facts panel or label makes comparison shopping between similar foods easier for the consumer.

Data from: U.S. Food and Drug Administration, Center for Food Safety and Applied Nutrition. *How to Understand and Use the Nutrition Facts Label.* 2004.

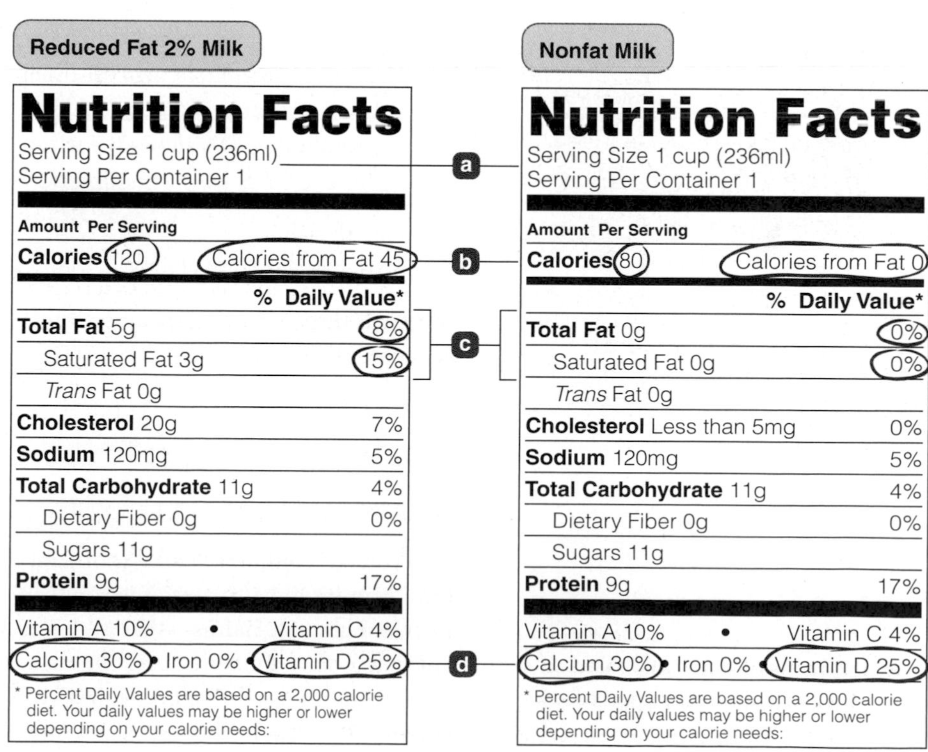

for both total and saturated fat (as well as cholesterol), so it isn't considered low in these nutrients. In fact, the saturated fat provides 15 percent of the DV, which is getting close to the definition of high (20 percent of the DV). In contrast, the nonfat milk doesn't contain any fat, saturated fat, or cholesterol.

d. Since foods that are low in fat aren't necessarily healthier, let's make sure that the nonfat milk is as nutritious as the reduced-fat variety. Comparing the remaining nutrients, especially calcium and vitamin D, confirms that the nonfat milk has all the vitamins and minerals that the reduced-fat milk does, but with fewer calories, no fat, and essentially no cholesterol. In fact, both milks provide a high amount of calcium and vitamin D, so, when it comes to choosing milk, the nonfat version is the smarter choice.

The Take-Home Message **The FDA regulates the labeling on all packaged foods. Every food label must contain the name of the food, its net weight, the name and address of the manufacturer or distributor, a list of ingredients, standardized nutrition information, and potential allergens. The Nutrition Facts panel identifies the nutrients in one serving of the food. The Daily Values are ballpark daily recommendations for the nutrients listed on food labels.**

Can Claims on a Food Label Be Trusted?

In the 1980s, the savvy Kellogg Company ran an ad campaign for its fiber-rich All Bran cereal, reminding the public of the National Cancer Institute's recommendation to eat low-fat, high-fiber foods, fresh fruits, and vegetables to maintain a healthy weight. According to the FDA, sales of high-fiber cereals increased over 35 percent within a year.[5] Manufacturers realized that putting nutrition and health claims on labels is effective in influencing consumer purchases. Supermarket shelves were soon crowded with products boasting various claims.

Currently, the FDA allows the use of three types of claims on food products:

- Nutrient content claims
- Health claims
- Structure/function claims

All foods displaying these claims on the label must meet specified criteria. Let's look at each of these claims closely.

Nutrient Content Claims Identify the Level of a Nutrient in the Food

nutrient content claim A claim on a food label that describes the level or amount of a nutrient in the food product.

Can you feel confident that a jar of light mayonnaise is really lower in calories and fat than regular mayonnaise? Yes, you can. That's because the FDA closely regulates **nutrient content claims**—that is, claims that describe the level or amount of a nutrient in a food. A food producer can make a claim about the amount of a nutrient the food contains (or doesn't contain) by using descriptive terms such as *free* (fat-free yogurt), *high* (high-fiber crackers), *low* (low saturated fat cereal), *reduced* (reduced-sodium soup), and *extra lean* (extra lean ground beef), as long as it meets the FDA's strict criteria. These terms can help you identify at a glance the food items that best meet your needs.

Jessie, the student with borderline high blood pressure from the beginning of this concept, could look for low-sodium claims on labels to help limit the amount of sodium in her diet. As you may remember, Jessie enjoys a mug of hot soup during her late-night studying. But she's probably sipping more sodium than she thinks.

Look at the labels of the canned soups in Figure 5.4. Jessie should be looking for the "low-sodium" label on her chicken soup, as that soup cannot contain more than 140 milligrams of sodium per serving. The next best choice would be the soup

Figure 5.4 Soup's On!
Nutrient claims on the food label can help you choose foods that meet your needs. **(a)** Because this can of chicken noodle soup displays the "low-sodium" nutrient claim, it can't provide more than 140 milligrams of sodium in a serving. **(b)** This can of soup has more than 25 percent less sodium than the classic version, so the term *less* may be displayed on its label. **(c)** The classic variety of chicken noodle soup has the most sodium per serving.

Table 5.1

What Does That Nutrient Claim Mean?

Nutrient	Free	Low	Reduced/Less	Light
Calories	< 5 calories (cal) per serving	≤ 40 cal per serving	At least 25% fewer calories per serving	If the food contains 50% or more of its calories from fat, then the fat must be reduced.
Fat	< 0.5 gram (g) per serving	≤ 3g per serving	At least 25% less fat per serving	Same as above
Saturated fat	< 0.5 g per serving	≤ 1 g per serving	At least 25% less saturated fat per serving	N/A
Cholesterol	< 2 milligrams (mg) per serving	≤ 20 mg per serving	At least 25% less cholesterol per serving	N/A
Sodium	< 5 mg per serving	≤ 140 mg per serving	At least 25% less sodium per serving	If the food is reduced by at least 50% per serving
Sugars	< 0.5 g	N/A	At least 25% less sugar per serving	N/A

Other Labeling Terms

Term	Definition
"High," "Rich in," or "Excellent source of"	The food contains 20% or more of the DV of the nutrient in a serving. Can be used to describe protein, vitamins, minerals, or fiber.
"Good source of"	A serving of the food provides 10–19% of the DV. Can be used to describe meals or main dishes.
"More," "Added," "Extra," or "Plus"	A serving of the food provides 10% of the DV. Can only be used to describe vitamins, minerals, protein, or fiber.
"Lean"	Can be used on seafood and meat that contains less than 10 g of fat, 4.5 g or less of saturated fat, and less than 95 mg of cholesterol per serving.
"Extra lean"	Can be used on seafood and meat that contains less than 5 g of fat, less than 2 g of saturated fat, and less than 95 mg of cholesterol per serving.

N/A = not applicable.

with the term *less sodium* on the label, which means that it must contain at least 25 percent less sodium than the regular variety. The classic can of chicken soup contains almost 900 milligrams for a serving, which is likely the same or even more sodium than Jessie consumed at dinner.

Table 5.1 lists some of the most common nutrient claims on food labels, the specific criteria that each claim must meet as mandated by the FDA, and examples of food products that carry these nutrient claims.

In a recent survey, **over 40 percent** of consumers said they bought foods claiming to reduce the risk of heart disease, and over 25 percent picked items claiming to reduce the risk of cancer. Health claims do influence food decisions!

Health Claims Identify a Food-Health Relationship

Suppose you are sitting at your kitchen table, eating a bowl of Cheerios in skim milk and staring at the front of the cereal box. You notice a claim on the front of the box that's as big as a newspaper headline. The claim states: "The soluble fiber in

Figure 5.5 A Structure/Function Label Claim
A structure/function claim describes how a nutrient or substance, such as the antioxidants that have been added to this cereal, support the immune system, which is a function in the body. The manufacturer can't claim that the food lowers a consumer's risk of a chronic disease or health condition.

Cheerios, as part of a heart healthy diet, can help you lower your cholesterol." Do you recognize this as a health claim that links Cheerios with better heart health?

A **health claim** must contain two important components:

- A food or a dietary compound, such as fiber
- A corresponding disease or health-related condition that is associated with the claim[6]

In the Cheerios example, the soluble fiber (the dietary compound) that naturally occurs in oats has been shown to lower blood cholesterol levels (the corresponding health-related condition), which can help reduce the risk of heart disease.

There are three types of health claims: (1) authorized health claims, (2) health claims based on authoritative statements, and (3) qualified health claims. The differences among them lie in the amount of supporting research backing them up, as well as the level of agreement among scientists about the strength of the relationship between the food or dietary compound and the disease or condition. See Table 5.2 for a definition of these claims and examples of each.

Some Claims Link Foods to Body Structure or Function

The last type of label claim is the **structure/function claim,** which describes how a nutrient or dietary compound affects the structure or function of the human body (Figure 5.5).[7] The claims "calcium builds strong bones" and "fiber maintains bowel regularity" are examples of structure/function claims. Notice that structure/function claims are more limited than health claims: They cannot state that the nutrient or dietary compound has any beneficial effect in preventing or treating a disease or condition.[8]

Unlike the other claims we've discussed, structure/function claims don't need to be preapproved by the FDA. They do need to be truthful and not misleading, but the manufacturer is responsible for making sure that the claim is accurate. Moreover, it's up to the consumer to recognize the difference between nutrient and health claims, which are supported by a significant amount of solid research and approved by the

health claim A claim on a food label that describes a relationship between a food or dietary compound and a disease or health-related condition.

structure/function claim A claim on a food label that describes how a nutrient or dietary compound affects the structure or function of the human body.

Table 5.2

Sorting Out the Health Claims on Food Labels

Type of Claim	Definition	Examples (Claims of links between . . .)
Authorized health claims (well established)	Claims based on a well-established relationship between the food or compound and the health benefit Food manufacturers must petition the FDA and provide scientific research to back up the claim. If there is significant agreement among the supporting research and a consensus among scientists and experts in the field that a relationship exists between the food or ingredient and the disease or health condition, the FDA will allow an authorized health claim. Specified wording must be used. The FDA has approved 12 authorized health claims.	■ Calcium and osteoporosis ■ Sodium and hypertension ■ Dietary fat and cancer ■ Dietary saturated fat and cholesterol and risk of coronary heart disease ■ Fiber-containing grain products, fruits, and vegetables and cancer ■ Fruits, vegetables, and grain products that contain fiber, particularly soluble fiber, and the risk of coronary heart disease ■ Fruits and vegetables and cancer ■ Folate and neural tube defects ■ Dietary sugar, alcohol, and dental caries ■ Soluble fiber from certain foods and risk of coronary heart disease ■ Soy protein and risk of coronary heart disease ■ Plant sterol/stanol esters and risk of coronary heart disease
Health claims based on authoritative statements (well established)	Claims based on statements made by a U.S. government agency, such as the Centers for Disease Control (CDC) and the National Institutes of Health (NIH) If the FDA approves a claim submitted by the manufacturer, the wording of the claim must include "may," as in "whole grains may help reduce the risk of heart disease," to show that other factors in addition to the food or dietary ingredient may play a role in the disease or condition. This type of health claim can be used only for foods and not for dietary supplements.	■ Whole-grain foods and risk of heart disease and certain cancers ■ Potassium and the risk of high blood pressure ■ Fluoridated water and the reduced risk of dental caries
Qualified health claims (less well established)	Claims based on evidence that is still emerging; however, the current evidence to support the claim is greater than the evidence suggesting that the claim isn't valid These claims are allowed in order to speed up the communication of potentially beneficial health information to the public. They must include the statement: "The evidence to support the claim is limited or not conclusive" or "Some scientific evidence suggests. . . ." Many experts, including the American Dietetic Association, don't support this type of health claim, since it is based on emerging evidence. Qualified health claims may be used on dietary supplements if approved by the FDA.	■ Selenium and cancer ■ Antioxidant vitamins and cancer ■ Nuts and heart disease ■ Omega-3 fatty acids and coronary heart disease ■ B vitamins and vascular disease ■ Monounsaturated fatty acids from olive oil and coronary heart disease ■ Unsaturated fatty acids from canola oil and reduced risk of coronary heart disease

What's in That Taco? Getting the Facts When Dining Out

In this concept, you've learned how to use the information on food labels to make healthier choices. But what if fast-food outlets, restaurants, and cafés were required to "label" the foods they serve? If you knew, for example, that the tuna sandwich at Subway had 530 calories, and the roast beef sandwich had 290, would that information change your choice?

Although it might sound far-fetched, lawmakers from New York to California have proposed legislation requiring food-service providers to post in a prominent place the calorie content of each menu item they offer. In Manhattan, calorie-posting regulations took effect in April 2008 and, although the New York State Restaurant Association immediately sued to block the law, the postings are still required.[1] Public opinion polls show that an overwhelming majority of customers support them. So do the Center for Science in the Public Interest, the American Heart Association, and the American Cancer Society, as well as many other health and nutrition organizations.[2]

Opponents say that legislators shouldn't interfere in matters of personal responsibility and claim that menu-labeling isn't effective, anyway. They argue that millions of people see the caloric and fat content of a chocolate bar and eat it, anyway. In contrast, supporters point out that consumers cannot make healthy menu choices unless they know what's in the foods they're considering. They contend that consumers often choose foods they think are lower in fat and calories, when, in fact, another choice would be more healthy.

What about you? Do you think you could spot the healthiest choices on restaurant menus without nutrition information? Let's find out! Answer the following questions to see if you have a realistic impression of the calorie and fat content of some common fast foods:

1. You're late for class, so you stop at Dunkin' Donuts for a quick breakfast. Which of the following options is the lowest in calories and fat?
   a. sugar raised doughnut
   b. plain bagel with a packet (2 ounces) of cream cheese
   c. corn muffin

Answer: A. Surprised? The doughnut has 190 calories and 9 grams of fat. Both the corn muffin and the bagel and cream cheese have over 450 calories each and almost twice the fat (the corn muffin has 17 grams and the bagel and cream cheese has 18)! But before you start celebrating with doughnuts, the even better choice at Dunkin' Donuts is the English muffin (160 calories and 1.5 grams of fat) with jelly. Grab a piece of fruit on the way out to add fiber and tons of nutrients to your morning meal!

2. You're in the mood for a burrito, so you decide to have lunch at Taco Bell. Which burrito would be the lowest in both calories and fat?
   a. grilled stuffed beef burrito
   b. grilled stuffed chicken burrito
   c. steak supreme burrito

Answer: C. While the word *grilled* is usually synonymous with a leaner preparation method, the word *stuffed* can signify that the burrito is bursting with cheese, which is high in fat. The Steak Supreme Burrito has 380 calories and 12 grams of fat, whereas the Grilled Stuffed Chicken Burrito has 650 calories and 23 grams of fat. The Grilled Stuffed Beef Burrito is the heftiest lunch, packing a whopping 690 calories and 30 grams of fat!

3. Tonight you're having dinner at Pizza Hut. Which of the following pizza slices would be the lowest in both calories and fat?
   a. italian sausage and red onion pizza
   b. cheese pizza
   c. veggie lover's pizza

Answer: C. Order the veggie pizza if you want the fewest calories and the least amount of fat: It has 200 calories per slice and 7 grams of fat. In contrast, the cheese pizza has 220 calories and 8 grams of fat. But the real porker here is the sausage pizza: It has 240 calories per slice and 50 percent more fat (10 grams versus 7) of the veggie pizza.

FDA, and structure/function claims, which don't need prior approval for use. Unfortunately, this burdens busy shoppers, who may not appreciate the differences between the two types of claims.

Manufacturers can also use structure/function claims to trick shoppers into assuming that their brand of a product is superior to another brand of the same product without the claim. For instance, a yogurt that says "Calcium builds strong bones!" on its label may be identical to another yogurt without the flashy label claim.

All foods that boast a health claim and/or a structure/function claim can also be marketed as "functional foods." Concept 26 discusses this trendy category of foods.

Although keeping the types of health and structure/function claims straight can be challenging, here's one way to remember them:

- Authorized health claims and health claims based on authoritative statements are the strongest, as they are based on years of accumulated research or an authoritative statement.
- Qualified health claims are less convincing. They are made on potentially healthful foods or dietary components, but because the evidence is still emerging, the claim has to be "qualified."
- Structure/function claims are the weakest claims, as they are just statements or facts about the role the nutrient or dietary component plays in your body. They can't claim that consuming the food or dietary component will lower your risk of developing a disease, such as cancer, or a condition, such as high blood pressure. As you become more expert at decoding the claims on food labels, you will come to see that those with structure/function claims have the weakest wording.

The Take-Home Message **The FDA allows and regulates the use of nutrient content claims, health claims, and structure/function claims on food labels. Any foods or dietary supplements displaying these claims on the label must meet specified criteria and be truthful.**

Check out these recipes and more suggestions at **www.pearsonhighered.com/blake**

UCook

Cheese & Broccoli Stuffed Potato

You'll be stuffed at dinner when you enjoy this healthy and hearty tater that's a meal in itself. You'll find the full recipe on our website displayed above.

UDo

Virtual Food Label Fun

Take this virtual shopping trip challenge to see how food label savvy you really are. Visit the link on our Companion Website for some comparison shopping fun!

The Top Five Points to Remember

1. The FDA regulates all packaged foods to ensure that they are labeled accurately. The Nutrition Facts panel on the food label must list the serving size of the food. It must also show the corresponding amounts of calories, fat, saturated fat, *trans* fat, cholesterol, sodium, sugars, protein, vitamins A and C, calcium, and iron that are contained in a serving of the food. Other nutrients may be added by the manufacturer voluntarily. If a food product makes a claim about a nutrient, it must be listed in the Nutrition Facts panel.
2. The Daily Values are reference levels of intakes for the nutrients listed on the food label. Unlike the DRIs, they are not specific, individualized, recommended intakes but, rather, reference points that allow you to assess how the nutrients in the foods you buy can fit into your overall diet.
3. A food product label can carry a nutrient content claim about the amount of a nutrient the food contains by using descriptive terms such as *free, high, low, reduced*, and *extra lean,* as long as it meets the strict criteria for each item designated by the FDA.
4. A health claim must contain a food component or a dietary ingredient and a corresponding disease or health-related condition that is associated with the claim. The FDA must approve all health claims.
5. Structure/function claims describe how a food or dietary component affects the structure or function of the body. These claims must be truthful and accurate

and do not need FDA approval before being used. They cannot be tied to a disease or health-related condition.

Test Yourself

1. By law, which of the following MUST be listed on the food label?
   a. calories, fat, and potassium
   b. fat, saturated fat, and vitamin E
   c. calories, fat, and saturated fat
   d. calories, sodium, and vitamin D
2. The bran cereal you eat in the morning carries a "high-fiber" claim on its label. This is an example of
   a. a nutrient claim.
   b. a structure/function claim.
   c. a health claim.
   d. none of the above.
3. The package of cheese crackers you buy in the vending machine states that "cheese provides calcium, which builds strong bones." This is an example of
   a. a nutrient claim.
   b. a structure/function claim.
   c. a health claim.
   d. none of the above.
4. The Nutrition Facts panel on a carton of yogurt that you enjoy as a morning snack states that a serving provides 30 percent of the Daily Value for calcium. How would you rate this amount of calcium?
   a. high
   b. moderate
   c. low
   d. Calcium is not listed on the Nutrition Facts panel.
5. "Oatmeal contains a soluble fiber that can help lower your cholesterol." Which of the following statements is/are true?
   a. This is an approved health claim.
   b. The total DV for dietary fiber is identified in the foot-note at the bottom of the Nutrition Facts panel.
   c. Oatmeal is considered a functional food.
   d. All of the above are true.

Answers

1. (c) The Nutrition Facts panel on the package must contain the calories, fat, and saturated fat per serving. Vitamins E and D do not have to be listed unless they have been added to the food and/or the product makes a claim about them on the label.
2. (a) This high-fiber cereal label boasts a nutrient claim and is helping you meet your daily fiber needs.
3. (b) This package boasts a structure/function claim.
4. (a) If you consume 20 percent or more of the Daily Value for a nutrient, it is considered high in that nutrient. If a nutrient provides 5 percent or less of the Daily Value, it is considered low in that nutrient. The FDA requires that the DV for calcium be listed on the label.
5. (d) All of the statements are true. Oats contain the soluble fiber beta-glucan, which has been shown to help reduce blood cholesterol levels; thus, this is an approved health claim, and oatmeal can be considered a functional food. The total DV for dietary fiber is listed in the footnote at the bottom of the Nutrition Facts panel found on larger food packages. See, for example, Figure 5.2.

Web Resources

- For more information on food labeling, visit the Food and Drug Administration at: www.fda.gov

6

1. The **GI tract** is essentially a long tube. **T/F**

2. You absorb only **75 percent** of the nutrients in your food. **T/F**

3. **Heartburn** occurs when stomach acid leaks into the chest cavity and "burns" heart muscle. **T/F**

4. We absorb most of the nutrients in foods via our **stomach. T/F**

5. Stool is mostly made up of food remnants and **bacteria. T/F**

Digestion

How Food Becomes Nutrition

Rafael hadn't eaten breakfast and was getting antsy for lunch as he sat in his 11 a.m. nutrition class. In spite of his churning stomach and vague discomfort, he was paying close attention to the instructor's lecture. Suddenly, a loud rumble came from his midsection. As the students near him glanced over, Rafael realized that the growling was heard throughout the room. His mild embarrassment quickly turned into distress as the professor stopped talking and asked the class if they had all heard the growling stomach, and if they knew what caused it.

Can you guess the reason for Rafael's belly rumblings? Would you know how to quiet your own noisy stomach in a similar situation? In this concept, we'll explore the process of digestion and the organs involved, as well as some common digestive ailments. And although a growling stomach isn't necessarily of great concern, we'll also discuss its causes and solutions.

Answers

1. True. The gastrointestinal, or GI, tract runs through the body and connects the mouth to the anus. Turn to page 2 to find out more. about the organs that make up the GI tract.
2. False. Your body is very efficient and absorbs over 90 percent of the nutrients in your food. To find out how this happens, turn to page 3.
3. False. Although it might feel like the heart is burning, heartburn is actually caused by a backflow of stomach acid into the lower esophagus. Turn to page 5 for details.
4. False. The small intestine is the primary organ responsible for nutrient absorption. Check it out on page 6.
5. True. Stool (or feces) contains leftover food residue, nondigestible fibers, bacteria, gases, and sloughed-off intestinal cells. Turn to page 7 to find out more.

What Is Digestion and Why Is It Important?

As much fun as it is to eat, you're not taking in food just for fun. Food satisfies a true physical need for the energy that fuels body functions and the components that build body tissues. But in order for food to fulfill these functions, it must be broken down into molecules small enough to be absorbed. Thus, the simple definition of **digestion** is the breakdown of foods into absorbable components in the **gastrointestinal (GI) tract.** Through a multistep digestive process, food is softened with moisture and heat, then broken down into smaller particles by chewing and exposure to enzymes. Recall from Concept 2 that enzymes are substances that assist chemical reactions; digestive enzymes help break down foods.

Digestion Occurs in the GI Tract

The GI tract is a tube about 23 feet long; stretched vertically, it would be about as high as a two-story building. Although one continuous structure, the GI tract consists of the mouth, esophagus, stomach, small intestine, large intestine, and other organs. The main roles of the GI tract are (1) to break down food into its smallest components, (2) to absorb the nutrients, and (3) to prevent microorganisms or other harmful compounds consumed with food from entering the tissues of the body.[1]

Digestion is both mechanical and chemical. Mechanical digestion involves chewing, grinding, and breaking food apart in the mouth, so that it can be swallowed comfortably. The muscular activity and rhythmic contractions, or *peristalsis,* that move food through the GI tract and mix it with enzymes are also part of mechanical digestion. Chemical digestion involves using digestive juices and enzymes to break down food into absorbable nutrients that are small enough to enter the cells of the GI tract, blood, or lymph tissue.

digestion The body's breakdown of foods into absorbable components using mechanical and chemical means.

gastrointestinal (GI) tract The digestive tract, extending from the mouth to the anus.

absorption The process by which digested nutrients move into the tissues, where they can be transported and used by the body's cells.

Digestion Allows You to Absorb Nutrients from Foods

Digestion is the forerunner of **absorption.** Once the nutrients have been broken down completely, they are ready to be used by the cells of the body. In order to reach the cells, however, they have to leave the GI tract and move to other parts of the body. To accomplish this, the nutrients are absorbed through the walls of the intestines and into the body's two transport systems: the circulatory and lymphatic systems. They are then taken to the liver for processing before moving on to their destination.

The body is remarkably efficient at absorbing nutrients. Under normal conditions, you digest and absorb 92 to 97 percent of the nutrients in your food.[2]

The Take-Home Message **Digestion is the mechanical and chemical breakdown of food into smaller units that can be absorbed for use by the body. Digestion takes place in the gastrointestinal tract, which includes the mouth, esophagus, stomach, small intestine, large intestine, and other organs. Absorption is the process by which the digested nutrients move into your tissues. You absorb over 90 percent of the nutrients that you take in from foods.**

The smell of food, such as freshly baked bread, often triggers the appetite. As you eat a piece of bread, its aroma contributes to its flavor.

How Does Digestion Happen?

Digestion begins even before we eat, when the sensation of either **hunger** or **thirst** drives you to seek food or fluids. These strong physical needs also influence the amount you consume and the timing of your meals. **Appetite** is another powerful drive, but it is often unreliable. That's because appetite may be influenced by environmental and psychological cues. In other words, you can become interested in food and experience the desire to eat too much food without actually needing nourishment or being hungry. For example, the smell of food is a powerful stimulant to appetite. How many times have you been tempted to eat by the aromas coming from a café or bakery as you passed by? Odors also heighten your ability to taste foods—that is, to discern their flavor. This explains why you lose your appetite when you have a stuffy nose: Food loses some of its appeal when you can't smell it.

The average person has about 10,000 **taste buds** on the tongue, as well as about 10 million to 20 million scent cells in the nasal cavities.

Once either hunger or appetite has induced us to eat, the organs of the GI tract get involved. As we'll see, each plays a unique and crucial role in digestion. Figure 6.1, next page, provides an overview of the digestive process.

You Begin Breaking Down Food in Your Mouth

The process of digestion begins when you first see, smell, or think about a food that you want to eat. Glands in your mouth release **saliva,** a watery fluid that helps moisten and soften the food you are about to eat. Once you take a bite and begin to chew, your teeth, powered by your jaw muscles, cut and grind the food into smaller pieces and, along with your tongue, mix it with saliva. Once you have chewed the food adequately, your tongue pushes it to the back of your mouth and into your *pharynx* (tongue).

Swallowing seems simple because you do it hundreds of times a day, but it is actually a complicated process. Pushing chewed food to the pharynx is a voluntary

hunger The physical need for food.

thirst The physical need for water.

appetite The psychological desire to eat or drink.

saliva Watery fluid secreted by the salivary glands in the mouth that moistens food and makes it easier to follow.

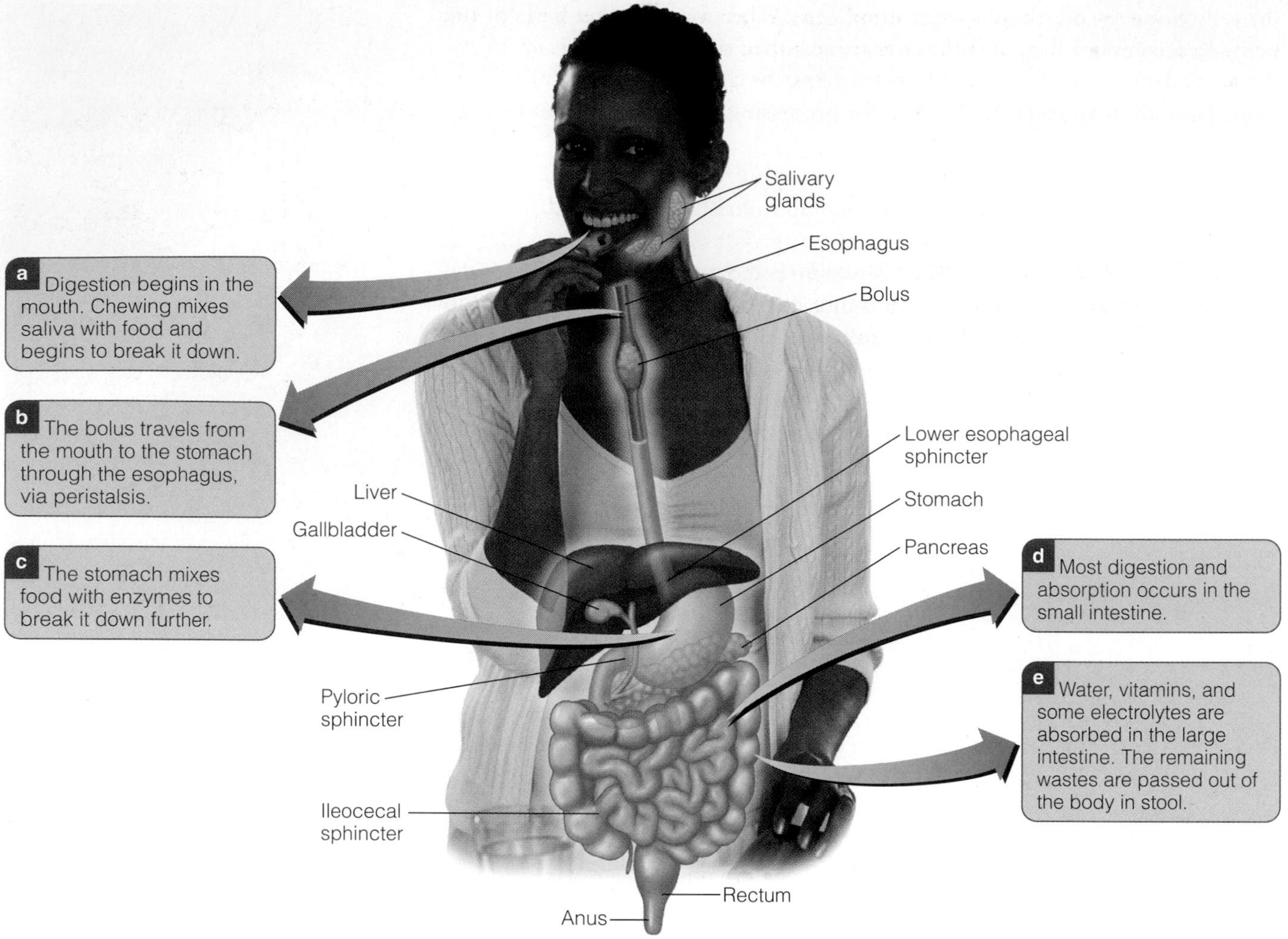

Salivary glands
Esophagus
Bolus
a Digestion begins in the mouth. Chewing mixes saliva with food and begins to break it down.
b The bolus travels from the mouth to the stomach through the esophagus, via peristalsis.
Lower esophageal sphincter
Stomach
Liver
Gallbladder
Pancreas
c The stomach mixes food with enzymes to break it down further.
d Most digestion and absorption occurs in the small intestine.
e Water, vitamins, and some electrolytes are absorbed in the large intestine. The remaining wastes are passed out of the body in stool.
Pyloric sphincter
Ileocecal sphincter
Rectum
Anus

Figure 6.1 Digestion and the Organs of the GI Tract

> You produce 1 to 1.5 liters of **saliva** every day.

act—that is, you control it. But once the food mass (called a *bolus*) enters the pharynx, the swallowing reflex kicks in, and you no longer control the action.

You have probably experienced an episode of "swallowing gone wrong," in which you've accidentally propelled food down the wrong "pipe." When this happens (and you find yourself in a coughing fit, trying to expel the item), it is because the mechanism that normally protects your larynx (the top part of your windpipe) hasn't engaged properly. Usually, a small flap called the *epiglottis* closes off your larynx during swallowing (Figure 6.2). The epiglottis ensures that food and

Bolus
Tongue
Epiglottis (up)
Larynx
Esophagus
Bolus
Tongue
Epiglottis (down)
Larynx (closed)
Esophagus

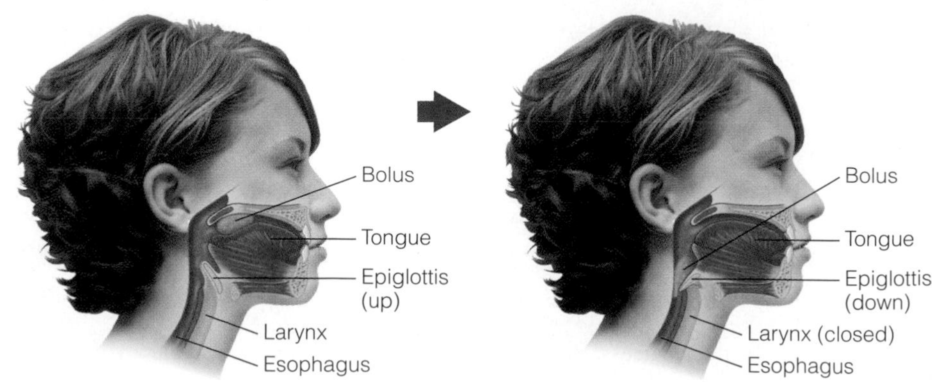

Figure 6.2 Epiglottis
The epiglottis prevents food from entering the larynx (the top part of the windpipe) when you swallow.

drink go down the correct pipe—the **esophagus.** When the epiglottis doesn't work properly, food can get lodged in the larynx, and potentially result in choking.

The Esophagus Propels Food into the Stomach

Once swallowed, a mass of food (a bolus) is pushed down your esophagus by the process of peristalsis (Figure 6.3). The esophagus narrows at the bottom (just above the stomach) and ends at a sphincter, a circular muscle, called the *lower esophageal sphincter (LES).* Under normal conditions, when you swallow food, the LES relaxes and allows the food to pass into the stomach. The stomach also relaxes to receive the food.[3] After food enters the stomach, the LES should close. If it doesn't, hydrochloric acid from the stomach may flow back into the esophagus and irritate its lining. This is called *heartburn* because it causes a burning sensation in the middle of the chest. Chronic heartburn and the reflux of stomach acids are symptoms of gastroesophageal reflux disease (GERD), which will be discussed later in this concept.

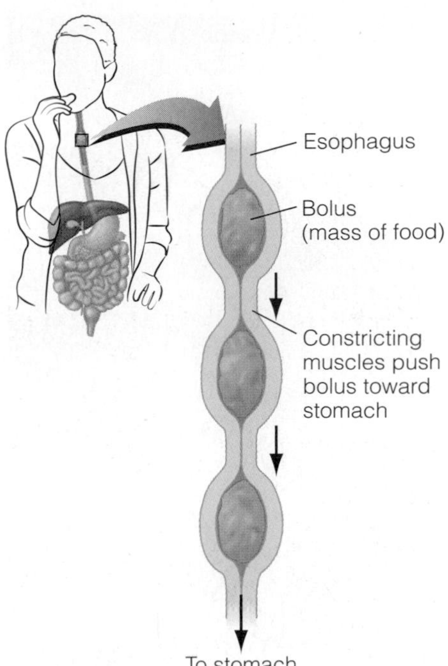

Figure 6.3 Peristalsis
Muscles around the organs of the GI tract constrict in a wavelike manner to help move food along.

The Stomach Stores, Mixes, and Prepares Food for Digestion

The **stomach** continues mechanical and chemical digestion by churning and contracting to mix food with digestive juices. These juices include *hydrochloric acid (HCl),* various enzymes, and other chemicals. The swallowed bolus of food soon becomes *chyme,* a semiliquid substance that contains digestive secretions plus the original food. The stomach can expand to hold 2 to 4 liters of chyme.

Hydrochloric acid has important digestive functions: activation of the protein-digesting enzyme *pepsin,* enhanced absorption of minerals, the breakdown of connective tissue in meat, and the destruction of some ingested microorganisms.[4] You might think that such a strong chemical would "digest" the stomach itself, but mucus—a thick, slippery secretion produced in the stomach—acts as a barrier between the HCl and the stomach lining, protecting the lining from irritation or damage.

Have you ever noticed that some foods keep you feeling full longer than others? Foods high in carbohydrate exit the stomach faster, and therefore make you feel less full, than foods high in protein, fat, or fiber. Similarly, low-calorie foods exit the stomach faster than high-calorie foods. This is because many low-calorie foods require minimal digestion. For example, a lightly sweetened cup of tea (a lower-calorie beverage) requires less digestion than a higher-calorie, nutrient-dense milkshake.

As digestion continues, G. I. tract contractions push the chyme toward the *pyloric sphincter,* the circular muscle that separates the stomach from the small intestine. As the sphincter relaxes, chyme gradually enters the small intestine. Approximately 1 to 5 milliliters (1 teaspoon) of chyme is released into the small intestine every 30 seconds during digestion.[5]

Most Digestion and Absorption Occur in the Small Intestine

The **small intestine** is a long, narrow, coiled chamber in the abdominal cavity. It extends from the pyloric sphincter to the beginning of the large intestine. The *small* in *small intestine* refers to its diameter, not its length; its length actually takes up about 20 of the 23 feet of the GI tract.

esophagus The tube that extends from the throat to the stomach.

stomach The digestive organ that receives food from the esophagus, mixes it with digestive juices, and stores it before it is gradually released into the small intestine.

small intestine The longest part of the GI tract where most of the digestion and absorption of food occurs.

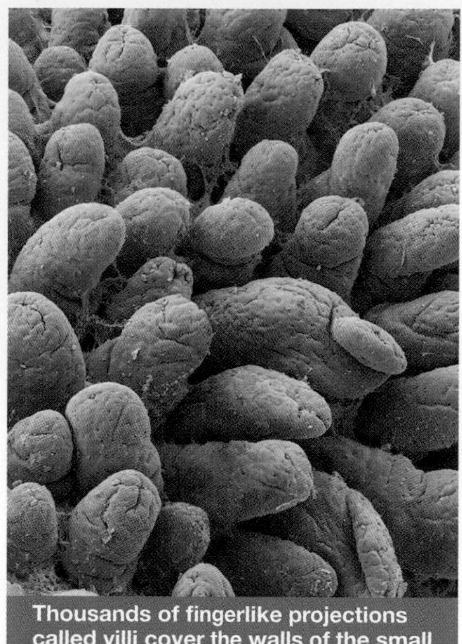
Thousands of fingerlike projections called villi cover the walls of the small intestine to increase its surface area.

The small intestine is the primary organ for digestion and absorption within the body. Here, carbohydrates, fats, and proteins are broken down into nutrients small enough to be absorbed by the cells in the intestinal lining (Figure 6.4).

The interior of the small intestine is not smooth and flat. If it were, partially digested food (chyme) would flow through it quickly, giving the lining cells little chance to absorb the nutrients it contains. Instead, the inner lining of the small intestine is covered with thousands of small projections called *villi* (Figure 6.4a). The villi greatly increase the surface area of the lining. As chyme flows past, more nutrients are exposed to lining cells, so more are absorbed. The villi also help mix the partially digested chyme with intestinal secretions.

The villi are covered by even smaller, hairlike projections called *microvilli* (Figure 6.4b), that provide additional surface area and maximize nutrient absorption. Blood vessels and lymphatic vessels, which carry a tissue fluid called *lymph,* pick up these absorbed nutrients and transport them throughout the body (Figure 6.4c).

The lining of the small intestine is arranged in circular folds that further increase its absorptive surface area. The circular folds cause the chyme to spiral forward through the small intestine, rather than merely moving in a straight line. Depending on the amount and type of food consumed, its contact time in the small intestine is about 3 to 10 hours.[6]

The Large Intestine Absorbs Water and Some Nutrients

By the time the chyme has passed through the small intestine, most of its nutrients have been absorbed. About 750 milliliters (3 cups) of unabsorbed residue enters the large intestine slowly each day through the *ileocecal sphincter*. The slow entry of this residue from the small to the large intestine enables the body to maximize nutrient absorption.[7]

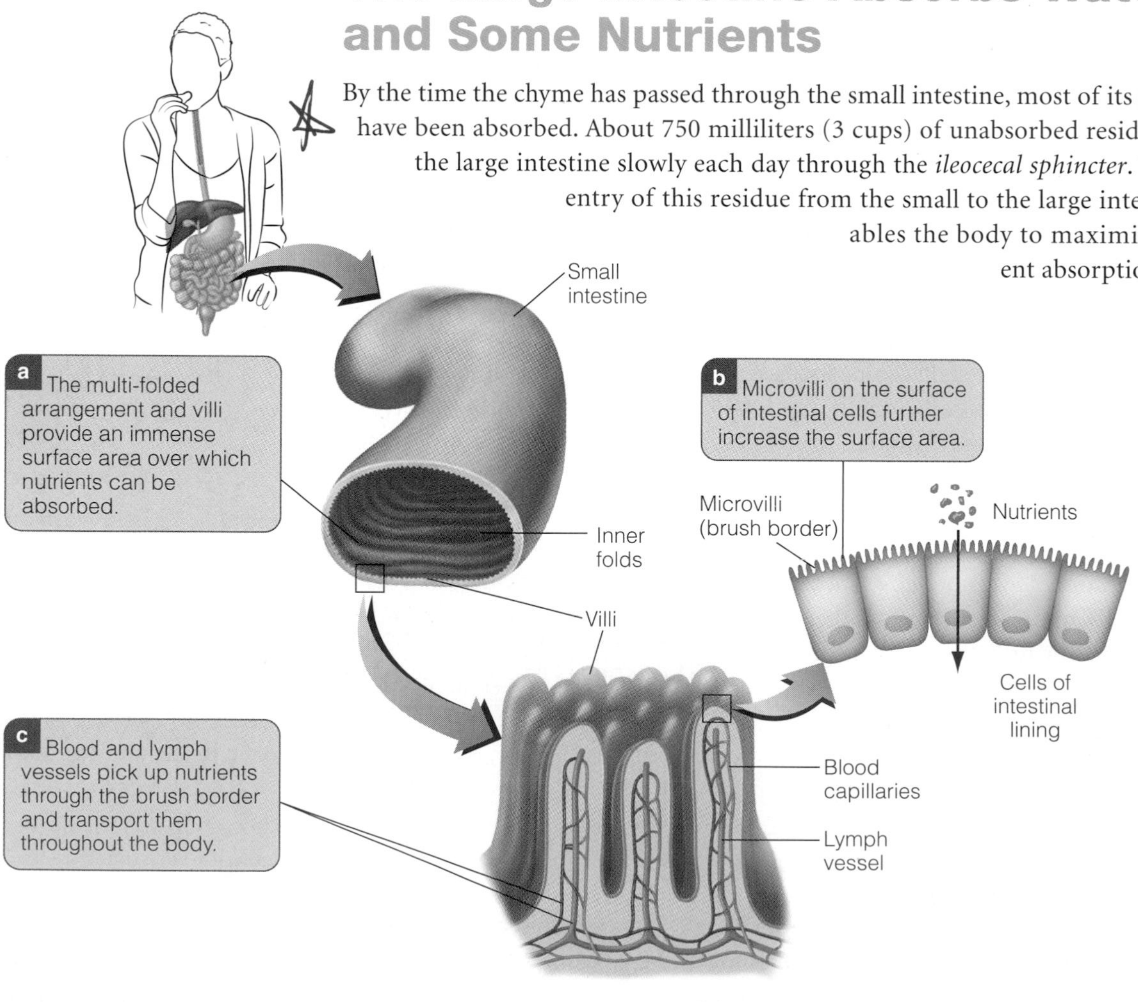

Small intestine

a The multi-folded arrangement and villi provide an immense surface area over which nutrients can be absorbed.

Inner folds

Villi

b Microvilli on the surface of intestinal cells further increase the surface area.

Microvilli (brush border)

Nutrients

Cells of intestinal lining

c Blood and lymph vessels pick up nutrients through the brush border and transport them throughout the body.

Blood capillaries

Lymph vessel

Figure 6.4 Surface Area in the Small Intestine

The **large intestine** looks and acts much differently than the small intestine because it does not contain villi or microvilli; it is wider, and it is not tightly coiled. Further, the chemical digestion that takes place in the large intestine is due not to digestive enzymes but to the helpful bacteria that live within it. These bacteria play a role in producing certain vitamins, breaking down fiber, and fermenting some of the undigested dietary carbohydrates into simpler compounds (methane gas, carbon dioxide, and hydrogen).

The cells of the large intestine absorb most of the fluids in the food residue that reaches them. This fluid absorption leaves a semisolid mass (about 7 ounces) of fecal matter (**stool,** or **feces**). Transit time through the large intestine can range from 12 to 70 hours, depending on a person's age, health, diet, and fiber intake.[8] The longer the food residue stays in the large intestine, the greater the amount of fluid that will be absorbed from it, and the harder the stool will be to pass.

There are more microorganisms than human cells in your body, and many of them are in your large intestine.

The stool is propelled forward until it reaches the **rectum,** the final portion of the large intestine, where it is stored. When stool stretches and extends the rectum, the action stimulates nerve endings, which then stimulate the defecation reflex. The result is relaxation of the internal sphincter of the *anus*. The elimination of stool is under voluntary control and is influenced by age, diet, prescription medicines, health, and abdominal muscle tone.

The Liver, Gallbladder, and Pancreas Are Accessory Organs

Although food doesn't pass through the liver, gallbladder, or pancreas during digestion, these three accessory organs are essential to the process. Weighing about 3 pounds, the **liver** is the largest abdominal organ in the body. It is so important that you couldn't survive without it. The liver helps regulate the metabolism of carbohydrates, fats, and proteins. It also stores nutrients, including some vitamins and minerals and a form of carbohydrate known as glycogen. The liver is also essential for processing and detoxifying alcohol. You'll learn about each of these functions in more depth later in this book. One of the liver's most important digestive functions is to make *bile*, a greenish yellow liquid that is important for fat digestion. Bile has two main functions:

- Bile breaks up large fat globules into small, suspended fat droplets. This action enhances the absorption of fats because it increases the surface area exposed to fat-digesting enzymes. The breakdown of fat also increases the rate of fat digestion.
- Bile acts as an emulsifier, dispersing fat throughout the chyme, thus helping enzymes make contact with the fat and digest it. This action is similar to the detergent activity of dishwashing soap on greasy dishes.

Bile is collected, drained, and released into the **gallbladder,** a small organ attached to the underside of the liver. The gallbladder stores approximately 1 to 2 ounces of concentrated bile at a time, releasing it into the small intestine in response to the ingestion of fat.

The **pancreas** is an organ about the size and shape of your hand that produces important digestive enzymes that are released into the small intestine. Enzymes from the pancreas are responsible for the digestion of 90 percent of the fat you ingest, as well as about 50 percent of the protein and carbohydrate.[9] The pancreas also produces sodium bicarbonate, a chemical that neutralizes the acids in the chyme that

large intestine The final organ of the GI tract. It is responsible for absorbing water and eliminating food residue as feces.

stool (feces) Waste product stored in the large intestine and then excreted from the body, consisting mostly of bacteria, sloughed-off gastrointestinal cells, water, unabsorbed nutrients, undigested fibers, and remnants of digestive fluids.

rectum The lowest part of the large intestine.

liver The largest abdominal organ in the body. The liver aids in digestion and is responsible for the metabolism of nutrients, the detoxification of alcohol, and some nutrient storage.

gallbladder A small, muscular organ that stores bile.

pancreas An accessory organ for digestion that produces enzymes and other substances. It is connected to the small intestine via the bile duct.

Table 6.1

Organs of the GI Tract and Their Functions

Organ	Function
Mouth	Begins breaking down food into smaller components through chewing
Esophagus	Transfers food from the mouth to the stomach
Stomach	Mixes food with digestive juices; breaks down some nutrients into smaller components
Small intestine	Completes the digestion of food and absorbs nutrients through its lining
Large intestine	Absorbs water and some nutrients; passes waste products out of the body
Sphincters (LES, pyloric, ileocecal)	Keep swallowed food from returning to the esophagus, stomach, or small intestine
Accessory organs (liver, gallbladder, pancreas)	Release bile, enzymes, and other chemicals to help break down food or direct digestive activity

enters the small intestine from the stomach. Without sodium bicarbonate, the tissues of the small intestine would be burned by the acidic chyme. Finally, the pancreas produces two hormones important in regulating the level of sugar in your blood.

Table 6.1 summarizes the organs of the GI tract and their functions.

The Take-Home Message **In the mouth, saliva mixes with food during chewing, moistening it and making it easier to swallow. Swallowed food that has mixed with digestive juices in the stomach becomes chyme. Maximum digestion and absorption occur through the villi and microvilli in the small intestine. Undigested residue next enters the large intestine, where additional absorption of water and minerals occurs. Eventually, the remnants of digestion reach the anus and exit the body in stool. The liver, gallbladder, and pancreas are important accessory organs. The liver produces bile and the gallbladder concentrates and stores it. The pancreas produces several enzymes essential for digestion.**

What Other Body Systems Affect Your Use of Nutrients?

Your body functions pretty well on its own. You don't have to worry constantly about keeping yourself nourished or distributing nutrients to your cells, because numerous body systems are continually doing this work behind the scenes. Let's take a quick look at four body systems that affect your use of nutrients.

The Nervous System Stimulates Your Appetite

The main role of the nervous system in keeping you nourished is to let you know when you need to eat and drink and when to stop. Your brain has a central role in communicating and interpreting messages of hunger and thirst and encouraging you to seek food and fluids. If you ignore the signals of hunger or thirst sent by your nervous system, you may experience a headache, dizziness, or weakness. The nervous system helps each of us make daily decisions regarding what to eat, when to eat, and, perhaps most important, when to stop eating.

The Circulatory and Lymphatic Systems Distribute Nutrients

The blood is the body's primary transport system, shuttling oxygen, nutrients, and many other substances throughout the body. The oxygen-rich blood that the heart receives from the lungs is pumped from the heart out to the body for its use (Figure 6.5). The blood picks up the nutrients absorbed through the lining of the small intestine and transports them to the liver, then to the cells of the body. Without the circulatory system, the nutrients you eat would not reach your cells. Equally important, the blood removes carbon dioxide, excess water, and waste products from the cells and takes these substances to the lungs (carbon dioxide) and kidneys (excess water and waste products) for excretion.

The lymphatic system is a complex network of small vessels, valves, lymph nodes, and ducts; it picks up lymph that has seeped into tissues, filters it, and returns it to the bloodstream. Fats and fat-soluble vitamins travel in lymph from the GI tract to the blood. Lymph eventually drains into two large veins near the heart.

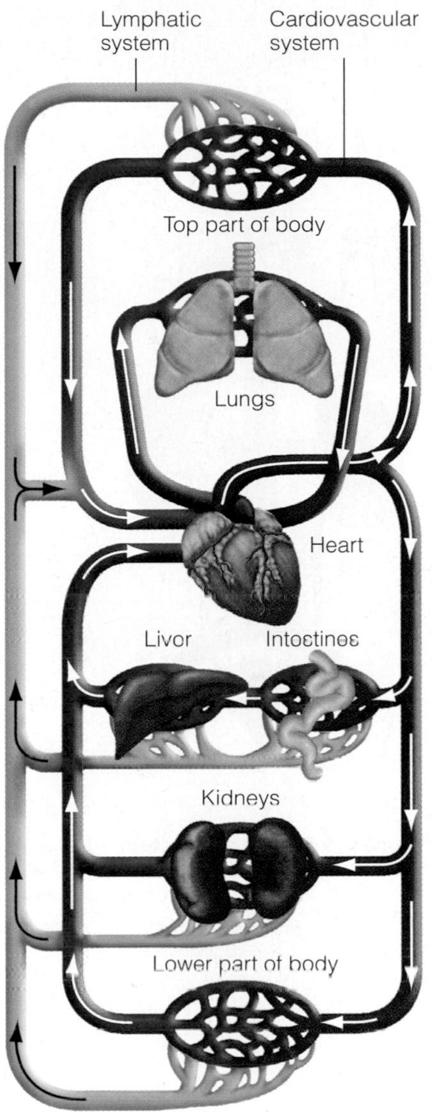

Figure 6.5 Circulatory and Lymphatic Systems
Blood and lymph are fluids that circulate throughout the body. They both distribute nutrients to cells, and blood picks up waste products from cells and delivers them to the kidneys for eventual excretion.

The Excretory System Passes Urine Out of the Body

The excretory system eliminates wastes from the circulatory system. After the cells have gleaned the nutrients and other useful metabolic components they need, waste products accumulate. The kidneys filter the blood, excreting the waste products into urine, which is stored in the bladder until it is released from the body (see Figure 6.6).

The Take-Home Message **In addition to the digestive system, other body systems help us use the nutrients we take in from foods. The nervous system lets us know when we need to eat or drink, the circulatory and lymphatic systems deliver absorbed nutrients to cells, and the excretory system helps filter and eliminate waste products from the blood.**

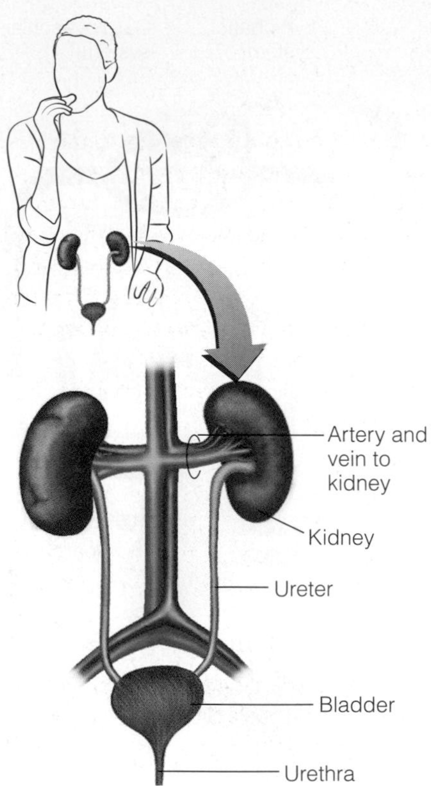

Figure 6.6 Excretory System
Water and waste products from cells are filtered from your blood in the kidneys and expelled from your body in urine.

What Are Some Common Digestive Disorders?

Generally, the digestive tract works just fine. As a matter of fact, it doesn't usually require tinkering or medications to be healthy. But sometimes the digestive tract gets "off track." Some of the problems such as occasional heartburn or indigestion, are minor; other problems, such as ulcers or celiac disease, are very serious.

Disorders of the Mouth and Esophagus

Oral health involves healthy teeth, gums, and supporting tissue. Maintaining a healthy mouth is important because its tissues are used to bite, chew, taste, speak, smile, swallow, and communicate through facial expressions. Properly nourishing yourself can be difficult if you have extensive tooth decay, gingivitis, or periodontal disease. *Gingivitis* involves gum swelling, bleeding, and oral pain. *Periodontal disease* is a more severe inflammation of the gums caused by infection or by plaque that accumulates on the surface of the teeth, causing teeth to loosen or partially separate from the gums and jawbone. Even though these conditions are serious, they are treatable through dental procedures, optimal food choices, and good oral hygiene.

One of the most common problems involving the esophagus is **heartburn.** About 7 percent of the population experience daily heartburn, and 25 to 35 percent of adults have occasional symptoms.[10] The condition is caused by hydrochloric acid flowing from the stomach back into the esophagus or even the throat. The acid causes a lingering, unpleasant, sour taste in the mouth, as well as nausea, bloating, belching, a vague burning sensation, and an uncomfortable feeling of fullness. Chronic heartburn can lead to a condition called *gastroesophageal reflux disease,* or *GERD.*

A weak lower esophageal sphincter is often the culprit in heartburn, because it can permit stomach acids to flow back into the esophagus. Certain foods, including chocolate, fried or fatty foods, coffee, soda, onions, and garlic, seem to be associated with this condition.[11] Lifestyle factors also play a role. For example, smoking cigarettes, drinking alcohol, wearing tight-fitting clothes, being overweight or obese, eating large evening meals, and reclining after eating may cause or worsen the condition. If dietary changes and behavior changes are insufficient to relieve heartburn, over-the-counter antacids or prescription drugs may help. Rarely, surgery may be required to treat severe, unrelenting heartburn.

Disorders of the Stomach

Everyone has had a stomachache at one time or another. Common causes are eating too much and eating too fast. Other possible causes are eating foods that are spicy, acidic, or high in fat or fiber and swallowing air while eating. For help in preventing minor episodes of discomfort, see the Table Tips.

A more serious cause of a stomachache is infection. Stomach flu, or *gastroenteritis* is an inflammation of the stomach or intestines caused by viruses or bacteria. Symptoms include nausea, vomiting, diarrhea, and abdominal cramping. Sometimes the problem requires medical intervention, but usually rest, oral rehydration therapy (intake of balanced fluids, such as Gatorade), and a soft-food diet are all that is needed.

heartburn A burning sensation originating in the esophagus, usually caused by the reflux of gastric contents from the stomach into the esophagus.

Celiac Disease: An Issue of Absorption

One of the more serious malabsorption conditions of the small intestine is **celiac disease.** A healthy small intestine is carpeted with villi and microvilli, small projections which efficiently absorb nutrients from food. In some people, these villi become eroded, and the lining of the small intestine flattens out, reducing the intestine's ability to absorb nutrients.

Although the exact cause of celiac disease is unknown, intestinal damage occurs when people with celiac disease consume gluten, a protein found in wheat, rye, and barley. When the gluten reaches the small intestine, the immune system attacks it as if it were a harmful invader, releasing inflammatory chemicals that destroy lining cells at the site. Since celiac disease is genetic, people with a close relative with the disease are at much higher risk of developing it. Interestingly, the risk for celiac disease may be decreased by breastfeeding, rather than bottle-feeding, infants.

Celiac disease is most common among people of European descent. Many Americans are descendants of European nationalities, and 1 out of 133 Americans is affected by celiac disease.[1] This is a larger percentage than previously thought.

The classic celiac symptoms are recurring abdominal bloating, cramping, diarrhea, gas, fatty and foul-smelling stools, weight loss, anemia, fatigue, bone or joint pain, and even a painful skin rash. Paradoxically, some people with celiac disease experience chronic constipation. Depending on the length of time between symptom development and diagnosis, the complications of celiac disease can be serious. They include increased incidence of osteoporosis due to poor calcium absorption, diminished growth because of nutrient malabsorption, and even seizures due to inadequate absorption of certain vitamins and minerals. Untreated celiac disease is also a significant risk factor for cancer of the small intestine.[2] Some people develop the symptoms of celiac disease in infancy or childhood. Others develop the disease later in life, sometimes during pregnancy or periods of severe stress or following a viral infection.

People with celiac disease cannot enjoy breads, bagels, pasta, and other foods containing gluten, a protein found in wheat, rye, and barley.

Diagnosing celiac disease is sometimes difficult, because it resembles other malabsorption diseases. Also, it is often confused with irritable bowel syndrome, food allergies, or food intolerances. A simple blood test can detect celiac disease, but the "gold standard" for diagnosis is surgical detection of the damaged villi.

The only treatment for celiac disease is a gluten-free diet. This should stop the symptoms from progressing, allow the intestine to heal, and prevent further damage. The symptoms often improve within several days of beginning the gluten-free diet. Within three to six months, the villi often return to normal functioning, if the diet is followed faithfully. Depending on the age at diagnosis and the progression of the disease, there may be some permanent health problems, such as stunted growth.

Adhering to a gluten-free diet—which means avoiding traditionally produced breads, pasta, and cereals, among other foods—can be challenging. However, many foods are naturally gluten-free, such as meats and beans, milk, eggs, fruits, and vegetables. These foods are permissible in any quantity. Rice, corn, and certain other grains are also acceptable because they do not contain gluten. Specially formulated gluten-free breads, pasta, and cereal products are also increasingly available in many supermarkets.

The biggest problem most people have in following a gluten-free diet is avoiding the many processed foods that contain latent, or hidden, sources of gluten. People with celiac disease need to read food labels carefully. Dining out can also be challenging, since even a trace of flour or a few bread crumbs can be enough to set off the immune reaction.

Nonetheless, celiac disease is a manageable condition. People with celiac disease can live normal lives and can learn about their condition by talking to health care professionals. Researchers are currently working to determine the exact component in gluten that causes the disease and to develop enzymes to destroy it.

celiac disease A malabsorption disease in which the consumption of the protein gluten causes an immune response that damages the lining of the small intestine.

TABLE TIPS 

Digest It Right!

Eat and drink slowly and chew your food thoroughly. This will cut down on the amount of air you take in, and it may reduce belching later on.

Watch your portion size and stop eating when you are full. You are less likely to feel uncomfortable and won't have to unbutton the top button of your jeans!

Set aside time to eat. Don't eat your meals while doing something else, such as watching television or driving. You will be more aware of your body's cues to stop if you are paying attention.

Be aware of foods that don't agree with you. If spicy foods irritate your stomach, eat them less frequently or in smaller amounts.

Get plenty of fiber and fluid. This will help keep you regular and help you avoid constipation.

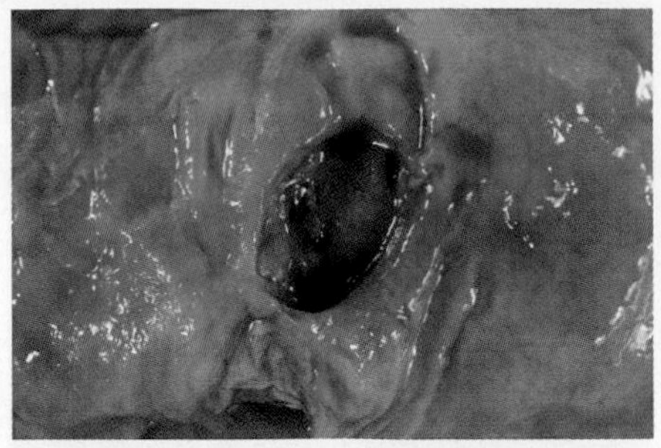

Figure 6.7 Peptic Ulcer
An ulcer is created when the mucosal lining of the GI tract erodes or breaks.

Figure 6.8 Gallstones
Gallstones result from the crystallization of salts and other compounds in bile. Luckily, most don't get this large.

A **peptic ulcer** is a sore, an erosion, or a break in the stomach lining caused by drugs, alcohol, or more often a bacterium (Figure 6.7). Symptoms of an ulcer are abdominal pain, vomiting, fatigue, bleeding, and general weakness. Medical treatments consist of prescription drugs and dietary recommendations, such as limiting intake of alcohol and caffeine-containing beverages and restricting spices and acidic foods.

Gallbladder Disease

One common type of gallbladder disease is the presence of **gallstones** (Figure 6.8). Most people with gallstones have abnormally thick bile, which forms crystals, then sludge, and finally gallstones. Some individuals with gallstones experience no pain or only mild pain. Others may have severe pain accompanied by fever, nausea, vomiting, cramps, and obstruction of the bile duct.

Medical treatment for gallstones may involve prescription medicine or shock-wave therapy (a type of ultrasound treatment) to break up the stones, or surgery to remove the gallbladder. After gallbladder removal, the liver secretes bile directly into the small intestine.

Disorders of the Intestines

The rumbling stomach that Rafael experienced at the beginning of this concept isn't really a problem (although if it's accompanied by pain or vomiting, it can be a sign of a disorder, such as a mechanical obstruction).[12] Rather, the gurgling is due to the gas and air pockets that form as the stomach contents are pushed through the GI tract. The best way to quiet the noise is to eat or drink something or to apply mild pressure to the abdomen.

More serious intestinal problems tend to involve nutrient malabsorption. As you can imagine, if the lining cells of your intestinal villi are unable to absorb nutrients, then no matter how much you eat, you'll become malnourished. The symptoms of malabsorption diseases vary, but they include abdominal pain, nausea, vomiting, bloating, loss of appetite, diarrhea, anxiety, weight loss, and fatigue. One of the more common causes of malabsorption is the intestinal damage resulting from celiac disease (see the box feature "Celiac Disease: An Issue of Absorption" earlier in this concept).

Common disorders of the large intestine are constipation, diarrhea, and irritable bowel syndrome:

- **Constipation** is caused by excessively slow movements of undigested residue through the colon, and it is often due to insufficient fiber or water intake, or both. Consuming an adequate amount of dietary fiber daily can help prevent it.

peptic ulcer A sore, erosion, or break in the lining of the stomach.

gallstones Small, hard structures formed in the gallbladder or bile duct due to abnormally thick bile.

constipation The condition of having difficulty passing stools caused by slow movement of undigested residue in the colon.

Stress, inactivity, certain medications, and various illnesses can also lead to constipation. It is usually treated with a high-fiber, high-liquid diet; exercise; and over-the-counter stool softeners.

- **Diarrhea** is the passage of frequent, loose, watery stools. It is considered more serious than constipation because it results in the loss of fluids, certain minerals, and other nutrients. There are many causes of diarrhea, including contaminated water, microorganisms, stress, and excessive fiber intake. Diarrhea is generally treated with oral rehydration therapy.
- **Irritable bowel syndrome** (**IBS**) is a disorder of bowel function; there is no underlying disease. Instead, in people with IBS, the large intestine appears to overrespond to stimuli. This results in alternating patterns of diarrhea, constipation, and abdominal pain. The exact cause of IBS is unknown, but low-fiber diets, stress, the consumption of irritating foods, and certain intestinal disorders are all suspected factors.[13] Effective responses to IBS may include changing your diet, managing stress, and in some cases taking prescription medications.

The Take-Home Message Gastrointestinal disorders include less serious conditions, such as heartburn, GERD, indigestion, and stomach flu, and more serious conditions, such as gallstones and gastric ulcers. Disorders of the small intestine can be the most dangerous, as they may result in malabsorption and/or malnutrition. Constipation, diarrhea, and irritable bowel syndrome are disorders of the large intestine.

diarrhea The condition of having frequent, loose, and/or watery stools.

irritable bowel syndrome (IBS) A bowel function disorder in which the large intestine is overly sensitive to stimuli.

Check out these recipes and more suggestions at www.pearsonhighered.com/blake

UCook

Apple Bran Muffins

These high-fiber muffins are music to your gastrointestinal tract and sweetly pleasing to your taste buds. You'll find the full recipe on our website and displayed above.

UDo

GI Tract Info!

Want to learn even more about the organs of the GI tract? Visit our website and slide through the organs and their functions.

The Top Five Points to Remember

1. Digestion is the process of breaking down food into absorbable nutrients. It takes place in the organs of the GI tract—particularly in the stomach, small intestine, and large intestine. Mechanical digestion includes chewing and peristalsis. Chemical digestion involves mixing consumed food with enzymes and gastric juices to break it down.
2. Hunger and thirst alert you to your basic physical need to take in food and fluid. Appetite is less about physical need and more about the psychological desire to eat. Digestion begins in the mouth as chewing breaks down food and mixes it with saliva. Swallowing is a coordinated process that involves the mouth, throat, and esophagus. The stomach mixes food with enzymes and stores it before propelling it into the small intestine, where most of the digestion and absorption occurs. The walls of the small intestine are covered with villi, which greatly increase its surface area and facilitate absorption. The large intestine absorbs water and some nutrients, before pushing waste out of the body via the anus. Several sphincters control the entry and exit of food and chyme through the organs of the GI tract.
3. In addition to producing bile, the liver processes and metabolizes several nutrients after they have been digested and absorbed. The liver also stores nutrients

and plays an important role in detoxifying alcohol. The gallbladder stores bile and releases it into the small intestine. The pancreas produces enzymes that play important roles in digestion.

4. Systems other than the digestive system help the body use nutrients. The nervous system signals hunger and thirst. The circulatory and lymphatic systems distribute nutrients to all the cells, and the excretory system filters waste products from the blood and passes them out of the body in urine.
5. Heartburn is an uncomfortable sensation of stomach acid seeping into the esophagus or throat. Peptic ulcers are sores, erosions, or breaks in the stomach lining. Celiac disease is a malabsorption disorder of the small intestine that can be treated with a gluten-free diet. Constipation is characterized by infrequent, difficult passage of stools. Diarrhea is characterized by frequent, loose, watery stools. It is often caused by exposure to microorganisms in food or water. People with irritable bowel syndrome often alternate between bouts of diarrhea and constipation.

Test Yourself

1. _____ is the process that breaks down food into absorbable units.
   a. Circulation
   b. Digestion
   c. Absorption
   d. Excretion
2. The protective tissue that covers the larynx when you swallow is the
   a. esophagus.
   b. tongue.
   c. pharynx.
   d. epiglottis.
3. The secretion produced in the stomach that helps break down protein and activates pepsin is
   a. sodium bicarbonate.
   b. hydrochloric acid.
   c. bile.
   d. chyme.
4. Which of the following is true regarding the small intestine?
   a. The small intestine has a vast digestive and absorptive surface area.
   b. The small intestine secretes bile, which breaks down fats.
   c. Intestinal cells have access to lymphatic vessels, but not to the bloodstream.
   d. The small intestine is relatively unimportant in the process of digestion.
5. What causes heartburn?
   a. improper relaxation of the lower esophageal sphincter
   b. improper contraction of the lower esophageal sphincter
   c. improper and rapid swallowing
   d. improper breathing and chest congestion

Answers

1. (b) Circulation is the process of distributing blood and lymph throughout the body. Absorption is the process of pulling nutrients from the GI tract into the body. Excretion is the passing of waste products out of the body.
2. (d) The esophagus is a tube that connects the mouth with the stomach. The tongue is a muscle that pushes food to the back of the mouth into the pharynx. The pharynx is a chamber that food passes through just before being swallowed.
3. (b) Hydrochloric acid (HCl) is part of the gastric juices that activate pepsin, break down protein, and destroy some ingested microorganisms. Sodium bicarbonate is a chemical produced in the pancreas that neutralizes the acid in chyme, which is the nutrient "soup" the stomach releases into the small intestine. Bile is made by the liver; it emulsifies fat.
4. (a) With numerous villi and microvilli along its interior wall, the small intestine has a vast surface area, which enhances digestion and absorption. Nutrients absorbed through these projections are transported through the blood and lymph throughout the body. Bile is produced in the liver and stored in the gallbladder, which releases it into the small intestine in response to the presence of fats. The small intestine is critical to the process of digestion.
5. (a) Heartburn occurs when a relaxed lower esophageal sphincter allows acid from the stomach to seep back into the esophagus.

Web Resources

- Go to www.medicinenet.com to learn more about GI concerns, disease, conditions, medicines, procedures, and treatments.
- To learn more about various digestive diseases, go to http://digestive.niddk.nih.gov
- Visit the National Library of Medicine for an abundant Internet resource for health care professionals, the public, researchers, and librarians at: www.nlm.nih.gov
- To learn about celiac disease, visit the American Celiac Disease Alliance at: www.americanceliac.org
- For more information about irritable bowel syndrome, go to www.ibs-research-update.org.uk/ibs/digestion1ie4. html

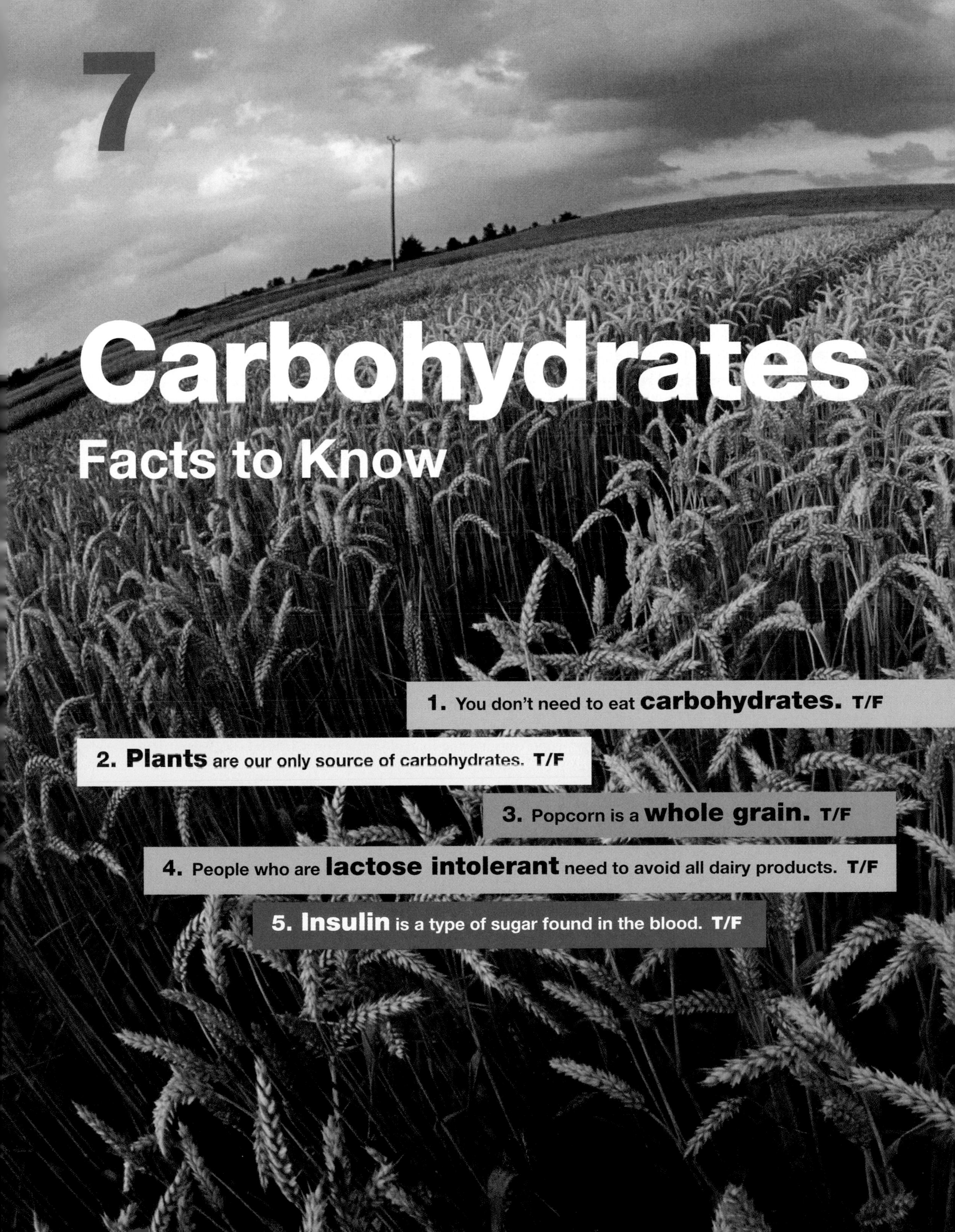

7 Carbohydrates

Facts to Know

1. You don't need to eat **carbohydrates.** T/F
2. **Plants** are our only source of carbohydrates. T/F
3. Popcorn is a **whole grain.** T/F
4. People who are **lactose intolerant** need to avoid all dairy products. T/F
5. **Insulin** is a type of sugar found in the blood. T/F

Emma is enjoying her first semester at college. She lives in a dorm and has made a ton of friends. She especially looks forward to hanging out on Sunday nights in the cafeteria for "Pizza and Sundae Night," when students get to choose their own pizza toppings and make their own ice cream sundaes. Because those are Emma's two favorite foods, she eats a small lunch on Sundays— just enough to tide her over until the big event. Unfortunately, within an hour after her last spoonful of cookie dough ice cream, she frequently has severe cramps and has to go back to her room to lie down. Her stomach bloats, and she finds herself running to the bathroom with diarrhea. What do you think is causing all this distress? Does she have to give up "Pizza and Sundae Night" because of her postdinner dilemma?

This concept discusses the unique role carbohydrates play in providing fuel for your body, the nutritional differences between simple and complex carbohydrates, and how your body digests and absorbs the carbohydrates you eat. We'll look into what's making Emma sick when she eats cheese and ice cream, as well as what she can do to feel better. We'll also talk about the role of an important body chemical, called *insulin*, in helping maintain just the right amount of carbohydrate fuel in your bloodstream.

Answers

1. False. You need a minimum amount of carbohydrates daily to fuel your brain. Turn to page 2 to find out what happens if you don't eat enough carbohydrates.
2. False. Dairy products also contain carbohydrates in the form of a sugar called lactose. Turn to pages 4 and 5 to learn about the different types of carbohydrates.
3. True! Who knew? Turn to page 6 to find more sources of whole grains!
4. False. Many people who are lactose intolerant are still able to enjoy some dairy products, especially if eaten with meals. In fact, dairy foods may be just what the doctor ordered. Turn to page 10 to learn why.
5. False. Insulin is a hormone produced by the pancreas. It helps regulate the level of sugar (glucose) in your blood. Check it out on page 11.

What Are Carbohydrates and Why Do You Need Them?

Carbohydrates are essential nutrients that make up the foundation of diets the world over. They are found mainly in plant-based foods, such as grains (rice and pasta), fruits, vegetables, nuts, and legumes (dry beans and peas). In Asia, rice accounts for 80 percent of people's calories daily. In Latin America, carbohydrate-laden bananas, chilies, beans, tubers, and nuts adorn most dinner plates. In the Mediterranean, grain-based pastas, breads, and couscous are plentiful, and here in the United States, many people consume the good old potato on a daily basis.[1] Carbohydrates are also found in dairy foods.

You need carbohydrates because they are the most desirable source of energy for your body. They supply fuel, mainly in the form of **glucose** (*ose* = carbohydrate), the primary sugar in high-carbohydrate foods, to your cells. Your brain, in particular, needs glucose to function, as do your red blood cells.

The carbohydrates you eat come mostly from plant foods. Plants make carbohydrates to store energy and to build their root and stem structures. Animals, including humans, also store energy as carbohydrates, but in limited amounts. These stored carbohydrates in animals break down when the animal dies, so eating meat and poultry does not supply carbohydrates to your diet.

Plants **synthesize** an estimated 140 billion tons of carbohydrates a year, about 20 tons per person worldwide!

Plants form the basic carbohydrate, glucose, in a process called *photosynthesis* (Figure 7.1). During photosynthesis, plants use a substance, called *chlorophyll,* (green pigment) in their leaves to absorb the energy in sunlight. The absorbed energy splits the water in the plant into two parts: hydrogen and oxygen. At the same time, the plant takes in carbon dioxide from the surrounding air. Glucose forms when the hydrogen released from the water joins with the carbon dioxide taken in from the air. The plant then produces oxygen as a waste product from water.

glucose The most abundant sugar in foods and the energy source for your body.

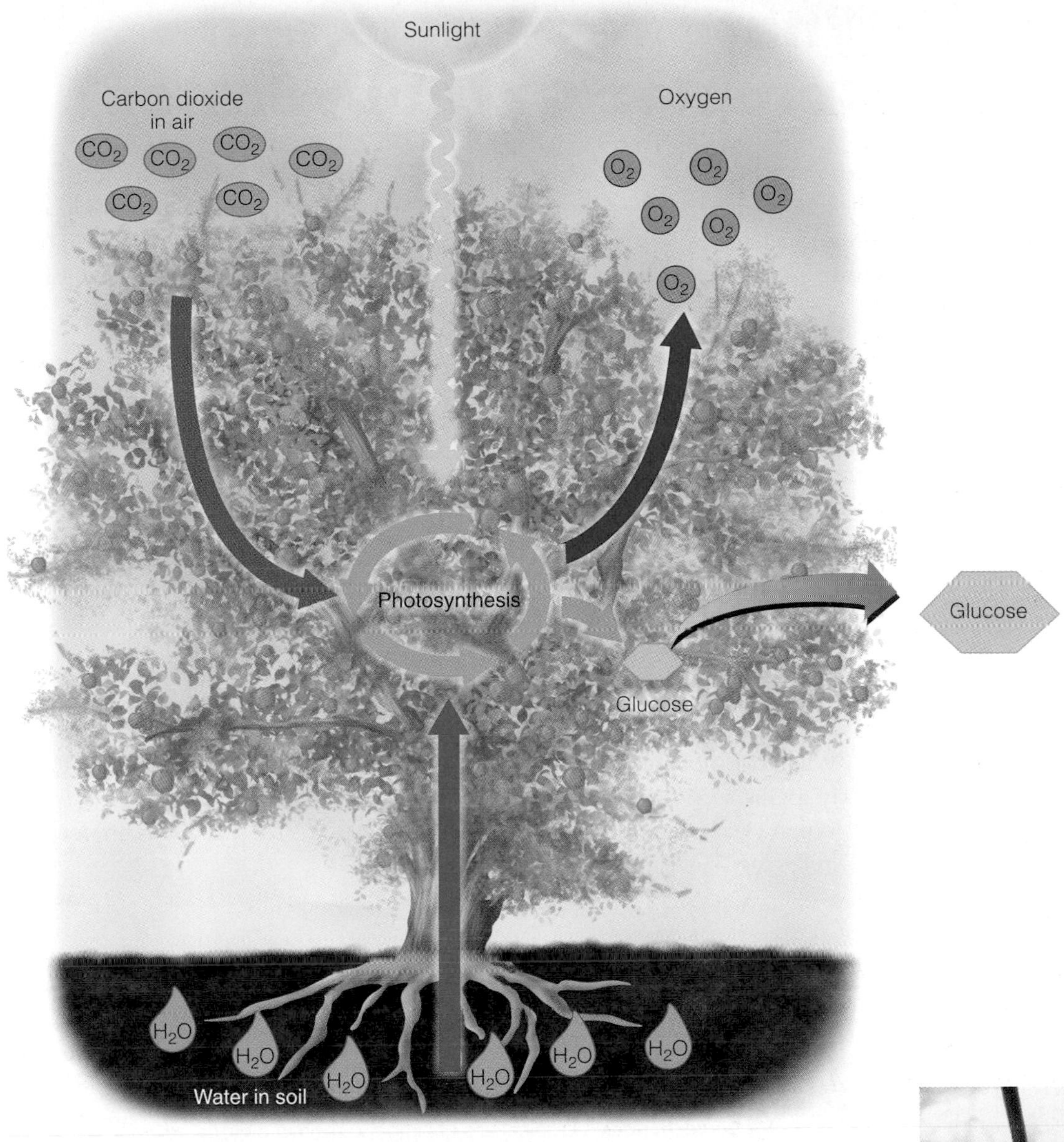

Figure 7.1 Photosynthesis: How Glucose Is Made
During photosynthesis, the leaves of green plants absorb energy from sunlight. This energy splits water into hydrogen and oxygen. The hydrogen combines with the carbon dioxide that the plant takes from the air to produce glucose. As a by-product of this process, oxygen is released into the air. Glucose is the most abundant sugar in nature and the optimal fuel for your body.

Glucose is the most abundant carbohydrate in nature, and plants use it as energy or combine it with minerals from soil to make other compounds, such as protein and vitamins. They also link glucose units together and store them in the form of starch. Plants can generate all the nutrients they need for their own health and maintenance from sunlight, water, and soil minerals.

The Take-Home Message **Carbohydrates are found most abundantly in plant-based foods. Your body cells, including brain cells and red blood cells, use them for energy. Many cultures around the world rely on carbohydrate-based foods as staples in their diets. Glucose is created in plants through the process of photosynthesis, and it is the most abundant carbohydrate in nature.**

Foods high in carbohydrates are staples in many of the world's cuisines.

What Are Simple and Complex Carbohydrates?

Carbohydrates are divided into two categories based on the number of sugar units, called saccharides (*saccharide* = sugar), joined together. **Simple carbohydrates** include **monosaccharides** (*mono* = one; "one sugar") and **disaccharides** (*di* = two; "two sugars"). **Complex carbohydrates** are **polysaccharides** (*poly* = many; "many sugars").

Monosaccharides and Disaccharides Are Simple Carbohydrates

Three monosaccharides are found in foods. We've already discussed one, glucose, which is produced by plants. The other two are *fructose* and *galactose* (Figure 7.2a). Fructose is the sweetest of the simple sugars and is found abundantly in fruit. For this reason, it is also known as *fruit sugar*. Galactose is a simple sugar found in dairy foods.

From various combinations of the monosaccharides glucose, fructose, and galactose, three disaccharides can be created (Figure 7.2b):

- When glucose and fructose combine, *sucrose,* or table sugar, is formed.
- When two glucose units combine, *maltose* is created. Maltose is the sugar found in grains, such as barley. It is used in the process of brewing beer.
- When glucose and galactose combine, *lactose* is created. Lactose is often called *milk sugar*, since it is found in dairy foods.

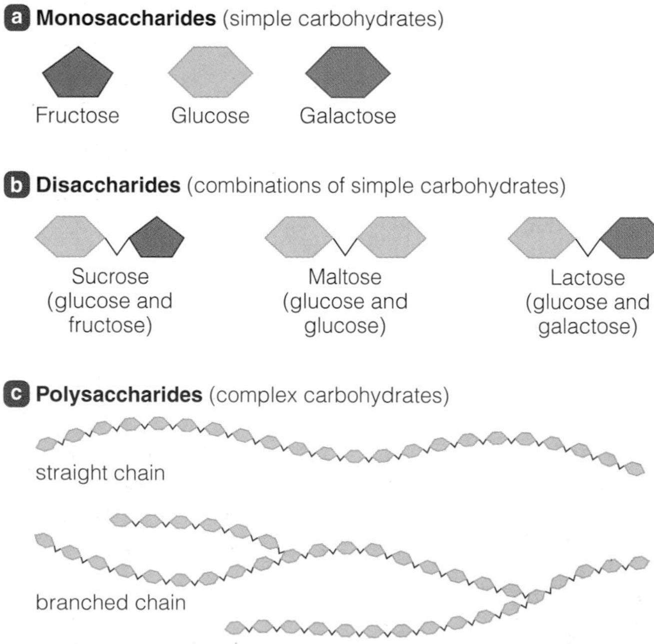

simple carbohydrates Carbohydrates that contain a single sugar unit or two sugar units combined. Monosaccharides and disaccharides are simple carbohydrates.

monosaccharides Simple carbohydrates that contain one sugar unit. There are three monosaccharides: glucose, fructose, and galactose.

disaccharides Simple carbohydrates that contain two sugar units combined. There are three disaccharides: sucrose, lactose, and maltose.

complex carbohydrates Carbohydrates that contain many sugar units combined. Polysaccharides are complex carbohydrates.

polysaccharides Complex carbohydrates that contain many sugar units combined. Starch, glycogen, and fiber are polysaccharides.

Figure 7.2 Monosaccharides, Disaccharides, and Polysaccharides
(a) Fructose, glucose, and galactose are the three simple carbohydrates (monosaccharides) found in nature. **(b)** Sucrose, maltose, and lactose are another form of simple carbohydrates (disaccharides), formed in foods as a result of bonding between two monosaccharides. **(c)** Polysaccharides (complex carbohydrates) are long chains of many glucose units, joined together in a straight chain or with "branches."

Polysaccharides Are Complex Carbohydrates

The three simple carbohydrates described previously—glucose, fructose, and galactose—are also the building blocks of all complex carbohydrates (polysaccharides). That is, polysaccharides consist of long chains of monosaccharides linked together. As you can see in Figure 7.2c, these chains contain many combined glucose units, which is why they are called complex carbohydrates. **Starch, fiber,** and **glycogen** are the three groups of polysaccharides.

Soluble fiber is found in legumes, as well as in many whole grains, fruits, and vegetables.

Starch Is Stored in Plants

One group of complex carbohydrates is starch, which is stored in plants in the form of thousands of glucose units strung together in a chain. These chains can be either straight or branched (Figure 7.2c), and both forms can be present in the same food. Pasta, rice, bread, and potatoes are all excellent sources of starch.

Fiber Is Not Digestible but Important

Humans lack the digestive enzyme needed to break down fiber, the second group of complex carbohydrates. In general fiber is the part of a plant that we eat but cannot digest. **Dietary fiber** is found naturally in foods, while **functional fiber** is added to food for a beneficial effect. For example, psyllium is a functional fiber derived from wheat husks; it can be added to breakfast cereals to help promote regular bowel movements. Together, dietary and functional fibers account for the *total fiber* that you eat.

Many fiber compounds can be classified as both dietary and functional, depending on how they are used. For example, pectin is a type of fiber found naturally in foods such as apples and citrus fruits, where it is considered to be a source of dietary fiber. However, pectin can also be isolated and added to foods, such as nonfat yogurt, to add texture; in this case, it is considered to be a functional fiber.

Unripe fruit tastes more starchy than sweet. As fruit ripens, its complex carbohydrates are broken down into **simple sugars,** including fructose. The more it ripens, the more fructose it has and the sweeter it tastes.

Fiber is also classified by its properties when combined with water. **Soluble fiber** dissolves in water, while **insoluble fiber** does not. Soluble fiber can be viscous; that is, it can have gummy or thickening properties. For example, the viscous soluble fiber in oats and beans thickens cooked oatmeal and bean chili. When you eat these foods, their soluble fiber is fermented (or digested) by bacteria in your large intestine. In contrast, insoluble fiber, found in foods such as bran flakes, is not viscous (gummy) and, so, is fermented less readily by bacteria.

A fiber's solubility affects how quickly it moves through the digestive tract. Since most foods contain both types of fiber and some fibers can have multiple effects in your body, this solubility effect isn't exact. In general, soluble fiber (from foods such as fruits and vegetables, oats and barley, legumes, and psyllium husks) is more viscous and moves more slowly through your intestinal tract. In contrast, insoluble fibers (found in some fruits and vegetables, seeds, cereal fiber, and whole-grain brans) typically move more quickly through your intestinal tract. However, viscous soluble fiber can also have a laxative effect by absorbing water.

Even though fiber is mostly nondigestible, it can have powerful health effects in your body. (See the box feature "Grains, Glorious Whole Grains" on how to enjoy more whole grains in your diet.) We will discuss some of these effects in depth in Concept 8. Do you have a whole-grain-friendly diet? Rate Yourself and find out!

starch The storage form of glucose in plants.

fiber A nondigestible polysaccharide.

glycogen The storage form of glucose in humans and other animals.

functional fiber A nondigestible polysaccharide added to foods because of a specific desired effect on human health.

dietary fiber A nondigestible polysaccharide found in foods.

soluble fiber A type of fiber that dissolves in water and is fermented by intestinal bacteria. Many soluble fibers are viscous, with gummy or thickening properties.

insoluble fiber The type of fiber that doesn't dissolve in water and is not fermented by intestinal bacteria.

Grains, Glorious Whole Grains

Grains are not only an important dietary staple but also a great source of nutrition. Americans' consumption of wheat, corn, oats, barley, and rye products has increased by nearly 50 percent since the 1970s. Most people in the United States consume around 140 pounds of flour and cereal products each year.[1]

A single kernel of grain has three edible parts: the bran, the germ, and the endosperm (see figure). The **bran,** or outer shell, of the wheat kernel is rich in fiber, B vitamins, phytochemicals, and minerals, such as chromium and zinc. The **germ,** or seed, of the kernel is a nutritional powerhouse, providing vitamin E, heart-healthy fats, phytochemicals, and plenty of B vitamins. The **endosperm,** or starchy part of the grain, has protein, B vitamins, and some fiber, but not as much as the bran.

Depending on which parts of the kernel are used, grain products can be divided into two categories: **refined grains** and **whole grains.** In refined grains, such as wheat or white bread and white rice, the grain kernel goes through a milling process that strips out the bran and germ, leaving only the endosperm of the kernel in the final product. As a result, some of the B vitamins, iron, phytochemicals, and dietary fiber are removed. **Enriched grains** are an attempt to restore some of the nutrition lost in the refinement process by adding folic acid, thiamin, niacin, riboflavin, and iron to them. This improves their nutritional quality somewhat, but the fiber and phytochemicals are still lost. Although refined grains can be a source of complex carbohydrates, you can think of *refined* as having left some of the nutrition *behind*. From a health standpoint, what is left behind may be the most important part of the kernel.

Whole-grain foods, such as whole-wheat bread, brown rice, and oatmeal, contain all three parts of the kernel. Whole grains are potential disease-fighting allies in your diet.[2] Research has shown that as little as one serving of whole grains every day may help lower the risk of dying from heart disease or cancer and reduce the risk of stroke.[3] In addition, the fiber in whole grains may also help reduce the risk of diabetes.[4] Because whole grains are abundant in vitamins, minerals, fiber, and phytochemicals, it's not clear which of these substances are the most important disease fighters, or if some or all of them work in a complementary way to provide protection.[5]

Typically, over 80 percent of Americans still choose refined grains over whole grains. While the current recommendation is to eat at least three servings of whole-grain foods every day, most Americans average only about one serving daily.[6]

The good news is that it's easy to incorporate more whole grains into your diet, because there are so many choices:

- Brown rice
- Bulgur (cracked wheat)
- Graham flour
- Oatmeal
- Popcorn
- Pearl barley
- Whole-grain cornmeal
- Whole oats
- Whole rye
- Whole wheat

bran The indigestible outer shell of a grain kernel.

germ In grains, the seed of a grain kernel.

endosperm The starchy part of the grain kernel.

refined grains Grain foods that are made with only the endosperm of the kernel; the bran and germ are not included.

whole grains Grain foods that are made with the entire edible grain kernel; the bran, the germ, and the endosperm.

enriched grains Refined grain foods to which folic acid, thiamin, niacin, riboflavin, and iron have been added.

RATE YOURSELF 

Do You Have a Whole-Grain-Friendly Diet?

On most days of the week:

1. I eat whole-grain cereals, like raisin bran, etc. **True** ☐ **False** ☐
2. I eat whole-wheat breads and/or English muffins. **True** ☐ **False** ☐
3. I eat brown rice instead of white rice. **True** ☐ **False** ☐
4. I snack on popcorn, rather than chips and pretzels. **True** ☐ **False** ☐
5. I consume whole-wheat pasta, rather than regular pasta. **True** ☐ **False** ☐

Answers

If you answered "true" to three or more questions, you have a whole-grain-friendly diet! If not, read on!

TABLE TIPS

Ways to Enjoy Whole Grains

Choose whole-grain cereals, such as shredded wheat, bran flakes, raisin bran, and oatmeal, in the morning.

Combine a 100 percent whole-wheat English muffin and low-fat cheddar cheese for a hearty breakfast cheese melt.

Enjoy your lunchtime sandwich made with a whole-wheat pita or 100 percent whole-grain bread.

Try instant brown rice for a quick whole-grain at dinner.

Snack on popcorn or 100 percent whole-wheat crackers for a high-fiber filler in the afternoon.

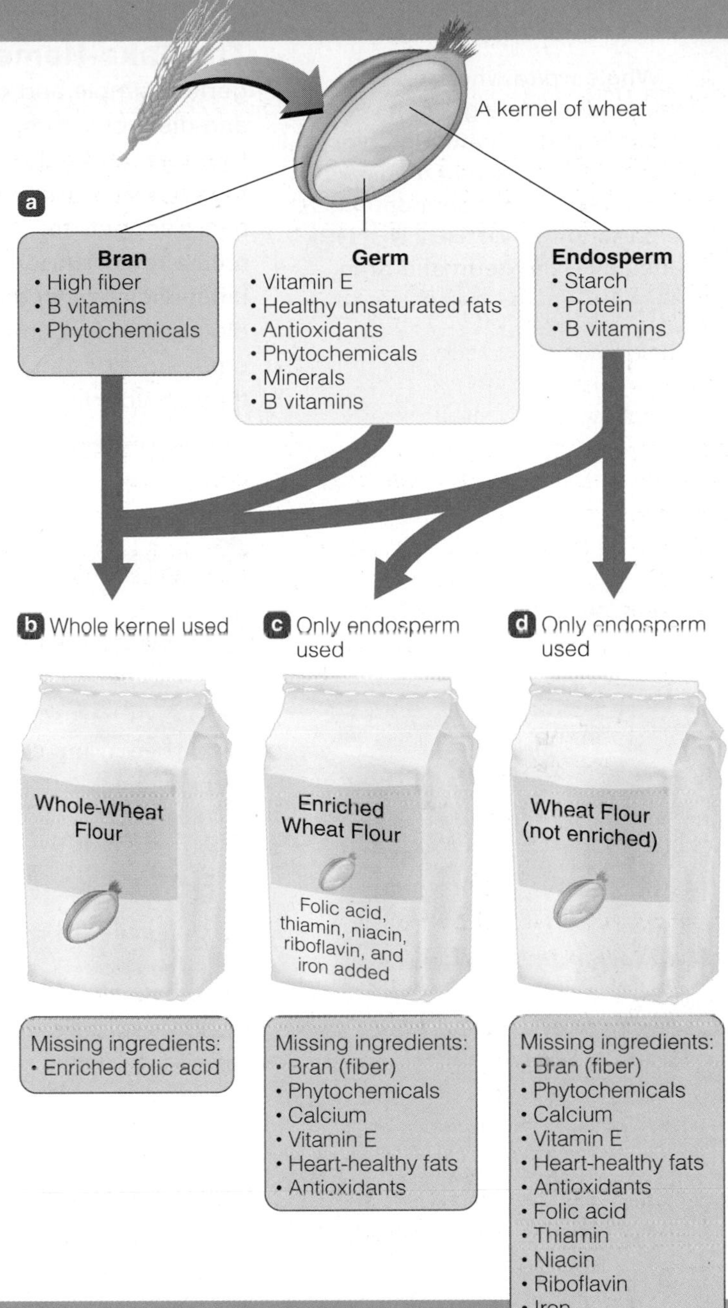

From Wheat Kernel to Flour
(a) The wheat grain kernel has three parts: the bran, the germ, and the endosperm. **(b)** Whole-wheat flour is made using the entire grain kernel. It is not enriched. **(c)** Enriched wheat flour doesn't contain the bran and germ, so it is missing some nutrients and phytochemicals. During an enrichment process, other nutrients are added back to the flour. **(d)** Wheat flour that is not enriched lacks not only the bran and germ but also many nutrients and phytochemicals

Glycogen Is Stored in Animals

Glycogen is the form of glucose stored in humans and other animals in the liver and in muscle cells. It is a complex carbohydrate similar to starch. Humans store only limited amounts of glycogen in their bodies, but it can be an important source of glucose for the blood. People can't access the carbohydrates stored in meats and poultry, however, because the glycogen stored in animals breaks down when the animals die.

Whole *white* wheat flour is considered a whole grain! It is made from wheat that is lighter in color and milder in flavor. Bread made with whole white wheat flour contains all the parts of the **wheat kernel**, including the germ and bran.

The Take-Home Message Carbohydrates are divided into two categories: simple and complex. Simple carbohydrates are monosaccharides and disaccharides; complex carbohydrates are polysaccharides. Glucose, fructose, and galactose are the three monosaccharides. They combine to form sucrose, maltose, and lactose—the three disaccharides. Starch, fiber, and glycogen are the three groups of polysaccharides. Dietary fiber occurs naturally in plant-based foods. Functional fiber is added to foods to achieve a beneficial, functional effect. The total fiber in your diet is a combination of dietary and functional fiber. Intestinal bacteria can break down soluble (viscous) fiber. It can have a beneficial laxative effect by moving more slowly through your intestinal tract than insoluble fiber.

Some People Cannot Digest Milk Sugar

Lactose, or milk sugar, is the main carbohydrate found in dairy products, such as milk, yogurt, and cheese. People who are deficient in the enzyme lactase cannot properly digest lactose.

Lactose Maldigestion Develops with Aging

Lactose maldigestion is a natural part of the aging process. In fact, as soon as children stop nursing, their bodies respond by making less lactase. About 25 percent of Americans, and 75 percent of adults around the world, do not digest lactose well. People of some ethnic origins—such as those from northern Europe, central Africa, and the Middle East—are less likely to develop lactose maldigestion. They are able to tolerate lactose better because they are genetically predisposed to having higher lactase levels throughout their adult lives.[2]

Although the term *lactose maldigestion* may sound serious, it doesn't mean that dairy foods need to be eliminated from the diet. In fact, many people continue to enjoy milk, yogurt, and cheese throughout their lives without any problems or unpleasant side effects.[3] This is good news, since dairy products provide over 70 percent of the calcium needed in the diet.[4]

Severe Lactase Deficiency Produces Lactose Intolerance

For some people, such as Emma, whom you read about at the beginning of this concept, the amount of lactase in their digestive tracts decreases so much that they experience distressing symptoms. The undigested lactose draws water into the digestive tract, causing diarrhea. To make matters worse, bacteria that normally live in the digestive tract can ferment the lactose and produce gases. Bloating, flatulence (gassiness), and cramps follow. People who regularly experience these symptoms within 2 hours after eating or drinking foods that contain lactose may have a condition called **lactose intolerance**.[5]

lactose maldigestion The inability to digest lactose in foods because of inadequate levels of the enzyme lactase.

lactose intolerance A significant deficiency in the enzyme lactase, resulting in symptoms such as nausea, cramps, bloating, flatulence, and diarrhea following the consumption of foods containing lactose.

What Happens to the Carbohydrates You Eat?

When you eat plant foods, your body breaks down the carbohydrates for energy. Let's look at how your body digests a meal of pasta (starch), milk (lactose), and a handful of cherries (sucrose and fiber). Each step is illustrated in the figure.

a. Cherries, pasta, and milk all contain carbohydrates.

b. The digestion of carbohydrates starts in your mouth. The act of chewing mixes the saliva in your mouth with the food. Your saliva delivers a powerful enzyme called amylase (*ase* = enzyme), which starts breaking down the starch in the pasta into smaller units. Some of the starch is broken down to the disaccharide maltose.

c. This mixture of starch and amylase, along with the disaccharides maltose, lactose (in the milk), and sucrose (in the cherries) and the fiber (in the cherries), travels down to your stomach. The amylase continues to break down the starch until your stomach acids deactivate this enzyme.

d. Once the food leaves your stomach, it moves through your small intestine. The food's arrival in the small intestine signals your pancreas to release another enzyme, pancreatic amylase. The pancreatic amylase breaks down the remaining starch units into maltose. Next, the disaccharides brush up against the lining of your digestive tract. There, they encounter a variety of enzymes, which break down the disaccharides into monosaccharides—specifically, glucose, fructose, and galactose. The monosaccharides are now ready to be absorbed into your blood.

e. The absorbed monosaccharides travel in your blood to your liver. There, the fructose and galactose are converted to glucose. If the glucose is not needed immediately, it is stored in your liver.

f. Glucose that is needed at once is shipped back out into your blood for delivery to cells throughout your body.

g. Meanwhile, the fiber, which was not absorbed in your small intestine, continues down to your colon. The bacteria in your colon can metabolize some of the fiber, but most of it is eliminated from your body as waste.

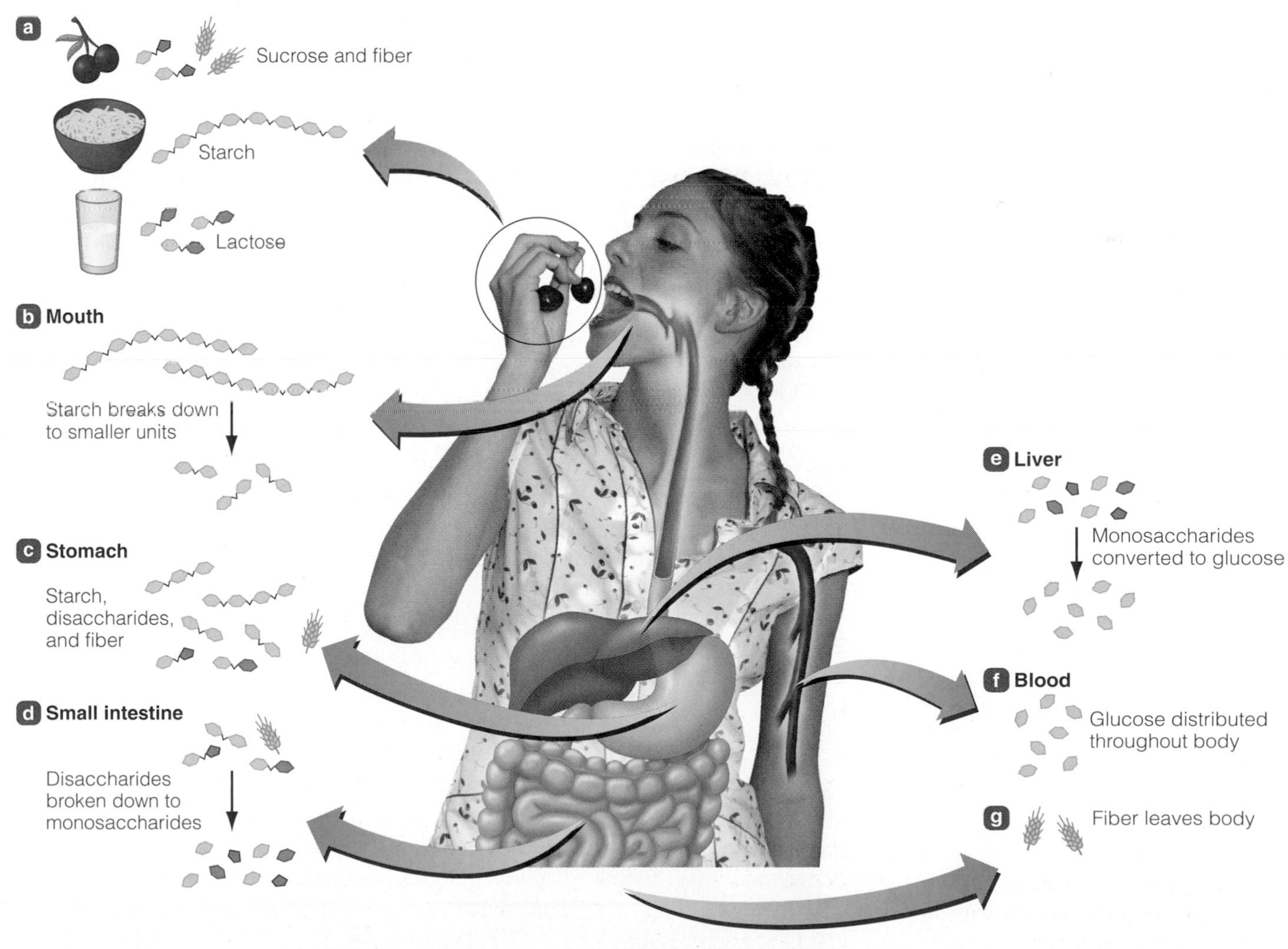

TABLE TIPS

Tolerating Lactose

Gradually add some dairy or other lactose-containing foods to your diet.

Eat smaller amounts of lactose-containing foods throughout the day, rather than eating a large amount at one time.

Enjoy your dairy foods with a meal or snack.

Try reduced-lactose milk and dairy products, such as cottage cheese.

Lactase pills can help with a lactose-laden meal or snack.

Lactose intolerance is not the same as an allergy to milk. A milk allergy is the immune system's response to one or more of the proteins in cow's milk. This condition typically affects only about 1 to 3 percent of children, and it rarely occurs in adults.[6] We'll talk more about food allergies in Concept 29.

You should never try to diagnose lactose intolerance, or any other medical condition, in yourself. Doing so may cause you to restrict your diet unnecessarily, potentially causing serious problems if your diagnosis is wrong. In fact, there are many documented cases of people who thought they were lactose intolerant but discovered they weren't, once the proper testing was done.[7] More seriously, an incorrect self-diagnosis may prevent you from getting an accurate diagnosis of potentially more serious medical conditions. It is always best to leave medical diagnosis to your doctor.

Some people with lactose intolerance can tolerate lactose-containing foods and beverages better than others (Table 7.1). Consuming smaller amounts of dairy foods throughout the day can be better tolerated than having a large amount at one time. Eating these foods with a meal or snack, rather than by themselves, can also influence how much lactose can be tolerated.[8] For instance, Emma might be able to eat both pizza and ice cream at the same meal if she simply eats less of each. But because she eats a small lunch, she is setting herself up for overindulging in these lactose-rich foods at dinner. She can also try starting her meal with a large salad to reduce her hunger and give her something to accompany the high-lactose foods.

People tend to tolerate some dairy foods better than others.[9] Whole milk tends to be better tolerated than skim milk. Cheeses (especially hard, aged cheeses, such as Swiss and cheddar) typically have less lactose than milk, so they are better tolerated. Yogurts that contain active cultures are also better tolerated than skim or low-fat milk.

Table 7.1

How Much Lactose Is in Your Foods?

	Lactose (grams)
Milk, whole, 1%, or skim, 1 cup	11
Ice cream, 1/2 cup	6
Yogurt, low-fat, 1 cup	5
Sherbet, 1/2 cup	2
Cottage cheese, 1/2 cup	2
Swiss, blue, cheddar, Parmesan cheese, 1 oz	1
Cream cheese, 1 oz	1
Lactaid milk, 1 cup	<1
Soy milk, 1 cup	0

Don't Forget These Hidden Sources of Lactose

Baked goods
Baking mixes for pancakes, biscuits, and cookies
Bread
Breakfast drinks
Candies
Cereals, processed
Instant potatoes
Lunch meats (other than kosher meats)
Margarine
Salad dressings
Soups

Data adapted from: The American Dietetic Association, *Manual of Clinical Dietetics 2000*; food manufacturers; and the National Digestive Diseases Information Clearinghouse, *Lactose Intolerance.* National Institutes of Health Publication No. 02-2751 (2002).

People with lactose intolerance who want to enjoy dairy foods without worrying about the unpleasant side effects can increasingly find lactose-reduced dairy products, such as milk, cottage cheese, and ice cream, in many supermarkets. Lactase pills are available that can be consumed before meals containing lactose. Emma can take some lactase pills prior to her pizza and ice cream dinner to prevent after-dinner discomfort. See Table Tips for more ideas on how to better tolerate lactose.

Many products are available to help those who are lactose intolerant enjoy dairy foods.

The Take-Home Message **Lactose maldigestion is the inability to absorb the milk sugar lactose properly due to a decrease in the amount of the enzyme lactase in your digestive tract. Lactose intolerance is a more significant lactase deficiency, resulting in symptoms such as intestinal cramps, gas, bloating, and diarrhea within 2 hours of consuming foods or beverages containing lactose.**

How Does Your Body Use Carbohydrates?

Your body uses carbohydrates—specifically, glucose—for energy. In this section, we'll see how.

Insulin Regulates Glucose in Your Blood

Chemical messengers called **hormones** regulate many important conditions in your body, including the amount of glucose in your blood. Hormones are like traffic cops, directing specific actions to keep your body working efficiently. After you eat a carbohydrate-heavy meal, your blood is flooded with glucose (Figure 7.3a). To lower your blood glucose level, your pancreas releases the hormone **insulin** into your blood. Insulin directs glucose into your cells and determines whether it will be used immediately as energy or stored for later use. If the amount of glucose in your blood exceeds your body's immediate energy needs, insulin directs it to be stored for later.

As mentioned earlier, your body stores unused glucose in long, branched chains called glycogen. (Recall that plants store glucose as starch. Humans and other animals store glucose as glycogen.) This storage occurs only in your liver and muscle cells. While plants have an unlimited capacity to store glucose as starch, people cannot store unlimited reserves of extra energy in the form of glycogen. However, insulin can direct your body to store energy from glucose in another form: fat! In fact, most of the energy stored in your body is in the form of fat. We'll discuss fat in detail in Concepts 10 and 11.

hormones Protein- or lipid-based chemical substances that act as "messengers" in the body to initiate or direct actions and processes. Insulin, glucagon, and estrogen are examples of bodily hormones.

insulin The hormone, produced in and released from the pancreas, that directs glucose from the blood into the body's cells.

Carbohydrates Fuel Your Body between Meals

Recall that both glycogen and fat are important sources of fuel stored to meet your body's energy needs. These storage forms come in handy between meals, when you aren't eating but your body continues to need fuel. Remember, your red blood cells and your brain, as well as the rest of your nervous system, rely on a steady supply of

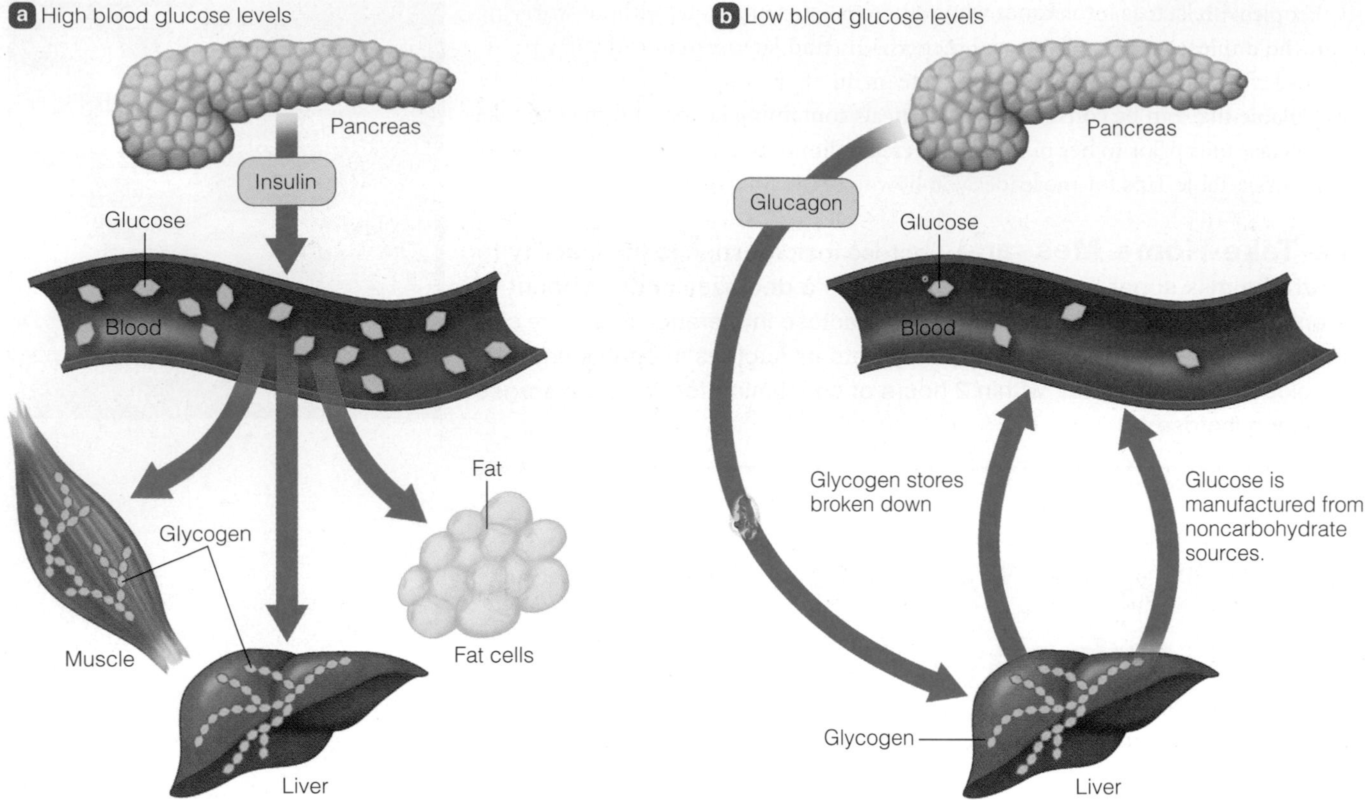

Figure 7.3 Insulin Directs Excess Glucose into Storage
(a) When your blood glucose levels are too high, your pancreas releases the hormone insulin into your blood to direct the excess glucose into storage. It is stored in your muscles and liver as glycogen, and in your fat cells as fat. **(b)** When your blood glucose levels drop too low, your pancreas releases the hormone glucagon, which directs the release of glucose from stored glycogen. Glucagon also prompts your liver to manufacture glucose from noncarbohydrate sources, such as protein.

glucose to function properly. When your blood glucose level dips too low—for instance, if it has been longer than 4 hours since your last meal—your body calls on its glycogen reserves to supply glucose to your blood (Figure 7.3b).

Let's say that your nutrition class is at 8 a.m., and you have overslept and have not eaten breakfast. The last time you ate was at dinner last night—over 12 hours ago. As your blood glucose level begins to drop, your pancreas releases another hormone, *glucagon,* which directs the release of glucose from the stored glycogen in your liver to help raise your blood glucose level. In addition, glucagon signals your liver to start manufacturing glucose from noncarbohydrate sources, mostly from protein. When your body dismantles protein, it frees up specific remnants (amino acids, which are discussed in Concept 13) to generate the glucose it needs. In short, if you don't feed your blood with glucose, your body will attempt to feed it. Once your blood glucose level returns to normal, glucagon is no longer released.

In addition to glucagon, other hormones can increase your blood glucose level. Epinephrine, commonly known as *adrenaline,* acts on your liver and muscle cells to stimulate the breakdown of glucose. Emotional and physical forms of stress, such as fear, excitement, and bleeding, increase your body's output of adrenaline. For example, if a ferocious dog were chasing you down the street, your body would pump out adrenaline to help provide the fuel you need to run. For this reason, it is referred to as the "fight-or-flight" hormone.

A low blood glucose level can also trigger the release of adrenaline. In fact, when you skip meals, some of the symptoms you may experience when your blood glucose level dips too low—such as anxiety, rapid heartbeat, and shakiness—are caused by the release of this hormone. This is one reason you need to eat regularly throughout the day.

During Fasting, Your Body Breaks Down Fat and Protein

Skipping breakfast is one thing; fasting, or not eating for long periods of time, is quite another. After about 18 hours of fasting, your liver's glycogen stores are depleted, so your body must rely solely on fat and protein for fuel.

To burn fat thoroughly, you need adequate amounts of glucose. Without it, *ketone bodies,* by-products of the incomplete breakdown of fat, are created and spill out into your blood. Because most ketone bodies are acids, they can cause your blood to become slightly acidic. After about two days of fasting, the number of ketone bodies in your blood is at least doubled, and you are in a state of *ketosis.* Individuals who fast or follow strict low-carbohydrate diets are often in ketosis because they consume inadequate amounts of carbohydrates. Although the term *ketosis* sounds scary, the condition is not necessarily harmful as long as you are otherwise healthy.

While your body continues to break down fat for fuel, it also uses protein to generate glucose. You can't store extra protein for this, so protein from your muscles and organs is broken down and some of its parts are used to make glucose. If you continue to fast, your body's protein reserves will reach a dangerously low level, causing death.

The Take-Home Message After a meal, when your blood glucose level begins to rise, the hormone insulin is released from your pancreas, directing glucose into your cells to be used for energy. Excess glucose is stored as glycogen or as fat. When your blood glucose level drops too low, the hormone glucagon directs the release of glucose from glycogen in your liver. Glucagon also signals the liver to begin producing glucose from noncarbohydrate sources, such as protein. That is, your body begins to break down protein-rich tissues to generate glucose. When you fast, stored fat and ketone bodies become the primary source of energy to fuel your body. If fasting continues, death is inevitable.

The upcoming Visual Summary Table reviews many of the functions, daily needs and consequences regarding Carbohydrates, along with some food sources that will be discussed more fully in Concept 8.

Carbohydrates

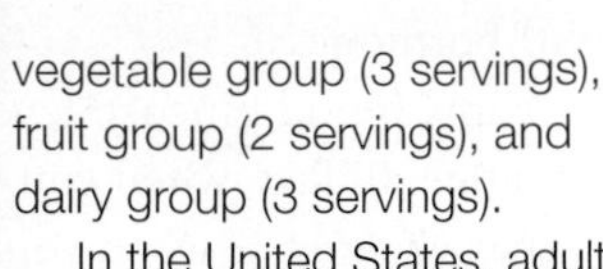

What Are Carbohydrates?

Carbohydrates are essential nutrients that are predominant in plant-based foods, and they make up the foundation of many diets around the world. You need carbohydrates on a daily basis because they are the most desirable source of energy for your body. Their main role is to supply fuel, primarily in the form of **glucose** (*ose* = carbohydrate), the predominant sugar in carbohydrate-rich foods, to your cells. Plants form glucose in a process called photosynthesis.

Simple and Complex Carbohydrates

Carbohydrates are divided into two categories based on the number of sugar units that are joined together. **Simple carbohydrates,** or sugars, include **monosaccharides** (*mono* = one, *saccharide* = sugar) and **disaccharides** (*di* = two), and **complex carbohydrates** include **polysaccharides** (*poly* = many).

There are three monosaccharides that are found in foods: glucose, *fructose,* and *galactose.* Fructose is the sweetest of the simple sugars and is found abundantly in fruit. For this reason, it is often referred to as fruit sugar. Galactose is found in dairy foods. From these three sugars, the other simple and complex carbohydrates can be created.

When two glucose units join together, the disaccharide *maltose* is created. Maltose is the sugar found in grains. When glucose and fructose pair up, the disaccharide *sucrose,* or table sugar, is formed. Galactose is joined with glucose to create lactose (often called milk sugar, as it is found in dairy foods).

Polysaccharides contain the most sugars so it makes sense that they are called complex carbohydrates. **Starch, fiber,** and **glycogen** are all polysaccharides.

Functions of Carbohydrates

Your body uses carbohydrates, specifically glucose, for energy, and there are chemical messengers called **hormones** that regulate the amount of glucose in your blood. To lower your blood glucose level, your pancreas releases the hormone **insulin** into the blood.

Surplus glucose is stored in long chains of glycogen. The process of generating glycogen for later use is call glycogenesis (*glyco* = sugar/sweet, *genesis* = origin). Glycogenesis occurs only in your liver and muscle cells. You can't squirrel away unlimited extra energy reserves in the form of glycogen. However, you can store excess energy in the form of fat.

Your pancreas releases another hormone, *glucagon,* when the body needs to direct the release of glucose from the stored glycogen in your liver to help raise your blood glucose level. This breakdown of glycogen is called glycogenolysis (*lysis* = loosening).

Fiber Has Many Health Benefits

Fiber has been shown to help lower your risk of developing constipation, diverticulosis, obesity, heart disease, cancer, and diabetes.

Meals high in fiber are typically digested more slowly, which allows the absorption of the nutrients to be extended over a longer period of time. Foods high in fiber, such as whole grains, fruits, and vegetables, can add to satiation so that fewer calories need to be eaten to feel full.

Viscous, soluble fibers have been shown to help lower elevated blood cholesterol levels. A high blood cholesterol level can increase the risk of heart disease.

Daily Needs

The latest Dietary Reference Intakes (DRIs) for carbohydrates recommend that adults and children consume a minimum of 130 grams daily. This is based on the estimated minimum amount of glucose your brain needs to function efficiently. A quick look at MyPyramid shows that 130 grams is less than the amount you would consume by eating the minimum recommended daily servings from the grain group (6 servings), vegetable group (3 servings), fruit group (2 servings), and dairy group (3 servings).

In the United States, adult males consume, on average, 220 grams to 330 grams of carbohydrates daily, whereas adult females eat 180 grams to 230 grams daily, well over the minimum DRI.

According to the latest DRIs, 45 to 65 percent of your total daily calories should come from carbohydrates. Adults in the United States consume about half of their calories from carbohydrate-laden foods, so they are easily meeting this optimal range.

Food Sources

In general, you want your diet to contain low to moderate amounts of simple carbohydrates and be high in fiber and other complex carbohydrates. This is the best strategy for long-term health.

Simple carbohydrates are found naturally in fruits, vegetables, and dairy foods. Though you can also get simple sugars from processed foods and sweets, the higher calorie and lower nutrient levels in these foods make them a less healthy option.

Complex carbohydrates, including starch and fiber, are found abundantly in grains, whole fruits, and vegetables. Starch is the primary complex carbohydrate found in grains and potatoes, while fiber is found in whole grains, whole fruits, vegetables, legumes, nuts, and seeds.

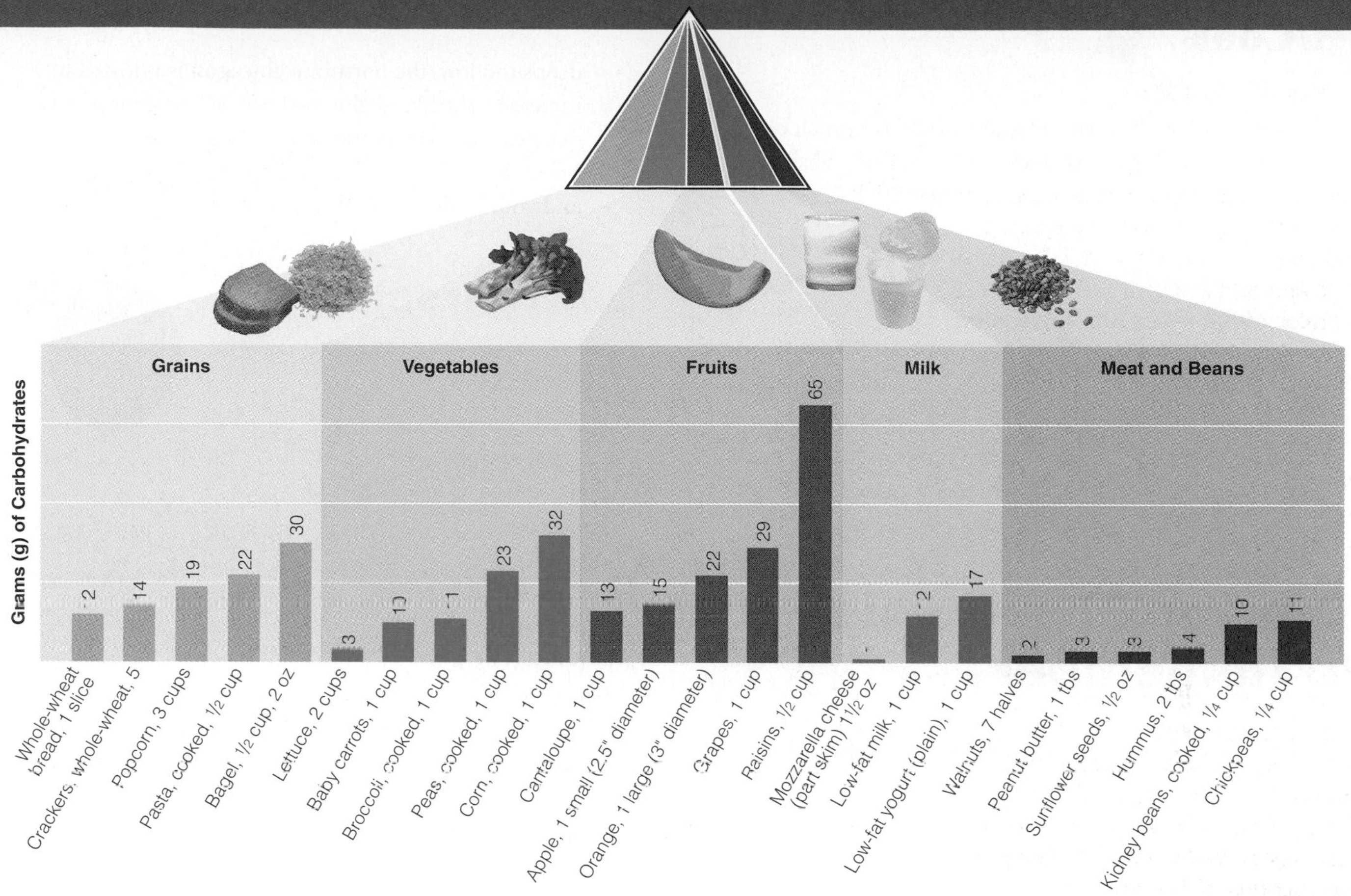

Food group	Food	Grams (g) of Carbohydrates
Grains	Whole-wheat bread, 1 slice	12
Grains	Crackers, whole-wheat, 5	14
Grains	Popcorn, 3 cups	19
Grains	Pasta, cooked, 1/2 cup	22
Grains	Bagel, 1/2 cup, 2 oz	30
Vegetables	Lettuce, 2 cups	3
Vegetables	Baby carrots, 1 cup	10
Vegetables	Broccoli, cooked, 1 cup	11
Vegetables	Peas, cooked, 1 cup	23
Vegetables	Corn, cooked, 1 cup	32
Fruits	Cantaloupe, 1 cup	13
Fruits	Apple, 1 small (2.5" diameter)	15
Fruits	Orange, 1 large (3" diameter)	22
Fruits	Grapes, 1 cup	29
Fruits	Raisins, 1/2 cup	65
Milk	Mozzarella cheese (part skim) 1 1/2 oz	1
Milk	Low-fat milk, 1 cup	12
Milk	Low-fat yogurt (plain), 1 cup	17
Meat and Beans	Walnuts, 7 halves	2
Meat and Beans	Peanut butter, 1 tbs	3
Meat and Beans	Sunflower seeds, 1/2 oz	3
Meat and Beans	Hummus, 2 tbs	4
Meat and Beans	Kidney beans, cooked, 1/4 cup	10
Meat and Beans	Chickpeas, 1/4 cup	11

Too Much or Too Little?

Adding too much carbohydrates in the diet can displace other essential nutrients, whereas consuming too little carbohydrates can create a diet that falls short of many vitamins, minerals, fiber, and phytochemicals. Both extremes will produce an unbalanced diet. Individuals with diabetes need to monitor their carbohydrate intake to maintain a healthy blood glucose level. Chronic, poor regulation of blood glucose levels can damage the body.

What Is Diabetes?

Individuals develop **diabetes** because they aren't producing enough insulin (type 1 diabetes) and/or they have developed **insulin resistance,** such that their cells do not respond to the insulin when it arrives (type 2 diabetes).

Type 1 diabetes is considered an autoimmune disease and is the rarer of the two forms. Type 2 is the more common form and is seen in people who have become insulin resistant. Type 2 diabetes accounts for 90 to 95 percent of diagnoses of the disease.

Diabetes, especially if it is poorly managed, increases the likelihood of a multitude of dire effects such as nerve damage, leg and foot amputations, eye diseases, including blindness, tooth loss, gum problems, kidney disease, and heart disease. Diabetes can also damage the tiny blood vessels in the retina of the eye, which can cause bleeding and cloudy vision, and eventually destroy the retina and cause blindness.

Good nutrition habits play a key role in both the prevention and management of diabetes. The ADA (American Diabetes Association) recommends that individuals with diabetes consume a diet that includes a combination of predominantly high-fiber carbohydrates from whole grains, fruits, and vegetables, along with low-fat milk, adequate amounts of lean protein sources, and unsaturated fats.

Terms to Know

glucose ■ simple carbohydrates ■ monosaccharides ■ disaccharides ■ complex carbohydrates ■ polysaccharides ■ starch ■ fiber ■ glycogen ■ hormones ■ insulin ■ diabetes ■ insulin resistance

UCook

Healthy Trail Mix

Looking for a healthy, whole-grain snack to munch on when you're hiking between classes? Visit our website for this tasty, filling, and easy-to-make Healthy Trail Mix.

UDo

How Much Fiber Are You Eating?

Do you think you have enough fiber in your diet? You may be surprised. Go to the website and fill out the daily food record for this concept. Then use Appendix A on the website or the MyDietAnalysis program to complete your record and see how you are really doing!

The Top Five Points to Remember

1. Glucose, fructose, and galactose are simple carbohydrates (monosaccharides). Glucose is the most abundant monosaccharide and the preferred fuel for your nervous system, including your brain, and your red blood cells.
2. When two monosaccharides are joined, a disaccharide is formed. The best-known disaccharide, sucrose (table sugar), is made of fructose and glucose. Lactose, or milk sugar, is made up of glucose and galactose. Maltose is two glucose units joined together.
3. When many glucose units are joined together, starch, a polysaccharide, is formed. Glycogen is the polysaccharide storage form of glucose in your body. Starch is the storage form of carbohydrate in plants. Fiber is a nondigestible polysaccharide.
4. Lactose maldigestion is the inability to absorb the milk sugar lactose properly because of a reduced amount of the enzyme lactase.
5. Your blood glucose level is maintained in a healthy range with the help of hormones. Insulin directs glucose into your cells. When your blood glucose level drops too low, the hormone glucagon is released to increase your blood glucose level. When your diet is deficient in carbohydrates, your body is not able to break down fat completely. Ketone bodies are created, and your body breaks down proteins.

Test Yourself

1. _______ is the storage form of glucose in your body.
   a. Glucagon
   b. Glycogen
   c. Galactose
   d. Glucose
2. Sucrose is a
   a. monosaccharide.
   b. disaccharide.
   c. polysaccharide.
   d. starch.
3. The hormone that directs the storage of glucose in body cells is
   a. galactose.
   b. glucagon.
   c. insulin.
   d. none of the above.
4. Soluble fiber can be
   a. found in oats.
   b. found in beans.
   c. viscous.
   d. all of the above.
5. Which of the following can improve the digestion of the milk sugar lactose?
   a. drinking milk with lactase added
   b. pouring milk over a cup of bran cereal
   c. enjoying cheese a little at a time and building up to larger servings
   d. all of the above

Answers

1. (b) Glycogen is stored in your liver and muscles, providing a ready-to-use form of glucose for your body. Glucagon is the hormone that directs the release of glucose from the stored glycogen. Galactose and glucose are monosaccharides.
2. (b) Sucrose contains two monosaccharides, glucose and fructose, and is therefore a disaccharide. Starch contains many units of glucose linked together and is therefore a polysaccharide.
3. (c) When your blood glucose level is too high, insulin is released from your pancreas to direct the uptake of glucose by your cells. Glucagon is a pancreatic hormone released when blood glucose is too low. Galactose is a monosaccharide found in dairy foods.
4. (d) Soluble fiber is found in oats and beans, and it is often viscous (gummy and thickening).
5. (d) All of these can help improve lactose absorption. The lactase-containing milk is pretreated to facilitate the breakdown of the lactose in the milk. Consuming lactose-containing foods, such as milk, with a meal or snack improves the digestion of lactose. Gradually adding dairy foods to the diet will lessen the symptoms of lactose intolerance.

Web Resources

- For more on fiber, visit the American Heart Association at: www.americanheart.org
- For more on lactose intolerance, visit the National Institute of Diabetes and Digestive and Kidney Disease (NIDDK) at: http://digestive.niddk.nih.gov/ddiseases/pubs/lactoseintolerance

8

1. You don't need to consume carbohydrates on a **daily basis.** T/F

2. Carbohydrates make you **fat.** T/F

3. Sugar consumption contributes to **tooth decay.** T/F

4. **Honey** is more nutritious than sugar. T/F

5. There is more **fiber** in dark-colored wheat bread than in white bread. T/F

Carbohydrates

Foods to Eat

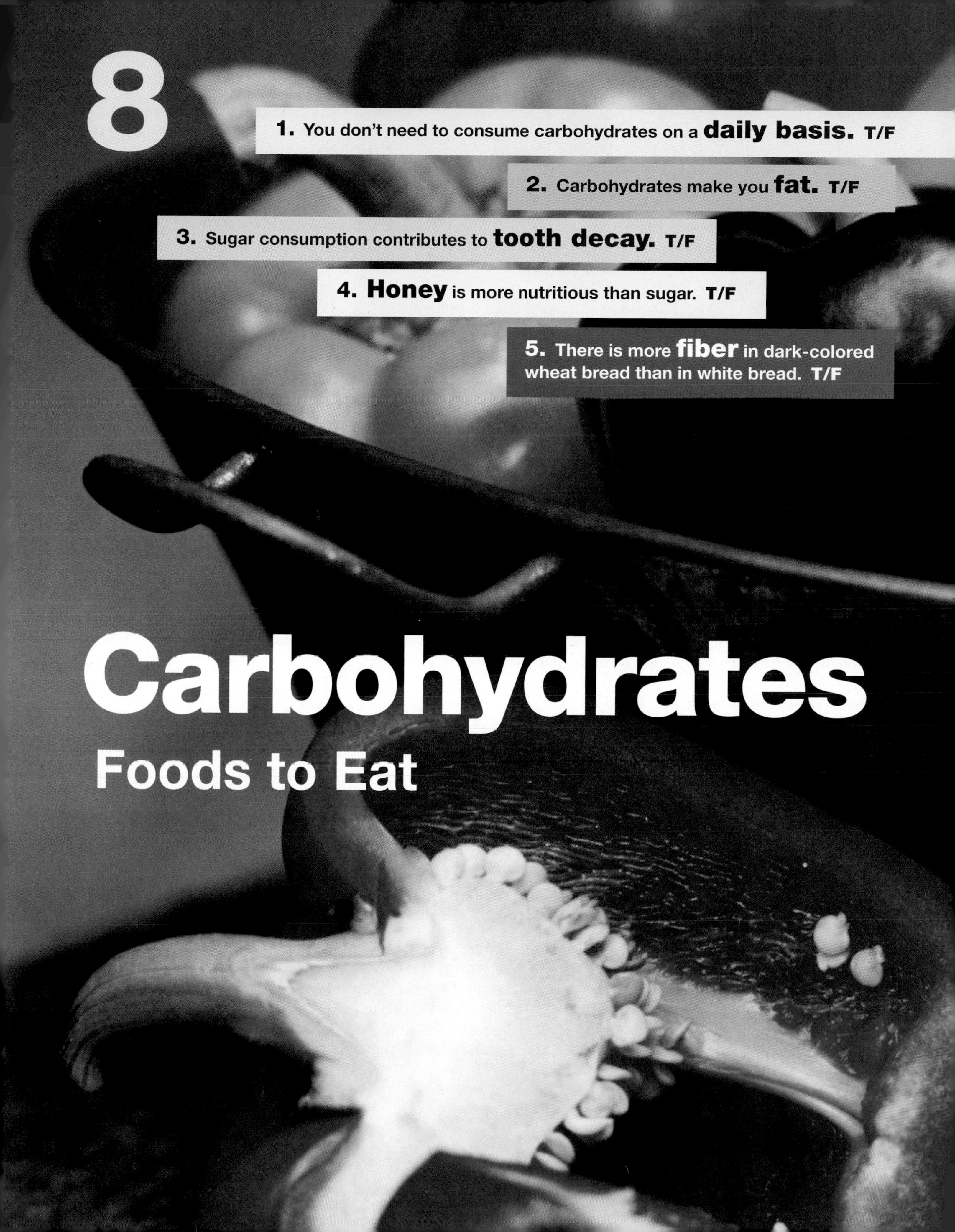

Marie's roommate, Celia, doesn't drink coffee. Instead, she starts her day off with a 20-ounce bottle of cola, and goes on to drink about two more every day. After reading a magazine article on healthy eating, Marie mentions to Celia that her cola habit may be adding a lot of sugar to her diet, and she might be better off drinking fruit juice or milk. Celia responds that there is sugar in fruit and milk, too. "Sugar is sugar!" she insists. "It doesn't matter where it comes from!" Who is right, Marie or Celia? Read on—the answer might surprise you!

In this concept, you'll learn about sugar: the ins and outs of natural sugars, added sugars, and sugar substitutes and where they are in the foods you eat. You'll also discover the powerful role that foods rich in fiber can play in fighting diseases such as obesity, heart disease, cancer, and diabetes. Most importantly, you'll learn how to change your diet to take full advantage of all the wonderful benefits of carbohydrates.

Answers

1. False. You need a minimum amount of carbohydrates daily. The answer is here on page 2!
2. False. Calories, not carbs, are what you need to monitor to avoid weight gain. In fact, some high-fiber carbohydrates can actually help you lose weight. Turn to page 4 to find out why.
3. True. The bacteria that cause cavities thrive on sugar. Turn to page 6 for details.
4. False. Honey contains a small amount of nutrients but not enough to make it nutritionally superior to sugar. Turn to page 6 to learn more.
5. False. Dark bread doesn't necessarily have more fiber than white bread. Learn why on page 16.

How Much Carbohydrate Do You Need and What Are Its Food Sources?

The question of how much carbohydrate you should consume every day has two answers. The first addresses the minimum amount of carbohydrate needed to fuel your body—specifically, your brain—in order to function efficiently. The second, more challenging answer relates to the best type and source of carbohydrates to choose for long-term health. We'll begin with the minimum amount of carbohydrates you need daily.

You Need a Minimum Amount of Carbohydrates Daily

The latest Dietary Reference Intakes (DRIs) for carbohydrates recommend that adults and children consume a minimum of 130 grams daily.[1] This is based on the estimated minimum amount of glucose your brain needs to function efficiently. This may sound like a lot, but 130 grams is less than what you would consume by eating the *minimum* recommended daily servings for each food group in MyPyramid—that is, six servings from the grain group, three servings each from the vegetable and dairy groups, and two servings from the fruit group.

If your diet is well balanced, feeding your brain should be a no-brainer. In the United States, men consume an average of 220 to 330 grams of carbohydrates daily, while women eat 180 to 230 grams daily, well over the minimum DRI.

Recall from Concept 4 that the acceptable macronutrient distribution range (AMDR) for carbohydrates is 45 to 65 percent of your total daily calories. Adults in the United States get about half of their calories from carbohydrate-rich foods, so they are easily within this optimal range.

The Best Carbohydrates Are Found in These Foods

Whole fruits and vegetables, whole grains, legumes, and lean dairy products are the best food sources of carbohydrates.

Now let's turn to the second part of our answer and look at the best type and source of carbohydrates to choose for long-term health. As with other nutrients, not all carbohydrate-laden foods are created equal. For example, eating high-sugar foods containing lots of calories and saturated fat, but few other nutrients, can lead to weight gain and promote heart disease. It's best to choose carbohydrates from a variety of nutrient-dense, low-saturated-fat foods whenever possible. In general, the best strategy for long-term health is to eat a diet with fewer (low to moderate amounts of) simple carbohydrates and more complex carbohydrates.

Simple carbohydrates are found naturally in fruits, vegetables, and dairy foods. Although you can also get simple sugars from processed foods and sweets, they typically have more calories and lower nutrient levels, making them a much less healthy option.

Complex carbohydrates include starch and fiber. Starch is the primary complex carbohydrate found in grains and potatoes, while fiber is found in whole grains, whole fruits vegetables, legumes, nuts, and seeds. You'll learn more about recommendations for fiber intake later in this concept.

The Take-Home Message You need to consume a minimum of 130 grams of carbohydrates daily to provide adequate glucose for your brain. It is recommended that 45 to 65 percent of your daily calories come from carbohydrates, which will provide more than the minimum amount needed daily. Whole fruits, vegetables, whole grains, legumes, and lean dairy products are the best food sources of carbohydrates.

What's the Difference between Natural and Added Sugars?

Finding the taste of sweet foods pleasurable is a natural response. A child being fed puréed applesauce for the first time will probably show his pleasure with a big smile. You're not likely to see the same smile when Junior is eating plain oatmeal.

You don't have to fight this taste for sweetness. A modest amount of sweet foods can easily be part of a well-balanced diet. However, some sources of sugar provide more nutrition than others.

Your taste buds can't distinguish between **naturally occurring sugars,** which are found in foods such as fruit and dairy products, and **added sugars,** which manufacturers add to foods such as soda and candy. From a nutritional standpoint, however, there is a big difference between these sugar sources. Foods that contain naturally occurring sugar tend to be nutrient dense and thus provide more nutrition per bite. In contrast, many foods that contain lots of added sugar provide little else. The calories in sugar-laden foods are often called **empty calories** because they provide so little nutrition.

naturally occurring sugars Sugars, such as fructose (in fruit) and lactose (in dairy products), that are found naturally in foods.

added sugars Sugars that are added to processed foods and sweets.

empty calories Calories that come with little nutrition. Jelly beans are an example of a food that provides lots of calories from sugar but few nutrients.

Many Foods Naturally Contain Sugar

Next time you have a yen for something sweet, reach for a piece of fresh fruit. You will be surprised how well a ripe peach, a crisp apple, or some chilled grapes can appease a craving for sweets. That's because fruit can contain more than 15 percent sugar by weight. Celia, the cola-guzzling student from the beginning of this concept, was right when she said that fruit provides sugar. However, like most Americans, she doesn't know about the many nutritional advantages of satisfying your sweet tooth with fruit, rather than sweets. To find out what those advantages are, compare slices from a fresh navel orange with candy orange slices (Figure 8.1).

Six slices of a navel orange provide about 65 calories, over 100 percent of the daily value for vitamin C, and 3.5 grams of fiber, which is more than 10 percent of the amount of fiber that most adults should eat daily. These juicy slices also provide fluid. In fact, over 85 percent of the weight of an orange is water. Their hefty amounts of fiber and water give orange slices bulk. This bulk can increase eating satisfaction, or satiation. When you eat fruit, you not only satisfy your urge for a sweet but also become full, lowering the chances that you'll overeat.

In contrast, six candy orange slices provide 300 calories, mostly from added sugar. Thus, the candy is quite energy dense. It provides more than four times as many calories as the fresh orange! However, since it doesn't provide any vitamins or other nutrients, it is nutrient poor. Moreover, six pieces of candy don't contain fiber, or much water, so they don't provide any bulk, which means you're not likely to feel satisfied after eating them, increasing the likelihood that you'll overeat. In contrast, you would have to eat more than four whole oranges to come close to the 300 calories found in the six pieces of candy.

Fiber-abundant whole fruits (and vegetables) are not only very nutritious, but they are also kind to your waistline, since their bulk tends to fill you up before they fill you out. In other words, it's hard to overconsume calories from fruits and vegetables because you will feel full and stop eating long before you take in too many calories. In fact, studies have confirmed that Americans who eat more fruit have

An orange has **four times** the fiber of 6 ounces of orange juice.

Figure 8.1 Fresh Orange Slices versus Candy Orange Slices
A fresh orange provides more nutrition for fewer calories and without any added sugars compared with candy orange slices. In addition, the fruit's bulk will fill you up and discourage overeating.

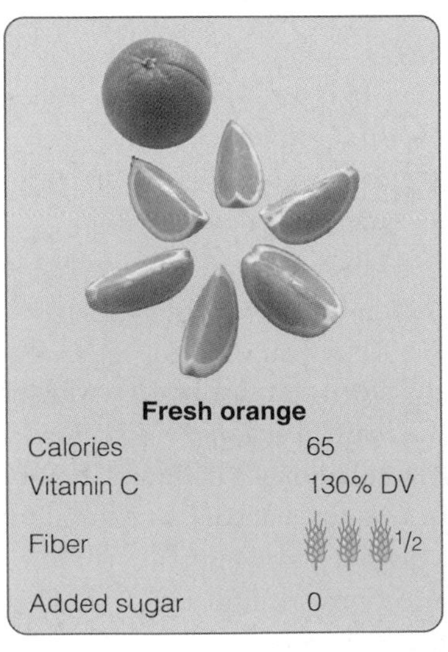

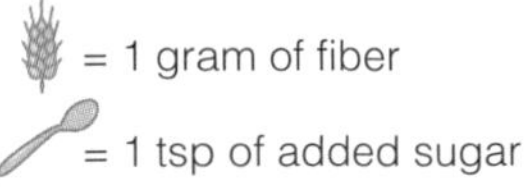

healthier body weights. According to USDA researchers, this may be due to the fact that fruit eaters tend to substitute fruit, with their lower calories and higher bulk, for high-calorie cakes and other sweets.[2]

Many Processed Foods Contain Added Sugars

Between 1980 and 2000, our yearly consumption of added sugars increased by more than 20 percent.[3] Sugars are added to foods for many reasons. In baked goods, they can hold on to water, which helps keep the product moist and soft. They help provide a golden brown color to the finished product. Added sugars also function as preservatives and thickeners in foods such as sauces. Fermenting sugars in dough produce the carbon dioxide that makes yeast breads rise. And, of course, sugars make foods taste sweet.

Are Added Sugars Bad for You?

Sugar has been blamed for everything from hyperactive children to diabetes, but are these claims myths or facts? Let's look at the most common claims:

- "Sugar causes hyperactivity in kids." Adults often point to sugary foods as the culprit behind the overly excited behavior of children at parties and holidays. However, research does not support the theory that sugar makes kids hyperactive.[4] The excitable behavior in kids is more likely due to their stimulation level than to the sweets they consume (this will be discussed in Concept 30).
- "Eating too much sugar causes diabetes." Contrary to popular thought, consuming lots of sugar doesn't necessarily cause diabetes. We'll explore what does in Concept 9.
- "Too much sugar can contribute to dental decay." This is certainly true, but so can other sources of carbohydrates. See the boxed feature, Avoiding a Trip to the Dentist, for information on how to prevent tooth decay.

Although these claims don't hold up, a high-sugar diet has been associated with some real health risks, including the following:

- Too much sugar in the diet can increase your blood level of triglycerides, the primary form of fat in your body. At the same time, it can lower the level of "good," HDL cholesterol. Together, these changes increase your risk for heart disease.[5] Luckily, you have choices and control over these bad effects: Reducing your intake of dietary sugar along with increasing your dietary fiber can significantly diminish this problem. (We'll discuss this in detail in Concept 12.)
- Consuming too much sugar can create weight-management challenges. Eating sugary foods won't automatically cause you to gain weight as long as you do not consume more than the total calories that you need daily. However, as many people already know, it is all too easy to overeat high-calorie, sugary foods and quickly add excess calories to your diet, as well as inches to your waist. Moderation and balance are the keys when it comes to added sugars.

Honey should **never be given** to children under the age of 1 year because it may contain microbe spores, which can germinate in babies' immature digestive tracts and cause deadly botulism. Older children and adults do not face this risk.

Finding the Added Sugars in Your Foods

While sucrose and fructose are the most common added sugars in foods, sugars can appear on the food label under many different names. Figure 8.2 shows some of the most common added sugars in foods.

Avoiding a Trip to the Dentist

Over the past 30 years, the incidence of tooth decay in the United States has decreased as the use of the mineral fluoride has increased.[1] (Fluoride will be covered in more detail in Concept 17.) Although dental health treatments have been improving, an estimated 20 percent of children from age 2 to 4 still have tooth decay. By the time these children reach age 17, almost 80 percent have experienced a cavity, the later stage of dental decay. *Dental caries* (tooth decay) are the cause of tooth loss in over two-thirds of adults age 35 to 44.[2] To avoid dental caries, you need to understand the role your diet plays in tooth decay.

Feeding into Tooth Decay

If you constantly eat carbohydrate-heavy foods, such as cookies, candy, and crackers, you are continually providing a buffet of easily fermentable sugars and starches to the bacteria bathing your teeth. A recent study of American diets revealed that adults who drank sugary sodas three or more times daily had 60 percent more dental caries than those who didn't drink any soda. To make matters worse, many soft drinks contain phosphoric acid and citric acid, which can erode teeth if consumed over a prolonged time.[3]

baby bottle tooth decay The decay of baby teeth due to continual exposure to fermentable sugary liquids.

remineralization The repair of teeth by adding back the minerals lost during tooth decay. Saliva can help remineralize teeth.

Eating several balanced meals daily is best for minimizing tooth decay. Snacks should be kept to a minimum, and you should choose fruit or vegetables over candies or pastries. Whole fruits and raw vegetables tend not to cause tooth decay, so snack on these to your teeth's content.[4]

Sticky foods, such as raisins and figs, can adhere to your teeth, so their fermentable sugars hang on to the teeth for longer periods. The longer the carbohydrate is in contact with your teeth, the more opportunity there is for the acids to do damage. Eating sticky foods in combination with other foods will discourage their ability to stick to your teeth. Drinking water after you eat will help by rinsing your teeth.

Fruit juice, even unsweetened juices, may be a problem for teeth, especially in small children. A child who routinely falls asleep with a bottle in her mouth that contains carbohydrate-laden beverages is at risk of developing **baby bottle tooth decay** because the baby's teeth are being exposed continually to fermentable sugars.[5] Children need adequate amounts of fluids, such as water, but they should not be given a continual supply of sweetened beverages.

Foods That Fight Tooth Decay

Some foods may help reduce the effects of acid on your teeth. For example, the texture of cheese stimulates the release of cleansing saliva. Cheese is also rich in protein, calcium, and phosphorus, all of which can help buffer the acids in your mouth following a meal or snack. The calcium can also assist in the **remineralization** of your teeth. Eating as little as ½ an ounce of cheese after a snack, or eating cheese with a meal, has been shown to protect your teeth.[6] Chewing sugarless gum can also be a healthy ending to a meal or snack if you can't brush your teeth. It encourages the production of saliva and provides a postmeal bath for your teeth. Xylitol, a sugar substitute often found in sugarless chewing gum, may even help with remineralization.[7]

With regular visits to your dentist, good dental hygiene, and a healthy diet, you can reduce your risk for tooth decay. Follow these Do's and Don'ts to keep your teeth healthy:

DO eat three solid meals but keep snacks to a minimum.
DON'T graze all day long!
DO snack, if necessary, on whole fruit, raw vegetables, and low-fat cheese, which tend to be friendlier to your teeth.
DON'T munch on sugary foods, such as candy, cookies, and other sweets.
DO drink plenty of water.
DON'T drink a lot of sugar-sweetened beverages. Not only are the calories hefty, but this constant flow of sugar can provide a continual meal for the acid-producing bacteria in your mouth.
DO chew sugarless gum or eat a piece of low-fat cheese after meals and snacks when you can't brush your teeth.
DON'T think that sugarless gum and cheese can replace a routine of brushing and flossing.
DO brush your teeth at least twice a day and floss daily.
DON'T forget this!

Over the years, some of these forms of added sugar, such as honey and fructose, have been publicized as being more nutritious than table sugar. This is an exaggeration. Honey provides a negligible amount of potassium, and it actually has more calories per teaspoon than sugar: 21 versus 16. Fructose can have a laxative effect on the body if you consume 20 grams or more in one day. That may seem like a generous amount, but keep in mind that a 12-ounce can of soda or 8 ounces of apple juice

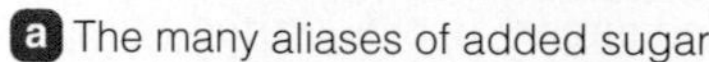

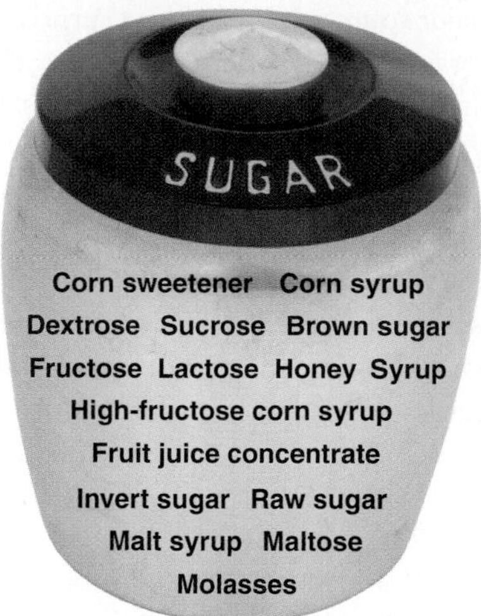

b

Nutrition Facts
Serving Size 1 Bar (24g)
Servings Per Container 10

Amount Per Serving	
Calories 90	Calories from Fat 20
	% Daily Value*
Total Fat 2g	3%
Saturated Fat 0.5g	3%
Trans Fat 0g	
Sodium 80 mg	3%
Total Carbohydrate 19g	6%
Dietary Fiber 1g	3%
Sugars 7g	
Protein 1g	
Calcium 8% • Iron	4%

Not a significant source of Cholesterol, Vitamin A, Vitamin C

* Percent Daily Values are based on a 2,000 calorie diet. Your Daily Values may be higher or lower depending on your calorie needs:

		Calories: 2,000	2,500
Total Fat	Less than	65g	80g
Sat Fat	Less than	20g	25g
Cholesterol	Less than	300mg	300mg
Sodium	Less than	2,400mg	2,400mg
Total Carbohydrate		300g	375g
Dietary Fiber		25g	30g

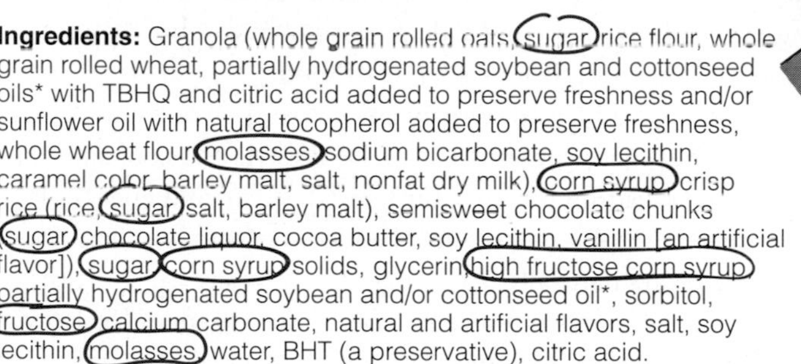
Ingredients: Granola (whole grain rolled oats, sugar, rice flour, whole grain rolled wheat, partially hydrogenated soybean and cottonseed oils* with TBHQ and citric acid added to preserve freshness and/or sunflower oil with natural tocopherol added to preserve freshness, whole wheat flour, molasses, sodium bicarbonate, soy lecithin, caramel color, barley malt, salt, nonfat dry milk), corn syrup, crisp rice (rice, sugar, salt, barley malt), semisweet chocolate chunks (sugar, chocolate liquor, cocoa butter, soy lecithin, vanillin [an artificial flavor]), sugar, corn syrup solids, glycerin, high fructose corn syrup, partially hydrogenated soybean and/or cottonseed oil*, sorbitol, fructose, calcium carbonate, natural and artificial flavors, salt, soy lecithin, molasses, water, BHT (a preservative), citric acid.

* Adds a dietarily insignificant amount of *trans* fat.

Figure 8.2 Finding Added Sugars on the Label
(a) Sugar can be referred to by a number of different names on ingredient lists and labels.
(b) Foods contain large amounts of sugar if added sugars appear first or second among the ingredients and/or if many varieties of added sugars are listed. Also, check the Nutrition Facts panel for the total grams of sugar the food contains per serving.

contains 14 to 22 grams of fructose.[6] As you can see, even though honey and fructose may have been glamorized in the media, they aren't nutritionally superior to sucrose.

To find the amount and type of added sugars in the foods you eat, read the ingredients on food labels. If added sugars appear first or second on the list or if the product contains many varieties of added sugars, it is very likely to be high in sugar. For example, as you can see in Figure 8.2, the ingredient label from a box of low-fat chocolate chip granola bars lists 10 types of added sugars!

The Nutrition Facts panel currently displayed on food packaging doesn't distinguish between naturally occurring and added sugars. For example, the nutrition label on raisin bran cereal lists 21 grams of sugars, and the label on low-fat milk lists 12 grams. The difference is that the number of grams of sugars listed for the raisin bran includes both the amount of naturally occurring sugars in the raisins and the amount of added sugars used to sweeten the cereal. For the milk, the sugar listed on the label includes the naturally occurring sugar, lactose. With the increased concern about the rising levels of added sugars in the diets of Americans, health professionals and organizations have pressured the Food and Drug Administration (FDA) to require that all added *sugars* be disclosed on the food label.

As you know, added sugars come from many sources and are found in many products. In fact, most Americans don't eat most of the added sugars in their diets—

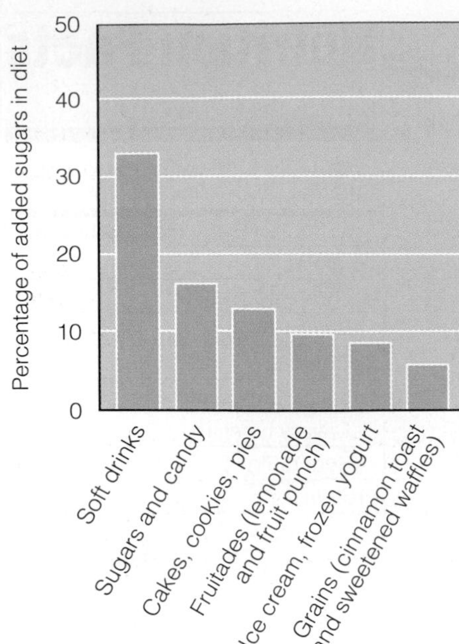

Figure 8.3 Where Are All These Added Sugars Coming From?
Soft drinks are the number-one source of added sugars in the diets of Americans. Sugar, candy, bakery items, fruitades, dairy desserts, and some grains are also sources of added sugars.

they drink them. The number-one source of added sugars in the United States is sweetened soft drinks (Figure 8.3).

Fruitades and sugary fruit drinks are also major sources. This fact isn't surprising when you look at the size of the sweetened beverages that Americans consume. The old, "classic" 8-ounce bottle of cola contained almost 7 teaspoons of added sugars. In most vending machines today, you will probably find 12-ounce cans or 20-ounce bottles. Because people typically drink the entire can or bottle, regardless of its size, they often underestimate how much added sugar they're consuming. (Figure 8.4).

At the beginning of this concept, Marie, Celia's roommate, was correct when she said that soda is loaded with sugar. As you can see from Figure 8.4, by drinking three 20-ounce bottles of cola daily, Celia is adding a whopping amount of sugar—and over 800 calories—to her diet. In addition to beverages, added sugars are hidden in many other foods (Table 8.1).

How Much Added Sugar Is Too Much?

The latest DRI recommends keeping your intake of added sugars to no more than 25 percent of your total daily calories.[7] However, this guideline may still be too high for many Americans who have lower daily calorie needs, including many women, sedentary people, and older adults. These individuals need to make sure they are getting a substantial amount of nutrition from each bite of food.

A recent report from the World Health Organization and the Food and Agriculture Organization recommends that people lead an active lifestyle and consume a diet abundant in fruits and vegetables and low in saturated fat, sugar, and energy-dense foods. The report recommends keeping calories from added sugars to less than 10 percent of the diet, including sugars naturally occurring in fruit juice. (In contrast, the 2005 *Dietary Guidelines for Americans* do not define fruit juice sugars as "added sugars.") These two agencies concur that this type of diet and lifestyle is one of the best strategies to fight chronic diseases, such as heart disease, diabetes, and obesity.[8]

This more conservative limit for sugar consumption means that a person who consumes 2,200 calories (roughly the number of calories active women need daily) should keep added sugar to about 8 teaspoons daily, or 9 percent of total calories. People consuming 2,800 calories daily (about the amount active men need daily) should consume no more than about 18 teaspoons of added sugar daily, or 10 percent of total calories.

Americans currently eat more than 30 teaspoons of added sugars daily.[9] Eating this much added sugar has a major impact on nutrition, and can wreck havoc on a diet, and is one of the many reasons Americans are overweight. The Table Tips on the next page can help you trim some added sugars from your diet.

Figure 8.4 The Many Sizes of Soft Drinks
A bottle or can of soda can provide from 6 to 17 teaspoons of added sugars, depending on the size of the container.

The Take-Home Message Your taste buds can't distinguish between naturally occurring and added sugars. Foods with naturally occurring sugars, such as whole fruit, not only provide more nutrition than empty-calorie sweets, such as candy, but because of their bulk, create a greater feeling of fullness and thus, less chance of overeating. Sugar can contribute to tooth decay, an elevated level of fat in your blood, and a lowering of the "good," HDL cholesterol. Foods with added sugars may displace more nutritious foods and quickly add excess calories to your diet. The current recommendation is to keep added sugars to no more than 25 percent of your daily calories; however, this amount may still be too high for people with lower daily calorie needs.

Table 8.1

Sugar Smacked!

Food Groups	Teaspoons of Added Sugar
Bread, Cereal, Rice, Pasta	
Bread, 1 slice	0
Cookies, 2 medium	1
Doughnut, 1 medium	1
Cake, frosted, 1/16 average	5
Pie, fruit, 2 crust, 1/6, 8" pie	6
Fruit	
Fruit, canned in juice, ½ cup	0
Fruit, canned in heavy syrup, ½ cup	4
Milk, Yogurt, and Cheese	
Milk, plain, 1 cup	0
Chocolate milk, 2% fat, 1 cup	3
Yogurt, low fat, plain, 8 oz	0
Yogurt, fruit, sweetened, 8 oz	7
Chocolate shake, 10 fl oz	9
Other	
Chocolate bar, 2 ounces	6
Fruit drink, ade, 12 fl oz	12

(spoon) = 1 teaspoon of sugar

Data from USDA, *Dietary Guidelines for Americans,* (5th ed., 2000).

TABLE TIPS

Lowering Your Intake of Added Sugars

Mix chocolate milk with an equal amount of regular low-fat milk.

Mix equal amounts of sweetened cereal with an unsweetened variety for a breakfast cereal with half the added sugar.

Drink water rather than soda or sweetened beverages throughout the day.

Buy sweets, such as candy and cookies, in individual-serving-size pouches rather than large packages. The less you buy, the less you'll eat.

Mix an ounce of 100 percent fruit juice with 10 ounces of sparkling water for a no-sugar-added "fruit" drink.

What Are Sugar Substitutes and What Forms Can They Take?

Since eating too much sugar can be unhealthy, what's a person with a sweet tooth to do? Many Americans look to beverages and foods containing sugar substitutes to limit their sugar intake while satisfying their taste for sugar. **Sugar substitutes** are substances that are as sweet, or sweeter, than sugar but contain fewer calories.

The FDA must approve all sugar substitutes and deem them safe for consumption before they are allowed in food products sold in the United States.[10] Of the several sugar substitutes presently available to consumers, all are either reduced in calories or are calorie free. See Table 8.2 for a comparison of available sweeteners.

Polyols Are Sugar Alcohols

Polyols are often called *sugar alcohols* because they have the chemical structure of sugar with an added alcohol component. Polyols, such as sorbitol, mannitol, and

sugar substitutes Alternatives to table sugar that sweeten foods while using fewer calories.

Table 8.2

Oh, So Sweet!

Sweetener	Calories/Gram	Trade Names	Sweetening Power	The Facts
Sucrose	4	Table sugar	—	Sweetens food, enhances flavor, tenderizes, and contributes browning properties to baked goods
Reduced-Calorie Sweeteners				
Polyols (Sugar Alcohols)				
Sorbitol	2.6	Sorbitol	50–70% as sweet as sucrose	Is found in foods such as sugarless chewing gum; may cause diarrhea when consumed in excess.
Mannitol	1.6	Mannitol	50–70% as sweet as sucrose	Is found in chewing gum and jams and is a bulking agent in powdered foods; may cause diarrhea
Xylitol	2.4	2.4	Equally as sweet as sucrose	Is found in foods such as chewing gum and candies; also in pharmaceuticals and hygiene products
Hydrogenated starch hydrolysates	3.0	HSH	50–70% as sweet as sucrose	Are found in confections and can be used as a bulking agent
Calorie-Free Sweeteners				
Saccharin	0	Sweet 'N Low	200–700% sweeter than sucrose	Retains its sweetening power at high temperatures, such as in baking
Aspartame	4*	Nutrasweet, Equal	Approximately 200% sweeter than sucrose	Loses some sweetening power at high temperatures, such as baking; can be added at the end stages of recipes if removed from the heat source; individuals with phenylketonuria need to monitor all dietary sources of phenylalanine, including aspartame
Acesulfame-K	0	Sunette	200% sweeter than sucrose	Retains its sweetening power at high temperatures, such as in baking
Sucralose	0	Splenda	600% sweeter than sucrose	Retains its sweetening power at high temperatures, such as in baking
Neotame	0	Neotame	7,000–13,000% sweeter than sucrose	Retains its sweetening power at high temperatures, such as in baking
Rebaudioside A	O	Truvia, Purevia	200% sweeter than sucrose	Retains its sweetening power at high temperatures, such as in baking

*Because so little aspartame is needed to sweeten foods, it provides a negligible number of calories.

xylitol, are found naturally in plants, but they are also produced synthetically and used as sweeteners in foods such as chewing gum and candies. They can be used tablespoon for tablespoon as a substitute for sucrose.

Chewing gum and candies containing sugar alcohols may be labeled "sugar free" and boast that they don't promote tooth decay. Keep in mind, however, that even though these products are sugar free, they are not necessarily calorie free. Even more importantly, because polyols are incompletely absorbed in the digestive tract, they can cause diarrhea. For this reason, they should be used in moderation.

Saccharin Is the Oldest Sugar Substitute

A variety of sugar substitutes are available to consumers.

Saccharin was first discovered in 1879. During the two World Wars, when sugar was being rationed, saccharin was widely used as a sugar substitute in the United States and Europe. Today, you probably recognize saccharin from its little pink packet, found on coffee shop counters and diner tables. It has been used in foods, beverages, vitamins, and pharmaceuticals. Because saccharin is not metabolized in your body, it doesn't provide any calories.

In 1977, the FDA banned saccharin, due to reports linking it to bladder cancer in rats. Congress then suspended this ban through the Saccharin Study and Labeling Act, which allowed saccharin to continue being used commercially but required saccharin-containing products to display a warning label stating that it was potentially hazardous to your health.

In 2000, the National Toxicology Program (NTP) removed saccharin from the list of substances that potentially cause cancer. After extensive review, the NTP determined that the bladder tumors in observed rats were actually caused by a biologic mechanism that wasn't relevant to humans.[11] (The lesson learned from this is that, although you can safely consume saccharin in moderation, you probably shouldn't feed it to your pet rat.) Today, saccharin is used in over 100 countries.

Aspartame Is Derived from Amino Acids

In 1965, a scientist named James Schlatter was conducting research on amino acids (components of proteins) in his search to find a treatment for ulcers. To pick up a piece of paper in his laboratory, he licked his finger and stumbled on a sweet-tasting compound.[12] Schlatter had discovered aspartame, a substance that would change the world of sugar substitutes.

Aspartame is composed of two amino acids providing 4 calories per gram, so it has the potential to provide calories to foods as an added sweetener. However, because aspartame is 200 times sweeter than sucrose, only a small amount is needed to sweeten food.

In 1981, the FDA approved aspartame for use in tabletop sweeteners, such as Equal and Nutrasweet, and in 1996, the FDA gave the food industry the OK to use aspartame in all types of foods and beverages. Although now found in over 6,000 foods, most of the aspartame consumed in the United States is in soft drinks.

The FDA considers aspartame to be one of the most thoroughly studied and tested food additives it has ever approved. The agency reevaluated the safety of aspartame more than 25 times since it first came on the market and each time concluded that it is safe to consume.[13]

The FDA has set an Acceptable Daily Intake (ADI) for aspartame at 50 milligrams per kilogram (mg/kg) of body weight. To exceed this, a 150-pound person would need to drink almost sixteen 12-ounce cans of "diet" (aspartame-containing) soda daily for a lifetime. Currently, most people consume well below that amount, an estimated 4 to 7 percent of the ADI.[14]

Some people with a rare, inherited disorder called phenylketonuria are unable to metabolize one of the amino acids (phenylalanine) in aspartame; therefore, they must monitor their aspartame consumption closely. Because of the seriousness of this disorder, the FDA mandates that all food products containing phenylalanine carry a label declaring its presence.

Foods and beverages that contain aspartame must carry a warning label that says phenylalanine is present.

Substituting sweeteners for sugar doesn't necessarily result in weight loss. Although the consumption of **low-calorie sweeteners** has tripled since 1980, the problem of overweight and obesity in Americans increased by 60 percent between 1985 and 2000.

Acesulfame-K Contains Potassium

Although less than sweet-sounding, acesulfame-K (the *K* refers to the potassium component) is about 200 times sweeter than sucrose. It is available as a tabletop sweetener, called Sunette, and is currently used in chewing gum, candy, desserts, yogurt, and alcoholic beverages. Your body does not metabolize acesulfame-K so it provides no calories.

Sucralose Is Made from Sucrose

Sucralose was developed in 1976 by slightly changing the structure of the sucrose molecule. Unlike sucrose, sucralose isn't absorbed by your body—it is excreted in your urine. In 1998, sucralose was approved as a tabletop sweetener, and it's available commercially as Splenda, which is now widely used in many foods and drinks.

Rebaudioside A Is from the Stevia Plant

The newest addition to the world of sugar substitutes is rebaudioside A, which combines an extract from the stevia plant with a sugar alcohol. Stevia is a native plant product from Brazil and Paraguay. Extracts from the stevia plant have been used abroad as a table-top sweetener and in some products, such as teas and yogurt. This zero-calorie sweetener is approximately 200 times sweeter than sugar and is now available as a tabletop sweetener in the United States under the trade names of Truvia and PureVia. It doesn't affect blood glucose levels so it may be used by people with diabetes.

Neotame Is Derived from Amino Acids

Neotame, which the FDA approved in 2002, comprises the same two amino acids as aspartame, but they are joined together in such a way that the body cannot break them apart. Thus, individuals with PKU can use neotame without concern (unlike aspartame). It has been approved as a sweetener for a variety of uses, including chewing gum, frostings, frozen desserts, puddings, fruit juices, and syrups.[15]

The Take-Home Message Millions of Americans consume reduced-calorie or calorie-free sugar substitutes. The FDA has approved the sugar substitutes of polyols, saccharin, aspartame, acesulfame-K, sucralose, rebaudioside A, and neotame to be used in a variety of foods. These do not promote dental decay, and they may benefit people with diabetes who are trying to manage their blood glucose.

How Much Fiber Do You Need and Why?

Even though fiber is a nondigestible substance that resists being broken down in your GI tract, it still plays many important roles in your body, so you need an adequate intake every day to stay on top of your game.

Fill Up on Fiber

The current DRIs recommend consuming 14 grams of fiber for every 1,000 calories you eat.[16] That means that people who need 2,000 calories daily to maintain their weight should consume 28 grams of fiber daily (Table 8.3). Because few people know

TABLE TIPS

High Five! Five Ways to Increase Fiber Daily

Choose only whole-grain cereals for breakfast.

Eat two pieces of whole fruit daily as snacks.

Use only 100 percent whole-wheat bread for your lunchtime sandwich.

Layer lettuce, tomatoes, or other vegetables on your sandwich.

Eat a large salad with dinner nightly.

Table 8.3

What Are Your Fiber Needs?

	Grams of Fiber Daily*	
	Males	**Females**
14 through 18 years old	38	36
19 through 50 years old	38	25
51 through 70+ years old	30	21
Pregnancy		28
Lactation		29

*Based on an Adequate Intake (AI) for fiber.

Data from: Institute of Medicine, *Dietary Reference Intakes for Energy, Carbohydrate, Fiber, Fat, Fatty Acids, Cholesterol, Protein, and Amino Acids* (Washington, D.C.: The National Academies Press, 2002).

RATE YOURSELF ★★★★★

Is Your Diet Fiber Rich?

Rate yourself below:

1. I eat at least 2 cups or 2 pieces of fruit daily. **True** ☐ **False** ☐
2. I eat at least 3 cups of raw or cooked veggies daily. **True** ☐ **False** ☐
3. I eat at least 4 servings of whole grains daily. (A serving = 1 cup whole-grain cereal, 1 slice whole-grain bread or 1 small roll, or ½ cup brown rice or whole-wheat pasta.) **True** ☐ **False** ☐
4. I eat at least ½ cup of legumes (such as kidney beans, chickpeas, lentils) on most days. **True** ☐ **False** ☐
5. I eat a handful of nuts (walnuts, almonds) or seeds (sunflower seeds) daily. **True** ☐ **False** ☐

Answers

If you answered "true" to at least 4 of the above, you are a fiber role model! If you answered "true" to fewer than 4 of the above, at least you're among friends. Most American adults fall short on their daily fiber needs. Read on to see how you can boost your fiber intake.

the exact number of calories they take in daily, the recommendations for fiber are categorized by age and gender. This way, you can quickly determine the estimated grams of fiber you need daily. Unfortunately, most Americans fall short of their goal and consume only a little over 15 grams of fiber a day.

Whole grains, fruits, vegetables, legumes, nuts, and seeds are fiber powerhouses. These foods should be included in your meals and snacks to meet your daily needs (Figure 8.5). See the "High Five!" Table Tips for five ways to add fiber to your diet.

A word of caution: Dramatically increasing the fiber in your diet can create negative side effects such as flatulence (gas) and bowel cramps. So make sure you increase the fiber in your diet gradually, rather than adding large amounts all at once. This will allow your body to adjust to the increased amount of fiber and minimize the side effects.

As you increase your fiber intake, you should also be increasing the amount of fluids you drink. A small, steady increase of fiber accompanied by increased fluids will be easier on your colon—and on those around you!

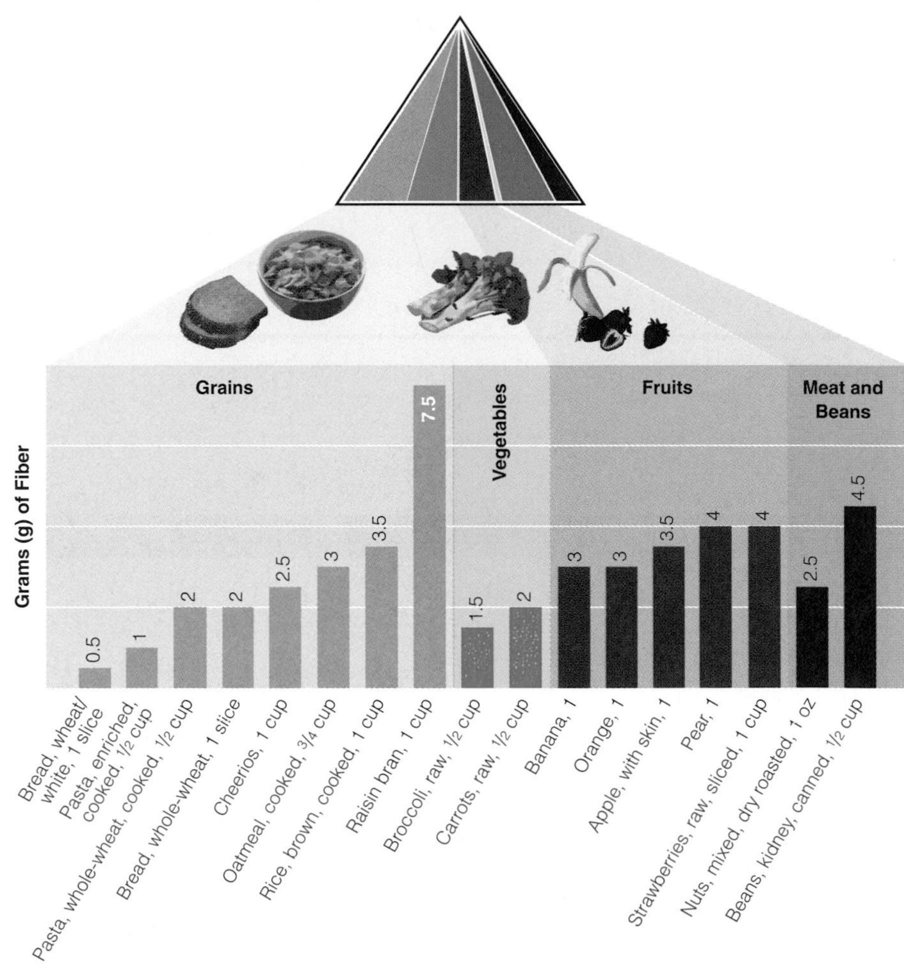

Figure 8.5 Food Sources of Fiber
Adults need to consume 20 to 38 grams of fiber daily.

Data from: Position of the American Dietetic Association, "Health Implications of Dietary Fiber," *Journal of the American Dietetic Association* 102 (2002): 993–1000; USDA National Nutrient Database for Standard Reference, www.nal.usda.gov/fnic.

A Diet High in Fiber Promotes Good Health

Fiber has been shown to help lower your risk of developing constipation, diverticulosis, obesity, heart disease, cancer, and diabetes mellitus (Table 8.4). Let's look closely at how fiber works.

Fiber Helps Prevent Constipation and Diverticulosis

Over 4 million Americans complain about being constipated, with women (especially pregnant women), children, and adults over 65 experiencing it most frequently. The uncomfortable, bloated, and sluggish feelings of constipation compel Americans seeking relief to spend over $700 million each year on laxative products.[17] A diet that lacks a sufficient amount of fiber (from whole grains, fruits, and vegetables, cheese, eggs, and meats) is setting the stage for problems associated with constipation. Many people would be better off spending more time in the produce and whole-grain aisles of the supermarket, rather than shopping for laxatives.

A diet providing insoluble fibers, such as bran, whole grains, and many fruits and vegetables, helps keep things moving along in your digestive tract and decreases the likelihood of your becoming constipated. As remnants of food move through your colon, water is absorbed, which causes the formation of solid waste products (stool). The contractions of the muscles in your colon push the stool toward your rectum to be eliminated. If these muscle contractions are sluggish, the stool may linger too long in your colon, allowing too much water to be reabsorbed into your colon and out of the stool. This can create hard, dry stools that are more difficult and painful to expel. (Some soluble fibers, such as psyllium, can also be an aid in constipation, since their water-attracting qualities allow the stool to increase in bulk and form a gel-like, soft texture, making it easier to pass.)

Long-term constipation can lead to an uncomfortable disorder called *diverticulosis* (*osis* = condition). It develops when constipation leads to increased pressure in the colon, causing weak spots along your colon wall to bulge out, forming small pouches called *diverticula* (Figure 8.6).

Table 8.4

Type-Casting Fiber

Type	Found in	Can Help Reduce the Risk of
Insoluble Fiber		
Cellulose Hemicellulose Lignins	Whole grains, whole-grain cereals, bran, oats, fruits, vegetables	Constipation Diverticulosis Certain cancers Heart disease Obesity
Soluble, Viscous Fibers		
Pectin Beta-glucan Gums Psyllium	Citrus fruits, prunes, legumes, oats, barley, brussels sprouts, carrots	Constipation Heart disease Diabetes Obesity

Infection of the diverticula, a condition known as *diverticulitis* (*itis* = inflammation), can lead to stomach pain, fever, nausea, vomiting, cramping, and chills. Though not proven, it is believed that the stool and its bacteria in the colon may get stuck in the diverticula and cause the infection.

Approximately 50 percent of Americans age 60 to 80 and most individuals over 80 years of age have diverticulosis.[18] The disorder is more common in developed countries, such as the United States and England, and is rarely found in areas where high-fiber diets are more commonplace, such as Asia and Africa. The best way to prevent both diverticulosis and diverticulitis is to eat a diet that is generous in fiber to avoid constipation and to keep things moving through your system.

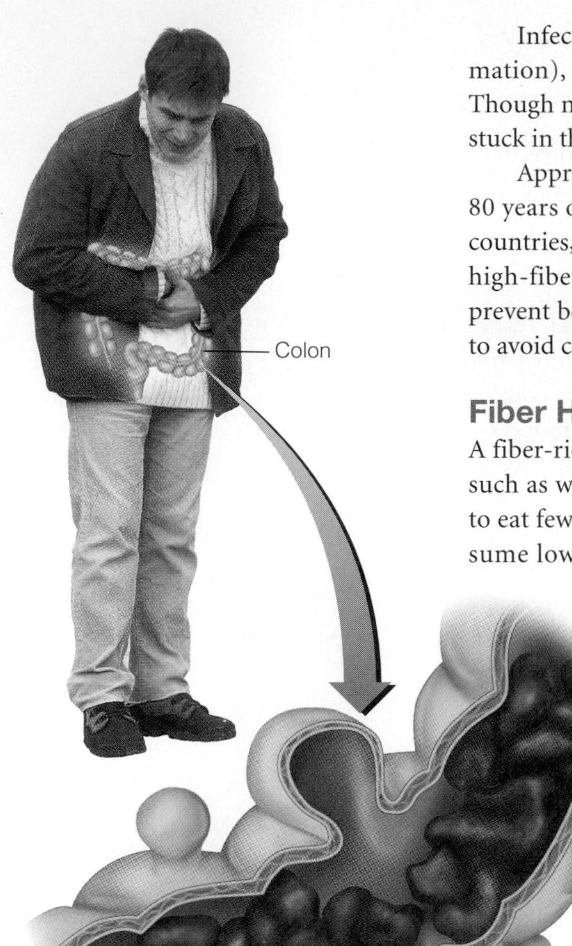

Figure 8.6 Diverticula
Diverticula are small pouches that can develop along your colon wall. When stool gets trapped in them, they can become inflamed, and this can lead to diverticulitis.

Fiber Helps Prevent Obesity

A fiber-rich diet can benefit your waistline. As mentioned earlier, high-fiber foods, such as whole grains, fruits, and vegetables, can add to satiation, so that you need to eat fewer calories to feel full. Research has shown that obese people tend to consume lower amounts of dietary fiber daily than their leaner counterparts. This lends credibility to the notion that fiber plays a key role in weight management.[19] Although some weight-loss diets restrict carbohydrates, these plans would work better if they actually recommended *increasing* high-fiber carbohydrates in the diet. Fiber can be a strong ally in weight management.

Fiber Helps Prevent Heart Disease, Diabetes, and Cancer

Viscous, soluble fibers have been shown to help lower elevated blood cholesterol levels, which put you at risk for heart disease. It is believed that viscous fiber in the gastrointestinal tract "grabs" cholesterol-carrying compounds before they can be absorbed. Instead, these compounds are excreted along with the fiber in your stool. Your body replaces the lost cholesterol by removing cholesterol from your blood, lowering your blood cholesterol levels.

Slow-moving, viscous, soluble fibers may also reduce the rate at which fat and carbohydrates are absorbed from your meals. Delayed absorption can lower the surge of fat into the blood after a meal and may help improve sensitivity to the hormone insulin. Both high levels of fat in the blood and a decreased sensitivity to insulin are risk factors for heart disease.

Viscous, soluble fiber may not be the only type of fiber that can promote heart health. Several research studies have shown that cereals and grains containing insoluble fiber may help lower the risk for heart disease.[20] A study of the dietary habits of over 65,000 women for 10 years found that the risk of developing heart disease was more than 30 percent lower in those consuming the highest amount of cereal fiber.[21]

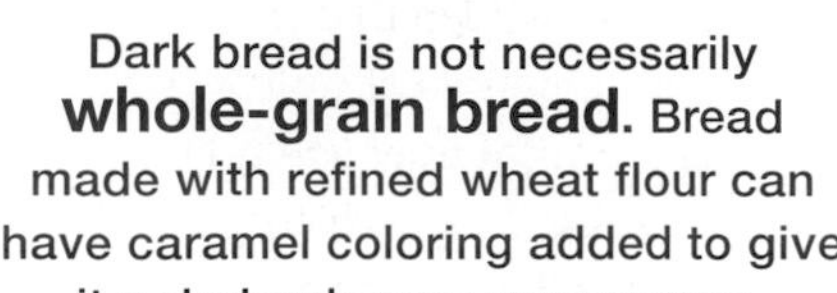

Dark bread is not necessarily **whole-grain bread.** Bread made with refined wheat flour can have caramel coloring added to give it a darker brown appearance.

Viscous, soluble fibers have also been shown to help individuals with diabetes. We'll discuss this in depth in Concept 9.

Fiber is also thought to have many positive and protective effects in the fight against certain cancers. For instance, fiber from cereals has been shown to help lower the risk for breast cancer.[22] Research also suggests that, as fiber consumption increases, the incidence of colorectal cancer is reduced. Four mechanisms may account for fiber's role in fighting cancer:

- Fiber increases the bulk of stool, which can dilute cancer-promoting substances in the colon.
- Fiber helps keep things moving through the digestive tract, so that potential cancer-promoting substances spend less time in contact with the intestinal lining.
- Fiber encourages the growth of friendly bacteria in the colon and their fermentation by-products, both of which have cancer-fighting potential.
- Fiber binds with acids in bile, a substance produced by the liver and important in fat breakdown. This causes the acids to be expelled from the body in the stool, rather than be reabsorbed. Because an increased amount of bile acids in the colon is thought to be associated with colon and rectal cancer, fiber's ability to reduce the concentration of these acids is viewed as a cancer deterrent.[23]

Over the years, however, some studies have challenged fiber's protective role against colon and rectal cancer. Several short-term studies failed to show a clear anti-cancer effect. These findings may have been due to several factors: The amount of fiber consumed in the studies may not have been large enough to make a difference; the studies may have been too short to show an effect; and the fiber used in the studies wasn't from a variety of sources.[24] We'll talk more about how you can fight cancer with a knife and a fork in Concept 20.

More current research supports the cancer-fighting potential of fiber. A large study involving over 500,000 people from 10 European countries showed that individuals who consumed the most fiber (35 grams of fiber, on average), compared with those eating the least amount of fiber daily (15 grams, on average), reduced their risk of colon and rectal cancer by about 40 percent.[25] The dietary sources of fiber were varied among the countries and included fiber from cereals, vegetables, fruits, and legumes.

The Take-Home Message **You should consume 14 grams of fiber for every 1,000 calories you eat. Whole grains, fruits, vegetables, legumes, nuts, and seeds are excellent sources. A fiber-rich diet can help reduce your risk for constipation, diverticulosis, heart disease, obesity, diabetes mellitus, and certain cancers.**

Check out these recipes and more suggestions at www.pearsonhighered.com/blake

UCook

Strawberry Yogurt Shake

Sip a serving of fruit through a straw with this refreshing Strawberry Yogurt Shake, which can be whipped together in minutes using fresh or thawed frozen strawberries and any 100 percent juice.

UDo

Sweet on Sweets

Visit our website to see one student's typical daily diet—high in added sugars and low in fiber. Use Table 8.1 ("Sugar Smacked!") and Figure 8.5 ("Food Sources of Fiber") in this concept and see if you can come up with healthier choices to satisfy a sweet tooth and provide fiber.

The Top Five Points to Remember

1. A minimum of 130 grams of dietary carbohydrates is needed daily. It's recommended that 45 to 65 percent of your daily calories come from carbohydrates. It's also recommended that your diet include only low to moderate amounts of simple carbohydrates and higher amounts of fiber and other complex carbohydrates.
2. Your body can't distinguish between naturally occurring and added sugars. Food sources of naturally occurring sugars tend to be more nutritious than foods

with a lot of added sugar. The major source of dietary added sugar is soft drinks. A diet too high in added sugar may increase the level of fat and decrease the level of the "good" cholesterol in your blood. Sugary foods contain calories but little else and can crowd out more nutritious food choices.

3. Polyols, saccharin, aspartame, acesulfame-K, sucralose, rebaudioside A, and neotame are sugar substitutes currently deemed safe by the FDA. Because aspartame contains the amino acid phenylalanine, individuals with phenylketonuria, a rare disorder, must limit their intake of all dietary sources of this amino acid.
4. Carbohydrates themselves don't cause weight gain. Consuming excess calories from any source on a regular basis is the culprit behind gaining weight. Meals containing whole grains, fruits, and vegetables are high in fiber and are processed more slowly in your body than low-fiber meals. This fact, along with the greater bulk of such meals, may cause you to eat less and help you feel satiated longer.
5. Adults should consume approximately 20 to 35 grams of fiber daily, depending on their age and gender. A high-fiber diet can help you avoid constipation and lower your risk for diverticulosis, obesity, heart disease, diabetes, and certain cancers.

Test Yourself

1. The minimum amount of carbohydrates needed daily is
   a. 100 grams.
   b. 120 grams.
   c. 130 grams.
   d. 150 grams.
2. Reducing the consumption of which item would have the biggest impact on decreasing the amount of added sugars that Americans consume?
   a. fruits
   b. soft drinks
   c. candy bars
   d. sweetened breakfast cereals
3. Your blood cholesterol level is too high, so you would like to eat additional viscous, soluble high-fiber foods to help lower it. A good choice would be
   a. low-fat milk.
   b. chocolate chip cookies.
   c. bananas.
   d. oatmeal.
4. The small, bulging pouches that sometimes develop along the intestinal lining are called
   a. diverticulosis.
   b. diverticulitis.
   c. diverticula.
   d. diabetes.
5. A high-fiber diet helps prevent
   a. obesity.
   b. diarrhea.
   c. flatulence.
   d. all of the above.

Answers

1. (c) You should consume at least 130 grams of carbohydrates daily to supply your body, particularly your brain, with the glucose it needs to function effectively.
2. (b) Soft drinks are the number-one source of added sugars in the American diet, so reducing the intake of these sugary beverages would go a long way in reducing the amount of added sugars that Americans consume. Reducing the consumption of candy or sweetened breakfast cereals would also help reduce the added sugars in the diet, but not as much as soft drinks. The sugars in fruits are naturally occurring sugars; fruits don't contain added sugar.
3. (d) Oatmeal is rich in viscous fiber that can help lower your cholesterol when eaten as part of a heart-healthy diet. Although nutrient dense, the bananas and milk do not contain fiber. Cookies won't help lower your cholesterol.
4. (c) Diverticula are a product of diverticulosis. When these pouches become inflamed, diverticulitis occurs. Diabetes is a chronic disease that results from poor regulation of blood glucose.
5. (a) A high-fiber diet can add to satiation and help with weight management. Diarrhea is typically caused by infection and is not prevented by consuming a high-fiber diet. Flatulence can occur if you adopt a high-fiber diet without allowing your body a chance to adjust.

Web Resources

- For more on dental caries, visit the National Library of Medicine at: www.nlm.nih.gov/medlineplus/ency/article/001055.htm
- For more on fiber, visit the American Heart Association at: www.americanheart.org

9

1. More than **10 percent** of American adults now have diabetes. **T/F**

2. Weight gain is a typical **symptom** of diabetes. **T/F**

3. **Obesity** increases your risk for diabetes. **T/F**

4. Women who develop diabetes during **pregnancy** risk giving birth to an abnormally small baby. **T/F**

5. Diabetes can cause **blindness. T/F**

Diabetes

A Growing Epidemic

Adam is a star hockey center on his college team and skates a minimum of 2 hours a day (and up to 4 hours daily when the team is in the throes of a hockey tournament). When not on the ice, Adam is in the library, maintaining a 3.7 GPA. Besides being a hockey star, Adam has had type 1, insulin-dependent diabetes ever since he laced up his first pair of skates at age 2.

Adjusting his daily diet and insulin injections to his demanding exercise schedule is no small feat. "Once when I was in a hockey league in high school, I buckled on the ice because I didn't eat enough before the game. I went to the hospital in an ambulance because my blood sugar dropped too low," recalls Adam. "Now, I work with the team trainer and the school's registered dietitian to make sure my pregame snack covers my ice time. Because of my diabetes, I probably eat better than anyone else on the team and have the most energy," Adam boasts. "I can outskate them all!"

Diabetes is a condition related to blood glucose levels, which are affected by diet, particularly carbohydrate intake. In this concept, you will learn why it's considered an epidemic, what forms it takes, and how it's treated. You'll also learn about some lifestyle changes you can make to prevent it or reduce its symptoms.

Answers

1. True. The number of Americans with diabetes is growing. Turn to page 3 to learn more.
2. False. To learn about the signs and symptoms of diabetes, turn to page 4.
3. True. Being overweight or obese can increase your chances of developing type 2 diabetes. Turn to page 5 to learn more.
4. False. The blood of diabetic mothers is high in glucose. This excessive glucose passes to the fetus. Thus, the newborns of women with diabetes are typically abnormally large. Turn to page 6 for details.
5. True. Diabetes can damage blood vessels in the eye and lead to irreversible blindness. Check it out on page 7.

What Is Diabetes and Why Is It Considered an Epidemic?

Diabetes (diabetes mellitus) is a group of diseases marked by the body's inability to regulate the level of glucose in the bloodstream. It results from problems with the pancreas's ability to produce the hormone insulin, problems with the way the body responds to insulin, or both.[1]

How Does Diabetes Develop?

Recall from Concept 7 that the hormone *insulin* directs glucose out of the bloodstream and into the cells to be used as immediate energy, or to be stored in another form for later use. When there isn't enough insulin to perform this job efficiently, glucose remains in the bloodstream. That's what happens in type 1 diabetes: The body's immune system destroys the cells in the pancreas that make insulin. In contrast, type 2 diabetes usually begins as **insulin resistance,** in which the pancreas produces insulin, but the person's cells do not respond to the insulin when it arrives.[2] In a sense, the cells put up a roadblock (Figure 9.1): Insulin is available in the blood, but the cells' decreased sensitivity to it means that they don't take in the glucose the way cells normally do. We'll distinguish between these two types of diabetes in more detail shortly.

Mellitus is Latin for "honey-sweet," reflecting the **higher glucose** level in the blood and urine of people with diabetes.

In both type 1 and type 2 diabetes, the bloodstream is flooded with glucose that can't get into the cells. The body interprets this situation as a fasting state and shifts into fasting mode. The liver then begins breaking down its glycogen stores and making glucose from noncarbohydrate sources in an attempt to provide glucose for the cells. This floods the blood with even more glucose. Eventually, the level of glucose in the blood becomes so high that some of it spills over into the urine and leaves the body.

diabetes The disease in which the body is unable to process blood glucose levels normally due to lack of the hormone insulin, or insulin resistance. Also known by the medical term *diabetes mellitus.* The three types of diabetes are type 1, type 2, and gestational diabetes. Type 2 is the most common form.

insulin resistance The inability of the body's cells to respond to the hormone insulin.

At the same time, the body calls on its energy reserve—fat—to be used as fuel. The body needs glucose to burn fat thoroughly. When glucose is unable to get into the cells, acidic ketone bodies build up in the blood to dangerous levels, causing a serious condition called *ketoacidosis*, which can cause nausea, confusion, and in some cases, if left untreated, coma or death. Although *ketosis* (an elevated level of ketone bodies in the blood) can develop in individuals who are fasting or consuming a low-carbohydrate diet, it is not life-threatening.

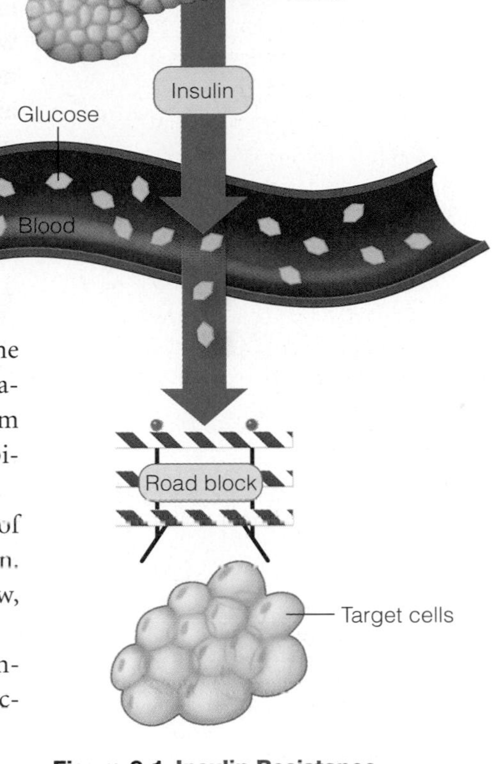

Figure 9.1 Insulin Resistance
In the early stages of type 2 diabetes, the pancreas secretes sufficient amounts of insulin into the bloodstream. However, the target cells resist its effects and, so, fail to take up glucose effectively.

Cases of Diabetes Are on the Rise

Diabetes is becoming so common that it would be rare if you *didn't* know someone who has it. Over 23 million American adults—over 10 percent of the adult population—have diabetes. This represents an increase of 15 percent in just 2 years (from 2005 to 2007).[3] As you can see in Figure 9.2, this dramatic increase suggests an epidemic that is spiraling out of control.

As the number of adult diabetes cases continues to rise, so does the number of children with diabetes. Type 1 diabetes used to be the only prevalent type in children. In fact, in 1990, less than 4 percent of diabetic children had type 2 diabetes. Now, however, up to 45 percent of the new cases of diabetes in children are type 2.[4]

If you're thinking that something in our contemporary lifestyle must be contributing to this recent surge in cases of diabetes, you're right. We'll identify the factors contributing to the diabetes epidemic shortly.

Over 200,000 Americans die from diabetic complications annually, and diabetes was the sixth leading cause of death in the United States in 2006.[5] Diabetes is also an extremely costly disease: Disability insurance payments, time lost from employment, and the medical costs associated with diabetes cost the United States more than $150 billion annually.[6]

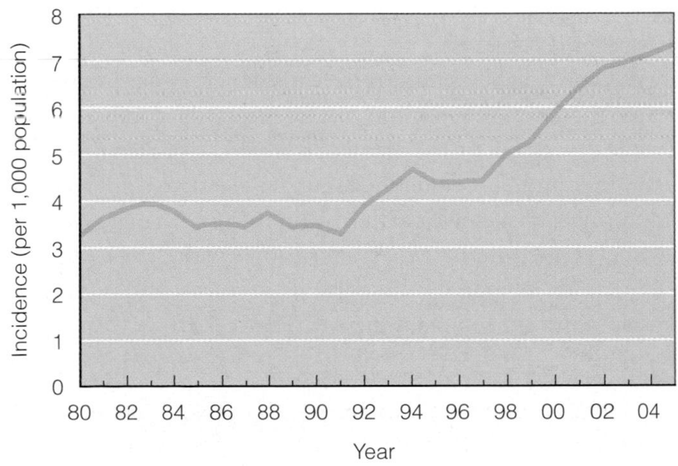

Figure 9.2 Incidence of Diabetes
Over the past few decades, the incidence of diabetes has risen dramatically in the United States.

Data from: United States Centers for Disease Control and Prevention, Diabetes Statistics, 2007. www.cdc.gov/diabetes/statistics/incidence/images/fig2.gif.

The Take-Home Message Diabetes is a group of diseases characterized by an inability to regulate blood glucose levels. It results from problems with the pancreas's ability to produce the hormone insulin, problems with the way the body responds to insulin, or both. The number of American adults and children with diabetes has skyrocketed in recent years. Diabetes is the sixth leading cause of death in the United States, and it costs the economy more than $150 billion annually.

What Are the Types of Diabetes?

All types of diabetes involve insulin and unregulated blood glucose levels. The most prevalent are type 1 and type 2. Type 1 diabetes is considered an *autoimmune disease*—that is, a disease in which the body's immune cells strike out against the body's own tissues. It is the rarer form of the two major types of diabetes. Type 2 is more common and is found in people who have become insulin resistant. Still another form occurs only during pregnancy. Let's discuss each of these forms separately.

Type 1 Diabetes Is Less Common

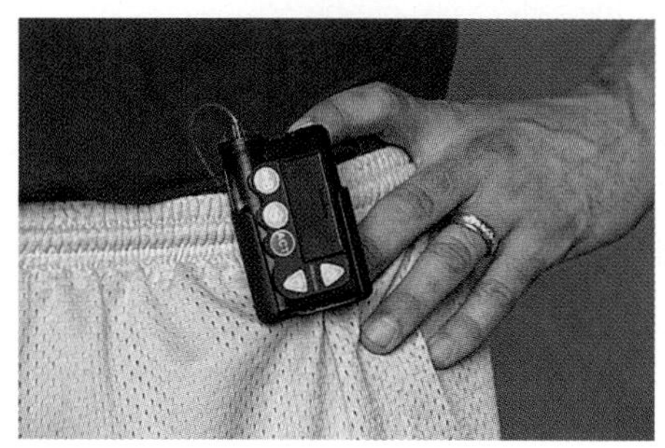

Figure 9.3 Insulin Pump
Today, many people with diabetes use an insulin pump to maintain their blood sugar at a healthy level throughout the day. The small pump shown here could easily pass for a cell phone or an iPod.

Recall from the beginning of this concept that Adam's diabetes was diagnosed when he was just 2 years old. This is typical of *type 1 diabetes:* It usually begins in childhood or the early adult years. This form of the disease accounts for only 5 to 10 percent of all cases in the United States.[7] The immune system in type 1 diabetics actually destroys the insulin-producing cells in the pancreas. Symptoms such as increased thirst, frequent urination, constant blurred vision, hunger, weight loss, and fatigue are typical, resulting from glucose being unable to get into the cells of the body. If a person with type 1 diabetes does not receive insulin, he or she will develop ketoacidosis and may become comatose.

People with type 1 diabetes must receive insulin every day in order to live a normal life. Because the hormone insulin is derived from the components of protein, it can't be taken orally—in pill form—because it would be broken down in the GI tract in the same way that protein-containing foods are digested. Until recently, most people have had to inject themselves with insulin using a syringe. Now, however, researchers have developed alternative ways for people with diabetes to self-administer insulin. New methods include insulin pens, jet injectors, and pumps, which infuse insulin in small amounts throughout the day (Figure 9.3).

Type 2 Diabetes Is the Most Prevalent Form

Type 2 diabetes accounts for 90 to 95 percent of cases of the disease. People with type 2 diabetes typically produce insulin, but their cells have become resistant to its effects. As a result, their pancreas produces more insulin. After several years of such overproduction, the pancreas's insulin-producing cells become exhausted, and their insulin production then decreases to the point where the person must take medication and/or insulin to manage his or her blood glucose level.

Why do people develop type 2 diabetes? The following are the two most significant risk factors:

Being overweight increases the risk for type 2 diabetes at any age.

- Overweight and obesity. The primary risk factor for type 2 diabetes is being overweight,[8] with obesity posing an even more significant risk. Since over 65 percent of American adults are overweight or obese[9] and 16 percent of American children and teens age 6 to 19 are overweight,[10] it's not surprising that diabetes is on the rise. Of children diagnosed with type 2 diabetes, as much as 85 percent are overweight or obese.[11] Super-size portions of sugary beverages, high-fat restaurant and fast-food meals, and low-fiber, high-calorie snacks are likely culprits in America's weight gain. At the same time, we engage in far less physical activity than earlier generations of Americans. Sedentary jobs, driving, and indoor activities, such as surfing the Web, watching TV, and playing video games, have replaced much of the physical labor, walking, biking, and outdoor play of earlier times.

RATE YOURSELF ★★★★★

Are You at Risk for Type 2 Diabetes?

This list contains the currently known risk factors for type 2 diabetes, but there may be others. If you have questions, ask your doctor.

First, do you have a body mass index (BMI) of 25 or higher?[a] **Yes** ☐ **No** ☐

If you answered no, you don't need to continue. If you answered yes, continue.

1. Does your mom, dad, brother, or sister have diabetes? **Yes** ☐ **No** ☐
2. Do you typically get little exercise? **Yes** ☐ **No** ☐
3. Are you of African-American, Alaska Native, Native American, Asian-American, Hispanic, or Pacific Islander–American descent? **Yes** ☐ **No** ☐
4. Have you ever given birth to a baby weighing more than 9 pounds at birth? **Yes** ☐ **No** ☐
5. Have you ever had diabetes during pregnancy? **Yes** ☐ **No** ☐
6. Do you have a blood pressure of 140/90 millimeters of mercury (mmHg) or higher? **Yes** ☐ **No** ☐
7. Do you have a high level of fatty triglycerides (fat) in your blood or too little of the "good," HDL cholesterol? **Yes** ☐ **No** ☐
8. Have you ever had a blood glucose test with results that were higher than normal? **Yes** ☐ **No** ☐
9. Have you ever been told that you have vascular disease or problems with your blood vessels? **Yes** ☐ **No** ☐

Answers

If you are overweight and answered "yes" to 1 or more questions, you could benefit from speaking with your doctor.

[a]BMI is a measure of your weight relative to your height. See Concept 20 for a chart to determine your BMI.

Data from: American Diabetes Association, "Report of the Expert Committee on the Diagnosis and Classification of Diabetes Mellitus", *Diabetes Care* 26 (2003): S5–S20.

Table 9.1

Interpreting Blood Glucose Levels

If a Fasting Blood Glucose Level Is	The Level Is Considered
<100 mg/dl	Normal
100 to 125 mg/dl	Prediabetic
≥126 mg/dl*	Diabetic

*There must be two "positive" tests, done on separate days, for an official diagnosis of diabetes.

Data from American Diabetes Association, "Diagnosis and Classification of Diabetes Mellitus," *Diabetes Care 29* (2006): S43–S48.

- Heredity. There is a strong genetic influence on your risk for type 2 diabetes. Certain ethnic groups, including Native Americans, African-Americans, Hispanics, and Asian-Americans, have significantly higher rates than Caucasian Americans.[12]

One of the major problems with type 2 diabetes is that the condition may go undiagnosed for a long time. While some people have potentially telltale symptoms, such as increased thirst, others do not. Consequently, diabetes can silently damage people's vital organs without their awareness. Because of this, the American Diabetes Association (ADA) recommends that everyone over the age of 45 undergo routine screening for diabetes. A simple blood test performed after fasting can reveal your fasting blood glucose level. A level of 126 milligrams/deciliter or higher suggests diabetes (Table 9.1). People at high risk for developing diabetes shouldn't wait until age 45 to be tested. Review the Rate Yourself feature on previous page to see if you are at risk.

Unhealthy Changes in Blood Glucose Are a Sign of Prediabetes

Prediabetes is a term used to characterize people who are at increased risk of developing diabetes but do not currently have the disease. The presence of either of the following conditions, both of which can be diagnosed by simple blood tests suggests prediabetes:[13]

Impaired fasting glucose. In this condition, the blood glucose level is higher than normal after an overnight fast, but it is not high enough to be classified as diabetes (Table 9.1).

Impaired glucose tolerance. In this condition, the blood glucose level is higher than normal after a 2-hour oral glucose tolerance test, but it is not high enough to be classified as diabetes.

About 16 million people over the age of 40 have prediabetes and are at a higher risk of developing not only diabetes but also heart disease.[14] When a person is in the prediabetic state, damage may already be occurring to the heart and circulatory system.

Gestational Diabetes Develops during Pregnancy

Some pregnant women develop high blood glucose levels during pregnancy and are diagnosed with **gestational diabetes** (*gestation* = pregnancy). This occurs in about 7 percent of the pregnancies in the United States and manifests itself after about the 20th week of pregnancy.[15] Pregnant women are routinely screened for gestational diabetes during this time.

Although the cause of gestational diabetes is unknown, pregnancy-related hormones appear to lead to insulin resistance in the mother. Her blood glucose levels rise, and as this blood circulates to her baby it stimulates changes that can lead to problems for the baby, such as an abnormally large size, difficulty breathing, or birth defects. As with type 2 diabetes, the risk for gestational diabetes is increased in pregnant women who are overweight.

prediabetes The condition in which a person's blood glucose levels suggest an increased risk of developing diabetes, but which are not high enough to confirm it.

gestational diabetes The form of diabetes that develops in women during pregnancy.

The Take-Home Message There are several types of diabetes. Type 1 diabetes, which accounts for only 5 to 10 percent of cases, usually begins in childhood or the early adult years. In this form, the immune system attacks and destroys the insulin-producing cells in the pancreas. Type 2 diabetes is far more common. In this form, the pancreas typically produces insulin but the body cells have become resistant to its effects. Being overweight is the primary risk factor for type 2 diabetes. Prediabetes is the term used to characterize people whose high blood glucose level indicates that they are at increased risk of developing diabetes but do not currently have the disease. Gestational diabetes develops during pregnancy.

What Are the Long-Term Consequences of Diabetes?

Constant exposure to high blood glucose levels can wreak havoc with tissues throughout the body. As you read earlier, diabetes, especially if it is poorly managed, increases the likelihood of a serious chemical imbalance called ketoacidosis, which can be life-threatening. In addition, poorly managed diabetes is associated with a number of serious long-term consequences:[16]

- Nerve damage. Nerve damage occurs in an estimated 50 percent of individuals with diabetes, and the longer the person has diabetes, the greater the risk for the damage. Numbness in the toes, feet, legs, and hands and changes in bowel, bladder, and sexual function are all signs of nerve damage. Moreover, nerve damage can affect the ability to feel changes in temperature or pain in the legs and feet. A cut or sore on the foot can go unnoticed until it becomes infected.
- Poor wound healing and decreased ability to fight infection. The poor blood circulation common in diabetics can make it harder for sores and infections to heal. It is not uncommon for an infection of the feet to infiltrate the bone, causing the need for amputation. People with diabetes are also more likely to die of respiratory infections, such as the flu, than people who don't have the disease.
- Impaired vision. Diabetes can damage the tiny blood vessels in the retina of the eye, the nerve tissue responsible for sensing light. Damage to these vessels can cause bleeding and cloudy vision and can eventually destroy the retina, leading to blindness.
- Dental problems. A high blood glucose level can cause tooth and gum problems, including the loss of teeth.
- Kidney problems. One job of the kidneys is to filter wastes and fluid from the blood to excrete in urine. If the blood is full of glucose, the microscopic tubes in the kidneys' filtration system can become damaged. As a result, protein can leak out into the urine, while causing a backup of wastes in the blood. Kidney failure can result.
- Heart disease and stroke. The excess amount of fat in the blood of many people with poorly managed diabetes is probably an important factor in their increased risk for heart disease and stroke.

The Take-Home Message Poorly managed diabetes can lead to severe and even life-threatening long-term complications, including nerve damage, poor wound healing, decreased ability to fight infection, impaired vision leading to blindness, dental problems, kidney problems, heart disease, and stroke.

Table 9.2

Glycemic Index of Some Commonly Eaten Foods

Food	GI
Potato, baked	121
Cornflakes	119
Jelly beans	114
Green peas	107
Cheerios	106
Puffed wheat	105
Bagel, plain	103
Carrots, cooked	101
White bread	100
Angel food cake	95
Ice cream	87
Bran muffin	85
Brown rice	79
Oatmeal	79
Popcorn	79
Corn	78
Banana, overripe	74
Carrots, raw	71
Chocolate	70
Baked beans	69
Sponge cake	66
Pear, canned in juice	63
Custard	61
Spaghetti	59
Rice, long grain	58
Apple	52
Pear	47
Banana, underripe	43
Kidney beans	42
Whole milk	39
Peanuts	21

How Can Diabetes Be Managed?

In the early 1990s, a groundbreaking study called the Diabetes Control and Complications Trial (DCCT) was published. It showed that controlling the level of blood glucose with an intense regimen of diet, insulin, and exercise, along with monitoring blood sugar levels and regularly visiting health care professionals, slowed the onset of some of the complications of diabetes. For example, reducing high blood glucose helped lower the risk for eye disease by 76 percent and the risk for kidney and nerve disease by at least 50 percent.

The nutrition and lifestyle choices advocated for people with type 1 or 2 diabetes are the same: Adopt a healthy, well-balanced diet and get regular physical activity in order to maintain a blood glucose level in a normal or close to normal range.

Adopt a Healthy, Well-Balanced Diet

The ADA recommends that people with diabetes eat a diet that includes a combination of mostly high-fiber carbohydrates from whole grains, fruits, and vegetables, along with low-fat milk, adequate amounts of lean protein sources, and unsaturated fats.[17]

In addition, the *glycemic index* (*GI*) and *glycemic load* (*GL*) can be used to classify the effects of carbohydrate-containing foods on blood glucose. The glycemic index is a measure of the rise, peak, and eventual fall of blood glucose following consumption of a carbohydrate-intense food. Some foods cause a sharp spike and rapid fall in blood glucose levels, while others cause a more gradual rise and decline.[18] The index ranks high-carbohydrate foods according to their effect on blood glucose levels, compared with that of an equal amount of white bread or pure glucose.

If a carbohydrate-rich food causes your blood glucose level to produce a curve with a larger area than the standard curve of white bread, the food is considered a high-GI food. A carbohydrate-containing food that produces a smaller blood glucose level curve is considered a low-GI food. For example, 50 grams of white bread have a glycemic index of 100. A 50-gram portion of kidney beans has a GI of 42, while the same amount of puffed wheat cereal has a GI of 105. So, the kidney beans are considered a low-GI food compared with the white bread, while puffed wheat is considered a high-GI food (Table 9.2).

The problem with using the GI is that it's not always practical. For instance, 50 grams of puffed wheat would be over 4 cups of cereal, an amount that you are unlikely to eat in one sitting. That's where the glycemic load (GL) comes in as a practical additional measurement. The GL adjusts the GI to take into account the amount of carbohydrate consumed in a typical serving of a food. In the case of puffed wheat cereal, a smaller, typical serving size would lower its effect on blood glucose dramatically.

A Healthy Diabetes Food Guide

People with diabetes need to consume a well-balanced diet that contains whole grains, fruits, and vegetables coupled with lean protein and dairy foods and some healthy fats. Sweets and treats need to be modest and balanced within the diet. The list here, which is adapted from the U.S. Department of Health and Human Services National Diabetes Education Program, provides the details.

Vegetables: Choose dark green and orange vegetables as often as you can.

Aim for 2½ to 3 cups a day. Here are choices that equal 1 cup:

- 1 cup cut-up raw or cooked vegetables
- 2 cups leafy salad greens
- 1 cup vegetable juice

Milk, Yogurt, and Cheese

Aim for 3 cups a day. Here are choices that equal 1 cup:

- 1 cup nonfat or low-fat milk or yogurt
- 1½ ounces cheese

Fruits: Choose fresh, whole fruits as often as you can.

Aim for 1½ to 2 cups a day. Here are choices that equal 1 cup:

- 1 cup cut-up raw or cooked fruit
- 1 cup fruit juice
- ½ cup dried fruit

Breads, Cereals, Rice, and Pasta: Choose whole-grain foods for at least 3 of your 6 choices.

Aim for 6 to 7 ounces a day. Here are choices that equal 1 ounce:

- ½ cup cooked, whole-grain cereal
- ½ cup cooked rice or pasta
- 1 cup ready-to-eat cereal
- 1 slice whole-grain bread
- ½ small bagel or 1 small muffin

Meat, Fish, Beans, Eggs, and Nuts

Aim for 5 to 6 ounces a day. Here are choices that equal 1 ounce:

- 1 ounce lean meat, fish, or chicken
- 1 egg
- 1 tablespoon peanut butter
- ½ ounce nuts
- ¼ cup cooked dry peas or beans, such as kidney, white, split, or blackeye
- ¼ cup tofu

Heart-healthy Fats

One serving is

- 1 teaspoon vegetable, olive, or canola oil
- 1 teaspoon tub margarine
- 5 large olives or ⅛ avocado
- 1 tablespoon low-fat mayonnaise
- 2 tablespoons low-fat salad dressing

Regular Soda, Cookies, and Desserts

How much should you eat?

You get most of the fat your body needs from other foods you eat, so choose only a few extra servings of these heart-healthy fats each day. If you choose to eat these foods, have a very small amount and not every day.

Adapted from the U.S. Department of Health and Human Services' National Diabetes Education Program. 2008. Your Healthy Food Guide. http://ndep.nih.gov/diabetes/youth/youthtips/youthtipseat.htm (accessed July 2008).

Figure 9.4 Eating Well with Diabetes
The ADA recommends that people with diabetes consume plenty of whole grains, fruits, vegetables, and adequate amounts of lean protein, like the foods shown here, along with low-fat milk, monounsaturated fats, and legumes.

Other factors can also affect the GI of a food. Overripe fruits have sugar that is more easily digested and a higher GI than underripe ones. Both cooking and food processing change the structure of foods and make them more easily digested, increasing the GI compared with raw, unprocessed equivalents. Larger chunks and bigger particles of food contribute to slower digestion and lower GI than the same foods chopped into smaller pieces. Foods with viscous, soluble fiber tend to be absorbed more slowly and, so, have a lower GI than refined carbohydrates. In general, whole grains, vegetables, whole fruit, and legumes tend to have a low GI.[19] Finally, eating carbohydrate-heavy foods with protein and/or fat can also lower the GI.[20]

While the overall amount of carbohydrate within a healthy diet, along with weight management, are key factors in managing diabetes, monitoring the GI and GL of the foods they eat may also help people with diabetes, according to the American Diabetes Association. As noted earlier, the ADA recommends a diet that provides high-fiber carbohydrates from whole grains, fruits, vegetables, and legumes, like the foods shown in Figure 9.4, along with low-fat milk, monounsaturated fat, and adequate amounts of lean protein sources, which also help control GI.[21]

Although sugar was once thought of as a "diabetic no-no," it can now be part of a diabetic's diet. Research has found that eating sucrose doesn't cause a rise in a person's blood glucose level to any greater extent than does starch, so completely avoiding sugar isn't necessary. However, because weight management is often a concern, especially for people with type 2 diabetes, there's little room for many sweets and treats in a diabetic diet (or any diet, for that matter).

Participate in Regular Physical Activity

People with diabetes can better manage their blood glucose levels and their weight by being physically active every day. All types of physical activity, from walking the dog and cleaning the house to structured exercise, such as going for a brisk walk or riding a stationary bicycle, are beneficial. Physical activity can also help lower your blood pressure, "bad" cholesterol level, and stress, and keep your heart healthy and your bones strong.

Nutrition and Exercise Can Help Prevent Type 2 Diabetes

Recent research has suggested that shedding excess weight, exercising regularly, and eating a balanced, high-fiber, healthy diet may be the best strategy to lower your risk of getting diabetes in the first place. These suggestions are supported by the findings of a landmark study by the Diabetes Prevention Program of over 3,000 people with prediabetes. It showed that people who made such lifestyle changes were 58 percent less likely to develop type 2 diabetes than those who did not. Specifically, the study's interventions included the following:

- Losing weight—as little as 5 to 7 percent of former body weight
- Exercising 2½ hours a week
- Eating a plant-based, heart-healthy diet
- Meeting with a health professional for ongoing support and education[22]

When it comes to winning the battle against diabetes, a healthful diet and lifestyle is the best game plan. Check out the accompanying Table Tips for simple steps to help you dodge diabetes.

The Take-Home Message **Weight loss; a plant-based, high-fiber diet; and regular exercise play important roles in managing and preventing diabetes.**

TABLE TIPS

Diet Tips to Dodge Diabetes

Sweeten your morning cereal with sliced bananas or berries rather than sugar.

Pack an individual-size can of juice-packed fruit and a spoon for an on-the-go snack.

Add fiber-rich beans to your dinner stir fry.

What Is Hypoglycemia?

While a high level of glucose in your blood on an ongoing basis isn't healthy, a blood glucose level that is too low, called **hypoglycemia**, can be unpleasant for many people and downright dangerous for those with diabetes. People who experience hypoglycemia may feel hungry, nervous, dizzy, light-headed, confused, weak, and shaky, and even begin to sweat. Eating or drinking carbohydrate-rich foods, such as hard candies, juice, or soda, can relieve these symptoms and quickly raise the blood glucose level to a normal range.

People with diabetes who need to use insulin and/or blood glucose–lowering medications daily need to eat regularly to maintain blood glucose levels that correspond to their medication. If they skip meals and snacks, or if they don't eat enough to cover the effects of the medication, they are at risk for hypoglycemia. If they ignore their symptoms, their blood glucose level can drop so low that they could faint or slip into a coma.[23] Vigorous exercise can also lower the blood glucose level, so people with diabetes need to check their blood glucose level before they exercise to determine if they need a snack.

Although not common, some people without diabetes also experience bouts of hypoglycemia after meals. This is commonly known as *reactive hypoglycemia* and may be hormone-related. The symptoms can occur within 4 hours after a meal and include shakiness, dizziness, hunger, and perspiration. A doctor can diagnose this

There are many ways to monitor blood glucose levels.

hypoglycemia A condition in which the blood glucose level drops to lower than 70 mg/dl. Hunger, shakiness, dizziness, perspiration, irritability, and light-headedness are common symptoms.

Drinking juice can help restore blood glucose levels to a normal range.

condition by testing a person's blood glucose level while he or she is experiencing these symptoms. Although the cause of reactive hypoglycemia is not known, one thought is that some people are overly sensitive to one or more of the hormones normally released when the blood glucose level begins to drop. Eating smaller, well-balanced meals throughout the day can help prevent reactive hypoglycemia.

Another type of hypoglycemia, called *fasting hypoglycemia*, can occur in the morning, after fasting throughout the night. It can also occur during long stretches between meals and after exercise. Some medications, certain illnesses, tumors, hormone imbalances, and too much alcohol consumption can cause this type of hypoglycemia.

The Take-Home Message **The symptoms of hypoglycemia include feeling hungry, nervous, light-headed, shaky, and sweaty. Those who take medication and/or insulin to manage their diabetes but don't eat properly are at a greater risk of experiencing hypoglycemia. People without diabetes can experience reactive hypoglycemia several hours after a meal. Fasting hypoglycemia can occur in the morning upon awakening and can be caused by certain medications, certain illnesses, tumors, hormone imbalances, or an excessive consumption of alcohol.**

Check out these recipes and more suggestions at www.pearsonhighered.com/blake

UCook

Pizza in a Pocket

If you love pizza (and who doesn't?), you'll enjoy this twist on a classic slice of pizza pie that's a snap to make.

UDo

Take a Virtual Grocery Store Tour

Need some help in choosing healthy foods at the supermarket? Visit the companion website for a virtual tour and advice about the best foods to put into your grocery cart.

The Top Five Points to Remember

1. Blood glucose level is maintained in a healthy range with the help of hormones. Insulin directs glucose into the cells. When the pancreas produces insufficient insulin, or the body's cells do not respond properly to insulin's effects, a person is said to have diabetes. This disease is becoming more prevalent in the United States, among adults and children.
2. Type 1 diabetes is a disease that typically arises in childhood or the early adult years. In this form, the immune system destroys the insulin-producing cells in the pancreas. In type 2 diabetes, the pancreas typically produces insulin but the body cells have become resistant to its effects. Being overweight is the primary risk factor for type 2 diabetes, but there is a strong genetic tendency toward the disease, especially in certain ethnic groups. Prediabetes is a term used to characterize people whose high blood glucose level indicates that they are at increased risk of developing diabetes but do not currently have the disease. Gestational diabetes develops during pregnancy.
3. If poorly managed, diabetes can result in diabetic ketoacidosis, and the individual may become comatose. The long-term consequences of poorly managed diabetes include nerve damage, poor wound healing, increased vulnerability to infection, vision impairment, dental problems, kidney problems, and heart disease and stroke.

4. People with diabetes should consume a well-balanced diet and exercise regularly to help maintain a blood glucose level within a healthy range. Medication and/or insulin as well as regular blood tests may also be needed to manage blood glucose. Those with diabetes can include a modest amount of added sugar in their diets as long as their weight is being managed. Prevention strategies include weight loss, a plant-based, high-fiber diet, and regular exercise. These strategies are key to halting the rising incidence of diabetes in the United States.
5. Hypoglycemia can occur in people with diabetes, especially if they are taking medication and/or insulin and are not eating properly or regularly. People without diabetes can also experience hypoglycemia, although this is less common.

Test Yourself

1. Which of the following disorders typically arises in childhood or adolescence?
   a. type 1 diabetes
   b. type 2 diabetes
   c. prediabetes
   d. gestational diabetes
2. The primary risk factor for developing type 2 diabetes is
   a. having high blood pressure.
   b. maintaining a sedentary lifestyle.
   c. being overweight.
   d. having a family history of type 1 diabetes.
3. Poorly managed diabetes can lead to which of the following long-term complications?
   a. nerve damage
   b. hair loss
   c. pancreatic cancer
   d. both a and c
4. Which of the following can help you reduce your risk for type 2 diabetes?
   a. avoiding sugar
   b. eating a plant-based, high-fiber diet
   c. exercising regularly
   d. both b and c
5. Which of the following disorders typically arises in the morning?
   a. reactive hypoglycemia
   b. fasting hypoglycemia
   c. impaired glucose tolerance
   d. ketosis

Answers

1. (a) Type 1 diabetes typically manifests itself during childhood or adolescence. Unlike type 2 diabetes and prediabetes, it is unrelated to lifestyle factors. Gestational diabetes arises during pregnancy.
2. (c) The primary risk factor for developing type 2 diabetes is being overweight.
3. (a) Nerve damage is a common long-term complication of poorly managed diabetes.
4. (d) Eating a plant-based, high-fiber diet and getting regular exercise, both of which can help you maintain a healthy weight, is the best approach to help reduce your risk of developing type 2 diabetes. Eating sugar doesn't cause diabetes, and avoiding it doesn't reduce your risk.
5. (b) Fasting hypoglycemia typically arises in the morning, after 8 or more hours without food. In contrast, reactive hypoglycemia typically occurs within 4 hours after a meal. Impaired glucose tolerance is a clinical sign of prediabetes. Ketosis is an increase of ketone bodies in the blood, which typically occurs with fasting and long-term carbohydrate restriction.

Web Resources

- For more on diabetes, visit the FDA's Diabetes Information site at: www.fda.gov/diabetes
- To learn more about diet, exercise, and other lifestyle choices you can make to prevent or reduce the symptoms of diabetes, visit the CDC's Diabetes & Me site at: www.cdc.gov/diabetes/consumer/index.htm

10

1. You need to eat **cholesterol** daily to meet your needs. **T/F**
2. Your body has an unlimited capacity to store **excess calories** as fat. **T/F**
3. The fats you eat are absorbed directly from your **GI tract.** **T/F**
4. If you never ate any fat, you'd become deficient in several **vitamins.** **T/F**
5. **Eating fish** can provide your body with essential fatty acids. **T/F**

Fats

Facts to Know

Talia loves her grandmother's homemade salad dressing of balsamic vinegar, canola oil, and basil. She uses it every night on her dinner salad, and every night her friend Misty gives her grief for using oil. "It adds calories but nothing else to your diet," Misty claims. "I don't go near it!" Is Misty right to advise her friend to skip the oil?

Do you know what fats really are, and how your body uses and stores them? Do you know which types of fats are more healthy, and why? Like Misty, would you consider avoiding all fat in your diet? In this concept, you will learn the facts you need to know about fats.

Answers

1. False. Your body *does* need cholesterol for important functions. However, you don't need to eat any to meet your needs. Turn to page 6 to find out why.
2. True. Fat cells enlarge as more fat storage is needed; if they fill to capacity, your body can make more! See page 6 to learn the details.
3. False. Fats consumed in foods must be broken down by stomach and pancreatic enzymes before they can be absorbed. Turn to page 7 for more on this.
4. True. Dietary fat allows you to absorb the fat-soluble vitamins A, D, E, and K. Turn to page 8 for details.
5. True! Turn to page 9 to find out why.

What Are Fats and Why Do You Need Them?

When you see the word *fat*, you may think of butter, mayonnaise, the cholesterol in meats and eggs, and even the fatty tissues in your own body. But technically speaking, these aren't all fats. Instead, they're examples of a broader category of substances known as **lipids**—compounds that contain carbon, oxygen, and hydrogen and which are *hydrophobic* (*hydro* = water, *phobic* = fear), meaning, they don't dissolve in water. If you were to drop lipids, such as butter or olive oil, into a glass of water, you would see them rise to the top and sit on the water's surface. This repelling of water enables lipids to play a unique role in foods and in your body.

To answer our original question, *fat* is the common name for just one type of lipid, known as a triglyceride. Because this is the type of lipid found most abundantly in foods, food labels and nutrition sources refer generally to this category as dietary *fat*—not dietary *lipid*—so that is the term we'll use throughout this book.

The most popular **salad dressing** in the United States is ranch, followed by Italian.

Fats Serve Multiple Functions in Foods and in Your Body

Fats perform a variety of functions in cooking. They give a flaky texture to pie crusts and other baked goods, and they make meat tender and soups and puddings creamy. The flavors and aromas that fats provide can make your mouth water as you eye crispy fried chicken or smell doughnuts frying. Foods that are higher in fats contribute to satiety, that feeling of fullness you experience after eating.

In your body, fats are essential for energy storage and insulation. Two other types of lipids are also important as components of the membranes surrounding your cells and play a key role in transporting proteins in your blood. We'll look in more detail at how your body uses lipids later in this concept.

Three types of lipids are found in foods and in your body: triglycerides (*fats*), phospholipids, and sterols. Two of the three, triglycerides and phospholipids, are built from a basic unit called a **fatty acid.** So let's start our discussion of the structure of lipids with the fatty acids.

Toasting chopped nuts in a fry pan or in an oven on a cookie sheet will intensify their **flavor.** This way, you can eat less but still add a rich flavor to your foods.

lipids A broad category of compounds, that contain carbon, hydrogen, and oxygen and which are insoluble in water.

fatty acid The most basic unit of lipids, composed of triglycerides and phospholipids.

Fatty Acids Are Found in Triglycerides and Phospholipids

Hydrophobic compounds, such as olive oil, don't dissolve in water. By repelling water in this way, lipids play a unique role in foods and in your body.

All fatty acids consist of a chain of carbon and hydrogen atoms, with an acid group (a group in which oxygen is attached to the carbon and hydrogen) at one end. If you study Figure 10.1, you'll notice that each link in the chain consists of a carbon atom (C) attached to hydrogen atoms (H) above and below, with another carbon atom on each side. Thus, each carbon has four attachments, which are also called *bonds*. The way carbon bonds occur in different types of fatty acids is what makes some fatty acids healthier than others.

There are three main types of fatty acids:

- *Saturated fatty acids.* When each carbon in a fatty acid chain is bonded with two atoms of hydrogen, as in Figure 10.1, the chain is considered saturated with hydrogen. It cannot hold any more. We therefore call such a fatty acid a *saturated fatty acid*. For example, stearic acid is a saturated fatty acid (Figure 10.2a), because its 18 carbons are all bound, or saturated, with hydrogen. Long fatty acids, such as stearic acid, are strongly attracted to one another and are relatively straight, which means they are able to pack tightly together within food and thus are solid at room temperature. Stearic acid can be found in cocoa butter (in chocolate) and in the fatty part of meat. Shorter saturated fatty acids (those with fewer than 12 carbons) have a weaker attraction to one another, so they do not pack tightly together. Because of this, foods containing them are liquid at room temperature. Whole milk contains short-chain saturated fatty acids. Fats made up of mostly saturated fatty acids are called **saturated fats**. As you will learn in Concept 11, you should limit your consumption of saturated fats because they are not healthy for your heart.

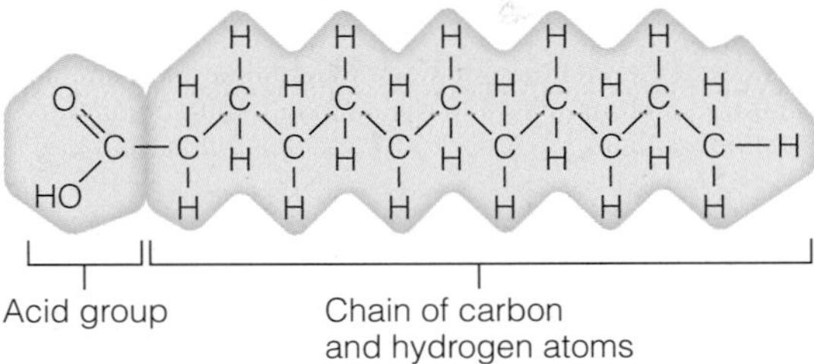

Figure 10.1 Structure of a Fatty Acid
Fatty acids are the building blocks of some lipids.

- *Monounsaturated fatty acids.* Take a look at the fatty acid shown in Figure 10.2b). Do you notice that, at one place in the chain, two carbons are each bound to only one atom of hydrogen and are joined twice to each other? This double carbon bond, indicated with an equal sign (=), means that the carbons are not "saturated" with hydrogen atoms at that point in the chain. This makes the chain unsaturated. Because a double bond occurs at just one point in the chain, the molecule is called a *monounsaturated fatty acid* (recall that *mono* means one). The example in Figure 10.2b is oleic acid. Like stearic acid, oleic acid contains 18 carbons, but two of them are paired with each other rather than hydrogen, so oleic acid has one double bond. This one double bond makes oleic acid a monounsaturated fatty acid. It also makes it crooked, because double bonds cause a "kink" in the chain of the fatty acid. This kink keeps unsaturated fatty acids from packing together tightly. Thus, unsaturated fatty acids are liquid at room temperature. For instance, oleic acid is found in olive oil. In Figure 10.3, you can see the effect of straight versus kinked fatty acid chains on foods. As you might expect, fats made up of mostly unsaturated fatty acids are called **unsaturated fats.** While saturated fats are unhealthy, unsaturated fats are considered important to your health.
- *Polyunsaturated fatty acids.* A polyunsaturated fatty acid (*poly* = many) contains more than one double bond and is even less saturated with hydrogen than are monounsaturated fatty acids. In the example shown in Figure 10.2c, linoleic acid contains two double bonds and is polyunsaturated. It is found in soybean oil. Like monounsaturated fats, polyunsaturated fats are also considered healthy. Incidentally, your body can make most of the fatty acids it needs, but there are two that it cannot make and both are polyunsaturated. Since you

saturated fats Fats in which the fatty acid chain is saturated with hydrogen. Foods high in saturated fats with long fatty acid chains are solid at room temperature, and are heart-unhealthy.

unsaturated fats Fats in which the fatty acid chain contains less hyrodgen. Foods with unsaturated fats are liquid at room temperature, and have health benefits.

Figure 10.2 Saturated and Unsaturated Fatty Acids
Fatty acids differ by the length of the fatty acid chain, whether there are double bonds between the carbons, and (if there are double bonds) how many double bonds they contain.

a Stearic acid, a saturated fatty acid

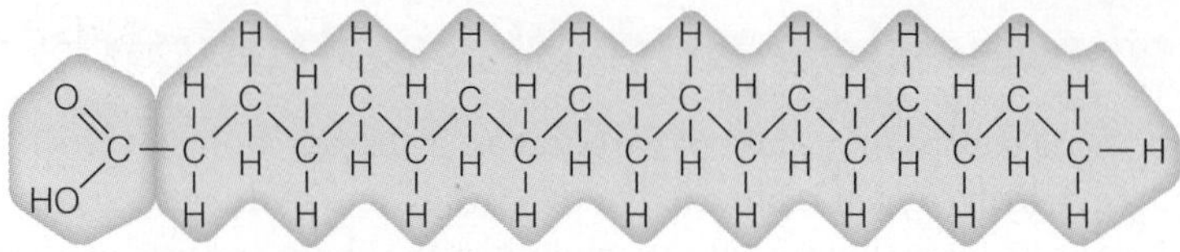

b Oleic acid, a monounsaturated fatty acid

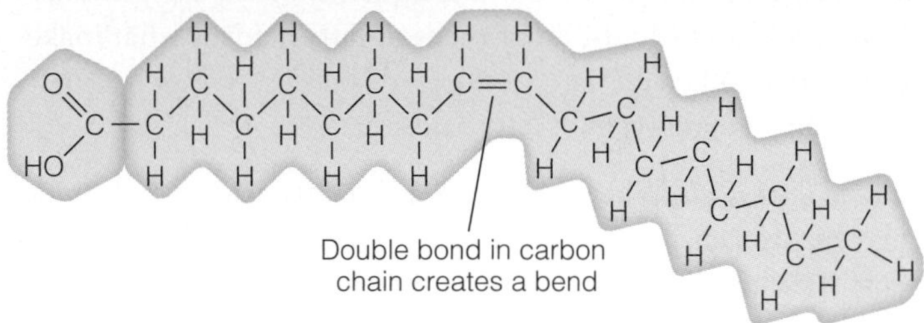

c Linoleic acid, a polyunsaturated omega-6 fatty acid

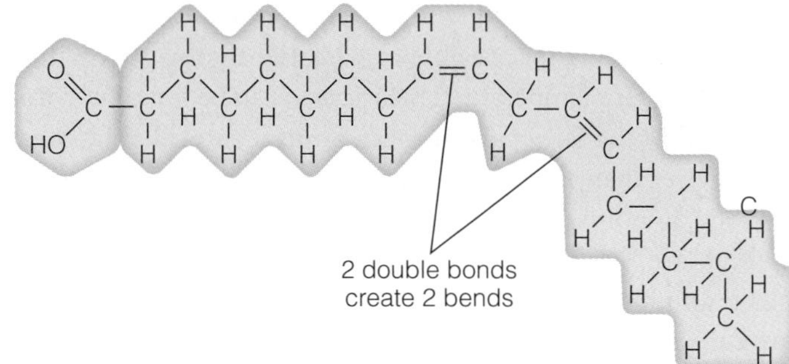

d Alpha-linolenic acid, a polyunsaturated, omega-3 fatty acid

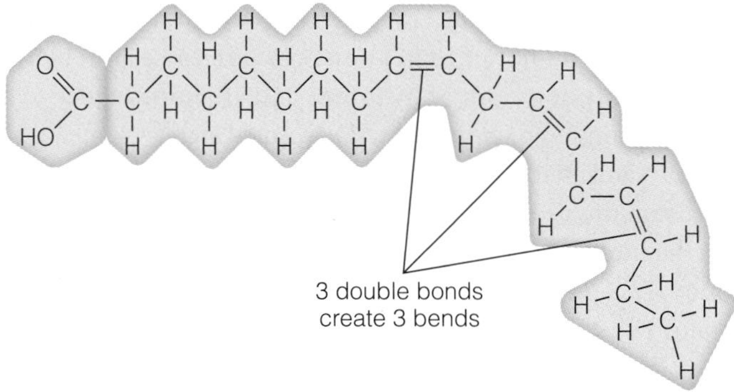

must consume them in your diet, they're known as **essential fatty acids**. They are *linoleic acid*, shown in Figure 10.2c, and *alpha-linolenic acid*, shown in Figure 10.2d. We'll discuss these essential fatty acids in more detail later in this concept.

essential fatty acids Fatty acids (linoleic acid and alpha-linolenic acid) which the body needs but cannot make, and therefore must be obtained from foods.

triglycerides The most common type of lipid found in foods and in your body; commonly known as *fats*.

Triglycerides Contain Three Fatty Acid Chains

Triglycerides are the most common lipid found in foods and in your body. Each triglyceride compound is made up of three fatty acid chains (*tri* = three) connected to a *glycerol* "backbone." Glycerol is a compound containing carbon, hydrogen, and a type of alcohol. The three fatty acids join to the glycerol backbone to form the triglyceride (Figure 10.4).

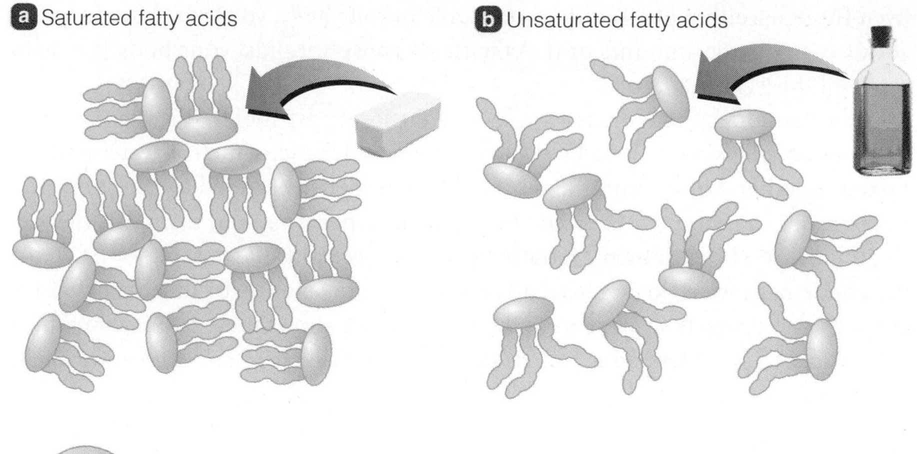

Figure 10.3 Saturated and Unsaturated Fatty Acids Help Shape Foods Saturated fatty acids are able to pack tightly together and most are solid at room temperature. The double bonds in unsaturated fatty acids cause kinks in their shape and prevent them from packing tightly together, so they tend to be liquid at room temperature.

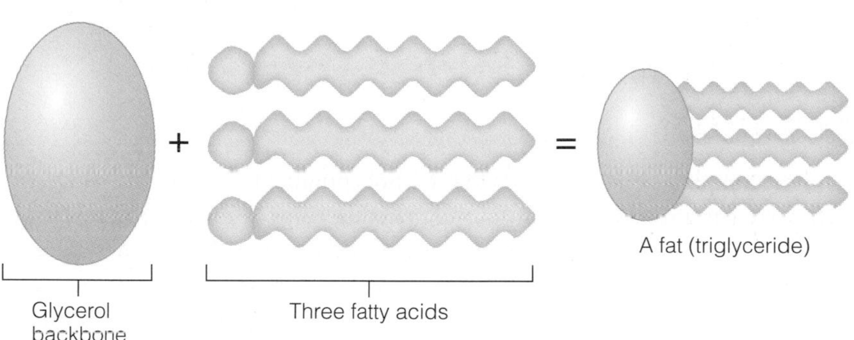

Figure 10.4 Structure of a Triglyceride A triglyceride consists of three fatty acids attached to a glycerol backbone.

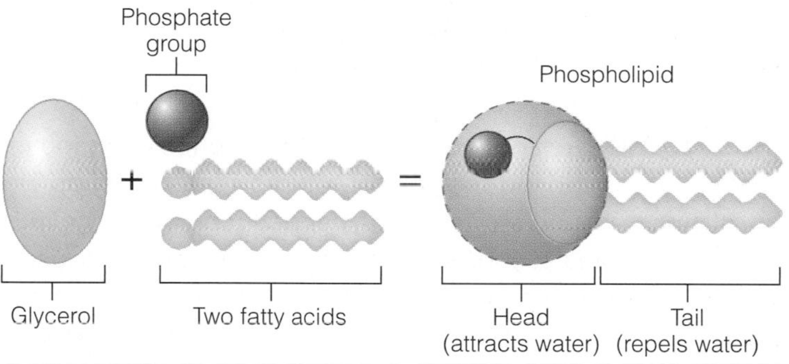

Figure 10.5 Structure of a Phospholipid Phospholipids have two fatty acids and a phosphate group connected to their glycerol backbone. This configuration allows phospholipids, such as lecithin, to be attracted to both water and fat.

Recall that triglycerides are commonly called *fats*, the term used throughout this concept and the rest of the book. Most of the lipids that you eat and that are in your body are in the form of fat. Many fatty foods, such as butter, lard, and the fat in meats, are solid at room temperature. **Oils** are lipids that are liquid at room temperature.

Phospholipids Contain Phosphate

Phospholipids, like fats, contain a glycerol backbone but instead of attaching to three fatty acids this backbone is attached to two fatty acids and a phosphate group (a compound containing the mineral phosphorus) (Figure 10.5). The portion where the phosphate is attached to the glycerol is referred to as the head, which is *hydrophilic* (*philic* = loving), so it is able to attract water. In contrast, phospholipids' fatty acid tails are hydrophobic.

Phospholipids are the primary component of the membranes surrounding your body cells; their water-attracting and water-repelling sides allow certain substances, such as water, to enter, while keeping others, such as protein, from leaking out. You can visualize this phospholipid layer as being like a picket fence, acting as a barrier surrounding each cell. The major phospholipid in your cell membranes is lecithin.

oils Lipids that are liquid at room temperature.

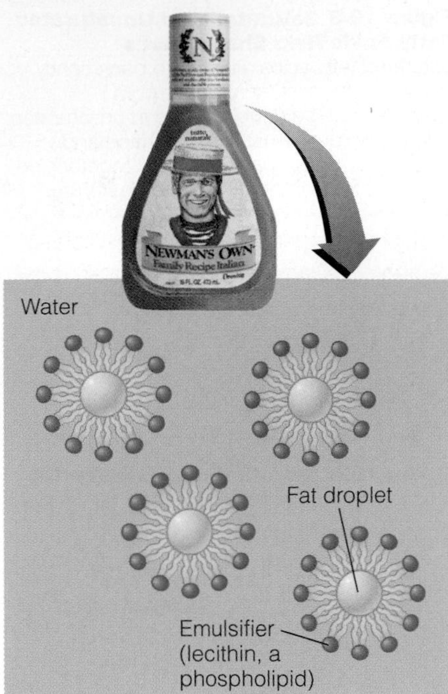

Figure 10.6 Keeping a Salad Dressing Blended
To prevent the fat from separating out in a salad dressing, an emulsifier is added. The emulsifier's fat-attracting tails surround the droplets of fat, whereas the water-attracting heads remain oriented toward the watery portion of the dressing. This allows the fat droplets to stay suspended and blended in the dressing.

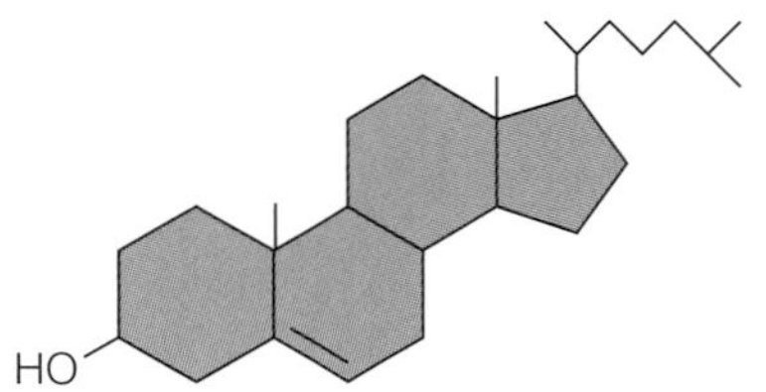

Figure 10.7 Structure of a Sterol
Rather than being made from fatty acids attached to a glycerol backbone, sterols have a carbon ring configuration. Cholesterol is the most commonly known sterol.

Even though lecithin plays an important role in your body, you don't have to worry about eating large amounts of it. As with all phospholipids, your body is able to make all the lecithin it needs.

Because of lecithin's unique water- and fat-loving attributes, it is used in many foods as an *emulsifier* to help keep incompatible substances, such as water and oil, mixed together. For example, an emulsifier is sometimes added to commercially made salad dressings to prevent the fat from separating and rising to the top (Figure 10.6). The emulsifier's fat-attracting tail surrounds the droplets of fat, while the emulsifier's water-loving head attracts the watery solution of the dressing. This keeps the fat droplets suspended in the dressing and allows these two incompatible substances to stay blended together. We'll see the process of emulsification again when we discuss how the body uses fat.

Sterols Have a Unique Ring Structure

Unlike phospholipids, *sterols* are lipids that do not contain glycerol or fatty acids. Instead, they are composed mainly of four connecting rings of carbon and hydrogen (Figure 10.7). The best known sterol is cholesterol. Although cholesterol's association with heart disease has blemished its reputation, it plays an important role in your cell membranes and is the *precursor* of some very important compounds in your body. A precursor is a substance that is converted into or leads to the formation of another substance. As with lecithin, don't be concerned about meeting your daily need for this important substance through your diet, since your tissues manufacture all the cholesterol you need.

The Take-Home Message **Lipids are hydrophobic compounds made up of carbon, hydrogen, and oxygen. The three types of lipids are triglycerides, phospholipids, and sterols. Triglycerides (commonly called fats) are the most prevalent lipids in your food and body. They are composed of three fatty acids attached to a glycerol backbone. Phospholipids have unique water- and fat-attracting properties, and they play important roles in your cell membranes and as emulsifiers in foods. Cholesterol is an important sterol in your cell membranes and is the precursor to other essential compounds.**

How Does Your Body Use Fat and Cholesterol?

Like Misty at the start of this concept, many people believe that fat plays no beneficial role in the body. This is a myth. Let's look at the facts.

Fat Is Used for Energy, Insulation, and the Absorption of Other Nutrients

At 9 calories per gram, compared with 4 calories per gram each for carbohydrates and proteins, fat is a major fuel source for your body. Your body has an unlimited ability to store excess energy (calories) as fat. In fact, your fat reserves have the

What Happens to the Fats You Eat?

The fats you eat must be broken down before they can be absorbed and used or stored for energy. Let's look at how your body digests the fats in a piece of cheese pizza. Each step is illustrated in Figure 10.8.

a. The digestion of fat starts in your mouth. While chewing mechanically breaks down the food, an enzyme called lingual lipase plays a minor role in beginning to break down some fat.

b. Once the food is swallowed and reaches your stomach, it is mixed with gastric lipase. This enzyme breaks some of it into a free fatty acid and a *diglyceride* (a compound with only two fatty acids left joined to the glycerol backbone).

c. The majority of fat digestion occurs in your small intestine. When fat reaches your small intestine, an enzyme released from your pancreas, pancreatic lipase, continues to break it down into two free fatty acids and a *monoglyceride* (the remnant of fat digestion, in which only one fatty acid is left joined to the glycerol backbone). Simultaneously, your gallbladder releases bile, an acid-containing compound that helps emulsify the fat into smaller globules within the watery digestive solution. This disperses the fat globules, so that pancreatic lipase can more easily reach and break down the fat.

d. Monoglycerides and fatty acids are next packaged with lecithin, which is in the bile, and other substances to create *micelles* (small transport carriers). Once close to the lining of your small intestine, the micelles travel through your intestinal cells. At this point, short-chain fatty acids enter your bloodstream and go directly to your liver. Long-chain fatty acids can't enter your bloodstream directly and need transport carriers, called *chylomicrons*, compounds in which the fatty acids are enveloped in phospholipids and proteins. Chylomicrons travel through your lymphatic system before entering your bloodstream. Once in your blood, they're further broken down by an enzyme located in the walls of your tiniest blood vessels. Your heart and muscles use fatty acids as energy or store them as an energy reserve in your fat cells.

Figure 10.8 Digesting and Absorbing Fat

a Mouth
Chewing begins the breakdown of fatty foods.

b Stomach
Fat digestion continues in the stomach with the aid of the enzyme gastric lipase.

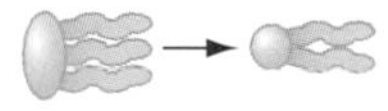

c Small intestine
Helps emulsify the fat into smaller globules, enabling pancreatic lipase to break it down more easily.

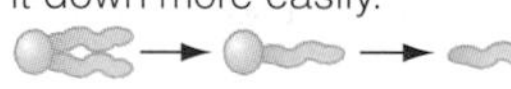

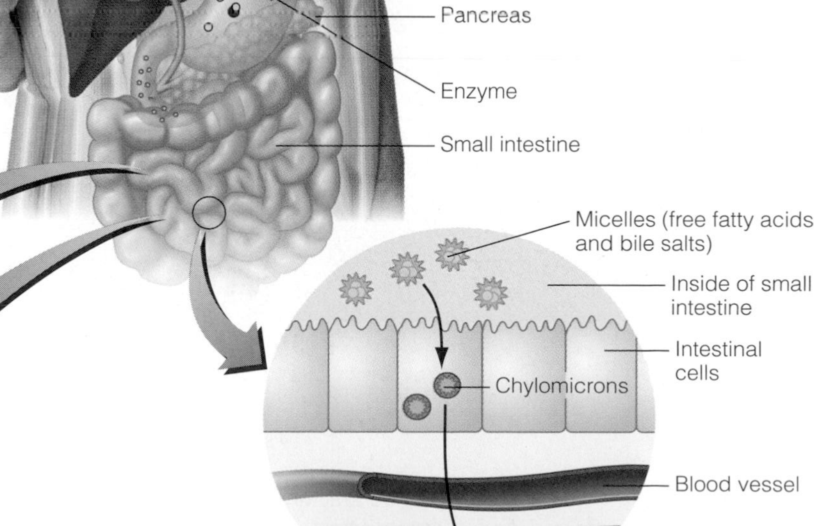

d Absorption
By-products of fat disgestion travel via micelles through your intestinal cells. Short-chain fatty acids enter your bloodstream directly. Long-chain fatty acids are reformulated into fats and carried by chylomicrons to your lymph before entering your blood.

capacity to enlarge to as much as 1,000 times their original size, as more fat is added. If your cells fill to capacity, your body can add more fat cells.

However, remember from Concept 7 that your body has only a limited ability to store glucose, which your brain and red blood cells need to function. When your blood glucose level begins to fall, a hormone promotes the release of more glucose from your liver in order to supply it to the blood and simultaneously helps release fat from fat cells to provide additional energy for your body. Your heart, liver, and resting muscles prefer fat as their fuel source, which allows glucose to be reserved for your nervous system and red blood cells. In fact, fat is your main source of energy throughout the day. This stored fat provides a backup source of energy between meals. In extreme situations, such a famines, individuals with significant fat stores could survive for months without eating, as long as they had adequate fluids.

The fat located just under your skin helps insulate your body and maintain your body temperature. Fat also acts as a protective cushion for your bones, organs, and nerves.

Dietary fat also allows you to absorb the fat-soluble vitamins A, D, E, and K, as well as carotenoids, compounds that can have beneficial antioxidant properties in your body.[1] People with disorders that impair their body's ability to absorb fat can develop deficiencies of these vitamins.

Although you may think that the fats you eat are all the same, different fats can have different effects on your health—specifically, the health of your heart. We'll talk more about this in Concepts 11 and 12. In the meantime, let's look at the role that essential fatty acids play in your body.

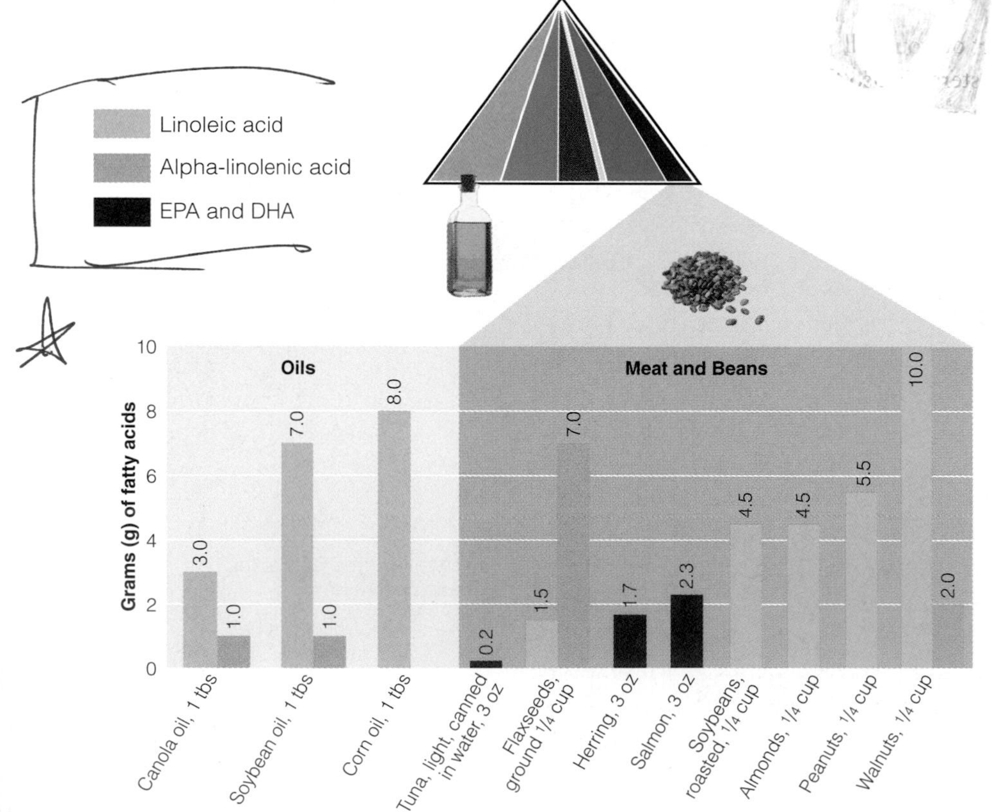

Figure 10.9 Food Sources of the Essential Fatty Acids
Many oils and nuts contain high amounts of the two essential fatty acids you need in your diet. Also, several types of fish, particularly fatty fish, are high in the heart-healthy omega-3 fatty acids EPA and DHA.

Essential Fatty Acids Create Key Compounds and Help Keep Cell Membranes Healthy

Recall that two polyunsaturated fatty acids, linoleic acid and alpha-linolenic acid, are essential (see Figure 10.2). This means that your body can't make them, so you need to get them from your diet. A deficiency of these essential fatty acids can interfere with normal cell membranes' function and growth and result in scaly skin. Essential fatty acids are also necessary to make other substances your body needs:

- Your body uses linoleic acid to make another polyunsaturated fatty acid, called arachidonic acid, which is important for the functioning of your cells and for making compounds that play a role in inflammation, blood clotting, and raising blood pressure.
- Your body can convert a limited amount of alpha-linolenic acid to two other important fatty acids: eicosapentaenoic acid (EPA) and docosahexaenoic acid

(DHA),[2] which prompt the production of eicosanoids and are very important for the health of your heart and blood vessels.

Linoleic acid is also referred to as *omega-6 fatty acid*, and alpha-linolenic acid is commonly called *omega-3 fatty acid*. If this sounds Greek to you, it should. The letters of the Greek alphabet help identify the placement of the carbons in fatty acid chains. Omega is the last letter of the Greek alphabet, and the omega carbon is the last carbon of the fatty acid chain. The place in each chain where the first double bond occurs identifies the omega number (see Figure 10.2).

Vegetables, nuts, and the oils derived from them are good sources of essential fatty acids (Figure 10.9). Talia, from the start of this concept, is smart to add vegetable oil to her salad because it adds essential fatty acids to her diet. If Misty purposefully avoids all sources of added fat in her diet, she may fall short of meeting her daily need for these important fatty acids. In addition, all fish contain EPA and DHA, with some fatty fish, such as salmon, herring, and sardines, as especially rich sources. Cod-liver oil is abundant in EPA and DHA, but also in the fat-soluble vitamins A and D, which can both be toxic if consumed in high amounts. Eating fish is a safer way to obtain the essential fatty acids.

How can you be sure you're eating enough of the heart-healthy essential fatty acids? Rate Yourself and find out!

Cholesterol Has Many Important Roles

Your body needs cholesterol, both as a part of your cell membranes and as the precursor for vitamin D and bile acids. Cholesterol is also the precursor for the reproductive hormones estrogen and testosterone, which help determine our sexual characteristics. As noted earlier in this concept, you don't need to consume cholesterol, because your liver can make all you need.

The confusion over cholesterol persists. While dietary cholesterol has been proclaimed to be unhealthy, the cholesterol that exists in your blood may be either "good" or "bad" cholesterol. How can one substance be both? In Concept 12, we'll look at the health effects of cholesterol and help you make some sense of this potentially confusing topic. For now, just keep in mind that dietary cholesterol isn't the only factor determining the levels of cholesterol in your blood.

The Take-Home Message **Fat contains 9 calories per gram and is an energy-dense source of fuel for your body. Fat cushions and protects your bones, organs, and nerves and insulates you to help maintain your body temperature. Your body also needs fat to absorb fat-soluble vitamins and carotenoids. Essential fatty acids must be consumed. The essential fatty acids linoleic acid (omega-6 fatty acid) and alpha-linolenic acid (omega-3 fatty acid) are important for cell health and growth, as well as for making other body compounds important to your health. Cholesterol is part of your cell membranes; it is needed to make vitamin D, bile acids, and reproductive hormones.**

The upcoming Visual Summary Table reviews many of the functions, daily needs and consequences regarding lipids. We have touched on some of the food sources for lipids contained in the table; others will be discussed more fully in Concept 11.

RATE YOURSELF 

Are You Eating Enough "Good" Fats?

Your body needs certain essential fatty acids daily to maintain good health. Rate yourself to see if your diet has enough of these good fats.

Every day, I eat:

1. At least a tablespoon of vegetable oil, such as canola, soybean, corn, or olive oil
   True ☐ **False** ☐
2. At least 2 tablespoons of salad dressing
   True ☐ **False** ☐
3. At least 1 cup green leafy vegetables
   True ☐ **False** ☐
4. At least a handful of nuts or a tablespoon of any nut butter
   True ☐ **False** ☐
5. At least 1 tablespoon of ground flaxseeds
   True ☐ **False** ☐

Answers

If you answered "true" to a minimum of three of the above, you are likely meeting your daily needs for essential fatty acids. If you didn't, you may be coming up short.

Lipids

What Are Lipids?

Lipids refer to a category of carbon, oxygen, and hydrogen compounds that are all hydrophobic (*hydro* = water, *phobic* = fear). In other words, they don't dissolve in water. There are three types of lipids: triglycerides, phospholipids, and sterols. Two of these, triglycerides and phospholipids, are built from a basic unit called a fatty acid.

Fatty Acids Vary in Length and Structure

All *fatty acids* consist of a chain of carbon and hydrogen atoms, with an acid group (OH) at one end. There are over 20 different fatty acids. They can vary by (1) the length of the chain, (2) whether or not the carbons have a single or double bond between them (C — C or C = C) and (3) the total number of double bonds.

If all the carbons have single bonds between each other in a fatty acid, they are also all bonded to hydrogen. When all of the carbons on a fatty acid are bound with hydrogen, it is called a *saturated fatty acid.* In contrast, if a fatty acid has carbons that are not bound to hydrogen, but rather to each other, which creates a double bond, it is called an *unsaturated fatty acid.*

Triglycerides Are More Commonly Known as Fat

Three fatty acids connected to a *glycerol* backbone create a *triglyceride,* which is the most common lipid found in foods and in your body. Glycerol is a three-carbon compound that contains three alcohol (OH) groups. The fatty acids join to each of the alcohol groups. The more common name for triglycerides is **fat.**

Phospholipids and Sterols Are More Complex

Like fats, phospholipids contain a glycerol backbone, but instead of being made up of three fatty acids, they contain two fatty acids and a phosphorus group. The phosphate-containing head is polar, which attracts charged particles, such as water, and the fatty acid–containing tail is nonpolar, so it mingles with other nonpolar molecules such as fats.

Unlike phospholipids, sterols do not contain glycerol or fatty acids. Sterols are comprised mainly of four connecting rings of carbon and hydrogen. The best known sterol is cholesterol.

Functions of Lipids

Fat provides fatty acids that are essential to your health and also allows you to absorb the fat-soluble vitamins, A, D, E, and K. Fat is also an important source of energy, helps insulate you, keeps you at a constant body temperature, and cushions your major organs.

Phospholipids make up the phospholipid bilayer in cell membranes. Lipoproteins, made of protein and phospholipids, are transport carriers that shuttle insoluble fat and cholesterol through your bloodstream and lymph to be used throughout the body.

Cholesterol is also an important part of your cell membranes. It is a precursor for vitamin D, bile acids, and sex hormones, such as estrogen and testosterone.

Daily Needs

The current AMDR recommendation is for 20 to 35 percent of your daily calories to come from fat. For some individuals, especially sedentary, overweight folks, a very low-fat diet (providing less than 20 percent of daily calories from fat) that's high in carbohydrates may cause an increase in fat in the blood and a lowering of the good HDL cholesterol. For others, consuming more than 35 percent of their total daily calories from fat could perpetuate obesity, which is a risk factor for heart disease.[72]

You Need to Consume the Essential Fatty Acids, Linoleic Acid and Alpha-Linolenic Acids, in Foods

A minimum of 5 percent and up to 10 percent of the total calories in your diet should come from linoleic acid, and alpha-linolenic acid should make up 0.6 percent to 1.2 percent of your total calories.[73]

Men aged 19 to 50 need 17 grams and women aged 19 to 50 who aren't pregnant or lactating need 12 grams of linoleic acid daily. For alpha-linolenic acid, men aged 14 to 70 need 1.6 grams daily, and women of the same age need 1.1 grams daily.

Linoleic and alpha-linolenic acids must also be consumed in the proper ratio. Too much linoleic acid in relationship to alpha-linolenic acid can inhibit the conversion of alpha-linolenic acid to DHA, while the inverse (too much alpha-linolenic acid and not enough linoleic acid) can inhibit the conversion of linoleic acid to arachidonic acid.

You Do Not Need to Consume Cholesterol or *Trans* Fat

Your body can make all the cholesterol that it needs, so you do not need to consume it in your diet, and you should limit your cholesterol intake for the sake of your heart and arteries. Healthy individu-

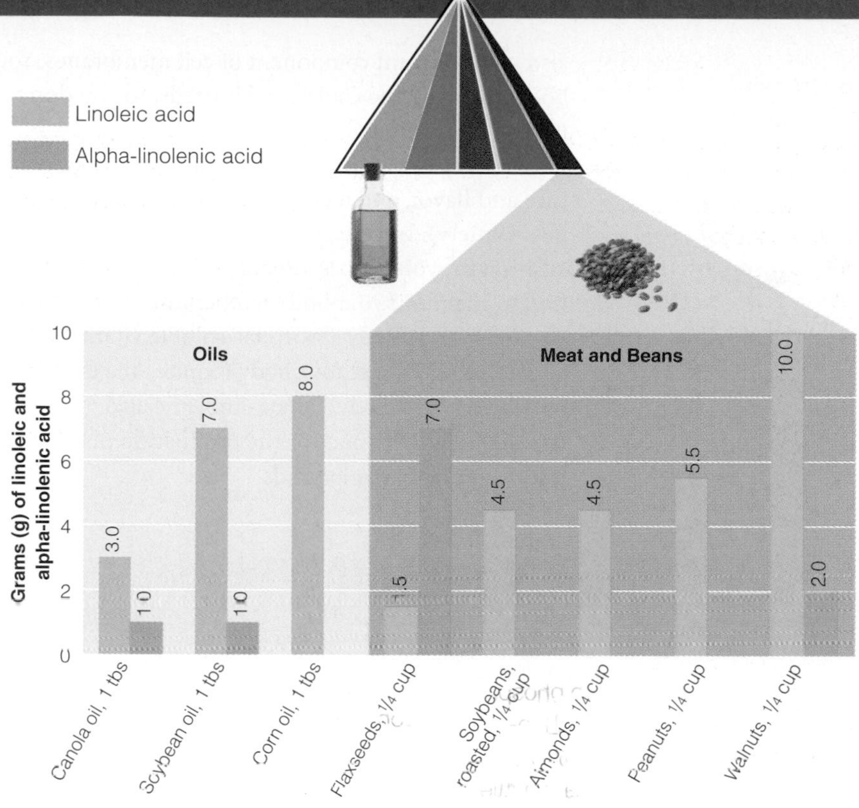

The best way to minimize both dietary cholesterol and saturated fat intake is to keep your portions of lean meat, skinless poultry, and fish to about 6 ounces daily, use only low-fat or nonfat dairy foods, use vegetable oils more often than butter, keep consumption of baked goods to a minimum, and fill up on fruits, vegetables and whole grains.

als over the age of 2 are advised to limit their dietary cholesterol to under 300 milligrams daily, on average.[74]

Trans fats are worse for heart health than saturated fat because they not only raise the LDL cholesterol levels, but they also lower HDL cholesterol in the blood. Therefore, *trans* fats should be limited in foods.

Food Sources

Unsaturated fats are abundant in vegetable oils, such as soybean, corn, and canola oils, as well as soybeans, walnuts, flaxseeds, and wheat germ, and these are also all good sources of essential fatty acids.

Foods high in cholesterol and saturated fat should be limited. Dietary cholesterol is found only in foods from animal sources, with egg yolks being a significant contributor. Because cholesterol is not found in foods from plant sources, you won't find it in vegetables, fruits, pasta, nuts, peanut butter, or vegetable oils.

Most saturated fat in the diet comes from animal foods such as fatty cuts of meat, whole-milk dairy products like cheese, butter, and ice cream, and the skin on poultry. Certain vegetable oils, such as coconut, palm, and palm kernel oils, are very high in saturated fat. Although food manufacturers now use these oils less often, they may still be found in foods such as candies, commercially made baked goods, and gourmet ice cream.

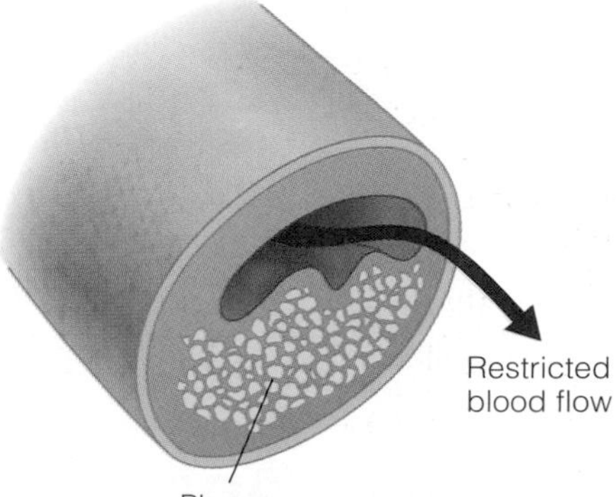

Too Much or Too Little

Overweight and Obesity

Your body has an *unlimited* ability to store excess energy (calories) as fat. In fact, your fat reserves have the capacity to enlarge as much as 1,000 times their original size, as more fat is added. If your cells fill to capacity, you can add more fat cells.

Heart Disease

Blood cholesterol levels are one of several factors that can affect your risk of heart disease. Eating foods low in saturated fat, dietary cholesterol, and *trans* fat, exercising regularly, and maintaining a healthy weight can help control your blood cholesterol levels and reduce your risk of heart disease. Quitting smoking, lowering high blood pressure, and controlling diabetes (if you have it) can also reduce your risk of heart disease.

In general, you want to lower your "bad" LDL cholesterol levels and raise your "good" HDL cholesterol levels. Having an LDL level of less than 100 milligrams per deciliter (mg/dl) is optimal. An HDL level less than 40 mg/dl increases your risk of heart disease, while a high level of HDL cholesterol, 60 mg/dl or higher, is considered a "negative" risk factor.

Too Little of the Essential Fatty Acids Can Result in These Symptoms

A deficiency of the essential fatty acids can interfere with normal cell membranes and growth and result in scaly skin.

Terms to Know

fatty acid ■ saturated fats ■ unsaturated fats ■ triglycerides ■ fat

Check out these recipes and more suggestions at www.pearsonhighered.com/blake

UCook

Sweet Greens Salad with Honey Mustard Dressing

If you have a sweet tooth, you'll love this tasty salad. Since it's high in essential fatty acids, your heart will love it, too.

UDo

A Virtual Trip to the Mediterranean

Do you want your diet to have more of a Mediterranean flavor? And benefit from a heart-healthier approach to fats and cooking? Visit an interactive guide to the Traditional Healthy Mediterranean Diet Pyramid on the link from our website to learn how!

The Top Five Points to Remember

1. Lipids are a broad category of hydrophobic (water-repelling) compounds made up of carbon, hydrogen, and oxygen. The three types of lipids are triglycerides, phospholipids, and sterols. Triglycerides (commonly called fats) are the most prevalent lipids in your body and in foods. A triglyceride contains three (*tri*) fatty acids joined to a glycerol backbone.
2. A fatty acid is the most basic unit of triglyercides and phospholipids. It is composed of a carbon and hydrogen chain with an acid group at one end. A fatty acid chain with no double carbon bonds is called a saturated fatty acid because the chain is said to be saturated with hydrogen. If one or more double bonds are present, it is called an unsaturated fatty acid because the fatty acid chain contains less hydrogen. Saturated fats are made up of mainly saturated fatty acids and tend to be solid at room temperature. Unsaturated fats have mostly unsaturated fatty acids, are liquid at room temperature, and are known as oils.
3. Phospholipids contain two fatty acids and a phosphate group attached to a glycerol backbone. Their phosphate-containing head attracts water, while their fatty acid tail attracts fat. They act as a barrier, allowing some substances in and keeping others out. Lecithin, the major phospholipid in cell membranes, is used as an emulsifier in foods to keep incompatible substances, such as water and oil, mixed together.
4. Sterols are lipids with unique structures; they do not contain glycerol or fatty acids. Cholesterol, the major sterol in your body and in foods, is the precursor of vitamin D, bile acids, and reproductive hormones. It is also an important component of cell membranes. Your body makes all the cholesterol it needs, so you don't have to consume it.
5. Fat can play beneficial roles. In food, it provides texture and flavor, and it contributes to a feeling of fullness (satiety). In your body, fat provides a protective cushion for your bones, organs, and nerves and insulation to maintain your body temperature. Fat in food also helps your body absorb fat-soluble vitamins. Not all fats are the same. Your body requires the essential fatty acids, linoleic and alpha-linolenic acid, for cell health and growth and for the production of other important body compounds.

Test Yourself

1. The primary lipid in your body is
   a. cholesterol.
   b. lecithin.
   c. triglyceride.
   d. stearic acid.
2. Fat provides
   a. a secondary source of energy.
   b. 4 calories per gram.
   c. assistance in absorbing fat-soluble vitamins.
   d. all of the above.
3. Fats contain
   a. a glycerol backbone.
   b. three fatty acids.
   c. a phosphate group.
   d. both a and b.
4. A hydrophilic compound
   a. has properties that attract water.
   b. uses water to dilute fats.
   c. has properties that repel water.
   d. changes in water.
5. Which of the following are good sources of the essential fatty acids linoleic acid and alpha linolenic acid?
   a. ground flaxseeds
   b. walnuts
   c. soybean oil
   d. all of the above

Answers

1. (c) The primary lipid in your body is triglycerides, or fats. Cholesterol is another type of lipid but is not as abundant as fat. Lecithin is a phospholipid found in your cell membranes and used as an emulsifier in some foods.

2. (c) Fat is required for the absorption of fat-soluble vitamins. It is your primary energy nutrient and your main source of energy. It provides 9 calories per gram, not 4.
3. (d) A fat contains a glycerol backbone with three fatty acids attached to it. The phosphate group is part of a phospholipid.
4. (a) *Hydro* = water, *philic* = loving. Hydrophilic compounds attract water.
5. (d) Ground flaxseeds, walnuts, and soybean oil are all good sources of essential fatty acids.

Web Resources

To learn more about essential fatty acids, visit

- Essential Fatty Acid Education at: http://efaeducation.nih.gov
- American Heart Association at: www.americanheart.org
- International Food Information Center at: www.ific.org/publications/factsheets/omega3fs.cfm

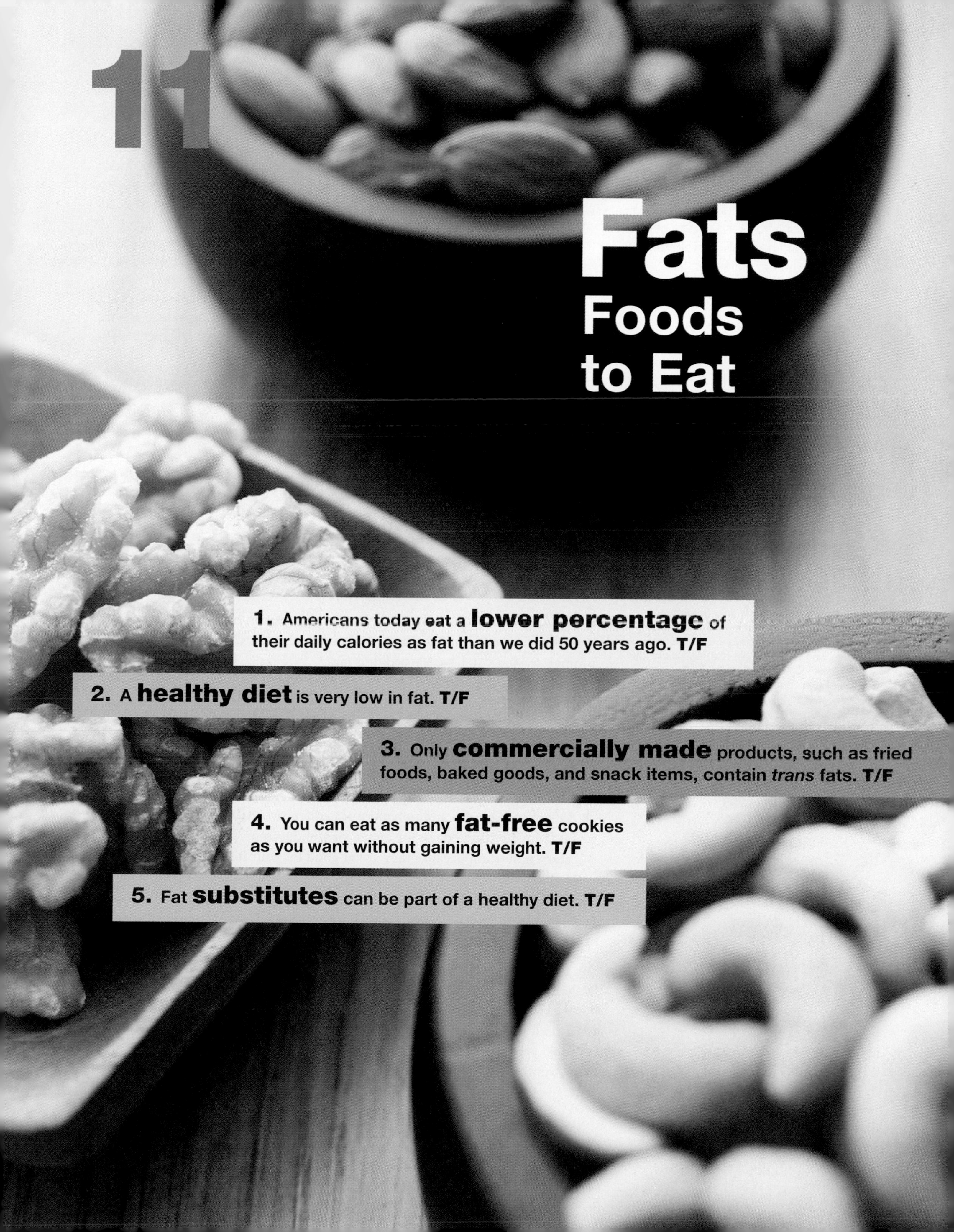

11

Fats
Foods to Eat

1. Americans today eat a **lower percentage** of their daily calories as fat than we did 50 years ago. **T/F**

2. A **healthy diet** is very low in fat. **T/F**

3. Only **commercially made** products, such as fried foods, baked goods, and snack items, contain *trans* fats. **T/F**

4. You can eat as many **fat-free** cookies as you want without gaining weight. **T/F**

5. Fat **substitutes** can be part of a healthy diet. **T/F**

Brian and Jim are college sophomores who play for their school's baseball team. One afternoon, they're sitting on a bleacher, waiting for their turns at bat. As usual, with their late afternoon practices, they're starving and need a quick snack to tide them over until they have time for a full meal. Luckily, Brian has brought along a package of light potato chips, and he's willing to share. As he pulls apart the top of the package, Jim notices a big, bright icon that says "Olean." He watches in mock horror as his friend reaches in to grab a handful.

"What are you doing?" he asks. "Don't you know those things give you the runs? Do you want to end up in the bathroom all night?" "Huh?" Brian replies in confusion. "These are good for me. Look, it says right here, they're fat free. How can they be bad?"

Who do you think has his facts straight, Brian or Jim? Have you heard reports that fat substitutes can cause digestive problems? Do you know what types of fats you should eat, how much, and how they affect your health? In this concept, we'll answer these questions, as well as debunk some popular myths about fat and fat substitutes. We'll also identify some foods containing different types of fats, and discuss which of them you should aim to eat during meals and snacks.

Answers

1. True. But because we're eating more calories overall, our daily average consumption of fat grams is actually up. See page 3 for details.
2. False. Whereas too much dietary fat may cause you to gain weight, eating too little isn't healthy, either. A diet low in fat but high in added sugars may increase the level of fat in your blood. To find out more, read page 3.
3. False. Although most *trans* fats are made from the hydrogenated oils that are found in commercially prepared, processed foods, *trans* fats also occur naturally in meat and dairy foods. Turn to page 9 to learn more.
4. False. Fat-free foods are not necessarily calorie free. Find out more on page 12.
5. True. Food containing fat substitutes can satisfy our taste buds while providing half the fat calories of regular versions of the same foods. See page 12.

How Much (and What Types of) Fat Do You Need and What Are Its Food Sources?

In the previous concept, we discussed many types of fats, but which ones should you eat and which ones you should try to limit in your diet? The following should help summarize what you have learned thus far:

- DO be sure to get enough of the two essential fatty acids, linoleic acid and alpha-linolenic acid, in your diet by eating plenty of polyunsaturated fats. Foods rich in these essential fatty acids are canola, soybean, and corn oils; soybeans and flaxseeds; and nuts, such as almonds, peanuts, and walnuts.
- DON'T worry about eating enough cholesterol because your body makes all that it needs.
- DO choose mono- and polyunsaturated fats over saturated fats when possible, as these unsaturated fats are better for you. Saturated fats should be kept to a dietary minimum because they aren't good for your heart or your blood cholesterol levels.
- DON'T add *trans* fats to your diet. As we'll explain shortly, *trans* fats are unhealthy for your heart and blood cholesterol levels and should be consumed as little as possible.

Over the years, Americans' fat intake appears to have been on a roller-coaster ride. In the 1930s, Americans were consuming about 34 percent of their calories from fat, but the figure climbed to around 42 percent by the mid-1960s. The amount of fat in the American diet then started a gradual descent and is currently at an all-time low of about 33 percent of calories consumed.[1] Although this reduction is promising, don't break out the hot fudge sundaes just yet. Measuring fat consumption only as a percentage of total calories can be misleading. That's because the total *grams* of fat we consume daily have increased about 4 percent since the early 1990s, and our total number of *calories* has increased about 10 percent.[2] In other words, Americans are eating more of both fat and calories, and the reason that the percentage of dietary fat has gone down is because the number of calories has gone up. The main source of this increase in calories is soft drinks, which are high in refined carbohydrates.

As you can see, the overall consumption of fat (and calories) in the United States is higher than it should be. But dietary fat is still essential for health, so how much should you eat?

You Need to Consume Some Fat Daily

The current Acceptable Macronutrient Distribution Range (AMDR) recommendation is that 20 to 35 percent of your daily calories should come from fat. Surprisingly, for some people—especially those who are sedentary or overweight—a very-low-fat diet (providing less than 20 percent of daily calories from fat) that is high in sugary carbohydrates may cause an *increase* in fat in the blood. For others, consuming more than 35 percent of their total daily calories from fat can perpetuate obesity, which is a risk factor for heart disease.[3]

As noted earlier, your body can make all the cholesterol it needs; therefore, you do not need to consume it. In fact, you should limit the amount of cholesterol you eat for the sake of your heart and arteries. Healthy individuals are advised to limit their dietary cholesterol to under 300 milligrams daily, on average.[6] That's only about 80 milligrams more than one egg. On average, men in the United States consume about 330 milligrams of cholesterol daily, whereas women eat slightly over 210 milligrams. Cholesterol is found in foods derived from animal sources, such as meats, eggs, milk, cheese, and butter. Margarine is made from plant oils; thus, it doesn't contain cholesterol. Table 11.1 lists a variety of foods and their cholesterol content.

Although consuming fat won't increase your weight unless you consistently eat more calories than you need, dietary fat has more than twice the calories per gram of carbohydrates or protein. Therefore, eating too many fatty foods can perpetuate a weight-management problem. Numerous studies have shown that reducing dietary fat can also reduce dietary calories, which can result in weight loss.[4] Consequently, controlling your fat intake can help control your weight.

According to the AMDR recommendation, if you need 2,000 calories daily to maintain your weight, you can consume between 44 and 74 grams of fat daily (Table 11.2). For heart health, you should consume no more than 10 percent of your calories, or 22 grams, from a combination of saturated fats and *trans* fats. (*Trans* fats are discussed later in this concept.)

To ensure that you are consuming enough linoleic acid and alpha-linolenic acid, a recommended amount has been set for these important nutrients. Five to 10 percent of the total calories in your diet should come from linoleic acid, and alpha-linolenic acid should make up 0.6 to 1.2 percent of your total calories.[5] These recommended amounts are based on estimated daily caloric needs, according to your gender and age. As you recall from Concept 10, adding a tablespoon of vegetable oil, such as canola or soybean oil, or a handful of nuts to your diet is an easy way to consume these important nutrients.

Table 11.1

How Much Cholesterol Is in Your Food?

	Cholesterol (mg)
Liver, 3 oz	324
Breakfast biscuit with egg and sausage, 1	302
Egg, 1 large	212
Shrimp, canned 3 oz	147
Fast-food hamburger, large, double-patty	122
Ice cream, soft-serve, vanilla, ½ cup	78
Beef, ground, cooked, 3 oz	77
Salmon, cooked, 3 oz	74
Chicken or turkey, breast, cooked, 3 oz	72
Lobster, cooked, 3 oz	61
Turkey, light meat, cooked, 3 oz	59
Egg noodles, 1 cup	53
Butter, 1 tbs	31
Cheddar cheese, 1 oz	30
Frankfurter, beef, 1	24
Milk, whole, 1 cup	24
Cheddar cheese, low-fat, 1 oz	6
Milk, skim, 1 cup	4

Data from: USDA National Nutrient Database for Standard Reference, Release 16. www.ars.usda.gov (accessed August 2003).

Table 11.2

Capping Your Fat Intake

If You Need This Many Calories to Maintain Your Weight	Eat No More Than This Much Daily	
	Fat (grams) (20–35% of total calories)	Saturated Fat and *Trans* Fat (grams) (<10% of total calories)
1,600	36–62	18
1,700	38–66	19
1,800	40–70	20
1,900	42–74	21
2,000	44–78	22
2,100	47–82	23
2,200	49–86	24
2,300	51–89	26
2,400	53–93	27
2,500	56–97	28
2,600	58–101	29
2,700	60–105	30
2,800	62–109	31

Sedentary women consume approximately 1,600 calories daily. Teenage girls, active women, and many sedentary men need approximately 2,200 calories daily. Teenage boys, many active men, and some very active women need about 2,800 calories daily. The percentage of calories from fat and the corresponding grams of fat can be calculated by multiplying your number of daily calories by 20% and 35% and then dividing those numbers by 9. (Fat provides 9 calories per gram.) To determine the amount of calories you should be eating daily, turn to Table 4.3 in Concept 4.

For example, if you consume 2,000 calories daily:

$$\underline{2{,}000} \times 0.20\ (20\%) = \underline{400}\ \text{calories} \div 9 = \underline{44}\ \text{grams}$$

$$\underline{2{,}000} \times 0.35\ (35\%) = \underline{700}\ \text{calories} \div 9 = \underline{78}\ \text{grams}$$

your range of fat intake should be 44 to 78 grams daily.

To find the maximum grams of saturated and *trans* fats that you should be consuming daily, repeat the process:

$$\underline{2{,}000} \times 0.10\ (10\%) = \underline{200}\ \text{calories} \div 9 = 22\ \text{grams}$$

The total amount of saturated fat and *trans* fat intake should be no more than 22 grams daily.

Eggs are an excellent source of protein, but egg yolks are high in cholesterol.

What Are the Best Food Sources of Fats?

Foods containing unsaturated fats are better for your health than foods high in saturated fat, cholesterol, and/or *trans* fat. (*Trans* fats will be discussed in the next section.) Where can you find the healthier fats in foods? Unsaturated fats are abundant in vegetable oils, such as soybean, corn, and canola oils, as well as soybeans, walnuts, flaxseeds, and wheat germ. Remember the figure showing the food sources of essential fatty acids in Concept 10 (Figure 10.9)? All of those foods are also excellent sources of unsaturated fats.

You should limit your intake of foods high in saturated fat. Most saturated fat in the diet comes from animal foods, such as fatty cuts of meat; whole-milk dairy products, such as cheese, butter, and ice cream; and the skin on poultry (Figure 11.1). Choosing lean meats and dairy foods, skinless poultry, and oil-based spreads can help you reduce the amount of saturated fat in your diet. Certain vegetable oils, such as coconut, palm, and palm kernel oils, are very high in saturated fat. Although food manufacturers now use these highly saturated tropical oils less often, they can still be found in foods such as candies, commercially made baked goods, and gourmet ice cream. Checking the ingredient label on food packages is the best way to find out if these oils are in the foods you eat.

Plant oils are rich in unsaturated fatty acids.

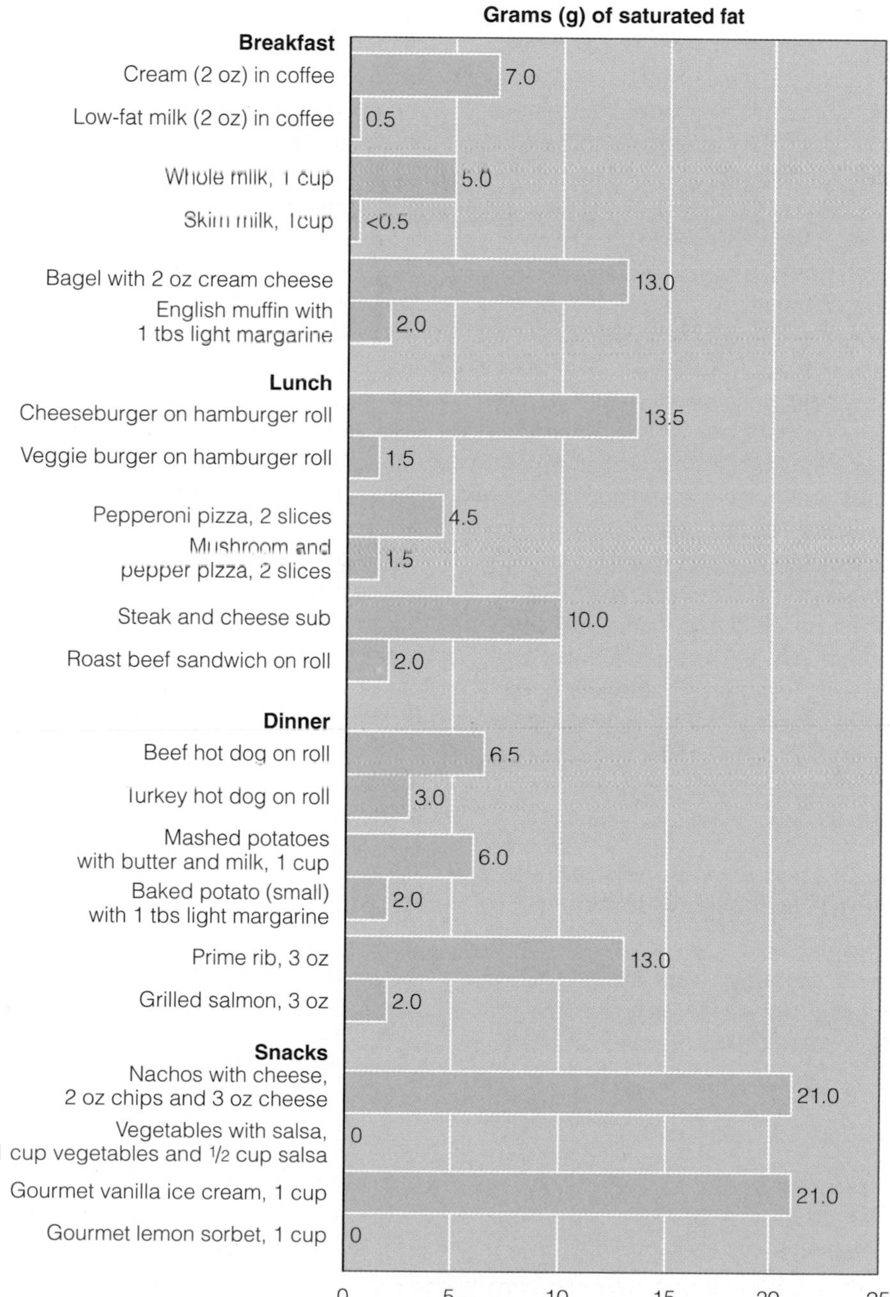

Figure 11.1 Where's the Saturated Fat in Your Food?
Choosing less-saturated-fat versions of your favorite foods and snacks can dramatically lower the amount of "sat" fat you consume.

The Mediterranean Diet: What Do People Living in the Mediterranean Do Differently?

The *Mediterranean Diet* doesn't refer to the diet of a specific country but, rather, to the dietary patterns found in several areas of the Mediterranean region—specifically, Crete (a Greek island), other areas of Greece, and southern Italy—in the early 1960s. Researchers were drawn to these areas because the people living there had very low rates of chronic diseases, such as heart disease and cancer, and a very long life expectancy. For example, the natives of Greece had a rate of heart disease that was 90 percent lower than that of Americans at that time.[1] Ironically, the people in Crete, in particular, were less educated, less affluent, and had less access to good medical care than Americans, so their health benefits could not be explained by education level, financial status, or a superior health care system.

Researchers found that, compared with the diets of affluent Americans, the diet in Crete was dramatically lower in foods from animal sources, such as meat, eggs, and dairy products, and higher in fat (mostly from olive oil and olives) and inexpensive grains, fruits, and vegetables. Because their diet was plant-based with few processed foods, their intake of heart-unhealthy *trans* fat was negligible. Research continues to support the benefits of a Mediterranean-style diet. A study in Greece showed that adherence to a traditional Mediterranean diet was associated with greater longevity. In another study, individuals who had experienced a heart attack, and then adopted a Mediterranean-style diet, had a 50 to 70 percent lower risk of recurrent heart disease compared with those following a more classic low-saturated-fat, low-cholesterol diet.[2]

The newly updated Mediterranean Diet Pyramid shown here was designed to reflect these dietary patterns and lifestyle habits.[3] Let's look a little closer at this pyramid, the dietary and lifestyle changes that support it, and some changes that you can make in your diet and lifestyle to reap similar benefits.

The Mediterranean Lifestyle

First, note that physical activity is front and center, at the base of this pyramid, reflecting the foundation of the Mediterranean way of life. This is an important concept, as the Mediterranean residents in the 1960s were very active and, not surprisingly, much leaner than Americans at that time. In addition to exercise, Mediterranean citizens enjoyed other lifestyle habits that have been known to promote good mental and physical health: they had a supportive community of family and friends; long, relaxing family meals, and afternoon naps.[4] Exercising daily, resting, and relaxing with family and friends are good health advice for all, no matter what diet you follow.

A Diet of Well-Seasoned Plants Fish, and Dairy Foods

Plant-based foods, such as whole grains, fruits, vegetables, legumes, and nuts, are the focus of the Mediterranean diet. In fact, over 60 percent of the calories of the diets in Crete in the 1960s were supplied by these high-fiber, nutritionally dense plant foods. In traditional Mediterranean-style eating, a combination of plant foods, such as vegetables and legumes ladled over couscous or pasta, was the focus of the meal.[5] Fresh bread, without margarine or butter, often accompanied the meal, and fruit was served as dessert. Herbs and spices provided rich, regional flavors to the cuisine.

Over 75 percent of the fat in the diets in Crete was supplied by olives and olive oil.[6] As previously discussed, vegetable oils are low in saturated fat, and olive oil, in particular, is high in monounsaturated fat.

Nonfat milk and yogurt and low- and reduced-fat cheeses can be enjoyed on a daily basis when eating a Mediterranean-style diet. A small amount of grated Parmesan cheese sprinkled over vegetables and a grain-based meal can provide a distinctly Mediterranean flavor. In addition, heart-healthy meals featuring fish and seafood should be enjoyed at least twice a week, following the Mediterranean example.

Occasional Poultry, Eggs, and Meat

Foods from animal sources were limited in the diet in Crete; local people consumed less than 2 ounces of meat and poultry daily.[7] They ate no more than four eggs a week, including those used in cooking and baking. Following this trend, the Mediterranean Diet Pyramid suggests eating limited amounts of poultry and eggs, and red meat on only an occasional basis.

Sweets, Water, and Wine

Historically, sweets were more prevalent during the holidays and fruit was the standard daily dessert.[8] Consequently, this pyramid recommends that the consumption of honey- or sugar-based sweets be limited. Water is recommended daily; the local population on Crete drank it throughout the day and with their meals. They also drank moderate amounts of wine, typically only with meals. Sometimes they mixed the wine with water, and many local women did not consume any alcohol. Although the pyramid depicts wine consumption on a daily basis, it is actually considered optional and based on personal preferences, family and medical history, and social situations.

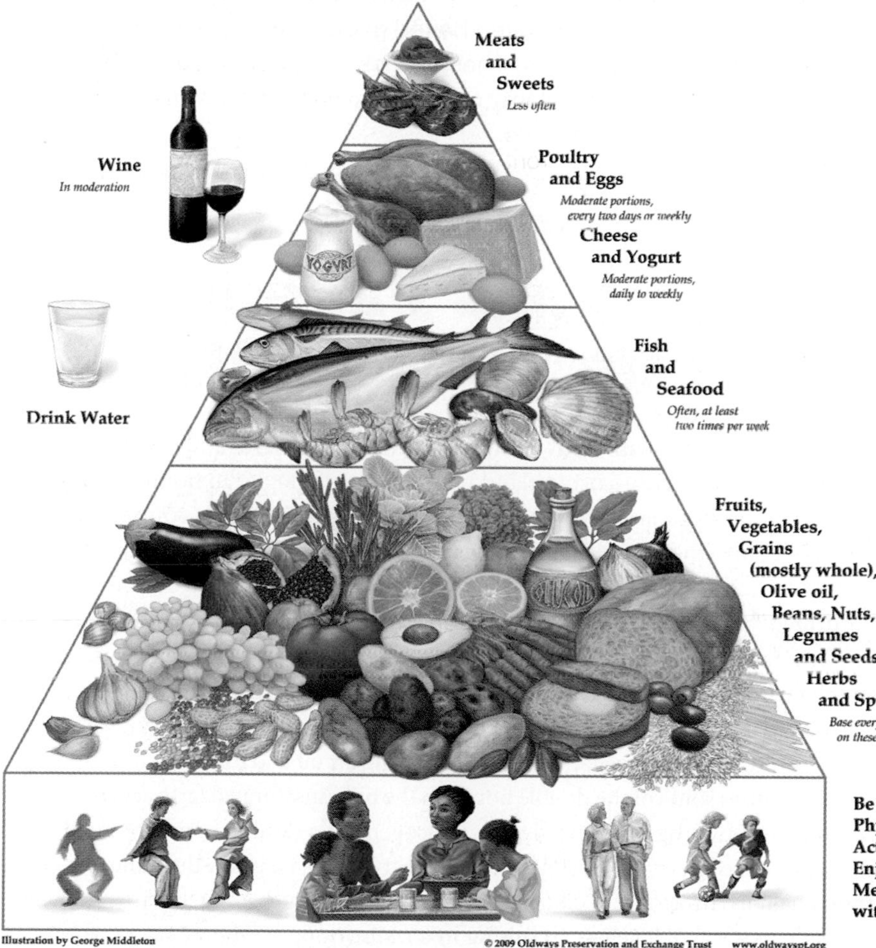

Traditional Healthy Mediterranean Diet Pyramid
A plant-based diet with minimal amounts of high-saturated-fat, high-sugar foods, coupled with daily physical activity, reflects the healthy habits of the Mediterranean lifestyle.

How Does the Mediterranean Diet Pyramid Compare with MyPyramid?

There are many food similarities between the Traditional Healthy Mediterranean Diet Pyramid and MyPyramid. Both emphasize the importance of regular physical activity, and both recommend a plant-based diet rich in grains, fruits, and vegetables and the daily consumption of dairy products. Mediterranean-style eating encourages the use of olive oil, a fat source that is rich in heart-healthy, unsaturated fat. Vegetable oils are also recommended by MyPyramid, but more modestly. Whereas the Mediterranean Diet Pyramid limits poultry, eggs and meat more than MyPyramid, both advise minimizing the intake of sweets. Both pyramids can be used as a foundation for a healthy diet. The key is to stick to the recommendations.

TABLE TIPS 

Nuts about Nuts?

Toss some nuts in your mealtime salad. Use less oil or salad dressing and more vinegar to adjust for the added calories.

Swap nuts for meat in meals, such as stir-fries. A third of a cup of nuts is equal to an ounce of red meat or chicken.

Add a tablespoon of nuts to your morning cereal, and use skim rather than reduced-fat milk to offset some of the extra calories.

Add a tablespoon of chopped nuts to your afternoon yogurt.

Add a handful of peanuts to your air-popped popcorn the next time you need a snack.

Because all fats and oils are a combination of fatty acids, however, it's not only impossible to eliminate saturated fat entirely from your diet; it's also unhealthy. Extreme avoidance of fats and oils can lead to the unnecessary elimination of certain foods—such as soybean and canola oils, lean meats, fish, poultry, and low-fat dairy foods—which can cause you to fall short of important nutrients, such as essential fatty acids, protein, and calcium. Rather, your goal should be to keep your dietary intake of saturated fat to less than 10 percent of your daily total calories.

Americans consume about 11 percent of their daily calories from saturated fat, so it's likely that you need to reduce your intake. Use Figure 11.1 to help you choose foods low in saturated fat at some of your meals and snacks.

The Take-Home Message **You need some fat in your diet, particularly the essential fatty acids, but you should limit saturated fats and *trans* fats. Your fat intake should range from 20 to 35 percent of your total calories. You do not need to eat cholesterol, since your body produces all it needs. Eating lean meats, skinless poultry, lean dairy products, and vegetable oils while limiting commercially prepared baked goods and snack items is a good strategy for overall good health. These foods will provide you with enough healthy unsaturated fats and plenty of essential fatty acids while limiting your intake of unhealthy, saturated fats.**

What Is *Trans* Fat and Where Do You Find It?

At one time, saturated fats from animal sources, such as lard, and highly saturated tropical plant oils, such as coconut and palm oils, were staples in home cooking and commercial food preparation. These saturated fats work well in commercial food products because they provide a rich, flaky texture to baked goods and are more resistant to **rancidity** than the unsaturated fats found in oils. (The double bonds in unsaturated fats make them more susceptible to being damaged by oxygen and thus becoming rancid.) Then, in the early twentieth century, a German chemist discovered the technique of **hydrogenation** of oils, which causes the unsaturated fatty acids in the oils to become more saturated; ***trans* fats** were born.

The process of hydrogenation involves heating an oil and exposing it to hydrogen gas, which causes some of the double bonds in the oil's unsaturated fatty acid to become saturated with hydrogen. Typically, the hydrogens of a double bond are lined up in what's called a *cis* (*cis* = same) configuration; that is, they are all on the same side of the carbon chain in the fatty acid. During hydrogenation, some hydrogens cross to the opposite side of the carbon chain, resulting in a *trans* (*trans* = cross) configuration (see Figure 11.2, next page). The newly configured fatty acid becomes a *trans* fatty acid.

rancidity The decomposition or spoiling of fats through oxidation.

hydrogenation Adding hydrogen to unsaturated fatty acids, making them more saturated and solid at room temperature, and resulting in *trans* fat.

***trans* fats** Fats primarily resulting from the hydrogenation of unsaturated fatty acids, a process used widely in commercially-made foods to add texture, longer shelf life and better resistance to rancidity. *Trans* fats are bad for heart health in numerous ways.

Trans Fats Are Found in Many Processed Foods

Trans fats provide a richer texture, a longer shelf life, and better resistance to rancidity than unsaturated fats, so food manufacturers use them in many commercially made food products. The first partially hydrogenated shortening, Crisco, was made from cottonseed oil; it became available in 1911.

Commercially made peanut butter doesn't have detectable levels of *trans* fatty acids. Although partially hydrogenated oil is used as a stabilizer in many peanut butter brands, the amount is insignificant.

Trans fats came into even more widespread commercial use when saturated fat fell out of favor in the 1980s. Research confirmed that saturated fat plays a role in an increased risk for heart disease, so food manufacturers reformulated many of their products to contain less saturated fat. The easiest solution was to replace the saturated fat with *trans* fats. Everything from cookies, cakes, and crackers to fried chips and doughnuts were made with *trans* fats to maintain their texture and shelf life. *Trans* fats were also frequently used for frying at fast-food restaurants.

We now know that *trans* fats are actually worse for heart health than saturated fat because they raise blood levels of the damaging type of cholesterol, called LDL cholesterol. At the same time, they lower the levels of healthy cholesterol, called HDL cholesterol, which protects your blood vessels and heart. We'll discuss this in more detail in Concept 12.

Trans fats provide an estimated 2.5 percent of the daily calories in the diets of adults in the United States. Of this amount, about 25 percent is from the naturally occurring *trans* fats found in meat and dairy foods.[7] It's unknown whether naturally occurring *trans* fats have the same heart-unhealthy effects as those that are created through hydrogenation; either way, the amount of *trans* fat in your diet should be kept as low as possible.

The major sources of *trans* fats are commercially prepared baked goods, margarines, fried potatoes, snacks, shortenings, and salad dressings.[8] Whole grains, fruits, and vegetables don't contain any *trans* fats, so eating a plant-based diet with few commercially prepared foods will go a long way toward preventing *trans* fat (and saturated fat) from overpowering your diet.

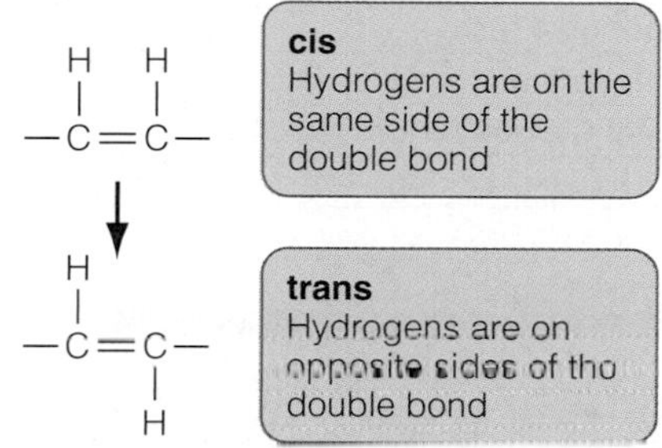

Figure 11.2 Creating *Trans* Fatty Acids Hydrogenation (adding hydrogen to an unsaturated fatty acid) creates a more saturated fatty acid. This process causes some double bonds to twist from a *cis* position to a *trans* position, thus creating a *trans* fatty acid.

Trans Fat Must Be Listed on Food Labels

To make consumers more aware of *trans* fats, in 2006 the Food and Drug Administration (FDA) mandated that most foods—and even some dietary supplements, such as energy bars—must list the grams of *trans* fats per serving on the Nutrition Facts panel on food labels.

The FDA estimates that providing this information to consumers to help them make healthier food choices will save between $900 million and $1.8 billion annually in reduced medical care costs, lost productivity, and pain and suffering.[9] The label allows you to quickly add up the amounts of saturated and *trans* fats listed, making it easier to monitor the amount of these fats that you consume. The FDA's labeling mandate had an effect on food producers as well: Hundreds of products were quickly reformulated to eliminate their *trans* fat content.

Now that you understand the importance of consuming adequate amounts of unsaturated fats, while limiting saturated and *trans* fats, you might be wondering how your own diet measures up. Table 11.1 displays a healthy range of recommended fat intake based on your daily caloric needs. (To figure out your approximate daily caloric needs, see Table 4.3 in Concept 4.) Rate Yourself to estimate how much fat, saturated fat, and *trans* fat you consume daily.

Krispy Kreme is just one of the many commercial bakeries to remove *trans* fat from their products.

Nutrition Facts
Serving Size 1 cup (228g)
Serving Per Container 2

Amount Per Serving	
Calories 250	Calories from Fat 110
	% Daily Value*
Total Fat 12g	18%
Saturated Fat 3g	15%
Trans Fat 3g	
Cholesterol 30g	
Sodium 470mg	
Potassium 700mg	20%
Total Carbohydrate 31g	10%
Dietary Fiber 0g	0%
Sugars 5g	
Protein 5g	
Vitamin A	4%
Vitamin C	2%
Calcium	20%
Iron	4%

* Percent Daily Values are based on a 2,000 calorie diet. Your Daily Values may be higher or lower depending on your calorie needs:

	Calories:	2,000	2,500
Total Fat	Less than	65g	80g
Sat Fat	Less than	20g	25g
Cholesterol	Less than	300mg	300mg
Sodium	Less than	2,400mg	2,400mg
Total Carbohydrate		300g	375g
Dietary Fiber		25g	30g

Data from: http://www.cfsan.fda.gov/-dms/transfat.html

The FDA requires that the *trans* fat content of foods be identified on the Nutrition Facts panel.

RATE YOURSELF 

How Much Fat Is in Your Diet?

Is your diet too overloaded with fat, saturated fat, and/or *trans* fat? Use the diet analysis software program, the Food Composition Table supplement, or food labels to track your fat consumption for a day. How does your actual intake compare with the amount recommended for you in Table 11.1?

Food Log

	Food/Drink	Amount	Fat (g)	Saturated Fat (g)	*Trans* Fat (g)
Breakfast					
Snack					
Lunch					
Snack					
Dinner					
Snack					
Total					

The Take-Home Message ***Trans*** **fats are made by heating oil and adding hydrogen gas to saturate the carbons of the fatty acids with hydrogen. They are actually more harmful to your heart and blood vessels than saturated fats.** ***Trans*** **fats are found in many commercially prepared foods and must be listed on food labels.**

What Are Fat Substitutes and How Can They Be Part of a Healthy Diet?

Although high in calories, nuts are an excellent source of antioxidants and essential fatty acids; they have no cholesterol and are low in saturated fat.

If you adore the taste and texture of creamy foods but don't adore the extra fat in your diet, you're not alone. A survey of Americans found that over 160 million people (79 percent of the adults in the United States) regularly choose lower-fat foods and beverages. The respondents cited their health as the major reason they were actively shopping for these foods.[10] To meet the growing demand, food manufacturers introduced more than 1,000 reduced-fat or low-fat products, from margarine to potato chips, each year throughout the 1990s.[11] Today, with few exceptions, you can probably find a lower-fat alternative for almost any high-fat food on the grocery store shelves. The keys to these products' containing less fat than their counterparts are **fat substitutes.**

Fat substitutes are designed to provide all the creamy properties of fat for fewer calories and total fat grams. Because fat has more than double the calories per gram of carbohydrates or protein, fat substitutes can reduce calories from fat by more than 50 percent without sacrificing taste and texture.

Fat Substitutes Can Be Carbohydrate-, Protein-, or Fat-Based

No single fat substitute works in all foods and with all cooking preparations, so there are several types of fat substitutes. As you can see in Table 11.3, they fall into three categories, depending on their primary ingredient: (1) carbohydrate-based substitutes, (2) protein-based substitutes, and (3) fat-based substitutes.[12]

fat substitutes Substances that replace added fat in foods by providing the creamy properties of fat with fewer calories and fewer total fat grams.

Table 11.3

The Lighter Side of Fat: Fat Substitutes

Name (trade name)	Calories (per gram)	Properties	How It's Used
Carbohydrate Based Substitute			
Fibers from grains (Betatrim)	1–4	Gelling, thickener	Baked goods, meats, spreads
Fibers, cellulose (cellulose gel)	0	Water retention, texture, mouthfeel	Sauces, dairy products, frozen desserts, salad dressings
Gums	0	Thickener, texture, mouthfeel, water retention	Salad dressings, processed meats
Polydextrose (Litesse)	1	Water retention, bulk	Baked goods, dairy products, salad dressings, cookies, gum
Modified food starch (Sta Slim)	1–4	Thickener, gelling, texture	Processed meats, salad dressings, frostings, fillings, frozen desserts
Protein-Based Substitute			
Microparticulated protein (Simplesse)	1–4	Mouthfeel	Dairy products, salad dressings, spreads
Fat-Based Substitute			
Mono- or diglycerides (Dur-Lo)	9*	Mouthfeel, moisture retention	Baked goods
Short-chain fatty acids (Salatrim)	5	Mouthfeel	Confections, baked goods
Olestra (Olean)	0	Mouthfeel	Savory snacks

*Less of this fat substitute is needed to create the same effect as fat, so the calories are reduced in foods using this product.

Data from: R. D. Mattes, "Fat Replacers," *Journal of the American Dietetic Association* 98 (1998): 463–468; J. Wylie-Rosett, "Fat Substitutes and Health: An Advisory from the Nutrition Committee of the American Heart Association," *Circulation* 105 (2002): 2800–2804.

Most fat substitutes are carbohydrate-based; they use plant polysaccharides, such as fiber, starches, gums, and cellulose, to help them retain moisture and to provide a fatlike texture.[13] For example, low-fat muffins might have fiber added to them to help retain the moisture that is lost when the fat content is reduced. Protein-based fat substitutes are created from the protein in eggs and milk. The protein is heated and broken down into microscopic "balls," which tumble over each other when you eat them, providing a creamy mouthfeel that's similar to that of fat. Fat-based substitutes are fats that have been modified either to provide the physical attributes of fat for fewer calories or to interfere with the absorption of fat in the body.[14] Mono- and diglycerides are used as emulsifiers in products such as baked goods and icings to provide moistness and mouthfeel. Although these remnants of fat have the same number of calories per gram as fat, fewer remnants are needed to create the same effect, so the total levels of calories and fat are reduced in the food product.[15]

One fat substitute, olestra (also known as Olean), is a mixture of sucrose and long-chain fatty acids. Unlike fat, which contains three fatty acids connected to a glycerol backbone, olestra contains six to eight fatty acids connected to sucrose. The enzymes that normally break apart fatty acids from their glycerol backbones during digestion cannot disconnect the fatty acids in olestra. Instead, olestra moves through the gastrointestinal tract intact and unabsorbed. Thus, it doesn't provide calories. Olestra is heat stable, so it can be used in baked and fried foods.

In 1996, the FDA approved olestra's use in salty snacks, such as potato and corn chips. An ounce of potato chips made with olestra can trim half the calories and all the fat. Because of olestra's inability to be absorbed in the body, there has been concern about its interference with the absorption of fat-soluble vitamins and carotenoids.[16] Consequently, the FDA has mandated that fat-soluble vitamins be added to olestra to offset these losses. Because olestra travels through your digestive tract untouched, there is also a concern that it may cause stomach cramps and loose stools. Although there have been anecdotal studies of individuals experiencing bouts of diarrhea and cramps after eating olestra-containing products, controlled research studies don't seem to support this claim.[17] Brian, the baseball player whom you read about in the beginning of this concept, can eat his light potato chips without developing the runs, although he should be concerned about consuming too many snacks that provide little nutrition.

Foods made with fat substitutes are not calorie free.

Reduced-Fat Products Are Not Calorie Free

The use of fat substitutes doesn't seem to be helping Americans curb their calories or weight, and one reason for this may be that people often overindulge in them. Another reason may be that many reduced-fat products actually have close to the same number of calories as their regular counterparts (Table 11.4). For example, some fat-free foods, especially baked goods, have reduced fat but increased carbohydrate, which adds back a significant number of calories. Similar to products containing sugar substitutes, reduced-fat and fat-free products still contain calories, and overconsuming calories leads to weight gain.

You should also be careful not to assume that fat-free foods are healthy, because many aren't. For example, jelly beans are fat free, but few people would agree that they're a healthy snack. Moreover, although choosing 4 ounces of fat-free chips will spare you half of the 600 calories found in the same amount of regular chips, those fat-free chips are displacing 300 calories of more nutritious foods,

Table 11.4

Fat-Free Doesn't Equal Calorie-Free

	Serving Size	Calories	Fat (g)	Carbohydrates (g)	Calories Saved
Fudgsicle Pop (Popsicle)	1 (1.65 fl oz)	60	1.5	12	
Fat-Free Fudgsicle Bar (Popsicle)	1 (1.75 fl oz)	60	0	13	**0**
Oatmeal Raisin Cookies (Archway)	1 (28 g)	120	3.5	20	
Fat-Free Oatmeal Raisin Cookies (Archway)	1 (31 g)	110	0	25	**10**
Fig Newtons (Nabisco)	2 (31 g)	110	2	22	
Fat-Free Fig Newtons (Nabisco)	2 (29 g)	90	0	22	**20**

Data from: Food manufacturers labels.

such as fruits, vegetables, and whole grains that you could and should be consuming in a balanced diet. If you want chips, enjoy just a handful rather than a full bag, alongside your whole-grain sandwich and large salad at lunch.

Fats impact more than your weight and waistline. They also impact the health of your heart. We'll discuss this in detail in Concept 12.

The Take-Home Message Fat substitutes are used in foods to provide the properties of fat for fewer grams of fat. Fat substitutes can be carbohydrate-based, protein-based, or fat-based. Some fat substitutes provide fewer calories and fat grams than regular fat, whereas others, such as olestra, aren't absorbed by the body and so are fat and calorie free. However, food products containing fat substitutes may provide almost as many calories as regular versions of these products. Reduced-fat and fat-free foods are not necessarily good for you and shouldn't displace naturally low-fat and healthy foods, such as fruits and vegetables, in your diet.

Check out these recipes and more suggestions at www.pearsonhighered.com/blake

UCook

Cranberry Turkey Wrap

Who said that turkey and cranberries are only for Thanksgiving? Try this festive and healthy wrap all year long.

UDo

Finding the Fat Content of Fast Foods

What has more saturated fat: a chocolate doughnut or a bagel with cream cheese? How much heart-unhealthy fat is in a large mocha coffee? Visit our website to test your assumptions—the answers may surprise you!

The Top Five Points to Remember

1. Approximately 20 to 35 percent of your total calories should come from fat. Your intake of saturated fat should be no more than 10 percent of your total calories. You do not need to consume cholesterol because your body makes what you need. Your diet should contain no more than 300 milligrams of cholesterol daily, on average.

2. Heart-healthy unsaturated fats are abundant in vegetable oils, such as soybean, corn, and canola oils; olive oil; and nut oils. Soybeans, nuts, avocados, and flaxseeds are also rich in unsaturated fats.

3. *Trans* fatty acids are created by hydrogenating unsaturated fatty acids; they have been used for decades in many processed foods. Your diet should be as low in *trans* fats as possible because they are harmful to your health. Thus, commercially prepared baked goods, snack items, and fried foods should be limited in your diet. The FDA requires that the level of *trans* fats in foods be listed on the Nutrition Facts panel.

4. Fat substitutes are designed to provide all the properties of fat but for fewer fat grams. Olestra is a fat substitute used in some snack items. It is not absorbed in the gastrointestinal tract and thus contributes no calories.

5. Fat substitutes can reduce calories from fat in a food by more than 50 percent. However, some fat-free foods, especially baked goods, have reduced fat but a similar number of calories as their traditional counterparts because carbohydrates have been added to the foods. Consequently, fat-free foods may not be lower in calories.

Test Yourself

1. Which of the following lunch and dinner combinations provides the greatest amount and variety of heart-healthy unsaturated fats for one day?
   a. a peanut butter sandwich at lunch and salmon at dinner
   b. a hamburger at lunch and macaroni and cheese at dinner
   c. a frozen yogurt parfait at lunch and a grilled chicken Caesar salad at dinner
   d. an egg salad sandwich at lunch and a pork chop at dinner
2. To be healthy, you need to consume how much cholesterol daily?
   a. over 300 milligrams
   b. 1,000 milligrams
   c. over 1,000 milligrams
   d. none
3. You should keep your dietary fat intake
   a. between 8 and 10 percent of your daily calories.
   b. between 20 and 35 percent of your daily calories.
   c. between 35 and 40 percent of your daily calories.
   d. under 500 milligrams daily.
4. *Trans* fats are
   a. a better choice in your diet than saturated fats.
   b. found only in commercially produced foods.
   c. known to have an unhealthy effect on your blood cholesterol levels.
   d. both a and c.
5. Olestra is
   a. a protein-based fat substitute.
   b. a fat substitute that does not provide any calories.
   c. highly unstable at high temperatures and cannot be used in fried or baked foods.
   d. a type of *trans* fat found in potato chips and other snack foods.

Answers

1. (a) The meal combinations of a peanut butter sandwich and salmon provide a greater amount and variety of healthy unsaturated fats than any of the other meal combinations.
2. (d) Because your body can make all the cholesterol it needs, you do not have to consume any dietary cholesterol. You should try to limit the amount of cholesterol you eat to no more than 300 milligrams daily.
3. (b) Your daily fat intake should be between 20 and 35 percent of your daily calories.
4. (c) Trans fats provide a double whammy for your heart because they raise the level of "bad" LDL cholesterol and lower the level of "good" HDL cholesterol in your body. They are thus considered more harmful to your health than saturated fats. We'll talk about heart health in more depth in Concept 12. Some foods, including meat and milk, contain naturally occurring trans fats.
5. (b) Olestra is a fat substitute that cannot be absorbed in the gastrointestinal tract and therefore does not provide any calories. It is made from sucrose and long-chain fatty acids, not proteins. Olestra is stable in heat, so it can be used in snack foods, such as chips, that are prepared at high temperatures.

Web Resources

- To learn more about *trans* fat and fat substitutes, visit the DA Q&A's Regarding Trans Fats at: www.cfsan.fda.gov/~dms/qatrans2.html
- Check out the Dietary Fats and Fat Replacers from the International Food Information Council. at: www.ific.org/nutrition/fats/index.cfm

12 Eat to Beat Heart Disease

1. Each year, **heart disease** kills more Americans than cancer and diabetes put together. **T/F**

2. **Smoking** increases the risk of heart disease. **T/F**

3. A high amount of **HDL cholesterol** in your blood is good for you. **T/F**

4. **Butter** is better for you than margarine. **T/F**

5. **Shellfish** contains more cholesterol than nuts. **T/F**

After his father suffered a heart attack last summer, Julio made some changes to his lifestyle to try to avoid his father's fate. He stopped smoking, began working out with weights, cut down on butter and eggs, and started taking fish-oil capsules every day. But he's still about 30 pounds overweight, and he finds it hard to resist the fatty meats and fried foods he grew up with. Then again, Julio is only 21. He has plenty of time to get fit, right?

What do you think of Julio's strategies to avoid heart disease? For instance, do you know how different types of foods affect your heart and what roles exercise, smoking, and other factors play? In this concept, you will learn some important facts about heart disease and debunk some common myths. You will also find out how to interpret blood cholesterol numbers, and learn some tips for keeping yours in the healthy range.

Answers

1. True. According to the National Center for Health Statistics, heart disease not only was the leading cause of death but also caused more deaths than cancer and diabetes put together. See page 1 to learn more.
2. True. Smoking damages the walls of blood vessels and increases the risk of having a heart attack. See page 4 for more.
3. True. High levels of HDL cholesterol can help reduce your risk for heart disease. Turn to page 7 to find out how.
4. False. Although stick margarines can contain heart-unhealthy *trans* fats, butter has more total cholesterol-raising fats than margarine and, so, is ultimately less healthy. Find out more on page 8.
5. True. Cholesterol is not found in foods from plant sources, including nuts. Check out page 9.

What Is Heart Disease and What Increases Your Risk?

Heart disease is a name that encompasses several disorders affecting the heart, including problems with heart valves, heartbeat irregularities, infections, and other problems. But the most common type of heart disease is *coronary heart disease*, which affects the blood vessels that serve the heart muscle and can lead to a heart attack.[1] That's the type we will focus on in this concept.

Heart disease has been the number-one killer of adults in the United States since 1918. Although it was once believed to be a greater danger to men than to women, heart disease actually takes the lives of more women than men. Each year, about 450,000 American women die from heart disease compared to about 400,000 deaths among men from the same cause.[2] Let's look at how heart disease develops, as well as the types of lipids that can accelerate it.

Heart Disease Begins with a Buildup in the Coronary Arteries

Heart disease develops when the coronary arteries—the blood vessels that supply oxygen and nutrients to the heart muscle—accumulate a buildup of substances, such as fat, cholesterol, and cellular materials, along their walls. This hardened buildup, called *plaque*, narrows the affected artery. As a result, blood flow through it becomes restricted, so less oxygen and fewer nutrients are delivered to nourish the tissue in that area. Without sufficient nourishment, that area of heart muscle can become damaged, and chest pains can result. If the vessel becomes completely blocked, the tissue in that area of heart muscle can die, and the person can experience a heart attack. Over 8 million Americans suffer a heart attack every year.

The condition in which the arteries become narrowed is called **atherosclerosis,** from the Greek word *athero-*, meaning a thick gruel or paste, plus *sclera*, meaning hardness (Figure 12.1). The exact cause of atherosclerosis is unknown, but researchers think it begins with an injury to the lining of the arteries. High blood levels of cholesterol and fat, high blood pressure, type 2 diabetes, and smoking likely contribute to this damage.

heart disease A term encompassing several disorders affecting the heart, of which coronary heart disease is the most common.

atherosclerosis Narrowing of the coronary arteries due to a buildup of debris along the artery walls.

Risk Factors for Heart Disease

There are many risk factors for heart disease (Table 12.1). You have control over some, but not all, of them.

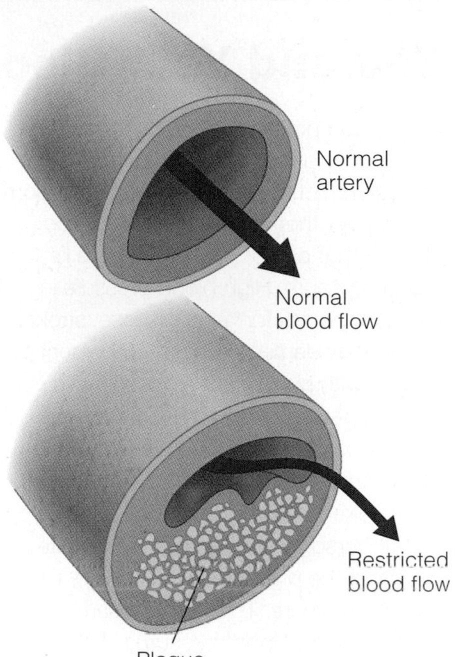

Figure 12.1 Atherosclerosis
When plaque builds up in a coronary artery, it narrows the passageway and reduces the flow of oxygen-rich blood to the heart.

Risk Factors You Can't Control

As your blood cholesterol level increases, so does your risk of developing heart disease and experiencing a heart attack. Your blood cholesterol level tends to rise with age until it stabilizes around the age of 65. Your gender also plays a role. Until menopause, which occurs around the age of 50, women tend to have a lower blood cholesterol level than men and a reduced risk for heart disease. After menopause, women's blood cholesterol levels tend to catch up and even surpass those of men of the same age. About one in eight American women between 45 and 64 years of age has heart disease, but this jumps to one in four women over the age of 65.[3]

High blood cholesterol levels can be partly determined by your genes. If your father or brother had signs of heart disease before age 55, or your mother or sister had them before age 65, then you are at a greater risk of getting heart disease. This means that Julio, in the opening story, has a higher than average risk for heart disease.

Having diabetes also increases your risk for heart disease. Although the less common form, type 1 diabetes, is not preventable, the more common form, type 2 diabetes, can be controlled.

Risk Factors You Can Control

For people with type 2 diabetes, keeping the disease under control can help dramatically lower their risk for heart disease.[4] As you read in Concept 9, type 2 diabetes can be managed, and even prevented, through diet and lifestyle changes. Sometimes, the use of prescription medication is also needed to control type 2 diabetes. Diseases of the heart and blood vessels are the cause of death of an estimated 75 percent of adults with diabetes.

Chronic high blood pressure can damage your arteries. Blood pressure is the force of your blood against the walls of your arteries. A blood pressure reading consists of two numbers. The top number, called the *systolic pressure*, is the pressure within your arteries when your heart contracts. The bottom number, called the *diastolic pressure*, is the pressure in your arteries a moment later, when your heart is relaxed. A *normal blood pressure* is considered less than 120 millimeters of mercury (Hg) for the systolic pressure and less than 80 millimeters Hg for the diastolic pressure. You might hear this referred to as "120 over 80." A blood pressure of 140/90 or higher is considered to be **hypertension,** or high blood pressure.

People with hypertension constantly have a higher than normal force pushing against the walls of their arteries. This is thought to damage the artery lining and accelerate the buildup of plaque. Chronic high blood pressure also causes the heart to work

Table 12.1
Risk Factors for Heart Disease

Factors You Cannot Control	Factors You Can Control
Your age and gender	Developing type 2 diabetes
Your family history of heart disease	High blood pressure
Having type 1 diabetes	Smoking
	Physical inactivity
	Excess weight
	A low HDL "good" cholesterol level
	A high LDL "bad" cholesterol level

hypertension High blood pressure, generally measured as a level of "140 over 90" or higher.

You and Your Blood Pressure

High blood pressure, or hypertension, is an increasing problem in the United States. In fact, if you were sitting in a room with three other adults, there is a good chance that one of you would have high blood pressure. High blood pressure increases the risk for heart disease, stroke, and kidney damage.[1] Up to 30 percent of people with high blood pressure have "white coat hypertension." This refers to the phenomenon whereby an individual's blood pressure measurement is elevated when taken at a doctor's office or clinic by a staff person (typically wearing a white lab coat) but the pressure is normal when taken elsewhere. This isn't the same as constant high blood pressure.

Why Is Hypertension a Silent Killer?

Hypertension, a blood pressure of 140/90 millimeters of mercury (Hg) or above, happens gradually. As blood pressure begins to rise above normal—that is, systolic pressure above 120 and diastolic pressure above 80—it is classified as *prehypertension*. Many individuals with prehypertension will develop hypertension if they don't lower their blood pressure.

Hypertension is referred to as the "silent killer" because there are no outward symptoms that your pressure is dangerously elevated, and you can have hypertension for years without knowing it. The only way to be sure you don't have it is to have your blood pressure checked regularly.

People with chronic high blood pressure have a higher than normal force pounding against the walls of their arteries, which makes the walls thicker and stiffer, contributing to atherosclerosis. The heart becomes enlarged and weakened, as it has to work harder to pump enough oxygen- and nutrient-laden blood throughout the body. This can lead to fatigue, shortness of breath, and heart attack. Hypertension can also damage the arteries leading to the brain, kidneys, and legs, which increases the risk for stroke, kidney failure, and partial amputation of a leg.[2]

Can You Control Your Hypertension?

There are factors that increase the chances of developing hypertension, some of which you can control and others you cannot.

Your family history, the aging process, and your race can all affect the likelihood that you will develop high blood pressure. These are the risk factors you can't control. If your parents, siblings, and/or grandparents have or had hypertension, you are at a higher risk of developing it yourself. Typically, the risk for hypertension increases with age. It is more likely to occur after the age of 35 for men, and women generally experience it after menopause. Hypertension is more prevalent in African-Americans and tends to occur earlier and be more severe than in Caucasians.[3]

The good news is that there are more risk factors you *can* control than those you can't. You can change a number of dietary and lifestyle habits to help reduce your risk. Chief among these are your weight and your physical activity level. Individuals who are obese are twice as likely to have hypertension as those at a healthy weight. Even a modest weight loss can have an impact. Losing as little as 10 pounds can reduce a person's blood pressure, and may actually prevent hypertension in

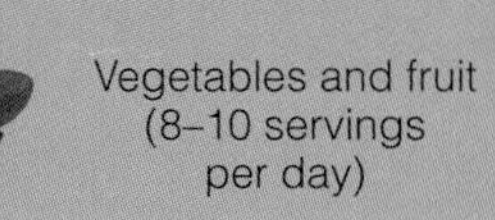

The DASH diet, which is rich in whole grains, fruits, vegetables, and low-fat dairy foods, can help lower blood pressure.

harder than normal and can lead to an enlarged heart. For more information on hypertension, check out the accompanying box feature, "You and Your Blood Pressure."

Smoking also damages the walls of the arteries and accelerates atherosclerosis and heart disease. In fact, women smokers are two to six times more likely to have a heart attack than women who don't smoke. Male smokers also increase their risk for heart disease.[5]

overweight individuals even if they haven't yet reached a healthy weight. Additional weight loss can have an even more dramatic effect. Regular physical activity can lower blood pressure even if weight loss hasn't occurred.[4]

You can also control your alcohol consumption, which affects your risk of developing high blood pressure. Studies have shown that drinkers who consumed three to six drinks daily and then reduced their alcohol consumption by 67 percent, on average, were able to reduce their systolic pressure by over 3 millimeters Hg and their diastolic pressure by 2 millimeters Hg.[5] Less drinking and more physical activity is the name of the game when it comes to keeping high blood pressure at bay.

Finally, eating a balanced diet is a proven strategy to lower your blood pressure. A large research study, called the Dietary Approaches to Stop Hypertension (DASH) study, followed people on three different diets. One group ate a typical American diet: low in fruits, vegetables, and dairy products and high in fat, saturated fat, and cholesterol. The second group ate a diet that was rich in just fruits and vegetables. The third group ate the DASH diet, which was a balanced diet lower in fat, saturated fat, cholesterol, and sweets and high in whole grains, fruits, vegetables, and low-fat dairy products. In fact, the DASH diet was very similar to the diet recommended by MyPyramid (see figure).

The individuals in the study who followed the DASH diet experienced a significant reduction in blood pressure compared with those following the other two diets. A follow-up to the DASH study, called the DASH-Sodium study, went one step further and showed that the overall best diet combination for lowering blood pressure is the DASH diet plus consuming only 1,500 milligrams of sodium daily.[6]

The table shows how effective each of these changes can be once you decide to take charge of your diet and lifestyle.

Take Charge of Your Blood Pressure!

Diet and lifestyle changes help reduce blood pressure and help prevent hypertension.

If You	By	Your Systolic Blood Pressure* May Be Reduced By
Reduce your sodium intake	Keeping dietary sodium consumption to no more than 2,400 mg daily	8–14 mm Hg
Lose excess weight	An amount that allows you to maintain a normal, healthy body weight	5–20 mm Hg for every 22 lbs of weight loss
Stay physically active	Partaking in 30 minutes of aerobic activity (brisk walking) on most days of the week	4–9 mm Hg
Drink alcohol moderately	Limiting consumption to no more than 2 drinks daily for men and 1 drink daily for women	2–4 mm Hg
Follow the DASH diet	Consuming a heart-healthy DASH diet that is abundant in fruits and vegetables and low-fat dairy products	8–14 mm Hg

*Controlling the systolic pressure is more difficult than controlling the diastolic pressure, especially for individuals 50 years of age and older. Therefore, it is the primary focus for lowering blood pressure. Typically, as systolic pressure goes down with diet and lifestyle changes, the diastolic pressure will follow.

Data adapted from: A. V. Chobanian et al., The Seventh Report of the Joint National Committee on Prevention, Detection, Evaluation, and Treatment of High Blood Pressure, *Journal of the American Medical Association,* 289 (2003): 2560–2572.

Being inactive and being overweight are risk factors for heart disease. Thus, regular exercise can help improve your blood cholesterol levels as well as help you manage your weight.

The last two risk factors listed in Table 12.1 are a low HDL cholesterol level and a high LDL cholesterol level. We'll explore these factors shortly.

Other Potential Risk Factors

Researchers are continually searching for clues, or "markers," in the blood, besides cholesterol levels, that signal the presence of heart disease. Here are a few:

- A high level of the amino acid homocysteine may injure arteries and promote the development of atherosclerosis.
- A high level of a protein called C-reactive protein can indicate inflammation in the walls of the arteries, which can lead to plaque formation.
- The presence in the blood of *Chlamydia pneumoniae*, a bacterium that can cause pneumonia and other respiratory infections, may also damage artery walls.
- A lipid-protein compound called Lp(a) is being investigated for its role in promoting heart disease.

Although the name sounds mysterious, *syndrome X*, also called *metabolic syndrome*, is a cluster of many factors that increase the risk for heart disease. These include abdominal obesity (too much weight around the middle) and insulin resistance, which we discussed in Concept 9. Being overweight and inactive increases the risk for insulin resistance, and exercise and weight reduction can help reduce all of the risk factors associated with this syndrome.

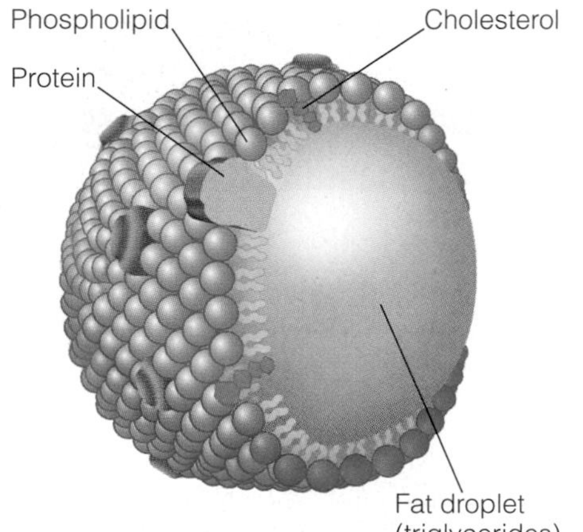

Figure 12.2 Chylomicron
A chylomicron is one type of lipoprotein.

The Take-Home Message **Heart disease, the leading cause of death in the United States, develops when atherosclerosis causes a narrowing of the coronary arteries that deliver oxygen and nutrients to the heart muscle. Risk factors you can't control are your age and gender, your family history of heart disease, and type 1 diabetes. Risk factors you can control are the prevention and control of type 2 diabetes, high blood pressure, smoking, physical inactivity, excess weight, a low HDL cholesterol level, and a high LDL cholesterol level. Syndrome X is a group of risk factors that collectively increase the risk for heart disease.**

What Is High Blood Cholesterol?

In Concept 10, you learned that fats are not soluble in watery blood, so if they are to travel in your bloodstream they need to be packaged inside a substance that is water soluble. For this job, the body uses proteins. The resulting molecule is called a **lipoprotein**. These capsule-shaped fat "carriers" have an outer shell high in protein and phospholipids and an inner compartment that carries the insoluble fat, as well as cholesterol, through your watery lymph and bloodstream. One example of a lipoprotein that you learned about in Concept 10 is a chylomicron (Figure 12.2). Recall that chylomicrons carry digested fat and other lipids through the lymphatic system into the blood. After the fat portion is removed from the chylomicron, the remnants go to the liver to be dismantled.

The liver produces other lipoproteins with different roles in your body:

- Very-low-density lipoprotein (VLDL)
- Low-density lipoprotein (LDL)
- High-density lipoprotein (HDL)

lipoprotein A capsule-shaped fat "carrier" that enables fats and cholesterol to travel through the lymph and blood.

low-density lipoprotein (LDL) A lipoprotein that deposits cholesterol in the walls of the arteries. Because this can lead to heart disease, LDL is referred to as the "bad" cholesterol carrier.

high-density lipoprotein (HDL) A lipoprotein that removes cholesterol from the tissues and delivers it to the liver to be used in the production of bile or to be excreted from the body. Because of this, it is known as the "good" cholesterol carrier.

Although all lipoproteins contain fat, phospholipids, cholesterol, and protein, the proportion of these substances differs in the various types. Protein is denser than fat, so the proportion of protein in these lipoproteins determines their overall density (Figure 12.3).

For example, *very low-density lipoproteins (VLDLs)* are composed mostly of triglycerides and have very little protein, so they are considered to be of very low density. **Low-density lipoproteins (LDLs),** which are mostly made up of cholesterol, have more protein than VLDLs but less than **high-density lipoproteins (HDLs)**, which have the highest density. The protein in the lipoproteins helps them perform their functions in your body. For example, the high protein content in HDLs not only helps remove cholesterol from your cells but also enables the HDLs to expand and contract according to the amount of fat and cholesterol being carried.

Why is the proportion of protein in a lipoprotein important? Each lipoprotein has a different role. The main role of the VLDLs is to deliver fat, made in the liver, to your tissues. Once the fat is delivered, the VLDL remnants are converted into LDLs. The LDLs deliver cholesterol to your cells. LDLs are often referred to as "bad" cholesterol because they deposit cholesterol in the walls of your arteries and thus can contribute to heart disease. To help you remember this, you may want to think of the **L** in **L**DL as meaning of "Little" health benefit.

The HDLs, as mentioned previously, are mostly protein. They remove cholesterol from dying cells and arterial plaques and deliver it to your liver to be used to make bile or to be excreted from your body. For this reason, HDLs are often referred to as "good" cholesterol. An easy way to remember this is to think of the **H** in **H**DL as referring to "Healthy" (Figure 12.4).

Studies have shown that a low amount of LDL cholesterol and a high amount of HDL cholesterol in your blood will reduce your risk for heart disease (see Table 12.1). Starting around age 20, you should have your blood tested at least once every five years to get your "lipoprotein profile" showing the total cholesterol, the LDL cholesterol, and the HDL cholesterol levels in your blood. Table 12.2 on the next page explains how to interpret your lipoprotein profile numbers.

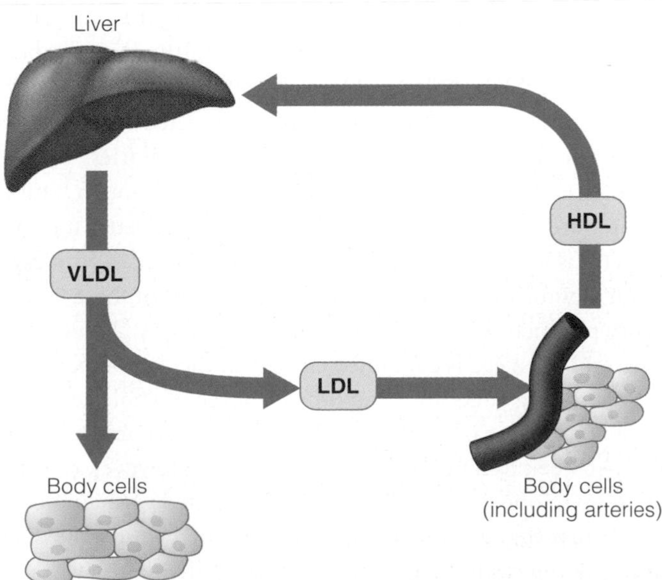

Figure 12.4 Roles of Lipoproteins
VLDLs deliver fat made in your liver to your cells. LDLs deposit cholesterol in the walls of your arteries. HDLs remove cholesterol from your cells and artery walls and deliver it to your liver.

Figure 12.3 Lipoproteins
Lipoproteins vary due to their composition.

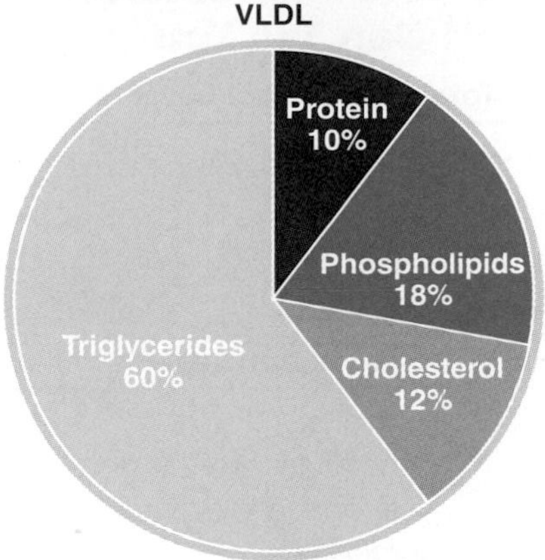

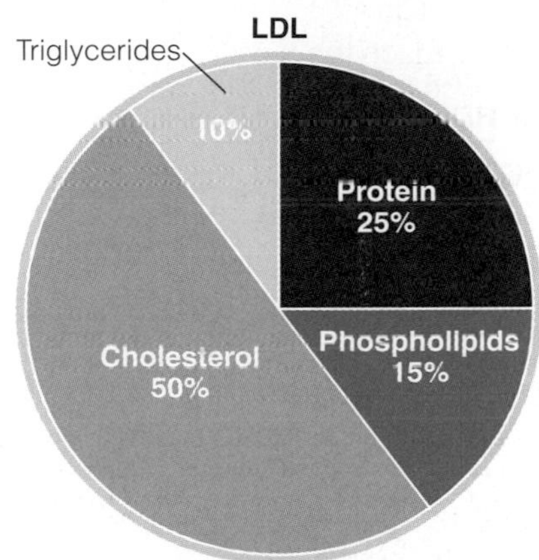

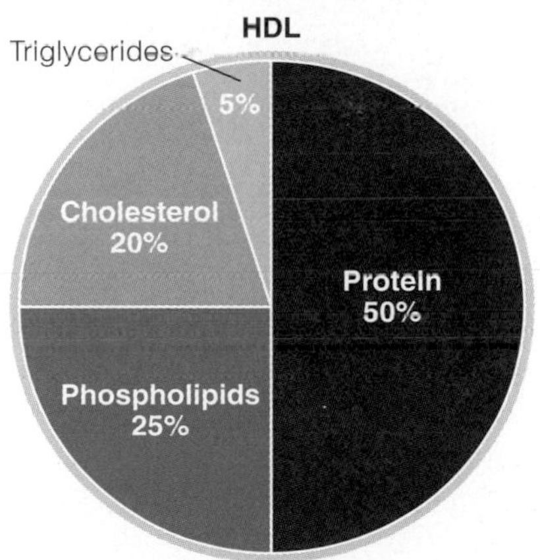

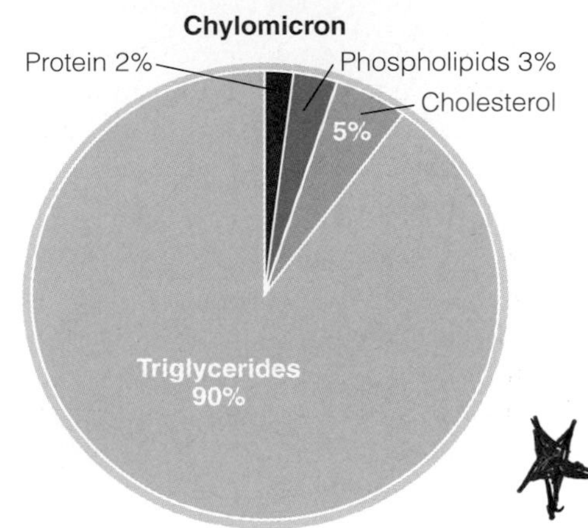

Table 12.2

What Your Cholesterol Level* Can Tell You

If Your Total Cholesterol Level Is	
<200	Fabulous! Keep up the good work!
200–239	Borderline high
≥240	High

If Your LDL Cholesterol Level Is	
<100	Fabulous! Congratulations!
100–129	Near or above optimal
130–159	Borderline high
160–189	High
190	Much too high!

If Your HDL Cholesterol Level Is	
≥60	Fabulous!
40–59	Good
>40	Too low

*All lipoprotein levels are measured in milligrams of cholesterol per deciliter of blood (mg/dl).

Data from: National Cholesterol Education Program, *Detection, Evaluation, and Treatment of High Blood Cholesterol in Adults (Adult Treatment Panel III)*. (National Institutes of Health Publication, May 2001, No. 01-3290).

The Take-Home Message Lipoprotein fat "carriers" include chylomicrons, VLDLs, LDLs, and HDLs. The VLDLs are converted to "bad" LDL cholesterol, which can deposit cholesterol in the walls of your arteries. The "good" HDL cholesterol removes cholesterol from your arteries and delivers it to your liver to be used to make bile or to be excreted from your body.

How Can You Improve Your Lipoprotein Profile?

The good news is that you can make diet and lifestyle changes to help lower your LDL cholesterol level. In this section, we'll discuss limiting saturated fats, *trans* fats, and dietary cholesterol, as well as adding foods to your diet that may help lower your LDL cholesterol levels. Other dietary and lifestyle factors can also affect both your LDL and your HDL cholesterol levels.

Minimize Saturated Fats, *Trans* Fats, and Cholesterol in Your Diet

In general, saturated fats raise your LDL cholesterol level, while unsaturated fats, when they replace saturated fats in your diet, have a cholesterol-lowering effect. (Note that saturated fats in your diet will raise your blood cholesterol level more than cholesterol in your diet will.) Typically, the more saturated fats you consume, the higher the LDL cholesterol levels in your blood.

Americans eat about five times more saturated fat than *trans* fat. A food that is low in *trans* fats can still be unhealthy for your heart if it is high in saturated fat. For example, years ago, many people switched from using stick margarine, which is high in *trans* fat, to butter, thinking that butter was better for their blood cholesterol levels. However, per Table 12.3 on page 9, although butter has less *trans* fat than stick margarine, if you combine the saturated fat and the *trans* fat in each spread, margarine is still better for your cholesterol levels. Decreasing the *trans* fats in your diet at the expense of increasing the saturated fat isn't healthy for your heart. When it comes to lowering your LDL cholesterol level, both types of fats should be limited in your diet. For your heart's sake, cholesterol-raising saturated and *trans* fats combined should contribute no more than 10 percent of your daily calories.

Dietary cholesterol raises your LDL cholesterol level, although saturated fats and *trans* fats raise it more. The less cholesterol in your diet, the better it is for your heart. Dietary cholesterol is found only in foods from animal sources, with egg yolks being a significant contributor in the diet.[6] Limiting the amount of these foods and choosing low-fat dairy products will cut down fat and trim dietary cholesterol.

The cholesterol in an egg is contained entirely in the yolk—the egg white is cholesterol free. Because egg yolks are a significant source of cholesterol in Americans' diets, the National Institutes of Health (NIH) recommends consuming no more than four egg yolks per week to help prevent heart disease. However, research now suggests that eating up to one egg daily may *not* be associated with an increased risk for heart disease. Because eggs are also a good source of many nutrients, such as protein and vitamin B_{12}, some health professionals suggest lifting the weekly cap on egg yolks for healthy individuals and focusing instead on keeping dietary cholesterol to no more than 300 milligrams daily, regardless of the source.[7] Hence, you can eat egg yolks more often if you avoid other sources of dietary cholesterol.

Table 12.3

The Cholesterol-Raising Effects of Popular Foods

Food	Total Fat	Saturated Fat	*Trans* Fat	Total Cholesterol-Raising Fats (saturated fats + *trans* fats)
Spreads				
Butter, 1 tbs	**11**	**7.0**	0.5	7.5
Margarine (stick), 1 tbs	**11**	**2.0**	3.0	5.0
Margarine (tub), 1 tbs	**6.5**	**1.0**	0.5	1.5
Commercially Prepared Foods and Snacks				
French fries, medium (fast-food)	**27**	**6.5**	8.0	14.5
Doughnut, 1	**18**	**4.5**	5.0	9.5
Potato chips, small bag	**11**	**2.0**	3.0	5.0
Cookies, 3	**6**	**1.0**	2.0	3.0

Data adapted from: Center for Food Safety and Applied Nutrition, Questions and Answers about *Trans* Fat Nutrition Labeling. CFSAN Office of Nutritional Products, Labeling and Dietary Supplements. www.cfsan.fda.gov/~dams/qatrans2.html (accessed 2006); U.S. Department of Agriculture, National Nutrient Database for Standard Reference, Release 15, 2002. www.nal.usda.gov/fnic/foodcomp/search.

Some shellfish, such as shrimp, are also high in cholesterol; however, they are very low in saturated fat and contain some heart-healthy omega-3 fatty acids. Lobster has less than one-third the amount of cholesterol of shrimp and is very low in total fat. Unfortunately, the relatively high price of these shellfish foods limits their consumption for many people.

Because cholesterol is not found in plant-based foods, you won't find it in vegetables, fruits, pasta, nuts, peanut butter, or vegetable oils. The best way to minimize your dietary cholesterol intake is to limit your portions of lean meat, skinless poultry, and fish to about 6 ounces daily, use only low-fat or nonfat dairy foods, use vegetable oils more often than butter, keep your consumption of baked goods to a minimum, and fill up on cholesterol-free fruits, vegetables, and whole grains.

Now that you've learned about the food sources of cholesterol, you might be wondering how your own diet measures up. Are you eating too much cholesterol? Rate Yourself and find out!

RATE YOURSELF 

Are You Eating Too Much Dietary Cholesterol?

On most days of the week:

1. I eat more than 6 ounces of meat or poultry.
   True ☐ **False** ☐
2. I drink whole or 2 percent milk.
   True ☐ **False** ☐
3. I eat full-fat cheese, such as cheddar, American, or feta.
   True ☐ **False** ☐
4. I use butter rather than margarine.
   True ☐ **False** ☐
5. I eat at least one egg.
   True ☐ **False** ☐

Answers

If you answered "true" to all of these questions, your diet could stand some cholesterol trimming.

If you answered "true" to fewer than three of these questions, congratulate yourself!

If you answered "true" to none of these questions, you are a superstar!

Eat More Fish

Over a decade ago, researchers studied the Greenland Eskimos' regular consumption of fatty fish (approximately 14 ounces a day), which is rich in two omega-3 fatty acids: eicosapentaenoic acid (EPA) and docosahexaenoic acid (DHA). These substances played a key role in the Eskimos' low incidence of death from heart disease.[8] Ongoing research supports the protective roles EPA and DHA may play in reducing the risk for heart disease and stroke. These omega-3 fatty acids may prevent irregular heartbeat, reduce plaque formation and atherosclerosis, mildly lower blood pressure, lower the level of fat in the blood, and modestly increase the amount of good HDL cholesterol in the blood, to name just a few benefits. In fact, studies have shown that eating slightly over an ounce or more of fish daily may help reduce your risk of dying from heart disease, and consuming even one fish meal per week may help reduce your overall risk for heart attack.

The American Heart Association (AHA) recommends that you eat at least two servings of fish (particularly fatty fish, such as salmon, sardines, or herring) per week

TABLE TIPS 

Easy Ways to Add Fish to Your Diet

Flake canned salmon over your lunch or dinner salad.

Add tuna to cooked pasta and vegetables and toss with a light salad dressing for a quick pasta salad meal.

Order baked, broiled, or grilled fish when dining out.

Try a shrimp cocktail on your next restaurant visit.

to obtain these omega-3 fatty acids. But, don't try to meet this quota at the fast-food drive-through. Fried fish that is commercially prepared tends to have few of these fatty acids and is often fried in unhealthy fat. Note also some precautions regarding fish consumption in the box feature "Mercury and Fish" on page 11.

Although consuming some omega-3 fatty acids is good, eating too much may not be wise. Because EPA and DHA interfere with blood clotting, consuming more than 3 grams—which typically happens only by taking supplements—can increase the risk for excessive bleeding and a certain type of stroke (blockage or rupture of a blood vessel in the brain).[9] Because of these potential negative effects, omega-3 fatty acid supplements (fish-oil supplements) should be taken only with the advice and guidance of a doctor. (Eating large amounts of fish-oil supplements can also leave a less than appealing fishy aftertaste in your mouth.) However, consuming approximately 1 gram of EPA and DHA daily from fish may provide some protection against heart disease without any known adverse risks.[10] In our opening story, Julio would be better off skipping the fish-oil capsules and eating at least two fish meals weekly. By eating more fish rather than meat, he would also reduce the heart-unhealthy saturated fat in his diet.

Americans currently consume only about 0.1 to 0.2 gram of EPA and DHA daily. The Table Tips on this page suggest a few quick ways to add fish to your diet. Think of fish as food for your heart!

Try substituting tofu for meat or poultry in your next stir-fry!

Eat More Plant Foods

In addition to fish, the AHA recommends that you consume plant foods, such as soybean and canola oils, walnuts, and flaxseeds, that are high in alpha-linolenic acid. As mentioned in Concept 10, some alpha-linolenic acid is converted in the body to heart-healthy omega-3 fatty acids.

Eating more plant foods high in viscous, soluble fiber may be one of the easiest ways to decrease your LDL cholesterol level. In reviewing over 65 studies, researchers found that each gram of viscous, soluble fiber consumed (in the range of 2 to 10 grams daily) from oatmeal, oat bran, legumes (such as dried beans), psyllium, or pectin, lowered LDL cholesterol levels over 2.0 mg/dl on average.[11] While the DRI for fiber ranges from 20 to 38 grams daily, consuming about half this amount—or 10 to 25 grams of viscous, soluble fiber—can help decrease high LDL cholesterol levels. Increasing the soy in your diet may also help reduce your risk for heart disease.[12] Soy, a protein source low in saturated fat, can be used in place of meat in many dishes.

Although all plant foods are cholesterol free, they do contain **phytosterols,** which are substances similar in structure to cholesterol that are found in the plant's cell membranes. Plant sterols can help lower LDL cholesterol levels by competing with cholesterol for absorption in the intestinal tract. With less cholesterol being absorbed, there is less in the blood. Plant sterols occur naturally in soybean oil, many fruits, vegetables, legumes, sesame seeds, nuts, cereals, and other plant foods.

In a study of over 150 people with mildly high cholesterol levels, a margarine containing a plant sterol was shown to reduce LDL cholesterol levels by approximately 14 percent after one year of use.[13] Products such as margarines and soft-gel tablets that contain plant sterols are now available.

phytosterols Naturally occurring substances found in plants. Phytosterols lower LDL cholesterol levels by competing with cholesterol for absorption in the intestinal tract.

Load Up on Antioxidants and Phytochemicals

You might think that a substance that starts with the prefix anti can't be good for you. However, the antioxidant vitamins C and E and beta-carotene appear to be "pro" heart health. Foods rich in vitamins C and E and beta-carotene also contain other important

Mercury and Fish

Although the health benefits of eating fish are well established, not everyone should be eating unlimited amounts of *all* types of fish. In fact, pregnant and nursing women, women of childbearing age who may become pregnant, and young children should avoid certain types of seafood that may contain high amounts of methylmercury. This form of mercury can be harmful to the developing nervous system, especially during the first trimester of pregnancy, a time when women may not even realize that they are pregnant.[7]

Although mercury occurs naturally in nature, it is also a by-product of industrial processes and pollution. The airborne form of mercury accumulates on the surface of streams and oceans and is transformed by bacteria in the water into the toxic form of methylmercury.[8] Fish absorb the methylmercury from the water or get it by eating the organisms that live in the water. Because the ingested methylmercury accumulates over time, larger fish, such as swordfish, shark, king mackerel, and tilefish (golden bass or golden snapper), have the highest concentration of methylmercury, as they have a longer life span and feed on other, smaller fish.

The Food and Drug Administration (FDA) recommends that women of childbearing age and young children avoid eating these four types of fish. Pregnant women and women of childbearing age can eat up to 12 ounces weekly of other types of cooked fish, including shellfish, and should choose from a variety of fish. Luckily, the 10 most popular types of seafood (canned *light* tuna, shrimp, pollock, salmon, cod, catfish, clams, flatfish, crabs, and scallops) contain low amounts of methylmercury. Canned albacore (white) tuna has more mercury than the light variety, so it should be limited to no more than 6 ounces weekly.[9]

While the FDA regulates all commercial fish, the Environmental Protection Agency (EPA) oversees all freshwater fish caught recreationally, such as by family members and friends. This agency recommends that women who are or may become pregnant, nursing mothers, and young children limit their consumption of freshwater fish to 6 ounces of cooked fish weekly for adults and 2 ounces of cooked fish weekly for children. If you eat noncommercial fish from local waters, you should always check with your state or local health department for specific advice, as there could be additional advisories based on your local waters. The EPA recommends that, if you want to eat coastal and ocean fish that is caught recreationally, you should check with your local or state health department and follow the FDA advice.[10]

Large fish, such as swordfish, shark, king mackerel, and tilefish, are likely to contain high levels of methylmercury, and should be avoided by women of childbearing years and children.

vitamins and minerals, some of which may help them work. Also, these foods are naturally low in saturated and *trans* fats and are cholesterol free and full of fiber. For all these reasons, your heart will benefit if you eat plant foods high in antioxidants at each meal.

Nuts are an example of a food that is rich in antioxidants, and they can have a beneficial effect on LDL cholesterol levels for other reasons. A study of over 80,000 women showed that those who ate nuts frequently—an ounce of nuts at least five times a week—had approximately a 35 percent reduction in their risk for heart disease compared with women who hardly ever ate nuts.[14] Because nuts come from plants, they are free of dietary cholesterol and low in saturated fat, which is a healthy combination for lowering LDL cholesterol level. They are also high in fiber, and they contain plant sterols. They also contain the B vitamin folic acid, which has been shown to help reduce homocysteine levels. As we mentioned earlier, high homocysteine levels are thought to increase your risk for heart disease.

Spreads and soft-gel tablets containing plant sterols (phytosterols) can be used as part of a heart-healthy diet to lower LDL cholesterol.

The primary downside to nuts is that they are high in calories. A mere ounce of nuts (about 24 almonds or 28 peanuts) can contribute a hefty 160 to 200 calories to your diet. Routinely sitting down with a jar of peanuts while studying can quickly have you overconsuming calories. If you don't adjust for these calories elsewhere, your weight may also be adjusted, upward. Remember, excess weight can increase your risk for heart disease.

Certain phytochemicals are also thought to boost heart health. Recall that phytochemicals are a large group of chemicals that occur naturally in plants and are considered to have protective properties. For instance, while garlic may not be perfume to your breath, its sulfur-containing phytochemicals are thought to be slightly protective of your heart. However, studies are not definitive, so, until more is known, your best bet is to enjoy garlic as one part of your heart-healthy meals.

Tea also contains phytochemicals that may reduce your risk for heart disease. Black and green tea are high in flavonoids, phytochemicals believed to have a beneficial effect on LDL cholesterol. In a study of over 800 elderly men, those who consumed the most flavonoids, mainly from tea, cut their risk of dying from heart disease by about half compared with those whose flavonoid consumption was low.[15]

Table 12.4

To Decrease Excess LDL Cholesterol

Dietary Changes	Lifestyle Changes
↓ Saturated fat *Trans* fats Dietary cholesterol	↓ Excess weight
↑ Soluble fiber-rich foods Plant-based diet	↑ Exercise

TABLE TIPS

Eating for a Healthy Heart

Choose only lean meats (round, sirloin, and tenderloin cuts) and skinless poultry and keep your portions of meat to about 6 ounces daily. Eat fish at least twice a week.

Use two egg whites in place of one whole egg when baking.

Use reduced-fat or nonfat dairy products, such as low-fat or skim milk, reduced-fat cheese, and low-fat or nonfat ice cream. Sprinkle cheese on top of your food rather than mixing it in, so that you use less. Be sure to keep ice cream servings small.

Substitute cooked beans for half the meat in chili, soups, and casseroles.

Use canola, olive, soybean, or corn oil and *trans* fat–free margarine instead of butter or shortening.

Get Plenty of Exercise and Manage Your Weight

Regular exercise can help reduce LDL cholesterol levels, high blood pressure, insulin resistance, and excess weight and improve HDL cholesterol level. A review of over 50 studies involving more than 4,500 people found that exercise training for more than 12 weeks increased HDL cholesterol level by about 4.5 percent. Currently, the AHA recommends that healthy people partake in 30 minutes or more of moderate exercise, such as brisk walking, on most days, if not every day.[16] This amount of physical activity is considered sufficient to help reduce the risk for heart disease, but exercising longer than 30 minutes or at higher intensity may offer even greater protection, especially when it comes to maintaining a healthy body weight.

Regular physical activity can also help accelerate weight loss. Losing excess weight helps to not only lower LDL cholesterol level, high blood pressure, and the risk of developing type 2 diabetes but also to raise HDL cholesterol level. Hence, sedentary individuals should exercise more, and people who are both sedentary and overweight should "move and lose" to lower their risk for heart disease. Table 12.4 summarizes the diet and lifestyle changes you can make to reduce your LDL cholesterol and risk for heart disease. In addition, the Table Tips on this page provide eating tips for a heart-healthy diet.

A Word About the Protective Effects of Red Wine

Drinking alcohol in moderation can reduce the risk for heart disease. Alcohol can increase the level of HDL cholesterol, and some studies suggest that the antioxidants in red wine and dark beer have heart-protective effects.[17] However, these benefits are reaped mainly by adults who are middle-aged or older. We will discuss alcohol in Concept 19. Although some alcohol may be good, more is definitely not better. People who consume three or more drinks per day increase their risk of dying prematurely.

The Take-Home Message Limiting your consumption of foods high in saturated fats, cholesterol, and *trans* fats and increasing your consumption of fish, fruits, vegetables, whole grains, and nuts can help reduce your risk for heart disease. Regular exercise and weight loss can also help lower LDL cholesterol level and raise HDL cholesterol level.

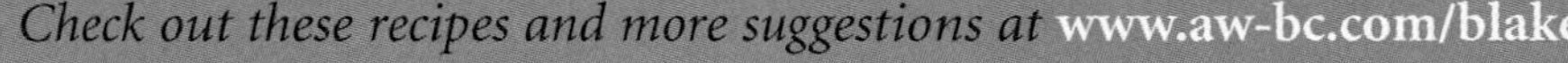

Check out these recipes and more suggestions at **www.aw-bc.com/blake**

UCook

Heavenly Angel Cake

For a light-as-a-feather dessert, try the Heavenly Angel Cake recipe we've posted at our website!

UDo

Eating Right and Light

Your challenge: Plan a lower-saturated-fat, fast-food meal (from places such as McDonald's, Taco Bell, or KFC) that includes at least one serving from four of the five food groups in MyPyramid. Can it be done? Visit our website to find out.

The Top Five Points to Remember

1. Heart disease occurs when atherosclerosis causes narrowing of the coronary arteries. When the arteries do not receive an adequate supply of oxygen and nutrients, the area of the heart wall they supply sustains damage and the tissue may die. Chest pain is an early symptom, and total blockage can result in a heart attack.
2. Lipoproteins have varying amounts of protein and lipid components, and thus varying levels of density. While a high level of LDL cholesterol is a major risk factor for heart disease, a high level of HDL cholesterol is protective. Having a family history of heart disease, being a man or a postmenopausal woman, having diabetes, smoking, being physically inactive, having high blood pressure, and being overweight can also increase your risk for heart disease.
3. Hypertension, the medical term for high blood pressure, is defined as a blood pressure of 140/90 millimeters of mercury or higher. High blood pressure increases the force of the blood against the artery walls and may increase the likelihood of vessel damage. Chronic high blood pressure also causes the heart to work harder than normal and can lead to an enlarged heart.
4. A heart-healthy diet is low in saturated and *trans* fats and cholesterol. It is high in plant-based foods and foods rich in soluble fiber, and it includes at least two servings of fish per week.
5. Engaging in regular physical activity and maintaining a healthy weight can reduce your risk for heart disease.

Test Yourself

1. The major dietary component that raises your LDL cholesterol level is
   a. viscous, soluble fiber.
   b. dietary cholesterol.
   c. saturated fat.
   d. plant sterols.
2. To raise your blood level of HDL cholesterol, you can
   a. increase the viscous, soluble fiber in your diet.
   b. exercise more.
   c. lose excess weight.
   d. do b and c only.
3. Eating fatty fish is good for your heart because it
   a. is rich in omega-3 fatty acids.
   b. is rich in linoleic acid.
   c. lowers HDL cholesterol levels.
   d. promotes blood clotting.
4. Hypertension is a blood pressure reading of
   a. 120/80 or higher.
   b. 140/90 or higher.
   c. 160/100 or higher.
   d. 180/110 or higher.
5. Which of the following is a controllable risk factor for heart disease?
   a. type 1 diabetes
   b. smoking
   c. advanced age
   d. high HDL cholesterol level

Answers

1. (c) Although dietary cholesterol does raise LDL cholesterol level in the blood, saturated fat is the bigger culprit. Viscous, soluble fiber and plant sterols can help lower LDL cholesterol.
2. (d) Increasing your exercise and losing excess weight can help increase your HDL cholesterol level. Increasing soluble fiber does not affect your HDL cholesterol level.
3. (a) Fatty fish is rich in omega-3 fatty acids. Linoleic acid is one of the omega-6 fatty acid group. Omega-3 fatty acids modestly increase the amount of good HDL cholesterol in the blood. Omega-3s interfere with blood clotting.
4. (b) Hypertension is clinically defined as a blood pressure of 140/90 or higher.
5. (b) Smoking is a risk factor for heart disease that is within your control. You cannot control your age or whether you develop type 1 diabetes. A low HDL cholesterol level is a risk factor for heart disease. A high HDL level is protective.

Web Resources

To learn more about heart disease and how to lower your risk, visit these websites:

- National Cholesterol Education Program: at www.nhlbi.nih.gov/chd
- American Heart Association at: www.americanheart.org.
- Centers for Disease Control and Prevention at: www.cdc.gov/nccdphp/dnpa/physical/index.htm

13 Proteins

Facts to Know

1. Proteins are made up of **amino acids.** T/F

2. Excess **dietary protein** is stored in the body as fat. T/F

3. Proteins provide **structural support** in your body. T/F

4. Most **enzymes** in your body are proteins. T/F

5. Your body can use protein as an **energy source.** T/F

Aaron, 19, had always been a lean guy, almost verging on skinny for most of his life. After graduating from high school and then working for a year, he decided to enlist in the military to get some training and qualify for college assistance when he got out.

When he came home for a visit after basic training his brother Isaac immediately noticed that Aaron had bulked up a lot while he was away. "What are they feeding you army guys out there?" he joked. "Raw meat?"

Aaron laughed. "Hey dude, I learned a few things while I was away. You don't have to eat a ton of protein to build muscle. You just have to work out, and that's what I did, every day!"

How does the body actually "bulk up," as Aaron did? Is Aaron right about just "working out" rather than also consuming protein? What role does dietary protein actually play in building lean muscle mass? And what are proteins, anyway, and why are they so important?

In this concept we'll explore some of these basic facts that you need to know about proteins, and their role in the body and your health.

Answers

1. True. Amino acids are the building blocks of protein. See page 2 for more details.
2. True. All excess calories are eventually stored as fat. See page 7.
3. True. Protein is need to "hold up" your body. Turn to page 9 to learn why.
4. True. There are thousands of unique enzymes in your body, and most are made of protein. Turn to page 10 to discover why you need so many specialized enzymes.
5. True. However, using proteins, rather than carbohydrates or fat, for energy is an inefficient way to use this precious nutrient. To learn why, turn to page 12.

What Are Proteins?

Proteins are the predominant structural and functional materials in every cell, and you have thousands of unique proteins in your body. Your protein-rich muscles enable you to swim, jog, walk, stand, and hold up your head. Without adequate protein, your immune system wouldn't be able to fight off infections, your hair wouldn't grow, your fingernails would be mere stubs, and you wouldn't be able to digest your food. In fact, proteins are involved in most of your body's functions and life processes; without them, you wouldn't survive.[1]

While proteins are critical for your existence, you don't need to make protein-rich foods the focus of your diet in order to meet your daily needs. In fact, too much protein, particularly if it comes at the expense of other nutrients, can be unhealthy for your heart, kidneys, and bones.

In this concept, you will learn about the building blocks of proteins, the vital role that proteins play in your body, and how your body uses this precious nutrient. Let's begin by exploring what proteins are and what they are made of.

The Building Blocks of Proteins Are Amino Acids

Proteins are made of important units called **amino acids.** To understand what amino acids are, think of the numbers 0 to 9 arranged in a long sequence. Your phone number, your Social Security number, and your bank PIN number are all derived from the same small pod of numbers arranged in different sequences of varying lengths, and each of these numbers has a specific purpose. Amino acids are similar to this because they, too, can be linked together to make unique sequences of varying lengths. Each amino acid sequence represents a unique protein that has a specific function in the human body (Figure 13.1).

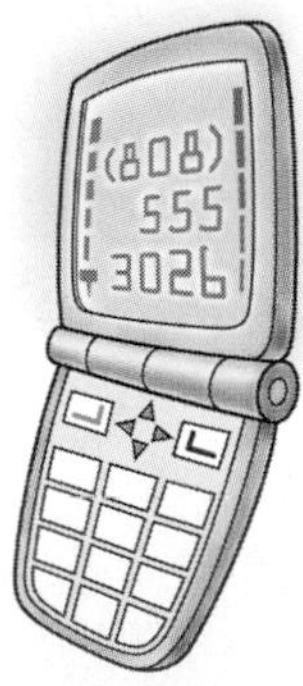

Figure 13.1 Amino Acids Are Like Digits They link together to form unique sequences with a specific purpose.

proteins Compounds in your body that consist of numerous amino acids and are found in all living cells.

amino acids The building blocks of protein. Amino acids contain carbon, hydrogen, oxygen, and nitrogen. All amino acids include a unique side chain.

As with carbohydrates and fats, amino acids contain carbon, hydrogen, and oxygen. Unlike carbohydrates and fats, however, amino acids also contain nitrogen. Every amino acid has a unique component, called a *side chain,* that gives the amino acid its distinguishing qualities. The side chain can be as simple as a single atom, or it can be a collection of atoms.

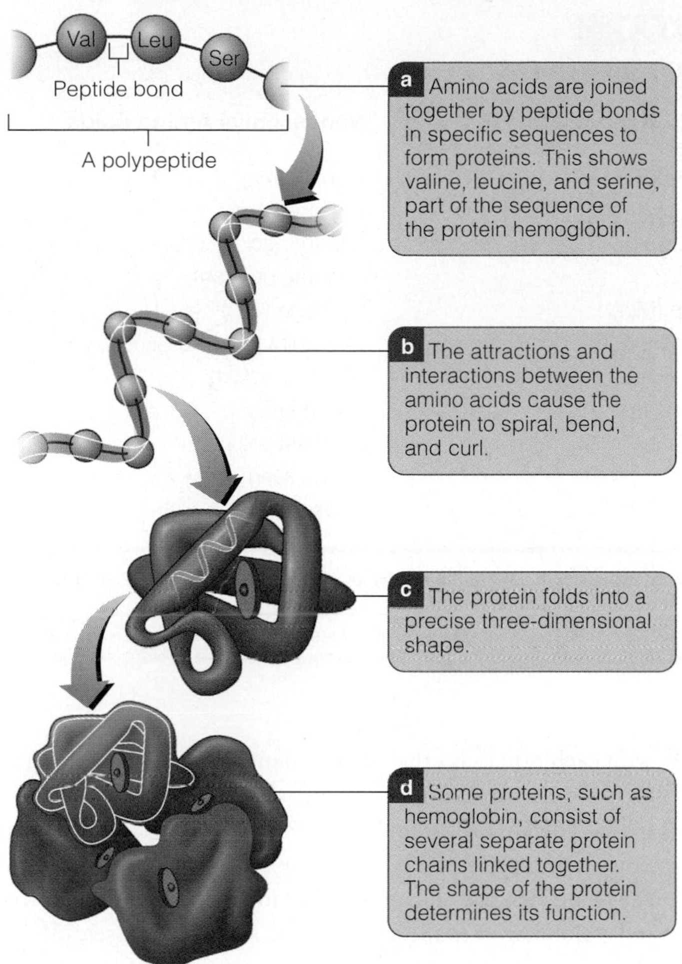

Figure 13.2 The Making of a Protein

There are 20 amino acids (thus, 20 different side chains), which your body combines to make all the proteins it needs (Figure 13.2). As you can see in Table 13.1 on the next page, amino acids are categorized as either essential or nonessential. Let's take a closer look at the differences between these two types.

Essential and Nonessential Amino Acids

There are nine amino acids that your body cannot make and that you must therefore get from the foods you eat. These are the **essential amino acids,** and you can find them in foods such as meat and milk. It is *essential* that you obtain them from your diet.

The remaining 11 amino acids are **nonessential amino acids** because your body can synthesize, or create, them. It is *not essential* that you consume them in your diet.

Now let's look at how amino acids are used to build proteins.

Building Proteins from Amino Acids

Amino acids are joined to each other by unique chemical bonds called *peptide bonds* (Figure 13.2). Two joined amino acids form a dipeptide; three joined amino acids form a tripeptide; and a polypeptide chain is many amino acids joined together. Proteins typically contain between 100 and 10,000 amino acids in a sequence. The protein that forms the hemoglobin in your red blood cells, for example, consists of close to 300 amino acids.

The unique nature of each amino acid side chain prevents a protein from remaining in an orderly straight line. Rather, each long chain folds into a precise, three-dimensional shape, such as a coil, based on the interactions of its amino acid

essential amino acids The nine amino acids that the body cannot synthesize, and must therefore be obtained through dietary sources.

nonessential amino acids The 11 amino acids that the body can synthesize.

Table 13.1

The Mighty 20

Essential Amino Acids	Nonessential Amino Acids
Histidine (His)*	Alanine (Ala)
Isoleucine (Ile)	Arginine (Arg)†
Leucine (Leu)	Aspartic acid (Asp)
Lysine (Lys)	Asparagine (Asn)
Methionine (Met)	Cysteine (Cys)†
Phenylalanine (Phe)	Glutamic acid (Glu)
Threonine (Thr)	Glutamine (Gln)†
Tryptophan (Trp)	Glycine (Gly)†
Valine (Val)	Proline (Pro)†
	Serine (Ser)
	Tyrosine (Tyr)†

*Histidine was once thought to be essential only for infants. It is now known that small amounts are also needed for adults.

†These amino acids can be "conditionally essential" if there are either inadequate precursors or inadequate enzymes available to create these in the body. This can happen in certain illnesses and in premature infants.

side chains with each other and the environment. Some side chains are attracted to other side chains; some are neutral; and some repel each other.

Additionally, side chains can be hydrophilic ("water-loving") or hydrophobic ("water-fearing"), and this affects how they react with their environment. Hydrophobic side chains tend to cluster together in the interior of the protein, causing the protein to be globular in shape. Hydrophilic side chains assemble on the outside surface of the protein, closer to the watery environments of blood and other body fluids.

The shape of a protein determines its function in your body. Therefore, anything that alters the bonds between the side chains alters its shape and thus its function.

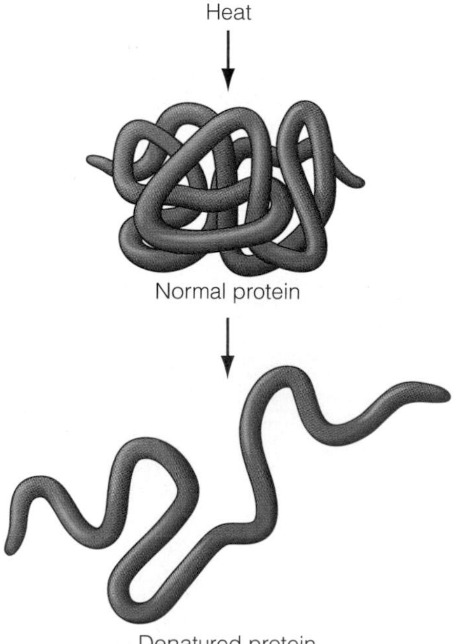

Figure 13.3 Denaturing a Protein
A protein can be denatured, or unfolded, by exposure to heat, acids, or salts. Any change in a protein's shape alters its function.

Protein Function Is Altered by Denaturation

Proteins can be *denatured,* or unfolded, by heat, acids, or salts (Figure 13.3). Denaturation doesn't alter the sequence of amino acids in the protein strand, but it does change the shape of the protein. Changing the protein's shape alters its function, sometimes permanently.

For example, when you fry a raw egg, which is high in protein, the heat denatures the protein to create a firmer, better-tasting egg. This happens because heat disrupts the bonds between the amino acid side chains, causing the protein in the egg to uncoil. New bonds then form between the amino acid side chains, changing the shape of the protein and the structure and texture of the egg. (This solidifying quality explains why eggs are a key ingredient in custards, puddings, and cakes.[2])

Acids and salts can also denature proteins. When you marinate a chicken or steak before cooking it, you might use a mixture that is high in lemon juice, vinegar, or salt to denature its protein. The result is meat that is juicier and more tender.[3] Your acidic stomach juices help denature and untangle proteins during digestion, so that digestive enzymes can break down and prepare proteins for absorption in your intestinal tract.

What Happens to the Protein You Eat?

When you enjoy a tasty peanut butter sandwich, what happens to the protein from the peanut butter once it's in your body? How is the protein in the peanuts broken down, so that the valuable amino acids can be digested, absorbed, and used efficiently to synthesize other proteins? Let's have a look at the process step-by-step (Figure 13.4).

a. Protein digestion begins after chewed food enters your stomach. Stomach acids denature the protein strands, untangling their bonds. This allows the digestive enzyme pepsin, which is produced in your stomach lining, to begin breaking down the proteins into shorter polypeptide strands and preparing them for absorption.

b. After entering the small intestine, the strands are broken down by other enzymes into tripeptides and dipeptides, as well as some amino acids. Pepsin is inactivated.

c. The protein remnants are then absorbed into the cells of the small intestine lining, where the remaining tripeptides and dipeptides are broken down into single amino acids, which enter the blood and travel to the liver.

d. The liver uses these amino acids according to your body's needs. For example, it might use them to make new proteins or, if necessary, to make glucose if you are not getting enough carbohydrate in your diet. Some amino acids pass through the liver and travel back out to the blood to be picked up and used by your cells.

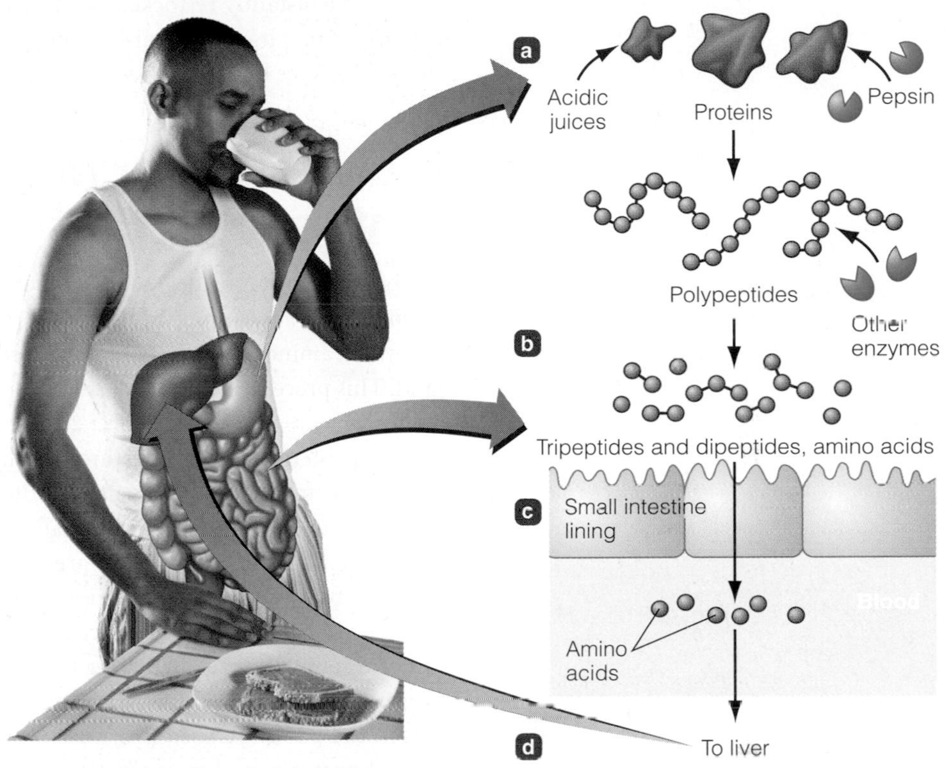

Figure 13.4 Digesting and Absorbing Proteins
(a) Stomach: Acidic juices denature proteins and activate pepsin, which breaks down proteins into polypeptides. **(b)** Small intestine: Other enzymes break polypeptides into tripeptides, dipeptides, and amino acids. **(c)** Intestinal lining: Protein remnants are absorbed and further broken down into amino acids, which enter the blood and travel to the liver. **(d)** Liver: The liver uses amino acids to make new proteins or glucose. Some amino acids return to the blood.

The Take-Home Message Proteins are made up of amino acids that contain carbon, oxygen, hydrogen, and nitrogen. An amino acid's side chain is the portion that makes it unique. The body needs 20 different amino acids to make proteins, but you don't have to consume all 20 in your diet. That's because 11 of these can be synthesized in your body and are thus nonessential. The remaining nine amino acids are the essential amino acids that your body cannot synthesize. Hence essential amino acids need to be obtained from your diet. Amino acids are joined together by peptide bonds to create proteins. The attractions and interactions between the side chains cause the protein to fold into a precise, three-dimensional shape that determines its function. Heat, acids, and salts can denature, or unfold, a protein, altering its shape and function.

Cooking, a form of protein denaturation, often improves the quality, structure, and texture of the protein-rich foods you eat. Raw eggs, meat, and poultry are basically inedible, but cooking greatly increases their palatability.

How Does Your Body Build Proteins?

Your diet provides both essential and nonessential amino acids. Your body stockpiles a limited amount of all these in *amino acid pools* in your blood and inside your cells (Figure 13.5). Because your body can't make the essential amino acids, the pools need to be constantly restocked. That means your body is always breaking down its proteins, so that it can replenish its stock of amino acids and build the new proteins it needs. Let's see how the process works.

Your Body Degrades and Synthesizes Proteins

Your body is constantly degrading its proteins—breaking them down into their component amino acids, some of which are released into your amino acid pools. At the same time, amino acids are being removed from the pools to create proteins on demand. This process of continually degrading and synthesizing protein is called *protein turnover* (Figure 13.5). In fact, over 200 grams of protein are turned over daily.

The proteins in your intestines and liver—two active areas of your body—account for as much as 50 percent of protein turnover.[4] The cells that make up the lining of your intestines are continually being sloughed off and replaced. The proteins in these sloughed-off cells are degraded, and most of the resulting amino acids are absorbed and recycled in your body, although some are lost in your stool and urine. Proteins and amino acids are also lost daily through sloughed-off skin, hair, and nails. Replacements for these proteins need to be synthesized, and the amino acid pools provide the building materials to do this. Some of the amino acids in the pools are used to synthesize other (nonprotein) substances, including certain hormones and melanin, the pigment that gives color to dark skin and hair.

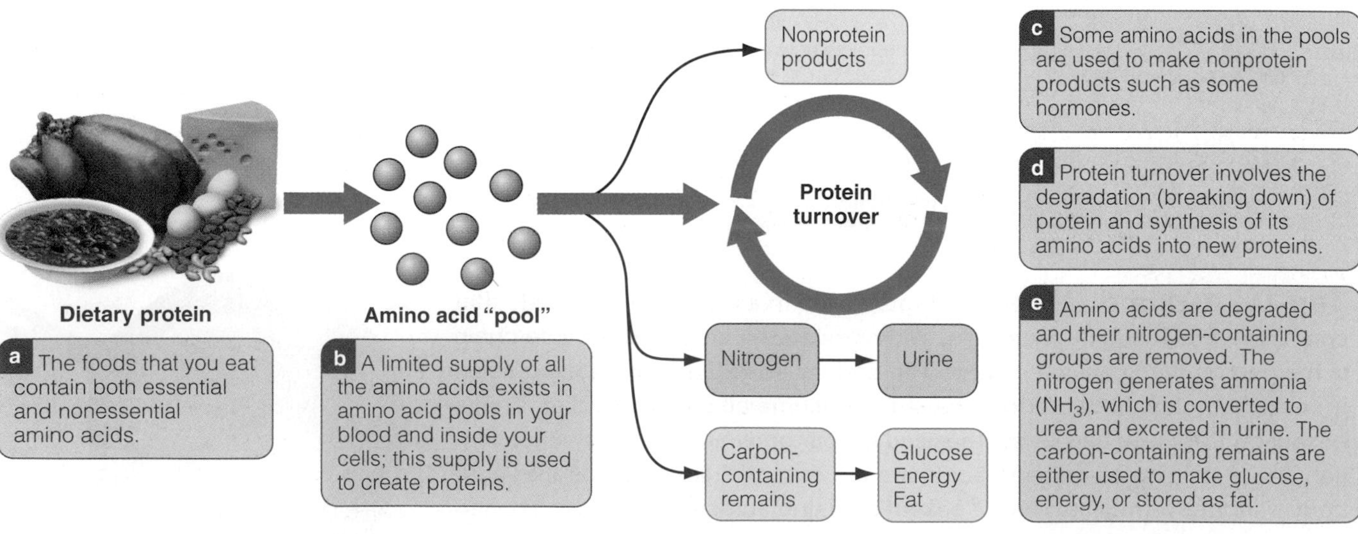

Figure 13.5 The Fate of Amino Acids in Your Body

Amino acids are also broken down into their component parts, which meet different fates. The nitrogen in amino acids forms ammonia (NH_2), which can be toxic to your cells in high amounts. Your liver converts the ammonia to *urea*, a waste product excreted in your urine via your kidneys. The carbon-containing remnants of the amino acids are converted to glucose, used as energy, or stored as fat, depending on your body's needs. When your diet is too low in carbohydrates, the amino acids are used to make glucose. When calories are inadequate, the amino acids can be utilized to create energy.

Surplus amino acids (beyond what is needed in the amino acid pools) from excess dietary protein can't be stored as protein and, so, must be stored mainly as fat. This helps explain why *all* excess calories—whether from carbohydrates, proteins, or fats—are stored as fat in your body.

Proteins don't have a mind of their own. How does your body know when to create more proteins? Let's look at how proteins are created—or "synthesized"—in your body.

DNA Directs the Synthesis of New Proteins

Protein synthesis in your body is directed by a molecule in the nucleus of each cell called **DNA** (***d**eoxyribo**n**ucleic **a**cid* (**DNA**). Each DNA molecule carries the code to synthesize every protein you need. However, your cells specialize in their protein-producing capabilities. For example, only cells in the pancreas make the hormone insulin, because no other cell in the body produces the **gene** (a DNA segment that identifies a specific protein) to make insulin.

DNA is a blueprint. It doesn't do the actual building or synthesizing, it only provides the instructions. DNA can't leave the nucleus of the cell, so it sends a messenger, another important molecule called *mRNA* *m*essenger *r*ibonucleic *a*cid (mRNA), to carry its instructions for building a protein out to the cell's "machinery." There, another specialized form of RNA, called *transfer RNA (tRNA)*, gathers the amino acids within the cell that are needed to make the desired protein. Figure 13.6 shows how protein synthesis takes place in a cell.

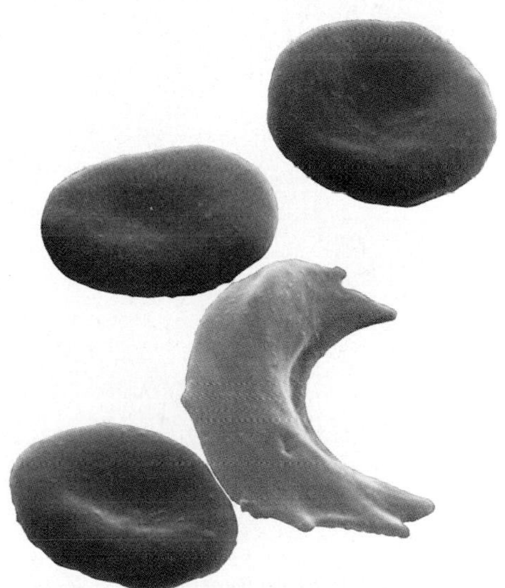

Red blood cells with normal hemoglobin, like the three similar ones, are smooth and round. A person with sickle-cell anemia has red blood cells like the one on the right; these cells are stiff and form a sickle (half-moon) shape when blood oxygen levels are low.

When abnormalities occur during protein synthesis, a serious medical condition can result. One example is sickle-cell anemia. The most common inherited blood disorder in the United States, sickle-cell anemia is caused by the abnormal formation of the protein hemoglobin, which is responsible for carrying oxygen in your red blood cells. According to the National Institutes of Health (NIH), approximately one in 12 African-Americans and one in 100 Hispanic Americans carry the mutated gene that causes the disease.[5]

In sickle-cell anemia, a mutation occurs in the affected gene that changes the normal sequence of amino acids in the polypeptide chains of the molecule resulting in abnormally shaped cell structures. The resulting abnormal sickle-shaped cells are easily destroyed, which can lead to anemia, and they can build up in blood vessels, causing painful blockages and damage to tissues and organs.

The box feature "Nutritional Genomics" explores the fascinating topic of nutritional genomics and the ways that your diet and genes can interact.

deoxyribonucleic acid (DNA) Genetic material within cells that develops and directs the synthesis of proteins in the body.

gene A DNA segment that identifies a specific protein.

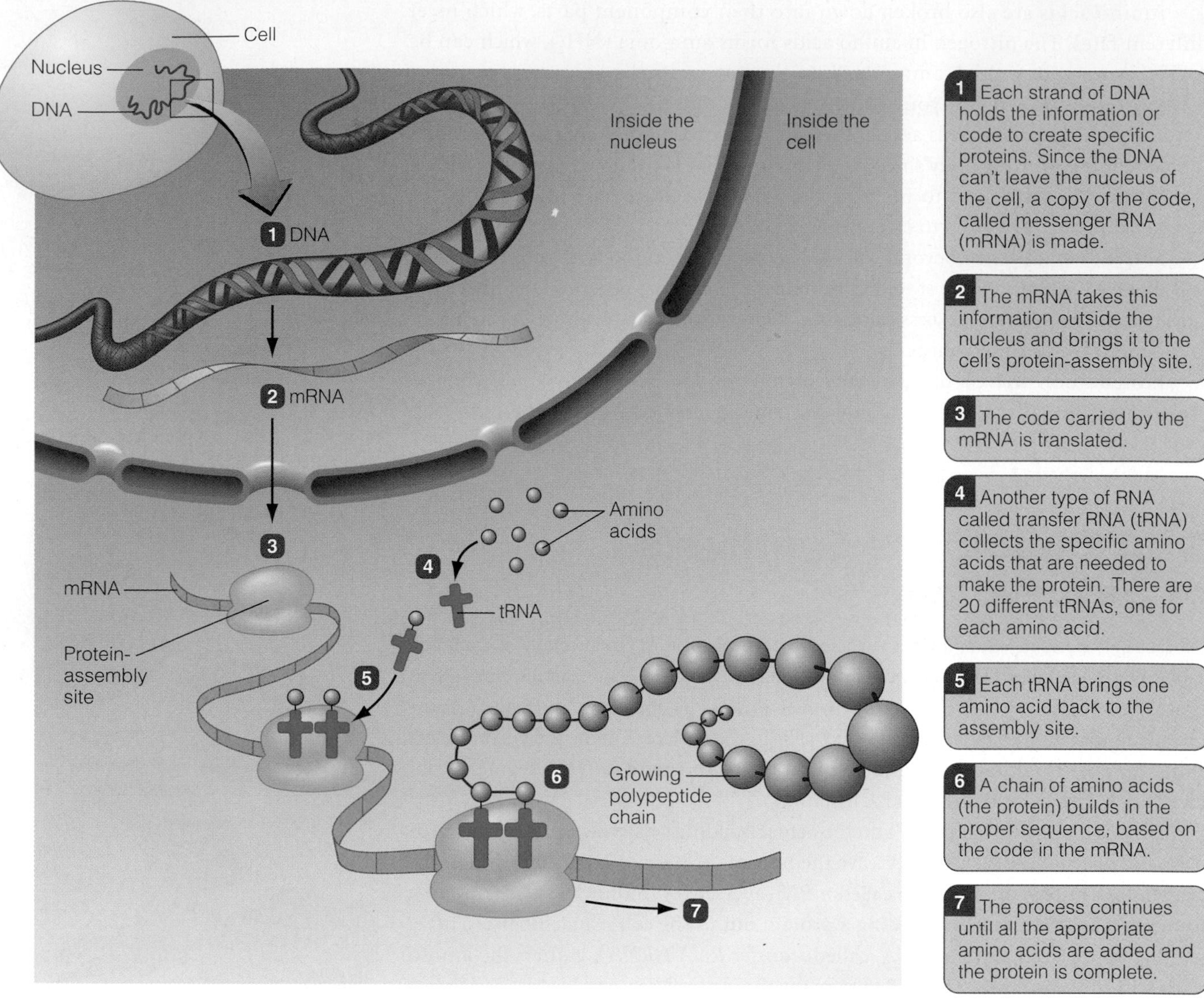

Figure 13.6 Protein Synthesis

The Take-Home Message A limited supply of amino acids exists in pools in your body and acts as a reservoir for protein synthesis as needed. Surplus amino acids are broken down, and the carbon-containing remnants can be used for glucose or energy, or they can be stored as fat, depending on your body's needs. The nitrogen in amino acids is eventually converted to the waste product urea and excreted in your urine. Amino acids can be used to create nonprotein substances, including certain hormones. The synthesis of proteins is directed in the cell nucleus by DNA, which carries the code for the amino acid sequences necessary to build the proteins your body needs.

Nutritional Genomics: You Are What You Eat

The Human Genome Project was a massive project to identify all of the 25,000 genes in the human body and determine their sequence. Thus, the entire sequencing of DNA in your cells is now known. Your DNA contains the genetic blueprint needed to assemble the proteins that direct your body's activities. While we all have the same set of genes needed to make our bodies function, each of us has slight variations in these genes. That's why some people have brown eyes and others blue, or why some runners are great sprinters and others excel at marathons. Researchers are only beginning to understand that genetic variations may also cause us to have slightly different nutrient needs. Your genetic makeup can also increase your potential for succumbing to a specific disease, as well as influence how the environment, including your diet, interacts with your genes.[1]

Welcome to the world of nutritional genomics. This area of research has the potential to help you personalize your diet according to your genetic makeup and thereby to reduce your risk for specific diseases. Nutritional genomics includes two different areas of genetic research—nutrigenomics and nutrigenetics:[2]

Nutrigenomics focuses on how the specific components in foods and beverages interact on a cellular level with the expression and regulation of genes.[2]

Nutrigenetics focuses on *your* unique response to these numerous dietary components based on your genetic makeup and its possible impact on *your* health.

A key claim of nutrigenetics is that certain nutrients and dietary components can exert different effects on your genes and thus initiate a very specific and unique response in your body, as opposed to the response the same components initiate in someone else. For example, you may enjoy a diet rich in wheat products, such as pasta, bread, and cereals. However, someone who has celiac disease (see Concept 6) must avoid these foods because she cannot tolerate gluten, a protein in wheat. If she consumes wheat, her immune system releases inflammatory chemicals, which damage the lining of her small intestine, reducing her ability to absorb the nutrients in her diet. In short, individuals with celiac disease have a genetic variation that makes them unable to tolerate gluten in their diet.

Your diet contains more than 2,500 active food components, many of which may influence the way that both normal cells and cancer cells develop. Research is beginning to sort out the role these food components may play in preventing or initiating diseases, such as cancer, and identifying specific populations that may be at risk.[3]

As research into nutritional genomics continues, nutrition professionals may be able to use the findings to make recommendations about your diet and your health. For example, registered dietitians with an expertise as nutrigenomics practitioners may work with you to design a personalized diet to help you reduce your risk for chronic diseases that run in your family.

How Does Your Body Use Proteins?

Without adequate amounts of proteins, you wouldn't be able to breathe, fight infections, or maintain your vital organs. This is because proteins play so many important roles in your body. Let's look at the most significant ones.

Proteins Provide Structural and Mechanical Support

Proteins provide much of the structural and mechanical support that keeps you upright, moving, and flexible. Just as wood, nails, and plaster are the behind-the-scenes materials holding up the room around you, fibrous proteins in your bones, muscles, and other tissues help hold up your body.

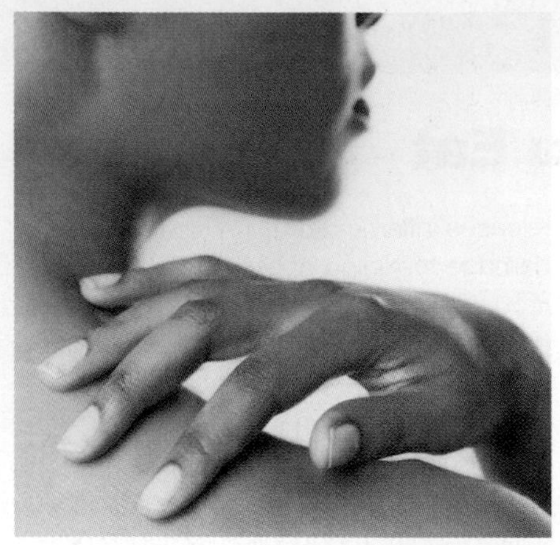

Proteins play an important role in keeping your skin healthy and your nails strong.

Collagen, the most abundant protein in your body, is found in all of your connective tissues, including the bones, tendons, and ligaments, that support and connect your joints and other body parts. Other proteins provide mechanical support by helping your muscles contract, so that you can run, walk, sit, and lie down. When you regularly engage in weight-bearing exercise, your body produces new muscle cells which fuse with existing muscle cells to make them larger. In our concept-opening story, that's why Aaron returned from three months of basic training looking "bulked up." That's right—eating extra protein won't make your muscles bigger, but exercise will. You'll learn about the foods you need to eat to support physical activity in Concept 26.

Proteins Help Maintain Body Tissues

Everyday wear and tear causes the breakdown of bodily tissues, and your body uses proteins to restore those tissues:

Your body produces about 250 billion new **red blood cells** each day.

- The protein-rich cells of your skin are constantly sloughing off, and proteins help create a new layer of outer skin every 25 to 45 days.[6]
- Because your trillions of red blood cells have a short life span—only about 120 days—new red blood cells must be regenerated continually.
- The cells that line the inner surfaces of your organs, such as your lungs and intestines, are constantly sloughed off, excreted, and replaced.

In addition to regular maintenance, extra protein is sometimes needed for "emergency repairs." Protein is essential in healing, and a person with extensive wounds, such as severe burns, may have dietary protein needs that are more than triple his or her normal needs.

Proteins Build Enzymes and Hormones

When your body needs a swift chemical reaction, such as the breakdown of carbohydrates after a meal, it uses substances called **enzymes** to get things going. Without enzymes, reactions would occur so slowly that you couldn't survive. Many enzymes are proteins, although some also have a *coenzyme,* such as a vitamin, that helps initiate a reaction.

Each of the thousands of enzymes in your body speeds up a specific reaction. Some enzymes, such as digestive enzymes, break compounds apart. (Recall from Concept 7 that the enzyme lactase is needed to break down the milk sugar lactose.) Other enzymes, such as those used to synthesize proteins, help compounds combine. Enzymes aren't changed, damaged, or used up in the process of speeding up a reaction. Figure 13.7 shows how an enzyme breaks apart two compounds yet isn't changed in the process. Thus, the enzyme is available to assist with additional reactions.

While enzymes help speed up reactions, **hormones** direct them, often by turning on or shutting off enzymes. Some hormones are lipids (fats), but hormones that come from amino acids form a larger group. Hormones are released from tissues and organs, and travel to target cells in other parts of your body to direct activities. All of the 70 trillion cells in your body interact with at least one of more than 50 known hormones.[7]

enzymes Substances (often proteins) that speed up reactions in the body without being changed or used up in the process.

hormones Protein- or lipid-based chemical substances that act as "messengers" in the body to initiate or direct metabolic actions and processes. Insulin, glucagon, and estrogen are examples of bodily hormones.

In Concept 7, you learned about the actions of two protein hormones, insulin and glucagon. When your blood glucose level rises after a meal or snack, your pancreas (an organ) releases insulin (a protein hormone) into your blood. Insulin, in turn, directs the uptake of glucose in your cells (an activity). If your blood glucose level drops too low, such as between meals, your pancreas releases the hormone glucagon, which promotes the release of glucose from your liver, which raises your blood glucose level.

Compound Enzyme

1 A compound approaches a specific enzyme.

2 The compound binds to the enzyme.

3 The enzyme changes shape.

Products

4 Two products are released and the enzyme is available for another reaction.

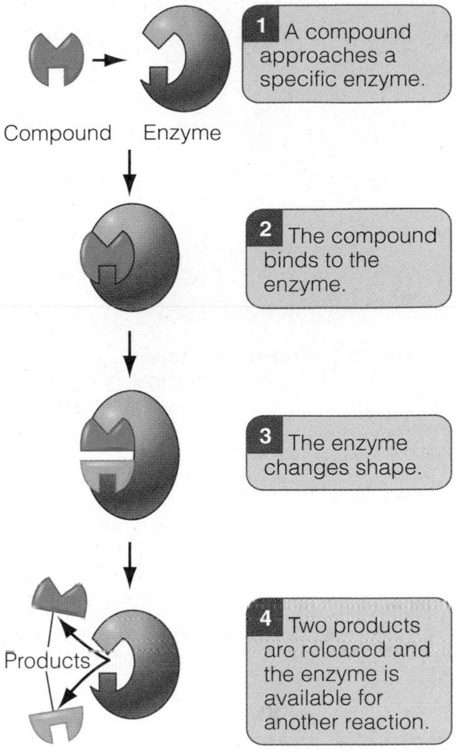

Figure 13.7 An Enzyme in Action
Enzymes speed up reactions in your body, yet they aren't changed, damaged, or used up in the process.

Proteins Help Maintain Fluid Balance

Your body is made up predominantly of water, which is distributed throughout various body compartments. Proteins help ensure that all this water is dispersed evenly, keeping you in a state of fluid balance.

Normally, your blood pressure forces the nutrient- and oxygen-rich fluids out of your tiniest blood vessels (capillaries) and into the spaces between your cells. While fluids can flow easily in these spaces, proteins can't because they are too big to cross the cell membranes. Proteins attract water, so the proteins remaining in the capillaries eventually draw the fluids back into the capillaries. Hence, protein plays an important role in the movement of fluids and in fluid balance among these compartments.

When fewer proteins are available to draw the fluid from between the cells back into the bloodstream, as during severe malnutrition, a fluid imbalance results. The spaces between the cells become bloated and the body tissues swell, a condition known as edema (Figure 13.8).

Proteins Help Maintain Acid-Base Balance

Proteins can alter the concentration of hydrogen ions (pH) of your body fluids. Normally, your blood has a pH of about 7.4, and the fluid in your cells has a pH of about 7.0. Even a small change in the pH of your blood in either direction can be harmful or even fatal. With a blood pH below 7.35, a condition called acidosis sets in and can result in a coma. A blood pH above 7.45, known as alkalosis, can cause convulsions.

Proteins act as buffers in your blood; that is, they minimize any changes in acid-base levels by picking up or donating hydrogen ions. Should your blood become too acidic, some of the amino acid side chains in the proteins pick up excess hydrogen ions. Other side chains can donate hydrogen ions to your blood if it becomes too basic.

Proteins Transport Substances throughout the Body

Transport proteins shuttle oxygen, waste products, lipids, some vitamins, sodium, and potassium through your blood and into and out of cells through the cell membranes. For example, hemoglobin acts as a transport protein, carrying oxygen from the lungs to the body cells. Hemoglobin also picks up carbon dioxide waste products from cells for transport to your lungs, to be exhaled from your body.

Transport proteins are also found in cell membranes, where they form a "doorway" allowing substances, such as sodium and potassium, to pass in and out of the cells

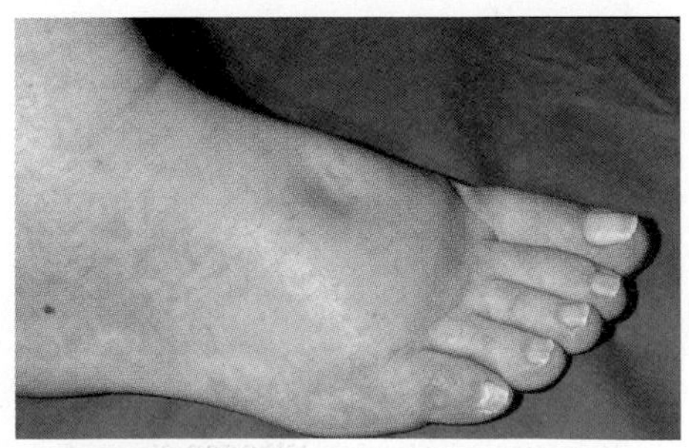

Figure 13.8 Edema
Inadequate protein in the blood can cause edema.

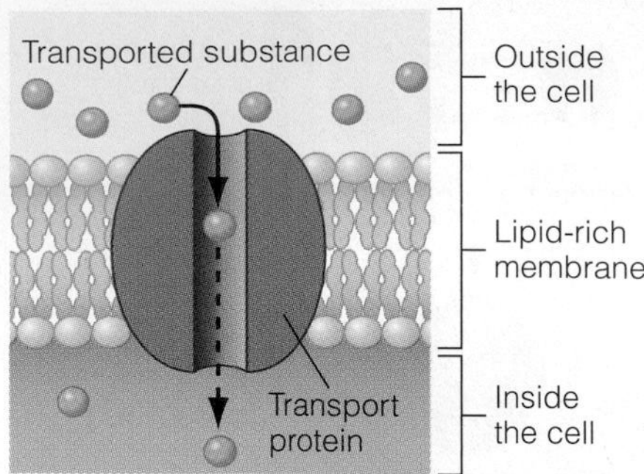

Figure 13.9 Protein Transport
Transport proteins form a channel, or doorway, through which substances, such as sodium and potassium, can move from one side of the cell membrane to the other.

(Figure 13.9). Substances that are not lipid-soluble or that are simply too big to pass through the lipid-rich membrane have to enter the cell through a protein channel.

Proteins Are Needed for Antibodies and the Immune Response

Your immune system works like an army to protect your body from foreign invaders, such as disease-causing bacteria and viruses. Specialized proteins called *antibodies* tag these potentially harmful substances for elimination from your body.

Once your body knows how to create antibodies against a specific invader, such as a particular virus, it stores that information, and you have immunity to that pathogen. The next time that invader enters your body, you can respond very quickly (producing up to 2,000 antibodies per second) to fight it. When this rapid immune response works efficiently, it prevents the virus or any other invader from multiplying to levels high enough to make you sick.

Sometimes, your body incorrectly perceives a nonthreatening substance as harmful and attacks it. This perceived enemy is called an *allergen*, and the response it provokes is called an allergic reaction. Food allergens are proteins in food that resist being broken down by heat during cooking or by the body's gastric juice and enzymes.[8] People who react to these allergens are diagnosed with food allergies. You will learn more about food allergies in Concept 29.

Proteins Can Provide Energy

Because proteins provide 4 calories per gram, they can be an energy source. However, the last thing you want to do is to use this valuable nutrient, which plays so many important roles in your body, as a regular source of fuel, especially since carbohydrates and fats are far better suited for providing energy. When your diet contains sufficient calories from carbohydrates and fat, your body uses proteins for their other important roles.

When your diet doesn't provide adequate calories—for example, in times of starvation—your body begins to break down its protein, mainly from muscles, into its amino acid components. The amino acids are used for energy and for gluconeogenesis, the creation of glucose from noncarbohydrate sources. (Remember that your brain and nervous system need a minimum amount of glucose to function properly.) However, when proteins are used for energy, they create waste products that must be eliminated from your body, which is a burden for your liver and kidneys.

Some hair conditioners deposit protein on damaged hair to give it **extra strength.** The protein is washed away with the next shampoo, so a new coating must be re-applied each time.

The best plan is to eat enough protein daily to meet your body's needs, along with a combination of carbohydrates and fats which will ensure that proteins won't be used as fuel for energy. In Concept 14, we'll discuss what your daily protein needs are and how you can meet them easily with a balanced diet.

Table 13.2

The Many Roles of Proteins

Roles of Proteins	How Proteins Work
Structural and mechanical support and maintenance	Proteins are your body's building materials, providing strength and flexibility to your tissues, tendons, ligaments, muscles, organs, bones, nails, hair, and skin. Proteins are needed for the ongoing maintenance of your body.
Enzymes and hormones	Proteins are needed to make most enzymes that speed up reactions in your body and many hormones that direct specific activities, such as regulating your blood glucose level.
Fluid balance	Proteins play a major role in ensuring that your body fluids are evenly dispersed in your blood and inside and outside your cells.
Acid-base balance	Proteins act as buffers to help keep the pH of your body fluids balanced within a tight range. A drop in pH causes your body fluids to become too acidic, while a rise in pH can make them too basic.
Transport	Proteins shuttle substances, such as oxygen, waste products, and nutrients (such as sodium and potassium), through your blood and into and out of your cells.
Antibodies and the immune response	Proteins create specialized antibodies that target germs and other invaders that can make you sick.
Energy	Because proteins provide 4 calories per gram, they can be used as fuel or energy in your body.

The Take-Home Message **Proteins play many critical roles in your body, as summarized in Table 13.2. Although proteins can provide energy, you should eat adequate amounts of all three macronutrients daily to keep proteins from being used as energy.**

The upcoming Visual Summary Table reviews many of the functions, daily needs and consequences regarding Proteins, along with some food sources that will be discussed more fully in Concept 14.

Protein

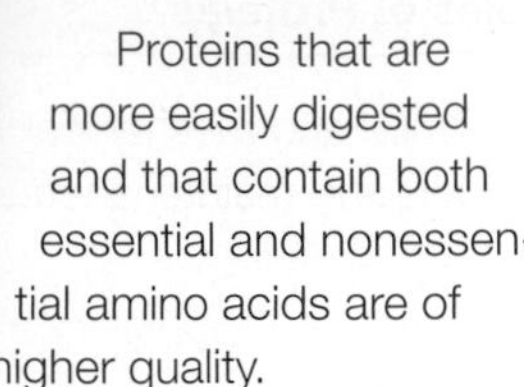

What Are Proteins?

Proteins are the predominant structural and functional materials in every cell in your body. Proteins are made up of **amino acids.**

As with carbohydrates and fats, amino acids are made up of carbon, hydrogen, and oxygen atoms. Unlike carbohydrates and fats, amino acid molecules also contain nitrogen.

The atoms that make up every amino acid molecule are clustered into three groups. The acid group contains carbon, hydrogen, and oxygen atoms (COOH), which is why it is called an amino "acid." The amine group (NH_2) contains the nitrogen. These two groups are the same for every amino acid. The third group, a unique side chain, varies from amino acid to amino acid and gives each its distinguishing qualities.

There are 20 different amino acids, 9 of which are **essential** and 11 of which are **nonessential.** Essential amino acids are not made in the body and need to be obtained through foods. Nonessential amino acids are synthesized in the body.

Proteins Are Built with Amino Acids

Amino acids are joined to each other by peptide bonds to build proteins.

Two amino acids joined together form a dipeptide. Three amino acids joined together form a tripeptide. And a polypeptide consists of many amino acids joined together.

The shape of a protein determines its function.

Shapes of Proteins Are Altered by Denaturation

The weak bonds between the side chains on the amino acids can be denatured, or broken apart, by temperature change or acids, bases, or salts. Although denaturation doesn't alter the sequence of amino acids in the protein strand, changing the protein's shape can alter its function, sometimes permanently.

Functions of Protein

- Proteins provide structural and mechanical support and help maintain body tissues.
- Proteins build enzymes and hormones.
- Proteins help maintain acid-base balance.
- Proteins transport substances throughout the body and act as channels in membranes.
- Proteins are needed for antibodies and the immune response.
- Proteins can provide energy.

Daily Needs

If you are 14 to 18 years old, you need 0.85 gram of protein per kilogram of body weight (g/kg) per day. If you are 19 years of age or older, you need 0.80 gram per kilogram daily.

Not all proteins are created equal. Protein quality is determined by two factors: your body's ability to digest the protein, which is unique to each person, and the types of amino acids (essential, nonessential, or both) that the protein contains.

Proteins that are more easily digested and that contain both essential and nonessential amino acids are of higher quality.

Food Sources

Protein is particularly abundant in meat, fish, poultry, dairy foods, and meat alternatives such as peanut butter and soy. A 3-ounce serving of cooked meat, poultry, or fish provides approximately 21 to 25 grams of protein, or about 7 grams per ounce.

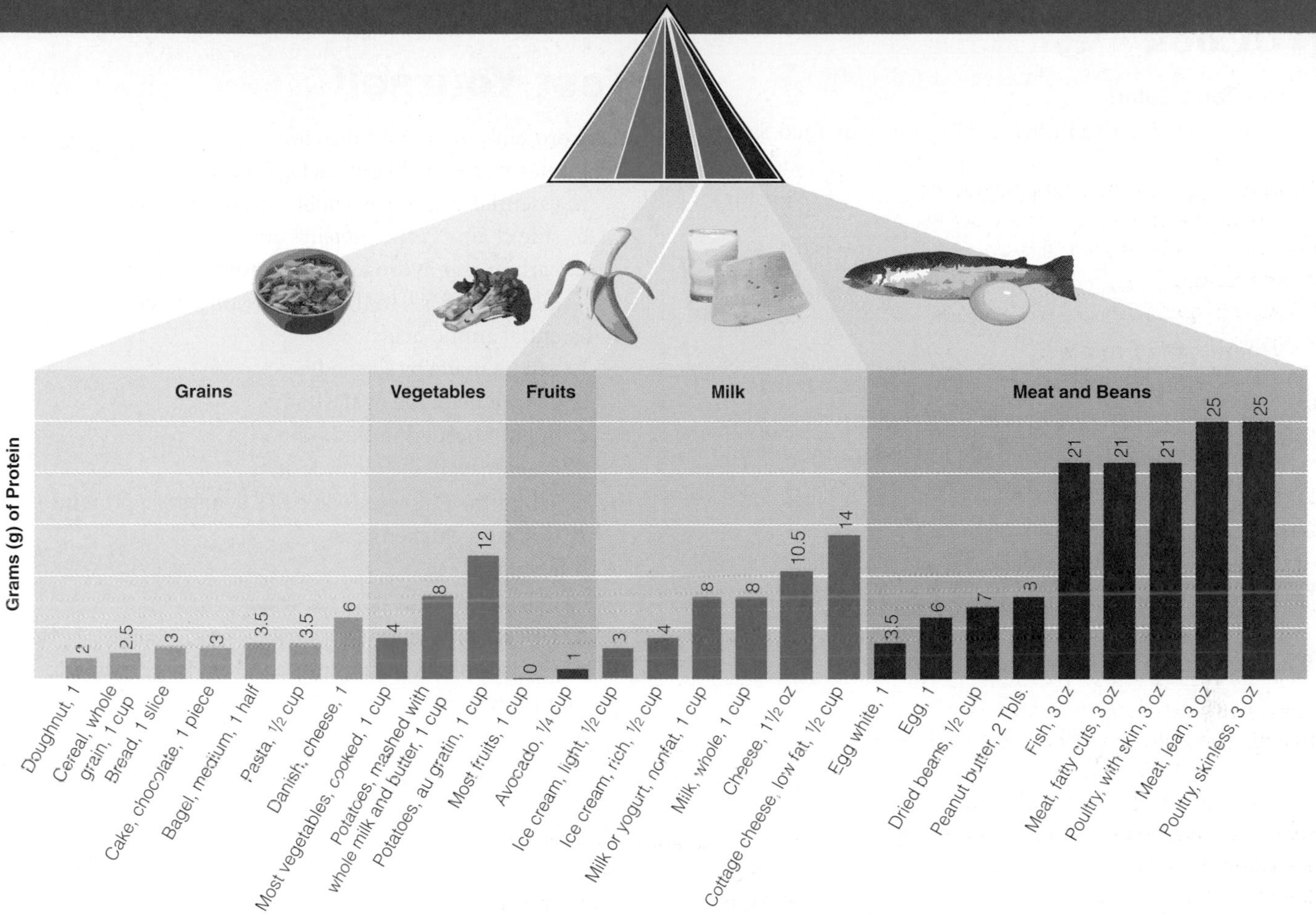

Food group	Food	Grams (g) of Protein
Grains	Doughnut, 1	2
Grains	Cereal, whole grain, 1 cup	2.5
Grains	Bread, 1 slice	3
Grains	Cake, chocolate, 1 piece	3
Grains	Bagel, medium, 1 half	3.5
Grains	Pasta, 1/2 cup	3.5
Grains	Danish, cheese, 1	6
Vegetables	Most vegetables, cooked, 1 cup	4
Vegetables	Potatoes, mashed with whole milk and butter, 1 cup	8
Vegetables	Potatoes, au gratin, 1 cup	12
Fruits	Most fruits, 1 cup	0
Fruits	Avocado, 1/4 cup	1
Milk	Ice cream, light, 1/2 cup	3
Milk	Ice cream, rich, 1/2 cup	4
Milk	Milk or yogurt, nonfat, 1 cup	8
Milk	Milk, whole, 1 cup	8
Milk	Cheese, 1 1/2 oz	10.5
Milk	Cottage cheese, low fat, 1/2 cup	14
Meat and Beans	Egg white, 1	3.5
Meat and Beans	Egg, 1	6
Meat and Beans	Dried beans, 1/2 cup	7
Meat and Beans	Peanut butter, 2 Tbls.	8
Meat and Beans	Fish, 3 oz	21
Meat and Beans	Meat, fatty cuts, 3 oz	21
Meat and Beans	Poultry, with skin, 3 oz	21
Meat and Beans	Meat, lean, 3 oz	25
Meat and Beans	Poultry, skinless, 3 oz	25

Nonmeat protein sources are also abundant and particularly important for vegetarians. Half a cup of cooked dried beans provides 7 grams of protein, whereas an egg or 2 tablespoons of peanut butter each provides 8 grams of protein.

Too Much or Too Little

A diet that is too high in protein has been linked to health problems such as cardiovascular disease, kidney stones, osteoporosis, and some types of cancer. Eating too little protein can also lead to compromised bone health.

Diets that are inadequate in protein, calories, or both lead to a condition know as **protein-energy malnutrition (PEM).** PEM is most common among infants and children living in poverty and unsanitary conditions. Because they are still growing, children have greater nutritional needs than most adults, making them more vulnerable to the effects of malnutrition. Two forms of PEM are marasmus and kwashiorkor.

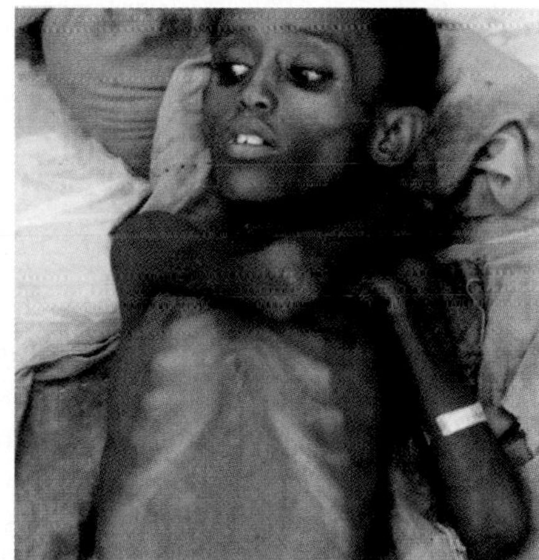

Child with marasmus.

Swollen belly characteristic of kwashiorkor.

Marasmus is a disease caused by insufficient intake of dietary protein. Marasmic individuals literally look as though they are starving and are often not even at 60 percent of their desirable body weight for their height.

Kwashiorkor occurs when a person consumes sufficient calories but not sufficient protein. A classic symptom of severe kwashiorkor is edema in the legs, feet, and stomach. Other symptoms include dry and peeling skin, rashes or lesions, and brittle hair that can be easily pulled out.

Terms to Know

proteins ■ amino acids ■ essential amino acids ■ nonessential amino acids ■ protein-energy malnutrition (PEM)

Check out these recipes and more suggestions at **www.pearsonhighered.com/blake**

UCook

Hot Taco Salad

Want a salad with a little kick? Try this Hot Taco Salad, loaded with lean, protein-rich ground turkey, kidney beans, and light cheddar cheese. Save the leftovers for the next day!

UDo

Where's the Protein?

After reading this concept, see if you can accurately guess how much protein is in the foods you eat. Go to our website above to match the foods with the amount of protein they provide.

The Top Five Points to Remember

1. Proteins are made of amino acids containing carbon, hydrogen, oxygen, and nitrogen. Each amino acid has a unique side chain. There are 20 side chains and hence, 20 amino acids in the human body.
2. The interactions between the side chains of amino acids cause individual proteins to fold into precise, three-dimensional shapes. The shape of a protein determines its function. Heat, acids, and salts denature these bonds and disrupt the shape and function of a protein.
3. Of the 20 amino acids, nine are essential, so you need to obtain them through your diet. Your body can synthesize the remaining 11 amino acids, so they are nonessential.
4. With the help of stomach juices and enzymes, your body digests and breaks down proteins into amino acids to make them available for use. A limited number of amino acids are readily available in pools in your body. The DNA in your cells directs the synthesis of proteins. Excess amino acids are also broken down and either stored in another form or used as energy, depending on your body's needs. The nitrogen is converted to the waste product urea and excreted in your urine.
5. Proteins play many roles in your body. They provide structural and mechanical support, supply materials for ongoing maintenance, form enzymes and hormones, maintain acid-base and fluid balance, transport nutrients, and aid your immune system. Proteins can provide energy, can be used to make glucose, and can be stored as fat.

Test Yourself

1. A protein's shape, and therefore its function in your body, is determined by the interactions of the
   a. essential and nonessential amino acids in the protein.
   b. side chains in the protein's amino acids.
   c. carbon and hydrogen in the protein's amino acids.
   d. DNA and RNA in the protein's amino acids.
2. Essential amino acids
   a. can be made by the body.
   b. cannot be made by the body.
   c. are not needed in the body.
   d. are not available in any foods.
3. Which of the following will NOT denature a protein?
   a. grilling a chicken breast
   b. frying an egg
   c. marinating a steak in red wine
   d. refrigerating milk
4. Limited amounts of surplus amino acids are stored in your body in your
   a. muscles.
   b. fat stores.
   c. amino acid pools.
   d. stomach.
5. Proteins play important roles in your body, such as
   a. helping you fight the flu.
   b. aiding in digesting the pizza you ate for lunch.
   c. transporting fat and cholesterol through your blood.
   d. all of the above.

Answers

1. (b) The interactions of amino acid side chains with each other and with their environment determine the shape, and thus the function, of the proteins in your body. Essential amino acids must be consumed in the diet, while nonessential amino acids can be synthesized by the body. Amino acids contain carbon and hydrogen, but these atoms are not present in all side chains, and their interaction does not direct denaturation. DNA is a compound in the nucleus of your cells, where, along with RNA, it directs protein synthesis.
2. (b) Essential amino acids cannot be made by the body and need to be obtained from foods. Many foods provide essential amino acids, and they are vital to your health and functioning.
3. (d) Heat and acids will denature proteins. Refrigeration does not alter the bonds between the amino acid side chains and does not denature proteins.

4. (c) Limited amounts of all the amino acids exist in amino acid pools in your blood and inside your cells, not in your stomach. Your muscles contain protein but don't store surplus amino acid. Your fat stores are the result of excess calories from carbohydrates, proteins, and fats.
5. (d) You need adequate amounts of protein to fight infections, such as the flu; to build enzymes that help you digest your food; and to transport substances, such as fat and cholesterol, through your blood.

Web Resources

- For information on specific genetic disorders, including those that affect protein use in the body, visit the National Human Genome Research Institute at: www.nhgri.nih.gov
- For more information on protein, visit the Centers for Disease Control and Prevention (CDC) at: www.cdc.gov/nccdphp/dnpa/nutrition/nutrition_for_everyone/basics/protein.htm

14 Proteins

Foods to Eat

1. **Soy** is a good source of protein. **T/F**

2. **Most Americans** do not meet their daily protein needs. **T/F**

3. Approximately one-half of your **daily calories** should come from dietary protein. **T/F**

4. **Active people** need to eat protein bars to meet their daily protein needs. **T/F**

5. Consuming too much **protein** may be unhealthy for your heart. **T/F**

Melissa, a 35-year-old college student, started struggling with her weight when she went back to school and had to juggle class time and homework with her family's needs. She often found herself eating on the run between classes or errands. After reading an article in a health magazine stating that a high-protein diet would help her lose weight, Melissa cut back on eating grains, fruits, and vegetables and started eating more hamburgers, steaks, cheese, and fried foods. While she dropped a few pounds in the first week, the bathroom scale didn't budge much thereafter. After about eight weeks of eating mostly high-protein foods, she began to have stomach pains. When she visited her doctor, a blood test revealed that she had higher than normal levels of some substances in her blood. Can you guess what problems Melissa was having as a result of her high-protein diet? In this concept, we will discuss why Melissa's steady diet of fatty beef, cheese, and fried foods is unhealthy for both her bowels and her heart.

Answers

1. True. Soy protein can be a good choice to help meet your daily protein needs. See page 3 for details.
2. False. Americans on the whole are actually exceeding the amount of protein they should consume daily. Turn to page 5 for more.
3. False. While proteins play a vital role in your body, a little can go a long way. For most healthy adults, less than one-fifth of their daily calories should come from dietary protein. For more on how to meet your protein needs, see pages 6 and 7.
4. False. Even an extremely active person or a competitive athlete can easily meet his or her protein needs through a well-balanced diet. To learn more about protein bars, turn to pages 10 and 11.
5. True. A high-protein diet that contains artery-clogging saturated fat and low amounts of whole grains, fruits, and vegetables is not heart-healthy. To learn more, turn to page 12.

What Is a High-Quality Protein?

You need to eat foods with enough of the essential amino acids and some nonessential amino acids every day. But before you can determine how much protein you need to eat to obtain these amino acids, you need to look at the quality of the protein you consume. Protein quality varies among food sources; that is, not all protein sources are the same.

Protein quality is determined by two factors: your body's ability to digest the protein (its *digestibility*) and the types and amounts of amino acids (essential, nonessential, or both) the protein contains. Proteins that are more easily digested and that contain both essential and nonessential amino acids are of higher quality.

A High-Quality Protein Is Digestible

The digestibility of proteins varies, depending on their sources. In general, animal proteins are more digestible than plant proteins. Some of the plant proteins, especially when consumed raw, are protected by the plant's cell walls and cannot be broken down by the enzymes in your intestinal tract. While 90 to 99 percent of the proteins from animal sources (cheese and other dairy foods, meat, poultry, and eggs) are digestible, only 70 to 90 percent of plant proteins, such as from chickpeas and other legumes, are typically digestible.[1]

Chickpeas are deficient in a certain amino acid, but the addition of sesame paste provides the missing ingredient and makes the protein complete. Season with garlic and lemon for a completely delicious hummus dip!

A High-Quality Protein Has a Complete Amino Acid Profile

The second factor that affects protein quality is the types and amounts of amino acids the protein contains, or its *amino acid profile.* A protein that provides all nine of the essential amino acids, along with some of the 11 nonessential amino acids, is considered a **complete protein.** A protein that is low in one or more of the essential amino acids is considered an **incomplete protein.** A complete protein is considered of higher quality than an incomplete protein. Protein from animal sources is typically a complete protein, while protein from plant foods tends to be incomplete.

Two exceptions to this generalization are gelatin and soy. Gelatin, an animal protein, is not a complete protein because it is missing the amino acid tryptophan. Soy, a plant protein, has an amino acid profile that resembles the protein needs in your body, making it a complete protein.

Any protein chain is only as strong as its weakest amino acid link. If a single essential amino acid is in low supply in your diet, and thus in your body, your ability to synthesize the proteins you need will be limited. The amino acid that is in the shortest supply in an incomplete protein is known as the *limiting amino acid.*

Imagine a jeweler trying to create a necklace. If the jeweler attempts to make a necklace using a diamond-ruby-emerald pattern with unlimited numbers of diamonds and rubies but only three emeralds, the emeralds are the limiting jewels in the pattern. After the third round of sequencing, the jeweler has run out of emeralds, and the necklace can't be completed as designed. Because the full chain can't be completed, the jewels have to be dismantled.

Similarly, when proteins are being synthesized in your body, all the amino acids have to be available at the same time to complete the protein. A half-synthesized protein can't wait for the needed amino acids to come along to complete the process. Rather, the unfinished protein will be degraded, and the amino acids will be used to make glucose, will be used as energy, or will be stored as fat.

Does that mean that plant proteins are of less value in the diet? Absolutely not. When incomplete proteins are coupled with modest amounts of animal proteins or soy, which have all the essential amino acids, or combined with other plant proteins that are rich in the incomplete protein's limiting amino acids, the incomplete protein becomes a **complemented protein.** In other words, its amino acid profile is upgraded to a complete protein. You don't have to eat the two food sources of the complementing plant proteins at the same meal to improve the quality of the protein source. As long as the foods are consumed in the same day, all the essential amino acids will be provided to meet your daily needs.

Once the digestibility and the amino acid profile of a protein are known, the quality of the protein can be determined. Let's look at how this is done.

The Take-Home Message **A protein's quality is determined by its digestibility and by the types and amounts of amino acids (essential versus nonessential) it contains. Protein from animal foods is more easily digested than protein from plant foods. A complete protein, which is typically found in animal foods and soy, provides a complete set of the essential amino acids, along with some nonessential amino acids. Plant proteins are typically incomplete, as they are missing one or more of the essential amino acids. Plant proteins can be complemented with protein from other plant sources or animal food sources to improve their quality.**

TABLE TIPS 

Protein Power

Melt a slice of reduced-fat cheese between slices of a toasted whole-wheat English muffin for a protein-packed, portable breakfast.

Spread peanut butter on apple slices for a sweet, stick-with-you morning snack.

Add high-fiber, protein-rich chickpeas to your lunchtime salad.

Roast beef is the best-kept lunchtime secret. It's naturally lean and makes a mean sandwich filler.

Stuff a baked potato with cottage cheese, steamed broccoli, and a sprinkling of Parmesan cheese for a meal filled with protein and good nutrition.

---

complete protein A protein that provides all the essential amino acids your body needs, along with some nonessential amino acids. Soy protein and protein from animal sources, in general, are complete.

incomplete protein A protein that is low in one or more of the essential amino acids. Protein from plant sources tend to be incomplete.

complemented protein An incomplete protein that is combined with small amounts of animal or soy proteins, or with other plant proteins, to create a complete protein.

How Much Protein Do You Need and What Are Its Food Sources?

Now that you've learned the important roles that protein plays in your body, and the variable quality of dietary protein, you're probably wondering how you can be sure you're eating the best amount and types of protein foods every day.

You Can Determine Your Personal Protein Needs

For healthy adults, the amount of dietary protein (amino acids) consumed every day should equal the amount of protein their bodies use. Because amino acids contain nitrogen, a person's nitrogen levels can be measured to determine the amount of protein in the body. Nitrogen balance studies, which measure nitrogen consumed against nitrogen excreted, have been used to find out how much dietary protein people need daily. If the nitrogen intake from dietary protein is equivalent to the amount of nitrogen excreted as urea in the urine, then the person is in nitrogen balance. He or she is consuming a balanced diet with adequate amounts of protein and excreting an equally balanced amount of nitrogen. Healthy adults are typically in nitrogen balance.

A body that retains more nitrogen than it excretes is in a state of positive nitrogen balance. When you were a rapidly growing baby, child, and teenager, you were in positive nitrogen balance. Your body excreted less nitrogen than it took in because your body was using nitrogen to aid your growth, build your muscles, and expand your supply of red blood cells. When your mother was pregnant with you, she, too, was in positive nitrogen balance because she was building a robust baby.

Individuals who are healing from a traumatic injury, such as a fracture or burn; fighting a fever caused by infection; or experiencing severe illness are often in negative nitrogen balance. These situations increase the body's need for both calories and protein. If the calories and protein in the diet are inadequate to cover these increased demands, then proteins from body tissues are broken down to meet the body's needs. Tissues are also broken down when otherwise healthy people are undernourished. Figure 14.1 summarizes some of the situations that contribute to nitrogen balance in your body.

There are two ways to measure your dietary protein intake: as a percentage of total calories or as grams of protein eaten per day. The latest dietary recommendation, based on data from numerous nitrogen balance studies, is to get from 10 to 35 percent of your total daily calories from protein. Currently, adults in the United States get about 15 percent of their daily calories from protein, which falls within this range.[2]

The current recommendation for the amount of protein you need daily is based on your age and your weight (Table 14.1). Adults age 19 and older should consume 0.8 gram (g) of protein for each kilogram (kg) of body weight. You can use the table to calculate your precise protein needs. For example, if you weigh 176 pounds (lbs), you should consume about 64 grams of protein a day. If you weigh 130 pounds, you

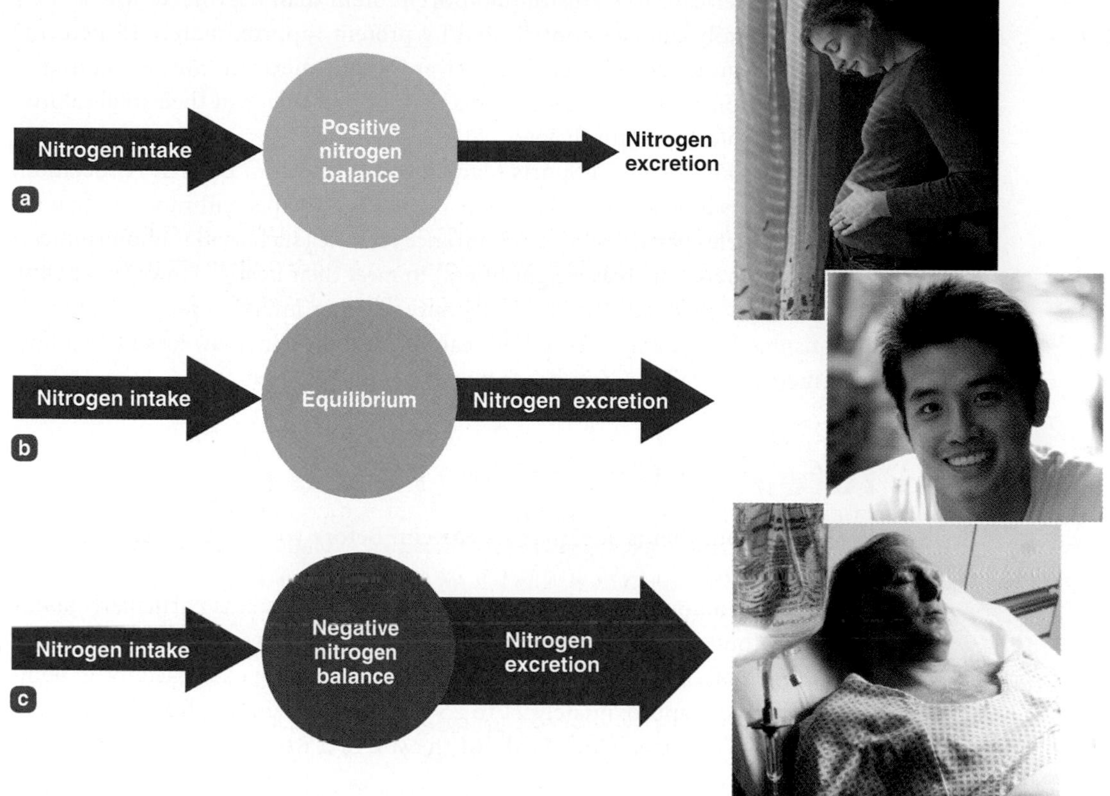

Figure 14.1 Nitrogen Balance and Imbalance
(a) Pregnant women, growing children and adolescents, and some athletes tend to be in positive nitrogen balance. (b) A healthy adult is typically in nitrogen balance. (c) An individual who is experiencing a medical trauma or is not eating a healthy diet is often in negative nitrogen balance.

should consume approximately 47 grams of protein daily (130 lbs ÷ 2.2 = 59 kg × 0.8 g = 47). In the United States, men typically consume 71 to 101 grams of protein daily, while women on average consume 55 to 62 grams. Americans are typically meeting, and even exceeding, their dietary protein needs.

Table 14.1

Calculating Your Daily Protein Needs

If You Are	You Need
14–18 years old	0.85 g/kg
≥19 years old	0.80 g/kg

To calculate your needs, first convert your body weight from pounds (lbs) to kilograms (kg) by dividing by 2.2:

Your weight in pounds: ______ lbs ÷ 2.2 = ______ kg

Then, multiply your weight in kilograms by 0.8 or 0.85:

Your weight in kilograms: ______ kg × 0.8 g = ______ g/day

Data from: Institute of Medicine, *Dietary Reference Intake for Energy, Carbohydrate, Fiber, Fat, Fatty Acids, Cholesterol, Protein, and Amino Acids* (Washington, D.C.: The National Academies Press, 2002).

If most Americans are consuming more protein than they need, why is their percentage of daily calories contributed by protein (approximately 15 percent) within the recommended range? The answer is that Americans are consuming so many calories from carbohydrates and fats that the percentage of their total calories coming from protein is relatively low.

The American College of Sports Medicine, the American Dietetic Association, and other experts have advocated an increase of 50 to 100 percent more protein for competitive athletes participating in endurance exercise (such as marathon runners) or resistance exercise (such as weight lifters) to meet their needs.[3] However, because of their active lifestyles, athletes typically have a higher intake of food and thus already consume higher amounts of both calories and protein. Now let's look at how you can meet your daily protein needs through a balanced diet.

Protein Is Found in These Foods

Do you think your diet is adequate in protein? Before you read this section, Rate Yourself to find out!

While some amount of protein is found in many foods, it is particularly abundant in dairy foods, meat, fish, poultry, and meat alternatives, such as dried beans, peanut butter, nuts, and soy (Figure 14.2). A 3-ounce serving of cooked meat, poultry, or fish provides approximately 21 to 25 grams of protein, or about 7 grams per ounce. This serving size, which is about the size of a woman's palm or a deck of

RATE YOURSELF ★★★★★

Do You Have a Protein-Friendly Diet?

Take this brief self-assessment to see if you have adequate amounts of protein-rich foods in your diet.

1. Do you eat at least 5 to 7 ounces of meat, fish, and/or poultry on most days of the week? **Yes** ☑ **No** ☐
2. Do you have at least 2 to 3 cups of milk, yogurt, soy milk, and/or soy yogurt daily? **Yes** ☑ **No** ☐
3. Do you enjoy at least 6 ounces of grains every day? (An ounce is considered one slice of bread, 1 cup of ready-to-eat cereal, or ½ cup of pasta or rice.) **Yes** ☐ **No** ☑
4. Do you eat at least 1 ounce of cheese or soy cheese daily? **Yes** ☑ **No** ☐
5. Do you eat at least 1 tablespoon of peanuts daily? **Yes** ☐ **No** ☑
6. Do you eat at least ½ cup of dried beans or peas, such as kidney beans or chickpeas, every day? **Yes** ☐ **No** ☑
7. Do you eat soy-based foods, such as soy burgers or tofu, daily? **Yes** ☐ **No** ☑

Answers

If you answered "yes" to at least the first three questions and are meeting your calorie needs on a daily basis, you have a *very* protein-friendly diet! If you answered "no" to question 1 but "yes" to most of the other questions, you are also likely meeting your protein needs if your daily calories are adequate. If you have more "no" than "yes" answers, your diet may be in need of a protein makeover. Read on to learn how you can easily add healthy sources of protein to your diet.

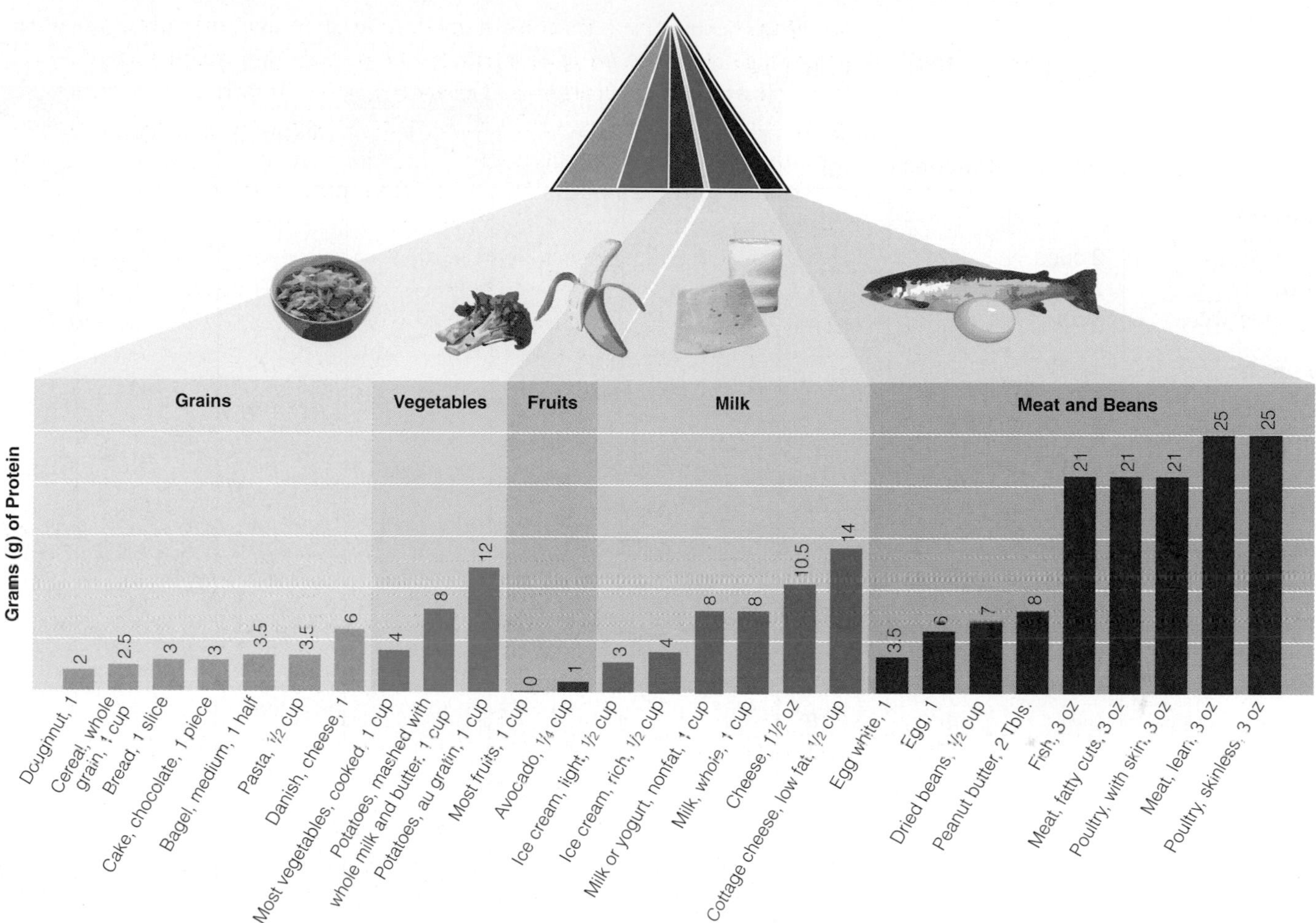

Figure 14.2 Food Sources of Protein
Food choices from the meat, poultry, fish, meat alternative, and milk groups are the most abundant sources of dietary protein. Grains and vegetables provide less protein per serving but, as part of a varied, balanced diet, can add significantly to your daily needs.

Data from USDA National Nutrient Database for Standard Reference. www.nal.usda.gov/fnic.

cards, contains plenty of protein for one meal. Grains and vegetables are less robust protein sources, providing about 3 to 4 grams per serving, but as part of a varied, balanced diet, they can aid significantly in meeting your daily needs.

Eating a wide variety of foods is the best approach to meeting your protein needs. A diet that consists of the recommended servings from the MyPyramid food guidance system based on 1,600 calories, which is far less than most adults consume daily, will meet the protein needs of adult women and most adult men (Table 14.2). In fact, many people meet their daily protein needs well before they even sit down to dinner.

Although most Americans are getting plenty of protein in their diets, there has recently been a boom in the consumption of high-protein energy bars. Are these a bargain? Are they necessary? The box feature "Protein Bars: Are They a Health Bargain?" on pages 10 and 11, takes a look at this hot topic.

Table 14.2
A Typical Day in the Life

Food	Amount	Calories	Protein* (g)	Grain Group (servings)	Vegetable Group (servings)	Fruit Group (servings)	Oil Group (tsp)	Milk Group (servings)	Meat Group (oz)
Breakfast									
Bran flakes	2 cups	256	7.5	2					
Milk, nonfat	1 cup	86	8					1	
Orange juice	8 oz	112	2			1			
Lunch									
Turkey and cheese sandwich:									
Turkey breast	2 oz	94	11						2
Cheese, low-fat	2 oz	98	14					1	
Whole-wheat bread	2 slices	138	5	2					
Tossed salad	3 cups	30	2		1.5				
Italian dressing	1 tbs	69	0				3		
Snack									
Yogurt, vanilla	8 oz	160	8					1	
Banana	1	109	1			1			
Dinner									
Chicken breast, skinless	3 oz	189	25						3
Brown rice	1 cup	216	5	2					
Broccoli, cooked	1 cup	52	6		1				
Margarine	2 tsp	68	0				2		
Totals		1,677	94.5	6	2.5	2	5	3	5

*Note: A 140-pound adult needs 51 g of protein daily. A 180-pound adult needs 65 g of protein daily.

Data from: MyPyramid.gov; J. Pennington and J. S. Douglass, *Bowes & Church's Food Values of Portions Commonly Used,* 18th ed. (New York: Lippincott Williams and Wilkins, 2005).

The Take-Home Message A balanced diet can easily fulfill your daily protein needs. Adults should consume 0.8 gram of protein for each kilogram of body weight. In the United States, men typically consume 71 to 101 grams of protein daily, while women consume 55 to 62 grams—in both cases, far more than is needed. The foods that are richest in high-quality protein are the milk group, and the meat and beans groups. Grains and vegetables do provide some protein. Choose heart-healthy, protein-rich foods that are also low in saturated fat (Figure 14.3). Table 14.3 recaps the three energy-providing nutrients and their recommended contributions to your diet. Most of your daily calories should come from carbohydrate-rich foods. Your fat intake should be no more than about one-third of your daily calories, and protein should provide the rest.

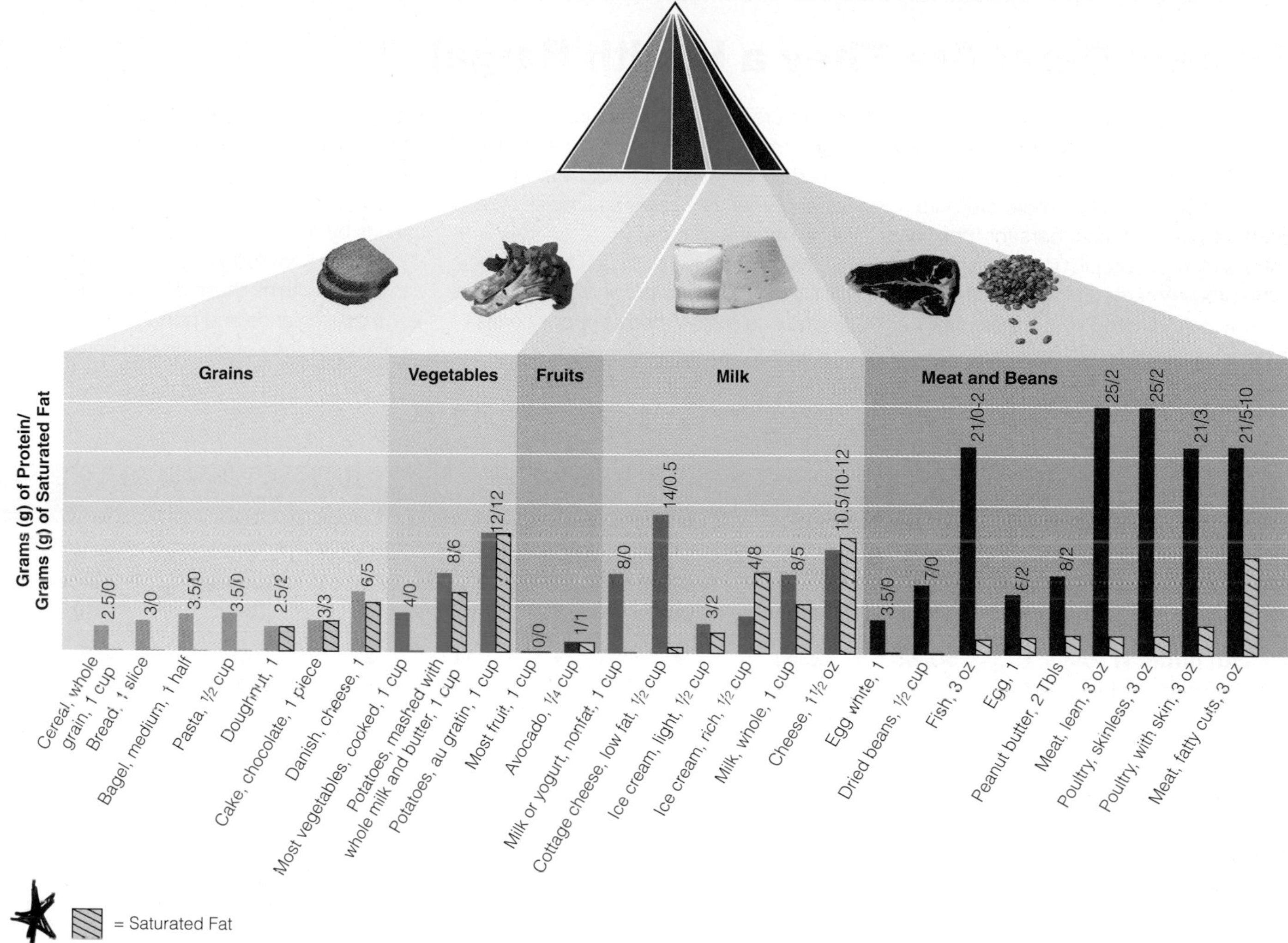

Figure 14.3 Where's the Protein and Saturated Fat in Your Foods?
While many foods—in particular, dairy foods and meats—can provide a hefty amount of protein, they can also supply a large amount of saturated fat. Choose nonfat and low-fat dairy foods, lean sources of meats, and skinless poultry to enjoy your protein without consuming too much saturated fat.

What Happens If You Eat Too Much or Too Little Protein?

While protein is essential to health and normal body function, eating too much or too little can be unhealthy. Let's look at what happens to the human body when it gets too much or too little protein.

Eating Too Much Protein Can Be Harmful

As you read in the beginning of this concept, Melissa switched to a high-protein diet to help her slim down. Unfortunately, her steady diet of low-fiber, fat-rich cheeses, hamburgers, and fried foods soon began to affect her health. The lack of fiber-rich

Table 14.3
Makeup of Your Diet

Nutrient	Current Adult Dietary Intake Recommendations*
Carbohydrates	45–65
Fats	20–35
Proteins	10–35

Nutrient	Example of a Healthy Diet*
Carbohydrates	55
Fats	30
Proteins	15
Total	100

*Percent of total calories.

Protein Bars: Are They a Health Bargain?

The sales of protein and energy bars have skyrocketed over the last decade, fueling an industry that now generates over a billion dollars annually.[1] There are bars advertised for women, bars for men, bars for the elderly, and junior bars for children. When they emerged in the 1980s, these bars were marketed as portable snacks to keep athletes fueled for long-distance or endurance outings. Manufacturers often claim that the bars are needed to fuel daily activities and build strong muscles, or that they serve as a quick meal in a cellophane wrapper.

As you learned from previous concepts, all foods provide energy in the form of calories. Whether your calories come from a balanced meal or a "balanced bar," your body will either use them as fuel or store them if they're not needed immediately. You also just learned that you can easily meet your daily protein needs by making wise food choices. Given this knowledge, what advantage, if any, do you think these bars provide?

If convenience and portability are the main attractions of protein and energy

Bar Hopping

Product	Price	Calories	Protein (g)	Total Carb. (g)	Total Fat (g)	Sat. Fat (g)	Sugars (tsp)	Fiber (g)
Peanut butter (1 tbs) on 2 slices whole-wheat bread	**$0.22**	**234**	**9**	**29**	**11**	**2**	**<1 (5%)***	**5**
Dr. Soy Double Chocolate	1.40	180	12	27	3	2.5	2.5 (22%)	1
Balance Chocolate	1.28	200	14	22	6	3.5	4.5 (36%)	<1
Zoneperfect Chocolate Peanut Butter	1.31	210	16	20	7	3	3.5 (25%)	1
EAS AdvantEdge Chocolate Peanut Crisp	1.10	220	13	32	6	3	5 (26%)	1
Atkins Advantage Chocolate Decadence	2.29	220	17	25	11	7	0	11
Genisoy Ultimate Chocolate Fudge Brownie	1.15	230	14	33	4.5	3	7 (49%)	2
Carb Solutions Creamy Chocolate Peanut Butter	2.24	240	24	14	10	3.5	0.5 (3%)	1

bars, then consider another classic, convenient, and portable food—the peanut butter sandwich. It can be made in a snap, and since it doesn't need to be refrigerated, it can travel anywhere. The accompanying table lets you do some comparison shopping to see how a peanut butter sandwich stacks up to a protein bar.

From a price standpoint, a peanut butter sandwich is a bargain, compared with bars that can cost more than $2.50 each, or 10 times as much as the sandwich. While the calorie and protein content of the sandwich are similar to that of many bars, the saturated fat and sugar contents are not. Some bars provide up to 7 grams of saturated fat, which is about one-third of the upper limit recommended for many adults daily. In contrast, the sandwich contains less saturated fat than all the bars listed. Since these bars can contain up to 7 teaspoons of sugar, which supplies up to 50 percent of the calories in the bar, much of the "energy" in an energy bar is simply sugar. The bars with the most sugar tend to have the least amount of fiber. Ironically, average consumers need more fiber in their diets. Because the peanut butter sandwich has less sugar and more fiber than most of the bars, it's the healthier food choice.

Product	Price	Calories	Protein (g)	Total Carb. (g)	Total Fat (g)	Sat. Fat (g)	Sugars (tsp)	Fiber (g)
PowerBar ProteinPlus Chocolate Fudge Brownie	1.99	270	24	36	5	3	5 (38%)	2
Met-Rx Protein Plus Chocolate Roasted Peanut	2.57	320	31	29	9	4.5	0.5 (3%)	1
PowerBar Pria Double Chocolate Cookie	0.94	110	5	16	3	2.5	2.5 ½ (36%)	0
Clif Luna Nutz Over Chocolate	1.40	180	10	24	4.5	2.5	3 (27%)	2
Kellogg's Krave Chocolate Delight	0.53	200	7	31	6	3.5	5.5 (44%)	2
Slim-Fast Meal Options Rich Chocolate Brownie	1.02	220	8	35	5	3	6 (44%)	2
Ensure Chewy Chocolate Peanut	1.13	230	9	35	6	4	6 (42%)	1

Key: = 1 tsp sugar
=1 g fiber
* = % of calories

Data adapted from: *Consumer Reports* 68 (June 2003): 19–21.

whole grains, fruits, and vegetables caused her to become extremely constipated and gave her bellyaches. As you recall from Concept 12, a diet high in saturated fat can raise the LDL ("bad") cholesterol level in the blood. Before Melissa switched to a high-protein diet, her LDL cholesterol was in the healthy range. But her steady diet of fatty foods caused her LDL cholesterol level to climb into the dangerously high range. Her doctor sent her to a registered dietitian (RD), who advised her to trim the fatty foods from her diet and add back the fiber-rich whole grains, fruits, and vegetables. Melissa's LDL cholesterol dropped to a healthy level within months, and the high-fiber foods helped "keep things moving" in her intestinal tract and eliminate the constipation. The dietitian also recommended that Melissa walk on campus between classes daily to help her better manage her weight.

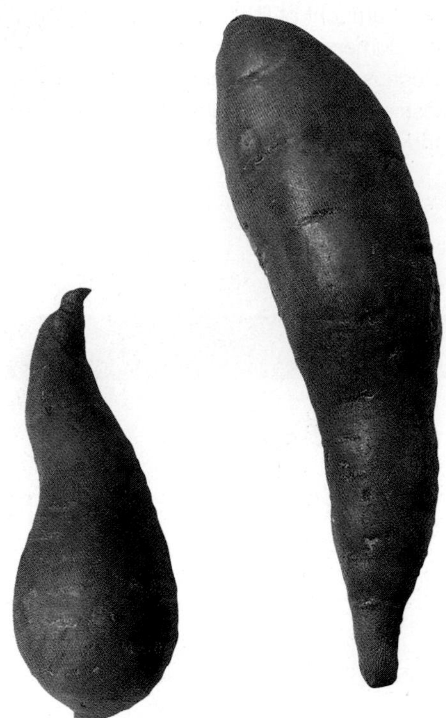

While consuming protein is a key to good health, eating more is not necessarily eating better. In fact, a diet that is too high in protein is associated with the following risks:

- *Heart disease.* A high-protein diet may increase your risk for heart disease. Many foods rich in protein are also rich in heart-unhealthy saturated fats. While lean meats and skinless poultry contain less saturated fat than some other cuts of meat, they are not completely free of saturated fat. Hence, a high protein intake can make a low saturated fat intake a challenge. As you read in Concept 12, lowering the saturated fat in your diet is important in lowering your risk for heart disease.
- *Kidney stones.* A high-protein diet may also increase your risk for kidney stones, which commonly contain calcium. Over 10 percent of Americans will likely suffer from a kidney stone at least once in their lives.[4]
- *Osteoporosis.* A high-protein diet may also increase your risk for osteoporosis (poor bone density). Although still a controversial issue, numerous research studies have shown that bones lose calcium when a person's diet is too high in protein. The loss seems to occur because calcium is taken from bone to act as a buffer, offsetting the acid generated when specific amino acids are broken down.[5] Other research has attempted to determine if calcium loss leads to osteoporosis when there is an adequate amount of calcium in a high-protein diet. If a higher dietary protein intake is coming from foods such as low-fat milk, yogurt, and cheese, it can add calcium to the diet.[6] Unfortunately, many American adults are falling short of their recommended calcium intake. If their diets are also high in protein, this isn't a healthy combination for their bones.
- *Cancer.* A high-protein diet may increase your risk for cancer; however, this relationship is also less than clear. While large amounts of meat, especially red and processed meats, may increase the risk for colon cancer, research doesn't necessarily support a connection between high amounts of total protein and increased colon cancer risk.[7]

An important health concern surrounding a high-protein diet is the displacement of other foods. If your diet is overloaded with protein-rich foods, such as meat, fish, and poultry, they will likely displace, or crowd out, other nutrient- and fiber-rich foods. As you know, a diet that contains high fiber and a wide variety of nutrient-rich foods can help you reduce your risk for several chronic diseases, such as cancer, heart disease, diabetes, and stroke. If you fill up on meat and milk at meals, you might be shortchanging yourself on foods, such as whole grains, fruits, and vegetables, that contain disease-fighting compounds.

More than **half the protein** in an egg is in the white. In fact, two egg whites provide 7 grams of protein, compared with only 6 grams in a whole egg.

While many individuals have the luxury of worrying about consuming too much protein, others are desperately trying to meet their daily needs. Let's look at the serious health implications of chronically eating too little dietary protein.

Eating Too Little Protein Can Be Harmful

Because protein is needed for so many body functions, it isn't surprising that a chronic protein deficiency can lead to many health problems. Two such problems are loss of bone mass and protein energy-malnutrition (PEM).

Loss of Bone Mass

We've said that a high-protein diet can increase the risk of bone loss, but some studies suggest that too little protein can have a similar effect! A study of more than 500 women over age 55 showed that eating higher amounts of protein is associated with denser bones. In another study, of over 2,000 men and women from ages 50 to 89, those under the age of 70 who ate more protein had 65 percent fewer hip fractures than those with the lowest protein intake. When it comes to our bones, protein balance is the key: Too much protein or too little can each be unhealthy.[8]

Protein-Energy Malnutrition (PEM)

Every day, almost 17,000 children around the world—approximately 6 million annually—die because they don't have access to enough food.[9] These children's diets are inadequate in protein, calories, or both, a condition known as **protein-energy malnutrition (PEM).** When calories and protein intakes are inadequate, the body uses dietary protein for energy, rather than reserving it for its numerous other roles in the body. Moreover, other important nutrients, such as vitamins and minerals, also tend to be in short supply, which further compounds PEM.

Many factors can lead to PEM, including poverty, poor food quality, insufficient food intake, unsanitary living conditions, ignorance of how to feed children properly, and stopping breast nursing (lactation) too early.[10] PEM is most frequently seen in infants and children compared with adults, growing infants and children have higher nutritional needs for their size. Also, they depend on others to provide them with food.

PEM can lead to life-threatening health problems. For example, without adequate dietary protein, the cells in the lining of the gastrointestinal tract aren't adequately replaced when they are routinely sloughed off. The inability to regenerate these cells inhibits their ability to function. The absorption of what little food may be available is reduced, and the bacteria that normally stay in the intestines can get into the blood and poison it. Many malnourished people have compromised immune systems, which can make fighting even minor infections, such as a respiratory infection, impossible. Malnourished children have died after exposure to measles, as well as after bouts of diarrhea caused by an infection.[11]

While deficiencies of calories and protein often occur simultaneously, sometimes one deficiency is more pronounced than the other. Let's look at two types of PEM, kwashiorkor and marasmus.

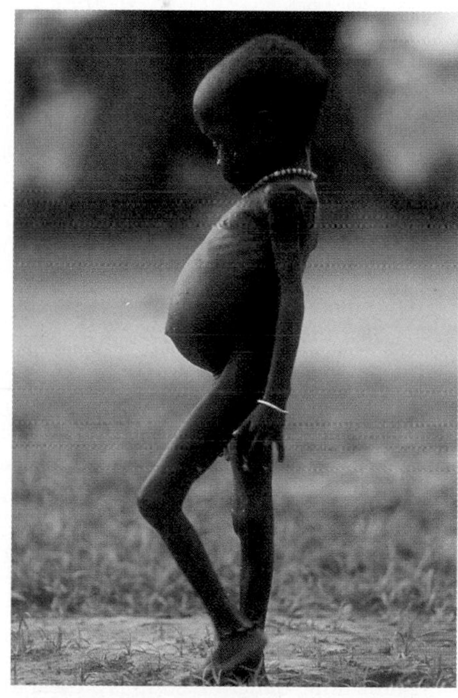

Figure 14.4 Kwashiorkor
The bloating in this child's belly is a classic sign of kwashiorkor.

Kwashiorkor

Kwashiorkor is a serious disorder caused by a severe deficiency of dietary protein. It was first observed in the 1930s in tribes in Ghana, West Africa, when a firstborn child became sick at the time that a new infant was born into the family. Typically, the newborn displaced the first child, usually around 18 months of age, from his or her lactating mother's nutritionally balanced breast milk. As a result, the older child consumed an inadequate and unbalanced diet high in carbohydrate-rich grains but severely deficient in protein, setting the stage for serious medical complications.

A classic symptom of kwashiorkor is edema in the legs, feet, and stomach (Figure 14.4). As you recall from Concept 13, edema is an abnormal accumulation of

protein-energy malnutrition (PEM) A lack of sufficient dietary protein and/or calories.

kwashiorkor A serious protein-energy malnutrition (PEM) disorder caused by a severe deficiency of dietary protein.

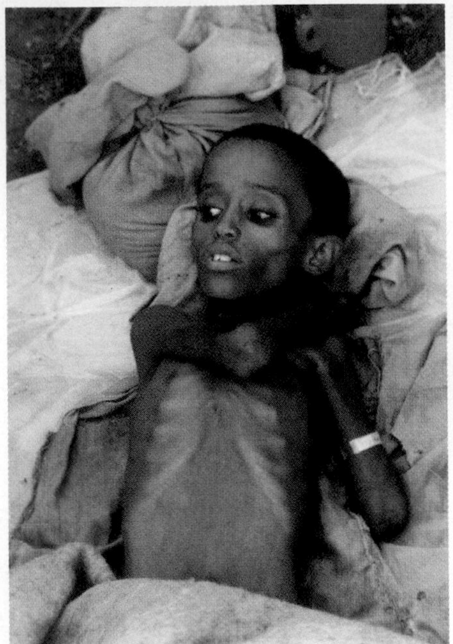

Figure 14.5 Marasmus
The emaciated appearance of this child is a sign of marasmus.

fluids beneath the skin, creating a bloated look. With a protein deficiency, fluid accumulates in the spaces surrounding the cells, causing swelling. As we've discussed, protein plays an important role in maintaining fluid balance in the blood and around the cells. As muscle proteins are broken down, the body wastes away, and muscle tone and strength diminish. Many children with kwashiorkor have skin that is dry and peeling, and their hair is brittle and can be pulled out easily. They are prone to infections, rapid heartbeat, excess fluid in the lungs, pneumonia, blood poisoning, and water and electrolyte imbalances—all of which can be deadly.[12]

Marasmus

The bloating seen in kwashiorkor is the opposite of the frail, emaciated appearance of **marasmus** (Figure 14.5). Because they are not consuming enough calories, many people with marasmus do not reach even 60 percent of their desirable body weight. Since the body is using all available calories to stay alive, growth is restricted. The person is weak and appears apathetic. Many can't stand without support. Children with marasmus look old beyond their years, since the loss of fat in the face—one of the last places the body loses fat during starvation—causes the disappearance of a robust, childlike appearance. Their hair is thin and dry and lacks the sheen found in healthy children. Their body temperature and blood pressure are low, and they are prone to dehydration, infections, and unnecessary blood clotting.[13]

marasmus A serious condition of protein-energy malnutrition (PEM) stemming from severe deficiency of calories, that results in wasting; commonly called *starvation.*

The Take-Home Message **A high-protein diet may play a role in increasing the risk for heart disease, kidney problems, and calcium loss from bone. Consuming too much protein from animal sources can increase the amount of heart-unhealthy saturated fat in your diet. Consuming too many protein-rich foods can displace whole grains, fruits, and vegetables, which have been shown to help reduce the risk for many chronic diseases. A low-protein diet has also been shown to lead to loss of bone mass. Protein-energy malnutrition (PEM) is caused by an inadequate amount of protein and/or calories in the diet. A severe disorder caused by protein deficiency is kwashiorkor. Marasmus results from a serious deficiency of calories. These conditions can be improved through proper nutrition and treatment.**

Check out these recipes and more suggestions at **www.pearsonhighered.com/blake**

UCook

Hearty Bean Soup
This filling, delicious soup is a meal in itself. Add whole-grain bread for a warm and lasting meal.

UDo

Plan Your Protein
Go to our website to plan a day of food choices that will allow you to meet your protein needs without exceeding your upper limits for saturated fat.
(Note: Use the MyDietAnalysis program to help you.)

The Top Five Points to Remember

1. A protein's quality is determined by its digestibility and by the types and amounts of amino acids it contains. Protein from animal foods is more easily digested than protein from plant foods. Proteins from animal foods and soy are typically complete proteins, providing all the essential amino acids, along with some nonessential amino acids. Plant proteins are typically incomplete, since they are missing one or more essential amino acids.

2. A healthy adult is typically in nitrogen balance; that is, intake balances excretion. Athletes, pregnant women, and growing children typically take in more nitrogen than they excrete because they are building tissues. In people who are starving or experiencing severe illness, tissues are breaking down and nitrogen excretion is increased.
3. Adults should consume 0.8 gram of protein for each kilogram of body weight. The typical American diet provides far more protein than they need.
4. In protein consumption, balance is important. Consuming too much protein from animal sources can increase the amount of heart-unhealthy saturated fat in the diet. A high-protein diet has been associated with the loss of calcium from the body and the development of kidney stones. An excess of protein-rich foods in the diet can displace whole grains, fruits, and vegetables.
5. Protein-energy malnutrition (PEM) is caused by an inadequate amount of protein and/or calories in the diet. Kwashiorkor is a severe deficiency of protein; marasmus is a severe deficiency of calories.

Test Yourself

1. Protein is found abundantly in
   a. the milk group and the fat group.
   b. the meat and beans group and the fruit group.
   c. the vegetable group and the milk group.
   d. the milk group and the meat and beans group.
2. Which of the following is a source of complete protein?
   a. kidney beans
   b. peanut butter
   c. soy milk
   d. pasta
3. Which of the following people is likely to be in nitrogen balance?
   a. a school-age child
   b. an adult who is battling cancer
   c. a healthy adult
   d. an adult who is malnourished
4. Kwashiorkor is a type of PEM that develops when
   a. there is a severe deficiency of protein in the diet but an adequate amount of calories.
   b. there are inadequate amounts of both protein and calories in the diet.
   c. there is an inadequate amount of animal protein in the diet.
   d. there are adequate amounts of both protein and calories in the diet.
5. High-protein diets are associated with an increased risk for
   a. constipation.
   b. heart disease.
   c. kidney stones.
   d. all of the above.

Answers

1. (d) Both the milk group and the meat and beans group are full of protein-rich food sources. While there is some protein in vegetables, there is little in fruits. Fats do not contain protein.
2. (c) Soy foods, such as soy milk, provide all the essential amino acids you need, along with some nonessential amino acids; thus, they are a source of complete protein. Kidney beans, peanut butter, and pasta are missing adequate amounts of the essential amino acids.
3. (c) Healthy adults are usually in nitrogen balance. Infants, children, and growing adolescents are typically in positive nitrogen balance, while individuals who are seriously ill or malnourished are typically in negative nitrogen balance.
4. (a) Kwashiorkor occurs when protein is deficient in the diet even if calorie intake is adequate. Marasmus occurs when calories are inadequate in the diet and the person is starving. Consuming protein from animal sources is not necessary, because people can meet their protein needs from a combination of plant proteins, such as soy, legumes, grains, and vegetables, as part of a well-balanced diet.
5. (d) High-protein diets are often low in fiber, increasing the risk for constipation. They are also associated with an increased risk for heart disease and kidney stones.

Web Resources

- For more information on protein bars and supplements, visit the Center for Science in the Public Interest at: www.cspinet.org/nah/12_00/barexam.html
- For more information on PEM, visit the World Health Organization (WHO) at: www.wpro.who.int/health_topics/protein_energy

15 Vegetarian Diets

What to Eat When You Don't Eat Meat

1. About 1 in every 100 Americans is a **vegetarian.** **T/F**

2. Farm animal production releases more **greenhouse gases** than transportation does. **T/F**

3. Vegetarian diets are always **healthier** than nonvegetarian diets. **T/F**

4. **Soy** food consumption is increasing. **T/F**

5. Athletes need to **eat meat** to compete. **T/F**

When Jackie moved away from home to start college, she did something she'd been wanting to do for years: She became a vegetarian. "If I had tried this at home," she explains to her roommate, "my parents would have freaked out—especially my dad, who thinks steak is an essential nutrient!"

Still, in the three months since starting her vegetarian diet, Jackie has noticed that her daily routine—her morning jog, classes, work-study job, and homework—seems to be getting harder to maintain, and she wonders if her new diet has anything to do with it.

When her roommate asks if she's been following a vegetarian diet plan, Jackie admits she hasn't. "I keep meaning to read up on it, but I just don't have the time. Anyway, how hard can it be? People all over the world are vegetarians, and I bet most of them never read a book about it!"

While it's true that people throughout the world stay healthy on a vegetarian diet, there are many variations, and some vegetarian diets are easier to follow than others. What are the different diets, and what are the benefits and challenges of a vegetarian lifestyle? Is Jackie putting her health in danger by failing to plan a vegetarian diet?

Answers

1. False. The figure is closer to about 3 out of every 100 Americans is a practicing vegetarian. See page 2 to learn more.
2. True. Animal husbandry produces significant amounts of carbon dioxide, methane, and other gases that contribute to global warming. Check out pages 3 and 4 for details.
3. False. While a well-planned vegetarian diet is quite healthy, one that isn't well balanced can lack nutrients. To learn about vegetarian diets, turn to page 5.
4. True. Consumption of soy-based foods in the U. S. has been increasing over the past two decades. Turn to page 10 to learn more.
5. False. Theoretically, competitive athletes do not need to eat meat, chicken or fish to fulfill their protein and nutrient needs. In practice, however, athletes who choose to avoid meat must be careful that their diet provides the nine essential amino acids and other nutrients they need, which is easier to do if they eat meat. See page 12 for more.

What Are Vegetarian Diets, and Why Do People Choose Them?

What do spaghetti topped with marinara sauce, veggie pizza, and lentil soup have in common? All these classic **vegetarian** meals lack meat, and you've probably eaten one or more of them—maybe even on a regular basis. From meal to meal, you may be eating as a vegetarian without realizing it. Does this mean that you are a vegetarian? According to the American Dietetic Association (ADA), a vegetarian is a person who does not eat meat, fish, poultry, or (sometimes) food products made from these animal sources.[1] The term has been adapted from the Latin word *vegetus,* meaning whole or sound, which did not originally refer to a diet based on vegetables!

An estimated 3 percent of American adults (about 6 million people) follow a vegetarian diet. In the United States, the vegetarian food market has grown into an industry generating over $1.5 billion, as manufacturers respond to the growing consumer demand with new vegetarian products each year.[2]

The supermarket is not the only place you can get a vegetarian meal. Over 70 percent of sit-down restaurants offer vegetarian options. Even some fast-food restaurants have added veggie burgers and other vegetarian fare to their menus. Vegetarianism is also increasingly common on college campuses, as schools offer more vegetarian options to meet growing student demand.[3]

Types of Vegetarian Diets

How vegetarian savvy are you? Before reading on, Rate Yourself and find out!

vegetarian A person who does not eat meat, fish, poultry, or (sometimes) food products made from these animal sources.

As you can see in Table 15.1, there are several types of vegetarians, each with its own range of acceptable foods. Semivegetarians, also called flexitarians, take a flexible approach to eating meat. For instance, they might avoid all red meat but eat poultry and fish several times a week. Some semivegetarians eat red meat a few times a

Table 15.1

The Many Types of Vegetarians

Type	Diet Restrictions: Does Eat	Diet Restrictions: Doesn't Eat
Lacto-vegetarian	Grains, vegetables, fruits, legumes, nuts, dairy foods	Meat, fish, poultry, eggs
Lacto-ovo-vegetarian	Grains, vegetables, fruits, legumes, seeds, nuts, dairy and eggs	Meat, fish, poultry foods
Ovo-vegetarian	Grains, vegetables, fruits, legumes, seeds, nuts, eggs	Meat, fish, poultry, dairy foods
Vegan	Grains, vegetables, fruits, legumes, seeds, nuts	Any animal foods, meat, fish, poultry, dairy foods, eggs
Semivegetarian	A vegetarian diet that occasionally includes meat, fish, poultry, and eggs	Meat, fish, and poultry on occasion

year. A subgroup of semivegetarians, called pesco (*pesce* = fish) vegetarians, avoid all meat and poultry but regularly eat fish.

Among true vegetarians, lacto-ovo-vegetarians are the broadest group: They eat dairy products and eggs, while avoiding meat, poultry, and fish. Lacto-vegetarians consume milk products but not eggs. Ovo-vegetarians consume eggs but not dairy products. Because their diets include some animal-based foods (eggs and dairy products), these vegetarians avoid many of the nutritional challenges seen with stricter vegetarians, called vegans, who eat no foods of animal origin. Some vegans are so strict that they even avoid honey.

Many vegetarians of all types also avoid using products made from parts of animals, including such items as leather and hair bristles. Many also avoid using products, such as toiletries and cosmetics, that have been tested on animals.

RATE YOURSELF 

How Vegetarian Savvy Are You?

1. A lacto-vegetarian can eat a slice of cheese pizza as a snack.
   True ☐ **False** ☐
2. A vegan can eat gelatin.
   True ☐ **False** ☐
3. A lacto-ovo-vegetarian can enjoy a cheese omelet for breakfast.
   True ☐ **False** ☐
4. An ovo-vegetarian can eat a chicken Caesar salad at lunch.
   True ☐ **False** ☐
5. A semivegetarian can have a shrimp stir-fry for dinner.
   True ☐ **False** ☐

Answers

1. True. Because lacto-vegetarians can eat dairy products, a cheese pizza is a perfect snack food. They will pass on the pepperoni, though.
2. False. Gelatin is derived from cows, so a vegan who avoids all animal products won't eat it.
3. True. Lacto-ovo-vegetarians can eat both eggs and dairy foods, so a cheese omelet is a "go" for breakfast.
4. False. Even though chickens come from eggs, ovo-vegetarians avoid poultry (but can eat eggs). An egg salad sandwich would be a better match.
5. True. A semivegetarian occasionally eats animal foods, so shrimp stir-fry would be a dinner they could enjoy from time to time.

Reasons for Choosing a Vegetarian Diet

The reasons for choosing a vegetarian diet can be as complex as the people who make that choice. Still, the following are some of the most commonly cited reasons:

- *Health concerns.* As we'll explain in more detail, a balanced vegetarian diet can help you maintain a healthy weight and reduce your risk for certain chronic diseases. In addition, many vegetarians are concerned that the hormones and antibiotics fed to animals to increase their milk or meat production might come with health risks. Others avoid animal-based foods because of concerns about infection from bacteria, worms, or the prions associated with mad cow disease. (For more information, see Concept 27.)
- *Environmental concerns.* According to the Food and Agriculture Organization (FAO) of the United Nations, farm animal production creates nearly a fifth of the world's greenhouse gases—more than what comes from cars and other forms of transportation.[4] A significant amount of carbon dioxide emissions is due to (1) the production of fertilizer to make the crops for feed, (2) the

Thousands of cows are confined for their lifetime in feedlots such as this one.

transportation of the feed, and (3) the energy required to maintain the animals and to process and transport the animal products.[5]

- *Compassion for animals.* Many people deplore the treatment of farm animals whose entire lives are spent confined in densely packed feedlots and windowless barns and are slaughtered without concern for their sense of fear or pain. These concerns prompt many people to choose meat and poultry from local farms where animals are free to range and humane practices are used at slaughter, while others choose a vegetarian diet to avoid harming animals entirely.
- *Religious convictions.* Various sects within many major religions, including Christianity, Buddhism, and Hinduism, forbid or discourage the consumption of animal-based foods.
- *Financial constraints.* Meat, poultry, and fish are relatively expensive foods, and many people worldwide simply cannot afford them. Typically, as countries transition from poverty to affluence, meat consumption rises. The staple dishes of many cultures, such as the Mexican bean burrito, the miso soup of Japan, and the rice and dal of India, combine complementary plant-based proteins that make low-cost complete-protein meals.

The Take-Home Message **A true vegetarian diet does not consume any meat, poultry, or fish; however, semivegetarians occasionally consume one or more of these foods, while focusing most of their diet on plant-based foods. About 3 percent of American adults follow a vegetarian diet. Reasons for adopting a vegetarian diet include health concerns, environmental concerns, compassion for animals, religious convictions, and financial constraints.**

What Are the Potential Benefits and Risks of a Vegetarian Diet?

As we have noted, many people choose a vegetarian diet because of the health benefits associated with it. If not planned carefully, however, a vegetarian diet can also carry some unique health risks. Let's look at both sides of the issue.

Health Benefits of a Vegetarian Diet

A plant-based diet can be rich in high-fiber whole grains, vegetables, fruits, legumes, and nuts and thus naturally lower in saturated fat and cholesterol. This type of diet contains the fundamentals for reducing the risk of the following diseases:

- *Heart disease.* Vegetarian food staples, such as soy, nuts, and soluble fiber–rich foods, such as beans and oats, have been shown to reduce blood cholesterol levels.

Numerous studies have shown that the rates of deaths from heart disease are about 25 percent lower among vegetarians than among nonvegetarians.[6]

- *High blood pressure.* Vegetarians tend to have lower blood pressure than meat eaters. The incidence of high blood pressure has been shown to be over two times higher in nonvegetarians.[7] High blood pressure is a risk factor not only for heart disease but also for stroke.
- *Type 2 diabetes.* You know from Concept 9 that a plant-based diet can help reduce the risk for type 2 diabetes, so it shouldn't surprise you that vegetarians tend to have a lower risk for diabetes. Diabetes is also a risk for heart disease. For people with diabetes, consuming foods rich in fiber and low in saturated fat and cholesterol makes eating a vegetarian diet an attractive strategy to better manage this disease.[8]
- *Certain types of cancer.* Vegetarian diets have been shown to reduce the risk for both prostate and colon cancer. Respected health organizations, such as the American Institute for Cancer Research and the American Cancer Society, advocate a plant-based diet to reduce the risk for cancer.[9]
- *Obesity.* A plant-based diet containing mostly fiber-rich whole grains and low-calorie, nutrient-rich vegetables and fruits tends to "fill you up before it fills you out," making you more likely to eat fewer calories overall. Hence, the plant-based foods of a vegetarian diet can be a healthy, satisfying strategy for those fighting the battle against obesity.

In India, many people consider cows sacred and decorate them with colorful paints and flowers for religious ceremonies.

Health Risks of a Vegetarian Diet

The biggest risk of a vegetarian diet is in not consuming enough of the nutrients that are found in abundance in animal foods. Table 15.2 identifies the key nutrients that can be missing from a vegetarian diet: protein, iron, zinc, calcium, vitamin D, vitamin B_{12}, vitamin A, and omega-3 fatty acids. Thus, strictly avoiding meat, fish, poultry, and food products derived from animal sources can be *unhealthy* if you don't consume these nutrients in nonmeat alternatives. Like Jackie in our opening story, vegetarians need to plan their meals with care to meet all their nutrient needs. Table 15.2 identifies food sources of these important nutrients, as well as Table Tips for adding them to your diet. We discuss vegetarian meal planning in the next section.

The Take-Home Message **The health benefits of a vegetarian diet include reduced risk for heart disease, high blood pressure, type 2 diabetes, certain types of cancer, and obesity. The risks associated with eating a vegetarian diet include not consuming enough of certain important nutrients, including protein, iron, zinc, calcium, vitamin D, vitamin B_{12}, vitamin A, and omega-3 fatty acids.**

Table 15.2

Nutrients That Can Be MIA (Missing in Action) in a Vegetarian Diet

Vegetarians need to take care in planning a diet that meets all their nutritional needs. Here are the nutrients that vegetarians could fall short of in their diet, some vegetarian food sources for these nutrients, and tips on how to enjoy these foods as part of a balanced diet.

Nutrient	Risks	Vegetarian Food Sources	Table Tips
Protein	A vegetarian's protein needs can be met by consuming a *variety* of plant foods. A combination of protein-rich soy foods, legumes, nuts, and/or seeds should be eaten daily.	Soybeans, soy burgers, tofu, tempeh, nuts, peanuts, peanut butter, legumes, sunflower seeds, milk, soy milk, yogurt, cheese	■ Add nuts to your morning cereal. ■ Add beans to your salads, soups, and main entrées. ■ Have a soy burger for lunch. ■ Use tofu in stir-fries, rice and pasta dishes, and casseroles. ■ Snack on a soy milk and banana or berry shake.
Iron	The form of iron in plants is not as easily absorbed as the type in meat, milk, and poultry. Also, phytate in grains and rice and polyphenols in tea and coffee can inhibit iron absorption. The iron needs of vegetarians are about 1½ times higher than those of nonvegetarians. Vitamin C enhances the absorption of the iron in plant foods.	Iron-fortified cereals, enriched grains, pasta, bread, oatmeal, potatoes, wheat germ, cashews and other nuts, sunflower seeds, legumes, soybeans, tofu, bok choy, broccoli, mushrooms, dried fruits	■ Make sure your morning cereal is iron fortified. ■ Add soybeans to your lunchtime salad. ■ Eat bread with your salad lunch or make a sandwich. ■ Pack a trail mix of dried fruits and nuts for a snack. ■ Add vitamin C–rich foods (broccoli, tomatoes, citrus fruits) to all your meals.
Zinc	The absorption of zinc is enhanced by animal protein. Eating a vegetarian diet means that you lose out on this benefit and are more likely to develop a deficiency. Phytate also binds zinc, making it unavailable to your body. A vegan's zinc needs may be as much as 50 percent higher than a nonvegetarian's.	Soybeans, soy milk, tofu, tempeh, fortified soy burgers, legumes, nuts, sunflower seeds, wheat germ, fortified ready-to-eat cereals, mushrooms, low-fat or nonfat milk, yogurt, and cheese	■ Douse your morning cereal with low-fat milk. ■ Add low-fat cheese and soybeans to your lunchtime salad. ■ Snack on sunflower seeds. ■ Top an afternoon yogurt with wheat germ. ■ Add soybeans to your dinner rice.
Calcium	Calcium is abundant in lean dairy foods, such as nonfat or low-fat milk, yogurt, and cheese, so obtaining adequate amounts shouldn't be difficult if you consume these foods. Calcium-fortified soy milk and orange juice as well as tofu can provide about the same amount of calcium per serving as is found in dairy foods.	Low-fat or nonfat milk, yogurt, and cheese; fortified soy milk, soy yogurt, and soy cheese; calcium-fortified orange juice; legumes; sesame tahini; tofu processed with calcium; bok choy; broccoli; kale; collard greens; mustard greens; okra	■ Add milk to your morning cereal and coffee. ■ Have at least one yogurt a day. ■ Have a glass of calcium-fortified orange juice with lunch. ■ Snack on low-fat cheese or yogurt in the afternoon. ■ Eat green vegetables often at dinner.

Nutrient	Risks	Vegetarian Food Sources	Table Tips
Vitamin D	Some vegetarians will need to consume vitamin D–fortified milk or soy products.	Low-fat or nonfat milk, egg yolk, fortified yogurt, soy milk, soy yogurt, ready-to-eat cereals, vitamin supplement	■ Have a glass of milk or soy milk at breakfast every day. ■ Make sure your morning cereal is vitamin D fortified. ■ Use fortified evaporated skim milk as a base for cream sauces. ■ Snack on fortified cereals. ■ Have a fortified yogurt each day.
Vitamin B_{12}	Animal foods are the only naturally occurring food source of B_{12}, so it is extremely important that vegetarians, especially strict vegans, look to fortified cereals and soy milk or a supplement to meet their daily needs.	Low-fat and nonfat milk, yogurt, or cheese, eggs, fortified soy milk, ready-to-eat cereals, soy burgers, egg substitutes, vitamin supplement	■ Make sure your morning cereal is fortified with vitamin B_{12}. ■ Drink a cup of milk or fortified soy milk with your meals. ■ Top an afternoon yogurt snack with a fortified cereal. ■ Try an egg substitute omelet for lunch. ■ Use fortified soy "meat" alternatives at dinner.
Vitamin A	Vitamin A is found only in animal foods. However, vegetarians can meet their needs by consuming the vitamin A precursor, beta-carotene.	Fortified low-fat or nonfat milk and soy milk, apricots, cantaloupe, mangoes, pumpkin, kale, spinach	■ Enjoy a slice or bowl of cantaloupe in the morning. ■ Snack on dried apricots. ■ Add spinach to your lunchtime salad. ■ Drink a glass of fortified milk or soy milk with dinner. ■ Try mangoes for a sweet dessert.
Omega-3 fatty acids	If your vegetarian diet doesn't include fish, you may not be consuming enough of the essential omega-3 fatty acid called alpha-linolenic acid.	Fish (especially fatty fish such as salmon and sardines), walnuts, flaxseed and flaxseed oil, soybean and canola oil	■ Add walnuts to baked breads and muffins. ■ Try canned salmon on top of your lunchtime salad. ■ Top your yogurt with ground flaxseeds. ■ Have fish regularly for dinner. ■ Cook with canola and flaxseed oil.

How Can You Be a Healthy Vegetarian?

To avoid nutrient deficiencies, vegetarians must eat adequate amounts of all nutrients by eating a wide variety of foods. A vitamin and mineral supplement may be necessary to help balance nutrients. The vegetarian food guide pyramid in Figure 15.1 can help you incorporate these nutrients in a vegetarian diet.

Many people considering adopting a vegetarian diet wonder whether plant foods can really supply all their nutrient needs. The two nutrients people are typically most concerned about—protein and vitamin B_{12}—are discussed in more detail in this section, including strategies for getting adequate amounts of these nutrients. Table 15.3 compares the nutrient composition of a traditional meat-based meal and a similar meal made solely from plant foods. Compare their nutrition profile as shown in Table 15.3. What you find may surprise you.

Figs are a sweet way to get some calcium. Five large figs provide over 10 percent of many adults' daily calcium needs.

Concerns about Consuming Adequate Amounts of Protein

Because vegetarians avoid meat and other animal foods that are high in protein, they need to be sure to get adequate protein from other food sources. Vegetarians can meet their daily protein needs by consuming a varied plant-based diet that contains protein-rich alternatives to meat, such as soy, dried beans and other legumes, and

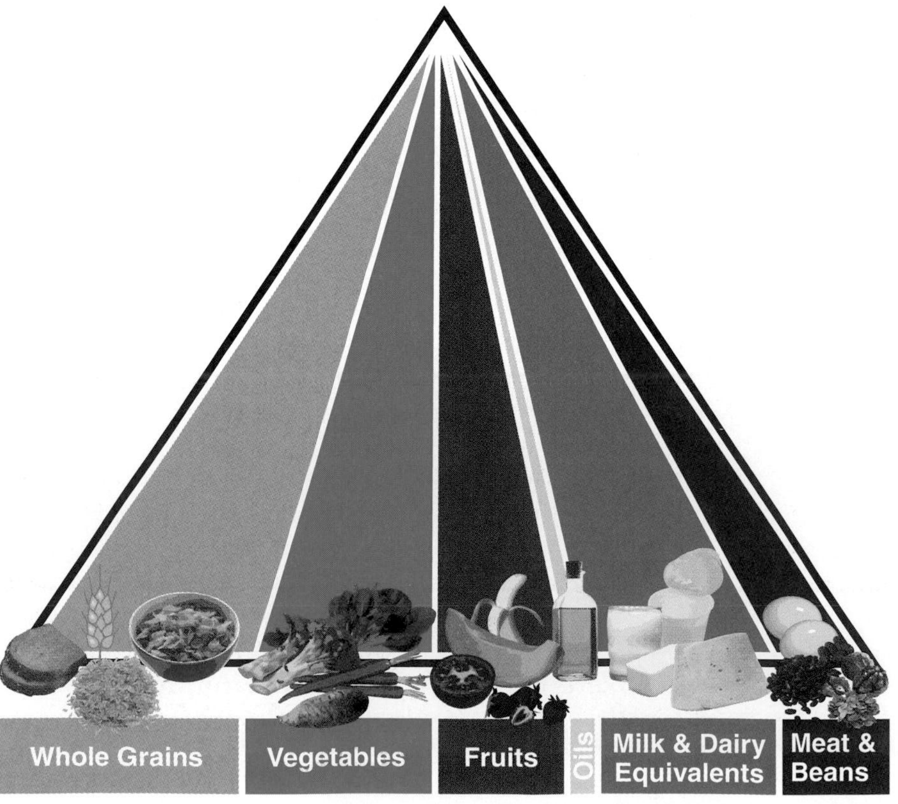

Figure 15.1 Vegetarian Food Guide Pyramid
Vegetarians should eat a variety of foods from each food group, especially legumes, nuts, and oils, to obtain essential fatty acids and adequate protein, calcium, and vitamin B_{12}.

Table 15.3

How Does a Vegetarian Meal Compare?

Similar to meat meals, vegetarian meals can provide a robust amount of protein and iron with less heart-unhealthy saturated fat and cholesterol. While a tofu stir-fry doesn't provide as much zinc or vitamin B_{12} as meat, it is a fabulous source of calcium, a mineral many adults are falling short of.

	Beef Stir-Fry (per Serving)	vs.	Tofu Stir-Fry (per Serving)
Protein	38 grams		26 grams
Saturated Fat	3.3 grams		1.8 grams
Dietary Cholesterol	105 milligrams		0
Iron	3.9 grams		5.1 grams
Calcium	34 milligrams		450 milligrams
Zinc	6.8 milligrams		2.9 milligrams
Vitamin B_{12}	2.5 micrograms		0

nuts. Combining many sources of protein at one meal is not necessary; however, as noted earlier, many vegetarian meals, such as rice with beans, lentil soup with barley, and even a peanut butter sandwich on whole-wheat bread, naturally combine foods with complementary proteins. Some vegetarians include protein-rich eggs, dairy foods, and fish as part of their diet.

We noted in Concept 14 that soybeans, and the foods made from them, provide all the essential amino acids and are thus a source of complete protein. For more information on soy, check out the feature box in this concept, The Joy of Soy. As shown there, and in the Table Tips in Table 15.2, you can substitute soy-based products for meat in many traditional meals. In addition, the following are some popular ways to add soy to your diet:

- For breakfast, grill a soy-based "sausage" patty instead of meat sausage.
- Switch your hot dog with a veggie dog.
- Mix soy "ground beef" into your pasta sauce or tacos.
- Use frozen soy "beef" or "chicken" strips in a stir-fry.
- Choose veggie "chicken" nuggets over traditional chicken nuggets.

Concerns about Consuming Adequate Amounts of Vitamin B_{12}

Vitamin B_{12} is derived only from foods with animal origins. Because lacto-ovo-vegetarians consume dairy products and eggs, both of which provide vitamin B_{12}, their diet is more likely than that of vegans to provide adequate amounts of this important nutrient. However, both lacto-ovo-vegetarians and vegans must be careful to consume adequate amounts of B_{12}. For vegans, that means consuming foods fortified with B_{12} or taking B_{12} supplements regularly. The ADA recommends including at least three good food sources of vitamin B_{12} in your diet every day.[10] For vegetarians who are not strict vegans, choices include eggs, yogurt, cheese, and cow's milk.

The Joy of Soy

Soy has been used as a dietary staple for centuries in Asia. Soy consumption in the United States, in foods ranging from soy milk to soy burgers, has been increasing since the 1990s. According to the United Soybean Board, 32 percent of Americans consume soy foods or soy beverages at least once a month.[1] The sales of soy-based beverages and foods are predicted to reach $1.5 billion in 2012.[2]

The popularity of soy foods is increasing among many age-groups and ethnic groups, including baby boomers, Asian populations in the U.S. looking for soy-based foods, and young adults with an interest in vegetarian diets[3].

isoflavones Naturally occurring plant estrogens, which function similarly to the estrogen hormone in the human body.

estrogen The hormone responsible for female sex characteristics.

What Is Soy?

Soy is a high-quality protein source derived from soybeans. It is low in saturated fat and, like many beans, provides iron. In addition, soy contains **isoflavones,** which are naturally occurring phytoestrogens. These plant estrogens have a chemical structure similar to human **estrogen,** a female sex hormone.[4] While isoflavones can also be found in other plant foods, such as grains, vegetables, and legumes, soybeans contain the largest amount found in food.

Soy and Your Health

Studies of health and disease in populations suggest that isoflavones may reduce the risk for chronic diseases, including heart disease and possibly breast cancer.

Eating soy protein may reduce the risk for heart disease by lowering cholesterol levels. A review of over 35 research studies showed that soy protein lowered total cholesterol, LDL ("bad") cholesterol, and triglycerides by about 10 percent. Another research review showed a less dramatic lowering of LDL cholesterol with no effect on triglycerides.[5] Originally, researchers theorized that isoflavones might play a major role in soy's cholesterol-lowering capabilities. However, nu-

What's on the Soy Menu?

Tofu ►
Cooked, puréed soybeans that are processed into a silken, soft or firm texture; has a neutral flavor, which allows it to blend well.
Use the silken version in dips, soups, and cream pies. Use the firm variety in stir-fries and on salads, or marinate it and then bake or grill it.

Soy milk ▲
A soy beverage made from a mixture of ground soybeans and water.
Use it in place of cow's milk. Combine soy milk with ice and fruit in a blender for a soy shake.

Edamame ▲
Tender, young soybeans; can be purchased fresh, frozen, or canned.
Use in salads, grain dishes, stir-fries, and casseroles.

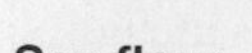

Soy flour ▲
Made from ground, roasted soybeans.
Use it in baked goods, such as pancakes, muffins, and cookies. It can also substitute for eggs in baked goods: Use 1 tbs soy flour combined with 1 tbs of water for each whole egg.

merous research studies have questioned isoflavones' effect on cholesterol and concluded that, if it does play a role, it is probably a minor one in comparison to the soy protein and/or another component in the soybeans.[6] Since soy products, such as tofu and soy nuts, are low in saturated fat, these protein-rich foods can replace other animal foods that provide heart-unhealthy dietary cholesterol and saturated fat at meals.

Interest in soy as a cancer fighter was sparked after researchers observed that Asian countries had lower rates of breast cancer than Western countries. Numerous studies suggest that the isoflavones in soy may help reduce the risk for cancer, as these weak estrogens may have anticancer functions in the body. Isoflavones compete with the hormone estrogen within the body. Since estrogen may increase the risk for breast cancer, inhibiting or blocking the actions of estrogen may help reduce the risk.[7]

Timing may be an important part in the preventive role that soy plays in breast cancer. A study of Chinese women revealed that those who ate the most soy during their adolescent years had a reduced risk for breast cancer in adulthood. The early exposure of soy foods may be protective by stimulating the growth of cells in the breast, enhancing the rate at which the glands mature, and altering the tissues in a beneficial way.

However, the anticancer role of isoflavones may also be a detriment.[8] There is some concern that, once the isoflavones are bound to the estrogen receptors, they can initiate the production of cancer cells, which can *raise* the risk for breast cancer. A recent review of over 200 research studies supports the safety of soy isoflavones when consumed as soy and soy products. However, this issue of potentially increasing the risk for breast cancer, especially for those who are at high risk of developing or who presently have breast cancer, isn't resolved as yet. The American Cancer Society advises women with breast cancer to avoid eating large amounts of soy without discussing it first with their doctor. If they do eat soy foods, they should limit consumption to no more than three servings daily.[9]

Soy can be an inexpensive, heart-healthy protein source that may also help lower your blood cholesterol. While soy may help lower the risk for certain cancers, it is currently unclear if it is beneficial or harmful for individuals at high risk of developing breast cancer.

Tempeh ►
Made from cooked whole soybeans that are condensed into a solid block.
Can be seasoned and used as a meat substitute.

Textured soy protein ▲
Defatted soy flour that has been compressed and dehydrated.
Use it as a meat substitute in foods such as meatballs, meatloaf, chili, tacos, and spaghetti sauce.

Miso 
A flavorful paste of fermented soybeans used to season foods.
Use in soups, stews, and sauces.

Soy meat analogs 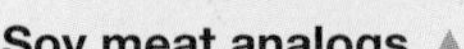
Products such as hot dogs, sausages, burgers, cold cuts, yogurts, and cheese can be made using soy.
Use as a meat substitute at meals and snacktimes.

For vegans, the choices are limited to plant-based sources that have been fortified with vitamin B_{12}, such as the following:

- 1 cup fortified soymilk
- 1 ounce fortified breakfast cereal
- 1.5 ounces fortified meat substitute made from soy
- 1 tbs high-quality nutritional yeast

If you don't consume at least three good food sources of vitamin B_{12} every day, you should take a supplement.

Veggie pizza (such as this spinach, feta, and onion slice) is a favorite among vegetarians and nonvegetarians alike!

Athletes Can Follow a Vegetarian Diet

Sports dietitians agree that athletes consuming a vegetarian diet can keep their competitive edge—with careful planning. Soy products, eggs, yogurt, cow's milk, cheese, and protein shakes can help a vegetarian athlete get needed amounts of protein, vitamin B_{12}, calcium, and vitamin D. Iron is a critical nutrient for athletes, because it carries oxygen to working muscles. Zinc is important to help tissues recover from the stress of training. Fortified foods can help increase the level of these minerals in a vegetarian diet, and a daily multivitamin/mineral supplement can provide added insurance. For athletes who don't consume fish, soy products, walnuts, flaxseeds, soybean oil, and canola oil provide omega-3 fatty acids. Vegetarian athletes should consult a registered dietitian to plan a nutritionally complete diet.

The Take-Home Message All vegetarians must take care in planning a varied diet that meets their nutrient needs, especially for protein, iron, zinc, calcium, vitamin D, vitamin B_{12}, vitamin A, and omega-3 fatty acids. Following the vegetarian Food Guide Pyramid and the Table Tips in Table 15.2 can help. Athletes can maintain their competitive edge on a vegetarian diet, but careful planning is required.

UCook

Mexican Mac and Cheese

If you like mac and cheese, try this Mexican Mac and Cheese, which adds a kick to your dish and is a snap to make!

UDo 

Hungry for More Vegetarian Advice?

Need some more help in planning a vegetarian diet? Click your way through a menu of more delicious vegetarian tips at our website, listed above.

The Top Five Points to Remember

1. Strictly speaking, a vegetarian is a person who doesn't eat meat, poultry, or fish. Whereas true vegetarians abstain from all animal foods, semivegetarians occasionally eat a limited amount. Strict vegetarians, called vegans, do not consume any foods from animal sources, including eggs and dairy products.
2. People choose vegetarianism for a variety of reasons. These include a desire to promote their personal health, concerns about the environment, compassion for animals, religious convictions, and financial constraints. As more and more countries transition out of poverty, the global demand for meat is increasing.
3. The health benefits of a vegetarian diet include a reduced risk for heart disease, high blood pressure, type 2 diabetes, certain types of cancer, and obesity.
4. One of the challenges of a vegetarian diet is obtaining complete protein. Protein from animal foods is more easily digested than protein from plant foods, and it is typically complete, providing all the essential amino acids along with some nonessential amino acids. Plant sources of proteins, other than soy, are typically incomplete, missing one or more essential amino acids. Other nutrients of concern in a vegetarian diet are omega-3 fatty acids, iron, calcium, zinc, vitamin A, vitamin D, and vitamin B_{12}.
5. All vegetarians must eat a varied diet that meets all their nutrient needs. Following the vegetarian Food Guide Pyramid and the Table Tips in Table 15.2 can help vegetarians meet their nutrient needs.

Test Yourself

1. A lacto-ovo-vegetarian is coming to your house for dinner. You need to make a meal that she will enjoy. An acceptable entrée would be
   a. stir-fry tofu and vegetables over brown rice.
   b. a cheese and broccoli omelet.
   c. baked ziti with ricotta cheese, spinach, and tomato sauce.
   d. all of the above.
2. You are a vegan and need a good source of vitamin B_{12}. You can get this vitamin from
   a. fortified soy milk.
   b. yogurt.
   c. raw nuts and seeds.
   d. all of the above.
3. Vegetarian diets are associated with a reduced risk for
   a. iron-deficiency anemia.
   b. type 1 diabetes.
   c. heart disease.
   d. all of the above.
4. Nutrients that may be limited in a vegetarian diet include
   a. protein and fiber.
   b. iron and omega-6 fatty acids.
   c. calcium and omega-3 fatty acids.
   d. all of the above.
5. Which of the following nutrients is found naturally in soy-based foods?
   a. protein
   b. iron
   c. omega-3 fatty acids
   d. all of the above

Answers

1. (d) Because a lacto-ovo-vegetarian avoids meat, poultry, and fish but eats a predominantly plant-based diet with dairy foods and eggs, the tofu stir-fry, cheese omelet, and baked ziti are all fine.
2. (a) Nuts and seeds do not provide vitamin B_{12}, which is derived from animal products. While yogurt is a source of vitamin B_{12}, vegans don't consume animal products. For them, fortified soy milk is a good option.
3. (c) Vegetarian diets are associated with a reduced risk for heart disease. They are also associated with a reduced risk for type 2 diabetes, but type 1 is inherited. The risk for iron-deficiency anemia is increased in vegetarians who are not careful to consume adequate dietary iron.
4. (c) Nutrients that may be limited in a vegetarian diet include calcium and omega-3 fatty acids. Fiber and omega-6 fatty acids are abundant in vegetables and many whole-grain foods; thus, these nutrients are unlikely to be deficient in a vegetarian diet.
5. (d) Foods produced from soybeans provide protein, iron, and omega-3 fatty acids.

Web Resources

- For tips and resources for following a vegetarian diet, check out the United States Department of Agriculture's MyPyramid website at: www.mypyramid.gov/tips_resources/vegetarian_diets.html
- For more information on vegetarian diets, visit the Vegetarian Research Group at: www.vrg.org
- For more information on soy foods, visit the United Soy Board at: www.talksoy.com

16 Vitamins

Small but Powerful

1. A hundred years ago, no one knew anything about **vitamins.** **T/F**

2. Taking vitamin supplements vitamin supplements is never harmful because **your body** eliminates any excesses that you don't need. **T/F**

3. Many vitamins can be destroyed by **exposure** to air. **T/F**

4. Taking vitamin C **supplements** can help you ward off the common cold. **T/F**

5. **Fortified foods** can help you meet your vitamin needs. **T/F**

Brendan is a college freshman and future track star. In addition to carrying a full course load and working part-time, Brendan works out at least 2 hours a day on the outdoor track. Within the first few weeks of school, Brendan caught a cold and had a stuffy nose and headache for a few days. As soon as he recovered, a second cold set in and lingered for more than a week.

Hoping to ward off another bout of illness, Brendan went online to find information on building up his immune system. He found websites that claimed vitamin C helps protect against colds. After a visit to his local health food store, Brendan began to take vitamin C tablets, and soon his daily intake was 3,500 milligrams, about 100 times his daily needs. Within a week, his long training sessions were interrupted by bouts of diarrhea. He visited the health center and complained to the doctor that the only training he was getting was running to the bathroom. The doctor recognized Brendan's symptoms as common in runners who take certain supplements. Can you guess what caused Brendan's intestinal discomforts?

Although vitamins (*vita* = vital) have always been in foods, they remained nameless and undiscovered substances as recently as 100 years ago.

In the twentieth century, improved diets meant that those earlier vitamin deficiencies were less of an issue for most Americans. Scientists shifted their focus from curing diseases to preventing them through the use of vitamins.[1] Today, research is being done to find out how vitamins affect and prevent everything from birth defects to cancer.

In this concept, we will look at how each vitamin functions in the body, how much you need to be healthy, which foods contain which vitamins, and the effects of consuming too much or too little of any these nutrients in your diet.

Answers

1. True. The importance of vitamins has been recognized only in the past century. See page 2.
2. False. Some vitamins are stored in the body and can build up to toxic levels if taken in excess. To find out more, turn to page 3.
3. True. Water, air, and heat can all promote the loss of water-soluble vitamin properties. We'll explain why on pages 5 and 6.
4. False. There is no clear evidence that vitamin C supplements protect you from the common cold. To find out what role it does play in combating colds, turn to page 32.
5. True. However, fortified foods are not always healthy foods. To find out how to tell the difference, turn to pages 36 and 37.

What Are Vitamins?

Vitamins are tasteless, organic compounds your body needs in small amounts for growth, reproduction, and overall good health. They are essential nutrients for well-being, and a deficiency of any one causes physiological symptoms. There are 13 vitamins, most of which come from foods, although the vitamins D, K, niacin, and biotin can also be synthesized in the body or by microorganisms in the intestinal tract.

A chronic deficiency of any of the essential vitamins can cause a cascade of symptoms, from scaly skin to blindness. However, consuming too much of some vitamins can cause adverse effects that can be just as damaging. Balance is always your best bet when it comes to meeting your vitamin needs.

vitamins Essential nutrients your body needs in small amounts to grow, reproduce, and maintain good health.

Vitamins Are Either Fat Soluble or Water Soluble

A vitamin is either fat soluble or water soluble, depending on how it is absorbed and handled in your body. Fat-soluble vitamins need dietary fat to be absorbed properly, while water-soluble vitamins are absorbed in water (Figure 16.1).

Vitamins A, D, E, and K are fat soluble. They are absorbed at the beginning of your small intestine (Figure 16.2). They are packaged with fatty acids and bile in micelles, small transport carriers that shuttle them close to your intestinal lining. Once there, the fat-soluble vitamins travel through the lining cells and are packaged with fat and other lipids in chylomicrons (one of the lipoprotein carriers, discussed in Concept 10). The vitamins then travel through your lymphatic system before they enter your bloodstream.

Fat-soluble vitamins are stored in your body and used as needed when your dietary intake falls short. Your liver is the main storage depot for vitamin A and, to a lesser extent, vitamins K and E, while vitamin D is stored mainly in your fat and muscle tissues. Because they are stored in your body, large quantities of some of the fat-soluble vitamins, particularly A and D, can build up to the point of **toxicity,** causing harmful symptoms and conditions.

The B vitamins and vitamin C are water soluble. They are absorbed in water and enter your bloodstream directly. Most water-soluble vitamins are absorbed in the upper portion of your small intestine, although vitamin B_{12} is absorbed in the lower part of your small intestine. Water-soluble vitamins are not stored in your body, and excess amounts are excreted in urine, so it's important to consume adequate amounts of them every day. Even though most water-soluble vitamins aren't stored in your body, dietary excesses can still be harmful.

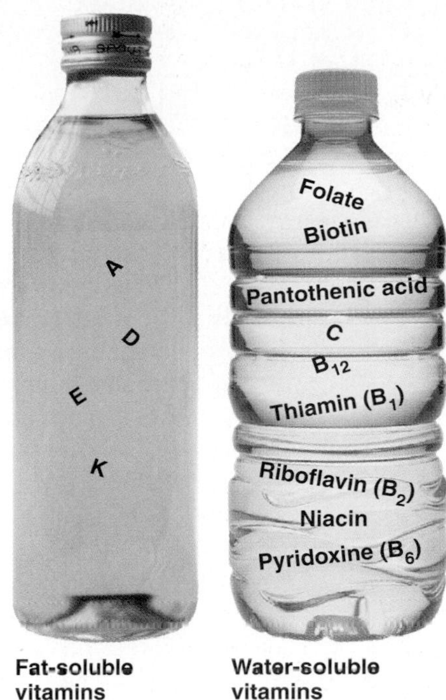

Figure 16.1 Categorizing the Vitamins Fat-soluble vitamins need dietary fat to be absorbed properly, while water-soluble vitamins are absorbed in water.

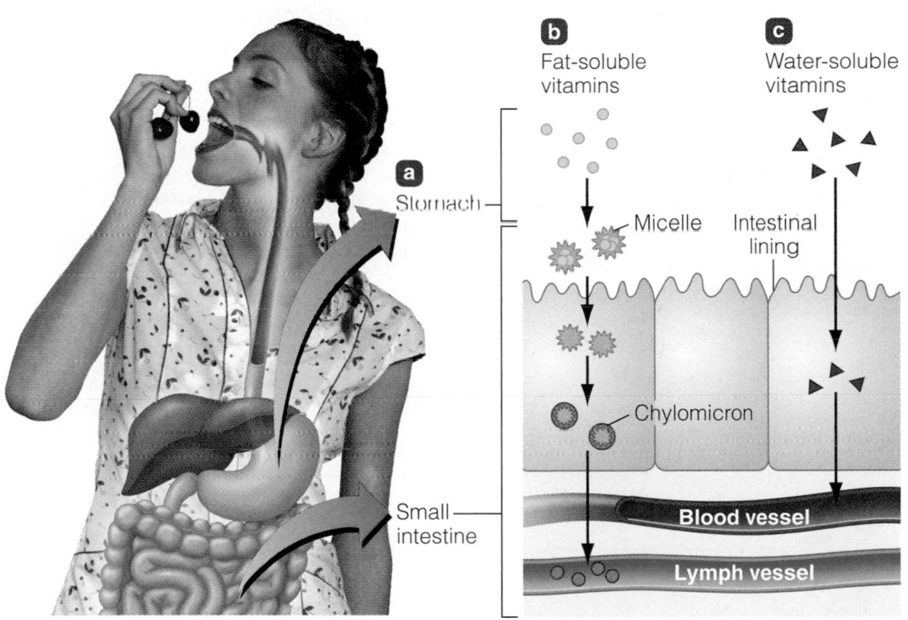

Figure 16.2 Digesting and Absorbing Vitamins (a) Vitamins are absorbed at the beginning of your small intestine. Vitamin B_{12} is absorbed in the lower portion of your small intestine. **(b)** In your small intestine, the fat-soluble vitamins are packaged with fatty acids and bile in micelles, which transport them to your intestinal wall. The fat-soluble vitamins travel through the cells in your intestinal wall and are packaged with fat and other lipids in chylomicrons. The chylomicrons travel through your lymphatic system and into your bloodstream. **(c)** The water-soluble vitamins are absorbed directly into your bloodstream from your small intestine.

toxicity The level at which exposure to a substance becomes harmful.

Some Vitamins Are Antioxidants

Antioxidants (*anti* = against; *oxidants* = oxygen-containing substances) are a group of compounds that includes vitamins E and C, the mineral selenium, and certain phytochemicals. Just as their name implies, antioxidants counteract **oxidation,** a chemical reaction involving oxygen that takes place in your cells.

Vitamins were originally called **vitamines.** When later discoveries found that nitrogen-containing amines weren't present, the *e* was dropped from the word.

During oxidation, harmful oxygen-containing molecules called **free radicals** damage your cells by altering their structure, their proteins, and even their DNA.[2] Free radicals are normal by-products of your body's metabolic reactions, which release energy from food. Free radicals can also result from exposure to chemicals in the environment (such as cigarette smoke and air pollution) and from the damaging effects of the sun's ultraviolet rays on unprotected skin.

Free radicals are very unstable. These restless molecules act as thieves on the prowl, looking to steal components of other molecules in order to stabilize themselves. Once such a robbery takes place, the victim becomes a new free radical and pursues another molecule to attack. This chain reaction, if not stopped, can significantly damage cells. Antioxidants are part of your body's natural defense system to harness free radicals and stop them from damaging cells (Figure 16.3).

If free radicals accumulate faster than your body can neutralize them, a condition known as *oxidative stress,* their damaging effects can contribute to various health problems, including heart disease, cancer, type 2 diabetes, arthritis, and Alz-

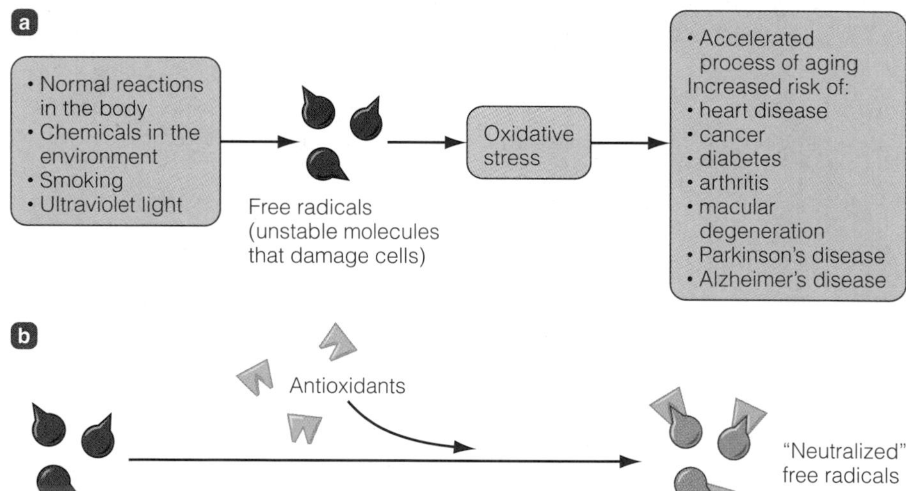

Figure 16.3 Free Radicals (a) Free radicals are the by-products of normal reactions in your body, as well as exposure to chemicals in the environment and the damaging effects of the sun's ultraviolet rays. Free radicals can damage cells and tissues and lead to chronic diseases. **(b)** Antioxidants help neutralize free radicals, limiting the damage that free radicals cause and helping reduce the risk for many chronic diseases.

antioxidants Substances that neutralize free radicals, which can cause cell damage. Vitamins A, C, and E and beta-carotene are antioxidants.

oxidation A chemical reaction in the body in which oxygen combines with other molecules.

free radicals Unstable oxygen-containing molecules that can damage the cells of the body and contribute to the increased risk for chronic diseases.

heimer's disease.[3] Free radicals can also be damaging to your eyes, contributing to age-related macular degeneration (AMD) and cataracts:

- **Age-related macular degeneration (AMD)** results from damage to the macula, a tiny area of the eye that is needed for central vision (the ability to see things that are directly in front of you). AMD can make activities such as reading, driving, and watching television impossible (compare Figure 16.4a with Figure 16.4b). It is usually the culprit when Americans 60 years of age or older experience blindness.[4] A study conducted by the National Eye Institute (NEI) discovered that supplements containing large amounts of antioxidants (vitamin C, vitamin E, and beta-carotene), with the minerals zinc and copper, are effective in reducing the risk for AMD, as well as the extent of vision loss.[5]
- A **cataract** is a disorder in which the lens of the eye becomes cloudy, resulting in blurred vision, as shown in Figure 16.4c. More than half of all Americans have experienced cataracts by the time they reach 80 years of age, and many undergo surgery to remove them. Some studies have suggested that specific antioxidants—including vitamins C and E and some phytochemicals—may help lower the risk for cataracts.[6] The NEI recommends consuming antioxidant- and carotenoid-rich fruits and vegetables, such as citrus fruits, broccoli, and leafy dark green vegetables, for the health of your eyes.[7]

There is no question that diets high in antioxidant-rich fruits, vegetables, and whole grains are associated with a lower incidence of some diseases. However, these foods contain other compounds that may work with antioxidants to provide protection. For example, phytochemicals (*phyto* = plant), naturally occurring plant compounds that give fruits and vegetables their vibrant colors, have many beneficial functions in the body, such as acting as antioxidants, stimulating the immune system, and interacting with hormones that may help prevent certain cancers.[8] Fruits, vegetables, and whole grains are also rich in fiber, and they are low in heart-unhealthy saturated fat. It is likely that all of these attributes work together to provide protection from chronic diseases.

Vitamins Can Be Destroyed by Air, Water, and Heat

Water-soluble vitamins can be destroyed by exposure to air, water, and heat. In fact, vegetables and fruits begin to lose their vitamins almost immediately after being harvested, and some preparation and storage methods can accelerate vitamin loss. While the fat-soluble vitamins tend to be more stable than the water-soluble vitamins, some food preparation techniques can cause the loss of these vitamins as well.

a Normal vision

b Age-related macular degeneration

c Cataract

Figure 16.4 Normal and Impaired Vision
(a) Normal vision is often taken for granted. **(b)** People with age-related macular degeneration (AMD) have difficulty seeing things directly in front of them. **(c)** Cataracts cause vision to become cloudy.

Data from: National Institutes of Health, National Eye Institute.

age-related macular degeneration (AMD) A disease that affects the macula area of the eye's retina, causing blurry vision.

cataract A common eye disorder that occurs when the lens of the eye becomes cloudy.

Cook your vegetables in a small amount of water. If you have to boil vegetables, use the leftover cooking liquid as a soup or gravy base.

Don't rinse rice before cooking it or pasta after cooking it. You'll wash away water-soluble vitamins.

Steam, microwave, or stir-fry vegetables to reduce the amount of time they are exposed to heat and therefore the amount of vitamins that are lost.

Store produce in the refrigerator and eat soon after purchasing.

Cut vegetables and fruits close to the time that they are going to be cooked and/or served.

Don't Expose Produce to Air

Air (oxygen) exposure can destroy the water-soluble vitamins and the fat-soluble vitamins A, E, and K. For this reason, fresh vegetables and fruits should be stored in airtight containers and used soon after being purchased. Cutting vegetables and fruits increases the amount of surface area exposed to the air, so cut your produce close to the cooking and serving time to minimize vitamin loss.

A Little Water Is Enough

When you toss out the water that cooks your vegetables, you are also tossing out some water-soluble vitamins. Soaking foods also causes water-soluble vitamins to leech out of the food and into the liquid. To reduce vitamin loss, cook vegetables in a minimal amount of liquid—just enough to prevent the pot from scorching and to keep your vegetables crisp.

In contrast, cooking rice in water doesn't diminish its nutrient content, because the water is absorbed by the grain, rather than discarded. However, washing the rice before cooking it will wash away the B vitamins that were sprayed on during the enrichment process.[9]

Reduce Cooking Time

Heat, especially prolonged heat from cooking, destroys water-soluble vitamins, especially vitamin C. Because they are exposed to less heat, vegetables cooked by microwaving, steaming, or stir-frying can have approximately 1½ times more vitamin C after cooking than if they were boiled.[10] The first three cooking methods are faster than boiling, reducing the length of time the food is in direct contact with the heat, and they all use less added water. (Stir-frying typically uses only oil.) Cooking vegetables until "just tender" is best, as it reduces the cooking time and heat exposure and preserves the vitamins. If you find yourself with a plate full of limp, soggy vegetables, it's a sure sign that vitamins have been lost.

Keep Food Cool

While heat causes foods to lose vitamins, cooler temperatures help preserve them. For this reason, produce should be stored in your refrigerator, rather than on a counter or in a pantry. A package of fresh spinach left at room temperature will lose over half of its folate, a B vitamin, after four days. Keeping the spinach in the refrigerator delays that loss until eight days.[11] See the Table Tips for more ways to preserve the vitamins in your foods.

The next several pages of this concept present the fat-soluble vitamins A, E, K, and D. Before we begin our discussion of these vitamins, Rate Yourself to see if your diet is rich in foods containing them.

RATE YOURSELF 

Are You Getting Enough Fat-Soluble Vitamins in Your Diet?

Rate Yourself to see if your diet contains enough food sources of the four fat-soluble vitamins.

1. Do you eat at least 1 cup of deep yellow or orange vegetables, such as carrots and sweet potatoes, or dark green vegetables, such as spinach, every day?
   Yes ☐ **No** ☐
2. Do you drink at least two glasses (8 ounces each) of milk daily?
   Yes ☐ **No** ☐
3. Do you consume a tablespoon of vegetable oil, such as corn or olive oil, daily? (Tip: Salad dressings, unless they are fat-free, count!)
   Yes ☐ **No** ☐
4. Do you eat at least 1 cup of leafy green vegetables in your salad and/or put lettuce in your sandwich every day?
   Yes ☐ **No** ☐

Answers

If you answered "yes" to all four questions, you are on your way to acing your fat-soluble vitamin needs! If you answered "no" to any one of the questions, your diet needs some fine-tuning. Deep orange and dark green vegetables are excellent sources of vitamin A, and milk is an excellent choice for vitamin D. Vegetable oils provide vitamin E, and if you put them on top of your vitamin K–rich leafy green salad, you'll hit the vitamin jackpot.

The Take-Home Message Vitamins are essential nutrients needed in small amounts for growth, reproduction, and overall good health. Vitamins are either fat soluble or water soluble. The fat-soluble vitamins, A, D, E, and K, need fat to be absorbed and are stored in your body, so chronic excesses of some fat-soluble vitamins can be toxic. The water-soluble vitamins B and C are absorbed in water. Excess water-soluble vitamins are excreted from your body, and surplus amounts generally aren't toxic. Antioxidants—such as vitamins E and C, the mineral selenium, and certain phytochemicals—help counteract the damaging effects of oxygen-containing molecules called free radicals. Many vitamins in foods can be destroyed or lost by exposure to air, water, and heat.

Vitamin A

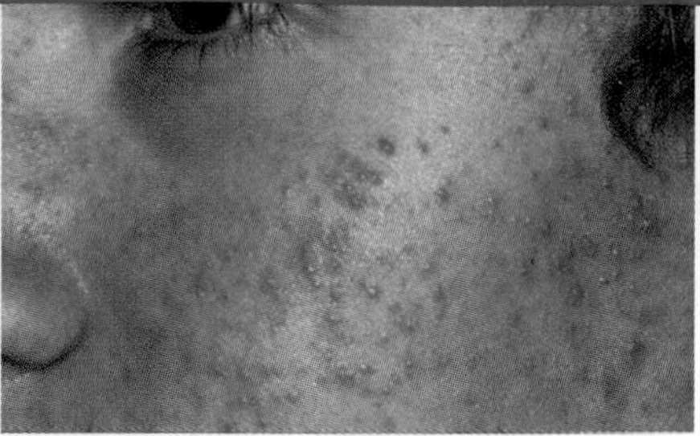
Vitamin A can help in the treatment of acne.

What Is Vitamin A?

Vitamin A is actually a family of substances called *retinoids.* Because retinoids exist in a form your body readily uses, they are also called *preformed* Vitamin A. **Retinol** is the most usable form of preformed Vitamin A because it can be converted into other forms in your body.[12]

Vitamin A is found only in foods from animal sources, such as liver and eggs, and is added to processed milk. Plant food sources don't contain vitamin A, but some contain substances called carotenoids, which can be converted to retinol in your body. *Carotenoids* are the pigments that give foods such as carrots their deep orange color.

There are over 600 carotenoids, and the most well-known is beta-carotene, which provides most of the vitamin A in our diets.[13]

Functions of Vitamin A

As you read this sentence, light enters your eye through the cornea and travels to the back to the macula and retina, as shown in the figure.

Vitamin A is essential for vision. Have you ever been outside on a sunny day and then entered a dark building? The adjustment period you had when you came inside happened because proteins in your eye were broken down ("bleached") in the bright outdoor sun and your eyes needed to regenerate them once you were in the dark room. Luckily, there is a pool of vitamin A in your retina to immediately help with this regeneration.

Vitamin A plays an important role in cell division and *differentiation,* the processes that determine what form cells take in your body.[14]

As cells divide and cluster together, they undergo changes that make them different from their original cells. This differentiation determines what form a cell takes in your body. For immature skin cells to become mature, for example, vitamin A acts as a signal to "turn on" genes to create the proteins needed to make healthy skin.

During the early stages of pregnancy, vitamin A signals cells to differentiate into tissues that form the baby's body. Vitamin A plays a very important role in the development of the limbs, heart, eyes, and ears. It may also help regulate the cells involved in bone growth.[15]

Vitamin A is important for keeping the mucous membranes of your lungs, intestinal tract, and kidneys healthy. If these linings become weak or damaged, bacteria and viruses can infiltrate and make you sick.

Vitamin A also helps keep your skin—which acts as another barrier to infections by preventing harmful bacteria from entering your body—healthy and functioning correctly. It also works with your immune system to create white blood cells that fight foreign "invaders" that may enter your bloodstream.

Daily Needs

Vitamin A in foods and supplements can be measured in two ways: in micrograms of *retinol activity equivalents (RAE)* and in *international units (IU).* The scientifically-preferred way to measure vitamin A in foods is by using RAE; however, most vitamin supplements and food labels use the older measure, IU. (One RAE in micrograms equals 3.3 IU.)

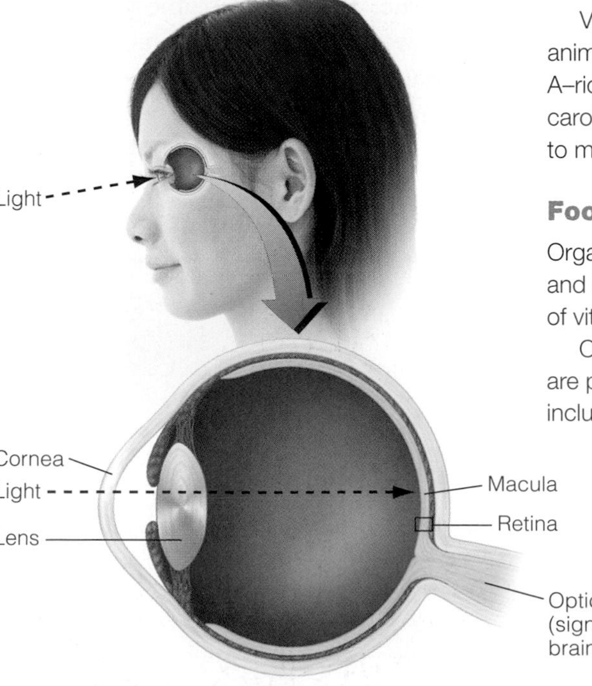

Most women need 700 mcg RAE of vitamin A daily, while men need 900 mcg RAE each day. This is the average amount needed to maintain adequate stores in your body.

A daily recommendation for beta-carotene hasn't been established, but the Institute of Medicine suggests consuming 3 to 6 milligrams of beta-carotene daily *from foods.*[17] You can meet this by eating five or more servings of fruits and vegetables daily. This amount of beta-carotene will provide about 50 percent of the recommended vitamin A intake. Choosing beta-carotene-rich foods will not only add antioxidants to your diet but also vitamin A.

Vegetarians or vegans who eat no animal-based foods (including vitamin A–rich milk and eggs) should consume carotenoids and beta-carotene rich foods to meet their daily vitamin A needs.

Food Sources

Organ meats (liver), milk, cereals, cheese, and eggs are the most common sources of vitamin A in the U.S. diet.

Carrots, spinach, and sweet potatoes are popular favorites for carotenoids, including beta-carotene. Like other fat-soluble vitamins, carotenoids are best absorbed when some fat is present in your intestinal tract. Adding as little as 1 tablespoon of vegetable oil to your diet can increase the absorption of carotenoids by as much as 25 percent.[18]

Too Much or Too Little

Because vitamin A is stored in your body, it can easily accumulate to toxic levels. The upper level for adults has been set at 3,000 milligrams daily.

People often take in too much vitamin A by taking supplements. Consuming more than 15,000 micrograms of vitamin A at once or over a short period of time can lead to nausea, vomiting, headaches, dizziness, and blurred vision.[19]

Chronic daily consumption of more than 30,000 micrograms of vitamin A (more than 300 times the amount adults need) can lead to extremely serious toxic liver damage, and even death.[20]

Consuming too much vitamin A during pregnancy, especially early on, can cause birth defects and damage a fetuses' central nervous system. Women who use retinoid products for acne or other skin conditions should avoid becoming pregnant, or stop using the product if they become pregnant.[21]

While vitamin A is needed for bone health, consuming too much may lead to osteoporosis (thinning bones), increasing the risk of fractures. Studies show a connection between high vitamin A intake and increased risks of fractures in both men and women.[22] As little as 1,500 micrograms (3,000 IU) of retinol (slightly more than twice the recommended daily amount for women) can be unhealthy for bones.[23] This level can be quickly reached if you are taking a supplement and also eating a diet high in vitamin A fortified foods.[24]

Eating too many carotenoids may also cause a nonserious condition called *carotenodermia* which results in orange-tinged skin, particularly on the palms of the hands and soles of the feet. Cutting back on carotenoid-rich foods will reverse this effect.

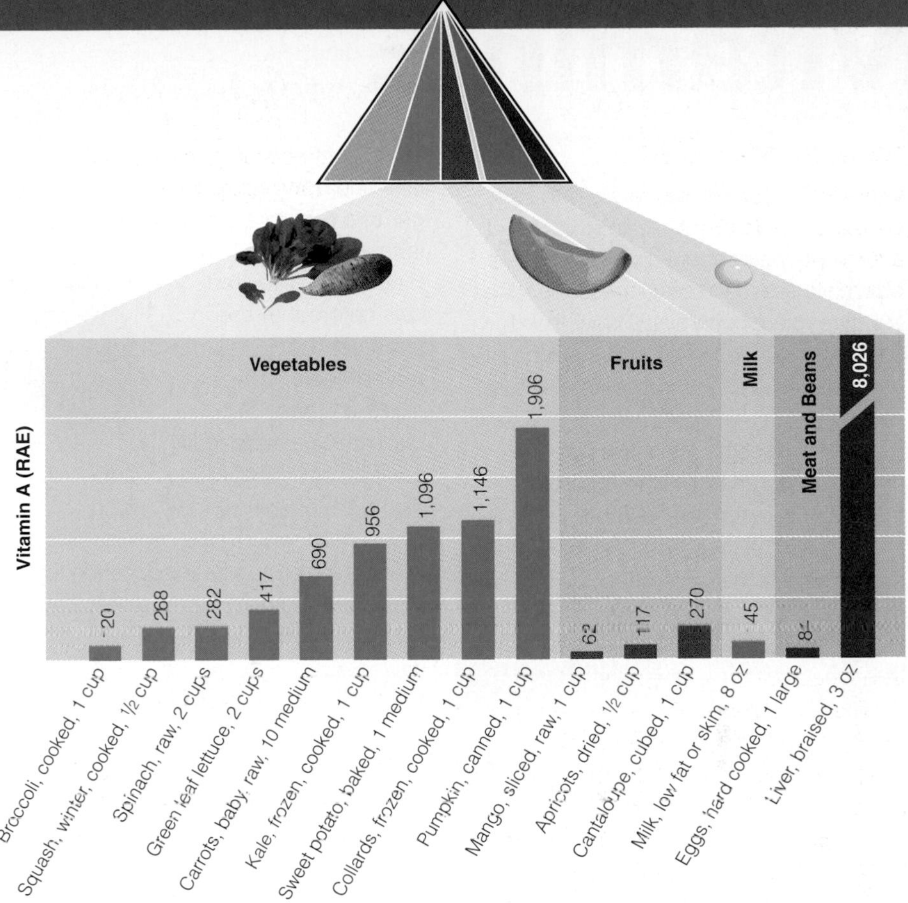

While a diet abundant in carotenoid-rich foods is not dangerous, carotenoid supplements may be.[25] Caution in taking excessive supplements is always a good idea. No established benefits are associated with taking beta-carotene supplements. Eating a variety of fruits and vegetables is still the safest way to meet your vitamin A needs.

Chronic vitamin A deficiency can lead to the condition of *night blindness.* People with night blindness have difficulty seeing at dusk, and may not be able to drive a car at that time of the day. If diagnosed early, night blindness can be reversed by taking vitamin A.

Prolonged vitamin A deficiency can also lead to permanent damage to the eye. As many as 500,000 children, mostly in developing countries, go blind every year because they don't get enough vitamin A in their diets. Vitamin A deficiency is the number one cause of preventable blindness in children, and is also associated with stunting of bones.[26]

TABLE TIPS

Score an A

Dunk baby carrots in a tablespoon of low-fat ranch dressing for a healthy snack.

Keep dried apricots in your backpack for a sweet treat.

Add baby spinach to a lunchtime salad.

Bake up sweet potatoes rather than white potatoes at dinner.

Buy frozen mango chunks for a ready-to-thaw beta-carotene-rich addition to cottage cheese or yogurt.

Vitamin E

What Is Vitamin E?

Vitamin E is sometimes referred to as a vitamin in need of a disease to cure. For almost 40 years after it was discovered, scientists searched unsuccessfully for a curative role for vitamin E. Now they have shifted their focus and begun looking at the vitamin's importance as an effective antioxidant.[27]

There are eight different kinds of naturally-occurring vitamin E, but one form, alpha-tocopherol is most active in your body. The synthetic form of vitamin E found in dietary supplements is only half as active as the natural form.[28]

Functions of Vitamin E

Vitamin E as an Antioxidant

Vitamin E's nutritional claim to fame is its role as a powerful antioxidant. This role is important in protecting cell membranes and preventing oxidation of "bad" LDL cholesterol.

As you recall from concept 10, phospholipids (lipids that contain phosphorus and two fatty acids) are critical components of cell membranes. Many phospholipids contain unsaturated fatty acids, which are vulnerable to the damaging effects of free radicals. (Free radicals and how antioxidants combat them are discussed in this concept.) Vitamin E neutralizes free radicals before they can harm cell membranes.

When "bad" LDL cholesterol is oxidized, it contributes to the buildup of artery-clogging plaque. *Anti*-oxidants, including vitamin E, help prevent LDL cholesterol from being oxidized and thus reduce the risk of cholesterol buildup in the arteries, which is called atherosclerosis.[29]

Other Functions of Vitamin E

Vitamin E is an anticoagulant (*anti* = against, *coagulant* = causes clotting), which means that it inhibits platelets (fragments of cells) from unnecessarily clumping together and creating a damaging clot in your bloodstream. Vitamin E also alters the "stickiness" of the cells that line your lymph and blood vessels. This decreases the ability of blood to stick to these walls and clog these passageways.

Studies are still under way to assess whether the long-term use of vitamin E supplements play a protective role against heart disease.[30]

Daily Needs

Adults need to consume 15 milligrams of vitamin E daily. Because alpha-tocopherol is the most active form of vitamin E in your body, your vitamin E needs are expressed in alpha-tocopherol equivalents.

Researchers speculate that healthy Americans, on average, consume more than the recommended 15 milligrams of vitamin E daily.[31]

Food Sources

Because vitamin E is fat-soluble, vegetable oils, foods that contain these oils, nuts, and seeds are good sources. *The Dietary Guidelines for Americans* specifically recommend consuming vegetable oils daily to meet your vitamin E needs. Some green leafy vegetables and fortified cereals can also contribute to your daily needs.

Too Much or Too Little

There currently isn't any known risk of consuming too much vitamin E from natural food sources. However, overconsumption of the synthetic form found in supplements and/or fortified foods could pose risks.

Because vitamin E acts as an anticoagulant and interferes with blood clotting, excess amounts in your body increase the risk of hemorrhage (severe bleeding). Because of this, the upper level from supplements and/or fortified foods is 1,000 milligrams for adults. This applies only to healthy individuals consuming adequate amounts of vitamin K. (Vitamin K also plays a role in blood clotting. A deficiency of vitamin K can heighten the anticoagu-

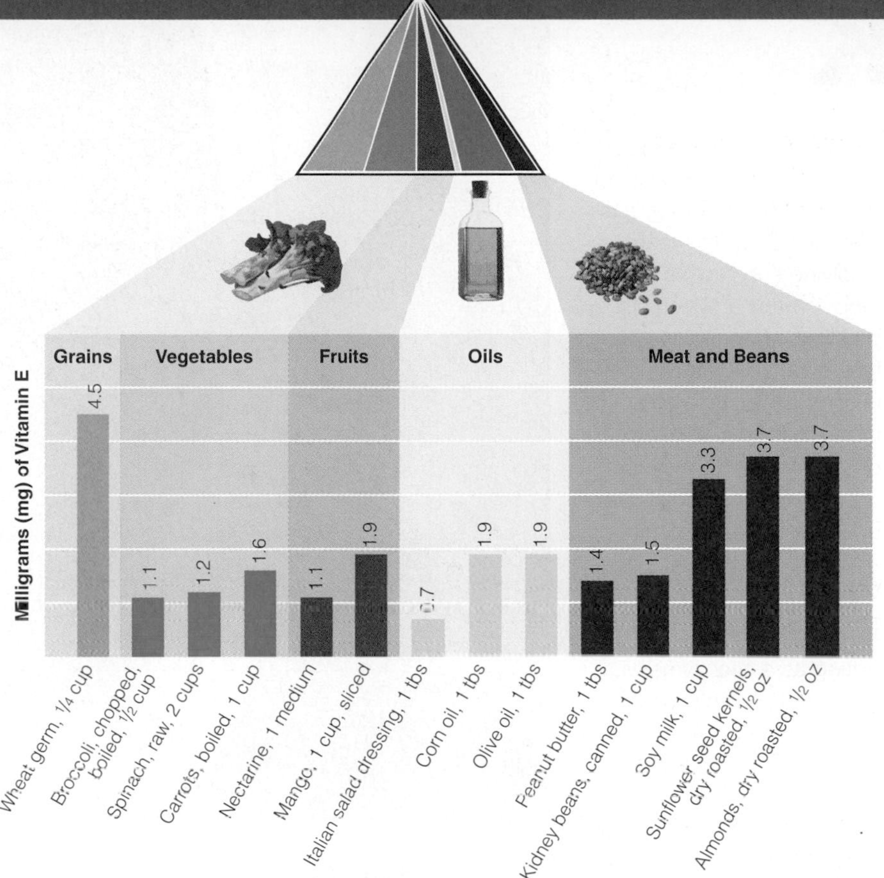

lant effects of vitamin E.) People taking anticoagulant medication and vitamin E supplements should be monitored by their doctor to avoid a potentially serious situation in which their blood can't clot quickly enough to stop the bleeding from a wound.

While the upper level of 1,000 milligrams was set to keep you safe, it may actually be too high. A recent study showed that people at risk for heart disease who took 400 IU or more of vitamin E daily for at least one year had an overall higher risk of dying. One theory suggests that too much vitamin E may disrupt the balance of other antioxidants in the body, causing more harm than good.[32]

Though rare, a chronic vitamin E deficiency can cause nerve problems, muscle weakness, and uncontrolled movement of body parts. Because vitamin E is an antioxidant and is found in the membranes of red blood cells, a deficiency can also increase the susceptibility of cell membranes to damage by free radicals.

Individuals who can't absorb fat properly may fall short of their vitamin E needs.

TABLE TIPS 

Enjoying Your Es

Add fresh spinach and broccoli to your lunch salad.

Add a slice of avocado or use guacamole as a spread on sandwiches.

Spread peanut butter on apple slices for a sweet treat.

Top low-fat yogurt with wheat germ for a healthy snack.

Pack a handful of almonds in a zip-closed bag for a mid-afternoon snack.

Vitamin K

What Is Vitamin K?

There are two forms of vitamin K: menaquinone and phylloquinone. Menaquinone is synthesized (created) by the bacteria that exist naturally in your intestinal tract. Phylloquinone is found in green plants, which is the primary source of vitamin K in your diet.

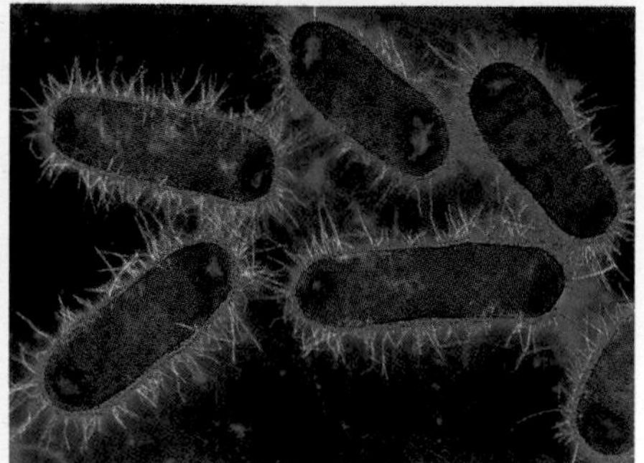

Bacteria in your GI tract synthesize one form of vitamin K.

Functions of Vitamin K

Vitamin K Is Essential for Blood Clotting

An easy way to remember vitamin K's major function is to associate the letter K with "klotting."

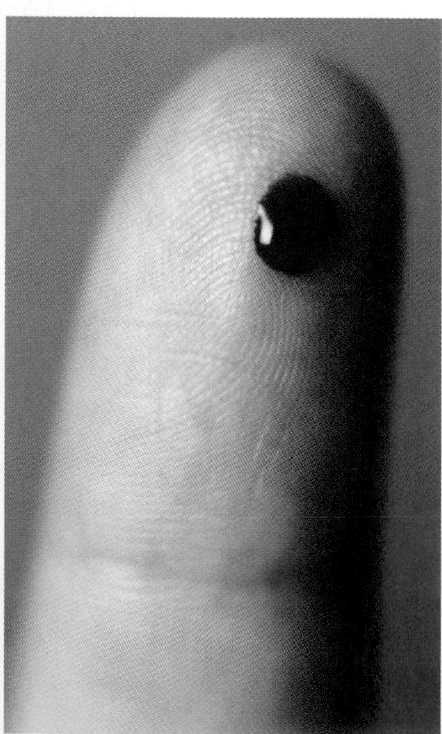

Vitamin K plays a major role in blood coagulation, or clotting. Blood clotting is a complex chain of events involving substances in your blood, many of which are proteins called clotting factors. Vitamin K plays a role in synthesizing some of these clotting factors. Without vitamin K, a simple cut on your finger could cause uncontrollable bleeding.

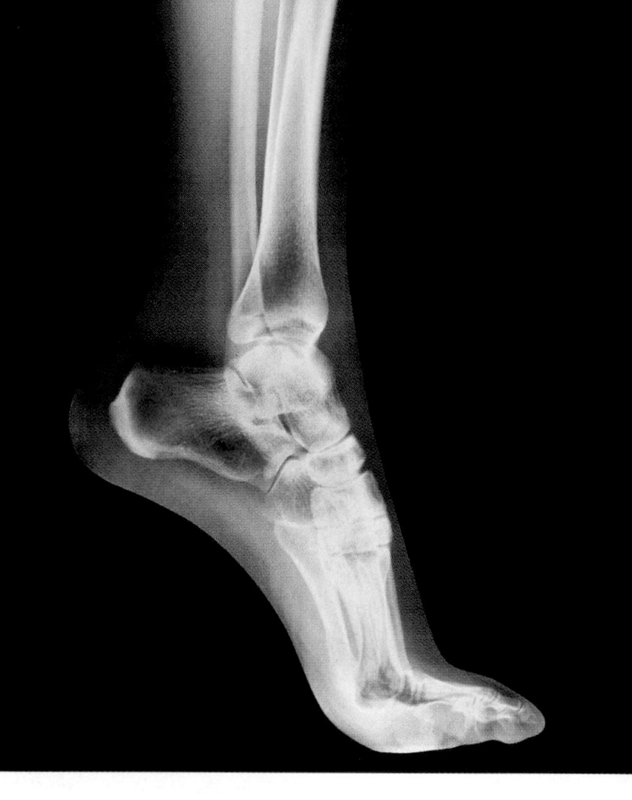

Vitamin K Is Important to Bone Health

Acting as a coenzyme, vitamin K aids an enzyme that alters the bone protein osteocalcin. Vitamin K enables osteocalcin to bind with the bone-strengthening mineral calcium.

Chronic inadequate amounts of dietary vitamin K may be a factor in osteoporosis. In a study of women over a ten-year period, researchers found that low dietary intake of vitamin K was associated with an increased risk of hip fractures.[33]

Research continues in the area of vitamin K and bone health.

Daily Needs

Currently, it is not known how much of the vitamin K made from bacteria in your intestinal tract actually contributes to meeting your daily needs. Thus, it is hard to pinpoint the exact amount you need to consume daily in your foods. Therefore, the recommendation for dietary vitamin K is based on the current amounts consumed, on average, by healthy Americans.[34]

Adult women need 90 micrograms of vitamin K per day, and men need 120 micrograms daily.

Food Sources

When it comes to meeting your vitamin K needs, think green. Vegetables like broccoli, asparagus, spinach, salad greens, brussels sprouts, and cabbage are all rich in vitamin K. Vegetable oils and margarine are the second largest source of vitamin K in the diet. A green salad with oil and vinegar dressing at lunch and ¾ cup broccoli at dinner will meet your vitamin K needs for the entire day.

Too Much or Too Little

There are no known adverse effects of consuming too much vitamin K from foods or supplements, so an upper intake level hasn't been set for healthy people. People taking anticoagulant (anticlotting) medications such as warfarin (also known as Coumadin) need to keep a consistent intake of vitamin K. This medication decreases the

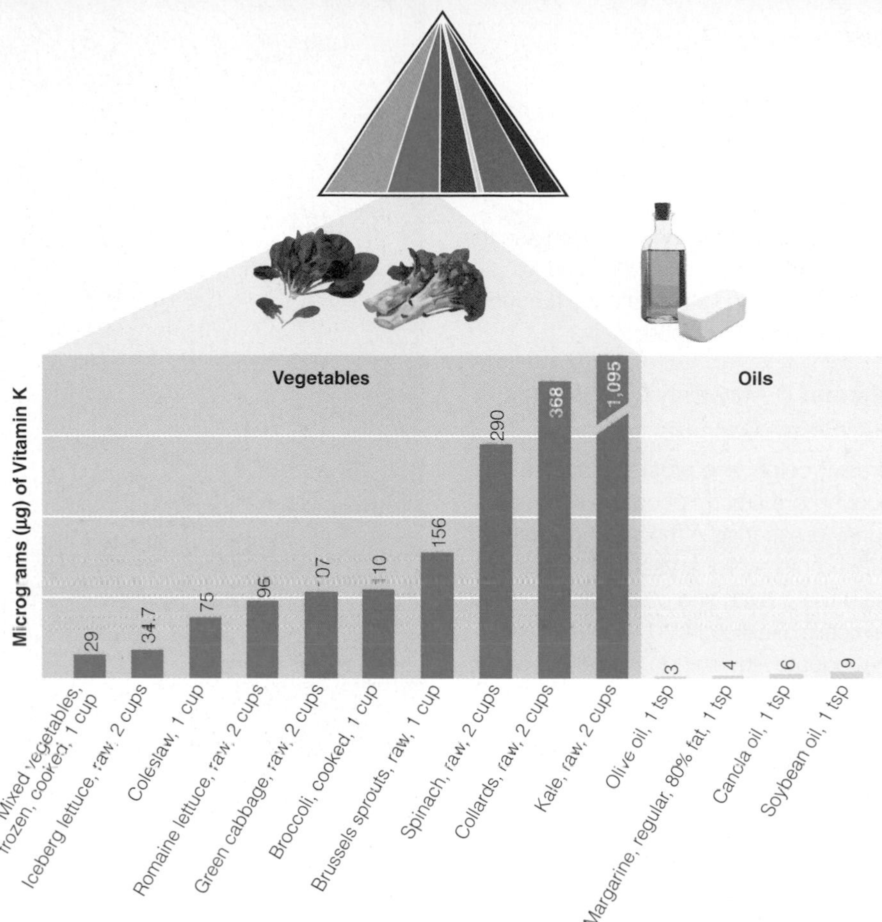

activity of vitamin K and prolongs the time it takes for blood to clot (compare normally clotted blood with blood treated with warfarin, in the photos below). If these individuals suddenly increase the vitamin K in their diets, the vitamin can override the effect of the drug, enabling the blood to clot too quickly. In contrast, a sudden decline in dietary vitamin K can enhance the effectiveness of the drug.[35]

A vitamin K deficiency severe enough to affect blood clotting is extremely rare in healthy individuals.[36] People with illnesses affecting absorption of fat in the intestinal tract, which is necessary to absorb fat-soluble vitamin K, may be at risk for not meeting their vitamin K needs.

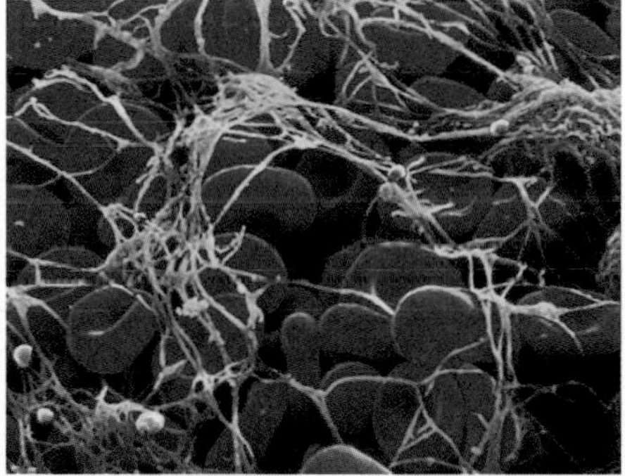

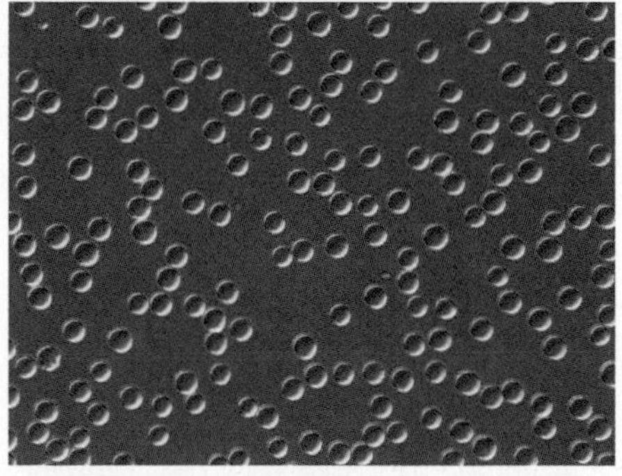

The photo at top shows normally clotted blood. The photo at bottom shows blood treated with warfarin.

TABLE TIPS 

Getting Your Ks

Have a green salad daily.

Cook with soybean oil.

Add shredded cabbage to your salad, or top it with a scoop of coleslaw.

Add a tad of margarine to your steamed spinach. Both will provide some vitamin K.

Dunk raw broccoli florets in salad dressing for two sources of vitamin K.

Vitamin D

What Is Vitamin D?

Vitamin D is called the "sunshine vitamin" because it is made in your body with the help of ultraviolet (UV) rays from sunlight. Most healthy people can synthesize all the vitamin D they need as long as they get adequate sun exposure.[37] People who don't get enough sun exposure must meet their Vitamin D needs through their diets.

Whether from food or sunlight, vitamin D enters your body in an inactive form. The ultraviolet rays of the sun convert a compound in your skin into previtamin D, which is then converted to an inactive form of vitamin D in your blood. The vitamin D in your foods is in this inactive form. It travels in your blood to your liver, where it is changed into a circulating form of vitamin D and released back into your blood. Once in your kidneys, it is converted to an active form of vitamin D.

Functions of Vitamin D

Vitamin D Helps Bone Health

Once in an active form, vitamin D acts as a hormone and regulates two important bone minerals, calcium and phosphorus. Vitamin D stimulates the absorption of calcium and phosphorus in your intestine, helping to keep levels of these minerals within a healthy range. Vitamin D also helps to build and maintain your bones.

Phosphorus deficiency is very rare, but dietary calcium deficiencies are common, causing blood levels of calcium to drop. When this happens, vitamin D and another hormone cause calcium to leave your bones in order to maintain the necessary levels in your blood. Vitamin D then signals your kidneys to decrease the amount of calcium excreted in urine. These actions help regulate the amount of calcium in your blood.

Vitamin D May Prevent Diabetes and Some Cancers

Breast, colon, and prostate cancers occur more among people living in less-sunny areas than in those living in regions with ample sunlight. Vitamin D helps regulate the growth and differentiation of certain cells. Researchers believe that inadequate vitamin D in the body may reduce the growth of healthy cells, allowing cancer cells to flourish.[38]

Vitamin D may also help prevent diabetes. Many people with type 2 diabetes have low blood levels of vitamin D. Vitamin D may play a role in insulin sensitivity.[39]

With growing awareness of the role vitamin D plays in disease prevention, some researchers suggest that the U.S. government add calcium and vitamin D to cereal and grain products as part of its food fortification program.[40]

Daily Needs

Not everyone can rely on the sun to meet their daily vitamin D needs. During the winter months in areas above latitudes of about 40 degrees north (Boston, Toronto, Salt Lake City) and below about 40 degrees south (Melbourne, Australia), sun exposure isn't strong enough to synthesize vitamin D in the skin.

In addition, people with darker-colored skin have more of the skin pigment melanin, which reduces vitamin D production from sunlight, so they need longer periods of sun exposure to derive the same amount of vitamin D.

Sunscreen can also block the body's ability to synthesize vitamin D by more than 95 percent.[41] Because of these variables in sun exposure, your daily vitamin D needs are based on the amount you need to derive from foods rather than on the synthesis of vitamin D in your skin from sunlight.

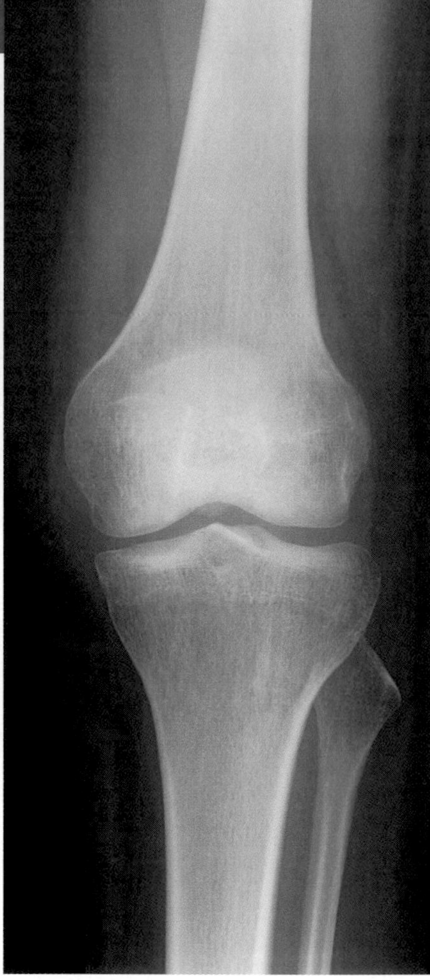

Adults need 5 to 15 micrograms (200 to 600 IU) of vitamin D daily, depending on their age. Keep in mind that the Daily Value (DV) on the Nutrition Facts panel on food labels is set at 400 IU, which is twice the amount recommended for children, teenagers, and many adults.

Food Sources

One of the easiest ways to get vitamin D from food is from fortified milk, which provides 100 IU of vitamin D per cup. Other than fortified milk, breakfast cereals and yogurt, and fatty fish (such as sardines and salmon), very few foods provide ample amounts of vitamin D. With this scarcity of naturally-occurring sources, it isn't surprising that many Americans are not meeting their daily vitamin D needs.[42]

Too Much or Too Little

Consuming too much vitamin D can cause loss of appetite, nausea, vomiting, and constipation. The upper level for vita-

Food	IU of Vitamin D
Grains	
Total Corn Flakes, 1 cup	26
Total Raisin Bran, 1 cup	40
Oils	
Margarine, fortified, 1 tbs	60
Milk	
Cheese, cheddar, 1½ oz	5
Tapioca pudding, prepared from mix and made with whole milk, ½ cup	49
Pudding, prepared with vitamin D-fortified milk, ½ cup	50
Yogurt, fortified with vitamin D, 8 oz	100
Milk, nonfat, vitamin D-fortified, 1 cup	102
Milk, 1% milk fat, vitamin D-fortified, 1 cup	127
Meat and Beans	
Egg, fried, 1 large	17
Soy milk, fortified, 1 cup	126
Tuna fish, light, canned in oil, 3 oz	201
Sardines, canned in oil, 3 oz	231
Salmon, 3 oz	309

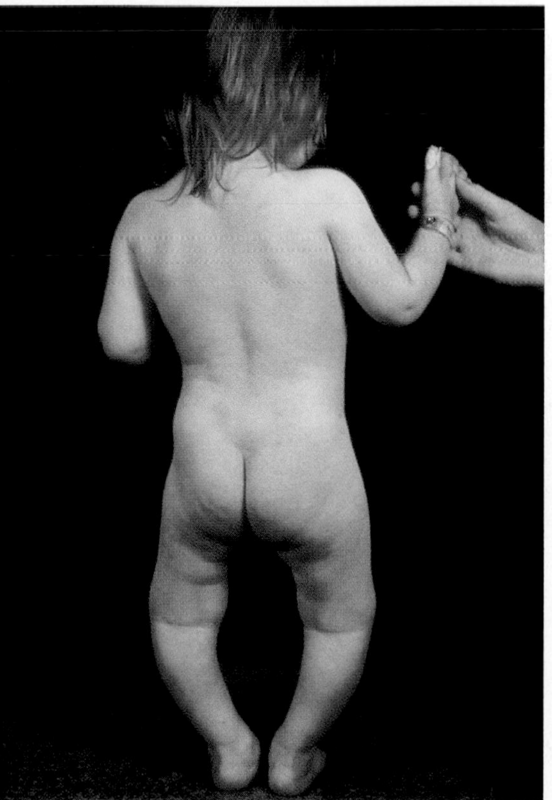

Child with rickets.

min D has been set at 2,000 IU, over three to ten times higher than the amount that is recommended daily.

As with other fat-soluble vitamins, excess vitamin D is stored in fat cells, and an accumulation can reach toxic levels, causing overabsorption of calcium from the intestines, and calcium loss from bones. When both of these symptoms occur, blood calcium levels can become dangerously high.

A chronically high amount of calcium can create damaging calcium deposits in the tissues of kidneys, lungs, blood vessels, and the heart. Excess vitamin D can also affect your nervous system and cause severe depression.[43]

The good news is that it is unlikely to get vitamin D toxicity *from foods,* even fortified foods. The exception is fish oils, specifically cod-liver oil, which contain very high levels. A more likely cause of toxicity is the overuse of vitamin D supplements.

Overexposing the skin to UV rays will eventually destroy the inactive form of vitamin D in the skin, causing the body to shut down its production of vitamin D, making toxicity from sun exposure unlikely.

Other Vitamin D Deficiency Disorders

Rickets is a vitamin D deficiency disease that occurs in children. The bones of children with rickets aren't adequately mineralized with calcium and phosphorus, which causes them to weaken.[44, 45] Because of their "soft bones," these children develop bowed legs, since they are unable to hold up their own body weight when they are standing upright.[46, 47, 48]

Osteomalacia is the adult equivalent of rickets and can cause muscle and bone weakness and pain.[49]

Vitamin D deficiency and its effect on decreased calcium absorption can lead to osteoporosis, a condition in which the bones there isn't enough calcium in the diet to maximize the bone density, or mass.

TABLE TIPS

Dynamite Ways to Get Vitamin D

Choose whole-grain cereal such as shredded wheat, bran flakes, raisin bran, and oatmeal in the morning.

Combine a 100% whole-wheat English muffin and low-fat cheddar cheese for a hearty breakfast cheese melt.

Enjoy your lunchtime sandwich made with a whole-wheat pita or 100% whole-grain bread.

Try instant brown rice for a quick whole grain at dinner.

Snack on popcorn or 100% whole-wheat crackers for a high-fiber filler in the afternoon.

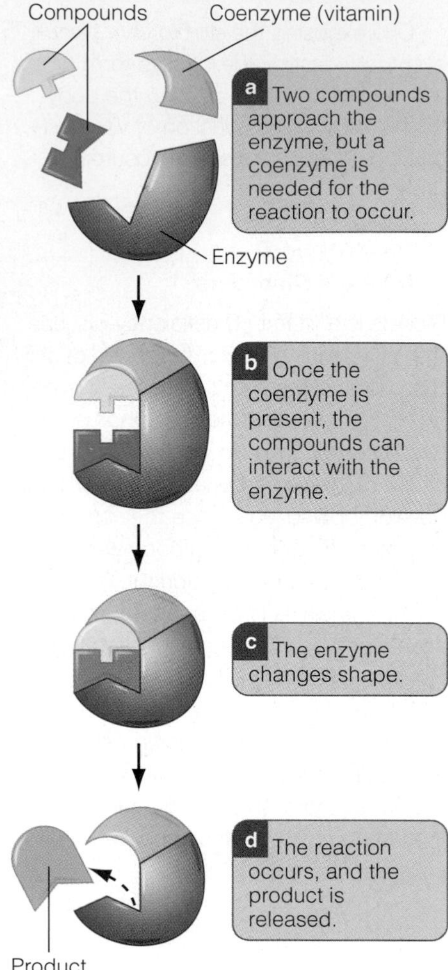

Figure 16.5 How B Vitamins Function as Coenzymes

coenzymes Substances needed by enzymes to perform many chemical reactions in your body. Many vitamins act as coenzymes.

The B Vitamins and Vitamin C Are Water Soluble

In contrast to fat-soluble vitamins, which can be stored in your body, excess water-soluble vitamins are excreted in your urine. Consumers who take large amounts of water-soluble vitamins in an attempt to "beef up" their vitamin stores literally end up flushing their vitamins, and their money, down the toilet.

Although water-soluble vitamins aren't stored in your body, routine intakes of excessive amounts can be harmful. In fact, Brendan's illness, described at the beginning of this concept, wasn't due to a vitamin deficiency but to overconsumption of the water-soluble vitamin C. In appropriate amounts, vitamin C plays important roles in the immune system and in bone health, in addition to its antioxidant and other functions.

When initially discovered in the early 1900s, the "water-soluble B" was thought to be one vitamin. After years of research, it became apparent that it is not a single substance but, rather, many vitamins, known collectively as the B vitamins. These B vitamins—thiamin, riboflavin, niacin, vitamin B_6, folate, vitamin B_{12}, pantothenic acid, and biotin—have a common role as **coenzymes,** helping numerous enzymes produce reactions in your cells. Without the B vitamins, many enzymes aren't able to function properly, and their reactions can't occur. As shown in Figure 16.5, once the coenzyme is present, the reaction can proceed and a new product can be released. Although vitamins don't provide calories and thus aren't a source of energy, many of the B vitamins are essential coenzymes in reactions that break down and allow your body to use the three energy-yielding nutrients—carbohydrates, proteins, and fats.

The roles of the water-soluble vitamins don't end there. Each vitamin has other important functions in your body, discussed in the following pages. Before we move on to the water-soluble vitamins, Rate Yourself to see if you are consuming foods that are rich in the B vitamins and vitamin C.

RATE YOURSELF 

Are You Getting Enough Water-Soluble Vitamins in Your Diet?

Rate Yourself to see if your diet is rich in the water-soluble B vitamins and vitamin C.

1. Do you consume at least 1/2 cup of rice or pasta daily?
   Yes ☐ **No** ☐
2. Do you eat at least 1 cup of a ready-to-eat cereal or hot cereal every day?
   Yes ☐ **No** ☐
3. Do you have at least one slice of bread, a bagel, or a muffin daily?
   Yes ☐ **No** ☐
4. Do you enjoy a citrus fruit or fruit juice, such as an orange, a grapefruit, or orange juice, every day?
   Yes ☐ **No** ☐
5. Do you have at least a cup of vegetables throughout your day?
   Yes ☐ **No** ☐

Answers

If you answered "yes" to all of these questions, you are a vitamin B and C superstar! Rice, pasta, cereals, bread, and bread products are all excellent sources of B vitamins. Citrus fruits are a ringer for vitamin C. In fact, all vegetables can contribute to meeting your vitamin C needs daily. If you answered "no" more often than "yes," read on to learn how to add more Bs and C to your diet.

Thiamin (B_1)

What Is Thiamin?

Thiamin, or vitamin B_1, was the first B vitamin to be discovered. The path to its discovery began in the 1890s in East Asia. A Dutch doctor, Christiann Eijkman, noticed that chickens and pigeons that ate polished rice (rice with the nutrient- and thiamin-rich outer layer and germ stripped away) developed *polyneuritis* (*poly* = many, *neur* = nerves, *itis* = inflammation). This debilitating nerve condition resulted in the birds not being able to fly or stand up. Eijkman noted that polyneuritis was also a symptom of **beriberi,** a similar disease that had been observed in humans.

When Eijkman changed the birds' diet to unpolished rice, with the outer layer and germ intact, the birds were cured.[50] While Eijkman realized that the unpolished rice eliminated the symptoms, he didn't know why. Finally, in 1911, Casimir Funk identified thiamin as the curative factor in the unpolished rice.

Functions of Thiamin

Thiamin Is Needed for Nerve Function and Energy Metabolism

Thiamin plays a role in the transmission of nerve impulses and so helps keep nerves healthy and functioning properly.

You also need thiamin for the metabolism of carbohydrates and certain amino acids. Thiamin also plays a role in breaking down alcohol in the body.

Daily Needs

The RDA for thiamin for adults is 1.1 milligrams for women and 1.2 milligrams for men. Currently, adult American men consume close to 2 milligrams of thiamin daily, whereas women, on average, eat approximately 1.2 milligrams daily, so both groups are meeting their daily needs.[51]

Food Sources

Enriched and whole-grain foods, such as bread and bread products, ready-to-eat cereals, pasta, and rice, and combined foods, such as sandwiches, are the biggest contributors of thiamin in the American diet. A medium-size bowl of ready-to-eat cereal in the morning and a sandwich at lunch will just about meet your daily thiamin requirement.

Pork is the richest source of naturally occurring thiamin.

Too Much or Too Little

There are no known toxicity symptoms from consuming too much thiamin from food or supplements, so no upper level has been set.

A disease that occurs in humans who are deficient in thiamin is beriberi. Symptoms of beriberi include loss of appetite and weight loss, memory loss, and confusion.

In the United States, refined grains are enriched with thiamin, so instances of beriberi are rare. (Recall that enriched grains have the B vitamins thiamin, riboflavin, niacin, and folic acid, as well as the mineral iron, added to them.)

The populations of poor countries with an inadequate food supply rely heavily

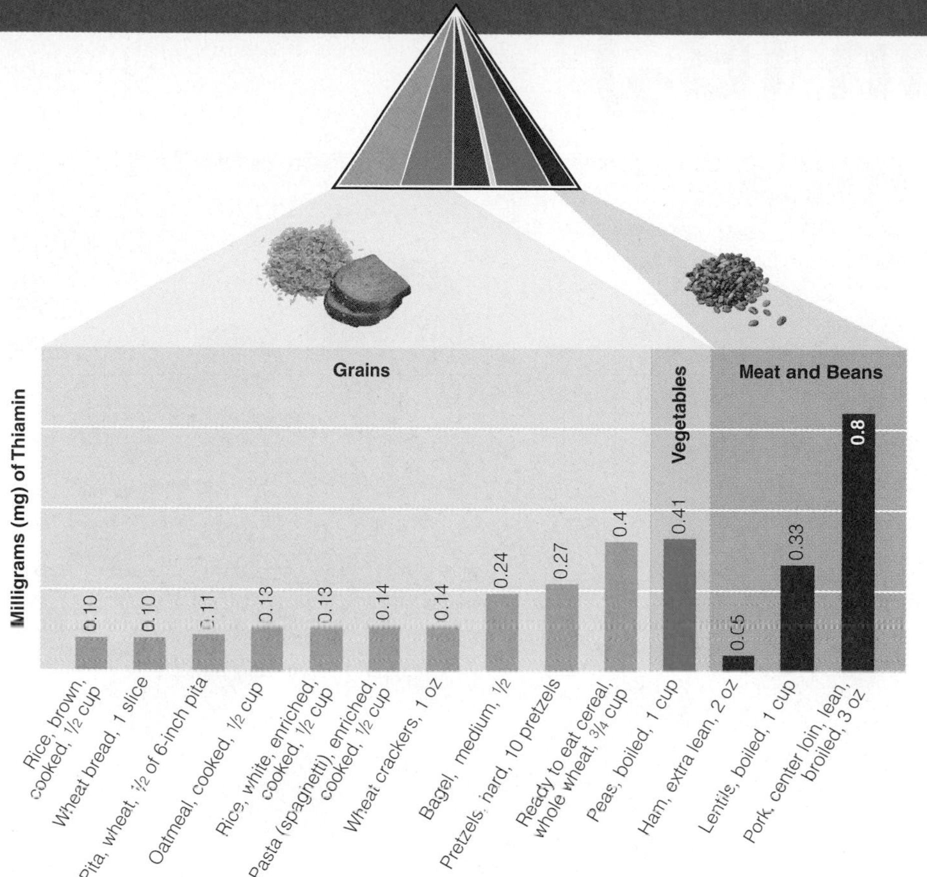

on refined grains that are not enriched. These people are more susceptible to a thiamin deficiency and the side effects of beriberi.

Americans, however, are not completely immune to thiamin deficiencies. Those who chronically abuse alcohol tend to have a poor diet that is probably deficient in thiamin. Alcohol consumption also interferes with the absorption of the small amounts of thiamin that may be in the diet, accelerating its loss from the body. Alcoholics may find themselves battling a thiamin deficiency, that can cause beriberi, and chronic alcohol abuse can lead to an advanced form of thiamin deficiency called Wernicke-Korsakoff syndrome. The syndrome is a progressively damaging brain disorder that can cause mental confusion and memory loss, difficulty seeing clearly, low blood pressure, uncontrolled movement of the arms and legs, and even coma. While some of these symptoms can be reversed after the person is medically treated with thiamin, some of the memory loss may be permanent.[52]

TABLE TIPS 

Thrive on Thiamin

Sprinkle cereal on your yogurt.

Toss pasta with peas. Both foods will boost your thiamin.

Add cooked rice to soups.

Have a sandwich daily.

Enjoy oatmeal for breakfast.

Riboflavin (B_2)

What Is Riboflavin?

Riboflavin, also known as vitamin B_2, is a light-sensitive B vitamin that is abundant in milk. One of the reasons that milk is packaged in opaque bottles or cardboard containers is to preserve its riboflavin content from being destroyed by light.

Not so long ago, milk made its way to a household not via the grocery store cooler, but by way of a daily visit from a milkman in the early hours of the morning. At each delivery, the milkman placed the clear glass milk bottles inside a covered "milk box" outside the home. The milk box helped protect the light-sensitive riboflavin in the milk from being destroyed by the morning sunlight. Sunlight destroys riboflavin quickly. In fact, just 30 minutes of midday summer sun will destroy over 30 percent of the riboflavin in glass-bottled milk.[53]

Functions of Riboflavin

Riboflavin Is Important for Energy Metabolism

Your body needs riboflavin to turn the carbohydrates, proteins, and fats that you eat into energy, and to keep the cells in your body healthy.[54] Riboflavin also enhances the functions of other B vitamins, such as niacin and B_{12}.

Daily Needs

You need to consume a little over 1 milligram of riboflavin daily to be healthy. Adult males should consume 1.3 milligrams

Milligrams (mg) of Riboflavin

Food group	Food	Milligrams (mg) of Riboflavin
Grains	Rice, white, enriched cooked, ½ cup	0.01
Grains	Pasta (spaghetti), enriched cooked, ½ cup	0.07
Grains	Pita, enriched, 6 inch, 1	0.2
Grains	Pizza, cheese, 1 slice, 100 g	0.26
Grains	Macaroni and cheese, 1 cup	0.41
Grains	Kellogg's Raisin Bran cereal, 1 cup	0.44
Vegetables	Mushrooms, raw, 1 cup	0.28
Vegetables	Spinach, boiled, 1 cup	0.43
Fruits	Prunes, (dried plums), ½ cup	0.12
Milk	dder cheese, reduced fat, 1½ oz	0.09
Milk	Feta cheese, 1½ oz	0.36
Milk	Yogurt, nonfat, 1 cup	0.44
Milk	Milk, low fat, 1% milk fat, 1 cup	0.47
Meat and Beans	Egg, scrambled, cooked, 1 large	0.27
Meat and Beans	Liver, beef, pan fried, 3 oz	2.91

and females, 1.1 milligrams of riboflavin every day.

Food Sources

Milk and yogurt are the most popular sources of riboflavin in the diets of American adults, followed by enriched cereals and grains. A breakfast of cereal and milk and a lunchtime pita sandwich and yogurt will provide your riboflavin needs for the day.

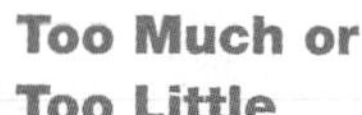

Too Much or Too Little

Your body has a limited ability to absorb riboflavin, so excessive amounts are excreted in urine. In fact, because riboflavin is a bright yellow compound, consuming large amounts through supplements will turn urine as yellow as a school bus. While this isn't dangerous to your health, it isn't beneficial either, so you should skip the supplements and pour yourself a glass of milk instead. No upper level for riboflavin has been determined.

If you don't consume enough of this B vitamin, the cells in the tissues that line your throat, mouth, tongue, and lips will be the first to signal a deficiency. Your throat would be sore, the inside of your mouth would swell, your tongue would be inflamed and look purplish red, and your lips will be dry and scaly. Deficiencies are rarely seen in healthy individuals who eat a balanced diet.

TABLE TIPS

Rally Your Riboflavin

Have a glass of milk with your meals.

A yogurt snack is a riboflavin snack.

Pizza is a good source of riboflavin.

Enriched pasta will enrich your meal with riboflavin.

Macaroni and cheese provides a double source of riboflavin from the pasta and cheese.

Niacin (B_3)

What Is Niacin?

Niacin, or vitamin B_3, is the generic term for nicotinic acid and nicotinamide, which are the two active forms of niacin that are derived from foods.

Functions of Niacin

Niacin Is Needed to Use the Energy in Your Food

Niacin is another nutrient your body needs to use carbohydrates, proteins, and fats. Without niacin, you wouldn't be able to create energy from the foods that you eat. Niacin is also needed to synthesize fat and cholesterol.

Other Functions of Niacin

Niacin is needed to keep your skin cells healthy and your digestive system functioning properly.

Niacin has been shown to lower the total amount of cholesterol in the blood and the "bad" LDL cholesterol carrier. It can also lower high levels of fat (triglycerides) in the blood and simultaneously raise the level of the "good" HDL cholesterol carrier. The nicotinic acid form of niacin is sometimes prescribed by physicians for patients with high blood cholesterol levels. When niacin is used to treat high blood cholesterol, it is considered a drug. The amount prescribed by a physician is often more than 40 times the upper level for niacin. Note that you should *never* consume high amounts of niacin unless a physician is monitoring you.

Daily Needs

The recommended daily amount for adults is 14 milligrams for women and 16 milligrams for men, an amount set to prevent the deficiency disease pellagra. American adults, on average, far exceed their daily niacin needs.[55]

While niacin is found in many foods, it can also be synthesized in the body from the amino acid tryptophan. For this reason, your daily niacin needs are measured in niacin equivalents (NE). It is estimated that 60 milligrams of tryptophan can be converted to 1 milligram of niacin or 1 milligram NE.

Food Sources

Niacin is found in meat, fish, poultry, enriched whole-grain breads and bread products, and fortified cereals. Protein-rich foods, particularly animal foods such as meat, are good sources of tryptophan and thus of niacin. However, if you are falling short of both your dietary protein and niacin, tryptophan will first be used to make protein in your body, at the expense of your niacin needs.[56]

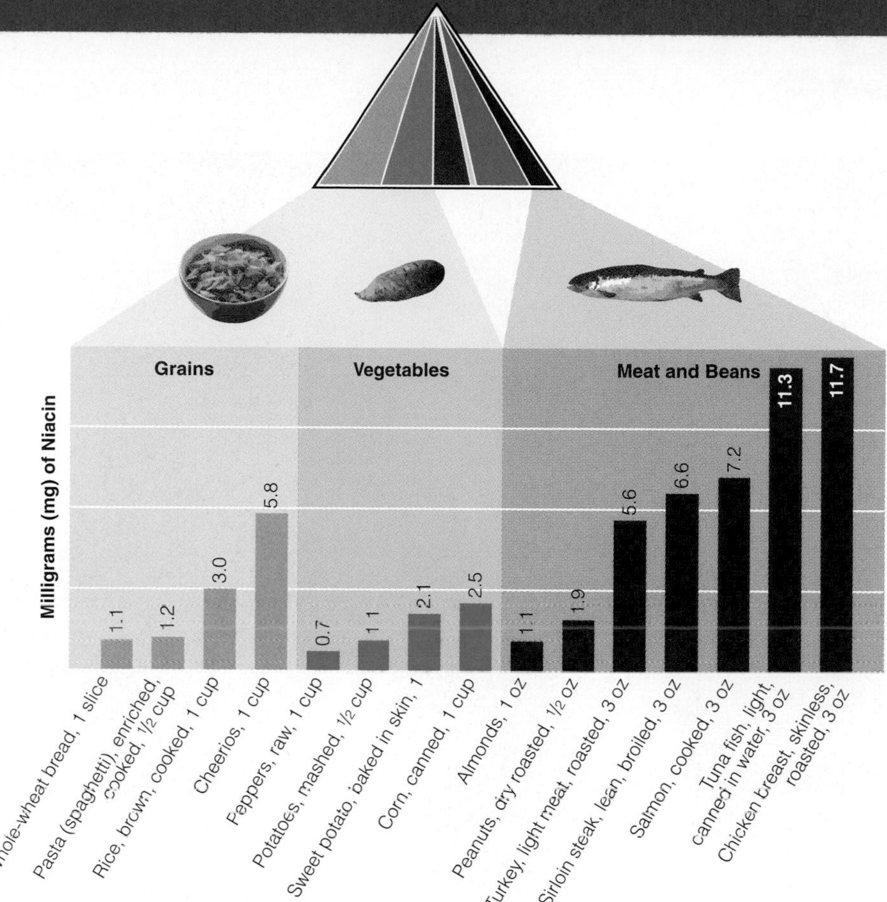

As with thiamin, your niacin needs are probably met after you eat your breakfast and lunch, especially since similar foods contain both vitamins.

Too Much or Too Little

As with most water-soluble vitamins, there isn't any known danger of consuming too much niacin from foods such as meat and enriched grains. However, overconsuming niacin by taking supplements or eating too many overly fortified foods can cause *flushing,* a reddish coloring of the face, arms, and chest. Too much niacin consumption can also cause nausea and vomiting, be toxic to your liver, and raise your blood glucose levels.

The upper level for niacin for adults is 35 milligrams to prevent flushing, the first side effect to be observed when too much niacin is consumed. This upper level applies only to healthy individuals; it may be too high for those with certain medical conditions, such as diabetes mellitus and liver disease.[57]

Too little niacin in the diet can result in the deficiency disease called pellagra. In the early 1900s, pellagra was widespread among the poor living in the southern United States, where people relied on corn—a poor source of niacin—as a dietary staple. The symptoms of pellagra—**d**ermatitis (inflammation or irritation of the skin), **d**ementia (loss of memory along with confusion and disorientation), and **d**iarrhea—led to its being known as the disease of the three Ds. A fourth D, **d**eath, was often associated with the disease.

Once other cereal grains were available, pellagra disappeared as a widespread disease in the United States. The niacin in the grains was later identified as the curative factor for pellagra. Although no longer common in the United States, pellagra does occur among individuals who abuse alcohol and have a very poor diet.

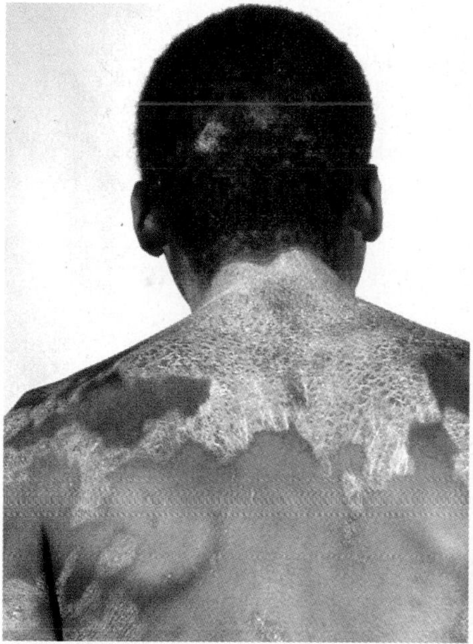

Inflamed skin (dermatitis) can result from pellagra.

TABLE TIPS

Nail Your Niacin

Have a serving of enriched cereal in the morning.

Dip niacin-rich peppers in hummus.

Enjoy a lean chicken breast at dinner.

Snack on peanuts.

Put tuna fish flakes on your salad.

Vitamin B_6

What Is Vitamin B_6?

Vitamin B_6 is a collective name for several related compounds, including pyridoxine, the major form found in plant foods and the form used in supplements and fortified foods.[58] Two other forms, pyridoxal and pyridoxamine, are found in animal food sources such as chicken and meat.

Functions of Vitamin B_6

Vitamin B_6 Is an Active Coenzyme

Vitamin B_6 acts as a coenzyme with over 100 enzymes involved in the metabolism of proteins. It is needed to create nonessential amino acids and to convert the amino acid tryptophan to niacin.[59] Vitamin B_6 also helps your body metabolize fats and carbohydrates and break down glycogen, the storage form of glucose.

Other Functions of B_6

Vitamin B_6 is needed to make the oxygen-carrying hemoglobin in your red blood cells and to keep your immune and nervous systems healthy.[60]

Finally, recent research indicates that vitamin B_6, along with two other water-soluble vitamins, folate and vitamin B_{12}, may help reduce the risk of heart disease (see the "B Vitamins for Your Heart" feature box on page 34).

Daily Needs

Adult women need 1.3 to 1.5 milligrams and men need 1.3 to 1.7 milligrams of vitamin B_6 daily depending on their age.

Food Sources

Because vitamin B_6 is found in so many foods, including ready-to-eat cereals, meat, fish, poultry, many vegetables and fruits, nuts, peanut butter, and other legumes, Americans on average easily meet their daily needs.

Too Much or Too Little

To protect against potential nerve damage, the upper level for vitamin B_6 is set at 100 milligrams daily for adults over the age of 19. Luckily, it would be extremely difficult to take in a dangerous level of vitamin B_6 from food alone.

However, taking vitamin B_6 in supplement form can be harmful. Over the years, vitamin B_6 has been touted to aid a variety of ailments, including carpal tunnel syndrome and premenstrual syndrome (PMS). But research studies have failed to show any significant clinical benefit for taking vitamin B_6 supplements for either of these syndromes.

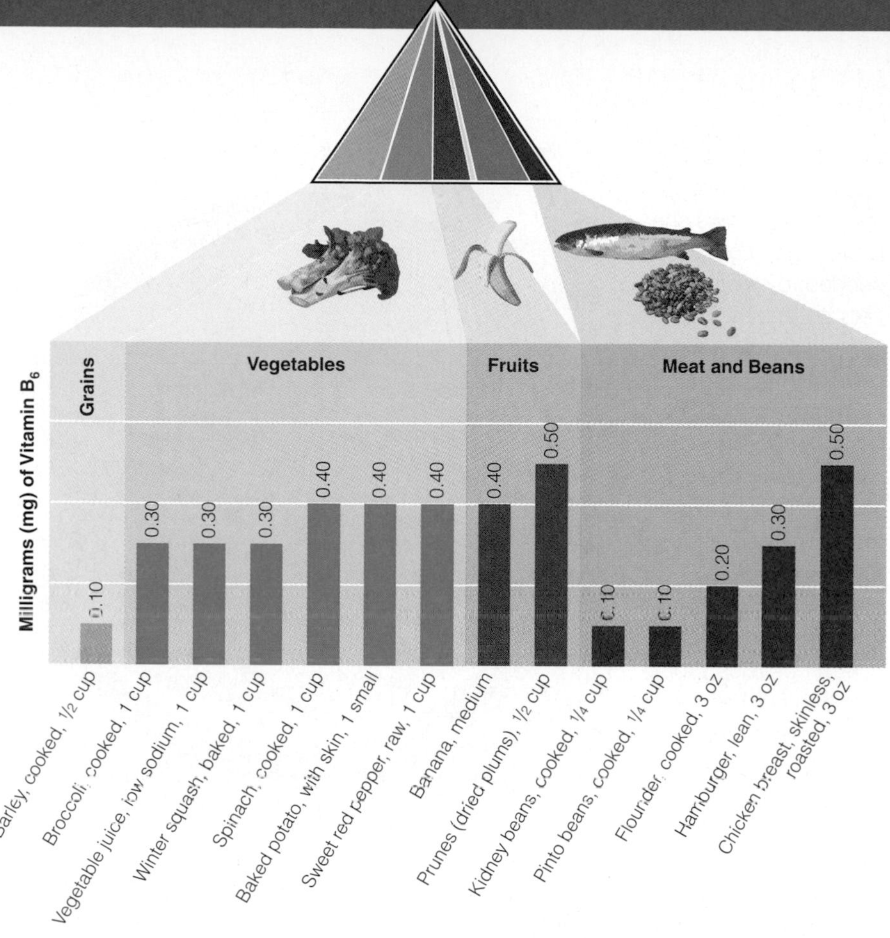

In fact, taking large amounts of vitamin B_6 through supplements may be associated with a variety of ill effects, including nerve damage. Individuals taking as little as 500 milligrams and as much as 6,000 milligrams of vitamin B_6 daily for two months experienced difficulty walking and tingling sensations in their legs and feet. These symptoms subsided once supplement consumption stopped.[61]

The telltale signs of a vitamin B_6 deficiency are a sore tongue, inflammation of the skin, depression, confusion, and possibly anemia.

Those who consume too much alcohol are more likely to fall short of their needs. Not only does alcohol cause your body to lose vitamin B_6, but those suffering from alcoholism are likely to have an unbalanced diet, with little variety.

TABLE TIPS 

Beam with B_6

Have a stuffed baked potato with steamed broccoli and grilled chicken for lunch.

Grab a banana for a midmorning snack.

Add cooked barley to your soup.

Snack on prunes.

Add kidney beans to your chili or salad.

Folate

What Is Folate?

There are two forms of the vitamin folate: the naturally occurring folate in foods and the synthetic form, folic acid, which is added to foods (such as ready-to-eat cereals and grains) and found in supplements. (A very small amount of folic acid can occur naturally in foods. But, for practical purposes in this book, folic acid will always refer to the synthetic variety.)

Functions of Folate

Folate Is Vital for DNA Synthesis

Folate is vital to making the DNA in your cells. If the synthesis of DNA is disrupted, your body's ability to create and maintain new cells is impaired.[62] For this reason, folate plays many important roles, from maintaining healthy blood cells and preventing birth defects to fighting cancer and heart disease. Folate also helps your body use amino acids and is needed to help red blood cells divide and increase in adequate numbers.

Folate Prevents Birth Defects

Folate plays an extremely important role during pregnancy, particularly in the first few weeks after conception, often before the mother knows she is pregnant. Folate is needed to create new cells so that the baby can grow and develop.

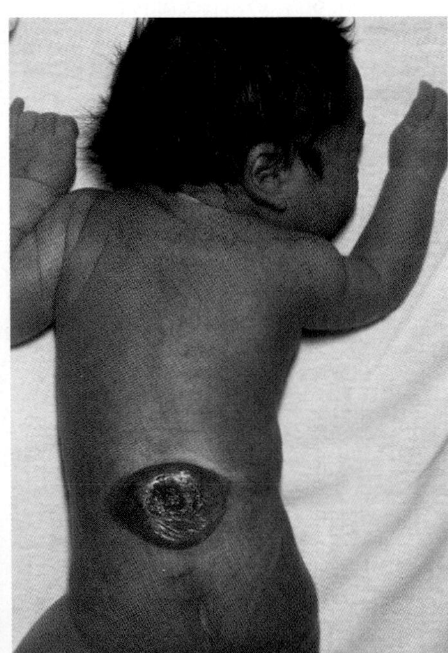

Infant with spina bifida.

A folate deficiency during pregnancy can result in birth defects called neural tube defects. The neural tube forms the baby's spine, brain, and skull. If the neural tube doesn't develop properly, two common birth defects, anencephaly and spina bifida, can occur. In anencephaly, the brain doesn't completely form so the baby can't move, hear, think, or function. An infant with anencephaly dies soon after birth. In spina bifida (see photo), the baby's spinal cord and backbone aren't properly developed, causing learning and physical disabilities, such as the inability to walk.[63]

Folic acid reduces the risk of these birth defects by 50 to 70 percent if consumed at least the month prior to conception and during the early part of pregnancy.[64]

Research studies to date suggest that synthetic folic acid has a stronger protective effect than the folate found naturally in foods. Since 1998, the FDA has mandated that folic acid be added to all enriched grains and cereal products. This enrichment program has reduced the incidence of neural tube defects by over 25 percent.[65]

Folate Reduces Some Cancer Risks

Folate has been shown to help reduce the risk of certain cancers, specifically colon cancer. Studies show that men and women taking a multivitamin supplement or otherwise consuming their recommended amounts of folate have a lower risk of developing colon cancer. Other studies show an association between diets low in folate and an increased risk of breast and pancreatic cancers. Inadequate amounts of folate in the body can disrupt the cell's DNA, potentially triggering the development of cancer.[66]

Daily Needs

Your body absorbs the synthetic folic acid more easily than it absorbs naturally occurring folate. In fact, synthetic folic acid, which is added to enriched grains and cereals, is absorbed 1.7 times more efficiently than folate that is found in foods such as orange juice.[67] Because of this, your folate needs are measured in dietary folate equivalents (DFE). Most adults should consume 400 micrograms DFE of folate daily.

While the foods in your diet analysis program database list the micrograms of folate as DFE, the Nutrition Facts panel on the food label doesn't make this distinction. To convert the micrograms of folic acid found on the food labels of foods with folic acid added, such as enriched pasta, rice, cereals, and bread, to

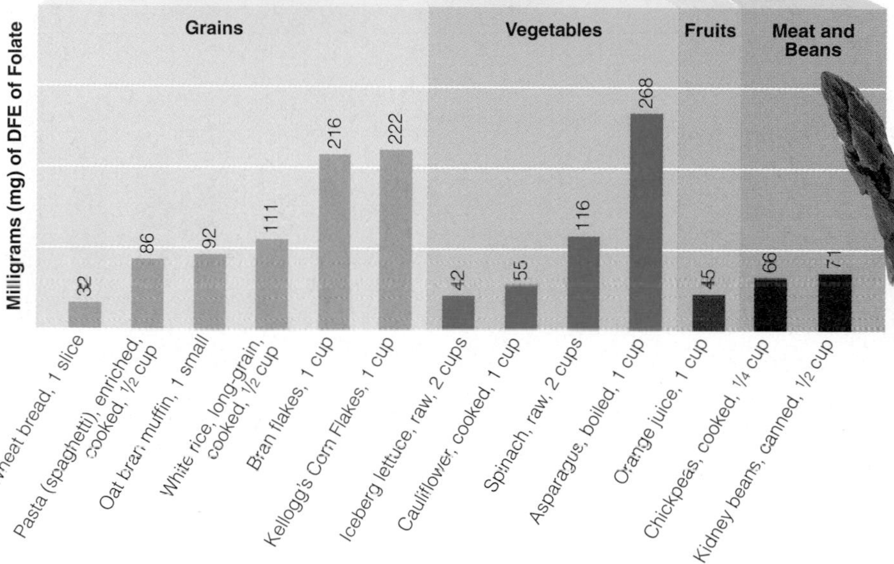

dietary folate equivalents, multiply the amount listed on the label by 1.7:

100 μg 31.7 5 170 μg DFE

Because 50 percent of pregnancies in the United States are unplanned, women at risk of becoming pregnant should consume 400 micrograms of synthetic folic acid daily from fortified foods or supplements, along with a diet high in naturally occurring folate. Women with a family history of neural tube defects should, under the guidance of their physicians, take even larger amounts.[68]

Food Sources

Enriched pasta, rice, breads and cereals, legumes (dried peas and beans), leafy green vegetables (spinach, lettuce, collards), broccoli, and asparagus are all good sources of this vitamin.

Too Much or Too Little

There isn't any danger in consuming excessive amounts of naturally occurring folate in foods. However, consuming too much folic acid, either through supplements or fortified foods, can be harmful for individuals who are deficient in vitamin B_{12}. A vitamin B_{12} deficiency can cause anemia and, more dangerous, crippling and irreversible nerve damage. Too much folate in the diet masks the symptoms of B_{12} deficiency anemia. Though folate can correct anemia, the nerve damage due to the vitamin B_{12} deficiency persists. This delays a proper diagnosis and corrective therapy with vitamin B_{12}. By the time the person is given the vitamin B_{12}, irreversible nerve damage may have occurred.[69]

A folate deficiency can also result in abnormally large and immature cells known as megaloblasts. Megaloblasts develop into abnormally large red blood cells, or macrocytes, that have a diminished oxygen-carrying capacity. Eventually, macrocytic anemia causes a person to feel tired, weak, and irritable and to experience shortness of breath. Because folate requires vitamin B_{12} to produce healthy red blood cells in the body, a deficiency of either vitamin can lead to anemia.

An upper level of 1,000 micrograms has been set for folic acid from enriched and fortified foods and supplements to safeguard those who may be unknowingly deficient in vitamin B_{12}.

TABLE TIPS 

Fulfill Your Folate Need

Have a bowl of cereal in the morning.

Add chickpeas to your salad.

Enjoy a tossed salad with your lunch.

Add fresh spinach leaves to your sandwich.

Have a handful of crackers as a late-afternoon snack.

Vitamin B_{12}

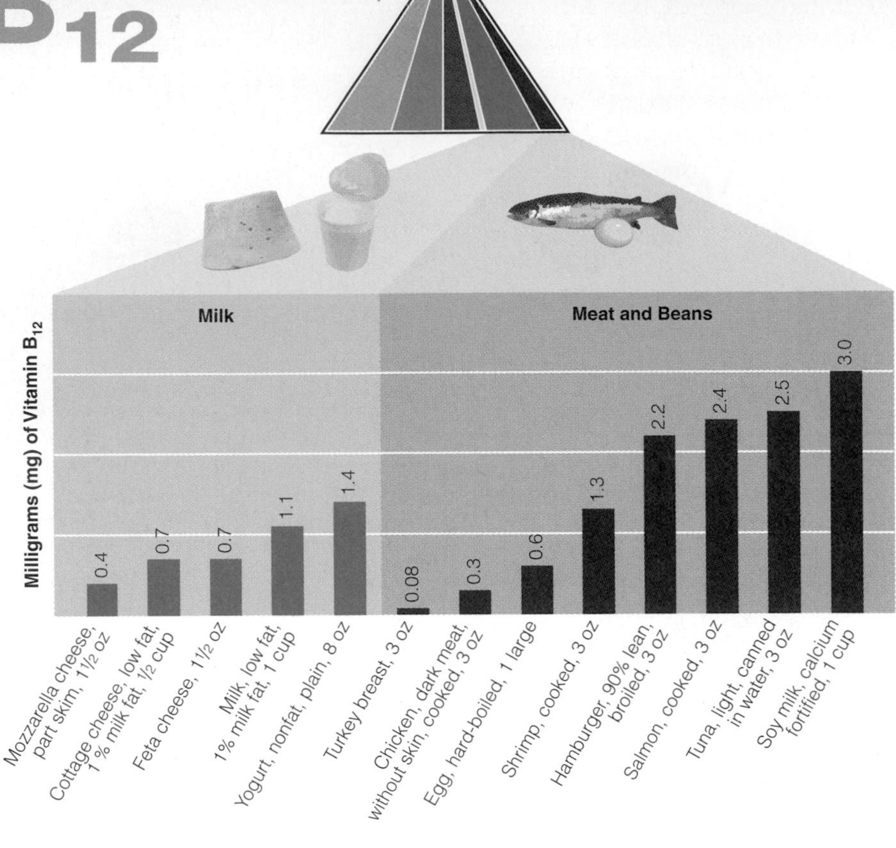

What Is Vitamin B_{12}?

The family of compounds referred to as vitamin B_{12} is also called cobalamin because it contains the metal cobalt.[70]

Vitamin B_{12} is the only water-soluble vitamin that can be stored in your body, primarily in your liver.

B_{12} Needs Intrinsic Factor to be Absorbed

A protein produced in your stomach called *intrinsic factor* is needed to promote vitamin B_{12} absorption. Intrinsic factor binds with vitamin B_{12} in your small intestine, where the vitamin is absorbed. People who cannot produce intrinsic factor are unable to absorb vitamin B_{12} and are diagnosed with pernicious anemia (*pernicious* = harmful). People with this condition, must be given regular shots of vitamin B_{12}, which injects the vitamin directly into the blood, bypassing the intestine.

Because your body stores plenty of vitamin B_{12} in the liver, the symptoms of pernicious anemia can take years to develop.

Functions of Vitamin B_{12}

Vitamin B_{12} Is Vital for Healthy Nerves and Red Blood Cells

Your body needs vitamin B_{12} to use certain fatty acids and amino acids and to make the DNA in your cells. Vitamin B_{12} is also needed for healthy nerves and tissues. Like folate, vitamin B_{12} plays an important role in keeping your cells, particularly your red blood cells, healthy.[71] It is also one of the three B vitamins that collectively could be heart-healthy (see "B Vitamins for Your Heart" feature box later in this concept).

Daily Needs

Adults needs 2.4 micrograms of vitamin B_{12} daily. American adults, on average, are consuming over 4 micrograms daily.

The body's ability to absorb naturally occurring vitamin B_{12} from foods diminishes with age. This decline appears to be due to a reduction in the acidic juices in the stomach, which are needed to

break the bonds that bind the B_{12} to the proteins in food. If the bonds aren't broken, the vitamin can't be released. Up to 30 percent of individuals over the age of 50 experience this decline in acidic juices in their stomachs. Not surprisingly, the pernicious anemia associated with a vitamin B_{12} deficiency occurs in about 2 percent of individuals over the age of 60.[72]

With less acid juice present, the bacteria normally found in the intestines aren't properly destroyed and so tend to overgrow. This abundance of bacteria feed on vitamin B_{12}, diminishing the amount of the vitamin that may be available. Luckily, the synthetic form of vitamin B_{12} that is used in fortified foods and supplements isn't bound to a protein, so it doesn't depend on your stomach secretions to be absorbed. (Synthetic vitamin B_{12} still needs intrinsic factor to be absorbed.)

Because the synthetic variety is a more reliable source, individuals over the age of 50 should meet their vitamin B_{12} needs primarily from fortified foods or a supplement.[73]

Food Sources

Naturally occurring vitamin B_{12} is found only in foods from animal sources, such as meat, fish, poultry, and dairy products. A varied diet including the minimum recommended servings of these food groups will easily meet your daily needs.

Synthetic vitamin B_{12} is found in fortified soy milk and some ready-to-eat cereals, which are ideal sources for older adults and strict vegetarians, who avoid all foods from animal sources.

If you are relying solely on fortified foods to meet your vitamin B_{12} needs, continually check the labels on these products to make sure they haven't suddenly been reformulated to exclude the vitamin.

Too Much or Too Little

At present, there are no known risks of consuming too much vitamin B_{12} from foods, fortified foods, or supplements, and no upper level has been set. There is also no known benefit from taking B_{12} supplements if your diet contains foods from animal sources and/or fortified foods.

A Vitamin B_{12} Deficiency Can Cause Macrocytic Anemia

Because vitamin B_{12} and folate work closely together to make healthy red blood cells, a vitamin B_{12} deficiency can cause macrocytic anemia, the same type of anemia, caused by a folate deficiency. In macrocytic anemia, due to a vitamin B_{12} deficiency, there is enough folate available for red blood cells to divide but the folate can't be utilized properly because there isn't enough vitamin B_{12} available. In fact, the true cause of macrocytic anemia is more likely a B_{12} deficiency than a folate deficiency.

Because pernicious anemia (caused by a lack of intrinsic factor) is a type of macrocytic anemia, its initial symptoms are the same as those seen in a folate deficiency: fatigue and shortness of breath.

Vitamin B_{12} is needed to protect nerve cells, including those in your brain and spine, so one long-term consequence of pernicious anemia is nerve damage marked by tingling and numbness in the arms and legs and problems walking. If diagnosed early enough, these symptoms can be reversed with treatments of vitamin B_{12}.

TABLE TIPS 

Boost Your B_{12}

Enjoy heart-healthy fish at least twice a week.

Sprinkle your steamed vegetables with reduced-fat shredded cheese.

Drink milk or fortified soy milk.

Try a cottage cheese and fruit snack in the afternoon.

Enjoy a grilled chicken breast on a bun for lunch.

Vitamin C

You don't have to go out of your way to ensure that your dog's daily chow contains enough vitamin C. Dogs and many other animals possess an enzyme that can synthesize vitamin C from glucose. Humans, however, lack the necessary enzyme for this conversion, and have to rely on food to meet their daily vitamin C needs.[74]

Functions of Vitamin C

Vitamin C Acts as a Coenzyme

Vitamin C, also known as ascorbic acid, acts as a coenzyme that is needed to synthesize and use certain amino acids. In particular, vitamin C is needed to make collagen, the most abundant protein in your body. Collagen is plentiful in your connective tissue, which supports and connects all your body parts, so this protein is needed for healthy bones, teeth, skin, and blood vessels.[75] Thus, a vitamin C deficient diet would affect your entire body.

Vitamin C Acts as an Antioxidant

Like beta-carotene and vitamin E, vitamin C acts an antioxidant that may help reduce the risk of chronic diseases such as heart disease and cancer (you will learn more about antioxidants later in the concept). It also helps you absorb the iron in plant foods such as grains and cereals and break down histamine, the component behind the inflammation seen in many allergic reactions.[76]

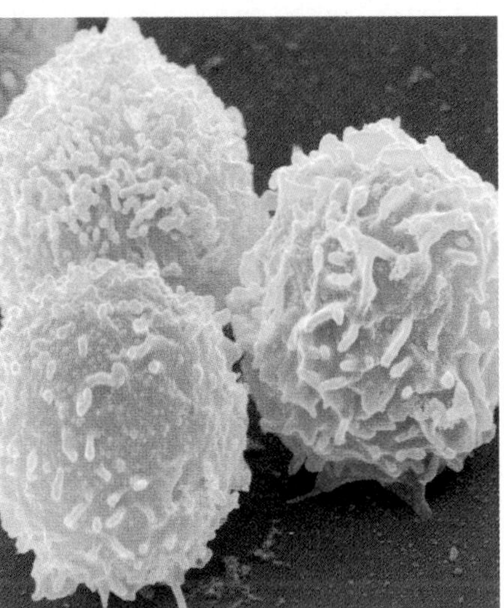

White blood cells.

Vitamin C Boosts Your Immune System

Vitamin C helps keep your immune system healthy by enabling your body to make white blood cells, like the ones shown in the photo above. These blood cells fight infections, and this immune-boosting role has fostered the belief that high doses of vitamin C can cure the common cold. (The "Gesundheit! Myths and Facts about the Common Cold" box takes a look at this theory.)

Daily Needs

Women need to consume 75 milligrams of vitamin C daily, and men need to consume 90 milligrams daily to meet their needs.

Smoking accelerates the breakdown and elimination of vitamin C from the body, so smokers need to consume an additional 35 milligrams of vitamin C every day to make up for these losses.[77]

Food Sources

Americans meet about 90 percent of their vitamin C needs by consuming fruits and vegetables, with orange and/or grapefruit juice being the most popular source in the diet. One serving of either juice will just about meet an adult's daily needs. Tomatoes, peppers, potatoes, broccoli, oranges, and cantaloupe are also excellent sources.

Too Much or Too Little

Brendan, the track athlete introduced at the beginning of this concept, attempted to ward off a cold by taking vitamin C supplements. His attempt to solve one medical dilemma created a worse one that impeded his training more than his sniffling and sneezing.

While excessive amounts of vitamin C aren't known to be toxic, consuming over 3,000 milligrams daily through the use of supplements has been shown to cause nausea, stomach cramps, and diarrhea. Brendan can attribute the diarrhea he experienced to his daily 3,500-milligrams supplement of vitamin C. Once he stopped taking the supplement, his diarrhea ended.

The upper level for vitamin C for adults is set at 2,000 milligrams to avoid the intestinal discomfort that excessive amounts

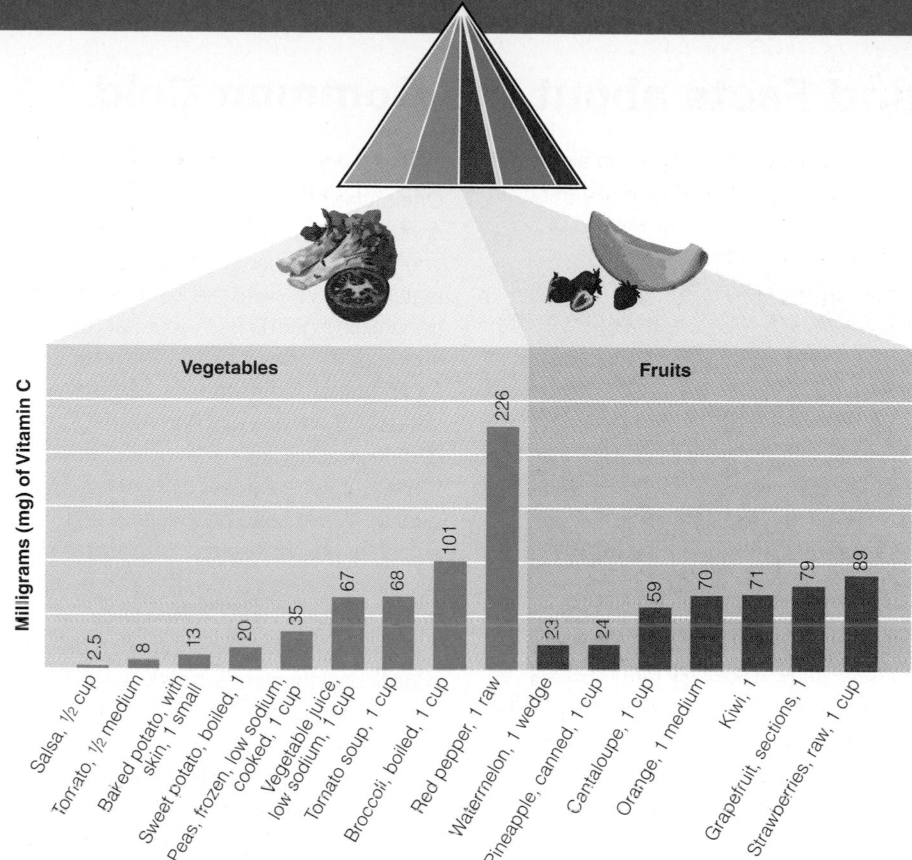

of the vitamin can cause. Too much vitamin C can also lead to the formation of kidney stones in individuals with a history of kidney disease.

Because vitamin C helps to absorb the form of iron found in plant foods, those with a rare disorder called hemochromatosis (*hemo* = blood; *chroma* = color; *osis* = condition), which causes the body to store too much iron, should avoid excessive amounts of vitamin C. Iron toxicity is extremely dangerous and can damage many organs in your body, including the liver and heart.

For centuries, scurvy, the disease of a vitamin C deficiency, was the affliction of sailors on long voyages. After many weeks at sea, sailors would run out of vitamin C–rich produce and then develop the telltale signs of scurvy: swollen and bleeding gums, a rough rash on the skin, coiled or curly arm hairs, and wounds that wouldn't heal.

In 1753, a British naval surgeon discovered that orange and lemon juice prevented scurvy. Decades later, the British government added lemon or lime juice to their standard rations for their sailors to thwart scurvy. In 1919, vitamin C was discovered as the curative factor in these juices.[78]

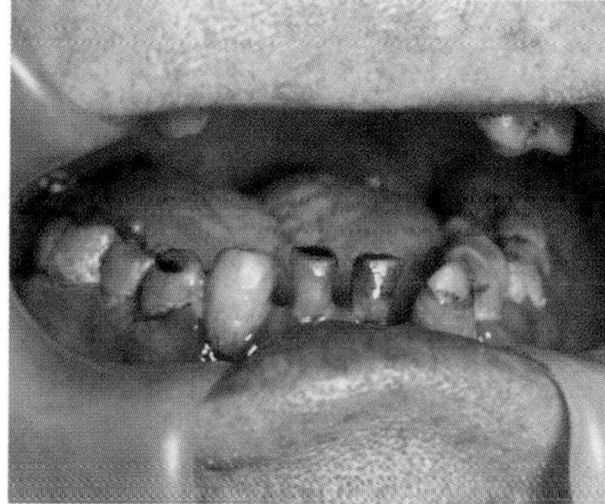

Swollen gums characteristic of scurvy.

TABLE TIPS 

Juicy Ways to Get Vitamin C

Have a least one citrus fruit (such as an orange or grapefruit) daily.

Put sliced tomatoes on your sandwich.

Enjoy a fruit cup for dessert.

Drink low-sodium vegetable juice for an afternoon refresher.

Add strawberries to your low-fat frozen yogurt.

Gesundheit! Myths and Facts about the Common Cold

You probably know the symptoms well. Your nose runs like a leaky faucet and turns beet red from constant wiping. Your head seems stuffed with cotton, and it feels as if someone is playing bongo drums under your scalp. Between coughing and sneezing, you can't catch the rest you need to relieve what feels like constant fatigue. The diagnosis? At least one of the more than 200 varieties of cold virus has invaded your body, and you have a cold that could last as long as two weeks.

You're never alone if you have a case of the common cold. Colds are the leading cause of doctor visits in the United States, and Americans will suffer a billion of them this year alone. Students miss over 20 million school days every year battling the common cold.

The Truth about Catching a Cold

Contrary to popular belief, you can't catch a cold from being outside on a cold day without a coat or hat. The only way to catch a cold is to come in contact with a cold virus. Contact can be direct, such as when you hug or shake hands with someone who is carrying the virus, or indirect, as when you touch an object, such as a keyboard or telephone, contaminated with a cold virus. The next time you touch your nose or rub your eyes, you transfer those germs from your hands into your body. You can also catch a cold virus by inhaling virus-carrying droplets from a cough or sneeze of someone with a cold.

The increased frequency of colds during the fall and winter is likely due to the fact that people spend more time indoors in the close quarters of classrooms, dorm rooms, and the workplace, which makes it easier to share germs. The low humidity of the winter air can also cause the inside of your nose to be drier and more permeable to the invasion of these viruses.

Vitamin C and the Common Cold

In the 1970s, a scientist named Linus Pauling theorized that consuming at least 1,000 milligrams of vitamin C would prevent the common cold. Since then, study after study has shown that megadoses of vitamin C are not effective in preventing colds. However, some research has suggested that vitamin C may help reduce the duration and severity of a cold in some individuals. This may be due to the antihistamine effect that vitamin C can have in the body when taken in large doses.[1]

Other Cold Remedies: The Jury Is Still Out

Recently, other dietary substances, such as the herb echinacea and the mineral zinc, have emerged as popular treatment strategies for the common cold. Echinacea was used centuries ago by some Native American populations to treat coughs and sore throats. Recent studies have shown that the herb comes up short in preventing or affecting the duration or severity of a cold and may contribute to side effects, such as a rash and intestinal discomfort. The results of a recent review of over 300 studies using echinacea were inconclusive. More research needs to be done to establish whether echinacea can help prevent or treat the common cold.[2]

Studies of zinc have also had mixed results. Too much zinc can be toxic and can suppress your immune system. You will learn more about zinc and its role in the immune system in Concept 17.

What You Can Do

One of the best ways to reduce your chances of catching a cold is to wash your hands frequently with soap and water. This will lower the likelihood of your transmitting germs from your hands to your mouth, nose, or eyes. One study found that children who washed their hands four times a day had over 20 percent fewer sick days from school than those who washed their hands less frequently. When soap and water aren't available, gel sanitizers or disposable alcohol-containing hand wipes can be an effective alternative.[3] Covering your mouth and nose when you cough or sneeze and then immediately washing your hands will help you keep from contaminating the people around you.

Finally, the Centers for Disease Control and Prevention recommends the following steps to take if you do get a cold:

- Get plenty of rest.
- Drink plenty of fluids. (Chicken soup and juices are considered fluids.)
- Gargle with warm salt water or use throat lozenges for a sore throat.
- Dab petroleum jelly on a raw nose to relieve irritation.
- Take aspirin* or acetaminophen (Tylenol) for a headache or fever.

*The American Academy of Pediatrics recommends that children and teenagers avoid consuming aspirin or medicine containing aspirin when they have a viral illness, as it can lead to a rare but serious illness called Reye's syndrome. This syndrome can cause brain damage or death.

Pantothenic Acid and Biotin

What Are Pantothenic Acid and Biotin?

Pantothenic acid and biotin are B vitamins.

Functions of Pantothenic Acid and Biotin

Pantothenic acid and biotin aid in the metabolism of the nutrients that provide you with energy—carbohydrates, proteins, and fats.

Daily Needs

Adults need 5 milligrams of pantothenic acid and 30 micrograms of biotin daily.

Food Sources

Both pantothenic acid and biotin are widely available in foods, including whole grains and whole-grain cereals, nuts and legumes, peanut butter, meat, milk, and eggs. Most Americans easily meet their needs.[79]

Biotin deficiency is so rare that an accurate list of the amount in foods is hard to find.

In addition to its abundance in foods, biotin can be synthesized by the bacteria in your intestinal tract, providing yet another avenue to meet your needs.

Eating a healthy diet to meet all of your other B vitamin needs will ensure that you meet your needs for pantothenic acid and biotin.

Too Much or Too Little

Like many of the other B vitamins, there are no known adverse effects from consuming too much pantothenic acid or biotin. An upper level has not been determined for either of these vitamins.

Although a pantothenic acid deficiency is rare, if you do fall short of your needs, your symptoms might include fatigue, nausea, vomiting, numbness, muscle cramps, and difficulties walking.

During World War II, prisoners of war in Asia experienced a "burning feet" syndrome. The symptoms ranged from heat sensations and tingling on the soles of their feet to a painful burning intense enough to disrupt sleep. Their diet consisted predominantly of nutrient-poor polished rice. A doctor in India who was studying an identical phenomenon in his patients discovered that when he gave them supplements of pantothenic acid, the condition stopped.[80] In both cases, the syndrome was later attributed to a diet deficient in pantothenic acid.

Consuming inadequate amounts of biotin can cause hair loss, skin rash, and feelings of depression, fatigue, and nausea.[81]

While deficiencies are rare, it can occur if you eat a lot of raw egg whites. The protein avidin, found in egg whites, binds with biotin and blocks it from being absorbed in your intestine. Cooking the egg denatures and inactivates the protein, eliminating the problem.[82]

B Vitamins for Your Heart

In the late 1970s, researchers made a curious discovery. They noticed that individuals with a very rare genetic disorder, in which they have too much of the amino acid homocysteine in their blood, suffer from a higher than average incidence of heart disease. Since then, approximately 80 research studies have found an association between high levels of homocysteine and the increased risk for heart disease. While it isn't known exactly how this amino acid contributes to heart disease, excessive amounts of homocysteine may injure the arteries, decrease the flexibility of the blood vessels, or increase the likelihood of clots forming in the blood. Since vitamin B_6, folate, and vitamin B_{12} are all involved in breaking down homocysteine in the body, researchers began studying the effect of these vitamins on this amino acid.[4]

Numerous studies have suggested that low blood levels of these B vitamins, especially folate, are associated with an increased level of homocysteine in the body. In fact, the mandatory addition of folic acid to enriched grains and grain products that began in the late 1990s to prevent certain birth defects may also fight heart disease. In a study of over 1,000 individuals, the average blood level of folate was higher and the level of the amino acid homocysteine lower in individuals seen in the time period after the implementation of the folic acid enrichment program, as compared with before the program began.[5]

Studies are currently underway to determine if taking supplements of these B vitamins will lower the risk for heart disease. Studies to date have had mixed results. Until more is known, you should eat a diet that is naturally rich in B vitamins.

Are There Other Important Nutrients?

Pantothenic Acid and Biotin Are B Vitamins

Pantothenic acid and biotin are B vitamins that aid in the breakdown of carbohydrates, proteins, and fats. Adults need 5 milligrams of pantothenic acid and 30 micrograms of biotin daily. Since both micronutrients are widely available in foods, including whole grains, nuts, legumes, meats, milk, and eggs, most Americans easily meet their needs. Although deficiency of either nutrient is rare, biotin deficiency can occur if you eat a lot of raw egg whites, which contain a protein that blocks biotin absorption. Cooking eggs deactivates the protein and eliminates the problem.

Choline Is an Essential Nutrient

Choline is essential for healthy cells and nerves, but it is not classified as a vitamin. Although your body can synthesize it, a study has shown that males given choline-deficient diets weren't able to synthesize enough of it to meet their needs and experienced liver damage. Research has not yet determined whether this can occur in women, infants, children, and older adults.[83] The current recommendation of 425 milligrams for women and 550 milligrams for men is based on the amount needed to protect your liver.

Choline is so widely available in foods, especially milk, liver, eggs, and peanuts, that it unlikely that your intake will ever fall short. However, too much choline from supplements can cause sweating and vomiting, as well as low blood pressure. Too much choline can also cause a person to emit an unpleasant fishy odor as the body tries to get rid of the excess. An upper level of 3,500 milligrams for choline has been set to prevent your blood pressure from dropping too low and to keep you from smelling like a fish!

Carnitine, Lipoic Acid, and Inositol Are Vitamin-like Substances

Certain vitamin-like substances are needed for overall health and important body functions, but they are not considered essential nutrients because your body can synthesize them in adequate amounts without consuming them in foods, and deficiency symptoms are not known to occur in humans.

Carnitine (*carnus* = flesh) is needed to utilize fat properly. It is abundant in foods from animal sources, such as meat and dairy products. Although there is no research to support the claim, carnitine supplements are sometimes advertised to promote weight loss and help athletes improve their performance.[84]

Similar to many B vitamins, lipoic acid helps your cells generate energy; in fact, it was initially thought to be a vitamin.[85] Lipoic acid is also being studied for its potential role as an antioxidant that could help reduce the risk for certain chronic diseases, such as type 2 diabetes and cataracts.

Inositol is needed to keep cell membranes healthy. Inositol can be found in foods from plant sources, and healthy individuals can synthesize enough to meet their needs.

The Take-Home Message Pantothenic acid and biotin are B vitamins widely available in foods. Choline is an essential nutrient that is needed for healthy cells and nerves. Carnitine, lipoic acid, and inositol are needed for important body functions and overall health, but they are not essential nutrients. Your body can synthesize them in adequate amounts, and there are no known deficiency symptoms.

How Should You Get Your Vitamins?

Once upon a time, eating unprocessed foods, such as fruits and vegetables, was the only way to get your vitamins. With advances in nutrition and food technology, however, fortified foods and supplements became available for meeting your nutrient needs. Let's look at the pros and cons of each of these next.

Foods Are the Best Way to Meet Your Vitamin Needs

As you learned earlier, foods provide more than just vitamins. Many are also rich in phytochemicals, antioxidants, minerals, fiber, water, and macronutrients, all of which are thought to work synergistically to fight disease. For example, the fat in your salad dressing helps you absorb the phytochemicals in the carrots in your salad. The vitamin C–rich tomatoes on your sandwich help you absorb the iron in the wheat bread. The

Table 16.1

You Can Meet Your Vitamin Needs with Healthy Food Choices

Nutrient	USDA Food Intake Pattern, 2,000 calories*	Institute of Medicine Recommendations, RDA/AI
Vitamin A, μ RAE	1,057.0	900.0
Vitamin E, mg AT	9.0	15.0
Thiamin, mg	2.1	1.2
Riboflavin, mg	3.0	1.3
Niacin, mg	23.0	16.0
Vitamin B_6, mg	2.4	1.3
Vitamin B_{12}, μg	7.9	2.4
Folate, μg	610.0	400.0
Vitamin C, mg	174.0	90.0

*The highest intake level for young adult men or women is stated.

Note: RDA = Recommended Dietary Allowance; AI = Adequate Intake; RAE = retinol activity equivalents; AT = α-tocopherol; mg = milligrams; μg = micrograms.

Data from: U.S. Department of Agriculture, *Report of the Dietary Guidelines Advisory Committee on the Dietary Guidelines for Americans,* 2005, www.health.gov/dietaryguidelines/dga2005/report (accessed February 2005).

whole is indeed greater than the sum of its parts, so eat whole foods to meet your vitamin needs. *Dietary Guidelines for Americans 2005* recommends eating a wide variety of foods from each food group. These recommendations are reflected in MyPyramid and increase the opportunity to meet your daily vitamin needs. Figure 16.6 illustrates the vitamins that each food group contributes to your diet.

A healthy 2,000-calorie diet based on the *Dietary Guidelines* provides adequate levels of most vitamins (Table 16.1). Vitamin E is the only nutrient that may be a challenge.[86] However, putting some margarine on your morning toast, a few nuts in your yogurt, and a little salad dressing on your dinner salad would likely do the trick. Refer to the Table Tips for vitamin E for more suggestions on meeting your needs for the day.

If you are falling short of some vitamins in your diet, fortified foods can help make up the difference.

Figure 16.6 Vitamins Found Widely in MyPyramid Eating a wide variety of foods from all food groups will ensure that you meet your vitamin needs.

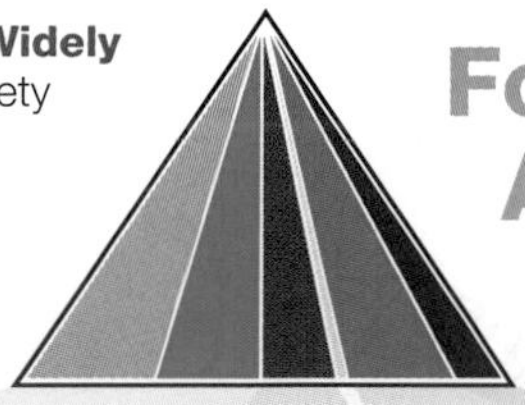

Grains	Vegetables	Fruit	Milk	Meat and Beans
Folic acid	Folate	Folate	Riboflavin	Niacin
Niacin	Vitamin A	Vitamin C	Vitamin A	Thiamin
Vitamin B_6	Vitamin C		Vitamin B_{12}	Vitamin B_6
Vitamin B_{12} (if fortified)	Vitamin E		Vitamin D	Vitamin B_{12}
Riboflavin				
Thiamin				

Fortified Foods Can Provide Additional Nutrients

When you pour your morning glass of orange juice, you know that you are getting a significant splash of vitamin C. However, depending on the brand of orange juice, you may also be meeting your vitamin E and vitamin D needs—two nutrients that are not (and never have been) naturally found in oranges. Welcome to the world of fortified foods.

Fortified foods are becoming more popular with the American consumer. Sales have tripled since 1997, topping $18 billion in 2001, and are expected to continue to grow.[87]

Fortified foods—that is, foods that have nutrients added to them—can be a valuable option for individuals whose diets fall short of some nutrients. For instance, someone who doesn't drink milk, such as a strict vegetarian or an individual who is lactose intolerant, can benefit from drinking vitamin D– and calcium-fortified soy milk. Older adults who are inactive and thus have lower calorie needs may choose fortified foods to add nutrients, such as vitamins B_{12} and E, to their limited dietary selections. Women in their childbearing years may look to folic acid–fortified cereals to help them meet their daily needs of this B vitamin.

However, fortified foods can do a disservice to the diet if they displace other vitamin- and mineral-rich foods. For example, a sugary orange drink that has vitamin C added to it should not replace vitamin C–rich orange juice. While the vitamin C content of the two beverages may be the same, the orange-flavored drink doesn't compare with the juice when it comes to providing other nutrients and phytochemicals. As you can see in Figure 16.7, the orange drink is basically orange-flavored water sweetened with 7 teaspoons of sugar and enriched with vitamin C.

A diet containing numerous fortified foods can put you at risk of overconsuming some nutrients. If a heavily fortified food, such as some cereals, energy bars, and beverages, claims to contain "100% of the vitamins needed daily," then eating several servings of the food or a combination of several fortified foods is similar to taking several multivitamin supplements. You are more likely to overconsume vitamins in fortified foods than in whole foods.

Fortified foods can give your diet a vitamin boost.

fortified foods Foods with added nutrients.

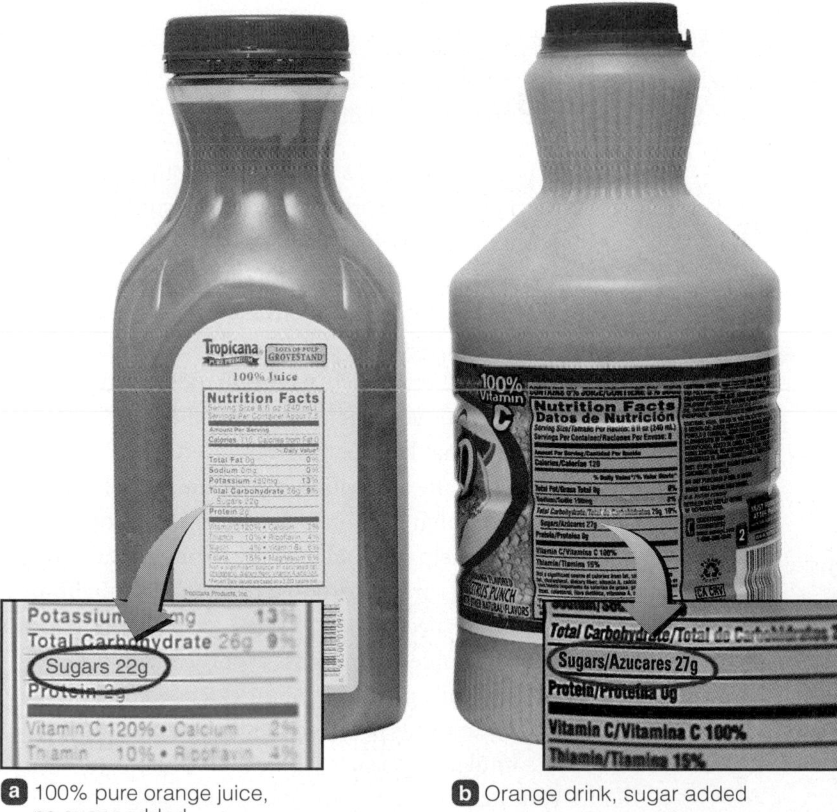

a 100% pure orange juice, no sugar added

Added sugar = 0

b Orange drink, sugar added

Added sugar =

= 1 tsp of added sugar

Figure 16.7 What Are You Pouring into Your Glass? While both of these beverages are a good source of vitamin C, they are worlds apart in their nutrition. **(a)** Pure orange juice is also an excellent source of the mineral potassium and doesn't contain any added sugar. **(b)** Orange drink is basically sugar water with vitamin C added to it. One glass contains the equivalent of 7 teaspoons of added sugar.

Vitamin Supplements Are Not a Substitute for Healthy Eating

Supplements should never be used to replace a healthy diet. A consistent diet of non-nutritious foods followed by a daily supplement won't transform your less than desirable eating habits into a healthy diet. The disease-fighting phytochemicals, fiber, and other substances that your body needs are all missing from a bottle of supplements. Moreover, the jury is out as to whether supplements provide the same health protection as nutrients consumed in foods. For example, studies are currently exploring the role of antioxidant supplements in fighting disease. At this time, the American Heart Association, American Dietetic Association, National Cancer Institute, and United States Preventive Services Task Force do not advocate taking supplements to reduce the risk for specific diseases, but they do encourage eating a phytochemical- and antioxidant-rich balanced diet.[88] Filling your plate with a colorful variety of plant-based foods is one of the best-known strategies to fight chronic diseases.

The Take-Home Message **A well-balanced diet that provides adequate calories can meet most people's daily vitamin needs. Fortified foods, as part of a healthy diet, can provide extra nutrients for those whose diets fall short. Vitamin supplements should not be used to replace a healthy diet.**

Check out these recipes and more suggestions at www.pearsonhighered.com/blake

UCook

Smashing Good Potatoes

For a satisfying meal or snack loaded with nutrients, try out this tasty recipe!

UDo

Are You Salad Bar Savvy?

A trip to your local salad bar can be a great way to add vitamin-rich vegetables to your diet. However, some of the food choices at a salad bar may also be high in saturated fat. To learn how to build a heart-friendly, vitamin-rich salad at the salad bar, visit our website.

The Top Five Points to Remember

1. Vitamins are essential nutrients needed by your body to maintain good health, to grow, and to reproduce. They are found naturally in foods, added to foods, or in pill form in dietary supplements.
2. Fat-soluble vitamins are stored in your body and need fat to be absorbed. They can accumulate to the point of toxicity if your intake is excessive. The fat-soluble vitamins are A, E, K, and D.
   Vitamin A is needed for strong vision, reproduction, and healthy fetal development. Vitamin E is an antioxidant that protects your cells' membranes. Vitamin K helps your blood to clot and to synthesize proteins that keep bones healthy. Vitamin D is necessary for the absorption of calcium and phosphorus. Although vitamin D can be made in your body with the help of ultraviolet rays from the sun, some individuals are not exposed to enough sunlight to meet their needs.
3. Water-soluble vitamins are absorbed with water and typically aren't stored for extended periods. Excess amounts of water-soluble vitamins do not accumulate to toxic levels but can be harmful if you routinely consume too much. The B vitamins thiamin, riboflavin, niacin, vitamin B_6, pantothenic acid, and biotin are water soluble, and all are coenzymes that help numerous energy-producing reactions.

Adequate amounts of folic acid can reduce the risk for certain birth defects. A prolonged vitamin B_{12} deficiency can cause nerve damage. Vitamin C is needed for healthy bones, teeth, skin, and blood vessels and for a healthy immune system. Excessive amounts can cause intestinal discomfort. Vitamin C doesn't prevent the common cold but may reduce the duration and severity of a cold in some people.

4. Antioxidants, such as vitamins E and C, the mineral selenium, and some phytochemicals, suppress harmful oxygen-containing molecules called free radicals. Free radicals can contribute to chronic diseases, such as cancer and heart disease, and accelerate the aging process. Diets abundant in antioxidant-rich fruits, vegetables, and whole grains are associated with a lower incidence of many diseases.
5. Whole foods are the best sources of the vitamins you need, in part because of the other nutrients and phytochemicals they provide. Fortified foods and vitamin supplements can help individuals with inadequate diets meet their nutrient needs. However, supplements should never replace a healthy diet.

Test Yourself

1. Which of the following is a water soluble vitamin?
   a. vitamin A
   b. vitamin C
   c. vitamin K
   d. choline
2. Vitamin D is
   a. a hormone.
   b. made in your body with the help of sunlight.
   c. found in fortified milk.
   d. all of the above.
3. Adam Craig is 55 years old. Which of the following might his body have difficulty absorbing?
   a. the vitamin B_{12} in a piece of steak
   b. the vitamin B_6 in liver
   c. the folate in spinach
   d. the riboflavin in milk
4. You are enjoying a breakfast of raisin bran cereal doused in skim milk and a glass of orange juice. The vitamin C in the orange juice will enhance the absorption of
   a. the calcium in the milk.
   b. the vitamin D in the fortified milk.
   c. the iron in the cereal.
   d. both a and b.
5. Folic acid can help reduce the risk for
   a. acne.
   b. neural tube defects.
   c. night blindness.
   d. pellagra.

Answers

1. (b) Vitamin C is water soluble (as are the B vitamins). Vitamins A and K are fat soluble. Choline is not classified as a vitamin.
2. (d) Vitamin D is a hormone and can be made in your body with the help of adequate exposure to the sun's ultraviolet rays. You can also obtain it by drinking fortified milk.
3. (a) Approximately 10 to 30 percent of adults over age 50 have reduced secretions of acidic stomach juices, which affects the absorption of the vitamin B_{12} that is found naturally in food. The other B vitamins should be absorbed regardless of Adam's age.
4. (c) Vitamin C will help your body absorb the iron in grain products and cereals. Vitamin C does not affect the absorption of calcium or vitamin D. However, the vitamin D in the milk will help you absorb the mineral calcium.
5. (b) If consumed prior to and during the first several weeks of pregnancy, adequate amounts of folic acid can reduce the risk for neural tube defects, birth defects that can occur early in pregnancy. Vitamin A–containing medication may be used to treat acne. Vitamin A can also help prevent night blindness. Consuming adequate amounts of niacin prevents pellagra.

Web Resources

- To learn more about phytochemicals, visit: www.5aday.com/html/phytochem/pic_home.php
- For more information on the disease-fighting capabilities of fruits and vegetables, visit: www.5aday.gov
- To find out the latest recommendations for vitamins, visit: http://ods.od.nih.gov/Health_Information/Vitamin_and_Mineral_Supplement_Fact_Sheets.aspx
- To learn more about preparing and cooking vitamin-rich fruits and vegetables, visit: www.cdc.gov/nccdphp/dnpa/5aday/month/index.htm

17 Minerals

Essential Elements

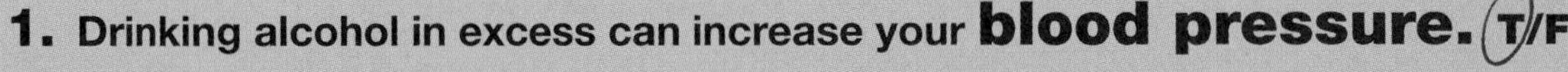

1. Drinking alcohol in excess can increase your **blood pressure.** T/F 

2. Most of your **dietary sodium** comes from the salt that you shake on your foods. T/F 

3. A serving of **milk** provides about one-third of an adult's daily calcium needs. T/F

4. **Trace minerals** are not as important to your body as major minerals. T/F

5. Meat is the major source of **iron** in the American diet. T/F

Colleen is a slender accounting major who used to claim that she "gave up drinking milk years ago." Starting in high school, she typically drank vitamin water or diet soda with her meals. But Colleen started rethinking her beverage of choice and switched back to milk after her 67-year-old grandmother fell and broke her hip. After surgery and two weeks in a rehabilitation clinic, her grandmother was moved to an assisted living center indefinitely because it was unclear whether her weak bones would be able to heal properly. Which physical factors and nutritional habits do you think put Colleen most at risk for following in her grandmother's footsteps?

Minerals play essential roles in your body. Iron, sodium, copper, and other rocky substances that come from the Earth are necessary for your day-to-day functioning. Minerals also help chemical reactions take place in your cells, help your muscles contract, and keep your heart beating. They are essential to your overall health and well-being.

In this concept, you will learn the many roles that minerals play in your body. You'll also learn how to make sure you're meeting your daily mineral needs and, equally important, how to avoid consuming toxic amounts.

Answers

1. True. Excessive alcohol is just one of many diet and lifestyle habits that can affect blood pressure. Turn to pages 4 and 5 to learn more.
2. False. Although seasoning your food with salt adds sodium, it is not the major culprit in sodium overload. Turn to page 10 to find out what is.
3. True. In fact, the recommended three servings of milk, yogurt, and/or cheese almost nails your calcium needs for the day. Unfortunately, most Americans' diets fall short of this amount. To find out how to meet your needs, turn to page 14.
4. False. Although needed in much smaller amounts, trace minerals are as indispensible as major minerals. See why on page 21.
5. False. While meat, fish, and poultry are fabulous sources of iron, they are not the main sources in Americans' diets. Turn to pages 22 and 23 to find out what contributes the most iron to our diets.

What Are Minerals?

Minerals are **inorganic** elements that your body needs in relatively small amounts. Inorganic compounds don't contain carbon and aren't formed by living things. Like vitamins, minerals don't provide calories, so they aren't a source of energy, but they work with other nutrients, such as protein and carbohydrates, to enable your body to function properly.

In Concept 18, which discusses water, you'll learn more about how the special properties of certain minerals help maintain your body's fluid balance. Like vitamins, minerals can be part of enzymes and work with your immune system to help it function. Finally, several minerals play an invaluable role in the growth and maintenance of your body's structure, including bones and blood cells.

Minerals are found in both plant and animal foods, but the best food sources are vegetables, legumes, milk, and meats. The mineral content of plants reflects the soil in which they are grown, since plants derive nutrients from the soil through their roots.

Mineral Absorption Depends on Bioavailability

The body's absorption of minerals from foods varies, depending on the *bioavailability* of the minerals. Some minerals compete with each other for absorption in your intestinal tract, and too much of one mineral can cause an imbalance in another. (For example, too much zinc in your diet can decrease the absorption of copper.) Also, minerals sometimes bind to other substances, reducing your body's ability to absorb them (for example, when they are eliminated from your body in your stool). One example of this is the calcium content in spinach. Spinach is technically high in calcium, but it is a poor food source of that nutrient because it contains oxalates, compounds that bind with calcium and render most of it unavailable for absorption. Similarly, substances in plant foods, known as phytates, inhibit your body's absorption of iron and zinc, and compounds in tea and coffee, called polyphenols, can inhibit your body's ability to absorb iron.

In contrast, some substances enhance mineral bioavailability. For instance, vitamin C enhances the absorption of the iron found in plant foods. Protein from ani-

minerals Inorganic elements essential to the nutrition of humans.

inorganic A characteristic of compounds that do not contain carbon and are not formed by living things.

mal foods enhances the absorption of zinc, and the vitamin D in fortified milk helps calcium absorption. All these factors affect the bioavailability of these nutrients.

Salt rations given to Roman soldiers were known as *salarium argentum,* which is Latin for "salt money" and led to our word *salary.*

Minerals Are Either Major or Trace

Minerals are categorized into two groups, depending on how much of them your body needs. The **major minerals** (known as macrominerals) are needed in amounts greater than 100 milligrams per day, while **trace minerals** (called microminerals) are needed in amounts less than 20 milligrams per day.

Major Minerals Are Needed in Larger Amounts

Minerals are considered to be major because you need more of them in your body; thus, you need more of them in your diet (Figure 17.1).[1] Your daily needs for the major minerals range from a few hundred milligrams daily to over a thousand. The seven major minerals are sodium, chloride, potassium, calcium, phosphorus, magnesium, and sulfur.

Many of the major minerals work together to perform important body functions. For example, sodium and chloride (located mainly outside your cells), as well as potassium, calcium, magnesium, and sulfur (which are mostly inside your cells), play a key role in maintaining fluid balance. And calcium, phosphorus, and magnesium work together to strengthen your bones and teeth.

Tables providing detailed visual summaries of the major minerals start on page 10 of this concept.

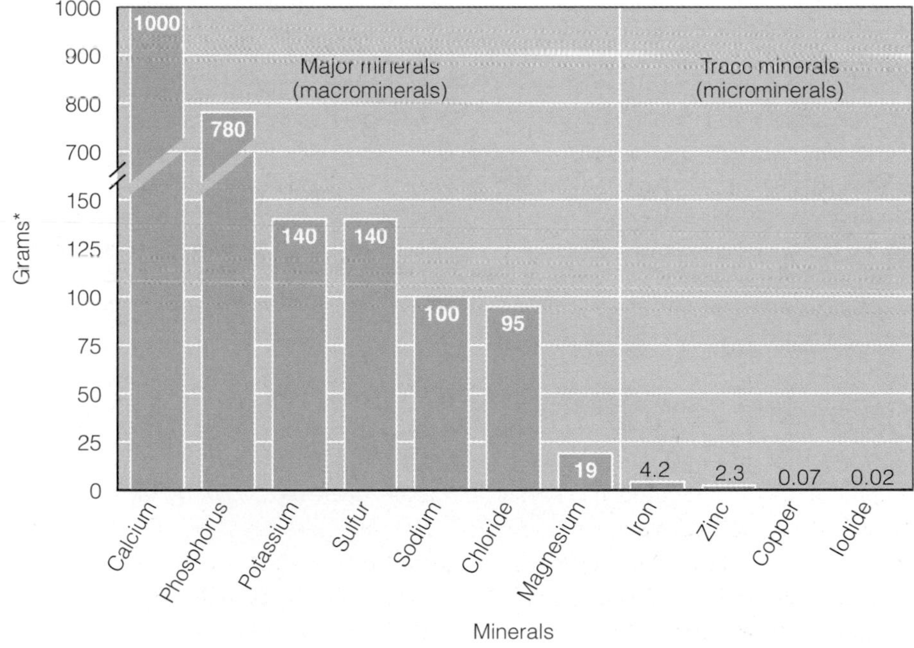

Figure 17.1 Minerals in the Body The major minerals are present in larger amounts than the trace minerals. However, all are equally important to your health.

The Take-Home Message Minerals are essential nutrients needed in relatively small amounts to enable your body to function properly. All minerals are inorganic elements. The body's absorption of minerals from foods varies, depending on their bioavailability. The seven major minerals are needed in amounts greater than 100 milligrams per day, and the nine trace minerals are needed in amounts less than 20 milligrams per day.

major minerals Seven key dietary minerals the body needs in amounts greater than 100 milligrams per day. The major minerals are sodium, chloride, potassium, calcium, phosphorus, magnesium, and sulfur.

trace minerals Nine dietary minerals the body needs in small amounts, less than 20 milligrams daily. The trace minerals are iron, zinc, selenium, fluoride, chromium, copper, iodine, manganese, and molybdenum.

You and Your Blood Pressure

High blood pressure, or **hypertension,** is an increasing problem in the United States. In fact, if you were sitting in a room with three other adults, there would be a good chance that one of you had high blood pressure. However, up to 30 percent of individuals with high blood pressure have "white coat hypertension." This term refers to the phenomenon in which an individual's blood pressure measurement is elevated when taken at a doctor's office or clinic by a staff person (typically, wearing a white lab coat) but the pressure is normal when measured elsewhere. This isn't the same as constant high blood pressure.

What Is Blood Pressure?

Your blood pressure is a measure of the force your blood exerts against the walls of your arteries. With every beat, your heart pumps blood into your arteries and thus to all the areas of your body. Blood pressure is highest at the moment of the heartbeat. This is your *systolic pressure*. Pressure is lower when your heart is at rest between beats. This is your *diastolic pressure.* Your blood pressure is expressed using these two measurements: the systolic pressure/diastolic pressure. Blood pressure of less than 120/80 millimeters of mercury (mm Hg) is considered normal. Your blood pressure rises naturally as you age, an effect that is believed to be due, in part, to the increased stiffness of the arteries.[1] However, if it rises too much, serious medical problems may occur. For example, high blood pressure increases your risk for heart disease, stroke, and kidney damage.[2]

hypertension High blood pressure, generally measured as a level of "140 over 90" or higher.

DASH diet A diet based on the DASH (Dietary Approaches to Stop Hypertension) study, that significantly reduces blood presure. The DASH diet is low in fat, saturated fat, cholesterol, and sweets, and high in whole grains, fruits, vegetables, and low-fat dairy products.

Why Is Hypertension a Silent Killer?

As blood pressure begins to rise above normal—that is, a systolic pressure of 120 or above and a diastolic pressure of 80 or above—it is classified as prehypertension. Many individuals with prehypertension will develop hypertension if they don't lower their blood pressure. A blood pressure of 140/90 mm Hg or above is considered hypertension.

Hypertension is referred to as the "silent killer" because there aren't any outward symptoms that your pressure is dangerously elevated. It develops gradually, and people can have it for years without knowing it. The only way to be sure you don't have it is to have your blood pressure checked regularly.

Individuals with chronic high blood pressure have a higher than normal force pounding against the walls of their arteries. This constant pressure makes the walls thicker and stiffer and contributes to atherosclerosis. The heart becomes enlarged and weakened, as it has to work harder to pump enough oxygen- and nutrient-laden blood throughout the body. This can lead to fatigue, shortness of breath, and heart attack. Hypertension can also damage the arteries leading to the brain, kidneys, and legs, which increases the risk for stroke, kidney failure, and partial amputation of a leg.[3]

Can You Control Your Hypertension?

You can control some of the factors that increase your risk of developing hypertension. Other factors are beyond your control.

Your family history, the aging process, and your race can all affect your chance of developing hypertension. These are the risk factors that you can't control. If your parents, siblings, and/or grandparents have or had hypertension, you are at a higher risk of developing it yourself. Typically, the risk for hypertension increases with age. It is more likely to occur after the age of 35 for men, and women generally experience it after menopause (after approximately age 50). Hypertension is more prevalent in African-Americans, among whom it tends to occur earlier and be more severe than in Caucasians.[4]

The good news is that there are more risk factors that you *can* control than those you can't. You can change several dietary and lifestyle habits to help reduce your risk, among them your weight and physical activity level. Obese individuals are twice as likely to have hypertension. Even a modest weight loss can have an impact. Losing as few as 10 pounds can reduce blood pressure and may prevent hypertension in overweight individuals, even if they haven't yet reached a healthy weight. Additional weight loss can have an even

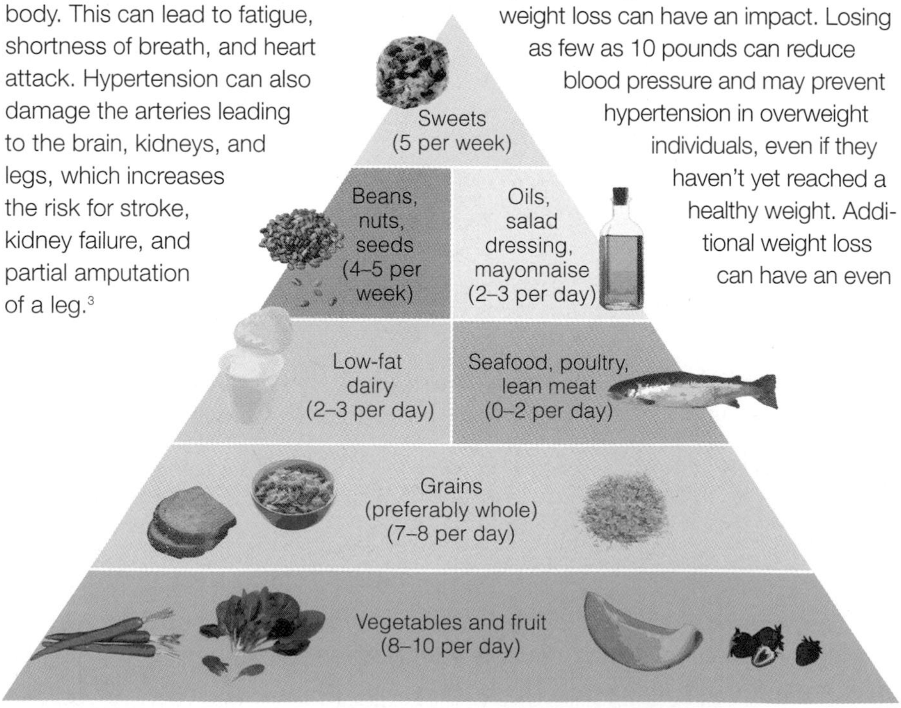

The DASH diet, which is rich in whole grains, fruits, vegetables, and low-fat dairy foods, can help lower blood pressure.

more dramatic effect. Regular physical activity can lower blood pressure even if weight loss hasn't occurred.[5]

You can also control your alcohol consumption, which affects your risk of developing high blood pressure. Studies have shown that drinkers who consumed three to six drinks daily and then reduced their alcohol consumption by 67 percent, on average, were able to reduce their systolic pressure by over 3 mm Hg and their diastolic pressure by 2 mm Hg.[6] Less drinking and more physical activity is the name of the game when it comes to keeping high blood pressure at bay.

Finally, eating a balanced diet is a proven strategy for lowering your blood pressure. A large research study, called the Dietary Approaches to Stop Hypertension (DASH) study, followed individuals on three different diets. One diet was a typical American diet: low in fruits, vegetables, and dairy products and high in fat, saturated fat, and cholesterol. A second diet was rich in fruits and vegetables. A third, the **DASH diet,** was low in fat, saturated fat, cholesterol, and sweets and high in whole grains, fruits, vegetables, and low-fat dairy products. In fact, the DASH diet was very similar to the recommended diet of MyPyramid (see the figure).

The individuals in the study who followed the DASH diet experienced a significant reduction in blood pressure, compared with those who followed the other two diets. Because the sodium content of all three diets was the same—about 3,000 milligrams, which is the approximate amount that Americans consume daily on average—the blood pressure lowering effect was attributed to some other substance or a combination of nutrients working together. For example, the DASH diet provides healthy doses of potassium, magnesium, and calcium, all of which can play a role in lowering blood pressure.[7]

A follow-up to the DASH study, called the DASH-Sodium study, went one step further and investigated whether reducing the amount of dietary sodium in each of the three diets could also help lower blood pressure. Not surprisingly, it did. In general, as a person's sodium intake increases, so does his or her blood pressure. Most importantly, the overall best diet combination for lowering blood pressure was the DASH diet plus consuming only 1,500 milligrams of sodium daily.[8] This study not only reinforced sodium's role in blood pressure but also showed that the DASH diet, along with a reduction in dietary sodium, is the best combination to fight hypertension.

The table shows how effective each of these changes can be, once you decide to take charge of your diet and lifestyle.

Calculating Your Risk for Hypertension

Would you like to find out YOUR risk for developing high blood pressure and learn how each lifestyle change you make will affect your personal risk? To check out the American Heart Association's interactive assessment, go to our website (see the end of this Concept for the url) and click on the link to the High Blood Pressure Health Risk Calculator. You're a click away from taking control of your blood pressure!

Take Charge of Your Blood Pressure!

Diet and lifestyle changes help reduce blood pressure and help prevent hypertension.

If You	By	Your Systolic Blood Pressure* May Be Reduced By
Reduce your sodium intake	Keeping dietary sodium consumption to no more than 2,400 mg daily	8–14 mm Hg
Lose excess weight	Losing an amount that allows you to maintain a normal, healthy body weight	5–20 mm Hg for every 22 lbs of weight loss
Stay physically active	Partaking in 30 minutes of aerobic activity (such as brisk walking) on most days of the week	4–9 mm Hg
Drink alcohol moderately	Limiting consumption to no more than two drinks daily for men and one drink daily for women	2–4 mm Hg
Follow the DASH diet	Consuming a heart-healthy DASH diet that is abundant in fruits and vegetables and low-fat dairy products	8–14 mm Hg

*Controlling the systolic pressure is more difficult than controlling the diastolic pressure, especially for individuals 50 years of age and older. Therefore, it is the primary focus for lowering blood pressure. Typically, as systolic pressure goes down with diet and lifestyle changes, the diastolic pressure will follow.

Data adapted from: A. V. Chobanian, et al., "The Seventh Report of the Joint National Committee on Prevention, Detection, Evaluation, and Treatment of High Blood Pressure," *Journal of the American Medical Association* 289 (2003): 2560–2572.

Osteoporosis: Not Just Your Grandmother's Problem

If you are fortunate enough to have elders, such as grandparents, in your life, you may have heard them comment that they are "shrinking" as they age. Of course, they aren't really shrinking, but they may be losing height as the tissues supporting their spine lose mass and elasticity and the joint capsules between the vertebrae of the spine lose their cushion of fluid. This is normal. In many older adults, however, the vertebrae themselves lose mass and begin to collapse, so that it becomes more difficult for the spine to hold the weight of the head and upper body. This leads to a gradual curvature of the spine, which affects their posture (see figure). As older individuals begin to hunch over, they can lose as much as a foot in height.[9]

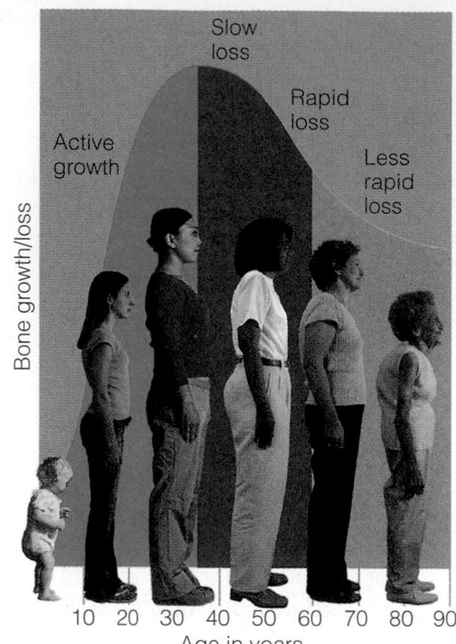

In your early years, more bone mass is added than lost in your body. In their mid-30s, women begin to slowly lose bone mass until menopause, when the rate of loss is accelerated for several years. Bone loss continues after age 60 but at a slower rate. Bone loss also occurs in men as they age.

Bones Are Constantly Changing

Bones are a dynamic, living tissue. Older layers of bones are constantly removed, and new bone is constantly added. In fact, your entire skeleton is replaced with new bone about once each decade. During childhood and adolescence, more bone is added than removed, as the bones are growing in length and mass. Although the growth of bone length typically ceases during the teenage years, bone mass continues to accumulate into the early years of young adulthood. *Peak bone mass*, which is the genetically determined maximum amount of bone mass an individual can build up, typically occurs when a person is in his or her 20s. Some additional bone mass can be added when an individual is in his or her 30s. After peak bone mass is reached, the loss of bone mass begins to slowly exceed the rate at which new bone is added.[10]

As bones lose mass, they become porous, and **osteoporosis** (*osteo* = bone; *porosis* = porous) can develop. The weakened, fragile bones are prone to fractures. A minor stumble can lead to a fall that results in a broken hip, ankle, rib, or arm. This is what happened to Colleen's grandmother, whom you read about at the beginning of this concept: She slipped off the bottom step of her porch, fell, and broke the top of her femur (thighbone) where it meets the pelvis. Hip fractures can be devastating because they often render a person immobile, which quickly affects quality of life. Feelings of helplessness and depression often ensue. Up to two-thirds of all individuals with hip fractures are never able to regain the quality of life they had prior to the injury and about 20 percent die within a year due to complications of the injury.[11] It is estimated that, by the year 2020, one out of every two Americans will either have or will be at risk for hip fractures due to osteoporosis and even more will be at risk for fractures of other bones.[12]

Adults can have their **bone mineral density (BMD)** measured with a bone scan. BMD is the amount of minerals—in particular, calcium—per volume in an individual's bone. The denser the bones, the stronger they are. A low measurement indicates *osteopenia* (*penia* = poverty), which signals low bone mass. A very low measurement indicates osteoporosis.

Ironically, although osteoporosis is often considered to be a condition of the elderly, it has its roots in childhood and should be prevented throughout adulthood. Preserving bone mass is like saving money for retirement. The more you save when you are young and throughout your adulthood, the more you will have for your later years. Conversely, if you don't save enough early in life, you may end up with little to fall back on when you need it later. If children don't reach their maximum bone mass by young adulthood, they will not have an adequate amount stored for their later years. If an adult doesn't have a healthy diet and lifestyle that includes regular exercise, he or she may experience accelerated bone loss after age 30.

It's never too late to try to reduce your risk for osteoporosis. To take a look at the risk factors involved, see page 8. Rate Yourself now!

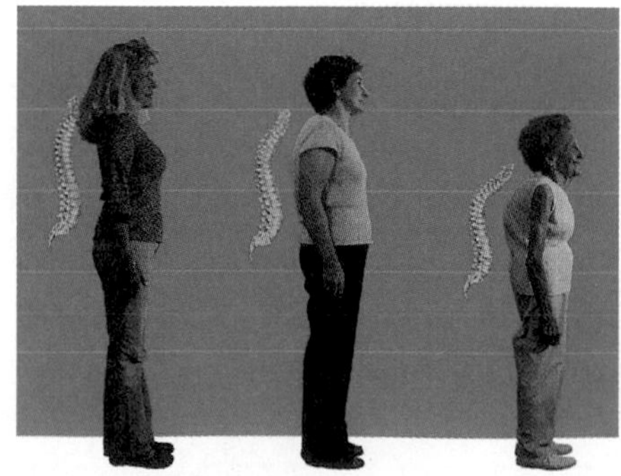

Weak bones cause the spine to collapse over time.

osteoporosis A condition in which the bones lose density, increasing the risk for bone fractures and breaks.

bone mineral density (BMD) The amount of minerals, particularly calcium, per volume in an individual's bone. The denser bones are, the stronger they are.

Other Minerals

A few other minerals—including arsenic, boron, nickel, silicon, and vanadium—exist in your body, but their nutritional importance has not yet been established. Limited research suggests that they may have a function in animals, but there isn't enough data at this point in time to confirm whether they play an essential role in humans.[2]

Table 17.1 summarizes these additional minerals, their potential role in animal health, their food sources, and the levels of deficiency and toxicity, if known, in humans.

Table 17.1

Additional Minerals

Mineral	Potential Role and Deficiency Symptoms	Food Sources	Potential Toxicity
Arsenic	Arsenic may be needed in the metabolism of a specific amino acid in rats. A deficiency may impair growth and reproduction in animals.	Dairy products, meat, poultry, fish, grains, and cereal products	There is no known adverse effect in humans from the organic form of arsenic in foods. The inorganic form is poisonous for humans.
Boron	A deficiency may be associated with reproductive abnormalities in certain fish and frogs, which suggests a possible role in normal development in mammals.	Grape juice, legumes, potatoes, pecans, peanut butter, apples, and milk	There is no known adverse effect of boron in food. Some research suggests that high amounts of boron may cause reproductive and developmental problems in animals. Because of this, the upper limit for human adults has been set at 20 mg daily, which is more than 10 times the amount American adults are consuming daily, on average.
Nickel	Nickel may be needed by specific enzymes in the body. It is considered an essential mineral in animals.	Grains and grain products, vegetables, legumes, nuts, and chocolate	There is no known toxicity in humans consuming a normal diet. In rats, large exposure to nickel salts can cause toxicity, with symptoms such as lethargy, irregular breathing, and a lower than normal weight gain. Because of this, the upper limit for adults is set at 1 mg daily for nickel salts.
Silicon	Silicon may be needed for bone formation in animals.	Grains, grain products, and vegetables	There is no known risk for silicon toxicity in humans from foods.
Vanadium	In animals, vanadium has insulin-like actions; a deficiency increases the risk for abortion.	Mushrooms, shellfish, parsley, and black pepper	There is no known risk for vanadium toxicity in humans from foods. Too much vanadium has been shown to cause kidney damage in animals. Vanadium can be purchased as supplements. Because of the toxicity in animals, the upper limit for adults is set at 1.8 mg daily.

Data from: Institute of Medicine, *Dietary Reference Intakes: Vitamin A, Vitamin K, Arsenic, Boron, Chromium, Copper, Iodine, Iron, Manganese, Molybdenum, Nickel, Silicon, Vanadium, and Zinc* (Washington, D.C.: The National Academies Press, 2001). www.nap.edu.

RATE YOURSELF

Are You at Risk for Osteoporosis?

Several factors increase your risk for osteoporosis and bone fractures. As with the factors that affect your risk for hypertension, you can control some of them, but not others. Take the following quiz to determine how many risk factors you have for osteoporosis. Shade in each part of the skeleton (on this page) based on your answers.

1. **Gender:** Are you female?
   Yes ☐ **No** ☐ (If you answered "no," shade in the left arm of the skeleton.)

   Females are at a higher risk for osteoporosis because they have smaller bones and thus less bone mass. Also, bone mass is lost at a faster rate right after menopause due to the decline of estrogen in women's bodies. However, men can suffer from osteoporosis and can experience it at a fairly young age.[13]

2. **Ethnicity:** Are you a Caucasian or Asian-American female?
   Yes ☐ **No** ☐ (If "no," shade in the right arm of the skeleton.)

   Caucasian and Asian-American women typically have lower bone mass than other women.

3. **Age:** Are you over 30 years of age?
   Yes ☐ **No** ☐ (If "no," shade in the left hand of the skeleton.)

   You begin to lose bone mass after about age 30, which increases your risk for osteoporosis and fractures.

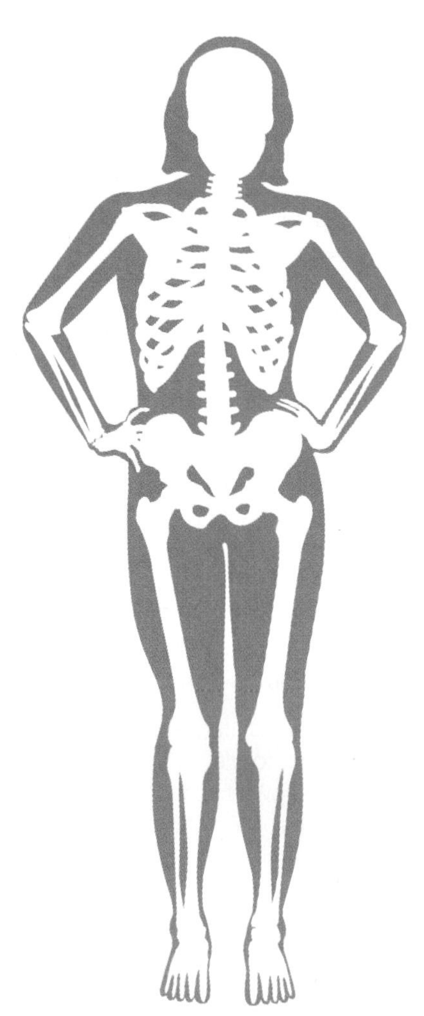

4. **Body type:** Are you a small-boned or petite woman?
   Yes ☐ **No** ☐ (If "no," shade in the right hand of the skeleton.)

   Women with slender bones have a lower bone mass and increased risk of fractures. Colleen, from the beginning of this concept, is slender and thus is at a higher risk for osteoporosis. In addition, women who are thin are at increased risk because higher body weight puts more weight-bearing, mechanical stress on bones, helping them stay healthy. A healthy body weight also means you'll have some padding, should a fall occur. Also, since most of the estrogen produced in menopausal women's bodies is formed in fat tissue, thinner women have less bone-protecting estrogen.[14]

5. **Family history of fractures:** Have your parents or grandparents ever experienced any bone fractures in their golden years?
   Yes ☐ **No** ☐ (If "no," shade in the left leg of the skeleton.)

   A family history of bone fractures in your relatives' later years increases your risk for osteoporosis. Because Colleen's grandmother had a hip fracture, this puts her at a higher risk.

6. **Level of sex hormones:** Are you a premenopausal woman who has stopped menstruating, a menopausal woman (with low estrogen levels), or a male with low testosterone levels?
   Yes ☐ **No** ☐ (If "no," shade in the right leg of the skeleton.)

   Women with amenorrhea (the absence of menstrual periods) experience hormonal imbalances, especially if they are at a dangerously low body weight.[15] Menopausal women, as well as men with low levels of sex hormones, which protect against bone loss, are also at a higher risk.

7. **Medications:** Are you taking certain medications, such as glucocorticoids (such as prednisone), antiseizure medications (such as phenytoin), aluminum-containing antacids, and/or excessive amounts of thyroid replacement hormones?
   Yes ☐ **No** ☐ (If "no," shade in the torso of the skeleton.)

The long-term use of glucocorticoids, antiseizure medicines, certain antacids, or too much thyroid hormone–replacing medication can lead to a loss of bone mass and increase the risk for fractures.[16] Certain cancer treatments can also cause bone loss. Although you shouldn't stop taking any prescribed medications, you should speak to your doctor about your bone health.

8. **Smoking:** Do you smoke?
   Yes ☐ **No** ☐ (If "no," shade in the left foot of the skeleton.)

   Smokers' bodies absorb less calcium. Women smokers have lower levels of estrogen in their bodies and begin menopause earlier than do nonsmokers.

9. **Physical activity:** Do you spend less than 30 minutes exercising daily?
   Yes ☐ **No** ☐ (If "no," shade in the left hip of the skeleton.)

   Regular physical activity contributes to higher peak bone mass in a person's early years, and strength and weight-bearing activities, such as walking, hiking, and tennis, help maintain bone mass during adulthood. These activities cause you to work against gravity, which helps your bones become stronger. Regular exercise also helps you maintain healthy muscles and improves your coordination and balance, which can help you prevent falls.[17]

10. **Alcohol:** Do you consume more than one alcoholic drink a day if you are a woman or consume more than two alcoholic drinks daily if you are a man?
    Yes ☐ **No** ☐ (If "no," shade in the right hip of the skeleton.)

    Heavy consumption of alcohol can reduce bone mass by inhibiting the formation of new bone, preventing the activation of vitamin D, and increasing the loss of calcium. It can also increase the risk of stumbling and falling.[18]

11. **Inadequate amounts of calcium and vitamin D:** Do you consume less than 3 cups daily of milk, yogurt, or soy or rice milk that has been fortified with calcium and vitamin D?
    Yes ☐ **No** ☐ (If "no," shade in the right foot of the skeleton.)

    Because your body needs calcium to build and maintain bone mass, and your body needs vitamin D to absorb this mineral, having inadequate amounts of either or both of these nutrients increases your risk for low bone mass, bone loss, and bone fractures.

After you have completed the self-assessment, look at the skeleton. If it has mostly shaded areas, you have fewer risk factors for osteoporosis, but the more risk factors you have, the higher your risk of developing osteoporosis. Many of these risk factors can be reduced by a healthy diet and lifestyle.

Although you cannot control your gender, ethnicity, age, bone structure, and family history, you can control many other risk factors. If your sex hormone levels are lower than they should be and/or if you are taking medications that may increase your risk for osteoporosis, talk to your doctor. Quitting smoking, exercising regularly, and limiting or avoiding alcohol consumption help reduce your risk. Finally, make sure you are consuming adequate amounts of vitamin D (Concept 16) and calcium (see the Visual Summary Table on page 10). If you can't meet your calcium needs through food, a supplement may be necessary.

Sodium

What Are Sodium and Salt?

Sodium is an electrolyte in your body. Most sodium in your body is in your blood and in the fluid surrounding your cells.

About 90 percent of the sodium you consume is in the form of sodium chloride. Sodium chloride is commonly known as table salt.

Functions of Sodium

Sodium's chief role is regulation of fluid balance. Sodium also plays an important role in transporting substances such as amino acids across cell membranes.

Salt is frequently added to foods to enhance flavor and as a preservative. It is also added to yeast breads to help the dough rise and to reduce the growth of bacteria and mold in many bread products and luncheon meats. Sodium phosphate, sodium carbonate, and sodium bicarbonate (baking soda) are food additives and preservatives that perform similar functions in foods.

Monosodium glutamate (MSG) is a common additive in Asian cuisines that is used to intensify the flavor of foods.

Sodium Balance in Your Body

The amount of sodium in your body is maintained at a precise level. When your body needs more sodium, your kidneys reduce the amount that is excreted in your urine. Likewise, when you take in too much sodium, you excrete the excess. For example, when you eat salty pretzels or popcorn, your kidneys will excrete the extra sodium you take in from these snacks.

Smaller amounts of sodium are lost in your stool and through daily perspiration. The amount of sodium lost through perspiration depends upon the rate you are sweating, the amount of sodium you have consumed (the more sodium in your diet, the higher the loss), and the intensity of heat in the environment. As you get acclimated to environmental heat, less sodium will be lost over time in your sweat. This built-in protective mechanism helps to prevent the loss of too much sodium from your body.

Daily Needs

The penny shown above is covered with about 180 milligrams of sodium. This is the bare minimum you need daily. It is based on the amount of sodium needed by individuals who live in temperate climates and those who have become acclimated to hotter environments.[3]

Planning a balanced diet with this small an amount of sodium is virtually impossible, so the recommended sodium intake for adults up to 51 years of age is set at 1,500 milligrams daily. This sodium recommendation allows you to eat a variety of foods from all the food groups so that you can meet your other nutrient needs. It also covers any sodium that is lost in sweat by moderately active individuals, or those who are not acclimated to the environmental temperature. Those who are very physically active and/or not acclimated to the heat will likely need to consume a higher amount of sodium. This can easily be obtained in the diet.

Sodium is so widely available in foods that you don't have to go out of your way to meet your needs.

Americans are currently consuming more than double the recommended amount, or over 3,400 milligrams of sodium daily, on average.[4]

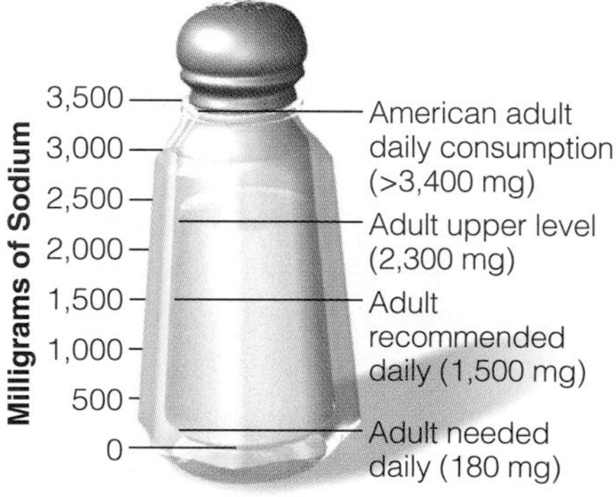

Food Sources

About 12 percent of Americans' consumption of sodium is from foods in which it occurs naturally, such as fruits, vegetables, milk, meat, fish, poultry, and legumes. Another 5 percent gets added during cooking and another 6 percent is used to season foods at the table.

Processed foods contribute a hefty 77 percent of the sodium in the diet of Americans. Comparing the amount of sodium in a fresh tomato (11 milligrams) to the amount found in a cup of canned tomatoes (355 milligrams) quickly illustrates just how much more sodium is found in processed foods.

Too Much or Too Little

There is a direct relationship between sodium and blood pressure in many people. In general, as a person's intake of sodium increases, so does their blood pressure. Blood

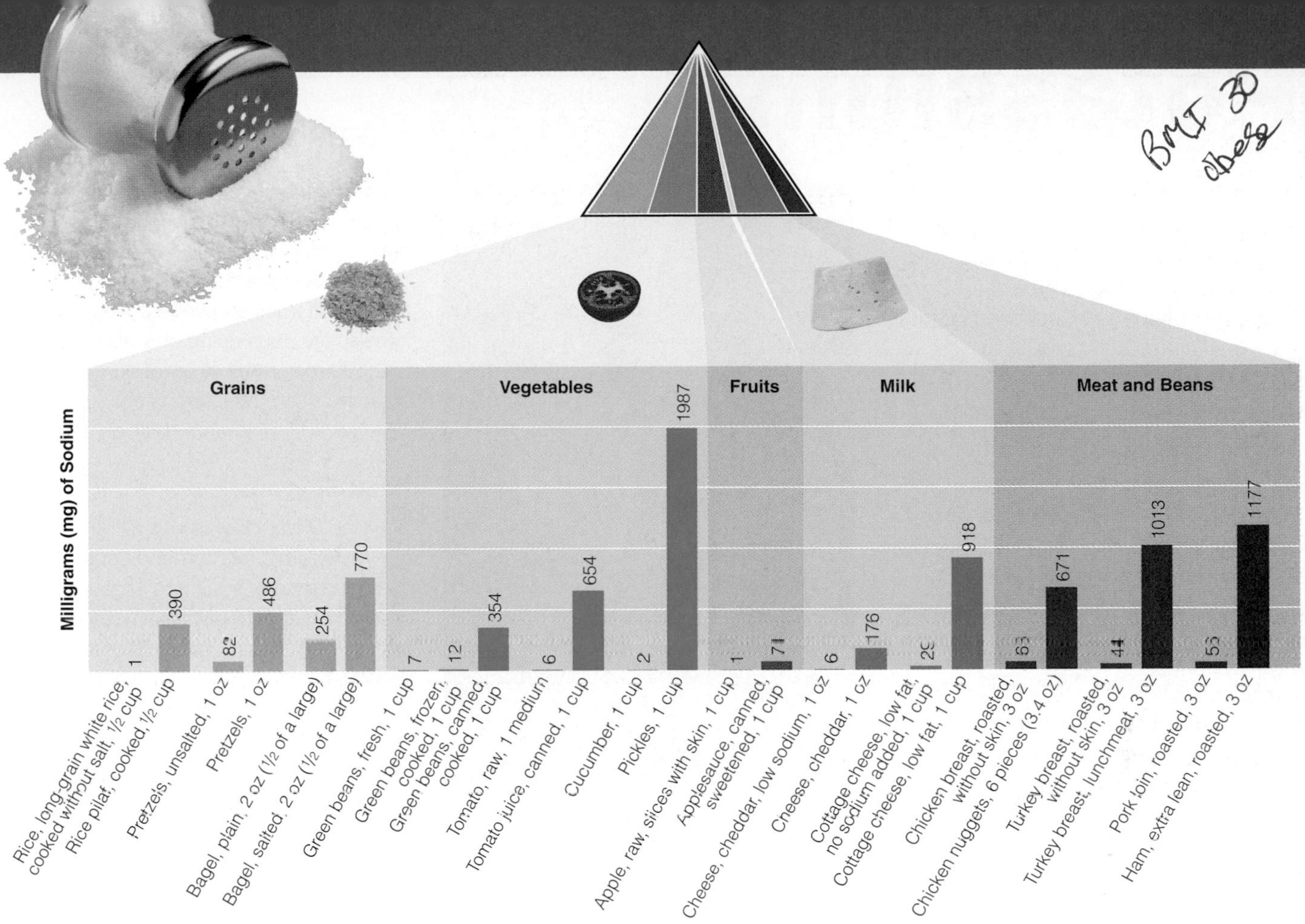

Milligrams (mg) of Sodium		
Grains		
	Rice, long-grain white rice, cooked without salt, ½ cup	1
	Rice pilaf, cooked, ½ cup	390
	Pretzels, unsalted, 1 oz	82
	Pretzels, 1 oz	486
	Bagel, plain, 2 oz (½ of a large)	254
	Bagel, salted, 2 oz (½ of a large)	770
Vegetables		
	Green beans, fresh, 1 cup	7
	Green beans, frozen, cooked, 1 cup	12
	Green beans, canned, cooked, 1 cup	354
	Tomato, raw, 1 medium	6
	Tomato juice, canned, 1 cup	654
	Cucumber, 1 cup	2
	Pickles, 1 cup	1987
Fruits		
	Apple, raw, slices with skin, 1 cup	1
	Applesauce, canned, sweetened, 1 cup	71
Milk		
	Cheese, cheddar, low sodium, 1 oz	6
	Cheese, cheddar, 1 oz	176
	Cottage cheese, low fat, no sodium added, 1 cup	29
	Cottage cheese, low fat, 1 cup	918
Meat and Beans		
	Chicken breast, roasted, without skin, 3 oz	63
	Chicken nuggets, 6 pieces (3.4 oz)	671
	Turkey breast, roasted, without skin, 3 oz	44
	Turkey breast, lunchmeat, 3 oz	1013
	Pork loin, roasted, 3 oz	53
	Ham, extra lean, roasted, 3 oz	1177

pressure that becomes too high, known as **hypertension,** increases the risk for heart disease, stroke, and kidney disease (see the boxed feature "You and Your Blood Pressure" for more about hypertension.) Unfortunately, many Americans will develop hypertension sometime during their life. To help reduce the risk of hypertension, the upper level for adults for sodium is set at 2,300 milligrams. Recall from Concept 2 that the current *Dietary Guidelines for Americans* also recommend that you limit your sodium intake for the same reason. Many Americans exceed the daily upper limit.

Because the majority of your sodium comes from processed foods, and a fair amount comes from the salt that you add to your foods, cutting back on these two sources is the best way to lower your intake.

When you buy processed foods, look for the terms "low," "reduced" or "sodium-free" on the labels to cut back on your sodium intake.

Bypass the salt shaker at the table. When cooking, season your foods with black pepper, Tabasco sauce, lemon juice, or a no-salt seasoning blend instead of salt.

Sodium deficiency is rare in healthy individuals consuming a balanced diet.

Terms to Know
hypertension

TABLE TIPS

Shake Your Salt Habit

Dilute and conquer. Combine a can of vegetable soup and a can of low-sodium vegetable soup for soup with less sodium. Add some cooked, frozen vegetables for an even healthier meal.

Keep your portions of deli meats to no more than 3 ounces and build a "meaty" sandwich by adding naturally low-sodium tomatoes, lettuce, cucumbers, and shredded cabbage.

Nibble on low-sodium dried fruits (apricots, raisins) and unsalted walnut pieces for a sweet and crunchy snack.

Use olive oil and balsamic vinegar for a salad dressing with less sodium than is in bottled dressings. Or, dilute equal portions of regular salad dressing with vinegar to cut the sodium.

Potassium

What Is Potassium?

Potassium is an important mineral with numerous functions in your body. Luckily, it is also found in many different foods, so it's not difficult to meet your needs for it.

Functions of Potassium

Potassium Is Needed for Fluid Balance and as a Blood Buffer

Over 95 percent of the potassium in your body is inside your cells, with the remainder in the fluids outside your cells, including your blood. As with other electrolytes, potassium helps maintain fluid balance and keeps your blood pH and acid-base balance correct.

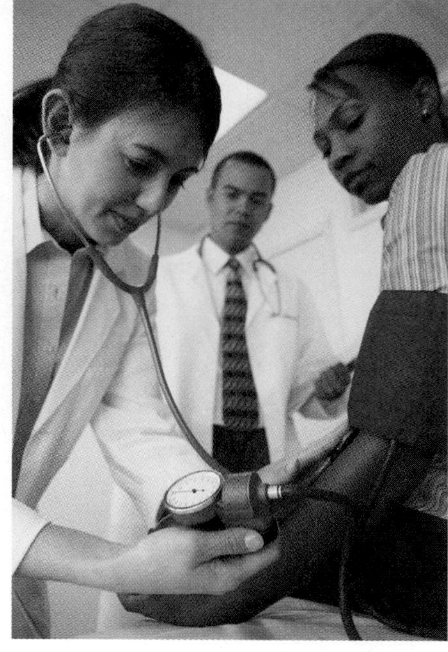

Potassium Is Needed for Muscle Contraction and Nerve Impulse Conduction

Potassium plays a role in the contraction of your muscles, including your heart, and the conduction of nerve impulses. Because of this, a dramatic increase of potassium in your body can lead to irregular heart beats or heart attack, while dangerously low levels could cause paralysis. Thus, potassium is tightly controlled and balanced in your body with the help of your kidneys.

Potassium Can Help Lower High Blood Pressure

A diet with plentiful potassium has been shown to help lower blood pressure, especially in salt-sensitive individuals who respond more intensely to sodium's blood pressure-raising capabilities. Potassium causes the kidneys to excrete excess sodium from the body, and keeping sodium levels low can help lower blood pressure. The DASH diet is abundant in foods with potassium.

Potassium Aids in Bone Health and Reduces Kidney Stones

Because potassium plays a buffering role in your blood, it helps keep the bone-strengthening minerals, calcium and phosphorus, from being lost from the bones and kidneys.[5] Numerous studies suggest that having plenty of potassium in your diet helps increase the density, and thus the strength, of your bones.

Potassium also helps reduce the risk of kidney stones by causing the body to excrete citrate, a compound that binds with calcium to form kidney stones, shown in the photo at right.

Daily Needs

Adults should consume 4,700 milligrams of potassium daily. This amount is recommended to help those with sodium sensitivity reduce their risk of high blood pressure. It is also beneficial to all Americans, in general, to lower their risk of developing kidney stones and preserve bone health.

Because Americans fall short of their servings of fruits and vegetables, adult females are consuming only about 2,200 to 2,500 milligrams of potassium, and adult males are consuming only 3,300–3,400 milligrams daily, on average.

Food Sources

Both the *Dietary Guidelines for Americans* and MyPyramid recommend consuming an abundance of fruits and vegetables in order to meet your potassium needs. A diet rich in at least 7 servings of fruits and vegetables, especially leafy greens, which is the *minimum* amount you should be consuming daily, can easily meet your potassium needs. Dairy foods, nuts, and legumes are also good sources (see figure).

Too Much or Too Little

There isn't any known danger from consuming too much potassium that occurs naturally in foods. These excesses will be excreted in your urine. However, consuming too much from supplements or salt substitutes (the sodium in some salt substitutes is replaced with potassium) can cause hyperkalemia (*hyper* = too much; *kalemia* = potassium in blood) for some individuals. Hyperkalemia can cause irregular heartbeats, damage the heart, and be life-threatening.

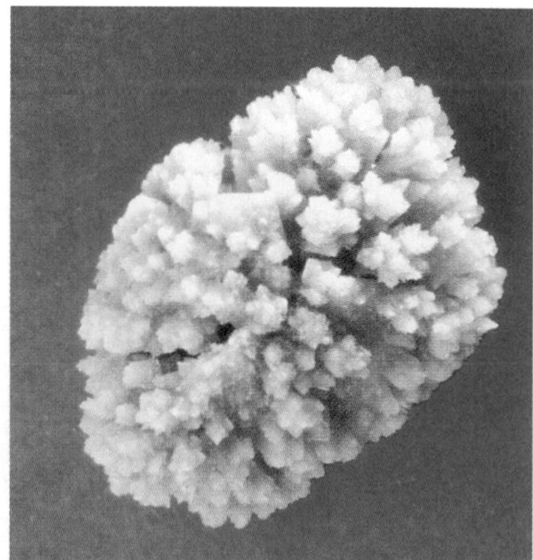

Kidney stone

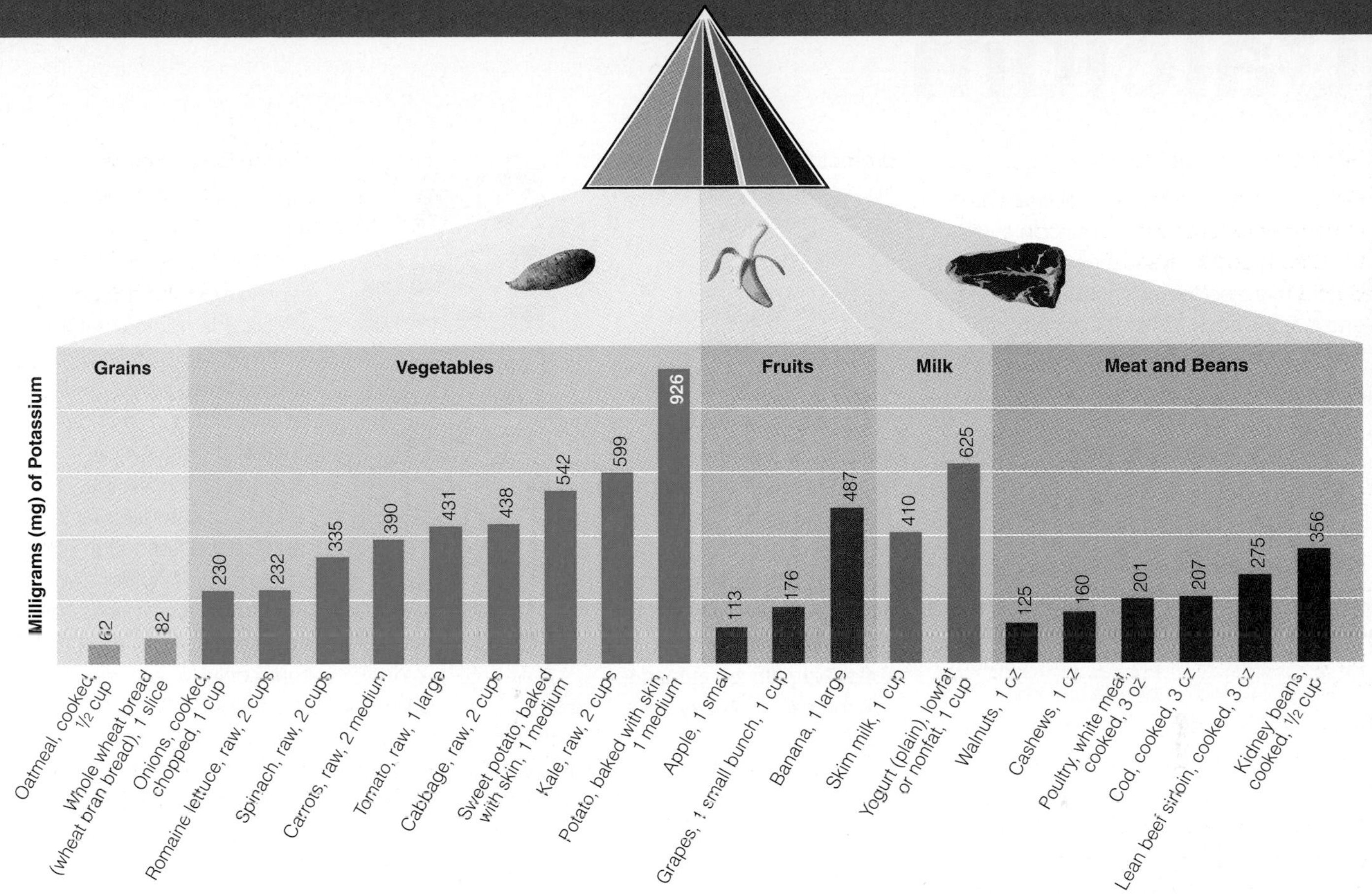

Milligrams (mg) of Potassium

Group	Food	Milligrams (mg) of Potassium
Grains	Oatmeal, cooked, ½ cup	62
Grains	Whole wheat bread (wheat bran bread), 1 slice	82
Vegetables	Onions, cooked, chopped, 1 cup	230
Vegetables	Romaine lettuce, raw, 2 cups	232
Vegetables	Spinach, raw, 2 cups	335
Vegetables	Carrots, raw, 2 medium	390
Vegetables	Tomato, raw, 1 large	431
Vegetables	Cabbage, raw, 2 cups	438
Vegetables	Sweet potato, baked with skin, 1 medium	542
Vegetables	Kale, raw, 2 cups	599
Vegetables	Potato, baked with skin, 1 medium	926
Fruits	Apple, 1 small	113
Fruits	Grapes, 1 small bunch, 1 cup	176
Fruits	Banana, 1 large	487
Milk	Skim milk, 1 cup	410
Milk	Yogurt (plain), lowfat or nonfat, 1 cup	625
Meat and Beans	Walnuts, 1 oz	125
Meat and Beans	Cashews, 1 oz	160
Meat and Beans	Poultry, white meat, cooked, 3 oz	201
Meat and Beans	Cod, cooked, 3 oz	207
Meat and Beans	Lean beef sirloin, cooked, 3 oz	275
Meat and Beans	Kidney beans, cooked, ½ cup	356

Those at a higher risk for hyperkalemia include individuals with impaired kidneys, such as people with type 1 diabetes mellitus, those with kidney disease, and individuals taking medications for heart disease or diuretics that cause the kidneys to block the excretion of potassium. These individuals may also need to consume less than the recommended amount of potassium daily as advised by their health care professional.

Although a deficiency of dietary potassium is rare, too little potassium can cause hypokalemia. This may occur during bouts of vomiting and/or diarrhea. It has been seen in individuals who suffer with anorexia and/or bulimia. Hypokalemia can cause muscle weakness, cramps, and in severe situations, irregular heartbeats and paralysis.[6]

Individuals who consume high-protein diets that don't contain an adequate variety of fruits and vegetables may be depriving themselves of the buffering actions of potassium. The breakdown of excessive amounts of dietary protein causes the formation of acids in the body. These acids are balanced by some of the actions of potassium, which can buffer, or diminish, the acidic effects. A diet too low in fruits and vegetables is setting the stage for an imbalance of acids and bases in the blood and the increased risk of kidney stones, loss of bone mass, and high blood pressure. As noted before and throughout this book, eating a variety of fruits, vegetables and other healthful foods is the best way to achieve a balance in your body.

TABLE TIPS 

Potassium Power!

Pour a 6-ounce glass of a citrus juice such as orange or grapefruit at breakfast to begin the day with a potassium boost.

Add leafy greens to all your sandwiches. Spinach in particular is a potassium dynamo!

Add a spoonful of walnuts to your midmorning yogurt for a one–two (nuts and dairy) potassium punch.

Include bean soup with your lunchtime sandwich for a warm way to enjoy your potassium.

Baked regular or sweet potatoes are potassium powerhouses on your dinner plate.

Calcium

What Is Calcium?

Calcium is one of the most abundant minerals in nature and is found in everything from pearls to seashells to eggshells. Calcium is also the most abundant mineral in your body. Over 99 percent of your body's calcium is located in your bones and teeth.

Functions of Calcium

Calcium Helps Build Strong Bones and Teeth

Calcium couples with phosphorus to form hydroxyapatite, providing strength and structure in your bones and the enamel on your teeth. Adequate dietary calcium is needed to build and maintain bone mass. Calcium makes up almost 40 percent of the weight of your bones.[7]

Calcium Plays a Role in Your Muscles, Nerves, and Blood

The remaining 1 percent of calcium is in your blood, in the fluids that surround your cells, in your muscles, and in other tissues. Calcium is needed to contract your muscles, dilate and contract your blood vessels, help your blood clot, secrete hormones and enzymes, and help your nervous system transmit messages. It must be maintained at a constant level for your body to function properly.[8]

Calcium May Help Lower High Blood Pressure

Studies have shown that a heart-healthy diet rich in calcium, potassium, magnesium, fruits, vegetables, and low-fat dairy products can help lower blood pressure. One example of such a diet, the DASH diet, contains three servings of lean dairy foods, the minimum amount of servings recommended to obtain this protective effect[9] (see the boxed feature "You and Your Blood Pressure" on page 4).

Calcium May Fight Colon Cancer

A diet with plenty of calcium has been shown to help reduce the risk of developing benign tumors in the colon that may eventually lead to cancer. Calcium may protect the lining of the colon from damaging bile acids and cancer-promoting substances.[10]

Calcium May Reduce the Risk of Kidney Stones

Approximately 2 million American adults visit their doctors annually with **kidney stones.** The majority of these stones are composed mainly of calcium oxalate.[11] Although health professionals in the past often warned those who suffer with kidney stones to minimize their dietary calcium, this advice has since been reversed. Research has shown that a balanced diet, along with adequate amounts of calcium, may actually reduce the risk of developing kidney stones. Calcium binds with the oxalates in foods in the intestines and prevents their absorption. With fewer oxalates filtering through the kidneys, fewer stones are formed.[12]

Calcium May Reduce the Risk of Obesity

Some preliminary research suggests that low-calcium diets may trigger several responses that stimulate fat production and its storage in cells, which increases the risk for obesity.[13] When dietary calcium is inadequate, the active form of vitamin D increases in the body in order to enhance calcium absorption from the diet. Parathyroid hormone is also increased, which causes less calcium to be lost from the body. These hormone responses may also cause a shift of calcium into fat cells, which is the mechanism that stimulates fat production and storage.[14]

Daily Needs

Adults need 1,000 to 1,200 milligrams of calcium daily, depending upon their age. Americans 20 years of age and older are consuming, on average, less than 800 milligrams of calcium daily.[15]

Food Sources

Milk, yogurt, and cheese are the major sources of calcium in the American diet. Each serving from the dairy group will provide approximately 300 milligrams of calcium. (Choose only nonfat and low-fat milk and yogurt and reduced fat or skim milk cheeses to reduce the amount of saturated fat in these foods.) Although three servings of dairy foods will just about meet many adults' daily needs, Americans consume only 1½ servings of dairy daily, on average.[16]

Broccoli, kale, canned salmon with bones (the calcium is in the bones), and tofu that is processed with calcium can also add calcium to the diet. Calcium-fortified foods, such as juices and cereals, are also excellent sources.

Too Much or Too Little

The upper level for calcium has been set at 2,500 milligrams daily to avoid *hypercalcemia,* or too much calcium in the blood, subsequent impaired kidneys, and calcium deposits in the body. Too much dietary calcium can also cause constipation and interfere with the absorption of other minerals, such as iron, zinc, magnesium, and phosphorus.

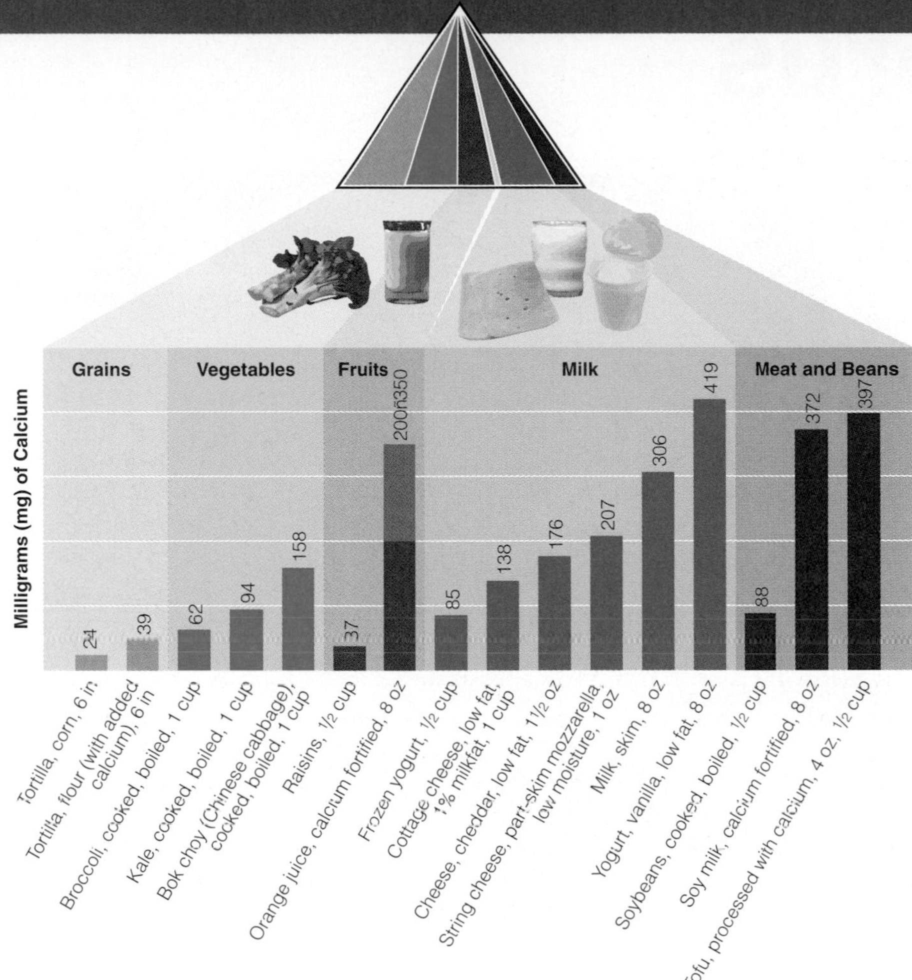

If your diet is low in calcium, calcium leaves your bones in order to maintain a constant level in your blood. A chronic deficiency of dietary calcium can lead to less dense, weakened, and brittle bones and increased risk for **osteoporosis** and bone fractures[17] (compare healthy bone, left in photo, with weakened bone at right). See the boxed feature "Osteoporosis" on page 8 for greater detail.

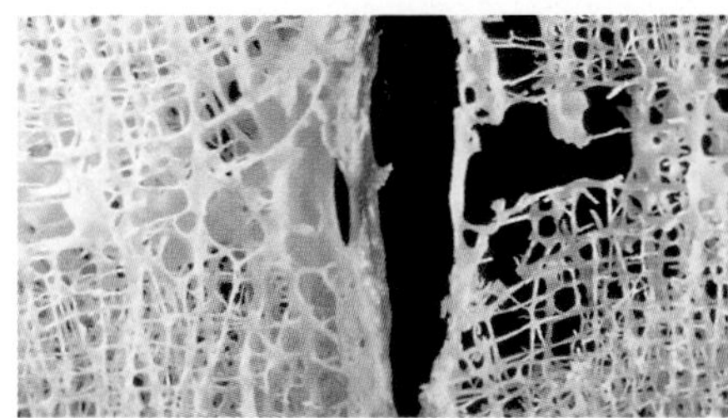

Healthy bone (left) vs weakened bone (right)

Calcium Supplements

Some individuals, based on their diet and/or medical history, are advised by their health care provider to take a calcium supplement. The calcium in these supplements is part of a compound, typically either calcium carbonate or calcium citrate. Calcium carbonate tends to be the least expensive and the most common form of calcium purchased. It is most effective when consumed with a meal, as the acidic juices in your stomach help with its absorption.[18] Calcium citrate can be taken any time throughout the day, as it doesn't need the help of acidic juices to be absorbed. Calcium citrate is a plus for those age 50 and older who may be producing less stomach acid as they age.

Regardless of the form, all calcium, whether from supplements or from fortified or naturally occurring foods, should be consumed in doses of 500 milligrams or less, as this is the maximum that your body can absorb efficiently at one time.[19] In other words, if a person has been advised to take 1,000 milligrams of calcium daily, 500 milligrams should be consumed in the morning and the other 500 milligrams in the afternoon or evening.

Calcium from unrefined oyster shell, bone meal, or dolomite (a rock rich in calcium) may also contain lead and other toxic metals. Supplements from these sources should state on the label that they are "purified" or carry the USP symbol to ensure purity. Because calcium can interfere with and reduce the absorption of iron, a calcium supplement shouldn't be taken along with an iron supplement.

Calcium supplements can sometimes cause constipation and flatulence (gas), especially when large amounts are taken. Increasing the fiber in the diet can help avoid these less-than-pleasurable side effects. There is an upper level set on the daily dosage of calcium; be cautious about adding a calcium supplement to your diet if you are already consuming plenty of lean dairy foods and/or calcium-fortified foods.

TABLE TIPS

Calcium Counts

Make cereal doused with skim or low-fat milk a morning habit.

Spoon a few chunks of tofu onto your salad bar lunch for extra calcium.

Use low-fat pudding or yogurt to satisfy a sweet tooth and get tooth-friendly calcium to boot.

Top your calcium-rich cheese pizza with calcium-rich broccoli for a pizza with calcium pizzazz.

Mozzarella string cheese sticks are an easy grab-as-you-go calcium snack.

Phosphorus

What Is Phosphorus?

Phosphorus is the second most abundant mineral in your body. The majority of phosphorus—about 85 percent—is in your bones. The remainder is in your cells and fluids outside your cells, including your blood.

Functions of Phosphorus

Phosphorus Is Needed for Bones and Teeth and Is an Important Component of Cells

As mentioned, phosphorus combines with calcium to form hydroxyapatite, the strengthening material found in bones and teeth.

Phosphorus is part of phospholipids, which give your cell membranes their structure. Phospholipids act as a barrier to keep specific substances out of the cells, while letting others in.

Phosphorus Is Needed during Metabolism

Phosphorus helps store, for later use, energy generated from the metabolism of carbohydrates, protein, and fat from food. Your body can draw upon these stores as needed.

Phosphorus Acts as a Buffer and Is Part of the DNA and RNA of Every Cell

If your blood becomes too acidic or too basic, phosphorus can act as a buffer to help return your blood pH to normal. Your blood pH must stay within a very narrow range to prevent damage to your tissues.

Phosphorus is part of your DNA and RNA. The instructions for your genes are coded in your DNA and transcribed in your RNA to make the proteins needed in your body.

Daily Needs

Adults, both male and female, need 700 milligrams of phosphorus daily. Americans, on average, are consuming over 1,000 milligrams of phosphorus daily.[20]

Food Sources

A balanced, varied diet will easily meet your phosphorus needs. Foods from animal sources such as meat, fish, poultry, and dairy products are excellent sources of phosphorus. Phosphorus is also part of many food additives.

Too Much or Too Little

Typically, consuming too much dietary phosphorus and its subsequent effect, hyperphosphatemia (*hyper* = over; *phosphat* = phosphate; *emia* = blood), is only an issue for individuals with kidney problems who cannot excrete excess phosphorus.

Constantly high phosphorus and low calcium intake can cause the loss of calcium from your bones and a subsequent decrease in bone mass. Loss of bone

Milligrams (mg) of Phosphorus

Group	Food	Phosphorus (mg)
Grains	Whole wheat bread, 1 slice	38
Grains	Shredded Wheat cereal, 1 cup	175
Grains	Raisin Bran cereal, 1 cup	259
Vegetables	Broccoli, cooked, 1 cup	105
Vegetables	Potato, baked with skin, 1 medium	121
Vegetables	Corn, cooked, 1 cup	169
Vegetables	Lentil, cooked, 1/2 cup	178
Vegetables	Green peas, cooked, 1 cup	187
Fruits	Banana, 1 medium	26
Fruits	Orange juice, 1 cup	27
Fruits	Strawberries, 1 cup	40
Milk	Milk, low fat, 1 cup	232
Milk	Yogurt, vanilla, low fat, 1 cup	331
Meat and Beans	Almonds, 1 oz	139
Meat and Beans	Chicken breast, cooked, 3 oz	194
Meat and Beans	Flank steak, cooked, 3 oz	198
Meat and Beans	Salmon, cooked, 3 oz	251

TABLE TIPS 

Fabulous Phosphorus

Layer sliced bananas, yogurt, and raisin bran cereal for a high-phosphorus breakfast that tastes like a dessert.

Blend together orange juice and slightly thawed frozen strawberries for a refreshing smoothie.

Skip the butter and sprinkle sliced almonds over your dinner vegetables for a crunchy topping.

Dunk raw broccoli florets in a spicy salsa for a snack with a kick.

Combine shredded wheat cereal, mixed nuts, and raisins for a sweet and crunchy snack mix.

mass increases the risk of osteoporosis. Hyperphosphatemia can also lead to calcification of tissues in the body. To protect against this, the upper level for phosphorus has been set at 4,000 milligrams daily for adults age 19 to 50 and 3,000 milligrams for those 50 years of age and older.

Too little phosphorus in the diet can cause its level in your blood to drop dangerously low and result in muscle weakness, bone pain, rickets, confusion, and, at the extreme, death. Because phosphorus is so abundant in the diet, a deficiency is rare. In fact, a person would have to be in a state of near starvation before experiencing a phosphorus deficiency.[21]

Magnesium

What Is Magnesium?

Magnesium is another abundant mineral in your body. While about half of the magnesium is in your bones, most of the remaining magnesium is inside your cells. A mere 1 percent is found in your blood and, like calcium, this amount must be maintained at a constant level.

Functions of Magnesium

Magnesium Aids Metabolism and Maintains Healthy Muscles, Nerves, Bones, and Heart

Magnesium helps over 300 enzymes produce reactions inside your cells. It is needed for the metabolism of carbohydrates, proteins, and fats. Magnesium is used during the synthesis of protein and to help your muscles and nerves function properly. It is also needed to help you maintain healthy bones and a regular heart beat.[22]

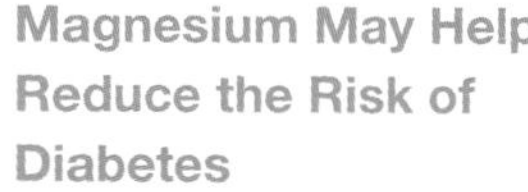

Magnesium May Help Lower High Blood Pressure

Studies have shown that magnesium may help regulate blood pressure and that a plant-based diet abundant in fruits and vegetables, which are rich in magnesium as well as other minerals, lowered blood pressure.[23]

The blood-pressure-lowering DASH diet, which has been clinically proven to lower blood pressure, is rich in magnesium as well as calcium and potassium (see the feature box "You and Your Blood Pressure" on page 4).[24]

Magnesium May Help Reduce the Risk of Diabetes

Some studies suggest that a diet abundant in magnesium may help decrease the risk of type 2 diabetes. Low blood levels of magnesium, which often occurs in individuals with type 2 diabetes, may impair the release of insulin, one of the hormones that regulates blood glucose. This may lead to elevated blood glucose levels in those with preexisting diabetes, and may contribute to higher than normal blood glucose levels in those at risk for type 2 diabetes.[25]

Daily Needs

Adult females age 19 to 30 need 310 milligrams of magnesium, whereas men of the same age need 400 milligrams daily. Females age 31 and over need 320 milligrams while men of this age need 420 milligrams of magnesium daily.

Currently, many Americans fall short of their magnesium needs. Females consume only about 70 percent of their needs, or about 220 milligrams daily, on average. Males consume approximately 320 milligrams daily, on average, which is only about 80 percent of the amount recommended daily. Because older adults tend to consume fewer calories, and thus less dietary magnesium, elders are at an even higher risk of falling short of their needs.

Food Sources

The biggest contributors of magnesium in Americans' diets are vegetables, whole grains, nuts, and fruits. Milk, yogurt, meat, and eggs are also good sources. Because the majority of the magnesium is in the bran and germ of the grain kernel, products made with refined grains, such as white flour, are poor sources.

It's not difficult to meet your magnesium needs. A peanut butter sandwich on whole-wheat bread, chased with a glass of low-fat milk and a banana, will provide over 200 milligrams, or about half of an adult's daily needs.

Too Much or Too Little

There isn't any known risk in consuming too much magnesium from food sources. However, consuming large amounts from supplements has been shown to cause intestinal problems such as diarrhea, cramps, and nausea. In fact, some laxatives purposefully contain magnesium because of its intestinal effects. Because

of this distress on the intestinal system, the upper level for magnesium from supplements, not foods, is set at 350 milligrams for adults. This level is to prevent diarrhea, the first symptom that typically arises when too much magnesium is consumed.[26]

Even though many Americans don't meet their magnesium needs, deficiencies are rare in healthy individuals because the kidneys compensate for low magnesium intake by excreting less of it.

However, some medications may cause magnesium deficiency. Certain diuretics can cause the body to lose too much magnesium, and some antibiotics, such as tetracycline, can inhibit the absorption of magnesium, both of which can lead to a deficiency. Individuals with poorly controlled diabetes or who abuse alcohol can experience excessive losses of magnesium in the urine, which could also cause a deficiency.

A severe magnesium deficiency can cause muscle weakness, seizures, fatigue, depression, and irregular heart beats.

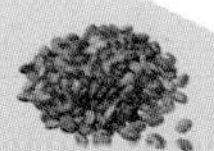

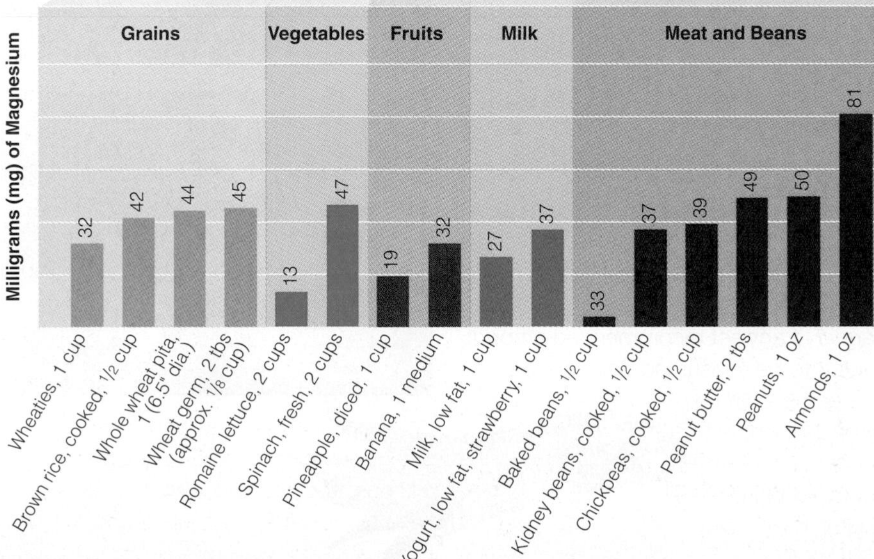

TABLE TIPS

Magnificent Magnesium

Sprinkle chopped almonds over your morning whole-grain cereal for two crunchy sources of magnesium.

Add baby spinach to your salad.

Add rinsed, canned black beans to salsa for a veggie dip with a magnesium punch.

Spread peanut butter on whole-wheat crackers for a satisfying afternoon snack.

Try precooked brown rice for an easy way to add whole grains to your dinner!

Chloride

What Is Chloride?

Chloride is a form of chlorine, a mineral you've surely smelled in bleach. Chlorine is a powerful disinfectant that if inhaled or ingested can be poisonous.

Fortunately, most of the chlorine in your body is in the nontoxic form of chloride. Chloride is part of hydrochloric acid, a strong acid in your stomach that enhances protein digestion and kills harmful bacteria that may be consumed with your foods.

Functions of Chloride

Chloride Helps Maintain Fluid Balance and Acid-Base Balance

Sodium and chloride are the major electrolytes outside your cells and in your blood. They help maintain fluid balance between these two compartments.

Chloride also acts as a buffer to help keep your blood at a normal pH.

Daily Needs and Food Sources

Adults aged 19 to 50 should consume 2,300 milligrams of chloride a day. Sodium chloride, which is 60 percent chloride, is the main source of chloride in your diet, so the food sources for it are the same as those for sodium.

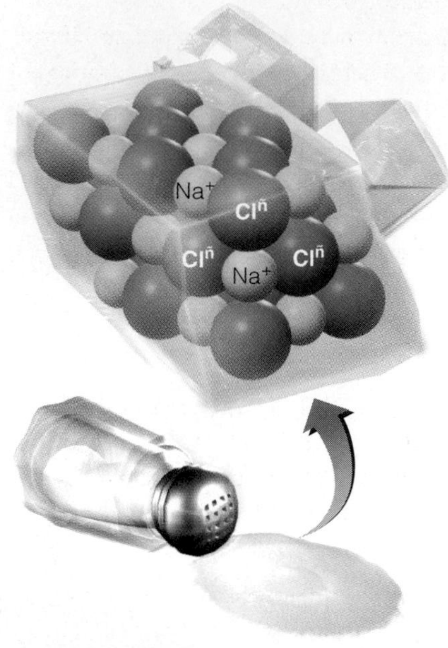

Because Americans consume plenty of salt, it is estimated that they are consuming, on average, 3,400 milligrams to just over 7,000 milligrams of dietary chloride daily.

Too Much or Too Little

Because sodium chloride is the major source of chloride in the diet, the upper level for adults for chloride is set at 3,600 milligrams to coincide with the upper level of sodium.[27]

A chloride deficiency rarely occurs in healthy individuals. Individuals who experience significant bouts of vomiting and diarrhea may become deficient as chloride is lost from the body.

Sulfur

What Is Sulfur?

Sulfur is typically found in your body as part of other compounds. For example, sulfur is part of vitamins, thiamin, biotin, and pantothenic acid.

Functions of Sulfur

Sulfur Helps Shape Some Amino Acids

The amino acids methionine and cysteine both contain sulfur. The sulfur part of these amino acids helps give some proteins their three-dimensional shape. This enables these proteins to perform effectively as enzymes and hormones.[28]

Sulfites Are Preservatives

Sulfur-based substances called sulfites are often used as a preservative by food manufacturers. They help prevent food spoilage and discoloration. We discuss sulfites further in Concept 14.

Food Sources

Foods that contain the two amino acids mentioned above are the major dietary sources of sulfur. A varied diet that contains meat, poultry, fish, eggs, legumes, dairy foods, fruits, and vegetables will provide sulfur.

Daily Needs and Too Much or Too Little

There isn't any set recommended amount of sulfur to be consumed daily, nor are there any known toxicity or deficiency symptoms. Most people get plenty of sulfur in their diet.

Trace Minerals Are Needed in Smaller Amounts

The trace minerals—iron, zinc, selenium, fluoride, chromium, copper, iodine, manganese, and molybdenum—are needed in much smaller amounts, less than 20 milligrams daily, compared with the major minerals. There are even smaller amounts of trace minerals in your body.[29] However, don't assume that this makes them less important. Trace minerals play roles that are as essential as those of the major minerals. Two (chromium and iodine) help certain hormones, including insulin and thyroid hormones, function. Trace minerals are necessary for maintaining healthy red blood cells (iron) and protecting your teeth (fluoride), and they can be cofactors (iron, zinc, copper, manganese, and molybdenum) that work with enzymes to ensure that critical chemical reactions occur.

The trace mineral molybdenum is part of several enzymes involved in the breakdown of certain amino acids and other compounds. Adult men and women need to consume 45 micrograms of molybdenum daily. Legumes, grains, and nuts are good sources.[30] Trace minerals, like major minerals, can be harmful if consumed in excess. In animal studies, too much molybdenum can cause reproductive problems. Because of this finding in animals, the upper level for molybdenum in humans has been set at 2 milligrams for adults.

A deficiency of molybdenum in healthy individuals is relatively rare, but when it occurs it can include rapid heartbeat, headaches, and night blindness.

For details on most of the essential trace minerals, review the visual summary tables coming up, starting on page 22.

Iron

What Is Iron?

Iron is the most abundant mineral on Earth, and the most abundant trace mineral in your body. A 130-pound woman has over 2,300 milligrams of iron in her body—about the weight of a dime—and a 165-pound man will have 4,000 milligrams of iron in his body—slightly less than two dimes.[31]

As a key component of blood, iron is highly valuable to the body. For the most part, iron is not excreted in the urine or stool, so once it's absorbed very little leaves the body. Approximately 95 percent of your body's iron is recycled and reused.[32] Whereas some iron is shed in hair, skin, and sloughed-off intestinal cells, most iron loss is due to bleeding.

Iron Occurs in Two Forms: Heme and Non-Heme

Foods from animal sources, such as meat, poultry, and fish, provide *heme iron* in your diet. Heme iron is part of the protein **hemoglobin** (in your red blood cells) and *myoglobin* in your muscles. Heme iron is easily absorbed by your body.

Plant foods such as grains and vegetables are the main sources of *non-heme iron* in your diet. Non-heme iron is not as easily absorbed as heme iron.

In general, your body absorbs only about 10–15 percent of the iron you eat. However, if your body stores are low, the amount of iron you absorb from foods will increase.

You can enhance your non-heme iron absorption by eating food high in vitamin C along with iron-rich foods (see the food source figure). As little as 25 milligrams of vitamin C—the amount in about one-quarter cup of orange juice—can double the amount of non-heme iron you absorb from a meal.

Another way to enhance non-heme iron absorption is to eat meat, fish, or poultry at the same time that you eat vitamin C-rich and iron-rich foods. The peptides (joined amino acids) in these animal-based foods are thought to enhance absorption. For example, the meat in a turkey sandwich will help enhance the absorption of the non-heme iron in whole-wheat bread.

Functions of Iron

About two-thirds of your body's iron is in hemoglobin. It binds with oxygen from your lungs and is transported to your tissues for their use. Hemoglobin also picks up carbon dioxide waste products from your cells and brings them to your lungs to be exhaled from your body. Similarly, iron is part of the myoglobin that transports and stores oxygen in your muscles.

Iron also helps enzymes in your brain send messages to the rest of your body. An iron deficiency in children can affect their ability to learn and retain information. Studies have shown that children in their early years with anemia (low levels of red blood cells) caused by iron deficiency can have persistent, decreased cognitive ability during their later school years.[33]

Daily Needs

Women between the age of about 19 to 50 need 18 milligrams daily to cover the iron lost during menstruation. After a woman stops menstruating, her daily iron needs drop to 8 milligrams.

Men need 8 milligrams of dietary iron daily. The recommendations for women and men are based on a typical American diet, which includes both heme and non-heme iron sources.

Men consume more than twice their recommended iron needs daily—over 16 milligrams, on average. However, premenopausal women consume only about 70 percent of their daily needs, or about 13 milligrams, on average. Postmenopausal women consume slightly over 12 milligrams of iron daily, so, like men, they are meeting their iron needs.

The iron needs of vegetarians are higher than those of nonvegetarians due to components in plant foods that inhibit iron absorption.

Food Sources

About half of Americans' dietary iron intake comes from enriched bread and other grain foods such as cereals. Meat, fish, and poultry contribute only 12 percent of people's dietary iron needs. Cooking foods in iron pans and skillets can increase the iron content in our diets because foods absorb iron from the pan.

Too Much or Too Little

Consuming too much iron (often from supplements) can cause constipation, nausea, vomiting, and diarrhea. The upper level for iron in adults is 45 milligrams daily, which is slightly less than the amount known to cause these intestinal symptoms. This upper level doesn't apply to people with liver or related diseases, because that level is already much too high for them.

In the United States the accidental consumption of supplements containing iron is the leading cause of poisoning deaths in children under age 6. Ingesting as little as 200 milligrams of iron has been shown to be fatal. Children who swallow iron supplements can experience symptoms such as nausea, vomiting, and diarrhea within minutes. Intestinal bleeding can also occur, which can lead to shock, coma, and even death. The FDA requires a warning about the risk of iron poisoning in small children on every iron supplement label, and pills containing 30 milligrams or more of iron must be individually wrapped.

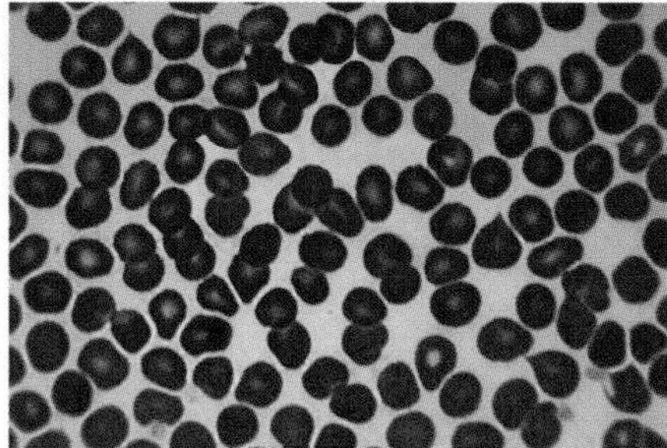

Normal red blood cells.

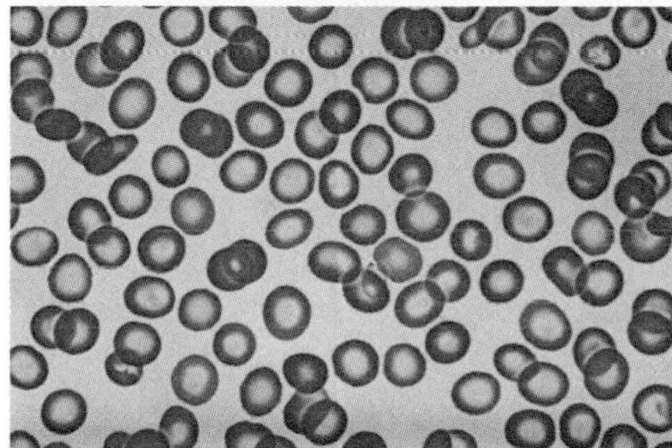

Blood cells affected by anemia.

Excessive storage of iron in the body over several years is called *iron overload* and can damage tissues and organs, including the heart, kidneys, liver, and nervous system. Hemochromatosis is a genetic disorder in which people absorb too much dietary iron, causing iron overload.

The role of iron in heart disease is still unclear. Some studies suggest that iron can stimulate free radical production in the body, which can damage the arteries leading to the heart. Unless you are medically diagnosed with iron deficiency, you should avoid consuming excessive amounts of iron.

Iron deficiency is the most common nutritional disorder in the world. Premenopausal and pregnant women, preterm and low-birth-weight infants, and older infants and toddlers are the groups that are most at risk of developing iron-deficiency anemia.

TABLE TIPS 

Ironing Out Your Iron Needs

Enjoy an iron-enriched whole-grain cereal along with a glass of vitamin C-rich orange juice to boost the iron absorption in your bowl of cereal.

Add plenty of salsa (vitamin C) to your bean burritos to enhance the absorption of the iron in both the beans and the flour tortilla.

Stuff a cooked baked potato (iron, vitamin C) with shredded cooked chicken (iron) and broccoli (vitamin C) and top it with melted low-fat cheese for a delicious dinner.

Eat a small box of raisins (iron) and a clementine or tangerine (vitamin C) as a sweet, iron-rich afternoon snack.

Add chickpeas (iron) to your salad greens (vitamin C). Don't forget the tomato wedges for another source of iron-enhancing vitamin C.

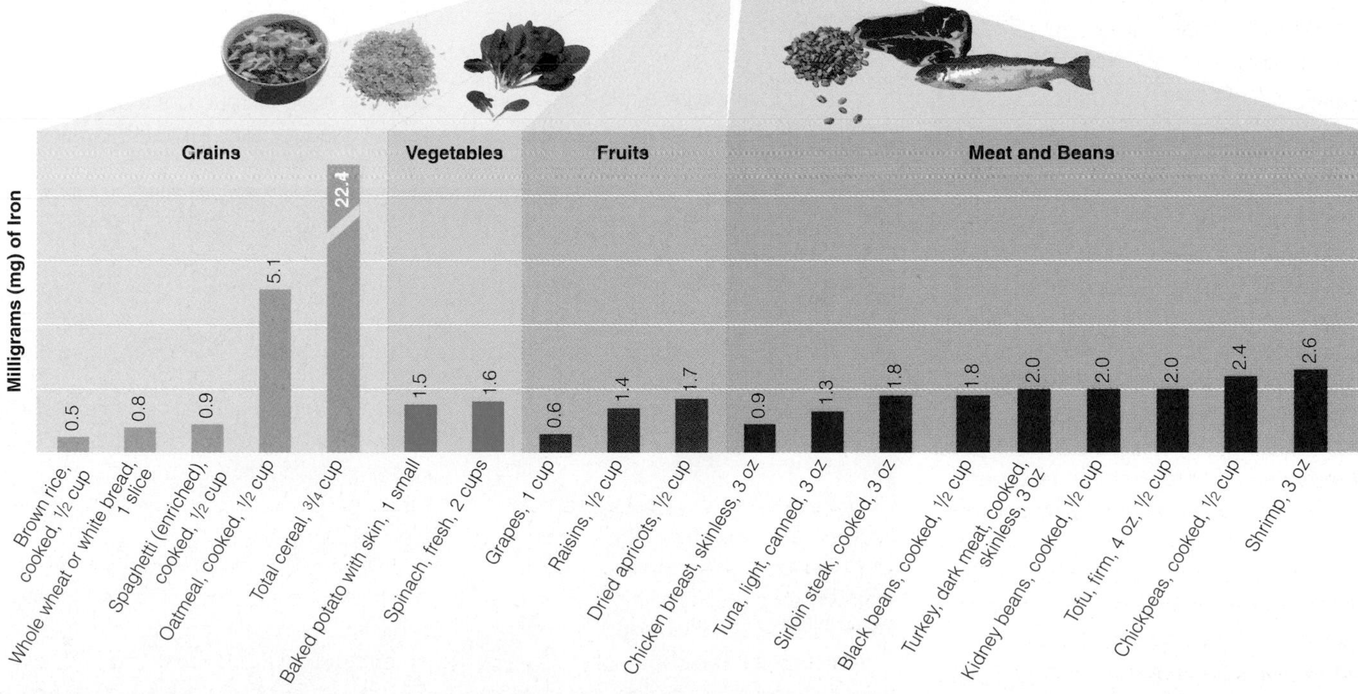

Zinc

What Is Zinc?

Zinc is found in almost every cell of your body. It is involved in the function of more than 100 enzymes, including those used for protein synthesis. As important as it is, it was not considered an essential nutrient until 1974.

Functions of Zinc

Zinc Is Needed for DNA Synthesis and Growth and Development

Zinc plays a role in the structure of both RNA and DNA in your cells and in gene expression.

Zinc is needed for adequate growth in developing infants and throughout the adolescent years.[34]

Zinc Helps Keep Your Immune System Healthy and Helps Wounds Heal

Zinc is needed for production of white blood cells, so it helps keep your immune system healthy.

Zinc helps reduce the inflammation that can accompany skin wounds. Zinc also helps in wound healing by being part of enzymes and proteins that repair and enhance the proliferation of skin cells.[35]

Zinc Brings Out the Best in Your Taste Buds

One lick of a chocolate ice cream cone or a forkful of cherry cheesecake will make you appreciate the role that zinc plays in taste acuity, which is the ability to savor the flavors of your foods. A deficiency of zinc has been shown to alter taste perceptions.[36]

The Truth about Zinc and the Common Cold

Zinc lozenges are sometimes advertised to help you reduce the severity and duration of the common cold. Unfortunately, the metallic taste of zinc may have cold sufferers fooled into thinking, as a team of researchers put it, ". . . anything tasting as bad as zinc and with as much aftertaste as zinc must be good medicine."[37] Don't let zinc's medicinal taste fool you.

Whereas a few studies have suggested that zinc intake, at high doses, may help fight against colds, a review of numerous studies has failed to find that it has any effect on sniffles and sneezes. In fact, the high dosages used in the studies often exceeded the recommended upper level. If consumed for too long, doses this high could put an individual at risk of more uncomfortable, medically worse problems than a stuffy nose.[38]

Zinc Plays a Role in Fighting AMD Disease

Research studies do support the assertion that zinc may play a role in reducing the risk of age-related macular degeneration (AMD), a condition that hampers central vision. Zinc may work with an enzyme in your eyes that's needed to properly utilize vitamin A for vision. Zinc may also help mobilize vitamin A from the liver to ensure adequate blood levels of this vitamin. Supplements that contain antioxidants along with zinc have been shown to reduce the risk of AMD. (See the section on antioxidants in Concept 16.)

Daily Needs

Adult males need 11 milligrams of zinc, whereas women need 8 milligrams daily. American adults, on average, are meeting their daily zinc needs. Men are consuming from 11 milligrams to over 14 milligrams and women are consuming 8 to 9 milligrams of zinc daily, on average.

Vegetarians, especially strict vegetarians, can have as much as a 50 percent higher need for zinc. Phytates in plant

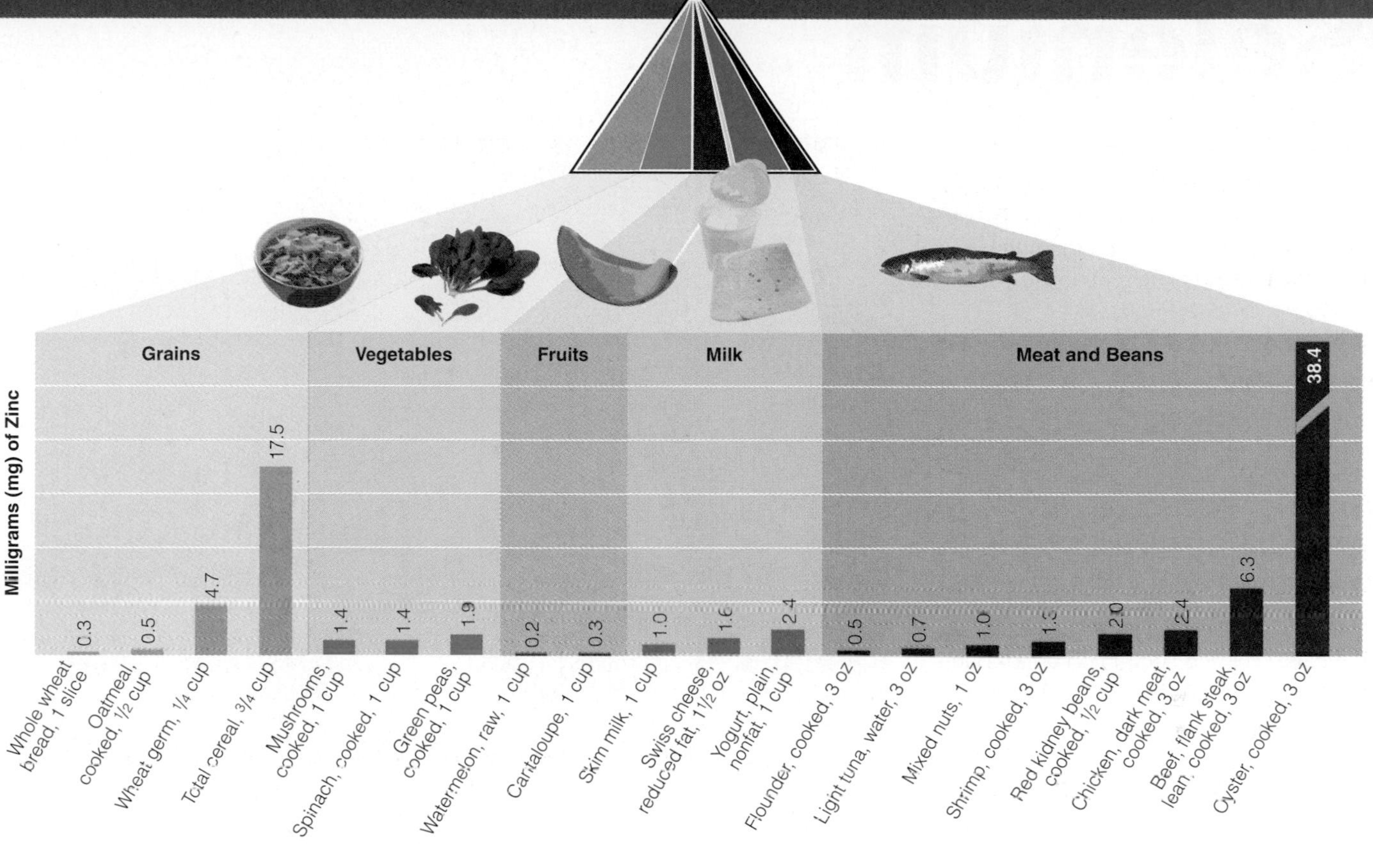

foods such as grains and legumes, which are staples of vegan diets, can bind with zinc, reducing its absorption in the intestinal tract.

Food Sources

Red meat, some seafood, and whole grains are excellent sources of zinc. Because zinc is found in the germ and bran portion of the grain, refined grains stripped of these components have as much as 80 percent less zinc than whole grains.

Too Much or Too Little

The upper level for zinc in food and/or supplements for adults is set at 40 milligrams daily. Consuming too much zinc, as little as 50 milligrams, can cause stomach pains, nausea, vomiting, and diarrhea. Approximately 60 milligrams of zinc daily has been shown to lower the level of copper in your body by competing with this mineral for absorption in the intestinal tract. This is an excellent example of how the overconsumption of one mineral can compromise the benefits of another.

Excessive amounts, such as 300 milligrams of zinc daily, have been shown to suppress the immune system and lower the HDL ("good") cholesterol.

A deficiency of zinc can cause hair loss, loss of appetite, impaired taste of foods, diarrhea, and delayed sexual maturation, as well as impotence and skin rashes.

Because zinc is needed during development, a deficiency can slow and impair growth. Classic studies of groups of people in the Middle East showed that people who consumed a diet mainly of unleavened bread, which is high in zinc-binding phytates, experienced impaired growth and dwarfism.[39]

TABLE TIPS

Zapping Your Zinc Needs

Enjoy a tuna fish sandwich on whole-wheat bread at lunch for a double serving (fish and bread) of zinc.

Kidney beans are often at cafeteria salad bars, so add a spoonful to your soup and salad lunch.

Pack a small handful of mixed nuts and raisins in a zip-closed bag for a snack on the run.

Selenium

What Is Selenium?

The mineral selenium is part of a class of proteins called selenoproteins, many of which are enzymes. Selenoproteins have important functions in your body.

Functions of Selenium

Selenium Is Needed by Your Thyroid

Selenium-containing enzymes help regulate thyroid hormones in your body.

Selenium Plays an Antioxidant Role

Selenoproteins can also function as antioxidants that protect your cells from free radicals. (See the section on antioxidants in Concept 16.) As you recall, free radicals are natural by-products of metabolism and can also result from exposure to chemicals in the environment. If free radicals accumulate faster than your body can neutralize them, their damaging effects can contribute to chronic diseases, such as heart disease.[40]

Selenium May Help Fight Cancer

Research studies have suggested that deaths from cancers, such as lung, colon, and prostate cancers, are lower in groups of people that consume more selenium. Selenium's antioxidant capabilities, and its ability to potentially slow the growth of tumors, are thought to be the mechanism behind its anticancer effects.

The FDA now allows a Qualified Health Claim on food labels and dietary supplements that states that "selenium may reduce the risk of certain cancers but the evidence is limited and not conclusive to date."[41]

A National Institutes of Health (NIH) study is currently under way to see if selenium alone or with vitamin E will reduce the risk of prostate cancer in men. The study is scheduled to end in 2013.

Daily Needs

Both adult females and males need 55 micrograms of selenium daily. American adults are more than meeting their needs—they consume about 80 micrograms to 160 micrograms daily, on average.

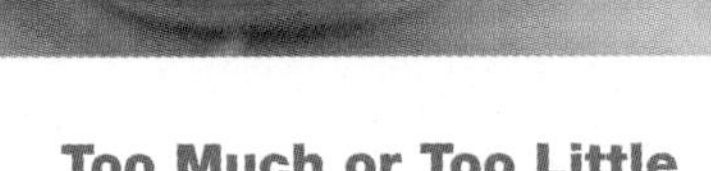

Food Sources

Meat, seafood, cereal, grains, dairy foods, and fruits and vegetables can all contribute to dietary selenium. However, the amount of selenium in the foods that you eat depends upon the soil where the plants were grown and the animals grazed. For example, wheat grown in selenium-rich soil can have more than a tenfold higher amount of the mineral than an identical wheat grown in selenium-poor soil.

Too Much or Too Little

Too much selenium can cause toxicity and a condition called selenosis. A person with selenosis will have brittle nails and hair, both of which may fall out. Other symptoms include stomach and intestinal discomfort, a skin rash, garlicky breath, fatigue, and damage to the nervous system. The upper level for selenium for adults is set at 400 micrograms to prevent the loss and brittleness of nails and hair, which is the most common symptom of selenosis.

While rare in the United States, a selenium deficiency can cause Keshan disease, which damages the heart. This disease typically only occurs in children who live in rural areas that have selenium-

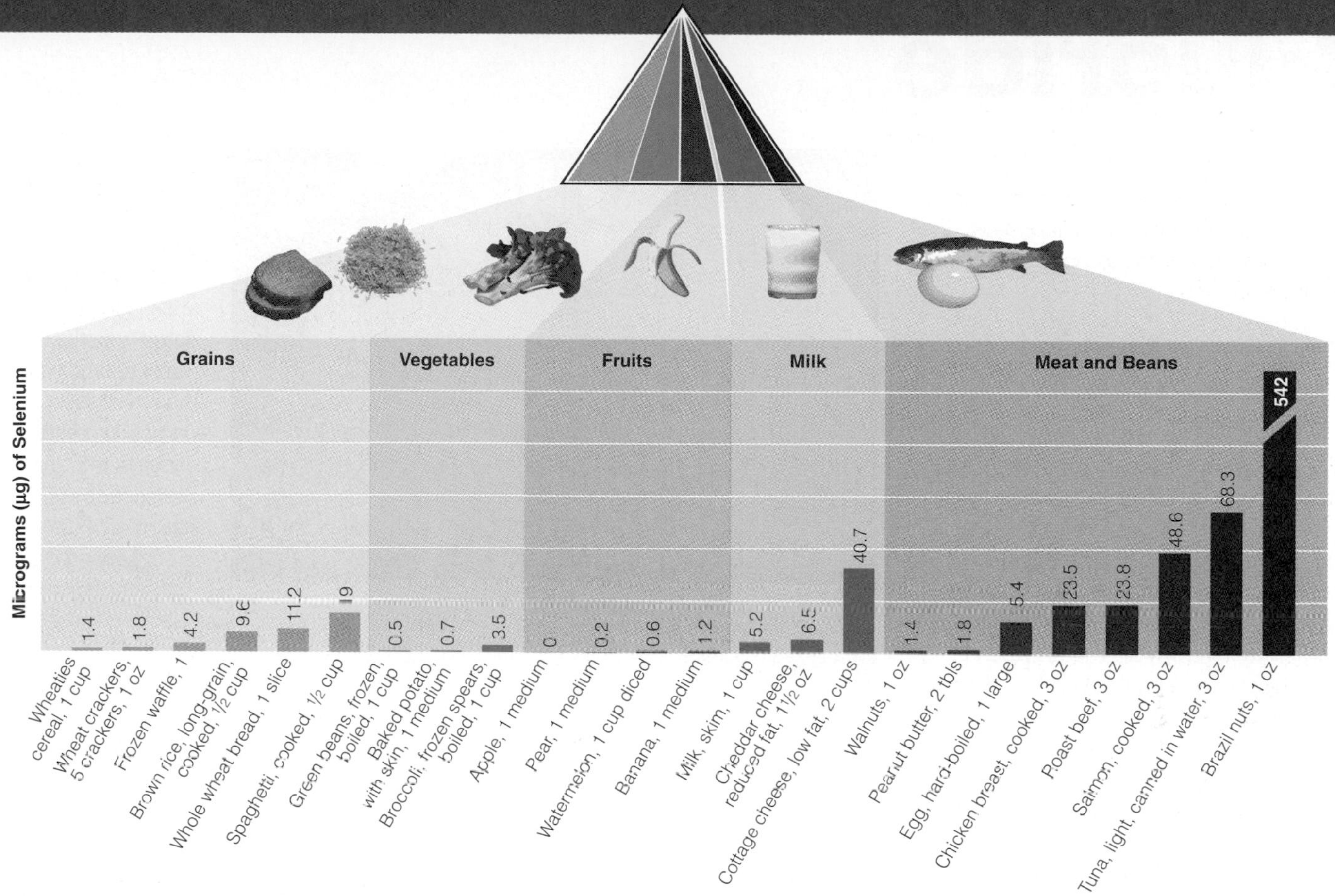

Micrograms (µg) of Selenium

Group	Food	µg
Grains	Wheaties cereal, 1 cup	1.4
Grains	Wheat crackers, 5 crackers, 1 oz	1.8
Grains	Frozen waffle, 1	4.2
Grains	Brown rice, long-grain, cooked, ½ cup	9.6
Grains	Whole wheat bread, 1 slice	11.2
Grains	Spaghetti, cooked, ½ cup	19
Vegetables	Green beans, frozen, boiled, 1 cup	0.5
Vegetables	Baked potato, with skin, 1 medium	0.7
Vegetables	Broccoli, frozen spears, boiled, 1 cup	3.5
Fruits	Apple, 1 medium	0
Fruits	Pear, 1 medium	0.2
Fruits	Watermelon, 1 cup diced	0.6
Fruits	Banana, 1 medium	1.2
Milk	Milk, skim, 1 cup	5.2
Milk	Cheddar cheese, reduced fat, 1½ oz	6.5
Milk	Cottage cheese, low fat, 2 cups	40.7
Meat and Beans	Walnuts, 1 oz	1.4
Meat and Beans	Peanut butter, 2 tbls	1.8
Meat and Beans	Egg, hard-boiled, 1 large	5.4
Meat and Beans	Chicken breast, cooked, 3 oz	23.5
Meat and Beans	Roast beef, 3 oz	23.8
Meat and Beans	Salmon, cooked, 3 oz	48.6
Meat and Beans	Tuna, light, canned in water, 3 oz	68.3
Meat and Beans	Brazil nuts, 1 oz	542

poor soil. However, some researchers speculate that selenium deficiency alone may not cause Keshan disease, but the selenium-deficient individual may also be exposed to a virus, which, together with the selenium deficiency, leads to the damaged heart.[42]

TABLE TIPS 

Seeking Out Selenium

Top a toasted whole-wheat bagel with a slice of reduced fat cheddar cheese for a smart way to start the day.

Spread peanut butter on whole-wheat crackers and top with a slice of banana.

Top your dinner pasta with broccoli for a selenium-smart meal.

Zap sliced apples, sprinkled with a little apple juice and cinnamon, in the microwave and top with vanilla yogurt.

Spoon a serving of low-fat cottage cheese into a bowl and top with canned sliced peaches and almonds for a fabulous dessert.

Fluoride

What Is Fluoride?

Fluoride is the safe ion form of fluorine, a poisonous gas. Calcium fluoride is the form that is found in your bones and teeth.

Functions of Fluoride

Fluoride Protects against Dental Caries

The best known function of fluoride is its role in keeping teeth healthy. Your teeth have an outer layer called enamel (see the figure below), which can become eroded over time by acids and result in dental caries. The acids are produced by the bacteria in your mouth when they feast on the carbohydrates that you eat. Continual exposure of your teeth to these acids can cause erosion and create a cavity.

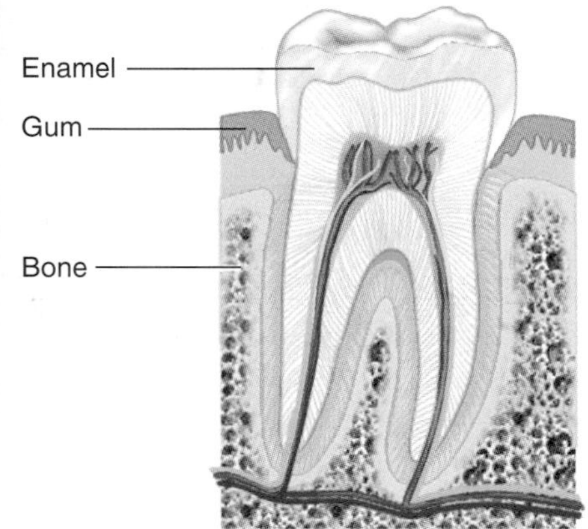

Fluoride from food, beverages, and dental products, such as toothpaste, helps protect your teeth in several ways. It helps to repair the enamel that has already started to erode.

Fluoride also interferes with the ability of the bacteria to metabolize carbohydrates, thus reducing the amount of acid they produce.

Finally, fluoride provides a protective barrier between your tooth and the destructive acids. As a component of saliva, it provides a continual fluoride bath to your teeth's surfaces.[43]

Consuming adequate amounts of fluoride is extremely important during infancy and childhood, when teeth are developing, and for maintenance of healthy teeth throughout your life.

Fluoride in Drinking Water Has Improved the Nation's Dental Health

In the 1930s, scientists noticed lower rates of dental caries among individuals whose community water systems contained significant amounts of fluoride. Studies confirmed that the fluoride was the protective factor in the water that helped fight dental decay. Since 1945, most communities have fluoridated their water, and today, 67 percent of Americans live in communities that have a fluoridated water supply.

The increase in access to fluoridated water is the major reason why there has been a decline in dental caries in the United States, and fluoridation of water is considered one of the ten greatest public health advances of the twentieth century.[44]

To find out if your community water is fluoridated and how much fluoride is added, visit the Centers for Disease Control and Prevention's website, My Water's Fluoride, at: http://apps.nccd.cdc.gov/MWF/Index.asp.

Daily Needs

Adult men should consume 3.8 milligrams and women 3.1 milligrams of fluoride daily to meet their needs. If the tap water in your community is fluoridated at 1 milligram/liter, you would have to

consume at least 13 cups of water daily, through either beverages or cooking, to meet your fluoride needs (1 liter = 4.2 cups).

Currently, adults are consuming 1.4 to 3.4 milligrams of fluoride daily if they are living in communities with fluoridated water. That number drops to only 0.3 to 1.0 milligrams consumed daily if the water isn't fluoridated.[45]

Food Sources

Foods in general are not a good source of fluoride. The best sources are fluoridated water and beverages and foods made with this water, such as coffee, tea, and soups. Another source of flouride can be juices made from concentrate using fluoridated tap water (remember, not all tap water contains fluoride).

Water and processed beverages, such as soft drinks, account for up to 75 percent of Americans' fluoride intake.

Tea is also a good source of fluoride, as tea leaves accumulate fluoride. Note that decaffeinated tea has twice the amount of fluoride as the caffeinated variety.[46]

If you shy away from tap water and drink and cook predominantly with bottled water, you may be robbing yourself of some cavity protection. Most bottled waters sold in the United States have less than the optimal amount of fluoride. It is difficult to determine the fluoride content of many bottled waters because currently, the amount of fluoride in bottled water only has to be listed on the label if fluoride has been specifically added. Check the label to see if your bottled water contains added fluoride. For more information about the differences between bottled and tap water, and their advantages and disadvantages, see the boxed feature "Tap Water or Bottled Water: Is Bottled Better?" in Concept 18.

Too Much or Too Little

Because of fluroide's protective qualities, too little exposure to or consumption of fluoride increases the risk of dental caries.

Having some fluoride is important for healthy teeth, but too much can cause fluorosis, a condition whereby the teeth become mottled (pitted) and develop white patches or stains on the surface. Fluorosis creates teeth that are extremely resistant to caries but cosmetically unappealing (see photo).

Fluorosis occurs when teeth are forming, so only infants and children up to 8 years of age are at risk. Once teeth break through the gums, fluorosis can't occur. Fluorosis results from overfluoridation of water, swallowing toothpaste, or excessive use of dental products that contain fluoride. Some research suggests that fluorosis may be reversable but more studies are needed to determine this.

Skeletal fluorosis can occur in bones when a person consumes at least 10 milligrams of fluoride daily for 10 or more years. This is a rare situation when water is mistakenly overly fluoridated. This can cause bone concentrations of fluoride that are up to 5 times higher than normal and result in stiffness or pain in joints, osteoporosis, and calcification of the ligaments.

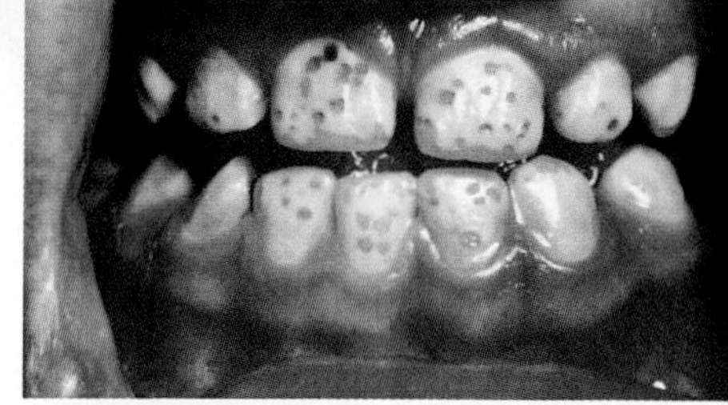

Teeth pitted by fluorosis

The upper level for adults has been set at 10 milligrams to reduce the risk of fluorosis in the bones. (Note, however, that the upper level for infants and children is much lower, to prevent fluorosis in teeth. See the inside cover of the textbook for this upper level.)

TABLE TIPS 

Fabulous Ways to Get Fluoride

Pour orange juice into ice cube trays and pop a couple of frozen cubes into a glass of tap water for a refreshing and flavorful beverage.

Use tap water when making coffee, tea, or juice from concentrate, and for food preparation.

Brew a mug of flavored decaffeinated tea, such as French vanilla or gingerbread, to keep you warm while you're hitting the books.

Chromium

What Is Chromium?

The most recent mineral to be found necessary in humans, chromium was identified as an essential mineral in 1977, although researchers have had an interest in chromium and its roles in the metabolism of glucose since the 1950s.[47]

Functions of Chromium

Chromium Helps Insulin in Your Body

The main function of this mineral is to increase insulin's effectiveness in cells. The hormone insulin plays an important role in the metabolism and storage of carbohydrates, fats, and protein in your body. Individuals who were intravenously fed a chromium-free diet experienced high blood levels of glucose, weight loss, and nerve problems—all telltale signs of uncontrolled diabetes and poor blood glucose control. The problems were corrected when chromium was provided.[48]

Chromium May Reduce Pre-Diabetes

Because it works with insulin, some researchers think that chromium may help individuals who have diabetes mellitus or pre-diabetes (glucose intolerance) improve their blood glucose control. There has yet to be a large research study in the United States that confirms this theory.

One small study suggests that a chromium supplement may reduce the risk of insulin resistance, and therefore, favorably affect the handling of glucose in the body. Improving the body's sensitivity to insulin and maintaining a normal blood glucose level can possibly lower the incidence of type 2 diabetes in individuals at risk.

Based on this one study, the FDA has allowed a Qualified Health Claim on chromium supplements. However, the supplement label must state that the evidence regarding the relationship between chromium supplements and either insulin resistance or type 2 diabetes is not certain at this time.[49]

Chromium Does Not Help Build Muscle Mass

Although advertisements have sometimes touted chromium supplements as an aid to losing weight and building lean muscle, the research doesn't support the claim. A review of over 20 research studies didn't find any benefits from taking up to

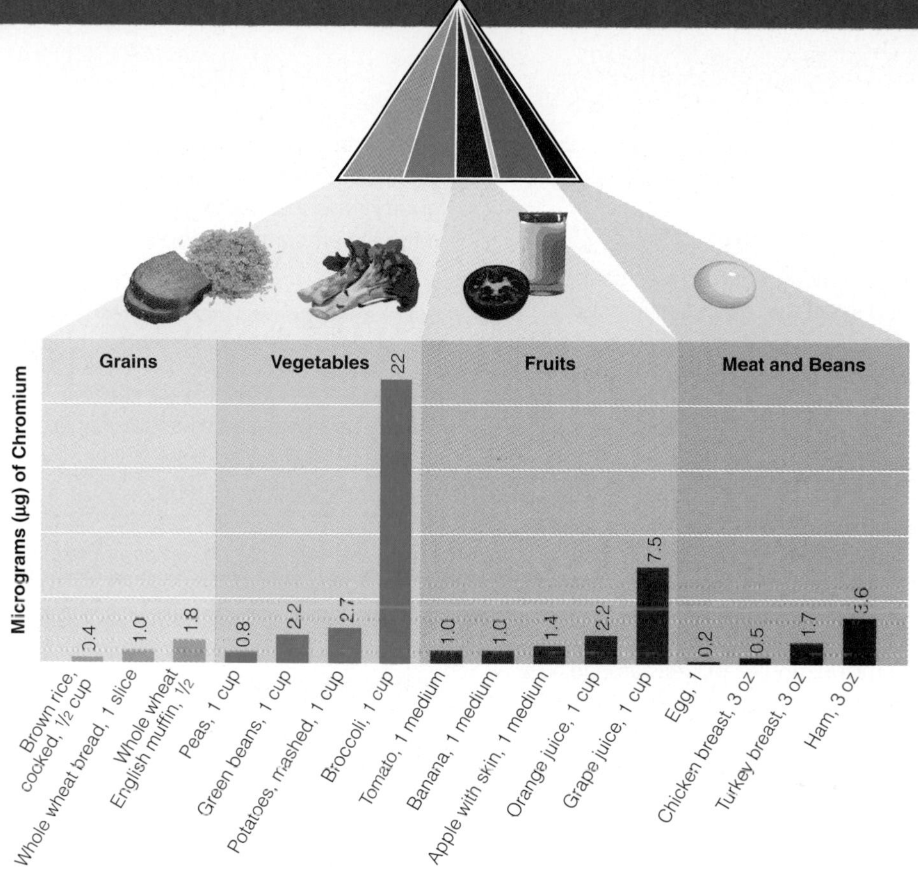

1,000 micrograms of chromium daily.[50] If you are trying to become lean and mean, taking chromium supplements isn't going to help.

Daily Needs

Adult men aged 19 to 50 need 30 to 35 micrograms of chromium daily, whereas women of the same age need 20 to 25 micrograms daily, on average, depending upon their age. It is estimated that American men consume 33 micrograms of chromium from foods, and women consume 25 micrograms, on average, daily.[51]

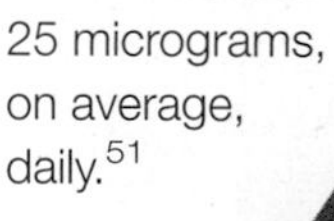

Food Sources

Grains are good sources of chromium. Meat, fish, and poultry and some fruits and vegetables can also provide chromium, whereas dairy foods are low in the mineral.

Too Much or Too Little

As yet, there is no known risk from consuming excessive amounts of chromium from food or supplements, so no upper level has been set.

A chromium deficiency is very rare in the United States. However, a study in China, where chromium deficiency has been shown to exist, determined that individuals with type 2 diabetes experienced lower blood glucose levels and less insulin resistance when they were given chromium supplements. Again, it is not clear if individuals with diabetes who did not have a chromium deficiency would benefit by taking a supplement.[52]

TABLE TIPS

Cram in the Chromium

Toast a whole-wheat English muffin and top it with a slice of lean ham for a meaty, chromium-rich breakfast.

Add broccoli florets to your salad for a chromium-packed lunch.

Try an afternoon glass of cold grape juice for a refreshing break. Add an apple for a double dose of chromium.

Combine mashed potatoes and peas for a sweet and starchy addition to your dinner plate and your chromium count.

Split a firm banana in half, lengthwise, and spread a small amount of peanut butter on each side.

Copper

What Is Copper?

Copper may bring to mind ancient tools, great sculptures, or American pennies (although pennies are no longer made of solid copper), but it is also associated with several key body functions.

Functions of Copper

Copper is part of many enzymes and proteins. It is important for iron absorption and transfer and the synthesis of hemoglobin and red blood cells.

Copper helps generate energy in your cells, synthesize melanin (the dark pigment found in skin), and link the proteins collagen and elastin together in connective tissue. It works with enzymes to protect your cells from free radicals.

Copper also plays an important role in blood clotting and in maintaining a healthy immune system.[53]

Daily Needs

Both adult women and men need 900 micrograms of copper daily. American women consume 1,000 to 1,100 micrograms, whereas men consume 1,300 to 1,500 micrograms daily, on average.

Food Sources

Organ meats such as liver, seafood, nuts, and seeds are abundant in copper. Bran cereals, whole-grain products, and cocoa are also good sources. Whereas potatoes, milk, and chicken are low in copper, they are consumed in such abundant amounts that they contribute a fair amount of copper to Americans' diets.

Too Much or Too Little

Too much copper can cause stomach pains and cramps, nausea, diarrhea, vomiting, and even liver damage. The upper level for copper for adults is set at 10,000 micrograms daily.

Copper deficiency is rare in the United States. It has occurred in premature babies fed milk formulas, malnourished infants fed cow's milk, and individuals given intravenous feedings that lacked adequate amounts of copper.

TABLE TIPS 

Counting Your Copper

Make your hot cocoa with milk, rather than water, for two sources (cocoa and milk) of copper in your mug.

Mix raisins into your brown rice at dinner.

Top chocolate pudding with a sprinkling of crushed walnuts for a dessert that is both sweet and crunchy.

Choose sunflower seeds for an afternoon snack.

Ladle black beans and salsa into a whole-wheat pita. Top with reduced fat cheddar cheese. Zap it in the microwave for a Mexican lunch with a copper kick.

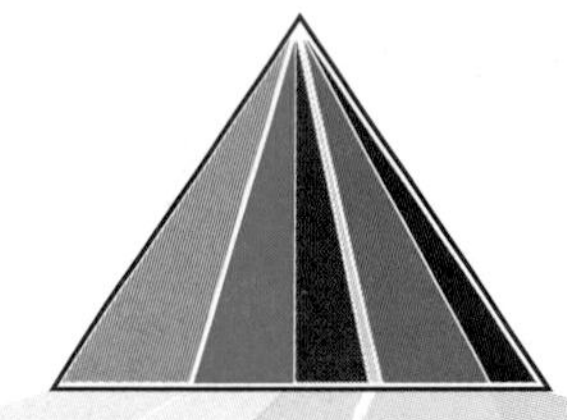

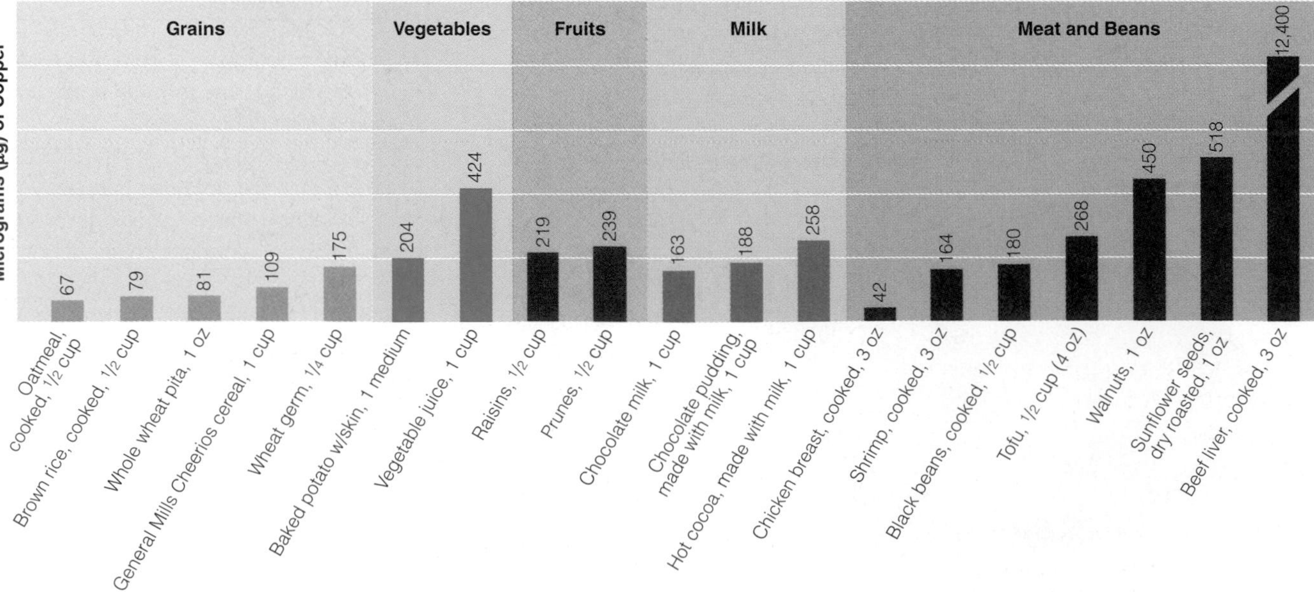

Iodine

What Is Iodine?

Like the fluoridation of community drinking water, the iodization of salt was a significant advance for public health in the United States. Prior to the 1920s, many Americans suffered from the iodine deficiency disease, goiter. Once salt manufacturers began adding iodine to their product, incidence of the disease dropped. Today, rates of the disease are very low in the United States, though not in other parts of the world.

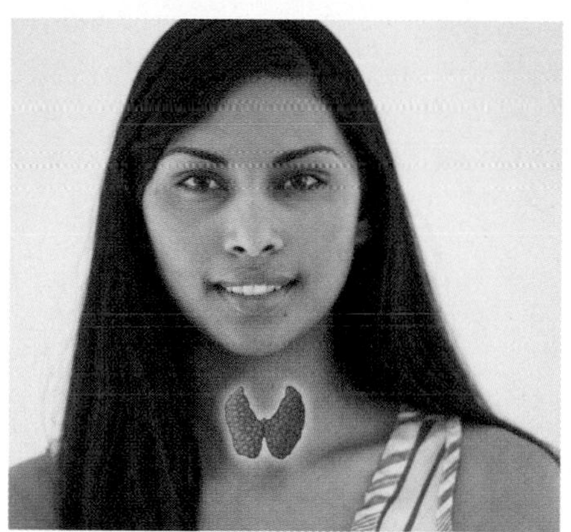

Functions of Iodine

Iodine is an essential mineral for your thyroid, a butterfly-shaped gland located in your neck. The thyroid needs iodine to make some essential hormones. In fact, approximately 60 percent of your thyroid hormones are comprised of iodine.

Thyroid hormones affect the majority of your cells, regulate your metabolic rate, and help your heart, nerves, muscles, and intestines function properly. Children need thyroid hormones for normal growth of bones and brain development.[54]

Daily Needs

Adult men and women need 150 micrograms of iodine daily to meet their needs. Americans are currently consuming 230 micrograms to 410 micrograms of iodine daily, on average, depending upon their age and gender.

Food Sources

The amount of iodine that occurs naturally in foods is typically low, approximately 3 to 75 micrograms in a serving, and is influenced by the amount of iodine in the soil, water, and fertilizers used to grow foods.

Fish can provide higher amounts of iodine, as they concentrate it from seawater. Iodized salt provides 400 micrograms of iodine per teaspoon. Note that not all salt has added iodine. Kosher salt, for example, has no additives, including iodine. Processed foods that use iodized salt or iodine-containing preservatives are also a source.

Too Much or Too Little

Consuming too much iodine can challenge the thyroid, impairing its function and reducing the synthesis and release of thyroid hormones. Because of this, the upper level for adults for iodine is 1,100 micrograms.

An early sign of iodine deficiency is *goiter,* which is an enlarged thyroid gland (see photo below). An iodine-deficient thyroid has to work harder to make the thyroid hormones, causing it to become enlarged.[55] A goiter epidemic in the midwestern United States is what prompted the campaign for mandatory iodization of salt. Based on the success of the campaign, the use of iodized salt spread rapidly throughout the United States.

MORTON IODIZED SALT

A deficiency of iodine during the early stages of fetal development can damage the brain of the developing baby, causing mental retardation. Inadequate iodine during this critical time can cause lower IQ scores. Depending upon the severity of the iodine deficiency, *cretinism,* also known as congenital hypothyroidism (*congenital* = born with; *hypo* = under; *ism* = condition), can occur. Individuals with cretinism can experience abnormal sexual development, mental retardation, and dwarfism (see photo below).

Early detection of an iodine deficiency and treatment in children is critical to avoiding irreversible damage.

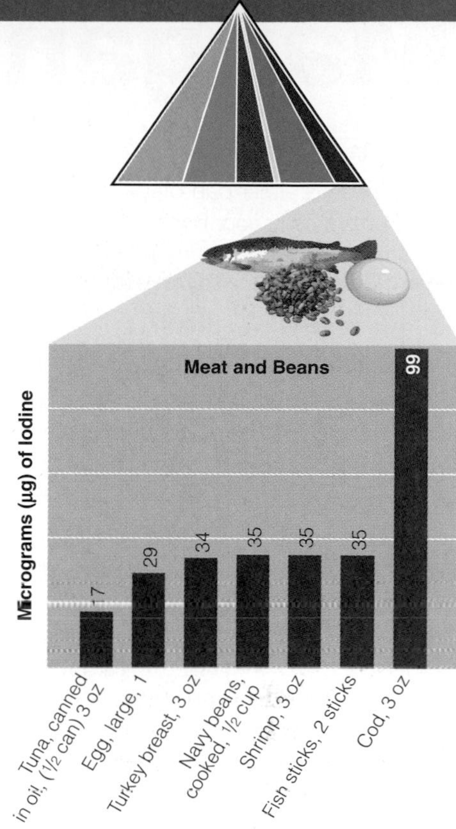

Goiter

Cretinism

Manganese

What Is Manganese?

Manganese is either part of, or activates, many enzymes in your body.

Functions of Manganese

Manganese Is Needed in Metabolism and for Healthy Bones

This mineral is involved in the metabolism of carbohydrates, fats, and amino acids. Manganese is needed for the formation of bone.

Daily Needs

Adult women need 1.8 milligrams, whereas men need 2.3 milligrams, of manganese daily. Americans are easily meeting their manganese needs. Adult women are consuming over 2 milligrams of manganese daily, and adult men are consuming over 2.8 milligrams daily, on average, from the foods in their diet.[56]

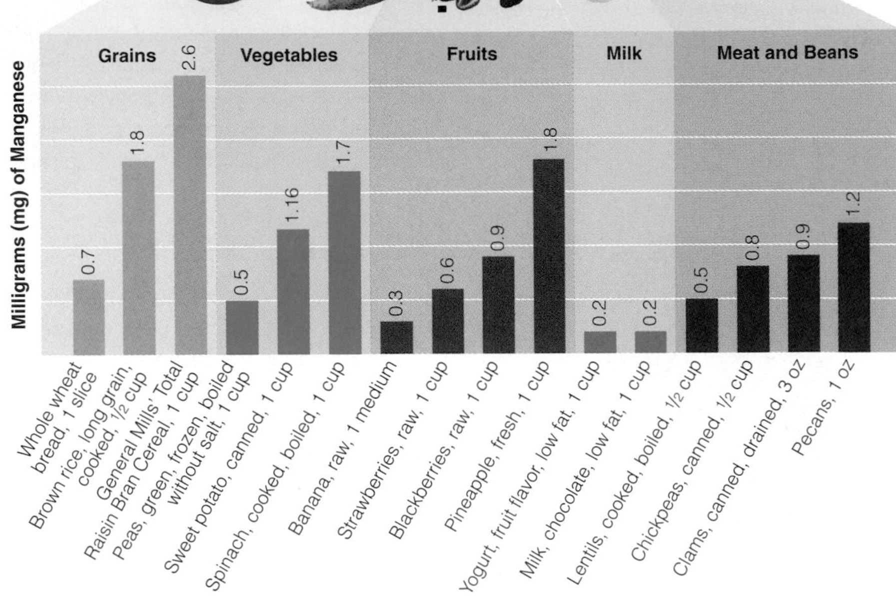

Food Sources

When it comes to meeting your manganese needs, look to whole grains, nuts, legumes, tea, vegetables, and fruits such as pineapples, strawberries, and bananas. A teaspoon of ground cinnamon provides just under 0.5 milligram of manganese.

Too Much or Too Little

Manganese toxicity, which has occurred in miners who have inhaled manganese dust, can cause damage to the nervous system and symptoms that resemble Parkinson's disease.[57]

A study of individuals who drank water with high levels of manganese showed that they also experienced Parkinson's disease-like symptoms.

To protect against this toxicity, the upper level has been set at 11 milligrams daily.

A deficiency of manganese is rare in healthy individuals who have a balanced diet. Individuals fed a manganese-deficient diet developed a rash and scaly skin.

TABLE TIPS 

Managing Your Manganese

Sprinkle your whole-wheat toast with a dusting of cinnamon to spice up your morning.

Combine cooked brown rice, canned and rinsed lentils, and chickpeas for a dinner in a snap.

Spoon vanilla yogurt over canned crushed pineapples and sliced bananas for a tropical snack.

UCook

Hearty French Toast

Try this delicious and satisfying delicacy for brunch, a filling snack, or even a special dinner!

UDo

Where's the Sodium in Your Foods?

Go online and take a virtual trip down the supermarket aisle to find the sodium content of some of your favorite foods. (Beware: If you're a ramen noodle fan, click with caution!)

The Top Five Points to Remember

1. Minerals are inorganic micronutrients that play many roles in your body. Many are part of enzymes. Minerals help maintain fluid and acid-base balance; play a role in nerve transmission and muscle contractions; help strengthen your bones, teeth, and immune system; and are involved in growth. Minerals are found in both plant and animal foods.
2. The major minerals are needed in amounts greater than 100 milligrams per day. The major minerals are sodium, potassium, calcium, phosphorus, magnesium, chloride, and sulfur.
3. Sodium plays an important role in balancing the fluid between your blood and your cells. Americans consume more than double the amount of sodium recommended daily. Potassium helps keep your heart, muscles, nerves, and bones healthy. The current recommendations to increase the fruits and vegetables in your diet will help you meet your potassium needs. Calcium, along with phosphorus and magnesium, provides your bones and teeth with strength and structure. A diet adequate in protein, vitamin K, calcium, and vitamin D, along with regular physical activity, is needed to build and maintain healthy bones.
4. The trace minerals are needed in amounts less than 20 milligrams per day. The trace minerals are iron, copper, zinc, selenium, fluoride, chromium, iodine, manganese, and molybdenum.
5. Iron is part of the oxygen-carrying hemoglobin in your red blood cells and myoglobin in your muscles. Heme iron is found in meat, poultry, and fish. Nonheme iron is found in plant foods, but it isn't absorbed as readily as heme iron. Copper, zinc, manganese, and molybdenum help enzymes function in your body. Selenium acts as an antioxidant and may help fight cancer. Chromium helps the hormone insulin function but has not been proven to enhance weight loss or build muscle mass during exercise. Iodine is essential in making thyroid hormones, which affect most of your body's cells and help regulate its metabolic rate.

Test Yourself

1. In your body, minerals can
   a. help maintain fluid balance.
   b. be part of enzymes.
   c. work with your immune system.
   d. do all of the above.
2. The recommendation for dietary sodium intake daily for adults up to age 51 is
   a. 3,400 milligrams.
   b. 2,300 milligrams.
   c. 1,500 milligrams.
   d. 180 milligrams.
3. How many servings of fruits and vegetables would you have to eat daily to meet your potassium needs?
   a. three
   b. four
   c. five
   d. seven
4. One cup of skim milk, 8 ounces of low-fat yogurt, and 1½ ounces of reduced-fat cheddar cheese EACH provide
   a. 100 milligrams of calcium.
   b. 200 milligrams of calcium.
   c. 300 milligrams of calcium.
   d. 400 milligrams of calcium.
5. You are having pasta for dinner. You want to enhance the absorption of the nonheme iron in the pasta. To do that, you can top your pasta with
   a. butter.
   b. olive oil.
   c. tomato sauce.
   d. nothing; eat it plain.

Answers

1. (d) Although you need only small amounts of minerals in your diet, they play critical roles in your body, such as helping maintain fluid balance, being part of enzymes, and working with your immune system to keep you healthy.
2. (b) The daily recommended amount of sodium for these adults is 1,500 milligrams. The upper level for sodium daily is 2,300 milligrams, while the absolute minimum that should be consumed is 180 milligrams per day. Unfortunately, Americans far exceed these recommendations and consume over 3,400 milligrams of sodium daily.
3. (d) Seven servings of fruits and vegetables daily will enable you to meet your potassium needs.
4. (c) Each of these servings of dairy foods provides 300 milligrams of calcium. Consuming the recommended three servings of lean dairy products daily will just about meet the amount recommended daily (1,000 milligrams) for many adults.
5. (c) Ladle the tomato sauce on your pasta—the vitamin C in it can enhance nonheme iron absorption. Though the butter and olive oil will give your spaghetti flavor, they won't help you absorb iron.

Web Resources

- For more on the DASH diet, visit DASH for Health at: www.dashforhealth.com
- For more on osteoporosis, visit The National Osteoporosis Foundation at: www.nof.org
- For more on high blood pressure, visit: www.nhlbi.nih.gov/hbp/index.html

18 Water

Facts to Know, Fluids to Drink

1. **Women** have more body water than men. **T/F**

2. Most of your **blood** is actually water. **T/F**

3. Quenching your **thirst** will provide enough water to avoid dehydration. **T/F**

4. Your morning cup of **coffee** counts toward your daily water needs. **T/F**

5. All bottled waters contain **fluoride.** **T/F**

Desiree, a college sophomore, stops off at the campus convenience store each morning to buy a bottle of water to take to her classes. Later in the day, she purchases another bottle before heading for the gym. Her mother sent her a reusable water bottle, which she could fill at on-campus water fountains, but Desiree scoffed at her mom's suggestion to drink tap water instead of bottled water, believing that bottled water is pure and safer to drink than tap water. But if Desiree does a little homework, she will find that her assumptions about the quality of tap water are incorrect. Also, her daily bottled water purchases are burning a hole in her wallet and adding plastic to landfills.

Everyone needs water to live, but is there really any benefit to drinking bottled water instead of tap water? Is bottled water really superior to the tap water in your home? These are a few of the questions we'll address in this concept.

Answers

1. False. It's the other way around: Muscle tissue holds more water than fat tissue, and men have a higher percentage of muscle mass, on average, than women. See page 2 for the facts.
2. True. About 45 percent of your blood is made up of red blood cells. Most of the rest is water. Check out page 3 on this.
3. False. Lack of thirst is not a reliable indicator that you're hydrated. Turn to page 7 to learn how to make sure you're getting enough fluid.
4. True. Your mug of java does contribute to your daily water needs, even though it may contain caffeine, a diuretic. Turn to page 8 to find out why.
5. False. In fact, few bottled waters contain flouride. Turn to pages 10 and 11 to find out why this could be a problem.

Why Is Water So Important?

Water is the most abundant substance in your body. The average healthy adult is about 60 percent water. However, the amount of water in your body depends on your age, your gender, and the amount of fat and muscle tissue you carry (Figure 18.1). Muscle tissue is approximately 65 percent water, while fat tissue is only 10 to 40 percent water.[1] Men have a higher percentage of muscle mass and a lower percentage of fat tissue than women of the same age, so men have more body water. For the same reason, muscular athletes have a higher percentage of body water than sedentary individuals.

Water is also essential for maintaining the fluid balance inside your body. Think about it: Your body cells are plump with fluid, and they float in the tissue fluid that surrounds them (Figure 18.2). Maintaining the equal distribution of all this body fluid is crucial to health, and water along with dissolved minerals play key roles.

The minerals important in fluid balance are called **electrolytes** (*electro* = electricity; *lytes* = soluble). They include sodium, potassium, phosphate, magnesium, calcium, and chloride. Electrolytes play a role in maintaining your body's fluid balance by attracting water into and out of your cells, somewhat as a magnet pulls metal toward it. Water in your body is drawn into and out of your cells by the "pull" of electrolytes: When cells have more electrolytes than the fluid outside them has, water flows in, and vice versa. We will talk more about the movement of fluids later in this concept.

~5% minerals and other nutrients

~14% protein

29% fat

52% water

Female, 137 lbs.

~5% minerals and other nutrients

~17% protein

20% fat

59% water

Male, 168 lbs.

Figure 18.1 The Composition of Your Body
Your body is mostly water. Protein, fat, and minerals make up most of the rest of you.

electrolytes Minerals important to bodily fluid balance that conduct an electrical current in a solvent such as water. Sodium, potassium, and chloride are examples of electrolytes in the body.

Water Is the Universal Solvent

Water is a wonderful *solvent*, a liquid in which substances dissolve. In fact, water is commonly known as the universal solvent. As a solvent, water is part of the medium in which molecules come in contact with each other. This contact between molecules allows chemical reactions to take place. For example, the combining of specific amino acids to synthesize a protein occurs in the watery medium inside your cells.

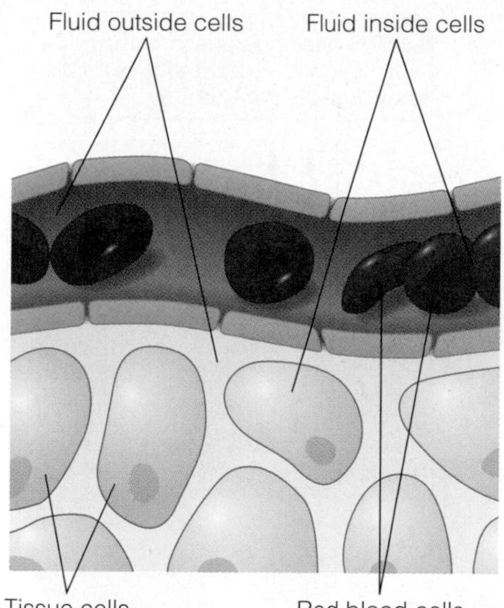

Figure 18.2 Water Inside and Outside Your Cells
Both tissue cells and blood cells contain water. Water is also the main component of the fluid that surrounds cells.

Water Is a Transport Medium

Recall our discussion of blood and lymph in Concept 6. The water in these two fluids helps transport substances throughout your body.

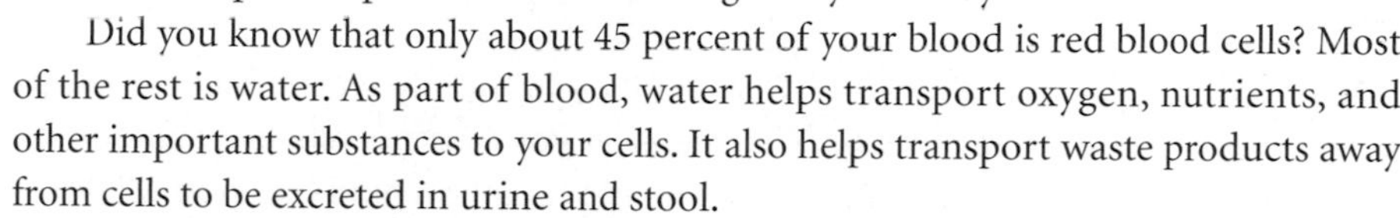

Did you know that only about 45 percent of your blood is red blood cells? Most of the rest is water. As part of blood, water helps transport oxygen, nutrients, and other important substances to your cells. It also helps transport waste products away from cells to be excreted in urine and stool.

Like the fluid in blood, lymph fluid is almost entirely water. Lymph transports proteins back to the bloodstream, and it is important in the absorption of fats. Lymph also transports wastes and microbes through "cleaning stations" called lymph nodes, where defensive cells consume these harmful substances before the lymph returns to the blood.

Water Helps Maintain Body Temperature

The water in your blood is like the coolant that runs through a car. They both absorb, carry, and ultimately release heat in order to keep a running machine from overheating. In a car, the coolant absorbs the heat from a running engine and carries it to the radiator for release. In your body, the water in your circulating blood absorbs the heat from your internal core—the center of your body, where your most important organs are located—and carries it to the skin for release (Figure 18.3). Water works so well as a coolant in both your car and your body because it has a unique ability to absorb and release a tremendous amount of heat.

Similar to a car, your body sometimes gets overheated. For instance, if you were to go jogging on a hot summer day, the enormous amount of internal heat that would be generated would probably overwhelm the heat-absorbing capacity of your body's water. The increasing heat would break apart the molecules of water on your skin, transforming them from a liquid (sweat) to a vapor. The evaporation of sweat from your skin would release the heat and cool you down, enabling you to maintain a safe body temperature.

When you are cold, less blood flows to your body surface, so that your core stays warm. That's why your hands, feet, and face can become so cool to the touch on a cold day.

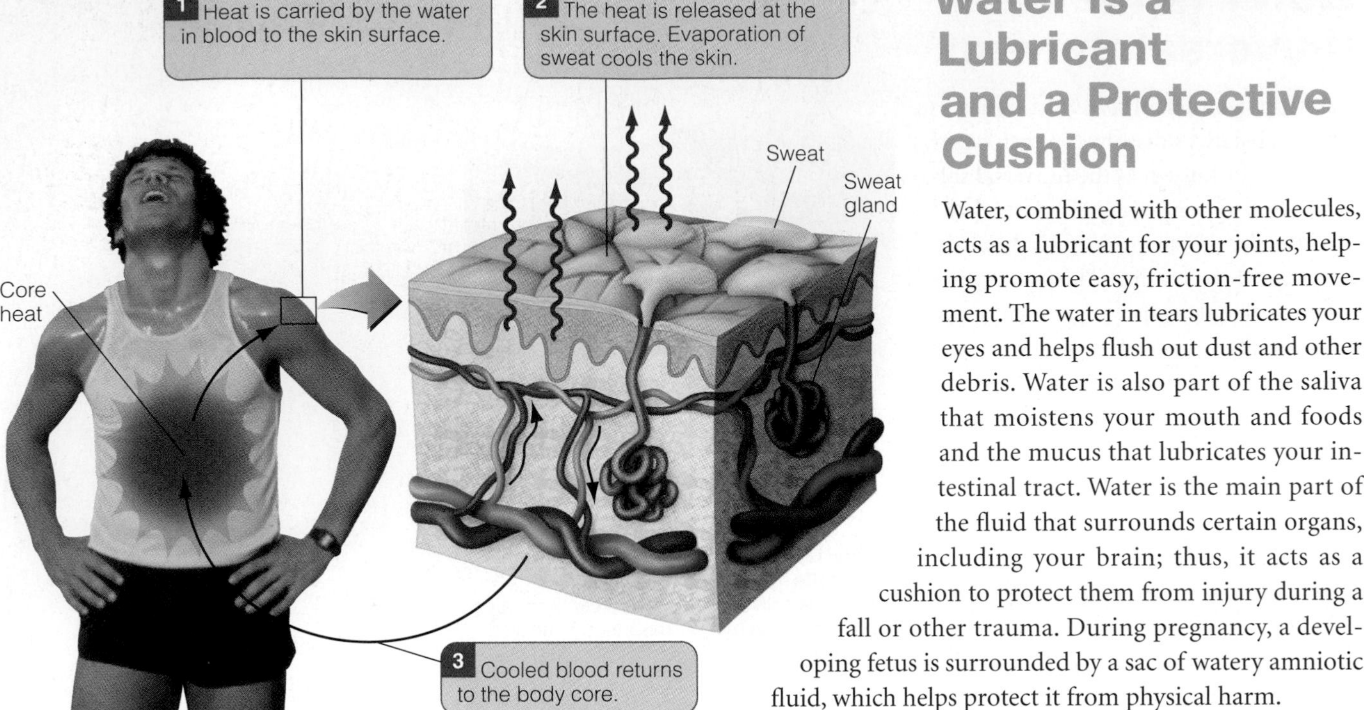

Figure 18.3 Water Helps Regulate Your Body Temperature

Water Is a Lubricant and a Protective Cushion

Water, combined with other molecules, acts as a lubricant for your joints, helping promote easy, friction-free movement. The water in tears lubricates your eyes and helps flush out dust and other debris. Water is also part of the saliva that moistens your mouth and foods and the mucus that lubricates your intestinal tract. Water is the main part of the fluid that surrounds certain organs, including your brain; thus, it acts as a cushion to protect them from injury during a fall or other trauma. During pregnancy, a developing fetus is surrounded by a sac of watery amniotic fluid, which helps protect it from physical harm.

The Take-Home Message **Your body is mostly water. Muscle tissue has more water than fat tissue. The water in your body cells is balanced by the water outside your cells. Electrolytes help maintain fluid balance. Water is a universal solvent that helps transport oxygen and nutrients throughout your body. It also absorbs and releases heat to regulate your body temperature, acts as a lubricant through saliva and mucus, and provides a protective cushion for your brain and other organs.**

What Is Water Balance and How Do You Maintain It?

When the amount of water you consume is equal to the amount you lose daily, you are in **water balance.** When you are not in water balance—that is, having too much or too little water in your system—health problems can occur. Thus, maintaining water balance is very important. There are several ways in which water is lost from your body and several mechanisms that help you replenish those losses. Let's look at how the whole process works.

water balance The state in which an equal amount of water is lost and replenished daily in the body.

You Take in Water through Beverages and Food

The first aspect of being in water balance is consuming enough water. You get most of your water from beverages, such as tap or bottled water, milk, juices, and soft drinks. You also get some water from the foods you eat, although much less in comparison (Figure 18.4). Even the driest foods, such as bread and uncooked oatmeal, provide some water. A small amount of water is also generated during metabolism.

A developing fetus is cushioned in a sac of watery amniotic fluid to protect it from physical harm.

You Lose Water through Your Kidneys, Large Intestine, Lungs, and Skin

The other aspect of water balance is excreting excess water, so that you don't have too much in your body. You normally lose water daily through these four routes:

- Via your kidneys in the form of urine
- Via intestinal fluids in your stool; the water lost in your stool is normally a small amount, unless you are experiencing diarrhea
- Via the water that evaporates when you exhale
- Via your skin when you release the heat produced in your body core

Loss of water through the evaporation of your breath and unconsciously through your skin is called *insensible water loss*, because it occurs without your noticing it. A person living in a moderate or temperate climate and doing little physical activity loses between ½ and 1 quart of water daily through insensible water loss.[2]

Insensible water loss doesn't include the water lost in sweat. As you learned earlier, sweating is your body's way of releasing a *higher than normal* amount of heat.

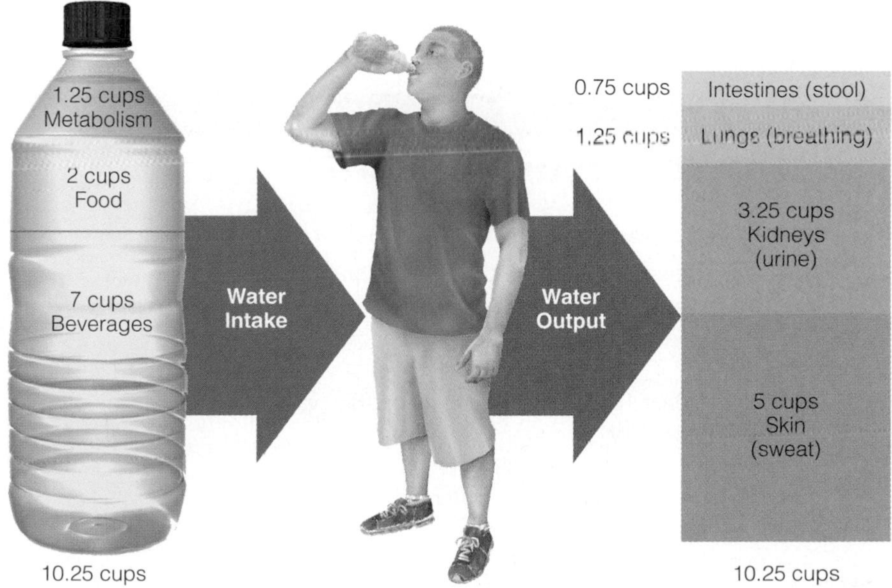

Figure 18.4 Water Intake and Output
You get most of your water from beverages and foods, although a small amount is also generated through the process of metabolism. You lose water in your urine, stool, sweat, and exhaled breath. If you are in water balance, the amount of water you take in is equal to the amount you excrete every day.

Water is vital for many body functions, but it isn't stored in your body, so it's important to take in enough water every day.

The amount of water lost during sweating varies greatly and depends on many environmental factors, such as the temperature, the humidity, the wind, the sun's intensity, the clothing you're wearing, and the amount of physical activity you're doing.[3] For example, if you jump rope in the noontime sun on a summer day wearing a winter coat, you'll soon be losing a lot of water as sweat. In contrast, little or no sweat will leave your body if you sit under a shady tree on a dry, cool day wearing a light T-shirt and slacks.

Losing Too Much Water Can Cause Dehydration

Dehydration is the state in which the body has too little water. It can result from not drinking enough fluids or from conditions that result in the loss of too much water (and sodium) from the body, such as diarrhea, vomiting, high fever, and the use of *diuretics* (substances that cause the body to lose water, such as alcohol or certain medications). If dehydration persists, a person can experience weight loss, dizziness, confusion, inability to perform normal physical activity, and, in extreme situations, death.[4]

Now that you know how serious dehydration can be, Rate Yourself to find out if you're getting enough fluid each day!

Your Thirst Mechanism Signals Dehydration

Have you ever been outside for a while on a hot day and noticed that your mouth was as dry as the Sahara Desert? The dry mouth is part of your **thirst mechanism** and is your body's way of telling you to find a water source—you are on the road to dehydration. The thirst mechanism plays an important role in helping you avoid dehydration and restore the water balance in your body.

The dry mouth that makes you thirsty when you are dehydrated is due to the increased concentration of electrolytes in your blood. As the concentration of these minerals increases, less water is available to your salivary glands to make saliva.[5] Thus, your mouth feels very dry.

RATE YOURSELF ★★★★★

How Are Your Fluid Levels?

Do you think you are consuming enough fluids each day? Rate Yourself to see.

1. Do you drink a glass (8 ounces) of orange juice or other juices in the morning? Yes ☐ No ☑
2. Do you have at least two cups (16 ounces) of coffee or tea daily? Yes ☐ No ☑
3. Do you drink at least 16 ounces (2 cups) of bottled water or water in a bottle daily? Yes ☑ No ☐
4. Do you drink 1–3 cups (8 ounces) of milk daily? Yes ☐ No ☑
5. Do you drink sports drinks, vitamin waters, or other "designer" waters daily? Yes ☑ No ☐

Answer

If you answered "yes" to at least four questions, it's likely that you are easily meeting your fluid needs.

dehydration The state in which there is too little water in the body due to too much water being lost, too little being consumed, or a combination of both.

thirst mechanism Various body reactions caused by dehydration, signaling you to drink fluids.

When you are dehydrated, the fluid volume in your blood decreases, resulting in a higher concentration of electrolytes—specifically, sodium—in your bloodstream. In response, the fluid inside your cells moves through the cell membrane to the outside of your cells and into your blood until the concentration of electrolytes inside and outside your cells is balanced (Figure 18.5). This causes your cells to shrink and can impair their function.

Your brain detects the increased concentration of electrolytes in your blood and triggers your thirst mechanism, reminding you to drink fluids. Your brain also triggers events that cause your kidneys to remove less water from your blood and thus concentrate your urine. These mechanisms work together to keep your body in water balance.

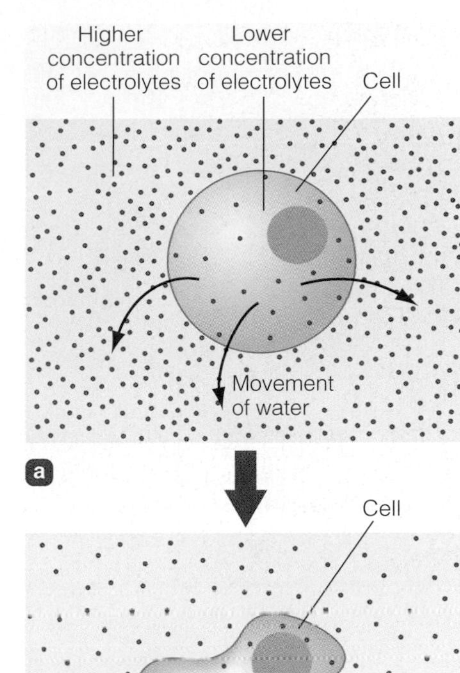

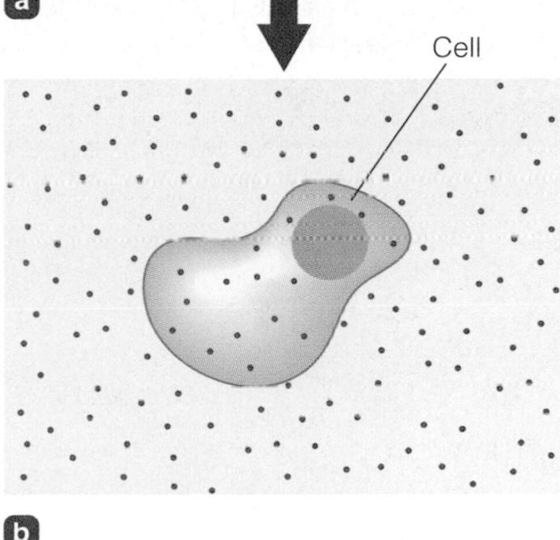

Figure 18.5 Dehydration
(**a**) Body cells become dehydrated when there are more electrolytes in the fluid surrounding them than in the fluid inside them. This high concentration of electrolytes attracts water. (**b**) As a result, water flows out of the cell. This restores balance to the concentration of electrolytes on each side of the cell but, in the process, dehydrates (dries out) the cell.

Other Ways to Tell If You Are Dehydrated

Just quenching your thirst will not necessarily provide enough fluids to remedy dehydration. In moderately active, healthy individuals, fluids from beverages and food throughout the day will eventually restore water balance.[6] However, elderly people, individuals who are very physically active or who have vigorous jobs (such as firefighters), and people who are experiencing certain conditions, such as fever, diarrhea, and/or vomiting, are at higher risk for dehydration. These individuals need to take additional steps to ensure that they are properly hydrated.

The cornerstone method to monitor hydration involves measuring body weight before and after long bouts of high physical activity or labor and noting any changes. If a person weighs less after an activity than before, the weight change is due to loss of body water, which must be replenished.

Urine color can also be used to assess hydration. When you are dehydrated, you produce less urine. The urine you do produce contains a higher proportion of metabolic wastes to a smaller volume of water. This causes the urine to be darker in color.[7] The National Athletic Trainers Association has created a chart to help individuals assess if they are drinking enough fluids to offset the amount of water lost through sweating (Figure 18.6).[8] If you are very physically active and the color of your urine darkens during the day, you likely need to drink more. (Note: Other factors, such as consuming excessive amounts of the B vitamin riboflavin and certain medications can also affect the color of urine.)

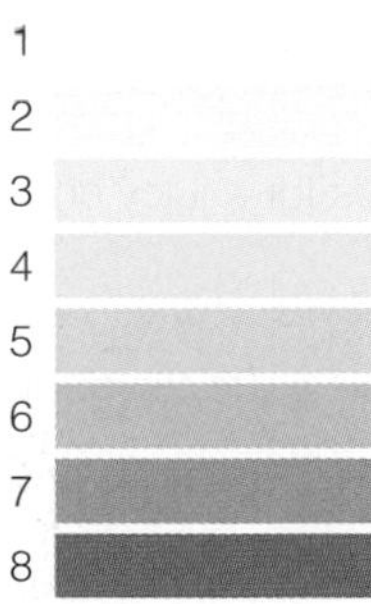

Figure 18.6 What the Color of Your Urine Can Reveal
The color of your urine can help you determine if you are drinking enough fluids to avoid dehydration. If you collect your urine in a cup and it looks like the color of 1 through 3 on the chart, you are well hydrated. If it resembles color 7 or is darker, you are dehydrated and need to drink more fluids.

Consuming Too Much Water Can Cause Hyponatremia

For healthy individuals who eat a balanced diet, it's hard to consume too much water, because the body will produce more urine to eliminate the excess. However, some people have experienced water toxicity in certain circumstances, particularly soldiers during military training and individuals who participate in endurance events, such as marathons.[9]

In an infamous example in April 2002, a 28-year-old woman named Cynthia Lucero was running the Boston Marathon. About 5 miles from the finish line, Lucero began to feel wobbly and told a friend that she felt dehydrated, even though she had been drinking fluids throughout her run. She suddenly collapsed and was taken to a nearby hospital. She died the next day—not of dehydration but of overhydration. The cause of her death was swelling of the brain brought on by too low a level of sodium in the blood, or *hyponatremia* (*hypo* = under; *natrium* = sodium; *emia* = blood).[10]

Although distance runners can overhydrate, dehydration is more common and a bigger challenge.

When swelling occurs in the brain, a person can experience symptoms similar to those of dehydration—fatigue, confusion, and disorientation.[11] Mistakenly treating these symptoms by taking in more fluids only makes matters worse.

Even though dehydration is more common and a bigger challenge to physically active people than overhydration, the seriousness of overhydration has prompted the USA Track & Field Association to revise its hydration guidelines for long-distance and marathon runners to avoid hyponatremia. Concept 26 will provide these guidelines and show you how to calculate how much fluid you need during exercise.

The Take-Home Message **You lose water daily through your kidneys, intestinal tract, lungs, and skin. If you lose more water than you take in, you will become dehydrated. Your thirst mechanism reminds you to drink fluids. Although rare, hyponatremia occurs and can be fatal.**

How Much Water Do You Need and What Are the Best Sources?

Your daily water requirements may be different from those of your grandparents, parents, and siblings, and even the classmate sitting next to you. The amount of water a person needs depends on environmental factors, such as the air temperature, as well as his or her diet and physical activity. (Recall from Concept 8 that, as you increase the fiber in your diet, you should increase your water consumption.)

The current recommendations for the amount of water you should consume daily are as follows:

- Healthy women should consume a total of about 12 cups of fluid daily, of which about 9 cups should be beverages. (The remaining 3 cups are provided in foods.)
- Healthy men should consume a total of about 16 cups of water daily, of which about 13 cups should be beverages.[12]

Very active people have higher water requirements because they lose more water by sweating.

If you think that sounds like a lot, keep in mind that a well-balanced 2,200-calorie diet that includes beverages at all meals and snacks provides about 12 cups of water.[13] Drinking milk, juices, and water, either from the tap or from a bottle, throughout the day can help you meet your needs. The box feature "Tap Water or Bottled Water: Is Bottled Better?" discusses some of the main differences and similarities between tap water and bottled water.

Contrary to popular belief, caffeinated beverages such as coffee, tea, and soft drinks contribute to your daily water needs. Caffeine is a diuretic, so it causes water to be excreted, but the water loss it causes is short lived. In other words, the caffeine doesn't cause a significant loss of body water over the course of a day. In fact, re-

TABLE TIPS

Bottoms Up

Drink low-fat or skim milk with each meal to add calcium as you meet your fluid needs.

Freeze grapes for a juicy and refreshing snack.

Add vegetable soup to your lunch for a fluid-packed meal.

Cool down with a sweet treat by spooning slightly thawed frozen strawberries onto low-fat vanilla ice cream or yogurt.

Add zip to a glass of water by adding a slice of fresh lemon or lime.

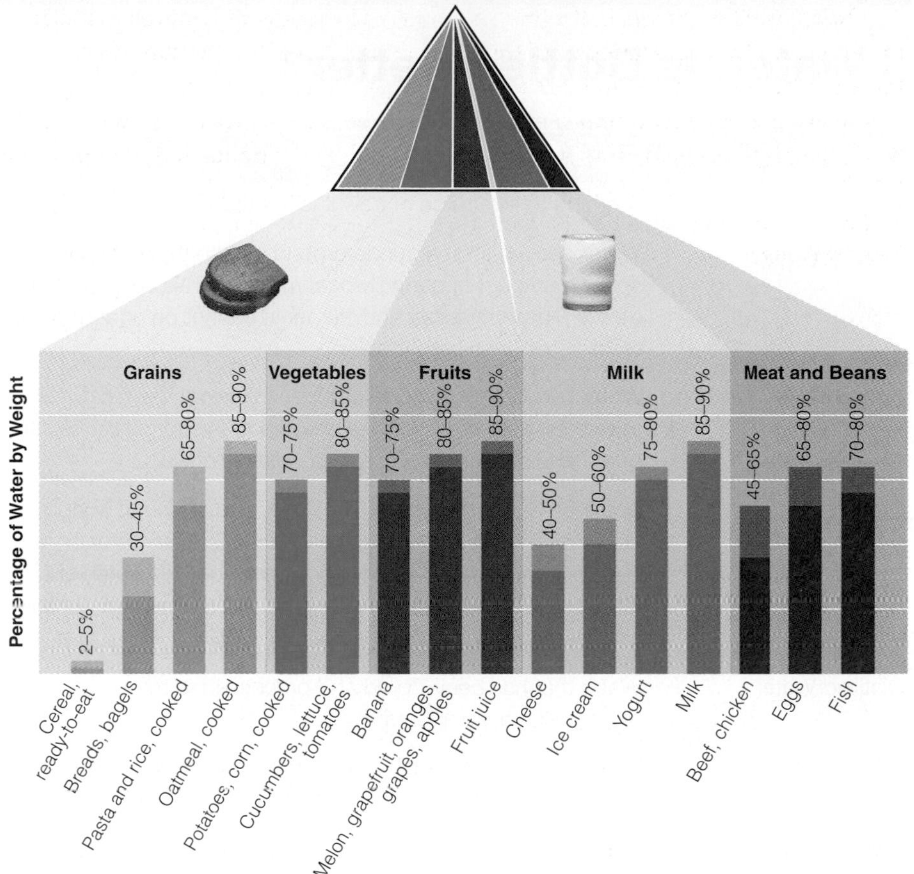

Figure 18.7 Water Content of Foods
Approximately 20 percent of the water you consume comes from foods. Cooked grains, fruits, and vegetables all contain a high percentage of water by weight.

Data from: A. Grandjean and S. Campbell, *Hydration: Fluids for Life* (Washington, D.C.: ILSI Press, 2004). www.ilsi.org.

search suggests that individuals who routinely consume caffeinated beverages develop a tolerance to its diuretic effect and experience less water loss over time.[14]

Even though caffeinated beverages can count as a water source, this doesn't mean you should start guzzling caffeinated colas and other soft drinks. Their high calorie and sugar contents can quickly have you drinking your way into a very unbalanced, high-calorie diet. These soft drinks also contain acids, which contribute to the erosion of tooth enamel.

The remaining 20 percent of your water can come from foods. All foods contain some water. Cooked hot cereals and many fruits and vegetables are robust sources of water (Figure 18.7).

The Take-Home Message **Healthy women should drink about 9 cups of water or other beverages daily, while healthy men should drink about 13 cups daily. Those who are very active will need more water to avoid dehydration. Caffeinated beverages contribute to your daily water needs.**

Tap Water or Bottled Water: Is Bottled Better?

What items do you *have* to have when you walk out the door in the morning? Your keys? Your student ID? Your wallet? What about a bottle of water? Would you ever leave home without it? Are you one of the many people, like Desiree from the beginning of this concept, who drink only bottled water because you think it is the only pure water? If you are, you're certainly not alone. But is bottled water really better or safer for you than tap water?

Desiree is wrong in her assumption that her bottled water is "pure." In fact, it's impossible to drink 100 percent *pure* water. Whether you fill your reusable water bottle from the tap or purchase bottled water, the water contains some impurities. However, this does not mean that the water is unsafe for most individuals to drink. (Individuals with a weakened immune system, such as those with HIV/AIDS, people with cancer undergoing chemotherapy, people who have undergone organ transplants, some elderly people, and infants can be particularly at risk from the contaminants in water. These individuals should ask their health care providers about drinking water. Precautions such as boiling their water—no matter the source—may be necessary.[1])

The source of any water, whether tap or bottled, varies from faucet to faucet and bottle to bottle, so it is virtually impossible to make a direct comparison. There are some basic points to understand about each type, though. Let's look at how tap and bottled water compare in terms of regulation, cost, and safety.

A Well of Sources for Bottled Water

Water can be classified according to its source or how it is treated prior to bottling.

Mineral Water	Water derived from an underground source that contains a specific amount of naturally occurring minerals and trace elements. These minerals and elements cannot be added to the water after it has been bottled.
Spring Water	Water obtained from underground water that flows naturally to the surface. The water is collected at the spring or the site of the well purposefully drilled to obtain this water.
Sparkling Water	Spring water that has carbon dioxide gas added to supply "bubbles" before it is bottled (also called seltzer water or club soda). This is not technically considered bottled water, but rather, a soft drink. Sparkling water does not have to adhere to FDA regulations for bottled water.
Distilled Water	Water that has been boiled and processed to remove most, but not all, contaminants.
Flavored Water	Water with a flavor, such as lemon or lime, added. It may also contain added sugars and calories.
Vitamin Water	Water with vitamins added to it. It may also contain added sugars and calories.

Data from: A. Bullers, "Bottled Water: Better Than Tap?" *FDA Consumer Magazine,* 2002 Center for Science in the Public Interest, "Water, Water . . . Everywhere," *Nutrition Action Health Letter* (June 2000).

Turn on the Tap

Most Americans obtain their drinking water from a community water system. The source of this municipal water can be underground wells or springs, rivers, lakes, or reservoirs. Regardless of the source, all municipal water is sent to a treatment plant, where any dirt and debris are filtered out, bacteria are killed, and other contaminants are removed. The Environmental Protection Agency (EPA) oversees the safety of public drinking water with national standards that set limits for more than 80 contaminants—either naturally occurring ones, such as bacteria, or humanmade ones, such as chemicals—that may find their way into your drinking water. Hundreds of billions of dollars have been invested in these treatment systems to ensure that the public water is safe to drink.[2]

Each year, the water supplier in your community must provide you with an annual report about the source and quality of your tap water. In fact, many of these regional reports can be accessed online at www.epa.gov.

Many municipalities add fluoride to their water. About two-thirds of the Americans who drink from public systems have fluoride in their water.[3] Fluoridation of public water has had a positive impact on the nation's dental health by reducing the incidence of dental caries.

Finally, tap water costs less than a penny a gallon, making it a very affordable way to stay hydrated.

Bottling Boom

Bottled water is second only to carbonated soft drinks in popularity among Americans. The per capita consumption of bottled water has doubled in the past decade and is expected to rise even more in the years to come.

Bottled water that is sold through interstate commerce is regulated by the Food and Drug Administration (FDA). Thus, as with other food products, manufacturers must adhere to specific FDA regulations, such as standards of identity. In other words, if the label on the bottle states that it is "spring water," the manufacturer must derive the water from a very specific source (see table). Interestingly, some bottled water may be from a municipal water source. (In fact, Desiree may be drinking municipal water in the bottles she purchases daily.) The bottled water must also adhere to a standard of quality set forth by the FDA, which specifies the maximum level of contaminants that can be in the water. The FDA sets its standards for bottled water based on the EPA's standards for public drinking water. However, water that is bottled and sold in the same state is not regulated by the FDA.[4]

The price of bottled water can be hefty, ranging from $1 to $4 a gallon. Desiree has a very expensive bottled water habit. She pays $1.50 per bottle and buys two bottles daily, so Desiree is shelling out over $20 a week and more than $80 monthly buying bottled water. Over the course of her nine months at college, she is spending over $750 on a beverage that she can get free from the campus water fountain. Finally, many bottled waters are not fluoridated, so you may be losing out on this important cavity fighter if this is your main source of drinking water.[5]

Keep in mind that reusing the bottles from bottled water is not advised. The plastic containers cannot withstand repeated washing and the plastic can actually break down, causing chemicals to leach into the water. Sturdier water bottles that are designed for reuse must be thoroughly cleaned with hot, soapy water after each use to kill germs.

The bottom line is that both tap water and bottled water can be safe to drink. Your choice is likely to come down to personal preference and costs. The following table summarizes the similarities and differences between the two types of water.

Bottled vs Tap Water: A Summary

Bottled Water	Tap Water
Cost to Consumers	
■ Bottled water costs about $1 to $4 per gallon.	■ Tap water costs about $0.003 per gallon.
Safety	
■ Bottled water is generally safe. ■ Some bottled water is not tested for contaminants. ■ Only bottled water sold across state lines is regulated by the FDA. ■ Bottled water not sold across state lines is regulated only by state and local agencies.	■ Municipal (tap) water is regulated and monitored by federal, state, and local agencies. ■ EPA guidelines require that the public have access to water quality reports and be notified if water quality falls outside established safety boundaries.
Benefits to Consumers	
■ The packaging of bottled water may make it more convenient than tap water. ■ Bottled water may taste better than tap water.	■ Tap water is freely available from the faucet. ■ Most tap water contains fluoride, which helps prevent tooth decay.

UCook

Vegetable Soup Italiano

Slurping some of your liquids as soup is a good way to help meet your fluid needs. Enjoy this easy-to-make soup to help you get there!

UDo

Is Your Wallet Water Logged?

Are you spending more than you think on bottled water? Log on to our website for a handy way to keep track of your bottled water spending.

The Top Five Points to Remember

1. Your body is mostly water. Both water and electrolytes contribute to fluid balance. Water is an important solvent that helps transport oxygen, nutrients, and other substances throughout your body and waste products away from your cells. It helps regulate your body temperature and cushion your organs. Combined with other substances to form saliva and mucus, it acts as a lubricant in your mouth and intestines.
2. You take in water through foods and beverages. You lose water in your urine, stool, and sweat. You also lose water through evaporation from your skin and through respiration, as part of your exhaled breath. This is called insensible water loss. When the amount of water you consume is equal to the amount you lose daily, you are in water balance.
3. Losing too much water can result in dehydration. Your body can be dehydrated even if you do not feel particularly thirsty. On the other hand, consuming too much water can result in hyponatremia, a condition caused by a dangerously low level of sodium in the blood.
4. Healthy women should consume 9 cups of beverages, and healthy men should drink approximately 13 cups of beverages, daily. Caffeinated beverages, juices, and milk all count toward meeting your fluid needs.
5. Both tap and bottled waters can be safe to drink. Fluoride is often added to water that comes from the tap, while bottled water typically does not contain added fluoride. In the United States, bottled water is no safer or more pure than tap water, but some people prefer the taste of bottled or specialty water.

Test Yourself

1. The most abundant substance in your body is
   a. magnesium.
   b. fat
   c. sodium.
   d. water.
2. In your body, minerals called electrolytes
   a. help maintain fluid balance.
   b. destroy harmful agents in lymph.
   c. make up as much as 14 to 17 percent of the body.
   d. do all of the above.
3. A source of insensible water loss is
   a. urine
   b. feces.
   c. sweat.
   d. none of the above.
4. Which of the following statements about daily fluid intake is true?
   a. Women should drink about 12 cups of water daily.
   b. Women should drink about 9 cups of beverages daily.
   c. Drinking coffee, tea, or cola drinks does not contribute to your daily fluid intake.
   d. Only beverages, not foods, count toward your daily fluid intake.
5. Which of the following statements about bottled water is true?
   a. All bottled water sold in the United States is regulated by the FDA.
   b. All bottled water is tested for contaminants.
   c. Bottled water can cost over a thousand times more than tap water.
   d. All of the above are true.

Answers

1. (d) Your body is 60 percent water. Water bathes the trillions of cells in your body and is part of the fluid inside your cells where reactions take place. Fats make up between 20 and 29 percent of your body. Both magnesium and sodium are major minerals in your body but are not as abundant as water.
2. (a) Minerals called electrolytes help maintain fluid balance in your body. Defensive cells in lymph nodes destroy harmful agents in lymph fluid. Proteins make up about 14 to 17 percent of your body. Minerals make up less than 5 percent.

3. (d) The sources of insensible water loss are respiration and the evaporation of moisture from the skin during the normal maintenance of body temperature. Urine, feces, and sweat are observable sources of water loss, and thus are not considered insensible.
4. (b) Although women need about 12 total cups of fluid daily, a portion of this is provided by the water in foods. They should drink about 9 cups of beverages daily. These beverages are not restricted to water. Other beverages, including coffee, tea, cola, and other caffeinated drinks, count toward meeting fluid needs.
5. (c) If you drink bottled water, you must have money to burn, because it can cost over a thousand times more than tap water: $1 to $4 per gallon versus less than a cent per gallon. Only bottled water sold across state lines is regulated by the FDA. Some bottled water is not tested for contaminants.

Web Resources

- For more on the FDA and its regulations regarding bottled water, visit: www.cfsan.fda.gov/~dms/ffbotwat
- For more on the EPA and its role in regulating water, visit: www.epa.gov/ow/

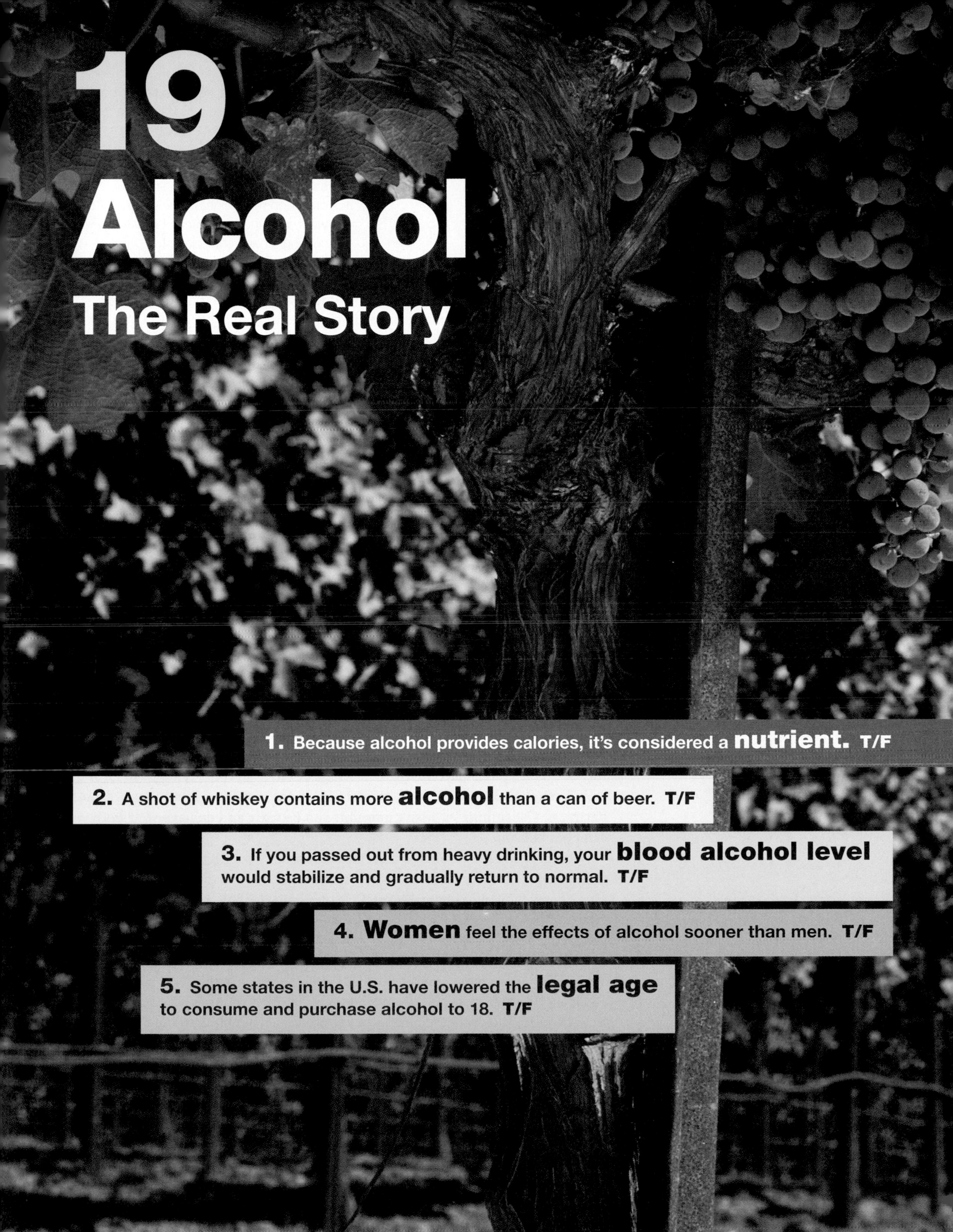

19 Alcohol

The Real Story

1. Because alcohol provides calories, it's considered a **nutrient.** T/F

2. A shot of whiskey contains more **alcohol** than a can of beer. T/F

3. If you passed out from heavy drinking, your **blood alcohol level** would stabilize and gradually return to normal. T/F

4. **Women** feel the effects of alcohol sooner than men. T/F

5. Some states in the U.S. have lowered the **legal age** to consume and purchase alcohol to 18. T/F

Twenty-one-year-old Leah's brother, Steve, says he needs a few drinks every day to relax. When he gets home from work, he is often anxious or grouchy but becomes "human" again, as Leah puts it, after several beers. Sometimes he drinks his dinner, making a meal out of a second six-pack instead of eating a real meal. His girlfriend broke up with him because he drank too much.

Steve has tried to cut back on the amount of beer he drinks, but once he gets started he can't seem to stop. When he tried to give up drinking cold turkey, he became anxious, shaky, and nauseated and broke out in cold sweats. He has become physically and emotionally dependent on alcohol to "steady his nerves." Leah knows these symptoms all too well. Steve's drinking patterns and behaviors mimic her father's, who died of cirrhosis of the liver when he was 62. And according to her mother, Steve and Leah's grandfather "drank himself to his grave."

Although Leah doesn't consider herself a heavy drinker, she has a beer after dinner on most nights. She's starting to worry that those weeknight beers is becoming a habit she can't stop.

Leah is right to be worried—her brother has the four classic symptoms of a drinking problem, and she is at increased risk of following in her brother's footsteps. Do you know what the four symptoms are and why she should be concerned about her own alcohol intake? In this concept, we will discuss some forms of alcohol use and abuse, and their potential health effects.

Answers

1. False. Your body doesn't need alcohol to survive; although it contains calories, it's not considered a nutrient. See page 2 for more.
2. False. A straight shot of liquor may look and taste more potent than a can of beer, but it isn't. To learn more, turn to page 3.
3. False. The alcohol in your stomach and small intestine would continue to be absorbed, your blood alcohol concentration would continue to rise, and you could die from alcohol poisoning. See pages 5 and 6 for details.
4. True. Women respond more quickly to the effects of alcohol than do men. To find out why, turn to page 6.
5. False. Decades ago, some states lowered their legal drinking age, but today you must be 21 to legally purchase and consume alcohol in the United States. You may be surprised why this age was selected. Turn to page 17 to learn more.

Your body doesn't need alcohol to survive. Therefore, alcohol is not an essential nutrient. Other than calories, you don't gain any nutrition from drinking alcohol. While it's legally sold in the United States to adults, teenagers often feel intense social pressure to consume it. Some medical reports say that, in moderation, it can be good for you, while others say that drinking too much of it can kill you. What's the real story about alcohol? Let's find out.

What Is Alcohol and Why Do People Drink It?

What is the first image that comes to your mind when you hear the word *alcohol*? Do you imagine a bottle of beer, a glass of wine, or a rum and coke? Technically, these beverages aren't alcohol by themselves, but they all contain a type of alcohol called **ethanol.** Although it's considered safe for consumption, ethanol is not harmless. Consuming excessive amounts can be toxic and damage your body. It can even kill you.

Ethanol is made through the **fermentation** of yeast and the natural sugars in grains and fruits. The yeast breaks down the sugar into ethanol and carbon dioxide. The carbon dioxide evaporates, leaving an alcohol-containing beverage. Grapes provide the sugar for making wine, whereas grains provide the sugar when producing beer.

Liquors, such as rum, scotch, and whiskey, are made through a process called *distillation* and are more accurately called distilled spirits.[1] In the distillation process, an alcoholic beverage is heated, causing the ethanol to vaporize. The vapor is collected, cooled, and condensed into a very concentrated liquid called liquor.

ethanol The type of alcohol in alcoholic beverages, such as wine, beer, and liquor.

fermentation The process by which yeast converts sugars in grains or fruits into ethanol and carbon dioxide, resulting in an alcoholic beverage.

People Drink Alcohol to Relax, Celebrate, and Socialize

People around the world drink alcohol in many different forms and for many different reasons. The sake (rice wine) of Japan is used during tea and Shinto ceremonies, while the dark beer of the Irish is consumed when pub patrons celebrate their favorite sport. Russian vodka and Napa Valley chardonnay are consumed for relaxation and pleasure. Globally, wine is part of many religious traditions, including the Catholic Mass and the Jewish Sabbath, and in some cultures, it's the beverage of choice during the main meal of the day.

In the United States, more than half of adults consume at least one alcoholic beverage per month.[2] Like many people around the world, Americans drink alcohol to relax, celebrate, and socialize. Alcohol helps us loosen up because it's a drug that affects the conscious mind. Within minutes of sipping an alcoholic beverage, a person feels more relaxed. After a few more sips, a mild, pleasant euphoria sets in and inhibitions begin to loosen. By the end of the first or second drink, a person will often feel more outgoing, happy, and social. This initial effect prompts many people to seek out more and continue to drink alcohol.

Having a drink with another person also symbolizes social bonding.[3] When celebrating a special occasion, pubs and restaurants are common gathering spots, and alcoholic drinks are usually served.

Beer is made from the fermentation of yeast and the natural sugars from grains.

Moderate Alcohol Consumption May Have Health Benefits

Some people drink alcohol because of its health benefits. That's right: Studies have suggested that *moderate alcohol consumption* may reduce the risk for heart disease, and the risk of dying in general, for middle-aged and older adults.[4] Moderate alcohol consumption is defined as up to one standard drink for women and up to two drinks daily for men. A standard drink is any one of the following:

- one 12-ounce serving of beer
- one 1.5-ounce shot of liquor
- one 5-ounce glass of wine

Each of these contains about half an ounce of alcohol (Figure 19.1).

The health benefits of alcoholic beverages have been linked to phytochemicals in red wine and dark beer, as well as to the alcohol itself. Red wine and dark beer contain flavonoids, phytochemicals, and antioxidants that can help reduce the build-up of LDL ("bad") cholesterol in arteries. Alcohol also helps inhibit the stickiness of platelets in the blood and increases the level of heart-protective "good" HDL cholesterol. However, some studies comparing various alcohol sources have found that most of the heart-protective effects are due to the alcohol content, regardless of the source.[5] In other words, a beer, a glass of cabernet, and a shot of scotch all may have similar heart-protective effects.

Figure 19.1 What Is a Standard Drink? One standard drink of beer (12 ounces), liquor (1.5 ounces), or wine (5 ounces) contains the same amount of alcohol.

Before you crack open a beer to celebrate, however, be aware that the people who gain the health benefits from moderate alcohol consumption are women age 55

Light beer has about the same amount of alcohol as regular beer.

and older and men age 45 and older. Alcohol consumption by younger people has not been shown to provide many—if any—health benefits. In fact, drinking alcohol during younger years increases the risk for injuries and violent, traumatic deaths, which offsets any possible health benefits of the alcohol.[6]

Moderate drinkers need to watch out for (1) the size of their drinks and (2) the frequency of their drinking. We've just said that a standard drink contains about .5 ounce of alcohol. If your 8-ounce wine glass gets filled to the brim, or you chug an oversize mug of beer, you could consume close to two standard drinks in one glass or mug (Figure 19.2). One rum and coke can provide the equivalent of over 2½ alcoholic drinks. Another important point to remember is that abstaining from drinking through the week and then having seven drinks on a single Friday night does not count as moderate drinking. When it comes to alcohol, no "banking" is allowed.

The Take-Home Message **Ethanol is the type of alcohol consumed in alcoholic beverages. Alcoholic beverages are made by the processes of fermentation and distillation. People drink alcohol to relax, celebrate, and socialize. Moderate alcohol consumption may provide health benefits to some older adults. Abstaining from alcohol for several days and then drinking a lot at once is not moderate drinking.**

12 oz
(1 drink)

16 oz
(1 1/3 drink)

5 oz
(1 drink)

8 oz
(1 1/2 drink)

Figure 19.2 When a Drink Is More Than a Drink
Depending on the amount, one drink may actually be the equivalent of 1⅓ to 1½ drinks.

What Happens to Alcohol in the Body?

Because alcohol is a toxin, the body quickly works to break it down and eliminate it. Let's follow a swallow of beer through your digestive system and see how it's handled along the way (Figure 19.3).

You Absorb Alcohol in Your Stomach and Small Intestine

Within seconds of your first sip of beer, alcohol enters your blood. This is because alcohol is one of those rare substances that can be absorbed directly into the bloodstream through the stomach. About 20 percent of the alcohol you consume is absorbed in your stomach. The rest, about 80 percent, is absorbed in your small intestine.

The amount and type of food in the stomach determine how long alcohol lingers there before entering your small intestine. Herein lies the logic behind advice to avoid drinking alcohol on an empty stomach. If your swallow of beer chases a bacon cheeseburger and fries, the alcohol will take longer to leave your stomach than if you drank the beer by itself. Fat also slows down the departure of food from the stomach, so the large amount of fat in the burger meal will help delay the alcohol's arrival into your small intestine.

Without food in your stomach, alcohol rapidly moves into and is absorbed through your small intestine and enters your blood. However, while a full stomach will delay the arrival of alcohol in the small intestine, the alcohol will still eventually get there. If a person drinks several glasses of beer with dinner, the alcohol will be absorbed once the stomach starts emptying. Intoxication could be an unexpected postdinner surprise.

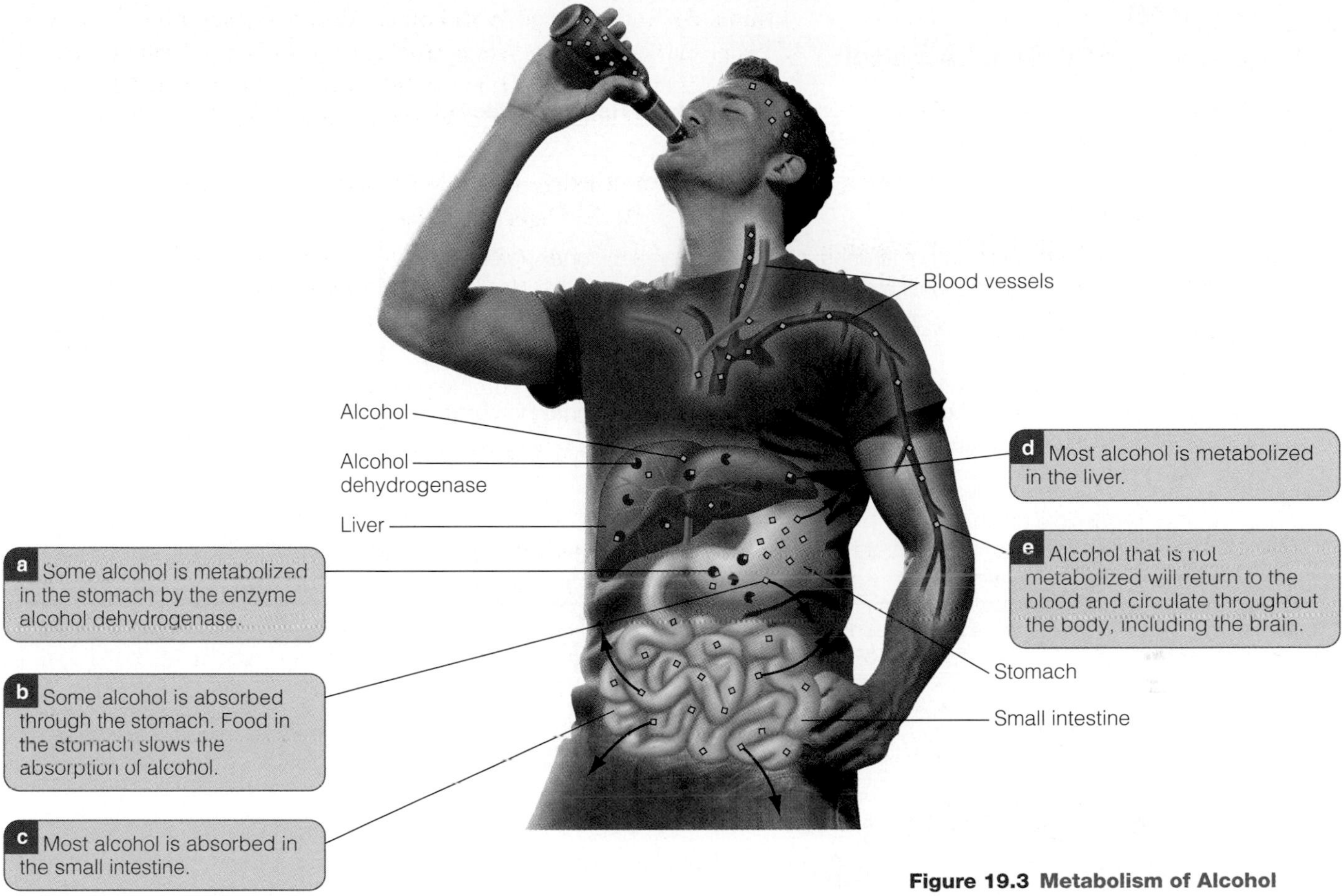

Blood vessels

Alcohol

Alcohol dehydrogenase

Liver

a Some alcohol is metabolized in the stomach by the enzyme alcohol dehydrogenase.

b Some alcohol is absorbed through the stomach. Food in the stomach slows the absorption of alcohol.

c Most alcohol is absorbed in the small intestine.

d Most alcohol is metabolized in the liver.

e Alcohol that is not metabolized will return to the blood and circulate throughout the body, including the brain.

Stomach

Small intestine

Figure 19.3 Metabolism of Alcohol

You Metabolize Alcohol Primarily in Your Liver

Some alcohol is metabolized in your stomach by an enzyme called *alcohol dehydrogenase.* But most of the alcohol is metabolized in your liver. Enzymes in the liver—most importantly, alcohol dehydrogenase—break down about one alcoholic drink in about 1½ to 2 hours. Regardless of the amount consumed, the metabolism of alcohol occurs at a steady rate in your body.

Alcohol Circulates in Your Blood

If your liver cannot handle the amount of alcohol you've consumed all at once, some of it will enter your bloodstream and be distributed in the watery tissues in your body. Although the liver will eventually metabolize most of the alcohol, a small amount will leave your body intact through your breath and urine.

Your **blood alcohol concentration** (**BAC**) is the amount of alcohol in your blood, measured in grams of alcohol per deciliter of blood, usually expressed as a percentage.[7] The more you drink, the higher your BAC. Because alcohol infiltrates your brain, as your BAC increases, so does your level of mental impairment and intoxication.

The amount of alcohol in your breath correlates with the amount of alcohol in your blood. For this reason, a Breathalyzer test can be used to measure a person's BAC. A Breathalyzer may be used by police officers who suspect that a person has consumed too much alcohol.

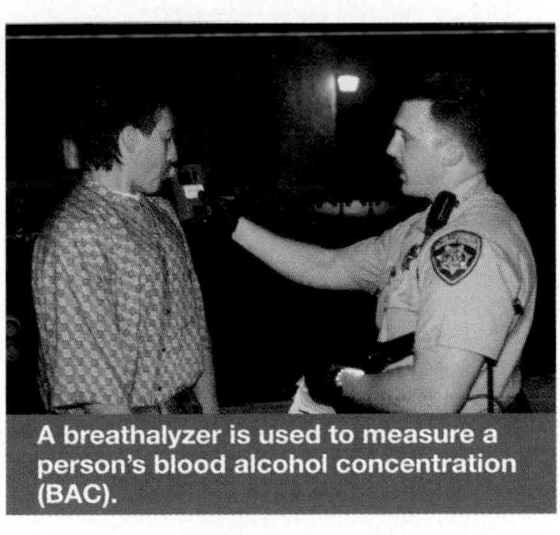

A breathalyzer is used to measure a person's blood alcohol concentration (BAC).

blood alcohol concentration (BAC) The measurement of the amount of alcohol in your blood. BAC is measured in grams of alcohol per deciliter of blood, usually expressed as a percentage.

Table 19.1

Progressive Effects of Alcohol

Blood Alcohol Concentration	Changes in Feelings and Personality	Brain Regions Affected	Impaired Functions (continuum)
0.01–0.05	Relaxation, sense of well-being, loss of inhibition	Cerebral cortex	Alertness, judgment
0.06–0.10	Pleasure, numbing of feelings, nausea, sleepiness, emotional arousal	Cerebral cortex, forebrain	Coordination (especially fine motor skills), visual tracking
0.11–0.20	Mood swings, anger, sadness, mania	Cerebral cortex, forebrain, cerebellum	Reasoning and depth perception, appropriate social behavior
0.21–0.30	Aggression, reduced sensations, depression, stupor	Cerebral cortex, forebrain, cerebellum, brain stem	Speech, balance, temperature regulation
0.31–0.40	Unconsciousness, coma, possible death	Entire brain	Bladder control, breathing
0.41 and greater	Death		Heart rate

Data from: National Institute on Alcohol Abuse and Alcoholism. 2003. Understanding Alcohol: Investigations into Biology and Behavior. http://science.education.nih.gov/supplements/nih3/alcohol/default.htm.

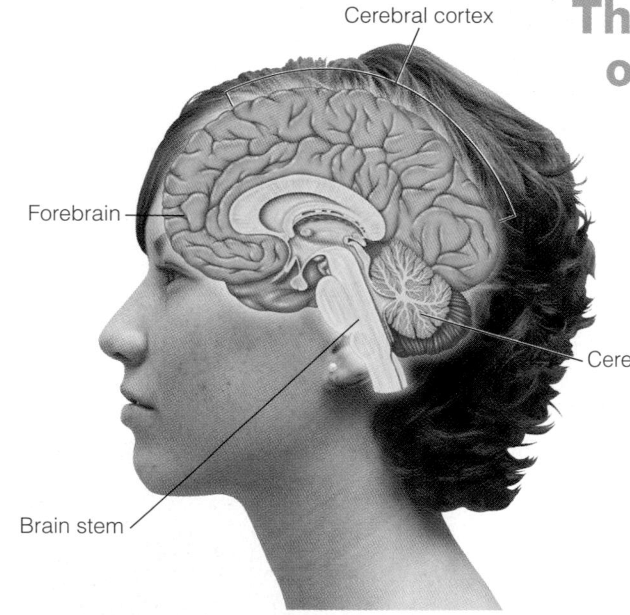

Figure 19.4 The Brain and Alcohol As you consume more alcohol, additional areas of your brain are affected. Your cerebral cortex is affected first, followed by your forebrain, cerebellum, and brain stem. The greater your alcohol intake, the greater the physical and behavioral changes in your body.

The Effects of Alcohol on Your Brain

Alcohol is a *depressant*, a substance that slows the transmission of nerve impulses. Your brain is very sensitive to the depressant effect of alcohol. For instance, alcohol slows down your reaction time to stimuli (such as a car coming toward you on the road), confuses your thoughts, impairs your judgment, and induces sleepiness.

The more you drink, the more areas of the brain are affected. Table 19.1 and Figure 19.4 show how increasing BAC levels impact specific areas of the brain, and how body movements and behaviors are affected. (Note: A person's BAC can continue to rise even after unconsciousness.) If enough alcohol has been consumed, the activities of the brain stem, which controls breathing and heart rate, can be suppressed, ultimately causing death.

Women Are More Susceptible Than Men to the Effects of Alcohol

In essence, every alcoholic beverage that a man consumes is equivalent to about 1⅓ alcoholic beverages for a woman. Two factors contribute to women's greater susceptibility to alcohol:

- Women have about 20 to 30 percent less alcohol dehydrogenase in their stomachs, so more alcohol enters the blood immediately through women's stomachs.[8]
- Women have less muscle mass, and thus less body water. (Recall from Concept 18 that muscle tissue has a higher percentage of water than fat.) Because alcohol mixes in water, people with more muscle are able to distribute more of the alcohol throughout their bodies than are people who have more fat.

Because of these factors, women will feel alcohol's effects sooner than men. Women take note: It's dangerous to try to keep up, drink for drink, with male companions. You will begin to feel the effects of alcohol long before they will.

The Take-Home Message **Alcohol is absorbed in your stomach and small intestine and is metabolized primarily in your liver. Your gender, your body type, the amount of food in your stomach, and the quantity of alcohol you consume, all affect the rate of absorption and metabolism in your body. Blood alcohol concentration (BAC) is the measurement of alcohol in your blood. Alcohol is a depressant. Because your brain is sensitive to alcohol, alcohol affects your behavior.**

How Can Alcohol Be Harmful?

Although alcohol is often advertised in magazines, on billboards, and in television commercials as a trendy and sexy way to relax and socialize (see the box feature "Alcohol and Advertising"), it can cause a number of problems for those who abuse it. Some of these problems merely cause temporary discomfort, but other long-term effects can be extremely damaging to health.

Alcohol Can Disrupt Sleep and Cause Hangovers

Many people wrongly think that a drink before bed will help them sleep better, but it will actually have the opposite effect. Although having a drink within an hour before bed may help you fall asleep sooner, it will disrupt your sleep cycle, cause you to awaken in the middle of the night, and make returning to sleep a challenge.[9] You will feel tired the next morning, which will make it harder for you to pay attention to what you are learning in class, and you may doze off by the end of the lecture. Even a moderate amount of alcohol consumed at dinner or even late in the afternoon during happy hour can disrupt that evening's sleep.

If you have a bad night's sleep, it's not a good idea to drink alcohol the next day. Studies have shown that a night of sleep disruption followed by even small amounts of alcohol the next day reduces the reaction time and alertness in individuals performing a simulated driving test. Being tired and then drinking alcohol exacerbates alcohol's sedating effect.[10]

A *hangover* is your body's way of saying, "Don't do that to me again." After a bout of heavy drinking, individuals can experience hangover symptoms ranging from a pounding headache, fatigue, nausea, and increased thirst to a rapid heartbeat, tremors, sweating, dizziness, depression, anxiety, and irritability. A hangover begins within hours of your last drink, as your BAC begins to drop. The symptoms will appear in full force once all the alcohol is gone from your blood, and these symptoms can linger for up to an additional 24 hours.[11] In other words, a few hours of excessive alcohol consumption on a Saturday night can not only ruin your entire Sunday but even disrupt part of your Monday.

There are several ways that alcohol contributes to the symptoms of a hangover. Alcohol is a diuretic, so it can cause dehydration and, thus, electrolyte imbalances.

Alcohol and Advertising

Advertising for alcoholic beverages is pervasive and persuasive. You need only drive down a major highway or turn on your television to see billboards or commercials for a beer or liquor brand. In some media, including popular magazines (such as *Rolling Stone* and *Sports Illustrated*), alcohol ads can outnumber nonalcohol ads by almost 3 to 1.[1]

Companies that make alcoholic beverages pay large sums of money to create and show these ads for one reason: They work. Studies have shown that advertisements for alcoholic beverages are associated with an increase in drinking among adolescents. Many ads emphasize sexual and social stereotypes. When targeted to underage drinkers, this type of message has been shown to increase adolescents' desire to emulate those portrayed in the advertisements.[2]

Alcohol ads need to be viewed with caution, as their messages are often misleading and in some cases blatantly false. Let's take a look at the messages and realities in a typical alcohol advertisement that might appear in a magazine.

Data from: Text courtesy of Dr. William R. Miller, University of New Mexico Center on Alcoholism, Substance Abuse and Addictions (CASAA).

Vomiting and sweating during or after excessive drinking further contribute to dehydration, and increased production of stomach acid and other digestive secretions can cause stomach pain, nausea, and vomiting.

Forget the old wives' tale of consuming an alcoholic beverage to "cure" a hangover. Drinking more alcohol, even if it is mixed with tomato or orange juice, only prolongs the recovery time. In fact, time is the only true remedy for hangover symptoms. Although aspirin and ibuprofen can ease a headache, these medications can also contribute to stomachache and nausea. Also, taking acetaminophen (Tylenol) during or after alcohol consumption, when the alcohol is being metabolized, has been shown to intensify this pain reliever's toxicity to the liver and may cause liver damage.[12] In short, time is the only true remedy for hangover symptoms. The best strategy is to avoid a hangover by limiting the amount of alcohol consumed.

Coffee will not **sober you up.** An intoxicated person who drinks coffee will end up being a stimulated drunk. It takes time to get sober because your liver has to metabolize the alcohol that was consumed.

Alcohol Can Interact with Hormones

Recall from Concept 7 that hormones are chemical messengers that regulate lots of important functions in your body. Alcohol negatively affects certain bone-strengthening hormones in a way that can increase your risk for osteoporosis.[13] In women, alcohol can also increase the levels of the reproductive hormone estrogen. This effect may increase the risk for breast cancer.[14] Drinking alcohol can also affect other reproductive hormones and is associated with both male and female sexual dysfunction.

Alcohol May Lead to Overnutrition and Malnutrition

At 7 calories per gram, alcohol provides fewer calories than fat (9 calories per gram) but more than either carbohydrates or protein (4 calories per gram each). And unless you are drinking a straight shot of liquor, your alcoholic beverages contain additional calories (see Figure 19.5). For example, a rum and coke contains the calories from both the rum and the coke, making the drink more than three times as high in calories as the rum itself. Depending on the mixers and ingredients added to your beverage, its calorie count can escalate to that of a meal. A mudslide, made with vodka, Irish cream, coffee liqueur, ice cream, and cream, should be ordered from the dessert menu and served with a spoon.

If you consistently add extra calories from alcoholic beverages—or any food or beverage source—to a diet that is already meeting your daily calorie needs, you will gain weight. Excessive consumption of alcohol has also been shown to increase fat and weight around the stomach. Although this is usually referred to as a "beer" belly, extra calories from any type of alcoholic beverage can contribute to a paunch. If high-calorie "bar foods" are consumed with the drinks, the calories can add up even more rapidly (Figure 19.6).

Compensating for calories in alcoholic beverages by cutting out more nutritious foods will cause you to fall short of your nutrient needs. If you drink a daily glass of beer instead of an equal amount of low-fat milk, your waist may not suffer, but your bones can. You will rob yourself of the calcium and vitamin D that the milk, but not the beer, provides. A chronic substitution of excessive amounts of alcohol for nutritious foods in the diet can lead to malnutrition.

Excessive alcohol consumption can also affect how the body handles the essential nutrients it actually gets. Routinely drinking too much alcohol can interfere with the absorption and/or use of protein, zinc, magnesium, and many vitamins. As you have learned, a chronic deficiency of nutrients can cause a cascade of ill health conditions and diseases.

Figure 19.5 Calories in Selected Alcoholic Drinks

Beer
Serving size: 12 oz
Alcohol servings: 1
Calories per drink: 150

Light Beer
Serving size: 12 oz
Alcohol servings: 1
Calories per drink: 110

Distilled Spirits (Whiskey, Vodka, Gin, Rum)
Serving size: 1.5 oz
Alcohol servings: 1
Calories per drink: 100

Red or White Wine
Serving size: 5 oz
Alcohol servings: 1
Calories per drink: 100–105

Cosmopolitan
Serving size: 2.5 oz
Alcohol servings: 1.7
Calories per drink: 131

Mudslide
Serving size: 12 oz
Alcohol servings: 4
Calories per drink: 820

◄ **Bloody Mary**
Serving size: 5.5 oz
Alcohol serving: 1
Calories per drink: 97

Margarita ►
Serving size: 6.3 oz
Alcohol servings: 3
Calories per drink: 327

◄ **Rum and Coke**
Serving size: 12 oz
Alcohol servings: 2.7
Calories per drink: 361

Note: Alcohol servings are per beverage.

Data from: U.S. Department of Agriculture. 2005. 2005 Report of the Dietary Guidelines Advisory Committee. www.health.gov/dietaryguidelines/dga2005/report/ (accessed January 2009).

Dinner 1

- 4 oz grilled chicken breast
- 3/4 cup mashed potatoes
- 1 1/2 cup steamed carrots
- 2 oz whole wheat dinner roll
- 4 tsp soft margarine
- 1 cup fat-free milk

Calories	724
Total fat (g)	28
Saturated fat (g)	8
Cholesterol (mg)	89

Dinner 2

- 5 12-oz beers
- 1 large serving nachos with cheese
- 8 BBQ chicken wings
- 1 handful goldfish crackers

Calories	1,719
Total fat (g)	51
Saturated fat (g)	16
Cholesterol (mg)	154

Figure 19.6 Too Much Alcohol Costs You Good Nutrition
A dinner of several alcoholic beverages and bar foods not only adds calories, fat, and saturated fat to your diet but also displaces healthier foods that would provide better nutrition.

Figure 19.7 Stages of Alcohol Liver Disease

Alcohol Can Harm Your Digestive Organs, Heart, and Liver

Alcohol inhibits the ability of the esophagus to contract. This enables the acidic juices in the stomach to flow back up into the esophagus, causing inflammation. Chronic inflammation can be a stepping-stone to esophageal cancer. If you smoke when you drink, your chances of developing esophageal cancer, as well as mouth and throat cancer, are even higher, as the alcohol enhances the ability of cigarettes to promote cancer.[15] Heavy drinkers also have increased incidences of *gastritis* (inflammation of the stomach) and stomach ulcers.[16]

Excessive amounts of alcohol can also affect the beating and rhythm of the heart, which likely plays a role in the sudden deaths of some alcoholics.[17] It can damage heart tissue and increase the risk for hypertension, which is a risk factor for both heart disease and stroke.

Alcohol can also damage your liver and cause *alcoholic liver disease.* The disease develops in three stages, although some stages can occur simultaneously (Figure 19.7):

- The first stage of the disease is *fatty liver*, which can result from just a few days of excessive drinking. Because alcohol metabolism takes top priority in the liver, the metabolism of other nutrients, including fats, is delayed. When the liver isn't able to metabolize all the fat that arrives, it builds up. Simultaneously, the liver uses certain by-products of alcohol metabolism to make even more fat. The net effect is a liver that has cells that are full of fat.[18] A fatty liver can reverse itself *if* the alcohol consumption is stopped.
- If the drinking doesn't stop, the second stage of the disease, *alcoholic hepatitis*, can develop. In alcoholic hepatitis, the liver becomes irritated by harmful by-products of alcohol metabolism. Nausea, vomiting, fever, jaundice, and loss of appetite are signs of alcoholic hepatitis.
- *Cirrhosis* is the third, and final, stage of the disease. In cirrhosis, the liver cells die and scar tissue forms. The liver becomes unable to perform its critical metabolic roles, such as filtering toxins and waste products in the blood and out of the

Figure 19.8 Fetal Alcohol Syndrome
People with fetal alcohol syndrome often have facial abnormalities.

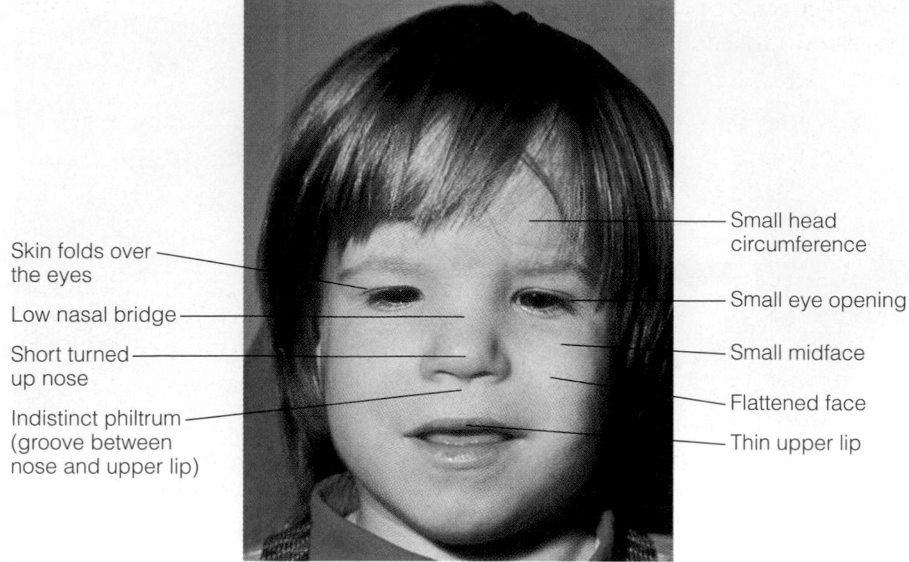

body. If these toxins and waste products build up, mental confusion, nausea, tremors or shakiness, and even coma can occur. More than 12,000 Americans die from alcoholic liver disease each year.[19]

Alcohol Can Put a Healthy Pregnancy at Risk

Over 30 years ago, researchers noticed an interesting trait among children in a clinic at the University of Washington School of Medicine. Some children looked alike, even though they weren't related. Many had facial abnormalities, such as eyes with very small openings and thin upper lips. These children also weren't growing as normally as other children their age, and they seemed to have some behavioral difficulties and learning disabilities. The doctors discovered that all these children had been born to women who drank alcohol during their pregnancy. The term **fetal alcohol syndrome (FAS)** was coined to describe the cluster of abnormalities affecting these children (Figure 19.8).[20] FAS is the leading cause of mental retardation and birth defects in the United States.

When a pregnant woman drinks, she is never drinking alone—her fetus is her drinking partner. Because the baby's body is developing, it isn't breaking down the alcohol as quickly as in the mother's body. The baby's BAC can become higher and stay higher longer than the mother's, causing serious damage to the baby's central nervous system, particularly the brain. Approximately 4 million U.S. infants each year experience prenatal exposure to alcohol, and up to 6,000 babies are born with FAS. The only proven safe amount of alcohol a pregnant woman can consume is *none*. Women should avoid alcohol if they think they are, or might soon become, pregnant.

fetal alcohol syndrome (FAS) A cluster of physical, mental, and behavioral abnormalities that can occur in children who are exposed to alcohol in utero.

The Take-Home Message **Excessive drinking can disrupt your sleep, cause hangovers, and add extra calories to your diet, which can lead to weight gain. Drinking too much alcohol can also interact with hormones; lead to malnutrition; harm your digestive organs, heart, and liver; and cause irreversible damage to a developing fetus. Individuals with alcohol**

liver disease can experience a fatty liver and deterioration of the liver that develops into alcohol-related hepatitis and cirrhosis.

What Are Alcohol Abuse and Alcoholism?

When people choose not to drink alcohol responsibly, they often end up abusing alcohol or suffering from a full-blown addiction. *Alcohol abuse* begins when people allow alcohol to interfere with their lives. They may have to call in sick to work or school due to a hangover or may have blank spots in their memory due to intoxication. At the extreme end of the spectrum is the disease of **alcoholism.** By the time people are addicted to alcohol, they are no longer in control of their drinking habits and are at serious risk of suffering long-term health damage. Approximately 17 percent of regular drinkers either abuse or are addicted to alcohol.[21]

Let's take a closer look at both of these categories of alcohol dysfunction.

Binge Drinking, Drinking and Driving, and Underage Drinking Are Forms of Alcohol Abuse

When people continue to consume alcohol even though the behavior has created social, legal, and/or health problems for them, they are abusing alcohol. Binge drinking and drunk driving are situations in which alcohol is being abused. Because 21 is the legal drinking age in the United States, anyone under this age who consumes alcohol is also abusing it. Are you at risk for alcohol abuse? Rate Yourself to discover the red flags.

alcoholism A chronic disease with genetic, psychological, and environmental components. Alcoholics crave alcohol, can't control their intake, and develop a high tolerance for it. Alcoholics also exhibit a dependency on alcohol, as abstaining from drinking will cause withdrawal symptoms.

RATE YOURSELF ★★★★★

Red Flags for Alcohol Abuse

Complete the following self-assessment to see if you may be at increased risk for alcohol abuse.

1. Do you fail to fulfill major work, school, or home responsibilities because of your consumption of alcohol? **Yes** ☐ **No** ☐
2. Do you drink in situations that are potentially dangerous, such as while driving a car or operating heavy machinery? **Yes** ☐ **No** ☐
3. Do you experience repeated alcohol-related legal problems, such as being arrested for driving while intoxicated? **Yes** ☐ **No** ☐
4. Do you have relationship problems that are caused or made worse by alcohol? **Yes** ☐ **No** ☐

Answers

If you answered "yes" to any of these questions, you should speak with your health care provider for insight and guidance.

Data adapted from: National Institute on Alcohol Abuse and Alcoholism. 2003. Understanding Alcohol: Investigations into Biology and Behavior. http://science.education.nih.gov/supplements/ nih3/alcohol/default.htm (accessed December 2005); U.S. Department of Health and Human Services, *Ninth Special Report of the U.S. Congress on Alcohol and Health* (Bethesda, MD: National Institute on Alcohol Abuse and Alcoholism, 1997).

Figure 19.9 Consequences of Binge Drinking on Campus
Alcohol use by college students results in numerous assaults, injuries, and deaths each year.

Data from: National Institute on Alcohol Abuse and Alcoholism, based on information from R. Hingson et al. "Magnitude of Alcohol-Related Mortality and Morbidity among U.S. College Students Ages 18–24: Changes from 1998 to 2001." *Annual Review of Public Health* 26 (2005): 259–279.

Binge Drinking

Binge drinking occurs when a man consumes five or more drinks or a woman consumes four or more drinks in a very short time. Approximately one in three American adults who drink alcohol fell into this category during the last month. College students who binge drink are more likely to miss classes, have hangovers, experience unintentional injuries (such as falling, motor vehicle accidents, and drowning), and even die (Figure 19.9). In 2005, a 21-year-old junior at Fairleigh Dickinson University in New Jersey died when, after an evening of drinking with friends, he fell four stories out of his dorm room window.[22] Binge drinking is also associated with hypertension, heart attack, sexually transmitted diseases, suicide, homicide, and child abuse.[23]

Research also indicates that binge drinkers engage in more unplanned sexual activity and fail to use safe sex strategies more frequently than non–binge drinkers.[24] Sexual aggression and assaults on campus increase when drinking enters the picture. Alcohol is involved in over 70 percent of the reported rapes on college campuses; the victims are often too drunk to refuse or defend themselves against the actions of the other person.

Binge drinking can also cause *blackouts*, which are periods of time that a person cannot remember, even though he or she may have been conscious. A research study of over 700 college students found that more than half of them had blacked out at least once in their lives, and many found out after the fact that they had taken part in activities such as vandalism, unprotected sex, and driving a motor vehicle during the blackout period.[25]

Binge drinking can lead to **alcohol poisoning.** Figure 19.10 documents the fate of Freya, a college student who nearly died of alcohol poisoning. Her BAC rose to such a high level that her breathing and heart rate were impaired (see Table 19.1). She passed out, yet the alcohol in her stomach and small intestine continued to be absorbed, so her BAC continued to rise as she slept. She could have stopped breathing, and ultimately died, if her friends hadn't gotten medical help.

alcohol poisoning A condition in which a person's BAC rises to such an extreme level that the central nervous system is affected and breathing and heart rate are interrupted.

Chronic binge drinking can lead to *alcohol tolerance,* which occurs over time as the body adjusts to long-term alcohol use. As the brain becomes less sensitive to alcohol, more is needed to get the same intoxicating effect.[26] People who've developed an alcohol tolerance should not think they can drink more without damaging their bodies. The harmful effects you read about in the previous section still occur.

Research shows that many college students have exaggerated perceptions of the amount of alcohol their peers consume. Binge drinking has been found to occur at rates ranging from almost never to nearly 70 percent of the students on a college campus.[27] Many of those who think binge drinking is just a normal part of the college experience have a circle of like-minded friends who reinforce their misperceptions.

Drinking in groups is associated with an increased intake of alcohol. For instance, joining a fraternity or sorority tends to increase alcohol consumption among college students. The box feature "Smashed: Story of a Drunken Girlhood," (page 16) describes the true story of Koren Zailckas, a college graduate, and her struggles with binge drinking.

Figure 19.10 Freya's Night of Binge Drinking

Data from: At-Bristol. www.at-bristol.org.uk/Alcoholandyou/effects/freya.html.

Freya goes to a party after having a few drinks at home to "warm up."

BAC = 0.01–0.05

She doesn't bother eating before she goes. As soon as she arrives she gets handed a glass of homemade punch—it tastes horrible, but makes her feel confident. She's chatty and having a good laugh with her friends.

BAC = 0.06–0.10

The first drinks have affected her judgment, Freya's friends are now having trouble talking to her. She's saying things without thinking, stopping mid-conversation, and disappearing or trying to drag people onto the dance floor.

BAC = 0.11–0.20

After a few more drinks, Freya is having trouble understanding and remembering things so conversation with her is even harder. Her reactions are slow and she's bumping into people. All her movements are uncoordinated and when she tries to dance she keeps losing her balance. She's having trouble recognizing people, and her vision is blurry.

BAC = 0.21–0.30

Freya has stopped drinking, but she's getting drunker as the last few drinks are absorbed into her body. She's sleepy and confused and unsure as to where she is or what she's doing. Freya is emotional and doesn't know whether to laugh or cry. Her vision has gotten worse and she's slurring her words so badly no one can understand her.

BAC = 0.31–0.40

Freya feels terrible, the room is spinning, and she feels sick. She's not sure what time it is as she keeps falling asleep.

BAC ≥ 0.40

Freya is unconscious. Her skin feels cooler than normal. Her breathing has slowed and is shallower than normal. Her friends give up trying to wake her and call an ambulance.

When it arrives, the EMTs tell them they did the right thing. She has poisoned herself by drinking too much alcohol and is taken to the hospital.

Smashed: Story of a Drunken Girlhood

Koren Zailckas was a shy, insecure girl raised in an upscale town in the Boston suburbs. She started drinking at the age of 14, and almost from her first sip, there was no turning back. During a socially awkward adolescence, Koren found it difficult to be at ease around other people, particularly girls her own age. When she drank, she became assertive and friendly. She bonded with other girls and met tons of guys. Throughout her high school and college years, alcohol was her crutch and best pal.

Koren didn't think of herself as an alcoholic, but she was a binge drinker. She drank herself into her first blackout with a thermos full of vodka at the age of 16. She woke up in her bedroom wearing a hospital Johnny and a pink plastic bracelet on her wrist that said "Zailckas, Koren." The bracelet was compliments of her local hospital emergency room. The Johnny had replaced her vomit-covered clothes the night before. Her stomach had been pumped. Her parents had carried her from the back seat of the family car to her bedroom in the middle of the night. They were devastated.

As a freshman entering college, Koren used beer and liquor to make friends and be accepted. She pledged a sorority for the sole purpose of sisterhood and booze. She frequently drank herself into a steady state of numbness and allowed sorority sisters and male friends to make many of her decisions. She was often the last girl to leave the party because she was too drunk to know that she should have left an hour before.

After college graduation, Koren continued her drunken lifestyle in the fast-paced mecca of New York City. She worked hard during the day and drank hard at night. One morning, she woke up in a strange bed, in a strange condo, next to a stranger from the cab ride the night before. For Koren, this was rock bottom. She realized that her chronic drinking was a magnet for like-minded people who also abused alcohol and were as damaged in life as she. But she wanted a good life. She wanted sound friendships and self-confidence, and she recognized that she wasn't going to achieve these goals with alcohol. At that moment, she decided to get help.

Through guidance from an addiction counselor and her own drive to quit drinking, Koren stopped her destructive behavior and began surrounding herself with a healthier circle of friends. Today, she is sober, and has a new lease on life.

You can read more about Koren's struggles and triumphs in her best-selling book, *Smashed* (Penguin, 2006), and on her website, www.korenzailckas.com.

Drinking and Driving

If you have spent any time behind a steering wheel, you know that you can't *just* drive. You need to drive defensively. Driving involves multitasking: You need to keep the car in your lane, stay within the speed limit, make constant quick decisions, and, of course, maneuver the car based on those decisions. Alcohol intake impairs all of these skills. It is illegal to drive in the United States with a BAC of 0.08 (some states have set their legal limit even lower), but the level of alcohol in the blood doesn't need to get that high to impair your driving. Even one alcoholic beverage impairs alertness, judgment, and coordination. In 2004, over 16,000 people died in automobile accidents that involved a driver with a BAC of .01 or higher.[28]

As the price of beer goes up, the number of people involved in fatal **traffic accidents** goes down.

Underage Drinking

The average age at which 12- to 20-year-old Americans take their first drink is 14 years old.[29] This means that many American youth are drinking alcohol when they

Drinking and driving can be deadly.

are not even tall enough to see over the bar. By high school, over 30 percent of teenagers are binge drinking at least one time a month.[30] Underage drinking not only increases the risk for violence, injuries, and other health risks, as previously discussed, but alcohol consumption at that age can also interfere with brain development and lead to permanent cognitive and memory damage.

Underage drinking, coupled with driving, is a disaster waiting to happen. Adolescent drivers are inexperienced behind the wheel to begin with, so it isn't surprising that automobile accidents are the number-one cause of death of young people between the ages of 15 and 20. Those between the ages of 16 and 20 who drink and drive are twice as likely to die in automobile accidents as those 21 and older who drink before getting behind the wheel.[31] In fact, that's why, by 1984, all states in the United States had adopted a minimum legal drinking age of 21.

There is another danger in consuming alcohol at a young age. The earlier in life a person starts drinking, the higher the chances that alcohol will become a problem later in life. A person who starts drinking at age 15 is four times more likely to suffer from alcoholism than an individual who doesn't start drinking until age 20.[32]

Alcoholism Is a Disease

At the beginning of this concept, you read that Leah is concerned about her daily alcohol habit. Her brother, Steve, currently suffers from alcoholism, and her father and grandfather both died of cirrhosis due to alcoholism.

Steve exhibits the four classic symptoms of alcoholism:

- He craves alcohol.
- He has developed a higher tolerance for alcohol.
- He can't limit his intake once he starts drinking.
- He has developed a dependency on alcohol because, if he stops drinking, his body reacts to the withdrawal.

An alcoholic's craving, loss of control, and physical dependency distinguish him or her as an "alcoholic," rather than a person who abuses alcohol but doesn't have the other three characteristics.[33]

TABLE TIPS

Keeping Your Drinking Moderate

Never drink on an empty stomach. The alcohol will be absorbed too quickly, which will impair your judgment and lower your willpower to decline the next drink.

At a party, make your first—and even your second—drink a tall glass of water. This will allow you to pace yourself and reduce the chance that you'll guzzle your first alcoholic drink because you are thirsty. Also, have a glass of water before you have a second alcoholic drink.

Try some fun nonalcoholic drinks, such as a Virgin Mary (a Bloody Mary without the vodka), a tame frozen Margarita (use the mix but don't add the tequila), or a Tom Collins without the gin (club soda, lemon, and sugar).

Become an alcohol snob. Rather than drinking excessive amounts of cheap beer or wine at parties, wait until you get home and have a microbrewed beer or a glass of quality wine. Don't drink a lot of junk; drink a little of the good stuff.

Become the go-to designated driver in your group and have your passengers reimburse you for the cost of the gasoline. You'll be everyone's best friend and have spare cash for things you really need.

Because the disease runs in her family, Leah is at a higher than average risk for alcoholism. Research has shown that approximately 50 percent of the risk for alcoholism is determined genetically.[34] Her risk for alcoholism is also influenced by her environment. Her home life, the drinking habits of her family and friends, social pressures, and access to alcohol will all impact whether she develops the disease. If Leah chooses to surround herself with friends and a lifestyle that don't focus on alcohol, she can reduce her risk of following in her brother's footsteps.

There is no cure for alcoholism. However, it can be treated with medication that helps reduce the craving, self-help therapies, and support groups. Because alcoholics can't limit their consumption once they start drinking, reducing the amount of alcohol consumed doesn't work for them. They must eliminate alcohol from their lives entirely to have a successful recovery. Alcoholics Anonymous (AA) is a worldwide fellowship of men and women who meet, bond, and support each other, with the sole purpose of remaining sober. AA's 12 steps for recovery and supportive group meetings help individuals maintain sobriety.[35] If you are interested in learning more about AA or finding a group in your area, look in your local telephone directory or online at www.alcoholics-anonymous.org. Everyone is welcomed at the meetings, including family members, friends, and coworkers.

The Take-Home Message **Individuals who abuse alcohol through binge drinking, drinking and driving, and underage drinking are putting themselves and others at risk for injuries, violence, and even death. Alcoholism is a disease that can't be cured, but it can be treated with medical help and psychological support.**

Who Should Avoid Alcohol?

According to the latest *Dietary Guidelines for Americans*, the following people should abstain completely from alcohol:[36]

- Women of childbearing age who may become pregnant
- Pregnant and lactating women
- Children and adolescents
- Those taking medications that can interact with alcohol, which include prescription and over-the-counter medications
- Those with specific medical conditions, such as stomach ulcers
- Those engaging in activities that require attention, skill, or coordination, such as driving or operating machinery
- Those who cannot restrict their alcohol intake

For these individuals, abstinence is the best option, as even modest amounts of alcohol can have detrimental health effects.

No one needs to drink alcohol. If you choose to do so, follow the guidelines for moderate drinking discussed earlier in this concept. The accompanying Table Tips can help.

The Take-Home Message **Many people, depending on their age, medical history, and lifestyle, would benefit from abstaining from alcohol.**

UCook

Cranberry Lime Spritzer

For this great-tasting nonalcoholic beverage you can enjoy on a night out out with friends, visit the companion website for the recipe.

UDo

How Much Alcohol Is Too Much?

If you drink alcohol, take the short survey based on the World Health Organization's Alcohol Use Disorders Identification Test (AUDIT), which will help you analyze your drinking habits. Go to our website (above) for the link.

The Top Five Points to Remember

1. For adults who choose to drink, moderate alcohol consumption is considered up to one drink for women daily and up to two drinks a day for men. A standard drink is 12 ounces of beer, 5 ounces of wine, or 1.5 ounces of liquor. Drinking alcohol in moderation may help reduce the risk for heart disease in older adults. Abstaining from drinking for several days and then drinking four or five drinks in one evening is not considered moderate drinking.
2. Alcohol is one of the rare substances that are absorbed in the stomach, as well as the small intestine. The presence of food slows the departure of alcohol from your stomach to your intestine, where the majority of the alcohol is absorbed. This is why drinking on an empty stomach is not a good idea. Most of the alcohol you consume is metabolized in your liver. Some alcohol is lost from your body in your breath and urine. Your liver can metabolize only about one standard drink per 1½ hours. As you drink more alcohol, your BAC goes up, as does your level of impairment and intoxication.
3. Although alcohol is often thought of as a stimulant, it is actually a depressant. Your brain is sensitive to the effects of alcohol; depending on the amount you consume, alcohol can cause numerous mental, behavioral, and physical changes in your body. Your alertness, judgment, and coordination are initially be affected. As you drink more alcohol, your vision, speech, reasoning, and balance are altered. An excessive amount of alcohol can interfere with your breathing and heart rate.
4. Alcohol can disrupt your sleep, cause hangovers, and add excess calories and/or displace healthier food choices from your diet. Chronically consuming excessive amounts of alcohol can harm your digestive organs, heart, and liver. The three stages of alcohol liver disease are fatty liver, alcoholic hepatitis, and cirrhosis. Many individuals die annually of alcohol-related liver disease. Alcohol can put a fetus at risk for fetal alcohol syndrome.
5. Alcohol abuse occurs when people continue to consume alcohol even though this behavior negatively affects their lives. Binge drinking, underage drinking, and drinking and driving are examples of alcohol abuse. Alcoholism, also called alcohol dependence, is a disease characterized by four symptoms: a craving for alcohol, a higher tolerance for alcohol, the inability to limit its intake, and a physical dependence on it. Although alcoholism can't be cured, it can be treated with medical and psychological support.

Test Yourself

1. Alcohol provides
   a. 9 calories per gram.
   b. 7 calories per gram.
   c. 4 calories per gram.
   d. 0 calories per gram.
2. The major site of alcohol metabolism in your body is your
   a. kidneys.
   b. lungs.
   c. liver.
   d. stomach.
3. Which of the following factors affect(s) your rate of absorption and metabolism of alcohol?
   a. whether you're male or female
   b. the amount of food in your stomach
   c. the time of day you drink
   d. both a and b
4. The *best* cure for a hangover is
   a. chicken soup.
   b. a light beer.
   c. time and abstinence.
   d. acetaminophen (Tylenol).
5. Drinking four to five alcoholic beverages in a very short time is called
   a. alcoholism.
   b. drunk driving.
   c. blackout.
   d. binge drinking.

Answers

1. (b) Alcohol serves up 7 calories per gram, which is less than fat, at 9 calories per gram, and more than carbohydrates and protein each of which provides 4 calories per gram. Alcohol isn't an essential nutrient—your body doesn't need it to survive—and it's not calorie free.
2. (c) Most alcohol in the body is metabolized in the liver. A small amount of alcohol is lost in your urine (kidneys) and in your breath (your lungs). Some alcohol is also metabolized in your stomach, although substantially less than in your liver.
3. (d) Both your sex and the amount of food in your stomach affect the rate of absorption and metabolism of alcohol. Women have less of the enzyme alcohol dehydrogenase in their stomachs, which means they metabolize less alcohol in the stomach, and more alcohol is absorbed into the blood. Drinking on a full stomach delays the arrival of alcohol in your small intestine, which is the primary site of absorption. The time of day doesn't have any effect on the absorption and metabolism of alcohol.
4. (c) The best cure is to stop drinking and let your body have the time it needs to recover from consuming too much alcohol. A warm bowl of chicken soup might be comforting, but it won't cure the fatigue or the other ill effects of drinking alcohol. Taking acetaminophen is not recommended, as its toxicity to your liver is enhanced if it is consumed while alcohol is being metabolized. The worst thing you can do for a hangover is to have another alcoholic beverage.
5. (d) Consuming that much alcohol in a very short time is considered binge drinking. Binge drinking can lead to alcoholism. Individuals who binge drink may experience blackouts and have a greatly increased risk for an automobile accident if they drive while drunk.

Web Resources

- For more information about drinking at college, visit: www.collegedrinkingprevention.gov
- For more information about alcohol and your health, visit the National Institute on Alcohol Abuse and Alcoholism (NIAAA) at: www.niaaa.nih.gov
- For more information about alcohol consumption and its consequences, visit the National Center for Chronic Disease Prevention and Health Promotion, Alcohol and Public Health, at: www.cdc.gov/alcohol/index.htm

20

A Healthy Weight

What Is It, and How Do You Maintain It?

1. Being **underweight** is always healthy. T/F

2. About one-quarter of a healthy **woman's body** is made up of fat. T/F

3. Fat around the hips is as unhealthy as fat stored around **the waist.** T/F

4. The number of **calories you burn** daily is affected by your body size, genes, and sex. T/F

5. Your body uses up about **10 percent** of the calories in foods just to process those foods. T/F

J. T., a freshman, is the youngest player on his university's baseball team, and he dreams of playing professionally someday. On top of classes and homework, he trains and practices every chance he gets, Monday through Saturday, so he frequently misses scheduled mealtimes at his dorm cafeteria and buys food at campus kiosks and vending machines to keep going. At his monthly weigh-in last week, his coach became concerned because J. T. had lost almost five pounds, so he scheduled an appointment for J. T. at the campus fitness lab. While there, he'll have an underwater weighing to determine his percentage of body fat, and he'll consult a sports dietitian for advice about maintaining a healthy weight. Meantime, he's still eating on the run.

With J. T.'s active schedule, it's no surprise that he's finding it challenging to maintain his weight. Truth is, he has no idea how many calories he should be eating each day, or even how to find this information. In this concept, you'll learn how to determine what weight is healthy for you, the importance of staying in energy balance, and how to calculate your energy needs.

Answers

1. False. Being very underweight can cause health problems. Turn to page 3 to learn more.
2. True. Healthy women between the ages of 20 and 49 carry about 22 to 26 percent of their weight as fat. See page 4 for more.
3. False. Fat around the belly puts a person at a higher health risk than fat stored on the hips and thighs. To find out why, turn to page 6.
4. True. But these aren't the only factors. Turn to pages 8 and 9 to find out the others.
5. True. To learn why this occurs, see page 9.

What Is a Healthy Weight and Why Is It Important?

A **healthy weight** is considered a body weight that doesn't increase your risk of developing weight-related health problems or diseases. Rather than a single number, it's a range of weight that is appropriate for your gender, height, and muscle mass, a weight at which you feel energetic and fit. A healthy weight is also a *realistic* weight, one that you can maintain naturally through consuming a nourishing diet and engaging in regular physical activity. As the U.S. Centers for Disease Control and Prevention puts it, a healthy weight is not a diet; it's a healthy lifestyle![1]

On each side of a healthy weight is overweight or underweight. Either extreme can be unhealthy, a red flag for undernutrition in some nutrients, overnutrition in others, and impending health problems. For instance, overweight is associated with high blood pressure, unhealthy blood lipid levels, and high blood sugar. At the other end of the scale, underweight is associated with a decreased ability to fight infections and other health problems. We'll talk about both overweight and underweight in Concepts 21 and 22.

To stay at a healthy weight, you need to be skilled in **weight management,** which simply means maintaining your weight within a healthy range. First, you need to know whether your current weight is healthy. If not, how does it need to change—and how much? You then need to understand the concept of energy balance, and how you can change your energy intake and output to achieve it. Maintaining energy balance is the key to maintaining a healthy weight, so let's figure it out and put it to work.

healthy weight A body weight in relation to your height that doesn't increase the risk of developing any weight-related health problems or diseases.

weight management Maintaining your weight within a healthy range.

The Take-Home Message **A healthy weight is a body weight that doesn't increase your risk of developing weight-related health problems or diseases. It's realistic for your gender and build, and achieving it doesn't require you to forego a nourishing diet. Being either overweight or underweight can be unhealthy. Weight management means maintaining a healthy weight to reduce your risk for specific health problems.**

How Do You Know If You're at a Healthy Weight?

Now that you know what constitutes a healthy weight, how can you determine if your body weight is within a healthy range? The following are a few methods you can use.

Determine Your BMI

One of the easiest ways to assess if you are at a healthy weight is to determine your **body mass index (BMI)**. The BMI is a calculation of your weight in relation to your height. It can be precisely calculated using a mathematical formula, but it's simpler to approximate using the graph in Figure 20.1. Find the horizontal line matching your height without shoes and the vertical line matching your weight without clothing. The point at which these two lines intersect is your approximate BMI.

Here's how to interpret your BMI:

- **Underweight.** If your BMI falls in the first part of the graph (shaded orange), it is below 18.5 and you are considered underweight. Although people who are underweight are at reduced risk for the chronic diseases associated with obesity, they are at increased risk for infection, and their overall risk of mortality is higher than for people of normal weight.

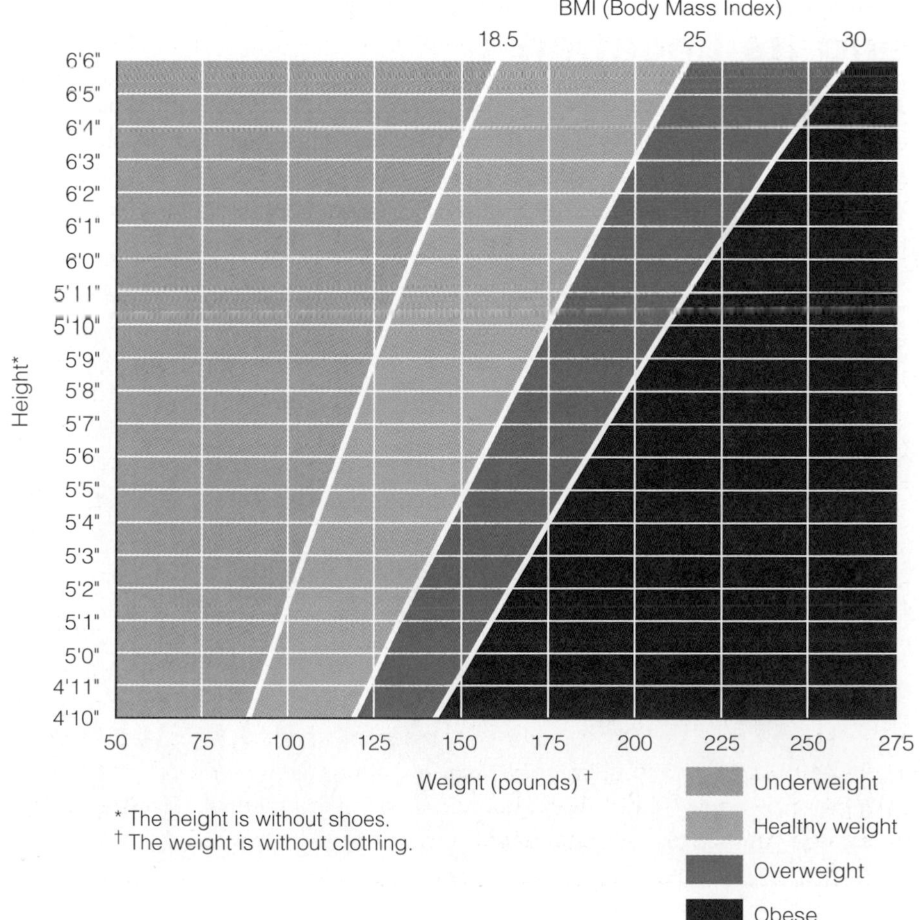

Figure 20.1 What's Your BMI?
A BMI between 18.5 and 24.9 is considered healthy. A BMI equal to or over 25 is considered overweight, and a BMI of 30 or above is obese. A BMI under 18.5 is considered underweight, which can also be unhealthy.

body mass index (BMI) A calculation of your weight in relation to your height. A BMI between 18.5 and 24.9 is considered healthy.

underweight Weighing too little for your height—specifically, a BMI below 18.5.

- Healthy weight. If your BMI falls within the "green zone," between 18.5 and 24.9, it is considered healthy.
- **Overweight.** If your BMI falls between 25 and 29.9 (the blue area of the graph), you are overweight. As the amount you are overweight increases, so does your risk of dying from certain chronic diseases, although research shows that the risk is modest until a person reaches a BMI of 30.
- **Obese.** If your BMI is 30 or over (the purple part of the graph), you are considered obese.[2] Obese individuals have a 50 to 100 percent higher risk of dying prematurely, compared with those at a healthy weight.[3]

Athletes with a high percentage of muscle mass have higher body weights. NBA player Shaquille O'Neal has a BMI of over 30 (obese). Although his BMI is high, his weight doesn't put him at an increased health risk.

As you can see, your BMI can help you determine if your weight is putting you at risk for health problems. Figure 20.2 shows you what various BMIs would look like.

As with any screening tool, the BMI may not be accurate for everyone. It is not a *direct* measure of your percentage of body fat, so it cannot help you assess if your body weight is predominantly muscle or fat. In fact, athletes and other people with a high percentage of muscle mass may have a BMI over 25 yet have a low percentage of body fat. Although these individuals are overweight based on their BMI, they are not "overfat" and unhealthy, and their muscular weight doesn't increase their health risk. Similarly, individuals who are short—under 5 feet—may have a high BMI but, like athletes, may not be unhealthy.[4]

In contrast, an elderly person may be in a healthy weight range but may have been steadily losing weight due to an unbalanced diet or poor health. This chronic weight loss is a sign of loss of muscle mass and the depletion of nutrient stores in the body, which increases health risks, even though the BMI seems healthy.

Measure Your Body Fat and Its Location

According to the American College of Sports Medicine, the average healthy adult male between the ages of 20 and 49 carries 16 to 21 percent of his weight as body fat. The average woman of the same age range carries 22 to 26 percent of her weight as body fat. There are several techniques you can use to measure total body fat (Figure 20.3),

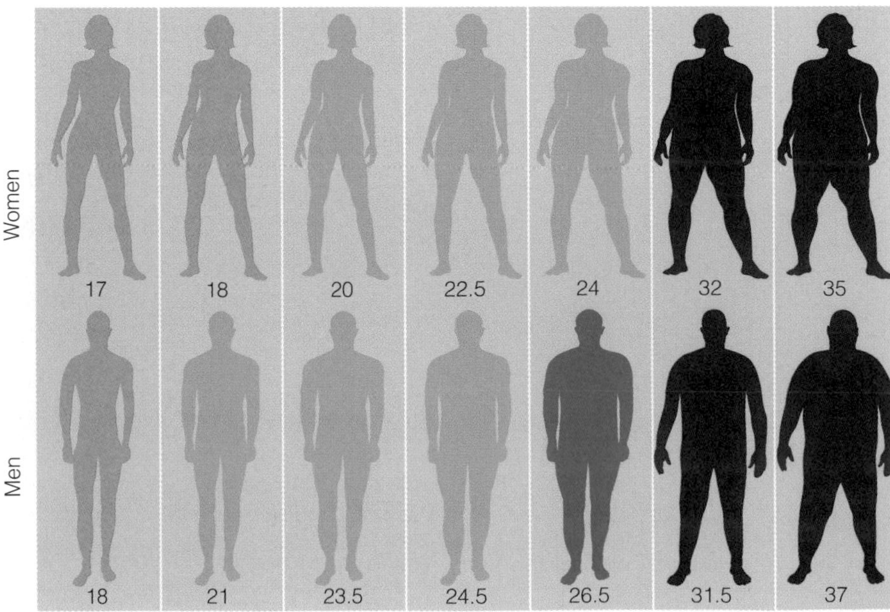

Figure 20.2 The Many Sizes of BMIs
People who look overweight or obese are likely to have a higher BMI.

overweight Weighing about 10 to 15 pounds more than a healthy weight for your height—specifically, a BMI between 25 and 29.9.

obese Having an unhealthy amount of body fat—specifically, a BMI of 30 or more.

Figure 20.3 Ways to Measure Percentage of Body Fat

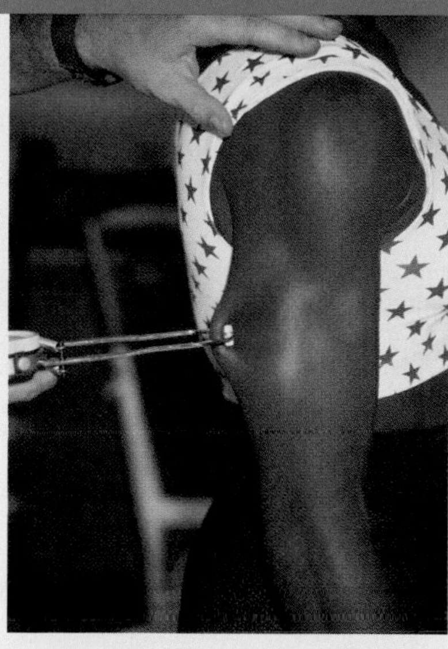

▲ **Skinfold Thickness Measurements**
How It Is Done: Calipers are used to measure the thickness of fat that is located just under the skin in the arm, in the back, on the upper thigh, and in the waist area. From these measurements, percent body fat can be determined.
Cost: $

Bioelectrical Impedance ►
How It Is Done: An electric current flows through the body and its resistance is measured. Lean tissue is highly conductive and less resistant than fat mass. Based on the current flow, the volume of lean tissue can be estimated. From this information, the percentage of body fat can be determined.
Cost: $

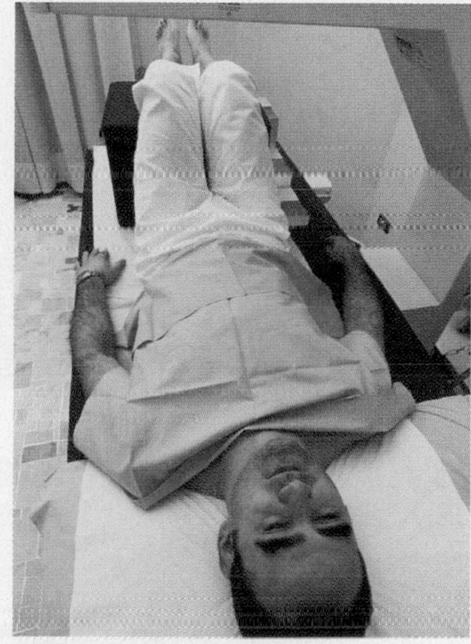

◄ **Dual-Energy X-Ray Absorptiometry (DXA)**
How It Is Done: A beam of energy is used to measure bone, fat, and lean tissue. The type of tissue that the beam passes through will absorb different amounts of energy. The amount of energy lost will allow the percentage of body fat to be determined.
Cost: $$$

▲ **Underwater Weighing**
How It Is Done: A person is weighed on land and while suspended in a water tank. This is done to determine the density of the body. Fat is less dense and weighs less than muscle mass and will be reflected as such when the person is weighed in the water. The difference of a person's weight in water and on land is then used to calculate the percentage of body fat.
Cost: $$

Air Displacement Using a BodPod ►
How It Is Done: A person's body volume is determined by measuring air displacement from a chamber. The person sits in a special chamber (called the BodPod) and the air displacement in the chamber is measured. From this measurement, the percentage of body fat can be estimated.
Cost: $$$

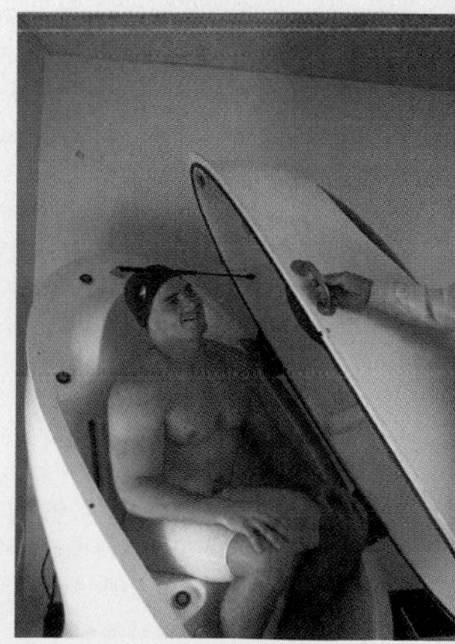

$ = very affordable
$$ = less affordable
$$$ = expensive

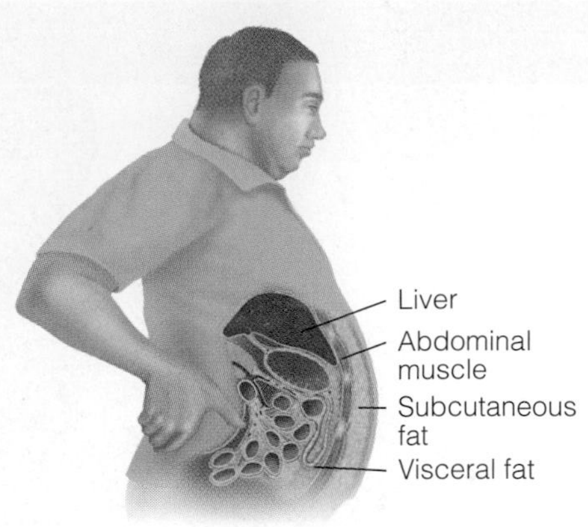

Figure 20.4 Visceral and Subcutaneous Fat Storage in the Body
Visceral fat stored around the waist is more likely to lead to health problems than subcutaneous fat stored elsewhere in the body.

including skinfold thickness measurements, bioelectrical impedance, dual-energy X-ray absorptiometry (DXA), underwater weighing, and air displacement. These methods need to be conducted by trained technicians and some of them can be expensive.

How much fat you carry isn't the only determinant of health risk—where you carry it also matters. Carrying excess fat around the waist versus carrying it around the hips and thighs has been shown to increase the risk for heart disease, diabetes, and hypertension.[5] *Central obesity* is due to storing too much **visceral fat** (the fat that surrounds organs in your chest and stomach and above your hips) around your waist. Another type of fat, called **subcutaneous fat,** is the fat sandwiched between your skin and your muscles (see Figure 20.4). As discussed in the accompanying box feature, some researchers believe that central obesity is a more important indicator of your health risks than is your BMI in general.

By measuring your waist circumference, you can find out quickly whether you are at risk. Figure 20.5 shows you how. A woman with a waist measurement of more than 35 inches or a man with a belly that's more than 40 inches around is at a higher risk for heart disease and other obesity-related disorders than people with slimmer middles.

Body Weight or Belly Fat: Which Matters More?

Your Uncle Victor has "chicken legs," as your Aunt Rose calls them, but also a protruding belly that hangs over his belt buckle. Your Aunt Rose, on the other hand, has a matronly figure, which she attributes to the fact that she "never lost the 25 pounds she gained during pregnancy." By BMI standards, both your uncle and aunt are considered overweight, but is one at a higher risk for health problems? If you study the accompanying figure, you'll see that Uncle Victor's belly puts him at a higher health risk than his wife's extra weight.

Research suggests that, in determining the health risks of overweight, it's necessary to look at measurements of both abdominal girth and BMI. According to research, among those with comparable BMIs, people whose waist circumference was just 2 inches larger had a greater risk for death.[1] Because visceral fat is located near the liver, it is believed that fatty acids released from the fat stored near the liver and can lead to insulin resistance, high levels of fat, low levels of the HDL ("good") cholesterol, and high levels of LDL cholesterol in the blood, which all increase the risk for heart disease and diabetes. Insulin resistance also increases the risk for hypertension. Men, postmenopausal women, and obese people tend to have more visceral fat than young adults and lean individuals.

Extremely High Risk
BMI 40+ and high waist circumference

Very High Risk
BMI 30–39.9 and high waist circumference

High Risk
BMI 25–29.9 and high waist circumference
or
BMI 30–34.9 and low waist circumference

Increased Risk
BMI 25–29.9 and low waist circumference

Low Risk
BMI under 25

How at Risk Are You?
Considering both your BMI and your waist circumference can give you a good idea of your level of risk for health problems.

Carrying extra fat around your waist can also increase your health risks even if you are not overweight. So, people at a healthy weight according to their BMI, but who have excess fat around their middles, are at a higher health risk. A person who has *both* a high BMI and a large waist circumference is at an even higher risk for health problems and early death (see the figure in this box).

In short, although *both* your body weight in general and your amount of abdominal fat are important in assessing your risk for chronic disease and early death, research suggests that waist circumference might matter more. Thus, even if you're maintaining a healthy weight, it's smart to keep the tape measure handy.

The Take-Home Message Body mass index (BMI) is a calculation of your weight in relation to your height and can be used to help you determine how weight influences your health risks. It is not a direct measure of body fat and may be inaccurate for people who are muscular, short, or frail due to illness. Skinfold thickness measurements using calipers, bioelectrical impedance, dual-energy X-ray absorptiometry, underwater weighing, and air displacement are all techniques that can be used to measure the percentage of body fat. Excess fat around the middle increases the risk for several chronic diseases, regardless of BMI.

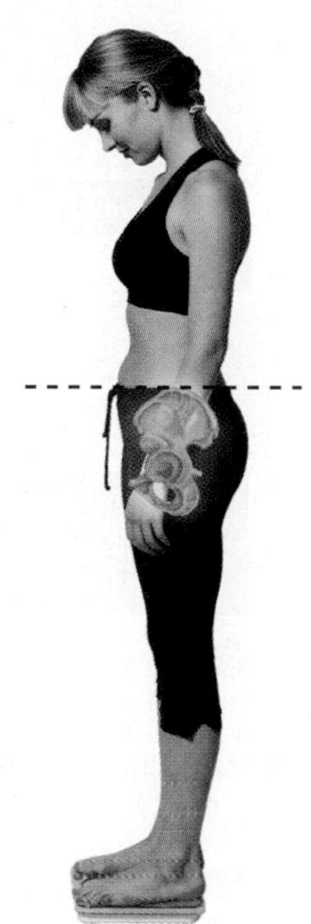

Figure 20.5 Measuring Waist Circumference
Measure your waist circumference just above your hip bone, as shown by the dashed line.

What Is Energy Balance and What Determines Energy Needs?

To maintain your weight, you need to make sure that you don't consume more calories than you expend daily. Spending as many calories as you take in is the concept behind energy balance.

Energy Balance Is Calories in versus Calories Out

Energy balance is the state at which your energy intake and your energy expenditure, both measured in calories, are equal (Figure 20.6a). When you consume more calories than you expend, you are in **positive energy balance** (Figure 20.6b). Routinely eating more calories than you expend will cause the storage of fat. When your calorie intake falls short of your needs, you are in **negative energy balance** (Figure 20.6c), and your body will break down stored body fat for fuel. Imbalances that occur over a long time period, such as weeks and months, are what change body weight.

You can determine whether you are in positive or negative energy balance by comparing the number of calories you take in with the number of calories you expend on a given day. Figuring out how many calories you take in is fairly straightforward. You can use the food labels or a diet analysis program (like the one available with this book) to find out how many calories are in the foods and beverages you eat and drink.

You can also use the grams of macronutrients in foods to calculate the number of total calories they contain. Recall that carbohydrates and protein each contain 4 calories per gram and fat contains 9 calories per gram. (Alcohol, at 7 calories per gram, can also contribute calories.) Multiplying the number of grams of carbohydrates, protein, or fat by the calories per gram and then adding up these numbers will provide the total amount of calories in the food. Adding together the calories in all the foods on your plate will provide you with the total calories for the meal. If you eat most of your meals in the campus dining hall, you probably don't need to do the math yourself. It is very likely that the dining hall food service manager has a complete list of the calories and nutrients in the foods available. Many colleges are posting these online to help students select foods that meet their health goals.

Calculating the number of calories you expend daily is a little more complicated. Let's start by determining your basic energy needs.

visceral fat The fat stored in the abdominal area.

subcutaneous fat The fat located under the skin and between the muscles.

energy balance The state at which energy (calorie) intake and energy (calorie) output in the body are equal.

positive energy balance The state whereby you store more energy than you expend. Over time, this results in weight gain.

negative energy balance The state whereby you expend more energy than you consume. Over time, this results in weight loss.

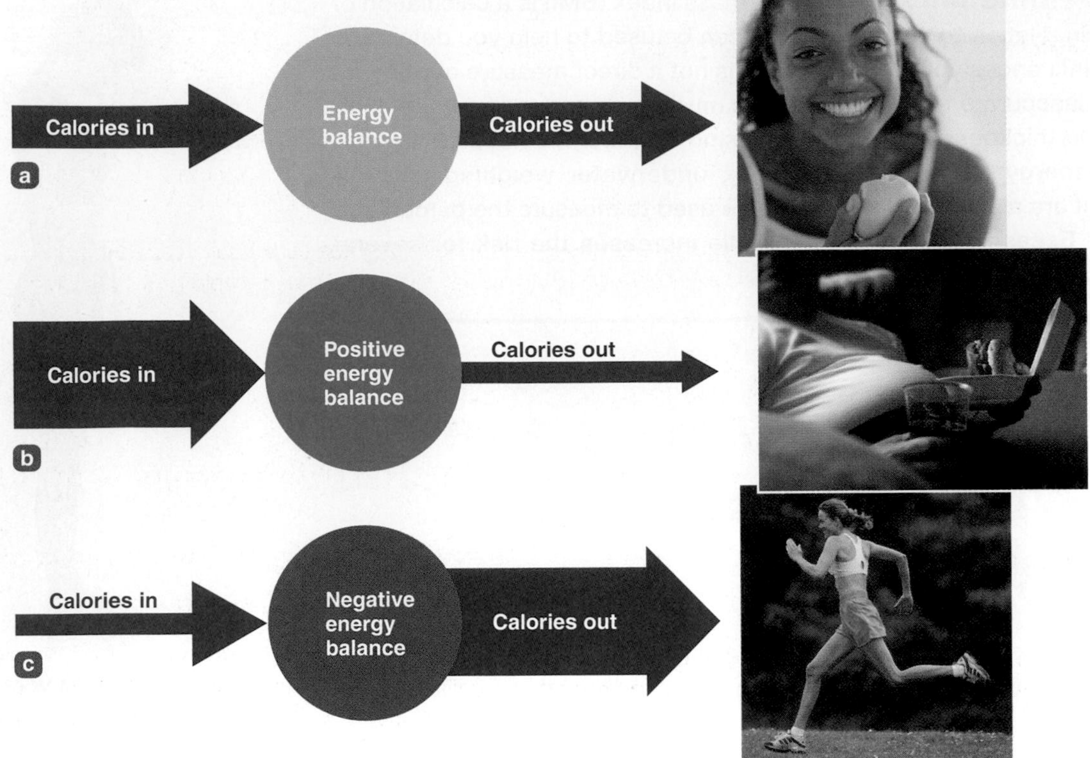

Figure 20.6 Energy Balance and Imbalance
(**a**) Energy balance: When the calories you consume meet your needs, you are in energy balance. Your weight will be stable. (**b**) Positive energy balance: When you take in more calories than you need, the surplus calories will be stored as fat. You will gain weight. (**c**) Negative energy balance: When you consume fewer calories than you expend, your body will draw upon your stored energy to meet its needs. You will lose weight.

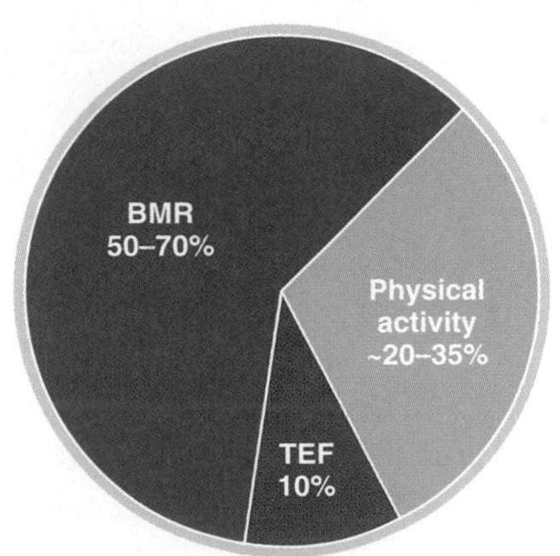

Figure 20.7 The Three Components of Your Energy Needs
The "calories out" side of the energy balance equation includes your basal metabolism (BMR), the thermic effect of food (TEF), and the energy you use to fuel your physical activity.

basal metabolism The amount of energy the body expends to meet its basic physiological needs; also referred to as basal metabolic rate (BMR).

Energy Needs Are Different for Everyone

Your energy needs are different from those of your 80-year-old grandparents, your 50-year-old parents, and even your marathon-running roommate. Your energy needs comprise your basal metabolism, the thermic effect of food (TEF), and the calories needed to fuel your physical activities (see Figure 20.7).

Your BMR Will Increase Your Energy Needs

Even when you're not at the gym or sprinting to class, your body is using energy. Pumping your blood, expanding your lungs, and using your brain all require energy every moment of your life. The **basal metabolism** is the amount of energy expended to meet the basic physiological needs that enable your organs and cells to function. Also referred to as the *basal metabolic rate (BMR),* it is the minimum energy needed to keep you alive.

Approximately 60 percent of your daily energy needs is determined by your BMR. The factor that most affects your BMR is your **lean body mass** (about 70 percent of your BMR). Age, gender, body size, genes, ethnicity, emotional and physical stress, thyroid hormones, nutritional state, and environmental temperature, as well as your caffeine and nicotine intake, affect your BMR. Table 20.1 explains each of these factors.

Table 20.1

Factors That Affect Your Basal Metabolic Rate

Factor	Explanation
Lean body mass	Lean body mass, which is mostly muscle mass, is more metabolically active than fat tissue, so more calories are needed to maintain it. Athletes who have a large percentage of lean body mass due to their increased muscle mass will have a higher BMR than individuals who aren't athletic.
Age	For adults, BMR declines about 1 to 2 percent per decade after the early adult years but it increases by 15 percent during pregnancy. For children, BMR increases during times of rapid growth, such as infancy and adolescence.
Gender	Women have less lean body mass and typically a higher percentage of body fat than men. This results in women having up to a 10 percent lower BMR. Women also tend to have a smaller body size. (See below.)
Body size	Taller individuals have a higher BMR due to increased surface area, compared with shorter individuals. More surface area means more heat lost from the body, which causes the BMR to increase to maintain the body's temperature.
Genes	Research suggests that genes may affect BMR, as individuals within families have similar metabolic rates.
Ethnicity	African Americans have BMRs that are about 10 percent lower than that of Caucasians.
Stress	Hormones such as epinephrine, which are released during emotional stress, increase BMR. Physiological stress on the body caused by injury, fever, burns, and infections also causes the release of hormones that raise BMR. Heat lost from the body through wounds, as well as the response of the immune system during infection, increases BMR.
Hormones	An increase in thyroid hormones increases BMR, while too little of these hormones lowers BMR. Hormonal fluctuations during a woman's menstrual cycle lower BMR during the phase before ovulation.
Starvation	Both starvation and fasting for more than about 48 hours lower BMR.
Environmental temperature	Being very cold or very hot can increase BMR, but the change is minimal if you make adjustments in your clothing or in the temperature of your surroundings.
Caffeine	Caffeine can raise BMR but only slightly when consumed regularly in moderate amounts.
Drugs	Nicotine may increase BMR.* Drugs such as amphetamine and ephedrine increase BMR.

*Institute of Medicine, *Dietary Reference Intakes for Energy, Carbohydrate, Fiber, Fat, Fatty Acids, Cholesterol, Protein, and Amino Acids*, 2002, www.iom.edu.

Data from: Smoking is not a weight-management strategy. Some people may think that replacing snacks with cigarettes helps them stay slim, but the health risks associated with smoking, such as lung cancer, emphysema, heart disease, and stroke, make it a foolish habit. Anyone concerned about weight gain when quitting smoking can minimize the chances of this with exercise (plus, you'll be able to run farther and faster with your cleaner lungs!).

The Thermic Effect of Food Affects Your Energy Needs

Your body uses energy to extract the calories from the foods you consume. The *thermic effect of food (TEF)* is the number of calories you expend to digest, absorb, and process your food. Approximately 10 percent of the calories in the food you eat is used for these functions. In other words, if you eat a 100-calorie cookie, about 10 calories will be used to process the cookie.

Physical Activity Will Increase Your Energy Needs

If you are very physically active, you need more energy than someone who is sedentary. For sedentary people, the amount of energy expended in physical activity is less than half of their BMR. For very physically active individuals, such as athletes, it can be as much as double their BMR. The more physical activity you routinely incorporate into your day, the more calories you will need to eat to meet your energy needs.

The amount of energy expended during physical activity goes beyond the activity itself. Exercise causes a small increase in energy expenditure for some time after the activity has stopped.[6]

lean body mass The body mass once the fat mass has been subtracted. It contains mostly muscle but also organs and fluids. Lean body mass is the metabolically active tissue in the body.

Calculating Your Energy Needs

Recall Table 4.3 from Concept 4, which helped you estimate your energy needs. This table was derived from the DRIs' **estimated energy requirement (EER).** The EER is the average calorie intake that is estimated to maintain energy balance based on a person's gender, age, height, body weight, and level of physical activity. (The physical activity levels are separated into categories ranging from sedentary to very active.) While Table 4.3 used a reference height and weight for each age grouping, you can calculate your own EER using your height and weight with the Rate Yourself feature, "What's Your Estimated Energy Expenditure (EER)?" Once you know your EER, you can start comparing the calories you consume on a daily basis with the calories you expend. With that information, you can take steps to change your diet or physical activities to achieve or maintain a healthy weight.

The Take-Home Message **Energy balance is the relationship between your energy intake and your energy expenditure, which are both measured in calories. Your basal metabolism, the thermic effect of food (TEF), and your physical activities all determine your daily energy needs.**

RATE YOURSELF 

What's Your Estimated Energy Expenditure (EER)?

Calculating your EER is a two-step process.

1. First, complete the information below.
   - **a.** My age is [30]
   - **b.** My physical activity during the day based on the chart below is [1.26]

Physical Activity	Male	Female
Sedentary (no exercise)	1.00	1.00
Low active (walks about 2 miles daily at 3–4 mph)	1.11	1.12
Active (walks about 7 miles daily at 3–4 mph)	1.26	1.27
Very active (walks about 17 miles daily at 3–4 mph)	1.48	1.45

   - **c.** My weight in pounds is 230 divided by 2.2 = [104.5] kg
   - **d.** My height in inches is 74 divided by 39.4 = [1.97] meters

2. Using your answers in each box in step 1, complete the following calculation based on your gender and age.

Males, 19+ years old, use this calculation:

662 − (9.53 × ______) + ______ × (15.91 × ______) + (539.6 × ______)
a b c d

= ______ (285.9 + 1.26) × 1662.5 + 1009

EER

Females, 19+ years old, use this calculation:

354 − (6.91 × ______) + ______ × (9.36 × ______) + (726 × ______)
a b c d

= ______

EER

estimated energy requirement (EER) The average calorie intake that is estimated to maintain energy balance based on a person's gender, age, height, body weight, and level of physical activity.

What Are the Effects of an Energy Imbalance?

At the start of this concept, you met J. T., who is so busy juggling studying with his team practices that he consumes fewer calories daily than he expends. At his monthly weigh-in, he had dropped almost five pounds from his already light frame. In short, J. T. is in negative energy balance. Now let's look at his classmate, Pam. Although she gets a few minutes of physical activity each day, walking from one class to another on campus, Pam gets no regular exercise. At the same time, the handful of cheese curls she eats every night while watching television is adding about 100 more calories than she expends daily. Since approximately 3,500 calories make up a pound of body fat, after three months, Pam's extra 100 calories a day has led to a weight gain of a little over 2 pounds.

As you can see, over time, a chronic energy imbalance results in a change in body weight. Let's look at what is happening inside your body when an energy imbalance occurs.

Too Few Calories Can Cause Underweight

Consuming fewer calories than you need daily will cause your body to draw upon its energy stores to overcome the deficit. Glycogen and fat will be used as fuel sources to meet your body's glucose and energy needs until the next time you eat. Amino acids from the breakdown of body protein, particularly muscle, can also be used to make glucose. As a result of these processes, if you continue in negative energy balance over time, then like J. T., you will lose weight.

Too Many Calories Can Cause Overweight

Eating more calories than you need, regardless of the foods they come from, will result in your body storing the excess as fat. Recall that you have a limited capacity to store glucose as glycogen and that you can't store extra protein. However, you have an unlimited capacity to store fat.

Your body contains about 35 billion **fat cells,** which can expand to accommodate a surplus of calories.

Although Americans spend millions of dollars on weight-loss supplements, diet programs, and other products and services to help them lose weight, a proven weight-loss strategy is available to everyone free of charge: Expend more calories than you consume. Maintaining a safe and sensible negative energy balance for a period of weeks or months will achieve weight loss. You'll learn more about how to do this in a healthful manner in Concept 21.

The Take-Home Message When you don't eat enough calories to meet your needs, your glycogen and fat stores, as well as muscle mass, will be broken down for fuel. A chronic deficit of calories will produce weight loss. When you chronically consume too many calories, the excess will be stored as fat, and weight gain will occur.

UCook 

The Best French "Fried" Potatoes

The best french fries aren't actually fried at all, but baked in the oven. Grab the ketchup because soon these will be your favorite, heart-healthier snack!

UDo 

An Estimated Energy Requirement Online Tool

To calculate a more precise EER, you'll need to record all of your physical activity over a single day. Visit the MyPyramid Tracker link from our website and enter your personal info to calculate your EER.

The Top Five Points to Remember

1. A healthy body weight is one that doesn't increase the risk of developing any weight-related health problems. Being very underweight increases the risk for nutritional deficiencies and related health problems. Being overweight increases the risk for chronic diseases, such as heart disease, cancer, and type 2 diabetes.
2. To assess if you are at a healthy weight, you can measure your BMI, which is your weight in relation to your height. A BMI below 18.5 is considered underweight. A BMI of 18.5 to 24.9 is considered healthy. If your BMI is 25 or up to 29.9, you are considered overweight. A BMI of 30 or higher is considered obese. As your BMI increases above 25, so does your risk of dying from many chronic diseases. Some individuals, such as athletes, may have a high BMI but their weight doesn't put them at a health risk because they are not overfat. In contrast, frail individuals may have a healthy BMI but be at risk. Excess weight around the middle, measured by your waist circumference, could put you at a higher health risk, regardless of your BMI.
3. When your energy intake equals your energy expenditure, you are in energy balance. When you consume more energy (calories) than you expend, you are in positive energy balance and weight gain occurs. When your calories fall short of your needs and/or you expend more energy, you are in negative energy balance and lose weight.
4. Your basal metabolic rate (BMR), the thermic effect of food (TEF), and your physical activities all factor into your daily energy needs. Your BMR is influenced mainly by your lean body mass but also by your age, gender, body size, genes, ethnicity, emotional and physical stress, thyroid hormones, nutritional state, and environmental temperature. Your caffeine intake and use of nicotine can also affect your BMR.
5. Consuming fewer calories than you expend daily over time will lead to weight loss. Consuming more calories than you expend daily over time will lead to weight gain.

Test Yourself

1. Kyle has a BMI of 27. He is considered
   a. underweight.
   b. at a healthy weight.
   c. overweight.
   d. obese.
2. Central obesity is
   a. the accumulation of excess fat in your hips and thighs.
   b. the accumulation of excess fat in your stomach area.
   c. the accumulation of excess fat in your arms and legs.
   d. none of these.
3. Your basal metabolic rate (BMR) is
   a. the amount of energy you expend during physical activity.
   b. the amount of energy you expend digesting your food.
   c. the amount of energy (calories) you consume daily.
   d. the amount of energy you expend to meet your basic physiological needs.
4. Which is an example of a factor that increases your BMR?
   a. growing older
   b. fasting for several days
   c. maintaining a lean body mass
   d. all of the above
5. Pam typically consumes about 100 calories more than she expends each day. Which of the following statements is true about Pam?
   a. Pam is likely to lose weight.
   b. Pam is currently in energy balance.
   c. Over six months, Pam is likely to gain a few ounces.
   d. Over six months, Pam is likely to gain a few pounds.

Answers

1. (c) Because Kyle's BMI falls between 25 and 29.9, he is considered overweight. If his BMI were under 18.5, he would be underweight, while a BMI of 18.5 to 24.9 would put him in the healthy weight category. A BMI of 30 and higher is considered obese.
2. (b) Central obesity is the accumulation of excess fat in the stomach area; it can be determined by measuring a person's waist circumference. Central obesity increases the risk for heart disease, diabetes, and hypertension.
3. (d) Your BMR is the minimum amount of energy (calories) needed to keep your blood circulating and lungs breathing so that you can stay alive. The amount of energy, or calories, you expend during physical activity is not factored into your BMR. The energy you expend digesting, absorbing, and processing food is called the thermic effect of food (TEF); it is also not part of your BMR. The amount of energy, or calories, you consume daily doesn't factor into your BMR.
4. (c) Since muscle tissue is more metabolically active than fat tissue, maintaining a lean body mass increases BMR. As you age, your BMR decreases. Fasting can actually reduce your BMR.
5. (d) Since Pam is consuming more energy than she is expending, she is likely to experience the effects of an energy imbalance, in this case gaining about 5 pounds in six months.

Web Resources

- For more information on weight management, visit the Weight-control Information Network (WIN) at: http://win.niddk.nih.gov/index.htm
- For more on achieving and managing a healthy weight, visit the CDC's website at: www.cdc.gov/nccdphp/dnpa/healthyweight/index.htm

21 Overweight and Obesity

Fighting the Factors That Put on Weight

1. The percentage of Americans who are overweight has more than **doubled** in the past 40 years. **T/F**

2. Your body weight is affected by your **genes** and your environment. **T/F**

3. Over **40 percent** of the homes in the United States have three or more televisions. **T/F**

4. Eating more vegetables and fruits can help you **lose** weight. **T/F**

5. The **nutrient** that has the most effect on satiety is fat. **T/F**

Eighteen-year-old Hannah is more nervous about the "freshman 15" than about her course load. After struggling with her weight for years, she was able to maintain a healthy 130 pounds during her senior year of high school by changing her eating habits and walking daily. She's continued those habits since then, but being away from home and surrounded by unhealthy foods makes her worry that she'll become another freshman statistic: the student who gains 15 pounds by the end of the first year of college. In contrast, her dorm mate, Jenna, rarely thinks about her weight—or her health. She skips breakfast, avoids exercise, and likes to snack on chips and cookies, especially in the evenings, when she's studying or watching TV.

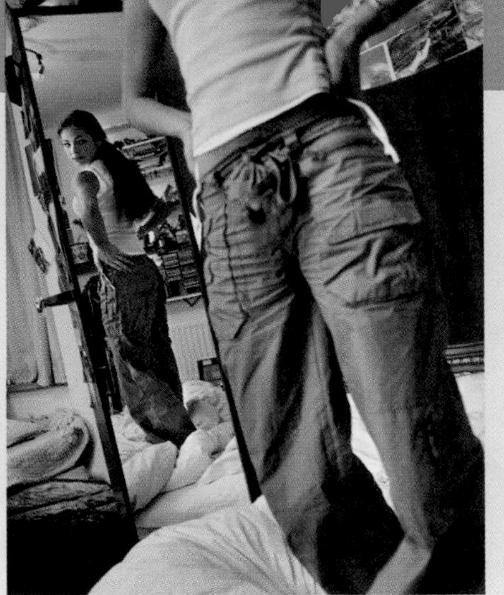

Hannah may be surprised to learn that the "freshman 15" is not as common as she thinks. However, Jenna has some habits that will make weight management difficult. In this concept, you'll learn why these habits are less than healthful, as well as strategies that college students and others can use to avoid unnecessary weight gain.

Answers

1. True. In the 1960s, about 32 percent of Americans were overweight. That percentage is now over 65 percent. See page 2 for more.
2. True. To find out why and how these factors interact with each other, turn to page 5.
3. True. Turn to page 8 to see how watching TV and other sedentary habits, can affect your weight.
4. True. Surprising as it may be, eating *more* of certain foods can help you lose weight. To find out why, turn to page 10.
5. False. Although fat makes food stay in the stomach longer, which slows its digestion and absorption, it isn't the nutrient that provides the greatest level of satiety. You may be surprised to learn what is. Turn to pages 11 and 12 to find out.

Flip through a magazine, watch television, or surf the Internet, and before long you'll find someone talking about weight loss. You may be accustomed to so much media attention to weight management, but it hasn't always been that way. In the early 1960s, fewer than 32 percent of Americans were overweight, so the topic didn't receive nearly as much media attention. Today, over 65 percent of Americans are overweight, so it's a hot topic.[1] In fact, in 2005, obesity was the most frequently covered health story in the media.[2]

Americans' expanding girths are shrinking their wallets. As a group, we spend over $45 billion—the highest amount ever—on everything from over-the-counter diet pills to books, magazines, online support groups, and commercial dieting centers to help shed the excess weight. Unfortunately, we aren't having much success, and the U.S. health care system bears over $92 billion in costs of treating the medical complications associated with being overweight.[3] No matter what you weigh, some of your tax dollars are supporting these costs. Despite spending so much money on the battle of the bulge, Americans are not winning the war on weight control.

What is causing this trend and how unhealthy is it? If you need to lose weight, what are the best strategies for doing so?

What Is Overweight and Why Is It a Problem?

As you learned in Concept 20, a healthy weight is a body weight that doesn't increase your risk of developing weight-related health problems or diseases.[4] In contrast, **overweight** is defined as a BMI between 25.0 and 29.9. It means that a person weighs as little as about 10 to 15 pounds more than a healthy weight.[5] Although 10 pounds may not sound like a lot, try this exercise: The next time you are in a supermarket, head to the produce aisle and pick up two 5-pound bags of potatoes. Try walking around with them for a while. Before long, your arms will probably be tired and you'll be ready to sit down for a rest. Can you imagine carrying this extra weight around every minute of your day?

overweight Weighing about 10 to 15 pounds more than a healthy weight for your height—clinically, a BMI between 25.0 and 29.9.

Being overweight is also a stepping-stone toward developing **obesity,** a BMI at or above 30.0. People who are obese carry 25 to 40 or more pounds of excess weight (the equivalent of carrying around a toddler or young child all day). Currently, 33 percent of Americans are obese.[6] Being overweight leads to numerous health problems. In addition to potentially leading to obesity, being overweight can increase your risk for the following:

- Hypertension, stroke, and heart disease. Generally, as a person's weight increases, so does his or her blood pressure. Overweight individuals can experience increased retention of sodium, which causes both increased blood volume and resistance in the blood vessels. This and additional demands on the heart likely contribute to high blood pressure.[7] High blood pressure increases the risk for stroke and heart disease. Overweight people also tend to have high blood levels of both fat and LDL ("bad") cholesterol, and less of HDL ("good") cholesterol, which is an unhealthy combination for the heart.
- Gallbladder disease. High blood cholesterol levels also increase the risk for gallstones and gallbladder disease. They are also more likely to contribute to an enlarged gallbladder, impairing its function.
- Type 2 diabetes. Over 80 percent of those with type 2 diabetes are overweight. Excess weight causes the body's cells to become insulin resistant. Over time, this resistance causes the pancreas to work harder to produce more insulin and can eventually cause the pancreas to stop producing insulin altogether.
- Certain cancers. Incidences of certain cancers, such as cancers of the colon and breast (in postmenopausal women), are higher in people who are overweight or obese.
- Osteoarthritis. Excess weight means extra stress on joints, especially in the knees, hips, and lower back, and contributes to osteoarthritis.
- Sleep apnea. A condition in which breathing stops for brief periods during sleep, sleep apnea disrupts a person's ability to obtain a restful slumber. The fat stored around the neck, as well as fat-induced inflammation in that area, may contribute to a smaller airway and interfere with breathing.[8]

Americans aren't the only ones getting bigger—our pets are too. According to the National Academy of Sciences, there has been an **epidemic of obesity** among pet dogs and cats.

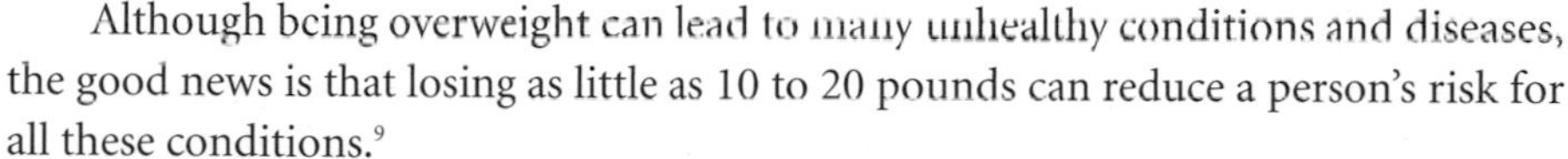

Although being overweight can lead to many unhealthy conditions and diseases, the good news is that losing as little as 10 to 20 pounds can reduce a person's risk for all these conditions.[9]

The Take-Home Message **Overweight is a BMI of 25.0 to 29.9. Obesity is a BMI of 30.0 or greater. Being overweight or obese can be unhealthy, increasing your risk for heart disease, certain cancers, and a variety of other serious health problems.**

obesity Having an unhealthy amount of body fat—clinically, a BMI of 30.0 or more.

The obesity trend is such a hot topic in the United States that it is frequently covered by the mainstream media.

What Factors Contribute to Overweight?

Many factors influence your body weight, starting with what and how often you eat. Physiology, genetics, and your environment also play a role.

Hunger and Appetite Affect What and When You Eat

Recall from Concept 6 that there is a difference between your physiological need for food (or hunger) and the psychological factors that prompt you to eat (your appetite.) Hunger is the physical need for nourishment that drives you to consume food. Once you start eating, hunger will subside and a feeling of satiety will arise. **Satiety** is the sensation that you have had enough to eat. Satiety determines the length of time between eating episodes.[10] That is, the longer you feel satiated, the longer you're likely to delay the start of your next eating episode. Anything that increases satiety is likely going to decrease weight gain—and vice versa. Scientists are currently studying the influence of various body chemicals, as well as certain foods and nutrients, on satiety.

Physiological Mechanisms Help Regulate Hunger and Satiety

Various physiological feedback mechanisms involving the mouth, stomach, intestines, and brain all work together to increase or decrease your hunger. For example, many hormones play a role. When your stomach is empty, the hormone *ghrelin,* which is produced mainly in the stomach, signals your brain that you need to take in food. Your body produces more ghrelin during fasting (such as between meals) in order to stimulate hunger, and it produces less after food is consumed. Another hormone, *leptin,* which is produced in fat tissue, helps regulate your body fat by affecting hunger. As your fat stores increase, leptin signals the brain to decrease your level of hunger and food intake.

Once food enters your mouth, sensory signals are sent to your brain that tell you whether to continue eating. The feedback mechanism is very much affected by your prior experience of tasting that food.[11] For example, a spoonful of your favorite ice cream is a pleasant stimulus, and your brain would encourage you to keep eating it. However, if you took a sip of sour milk, this stimulus would be unacceptable to the brain, especially if the last time you drank sour milk it made you sick. Your brain will instruct you to spit out the sour milk, so that you don't swallow it.

Once food is in your stomach, other factors, such as the size of the meal, come into play. After you eat a large meal, your stomach becomes distended. This will signal the brain to decrease your hunger, and you will stop eating. A distended stomach also causes the release of *cholecystokinin,* a hormone that will decrease your hunger and help you feel satiated.[12]

satiety The sensation that you feel when you have had enough to eat. Satiety determines how long you may go between meals and/or snacks.

When the food reaches your small intestine, the protein, fatty acids, and monosaccharides all stimulate feedback to the brain to decrease your hunger. Once these nutrients are absorbed, the hormone insulin is released, which also causes the brain to decrease your hunger.[13]

In a perfect world, all these physiological mechanisms would keep you in perfect energy balance. When you were hungry, you'd eat, and when you were satiated, you'd stop. The reality, however, is that many people override these mechanisms and end up in energy imbalance.

Just as we inherit different genes that give us our unique facial features, skin color, and bone structure, our genes influence our bodies' responses to food.

Genetics Plays a Role in Determining Body Weight

Genetics has such a strong influence on your body weight that, if your mother and father are overweight (with a BMI over 25), your risk of becoming obese approximately doubles, and your risk triples if they are obese (having a BMI of 30 or higher). If your parents are severely obese (with a BMI over 40), your risk of also being severely obese is five times greater than if they were not.[14] Studies on separated identical twins raised in different home environments have confirmed this, as both twins showed similar weight gain and body fat distribution.[15]

Research suggests that genetic differences in the level or the functioning of some hormones can influence a person's body weight and appetite. For example, genetically high levels of ghrelin may cause some people to overeat and become obese.[16] Individuals who are genetically prone to being leptin deficient become massively obese, yet when they are given leptin, their appetite decreases and their weight falls to within a healthy range.[17] Ironically, many obese people have adequate amounts of leptin but the brain has developed a resistance to it, rendering its appetite control ineffective.[18] For these individuals, other mechanisms are coming into play that prevent leptin from functioning as a regulator of their appetite.

Genetics may also affect how calories are expended in the body by affecting *thermogenesis* (*thermo* = heat, *genesis* = origin), which is the production of heat in body cells. Genes may cause different rates of *nonexercise-associated thermogenesis (NEAT),* which is the energy you expend during fidgeting, standing, chewing gum, getting up and turning off the television, and engaging in other nonexercise movement throughout the day. When some individuals overeat, they are able to rev up their NEAT to expend some of the excess calories and are thus better able to manage their energy balance.[19] Many overweight individuals don't appear to have this compensatory mechanism.

Some researchers have described a genetic "set point" that determines body weight. This theory holds that the body fights to remain at a specific body weight with mechanisms that oppose significant weight loss or gain. In other words, a person's weight remains fairly constant because the body "has a mind of its own." Given that the weight of Americans has disproportionately increased over the last few decades relative to previous decades, either this theory isn't true or the set point can be overridden.[20]

RATE YOURSELF ★★★

Does Your Environment Impact Your Energy Balance?

1. Do you eat out at least once a day?
   Yes ☐ **No** ☐
2. Do you often buy snacks at convenience stores, coffee shops, vending machines, sandwich shops, or other eateries?
   Yes ☐ **No** ☐
3. Do you buy the super-size portions of fast foods or snacks because you think you're getting more for your money?
   Yes ☐ **No** ☐
4. When you order pizza, do you have it delivered?
   Yes ☐ **No** ☐
5. Do you drive around a parking lot to get the closest parking space to the store entrance?
   Yes ☐ **No** ☐
6. Do you get off at the subway or bus stop that is nearest your destination?
   Yes ☐ **No** ☐
7. Do you take the elevator when stairs are available in a building?
   Yes ☐ **No** ☐
8. Do you e-mail, text, or call your friends and neighbors, rather than walk over to talk to them in person?
   Yes ☐ **No** ☐

Answer

All of these habits contribute to an obesity-promoting environment. If you answered "yes" to more than half, you should think about how you can improve your lifestyle habits.

Genetics Interact with Your Environment to Influence Your Weight

Research suggests that people with a genetic propensity to become overweight experience greater challenges to preventing obesity in an environment that is conducive to gaining weight. This relationship is referred to as a *gene-environment interaction.* To explain how these two entities interact with each other, researchers have used the analogy that genes load the gun but an obesity-promoting environment pulls the trigger.[21] For instance, if a person's lifestyle stays the same, his or her weight should remain fairly stable. However, if the environment shifts to make it easier to gain weight, the body will also shift, but it will shift upward. This means that an environment in which people can easily and cheaply obtain endless amounts of energy-dense food may be one of the biggest culprits in the current obesity epidemic. In one study, rats, which should genetically be able to maintain a healthy body weight, were shown to overeat and become fat when they had access to unlimited fatty foods and sweets.[22]

The same effect has been observed in human populations. For instance, Pima Indians of the southwestern United States have a high rate of obesity. Research comparing Pimas in Mexico with Pimas living in Arizona suggested that the environment promoted weight gain in this weight-susceptible population. The traditional Mexican Pimas whom the researchers studied lived an active lifestyle and ate a diet rich in complex carbohydrates and lower in animal fats than that of the "Americanized" Pimas in Arizona, who had a more sedentary lifestyle and fatty diet. The overweight Mexican Pimas, on average, had a BMI of about 25, compared with the obese Arizona Pimas, who had, on average, a BMI of over 33.[23] The traditional Pimas had a better chance of avoiding obesity because they lived in a healthier environment. As this study suggests, even if you have a genetic predisposition to being overweight, it's not a done deal. If you are determined to make healthy dietary choices and engage in regular physical activity, you can "outsmart" your genes!

Environmental Factors Can Increase Appetite and Decrease Physical Activity

How many times have you eaten a satisfying meal before going to the movies but bought a bucket of popcorn at the theatre, anyway? You didn't buy the popcorn because you were hungry. You just couldn't resist the buttery smell and the allure of munching during the film.

Many environmental stimuli can drive your appetite. In addition to aromas and certain venues (such as movie theatres), events, such as holidays and sporting events; people, such as your friends and family; and even the convenience of obtaining food can all encourage you to eat even when you're not hungry.

The average weight gain between Thanksgiving and New Year's Day is **about a pound.** Many people don't lose this extra weight and add to it every year.

Over the past few decades, our environment has changed in ways that have made it easier for many of us to incur an energy imbalance and a propensity to gain weight. Does your environment affect your energy balance? Rate Yourself to find out how your environment may influence the lifestyle decisions that you make throughout your day.

Let's look at some of the most significant environmental issues that are feeding Americans' energy imbalance.

We Work More and Cook Less

One reason Americans are getting larger is that they're not eating at home as much. Research shows that adults today spend more time traveling to work and devote more of their daily hours to work than in previous decades.[24] This longer workday means there is less time to devote to everyday activities, such as food preparation. Although they might seem insignificant, tasks such as preparing a meal and cleaning up afterward burn more calories than sitting in your kitchen, waiting for the pizza delivery van to arrive. More importantly, the calorie content of restaurant meals is much higher than that of meals we prepare for ourselves at home. Today, almost one-third of Americans' daily calories come from ready-to-eat foods that are prepared outside the home.[25]

Between 1972 and 1995, the prevalence of eating out in the United States increased by almost 90 percent, a trend that is expected to increase steadily to the year 2020.[26] To accommodate this demand, the number of eateries in the United States has almost doubled, to nearly 900,000 food service establishments, during the last three decades.[27] In light of these factors, it's no surprise that dining out frequently is associated with a higher BMI.[28] The top three foods selected when eating out, especially among college-age diners, are energy-dense french fries, hamburgers, and pizza. Less-energy-dense, waist-friendly vegetables, fruits, and salads don't even make the top five choices on the list among college-age diners. For many people, dining out often is harming their diet by making energy-dense foods too readily available and displacing less-energy-dense vegetables and fruits.

We Eat More (and More)

In the United States, food is easy to get, there's a lot to choose from, and portion sizes are generous. All these factors are associated with consuming too many calories.[29]

High-calorie, high-fat pizza is just one of the foods that college students commonly order when eating out.

Years ago, people went to a bookstore for the sole purpose of buying a book. Now they go to a bookstore to sip a mocha latte and nibble on biscotti while they ponder which book to buy. Americans can grab breakfast at a hamburger drive-through, lunch at a museum, a sub sandwich at many gas stations, and a three-course meal of nachos, pizza, and ice cream at a movie theatre. At any moment of your day, you can probably easily find a bundle of calories to consume.

This access to a variety of foods is problematic for weight-conscious individuals. While the appeal of a food diminishes as it continues to be eaten (that is, the first bite tastes the best but each subsequent bite loses some of that initial pleasure), having a variety of foods available allows the eater to move on to another food once boredom sets in.[30] The more good-tasting foods that are available, the more a person will eat. For example, during that three-course meal at the movie theatre, once you're tired of the nachos, you can move on to the pizza, and when that loses its appeal, you can dig into the ice cream. If the pizza and ice cream weren't available, you would have stopped after the nachos and consumed fewer calories.

Research shows that women who eat out five or more times weekly consume close to 300 calories more on those days than do women who eat at home.

The portion sizes of many foods, such as french fries and sodas, have doubled, if not tripled, over the past 20 years and are much higher than the standard portions listed on food labels. Because the "supersized" portions often cost only slightly more than the regular size, consumers perceive them as bargains. From the restaurant's point of view, the cost of increasing the portion size is outweighed by the extra money the consumer pays for the larger size. Hence, at many restaurants, movie theatres, and elsewhere, supersizing is common. Research shows that people tend to eat more of a food, and thus more calories, when larger portions are served.[31]

When you serve yourself a food item at home, you are influenced by the size of the serving bowl you use and the size of the package of food. Serving yourself from a large bowl or package has been shown to increase the amount of the food you put on your plate by more than 20 percent.[32] This means that you are more likely to scoop out (and eat) a bigger serving of ice cream from a half-gallon container than from a pint container. To make matters worse, most people don't compensate for these extra calories by reducing their portions at the next meal.[33]

We Sit More and Move Less

Americans are not only eating more calories—about 300 calories more daily since 1985—but also expending less energy during the day.[34] The resulting increase in "calories in" and decrease in "calories out" is a recipe for an energy imbalance and weight gain. Compared with years past, Americans are expending less energy both at work and during their leisure time.

When your great-grandparents went to work in the morning, chances are they headed out to the fields or off to the factory. Your parents and older siblings, though, are more likely to head off to an office and sit in front of a computer, and you probably sit at a desk for much of your day. This shift in work from jobs that required manual labor to jobs that are more sedentary has been shown to increase the risk of becoming overweight or obese.[35] One study found that men who sit for more than 6 hours during their workday are at higher risk of being overweight than those who sit for less than an hour daily.[36]

Technology in the workplace allows us to communicate with everyone without having to leave our desks. This means that people no longer have to get up and walk to see a colleague down the hall or a client across town. Researchers have estimated that a 145-pound person expends 3.9 calories for each minute of walking, compared with 1.8 calories per minute of sitting. Thus, walking 10 minutes during each workday to communicate in person with coworkers would expend 5,000 more calories annually than would be expended if the person sat in the office, sending e-mails or calling colleagues on the phone.[37]

Labor-saving devices also affect energy expenditure outside of work. Driving short distances is now the norm, while walking and biking have decreased over the years.[38] Many Americans have stopped pushing lawn mowers and are riding them instead. Leaf blowers and snow blowers have replaced rakes and shovels. Dishes aren't washed by hand but are stacked in a dishwasher.[39] All of these labor-saving devices add up, and the cumulative reduction in energy expenditure can total more than 100 calories a day.[40] As technology continues to advance and allows you to become more energy efficient in your work and lifestyle habits, you need to offset this conservation of energy with planned physical activity at another time of the day.

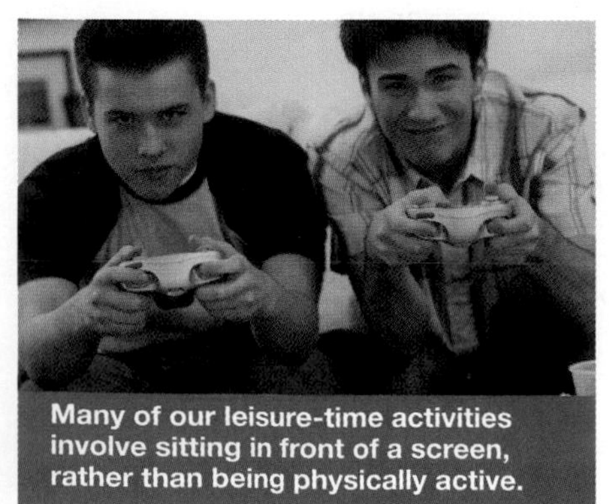

Many of our leisure-time activities involve sitting in front of a screen, rather than being physically active.

More than half of all Americans do not accumulate even the recommended minimum of 30 minutes of moderate-intensity activity on most days weekly.[41] In fact, over 20 percent of Americans report no leisure-time physical activity daily, due partly to the fact that leisure and social activities have become more sedentary.[42] Currently, 98 percent of the homes in the United States own at least one television, and over 40 percent have three or more.[43] With so many TVs in the house, everyone can retreat to different rooms to watch shows for hours on end. Other sedentary activities, such as playing video games and surfing the Web, have also increased. Research shows that 2- to 18-years-olds spend over 5 hours daily, on average, on a combination of "screen time" activities. These include watching TV, playing video games, and spending time on nonwork/school-related computer activities—even though experts have suggested limiting screen time to 2 hours daily.[44]

In short, we are moving less, both at work and at home. Combine this reduction in energy expenditure with an environment that is conducive to eating and it's not difficult to see why so many Americans are overweight or obese. Diet and lifestyle changes can help an individual lose weight, or at the very least, prevent further weight gain. Let's find out how.

The Take-Home Message **Your appetite is influenced by physiological mechanisms, your genes, and your environment. Physiological mechanisms, such as hormones, signal your brain to increase your hunger when you are hungry and decrease it after you have eaten. Genetics can make it more difficult for some individuals to manage their weight. The current environment—which provides easy access to a variety of excessive amounts of energy-dense foods and at the same time decreases energy expenditure—encourages obesity.**

TABLE TIPS

Eat More to Weigh Less

Eat more whole fruit and drink less juice at breakfast. An orange has more fiber and bulk than OJ.

Make the vegetable portion on your dinner plate twice the size of your meat portion. Have a side salad with low-fat dressing with your lunch sandwich instead of a snack bag of chips.

Order your next pizza with less pepperoni and more peppers, onions, and tomatoes. A veggie pizza can have 25 percent fewer calories and about 50 percent less fat and saturated fat than a meat pie.

Cook whole-wheat-blend pasta instead of enriched pasta for your next Italian dinner. Ladle on plenty of tomato sauce, and don't forget a big tossed salad as an appetizer.

How Can You Lose Weight Healthfully?

According to the National Institutes of Health, overweight individuals should aim to lose about 10 percent of their body weight over a six-month period.[45] This means that the goal for an overweight 180-pound person should be to shed 18 pounds over six months, about 3 pounds a month, or 3/4 pound weekly.

Because a person must have an energy deficit of approximately 3,500 calories over time to lose a pound of fat, a deficit of 250 to 500 calories daily will result in a weight loss of about ½ to 1 pound weekly. This is a healthy rate of weight loss that you can sustain. Although fad diets promise dramatic weight loss "overnight," don't be fooled. These plans are not based on legitimate science, and some can endanger your health. We'll talk more about fad diets in Concept 22.

Although there is no single diet approach that has been universally embraced, many health experts agree that a person needs to adjust three areas of life for successful, long-term weight loss (Figure 21.1):

- Diet
- Physical activity
- Behavior modification

Let's start with the diet.

Eat Smart Because Calories Count

When it comes to losing weight, there are two important words that need to be remembered: *calories count*—no matter where they come from. Because an energy imbalance of too many calories in and not enough calories out causes weight gain, reversing the imbalance will cause the opposite. That is, taking in fewer calories and burning off more will result in weight loss.

However, cutting back too drastically on calories often results in a failed weight-loss attempt. If a person skips meals or isn't satiated at each meal because of skimpy portions, he or she will experience hunger between meals and be more inclined to snack on energy-dense foods.

Figure 21.1 Three Pieces of the Long-Term Weight Loss Puzzle
Diet, physical activity, and behavior modification are all necessary for long-term weight management.

Thus, a key strategy during the weight-loss process is to eat a healthy, balanced diet that is not only lower in calories but also *satisfying.* One way you can add heft and satiation to your lower-calorie meals is by including higher-volume foods.

Eat More Vegetables, Fruit, and Fiber

People tend to eat the same amount of food regardless of its energy density—that is, the number of calories in the meal.[46] In other words, you need a certain volume of food in order to feel full. It is very easy to overeat energy-dense, low-volume foods such as candy, which can easily fill you *out* before they fill you *up.* You'll overeat them before you become satiated. The reverse of this—eating high-volume, low-energy-density foods that fill you *up* before they fill you *out*—can help in weight management. High-volume foods include fruits and vegetables, which are bulked up because of their water content, and whole grains, which contain a lot of fiber. These foods are also low in fat (which contains 9 calories/gram) and high in carbohydrate (which contains only 4 calories/gram). Research shows that these foods are associated with increased satiety and reduced feelings of hunger and calorie intake.[47]

In fact, consuming a large, high-volume, low-energy-density salad before a meal can reduce the calories eaten at that meal by more than 10 percent.[48] Adding vegetables to sandwiches and soups increases both the volume of food consumed and meal satisfaction and helps displace higher-calorie items (Figure 21.2). If you are full after eating a sandwich loaded with vegetables, you'll eat less from a bag of energy-dense chips. This is important because you don't need to eliminate chips from your diet if you enjoy them. Any food—from chocolate to chips—can be modest in calories if you eat modest amounts. Figure 21.3 provides examples of low-, moderate-, and high-energy-density foods. See the Table Tips for ways to increase the volume of foods you consume, while decreasing your overall calorie intake.

Change low-volume . . .

Sandwich	Calories
Whole-wheat bread, 2 slices	138
Ham, 4 oz	125
American cheese, 2 oz	213
Total	**476**

Change low-volume . . .

Soup	Calories
Chicken broth, 3/4 cup	29
Chicken (white meat), 1/2 cup	106
Noodles, 1 cup	212
Total	**347**

. . . to high-volume

Sandwich	Calories
Whole-wheat bread, 2 slices	138
Ham, 2 oz	63
American cheese, 1 oz	106
Tomato, 2 slices	7
Romaine lettuce, 2 leaves	10
Total	**324**

. . . to high-volume

Soup	Calories
Chicken broth, 3/4 cup	29
Chicken (white meat), 1/2 cup	106
Noodles, 1/2 cup	106
Mixed vegetables, 1/2 cup	59
Total	**300**

Figure 21.2 Adding Volume to Your Meals
Adding high-volume foods, such as fruits and vegetables, to your sandwiches, soups, and meals can add to satiety and displace higher-calorie foods, two factors that can help in weight management.

Figure 21.3 The Energy Density of Foods

▲ **Low**
These foods provide 0.7 to 1.5 calories per gram and are high in water and fiber. Examples include most vegetables and fruits—tomatoes, cantaloupe, strawberries, broccoli, and cauliflower—as well as broth-based soups, fat-free yogurt, and cottage cheese.

▲ **Medium**
These foods have 1.5 to 4 calories per gram and contain less water. They include bagels, hard-cooked eggs, dried fruits, lean sirloin steak, hummus, whole-wheat bread, and part-skim mozzarella cheese.

▲ **High**
These foods provide 4 to 9 calories per gram, and are low in moisture. They include chips, cookies, crackers, cakes, pastries, butter, oil, and bacon.

Data adapted from: Centers for Disease Control and Prevention, Can Eating Fruits and Vegetables Help People to Manage Their Weight? 2005, www.cdc.gov/nccdphp/dnpa/nutrition/pdf/rtp_practitioner_10_07.pdf (accessed July 2006).

Fiber also contributes to the bulk of vegetables and fruits and their ability to prolong satiety.[49] Overweight individuals have been shown to consume less dietary fiber and fruit than normal-weight people.[50] For these reasons, high-fiber foods, such as vegetables, fruit, and whole grains, are a key part of a weight-loss diet.

Include Some Protein and Fat in Your Meals

Of all the dietary substances that increase satiety, protein has the most dramatic effect. Even though the mechanism is unknown, this is likely one of the reasons high-protein diets tend to reduce hunger and can help in weight loss.[51] Because fat slows the movement of food out of the stomach into the intestines, it can also prolong satiety. Therefore, including some lean protein and fat in all meals and even with snacks can help increase satiety between meals.

However, you don't want to add high-saturated-fat foods, such as full-fat cheeses, whole milk, fatty cuts of meat, and butter, because eating these foods to feel full will come at the expense of your heart. It would be better to add lean meat, skinless chicken, fish, nuts, and oils, which are kinder to a person's waist and heart. (Unsaturated fat still contains 9 calories per gram, so excessive amounts of nuts and oils, even though they are heart-healthy, can quickly add excess calories to the diet.)

Look at the difference among the foods shown in Figure 21.4. The snack and dinner on the left are low in volume but high in calories. The foods on the right are

Figure 21.4 The Volume of Food You Eat
Low-volume, high-calorie foods can be much less satisfying than higher-volume, lower-calorie foods.

high in volume but have almost 500 fewer calories combined! These higher-volume foods are more satisfying for fewer calories.

Use MyPyramid as a Weight-Loss Guide

Meals that contain a high volume of fruits and vegetables, whole grains, some lean protein, and modest amounts of fat are a smart combination for weight loss, so a diet that contains all the food groups in MyPyramid can be used to lose weight. Most importantly, this type of diet is well balanced and will meet your daily nutrient needs.

Reducing calorie intake a little at a time can add up to healthy weight loss. A 180-pound, overweight person who consumes 2,800 calories daily can reduce his or her intake to 2,400 to 2,600 calories for a calorie deficit of 200–400 calories per day. He or she will then lose 10 pounds in about three months. Small changes, such as switching from full-fat to nonfat dairy products or replacing an afternoon soda with a glass of water, will contribute to this calorie reduction. Following the recommendations in MyPyramid to eat a variety of foods, but replacing higher-calorie foods with lower-calorie options within each food group, results in a satisfying diet while losing weight. Adding some physical activity can further increase that daily calorie deficit. Let's now look at the second piece of the weight-loss puzzle: physical activity.

Move to Lose

Research shows that regular physical activity is associated with a healthier body weight. Devoting up to 60 minutes daily to moderate-intensity activities can help prevent people at a healthy weight from becoming overweight and can aid in weight loss for those who need to lose weight.[52] Moderately intense physical activity is the equivalent of walking 3.5 miles per hour (Table 21.1).

Regular physical activity not only adds to the daily energy deficit needed for weight loss but also displaces sedentary activity, such as watching television, which often leads to mindless snacking on energy-dense foods.[53] Going for a walk and expending calories rather than watching television while snacking on a bag of chips will provide calorie benefits beyond the exercise alone.

Table 21.1

Calories Used During Activities

Moderate Physical Activity	Approximate Calories/Hour for a 154-lb Person*	Vigorous Physical Activity	Approximate Calories/Hour for a 154-lb Person*
Hiking	370	Running/jogging (5 mph)	590
Light gardening/yard work	330	Bicycling (<10 mph)	590
Dancing	330	Swimming (slow freestyle laps)	510
Golf (walking and carrying clubs)	330	Aerobics	480
Bicycling (<10 mph)	290	Walking (4.5 mph)	460
Walking (3.5 mph)	280	Heavy yard work (chopping wood)	440
Weight lifting (general light workout)	220	Weight lifting (vigorous effort)	440
Stretching	180	Basketball (vigorous)	440

*Calories burned per hour will be higher for persons who weigh more than 154 lbs (70 kg) and lower for persons who weigh less.

Data adapted from: Centers for Disease Control and Prevention, at: cdc.gov/healthyweight/physicalactivity/index.html

TABLE TIPS

Get UP and MOVE

The next time you want to chat with a dorm mate, skip the text message and go knock on his door.

Don't go to the closest coffee shop for your morning latte. Walk to the java joint that is a few blocks farther away.

Take a 5-minute walk at least twice a day. A little jolt of exercise can help break the monotony of studying and work off some stress.

Accomplish two goals at once by scrubbing down your dorm room or apartment. A 150-pound person can burn about 4 calories for every minute spent cleaning. Scrub for 30 minutes and you can work off about 120 calories.

Offer to walk your neighbor's dog daily.

A way to assess if you are incorporating enough physical activity into your day is to count your steps (such as with a pedometer). Research suggests that accumulating 10,000 steps daily, which is the equivalent of walking 5 miles, can help reduce the risk of becoming overweight.[54] Americans, on average, accumulate only 900 to 3,000 steps daily.[55] To reach 10,000 steps, most people need to make a conscious commitment to keep moving. See the Table Tips for some ideas for fun ways to expend more energy during the day.

Break Bad Habits

Hannah, the freshman you read about at the beginning of this concept, will be relieved to find out that a 15-pound weight gain is not inevitable for college freshmen. In fact, research to support the "freshman 15" is rather slim. Some research found that weight gain didn't occur at all or didn't occur in the majority of the students.[56] In other studies, the students gained less than 5 pounds, on average, and one study showed that certain behaviors, such as snacking in the evening; the consumption of junk foods; and the number of meals eaten on weekends were associated with weight gain.[57]

While Hannah can rest assured that, as long as she continues her good habits, she won't pack on those extra pounds, her roommate, Jenna, is another story. If Jenna continues with her habits, she may find weight management during her freshman year to be an uphill struggle. Jenna would benefit from some behavior modification.

Behavior modification consists of changing the behaviors that contribute to weight gain or impede weight loss. Several behavior modification techniques can be used to identify and change poor eating behaviors: self-monitoring the behaviors by keeping a food log, controlling environmental cues that trigger eating when not hungry, and learning how to better manage stress.[58]

Do you really know when, where, what, and why you eat? Understanding the habits and emotions that drive your eating patterns can help you change your less-than-healthy behaviors. Keeping a food log is one way to track the kinds of foods you eat during the day, when and where you eat them, your moods, and hunger ratings. You can use this information to minimize or eliminate the eating behaviors that interfere with weight management.

For example, if Jenna were to keep a food record, a typical day's log may be similar to the one in Figure 21.5. Jenna has habits that are common to people who struggle with their weight. She skips breakfast daily, which causes her to be very hungry in the late morning and increases her impulsive snacking on energy-dense, low-nutrition foods from the vending machine. A study of overweight women who typically skipped breakfast showed that, once they started consuming cereal for breakfast, they indulged in less impulsive snacking.[59] Eating a bowl of high-fiber whole-grain cereal (approximately 200 calories) will likely appease Jenna's morning hunger and help her bypass her 11 a.m. vending machine snack of 270-calorie cookies and a 210-calorie sports drink. This one behavior change would not only save her 280 calories in the morning but also reduce her added sugar intake and add more nutrition to her day. Similarly, adding a less-energy-dense salad at lunch could help increase her satiety and displace at least one of the cookies that she often eats with her sandwich.

behavior modification The process of changing behavior to improve health, including identifying and altering eating patterns that contribute to weight gain or impede weight loss.

Food Log

For: Jenna

Date: Monday, September 6

Food and drink	Time eaten	What I ate/ Where I ate it	Hunger level*	Mood †
Breakfast		Skipped it	3	G
Snack	11 a.m.	Oreo cookies, PowerAde from vending machine during morning class.	5	E
Lunch	1:30 p.m.	Ham and cheese sandwich, 2 large M&M cookies in student union cafeteria.	4	B
Snack				
Dinner	6:30 p.m.	Hamburger, french fries, salad at kitchen table	4	F
Snack	7 p.m. to 10 p.m.	Large bag of tortilla chips and entire bag of Pepperidge Farm Milano cookies while studying at kitchen table	1	I

*Hunger levels (1–5): 1 = not hungry; 5 = super hungry

† **Moods:**
A = Happy; B = Content; C = Bored; D = Depressed; E = Rushed; F = Stressed; G = Tired; H = Lonely; I = Anxious; J = Angry

Figure 21.5 Food Log
Keeping track of when, where, what, and why you eat can yield some surprising information. Do you think you sometimes eat out of boredom or stress, rather than because you're hungry?

Because studying for exams stresses her out and causes her to munch even though she isn't hungry, Jenna shouldn't study in her dorm, where she is surrounded by snacks, but should go to the campus library, where eating is prohibited. Exercising before or after studying would be a healthier way to relieve her stress than eating her way through a bag of snacks.

Changing behaviors that have become unhealthy habits is another important piece of improving weight management. Individuals who eat "out of habit" and in response to their emotions need to replace this unnecessary eating to better manage their weight. The Table Tips lists some healthy behaviors that can easily be incorporated into your life.

The Take-Home Message **For successful, long-term weight loss, people need to reduce their daily calorie intake, increase their physical activity, and change their behavior. Increasing the consumption of vegetables, fruits, and fiber, along with some lean protein and healthy oils, helps with satiety and reduces unplanned snacking. Incorporating approximately 60 minutes of physical activity daily can also help with weight loss. Changing unhealthy habits by restructuring the environment can help minimize or eliminate the eating behaviors that interfere with weight loss.**

TABLE TIPS

Adopt Some Healthy Habits

Don't eat out of boredom; go for a jog instead. If we ate only when hungry, we would probably be a lot leaner.

Shop for food with a full stomach and a grocery list. Walking around aimlessly while hungry makes you more likely to grab items on a whim.

When you feel stressed, lace up your sneakers and go for a walk.

The next time you pass a difficult course, or get a long-awaited raise, celebrate without a plate. Replace the traditional restaurant dinner with a no-calorie reward, such as a new music download or the latest best-seller.

Declare a vending machine–free day at least once a week and stop the impulsive snacking. On that day, pack two pieces of fruit as satisfying snacks.

Extreme Measures for Extreme Obesity

A BMI greater than 40 is considered **extreme obesity.** People who are extremely obese are at such a high risk for conditions such as heart disease, stroke, and even death that an aggressive weight-loss treatment is necessary. Treatments that go beyond eating less and exercising more, such as a very-low-calorie diet, medications, and/or surgery, are often recommended. Let's look at each of these.

A Very-Low-Calorie Diet

On her television show in 1988, a petite-looking Oprah Winfrey beamed after having lost 67 pounds using a very-low-calorie diet. Oprah achieved her weight loss by consuming a liquid protein diet. Such protein-rich diets provide fewer than 800 calories daily, are very low in or have no carbohydrates, and have minimal amounts of fat. They are designed to help people at a high risk for disease drop a substantial amount of weight in a short amount of time. However, they are not a long-term solution. After consuming the diet for 12 to 16 weeks, the dieter is switched to a well-balanced, low-calorie diet.

Very-low-calorie diets need to be supplemented with vitamins and minerals and must be medically supervised, since they can cause dangerous electrolyte imbalances, as well as gallstones, constipation, fatigue, hair loss, and other side effects. The National Institute of Health don't recommend very-low-calorie diets because well-balanced, low-calorie diets are just as effective in producing a similar amount of weight loss after one year and are less dangerous.[1]

In the 1980s Oprah Winfrey reached her goal weight by consuming a very low-kilocalorie, liquid protein diet. She has since regained the weight, and often publicly discusses the challenges of maintaining weight loss.

After all her effort, Oprah ultimately regretted her very-low-calorie diet: "I had literally starved myself for four months—not a morsel of food—to get into a pair of size 10 Calvin Klein jeans," claims Oprah. "Two hours after that show, I started eating to celebrate—of course, within two days those jeans no longer fit!"[2]

Medications

Some prescription medications can help a person lose weight. The drugs either suppress the appetite or inhibit the absorption of fat in the intestinal tract.

The drug sibutramine (trade name Meridia) reduces hunger and increases thermogenesis, which increases energy expenditure. Because it can also increase heart rate and blood pressure, it may not be appropriate for those who have hypertension, which tends to occur in overweight individuals.

Orlistat (trade name Xenical and its over-the-counter version, Alli) inhibits an intestinal enzyme that is needed to break down fat. If the fat isn't broken down, it (and its calories) is not absorbed by the body. Instead, about 25 to 30 percent of the dietary fat is expelled in the stool. Because fat is lost in the stool, the drug can cause oily and more frequent stools, flatulence, and oily discharge.[3] Ironically, these side effects may help an individual adhere to a low-fat diet, as these effects are more pronounced if a high-fat meal is consumed.

Some nonprescription weight-loss supplements have caused such serious side effects that these products had to be withdrawn from the market. For instance, the FDA has prohibited the sale of supplements that contain ephedra (also called *Ma Huang*), the plant source for ephedrine. Ephedrine has been shown to cause chest pains, palpitations, hypertension, and an accelerated heart rate and may lead to death.[4]

Surgery

In 1998, approximately 13,000 obese patients went under the knife to reduce the size of their stomachs. Four years later, more than five times as many **gastric bypass surgeries,** or over 71,000, were done.[5] During this surgery, most of the stomach is stapled shut. This leaves a small pouch of stomach that can expand to a maximum of only about 5 ounces, the size of a woman's fist. Food leaving the small stomach pouch bypasses the rest of the stomach and the uppermost portion of the small intestine (see the figure). After the surgery, patients not only eat less because of their smaller stomachs but also have higher levels of satiety and lower levels of hunger. This effect on their appetite is thought to be associated with lower levels of ghrelin due to the loss of stomach area after the surgery.[6]

Because most of the stomach and the upper part of the small intestine are both bypassed after the surgery, individuals can experience deficiencies of vitamin B_{12}, iron, and calcium. Supplements

extreme obesity Having a BMI greater than 40.

gastric bypass surgeries Surgical procedures that reduce the functional volume of the stomach, so that less food is eaten.

liposuction The surgical removal of subcutaneous fat with a penlike instrument.

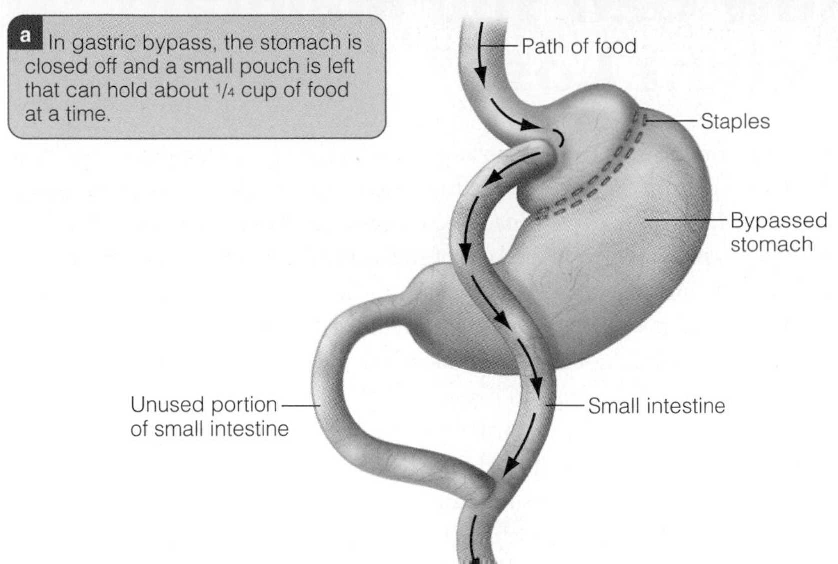

Liposuction is a surgical procedure that removes subcutaneous fat. Unlike gastric banding and bypass surgeries, liposuction is purely cosmetic and does not result in clear health benefits.

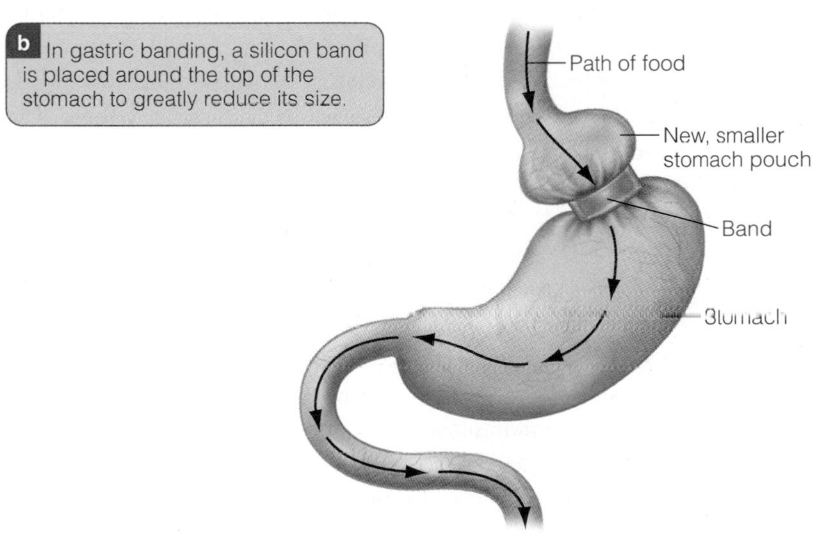

Gastric Bypass and Gastric Banding.

must be taken because of these deficiencies.

A type of gastric surgery that's becoming more popular is gastric banding, in which a silicon band is placed around the top of the stomach to create a small pouch with a very narrow opening at the bottom for the food to pass through. This delays the emptying of the stomach contents, so that the person feels fuller longer.

Although dramatic weight loss can occur and research has shown that incidences of hypertension, diabetes, high blood cholesterol levels, and sleep apnea have been reduced among people who've had the surgery, significant risks are involved. About 10 percent of those undergoing gastric bypass surgery experience complications, such as gallstones, ulcers, and bleeding in the stomach and intestines. Approximately 1 to 2 percent die.[7] After surgery, people need to be monitored long-term by their doctors and nutrition professionals to ensure that they remain healthy and meet their nutritional needs.

Another type of surgery, **liposuction,** is less about health and more about physical appearance. During liposuction, a doctor removes subcutaneous fat from the abdomen, hips, or thighs (and sometimes other areas of the body) by suctioning it out with a penlike instrument. People often undergo liposuction to get rid of *cellulite*, which isn't a medical term but refers to the fat cells that give the skin a dimpled appearance. Complications, such as infections, scars, and swelling, can arise after liposuction. Fat can also reappear at the site where it was removed, so the results of liposuction may not be permanent.

The Bottom Line

Very-low-calorie diets, medications, and surgery may be options for people who are extremely obese, but they are not without risks. For people who are overweight, the safest route to a healthy weight is to make incremental diet and lifestyle changes to take in fewer calories and expend more. Of course, the best overall strategy for weight management is to avoid becoming overweight in the first place.

How Can You Maintain Weight Loss?

You, or someone you know, may be familiar with the typical fad diet experience: the triumphant rush associated with the dropping of 10 pounds, the disappointment that sets in when 15 pounds are regained, then a new round of hope when 10 of them are re-shed. An estimated 90 to 95 percent of individuals who lose weight regain it within several years.[60] This fluctuation is known as *weight cycling,* and some research suggests that it can lead to problems such as hypertension, gallbladder disease, and elevated blood cholesterol levels, not to mention depression and feelings of frustration.[61]

However, there is some good news. Recent research suggests that weight cycling may not be as common as previously thought. A study of 800 people who had lost a substantial amount of weight showed that they were able to keep off at least 30 pounds for five years. These people were successful because they maintained their physical activity habits and positive behavior changes after they reached their weight goal.[62] They commonly limited their intake of fatty foods, monitored their calorie intake, and ate nearly five times a day, on average. (For many people, eating smaller meals allows them to avoid becoming ravenous and overeating at the next meal.) Most weighed themselves weekly and maintained a high level of daily physical activity, expending the energy equivalent of walking 4 miles a day.[63] This suggests that weight loss can be maintained as long as the individual doesn't abandon the healthy habits that promoted the weight loss and revert to the unhealthy habits that caused the excess weight in the first place.

Notice that these individuals participated in a high level of physical activity. Research suggests that physical activity can help those who've lost weight close the *energy gap.* After weight loss, a person has lower overall energy needs, because there is less body weight to maintain. The energy gap is the difference in the number of daily calories needed for weight maintenance before weight loss as compared with the number of calories needed after weight loss.[64] Researchers have estimated that the energy gap is about 8 calories per pound of lost weight.[65]

For example, someone who has lost 30 pounds needs approximately 240 fewer calories a day to maintain the new, lower body weight. This person can eat 240 fewer calories, expend 240 calories through added physical activity, or do a combination of both. Because the environment we live in seems to encourage eating more than discourages it, researchers feel that increasing daily physical activity is likely the easier way to close the energy gap.[66] *Adding* something (physical activity) to your lifestyle is often easier than *removing* something (calories). Individuals who lose weight are advised to engage in 60 to 90 minutes of moderate physical activity daily in order to maintain their weight loss.[67]

Some people are candidates for extreme treatment to help them shed their unhealthy excess weight. The box feature "Extreme Measures for Extreme Obesity" on pages 16 and 17 discusses treatment options for those with BMIs greater than 40.

The Take-Home Message People who lose weight are most likely to keep it off if they maintain the positive diet and lifestyle habits that helped them lose the weight. Eating less and/or exercising more will help close the energy gap after weight loss.

UCook

Green Beans with Sun Dried Tomatoes

Since veggies are waist-friendly, "filling you up before they fill you out," double this recipe so that you'll have a healthy snack for the next day.

UDo

Portion Distortion?

Over the last few decades, the portion sizes of many commercially prepared and fast foods have increased greatly, and so have the number of calories in a serving. Can you guess the calorie differences between the servings of yesteryear and those of today? Go online at our website to find out.

The Top Five Points to Remember

1. A healthy body weight is a body weight that doesn't increase the risk of developing any weight-related health problems. In contrast, being overweight increases the risk for chronic diseases, such as heart disease, cancer, and type 2 diabetes. If your BMI is 25 or up to 29.9, you are considered overweight. A BMI of 30 or higher is considered obese. As your BMI increases above 25, so does your risk of dying from many chronic diseases.
2. Appetite is your psychological desire for food and is affected by hunger, satiety, your emotions, and your environment. Hunger will subside as the feeling of satiation sets in after you start eating. Physiological mechanisms, such as hormones, sensory signals, and a distended stomach, as well as the size of the meal and the nutrients in your foods, influence your food intake. Genetics and your environment also play a role in your appetite and weight. If your parents are overweight, you are at a higher risk of developing obesity. An environment that enables easy access to a variety of large portions of foods, and encourages you to be sedentary, also promotes obesity.
3. Losing 10 percent of your body weight over a six-month period is considered a reasonable rate of weight loss. Losing weight rapidly can cause a person to fall short of meeting nutrient needs. Calories count. Eating more low-energy-density, high-volume foods, such as vegetables and fruit, can help you lose weight because you will feel full for fewer calories. Fiber also promotes satiation. Because protein has the most dramatic effect on satiety, eating high-protein lean meats, chicken, and fish at meals can help reduce hunger between meals. Because fat slows the movement of food out of the stomach into the intestines, it can also prolong satiety.
4. Routine physical activity can add to the daily energy deficit needed for weight loss. To aid in weight loss, overweight individuals should partake in 60 minutes of moderate-intensity exercise daily and continue at least this amount of activity daily to maintain the weight loss.
5. Changing the eating behaviors that contribute to weight gain or impede weight loss is necessary for long-term weight-loss success. Self-monitoring these behaviors by keeping a food record, controlling environmental cues that trigger eating when not hungry, and learning how to better manage stress are all behavior modification techniques that can be used by individuals who eat "out of habit" and in response to their environment.

Test Yourself

1. Being overweight can increase your risk for
   a. heart disease.
   b. osteoarthritis.
   c. gallbladder disease.
   d. all of the above.
2. You just ate a large plate of pasta and tomato sauce, so your stomach is rather full and quite distended. Which hormone is released because of the distention of your stomach?
   a. cholecystokinin
   b. insulin
   c. thyroid hormone
   d. none of the above
3. Which of the following can increase your risk of becoming overweight?
   a. having parents who are overweight
   b. having a high rate of NEAT
   c. living on your own away from home
   d. all of the above
4. Which are examples of low-energy-density, high-volume foods that can aid in weight loss?
   a. raw vegetables and salsa
   b. tomato soup
   c. fruit salad
   d. all of the above

5. Mary Ellen was obese and lost 30 pounds last year by eating a well-balanced, reduced-calorie diet and being physically active daily. To maintain her weight loss, she should continue to eat a healthy diet, monitor her eating behaviors, and
   a. accumulate 30 to 45 minutes of physical activity daily.
   b. accumulate 45 to 60 minutes of physical activity daily.
   c. accumulate 60 to 90 minutes of physical activity daily.
   d. do none of the above.

Answers

1. (d) Being overweight increases your risk for all these diseases and conditions, as well as type 2 diabetes, some cancers, and sleep apnea.
2. (a) A distended stomach causes the release of cholecystokinin, which is associated with the feeling of satiation and the ending of eating. Insulin will be released once this carbohydrate-heavy meal is digested and absorbed into the blood. Thyroid hormone affects your BMR and is not associated with your stomach being distended.
3. (a) Having parents who are overweight or obese can increase your risk of becoming overweight. Nonexercise-associated thermogenesis (NEAT), which is the energy you expend during fidgeting and other nonexercise movement throughout the day, can contribute to your total energy expenditure and help decrease your risk for weight gain. Moving out of your home and living on your own won't necessarily cause you to gain weight unless you consume more calories than you need daily.
4. (d) Vegetables, including salsa and vegetable soups, and fruit are all low-energy-density, high-volume foods. These foods increase satiation, contain few calories per bite, and can displace more energy-dense foods in the diet, all of which can help promote weight loss.
5. (c) If Mary Ellen would like to keep the weight off, she should try to accumulate 60 to 90 minutes of physical activity daily.

Web Resources

- For more on overweight and obesity, visit the Centers for Disease Control and Prevention at: www.cdc.gov/nccdphp/dnpa/obesity/index.htm
- For more information on weight control and physical activity, visit the Weight-control Information Network (WIN) at: http://win.niddk.nih.gov/index.htm
- For more weight-loss shopping tips, recipes, and menu makeovers, visit the USDA's Nutrition and Weight Management website at: www.nutrition.gov

22

1. Fashion models are about 8 percent thinner than the **average** woman. **T/F**

2. Being **skinny** is always healthy. **T/F**

3. Both men and women struggle with **eating disorders. T/F**

4. Eating disorders can be **fatal. T/F**

5. Most people **recover fully** from eating disorders. **T/F**

Underweight and Disordered Eating

When Eating Enough Is a Challenge

When her friends asked her why she hadn't been to the cafeteria lately, Kiko would say she was "on a new diet." Each day, she ate an apple for breakfast, a packet of melba toast for lunch, and a container of nonfat yogurt for dinner, along with lots of diet sodas. She also began each day with 100 sit-ups, 50 push-ups, and 10 minutes of rope skipping, then went for a 4-mile run after classes. In the evening, she rewarded herself after studying with a cup of herbal tea and a graham cracker.

After several weeks on her new diet, Kiko fainted in her yoga class. Her instructor called the university health services, and put her in the hospital for observation. Her physician informed Kiko that, at 5′ 6″ and 104 pounds, her BMI is 16.8, which means she's dangerously underweight. The doctor then told Kiko that she's going to help her gain weight. "Gain weight!" Kiko gasps. "I can't do that! I'm still too fat!"

Decades ago, Wallis Simpson, an American woman who became the Duchess of Windsor, famously claimed that one can't be "too rich or too thin." Is this true? Should we strive to be thin at all costs—or can underweight be as unhealthy as overweight? And if you are underweight, what's the best way to stay fit and healthy while you gain? We'll answer these questions in this concept.

Answers

1. False. That was true back in the 1980s. Today, fashion models are more than 20 percent thinner than the average woman. See page 3 to learn more.
2. False. Being underweight due to a poor diet can have serious health risks. Turn to page 3 to find out why.
3. True. About 10 percent of cases of eating disorders occur in men. Turn to page 10 to learn more.
4. True. Some eating disorders can be life-threatening. Turn to pages 14 and 15 to learn about the health effects of eating disorders.
5. True. And when treatment is obtained in the early stages, chances of recovery are excellent. For more, turn to page 15.

What Is Underweight and Why Can It Be a Problem?

For some, being very slender is their natural, healthy body shape, but for others, it's a sign of malnutrition. As you learned in Concept 20, **underweight** is a BMI below 18.5. People who are underweight don't have enough weight on their bodies for their height.

A Variety of Factors Can Lead to Underweight

What contributes to underweight? Sometimes the culprit is an underlying medical condition, such as cancer or an intestinal disorder; alcoholism; a psychiatric disorder, such as depression or dementia; or chronic emotional stress.[1] Poverty, which we'll discuss in Concept 28, can also be a factor. For instance, seniors living on a fixed income may not be able to afford adequate food or transportation to a supermarket. A single mother living in poverty might go hungry so that her children can have more food. Sometimes excessive physical activity can lead to significant energy imbalance. For instance, competitive athletes can lose weight simply because their energy expenditure is so high.

Of course, one of the most common reasons for underweight is excessive calorie restriction due to dieting. There are more than 3,000 diet books on the market, written by everyone from popular TV show therapists to celebrity advisers and self-proclaimed experts with dubious credentials. Many of these plans promise quick, dramatic results, but the reality is that few are based on legitimate science and some, such as those that encourage severe calorie restriction, can even put your health at risk. (See the box feature "Fad Diets Are the Latest Fad" on page 4 for more on how the various diet plans compare.)

You probably know someone who resorts to fad diets to maintain an idealized body image that's unrealistic—and unhealthy—for him or her. Over the years, varying body shapes have trended in and out of the media spotlight (Figure 22.1). In the 1980s, fashion models were 8 percent thinner than the average woman. Today, the typical cover girl is over 20 percent thinner. The male physique is being held up to a similarly unattain-

underweight Weighing too little for your height—clinically, a BMI below 18.5.

a The male physique depicted in popular action figures in the 1970s, like Luke Skywalker and Han Solo from *Star Wars*, was more realistic than the bulked-up versions of the late 1990s.

Figure 22.1 Is Beauty Timeless?
Our perception of beauty is influenced by our culture. **(a)** The male physique depicted in popular action figures in the 1970s, such as Luke Skywalker and Han Solo from *Star Wars,* was more realistic than the bulked-up versions of the late 1990s. **(b)** Over the years, the idealized model look has gone from curvy to stick thin to sporty and back to waiflike. Today, super-slender women are the norm in magazines and movies.

able standard. Witness the change from scrawny to beefy in toy action figures over the years.[2] Although models, celebrities, and dolls may reflect the "in" look, they don't necessarily correlate with good health, nor should they be your reference for the body weight that *you* should strive to obtain.

Underweight Contributes to Poor Health

Underweight increases your risk for many health problems:

- Anemia, hair loss, irregular heartbeat, impaired nerve function, low bone density, and other disorders related to nutrient deficiencies
- Increased risk for fracture due to low bone density
- Reduced immune defenses, resulting in increased vulnerability to infection and delayed wound healing. Undernourished elderly people, in particular, are at risk for low body protein and fat stores and a depressed immune system, which makes it more difficult to fight infections. Injuries, wounds, and illnesses that would normally abate in healthy individuals can cause serious medical complications, including death, in these individuals.[3]
- In women, loss of menstrual periods and an increased risk for miscarriage. A minimum level of body fat is necessary to maintain normal reproductive functions. Underweight women who do become pregnant are 72 percent more likely to suffer a miscarriage during the first three months of pregnancy.[4]

b Over the years, the idealized model look has gone from curvy to stick thin to sporty and back to waiflike again. Today, superslender women are the norm in magazines and movies.

Fad Diets Are the Latest Fad

Americans spend over $30 billion annually on weight-loss programs, products, and pills and are more than willing to keep reaching into their wallets for the next quick diet fix.[1] Although it may seem that there is a new fad diet around every corner, many of these diets have actually been around for years.

The low-carbohydrate, high-protein and high-fat diets of the 1970s (Dr. Atkins' Diet Revolution) were replaced by the very-high-carbohydrate and very-low-fat diets of the 1980s (Pritikin diets) and continued into the early 1990s (Dr. Ornish's diet). These diets led the way to the more carbohydrate-restricted, moderate protein and fat diets of the late 1990s (The Zone diet), only to flip back to the low-carbohydrate, high-protein and high-fat diets in the early 2000s (Dr. Atkins' New Diet Revolution, South Beach). The "Battle of the Diet Books" on page 6 summarizes how these diets compare with the DRIs, as well as how they compare with each other.

After four decades of clashing diet books, does one emerge as the clear winner in the battle of the bulge? The answer is no. Researchers who analyzed close to 200 weight-loss studies using a variety of these diets concluded that it's the calories, not the composition of the diet, that count when it comes to losing weight.[2] In fact, a study comparing the Atkins, Ornish, Weight Watchers, and Zone diets showed that, no matter what diet the individuals followed, they had all lost about the same amount of weight, on average, by the end of one year. Although each of these diets provides a different percentage of carbohydrates, protein, and fat, they all had one important thing in common: They all reduced calories.

A very interesting point emerged from this study: The people who were the most diligent about adhering to the diet—no matter which one—experienced the most weight loss. However, over 20 percent of the dieters called it quits only two months into the study, and more than 40 percent of them dropped out after one year. The highest dropout rates occurred among followers of the Atkins and Ornish diets. The researchers speculate that the rigidity of these extreme diets may have caused the higher dropout rates.[3] Some extreme diets may also be unhealthy in the long term. In fact, the high dropout rate for some fad diets has probably protected many individuals from serious ill health effects and long-term nutrient deficiencies.

A fad diet doesn't fix anything long-term. If it did, there wouldn't be new (or recycled) fad diets continually appearing on the market. The two major points of this research are that (1) any diet can result in weight loss as long as calories are reduced and (2) the more realistic and doable the diet, the more likely people will stick with it long enough to lose weight.

Marketers often make sensational claims about fad diets and weight-loss products. These red flags can often tell you if a diet is questionable.

Red Flags for Diet Hype

It's the Carbs, Not the Calories, That Make You Fat!

Many fad diet ads claim that you can eat as much protein and fat as you want, as long as you keep away from the carbs. These diets claim that your consumption of pasta, breads, rice, and many fruits and vegetables should be limited, but fatty meats, such as ribs, salami, bologna, and poultry with skin, as well as butter, bacon, and cheeses, should be on the menu often.

The Truth behind the Hype

Diets that severely limit carbohydrates (<100 grams daily) eliminate so many foods, as well as sweets and treats, that it is impossible for a person not to consume at least 500 fewer calories daily. Theoretically, this will produce about 1 pound of weight loss per week.[4] When you curtail the carbohydrates, you likely will also cut back on fat.[5] When you stop eating the bagel (carbs), you'll also elimi-

What's in the Fad Diets?

Type of Diet	Source of Calories (%) Carbohydrate	Protein	Fat
Low-carbohydrate, higher-protein, high-fat (example: Atkins Diet, South Beach Diet)	<20	25–30	55–65
Very-high-carbohydrate, moderate-protein, very-low-fat (example: Dr. Ornish's Diet, Pritikin Diet)	>65	10–20	<10–19
Carbohydrate-restricted, higher-protein, moderate-fat (example: Zone Diet)	40	30	30
Compared with DRI Dietary Recommendations	**45–65**	**10–35**	**20–35**

Data adapted from: M. Freedman, J. King, and E. Kennedy, "Popular Diets: A Scientific Review," *Obesity Research* 9 (2001): 1S–40S.

nate the cream cheese (fat) you slather on each half. The monotonous nature of these diets causes people to become "bored" with eating, so they *quit the diet*. Because carbohydrates such as bread, mashed potatoes, and corn are off limits at dinner, the dieter is limited to fatty steak and not much else. Most people can eat only so much of this before it loses its appeal, so they're likely to stop eating sooner. As always, putting down the fork will cut calorie consumption.

Buyer Beware

A diet high in saturated fat and low in fiber and phytochemicals because it is low in whole grains, fruits, and vegetables is a recipe for heart disease, cancer, constipation, elevated blood cholesterol levels, and deficiencies in many vitamins such as vitamins A, E, and B_6; folate; and minerals such as calcium; iron; zinc; and potassium.[6] Thus, each time you follow a diet low in whole grains, fruits, and vegetables and high in animal fats, you are robbing your body of the protection of plant foods and overfeeding it the wrong type of fat. The high protein content of these diets may also cause the loss of calcium, thus increasing your risk for osteoporosis and kidney stones.

Lose 7 Pounds in One Week!

Many diets guarantee rapid weight loss. This may happen on a low-carbohydrate diet—but only during the first few days, and only temporarily.

The Truth behind the Hype

The 4- to 7-pound weight loss during the first week of low-carbohydrate dieting is due to a loss of body water that results from two physiological processes. First, because the reduced amount of carbohydrates can't support the body's need for glucose, the stored glycogen in the liver and muscle is broken down. Each gram of glycogen removed from storage causes the loss of 2 grams of water with it. Because you store about 500 grams of glycogen in your body, you can expect to lose approximately 2 pounds of water weight during the first week of a low-carbohydrate diet. Second, the ketone bodies generated by the breakdown of fat are lost from the body through the kidneys. This also causes the body to lose sodium. Where sodium goes, water follows. Therefore, the ketone bodies that cause you to lose sodium also cause you to lose water.[7]

Buyer Beware

Although water weight may be lost during the first week, the rate of weight loss after that is determined by the energy imbalance in the body, as in any calorie-reducing diet. As soon as carbohydrates are added back to the diet, the body will retain water and some water weight will come back on. When it comes to shedding weight, quick loss usually means quick regain.

Celebrity-Endorsed Miracle Weight-Loss Products with a Money-Back Guarantee!

Just because a celebrity tries to sell you a product doesn't mean that the product is valid. It just means that the celebrity is being paid to do what he or she does best—act.

The Truth behind the Hype

No cream, shake, or potion will magically melt away body fat. The Federal Trade Commission (FTC) has charged many firms that sell dubious products with public deception and have fined them as much as $10 million.[8]

Buyer Beware

Forget about getting your money back. The FTC has received numerous complaints from dissatisfied customers who have unsuccessfully tried to get a refund. The more miraculous the claim, the more likely you are to lose (money, that is, not weight).

Naturally Occurring Plants, Herbs, and Other Substances Will Help You Lose Weight without Risk!

"Natural" substances, such as glucomannan, guar gum, chitosan, and bitter orange, are not necessarily safer or more effective for weight loss.

The Truth behind the Hype

Glucomannan is a compound found in the root of the starchy konjac plant, and guar gum is a type of dietary fiber found in a specific bean. Both are ineffective in weight loss. Chitosan is produced from a substance found in shellfish. Although the claim is that these substances decrease the absorption of fat in the body, research doesn't back up the claim. Bitter orange is a plant that is being touted as a substitute for ephedra (discussed in the box "Extreme Measures for Extreme Obesity" in Concept 21), yet the research is not definitive on its ability to stimulate weight loss.[9]

Buyer Beware

Guar gum has been shown to cause diarrhea, flatulence, and gastrointestinal disturbances. Chitosan may cause nausea and flatulence.[10] Bitter orange can increase blood pressure and interfere with the metabolism of drugs in the body.[11] Naturally occurring substances are not necessarily safe to consume, and there's no evidence that they help you lose weight.

(continued)

Fad Diets Are the Latest Fad, continued

Battle of the Diet Books

Name	Claim	What You Eat
The South Beach Diet by Arthur Agatson	Switching to "good carbs" stops insulin resistance, cures cravings, and causes weight loss. "Good fats" protect the heart and prevent hunger.	**Yes:** Seafood, chicken breast, lean meat, low-fat cheese, most veggies, nuts, oils; (later) whole grains, most fruits, low-fat milk or yogurt, beans **Less:** Fatty meats, full-fat cheese, refined grains, sweets, juice, potatoes
The Ultimate Weight Solution by Phil McGraw	Foods that take time to prepare and chew lead to weight loss. Other "Keys to Weight Freedom" include "no-fail environment," "right thinking," "healing feelings," and "circle of support."	**Yes:** Seafood, poultry, meat, low-fat dairy, whole grains, most veggies, fruits, oils (limited) **Less:** Fatty meats, refined grains, full-fat dairy, microwaveable entrées, fried foods
Dr. Atkins' New Diet Revolution by Robert C. Atkins	A low-carb diet is the key to weight loss (and good health) because carbs cause high insulin levels.	**Yes:** Seafood, poultry, meat, eggs, cheese, salad veggies, oils, butter, cream; (later) limited amounts of nuts, fruits, wine, beans, veggies, whole grains **Less:** Sweets, refined grains, milk, yogurt
Enter the Zone by Barry Sears	Eating the right mix of the right fats, carbs, and protein keeps you trim and healthy by lowering insulin.	**Yes:** Seafood, poultry, lean meat, fruits, most veggies, low-fat dairy, nuts **Less:** Fatty meats, full-fat dairy, butter, shortening, grains (limited), sweets, potatoes, carrots, bananas
Eat More, Weigh Less by Dean Ornish	Slashing the fat in foods is the key to weight loss.	**Yes:** Beans, fruits, veggies, grains, nonfat dairy (limited) **Less:** Meat, seafood, poultry, oils, nuts, butter, dairy (except nonfat), sweets, alcohol

Data from: D. Schardt, *Nutrition Action Healthletter* (January/February 2004): 6–7.

Is the Science Solid?	Is the Diet Healthy?	Worst Feature	Most Preposterous Claim
A healthy version of Atkins diet that's backed by solid evidence on fats and heart disease	**Pro:** Mostly healthy foods **Con:** Restricts some nutritious foods	Restricts carrots, bananas, pineapple, watermelon	You won't ever be hungry (despite menus that average just 1,200 calories a day).
A tough-love manual that relies more on Dr. Phil's opinion than science	**Pro:** Mostly healthy foods. **Con:** Gives no menus, recipes, or advice on how much of what to eat	It pushes Dr. Phil's name-brand expensive, questionable supplements, bars, and shakes	"Each of these nutrients [in his supplements] has solid clinical evidence (and a record of safety) behind it."
This low-carb "bible" overstates the results of weak studies and the evidence on supplements (however, in recent small studies, people lost more weight after six—but not 12—months on Atkins than on a typical diet)	**Con:** Too much red meat may raise risk for colon or prostate cancer. **Con:** Lack of fiber, vegetables, and fruits may raise risk for heart disease, stroke, cancer, diverticulosis, and constipation.	The long-term safety of this approach not established	"Only by doing Atkins can you lose weight eating the same number of calories on which you used to gain weight."
It exaggerates evidence that the Zone Diet is the key to weight loss and implies that the diet can cure virtually every disease	**Pro:** Mostly healthy foods **Con:** Few recipes or menus	It may convince people to use the diet to treat cancer, AIDS, chronic pain, impotence, depression, arthritis	"I believe that the hormonal benefits gained from a Zone-favorable diet will be considered the primary treatment for all chronic disease states, with drugs being used as secondary backup."
This diet worked (when combined with exercise and stress reduction) in a small but long-term study.	**Pro:** Mostly healthy foods **Con:** Too many carbs may raise triglycerides and lower HDL ("good") cholesterol if people don't exercise, lose weight, and reduce stress.	It unnecessarily restricts seafood, turkey and chicken breast, oils, nuts, and fat-free dairy	Eating a very-low-fat vegetarian diet is easy.

The Take-Home Message Underweight is a BMI below 18.5. Physical and psychiatric disorders, poverty, excessive physical activity, and excessive calorie restriction can lead to underweight. The risk for many health problems and even premature death is increased in those who are underweight.

How Can You Gain Weight Healthfully?

For people who are naturally underweight, weight gain can be as challenging and frustrating as weight loss is for those who are overweight. The major difference is that thin people rarely get sympathy from others. In fact, their efforts to eat more can sometimes be met with disparaging comments from those who don't understand their experience.

Like overweight individuals, those who are underweight experience an energy imbalance. In their case, however, they consume fewer calories than they expend, so people who want to gain weight need to do the opposite of those who are trying to lose weight. Instead of hunting for lower-calorie foods, they need to make each bite more energy dense. These individuals should add at least 500 calories to their daily energy intake. This will enable them to add about a pound of extra body weight weekly.

Of course, people who want to gain weight should not just load up on junk foods. Snacking on an extra 500 calories of jelly beans will add 500 calories of sugar but very little nutrition. The quality of the extra calories is very important, so people who are underweight should choose calorie-dense, nutritious foods from each food group. Figure 22.2 contrasts more- and less-energy-dense choices for each food group. For example, instead of eating a slice of toast in the morning, they should choose a waffle. In a salad bar lunch, adding coleslaw rather than cabbage will increase the calories more than tenfold.

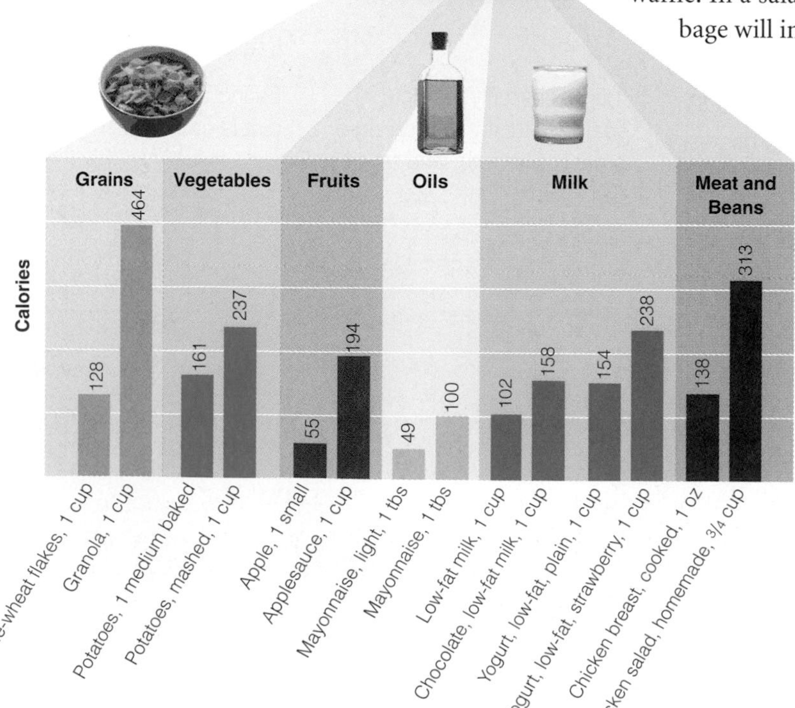

Figure 22.2 More- and Less-Energy-Dense Food Choices, by Food Group Choosing more energy-dense, but still nutritious, foods can help those who are underweight gain weight.

Here are some additional ways to add extra calories healthfully:

- Make sure your meals and snacks provide plenty of healthy unsaturated fats, including omega-3 fatty acids. Choose nuts, nut butters, and vegetable oils, such as olive oil and canola oil, and eat fish, especially fatty fish, at least twice a week.
- Sneak extra calories into your regular meals. For instance, add ground flaxseed to your yogurt, toss some walnuts onto your garden salad, or put a dollop of guacamole on your burrito.
- Beverages, especially carbonated sodas, can fill you up, so limit your intake of beverages that aren't rich in nutrients. For instance, choose low-fat milk, soy milk, 100 percent juices, and plain water over diet or regular sodas. Also, limit beverages for about 30 minutes before a meal, so that you don't spoil your appetite.
- Increase the variety of foods you eat at one meal. You learned in Concept 21 that it's easier to stop eating when your taste buds tire of one food. To help keep you going, eat a few bites of the whole-grain roll; then move on to the chili.
- Eat five or six small meals, rather than three large meals. This recommendation is especially helpful if you feel satiated very quickly.
- Finally, don't forget to snack throughout the day. You can even have a nutritious bedtime snack, such as a bowl of cereal or some peanut butter on toast and a glass of milk. The Table Tips provide more easy and portable snack ideas.

The Take-Home Message **People who want to gain weight need to add energy-dense foods to their diets, so that they take in more energy than they expend. Eating nutrient-dense snacks between meals is an easy way to increase the number of calories consumed daily.**

TABLE TIPS 

Healthy Snacks for Healthy Weight Gain

For healthy snacks that travel well and don't need refrigeration, stash an 8-ounce can or box of 100 percent fruit juice (about 100 calories) in your bag, along with one of the 150-calorie snacks listed below for a quick 250-calorie combined snack between meals.

Graham crackers, 5 (2½" square)

Mixed nuts, 1 oz

Fig bars, 2-oz package

Pudding, individual serving sizes, 4 oz

Peanut butter on whole-wheat crackers (1 tbs peanut butter on 6 crackers)

What Is Disordered Eating and How Can You Identify It?

Attaining a healthy weight, whether it means gaining or losing a few pounds, is a worthwhile goal that can result in lowered risk for disease and a more productive life. However, it's also important to maintain your weight in a healthy way. Patterns of eating that involve severe calorie restriction, purging, or other abnormal behaviors can be severely damaging to your health. Although disordered eating and eating disorders are often classified as psychological rather than nutrition-related topics, it's important to be aware of them and recognize their symptoms.

The term **disordered eating** is used to describe a variety of eating patterns considered abnormal and potentially harmful. Refusing to eat, compulsive eating, **binge eating,** restrictive eating, vomiting after eating, and abusing diet pills, laxatives, or diuretics are all examples of disordered eating behaviors. In contrast, health care providers diagnose **eating disorders** in patients who meet specific criteria, identified by the American Psychiatric Association, that include disordered eating behaviors as well as other factors (see Table 22.1, page 12). It is possible for someone to engage in disordered eating patterns without having an actual eating disorder.

In the United States, approximately 11 million people struggle with eating disorders.[5] Adolescent and young adult females in predominantly white upper-middle- and middle-class families are the population with highest prevalence. However,

disordered eating Abnormal and potentially harmful eating behaviors that do not meet the criteria for anorexia or bulimia.

binge eating A form of disordered eating marked by eating large amounts of food in a short period of time.

eating disorders Psychological illnesses that involve specific abnormal eating behaviors: anorexia (self-starvation) and bulimia (bingeing and purging).

about 12 percent of eating disorders occur in men.[6] These statistics may underestimate the extent of the problem, though, because many men and women feel ashamed or embarrassed and may hide their illness. In general, eating disorders and disordered eating among males, minorities, and other age groups are increasing.[7] Anyone can develop one of these conditions, regardless of gender, age, race, ethnicity, or social status.

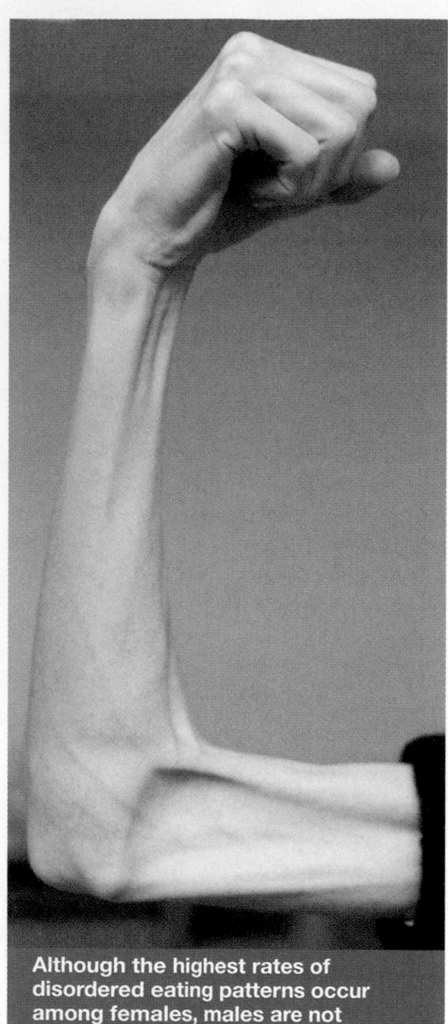
Although the highest rates of disordered eating patterns occur among females, males are not immune. Adolescents, in particular, can feel pressure to achieve a certain body image.

No Single Factor Causes Eating Disorders

Current research suggests that eating disorders are prompted by a complex network of factors, including sociocultural factors, physical factors, and preexisting psychological factors.

Sociocultural Factors

Some researchers theorize that the higher prevalence of eating disorders in females is due in part to the greater societal pressure they experience to be thin and have a "perfect" figure. Thinness is too often associated with beauty, success, and happiness in our society, as evidenced by images in magazines and on billboards of fashion models and celebrities with abnormally low body weights. Many young women don't realize that these images have been digitally enhanced and do not depict the people as they appear in real life. Instead, they come to believe that extreme thinness is both possible and desirable and that they cannot be beautiful, successful, or happy unless they achieve it. These young women may feel such extreme body dissatisfaction that they try to lose weight at any cost, including engaging in disordered eating behaviors.

Physical Factors

Researchers have not found a gene or genes that promote eating disorders; however, they theorize that a combination of genetic predisposition and environmental factors can increase an individual's risk. Certainly, eating disorders have been observed to "run in families." For example, an adolescent female has a greatly increased risk of developing an eating disorder if she has a sibling with an eating disorder, even if she does not live with that sibling.[8]

Psychological Factors

Depression and anxiety are common in people with an eating disorder, as is obsessive-compulsive disorder (OCD), a psychiatric illness characterized by intrusive thoughts that something bad will happen if a certain behavior is not repeated in a certain way. OCD is also more common in family members of people with an eating disorder.[9] Not only women but men diagnosed with eating disorders have higher rates of other psychiatric illness, compared with men who do not have eating disorders.[10]

A personality trait that can contribute to eating disorders is perfectionism, as an inability to reach unrealistic standards (such as in school, or in athletic competition) can lead to a sense of failure and lowered self-worth. Many people who struggle with eating disorders are trying to gain some control in their lives. When external factors feel out of control, the person with an eating disorder gets a sense of security from being able to control food intake and body weight. Other common psychological factors include lack of self-esteem, high family expectations, and family dysfunction.

The most common eating disorders are anorexia nervosa, bulimia nervosa, binge eating disorder, and night eating syndrome. Let's take a look at each type of disorder and the characteristics that make each one unique.

Anorexia Results from Severe Calorie Restriction

Anorexia (also known as *anorexia nervosa*) is a serious, potentially life-threatening eating disorder characterized by self-starvation and excessive weight loss. People who suffer from anorexia have an intense fear of gaining weight or being "fat." This fear causes them to control their food intake by restricting the amount of food they consume, resulting in significant weight loss.

Many people with anorexia have a distorted sense of body image and see themselves as fat even though they are underweight. This misperception of body size contributes to the behavior of restricting food intake in order to lose (more) weight. For instance, someone with anorexia might eat only a piece of fruit and a small container of yogurt in an entire day. They may also have a fear of eating certain foods, such as those that contain fat and sugar. They believe that these foods will make them fat, regardless of how much they eat. Some also exercise excessively as a means of controlling their weight. Recall that Kiko, in our opening story, engaged in excessive calorie restriction and exercise, and despite being underweight, perceived herself as fat.

Depression, low self-esteem, and a history of physical or sexual abuse often accompany eating disorders.

Of the numerous health consequences that can occur with anorexia, some can be fatal. One of the most serious health effects is an electrolyte imbalance—specifically, low blood potassium—which can occur if someone with anorexia engages in episodes of self-induced vomiting. An electrolyte imbalance can lead to an irregular heart rhythm, which can be fatal. Someone who's lost an extreme amount of body fat may experience a drop in body temperature and feel cold even when it's hot outside. In an effort to regulate body temperature, his or her body may begin to grow *lanugo* (downy hair), particularly on the face and arms.

Because someone with anorexia is not getting enough calories, the body begins to slow or shut down some processes in an effort to conserve energy for its most vital functions. The person may experience a decrease in heart rate and blood pressure, overall weakness and fatigue, and hair loss. In women, reproductive ability ceases. The digestive process also slows down, which often results in constipation, bloating, and delayed gastric emptying. Dehydration, iron deficiency, and osteoporosis are also negative health effects caused by anorexia.

Kirsten Haglun, Miss America 2008, was diagnosed with anorexia by her pediatrician. She was so fatigued and depressed that it was hard for her to get out of bed in the morning. Once she came to the realization that she had this condition, she was determined to recover, and she did! She devoted a major part of her reign as Miss America to speaking publicly and raising awareness of eating disorders.

Bulimia Involves Cycles of Binge Eating and Purging

Bulimia (also known as *bulimia nervosa*) is another type of eating disorder that can be life-threatening. During times of binge eating, the person lacks control over eating and consumes larger than normal amounts of food in a short period of time. Following the binge, the person counters the binge with some type of **purging.** Many people assume that bulimics purge by vomiting, but self-induced vomiting is only one form. Purging is any behavior that assists someone in "getting rid" of food to prevent weight gain or to promote weight loss. This includes excessive exercise; abuse of diet pills, laxatives, or diuretics; and strict dieting or fasting.

Most of the health consequences of bulimia nervosa are associated with self-induced vomiting, such as tears in the esophagus, swollen parotid glands, tooth

anorexia A serious, potentially life-threatening eating disorder characterized by self-starvation and excessive weight loss.

bulimia A serious, potentially life-threatening eating disorder characterized by binge eating followed by **purging**.

purging Behavior that assists in removing eaten food in order to prevent or lose weight, including self-induced vomiting, laxatives, diuretics (water pills), excessive exercise, and/or fasting.

decay and gum disease (caused by stomach acid), and broken blood vessels in the eyes (due to pressure from vomiting). Electrolyte imbalance also occurs with bulimia nervosa and can be fatal. People with bulimia nervosa may also experience dehydration and constipation due to frequent episodes of binge eating and purging.

Laxative abuse can also cause serious medical complications, depending on the type, amount, and length of time the person has used them. Laxatives used repeatedly can cause constipation, dehydration due to fluid loss in the intestines, electrolyte imbalances, fluid retention, bloody stools, and impaired bowel function.

Binge Eating Disorder Involves Compulsive Overeating

Binge eating disorder is characterized by recurrent episodes of binge eating without purging. People who have binge eating disorder eat without regard to physiological cues. They may eat for emotional reasons and feel out of control while eating. The overeating results in physical and psychological discomfort. Many people who struggle with this type of eating disorder binge in secret and feel ashamed about their behaviors.

The health effects of binge eating disorder are commonly those that are associated with overweight and obesity because most people who struggle with binge eating disorder are of normal or heavier than average weight. The health effects include

Table 22.1

Diagnostic Criteria for Eating Disorders

Eating Disorder	Diagnostic Criteria
Anorexia nervosa	■ Consistent body weight under the minimally normal weight for age and height (less than 85% of expected) ■ Intense fear of gaining weight or becoming fat, even though underweight ■ Disturbance in the way one's body weight or shape is experienced, excessive influence of body weight or shape on self-esteem, or denying seriousness of the current low body weight ■ Absence of at least three consecutive menstrual cycles
Bulimia nervosa	■ Recurrent episodes of binge eating, which is characterized by eating larger than normal amounts of food in a short period of time; and a lack of control over eating during the binge ■ Recurrent purging in order to prevent weight gain, such as by self-induced vomiting; misuse of laxatives, diuretics, enemas, or other medications; fasting; or excessive exercise ■ Bingeing and purging that occur, on average, at least twice a week for three months ■ Persistent overconcern with body shape and weight, which may influence self-esteem
Eating disorder not otherwise specified	■ Disordered eating behaviors that do not meet the criteria for anorexia nervosa or bulimia nervosa, including binge eating disorder and night eating syndrome

Data adapted from: American Psychiatric Association, *Diagnostic and Statistical Manual of Mental Disorders,* 4th ed. (Washington, D.C.: American Psychiatric Association, 1994).

People with binge eating disorder often eat in secret.

high blood pressure, high cholesterol levels, heart disease, type 2 diabetes, and gallbladder disease.

Binge eating disorder has specific signs and symptoms; however, it does not have its own diagnostic criteria, nor does it meet the diagnostic criteria for anorexia or bulimia. Instead, it falls into the diagnostic category of "Eating Disorders Not Otherwise Specified (EDNOS)." Other behaviors in this category include purging without bingeing, restrictive eating by people who are in a normal weight range despite having significant weight loss, bingeing and purging but not frequently enough to meet the criteria for bulimia, and chewing and spitting out food instead of swallowing it.

Some people with night eating syndrome consume more than half their day's calories between 8 p.m. and 6 a.m.

Night Eating Syndrome

Night eating syndrome is of EDNOS, in which a person consumes most of his or her daily calories after the evening meal and wakes up during the night, possibly even several times, to eat. In addition, the person typically does not have an appetite during the morning hours and consumes very little throughout the day. One study found that people with night eating syndrome consume 56 percent of their 24-hour calorie intake between 8:00 p.m. and 6:00 a.m. This study also found that people with night eating syndrome generally do not binge eat with each awakening; rather, they eat small portions of food several times throughout the night.[11] This disorder is most common among obese individuals, although people of normal weight can also develop night eating syndrome.[12]

Night eating syndrome appears to be a unique combination of disordered eating, a sleep disorder, and a mood disorder.[13] Research has shown that night eating syndrome is associated with low self-esteem, depression, reduced daytime hunger, and less weight loss among obese patients.[14] Stress also appears to be a contributing factor in the development and continuation of night eating syndrome.[15] Someone may feel guilty, ashamed, or embarrassed while eating during the night, as well as the next morning. Some may not even remember their nighttime eating bouts.

Learn the Warning Signs of Disordered Eating

Many people may know someone with an eating disorder but not know how to help the person. Learning about eating disorders will help you understand why a friend or loved one can have destructive eating behaviors and be seemingly unaware of the damage, pain, or danger they can cause. You also need to know the warning signs, so that you can identify disordered eating behaviors that could progress into more serious eating disorders (see Table 22.2 on page 14).

Both physical and behavioral signs can warn of disordered eating and eating disorders. Hair loss is very common among people with anorexia nervosa and bulimia nervosa, as the body does not receive adequate nutrients for hair maintenance and growth. You may also notice significant weight changes, such as sudden weight loss in anorexia nervosa and sudden weight gain in bulimia nervosa, binge eating disorder, or night eating syndrome. *Russell's sign*, which is scar tissue on the knuckles of fingers used to induce vomiting, is one indicator of bulimia nervosa. This is caused by scraping the knuckles when removing the fingers from the mouth during purging.

People with disordered eating often avoid social situations because they know food will be present and do not feel comfortable eating around others. People with eating disorders also have a preoccupation with food and body weight, such as weighing several times a day or severely limiting calorie intake. They may also deny unusual eating behaviors if confronted about them.

Table 22.2

Warning Signs for Eating Disorders

Symptom	Explanation/Example
Weight below 85% of ideal body weight	Refuses to accept and maintain body weight (even if it is within normal range)
Excessive exercise	Often exercises daily for long periods of time to burn calories and prevent weight gain; may skip work or class to exercise
Preoccupation with food, weight, and diet	Constantly worries about the amount and type of food eaten May weigh themselves daily or several times per day
Distorted body image	Does not see themselves as they truly are; may comment on being fat even if underweight
Refusal to eat	Avoids food in order to lose weight or prevent weight gain; may avoid only certain foods, such as those with fat and sugar
Loss of menstrual period	Has periods that are irregular or completely absent
Diet pill use or laxative use	Shows evidence of having pill bottles, boxes, or packaging
Changes in mood	May become more withdrawn, depressed, or anxious, especially around food
Hair loss	Has thinning hair that falls out in large quantities
Solitary eating	Wants to eat alone; Make excuses to avoid eating with others

If you are concerned about someone, find a good time and place to express your concerns gently without criticism or judgment. Realize that you may be rejected or your friend may deny the problem. Be supportive and let the person know that you are available if he or she wants to talk to you at another time. You should also realize that there are many things that you cannot do to help a loved one or friend get better. You cannot force an anorexic to eat, keep a bulimic from purging, or make a binge eater stop overeating. It is up to the individual to decide when he or she is ready to deal with the issues in life that led to the eating disorder.

The best thing you can do is learn to listen. Find out about the resources in your area for treating eating disorders, so that you can refer someone there when that person is ready to get help. See the Web Resources section on page 17.

How Are Eating Disorders Treated?

The most effective treatment for eating disorders is a multidisciplinary team approach, including psychological, medical, and nutrition professionals. All members of the team must be knowledgeable about and experienced with eating disorders because it is a complex area that some health care professionals do not feel comfortable treating. A psychologist can help the person deal with the emotional and other psychological issues that may be contributing to the eating disorder. Anyone who

RATE YOURSELF ★★★★★

Are You at Risk for an Eating Disorder?

Check the appropriate box in the following statements to help you find out.

1.	I constantly think about eating, weight, and body size.	**Yes** ☐	**No** ☐
2.	I'm terrified about being overweight.	**Yes** ☐	**No** ☐
3.	I binge eat and can't stop until I feel sick.	**Yes** ☐	**No** ☐
4.	I weigh myself several times each day.	**Yes** ☐	**No** ☐
5.	I exercise too much or get very rigid about my exercise plan.	**Yes** ☐	**No** ☐
6.	I have taken laxatives or forced myself to vomit after eating.	**Yes** ☐	**No** ☐
7.	I believe food controls my life.	**Yes** ☐	**No** ☐
8.	I feel extremely guilty after eating.	**Yes** ☐	**No** ☐
9.	I eat when I am nervous, anxious, lonely, or depressed.	**Yes** ☐	**No** ☐
10.	I believe my weight controls what I do.	**Yes** ☐	**No** ☐

Answers

These statements are designed to help you identify potentially problematic eating behavior; they do *not* tell you if you have an eating disorder. Look carefully at any statement you marked as "yes" and decide if this behavior prevents you from enjoying life or makes you unhealthy. Changing these behaviors should be done gradually, making small changes one at a time. Contact your student health services or your health care provider if you suspect you need help.

struggles with an eating disorder should be closely monitored by a physician or another medical professional, as some eating disorders can be life-threatening. A registered dietitian can help someone with an eating disorder establish normal eating behaviors.

At least half of those who seek **professional help** recover from an eating disorder.

Some nutritional approaches to eating disorders involve identifying binge triggers, safe and unsafe foods, and hunger and fullness cues. Food journals are often helpful to identify eating patterns, food choices, moods, eating disorder triggers, eating cues, and timing of meals and snacks. Meal plans are also used to ensure that anorexics have an adequate intake of calories and nutrients and to help bulimics and binge eaters avoid overeating.

Most people recover fully from eating disorders. When treatment is sought in the early stages, the person has a better chance of recovering fully and in less time than someone who begins treatment after many years. Some people continue to have the desire to engage in disordered eating behaviors; however, they are able to refrain from doing so. Unfortunately, some individuals never fully recover from an eating disorder. Caregivers must recognize that recovery is a process that can take years and has no "quick fix."

The Take-Home Message **Anorexia is characterized by self-starvation and excessive weight loss. Bulimia involves repeated cycles of binge eating and purging. Binge eating disorders are characterized by binge eating without purging. Night eating syndrome is described as excessive calorie intake in the evening and waking up during the night to eat. The most effective treatment for someone with an eating disorder involves a multidisciplinary team approach, including psychological, medical, and nutrition professionals.**

UCook

Three-Apple Waldorf Salad

This crunchy salad combines the sweetness of apples and raisins with a sprinkling of nutrient-rich nuts. Make extra and refrigerate the leftovers; it tastes even better the next day!

UDo

Beefing Up Your Diet

If you are in need of gaining some weight, visit our website above for a handy tracking tool to help you add some extra calories into your meals and snacks.

The Top Five Points to Remember

1. A BMI of less than 18.5 is considered underweight. The factors contributing to underweight are underlying physical and psychiatric disorders, poverty, excessive physical activity, and excessive calorie restriction. Many fad diets promise quick results but can be unhealthy for the long term. Being very underweight increases the risk for nutritional deficiencies and related health problems and is associated with an increased risk for premature death.
2. Weight gain can be challenging. Experts advise adding 500 calories per day to the normal energy intake. The quality of calories is important. Food choices should be energy dense but nutritious, and healthy snacking is recommended.
3. Disordered eating includes a variety of abnormal eating patterns, such as restrictive eating, binge eating, vomiting after eating, and abuse of laxatives or diet pills. In contrast, eating disorders are psychiatric disorders and are diagnosed using specific criteria identified by the American Psychiatric Association. In the United States, 11 million men and women struggle with eating disorders.
4. Anorexia nervosa is characterized by self-starvation and excessive weight loss. Bulimia nervosa involves repeated cycles of binge eating and purging. Binge eating disorders are characterized by binge eating without purging. Night eating syndrome is described as excessive calorie intake in the evening and waking up during the night to eat.
5. Numerous health consequences can occur with eating disorders, such as hair loss, digestive problems, electrolyte imbalances, changes in heart rate and blood pressure, dehydration, and nutrient deficiencies. The most effective treatment for someone with an eating disorder involves a multidisciplinary team approach, including psychological, and medical, nutrition professionals.

Test Yourself

1. Cecile is a gymnast. Her BMI is 17.5. She is at increased risk for
   a. heart disease.
   b. type 2 diabetes.
   c. fracture.
   d. all of the above.
2. Which example of high-calorie, nutrient-dense meals can aid in healthy weight gain?
   a. a bowl of granola with walnuts, topped with banana slices and a cup of milk
   b. a Caesar salad with dressing, topped with croutons, avocado slices, a scoop of chicken salad, and shredded Parmesan cheese
   c. a bowl of chili made with lean ground beef, beans, and tomatoes and a whole-grain roll with a spread
   d. all of the above
3. Which of the following is a warning sign of an eating disorder?
   a. eats three balanced meals daily
   b. will only eat with others
   c. takes diet pills
   d. none of the above
4. A form of purging in bulimia nervosa is
   a. self-induced vomiting.
   b. fasting.
   c. exercise.
   d. all of the above.
5. Lanugo, or downy hair growth, is common in what type of eating disorder?
   a. anorexia nervosa
   b. bulimia nervosa
   c. binge eating disorder
   d. night eating syndrome

Answers

1. (c) Being overweight increases the risk for heart disease and diabetes, but Cecile is underweight. This puts her at increased risk for low bone density and fractures.

2. (d) All of these meals are rich in calories, as well as nutrients, fiber, and phytochemicals.
3. (c) Taking diet pills is one of many warning signs of an eating disorder. Other signs include failing to eat regular meals and avoiding eating around others.
4. (d) Self-induced vomiting, fasting, and exercise are all forms of purging, as they assist in "getting rid" of food.
5. (a) Lanugo grows typically on the face and arms of people with anorexia nervosa as a way of regulating body temperature.

Web Resources

- For more on eating disorders, visit the National Eating Disorder Association at: www.nationaleatingdisorders.org
- To find a therapist or support group who can help someone with an eating disorder, visit the National Association of Anorexia Nervosa and Associated Disorders (ANAD) at: www.anad.org

23 Fighting Cancer with a Knife and Fork

1. The majority of cancers that affect Americans are caused by **agents** that can't be controlled. **T/F**

2. The most common type of cancer among **American adults** is lung cancer. **T/F**

3. Grilling meats at high temperatures can increase cancer risk. **T/F**

4. Being **overweight** increases your risk of cancer. **T/F**

5. Watching more than 2 hours of **television daily** can increase your risk for cancer. **T/F**

Gardner and Dalton are dorm buddies who eat dinner together almost every night. Dalton always gets a chuckle out of Gardner's dinner tray. No matter what Gardner chooses for dinner, he always takes a side dish of ketchup to use as a dipping sauce. "What can I say?" shrugs Gardner. "My mother told me to eat more foods made with tomatoes. It has something to do with my grandfather having prostate cancer." Do you know why Gardner's mom might have given him this advice?

Cancer—it's such a simple word, yet it inspires so much fear. In fact, in a recent survey conducted by the American Cancer Society, a majority of participants said they believed that the risk of dying of cancer is increasing. The good news is that the opposite is true. You have less chance of dying from cancer today than people did years, even decades, ago (see Figure 23.1). The even better news is that it is estimated that up to 75 percent of cancer deaths are caused by lifestyle behaviors that *you* can control.[1] In this concept we'll look at how cancer occurs and what behaviors you can change to reduce your risk.

Answers

1. False. You have more control over your risk of developing cancer than you may think. Turn to pages 2 and 3 to learn more.
2. True. Surprised? See page 3 to learn more.
3. True. Turn to page 4 to find out why.
4. True. To learn more about the link between overweight and cancer, turn to pages 7–9.
5. True. To learn more about the link between television viewing and cancer, turn to page 9.

What Is Cancer, and Why Does It Occur?

Cancer is the single name used to identify a group of diseases that are all characterized by the uncontrolled growth and spread of abnormal cells.[2] Your body is made of trillions of cells. Most of these grow, function for a while, then divide, die, and are replaced in a natural process that allows your body to stay healthy. If a cell happens to become damaged, it is quickly repaired or destroyed, so that it cannot reproduce (Figure 23.2a). Cancer begins when a small number of abnormal cells don't follow this process. Instead of dying a natural death, these abnormal cells hang around, multiply, and, if they're still not stopped, form a tumor (Figure 23.2b). Sometimes cells break off from the tumor and spread to other parts of the body. We'll explore the details of this process shortly.

Of the more than 100 different types of cancer, most are named for their location in the body—for example, prostate, breast, or lung cancer. Prostate cancer is the

cancer The name used to identify a group of diseases that are characterized by the uncontrolled growth and spread of abnormal cells.

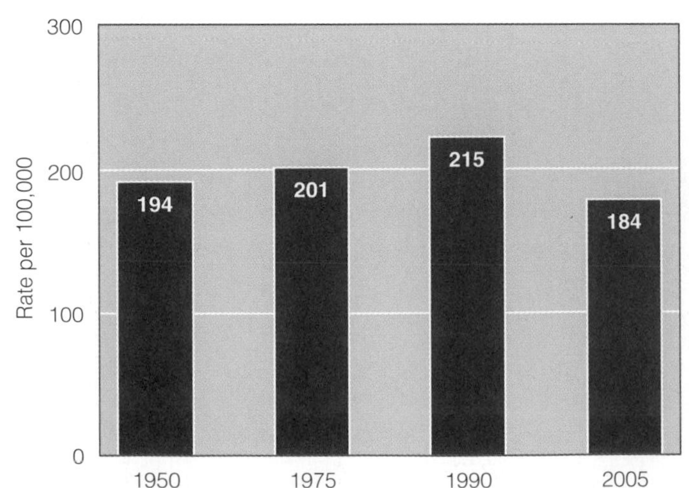

Figure 23.1 Decline in the U.S. Death Rate for All Cancers
The number of cancer deaths has been decreasing for decades. (Numbers represent deaths per 100,000 Americans. All numbers rounded off to nearest whole number.) Data from: National Cancer Institute. 2007. Cancer Trends Progress Report—2007 Update. http://progressreport.cancer.gov/doc_detail (accessed July 2008).

most common cancer among American men. It occurs in a gland that is present only in males and that sits just below the bladder. Breast cancer is the most prevalent type among women; however, some males develop breast cancer. The second most common cancer in both males and females is lung cancer. Lung cancer's rate of occurrence in both genders makes it the most prevalent cancer throughout the adult population. Figure 23.3 identifies the most common cancers by gender.

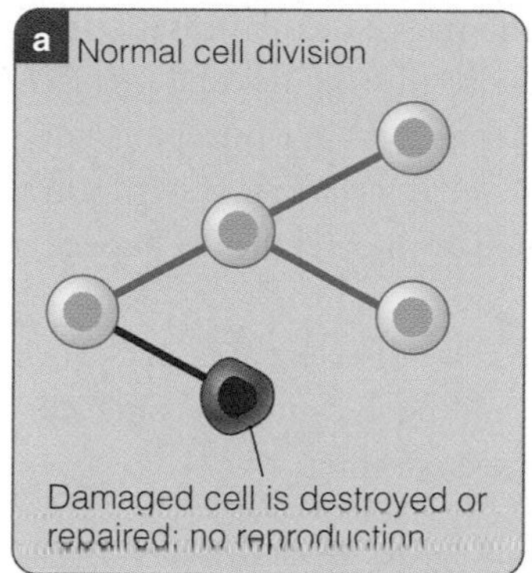

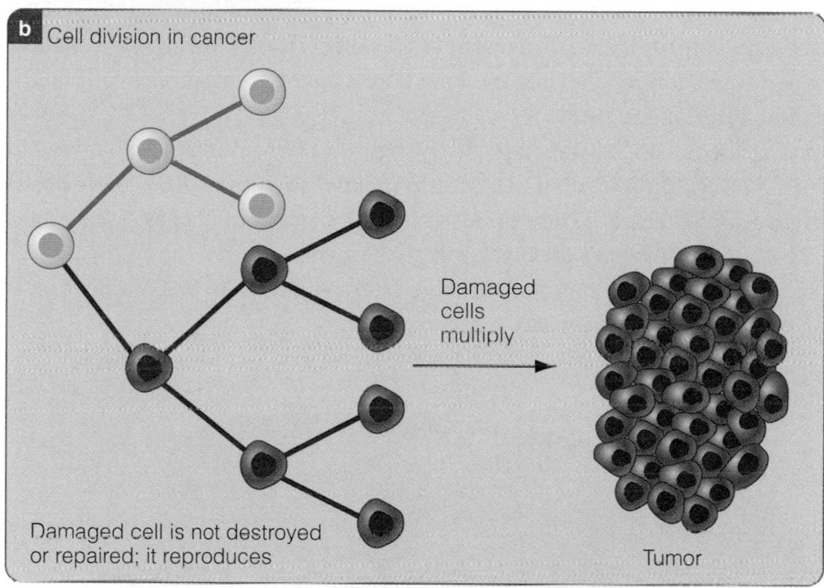

Figure 23.2 Cancer Occurs When Abnormal Cells Reproduce
Cancer begins with cell damage. If the abnormal cell is not repaired or destroyed, it can begin to reproduce rapidly, and all of its offspring will also be abnormal.

Men 745,180		Women 692,000	
Prostate	25%	26%	Breast
Lung & bronchus	15%	14%	Lung & bronchus
Colon & rectum	10%	10%	Colon & rectum
Urinary bladder	7%	6%	Uterine corpus
Non-Hodgkin lymphoma	5%	4%	Non-Hodgkin lymphoma
Melanoma of skin	5%	4%	Thyroid
Kidney & renal pelvis	4%	4%	Melanoma of skin
Oral cavity	3%	3%	Ovary
Leukemia	3%	3%	Kidney & renal pelvis
Pancreas	3%	3%	Leukemia
All other sites	20%	23%	All other sites

Figure 23.3 Estimated Cases of Cancer in the United States by Gender and Type: 2008

Data from: American Cancer Society. 2008. Cancer Facts and Figures 2008. www.cancer.org/downloads/STT/2008CAFFfinalsecured.pdf (accessed July 2008).

Most Cancers Start with Alterations in DNA

We've said that cancer starts with abnormal cells, but what makes the cells abnormal in the first place? Recall from Concept 13 that DNA is the blueprint for making all body proteins. Cancer starts when a cell's DNA gets altered or damaged. This damage (called a *mutation*) can be caused by harmful changes inside the body, such as a hormone imbalance or the presence of a virus. Damage also commonly arises during normal metabolism (see the discussion of oxidative stress in Concept 16). Although many people think that cancer is largely genetic, only about 5 to 10 percent of cancers are thought to be related to the presence of a specific "cancer gene."[3]

One in four **American women** die of heart disease, compared with one in 30 who die from cancer.

Much more commonly, DNA mutations occur because of external factors, such as long-term exposure to tobacco or industrial chemicals. Such cancer-causing substances are called **carcinogens.** Here are some of the most common:

- Tobacco. At least 80 chemicals in tobacco (including both smoking and chewing tobacco) are carcinogens. Smoking is the primary cause of lung cancer, and tobacco is the culprit behind 20 percent of all cancer deaths worldwide.[4] In addition, each year, about 3,000 nonsmoking adults die of lung cancer as a result of breathing secondhand smoke.[5]
- Industrial chemicals. Substances such as asbestos (a fibrous material that used to be found in building insulation), certain metals (such as nickel), some pesticides, and some chemical compounds (such as benzene) can act as carcinogens. Workers exposed for long periods are at greatest risk.
- Ultraviolet (UV) radiation from the sun. Excessive exposure to UV radiation is associated with an increased risk for skin cancer.

TABLE TIPS

Eat to Beat Cancer

Grind whole flaxseeds before eating them to reap their nutritional benefits. Whole flaxseeds can pass through your gastrointestinal tract intact, keeping their essential fatty acids and vitamin E enclosed in the shell.

Grilling meats, fish, or poultry (but not vegetables!) at high temperatures can cause the formation of several kinds of cancer-causing agents. For a healthier meal, grill smaller amounts of lean animal foods in foil pans poked with holes to avoid flare-ups, and grill more veggies!

Steeping antioxidant-rich black or green tea for about 5 minutes will allow over 80 percent of the cancer-fighting catechins to seep into your cup. Steeping is key!

Charred portions of grilled meats can contain carcinogens.

carcinogen Any substance capable of initiating the cell changes that can lead to cancer.

- Radiation from other sources. Frequent exposure to other types of radiation—for instance, from X-rays—has long been associated with an increased risk for certain types of cancer.
- Cancer-causing agents in foods and beverages. These include chemicals that form in charred portions of barbecued meat, poultry, and fish; molds, especially in stored foods; pollutants that enter foods from the environment; and excessive alcohol.

In addition to these carcinogens, other factors appear to increase cancer risk. For instance, overweight and obesity are thought to increase the risk for many types of cancer and contribute to 14 to 20 percent of all cancer-related deaths.[6] Physical inactivity and poor nutrition contribute to overweight; thus, these factors are also linked to increased cancer risk.

Although the average pack of cigarettes costs about $5, it costs 1½ times that much in medical care to keep a smoker healthy.

Cancer Develops in Stages

Imagine that you were building a home using a blueprint you received from an architect. However, by accident, you spilled a large mug of coffee all over the print, making it illegible. If you were to attempt to build the house according to this damaged blueprint, you might put supporting beams, pipes, and wiring in the wrong places, making the house structurally unsound. If these alterations weren't quickly noticed and repaired, the home could eventually collapse. Cancer develops in a similar way, beginning with damage to the initial blueprint and progressing to serious illness:

- Initiation. During the **initiation stage,** a body cell is exposed to an agent that damages a part of its DNA (blueprint), which controls cell growth and division (Figure 23.4a). Cancer does not necessarily develop after this stage because the damage can be repaired or the damaged cell destroyed (see Figure 23.2a).
- Promotion. If the damage is not repaired, an altered cell can reproduce itself rapidly during the **promotion stage** (Figure 23.4b). This name reflects the fact that the exposure of altered cells to certain agents or conditions, such as excessive alcohol, can promote their growth. The greater number of these cells that develop, the more likely it is that they will eventually cause disease.
- Progression. In the **progression stage,** these damaged cells reproduce uncontrollably, forming a tumor that invades surrounding tissues (Figure 23.4c). Often, cells from the original tumor break off and travel to other sites in the body. This process, called *metastasis*, makes cancers more challenging to treat successfully.

The Take-Home Message **Most cancers are caused by lifestyle behaviors that you can control. Cancer occurs when cells become altered and then multiply. Internal factors, such as genes, hormones, and infections, can promote cancer, but external factors, such as tobacco use, exposure to industrial chemicals or UV radiation, alcohol abuse, overweight, and physical inactivity, are more common. The three stages of cancer development are initiation, promotion, and progression. Metastasis, the spread of cancer cells to other parts of the body, can complicate cancer treatment.**

initiation stage The first stage in the cancer process, in which a body cell is exposed to an agent that damages its DNA.

promotion stage The second stage in the development of cancer, in which damaged body cells are exposed to agents or conditions that promote their rapid reproduction.

progression stage The third stage in the development of cancer, in which damaged cells progress to form a tumor that invades surrounding tissues.

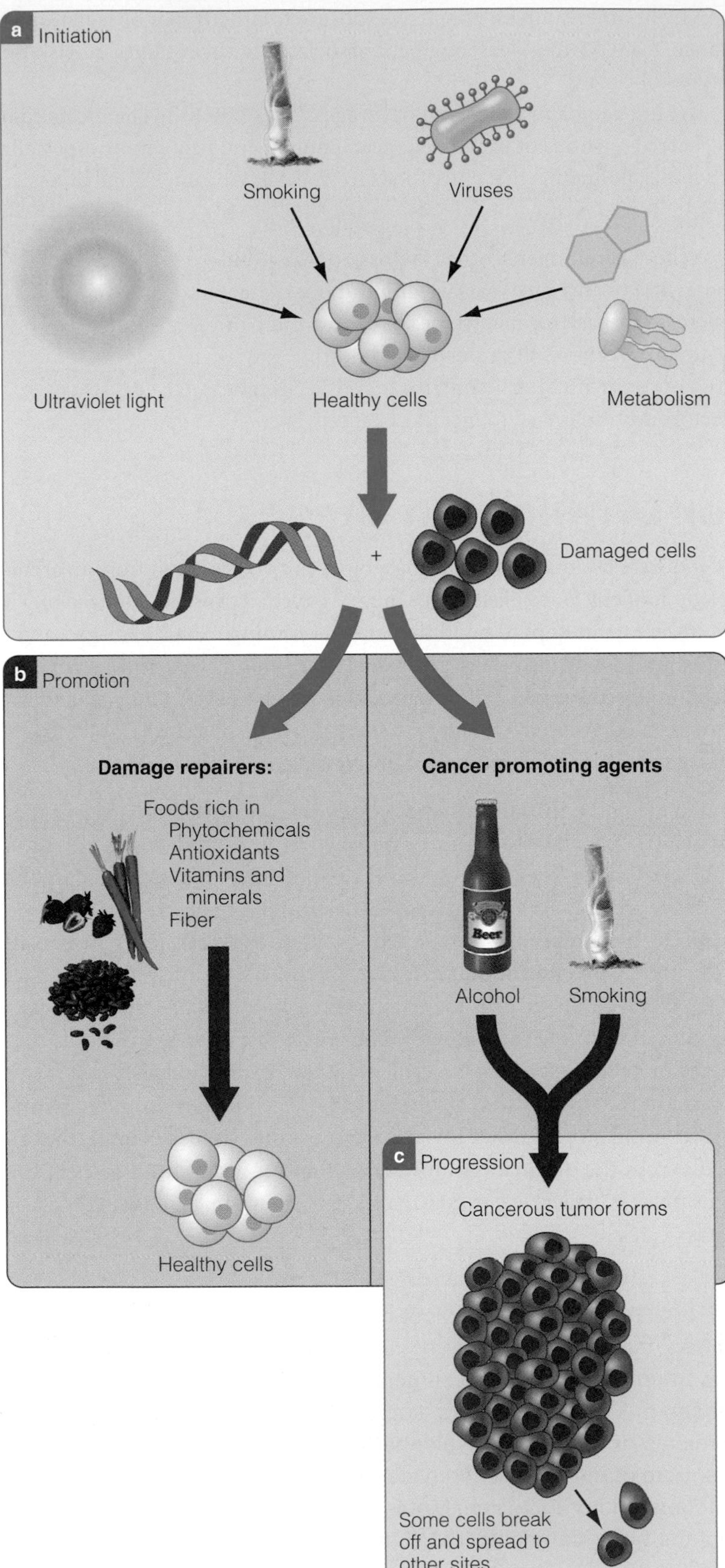

Figure 23.4 The Stages of Cancer
(a) During initiation, internal or external factors damage cells' DNA. **(b)** During promotion, abnormal cells that are not repaired or destroyed multiply. Foods rich in phytochemicals, antioxidants, and certain other nutrients can help prevent promotion, while smoking, alcohol abuse, pollutants, radiation, obesity, and other factors can encourage it. **(c)** During progression, the abnormal cells multiply uncontrollably and form a tumor. Some cells can break off and metastasize to other body sites.

How Can You Reduce Your Risk for Cancer?

In 2007, a review of over 7,000 research studies and input from hundreds of scientists worldwide culminated in the publication of a landmark report entitled *Food, Nutrition, Physical Activity, and the Prevention of Cancer: A Global Perspective.* This report identified changes that you can make to help reduce your risk for cancer (see Table 23.1). For example, maintaining a healthy weight, staying physically active, and consuming a healthy diet can reduce your risk of developing cancer by 30 to 40 percent.[7]

Rate yourself to see if your food choices are helping you to avoid cancer.

Regular physical exercise helps reduce the risk for several types of cancer, partly through healthy weight maintenance.

RATE YOURSELF ★★★★★

Fighting Cancer through Food

Are you a cancer-fighting superstar? Rate Yourself to see how you score!

1. I eat at least five servings of fruits and vegetables every day. **Yes** ☐ **No** ☐
2. I eat at least three servings of whole-grain bread, rice, pasta, and cereal every day. **Yes** ☐ **No** ☐
3. I rarely eat processed and red meat, such as bacon, hot dogs, sausage, steak, ground beef, pork, or lamb. **Yes** ☐ **No** ☐
4. I take it easy on high-calorie baked goods, such as pies, cakes, cookies, sweet rolls, and doughnuts. **Yes** ☐ **No** ☐
5. I rarely (less than twice a week) eat fried foods. **Yes** ☐ **No** ☐
6. I try to maintain a healthy weight. **Yes** ☐ **No** ☐
7. I get at least 30 minutes of moderate to vigorous physical activity on five or more days of the week. **Yes** ☐ **No** ☐
8. I usually take the stairs instead of waiting for an elevator. **Yes** ☐ **No** ☐
9. I try to spend most of my free time being active, instead of watching television or sitting at a computer. **Yes** ☐ **No** ☐
10. I never, or only occasionally, drink alcohol. **Yes** ☐ **No** ☐

Answers

Add up the number of your "yes" answers. If you have seven or more, you are a cancer-fighting superstar. If you have fewer than seven, read on to find out how you can reduce your risk for cancer.

Data adapted from: The American Cancer Society, 2008. With permission. www.cancer.org/docroot/PED/Ped_3_1x_Nutrition_and_Activity_Quiz.asp?sitearea=&level=.

Table 23.1

Recommendations for Preventing Cancer

<table>
<thead>
<tr><th>Recommendation</th><th>What to Do</th><th>How to Do It</th></tr>
</thead>
<tbody>
<tr><td>1. Be as lean as possible within the normal range of body weight.</td><td>■ Maintain a BMI between 21 and 23.*
■ Avoid weight gain, especially around your middle, as you age.</td><td>■ Your pants are your best predictor of weight gain. If they begin to feel snug, assess your diet: Is it heavy on the junk food? See recommendation 3.
■ Review Concepts 22 and 23 for the best strategies to obtain and maintain a healthy BMI.</td></tr>
<tr><td>2. Be physically active as a part of everyday life.</td><td>■ Incorporate at least 30 to 60 minutes of physical activity into your day.
■ Reduce the amount of screen time (TV, DVDs, computer, video games) spent daily.</td><td>■ Set a timer at your computer and get up and move for at least 5 minutes every hour.
■ Watch one less TV show or play one less computer game daily. Spend that time cleaning, doing laundry, or running errands.</td></tr>
<tr><td>3. Limit consumption of energy-dense foods. Avoid sugary drinks.</td><td>■ Cut back on sweets and treats that are energy (calorie) dense and serve up little nutrition.
■ Don't drink your calories by guzzling sodas, sports drinks, fruit juices, or sweetened coffee beverages.</td><td>■ If you want to snack on goodies, eat no more than about 100 calories of the item. That's typically a small handful of chips, cookies, and candy.
■ Drink one less sweetened beverage and one more glass of water daily.</td></tr>
<tr><td>4. Eat mostly foods of plant origin.</td><td>■ Eat at least 5 cups of a variety of colorful fruits and veggies for phytochemicals, fiber, and nutrients.
■ At least half of your daily grain choices should be whole grains.
■ Eat dried peas and beans (legumes) as often as you can.</td><td>■ Eat at least one salad with a minimum of three different-colored veggies daily.
■ Choose only whole-grain cereals, such as raisin bran, oatmeal, and shredded wheat, in the morning.
■ Add kidney beans and/or chickpeas to the daily salad that you are now going to be eating.</td></tr>
<tr><td>5. Limit intake of red meat and avoid processed meat.</td><td>■ Limit beef, lamb, and pork to no more than 18 ounces a week.
■ Avoid processed meats, such as ham, bacon, salami, hot dogs, and sausages.</td><td>■ Eat red meat only at lunch in a sandwich, as the portion size will be only about 3 ounces.
■ Try veggie or turkey sausages.</td></tr>
<tr><td>6. Limit alcoholic drinks.</td><td>If you choose to drink,
■ Women should consume no more than one alcoholic drink daily.
■ Men should consume no more than two alcoholic drinks daily.</td><td>■ Make a glass of water the first drink, rather than alcohol, when you are socializing.
■ Alternate alcoholic beverages with nonalcoholic drinks to pace your evening. Make the nonalcoholic drink twice as big as the one containing the booze.</td></tr>
<tr><td>7. Limit salt consumption.</td><td>■ Avoid salt, salt-preserved, and salty foods.
■ Limit sodium to no more than 2,400 mg daily.</td><td>■ Remove the salt from your salt shaker and fill it with a no-salt seasoning blend, such as Mrs. Dash, to accompany the pepper shaker.</td></tr>
<tr><td>8. Aim to meet nutritional needs through diet alone.</td><td>■ Look to food, not supplements, to fight cancer.
■ Eat at least three meals a day to increase the variety and all the potential cancer-fighting compounds in food.</td><td>■ Don't skip meals.
■ Eat at least three pieces of fruit daily. Use a stoplight as your guide. Choose one fruit from each of the following colors: (1) red (apple, watermelon, red grapes), (2) yellow (banana, pineapple, citrus fruit), and (3) green (green grapes, Granny Smith apple, kiwi).</td></tr>
</tbody>
</table>

Other Recommendations

- If you are pregnant, plan to breast-feed exclusively for up to six months and continue with complementary breast-feeding afterward to reduce your risk for breast cancer. Being breast-fed may also protect your child from becoming overweight.
- Cancer survivors should obtain nutritional recommendations from an appropriately trained professional, such as a registered dietitian and should eat a healthy diet, maintain a healthy weight, and be as physically active as they are able.

*See Concept 20 to determine your BMI.

Data adapted from: World Cancer Research Fund/American Institute for Cancer Research (AICR). *Food, Nutrition, Physical Activity, and the Prevention of Cancer: A Global Perspective* (Washington, D.C.: AICR, 2007).

Engage in Lifestyle Habits That Reduce Your Risk for Cancer

As you recall from the discussion of nutritional genomics in Concept 13, your diet—specifically, certain food components—can affect your DNA and genes. These components can help reduce your risk for numerous cancers. Here's how:

- A diet rich in certain phytochemicals, which are found in colorful vegetables and fruits, can help reduce the risk for cancer. For example, a phytochemical called lycopene is abundant in tomatoes and tomato products. The consumption of lycopene-rich foods is thought to help prevent certain cancers, including prostate cancer. This is why Gardner's mom, as you read in the beginning of this concept, wants him to eat lycopene-rich ketchup and other tomato-based foods. See the box feature for more information on phytochemicals.
- Antioxidant vitamins and minerals help squelch free radicals, which are unstable compounds in your body that can damage your cells, including your DNA. Many phytochemicals, such as carotenoids and ß-carotene, are also antioxidants. In addition, vitamins C and E and the mineral selenium may help prevent cancer from spreading to nearby tissues.
- Retinoids (vitamin A), vitamin D, folate, and selenium can help repair DNA in the initiation stage and stop the development of cancer in its tracks by inhibiting the progression of damaged cells.
- Omega-3 fatty acids may help reduce cancer cell growth.
- Fiber helps dilute waste products, which may contain cancer-promoting agents, in your intestinal tract and quickly move these out of your body. The less time these agents are exposed to your intestines, the better. Also, the healthy bacteria that live in your colon feast on the fiber, creating a by-product that may also help in the fight against cancer, especially colorectal cancer. Fiber-containing fruits and vegetables are also low in calories and high in bulk, so they fill you up before they fill you out. Thus, a fiber-rich diet can help you reduce excess weight to maintain a healthy body weight. Being overweight increases the risk for several cancers.

Colorful vegetables and fruits contain phytochemicals that can help reduce the risk for cancer.

People who watch more than 2 hours of **television daily** are more likely to be overweight. When you sit and watch TV, you're not only physically inactive but also more likely to munch on high calorie snacks.

In addition, routine physical activity reduces the risk for several types of cancer, in part by helping you maintain a healthful weight. Taken together, a varied, healthy diet and an active lifestyle can reduce your cancer risk. Since many cancers take years, if not decades, to develop after the initial DNA damage, making these changes *right now* can help you avoid cancer later in life.

Avoid Lifestyle Habits That May Increase Your Risk for Cancer

Now that you've seen which dietary components can help reduce your risk for cancer, you'll want to be aware of some foods and beverages that may not be so beneficial:

- A diet high in red meats, which include beef, pork, and lamb, can increase your risk for cancer. Meats processed by smoking, curing, salting, and/or with the addition of chemical preservatives, such as bacon, pastrami, salami, and hot dogs, may also increase your risk. **Nitrite,** which gives cured meat its pink color, is commonly used to preserve processed meats. Nitrite can react with the amino

nitrite A food additive that acts as a preservative and alters the color of the food. Also known as *nitrate.*

Phytochemicals: Powerful Ammunition for Your Health

We introduced **phytochemicals** briefly in Concept 2, so you may remember what they are: naturally occurring plant chemicals (*phyto-* means plant) that are thought to play a role in supporting your health. Unlike carbohydrates or vitamins, phytochemicals are not true nutrients, but they do help maintain and repair your body and thereby help prevent chronic diseases, such as heart disease, diabetes, and cancer.

Fruits, vegetables, beans, and even some whole grains are excellent sources of phytochemicals. Cooking the food does not typically destroy the phytochemicals and may actually enhance the absorption of some phytochemicals in the body. For example, the phytochemical lycopene, which is found in tomatoes, is better absorbed from tomato soups and sauces than from fresh tomatoes! On the other hand, research does not support claims that taking phytochemical supplements is as helpful as consuming whole food sources.[1] Plant foods contain not only a variety of phytochemicals but also vitamins and minerals that may work in concert to help fight cancer.

Of the thousands of phytochemicals that have been identified, many are pigments that give fruits and vegetables their vibrant colors. For instance, carotenoids are phytochemical pigments found in carrots, apricots, pumpkin, and several other yellow-orange and red fruits and vegetables. Table 23.2 is a color guide to help you choose a healthy variety of disease-fighting phytochemicals.

You might be wondering how phytochemicals work. We know that they develop naturally in the plant as it protects itself against pests and other aspects of the environment. It's thought that, when you consume phytochemicals, their protective properties help you stay healthy, too. A few of the ways that different phytochemicals seem to benefit your health are by

- Imitating the actions of natural hormones
- Protecting cells against chemical reactions that can lead to cancer
- Preventing the formation of carcinogens
- Blocking the actions of carcinogens[2]

Thus, if you want to fight cancer, make phytochemicals part of your ammunition!

phytochemicals Naturally-occuring substances in fruits, vegetables, beans, and whole grains that help protect against chronic diseases.

Table 23.2

Phytochemical Color Guide

The National Cancer Institute recommends eating a variety of colorful fruits and vegetables daily to provide your body with valuable vitamins, minerals, fiber, and disease-fighting phytochemicals. Whole grains also have phytochemicals and are included in this list.

Color	Phytochemical	Source
Red	Anthocyanins	Apples, beets, cabbage, cherries, cranberries, red cabbage, red onion, red beans
Yellow/orange	β-carotene	Apricots, butternut squash, cantaloupe, carrots, mangoes, peaches, pumpkin, sweet potatoes
	Flavonoids	Apricots, clementines, grapefruits, lemons, papaya, pears, pineapple, yellow raisins
White	Alliums/allicin	Chives, garlic, leeks, onions, scallions
Green	Lutein, zeaxanthin	Broccoli, collard greens, honeydew melon, kale, kiwi, lettuce, mustard greens, peas, spinach
	Indoles	Arugula, broccoli, bok choy, brussels sprouts, cabbage, cauliflower, kale, Swiss chard, turnips
Blue/purple	Anthocyanins	Blackberries, black currants, elderberries, purple grapes
	Phenolics	Eggplant, plums, prunes, raisins
Brown	β-gluton lignans, phenols, plant sterols, phytoestrogens, saponins, tocotrienols	Barley, brown rice, oats, oatmeal, whole grains, whole-grain cereals, whole wheat

Data adapted from: The National Institute of Health, National Cancer Institute's The Color Guide. www.5aday.gov/color.

acids in the meat or in your stomach to form potential cancer-promoting compounds called nitroasamines and nitroamides.

- Alcohol, especially when consumed excessively, can increase the risk for cancer of the mouth, pharynx, larynx, and esophagus, as well as breast cancer in women and colorectal cancer in men. The more you drink, the higher your cancer risk. While the jury is still out as to how alcohol may promote cancer, it is thought to damage your DNA. By-products of the breakdown of alcohol in your body may also promote cancer. If you are a smoker and you drink, you subject your body to a double whammy: The alcohol enhances the damaging effects of the carcinogens in tobacco.
- Research has also shown that high salt consumption, whether from the salt shaker or from salty foods, can damage the lining of the stomach, paving the way for stomach cancer. As you read in Concept 17, watching the salt in your diet can also help lower high blood pressure. High blood pressure increases your risk for heart attack and stroke.

The best strategy to reduce your risk for cancer is to follow the cancer-fighting recommendations listed in Table 23.1, on page 8.

The Take-Home Message **Maintaining a healthy weight, staying physically active, and consuming a healthy diet can reduce your risk of developing cancer by 30 to 40 percent. A healthy diet that is rich in whole grains, fruits, vegetables, nuts, and beans provides numerous cancer-fighting components, such as phytochemicals, antioxidants, vitamins, minerals, and fiber. Drinking too much alcohol and eating too much red meat, processed meats, and salty foods can increase your risk for cancer.**

Cancer Scams: How Can You Avoid Them?

Snake oil salesmen may no longer be selling door-to-door, but that doesn't mean they've gone out of business. In fact, they're doing better than ever, because they've moved their business onto the Internet. Of all the fraudulent claims you'll encounter on the Internet, claims for cancer "miracle cures" are among the most common—and the most heartbreaking. Cancer scams prey on cancer patients' hopes and fears with advertisements promoting useless products as miracle cures. Some of these creams, tonics, salves, and pills can even be harmful, either because they include tainted or unapproved ingredients or because they produce dangerous side effects. What's more, belief in their effectiveness can cause consumers to delay seeking legitimate treatment from health care providers.

All medicines, medicinal products, and devices promoted to treat cancer must be approved by the United States Food and Drug Administration (FDA) prior to their availability to the public, so how do these fraudulent websites get away with it? The answer lies partly in the sheer number of such sites: So many fraudulent products are being sold via the Internet that many manage to escape FDA notice. To address this problem, the FDA has joined forces with the Federal Trade Commission (FTC) in the fight against cancer fraud. The FDA has also listed over 120 fake cancer "cures" on its website: www.fda.gov/bbs/topics/factsheets/fakecancercures.html.[8]

FDA Consumer Health Information

Beware of Online Cancer Fraud

FDA Press Release

187 Fake Cancer 'Cures' Consumers Should Avoid

CDER: Fake Cancer Cures

While health fraud is a cruel form of greed, fraud involving cancer treatments can be particularly heartless—especially because fraudulent information can travel around the Web in an instant.

"Anyone who suffers from cancer, or knows someone who does, understands the fear and desperation that can set in," says Gary Coody, R.Ph., the National Health Fraud Coordinator and a Consumer Safety Officer with the Food and Drug Administration's (FDA) Office of Regulatory Affairs. "There can be a great temptation to jump at anything that appears to offer a chance for a cure."

Medicinal products and devices intended to treat cancer must gain FDA approval before they are marketed. The agency's review process helps ensure that these products are safe and effective.

Nevertheless, it's always possible to find someone or some company hawking bogus cancer "treatments." Such "treatments" come in many forms, including pills, tonics, and creams. "They're frequently offered as natural treatments and 'dietary supplements,'" says Coody. Many of these fraudulent cancer products even appear completely harmless, but may cause indirect harm by delaying or interfering with proven, beneficial treatments.

"Advertisements and other promotional materials touting bogus cancer 'cures' have probably been around as long as the printing press," says Coody. "However, the Internet has compounded the problem by providing the peddlers of these often dangerous products a whole new outlet."

Promotions for bogus cancer 'cures' are nothing new, but the Internet is providing a whole new outlet. Shown: two bogus treatments recently purchased online by FDA staff, and a 1957 FDA warning.

Unproven 'Remedies,' False Promises

Coody cites black salves as one of the fake cancer "remedies" that indeed have proven to be harmful. "Although it is illegal to market these salves as a cancer treatment, they are readily available online," he says.

The salves are sold with false promises that they will cure cancer by "drawing out" the disease from beneath the skin. "However, there is no scientific evidence that black salves are effective," says Janet Woodcock, Director of FDA's Center for Drug Evaluation and Research (CDER). "Even worse, black salves can cause direct harm to the patient."

The corrosive, oily salves "essentially burn off layers of the skin and sur-

The FDA is working to protect Americans from online cancer fraud.

To further help you, the FDA has developed seven red flags that serve as a tipoff that the cancer claim on a product or an advertisement is bogus. If you see these claims on a site, let the buyer beware:

- "Treats all forms of cancer"
- "Skin cancers disappear"
- "Shrinks malignant tumors"
- "Non-toxic"
- "Doesn't make you sick"
- "Avoid painful surgery, radiotherapy, chemotherapy, or other conventional treatments"
- "Treat non melanoma skin cancers easily and safely"

The Take-Home Message **Bogus claims for products marketed to prevent or treat cancer abound on the Internet. The FDA and FTC prosecute such fraudulent claims, but new websites continue to pop up. Let the buyer beware!**

Check out these recipes and more suggestions at **www.pearsonhighered.com/blake**

UCook

Berry Good Chicken Salad

Make this lean chicken salad with sweet cancer-fighting dried cranberries, which are rich in antioxidants and fiber. And it's so easy to make! Use leftover grilled or baked chicken.

UDo

Cancer-Fighting Meals

Do you know what it takes to plan and prepare cancer-fighting meals? Visit our website to analyze your plate.

The Top Five Points to Remember

1. Cancer occurs when abnormal cells, due to an alteration of the cell's DNA, multiply and form a tumor. These cancerous cells can also spread to other parts of the body, known as metastasis. There are over 100 different types of cancer.
2. Only about 5 to 10 percent of cancers are thought to be genetic. Tobacco, industrial chemicals, ultraviolet (UV) radiation, other types of radiation, and cancer-causing agents in foods and beverages can all damage the DNA in cells and promote cancer.
3. Cancer develops in three stages. During the initiation stage, a body cell is exposed to an agent that damages its DNA. If the damage is not repaired, an altered cell can reproduce itself during the promotion stage. In the progression stage, these damaged cells reproduce and form a tumor. The cancer can metastasize when these cancerous cells travel to other sites in the body.
4. You can reduce your risk for cancer by eating a well-balanced diet that contains adequate amounts of phytochemicals, antioxidants, vitamins, minerals, omega 3 fatty acids, and fiber. Routine physical activity and maintaining a healthy weight can also help reduce your risk for cancer.
5. A diet high in red meats, smoked, cured, and salted meats, processed meats made with chemical preservatives, foods made with nitrates, alcohol, and salt can all increase your risk for cancer. Smoking also increases your cancer risk.

Test Yourself

1. The stage during which the DNA in a cell becomes damaged is known as
   a. initiation.
   b. promotion.
   c. progression.
   d. metastasis.
2. Which of the following can reduce your risk of developing cancer?
   a. walking at least 30 minutes daily
   b. eating more fruit
   c. reducing your intake of red meat
   d. all of the above
3. Fiber can help fight cancer because
   a. it helps keep wastes moving through your intestinal tract.
   b. it provides food for helpful bacteria in your colon.
   c. both a and b.
   d. none of the above.
4. You are going to a sub shop for lunch. You want to order a healthy sandwich. Which of the following would be your best bet?
   a. an Italian sub with pastrami, salami, and provolone cheese
   b. a turkey breast sub with lettuce, tomato, and mayo
   c. a bacon, lettuce and tomato (BLT) sub
   d. a hot dog with mustard and relish
5. Which of the following protects against certain cancers?
   a. vitamins C and E
   b. retinoids (vitamin A)
   c. folate
   d. all of the above

Answers

1. a. The stage in which the initial damage occurs is called initiation. If the damage is not repaired, the cells can begin to reproduce. This stage, called promotion, can go on for many years before progression to a tumor and metastasis to other body sites.
2. d. Incorporating daily physical activity as well as eating more fruit and less red meat can help reduce your cancer risk.
3. c. Both are correct, as fiber helps move waste products that may contain cancer-promoting agents out of your body. Fiber is also a favorite food for bacteria that live in your colon. A by-product produced when bacteria feast on fiber may also help fight cancer.
4. b. Go with the turkey sub (and order extra cancer-fighting veggies!). The salami and pastrami on the Italian sub are both processed meats and should be avoided, as should the hot dog.
5. d. All of the listed vitamins can help fight cancer.

Web Resources

- For more tips on increasing fruits and veggies in your diet, visit: www.fruitsandveggiesmatter.gov/index.html
- For information on specific cancers, visit the National Cancer Institute at: www.cancer.gov
- For the FDA list of over 120 fake cancer "cures," visit its website at: www.fda.gov/bbs/topics/factsheets/fakecancercures.html

24 Focus on Fitness

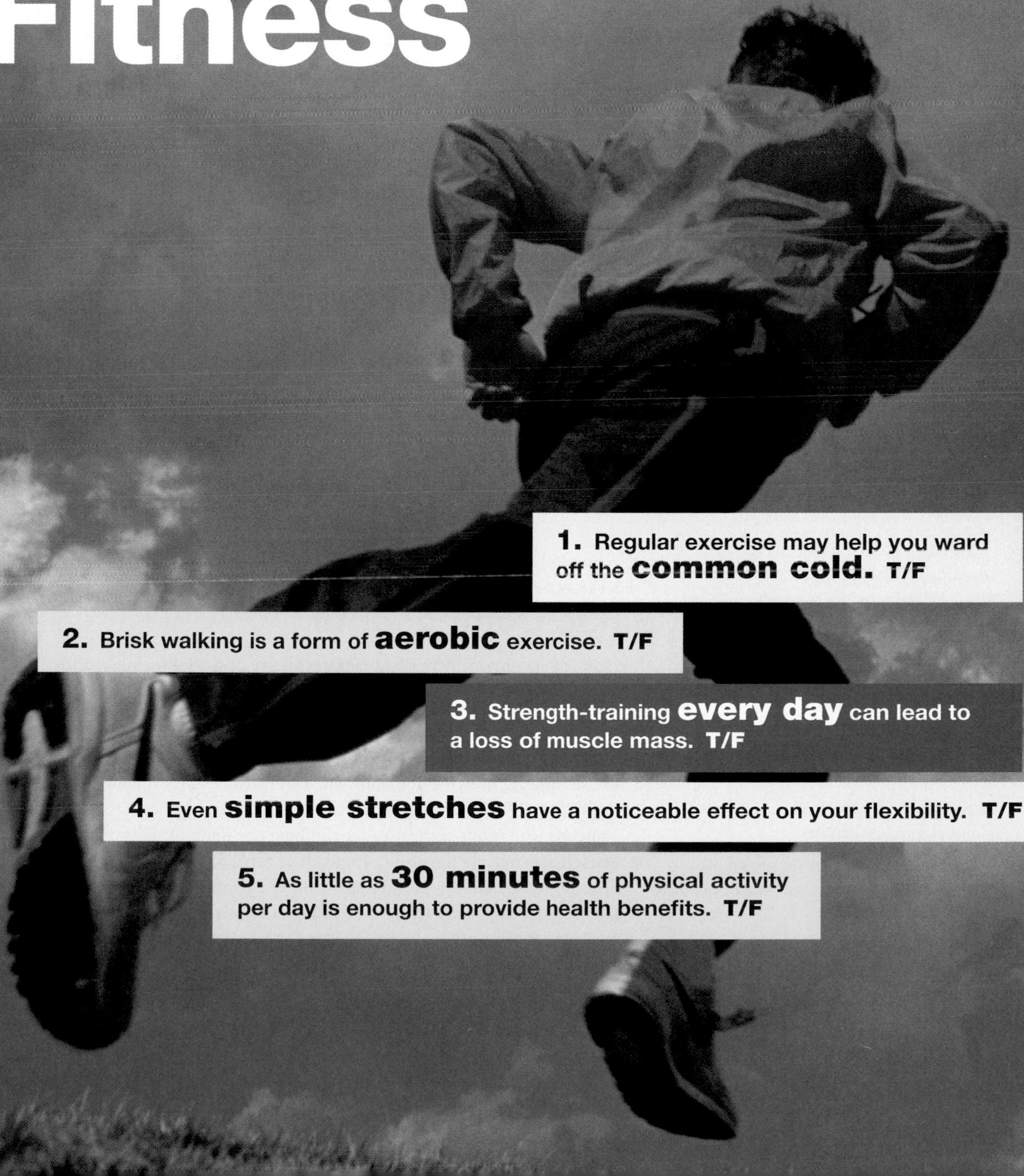

1. Regular exercise may help you ward off the **common cold.** **T/F**

2. Brisk walking is a form of **aerobic** exercise. **T/F**

3. Strength-training **every day** can lead to a loss of muscle mass. **T/F**

4. Even **simple stretches** have a noticeable effect on your flexibility. **T/F**

5. As little as **30 minutes** of physical activity per day is enough to provide health benefits. **T/F**

When they moved from Costa Rica to the United States to work in the high-tech industry, Daria's parents were both slender. Now, nine years later, both are overweight, and Daria's mother was recently diagnosed with type 2 diabetes. Determined to stay fit, Daria starts each day with a 90-minute workout in her school's fitness center. She runs on the treadmill, then switches to the stair-climber, and finishes with a circuit on the weight-training machines. Although she's maintained her program for months, Daria is disappointed that her strength hasn't improved, and she still experiences muscle soreness.

Although Daria's determination to maintain her physical fitness is productive, she might end up with an injury if she continues with her current program.

What is physical fitness? Is intensive daily exercise necessary to achieve and preserve it? In this concept, we'll explore these questions and help you design a fitness program that's right for you.

Answers

1. True. Regular exercise can help keep your immune system humming, and a healthy immune system is more effective in fighting off infections, such as colds. To learn more benefits of regular exercise, see page 4.
2. True. Any activity that gets your heart beating faster and increases oxygen exchange is considered aerobic. To learn more, see p. 5.
3. True. Rest periods during strength-training sessions are essential to allow your muscles time to recover. Turn to page 5 for details.
4. True. Turn to pages 6 and 7 to learn about different types of stretches.
5. True. You don't have to be an Olympian to enjoy the health benefits of exercise. With just 30 minutes each day, you can burn more calories and lower your risk for certain diseases. Turn to pages 8 and 9 for more information.

What Is Fitness, and Why Is It Important?

Physical fitness can be defined most simply as a state of being in good physical condition. Being physically active and consuming a healthy diet are the two behaviors that contribute most significantly to physical fitness. You will not achieve optimal fitness if you ignore either of these healthy habits.

Some people think of physical activity and exercise as the same thing, but this isn't technically the case. **Physical activity** refers to voluntary body movement that results in expending calories. Activities such as gardening, walking the dog, and playing with children can all be regarded as physical activity. **Exercise** is defined as structured or planned physical activity, such as step aerobics, running, or weight lifting. For our purposes, the terms *physical activity* and *exercise* are used interchangeably.

We've loosely defined physical fitness as a state of being in good physical condition. But what exactly does this entail?

physical fitness The ability to perform physical activities requiring cardiorespiratory endurance, muscle endurance, and strength and/or flexibility. Physical fitness is acquired through physical activity and adequate nutrition.

physical activity Voluntary movement that results in energy expenditure (burning calories).

exercise Any type of structured or planned physical activity.

cardiorespiratory endurance The body's ability to sustain prolonged cardiorespiratory exercise.

muscle strength The ability of a muscle to produce force for a brief period of time.

Fitness Has Five Basic Components

A person who is physically fit demonstrates all five of the following qualities:

- **Cardiorespiratory endurance** is the ability to sustain cardiorespiratory exercise, such as running and biking, for an extended length of time. This requires that the body's cardiovascular and respiratory systems provide enough oxygen and energy to the working muscles. Someone who can run a leisurely mile without being too out of breath to talk has good cardiorespiratory endurance. On the other hand, someone who is out of breath after climbing one flight of stairs does not.
- **Muscle strength** is the ability to produce force for a brief period of time. You probably associate muscle strength with bodybuilders or weight lifters, and it's true that these people train to be particularly strong. However, other athletes and performers, such as cheerleaders and ballet dancers, also work hard to strengthen their muscles. Consider the strength it takes to lift another person above your head!

- **Muscle endurance** is the ability to exert force over a long period of time without fatigue. If you could hold a person above your head for several minutes, that would show exceptional muscle endurance. Together, muscle strength and endurance are referred to as *muscular fitness.*
- **Flexibility** is the range of motion around a joint. Athletic performance and joint and muscular function are all enhanced with improved flexibility, which also reduces the likelihood of injury. A gymnast exhibits high flexibility when performing stunts and dance routines. In contrast, someone with low flexibility would not be able to bend over and touch his or her toes from a standing or sitting position.
- Finally, **body composition** is the relative proportion of muscle, fat, water, and other tissues in the body. Together, these make up your total body weight. Your body composition can change without your total body weight changing, due to the fact that muscle takes up less space (per pound) than does body fat. This is why you can lose inches on your body without losing pounds of weight when you increase your lean muscle mass and decrease body fat.

Running is one way to improve cardiorespiratory fitness.

Fitness Provides Numerous Benefits

We have long heard that eating a balanced diet and exercising regularly help prevent diseases and maintain health. The question is, how? In addition to reducing your risk of developing several diseases, being physically fit can improve your overall health in other ways, such as helping you get restful sleep and reducing stress. Figure 24.1 on page 4 identifies some of the numerous health benefits that result from being physically fit.

The Take-Home Message **Physical fitness is the state of being in good physical condition through proper nutrition and regular physical activity. The five components of physical fitness are cardiorespiratory endurance, muscle strength, muscle endurance, flexibility, and body composition. For optimal fitness, all five components must be present. The numerous health benefits of physical fitness include reduced risk for several chronic diseases and better overall health.**

Ask a friend or coworker to exercise with you. Many people are more likely to exercise if they have a partner to **motivate** them.

What Does a Sound Fitness Program Look Like?

At the opening of this concept, you met Daria, who is frustrated because her 90-minute daily workouts are not producing the increased strength she desires and are leaving her with persistent muscle soreness. If she were to seek out a certified fitness trainer in her school's fitness center, she would obtain sound exercise advice. The trainer would likely recommend a fitness program that incorporates cardiorespiratory exercise, weight training, and stretching in periods of varying duration and frequency. Let's take a look.

muscle endurance The ability of a muscle to produce prolonged effort without fatigue.

flexibility The range of motion around a body joint.

body composition The relative proportion of muscle, fat, water, and other tissues in the body.

Figure 24.1 Benefits of Physical Fitness

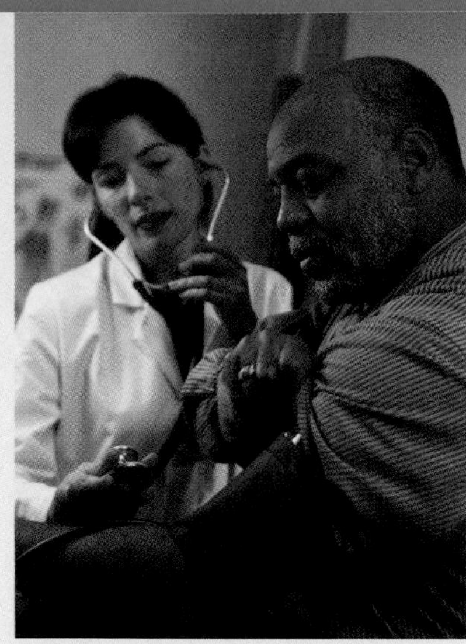

▲ **Reduced Risk for Cardiovascular Disease**

How It Works: Research has shown that moderate physical activity lowers blood pressure.[1] In addition, exercise is positively associated with high-density lipoprotein cholesterol (HDL).[2]

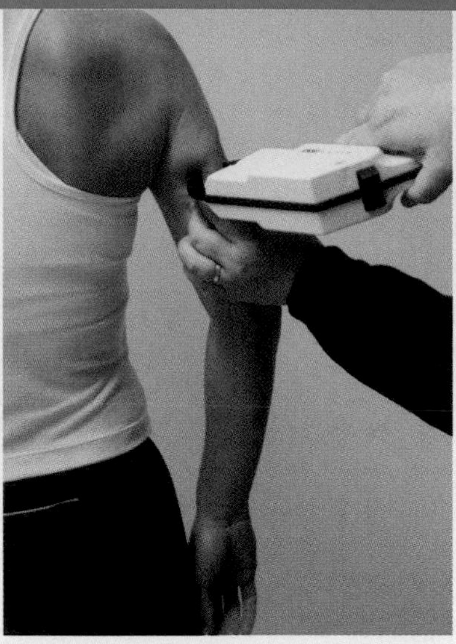

▲ **Improved Body Composition**

How It Works: Individuals with moderate cardiorespiratory fitness have less total fat and abdominal fat, compared with people with low cardiorespiratory fitness.[3]

▲ **Reduced Risk for Type 2 Diabetes**

How It Works: Exercise helps control blood glucose levels by increasing insulin sensitivity.[4] This not only reduces the risk for type 2 diabetes but also improves blood glucose control for those who have been diagnosed with type 2 diabetes.

▲ **Improved Bone Health**

How It Works: Bone density has been shown to improve with weight-bearing exercise and resistance training, thereby reducing the risk for osteoporosis.[5]

▲ **Improved Immune System**

How It Works: Regular exercise can enhance the immune system, which may result in fewer colds and other infectious diseases.[6]

▲ **Improved Sleep**

How It Works: People who engage in regular exercise often have better quality of sleep. This is especially true for older adults.[7]

Cardiorespiratory Exercise Can Improve Cardiorespiratory Endurance and Body Composition

Cardiorespiratory exercise often involves continuous activities that use large muscle groups, such as high-impact aerobics, stair climbing, and brisk walking. This type of exercise is predominantly **aerobic** because it uses oxygen. During cardiorespiratory exercise, your heart beats faster and more oxygen-carrying blood is delivered to your tissues. Your body also redistributes blood from your internal organs to maximize the volume of blood that is delivered to the muscles during exercise.

Walking is one of the best activities you can do to improve your **cardiovascular health** and maintain a healthy weight. In your lifetime, you will walk about 70,000 miles!

Cardiorespiratory exercise benefits your heart, blood, and blood vessels, thereby improving your cardiorespiratory endurance. In addition, it reduces stress, and it lowers your risk for heart disease by maintaining normal cholesterol levels, heart rate, and blood pressure. Cardiorespiratory exercise also helps you maintain a healthy weight and improve your body composition by reducing body fat. Over time, your body's amount of lean tissue will increase.

Weight Training Can Improve Muscular Fitness and Body Composition

Weight training has long been known to increase muscle mass, strength, and endurance. But working out with weights does not necessarily mean that you will develop large, bulky muscles. Maintaining adequate muscle mass and strength is important for everyone, and many females, as well as males, use weight training to tone and define their muscles to improve their physical appearance and body composition.

If you want to increase your muscle strength, you should perform a low number of repetitions using heavy weights. If you want to increase your muscle endurance, you should perform a high number of repetitions using lighter weights. However, you can also use heavier weights to improve muscle endurance, as long as you allow short rest intervals between repetition sets.

Rest periods between sets of an exercise and between workouts are important, so that you do not overwork your muscles and increase your risk for muscle strains or other injury. If you don't allow time for your muscles to rest, your muscles may break down and not recover, leading to a loss of muscle mass. That is what happened to Daria: Her daily full-body weight-training sessions left her muscles weak and sore. The amount of rest you need depends on your fitness goals and level of conditioning:

- Between sets, you should allow long rest periods of 2 to 3 minutes if you're using heavy weights to increase strength. If you're using lighter weights to increase muscle endurance, shorter rest periods of 30 seconds or less are recommended.
- Between workouts, the general guideline for rest periods is two days, or a total of 48 hours. However, Daria can continue her daily weight training as long as she trains different muscles on consecutive days. For instance, she can work her upper body one day and her lower body the next.

Weight training improves muscle strength and endurance.

aerobic With oxygen.

weight training Exercising with weights to build, strengthen, and tone muscle to improve or maintain overall fitness; also called *resistance training.*

Stretching Can Improve Flexibility

When you think about your degree of flexibility, you are likely referring to how far you can stretch in a particular way without feeling pain or discomfort. Stretching is the most common exercise used to improve your flexibility, or range of motion. Improving flexibility can reduce muscle soreness and your risk for injury, as well as improve your balance, your posture, and the circulation of blood and nutrients throughout your body.

There are several types of stretching. The most common form is static stretching, which consists of relaxing a muscle, then extending it to a point of mild discomfort and holding for about 10 to 30 seconds before relaxing it again. You can use static stretching exercises to stretch one muscle at a time, or you can stretch more than one muscle or muscle group at the same time. A form of stretching used by many professional athletes as a pre-event warm-up is dynamic stretching, which stretches muscles while moving, for example, by performing arm swings, kicks, or lunges. If you are performing any stretches for the first time, you need to consult a qualified trainer, coach, or physician on proper techniques to reduce your risk for injury.

Be adventurous—try new activities! Mixing up your routine will help **prevent boredom** and make you more likely to keep moving.

A form of exercise called *yoga* incorporates aspects of both static and dynamic stretching, and individuals who perform yoga on a regular basis can significantly improve their flexibility. Check out the box feature "Yoga: Ancient Workout for a New Age" to see whether yoga is right for you. Other, less common forms of stretching are types that involve a partner or machine to create the force needed to stretch the muscle and controlled stretches that use momentum to create the force needed to extend the muscle.

Rate yourself to see if you're meeting these fitness recommendations.

RATE YOURSELF 

Are You Meeting Your Fitness Recommendations?

Now that you know how to plan an effective fitness strategy, think about your current exercise habits. Take this brief assessment to find out if your daily habits are as healthful as they could be.

1. Do you participate in 30 minutes of moderately intense physical activity most days of the week? **Yes** ☐ **No** ☐
2. Do you engage in cardiorespiratory exercise at least three to five days per week? **Yes** ☐ **No** ☐
3. Do you participate in weight training two or three times per week? **Yes** ☐ **No** ☐
4. Do you perform stretching exercises two or three times per week? **Yes** ☐ **No** ☐

Answers

If you answered "yes" to all of the questions, you are well on your way to optimal fitness. Participating in regular exercise, including aerobic exercise, weight training, and stretching, helps you maintain health and improve your level of fitness. If you answered "no" to any of the questions, review this concept to learn more about fitness.

By improving your flexibility, yoga can help you reduce muscle soreness and lower your risk for injury.

Yoga: Ancient Workout for a New Age

Even if you're not among the 6 million Americans currently practicing yoga, you probably have a friend or relative who is. Virtually unknown in the United States 50 years ago, yoga has grown steadily in popularity, especially since celebrities such as basketball player Kareem Abdul Jabar, rock star Madonna, and actress Michelle Pfeiffer have endorsed it.[1] Is yoga just a new fad? What are the benefits behind its success? And is it right for you?

The word *yoga* is derived from the word *yuj* in Sanskrit, the ancient language of India. It means "to yoke" or "to unite" and signifies a path to enlightenment, or union with the divine. Other paths to enlightenment are also called yoga. For example, *karma yoga* is a path involving service to humankind. The type of yoga best known outside of India is *hatha yoga*, a path involving the practice of physical postures, controlled breathing, meditation, and sometimes chanting, moral behavior, and a pure (typically vegetarian) diet. Although you might think of yoga as the latest fad, ancient artifacts suggest that yoga may have been practiced as early as 5,000 years ago.[2]

Although many styles of yoga are practiced in the United States today, all teach students basic postures called *asanas*. In traditional hatha yoga, students move into these postures, then hold them, achieving a gentle stretch of the involved muscles, before moving to a new posture. In a yoga session of 60 to 90 minutes, the full body is stretched. In addition, several postures can be linked together in one seamless sequence of dynamic stretching, such as the Sun Salutation. Throughout the yoga session, students practice controlled breathing, coordinating their inhalations and exhalations with their movements. For example, students might be instructed to inhale as they arch their backs in the cat-stretch, then exhale as they round their backs and move into the child's pose.

So many different styles of yoga have become popular in the United States that it is impossible to mention them all. Some examples are:

- *Power yoga.* This is a vigorous style in which students move at a fast pace from one asana to the next.
- *Hot yoga.* In this style, students practice in a heated room. As they work, their muscles slacken and they sweat profusely, a response thought to cleanse the body of toxins.
- *Kundalini yoga*. Students may be drawn to kundalini yoga because of its focus on freeing *kundalini* energy (the body's life-force, thought to be stored at the base of the spine). As students explore the influence of their breath in different postures, usually with a straight spine, they may experience their kundalini energy rising through the seven *chakras*, or energy centers, located from the pelvis to the crown of the head.

For thousands of years, adherents have practiced yoga to integrate body, mind, and spirit and achieve union with the divine. If this goal sounds overly ambitious, you might still enjoy yoga for its many health benefits. According to the National Center for Complementary and Alternative Medicine, research suggests that yoga might:

- Improve mood and sense of well-being
- Counteract stress
- Help with conditions such as anxiety, depression, and insomnia
- Positively affect levels of certain brain or blood chemicals
- Reduce heart rate and blood pressure
- Increase lung capacity
- Improve muscle relaxation and body composition
- Improve overall physical fitness, strength, and flexibility[3]

Yoga is safe for healthy people when practiced appropriately, but if you have a medical condition, check with your primary health care provider before signing up. Also discuss with your instructor prior to the first class any health or functional limitations you have. This will help ensure that your exploration of yoga is safe, effective, and fun!

The FITT Principle Can Help You Design a Fitness Program

Now that you know the components of a fitness program, you may be wondering how to design a program that ensures that you become physically fit. One easy way to do this is to follow the FITT principle. FITT is an acronym for frequency, intensity, time, and type. Let's take a closer look at each of these components of a well-rounded fitness program:

- **Frequency** is how often you do an activity, such as the number of times per week.

- **Intensity** is the degree of difficulty at which you perform the activity. Common terms used to describe intensity are *low, moderate,* and *vigorous* (*high*). For example, if you're out walking on a cold day and you start to feel warm but don't break a sweat, your activity's level of intensity is likely moderate. If you're walking so briskly that you start to sweat and find it difficult to hold a conversation, then you're exercising at a vigorous intensity.
- **Time,** or duration, is how long you perform the activity, such as a 30-minute run.
- **Type** is the specific activity you are doing, such as step aerobics versus cycling.

The frequency, intensity, time (duration), and type of exercise that are right for you depend partly on what goal you are trying to achieve. For moderate health benefits, the *Dietary Guidelines for Americans 2005* suggests at least 30 minutes of moderate-intensity physical activity, such as brisk walking or dancing, most days of the week. Engaging in more vigorous-intensity activities, such as jogging or fast-paced swimming, for longer duration will result in even greater health benefits. Unfortunately, over half of adults living in the United States do not meet these recommendations for regular physical activity.[8]

You don't have to do an activity for 30 consecutive minutes to get health benefits. Break the time up into three 10-minute bouts of activity and you'll still receive the same benefits.

To maintain your body weight and prevent gradual weight gain, you should participate in approximately 60 minutes of moderate- to vigorous-intensity activity on

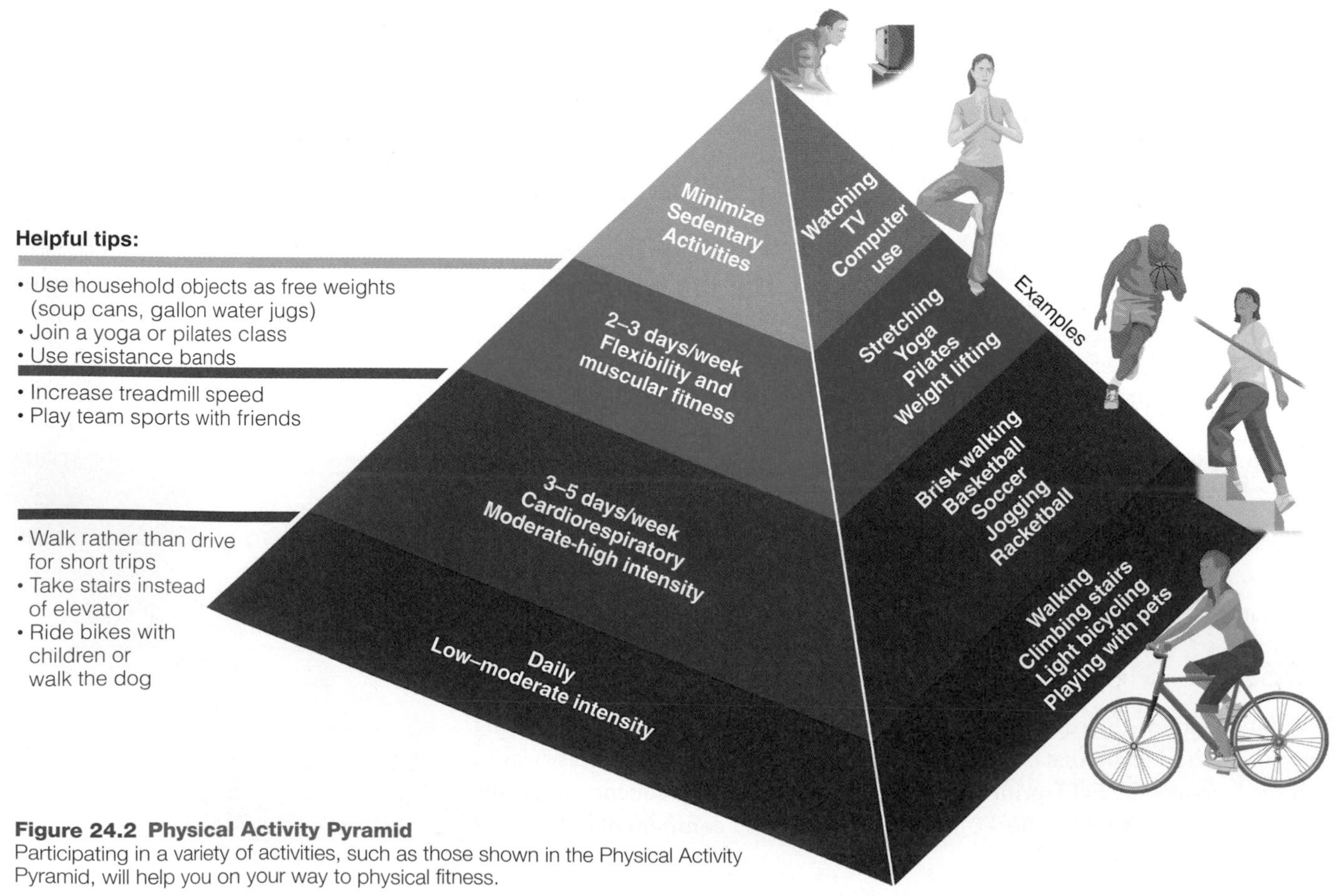

Figure 24.2 Physical Activity Pyramid
Participating in a variety of activities, such as those shown in the Physical Activity Pyramid, will help you on your way to physical fitness.

Table 24.1

Using FITT to Improve Fitness

	Cardiorespiratory Fitness	Muscular Fitness	Flexibility
Frequency	3–5 days per week	2–3 days per week	2–3 days per week
Intensity	55–90% of maximum heart rate	8–12 RM*	Enough to develop and maintain range of motion
Time	20–60 minutes, continuous or intermittent (minimum of 10-minute bouts)	8–10 different exercises performed in 1–3 sets	At least 4 repetitions for each muscle group; hold static stretch for 10–30 seconds
Type	Brisk walking, jogging, biking, step aerobics	Weight training	Stretching

*Revolutions per minute.

Data adapted from: American College of Sports Medicine. Position Stand: The Recommended Quantity and Quality of Exercise for Developing and Maintaining Cardiorespiratory and Muscular Fitness, and Flexibility in Healthy Adults. *Medicine & Science in Sports & Exercise* 30 no. 6 (June 1998). Used by permission of Lippincott Williams & Wilkins.

most days of the week while not consuming excess calories. To lose weight effectively, you should participate in at least 60 to 90 minutes of daily moderate-intensity physical activity and make calorie adjustments to your diet. You can use the Physical Activity Pyramid to help you become more physically active or improve your current level of fitness (Figure 24.2). People with diabetes, high blood pressure, and other types of heart disease should consult with a health care provider before participating in any exercise program, especially one to be performed at a vigorous intensity.

The key to being physically active is to find activities that you enjoy, so that you continue to do them on a regular basis. If you don't like jogging, you don't have to do it! Just find other activities you like. Maybe you enjoy playing basketball, going for a walk, or hiking. It doesn't really matter what the activity is, as long as you take pleasure in what you are doing and do it regularly.

Track your exercise in a log or journal, so that you see how much you are getting and note your **improvements** over time.

You can use the FITT approach to meet the American College of Sports Medicine's guidelines for cardiorespiratory endurance, muscular fitness, and flexibility for healthy adults, which are summarized in Table 24.1. For example, on your FITT program, you may want to jog three days a week for 30 minutes to attain your cardiorespiratory fitness. On other days, you may want to lift weights for muscular fitness or take a yoga class to improve your flexibility.

The Take-Home Message **Cardiorespiratory exercise improves cardiorespiratory endurance and body composition. Weight training can improve muscle strength and endurance, as well as body composition. Flexibility can be enhanced by stretching. An effective training program can be designed using the FITT principle, which stands for frequency, intensity, time, and type of activity. Most people should aim for 30 minutes of moderate activity most days of the week for health. Greater amounts of exercise are needed for weight management and improved physical fitness.**

Check out these recipes and more suggestions at www.pearsonhighered.com/blake

UCook 

Ziti with Chicken and Broccoil in a Creamy Sauce

This crowd-pleasing dish will fuel even the busiest folks on the go. Don't let the cream sauce fool you. Since it's made with evaporated milk, it's luscious but light!

UDo 

Get Ready to Get FITT!

Are you ready to incorporate more "FITTness" into your physical activity program? Go to our website and use the FITT worksheet to assess your regular physical activities for frequency, intensity, time, and type. Track your activities for a week, and see where you need to make adjustments to optimize your workouts.

The Top Five Points to Remember

1. Physical fitness is the state of being in good physical condition, especially as a result of regular physical activity and proper nutrition. The five basic components of fitness are cardiorespiratory endurance, muscle strength, muscle endurance, flexibility, and body composition.
2. Engaging in regular physical activity provides several health benefits: reducing the risk for chronic diseases, such as cardiovascular disease and type 2 diabetes; improving sleep; reducing stress; and improving body composition, immunity, and bone health.
3. A sound fitness program includes three components. Cardiorespiratory exercise, such as aerobics, stair climbing, brisk walking, jogging, running, tennis, and swimming is important for cardiorespiratory endurance and healthy body composition. Weight training is important for muscular fitness. Stretching improves flexibility.
4. The FITT principle can help you design a sound fitness program. FITT stands for frequency, intensity, time, and type of activity. Table 24.1 shows you how to use FITT to improve your fitness.
5. Thirty minutes of moderately intense activity most days of the week will benefit your health. If you want to prevent weight gain, you should engage in 60 minutes of moderate- to vigorous-intensity exercise on most days of the week. If you want to lose weight, 60 to 90 minutes of daily moderate- to vigorous-intensity exercise is recommended, along with adjustments to your calorie intake.

Test Yourself

1. Which of the following is *not* a component of physical fitness?
   a. muscle strength
   b. cardiorespiratory endurance
   c. stress
   d. body composition
2. Which of the following is a benefit of physical fitness?
   a. improved bone health
   b. reduced risk for type 2 diabetes
   c. better quality of sleep
   d. all of the above
3. If you are able to do 100 consecutive push-ups without taking a break, you are exhibiting great
   a. cardiorespiratory endurance.
   b. muscle endurance.
   c. flexibility.
   d. muscle strength.
4. If you want to increase your muscle endurance but avoid developing large, bulky muscles, you should
   a. use lighter weights and perform a higher number of repetitions.
   b. use lighter weights and perform a lower number of repetitions.
   c. use heavier weights and perform a higher number of repetitions.
   d. use heavier weights and perform a lower number of repetitions.
5. If you want to lose weight, in addition to adjusting your calorie intake, you should engage in
   a. at least 20 to 30 minutes of moderate-intensity activity daily.
   b. at least 30 to 60 minutes of moderate-intensity activity daily.
   c. at least 60 to 90 minutes of moderate-intensity activity daily.
   d. at least 90 to 120 minutes of moderate-intensity activity daily.

Answers

1. (c) Muscle strength, cardiorespiratory endurance, and body composition, along with muscle endurance and flexibility, are the five basic components of physical fitness. Stress is not a component of physical fitness.
2. (d) All of these are benefits of physical fitness.
3. (b) Performing 100 consecutive push-ups without resting shows great muscle endurance because you are able to

exert the force needed to push yourself up over a long period of time without getting tired.

4. (a) To increase your muscle endurance but avoid developing large, bulky muscles, you should work out with lighter weights and perform many repetitions.
5. (c) If you want to lose weight, in addition to adjusting your calorie intake, you should engage in at least 60 to 90 minutes of moderate-intensity activity daily.

Web Resources

For more on nutrition and fitness, visit

- The President's Council on Physical Fitness and Sports: www.fitness.gov
- American Council on Exercise: www.acefitness.org
- American College of Sports Medicine: www.acsm.org
- American Dietetic Association: www.eatright.org

25

Eat to Compete

1. Carbohydrate, fat, and protein all **provide energy** during exercise. **T/F**

2. The amount of carbohydrate needed to fuel **daily activities** depends greatly on the duration of your actions. **T/F**

3. Athletes should eat immediately **after training.** **T/F**

4. Low-fat **chocolate milk** is an ideal post-exercise drink. **T/F**

5. If you don't **feel thirsty,** then you can't be dehydrated. **T/F**

Greg, a college junior, is the starting point guard for the men's basketball team. Greg starts his day early, with 1 hour of basketball practice before heading off to his 9:00 a.m. class. Because he likes to get as much sleep as possible, Greg usually doesn't eat breakfast before practice, but sometimes has an energy bar on his way to class. He finishes his last class at 2:00 p.m. and then goes to practice again for several more hours.

Greg has difficulty finding time in his busy schedule to eat anything, much less healthy foods, so he usually grabs a fast-food burger and fries before his afternoon practice. Despite the fact that he's in great shape and considers himself to be healthy, Greg is often tired and cranky by the time he gets home in the evening.

What Greg doesn't realize is that his poor eating habits, including irregular meals and the kinds of foods he's eating, are compromising his athletic performance.

Do you think your eating habits have a significant impact on your fitness level? We'll explore this question, and other aspects of nutrition and how it relates to physical fitness and athletic performance, in this concept.

Answers

1. True. The body does use carbohydrate, fat, and protein for energy during exercise, but the amount that is used depends partly on the intensity of the exercise. Turn to pages 3 and 4 to learn about energy sources during exercise.
2. True. Your activity level has a definite bearing on the amount of energy you need to consume. Turn to page 4 for more information.
3. True. Consumption of specific nutrients immediately after stopping exercise will improve recovery. Find out more on page 9.
4. True. Low-fat chocolate milk is a less expensive source of carbohydrate and protein than specialty protein drinks. Turn to page 10 for more.
5. False. You can dehydrate without feeling thirsty. See page 14 for details.

How Are Carbohydrate, Fat, and Protein Used during Exercise?

In addition to regular physical activity, you need the right foods and fluids in order to be physically fit. When you eat and drink, you support physical activity in two ways: (1) You supply the energy, particularly from carbohydrate and fat that your body needs for the activity and (2) you provide the nutrients, particularly carbohydrate and protein, that will help you recover properly, so that you can repeat the activity.

In Concept 24, you saw that energy production during cardiorespiratory exercise is primarily *aerobic* because it uses oxygen. But during the first few minutes of exercise, energy production occurs under **anaerobic** conditions, or without oxygen. For the anaerobic production of energy, the body relies heavily on two high-energy molecules in muscle cells:

- *Adenosine triphosphate (ATP)* is a compound composed of a molecule called adenosine attached to a "tail" of three phosphates (*tri* = three). When one of these phosphates is removed from ATP, energy is released as a by-product (Figure 25.1a). The remaining compound is called *adenosine diphosphate (ADP)*, because it contains only two phosphates (*di* = two). The amount of ATP (energy) in cells is limited, so its breakdown can support only a few seconds of intense exercise.
- *Creatine phosphate* is a compound containing the molecule creatine attached to a single phosphate. Your body produces creatine with the help of the liver and kidneys and then stores it in skeletal muscle and other tissues. Your body also gets some creatine from foods, including meat and fish. Creatine phosphate has a dual role in energy production (Figure 25.1b). Direct energy is produced when the phosphate is split off from the creatine, and indirect energy is produced when the phosphate is donated to ADP, thereby regenerating ATP. The amount of creatine that can be stored in the muscles is very limited and becomes depleted after about 10 seconds of high-intensity activity.

anaerobic Without oxygen.

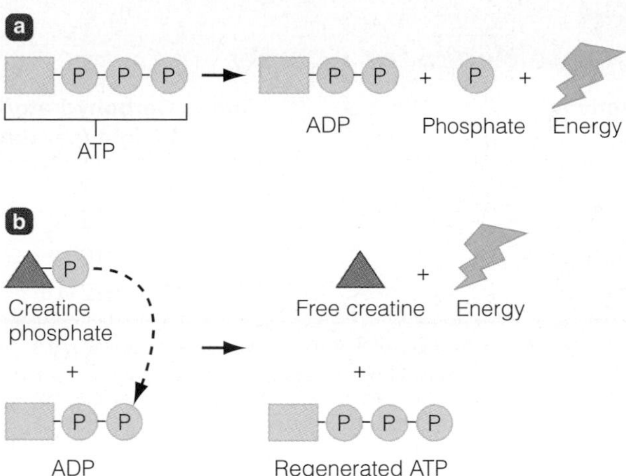

Figure 25.1 Energy Metabolism During anaerobic metabolism, energy is derived from the breakdown of ATP and creatine phosphate.

As you continue exercising beyond a few minutes, you will breathe more heavily and take in more oxygen. At this point, your body begins to rely more on aerobic energy production from the breakdown of carbohydrate (glucose) and fat (fatty acids).

Your body relies on carbohydrate, fat, and protein for energy during exercise, but the type and amount of energy it uses depend highly on the intensity and duration of the exercise, your nutritional status, and your level of physical fitness. Carbohydrate and fat contribute most of the energy needed for activity, while protein is best used to promote muscle growth and recovery. The following section discusses the roles of carbohydrate, fat, and protein during exercise.

Carbohydrate Is the Primary Energy Source during High-Intensity Exercise

During exercise, you obtain energy from carbohydrate through blood glucose and stored glycogen in your muscles and liver. In an average-sized man, the total amount of energy stored as carbohydrate in the body is about 2,600 calories, of which 2,000 calories can be used. This is enough energy to perform about 2 hours of moderate exercise, before glycogen stores are almost completely depleted.

Glycogen stores are continuously being depleted and replenished. If you exercise often, eating carbohydrate-rich foods on a regular basis is important, so that you provide your muscles with adequate glycogen. When glycogen stores are inadequate, the muscles no longer have the energy to support the activity. This reduces athletic performance and promotes fatigue.[1] Does this mean that, if you eat a large amount of carbohydrates every day you will have more energy? Not exactly. The glycogen storage capacity of both the muscles and the liver is limited. Once your muscles and liver have stored all of the glycogen possible, any excess glucose will be stored as body fat.

The cofounder of the company Nike poured rubber into his waffle iron to create ridges for the bottom of shoes to increase traction and improve athletic performance among runners.

Athletic training can increase the amount of glycogen that the muscles can hold.[2] When muscles are well trained, they can store 20 to 50 percent more glycogen than untrained muscles. More stored glycogen means more fuel for working muscles to use, which means you can exercise for a longer period of time and increase your endurance. However, just eating a high-carbohydrate meal before competition will

Table 25.1

Carbohydrate Needs for Activity

Duration of Activity (per day)	Grams Carbohydrate/Kg Body Weight (per day)
1 hour	6–7
2 hours	8
3 hours	10
4 hours or more	12–13

Note: To convert your body weight into kilograms (kg), divide your weight in pounds by 2.2.

Data from: C. Rosenbloom, ed. *Sports Nutrition: A Guide for the Professional Working with Active People.* 3rd ed. (Chicago: The American Dietetic Association, 2000), 16. © 2000 American Dietetic Association. Adapted with permission.

not help you perform at your best. You need to train your muscles *and* eat a high-carbohydrate diet regularly to improve endurance.

Although stored muscle glycogen is the preferred source of energy during exercise, liver glycogen stores are also important. Glycogen provided by the liver is converted into glucose and delivered to the bloodstream in order to maintain normal blood glucose levels, both during times of activity and while you are at rest.

While muscle glycogen provides energy for your muscles during activity, blood glucose is the energy source for your brain. If you are not supplying your brain with the energy it needs, you may feel a lack of coordination or concentration—two things you especially *don't* want to experience during exercise or a sport competition.

When glucose is broken down at a very high rate, the muscles produce a by-product called *lactate*. Muscles use lactate as an energy source when it is produced at a low rate. For example, during low-intensity exercise, the body oxidizes the lactate for energy. Therefore, lactate does not accumulate in the working muscle tissue. For many years, lactate "buildup" in muscles was thought to be a cause of muscle fatigue, but now researchers believe that lactate can also be an important fuel during exercise.[3]

Exercise Intensity Affects How Much Glucose and Glycogen You Use

Your muscles will use carbohydrates for energy no matter how intense the exercise. However, the *amount* of carbohydrate used is affected by exercise intensity, as well as your level of fitness, your initial muscle glycogen stores, and whether you're consuming carbohydrates during exercise. Research shows that, as the intensity of exercise increases, so does the use of glucose and glycogen for energy.[4] At very high exercise intensity, most of the energy is supplied by carbohydrates in the form of muscle glycogen. Although carbohydrate is not the main energy source during exercise of low to moderate intensity, it still provides some energy for the working muscles.

Exercise Duration Affects How Much Glucose and Glycogen You Use

The amount of carbohydrate needed per day to fuel activity depends greatly on the duration of the activity, in addition to the activity intensity. Table 25.1 identifies the amount of carbohydrate needed for different durations of physical activity.[5] **Carbohydrate loading** is a diet and training strategy that athletes use before a competition. The goal of carbohydrate loading before an endurance event is to maximize the storage capacity of muscle glycogen. Increasing the amount of stored muscle glycogen can improve an athlete's endurance performance by providing the energy to fuel activity at an optimal pace for a longer period of time.

carbohydrate loading A diet and training strategy that maximizes glycogen stores in the body before an endurance event.

Not all athletes or physically active people will have improved performance with carbohydrate loading. The people who are likely to benefit the most from this strategy are those who participate in endurance events or exercise that lasts more than 90 minutes. Examples of endurance events include marathons, triathlons, cross-country skiing, and long-distance cycling and swimming. Research has also shown that women are less likely than men to have improved performance with carbohydrate loading because women oxidize significantly more fat and less carbohydrate and protein than men during endurance exercise.[6]

The best types of carbohydrates to eat during and/or after exercise are carbohydrate-rich foods, such as baked potatoes, bagels, or corn flakes, that are absorbed and enter the bloodstream quickly and thus can be used immediately for energy (glucose) or to replenish glycogen stores. Carbohydrate-rich foods such as rice, oatmeal, pasta, and corn are ideal a couple of hours before exercise, as their carbohydrate content enters the bloodstream much more slowly and provides a sustained source of energy. You'll learn more about timing your nutrient intake shortly.

Carbohydrate-rich foods are ideal a couple of hours before exercise.

Fat Is the Primary Energy Source during Low- to Moderate-Intensity Exercise

Fat supplies nearly all the energy required during low- to moderate-intensity activity. Even at rest, your body uses fat as its main energy source. Unlike glycogen, fat does not contain water, so the amount of energy stored as body fat is far greater, and more concentrated, than the amount of energy stored as glycogen.

Endurance training increases your body's utilization of fat for energy, which spares glycogen. When you use more fat for energy, you "save" your glycogen stores for energy use later on.

Intensity and Training Affect How Much Fat You Use

The duration and intensity of exercise affect how much fat is used for energy. Your body typically begins to break down fat for energy after about 15 to 20 minutes of aerobic exercise. The process of converting fatty acids into energy is quite slow, so fat is the preferred energy source during activities that are of low to moderate intensity. For high-intensity exercise, fatty acids cannot be converted into energy fast enough to meet the demand. Therefore, fat use decreases and carbohydrates become the preferred energy source. So, if you are trying to lose weight and body fat, should you reduce the intensity of your workout? The box feature "The Truth about the Fat-Burning Zone" discusses this interesting issue.

Your level of training can also affect how much fat your body will use for energy. Muscles that are well trained burn more fat than muscles that are not as well trained.

How Much Fat Do I Need for Exercise?

Dietary recommendations for fat intake are generally the same for active people as for the average adult population, with approximately 25 to 30 percent of calories coming from fat.[7] Recall that high intakes of saturated and *trans* fats have been linked to high blood cholesterol levels and heart disease. Physically active people sometimes assume that, because they're in shape, they don't have to worry about these diseases. While it is true that physical activity grants some protection against heart disease, athletes and other fit people can also have high blood cholesterol levels, heart attacks, and strokes. Everyone, regardless of activity level, should limit their saturated fat intake to no more than 10 percent of total calories, and consume unsaturated fats in foods to meet the body's need for dietary fat.[8]

Some athletes, such as endurance runners and those in sports in which low body weight is important, such as gymnasts and figure skaters, feel they can benefit from a

The Truth about the Fat-Burning Zone

Many people recognize the importance of exercise, especially of the cardiovascular system, for weight loss. They head off to the gym and jump on an exercise machine to start their workout. Once on the machine, they hook up to a device that monitors their heart rate, which lets them know if they are in the fat-burning zone (65 to 73 percent of maximum heart rate) or the "cardio" zone (more than 73 percent of maximum heart rate). Because most people seek to lose body fat, they exercise in the fat-burning zone because they believe that this is the most effective way to lose weight. After all, it is true that the body burns more fat at lower intensities and burns more carbohydrate as the intensity increases. So, is staying in the fat-burning zone the best advice to follow if you are trying to lose weight? The simple answer is no. Let's look at some calculations to better understand why.

If you are trying to lose weight, you need to burn more calories than you consume. Working out is an excellent way to do this, but you need to be aware of how many calories you are burning, and aim to work off as many as possible. In the fat-burning zone at 65 percent of maximum heart rate, a moderately fit person burns an average of 220 calories during 30 minutes of exercise. Also at this intensity, fat supplies about 50 percent of the total calories burned for energy. This means that the person is burning an average of 110 fat calories (50 percent of 220). As the intensity increases to about 85 percent of maximum heart rate, this person burns an average of 330 calories during 30 minutes of exercise, with fat supplying only about 33 percent of the total calories burned. Guess what? The person burns the same number of fat calories (33 percent of 330) but is burning more total calories (330 calories) at a higher intensity, which will help meet the weight-loss goal sooner than exercising at a lower intensity (burning 220 calories). The bottom line is that you don't need to stay in the fat-burning zone to lose body fat. You just need to burn enough calories for an overall calorie deficit.

If you prefer not to exercise at a high intensity, there is an advantage to exercising at a lower intensity. If you have time for a long workout, you can probably exercise at a lower intensity for a longer period of time without getting tired. In other words, if you are jogging (high-intensity) you may get tired after you cover 3 miles. However, if you are walking briskly (lower-intensity), you may be able to cover 4 miles because you aren't as fatigued. Covering that extra mile allows you to expend more calories overall during your outing. But if you have a busy lifestyle and feel pressed for time to exercise, don't be afraid to go out of the fat-burning zone to get the most out of your workout and lose weight!

very-low-fat diet (less than 20 percent). Although consuming too much dietary fat is a concern, you don't want to limit your fat intake too much. When you consume less than adequate amounts of fat, you may not get enough calories, essential fatty acids, and fat-soluble vitamins, which can negatively affect athletic performance.[9]

Protein Is Needed Primarily to Build and Repair Muscle

Muscle damage is one of the most significant physiological effects of exercise, especially in weight training. Although it sounds negative, muscle damage stimulates remodeling of the muscle cells, which increases muscle strength and mass. Amino acids obtained from protein are the main nutrients needed to promote muscle growth and recovery. By supplying your muscles with adequate protein, you help ensure that muscle damage does not result in decreased muscle mass and strength.

The Body Can Use Protein for Energy

Your body prefers to use carbohydrate and fat as its main energy sources during exercise (Figure 25.2). It uses small amounts of protein for energy only when your calorie intake and carbohydrate stores are insufficient. If your body has to use a significant amount of protein for energy, that protein is not available to build and repair tissues. If this occurs too often, a loss of muscle mass will likely result.

Muscle protein is converted into energy by being broken down into amino acids, which are then released into your bloodstream. The amino acids are carried to your liver, where they are converted into glucose, which supplies the working muscles with energy.

How Much Protein Do You Need for Exercise?

Many athletes and exercisers assume that they need substantially more protein than non-exercisers. In truth, their needs are not significantly higher. Recall from Concept 14 that the RDA for protein for most healthy adults is 0.8 gram per kilogram of body weight per day, and most people, including athletes, far exceed this. Endurance athletes are advised to consume 1.2 to 1.4 grams of protein per kilogram of body weight. People who participate primarily in resistance and strength activities may need to consume as much as 1.6 to 1.7 grams per kilogram of body weight.[10]

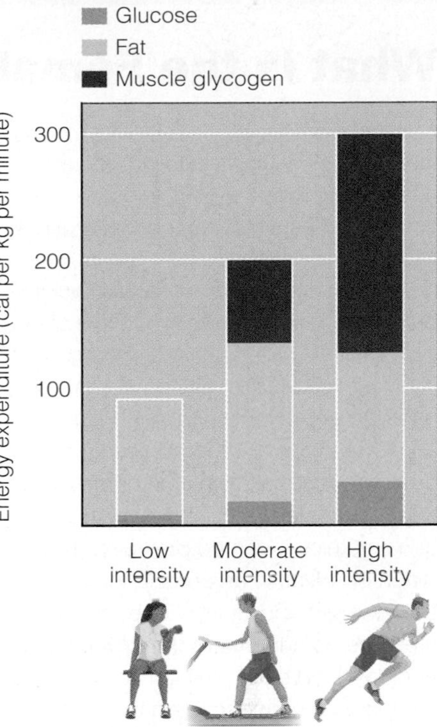

Figure 25.2 Energy Use during Varying Intensities of Exercise
During exercise, your body prefers to use carbohydrate and fat for energy. The intensity of the exercise will determine how much of these is used.

Data adapted from: J. A. Romijn et al., Regulation of Endogenous Fat and Carbohydrate Metabolism in Relation to Exercise Intensity and Duration, *American Journal of Physiology Endocrinology and Metabolism* 265 (September 1993): E380–E391.

Total Calorie Needs Depend on the Type and Schedule of Exercise

Your daily calorie needs depend on the type of exercise (swimming, volleyball, tennis, etc.) you choose and your training schedule. Playing an hour of Frisbee with your friends will use a little over 200 calories (based on a 150-pound person). Compare that with an hour of downhill skiing, which will burn over 500 calories. When eight-time Olympic gold medal champion Michael Phelps is training, he needs to consume over 10,000 calories daily to fuel his activities and maintain his weight. The best way to determine if you are consuming enough calories is to monitor your weight. If your weight doesn't decrease, you are consuming enough calories.

Unfortunately, some female athletes in certain "lean-build" sports are under pressure to maintain a low weight that's not conducive to good health. As discussed in the accompanying box feature, this pressure can contribute to a complex state known as the female athlete triad.

Timing of Food Intake Affects Fitness and Athletic Performance

Timing the foods that you eat around exercise has a significant impact on energy levels and recovery time. During exercise, especially weight training, muscles are under a great deal of stress. After exercise, the body is in a catabolic (breaking down) state. Muscle and liver glycogen stores are low or depleted, muscle protein is broken down, and the immune system is suppressed. Therefore, supplying the body with the nutrients it needs to reverse this catabolic state into an anabolic (building up) state is crucial for optimal fitness.

Michael Phelps won eight gold medals in swimming at the 2008 Beijing Olympics.

What Should You Eat before Exercise?

You need to eat before exercise or a competition so that you have enough energy for optimal performance. However, you also need to allow sufficient time for the food to digest, so that it doesn't negatively affect your performance. In general, larger meals (making you feel quite full) take 3 to 4 hours to digest, while smaller meals (making you feel satisfied but not overly full) take only 2 to 3 hours to digest. If you are drinking a liquid supplement or having a small snack, you should allow about 30 minutes

What Is the Female Athlete Triad?

Christy Henrich joined the U.S. gymnastics team in 1986 weighing 95 pounds at 4 feet, 11 inches tall. Christy soon succeeded as a gymnast, but after a judge told her she needed to lose weight, she developed anorexia nervosa. Her weight plummeted to 47 pounds, and she died from multiple organ failure at the age of 22.

The anorexia that Christy battled is one part of the *female athlete triad,* a combination of disordered eating, amenorrhea (abnormal cessation of menstruation), and osteoporosis. In certain sports, female athletes can be pressured to reach or maintain an unrealistically low body weight and/or level of body fat. This pressure contributes to the development of disordered eating, which helps initiate the triad. Of major concern with this disorder is that it not only reduces the athlete's performance but also has serious medical and psychological consequences.

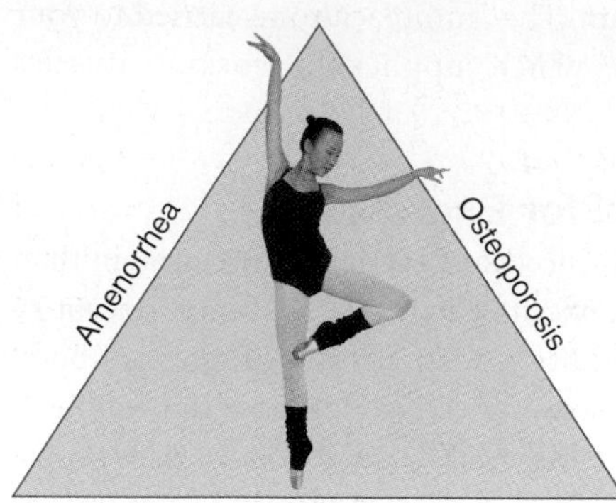

Female dancers and athletes for whom body size or appearance is an issue, such as gymnasts and skaters, are often particularly vulnerable to the female athlete triad.

Disordered Eating

Athletes who have disordered eating engage in abnormal, and often harmful, eating behaviors to lose weight or maintain a low body weight. At one extreme are those who fulfill the diagnostic criteria for anorexia nervosa or bulimia nervosa. At the other are those who unintentionally take in fewer calories than they need. They may appear to be eating a healthy diet—one that would be adequate for a sedentary individual—but their calorie needs are higher due to their level of physical activity. Many athletes mistakenly believe that losing weight by any method enhances performance, and that disordered eating is harmless. Disordered eating is most common among athletes in sports in which appearance is important, such as figure skating and gymnastics, but can occur in athletes in all types of sports.

Amenorrhea

Amenorrhea, the absence of three to six consecutive menstrual cycles, is the most recognizable component of the triad. It is prompted by a failure to consume enough energy to compensate for the "energy cost" of the exercise. Insufficient body fat reduces levels of the female hormone estrogen, which helps maintain healthy bone. Unfortunately, many women welcome the convenience of not menstruating and do not report it. However, this may put them at risk for reduced bone mass and fractures.

Osteoporosis

Osteoporosis is the loss of bone mineral density and the inadequate formation of bone. Premature osteoporosis, which is perpetuated by poor nutrition and amenorrhea, puts the athlete at risk for stress fractures, hip and vertebral fractures, and the loss of bone mass, which may be irreplaceable.

Unfortunately, the triad components are very often not recognized, not reported, or denied. Thus, all individuals, including friends, teachers, and coaches, involved with female athletes should be aware of the warning signs. These include weight changes, disordered eating patterns, depression, and stress fractures. People working with female athletes should provide a training environment in which athletes are not pressured to lose weight. They also should be able to recommend appropriate nutritional, medical, and/or psychological resources if needed.

to 1 hour for digestion. These are general guidelines and may not apply to everyone, so be sure that you experiment with your own eating and exercise schedule well before a workout or competition, so that you know how long you need to wait before starting your activity.

You just learned that carbohydrates are one of the main sources of energy during exercise. Thus, your preexercise meal should contain adequate amounts of carbohydrate, so that you maximize muscle and liver glycogen stores and maintain normal blood glucose levels. In general, your preexercise meal should contain 1 to 4.5 grams of carbohydrate per kilogram of body weight and be consumed 1 to 4 hours prior to exercise.

Consuming some carbohydrate, such as a piece of fruit or a fruit cup, immediately before exercise (about 15 to 30 minutes prior to the start) provides an advantage because it gives your muscles an immediate source of energy (glucose) and spares your glycogen stores, so that you can exercise longer or at a higher intensity without becoming tired.[11] Carbohydrate intake before exercise can also help reduce muscle damage by causing the release of insulin, which promotes muscle protein synthesis.

Including some protein in a preexercise meal benefits your body by causing a greater increase in muscle glycogen synthesis than consuming carbohydrate alone. With more glycogen in your muscles, you can increase endurance. Another benefit of consuming both protein and carbohydrate before exercise is that it results in greater protein synthesis after the exercise, compared with either protein or carbohydrate alone.[12] Foods with a higher fat content take longer to digest than foods that are higher in carbohydrate and protein. For this reason, high-fat foods should generally be avoided several hours before exercise. If you eat high-fat foods before exercise, you may feel sluggish or have stomach discomfort, which can impair your performance. Of course, this is a general guideline, and not all active people experience these effects. However, eating a high-fat fast-food meal before basketball practice was probably the reason Greg, the basketball player we met at the beginning of this concept, was feeling tired and cranky afterward.

What Should You Eat during Exercise?

For exercise lasting longer than 1 hour, carbohydrate intake should begin shortly after the start of exercise and continue at 15- to 20- minute intervals throughout. For long-lasting endurance activities, a total of 30 to 60 grams of carbohydrate should be consumed per hour to prevent early fatigue. Sports drinks and gels are one way to take in carbohydrate immediately before and/or during activity, but foods such as crackers and sports bars are also commonly eaten.

Sports drinks can be a good source of carbohydrate during exercise.

The best types of carbohydrate to consume during exercise are glucose, sucrose, and maltodextrin because they are absorbed by the body more quickly than other carbohydrates. Fructose, the sugar found in fruit and fruit juice, should generally be avoided because it may cause gastrointestinal problems, such as stomach discomfort.

Many sports drinks and gels contain only carbohydrate and electrolytes; others also contain protein. For endurance athletes, consuming both carbohydrate and protein during exercise has been shown to improve the protein balance at rest as well as during exercise and postexercise recovery.[13] In turn, this has an effect on muscle maintenance and growth.

What Should You Eat after Exercise?

What you eat after exercise will affect how fast you recover, which may affect how soon you're ready for your next workout or training session. This is especially important for competitive athletes who train more than once per day. Some people who load up on high-fat foods after a workout or competition experience fatigue that often results in less-than-optimal performance during the next workout.

The best postexercise meal is consumed quickly and contains both carbohydrate and protein. The muscles are most receptive to storing new glycogen within the first 30 to 45 minutes after you have finished exercising, so this is a crucial time period in which to provide the body with carbohydrate.[14] Research also shows that consuming carbohydrate immediately after exercise results in a more positive body protein balance.[15] In addition, protein intake immediately after exercise rather than several hours later results in greater muscle protein synthesis. Finally, the consumption of protein with carbohydrate causes an even greater increase in glycogen synthesis than carbohydrate or protein alone.[16] In short, both nutrients should be consumed shortly after exercise.

Low-fat chocolate milk is a low-cost option for providing the whey protein and carbohydrate that help with muscle and glycogen synthesis after exercise.

What is the best way to get these two nutrients? Studies have shown that the consumption of carbohydrate and protein in a ratio of approximately 3:1 (in grams) is ideal to promote muscle glycogen synthesis, protein synthesis, and faster recovery time.[17] Whey protein, such as in milk, is the preferred protein source because it is rapidly absorbed and contains all of the essential amino acids your body needs. You can use commercial shakes and drinks containing these nutrients, but they can be expensive. A cheaper alternative is low-fat chocolate milk, which will provide you with adequate amounts of carbohydrate and protein to help you recover after exercise.[18] If you consume a liquid supplement or small snack after exercise, it should be followed by a high-carbohydrate, moderate-protein, low-fat meal within the next 2 hours.

If you are a competitive athlete, always experiment with timing your nutrient intake and consuming new foods and beverages during practice, not on the day of competition. You don't want to be unpleasantly surprised to find that a particular food doesn't agree with you a few hours before an important race or other event.

The Take-Home Message **Carbohydrate and fat are the primary sources of fuel during exercise. Carbohydrate provides energy in the form of blood glucose and muscle and liver glycogen. Carbohydrate is also the main energy source during high-intensity exercise. Fat is the primary energy source during low-intensity exercise. Protein provides the amino acids that are necessary to promote muscle growth and repair muscle damage caused by exercise. Consuming the right balance of nutrients at the right time can improve exercise performance and recovery time.**

What Vitamins and Minerals Are Important during Exercise?

Vitamins and minerals play a major role in the metabolism of carbohydrate, fat, and protein for energy during exercise. Many athletes mistakenly believe that vitamins and minerals themselves supply energy and often consume extra vitamins and minerals, so that they can perform better. In fact, studies have shown that multivitamin and mineral supplements are the most commonly used supplements by college athletes.[19] Can taking these supplements really improve athletic performance? Not unless you are experiencing a deficiency. For people who consume enough vitamins and minerals in their diet, taking more than the RDA will not result in improved performance.[20] Eating a wide variety of foods to meet your calorie needs will likely provide your body with plenty of vitamins and minerals; thus, it is probably a waste of money to take vitamin and mineral supplements.

Antioxidants Protect Cells from Damage Caused by Exercise

Your muscles use more oxygen during exercise than while you are at rest. Because of this, your body increases its production of free radicals, which damage cells, especially during intense, prolonged exercise. Antioxidants, such as vitamins E and C, protect cells from the damage of free radicals. You do not need to consume more than the RDA for these vitamins, but you do need to be sure to consume adequate amounts from foods such as nuts, vegetable oils, broccoli, and citrus fruits.

Two Minerals Are of Concern in Highly Active People

Although active people do not need more minerals than less active individuals, two minerals they must be careful to consume in adequate amounts are iron and calcium.

Iron

Iron is necessary for energy metabolism and oxygen transport. If iron levels are low, the blood's ability to carry oxygen to the cells is reduced. If this occurs during exercise, you will experience early fatigue. (You can also feel tired if iron levels are low and you are not exercising.) Iron supplementation can improve the aerobic performance of people with depleted iron stores.[21]

Active people can experience iron-deficiency anemia, a state in which iron levels are so low that oxygen delivery through the body suffers, and the person experiences weakness and fatigue. Female athletes, long-distance runners, and athletes in sports in which they must "make weight" are at higher risk for iron-deficiency anemia.

Low iron levels can be a result of poor dietary intake or increased iron losses. Women can lose a lot of iron during menstruation, depending on their iron status and menstrual blood flow. Iron is also lost in sweat, but not in amounts significant enough to lead to iron deficiency.

Whether you exercise or not, you can maintain your iron status by consuming adequate amounts of iron-rich foods, and supplements if necessary. However, many female athletes do not consume enough iron to meet their needs, which often leads to low iron levels. Vegetarian athletes are especially susceptible to iron deficiency and need to plan their diets appropriately.

Calcium

Athletes are particularly susceptible to broken bones and fractures. Therefore, they need to consume enough calcium to keep their bones healthy. Calcium also affects skeletal and heart muscle contraction, as well as hormone and neurotransmitter activity, during exercise. It also assists in blood clotting when you have a minor cut.

Many people may not be aware that calcium is lost in sweat, and the more you sweat the more calcium you lose. Research suggests that exercise can increase bone mineral content (the mass of all minerals in bone) only when calcium intake is sufficient to compensate for what is lost through sweating.[22]

Calcium supplements are not recommended unless your intake from food and beverages is inadequate and you are not meeting your daily needs. Choosing foods that are high in calcium, including fortified foods, can ensure that athletes meet their needs.

Yogurt is an excellent source of calcium.

The Take-Home Message **Athletes need to consume adequate amounts of the micronutrients. Antioxidants, such as vitamins E and C, protect cells from the damage of free radicals but are not needed in excessive amounts. Iron is important because of its role in transporting oxygen in blood and muscle, and deficiency is prevalent among athletes, especially females and vegetarians. Calcium intake is important for bone health, muscle contraction, and blood clotting. Adequate amounts of all nutrients can be consumed in foods, so supplements are not usually necessary.**

How Does Fluid Intake Affect Vigorous Activity?

As basic as it sounds, water is one of the most important nutrients during physical activity. When you drink too little fluid, or you lose too much fluid and electrolytes through sweating, physiological changes occur that can cause you to experience early fatigue or weakness, and impair your athletic performance or health. Consuming adequate fluids on a regular basis, as well as monitoring fluid losses during physical activity, is key to maintaining optimal performance and preventing **dehydration** and electrolyte imbalance.

Fluid Balance and Body Temperature Are Affected by Exercise

You learned in Concept 18 that adequate amounts of water and electrolytes are necessary to maintain the fluid balance in your body. When you are physically active, your body loses more water via sweat and exhalation of water vapor than when you are less active, so you need to replace the water lost during exercise to maintain a normal fluid balance. Sweating also causes you to lose electrolytes—primarily, sodium and chloride, and to a lesser extent potassium. An electrolyte imbalance can cause heat cramps, as well as nausea, lowered blood pressure, and edema in your hands and feet. When electrolyte losses are within the range of normal daily dietary intake, they can easily be replaced by a balanced meal within 24 hours after exercise. Electrolytes can also be replaced by beverages that contain them, such as sports drinks, if food is not available.

The sweat you produce during exercise releases heat and helps keep your body temperature normal. However, if the air is very humid (that is, it contains a lot of water), sweat may not evaporate off the skin, and the body doesn't cool down. This can cause heat to build up in your body, placing you at risk for heat exhaustion, which can progress to an even more serious state called heat stroke. One significant warning sign of heat stroke is dry skin: You are *not* sweating when you should be. This happens when you are so dehydrated that your body cannot produce sweat. Loss of the sweating mechanism means that your body cannot release heat, so your temperature will continue to rise. Heat stroke is often fatal. The warning signs of heat exhaustion and heat stroke are shown in Table 25.2.

Table 25.2

Warning Signs of Heat Exhaustion and Heat Stroke

Heat Exhaustion	Heat Stroke
Profuse sweating	Extremely high body temperature (above 103°F [39.4°C] orally)
Fatigue	Red, hot, dry skin (no sweating)
Thirst	Rapid, strong pulse
Muscle cramps	Rapid, shallow breathing
Headache	Throbbing headache
Dizziness or light-headedness	Dizziness
Weakness	Nausea
Nausea and vomiting	Extreme confusion
Cool, moist skin	Unconsciousness

dehydration The state in which there is too little water in the body due to too much water being lost, too little being consumed, or a combination of both.

You Need Fluids before, during, and after Exercise

Staying hydrated during physical activity is important to maintain electrolyte balance and help regulate body temperature.

Many active people are aware that it's important to stay hydrated during exercise, but your need for water doesn't begin with your first sit-up or lap around the track. Meeting your fluid needs before and after activity is also important to maintain fluid and electrolyte balance and optimize performance.

You should consume adequate fluid every day. Most healthy women need approximately 9 cups of beverages daily, while most healthy men need about 13 cups. This is a general guideline for adequate hydration. Another way to determine your estimated daily fluid needs is to divide your body weight in pounds by 2. This tells you the number of ounces of fluid you need (8 ounces = 1 cup) on a daily basis, not including the additional needs associated with exercising.

You can determine your additional fluid needs by weighing yourself both before and after exercise because the amount of weight that is lost is mainly due to losses in body water. Drink 16 to 24 fluid ounces (about 2 to 3 cups) of fluid for every pound of body weight lost.[23] The American College of Sports Medicine (ACSM) has specific recommendations for how much fluid to drink before and during exercise (Table 25.3).

Some Beverages Are Better Than Others

Beverages such as tea, coffee, soft drinks, fruit juice, and, of course, water contribute to your daily fluid needs. But what is the best type of fluid for preventing dehydration prior to and during activity? For rehydrating your body after activity? For these varied purposes, not all beverages are equal.

Sports drinks are popular in the fitness world, and many are marketed as tasty beverages to all groups of people, not just athletes. They typically contain 6 to 8 percent carbohydrate, as well as sodium and potassium, two electrolytes that are critical in muscle contraction and the maintenance of fluid balance. One purpose of sports drinks is to replace the fluid and electrolytes that are lost through sweating. These drinks have been shown to be superior to water for rehydration, mostly because their flavor causes people to drink more than they would of plain water.[24]

Sports drinks also provide additional carbohydrate to prevent glycogen depletion. This is beneficial if you engage in long endurance events or exercise when your glycogen stores are running low. When you consume a sports drink during exercise, you provide your body with glucose to be used as an immediate energy source and prevent further decline in muscle glycogen stores.

Table 25.3

ACSM Hydration Recommendations

When?	How Much?
2 to 3 hours before exercise	14–22 fluid ounces (2–3 cups)
5 to 10 minutes before exercise	4–8 fluid ounces (½–1 cup), as tolerated
At 15- to 20-minute intervals after exercise has begun	6–12 fluid ounces (¾–1½ cups)

Fluids such as milk, and fruit and vegetable juices, can help meet your daily water needs. Whole fruits and many other foods are also good sources of water.

However, not everyone needs sports drinks to stay adequately hydrated. For exercise that lasts less than 60 minutes, water is sufficient to replace the fluids lost through sweating, and food consumption following exercise will adequately replace electrolytes. A sports drink is most appropriate when physical activity lasts longer than 60 minutes.[25]

Other beverages may be less than optimal for hydration during physical activity. Fruit juice and juice drinks contain a larger concentration of carbohydrate and do not hydrate the body as quickly as beverages with a lower concentration of carbohydrate (such as sports drinks). Carbonated drinks contain a large amount of water; however, the carbonation can cause stomach bloating and may limit the amount of fluid consumed.

Beware of choosing alcoholic beverages, such as beer, to quench your thirst. Because alcohol is a diuretic, it can contribute to dehydration. Alcohol during performance can also impair your judgment and reasoning, which can lead to injuries, not only for you but also for those around you.

Another diuretic, the caffeine found in coffee and some soft drinks, should be consumed only in moderate amounts because excessive intake can cause increased heart rate, nausea, vomiting, excessive urination, restlessness, anxiety, and difficulty sleeping. Moderate caffeine intake is about 250 milligrams (the amount found in about three 8 ounce cups of coffee) per day.[26]

Consuming Too Little or Too Much Fluid Can Be Harmful

As your body loses fluid through sweating and exhalation during physical activity, it will let you know that you need to replace these fluids by sending a signal of thirst. However, by the time you're thirsty, you may already be dehydrated. Figure 25.3 shows the effects of dehydration on exercise performance. As you can see in the figure, thirst is not a good

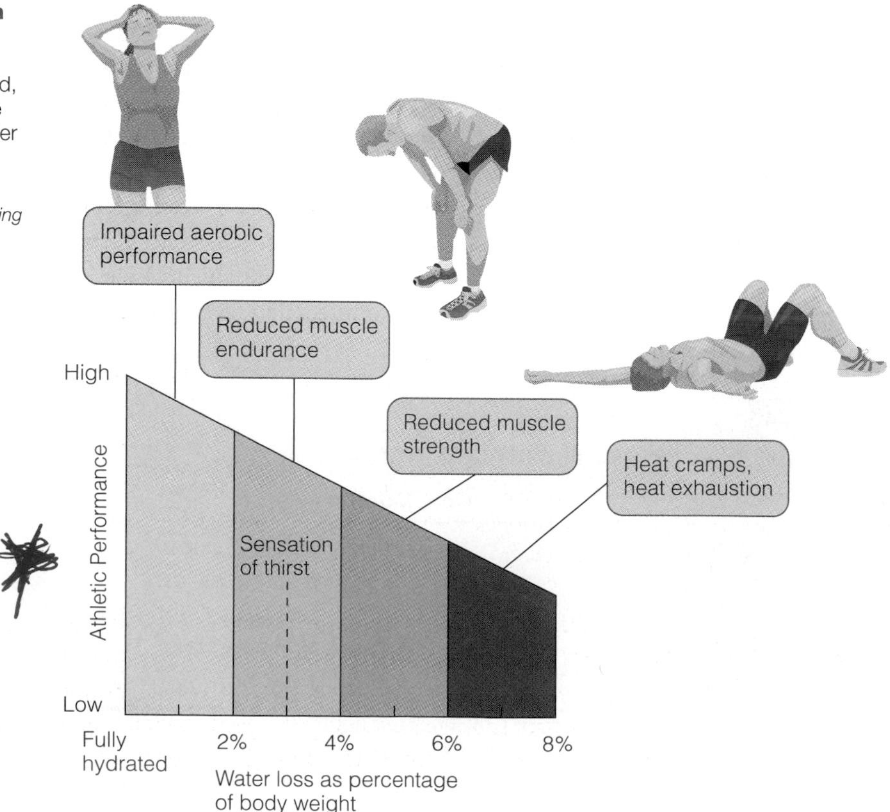

Figure 25.3 Effects of Dehydration on Exercise Performance
Failing to stay hydrated during exercise or competition can result in fatigue, cramps and, in extreme cases, heat exhaustion. Because the thirst mechanism doesn't kick in until after dehydration has begun, replacing fluids throughout physical activity is important.

Data adapted from: E. Burke and J. Berning, *Training Nutrition* (Travers City, MI: Cooper, 1996).

RATE YOURSELF 

Calculating Your Fluid Needs for Endurance Exercise

The next time you take a 1-hour training run, use the following process to determine your fluid needs.

1. Make sure you are properly hydrated before the workout. Your urine should be clear.
2. Do a warm-up run to the point where you start to sweat; then stop. Urinate if necessary.
3. Weigh yourself on an accurate scale.
4. Run for 1 hour at an intensity similar to your targeted race.
5. Drink a measured amount of a beverage of your choice during the run to quench your thirst. Be sure to keep track of how much you drink.
6. Do not urinate during the run.
7. After you have finished the run, weigh yourself again on the same scale you used in step 3.
8. Calculate your fluid needs using the following formula:

a. Enter your body weight in pounds from step 3.		______
b. Enter your body weight in pounds from step 7.	−	______
c. Subtract b from a.	=	______
d. Convert the pounds of weight in c to fluid ounces by multiplying by 15.3.	× 15.3	______
e. Enter the amount of fluid, in ounces, you consumed during the run.	+	______
f. Add e to d.	=	______

The final figure is the number of ounces of fluid you must consume per hour to remain well hydrated.

Data adapted from: D. Casa, *USA Track & Field Self-Testing Program for Optimal Hydration for Distance Running*. www.usatf.org/groups/Coaches/library/2007/hydration/USATFSelfTesting-ProgramForOptimalHydration.pdf.

indicator of fluid needs for most athletes and physically active people. To prevent dehydration, follow a regimented hydration schedule using water or sports drinks to hydrate before, during, and after exercise sessions and/or competition.

When speaking of hydration and physical activity, we are usually concerned about consuming *enough* fluids, so that we do not become dehydrated. But as you recall from Concept 18, consuming too much water without sufficient electrolytes can result in hyponatremia. Due to the growing concern about hyponatremia, USA Track & Field (USATF) recommends consuming 100 percent of fluids lost due to sweat while exercising and being sensitive to the onset of thirst as the signal to drink, rather than attempting to "stay ahead of thirst."[27]

If you are a distance runner, Rate Yourself to determine your fluid needs during long-distance races. Keep in mind that you should perform this hydration test well before a competition or an event and perform the test again if your level of fitness improves or if the climate changes from when you initially determined your fluid needs.

The Take-Home Message **Being adequately hydrated before, during, and after exercise is important to sustain fluid and electrolyte balance and a normal body temperature. Inadequate hydration can impair performance. Water is the preferred beverage for hydration, but sports drinks can be beneficial during moderate-intensity or vigorous exercise that lasts longer than 60 minutes.**

UCook

Chocolate Energy Shake

For a satisfying drink that is supernutrient-rich, try this easy-to-make Chocolate Energy Shake. Your bones and muscles will thank you for it!

UDo

Stay Hydrated for Fitness

How much fluid should you drink before, during, and after your workout? Go to the link on our website to find out.

The Top Five Points to Remember

1. All athletes and physically active people must consume adequate calories, carbohydrate, protein, fat, vitamins, minerals, and fluids to achieve optimal fitness and athletic performance.
2. The source of energy needed to fuel exercise depends on the intensity of the activity. Carbohydrate—specifically, muscle glycogen—is the main energy source for high-intensity activity. Fat is the preferred source of energy during low- to moderate-intensity activity. Protein is important because it maintains, builds, and repairs tissues, including muscle tissue. Only small amounts of protein are used for energy during exercise.
3. Vitamins and minerals assist in energy metabolism and are necessary for fitness. Athletes do not have greater needs for vitamins and minerals than do nonathletes, and intakes of vitamins and minerals above the RDA do not improve athletic performance.
4. Female and vegetarian athletes are at greater risk of developing an iron deficiency and should consume iron-rich foods regularly. Athletes also need to be sure their calcium intake is adequate to help reduce their risk for bone fractures during physical activity.
5. Being adequately hydrated before, during, and after exercise is important to both health and athletic performance. Staying hydrated helps maintain fluid and electrolyte balance and normal body temperature. Water is the best fluid for hydration during exercise, although sports drinks can be beneficial for moderate-intensity to vigorous exercise that lasts longer than 60 minutes.

Test Yourself

1. During low-intensity activity, your body obtains most of its energy from
   a. muscle glycogen.
   b. liver glycogen.
   c. muscle protein.
   d. fatty acids.
2. Under what conditions will the body use significant amounts of protein for energy during exercise?
   a. inadequate calorie intake
   b. inadequate carbohydrate stores
   c. inadequate fluid intake
   d. both a and b
3. A preexercise meal should be
   a. high in carbohydrate, low in fat.
   b. high in carbohydrate, high in fat.
   c. low in carbohydrate, low in fat.
   d. low in protein, high in fat.
4. A commercial sports drink can be beneficial after 60 minutes or more of exercise because it
   a. contributes to hydration.
   b. provides electrolytes.
   c. provides carbohydrate.
   d. does all of the above.
5. An appropriate exercise recovery beverage is
   a. a soft drink.
   b. coffee.
   c. low-fat chocolate milk.
   d. orange juice.

Answers

1. (d) Fatty acids are the main source of energy during low-intensity activity. As the intensity increases, the body uses less fatty acids and more glycogen for energy.
2. (d) The body will use larger amounts of protein for energy if overall calorie intake is inadequate and if carbohydrate stores are low.
3. (a) A meal before a game or workout should be high in carbohydrate to maximize glycogen stores and low in fat to prevent feelings of fatigue or discomfort.
4. (d) Sports drinks supply fluids to rehydrate the body during and after exercise, electrolytes to replace those lost during sweating, and carbohydrate, which acts as an immediate source of energy that can improve performance.
5. (c) Low-fat chocolate milk is a good exercise recovery beverage because it contains an appropriate ratio of carbohydrate to protein that is necessary for optimal recovery. Soft

drinks, coffee, and orange juice provide your body with fluids but lack other nutrients that are ideal for recovery after exercise.

Web Resources

For more on nutrition for exercise and athletic performance, visit

- American Council on Exercise at: www.acefitness.org
- American College of Sports Medicine at: www.acsm.org
- American Dietetic Association at: www.eatright.org
- Sports, Cardiovascular, and Wellness Nutritionists: A Dietetics Practice Group of the American Dietetic Association at: www.scandpg.org
- Gatorade Sports Science Institute at: www.gssiweb.org

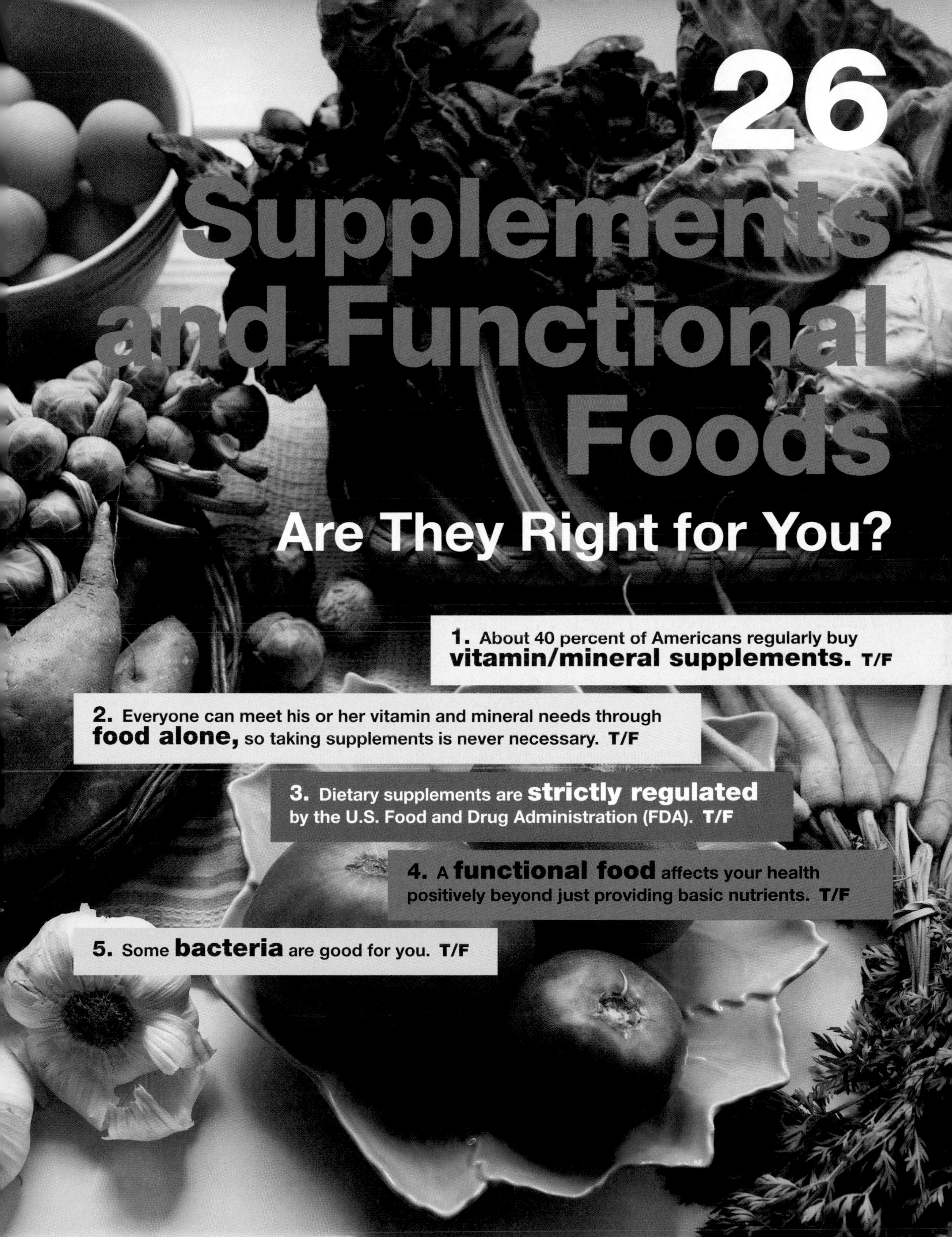

26 Supplements and Functional Foods

Are They Right for You?

1. About 40 percent of Americans regularly buy **vitamin/mineral supplements.** **T/F**

2. Everyone can meet his or her vitamin and mineral needs through **food alone,** so taking supplements is never necessary. **T/F**

3. Dietary supplements are **strictly regulated** by the U.S. Food and Drug Administration (FDA). **T/F**

4. A **functional food** affects your health positively beyond just providing basic nutrients. **T/F**

5. Some **bacteria** are good for you. **T/F**

Mariela is a 25-year-old recent community college graduate who's studying to qualify as a certified aerobics and fitness instructor. She considers herself a "health nut" and enjoys exploring the aisles of the health food store for regular food staples, as well as for new nutritional ideas. She enjoys experimenting with new products she finds in addition to scouring the health magazine section.

She's been looking for a "natural" way to treat her occasional insomnia, and after doing some research she's decided to give the herb kava a try. She read online that kava is a natural way to help people who toss and turn in bed at night to sleep more soundly. Because it's an herb, rather than a traditional supplement, Mariela assumes it's unlikely to have any harmful side effects and that it will work as expected. She also believes that treating her insomnia directly by using a "natural" supplement will be the best way to improve her sleep.

Do you think it's a good idea for Mariela to treat her insomnia with kava? What would your own expectations for an herb supplement be? Are all products made from plant sources inherently safe? What does "natural" really mean? In this concept, you'll learn about supplements and what they can and cannot do for you, as well as the role that functional foods play in your diet.

Answers

1. True. Micronutrient supplements are purchased by roughly 40 percent of American consumers. See page 2 to learn how much they are spending.
2. False. While the foods we eat are excellent sources of vitamins, some people need extra vitamin support from a supplement. To find out who would benefit from supplements, turn to page 3.
3. False. Supplements do not have to meet the same standards as drugs for safety or effectiveness. Turn to page 4 to find out why.
4. True. Eating certain functional foods can lower a person's risk for heart disease and some cancers. To learn more about functional foods, turn to page 9.
5. True. Probiotics are health-promoting bacteria found in foods such as yogurt. Some strains are thought to improve immunity, relieve allergies, and reduce GI tract inflammation. See page 12 for more.

What Are Supplements and Who Needs Them?

Dietary supplements got their name for a reason: They are products, such as multivitamin/mineral pills, flaxseed oil, and protein powders, used to supplement your diet by providing nutrients you might not be getting in adequate amounts from foods. In fact, many supplements contain herbs, a botanical, which are not essential nutrients your body needs. Some other dietary supplements are made from certain amino acids, such as lysine.[1]

In this section, we focus on vitamin and mineral supplements. For information on botanical supplements, check out the box feature "Botanicals: The Original Pharmaceuticals" on page 10. In addition to looking at the role of botanicals, we'll examine the common practice by many athletes of using amino acid supplements and other products to improve athletic performance. We'll explore this group of supplements, called *ergogenic aids*, later in this concept.

Who Might Benefit from a Micronutrient Supplement?

An estimated 40 percent of Americans spend over $1 billion a year on vitamin and mineral supplements. In a survey in the United States, the most popular reason for taking supplements was for good health and because they are considered "good for you."

dietary supplements Products containing nutrients, botanicals, amino acids, or enzymes intended to supplement the diet, but not intended as a substitute for conventional food or as a stand-alone item in a meal or the diet.

Does the popularity of vitamin and mineral supplements mean that you should be taking them? The answer depends partly on the reasons behind your choice. If you're hoping that, by taking a supplement, you can avoid eating a healthy diet, you're wrong. A consistent diet of nonnutritious foods followed by a daily supplement won't make up for poor eating habits. The important disease-fighting phytochemicals, fiber, and other substances your body needs can't be derived from a bottle of supplements.

On the other hand, supplements are often useful for people who, for various reasons, can't meet their nutrient needs through a regular and varied diet. Among those people who can benefit from taking a dietary supplement are[2]:

- Women of childbearing age who may become pregnant, since they need to consume adequate amounts of folic acid to prevent certain birth defects.
- Pregnant and lactating women who can't meet their increased nutrient needs with foods.
- Older people who need adequate amounts of synthetic vitamin B_{12} and/or calcium.
- People who don't drink enough milk and/or don't have adequate sun exposure to meet their vitamin D needs.
- People on low-calorie diets that limit the amount of vitamin and minerals they can consume through food.
- Strict vegetarians, who have limited dietary options for vitamins B_{12} and D and other nutrients.
- People with food allergies or a lactose intolerance that limits their food choices.
- People who abuse alcohol, who have medical conditions such as intestinal disorders, or who take medications that increase their need for certain vitamins.

It's always a good idea to talk to your health care professional or a registered dietitian (RD) before taking a vitamin or mineral supplement to make sure it's appropriate for you, based on your medical history. Supplements can interact or interfere with certain medications, so you'll also need to check with your doctor if you take over-the-counter or prescription medications. If you regularly eat a lot of fortified foods, the addition of a supplement might cause you to overconsume some nutrients. Meeting with an RD to review your diet, medications, and habits can help you decide if you need a supplement.

Is taking a dietary supplement the right choice for you? Rate Yourself in the nutrition assessment to find out!

RATE YOURSELF 

Should You Take a Dietary Supplement?

Use this checklist from the Center for Food Safety and Applied Nutrition to find out whether taking a dietary supplement is right for you.

Nutrition Assessment

1. I eat fewer than two meals a day. **Yes** ☐ **No** ☐
2. My diet is restricted (e.g., don't eat dairy, meat, and/or fewer than five servings of fruits and vegetables). **Yes** ☐ **No** ☐
3. I eat alone most of the time. **Yes** ☐ **No** ☐
4. Without wanting to, I have lost or gained more than 10 pounds in the last six months. **Yes** ☐ **No** ☐
5. I take three or more prescription or OTC medicines a day. **Yes** ☐ **No** ☐
6. I have three or more drinks of alcohol a day. **Yes** ☐ **No** ☐

Answers

If you answered "yes" to one or more of these above statements, you may benefit from taking a dietary supplement. Talk to your health care provider or registered dietitian.

Data from: CFSAN/Office of Nutritional Products, Labeling and Dietary Supplements (December 2004). What Dietary Supplements Are You Taking? www.cfsan.fda.gov/~dms/ds~take.html.

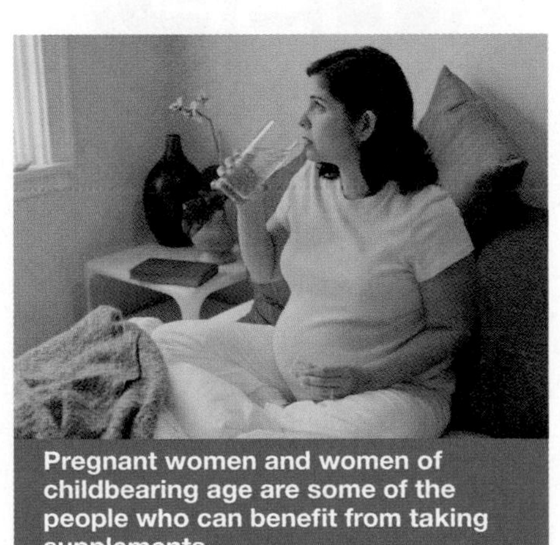

Pregnant women and women of childbearing age are some of the people who can benefit from taking supplements.

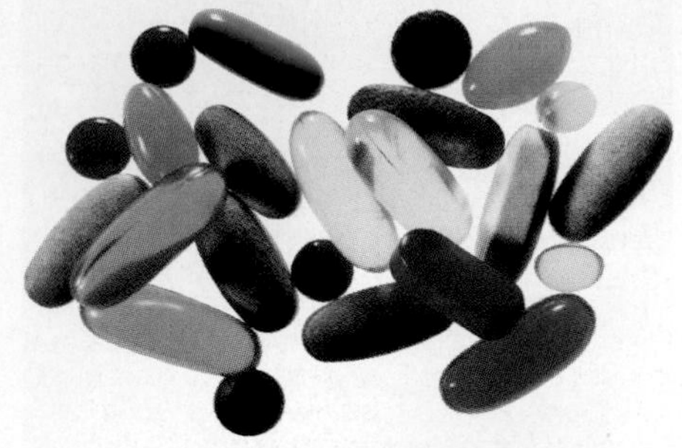

Who's Minding the Supplements Store?

The Food and Drug Administration (FDA) regulates dietary supplements less strictly than drugs. In 1994, Congress passed the Dietary Supplement Health and Education Act, which shifted the responsibility for assessing the quality, effectiveness, and safety of dietary supplements from the FDA to the supplement manufacturers. Unlike drugs, dietary supplements do not need FDA approval from the FDA before they can be marketed and sold to the public unless they contain a new ingredient that hadn't been used before 1994. Recall from Concept 5 that supplement manufacturers are legally permitted to make health or nutrition claims on the labels of dietary supplements. The FDA cannot remove a supplement from the marketplace unless it has been proven to be unsafe or harmful to consumers.[3] This provides a good example of the wisdom of the common expression "Buyer beware," meaning in this case that dietary supplements are relatively loosely regulated, and consumers should learn about their benefits and drawbacks.

The FDA is trying to tighten its regulation of dietary supplements to better safeguard the public against harmful products and misleading claims. One way it plans to do this is by improving the criteria it uses to make enforcement decisions about dietary supplements. The FDA is also trying to improve its process for evaluating possible safety concerns and addressing reports of problems that arise from various sources, including consumers, media reports, consumer groups, and experts.

The U.S. Pharmacopoeia (USP) is an independent nonprofit organization that provides some guidance for consumers on labeling dietary supplements.[4] Although it does *not* endorse or validate the health claims of supplement manufacturers, it does test supplement to ensure that they:

- Contain the ingredients in the amounts stated on the label.
- Disintegrate and dissolve in the body in a reasonable amount of time for proper absorption.
- Are free of contaminants.
- Have been manufactured using safe and sanitary procedures.

Supplement manufacturers may voluntarily submit their products to the USP's science staff for review. Products that meet the listed criteria can then display the USP's seal on their labels (Figure 26.1).

Figure 26.1 USP Seal
The presence of this seal on a supplement label verifies that the supplement has met certain minimum quality standards.

What's a Consumer to Do?

With hundreds of bottles of dietary supplements available on store shelves, you could get dizzy trying to find one that's right for you. The best place to start when picking a supplement is to read the label carefully. The FDA has strict guidelines for claims that appear on any supplement label. For example, the term "high potency" can be used only if at least two-thirds of the nutrients in the supplement contain at least 100 percent of the daily value (Figure 26.2). However, keep in mind that, although a supplement label may bear an approved claim, the supplement itself doesn't have formal FDA *approval*, even if it has the USP seal of quality and purity.

The FDA also requires that several other types of information appear on the labels of dietary supplements:

- The label must clearly identify the contents of the bottle.
- All the ingredients must be listed.
- The label must display a Supplement Facts panel, which lists the serving size, the number of tablets in the bottle, the amount of the micronutrient(s) or other active ingredient in each serving, and the percentage of the Daily Values.

Figure 26.2 Supplement Smarts
The FDA has strict guidelines for the information that must appear on any supplement label. **(a)** The FDA allows the term "high potency" to be used as long as at least two-thirds of the nutrients contain at least 100 percent of the daily value. **(b)** All supplements must clearly identify what is in the bottle. **(c)** Always look for the USP seal of approval for quality and purity. Choose the cheapest supplement with the seal to save a few dollars. **(d)** The FDA disclaimer is a reminder that this doesn't have the FDA seal of approval for effectiveness. **(e)** The structure/ function claim explains that vitamin C is beneficial for your immune system. **(f)** The net quantity of contents must be listed. The Nutrition Facts panel lists the serving size, the vitamins in the supplement, and the amount of the vitamin in each capsule. **(g)** The amount of each supplement is also given as a percentage of the daily value. Remember, the daily value may be higher than you actually need. **(h)** All the ingredients must be listed in descending order by weight. **(i)** The name and address of the manufacturer or distributor must be provided.

In addition to checking the supplement label, the FDA recommends that you reconsider your assumptions:[5]

- "Even if this supplement might not help me, at least it won't hurt me." This may not be true. When consumed in high enough amounts, for a long enough time, or in combination with certain other substances, many supplements can be toxic.
- "When I see the term *natural*, it means that the supplement is healthful and safe." Not necessarily—the term *natural* is not legally defined and does not guarantee safety.
- "A product is safe when there is no cautionary information or warnings on the label." Supplement manufacturers might not include warnings about possible bad effects on the labels of their products.
- "A recall of a harmful product guarantees that it will be immediately and completely removed from the marketplace." A recall of a dietary supplement is voluntary and does not ensure that all harmful products are removed from the marketplace.

The Take-Home Message **A dietary supplement is a product containing nutrients, botanicals, or amino acids intended to supplement the diet. A well-balanced diet that provides adequate calories can meet most individuals' daily micronutrient needs. A vitamin/mineral supplement is an option for individuals unable to meet their needs. Although the FDA has strict guidelines for the claims and information that appear on any supplement label, the responsibility for determining the quality, effectiveness, and safety of dietary supplements rests with the manufacturers. Consumers need to take care when selecting a dietary supplement and should seek guidance from a qualified health professional.**

Can Dietary Supplements Contribute to Fitness?

Competitive athletes are always looking for an edge, and many turn to supplements in hopes of improving their performance. The pill and powder manufacturers may claim that their products enhance immunity, boost metabolism, improve memory, or provide some other physical advancement, but since dietary supplements are not strictly regulated by the FDA, their manufacturers do not have to prove the truth of any of these claims. As a result, many athletes risk their health and, in some cases, eligibility for competition by taking supplements that can be ineffective or even dangerous.

Ergogenic Aids May Improve Performance but Can Have Side Effects

An **ergogenic aid** is any substance used to improve athletic performance, including dietary supplements. Although the makers of dietary supplements do not have to prove their effectiveness, researchers have examined several supplements and their effects on athletic performance. Studies have indicated that some dietary supplements have a positive effect on performance, while others do not. Further, some ergogenic aids cause serious side effects. Let's take a closer look at some of the most popular aids.

Athletes sometimes take supplements, such as creatine phosphate or caffeine, to enhance their athletic performance. Supplements are not strictly regulated by the FDA, so their quality and effectiveness can vary widely.

Creatine

Recall from Concept 25 that creatine is a substance involved in energy production that your body produces naturally and stores in skeletal muscle and other tissues. You also get a small amount of creatine from foods, including meat and fish. In the early 1990s, research showed that creatine supplementation increased creatine stores in the muscles (in the form of creatine phosphate), which increased the amount of ATP generated and improved performance during high-intensity, short-duration exercise.[6] (We explored some of these connections in Concept 25.) Creatine has since become one of the best-known dietary supplements in the fitness industry.

However, the data on whether creatine enhances performance are mixed. Newer studies have supported the claim that creatine supplementation improves athletic performance in *high-intensity, short-duration* activities, such as weight training, when the body relies on anaerobic energy metabolism. Creatine supplementation has been shown to increase muscle strength and muscle mass. However, research has shown mixed results in creatine supplementation improving sprinting performance.[7] And creatine has not been shown to improve performance in activities of *lower intensity and longer duration.*

To date, creatine has not been found to have negative effects on blood pressure or kidney or liver function among healthy people.[8] One case of kidney problems following the use of creatine has been documented, but it is unclear if the kidney problems existed prior to taking the supplement.[9] Because some of the findings on creatine have been mixed, and research is ongoing, anyone considering taking creatine supplements should check with their health care provider first.

ergogenic aid A substance, such as a dietary supplement, used to enhance athletic performance.

Caffeine

Caffeine is a popular ergogenic aid among athletes, trainers, and coaches. Caffeine may decrease a person's *perception of effort* by stimulating the central nervous system; it also affects the breakdown of muscle glycogen and increases the availability of fatty acids during exercise. Studies of caffeine's effects on exercise have shown that caffeine can enhance athletic performance, mostly during endurance events.[10] However, research has not proven that caffeine provides any benefit during short-duration activities, such as sprinting.[11] Some athletic associations consider caffeine a banned substance when consumed in high amounts. For example, the National Collegiate Athletic Association (NCAA) classifies caffeine as a banned substance when urine concentrations exceed 15 micrograms per milliliter. This is the equivalent of drinking four or five cups of coffee.

Anabolic Steroids

Anabolic steroids (*anabolic* = to stimulate growth) are substances designed to mimic the bodybuilding traits of testosterone, a male reproductive hormone. The primary effect of anabolic steroids, which is the one users are seeking, is the promotion of protein growth and muscle development, which leads to bigger muscles and greater strength. Most athletes want to be stronger, and some turn to anabolic steroids to build up muscle to a level that's not possible naturally.

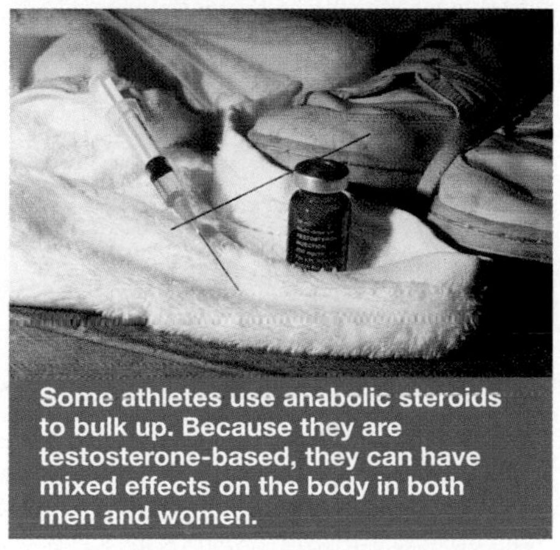
Some athletes use anabolic steroids to bulk up. Because they are testosterone-based, they can have mixed effects on the body in both men and women.

A secondary, undesirable effect of anabolic steroids is *androgenic* (testosterone-promoting). Taking in testosterone causes the body to decrease its own production of the hormone, leading to a hormone imbalance. In men, this can cause shrinkage of the testicles, decreased sperm production, impotence, painful urination, severe acne (especially on the back), and changes in hair growth (an increase in facial hair and a decrease in hair on the head). Men may also experience psychiatric side effects, such as extreme mood swings and aggressiveness, which can lead to violence.

Women who use anabolic steroids also experience androgenic effects, including severe acne, increased facial and body hair, and loss of hair on the head. Additionally, women may develop a lower voice, increased aggressiveness, increased sex drive, and their menstrual periods may become irregular or stop altogether.

In both sexes, using anabolic steroids can lead to severe health consequences, such as liver and kidney tumors, high blood pressure, and increases in LDL cholesterol. Although anabolic steroids can increase muscle mass and strength, their use among collegiate and professional athletes is prohibited by most agencies.

Growth Hormone

Growth hormone is naturally produced by the pituitary gland to stimulate growth in children. Synthetic (humanmade) growth hormone was originally created for children with growth hormone deficiency to enable them to grow to their full height. It targets numerous tissues, including bones, skeletal muscle, fat cells, immune cells, and liver cells. Growth hormone increases protein synthesis by increasing amino acid transport across cell membranes. This causes an increase in muscle mass, but not strength. Nevertheless, growth hormone has been promoted with claims of increasing both muscle mass and strength, and some athletes use it. Unfortunately, increasing muscle mass without strength can actually impair performance by reducing the athlete's power, speed, and endurance.

Growth hormone also decreases glycogen synthesis and the use of glucose for energy, causing an increase in fat breakdown and the use of fatty acids for energy. This can improve body composition by decreasing body fat. However, the results of studies on the effects of growth hormone for strength or athletic improvement have been mixed. Some research suggests that growth hormone reduces body fat and increases fat-free mass in well-trained adults.[12] Other studies show that it does not improve muscle strength or lean body mass in healthy adult athletes or the elderly.[13] It also appears to have no positive effect on cardiovascular performance in adults with growth hormone deficiency.[14]

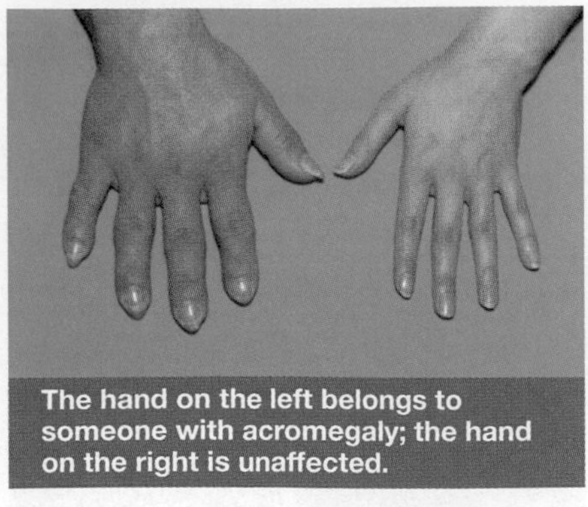
The hand on the left belongs to someone with acromegaly; the hand on the right is unaffected.

The abuse of growth hormone can have serious health effects, including the development of diabetes, atherosclerosis (hardening of the arteries), and hypertension (high blood pressure). Excess growth hormone can also cause *acromegaly*, a condition in which tissues, bones, and internal organs grow abnormally large.

Erythropoietin

Erythropoietin is a hormone the kidneys produce when there is a decrease in blood oxygen levels. Athletes use synthetic versions of erythropoietin as ergogenic aids because it increases the number of red blood cells increases the blood's oxygen-carrying capacity. This results in the athlete's being able to train at a higher intensity without becoming fatigued as quickly,[15] thereby having the potential to improve performance and overall physical fitness. Despite its popularity among competitive athletes, synthetic erythropoietin is a banned substance in most athletic organizations.

Synthetic erythropoietin can be dangerous because it increases blood viscosity (thickness). If the blood becomes too thick, it moves slowly and can clog capillaries. If this occurs in the brain, it results in a stroke. If there is a blood clot in the heart, it causes a heart attack. Both of these can be life-threatening. Erythropoietin can also cause sudden death during sleep and is believed to have contributed to several deaths among professional European cyclists in recent years.

Sports Bars, Shakes, and Meal Replacers May Provide Benefits

Peanut butter on whole-wheat bread is a nutritious, inexpensive, and easy snack.

Sports bars and shakes are not considered dietary supplements because they are foods and contain one or more macronutrients. If you're a supremely busy person, these products may be a convenient alternative to meals or snacks prepared at home. However, keep in mind that most of these items are expensive. An energy bar may be trendy and easy to stash in your book bag, but an old-fashioned peanut butter sandwich on whole-grain bread costs less and is just as easy to carry. (See the feature box on protein and energy bars in Concept 14, pages 10 and 11).

The ratio of the macronutrients in these foods varies depending on their purpose. Bars and shakes that are intended to provide energy for and recovery from exercise have a greater proportion of energy supplied by carbohydrates. Those that are promoted for muscle protein synthesis typically contain more protein than carbohydrate and fat. Bars and shakes that are high in protein are often used by vegetarians and some athletes who need additional sources of protein in their diet. Most bars and shakes also contain a variety of vitamins and minerals. Of course, these vitamins and minerals may not be necessary if you are consuming balanced meals regularly or taking a daily multivitamin.

The Take-Home Message **Dietary supplements and ergogenic aids, such as creatine, caffeine, anabolic steroids, growth hormone, and erythropoietin, may enhance performance but can have serious health effects. Sports bars and shakes are convenient sources of energy but are more expensive than whole foods and should be included only as a minor part of an overall healthy diet.**

What Are Functional Foods and What Role Do They Play in Your Diet?

Because of their beta-carotene, carrots qualify as a functional food.

Have you ever snacked on carrots? Did you know at the time that you were eating a functional food? A **functional food** is one that has been shown to have a positive effect on your health beyond its basic nutrients. Carrots are a functional food because they are rich in beta-carotene, which, in addition to being a key source of vitamin A, is an antioxidant that helps protect your cells from damaging substances that can increase your risk for some chronic diseases, such as cancer. In other words, the beta-carotene's function goes beyond its basic nutritional role as a source of vitamin A because it may also help fight cancer. Oats are another functional food because they contain the soluble fiber beta-glucan, which has been shown to lower blood cholesterol levels. This can in turn lower the risk for heart disease.[16]

If the beneficial compound in the food is derived from plants, such as in the case of beta-carotene and beta-glucan, it is called a phytochemical, (*phyto* = plant), a term you may recall from Concept 1. If it is derived from animals, it is called a **zoochemical** (*zoo* = animal). Heart-healthy omega-3 fatty acids, found in fatty fish, such as salmon and sardines, are considered zoochemicals. Manufacturers are promoting foods containing naturally occurring phytochemicals and zoochemicals and have also begun fortifying other food products with these compounds. You can buy margarine with added plant sterols and cereal with the soluble fiber psyllium, both of which help lower blood cholesterol levels, as well as pasta that has omega-3 fatty acids added to it. Table 26.1 identifies just a few of the currently known compounds in foods that have been shown to have positive health benefits.

functional food A food that has a positive effect on health beyond providing basic nutrients.

zoochemical A compound found within animal food products that is beneficial to human health, such as omega-3 fatty acids.

Table 26.1

Your Guide to Functional Foods

This Functional Food/Food Source	Contains This Compound	And May Have This Health Benefit	If Taken in This Amount
Psyllium in Kellogg's All Bran	Soluble fiber	Lower blood cholesterol	1 g daily
Soy in soy milk	Protein	Lower blood cholesterol	25 g daily
Oats in oatmeal	Beta-glucan	Lower blood cholesterol	3 g daily
Fortified margarines, such as Benecol spreads	Plant sterol and stanol esters	Lower blood cholesterol	1.3 g daily of sterols or 1.7 g daily of stanols
Cranberries in cranberry juice	Proanthocyanidins	Reduce urinary tract infections	1¼ cup daily
Fatty fish, such as salmon and sardines	Omega-3 fatty acids	Reduce the risk for heart disease	2 fish meals weekly
Garlic	Organosulfur compounds	Lower blood cholesterol	1 fresh clove daily
Cruciferous vegetables, such as cabbage and broccoli	Glucosinolates indoles	Reduce the risk for certain cancers	>½ cup daily
Tomatoes in processed tomato products, such as sauce and paste	Lycopene	Reduce the risk for prostate cancer	½ cup daily
Active cultures in products such as yogurt	Probiotics	Support intestinal health	Daily

Data adapted from: C. M. Hasler, A. S. Bloch, C. A. Thomson, E. Enrione, and C. Manning, Position of the American Dietetic Association: Functional Foods, *Journal of the American Dietetic Association* 104 (2004): 814–826; C. M. Hasler, The Changing Face of Functional Foods, *Journal of the American College of Nutrition* 19 (2000): 499S–506S.

Botanicals: The Original Pharmaceuticals

What do aloe vera, garlic, and chamomile have in common? They are all **botanicals**, products that have been made from plants and used for cosmetic, culinary, or therapeutic purposes. Aloe vera has been used to heal wound and skin conditions, garlic has been used as a seasoning for centuries, and chamomile has been touted to aid in sleep. Growing in nature rather than being dispensed by a pharmacist, botanicals are humankind's original pharmaceuticals. Ancient cultures from China to Egypt have used botanicals for healing. In fact, many of the medications prescribed today are derived from plants used since ancient times. For example, thousands of years ago, headaches were relieved with willow bark, a botanical source of the substance acetylsalicylic acid, which is similar to aspirin. Benign-looking flowering poppies are the source of morphine, codeine, and other medical forms of opium.

While any part of a plant—flowers, berries, bark, seeds, stems, or roots—can be used in botanicals, each part of the plant may have a different effect in the body. For example, dandelion root is considered a laxative, while the leaves of the dandelion plant act as a diuretic.[1] After harvesting, the plant part is typically processed. For instance, it may be dried and made into tea or tablets or crushed and the oil extracted to make capsules, ointments, or creams. Some botanicals, such as garlic and ginger, may be used fresh.

Are Botanicals Effective?

Many botanicals have a long history of claimed health benefits, but few of these claims are backed by scientific evidence. That doesn't mean that botanicals don't work, but simply that more research needs to be done. The National Center for Complementary and Alternative Medicine (NCCAM) funding numerous studies to further our understanding of the effectiveness of a variety of botanicals.[2] Table 26.2 identifies a few of the most commonly used botanicals, the claims for their use, and the current state of scientific knowledge of each.

botanicals Products made from herbs or woody plants and used for cosmetic, culinary, or therapeutic purposes.

Are Botanicals Safe?

Like any pharmaceutical, botanicals can cause health problems if used inappropriately, and some are even considered dangerous. Here are some warnings about herbal safety[3]:

- Beware of the term *natural,* which doesn't automatically mean *safe.* Mariela, the student you read about in the beginning of this concept, is dangerously mistaken about the low risk of taking herbs. The natural herbs kava and comfrey have been linked to liver damage.
- Even though they come from plants, herbal supplements can have druglike effects in your body. Because they can interact with both prescribed and over-the-counter medication, they can promote unforeseen medical issues. For example, St. John's wort can interact with birth control pills, resulting in an unwanted pregnancy. Taking more than the suggested amounts, of course, adds another level of danger.
- Since herbals are considered dietary supplements and are not regulated by the FDA, they do not have to meet the same strict standards for safety and effectiveness as prescription drugs and over-the-counter medications. In fact, research has uncovered differences between the amount of herb listed on the label and what's really in the bottle. Some bottles have been shown to contain contaminants, such as unwanted metals.
- Never take herbs unless you have consulted your health care provider. The active ingredient in many herbs is not known, and serious health problems can occur as a result of their use. It is especially important that women who are pregnant consult their health care provider before taking herbs, as some are known to promote spontaneous abortion.

Table 26.2

Botanicals Commonly Used as Supplements

Name of Herb	How It Is Used	What the Science Says	Side Effects and Cautions
Black Cohosh	Stems and roots are used to treat joint and muscle pain, menstrual irregularities, PMS, and menopausal symptoms.	Study results are mixed on whether black cohosh effectively relieves menopausal symptoms or other conditions.	Side effects are headaches, stomach discomfort, and reports of liver disease.
Chamomile	Flowering tops are used to treat insomnia, anxiety, upset stomach, and diarrhea.	Chamomile has not been well studied in humans, and there is little evidence to support its use for any condition.	Side effects are rare but may include allergic reactions.
Echinacea	Both plant and root parts are used to treat or prevent colds, flu, and other infections.	Most studies indicate that echinacea does not appear to prevent colds or other infections.	Side effects are rare but include rashes, asthma, and other allergic reactions.
Garlic	Garlic cloves are used to treat high cholesterol, high blood pressure, and heart disease and to prevent certain cancers.	Limited evidence suggests that garlic may slightly lower blood cholesterol and blood pressure, slow hardening of the arteries, and lower the risk for certain cancers.	Rare side effects include heartburn, upset stomach, and allergic reactions. Garlic can thin the blood and should be avoided before dental work or surgery. Garlic interferes with the actions of certain drugs.
Ginger	Underground stems are used to treat nausea, colds, flu, and joint pain.	Studies suggest short-term use can safely relieve pregnancy-related nausea and vomiting. It is unclear whether ginger is effective for joint pain.	Gastrointestinal side effects are rare and typically associated with powdered ginger.
Ginkgo	Ginkgo leaf extract is used to improve memory and treat many health conditions, such as asthma, bronchitis, and dementia.	Study results on the effectiveness of ginkgo have been mixed.	Side effects are varied and include occasionally severe allergic reactions. Ginkgo can increase bleeding, so use should be avoided before dental work or surgery and by people taking anticoagulant drugs.
Ginseng	The root is dried and used to boost the immune system, lower blood glucose, and treat various other conditions.	Ginseng may lower blood glucose and improve immune function, but research is not conclusive.	The most common side effects are headaches and sleep and gastrointestinal problems.
Hoodia	Stems and roots are used to suppress the appetite and promote weight loss.	There is no reliable research to support hoodia's use. No human studies using the herb have been published.	Hoodia's safety is unknown.
Kava	Roots and underground stems are used to treat asthma, anxiety, insomnia, and menopausal symptoms.	Kava may be beneficial for the management of anxiety but is not a proven therapy for other uses.	The FDA has issued a warning that using kava has been linked to a risk for serious liver damage.
Saw Palmetto	Berries are used to treat an enlarged prostate, urinary problems, pelvic pain, hair loss, and hormone imbalances.	There is not enough evidence to support the use of saw palmetto for any conditions.	Mild side effects include stomach discomfort and, in men, decline in libido.
St. John's Wort	Flowering tops are used to treat depression, anxiety, and sleep disorders.	Some evidence suggests St. John's wort *may* be useful in treating mild to moderate depression. Its use can dangerously delay obtaining medical treatment for major depression.	Side effects include increased sensitivity to sunlight, headaches, and other symptoms. It can interact with drugs, such as blood clotting medicine and birth control pills.

Data from: National Center for Complementary and Alternative Medicine. Herbs at a Glance. http://nccam.nih.gov/health/herbsataglance.htm (accessed December 2008).

Are People Buying Functional Foods?

Americans spend an estimated $25 billion annually on functional foods, and the market is predicted to grow as more consumers take a self-care approach to their health.[17] In a survey of more than 1,000 Americans, over 70 percent of the participants believed that food and nutrition play a key role in maintaining and improving their health.[18]

Baby boomers (people born roughly between 1946 and 1964) are reaching age 50 at the rate of one every 7.7 seconds.

Baby boomers (the generation born between roughly 1946 and 1964) are particularly interested in trying to hedge against the aging process and age-related diseases through their diets. With an estimated $150 billion in discretionary income, these adults can afford foods that are promoted as having a health advantage.[19]

What Are the Benefits of Functional Foods?

Functional foods are used by health care professionals to help alleviate and even treat some chronic diseases. For example, many doctors send their patients to a registered dietitian for advice to treat specific medical conditions, such as an elevated blood cholesterol level, rather than automatically putting them on cholesterol-lowering medication. Eating a diet that contains a substantial amount of cholesterol-lowering oats or plant sterols is less expensive, and often more appealing, than taking costly prescription medication, and it can be an effective tool in treating preventable conditions.

Another group of functional foods includes products, such as yogurt, that contain **probiotics,** live microorganisms that can have beneficial health effects. For example, these "healthy bacteria" partially digest the milk sugar lactose, enabling people with lactose intolerance to eat yogurt or other dairy products without incurring intestinal distress, such as diarrhea. While more research is needed regarding the type and amount of probiotics needed for good health, some probiotic strains are thought to positively affect the immune system, relieve certain allergies, relieve constipation, and reduce intestinal inflammation.[20]

Oat products, such as oatmeal and certain other cereals, contain beta-glucan, which has been shown to lower blood cholesterol levels.

What Concerns Are Associated with Functional Foods?

With so many labeling claims adorning products on supermarket shelves, consumers have an array of enhanced functional foods from which to choose. Having so many options can be confusing. Consumers often cannot tell if a pricey box of cereal with added "antioxidants to help support the immune system" is really better than an inexpensive breakfast of oatmeal and naturally antioxidant-rich orange juice. There is also a concern that, by eating a bowl of this antioxidant-enhanced cereal, consumers may think they are "off the hook" about eating healthfully the rest of the day. Often, more than one serving of a functional food is needed to reap the beneficial effect of the food compound, but the consumer hasn't been educated appropriately about how much of such a food to consume.

probiotics Live microorganisms (sometimes called "healthy bacteria") that can have beneficial health effects.

Functional beverages, such as vitamin waters, have recently flooded the market as well. These products have catchy names, but they are often produced simply by adding sugar and vitamins to water. Such beverages can contain as many calories—

all from the sugar—as do soft drinks and provide vitamins that can easily be obtained from the diet. In addition, many have a hefty price tag.

As with most dietary substances, problems may arise if too much is consumed. For example, while consuming some omega-3 fatty acids can help reduce the risk for heart disease, consuming too much can be problematic for people on certain medications or for those at risk for a specific type of stroke.[21] A person can unknowingly overconsume a dietary compound if his or her diet contains many different functional foods enhanced with the same compound.[22]

How Can Functional Foods Be Used?

Although functional foods can be part of a healthy diet, consumers would benefit from more research, regulation, and education. For now, keep in mind that whole grains, fruits, vegetables, healthy vegetable oils, lean meat and dairy products, fish, and poultry all contain varying amounts of naturally occurring phytochemicals and zoochemicals and are the quintessential functional foods. If you consume other, packaged functional foods, be careful not to overconsume any single compound. Balance is key.

Ideally, a registered dietitian (RD), who is trained in the area of nutrition, can recommend the addition of functional foods to a person's diet based on his or her medical history and nutritional needs. Look to an RD for sound nutrition advice on whether you would benefit from added functional foods and, if so, how to balance them in your diet. Visit the American Dietetic Association (ADA) website listed at the end of this concept for help finding an RD in your area.

The Take Home Message **A functional food is one that has been shown to have a positive effect on your health beyond its basic nutrients. Both whole and processed foods—for example, both carrots and carrot juice—can qualify as functional foods. A registered dietitian can recommend the addition of functional foods to the diet based on the person's medical history and nutritional needs.**

Check out these recipes and more suggestions at www.pearsonhighered.com/blake

UCook

Good 'n' Crunchy Slaw

If you are looking for a crunchy coleslaw that can double as a sweet snack, try this easy-to-prepare cruciferous salad blend!

UDo

Summing Up Your Daily Dietary Supplements

Visit our website and check out the link for this great Dietary Supplement Assessment to help you determine whether taking a supplement is right for you.

The Top Five Points to Remember

1. Dietary supplements are products containing nutrients, amino acids, enzymes, or botanicals intended to supplement the diet. The FDA does not strictly regulate dietary supplements for their safety and efficacy; those who choose to use them may be placing their health at risk. The USP seal on a supplement label indicates that the supplement has been tested and meets certain criteria for purity and other qualities.

2. Vitamin and mineral supplements can help individuals with inadequate diets or medical concerns meet their nutrient needs. However, supplements should never replace a healthy diet. If you choose to use a dietary supplement, you should inform your health care provider.
3. All athletes and physically active people must consume adequate calories and nutrients to achieve optimal fitness and athletic performance. Some dietary supplements are used as ergogenic aids to improve athletic performance; however, well-balanced meals and snacks consisting of whole foods should be the basis of an athlete's diet, with sports bars, shakes, and other supplements used only when necessary.
4. Creatine has been shown to increase both muscle strength and mass, but research is mixed on its role in athletic performance. Caffeine has been shown to improve endurance performance but has not shown any benefit in activities of short duration. Anabolic steroids can increase muscle mass and strength but also causes undesirable androgenic side effects for both men and women. Growth hormone may increase muscle mass and decrease body fat, but it also has serious health effects. Synthetic erythropoietin can improve endurance but can also thicken the blood, which may lead to a stroke or heart attack.
5. Functional foods have been shown to have a positive effect on health beyond providing basic nutrients. Some foods are deliberately enhanced with compounds and marketed as functional foods. Probiotics are live and active cultures of beneficial bacteria found in fermented milk products, such as yogurt.

Test Yourself

1. The USP seal on the label of a multivitamin/mineral supplement means that the product has been tested and shown to be
   a. effective.
   b. free of contaminants.
   c. safe to use.
   d. all of the above.
2. Which of the following statements about dietary supplements is true?
   a. Women of childbearing age who may become pregnant may benefit from taking a folic acid supplement.
   b. The term *natural* on a supplement label means that the supplement is healthful and safe.
   c. The FDA is responsible for determining the quality, effectiveness, and safety of dietary supplements.
   d. All of the above are true.
3. Acromegaly can be caused by abuse of which ergogenic aid?
   a. creatine
   b. growth hormone
   c. anabolic steroids
   d. erythropoietin
4. The use of anabolic steroids
   a. can promote protein growth and muscle development.
   b. can lead to severe physical and psychiatric problems.
   c. is prohibited among most collegiate and professional athletic associations.
   d. all of the above.
5. Yogurt contains beneficial bacteria that can support digestive function. Yogurt is considered
   a. a dietary supplement.
   b. a functional food.
   c. a zoochemical.
   d. all of the above.

Answers

1. (b) The USP seal guarantees that a supplement has been tested and shown to be free of contaminants, but it doesn't endorse or validate claims of effectiveness or guarantee that a product is safe to use.
2. (a) Women of childbearing age who may become pregnant need to consume adequate folic acid to prevent neural tube defects, which can develop early in a pregnancy before the woman even realizes she is pregnant. The term *natural* on a supplement does not guarantee product effectiveness or safety. Dietary supplement manufacturers, not the FDA, are responsible for ensuring the quality, effectiveness, and safety of their products.
3. (b) Abusing growth hormone causes acromegaly, a disease in which tissues, bones, and internal organs grow abnormally large.
4. (d) All of the statements about anabolic steroids are true.
5. (b) Yogurt is considered a functional food. A dietary supplement is not intended for use as a conventional food. A zoochemical is a beneficial compound found in animal food products; it is not a whole food, such as yogurt.

Web Resources

- To discover the facts about vitamin and mineral supplements, check the Office of Dietary Supplements' Fact Sheets at: http://ods.od.nih.gov/Health_Information/Vitamin_and_Mineral_Supplement_Fact_Sheets.aspx
- To find out whether a product is a waste of money before you buy, visit: www.quackwatch.org, a site that monitors false medical claims.
- To find an RD in your area, visit the American Dietetic Association (ADA) website at: www.eatright.org

27 Food Safety

1. **Viruses** can't survive on their own without an animal, plant, or human host. **T/F**

2. Foods that can make you sick always **smell bad. T/F**

3. Children are **less vulnerable** than adults to foodborne illnesses. **T/F**

4. Freezing foods **kills bacteria. T/F**

5. **Organic foods** can sometimes contain synthetic pesticides. **T/F**

The summer after his sophomore year in college, 20-year-old Miguel decided to take a backpacking trip through Mexico. He wanted to explore the distinct cultures, spend some time with his cousins, and experience an adventure or two. After a few days of hiking in the Sierra Madre, he made his way south toward Mexico City. One night, he bought a fish taco from a street vendor near the hostel where he was staying. Several hours later, he woke up with horrible cramps. After running to the bathroom and experiencing a painful bout of diarrhea, he headed to a local clinic to seek some help.

Although the United States enjoys one of the safest food supplies in the world, millions of Americans still suffer annually from some type of foodborne illness. In fact, foodborne illness causes about 325,000 hospitalizations (and 5,200 deaths) per year.[1] These illnesses often result in distressing gastrointestinal symptoms, such as the cramps and diarrhea Miguel experienced. Efforts to prevent foodborne illnesses have led to extensive food safety practices and guidelines. Several government agencies now work together to ensure that America's foods, from the farm to the table, are safe. You also play an important role in making sure that these foods remain safe once they are in your home. In this concept, you'll learn about a variety of food safety practices involving food storage and preparation. You will also learn about food additives, pesticides, and the increasingly hot topics of biotechnology and organic foods, and we'll find out the real deal when it comes to their benefits and drawbacks.

Answers

1. True. Viruses can't reproduce themselves outside of living hosts. See page 3 for more.
2. False. A food can contain disease-causing bacteria that can make you ill, yet smell perfectly fine. An off smell in food is more likely a sign of *spoilage*. Turn to page 3 to find out more.
3. False. Children's immune systems are underdeveloped, and they weigh less than adults, so they're at higher risk. Learn more on page 6.
4. False. Freezing doesn't kill bacteria but puts them in a dormant state. Find out what happens once the food is thawed, on page 10.
5. True. Some synthetic pesticides have been approved for use on organic crops. To find out more about organic foods, turn to page 23.

foodborne illness Sickness caused by consuming contaminated food or beverages; also known as *foodborne disease* or *food poisoning.*

pathogens Disease-causing microorganisms (microbes). Viruses, bacteria, and parasites are the pathogens most likely to cause foodborne illness.

viruses Microscopic organisms that must have a living "host," such as a plant or an animal, to survive. Viruses can infect a host and cause illness.

bacteria Microscopic organisms that can exist and flourish on both living and nonliving surfaces. Many bacteria are harmless, and some are beneficial. Pathogenic bacteria can cause illness.

What Causes Foodborne Illness and How Can It Make You Sick?

In 1906, an eye-opening book called *The Jungle*, written by a young author named Upton Sinclair, shocked the world with its descriptions of the filthy conditions in the meatpacking plants of Chicago.[2] The report, which described rodent droppings and body parts making their way into consumer-bound meat products, so horrified the public that meat sales dropped by half. An enraged President Theodore Roosevelt incited the United States Congress to pass the Meat Inspection Act.[3] The act mandated ongoing inspections of all meat processing plants in the United States.[4]

Before long, these food safety precautions had very positive effects on the nation's overall health. By 1920, instances of typhoid fever, a dangerous foodborne illness of the time, had declined by about two-thirds, and by the 1950s, it had virtually disappeared in the United States.[5]

Even with strict regulations in place, however, bouts of foodborne illness still happen. Let's look at the causes of foodborne illness.

Many Foodborne Illnesses Are Caused by Pathogens

If you consume foods or beverages that contain harmful agents, you might contract a foodborne illness. The agents of transmission may be chemicals (such as toxins in certain mushrooms), but most cases of foodborne illness are due to disease-causing microbes known as **pathogens,** such as **viruses, bacteria,** and parasites. Pathogens can be found on the skin or in the stool and droppings of infected humans and animals. Drinking water that has been contaminated with infected droppings and putting anything in your mouth (such as unwashed hands or contaminated food) that has been in contact with fecal matter are common ways to become infected. This is known as *fecal-to-oral transmission,* and it's why people should always wash their hands after using the bathroom and before preparing foods. Eating raw or undercooked meat, poultry, and fish from an infected animal can also expose you to pathogens.

Pathogenic viruses and bacteria are the most common causes of foodborne illness in the United States. Parasites are a less common cause. Here's how they differ:

- Viruses are microscopic organisms that must have a living "host," such as a plant or an animal, to survive. If you eat a contaminated plant or animal, the pathogen can invade the cells of your stomach and intestinal walls. The virus can then cause your cells' genetic material to start producing more viruses, ultimately leading to illness.[6] One serious foodborne virus, hepatitis A, caused an outbreak in 2003 among young people attending multi-day concerts at campgrounds. This type of environment, in which people are living, cooking, and eating close together in unsanitary conditions is an ideal breeding ground for a viral outbreak. Approximately 300 people had to be vaccinated against hepatitis A.[7]
- While viruses need a host to survive, bacteria are microscopic organisms that can exist and flourish on both living and nonliving surfaces. They live on your body, clothing, computer keyboard, and cell phone—on the surfaces in every room of your house. Most of the bacteria around you are harmless, and some are even essential, such as the ones in your intestine that synthesize biotin and vitamin K. A few bacteria are harmful, however, and can cause food spoilage or illness. The bacteria that cause food spoilage are not the same as those that cause foodborne illness. Although most people won't become seriously ill after eating slightly spoiled foods, these items can cause nausea and shouldn't be eaten. In contrast to spoiled foods, contaminated foods that contain more serious bacterial pathogens may look and smell perfectly fine.
- *Parasites* are microscopic organisms that, like viruses, take their nourishment from hosts. They can be found in food and water and are often transmitted through the fecal-to-oral route.[8] The most common parasitic illness outbreaks in the United States have been caused by only a few types of parasites.[9]

Table 27.1 identifies the most common viruses, bacteria, and parasites implicated in foodborne illnesses. One of these, a type of bacteria called *E. coli,* was the culprit in Miguel's bout of traveler's diarrhea. The accompanying Table Tips provides some advice for avoiding traveler's diarrhea.

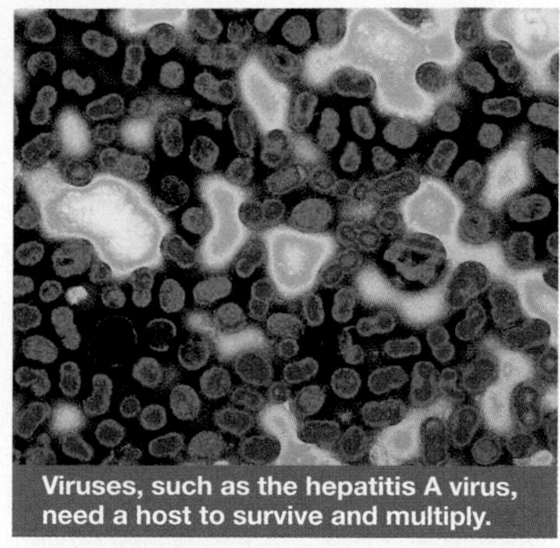

Viruses, such as the hepatitis A virus, need a host to survive and multiply.

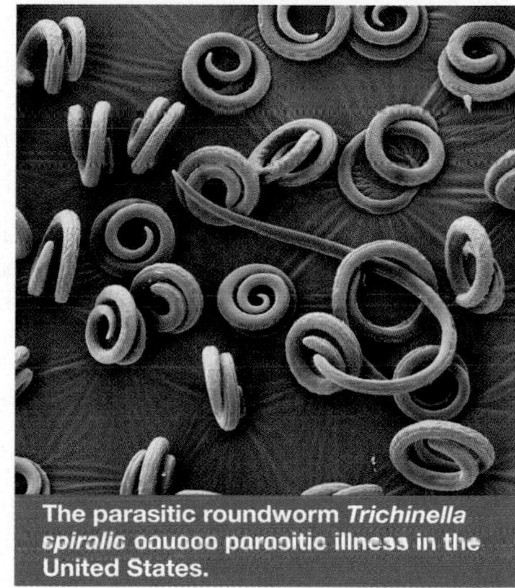

The parasitic roundworm *Trichinella spiralis* causes parasitic illness in the United States.

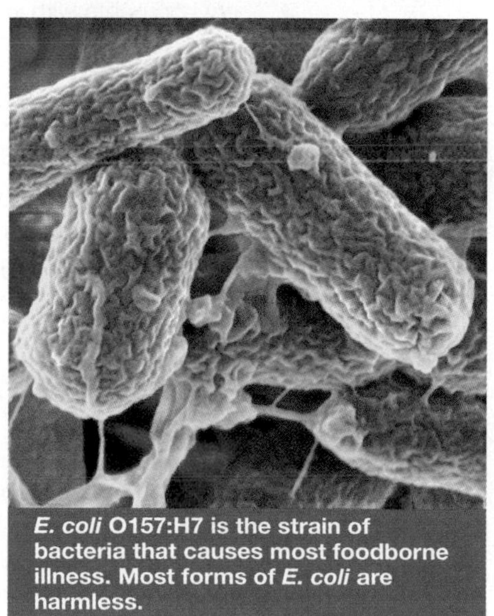

E. coli O157:H7 is the strain of bacteria that causes most foodborne illness. Most forms of *E. coli* are harmless.

Chemical Agents Can Also Cause Illness

As just noted, foodborne illnesses can also be caused by chemical agents that exist naturally in foods, such as the toxins in poisonous mushrooms and some fish. *Toxins* are harmful chemicals produced by living organisms; they can be produced by bacteria that have invaded and multiplied in foods. Industrial chemicals, such as antibiotics and pesticides that are intentionally added to foods, can also cause foodborne illness. We'll discuss this class of chemical agents shortly.

Table 27.1

Pathogens That Cause Foodborne Illness

Microbe	Where You Find It	How You Can Get It	What You May Experience
Viruses			
Noroviruses	Stool or vomit of infected individuals	Fecal-to-oral transmission; eating ready-to-eat foods or drinking liquids contaminated by an infected person; eating contaminated shellfish; touching contaminated objects and then putting hands in mouth	Watery diarrhea, nausea, vomiting, flulike symptoms, possible fever Can appear 24–48 hours after onset and last 24–60 hours Typically not serious
Hepatitis A	Stool of infected individuals	Fecal-to-oral transmission; eating raw produce irrigated with contaminated water; eating raw or undercooked foods that have not been properly reheated; drinking contaminated water	Diarrhea, dark urine, jaundice, flulike symptoms that can appear 30 days after incubation Can last 2 weeks to 3 months
Bacteria			
Campylobacter jejuni	Intestinal tracts of animals and birds, raw milk, untreated water, sewage	Drinking contaminated water or raw milk; eating raw or undercooked meat, poultry, or shellfish	Fever, headache, and muscle pain followed by diarrhea (sometimes bloody), abdominal pain, nausea Appears 2 to 5 days after eating; may last 7 to 10 days Guillain-Barré syndrome may occur
Clostridium botulinum	Widely distributed in nature in soil, in water, on plants, in the intestinal tracts of animals and fish; Grows only in environments with little or no oxygen	Eating improperly canned foods, garlic in oil, vacuum-packaged and tightly wrapped food	Bacteria produce toxin that causes illness by affecting the nervous system Symptoms usually appear after 18 to 36 hours; may experience double vision, droopy eyelids, trouble speaking and swallowing, difficulty breathing Fatal in 3 to 10 days if not treated
Clostridium perfringens	Soil, dust, sewage, intestinal tracts of animals and humans; grows only in little or no oxygen	Called "the cafeteria germ" because many outbreaks result from eating food left for long periods in steam tables or at room temperature; bacteria are destroyed by cooking, but some spores may survive	Bacteria produce toxin that causes illness Diarrhea and gas pains 8 to 24 hours after eating; usually last about 1 day, but less severe symptoms may persist for 1 to 2 weeks
Escherichia coli O157:H7	Intestinal tracts of some mammals, raw milk, unchlorinated water; one of several strains of *E. coli* that can cause human illness	Drinking contaminated water, unpasteurized apple juice or cider, or raw milk; eating raw or rare ground beef or uncooked fruits and vegetables	Diarrhea or bloody diarrhea, abdominal cramps, nausea, weakness Can begin 2 to 5 days after food is eaten, lasting about 8 days Small children and elderly adults may develop hemolytic uremic syndrome (HUS), which causes acute kidney failure; a similar illness, thrombotic thrombocytopenic purpura (TTP), may occur in adults

Table 27.1 continued

Pathogens That Cause Foodborne Illness

Microbe	Where You Find It	How You Can Get It	What You May Experience
Bacteria, continued			
Enterotoxigenic *Escherichia coli* (major cause of traveler's diarrhea)	Intestinal tracts of some mammals and unpasteurized dairy products; more common in developing countries	Fecal-to-oral transmission; consuming stool-contaminated water and foods from unsanitary water supplies and food establishments	Diarrhea, nausea, vomiting, stomach cramping, bloating, fever, weakness
Listeria monocytogenes	Intestinal tracts of humans and animals, milk, soil, leafy vegetables; can grow slowly at refrigerator temperatures	Eating ready-to-eat foods, such as hot dogs, luncheon meats, cold cuts, fermented or dry sausage, other deli-style meat and poultry, soft cheeses; drinking unpasteurized milk	Fever, chills, headache, backache, sometimes upset stomach, abdominal pain, and diarrhea May take up to 3 weeks to become ill; may later develop more serious illness in high-risk individuals
Salmonella (over 2,300 types)	Intestinal tracts and feces of animals, *Salmonella enteritidis* in eggs	Eating raw milk and other dairy products, seafood, or raw or undercooked eggs, poultry, and meat; also spread by infected food handlers	Stomach pain, diarrhea, nausea, chills, fever, headache Symptoms usually appear 8 to 72 hours after eating; may last 1 to 2 days
Shigella (over 30 types)	Human intestinal tract; rarely found in other animals	Fecal-to-oral transmission by consuming contaminated food and water; most outbreaks result from eating food, especially salads, prepared and handled by workers with poor personal hygiene	"Shigellosis," or bacillary dysentery; diarrhea containing blood and mucus, fever, abdominal cramps, chills, vomiting Begins 12 to 50 hours from ingestion of bacteria; can last a few days to 2 weeks
Staphylococcus aureus	On humans (skin, infected cuts, pimples, noses, and throats)	Consuming foods contaminated by being improperly handled; bacteria multiply rapidly at room temperature	Bacteria produce toxin that causes illness; severe nausea, abdominal cramps, vomiting, diarrhea Occurs 1 to 6 hours after eating; recovery within 2 to 3 days, longer if severe dehydration occurs
Parasites			
Crytosporidium parvum	Intestines of humans and animals	Fecal-to-oral transmission; drinking contaminated water; eating contaminated vegetables and fruits	Stomach pains, diarrhea, cramps, fever, vomiting
Cyclospora cayatenensis	Human stool	Fecal-to-oral transmission; drinking contaminated water; eating contaminated produce	Diarrhea, flatulence, stomach cramps, vomiting, fatigue
Giardia lamblia	Intestines of humans and animals	Fecal-to-oral transmission; drinking contaminated water; eating contaminated produce	Diarrhea, stomach pains, flatulence
Trichinella spiralis	Undercooked or raw meats containing *Trichinella* worms	Eating raw or undercooked contaminated meat, usually pork or game meats	Nausea, vomiting, diarrhea, fever, aching joints and muscles

Data from: Centers for Disease Control and Prevention (CDC). 2004. Diagnosis and Management of Foodborne Illness: A Primer for Physicians; CDC. Norovirus: Food Handlers; CDC. 2003. Viral Hepatitis A; CDC. 2004. Travelers' Diarrhea; MMWR "Recommendations and Reports" 50 (January 2001): 1–69; CDC. 2004. Parasitic Disease Information. All available at www.cdc.gov; Food Safety and Inspection Service. 2006. Foodborne Illness: What Consumers Need to Know; Food Safety and Inspection Service. 2001. Parasites and Foodborne Illness. Both available at www.fsis.usda.gov.

TABLE TIPS

Don't Let Bad Bugs Ruin Your Trip

A type of *E. coli* bacterium is a common cause of traveler's diarrhea primarily caused by contaminated food or water. People visiting countries where proper sanitation is questionable are at higher risk.[1] If you are traveling abroad, find out about any specific health advisories for that area.

Do not eat raw or undercooked meat or seafood.

Do not consume raw fruits and vegetables unless you peel them. Thoroughly cooked fruits and vegetables should be safe to eat.

Do not consume foods or beverages from street vendors or restaurants that appear to be unsanitary.

Do not drink tap water or use ice made from tap water unless it has been boiled or treated with iodine or chlorine. Bottled water with its original seal in place should be safe.

Do not consume unpasteurized milk or other unpasteurized dairy foods.

Data from: Centers for Disease Control Division of Bacterial and Mycotic Diseases. Updated 2004. Travelers' Diarrhea. www.cdc.gov/ncidod/dbmd/diseaseinfo/travelersdiarrhea_g.htm.

Some People Are at Higher Risk for Foodborne Illness

Older adults, young children, and people with compromised immune systems are more susceptible to the bad effects of foodborne illness.

In older adults, age-related deterioration of the immune system increases their risk for foodborne illness. Also, because less gastric juice is produced in the stomach as people age, fewer foodborne pathogens are destroyed during digestion.

Because of their underdeveloped immune systems, young children are also more vulnerable to foodborne illness. Children are also smaller and weigh less than adults and, so, can become sickened by exposure to a smaller amount of pathogens.

Any condition that weakens a person's immune system can increase his or her risk of contracting foodborne illness. This applies to people with HIV, AIDS, cancer, diabetes and other diseases.[10] Also, the hormonal shifts that occur during pregnancy can affect a pregnant woman's immune system, making her more vulnerable to certain foodborne illnesses.

People living in institutional settings (such as nursing homes, hospitals, and colleges and schools), where groups of people eat foods from the same source, are also at higher risk of contracting foodborne illnesses. Improper handling of foods and poor hygiene practices among food-service workers are often the cause of foodborne disease outbreaks in institutional settings.

The Take-Home Message **Foodborne illness is caused by consuming pathogens in contaminated food or drinks. Viruses and bacteria are the most common causes of foodborne illness in the United States, although parasites can also cause foodborne illness. Chemical agents, such as toxins, can also cause illness. Certain populations, including the elderly, children, pregnant women, and people with compromised immune systems, are at higher risk of contracting a foodborne illness.**

What Can You Do to Reduce Your Risk for Foodborne Illness?

One way to reduce your risk for foodborne illness is to keep the pathogens that cause it from flourishing in your foods. Bacteria, for instance, thrive and multiply in an environment with the following characteristics:

- *Adequate nutrients.* Protein- and nutrient-rich animal foods, such as raw and undercooked meat, poultry, seafood, eggs, and unpasteurized milk, are the most common havens for bacterial growth.
- *Moisture.* Bacteria thrive in moist environments, such as in raw chicken that is sitting in its juices.
- *A low level of acidity (pH).* Bacteria don't thrive in acidic foods, such as citrus fruits, but can flourish in less acidic foods, such as meat, fish, and poultry.
- *The correct temperature.* Bacteria multiply most abundantly between the temperatures of about 40°F and 140°F.
- *Time.* At body temperature, 98.6°F, bacteria can divide and double within 30 minutes, and they multiply to millions in about 12 hours.[11] Perishable food,

Figure 27.1 **A Bulk Recipe for Bacteria.**

A Bulk Recipe for Bacteria

Ingredients:

1. Nutrients (such as those contained in raw meat)
2. Moisture
3. Proper pH
4. Temperature (from 41°F–140°F)
5. Time (over 2 hours)

Directions:

Remove raw meat [nutrients] from the refrigerator. Let the juicy meat [moisture, proper pH] sit on your counter at room temperature (70°F) for more than 2 hours [time]. Watch the meat turn colors—the bacteria are having a field day multiplying.

Serving size:

Makes millions of bacteria, so don't eat or even handle the meat once it's been out for a while. Toss it immediately.

such as raw meat, left at room temperature for an extended period can become a feast for bacterial growth.

Figure 27.1 summarizes the conditions that enable bacteria to thrive.

You can reduce your risk for foodborne illness by practicing proper food handling and storage strategies. They're easy to remember as the "four *C*s" of food safety: cleaning, combating cross-contamination, cooking, and chilling (Figure 27.2). Let's look at each of these four steps individually.

Figure 27.2 Fight BAC!
The Fight BAC! symbol sums up the four *C*s of keeping food safe in your kitchen: *C*lean, *c*ombat cross-contamination (separate meats from ready-to-eat foods), *c*ook thoroughly, and *c*hill to a cold enough temperature.

Clean Your Hands and Wash Produce

You were probably taught as a child to wash your hands before eating, and guess what? Your parents were right! Hand washing is one of the most important strategies for preventing foodborne illness. In fact, if everyone practiced proper handwashing techniques, the incidences of foodborne illness could decrease by about half.[12] Washing your hands thoroughly is as important as washing your hands regularly, and this is where many people fall short. You should wash with warm, soapy water and rub your hands together vigorously for at least 20 seconds. Just rinsing your hands in water, or using cold water, is not nearly as effective.

In addition to your hands, you should thoroughly clean anything that touches your food, such as knives, utensils, and countertops, between uses. Cutting boards should be placed in the dishwasher or scrubbed with hot, soapy water and rinsed after each use. You can sanitize your cutting board by flooding it in your sink in a solution of 1 teaspoon of bleach in 1 quart of warm water. Let the board sit in the sanitizing liquid for a few minutes to kill the microbes; then rinse it thoroughly. Sponges and dishcloths should also be washed often in the hot cycle of your washing machine, preferably with bleach in addition to laundry soap. Sponges can also be cleaned effectively in your dishwasher.

One study of over 300 school children found that those who washed their hands four times a day had over 50 percent fewer sick days due to stomachaches.

Fruits and vegetables should be washed thoroughly under cold running tap water before eating. This will help remove any dirt or microbes on their surface. Produce with a firm surface can be scrubbed with a vegetable brush. The Table Tips summarize the cleaning strategies you should apply when preparing food.

Your countertop sponge may be the most contaminated item in your kitchen. Food scraps, moisture, and room temperature can lead to a thriving bacterial colony on this common cleaning item.

Combat Cross-Contamination

Produce, especially if it's going to be eaten raw, should never come in contact with raw meat, poultry, or fish during the food preparation process. If these items do come in contact, they might *cross-contaminate* each other, meaning that microbes from one might move back and forth between several surfaces or items. You should pay special attention to microbe-containing raw meat, poultry, and fish. Raw foods such as these should be kept separate from ready-to-eat foods during food preparation, and stored separately in your refrigerator. You should even keep these products from contact with others on the trip home from the grocery store.

Marinades that have been used to tenderize and flavor meats, poultry, or fish shouldn't also be used as a serving sauce unless they have been boiled for several minutes to kill any pathogens. A better bet is to discard used marinade and create a fresh batch to use as the sauce.

The knife and cutting board used to cut and prepare raw meat, poultry, or fish shouldn't be used to slice vegetables or bread unless both have been cleaned thoroughly. An ideal practice is to set aside one board for slicing only raw meats, poultry, and fish and use another one for cutting fresh, washed, produce, breads, rolls, and other ready-to-eat foods.

All plates and bowls that have contained raw meats, poultry, and fish should be washed thoroughly before using them again. For example, at a barbecue, a plate that held raw hamburgers should *never* be used to serve cooked burgers unless it has been washed thoroughly between each use.

Soiled dishtowels shouldn't be used to dry clean dishes or utensils. A towel that was used to wipe up raw meat juices or your hands can transfer those microbes to clean dishes or utensils. Figure 27.3 provides more ways to combat cross-contamination when you prepare food.

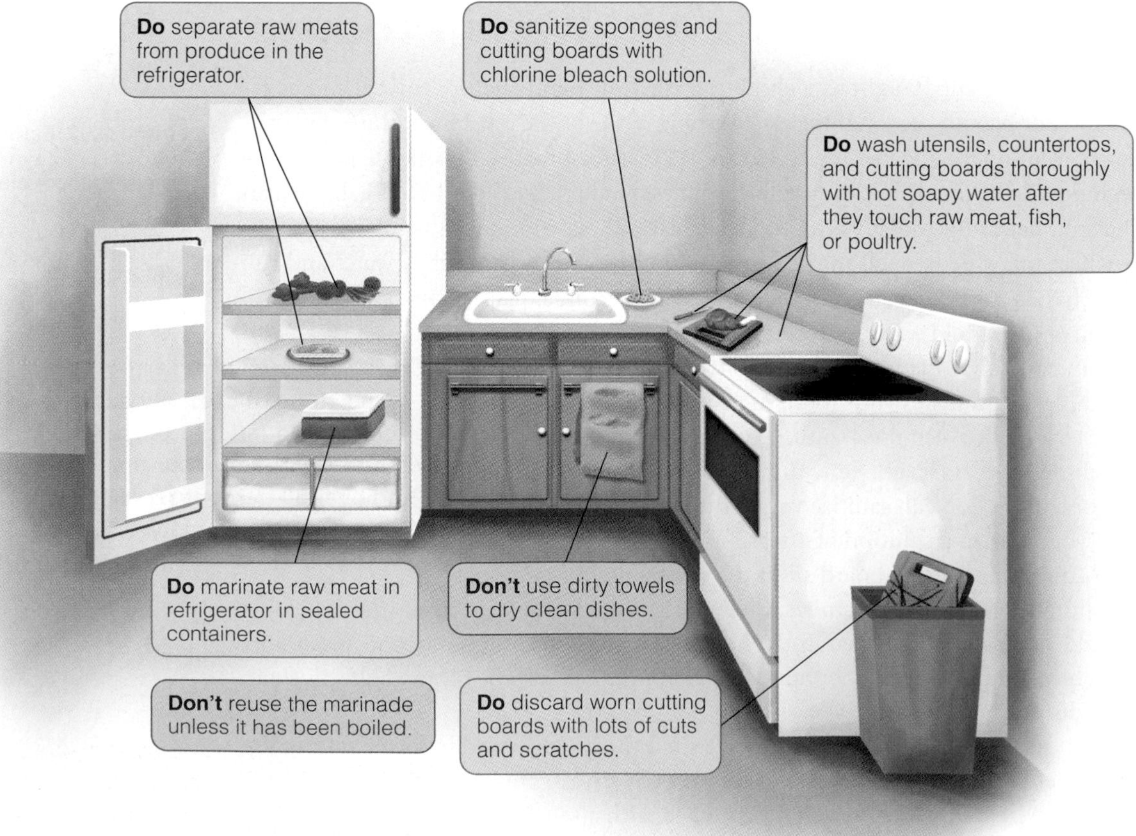

Figure 27.3 Do's and Don'ts of Cross-Contamination.

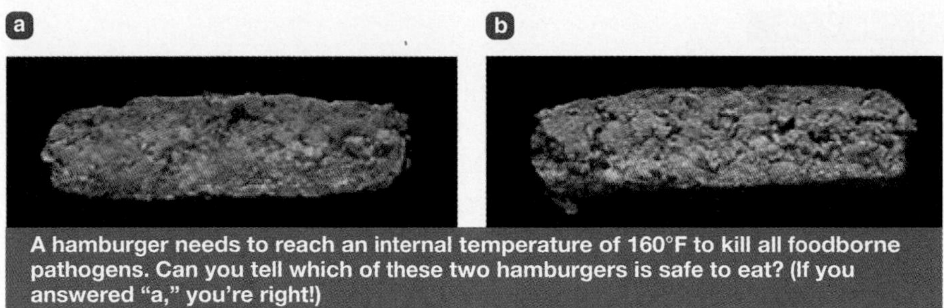

A hamburger needs to reach an internal temperature of 160°F to kill all foodborne pathogens. Can you tell which of these two hamburgers is safe to eat? (If you answered "a," you're right!)

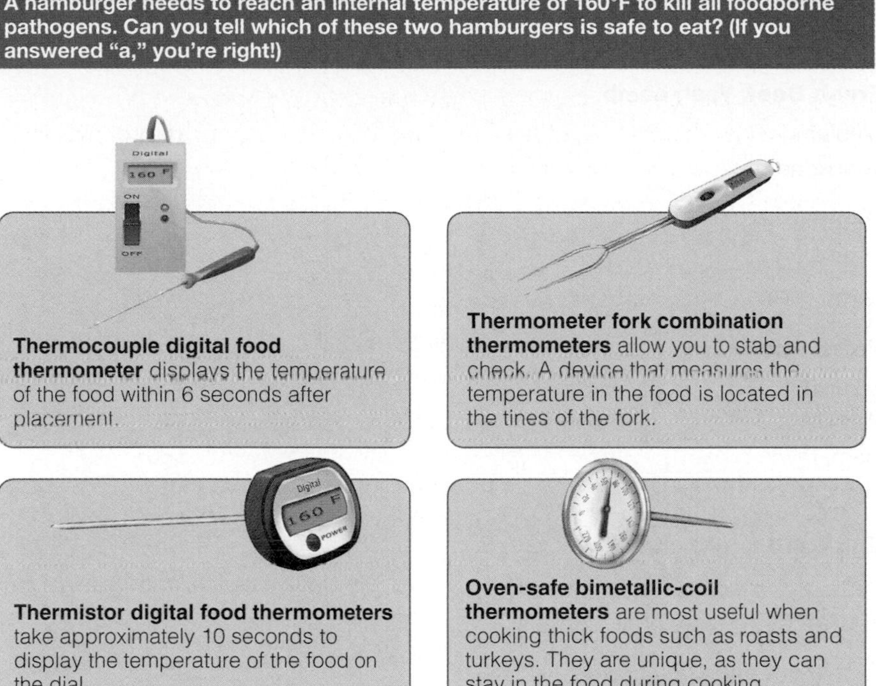

Thermocouple digital food thermometer displays the temperature of the food within 6 seconds after placement.

Thermometer fork combination thermometers allow you to stab and check. A device that measures the temperature in the food is located in the tines of the fork.

Thermistor digital food thermometers take approximately 10 seconds to display the temperature of the food on the dial.

Oven-safe bimetallic-coil thermometers are most useful when cooking thick foods such as roasts and turkeys. They are unique, as they can stay in the food during cooking.

Figure 27.4 Food Thermometers
There are several types of food thermometers you can use to tell if your food is safe to eat. The thermometer should be inserted at least ½ inch into the food. It should be washed thoroughly after each use, before it is inserted back into the food.

Cook Foods Thoroughly

Although you might assume that brown meat is cooked well, this is often not the case. Look at the two hamburger patties accompanying Figure 27.4. Which one do you think is safe to eat? The answer may surprise you. The patty on the right looks as though it is more thoroughly cooked than the patty on the left, but it's actually not. Meat can lose its pink color before it is safe to eat, while some lean varieties of beef can remain pink even though they have reached an internal temperature of 160°F (high enough to kill potential pathogens). Research has shown that hamburgers can look "well done" while only having reached an internal temperature of approximately 135°F.[13]

As you can see, color is not a reliable indicator that food is safe to eat. The only way to determine if your food has reached an appropriate internal temperature, high enough to kill pathogens, is to use a food thermometer. Table 27.2 provides a list of the internal temperatures that your foods should reach to ensure that they are safe to eat.

Chill Foods at a Low Enough Temperature

Just as cooking foods to a high enough temperature to kill pathogens is essential, chilling foods at a low enough temperature to inhibit the growth of pathogens is also important. Foodborne bacteria multiply most rapidly in temperatures between 40°F

TABLE TIPS
Scrub Away Pathogens

Wash your hands before eating, before and during cooking, and especially after visiting the bathroom or changing diapers.

Wash your hands with warm, soapy water for at least 20 seconds and use plenty of agitation. Dry with a clean towel, or better yet, a paper towel, which lets you toss away the germs.

Wash sponges and dishcloths at least weekly in the hot water cycle of the washing machine. Sponges can also be run through the dishwasher cycle. Otherwise, replace them regularly.

Wash all fruits and vegetables under cold, running tap water to remove dirt and microbes. Use a vegetable brush for firmer produce, such as apples, cucumbers, and potatoes. Do not use detergents or soaps, as these can leave a residue or be absorbed into the produce.

You don't need to wash meat, poultry, fish, or eggs. Proper cooking will destroy foodborne pathogens in these foods.

Table 27.2

Cook It Until It's Done!

If You Are Cooking . . .	The Food Thermometer Should Reach (°F)* . . .
Ground Meat and Meat Mixtures	
Beef, pork, veal, lamb	160
Turkey, chicken	165
Fresh Beef, Veal, Lamb	
Medium	160
Well done	170
Poultry	
Chicken, turkey (whole or parts)	165
Duck, goose	165
Fresh Pork	
Medium	160
Well done	170
Ham, raw	160
Ham, precooked (to reheat)	140
Eggs and Egg Dishes	
Eggs	Cook until yolk and white are firm
Egg dishes	160
Leftovers and Casseroles	165

*The thermometer should be placed in the thickest part of the food item.
Data from: USDA Food Safety and Inspection Service. Use a Food Thermometer. Updated 2008. www.fsis.usda.gov/Fact_Sheets/Use_a_Food_Thermometer/index.asp.

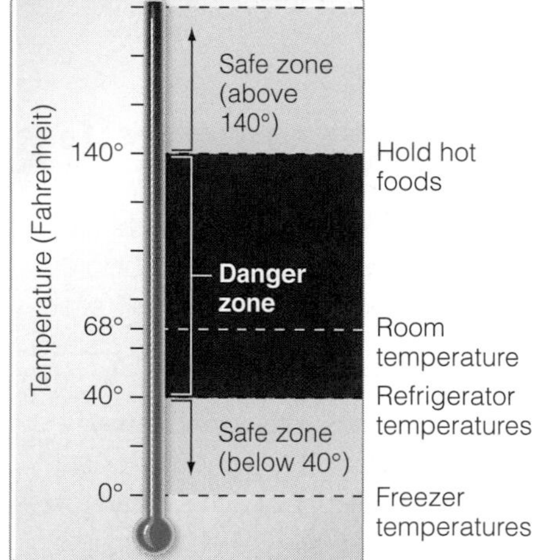

Figure 27.5 Danger Zone
Bacteria multiply rapidly in the "danger zone," between 41°F and 140°F.

and 140°F (or 5°C to 60°C), a range known as the "danger zone." To keep foods out of the danger zone, make sure that you keep hot foods *hot*, above 140°F, and cold foods *cold*, 40°F or below (Figure 27.5). In other words, lasagna on a buffet table should be sitting on a hot plate or other heat source that keeps its temperature above 140°F, while potato salad should be sitting on ice to keep it chilled and at 40°F or below at all times.

Cold temperatures will slow down most microbes' ability to multiply to dangerous levels. Because of this, the temperature in your refrigerator should be set at or below 40°F. The temperature for the freezer should be set at 0°F or below. The only way to know if the temperature in your refrigerator or freezer is low enough is to use a thermometer. While most microbes become dormant and are unable to multiply when they are frozen, they aren't destroyed by freezing temperatures. In fact, once the frozen foods are defrosted, the microbes can "thaw out" and thrive under the proper conditions.

Raw eggs and other perishables should not be stored in your refrigerator door. Store perishables in the back of the refrigerator, where it's colder and the temperature is more constant.

Perishables, such as raw meat and poultry, shouldn't be left out at room temperature (a temperature within the danger zone) for more than 2 hours. The same is true for leftovers. In temperatures above 90°F, foods shouldn't be left out for more than 1 hour.[14] Large roasts and pots of soup or stews should be divided into smaller batches in order to cool down more quickly in the refrigerator. If these items are left in the danger zone for too long or have been mishandled, not

Table 27.3

Keeping It Cool!

Follow these guidelines to keep your perishable foods safe after purchase*.

	Storage Time Limit	
Raw Foods		
Poultry	1 or 2 days	
Beef, veal, pork, lamb	3 to 5 days	
Ground meat, ground poultry	1 or 2 days	
Fresh variety meats (liver, tongue, brain, kidneys, heart, intestines)	1 or 2 days	
Cured ham, cook-before-eating	5 to 7 days	
Sausage from pork, beef, or turkey, uncooked	1 or 2 days	
Eggs	3 to 5 weeks	
Processed Products Sealed at Plant	**Unopened**	**After Opening***
Cooked poultry	3 or 4 days	3 or 4 days
Cooked sausage	3 or 4 days	3 or 4 days
Sausage, hard/dry, shelf-stable	6 weeks/pantry	3 weeks
Corned beef, uncooked, in pouch with pickling juices	5 to 7 days	3 or 4 days
Vacuum-packed dinners, commercial brand with USDA seal	2 weeks	3 or 4 days
Bacon	2 weeks	1 week
Hot dogs	2 weeks	1 week
Luncheon meat	2 weeks	3 to 5 days
Ham, fully cooked, whole	7 days	3 days
Ham, canned, labeled "keep refrigerated"	9 months	3 or 4 days
Ham, canned, shelf-stable	2 years/pantry	3 to 5 days
Canned meat and poultry, shelf-stable	2 to 5 years/pantry	3 or 4 days
Leftovers		3 or 4 days

*Based on refrigerator home storage (at 41°F or below).

Data from: Food Safety and Inspection Service. 2005. Keep Foods Safe! Food Safety Basics. www.fsis.usda.gov/Fact_Sheets/Keep_Food_Safe_Food_Safety_Basics/index.asp.

only can bacteria multiply but they can also produce toxins that are heat resistant. These toxins won't be destroyed even if the leftover food is reheated thoroughly, and could make you sick if consumed.[15]

Even stored at a proper temperature, leftovers should remain in the refrigerator for no more than four days. Here's an easy way to remember this: After *four* days in the refrigerator, leftovers are ready *for* the disposal. Raw meats and poultry can be kept for a maximum of two days in the refrigerator. Food will stay safe in the freezer indefinitely, although its quality may deteriorate. Table 27.3 shows the storage times for various foods. If you are unsure about the safety of a food, remember this: *When in doubt, throw it out.*

Now that you've read about how cleaning, avoiding cross-contamination, cooking, and chilling can help keep your foods safe, think about how many of these strategies you use in your own kitchen. Rate Yourself to discover ways in which you may need to improve your food safety habits.

RATE YOURSELF 

How Do Your Food Safety Habits Stack Up?

Take the following quiz to find out.

How Often Do You	Always	Sometimes	Never
Wash your hands before preparing food?			
Scrub your fruits and vegetables under cold, running water before eating them?			
Use an insulated pouch with an ice pack to carry your perishable lunches and snacks, such as meat-filled sandwiches and/or yogurt and cheese?			
Wash your hands after using the bathroom?			
Throw out refrigerated leftovers after four days?			
Chop raw vegetables on a clean chopping board, rather than the one you just used for raw meat, fish, or poultry?			
Use a thermometer to determine if meat or poultry is thoroughly cooked?			

Answers

If you answered "Always" to all of the questions, you are a food safety superstar! If you didn't, use the information in this concept to improve your food safety habits.

The Take-Home Message Proper food handling and storage strategies, particularly cleaning, combating cross-contamination, cooking, and chilling, can help reduce your risk for foodborne illness. Anything that comes in contact with your foods, including your hands, should be washed thoroughly. You should always wash produce before eating it, and separate raw meats, poultry, and fish, plus any utensils that touch them, from ready-to-eat foods to prevent cross-contamination. Using a food thermometer is the only accurate way to tell if your cooked food is safe to eat. Perishables should be chilled properly and promptly to minimize the growth of bacteria.

Who Protects Your Food and How Do They Do It?

Foods don't originate in the grocery store. Whether in a bag, box, or bin, every food you buy starts life on a farm. From the farmer to the consumer, everyone involved in the production and preparation of food plays a role in making sure the food we eat is safe. The *farm-to-table continuum* shows how farmers, food manufacturers, food transporters, retailers, and you, the consumer, can help ensure a safe food supply. Figure 27.6 shows the steps in this continuum. In this section, we'll look at the regulations, food preservation techniques, product dating, and irradiation that are done during various steps between the farm and the table. We'll start by looking at the government agencies that keep an eye on the food supply.

Figure 27.6 Farm-to-Table Continuum
Every step in the farm-to-table continuum plays an important role in reducing microbes and the spread of foodborne illness.

1 Farm: Use good agricultural practices. Farmers grow, harvest, sort, pack, and store their crops in ways that help reduce food safety hazards.

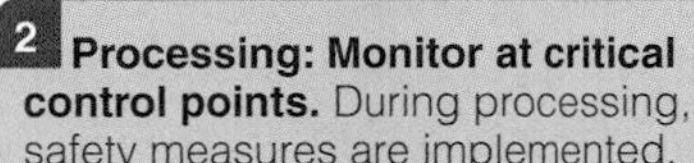

2 Processing: Monitor at critical control points. During processing, safety measures are implemented.

3 Transportation: Use clean vehicles and maintain the proper temperature. Food is kept at a proper temperature during transportation to reduce the growth of foodborne microbes.

4 Retail: Follow the Food Code guidelines. Retail outlets, including restaurants, grocery stores, and institutions (such as hospitals) use the Food Code guidelines to reduce the risk of foodborne illness.

5 Consumer: Always follow the four Cs of food safety (clean, combat cross-contamination, cook, chill). The consumer uses the four Cs to reduce the risk of foodborne illness.

Mad Cow Disease

Charlene Singh was 13 years old when she moved from the United Kingdom to sunny Florida in 1992. Nine years later, Charlene suddenly became forgetful and depressed. Baffled about her condition, her doctor referred her to a psychologist for help. Within a few weeks, Charlene had problems walking and difficulty dressing. She started to experience involuntary movements in her muscles, and incontinence. She visited her local hospital emergency room, and the medical staff concluded that she was suffering from panic attacks. She was sent home with a prescription for antianxiety medication.

In January 2002, a frustrated Charlene and her mother went to England in search of answers. During the three months of extensive medical evaluations that followed, Charlene's memory loss and other neurological symptoms became progressively worse. She couldn't remember routine numbers, such as her phone number, and couldn't perform simple mathematical problems. She fell often. She became confused, began to hallucinate, and started having difficulties communicating with her mother.

Charlene was referred to a neurologist, who had a hunch, which unfortunately turned out to be correct. Charlene had been exposed to bovine spongiform encephalopathy (BSE), more commonly known as mad cow disease. BSE is a slow, degenerative, and deadly disease that attacks the central nervous system of cattle. People who are exposed to BSE by eating infected beef also experience neurological damage and symptoms. Because the symptoms don't appear until 9 to 21 years after exposure, Charlene was probably exposed to BSE as a small child in the UK. By September 2002, Charlene had been confined to her bed, and she died in 2004.[1]

Bovine spongiform encephalopathy is caused by protein called a *prion*. Cattle can become infected by consuming feed contaminated with BSE.[2] The contaminant that causes BSE in animals is thought to cause a similar disease, called variant Creutzfeldt-Jakob disease (vCJD), in humans. Currently, there are approximately 150 cases of documented vCJD in people throughout the world.[3]

Although no one has acquired vCJD from cattle in the United States, a cow that tested positive for BSE was slaughtered in a meat plant in the state of Washington in 2003. Trace-back investigations confirmed that this BSE-infected cow had been imported from Canada. A recall was made of all the meat plant's production for that day, and the affected animal's herd was quarantined. Because all the tissues related to the central nervous system of the cattle slaughtered at the Washington meat plant were removed from the plant, any meat that left the plant for human consumption did not contain these at-risk components. Consequently, the USDA was confident that the recalled beef products posed no significant risk to the public.[4]

Since the late 1980s, the United States has taken steps to protect the public from beef contaminated with BSE. First and foremost, *ruminant animals* (those with four stomach chambers for digesting coarse food), such as cattle and sheep; meat and meat products from ruminant animals; and animal feed that contains animal protein derived from countries that are at risk for BSE, can no longer be imported into the United States. Also, feed for ruminant animals that is sold in North America is banned from containing any ruminant protein.

Since the BSE incident in Washington, additional precautions have been implemented in the United States to ensure a safe food supply. The CDC has improved its ability to investigate potential cases of vCJD through enhanced coordination of state and local health departments. The National Institutes of Health (NIH) has more than doubled its budget to allow for greater spending in the area of BSE and vCJD research.[5] Sick or lame cattle and specific tissues of those cattle (such as the small intestine and spinal cord tissue), which have the greatest risk of containing the BSE agent, are also banned from the food supply. Finally, techniques previously used when slaughtering cattle and separating the meat, which likely increased the potential for the meat to become contaminated, have been prohibited.[6]

Several Government Agencies Police the Food Supply

Several federal agencies share the responsibility for food safety in the United States.[16] Table 27.4 lists these agencies and summarizes the roles they play in safeguarding your foods. This shared responsibility has paid off; there was a 16 percent decline in foodborne illness from 1996 to 2002.[17]

Table 27.4

Who's Policing the Food Supply?

Agency	Responsibility
USDA Food Safety and Inspection Service (FSIS)	Ensuring safe and accurately labeled meat, poultry, and eggs
Food and Drug Administration (FDA)	Ensuring the safety of all other foods besides meat, poultry, and eggs
Environmental Protection Agency (EPA)	Protecting you and the environment from harmful pesticides
Animal and Plant Health Inspection Service (APHIS)	Protecting against plant and animal pests and disease

Data from: Food and Drug Administration and U.S. Department of Agriculture. 2000. A Description of the U.S. Food Safety System. www.fsis.usda.gov/OA/codex/system.htm.

Food Manufacturers Use Preservation Techniques to Destroy Contaminants

In addition to government efforts to help prevent foodborne illness, food manufacturers work to safeguard food. One way to control foodborne hazards is to use food preservation methods. Pickling (adding an acidic substance, such as vinegar, to the food), salting, drying, heating, freezing, and canning are all familiar methods of food preservation. You use some of these yourself when you cook (apply heat to) or freeze (apply cold to) foods. These methods have been in use for centuries, although today they're more often used by food manufacturers than home cooks.

Pasteurization is the technique of heating foods and liquids to a high enough temperature to kill pathogens. In addition to dairy foods, most juices (about 98 percent) consumed in the United States are pasteurized. Juices that aren't pasteurized must display a warning on the label.[18] *Canning* goes a step beyond pasteurization by packing food in airtight containers after heating it to a temperature high enough to kill most bacteria.

Two newer preservation methods are *modified atmosphere packaging (MAP)* and *high-pressure processing (HPP)*. In the MAP process, the manufacturer changes the composition of the air surrounding the food in a package. Usually, the amount of oxygen is reduced, which delays the decay of fruits and vegetables. MAP is used in foods such as packaged fruits and vegetables to extend their shelf life and preserve their quality.[19] HPP is a newer method, in which foods are exposed to pulses of high pressure, which destroys microorganisms. Foods such as jams, fruit juices, fish, vacuum-packed meat products, fruits, and vegetables can be treated with HPP.[20]

Some Foods Undergo Irradiation

After foods have been packaged by a manufacturer, they may undergo **irradiation,** at either the manufacturing plant or another facility. During this process, foods are subjected to a radiant energy source within a protective, shielded chamber. Most of the energy passes through the food and the packaging without leaving any residue.[21] This level of energy damages the DNA of any harmful microorganisms that are present, thus reducing the risk for foodborne illness.[22] Irradiation can also stop the ripening process in some fruits and vegetables and reduce the number of food spoilage bacteria. Irradiated strawberries can last up to three weeks before spoiling, while nonirradiated strawberries typically stay fresh for three to five days.[23]

pasteurization The process of heating liquids or food at high temperatures to destroy foodborne pathogens.

irradiation The process in which foods are subjected to a radiant energy source that kills specific pathogens by breaking up their cells' DNA.

Figure 27.7 International Radura Symbol
The radura symbol must appear on all irradiated foods.

Foods that have been irradiated are not radioactive and don't undergo harmful or dangerous chemical changes.[24] The temperature of the food isn't significantly raised during irradiation, which helps prevent nutrient losses. In fact, pasteurization, canning, and drying often destroy more nutrients, such as certain vitamins, than does irradiation.[25] Foods that are irradiated must bear the "radura" logo, along with the phrase "treated by irradiation" or "treated with radiation" on the package (Figure 27.7).

Although irradiation has many advantages, it doesn't guarantee that a food is safe. Proper food handling, preparation, and—especially—cooking techniques must still be used for foods that have been irradiated.

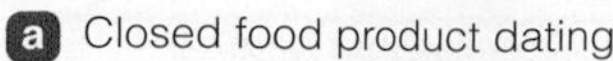

a Closed food product dating

b Open food product dating

(a) ***Closed food product dating*** **refers to the coded packing numbers that you often see on nonperishable foods, such as canned soups.**
(b) ***Open food product dating*** **must contain a calendar date and is used on perishable food items, along with information on how to use the date.**

Product Dating Can Help Determine Peak Quality

Although food product dating isn't federally mandated, except for infant formula and some baby foods, more than 20 states in the United States require some form of food product dating. There are two types of food product dating: closed dating and open dating. *Closed* (or *coded*) *dating* refers to the packing numbers manufacturers use, which are often found on nonperishable, shelf-stable foods, such as cans of soup and fruit (see photo). Manufacturers use this type of dating to keep track of product inventory, rotate stock, and identify products that may need to be recalled.[26]

Open dating is typically found on perishable items, such as meat, poultry, eggs, and dairy foods, and is more useful for consumers. Open dating must state a calendar date, which includes at least a month and day. You can use open dating to help you decide when to buy and consume a product while it is at its peak quality. This date does not refer to food safety, but to the *quality* of the food. For example, a carton of yogurt that has been mishandled and not refrigerated for several hours may be unsafe to eat even though the date on the container hasn't passed.

When open dating is used, there must be a phrase next to the date that tells you how to interpret it. If there is "Sell By" next to the date, you should purchase the product on or before that date. If there is "Best If Used By" or "Use By" next to it, this refers to the date by which you should consume the product in order to enjoy it at its best.[27] If you don't plan to consume a product by its Use By date, you can freeze it; once the food has been frozen, the Use By date doesn't apply.

What Are Food Additives and How Are They Used?

In addition to preservation techniques, irradiation, and product dating, food manufacturers sometimes use *food additives* to enhance the safety of foods. One of the earliest food additives was salt, which our ancestors quickly discovered did a great job of preserving meat and fish through a long winter. Later came spices, and today, when you get to the last heel of your bread loaf without encountering mold, you're enjoying the benefits of the additives and/or preservatives that the bread manufacturer included in the production process.

Table 27.5

Commonly Used Food Additives

Additives	Functions	Where You'll Find Them
Alginates, carrageenan, glyceride, guar gum, lecithin, mono- and diglycerides, methyl cellulose, pectin, sodium aluminosilicate	Impart/maintain desired consistency	Baked goods, cake mixes, coconut, ice cream, processed cheese, salad dressings, table salt
Ascorbic acid (vitamin C), calcium carbonate, folic acid, thiamin (B_1), iron, niacin, pyridoxine (B_6), riboflavin (B_2), vitamins A and D, zinc oxide	Improve/maintain nutritive value	Biscuits, bread, breakfast cereals, desserts, flour, gelatin, iodized salt margarine, milk, pasta, salt
Ascorbic acid, benzoates, butylated hydroxyanisole (BHA), butylated hydroxytoluene (BHT), citric acid, propionic acid and its salts, sodium nitrite	Maintain palatability and wholesomeness	Bread, cake mixes, cheese, crackers, frozen and dried fruit, lard, margarine, meat, potato chips
Citric acid, fumaric acid, lactic acid, phosphoric acid, sodium bicarbonate, tartrates, yeast	Produce light texture and control acidity/alkalinity	Butter, cakes, cookies, chocolates, crackers, quick breads, soft drinks
Annatto, aspartame, caramel, cloves, FD&C red No. 40, FD&C blue No. 1, fructose, ginger, limonene, MSG, saccharin, turmeric	Enhance flavor or provide desired color	Baked goods, cheese, confections, gum, spice cake, gingerbread, jams, soft drinks, soup, yogurt

Data from: FDA. Food Additives. 2001. www.cfsan.fda.gov/~lrd/foodaddi.html.

While preserving freshness is a common aim of today's additives, they are also used for many other reasons.[28] For example, food additives can help maintain a product's consistency, enhance a product's nutritional content, and prevent rancidity. Table 27.5 provides a list of commonly used additives and their functions in your foods.

The use of food additives is strictly regulated by the Food and Drug Administration (FDA), which since 1958 has mandated that food manufacturers must document a food additive's safety and get FDA approval to use it in foods.[29] However, two categories of food additives are exempt from the FDA's approval process:

- Substances that were known to be safe before 1958 were given *prior-sanctioned* status. For example, because **nitrates** (also called **nitrites**) were used to preserve meats before 1958, they have prior-sanctioned status, but only for use in meats. These preservatives can't be used in other foods, such as vegetables, without FDA approval.[30]
- Substances that are "generally recognized as safe" (GRAS), such as salt, sugar, spices, and vitamins, either have a long history of being safe to consume or have extensive research documenting that they are safe to eat.[31]

The FDA continually monitors both prior-sanctioned additives and those with GRAS status to ensure that current research supports their safety. If an additive is suddenly called into question, the FDA may prohibit its use or require that the food manufacturer conduct additional studies to demonstrate its safety.[32]

Even with these safeguards in place, some additives, such as the common flavor enhancer *monosodium glutamate (MSG)* and a class of preservatives called *sulfites*, cause unwanted effects in some people. The FDA requires that the labels of foods containing MSG or sulfites identify the presence of these additives, so that they can be avoided by those who are sensitive to them.

The Take-Home Message **Manufacturers use food additives to preserve foods, enhance their color or flavor, and add to their nutrient content. Some additives, such as MSG and sulfites, cause symptoms in sensitive individuals, but all additives are strictly regulated by the FDA.**

nitrates (nitrites) Chemical food additives that act as preservatives, in addition to enhancing the color of foods.

What Chemical Agents Affect Food Safety?

In addition to the toxins that certain types of bacteria can produce, other toxins can develop naturally as a plant or an animal grows, and industrial chemicals can accumulate in foods. In this section, we'll discuss these agents.

Toxins Occur Naturally

As noted earlier, toxins are harmful chemicals produced by living organisms. They occur frequently under natural circumstances to help a plant or an animal fend off predators or capture its meals. In many cases, toxins in foods exist in amounts too small to harm humans, but high levels of toxins in plant and animal foods can make a person ill, or worse. We noted earlier that thorough cooking kills many harmful bacteria, viruses, and parasites found in foods, but it doesn't destroy toxins.

For instance, some large fish naturally contain high levels of *marine toxins*. These harmful chemicals originate in microscopic sea organisms, which are then eaten by small tropical fish. As larger fish eat the smaller fish, the toxins *bioaccumulate* (build up in an organism over time) and thus become more concentrated in the larger fish.[33] Figure 27.8 shows how these kinds of toxins can accumulate in the food chain. In addition, certain shellfish, such as mussels, clams, scallops, oysters, crabs, and lobsters, can be contaminated with *neurotoxins* (toxins that affect the nervous system). Neurotoxins are also produced by microscopic sea organisms known as dinoflagellates, and the particular reddish-brown-colored dinoflagellates that contain them can become so abundant that the ocean appears to have red streaks, creating a phenomenon known as "red tides." Eating contaminated shellfish can lead to serious physical and health problems, including muscle paralysis, inability to breathe, and even death.[34]

Toxins can also occur in other foods. For instance, potatoes that have been exposed to light and have turned green contain increased amounts of solanine, a toxin that can cause fever, diarrhea, paralysis, and shock. (Peeling potatoes usually removes the green layer and the potato may be safely eaten. If it tastes bitter, however, throw it out.) The root vegetable known as cassava contains chemicals that have been known

Level 1 Dinoflagellates produce toxin and/or other microscopic organisms become contaminated with toxins.

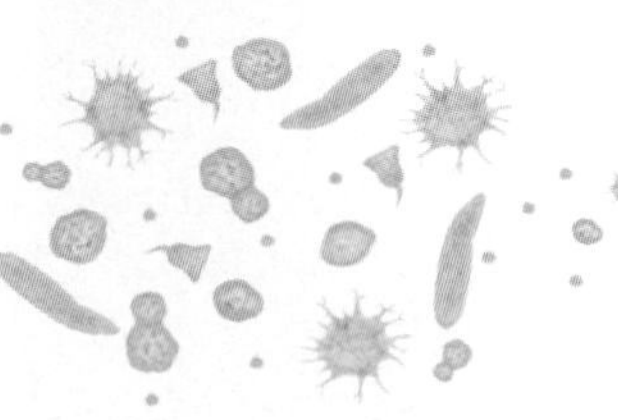

Level 2 Small fish eat the dinoflagellates. Over time, the toxins accumulate and become more concentrated in their bodies.

Level 3 Large, predatory fish consume the smaller contaminated fish, which increases their toxin concentration.

Level 4 Fishermen catch the larger fish for human consumption.

Increasing accumulation of biotoxins

Figure 27.8 Bioaccumulation of Toxins.

to cause cyanide poisoning in people who eat large amounts. And certain wild mushrooms are famously poisonous; they contain toxins that can cause nausea, vomiting, liver damage, and death.

Contamination Is Sometimes Due to Pollution

One person's trash can become another person's illness. Although industrial and household chemicals have useful purposes, if traces of these substances end up in the food supply, they can have negative health effects. Two pollutants of concern are PCBs and methylmercury.

Polychlorinated biphenyls (PCBs) are chemicals that occur in the food supply due to industrial pollution. A few decades ago, these chemicals were used as coolants and lubricants because they are good insulators and don't burn easily. They were banned in 1977 due to concerns about their toxicity.[35] For example, they may be responsible for promoting cancer in humans. (See Concept 24 for more about cancer.) Although PCBs are no longer manufactured in the United States, they can still make their way into the environment through hazardous waste sites, the burning of wastes, and the improper disposal of consumer products, such as old television sets and other electrical fixtures and devices.[36] PCBs have been shown to contaminate the sediments in rivers and lakes. Because PCBs don't break down over time, they bioaccumulate in small organisms and fish. In fact, PCBs are the major chemical risk associated with eating fish.[37]

Mercury occurs in nature, but it is also a by-product of industrial pollution. An airborne form of mercury can accumulate on the surface of streams and oceans and be transformed by the bacteria in the water into the toxic form of methylmercury. As fish either absorb the methylmercury from the water or eat smaller fish that contain methylmercury, they can bioaccumulate the substance to high levels.

TABLE TIPS 

Ways to Avoid Toxins and Chemical Agents in Your Food

Keep fish—especially fresh tuna, mackerel, grouper, and mahi mahi—chilled in the refrigerator to prevent spoilage and the formation of toxins.

Never consume fish or shellfish that is sold as bait, since they do not meet food safety regulations.

Observe all fish consumption advisories and warnings. To learn if an advisory exists for fish in your area, visit the EPA's Fish and Wildlife Consumption website: www.epa.gov/waterscience/fish/states.htm.

If you fish recreationally, always check with the local or state health department for specific advice for your local waters to avoid eating fish containing PCBs.

Eat a variety of types of fish to minimize your exposure to a particular toxin.

(Data from: Centers for Disease Control and Prevention. 2002. Marine Toxins. www.cdc.gov/ncidod/dbmd/diseaseinfo/marinetoxins_g.htm; Agency for Toxic Substances and Disease Registry. Updated 2008. ToxFAQ for Polychlorinated Biphenyls (PCBs). www.atsdr.cdc.gov/tfacts17.html; Environmental Protection Agency Persistent Bioaccumulative and Toxin (PBT) Chemical Program. www.epa.gov/pbt/pbtsandyou.htm.)

Some Chemicals Are Used Intentionally to Enhance the Food Supply

Chemicals are sometimes used to improve the health or output of food-producing animals. Two chemicals commonly used for this purpose are growth hormone and antibiotics.

Growth Hormone

Scientists and dairy farmers have known for years that cows injected with the naturally occurring bovine *growth hormone* produce more milk. Although consumer groups and Health Canada (the FDA equivalent in Canada) have questioned the safety of bovine growth hormone, the FDA's extensive review has found no evidence that it poses any long-term health threat to humans.[38]

Cows injected with a synthetic version of bovine growth hormone can produce up to 25 percent more milk than untreated cows.

Other steroid hormones are sometimes used to increase the amount of weight cattle gain and the amount of meat they produce. The FDA has approved the use of these hormones in beef cattle, as they have been shown to be safe at their approved level of use and not a health concern to consumers.[39]

Farmers use pesticides on food crops to diminish the damage from pests.

Antibiotics

Antibiotics are drugs that kill or slow the growth of bacteria, and are used in food-producing animals for three purposes: (1) to treat sick animals; (2) to preventively treat animals that may be at risk of becoming sick (for example, if one animal becomes ill, the entire herd may be given antibiotics); and (3) to promote growth. For the first two purposes, antibiotics are used for a relatively short period of time. This isn't true when antibiotics are used for the third purpose. Low-dose antibiotics are routinely put into animal feed, because animals that consume this feed gain more weight than do animals fed antibiotic-free feed.[40]

Pathogenic bacteria are commonly found in the gastrointestinal tracts of animals without making them sick. However, when animals are consistently given antibiotics, strains of *antibiotic-resistant bacteria* can reproduce in their intestinal tracts. If someone contracts a foodborne illness from this animal food source, treatment with the same antibiotic used in the feed, which killed the bacteria in the past, may no longer be effective.

An animal's chronic intake of antibiotics can also cause the "overgrowth" of other bacteria, which can evade the effects of the antibiotic. These bacteria can flourish and multiply to high levels. Treatment with typical antibiotics to control these surviving, resistant bacteria may be unsuccessful, perpetuating the need for a higher dose of medication and/or a longer treatment period.

Pesticides Are Widely Used in Agriculture

You have probably been handling *pesticides* (substances that kill or repel various pests) for years. If you use disinfectant to control the mold in your shower, bug spray to ward off mosquitoes, or a flea collar to keep your pet itch-free, you're making use of chemicals that destroy or mitigate pests. Different types of pesticides are used to destroy pests that threaten the food supply.

Pesticides Can Be Synthetic or Natural

Pests that can diminish or destroy crop yields include insects, weeds, bacteria, viruses, molds, and rodents. Pesticides used to combat such pests can be synthetically produced or derived from natural sources, such as animals, plants, bacteria, and some minerals.[41]

Of the numerous synthetic pesticides, *organophosphates* make up about half of all the insecticides used in the United States.[42] Organophosphates affect the nervous systems of the pests they destroy. These pesticides are used on fruits, nuts, vegetables, corn, wheat, and other crops, as well as commercial and residential lawns and plants. They are also used to help control mosquitoes and termites.[43] The Environmental Protection Agency (EPA) has reviewed the safety of organophosphates and concluded that they do not pose a health risk based on current human exposure in food and water.[44]

Naturally occurring pesticides are called *biopesticides*. Unlike synthetic pesticides, biopesticides curtail only a specific pest, and thus are not harmful to birds and other animals that come in contact with them.[45] For example, baking soda (sodium bicarbonate) can be diluted with water and sprayed on plants to inhibit the growth

antibiotics Drugs that kill or slow the growth of bacteria.

of fungi without any known risk to humans.[46] Insect hormones can be used in agriculture to interfere with the mating of pests. Scented extracts from plants can also be used to lure and then trap insects.[47]

Pesticides Have Both Benefits and Risks

Pesticides can be extremely helpful in preventing the growth of harmful fungi, controlling damaging insects, and stopping rampant weeds from contaminating crops with their natural toxin. Because of the pesticides used on agricultural crops, food plants can flourish and produce a hearty bounty. This enables farmers to offer affordable crops to the market.[48] The consumer then benefits by being able to buy a variety of nutrient-dense foods.

The benefits of pesticides must be weighed against their risks. Synthetic pesticides are strong chemicals that can cause unintended harm to animals, the environment, and even humans. Research has shown that some pesticides, depending on their level of toxicity and how much is consumed, may cause serious health problems, such as cancer, birth defects, and nerve damage.[49] To prevent potential harm to consumers, pesticide use is heavily regulated in the United States.

Regulating Pesticides: Who's Watching the Crops?

The EPA evaluates all food pesticides to ensure that they can be used with "a reasonable certainty of no harm." Because there are potential differences between a pesticide's effects on animals and its effect on humans, as well as differences among humans, the EPA builds in a margin of safety when determining the health risk. An extra tenfold safety factor is added (unless there is evidence that a lesser margin of safety is adequate) to protect the most vulnerable groups, such as infants and children, who might be exposed to the pesticide.[50] Thus, much effort goes into ensuring that the foods you eat are safe, yet affordable, in order for you to reap their health benefits and minimize any known risks.

If you swab your kitchen sink and look at the results under a microscope, you would find over **16 million** bacteria living there.

In addition to the EPA, the U.S. Department of Agriculture (USDA) and the FDA are involved in regulating pesticides. Once the EPA approves pesticides for their specific use, regulates how much of each pesticide can be used, and establishes the pesticides *acceptable tolerance levels,* the tolerances are enforced by the USDA for meat, poultry, and eggs and by the FDA for all other foods.[51]

You Can Minimize Pesticides in Your Diet

Washing your fruits and vegetables with clean, running water while using a vegetable brush can remove up to 81 percent of pesticide residue, according to one study by the University of California. Also, in this study, there wasn't a significant difference in the amount of residue removed when the fruit was washed with plain water or with a commercial produce wash.[52] (Because of the strict pesticide guidelines in the United States, the amount of pesticide residue found on all the fruits studied was below the EPA acceptable tolerance level, even before the researchers washed it.) Peeling the skin from fruits and removing the outer layers of some vegetables can also help remove pesticide residues. Eating a variety of produce also minimizes the consumption of any one type of pesticide. People who eat more fruits and vegetables, and therefore potentially increase their exposure to pesticides, still typically have a lower risk for cancer than those who eat fewer fruits and vegetables.[53] See Figure 27.9 for a summary of strategies you can use to minimize the amount of pesticides in your diet.

Figure 27.9 Reducing Pesticides in Your Foods.

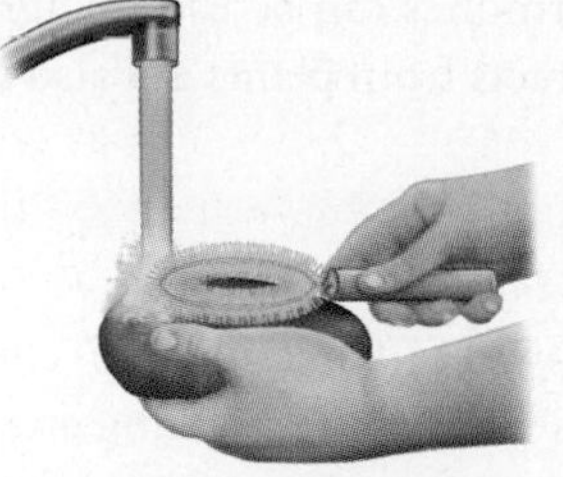

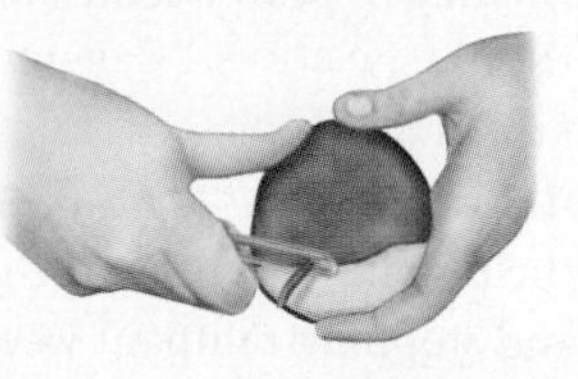

Wash: Thoroughly wash and scrub all fresh fruits and vegetables with a vegetable brush with sturdy surfaces under running water to dislodge bacteria and some of the pesticide residue. Running water is more effective for this purpose than soaking the fruit and vegetables.

Peel and trim: Peeling fruits and vegetables and tossing the outer leaves of leafy vegetables helps reduce pesticides. Trimming the visible fat from meat and the fatty skin from poultry and fish helps reduce some of the pesticide residue that remains in the fatty tissue of the animal.

Eat a variety of foods: Eating a variety of foods reduces your chances of being overexposed to any particular pesticide.

The Take-Home Message **Some toxins occur naturally in foods and can harm humans. Chemicals can also be in the food supply as a result of environmental pollution. Growth hormone can be given to dairy cows to increase milk production. Animal feed containing low doses of antibiotics has been used to increase the growth of cattle, poultry, and pigs. Chronic antibiotic exposure in animals can lead to antibiotic-resistant strains of bacteria. Pesticides are used to destroy or mitigate pests; they are regulated in the United States by several government agencies. You can minimize your exposure to plant pesticides by washing your produce under running tap water before consuming it.**

What Is Organic and How Do You Find Organic Foods?

Organic farming involves growing crops without the use of *some* synthetic pesticides, synthetic fertilizers, bioengineering (this will be discussed in the next section), or irradiation. Similarly, only antibiotic-free or growth hormone–free animals can be used to produce organic meat, poultry, eggs, and dairy foods.[54] The popularity of **organic foods** has soared in recent years. By 2025, the market for organic foods in the United States is projected to reach over $50 billion annually, compared with $20 billion in 2007.[55]

organic foods Foods that are free of most (but not all) chemical-based pesticides, synthetic fertilizers, irradiation, and bioengineering. A USDA-accredited certifying inspector must certify organic foods.

This growing interest in organic foods prompted the USDA to develop National Organic Standards (NOS) as part of their National Organic Program. These standards provide specific criteria that food producers must meet during production, handling, and processing to label their products "organic." As a result of these standards, you can be confident that, if the food is labeled as organic, it was produced and handled using specific guidelines and certified by a USDA-accredited inspector.[56]

Contrary to popular belief, organic foods are not necessarily free of all pesticides. Organically grown crops may come in contact with chemicals due to drift from wind and rainwater. Also, the National Organic Program allows several synthetic pesticides, such as insecticidal soaps, to be used in organic farming, while some natural substances, such as ash from the burning of manure, cannot be used.[57]

The USDA and recent research haven't found that organic foods are safer or nutritionally superior to those grown in a conventional manner.[58] The National Organic Trade Association confirms that there isn't any conclusive evidence that organic foods are more nutritious than conventionally grown foods.[59] Organic foods may also cost more than those that are conventionally grown.

You can identify organically produced foods in your supermarket by looking for the USDA Organic Seal (Figure 27.10). Foods that display this seal or otherwise state that they are organic must contain at least 95 percent organic ingredients. However, organic food producers can choose whether to display this seal, so it may not be on all such products. There are other label claims and standards for foods that are 100 percent organic, or that use organic ingredients. Figure 27.11 identifies the standards that organic label claims must meet.

Figure 27.10 USDA Organic Seal
Foods that are labeled or advertised with the USDA Organic Seal must contain at least 95 percent organic ingredients.

Figure 27.11 Various Levels of Organic Labelling

▲ **If the label says**
"100% Organic"
Then: The food must be composed entirely of organic ingredients. Note: These foods cannot contain sulfites and must declare the certifying agent. The USDA Organic Seal may be displayed.

If the label says ▶
"Organic" and/or displays the USDA Organic Seal
Then: The food contains at least 95 percent organic ingredients.

◀ **If the label**
makes no organic claims
Then: The food contains less than 70 percent organic ingredients.

◀ **If the label says**
"Made with Organic Ingredients"
Then: The food contains at least 70 percent organic ingredients.

The apples of today are larger and sweeter than their ancestors, thanks to hundreds of years of selective breeding.

The Take-Home Message Organic foods are grown without the use of some synthetic pesticides, synthetic fertilizers, bioengineering, or irradiation. The National Organic Standards provide specific criteria and guidelines for the production, handling, processing, and labeling of organic foods, as well as mandatory certification by an accredited inspector. Organic foods may cost more than conventionally grown foods, and there is no conclusive evidence that they are more nutritious than conventionally grown foods.

What Is Biotechnology and Why Is It Used?

Humans have been using **biotechnology** by selectively breeding plants and animals for generations. Historically, farmers have crossbred plants by trial and error, hoping for the best results and using the best offspring to further breed more desirable plants. Within the last century, however, as scientists came to understand more about the workings of DNA and how to manipulate it, the process has become faster and more controlled. Today, farmers routinely use selectively bred, *genetically modified* plants to create bigger and better produce and disease-resistant crops.

a Traditional plant breeding

Desired gene

X (cross)

Donor DNA

Recipient DNA

Desired gene

Undesired new DNA

Result

b New plant breeding using genetic engineering

Desired gene

Isolate gene

Donor DNA

Recipient DNA

Desired gene

Result

Figure 27.12 Plant Breeding versus Genetic Engineering
(a) Traditional plant breeding involved crossing two plants of the same species to produce DNA with more desirable traits. The process was imprecise, however, and achieving the desired result could take years. **(b)** Today, genetic engineering allows scientists to precisely manipulate plant DNA and impart the desirable qualities of one plant to its offspring much more quickly.

Genetic Engineering Is the Latest Form of Biotechnology

Today's versions of biotechnology include techniques, such as *genetic engineering (GE)*, to alter the genetic makeup of organisms. In genetic engineering, or bioengineering, a gene or genes from the DNA of a plant cell are isolated and inserted into the DNA of another cell to create a genetically modified product (Figure 27.12). This cutting and splicing of genes into the DNA of another cell is called recombinant DNA (rDNA) technology. Organisms that have been genetically engineered to contain both original and foreign genes are called *genetically modified organisms (GMOs)*. These GMOs are used to grow GE plants that produce GE foods. In 2003, 100 million acres of GE crops, including corn, cotton, canola, and soybeans, were cultivated on U.S. soil.[60]

Genetic Engineering Can Produce More and Better Foods

Proponents of GE products believe that they can be good for the environment, help feed countries that have an inadequate food supply, improve the quality and quantity of foods available all year round, and create new uses for plants in industries such as pharmaceuticals and manufacturing.

biotechnology The application of biological techniques to living cells, which alters their genetic makeup.

The original purpose of GE plants was to reduce the amount of pesticides used on food crops.[61] For example, the bacterium *Bacillus thuringiensis (Bt)*, which is found naturally in soil, produces a toxin that is poisonous to certain pests but not to humans or animals. When the gene for this toxin is inserted into a crop plant, the plant becomes resistant to these pests.[62] Some corn crops in the United States contain the *Bt* gene, which makes them resistant to some insect pests (see photo).

First-generation GE products were also created to improve a crop's tolerance to pesticides. With a resistant version of a desired crop, a farmer can spray pesticide over a field to kill a variety of weeds without harming the crop.[63] The second-generation GE products were designed to provide consumers with added nutritional value as well as increase the crop's shelf life.[64] For example, "golden" rice contains foreign gene segments that encode the rice grain to make beta-carotene and to stockpile extra iron (see photo). This "super" rice, if planted by farmers and accepted by consumers in Southeast Asia, could help eliminate the epidemic of vitamin A and iron deficiency in children there.[65] Genetically modified, high oleic–acid soybean oil is less prone to becoming rancid and, thus, is more stable when used for frying foods.

Third-generation GE products hold promise in the pharmaceutical, environmental, and industrial arenas. For instance, human insulin (needed by diabetics) can be produced by genetically engineered *E. coli.*[66] In addition, plants can be genetically modified to create substances with numerous medical uses, such as vaccines, antibiotics, anticlotting drugs, hormones, and substitutes for certain blood substances.[67] Scientists are experimenting with the concept of "growing" vaccines for measles, hepatitis B, and Norwalk virus in produce.[68] Imagine how much easier it would be to give the measles vaccine to a small child in a spoonful of puréed fruit rather than a needle!

Bt **corn has been genetically engineered to be resistant to the corn borer.**

"Golden" rice, a product of genetic engineering, is rich in both beta-carotene and iron.

Some Concerns about Genetically Engineered Foods

Some opponents of GE products fear that biotechnology might cause everything from "Frankenstein" foods to genetically-damaged monarch butterflies. A study at Cornell University in the late 1990s raised concerns that, when milkweed leaves, which are the sole diet of monarch caterpillars, were heavily dusted with pollen from *Bt* corn and then *exclusively* fed to monarch butterfly caterpillars, many of them died. Critics of this finding said that this experiment didn't mimic a "real-life" setting. Most milkweed doesn't grow close enough to cornfields to collect significant amounts of corn pollen, especially since this heavy pollen typically doesn't travel far from its place of origin. Hence, it is unlikely that monarch caterpillars would feed primarily on milkweed that contained such an enormous amount of GE corn pollen.[69] After conducting extensive research coordinated by the USDA, researchers concluded that the monarch butterflies' exposure to GE corn pollen in a natural setting is minimal and, so, is not likely to be dangerous to them.[70]

If you are concerned about "Franken-foods," you should know that the risk of creating an abnormal plant is smaller in GE foods than in foods cultivated through plant breeding. In fact, because genetic engineering involves precise cutting and splicing of specific genes, its end products are less likely to have undesirable traits.

Genetic engineering is also more tightly regulated than any other technology, so there are safeguards in place to halt or prevent undesirable outcomes, such as the introduction of a known food allergen into a GE product.[71]

Genetically Engineered Foods Are Regulated in the United States

In the United States, GE foods are regulated by the same three government agencies that regulate pesticides: the FDA, USDA, and EPA. The FDA ensures that GE foods are safe to eat. The USDA ensures that the plants are safe to grow, while the EPA makes certain that the gene for any pesticide, such as that for *Bt* toxin, inserted into a plant is safe and won't hurt the environment. Although these agencies work together to ensure the safety of GE foods, the FDA has the overall authority to remove from the marketplace any GE food that doesn't meet the same high safety standards that are set for its conventionally grown equivalent.[72]

The FDA has evaluated more than 50 GE foods, including canola oil, corn, cottonseed oil, potatoes, soybeans, squash, and tomatoes, and are considered as safe as their conventional counterparts.[73] Your supermarket shelf is likely littered with foods with GE ingredients. The FDA has concluded that, because there is no scientific evidence that GE foods differ from their conventionally grown counterparts, labeling is not warranted.[74] Thus, you have probably eaten them without being aware of it.

The public seems to be warming up to GE foods because of their health benefits and improved quality. In a survey of approximately 1,000 American adults conducted in January 2004, almost 60 percent felt that biotechnology would benefit them and their families in the future. Only 1 percent identified biotechnology as their top worry. The majority also stated that they would be likely to use GE produce that was modified to protect against insect damage, required less pesticide application during growing, or had improved taste or freshness.[75]

The Take-Home Message **Plant breeding and genetic engineering are types of biotechnology that alter the genetic makeup of an organism's cells to create a new plant with more desirable traits. Genetically engineered crops can be developed to be pest resistant and to provide additional nutrients and enhanced flavor and quality. GE products are heavily regulated to minimize undesirable genetic modifications, toxic substances, and nutrient changes in food, as well as potential food allergens and the creation of unsafe feed for animals. Labeling is not mandatory for GE foods.**

What Is Bioterrorism and How Can You Protect Yourself?

Food and water supplies are potential targets for *bioterrorism.* Chemical agents such as the bacterium that causes anthrax and the virus that causes smallpox are possible bioterrorist weapons. Until recently, scenarios of human-caused outbreaks of these diseases were thought to exist only in Hollywood movies. Today, Americans face a real threat that someone will use plant or animal food supplies, or drinking water sources, to cause harm.[76]

Food can be the primary agent of bioterrorism by being contaminated with a biologic or chemical toxin. In fact, the Centers for Disease Control and Prevention

(CDC) lists several foodborne pathogens, such as botulism, *Salmonella, E. coli*, and *Shigella*, as potential bioterrorism agents.[77] Several years ago, London police arrested a group of people involved in a plot to add poison to the food served at a British military base, and in Jerusalem, people were arrested for planning to poison customers at a local restaurant.[78]

To combat these threats, government agencies have made bioterrorism a national priority. Under the direction of the Department of Homeland Security, numerous local, state, and federal agencies, such as the Federal Emergency Management Agency (FEMA), FDA, and USDA, work together at each stage of the food continuum—from the farm to the table—to protect your food.

As a consumer, you need to be aware of strategies to employ if you should come in contact with suspicious-looking food items. Although *food tampering* is rare in the United States, a watchful consumer can spot it and avoid it. You can use the Table Tips to identify tampered food items and to learn how to report suspicious items.

The Take-Home Message **Food and water can be primary agents of bioterrorism by being contaminated with a biologic or chemical toxin. If you come in contact with a tampered food, you should report the suspicious items to the store manager or other authority.**

TABLE TIPS 

Avoid Potentially Tampered Foods

Don't purchase a food product if the outer seal is broken, if the package is torn or damaged, or if the safety button on the jar lid is up.

Purchase your foods before the "Sell By" dates.

Don't buy canned items that are bulging or leaking.

Don't buy frozen items if they look as if they have been thawed and refrozen.

Report any suspicious store items to the store manager.

(Data from: FDA. 2003. Food Tampering. www.cfsan.fda.gov/~dms/fstamper.html.)

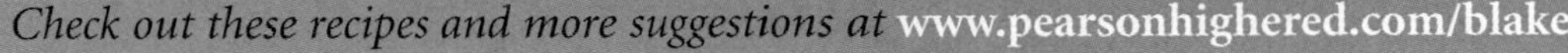

Check out these recipes and more suggestions at **www.pearsonhighered.com/blake**

UCook

Marvelous Microwave Meatballs

With these easy meatballs, your microwave does all the work! Use a cooking thermometer to make sure the internal temperature of each meatball reaches 165°F and they're ready to eat!

UDo

Real Food Safety Decisions

Now that you've read about how to minimize your risk for foodborne illness, put your new knowledge to the test. Go to our website and click on the link to test your food safety savvy in five real-world scenarios.

The Top Five Points to Remember

1. Pathogens (viruses, bacteria, and parasites) are the primary causes of foodborne illness. Older adults, young children, pregnant women, and those with a compromised immune system are at a higher risk for foodborne illness.
2. Animal foods, such as raw and undercooked meat, poultry, seafood, eggs, and unpasteurized milk and cheese, are the most common havens for bacterial growth. Proper food handling techniques during four critical steps—cleaning, combating cross-contamination, cooking, and chilling—can help reduce your risk for foodborne illness. Numerous U.S. government agencies work together to safeguard America's food supply against foodborne pathogens. Everyone, from the farmer to the consumer, plays an important role in food safety. Food irradiation exposes a food item to a radiant energy source that kills or greatly reduces some pathogens.
3. Food additives are used as preservatives, antioxidants, flavoring, coloring, and leavening agents. They are used to maintain a food's consistency and to add nutrients. The FDA must approve most additives before they can be used in foods, and all additives must be listed on the food label. Some additives are exempted from obtaining FDA approval by having attained GRAS or prior-sanctioned status based on their long history of being safely consumed.
4. In addition to pathogens, toxins and other chemical agents, such as marine toxins, polychlorinated

biphenyls, and mercury, can cause foodborne illness. The antibiotics and pesticides farmers use to boost food production can also be found in foods. Washing all fresh fruits and vegetables, peeling fruits and vegetables, and discarding the outer leaves of leafy vegetables can help reduce the amount of pesticides left on your foods. Although organic foods are grown without the use of some synthetic pesticides, synthetic fertilizers, bioengineering, and irradiation, approved synthetic pesticides may be used. All foods advertised as "organic" must meet specific standards and be certified by a USDA-accredited inspector.

5. Biotechnology is the application of biologic techniques to alter the genetic makeup of living cells in order to create a desired trait in an organism. Plant breeding has evolved over the years to create disease-resistant crops and increase the yield of crops. Genetic engineering is a more precise technique in which a specific gene or genes are inserted into the DNA of another cell to create a genetically modified product. Genetic engineering improves crop yields, reduces the need for pesticides, and may have other benefits. Concerns about GE include that it may harm plants, animals, or humans. To protect the consumer, genetically engineered foods are heavily regulated in the United States.

Test Yourself

1. Which of the following is *not* a potential cause of foodborne illness?
   a. parasites
   b. viruses
   c. toxins
   d. food additives
2. Which group is at greatest risk of contracting a foodborne illness?
   a. a 70-year-old grandmother, a 2-year-old toddler, and a teenage boy
   b. a 35-year-old basketball coach, a 70-year-old grandmother, and a 45-year-old professor
   c. a 70-year-old grandmother, a 2-year-old toddler, and a middle-aged woman who has diabetes
   d. a 45-year-old professor, a middle-aged woman who has diabetes, and a teenage boy
3. The danger zone is the temperature at which bacteria multiply most rapidly. The temperature range of the danger zone is
   a. 40°F to 140°F.
   b. 45°F to 140°F.
   c. 40°F to 145°F.
   d. 50°F to 150°F.
4. There are four critical steps in the food handling process that you need to take to prevent foodborne illness. These four steps are
   a. cutting, cleaning, chopping, and chilling.
   b. cleaning, combating cross-contamination, cutting, and chilling.
   c. clearing, combating cross-contamination, cutting, and chilling.
   d. cleaning, combating cross-contamination, cooking, and chilling.
5. You are in the supermarket, shopping for cereal, and find a package of raisin bran that has the USDA Organic Seal on its label. You can be assured that this cereal is made with
   a. at least 95 percent organic ingredients.
   b. 70 percent organic ingredients.
   c. 60 percent organic ingredients.
   d. 50 percent organic ingredients.

Answers

1. (d) Parasites, viruses, toxins, and naturally occurring toxins and chemicals can cause foodborne illness. Food additives do not. In fact, they are either approved by the FDA prior to their use or have GRAS or prior-sanctioned status based on a history of safe consumption.
2. (c) Older adults, young children, and individuals with a compromised immune system, such as those with diabetes, are at a higher risk of contracting foodborne illness. A healthy teenager and a professor (even a tired one around exam time) aren't at an increased risk.
3. (a) The danger zone is 40°F to 140°F.
4. (d) To prevent foodborne illness, it's important to employ proper food handling strategies when cleaning, combating cross-contamination, cooking, and chilling the foods in your meal.
5. (a) Only foods made with at least 95 percent organic ingredients can display the USDA Organic Seal. If a product is made with at least 70 percent organic ingredients, an organic statement can be made, but the seal cannot be displayed.

Web Resources

- For food safety education, visit: www.fightbac.org/main.cfm
- For foodborne illness fact sheets, visit: www.fsis.usda.gov/fact_sheets/Foodborne_Illness_&_Disease_Fact_Sheets/index.asp
- For more information on organic foods, visit: www.ams.usda.gov/nop/indexIE.htm
- For information on biotechnology, visit: www.cfsan.fda.gov/~lrd/biotechm.html
- For advance information on travel to other countries where sanitation may be an issue, visit the CDC'S National Center for Infectious Diseases Travelers' Health Destination website at: www.cdc.gov/travel/destinat.htm

28 Food Insecurity

1. **Food insecurity** is not an issue in the United States. **T/F**

2. The world produces **enough food** to feed everyone. **T/F**

3. "Hidden hunger" is energy deprivation among people who look **well nourished.** **T/F**

4. Over 1 billion people worldwide **lack access** to safe drinking water. **T/F**

5. There is nothing you can do to help **eradicate** hunger. **T/F**

Anna is in her early 30s, single, and has a 4-year-old son named Greg. She is going back to school to become a nurse and attends classes at her local community college part-time. To support herself and her son, she works part-time at a local restaurant every evening. The restaurant allows Anna to eat one daily meal there at a reasonable cost.

With her limited income and time constraints, Anna frequently finds herself unable to buy enough food, or prepare nutritious meals, for her and her son. Even with the affordable daily meal she's provided with at work, food costs still greatly exceed her limited income.

Greg is at day care during the day and spends his evenings with his grandmother. His noon meal at the day-care center is well balanced and nutritious, but his evening "meal" usually consists of snacks, sodas, and sweets, which his grandmother also eats. Greg usually doesn't eat anything nourishing while he is at his grandmother's house but Anna doesn't want to complain about her mother's food habits. She is thankful for the free child care, but worries about the poor nutrition he's getting while away from her.

Do you think Anna is compromising her and her son's nutritional health? What suggestions would you make to help improve her situation? In this concept, we'll explore the conditions of hunger and malnutrition, their causes and effects, and the steps you can take to help the hungry in your own community, as well as around the world.

Answers

1. False. Despite living in a wealthy nation, many people in the United States grapple with food insecurity. See page 2 to find out why.
2. True. The world's agricultural producers grow enough food to meet the world's needs. The challenge is in distributing food products evenly. Learn more on page 6.
3. False. The term refers to a micronutrient deficiency (such as vitamin A or iron) that occurs in about one-third of the world's population. See page 10 for more.
4. True. Lack of access to clean water contributes to most diseases linked to diarrhea, a leading cause of death in children. Turn to page 13 for more details.
5. False. You can help the hungry in your own area by volunteering your time or making a donation to your local food bank. Learn more on page 14.

What Is Food Insecurity and Why Does It Exist?

The U.S. Department of Agriculture (USDA) describes an American household as *food secure* if it has access at all times to enough food for an active, healthy life for all household members.[1] In contrast, **food insecurity** is a situation in which members of a household are uncertain whether they will have the resources they need to get adequate amounts of nutritious food. Thus, people who experience food insecurity may be at risk for **undernutrition,** a form of malnutrition caused by insufficient energy (calories and nutrients) in the diet. Because the United States is the wealthiest country in the world, it seems unlikely that some of its citizens would be unable to visit a local grocery store and buy an adequate supply of healthy foods. However, food insecurity in the United States is a major problem: In 2007, 11.1 percent of American households—representing 36.2 million people—were food insecure at least sometime during the year.[2] Figure 28.1 is a map of food insecurity in the United States.

Also in 2007, about one-third of these food insecure households (4.1 percent of all U.S. households) experienced *very low food security*, meaning that the food intake of one or more adults was reduced and their eating patterns were disrupted at times during the year.[3] People who have very low food security are at significant risk for hunger, a physical need for food. Prolonged hunger can lead to starvation, a state in which the body breaks down its own tissues for fuel. As shown in Figure 28.2, you can think of these states—from food security to starvation and death—as occurring along a continuum.

Although the percentage of Americans who experience food insecurity might surprise you, it is much lower than in many countries of the world. That's because the United States is a developed country with a high rate of industrial capacity, technological sophistication, and economic productivity. In contrast, in developing and underdeveloped countries where there are low levels of economic productivity, the rates of food insecurity and very low food security are higher. Worldwide, the Food and Agriculture Organization of the United Nations (FAO) estimates that, in 2007,

food insecurity Circumstances in which people have uncertain access to enough food to meet their nutritional needs due to lack of financial or other resources.

undernutrition A state of malnutrition in which a person's nutrient and/or calorie needs aren't met through the diet.

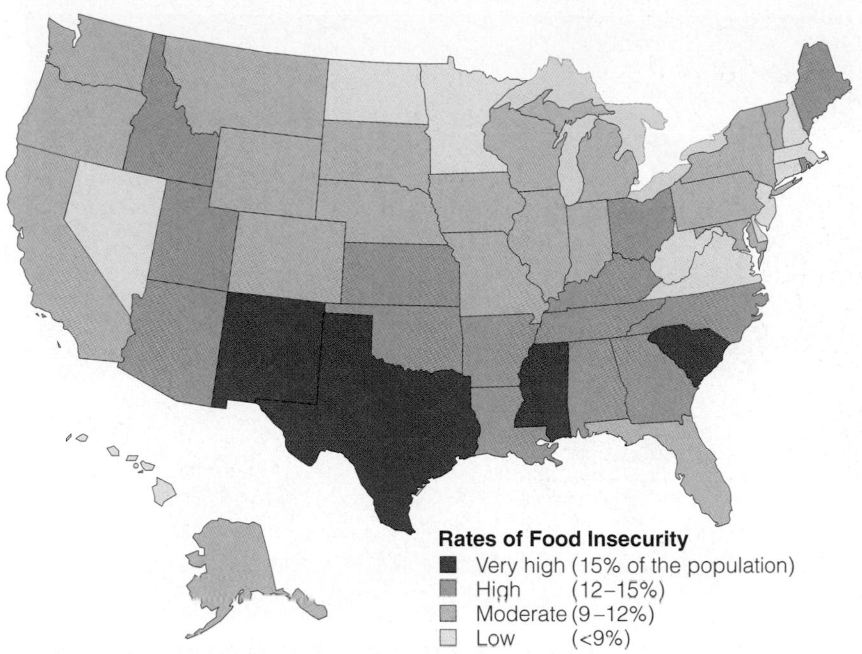

Figure 28.1 Food Insecurity in the United States
Although some regions of the United States have higher rates of food insecurity, the conditions that produce it can happen anywhere.

Data from: Household Food Security in the United States. 2005. www.ers.usda.gov/Publications/err29.

923 million people were hungry.[4] This number represents about one-seventh of the world's population. In underdeveloped countries, such as those in central Africa, more than 50 percent of the population is undernourished.[5] Figure 28.3 identifies developed, developing, and underdeveloped countries around the world.

In developed countries, food insecurity typically results from factors affecting individuals, such as poverty or poor health. In developing and underdeveloped countries, regional problems, such as discrimination, armed conflict, natural disasters, and population overgrowth, can be as significant as individual hardships. Let's take a closer look at these factors, beginning with those contributing to food insecurity in the United States.

In the United States, Food Insecurity Is Often Caused by Poverty

Poverty levels in the United States are defined according to strict guidelines. A family of four is considered impoverished if its annual income is at or below $22,050. In 2007, about 12.5 percent of the U.S. population lived at or below the poverty level, including 13.3 million children.[6]

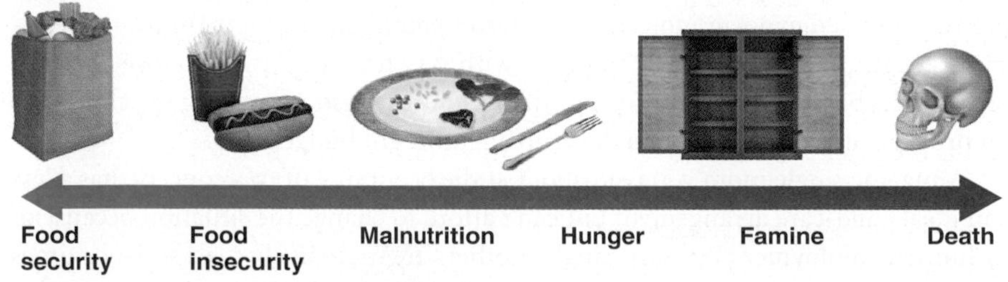

Figure 28.2 Continuum of Food Insecurity
Food insecurity and hunger are points along a continuum between food security and death from starvation.

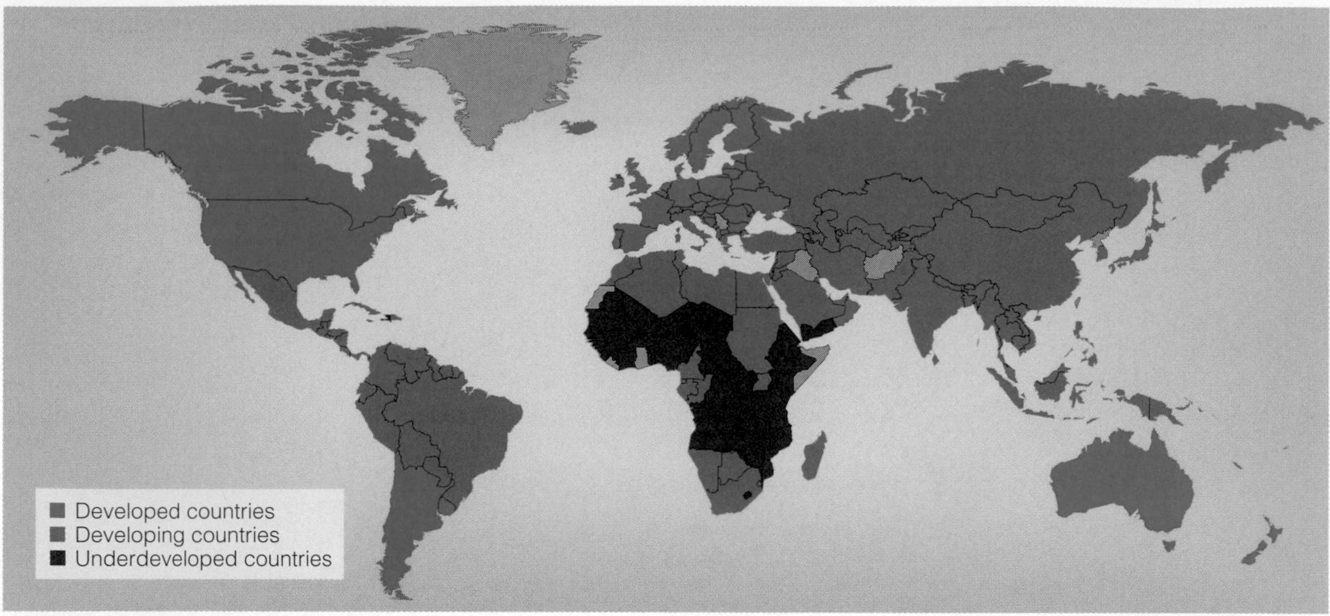

Examples of developed countries	Examples of developing countries	Examples of underdeveloped countries
United States	China	Ethiopia
Canada	India	Sudan
Japan	Mexico	Angola
Australia	Brazil	Haiti
New Zealand	Mongolia	Sierra Leone
Most Western European nations	Saudi Arabia	Yemen

Figure 28.3 Developed, Developing, and Underdeveloped Countries around the World
Hunger is a global problem. In developed countries, such as the United States, Canada, and the countries of Western Europe, many people experience hunger because of personal factors, such as economic hardship, unemployment, and disability. In underdeveloped countries, such as many in central Africa, war, civil conflict, and natural disasters can lead to chronic hunger.

Data from: United Nations Development Programme, *United Nations Human Development Report* (New York: Palgrave Macmillan, 2006).

In the United States, poor single parents and their children can experience food insecurity due to unemployment, low wages, or other circumstances that lead to financial hardship.

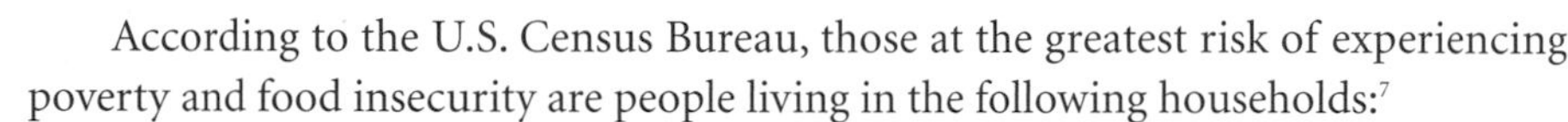

According to the U.S. Census Bureau, those at the greatest risk of experiencing poverty and food insecurity are people living in the following households:[7]

- Households headed by a single woman
- Households with children
- Households with members in a minority group
- Households located in the inner city

These circumstances contribute to poverty because they contribute to disadvantages, such as increased exposure to crime and fewer employment opportunities. For example, single mothers may feel "trapped" with very few options to explore different career paths because of obligations to their children. Also, arranging for child care can prompt additional stress and drain an already tight budget.

Anna, the single mom you read about at the beginning of this concept, has a less than ideal child-care arrangement but can't afford to change the situation because of her limited employment options. Single mothers are more likely to experience times without adequate amounts of food than are families headed by a married couple.[8]

Steady employment does not guarantee that an individual or a family won't experience food insecurity. Even people with an excellent job may experience food insecurity if they are laid off. Additionally, people can be steadily employed in a low-wage full-time job, in a series of seasonal jobs, or in several part-time jobs and

Table 28.1

Comparing Two Shopping Lists

(sample prices from one Boston supermarket)

Meal	Low-Cost Shopping List	Cost	Healthy Shopping List	Cost
Breakfast	Frozen waffles (10)	$1.19	Cereal (10 oz)	$2.69
	Syrup (12 fl oz)	$1.89	Skim milk (1 gal)	$2.79
	Fruit punch (1 gal)	$2.78	Orange juice (1 gal)	$5.32
Snack	Potato chips (1 lb)	$2.46	All-natural popcorn (1 lb)	$5.31
Lunch	Bologna (1 lb)	$2.18	Solid white tuna (1 lb)	$3.44
	White bread (1 lb)	$0.68	Whole-wheat bread (1 lb)	$1.73
Dinner	Pasta sauce with meat (1 lb)	$1.16	Chicken breast (1 lb)	$3.29
	Pasta (1 lb)	$0.79	Broccoli (1 lb)	$1.19
Dessert	Ice cream (½ gal)	$2.39	Strawberries (2 lbs)	$6.98
Total		$15.52		$32.74

Data from: Project Bread: The Link between Hunger and Obesity, 2004. www.projectbread.org/site/DocServer/TheLinkBetweenHungerAndObesity_2004.pdf?docID=104.

still experience food insecurity. In fact, in 2003, about 7.4 million individuals were classified among the **working poor.** In these households, once the monthly expenses are paid, there is often too little money available to feed everyone adequately.

People living in poverty often shop for "volume" rather than "value." Many less nutritious foods cost less than higher-quality foods and therefore are more appealing to those with severe financial constraints. For example, although fruit punch is nutritionally inferior to orange juice, it is about half the price (Table 28.1).

Health Problems Contribute to Food Insecurity among Americans

A variety of health issues can set the stage for food insecurity:

- *Chronic illness.* Adults who are chronically ill are less likely to earn a steady income and therefore are at risk of having a poor diet. Chronic illness in an elderly person can reduce mobility, making it difficult to get to a grocery store or to prepare nourishing meals.
- *Disability.* Many adults who are disabled lead highly productive lives, but others are limited to low-skilled, low-wage jobs. Some cannot work at all and must depend on disability income, which may not provide adequate money for nourishing food. Similar to chronic illness, disability can make it difficult for a person to shop for food and prepare meals.
- *Substance abuse.* Drug and alcohol abuse are common causes of food insecurity, in part because of the challenge these problems create in maintaining steady employment. Many people who abuse substances become unable to keep up their mortgage or rent, and they descend into homelessness. In fact, an estimated 85 percent of all homeless men and women in urban areas abuse substances and/or have a mental illness.
- *Mental illness.* Many mentally ill people, often including the homeless, are forced to rely on charity, church meals, or public assistance programs for most of their food. Even people with homes and jobs who suffer from mental illness can lose interest in eating or have decreased ability to prepare meals. For example, clinical

working poor The term used for people or families who are steadily employed but still experience poverty due to low wages or high dependent expenses.

Thanks to agricultural advances, the world's farmers can grow plenty of food. However, distribution problems and other factors keep some people from getting enough to stave off hunger.

depression among mothers, particularly those in low-income families, has been associated with food insecurity in households.[9]

Now that you've learned about the factors contributing to food insecurity in the United States, you may be wondering if you're at risk. If so, Rate Yourself to find out.

Global Hunger Is Often Caused by Regional Issues

Worldwide, food insecurity persists despite the fact that global food production exceeds the needs of the world's population. This sobering reality tells us that agricultural production is not the problem, and increasing it is not the sole solution. What are the real culprits in global hunger?

Discrimination

Various forms of discrimination, including racial, gender, and ethnic discrimination, contribute to reduced employment, lower educational achievement, and fewer business opportunities in some cultures.[10] Vulnerable groups include women, the elderly, people with disabilities, refugees, orphans, migrant workers, and people who are illiterate.

> Enough food is available to provide at least 4.3 pounds of food per person per day **worldwide.**

In many countries, such as Sudan, Afghanistan, Angola, and Ethiopia, discrimination exists at both the national and local levels. For example, at the national level, control over land and other assets is often unequal. At the local or household level, access to food is influenced by factors such as gender, control over income, education, birth order, and age.[11] Much of the inequity is due to educational inequalities between boys and girls. Two-thirds of the almost 900

RATE YOURSELF ★★★★★

Are You at Risk for Hunger?

Take this quiz to find out if you are at risk for hunger.
In the past 12 months:

1. Have you run out of money to buy food? **Yes** ☐ **No** ☐
2. Have you eaten less than you felt you should because there was not enough money to buy food or enough food to eat? **Yes** ☐ **No** ☐
3. Have you completely depleted your food supply because there was not enough money to buy replacement groceries? **Yes** ☐ **No** ☐
4. Have you gone to bed hungry because there was not enough food to eat? **Yes** ☐ **No** ☐
5. Have you skipped meals because there was not enough money to buy food? **Yes** ☐ **No** ☐
6. Have you relied on a limited number of foods to feed yourself because you were running out of money to buy food? **Yes** ☐ **No** ☐

Answers

If you had no "yes" replies, you are considered "food secure." If you had one to three "yes" replies, you are at risk for hunger. If you had four or more "yes" replies, you are classified as "hungry."

Data adapted from: The Community Childhood Hunger Identification Project Survey, July 1995; R. E. Kleinman et al., "Hunger in Children in the United States: Potential Behavioral and Emotional Correlates," *Pediatrics* 101 (1998): 3–10.

million illiterate adults in the world are women. Thus, it's not surprising that, worldwide, 70 percent of the 1.2 billion people who live in extreme poverty are female.[12]

Political Sanctions and Armed Conflicts

Political sanctions, such as boycotts and trade embargoes, may be used by one government or country to force political change on another. Sometimes the goal of sanctions is to postpone or replace possible military actions. Other goals include restoring democracy, condemning the abuse of human rights, and punishing groups that protect terrorists or international criminals. Although the goals of the sanctions may be noble, the outcomes—such as shortages in food, fuel, or medicine—often harm innocent people, affecting "the poor, not the powerful."[13]

Agricultural embargoes create food shortages by decreasing access to agricultural supplies, fuel, or crops. As with sanctions, embargoes are more likely to hurt the average citizen than affect government authorities.[14]

War, armed conflict, and civil unrest cause hunger because of the disruption to agriculture, food distribution, and normal community activities. During wars and regional conflicts, government money is often diverted from nutrition programs and food distribution efforts and redirected toward weapons and military support. Conflicts have caused increases in hunger and overwhelmed the humanitarian safety network. Political turbulence can compromise food distribution programs.[15]

Many hunger relief programs work to provide food aid to needy nations. However, successfully delivering the food to those who need it is often challenging.

Crop Failure, Natural Disasters, and Wasteful Agricultural Practices

Natural disasters, such as drought, floods, crop diseases, and insects, can occur in any country, on any continent. However, the impact of natural disasters is much greater on underdeveloped countries than on developed countries. There are several reasons for this, including the population's inability to relocate away from disaster-prone areas and their inability to make their homes and farms less vulnerable to destructive weather forces. Additionally, the local economy and infrastructure tend to be unstable in underdeveloped areas, so a natural disaster can quickly become devastating.[16]

Drought is the leading cause of food shortages in developing and underdeveloped countries.

Drought is the leading cause of severe food shortages in developing and underdeveloped countries. Because of water's essential role in growing crops, water and food security are closely linked. Lack of water is a major cause of **famine** and undernutrition. However, floods can also destroy food crops, and are major causes of food shortages.

Approximately 33 percent of the world's food supply is destroyed each year by insects.[17] A good example of how destructive insects can be was the locust infestation of 2004, in which locusts devastated pastures and crops in the northern regions of Africa.

Wasteful agricultural practices also threaten limited resources. The depletion of natural resources through practices such as improper land plowing, overgrazing of livestock, aggressive timber harvesting, and the misuse of fertilizers, pesticides, and water may increase yield in the short term but inhibit production in the long term.[18]

World-wide, roughly eighty percent of the people who suffer from **chronic hunger** make their living from the land in one way or another; of these, about half are farmers.

Lack of irrigation also contributes to crop failures and low yields. The proper use of irrigation can increase crop yield by 100 to 400 percent. Surprisingly, only 17 percent of the world's land is irrigated, yet this small amount disproportionately produces 40 percent of the world's food.[19]

Population Overgrowth

The human population is growing by more than 80 million people per year, and the projected world population for 2020 is 7.7 billion people.[20] By 2050, the United Nations estimates, the world population will reach 8 to 12 billion people. Most of this growth is

famine A severe shortage of food caused by crop destruction due to weather, pestilence, war, or civil unrest within a region.

occurring in developing and underdeveloped countries. Whenever rapid population growth occurs in areas that are strained for food production, the resulting overpopulation can take a toll on the local people's nutritional status.

The Take-Home Message **The causes of food insecurity in the United States include individual hardships, such as poverty and health problems. Food insecurity is particularly prevalent in households headed by a single mother, households with children, minority households, and households in inner cities. The causes of hunger in other parts of the world also include poverty, as well as discrimination, political sanctions and conflicts, crop failures, natural disasters, wasteful agricultural practices, and overpopulation.**

Who Is at Increased Risk for Undernutrition?

The following populations are at increased risk for undernutrition:

- *Pregnant and lactating women.* Pregnant women need extra calories and nutrients—in particular, protein, vitamins, and minerals—to support their own health and their growing baby. Many inadequately nourished pregnant women give birth to undernourished infants. Lactating women need even more calories than pregnant women if they are to maintain their weight and produce an adequate, nourishing milk supply. The global recommendation is for women to nurse their babies for the first six months and to continue nursing with supplemental foods into the second year of life.[21]
- *Infants.* Infants are vulnerable to undernutrition because they are growing rapidly, have high nutrient requirements (per unit of body weight), and may be breast-fed by mothers who are undernourished themselves. Because they are dependent on their caregivers to give them adequate breast milk, formula, or foods, they are particularly vulnerable to neglect. From 6 to 12 months of age, as an infant transitions from breast milk to a diet of breast milk plus solid foods, inadequate feeding can lead to diminished growth and the potential for severe undernutrition during the second year of life.[22]

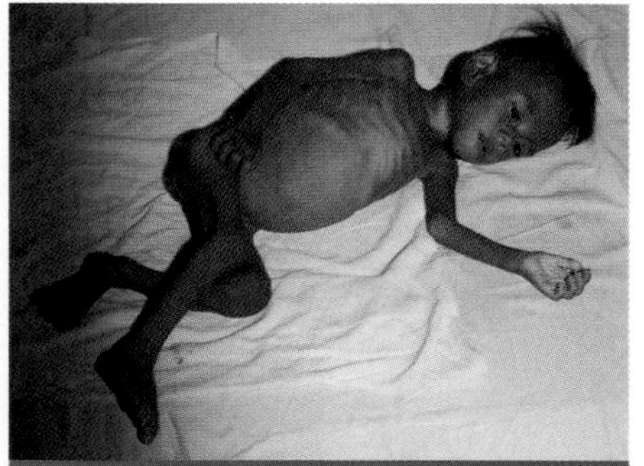

Infants and children are highly vulnerable to the effects of undernutrition.

- *Children.* The risk for undernutrition continues into childhood if the family experiences food shortages or chronic disease. For example, AIDS can result in the death, and loss of income, of one or both parents. An estimated 13 million children worldwide have become orphaned by AIDS.[23]
- *The critically ill.* Liver and kidney disease can impair the body's ability to process and use some nutrients. Some cancer patients, and most people with AIDS, experience loss of appetite, which further complicates their treatment and their ability to eat.[24]
- *Older adults.* Older adults are at increased risk for undernutrition because of a decreased sense of taste and smell, dental problems, immobility, malabsorption, or chronic illnesses.[25] In addition, loneliness, isolation, confusion, or depression can diminish appetite or cause a person to lose interest in cooking and eating.

Now let's take a look at the effects an inadequate diet can have on the body.

What Are the Effects of Chronic Undernutrition?

Once people move along the continuum from food insecurity to malnutrition and hunger, it can be extremely difficult to get ahead again. That's because lack of food can lead to physical problems that interfere with a person's ability to earn an adequate income, a situation that leads to continued poverty and lack of adequate food (Figure 28.4).

In general, whenever the body experiences a fasting state, it attempts to conserve energy and preserve body tissues. Over an extended period of time, however, the body breaks down its own tissue as a source of energy. This results in the deterioration of internal organs and muscle mass and the reduction of stored fat. In prolonged starvation, adults can lose up to 50 percent of their body weight. The greatest amount of deterioration occurs in the intestinal tract and the liver. The loss is moderate in the heart and kidneys, and the least damage occurs in the brain and nervous system.[26]

Now let's look at some of the specific effects of undernutrition.

Lack of food
Fatigue, apathy, no ambition
Weight loss
Compromised health and disease
Anemia
Decreased growth
Malabsorption in GI tract
Loss of muscle mass

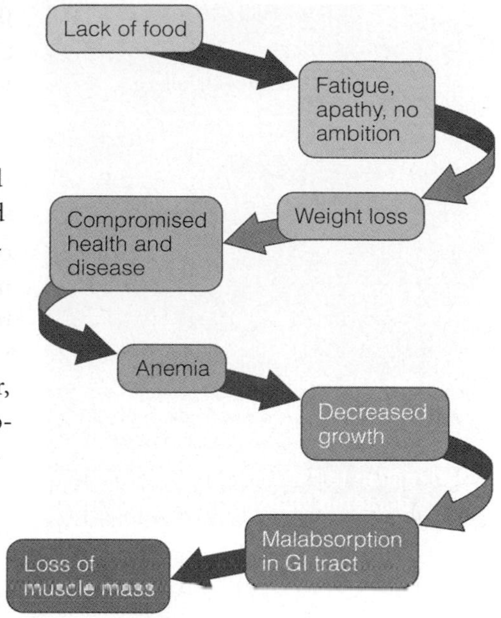

Figure 28.4 Downward Spiral of Hunger
Lack of food can lead to numerous other symptoms that compound the problem of hunger.

Impaired Growth and Development

When children do not receive the nutrients they need to grow and to develop properly, they are likely to experience both physical and mental problems, including physical *wasting* (low weight for one's height), improper muscle development, *growth stunting* (low height for one's age), and impaired brain development (Figure 28.5).[27] Children are also more likely to show behavioral, emotional, and academic problems if they come from families that experience hunger and food insecurity, rather than

Figure 28.5 Effects of Undernutrition
As undernutrition persists, physical symptoms set in and lead to further complications.

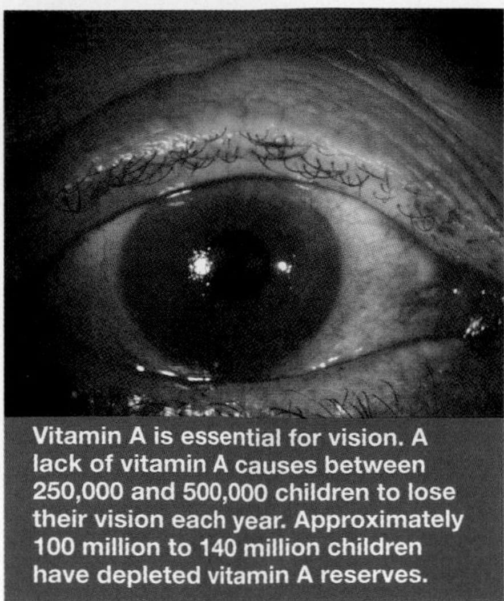

Vitamin A is essential for vision. A lack of vitamin A causes between 250,000 and 500,000 children to lose their vision each year. Approximately 100 million to 140 million children have depleted vitamin A reserves.

families that do not report such experiences.[28] Growth stunting has also been associated with long-term negative effects on fertility and the ability to perform physical work.[29] Globally, an estimated 225 million children experience growth stunting because of deficiencies in protein and other nutrients.[30]

Impaired Immunity and Disease

An undernourished individual has a weakened immune system, which increases his or her vulnerability to various infections. Fever, parasitic disease, pneumonia, measles, and malaria are examples of conditions that occur because of weakened immune systems and chronic undernutrition.

Approximately 12 million children younger than 5 years of age die each year in developing countries from preventable causes, such as diarrhea, measles, and malaria. Malnutrition is linked to more than half of these childhood deaths.[31] For example, diarrhea is a common infectious illness that rarely poses a serious threat to well-nourished children. But because undernourished children lack adequate immune protection, physical strength, and nutrient reserves, more than 2 million die each year from diarrhea.[32] Table 28.2 identifies other illnesses that can be fatal in undernourished children.

Vitamin and mineral deficiencies and their resulting diseases are serious concerns for people living in developing countries and in the United States. For example, more than 2 billion people, or greater than one-third of the world's population, live with a vitamin A, iron, or iodine deficiency. These micronutrient deficiencies are referred to as "hidden hunger." Table 28.3 lists the most common vitamin and mineral deficiencies worldwide.

Increased Rates of Maternal, Infant, and Child Mortality

As mentioned, undernutrition is part of a vicious cycle that passes hunger from one generation to the next. Unfortunately, many young women experience undernutrition during their own infancy and childhood. Girls who were born prematurely, were underweight at birth, or were undernourished during the first five years of their lives may be less able to support a healthy pregnancy when they become

Table 28.2

Common Illnesses in Malnourished Children

Illness	Cause	Effect
Diarrhea	Pathogenic infections	Severe dehydration
Acute respiratory infection	Virus or bacterium	Pneumonia, bronchitis, colds, fast breathing, coughing, fever
Malaria	Parasite (transmitted by mosquito)	Flu, weakness, sweating, shivering, shaking, nausea, liver failure, infected red blood cells, kidney failure or bleeding in the kidneys
Measles	Respiratory illness caused by a highly contagious virus, from airborne droplets (coughing/sneezing)	Pneumonia, brain inflammation, infection, diarrhea, seizures

Table 28.3

Most Common Micronutrient Deficiencies Worldwide

Vitamin or Mineral	Effects	Incidence
Vitamin A	Eye disease, blindness	Vitamin A deficiency is the leading cause of preventable blindness in children in developing countries.
Iron	Iron-deficiency anemia	Iron deficiency is extremely common worldwide. Anemia is most common among 7- to 12-month-old infants; toddlers and young children (less than 8 years of age); women of reproductive age; and anyone who has lost large amounts of blood.
Iodine	Goiter, cretinism	Up to 790 million people (13% of the world's population) have some form of iodine deficiency, goiter, or mental impairment caused by lack of iodine.
B vitamins (folic acid, B_{12})	Folic acid: macrocytic anemia	Folic acid deficiency is common among women of reproductive age; people with limited diets and reduced vegetable consumption; people who abuse alcohol; and obese individuals.
Vitamin B_{12}	Pernicious anemia	B_{12} deficiency is common among elderly men and women (over 50 years of age); African-American adults; individuals who have malabsorption syndromes; and people who practice extreme vegetarianism.

Data from: World Health Organization. 1991. Micronutrient Deficiencies. www.who.int/nutrition/topics/micronutrients/en/index.html.

adults. Undernourished women are also more likely to die during the postpartum period, often because of infection or blood loss.[33] Infants born to undernourished women are more likely to be undernourished themselves, to experience chronic illness, and to have an increased risk for premature death. Finally, the World Health Organization estimates that 60 percent of all childhood deaths in developing countries are associated with chronic hunger and malnutrition.[34]

The Take-Home Message **Pregnant and lactating women, infants and children, and the ill and elderly are at increased risk for undernutrition. In a fasting state, the body will try to conserve nutrients and preserve its own organs, but eventually irreversible organ damage will occur. The physical effects of undernutrition include physical wasting; growth stunting; impaired mental development; behavioral, emotional, and academic problems; increased risk for infection; micronutrient deficiency diseases; and increased maternal, infant, and child mortality.**

How Can We Reduce Food Insecurity?

Throughout the United States, faith-based organizations, corporations, and community relief agencies assist people who have insufficient resources. From free food and meals to education and job training, there are numerous ways such organizations help alleviate food insecurity. At the federal level, the USDA provides food aid through a variety of programs. (See the box feature "Food Assistance Programs in the United States.")

Everyone—from children to adults—can help eradicate hunger.

Food Assistance Programs in the United States

In 2003, the USDA spent over $41.5 billion on numerous food assistance programs to feed Americans in need. Some of the main programs are reviewed below.

- The federally subsidized Supplemental Nutrition Assistance Program (SNAP), formerly called the Food Stamp Program, services more than 26 million people.[1] Individuals who are eligible for food stamps can use coupons to purchase specified foods, such as fruit, vegetables, cereals, meats, and dairy products, at their local authorized supermarket. (Items such as alcohol, tobacco products, and household items are not covered.) When added to the monthly household income of a needy family, food stamps can help reduce child poverty by an estimated 20 percent or more.[2]
- The Women, Infants, and Children (WIC) Nutrition Program provides nutritious food to at-risk women and children to supplement their diets. The program also emphasizes nutrition education and offers referrals to health care professionals.
- Under the National School Lunch Program, over 16 million schoolchildren receive free or reduced-price lunches each year. A subsidized breakfast is sometimes also available at schools.
- The Summer Food Service Program is a federal program that combines a meal or feeding program with a summer activity program for children. It is available to communities based on income criteria.
- The Child and Adult Care Food Program provides nutritious meals to low-income children and senior adults who receive day care or adult care outside the home. There are income guidelines and specific menu requirements for program participation.
- Congregate meals for the elderly and Meals On Wheels are two programs that provide meals at a community site or delivered to the home.

Thanks to the National School Lunch Program, over 16 million American schoolchildren receive free or reduced-price lunches each year.

- Additional programs are available for low-income American Indians or for individuals living on a reservation or members of a federally recognized tribe. Some communities also have special feeding or church programs for new immigrants, guest workers, or children of immigrants. College towns often sponsor special programs for international students and their families.

Biotechnology, Better Land Management, and Proper Sanitation

In addition to the human (person-to-person) help provided by people and organizations, technology is also playing a role in alleviating malnutrition. The latest developments in biotechnology are already helping reduce hunger in some areas. Some of the most successful new biotechnologies enhance agricultural productivity and improve human nutrition at an affordable cost. For example, genetically engineered crops are providing some of the common nutrients (iron, vitamin A, and iodine) that are in low supply in current crops. And as mentioned in Concept 27, biotechnology is creating crops with increased yields, pest resistance, and a longer shelf life.

Better land management, appropriate crop selection, and biotechnology can all help eliminate hunger.

Proper land management and appropriate crop selection can also help increase agricultural production. For example, productive land is frequently used for nonconsumable crops, such as flowers, for sale to industrialized nations. Raising edible, nutritious plants such as high-protein beans, vegetables, grains, seeds, nuts, or fruit instead of planting export crops like tea, coffee, and cocoa, or raising animal feed for livestock, helps increase food security.[35]

Food security and land access are directly related, even if the land is not irrigated or of the highest quality. Ownership of even a few acres provides incentive for improved land decisions regarding irrigation, crop rotation, land fallowing (plowed, but unplanted, land), and appropriate soil management.[36] Landownership is part of a long-term solution to a very complex problem. However, in the short term, remarkable progress is being made by providing access to land for women and their families for vegetable gardens.

Access to clean drinking water is just as important as adequate nutrition for human health.

Most people think providing food is the primary means of reducing hunger, but safe water is equally important. More than 2.6 billion people (40 percent of the world's population) lack basic sanitation facilities, and over 1 billion people drink unsafe water.[37] The consequences of unsanitary conditions are enormous. The World Health Organization estimates that 88 percent of all diarrheal illnesses in the world are attributable to inadequate water or sanitation.[38] Entire communities are often at risk for health problems from drinking contaminated water.

Some innovative solutions are being proposed to alleviate the world's water problems. For example, in some African villages, solar energy is used to thermally purify the water supply. Water is poured into plastic jugs, then the jugs are placed on black-covered roofs and allowed to heat for several hours. If the temperature of the water exceeds 50°C (122°F), it becomes safe to drink. The heat from solar radiation effectively destroys common waterborne bacteria which can cause disease such as cholera, typhoid, and dysentery.[39] This technology is available, inexpensive, and accessible in many countries with a warm climate. Other water sanitation solutions include chlorination of water, irrigation technology, river diversion projects, piped water systems, and community wells.

Fortification of Foods Can Ensure Adequate Intake of Some Nutrients

Food fortification can help alleviate micronutrient deficiencies. Because they are the most commonly deficient, iodine, iron, and vitamin A are the three nutrients most often added to foods. For fortification to work, the foods chosen to carry these extra nutrients must be a staple in the community's food supply (and therefore eaten often) and consistently available. The food should also be shelf-stable and affordable. Rice, cereals, flours, salt, and even sugar are examples of foods that can be fortified.

Because food fortification is inexpensive, yet enormously beneficial, fortification programs are being developed and implemented worldwide. Countries such as China, Vietnam, South Africa, and Morocco are fortifying foods—for instance, salt, flour, oil, sugar, and soy sauce—with iron, iodine, and vitamin A.[40]

Education Is Key

Education plays an important role in ensuring food security (Figure 28.6). Educated people are more likely to have increased economic and career opportunities, and they are less likely to fall into the trap of poverty. Literacy and education also build self-esteem and self-confidence, two qualities that help people overcome life's challenges. Agricultural education can lead to increased agricultural production. This not only increases the food supply but also helps create jobs and lifts people out of poverty.[41]

Education also reduces poverty in other ways. For example, one study found that societies with a more educated population enjoyed the following:[42]

- Higher earning potential
- Improved sanitation
- More small businesses/rural enterprises
- Lower rates of infant mortality and improved child welfare
- Higher likelihood of technological advancement

Food security
Land management
Biotechnology
Fortification of foods
Water sanitation
Education

Figure 28.6 Factors Contributing to Food Security

You Can Help

When it comes to fighting food insecurity in America, everyone's efforts are welcome, including yours. You can help your needy neighbors in three ways: give funds, give food, and/or give time. For example, you can donate funds in person to a local food bank or online to a national organization, such as Feeding America (formerly called American's Second Harvest), the largest hunger relief organization in the United States (www.feedingamerica.org). Every dollar donated to Feeding America can provide up to four bags of groceries for an individual in need. You can also donate food by hosting a food drive, then delivering the food to a local food bank. Finally, you can volunteer your time by helping out at a local food pantry, cooking for a soup kitchen, or transporting food to the hungry.

To find out where you can help, visit the Feeding America's website and search for opportunities in your area using the Volunteer Match service.

The Take-Home Message **Local charities, faith-based organizations, corporate and community groups, and government programs can provide aid to increase food security. Biotechnology and food fortification are two strategies that can provide healthier, hardier food crops with additional nutrients. Education of the world's population is also important, along with proper land management and proper crop selection. You can help increase food security in your community by donating funds, food, or time.**

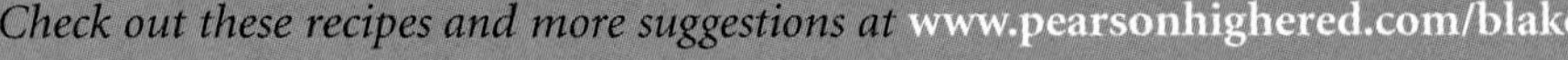

Check out these recipes and more suggestions at www.pearsonhighered.com/blake

UCook

Pasta Bean Toss

If you're on a limited food budget, you can still eat a healthy meal by filling your plate with beans, vegetables, and pasta. This recipe is inexpensive to make and guaranteed to supply leftovers for another meal!

UDo

Helping Others to Stay Food Secure

Would you know what advice to give someone who experiences food insecurity? Consider the scenarios on our website link and put your nutrition knowledge to work!

The Top Five Points to Remember

1. Food insecurity is a situation in which households are uncertain of having access to enough food to meet the needs of all members. Food insecurity can lead to hunger, a physical need for food, and undernutrition, a form of malnutrition caused by inadequate energy in the diet. Despite abundant food production, many people in the United States and around the world suffer from food insecurity, hunger, and undernutrition.
2. The causes of food insecurity in the United States include poverty, chronic disease or disability, substance abuse, and mental illness. Individuals who are employed but still fall below the poverty line are sometimes referred to as the working poor. Globally, discrimination, political sanctions, armed conflicts, crop failures, natural disasters, wasteful agricultural practices, and overpopulation contribute to food insecurity.
3. The populations at increased risk for food insecurity and undernutrition include pregnant and lactating women, infants and children, the ill, and the elderly.
4. The effects of chronic hunger include growth stunting, wasting, impaired immune function, increased risk for infections, micronutrient deficiencies, and increased rates of maternal, infant, and child mortality.

5. Biotechnology and food fortification are helping reduce hunger worldwide by providing larger and more nutrient-dense food crops. Corporate, community, and faith-based organizations combat food insecurity by providing free food and meals and assistance programs to help people overcome poverty and hunger. The federal government's food assistance programs, such as SNAP, WIC, and the National School Lunch Program, in addition to others, provide assistance to Americans who experience food insecurity.

Test Yourself

1. Hunger exists because
   a. there is not enough food produced in the world to feed everyone adequately.
   b. food distribution is uneven, and some people do not have access to enough food.
   c. the world is overpopulated.
   d. all of the above factors are true.
2. What causes famine?
   a. poverty
   b. lack of education and economic opportunity
   c. natural disaster, war, or civil unrest
   d. the use of inappropriate farm machinery
3. Which of the following states has a food insecurity rate above 10 percent of the population?
   a. Maine
   b. South Carolina
   c. Texas
   d. all of the above
4. Which of the following is an example of the use of biotechnology to help alleviate global food insecurity?
   a. production of genetically engineered rice that provides beta-carotene
   b. production of genetically engineered tomatoes that taste sweeter
   c. fortification of salt with iodine
   d. cloned sheep
5. Which nutrients are most likely to be used to fortify food?
   a. vitamins A, D, E, and K
   b. sodium, potassium, and chloride
   c. magnesium, phosphorus, and sulfur
   d. iron, iodine, and vitamin A

Answers

1. (b) Enough food is produced to feed the entire population of the world, but because the distribution of the world's food supply is uneven, people in some parts of the world do not have access to adequate food.
2. (c) Famine is a severe shortage of food caused by crop destruction due to natural disaster, war, or civil unrest. Poverty and lack of education are factors that can lead to individual hunger, but they don't generally cause crop failure.
3. (d) All of these states, and many more, have a food insecurity rate above 10 percent of the population. Although the United States has a higher standard of living and lower rates of hunger than many other countries, many Americans are still poor and lack a dependable supply of adequate, nourishing food.
4. (a) Producing enriched versions of staple foods, such as rice, is a biotechnological technique that can help reduce malnutrition. Biotechnology is also used to improve the taste, look, and hardiness of produce, but this isn't necessarily a nutritional advantage. The fortification of salt with iodine is important for combating iodine deficiency but is not considered a method of biotechnology. Cloning food animals is not a common practice.
5. (d) Iron, iodine, and vitamin A are frequently used to fortify food because deficiencies of them are linked to many common and serious illnesses. Many of the other nutrients listed are important but are not generally part of food fortification programs.

Web Resources

- For more on the state of hunger in the United States and around the world, visit the Bread for the World Institute at: www.bread.org
- To learn more about one organization that is fighting global poverty, visit CARE at: www.care.org
- To find out how the Food and Agriculture Organization of the United Nations leads international efforts to defeat hunger, visit: www.fao.org
- To learn more about an international children's group, visit the UNICEF website at: www.unicef.org
- For more about the World Health Organization, visit: www.who.org
- To learn more about how biotechnology is improving food production in developing countries, visit: www.sustaintech.org

29

1. A father's health has **no impact** on the health of a developing fetus. **T/F**

2. Women who are obese may have more trouble becoming **pregnant** than women who are normal weight or only somewhat overweight. **T/F**

3. Pregnant women shouldn't **exercise.** **T/F**

4. **Breast milk** helps boost a baby's immune system. **T/F**

5. Honey is an appropriate **sweetener** to provide infants. **T/F**

Life Cycle Nutrition

Pregnancy through Infancy

Kathy, a young mother in her mid-20s, is in the middle of a career change. Although she gets satisfaction from her job in nonprofit social work, she's decided that technology would be a better career direction, so she has enrolled in several computer science classes at her local community college. Kathy and her husband had expected to start their family after she finished her undergraduate degree, but they were thrilled when she unexpectedly became pregnant. She delivered a beautiful baby boy during the middle of spring semester.

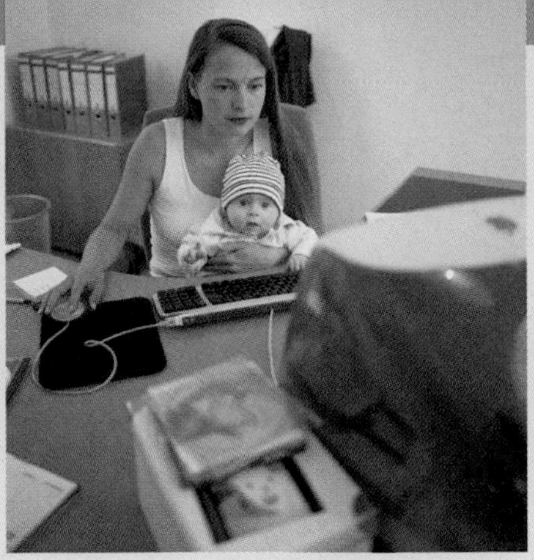

Kathy wants to finish the semester, so that she can get a part-time job in a high-tech company. She also wants to breastfeed her baby, even though she'll be attending morning classes on campus. Her hectic schedule and many demands keep her in constant motion, and she sometimes finds it hard to keep up with everything she needs to do.

How can Kathy ensure that both she and her newborn son both receive adequate nutrition? How might she overcome the challenges of nursing a baby while working to finish a college degree program? What are some of the unique nutritional needs for both her and her baby?

In this concept you'll learn about the nutritional needs of infants, as well as those of parents and parents-to-be.

Answers

1. False. Fathers need to eat healthy diets and avoid certain substances to help produce a healthy baby. See page 2 to find out why this is the case.
2. True. Obese women may have more difficulty conceiving, possibly because of irregular menstrual cycles. See page 3 for details.
3. False. Physical activity can be good for mothers-to-be, although some activities should be avoided. To find out which activities are safe, turn to pages 10 and 11.
4. True. Antibodies in breast milk are passed from the mother to the baby, giving the baby an immunity boost. To learn about the other benefits of breast milk, turn to page 14.
5. False. Honey should never be given to infants because it can carry a bacterium that can cause fetal botulism. However, infants don't need to have their food sweetened with anything, so sugar should also be avoided. See page 22 for more.

What Nutrients and Behaviors Are Important before Attempting Pregnancy?

You're probably aware of at least a few things that women should do during pregnancy to support their baby's health. For instance, you probably know that pregnant women shouldn't smoke or drink alcohol. But it might surprise you to learn that, even before a couple attempts pregnancy, they should both adopt some healthy behaviors, including several by the father-to-be. Let's review these now.

A Man's Diet and Lifestyle Affect the Health of His Sperm

The moment when a sperm fertilizes an egg is called **conception.** In order for conception to occur, the male's sperm has to be plentiful and motile: able to swim against obstacles to reach the waiting egg. Thus, men who hope to father a child should take note: Their lifestyle and dietary habits may affect the number and motility of their sperm. Smoking, alcohol and drug abuse, and obesity have been associated with the decreased production and function of sperm.[1] Stopping smoking, abstaining from alcohol and other drugs or drinking only in moderation, and striving for a healthy body weight are all beneficial behaviors.

The average male produces between 20 and 150 million sperm per milliliter!

An adequate intake of zinc and folate has been associated with the production of healthy sperm. In addition, antioxidants, such as vitamins E and C and carotenoids, may help protect sperm from damage by free radicals.[2] Men should make sure to eat a balanced diet that contains adequate amounts of fruits and vegetables (containing antioxidants and folate), as well as whole grains, lean meats and dairy foods, legumes, and nuts (containing zinc).[3]

conception The moment when a sperm fertilizes an egg.

Women Need to Adopt a Healthy Lifestyle before Conception

A well-balanced diet and healthy lifestyle are important for both men and women prior to conception.

If you have ever run a marathon or know someone who has, you know that a tremendous amount of effort and diligence goes into training for the event. Your commitment doesn't begin on the day of the race, but as far as a year in advance. In fact, the more time and effort the runner puts into preparing for the race, the better the results are likely to be.

Ask any woman who has had a baby and she will tell you that planning, carrying, and delivering a healthy child was the marathon of her life. The commitment to change not-so-healthy behaviors is an extremely important part of prepregnancy preparation.

Let's look at the specific nutritional and lifestyle adjustments a woman needs to make to improve her chances of conceiving a healthy baby.

Attain a Healthy Weight

Women who want to get pregnant should strive for a healthy weight *before* conception. Women who begin pregnancy at a healthy weight are likely to conceive more easily, have an uncomplicated pregnancy, and have an easier time nursing the baby.[4]

In contrast, both women who are obese and women who are underweight may have a harder time getting pregnant, possibly because of irregular menstrual cycles. When they do become pregnant, they are at increased risk for a variety of health problems, some of which can affect their baby.

Get Plenty of Folic Acid

Folic acid is needed to create new cells and help the baby grow and develop properly. To reduce the risk for neural tube birth defects in infants, the mother-to-be should consume adequate amounts of folic acid at least one month prior to conception and during the early weeks of pregnancy. These birth defects occur very early in the pregnancy, typically three to four weeks after conception—a time when few women even know they are pregnant. For this reason, women who are capable of becoming pregnant and are planning to conceive should consume 400 micrograms of folic acid through supplements or fortified foods.

Moderate Fish and Caffeine Consumption

The Food and Drug Administration (FDA) recommends that women of childbearing age who may become pregnant avoid certain fish that may contain high amounts of the toxin *methylmercury*. This form of mercury can harm the nervous system of a developing fetus, especially during the first trimester of pregnancy. All fish contain some methylmercury, and Table 29.1 summarizes the fish consumption guidelines for prepregnant, pregnant, and lactating women.

Caffeine consumption may affect a woman's fertility. Research suggests that consuming 500 milligrams or more of caffeine daily may delay conception.[5] Although the mechanism by which caffeine affects fertility is unknown, to be safe, women who are trying to get pregnant should consume less than 300 milligrams of caffeine per day. This means limiting brewed coffee and energy drinks to no more than three 8-ounce servings a day—or better yet, switching to decaffeinated versions of these drinks. See Table 29.2 for other common sources of caffeine in the diet.

Avoid Cigarettes and Other Toxic Substances

Cigarette smoking increases the risk for infertility, making conception more difficult.[6] If a female smoker is able to conceive, she'll face the difficulty of needing to quit smoking along with the many other challenges of pregnancy. The risks of maternal smoking will be discussed later in this concept.

In addition to other beneficial habit changes, abstaining from alcohol or drinking only moderately can help both men and women conceive.

Table 29.1

Fishing for a Healthy Baby

Women of childbearing age who may become pregnant, as well as pregnant and nursing women, should follow these guidelines for eating fish.

Do Not Eat	Limit	Enjoy
Shark Swordfish King mackerel Tilefish (golden bass or golden snapper)	Albacore (white) tuna to no more than 6 oz weekly Locally caught fish from nearby lakes, rivers, and coastal areas. Check local safety advisories before consuming fish. If no advice is available, eat up to 6 oz weekly. Don't consume any other fish during that week.	Up to 12 oz weekly of fish with low levels of methylmercury, such as canned light tuna, cod, catfish, crab, pollack, salmon, scallops, and shrimp

Table 29.2

A Jolt of Caffeine

Beverage	Caffeine (mg)
Coffee (8 oz)	
Brewed, drip	85
Brewed, decaffeinated	3
Espresso (1 oz)	40
Tea (8 oz)	
Brewed	40
Iced	25
Soft drinks (8 oz)	24
"Energy drinks" (8 oz)	80
Hot cocoa (8 oz)	6
Chocolate milk (8 oz)	5
Milk chocolate (1 oz)	6

Data from: National Toxicology Program, www.cerhr.niehs.nih.gov; International Food Information Council (IFIC). www.ific.org.

Alcohol can affect a baby within weeks of conception, before a woman is aware that she is pregnant. For this reason, the surgeon general has recommended that all women who may become pregnant abstain from alcohol.[7]

Smoking marijuana can reduce fertility in both men and women. Women who use it should speak with their health care provider about how to stop. They can also visit the National Drug and Alcohol Treatment Referral Routing Service at the website listed in the Web Resources section at the end of this concept.

Now that you've learned the health habits that are important to establish before trying to become parents, are you ready for a healthy pregnancy? Rate Yourself and find out!

RATE YOURSELF ★★★★★

Are You Ready for a Healthy Pregnancy?

Both men and women should practice healthy habits before becoming parents. Take the following self-assessment to see if you need some diet and lifestyle fine-tuning before trying to get pregnant.

For Both Men and Women

1. Are you overweight? **Yes** ☐ **No** ☐
2. Do you smoke? **Yes** ☐ **No** ☐
3. Do you abuse alcohol? **Yes** ☐ **No** ☐
4. Do you consume less than 400 micrograms of folic acid daily? **Yes** ☐ **No** ☐
5. Do you use any illicit drugs, such as marijuana, cocaine, or ecstasy? **Yes** ☐ **No** ☐

Additional Questions for Women Only

1. Do you drink alcohol? **Yes** ☐ **No** ☐
2. Do you drink more than 12 ounces of caffeinated coffee or energy drinks or four cans of caffeinated soft drinks daily? **Yes** ☐ **No** ☐
3. Do you eat albacore tuna, swordfish, mackerel, tilefish, and/or shark? **Yes** ☐ **No** ☐

Answers

If you answered "yes" to any of these questions, read on to find out how diet and lifestyle habits can affect a pregnancy.

The Take-Home Message Good nutrition and healthy lifestyle habits are important for both men and women before conception. Smoking, alcohol abuse, and obesity are associated with the decreased production and function of sperm. Conception is easier for women when they are at a healthy weight. Women should consume adequate amounts of folic acid prior to getting pregnant and continue to take it during pregnancy. Women should also avoid consuming fish that may contain high amounts of methylmercury and should consume caffeine only in moderation. They should not smoke, drink alcohol, or take recreational drugs.

What Nutrients and Behaviors Are Important in the First Trimester?

When a woman is pregnant, her diet must not only maintain her own health but also foster the health and growth of her baby. She is truly eating for two. To help you appreciate the increased nutrient needs of pregnancy, let's examine how a pregnancy begins and how the developing child obtains nutrients from the mother.

During the First Trimester, the Fertilized Egg Develops into a Fetus

A full-term pregnancy is approximately 40 weeks long and is divided into **trimesters** (three time periods). The moment of conception marks the beginning of the first trimester. During the first few days of this 13-week period, the fertilized egg travels down the fallopian tube to embed itself in the lining of the woman's uterus (Figure 29.1). Once attached, it immediately begins obtaining nutrients from the mother. This enables the developing **embryo** to obtain nutrients via the *placenta*, an organ of common tissue between the mother and the growing embryo that develops in the mother's uterus (Figure 29.1). The placenta is attached to the fetus via the *umbilical cord.*

After the eighth week of pregnancy, the developing embryo is called a **fetus**. As the fetus develops, the mother's diet and lifestyle habits are critical in supporting and nurturing it.

By the end of the first trimester, the baby's liver is already forming red blood cells, the heart is pumping blood, the limbs are taking shape, and the brain is growing rapidly. With all this activity taking place, the fetus still weighs just ½ ounce and measures about 3 inches long. It has a lot more growing to do before being born.

Morning Sickness and Cravings Are Common

During this period, the mother's body is also changing rapidly. She's beginning to notice some breast tenderness, a newly heightened sense of taste or smell, and perhaps some morning sickness or food cravings.

trimesters The three time periods of pregnancy.

embryo A fertilized egg during the third through the eighth week of pregnancy.

fetus A developing baby in the womb after the eighth week of pregnancy.

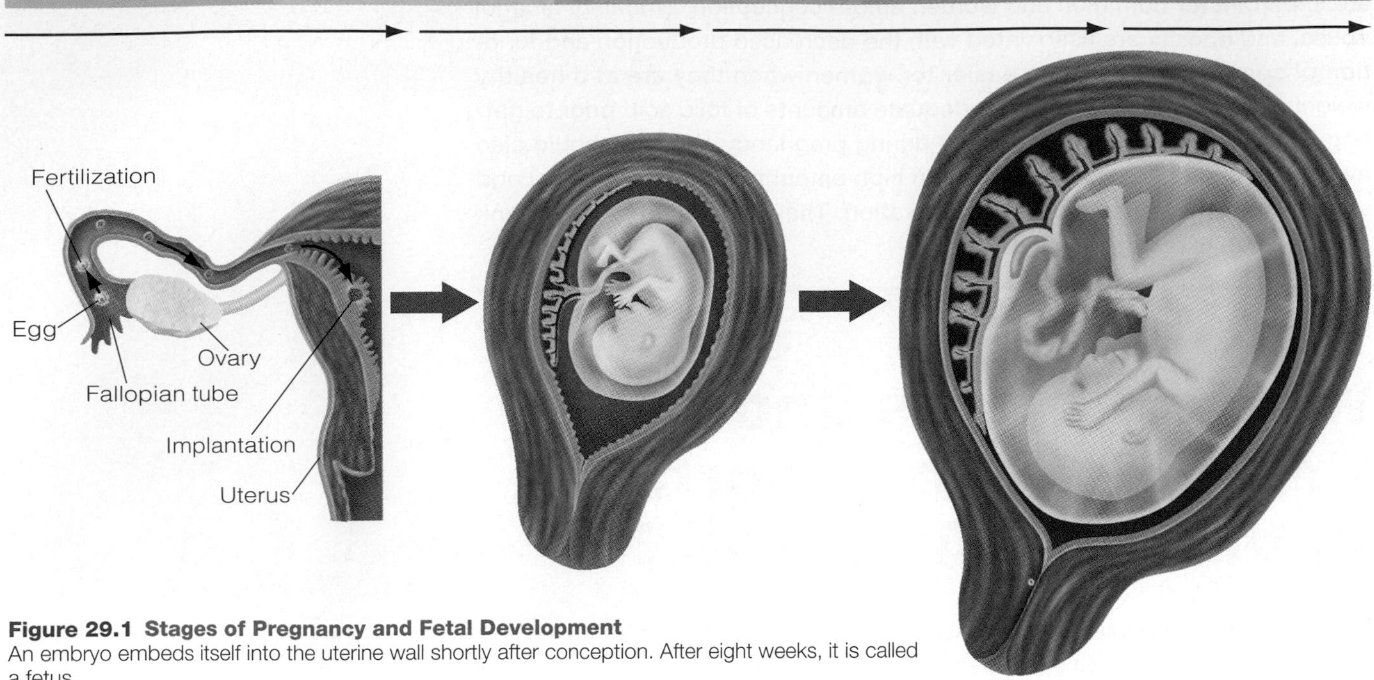

Figure 29.1 Stages of Pregnancy and Fetal Development
An embryo embeds itself into the uterine wall shortly after conception. After eight weeks, it is called a fetus.

One of the biggest myths of pregnancy is that morning sickness happens only in the morning. Ask any of the 80 percent of women who experience nausea and vomiting during pregnancy and many will tell you that they wish their symptoms ended by noon. The causes of morning sickness are unknown, but fluctuating hormone levels may play a role.[8] Although there are no known dietary deficiencies that cause, or diet changes that can prevent, morning sickness, some women find relief in eating small, frequent meals that are high in carbohydrates, such as pasta, rice, and crackers, and avoiding an empty stomach.

While some pregnant women have an aversion to certain foods, such as coffee, tea, or fried or spicy foods, other women can have cravings for specific foods. Chocolate, citrus fruits, pickles, chips, and ice cream are foods that women commonly want when they are pregnant.[9] Sometimes women even crave and consume nonfood substances, such as cornstarch, clay, dirt, or baking soda. This condition, called *pica*, can lead to iron deficiency or the ingestion of toxic substances, such as lead.

Table 29.3

Recommended Weight Gain during Pregnancy

Body Mass Index (BMI)	Recommended Weight Gain (lbs)
<19.8	28–40
19.8 to 26	25–35
>26 to 29	15–25
>29	at least 15

Data from: Institute of Medicine, *Nutrition during Pregnancy, Part 1: Weight Gain* (Washington, D.C.: The National Academies Press; 1990); L. Kaiser and L. Allen, "Position of the American Dietetic Association: Nutrition and Lifestyle for a Healthy Pregnancy Outcome," *Journal of the American Dietetic Association* 102 (2002): 1479–1490.

Adequate Weight Gain Supports the Baby's Growth

Healthy women gain, on average, 27.5 pounds during the entire pregnancy.[10] Coincidentally, this is the approximate amount of weight that is needed to support the growth of the baby (Figure 29.2). Table 29.3 identifies recommendations for weight gain that provide for adequate growth, so that the baby will healthfully weigh about 6.5 to 8.5 pounds, yet do not increase the risk for complications during delivery or cause excess weight gain for the mother.[11] Gaining excess weight will make it more difficult to lose the weight once the baby is born and increases the likelihood of the mother's remaining overweight many years after childbirth.[12]

Because pregnant women typically gain only about 2 pounds in the entire first trimester, they do not yet need an increased intake of calories. However, a pregnant woman does have an increased need for certain nutrients immediately after conception.

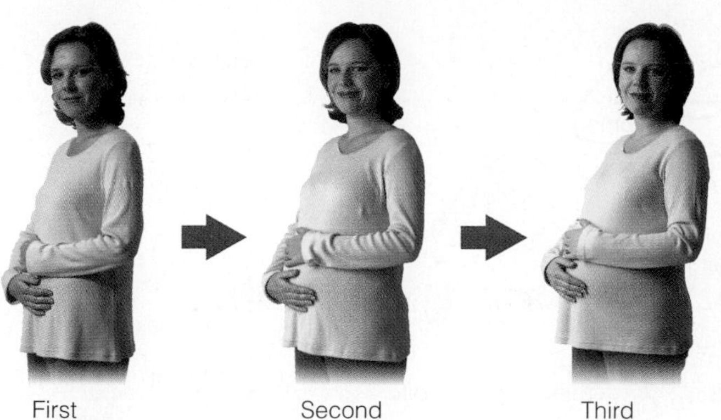

Figure 29.2 Components of Weight Gain during Pregnancy
Healthy-weight women gain 27.5 pounds, on average, during pregnancy.

The Need for Certain Nutrients Increases

In the first trimester, a pregnant woman needs up to 50 percent more folate, iron, zinc, and copper than before she was pregnant:

- *Folate.* If a woman is conscientious about taking folic acid prior to conception and continues to take a supplement and/or consume folic acid–fortified foods, she should be able to meet her increased needs for this vitamin. Foods high in folate include green leafy vegetables, citrus fruits and juices, and whole-grain products.
- *Iron.* Pregnant women need extra iron to make additional red blood cells, prevent anemia, and provide for fetal growth and development.[13] Although meat, fish, poultry, and enriched grains supply iron, the amount recommended during pregnancy is unlikely to be met from food alone, so a supplement is needed.[14] Many women are prescribed a prenatal supplement to help them meet their iron and other increased nutrient needs.
- *Zinc and copper.* Because iron can interfere with the absorption of other minerals, if a woman is taking more than 30 milligrams of iron daily, she should also take 15 milligrams of zinc and 2 milligrams of copper.[15] Zinc is needed in protein metabolism and in the synthesis of DNA. Copper, as part of enzymes, is needed in the production of energy, the synthesis of connective tissues, and the transport and utilization of iron.

Other nutrients are also of concern during pregnancy, especially if the mother is a vegetarian or vegan. Pregnant women, especially vegetarians, should be mindful about meeting their need for essential fatty acids, which are important in the formation of new tissues, particularly those of the central nervous system.[16] Vegans who don't consume any animal products need to make sure that they are getting a reliable source of vitamin B_{12}. A pregnant woman will absorb more calcium from foods during pregnancy to offset the amount of calcium needed by the growing fetus, but she still needs to meet her daily needs for calcium, as well as for vitamin D, to preserve bone mass and to prevent osteoporosis later in life. One way to ensure an adequate calcium and vitamin D intake during pregnancy is to drink nutrient-dense milk as the beverage of choice, rather than nutritionally empty sodas.

While it's important that pregnant women meet their nutrient needs, it is equally important that they not consume too much of some nutrients. Too much vitamin A can be toxic and increase the risk for birth defects, especially when taken during the first trimester. Pregnant women who take a supplement should consume no more than 5,000 IU (1,500 micrograms) of preformed vitamin A daily, which is

Fortified whole-grain cereals are a good source of folic acid, iron, zinc, and copper, and milk provides calcium and vitamin D.

Figure 29.3 Nutrient Needs during Pregnancy
A balanced 2,000-calorie diet can meet most of a pregnant woman's increased nutrient needs even before she adds calories in her second and third trimesters.

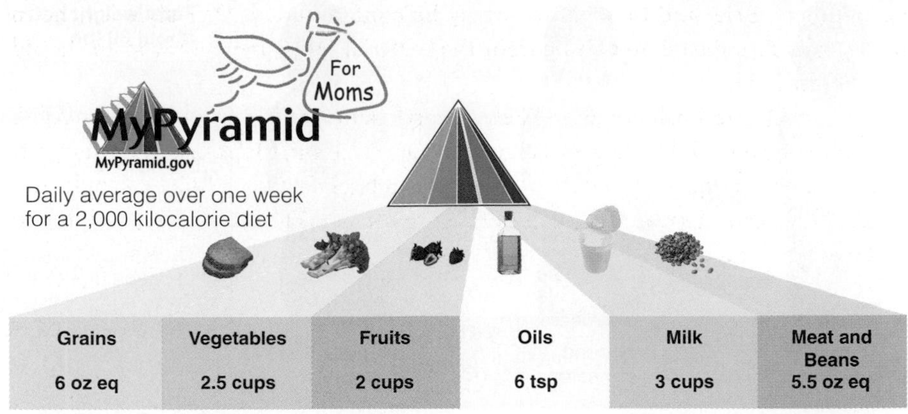

Nutrient	Recommended DRI for Nonpregnant Women Age 19–50 Years	Recommended Nutrient Intake During Pregnancy
Protein	46 g	71 g
Carbohydrates	130 g	175 g (minimum)
Linoleic acid	12 g	13 g
Alpha-linolenic acid	1.1 g	1.4 g
Dietary folate equivalents	400 mcg	600 mcg*
Thiamin	1.1 mg	1.4 mg
Riboflavin	1.1 mg	1.4 mg
Niacin equivalents	14 mg	18 mg
Vitamin B_6	1.3–1.5 mg	1.9 mg
Vitamin B_{12}	2.4 mg	2.6 mg
Vitamin C	75 mg	85 mg
Vitamin E	15 mg	15 mg
Vitamin A	700 mcg	770 mcg
Calcium	1,000 mcg	1,000 mcg
Magnesium	310–320 mg	350–360 mg
Copper	0.9 mg	1.0 mg
Iron	18 mg	27 mg†
Phosphorus	700 mg	700 mg
Zinc	8 mg	11 mg
Kilocalories	**2,000–2,200‡**	**§**

* Supplemented and/or fortified foods are recommended.
† A supplement is recommended.
‡ Varies depending upon activity level and weight.
§ Doesn't increase until second and third trimester.

100 percent of the Daily Value (DV) listed on the label. Figure 29.3 summarizes the nutrient needs of pregnant women and compares them with a well-balanced diet. As you can see, a balanced diet can meet the majority of a pregnant woman's nutrient needs.

Food that may carry pathogens, such as sushi or sashimi, should be avoided by pregnant women for their own safety and the safety of their fetus.

Pregnancy Increases the Risk for Foodborne Illness

During pregnancy, a woman's immune system is weakened and the fetus's immune system is undeveloped, both of which set the stage for potential difficulties in fighting off pathogens that can cross the placenta. The bacterium *Listeria monocytogenes*, for example, may cause miscarriages, premature labor, low birth weight, developmental problems, and even infant death. Meat and dairy foods are most likely to be contaminated. Pasteurization kills *Listeria*, but unpasteurized soft cheeses, such as

Camembert, Brie, and blue cheeses, may be contaminated. Deli-style luncheon meats, salami, and paté may also harbor the bacteria. Thus, pregnant women should avoid these foods.

Raw meats and fish are more likely to carry pathogens and need to be handled with care or avoided during pregnancy. Sushi and sashimi, for example, contain raw fish and are more likely to contain parasites or bacteria. Pregnant women should also avoid undercooked meat, fish, or poultry; unpasteurized milk, cheese, and juices; and raw sprouts.

Smoking during pregnancy can seriously harm the fetus.

Pregnant Women Should Avoid Many Other Substances

We noted earlier that smoking decreases the chance that a woman will conceive. When a woman continues smoking during pregnancy, her infant will weigh a ½ pound less, on average, than infants of nonsmokers, and will be at an increased risk of being born prematurely or dying. Prenatal exposure to smoke can also increase the risk for *sudden infant death syndrome (SIDS)*—the unexplained death of an infant less than 1 year of age—and may stunt the infant's growth.[17]

Even secondhand smoke can affect the health of a mom-to-be and her infant. Exposure to passive smoke can affect the infant's ability to grow properly.[18] Thus, pregnant women and new mothers should avoid work, home, or social environments where they are exposed to secondhand smoke.

As you read in Concept 19, drinking alcohol during pregnancy can lead to fetal alcohol syndrome (FAS) in the baby. Children exposed to even low levels of alcohol during pregnancy can be born with learning and behavioral disabilities. Because there is no known safe level of alcohol consumption, pregnant women need to abstain completely to eliminate the chance of harming the baby.

When used during pregnancy, illicit drugs can increase the risk for miscarriage, preterm labor, a low birth weight baby, and birth defects.[19] After birth, the baby may experience drug withdrawal symptoms, such as excessive crying, trembling, and seizures, as well as long-term health problems, such as heart defects and behavioral and learning problems.

Pregnant women should restrict their intake of caffeine, which can be passed on to the fetus (as can anything else consumed). Research studies to date suggest that caffeine intake of less than 150 milligrams daily, or the amount in 12 ounces (1½ cups) of coffee, doesn't increase the risk for miscarriage or birth defects. However, some studies suggest that intakes greater than 200 milligrams (found in about two cups of coffee) daily, especially if the pregnant woman is also smoking and/or drinking alcohol, may increase the risk for miscarriages.[20]

The Take-Home Message A pregnancy is divided into trimesters. During the first trimester, the fertilized egg develops into an embryo and eventually into a fetus. Many women experience morning sickness and cravings during this trimester. Women should gain from 25 to 35 pounds during pregnancy, depending on their prepregnancy weight. The needs for folate, iron, and zinc increase significantly during pregnancy. Pregnant women should avoid excess amounts of preformed vitamin A. They also need to avoid foods that may contain pathogens. Tobacco, alcohol, and illicit drugs should be avoided during pregnancy. Caffeine intake should be limited to no more than 150 milligrams daily.

As with smoking, drinking alcohol during pregnancy exposes the fetus to potentially toxic substances.

1 whole-wheat English muffin
2 tbs peanut butter
+ 5 baby carrots
340 calories

The extra calorie and nutrient needs of the second and third trimesters can be met with nutrient-dense additions to the diet.

What Nutrients and Behaviors Are Important in the Second Trimester?

For many pregnant women, the nausea and fatigue of the first trimester subside during the second trimester, and their appetite begins to increase. The baby is growing rapidly, and the mother's body is changing to accommodate this growth (see Figure 29.2). The fetus is just under 2 pounds and about 13 inches long by the end of this trimester. During this period of growth, the mother needs to focus on consuming adequate calories and nutrients; to exercise, if possible; and to be aware of potential complications.

Pregnant Women Need to Consume Adequate Calories, Carbohydrate, and Protein to Support Growth

Pregnant women should consume an additional 340 calories daily during the second trimester and gain slightly less than a pound per week. A whole-wheat English muffin topped with peanut butter and a few baby carrots fits these requirements nutritiously, as do many other meal combinations. This combination of foods also provides plenty of essential fatty acids, carbohydrates, fiber, zinc, iron, and protein—the nutrients that a woman needs more of during pregnancy.

Pregnant women need a minimum of 175 grams of carbohydrates per day (versus 130 grams for nonpregnant women) to cover the amount of glucose needed for both the developing brain and the energy needs of the fetus. Protein needs also increase by about 35 percent, to about 71 grams daily, during the second and third trimesters. As you can see from Figure 29.3, women usually meet this higher protein demand by eating a balanced diet.

Walking is one form of exercise that is safe for both mother and baby.

Daily Exercise Is Important

Daily exercise during pregnancy can help improve sleep, lower the risk for hypertension and diabetes, prevent backaches, help relieve constipation, shorten labor, and allow women to return more quickly to their prepregnancy weight after delivery. Exercise can also help provide an emotional boost by reducing stress, depression, and anxiety.[21] The American College of Obstetricians and Gynecologists recommends 30 minutes or more of moderate exercise on most, if not all, days of the week, as long as the woman doesn't have any medical issues or complications.[22] Pregnant women should check with their health care provider before exercising to see if it is appropriate. Low-impact activities, such as walking, swimming, and stationary cycling, are recommended (Table 29.4). See the Table Tips for more on exercising while pregnant.

Potential Complications: Gestational Diabetes and Hypertension

gestational diabetes The type of diabetes that develops in women during pregnancy.

Sometimes a pregnant woman develops high blood glucose levels and is diagnosed with **gestational diabetes** (*gestation* = pregnancy-related). This type of diabetes occurs in about 7 percent of pregnancies in the United States and manifests itself after

Table 29.4

Safe and Unsafe Exercises during Pregnancy

Safe Activities	Unsafe Activities (contact sports and high-impact activities)
Walking	Hockey (field and ice)
Stationary cycling	Basketball
Low-impact aerobics	Football
Swimming	Soccer
Dancing	Gymnastics
	Horseback riding
	Skating
	Skiing (snow and water)
	Vigorous racquet sports
	Weight lifting

Data from: T. Wang and B. Apgar, "Recommendations for Sports Activities during Pregnancy," *American Family Physician* 57 (1998): 1846–1856.

TABLE TIPS 

Exercising While Pregnant

Consult your health care provider before starting an exercise program.

Begin slowly to avoid excessive fatigue and shortness of breath.

Exercise in the early morning or evening to avoid becoming overheated.

Drink plenty of fluids to stay hydrated.

Report problems or unusual symptoms, such as chest pain, contractions, dizziness, headache, calf swelling, blurred vision, vaginal discharge or bleeding, or abdominal pain, immediately to your health care provider.

(Data adapted from: The National Women's Health Information Center, "Healthy Pregnancy: Have a Fit Pregnancy," 2006. Available at: www.womenshealth.gov/pregnancy)

approximately the twentieth week.[23] A pregnant woman should be tested for gestational diabetes during her second trimester. Untreated gestational diabetes can lead to the birth of a baby who is excessively large, or one who has breathing or other problems.

Hypertension (high blood pressure) during pregnancy can damage the woman's kidneys and other organs and increase the risk for low birth weight and premature delivery.[24] It occurs in about 8 percent of pregnancies in the United States.[25] Some women have hypertension prior to conceiving, but others develop it during their pregnancy.

The Take-Home Message **Pregnant women need to consume an additional 340 calories daily during the second trimester. A varied selection of nutrient-dense foods will easily meet increased calorie needs. Exercise can provide numerous benefits during pregnancy. Some women develop gestational diabetes and pregnancy-induced high blood pressure and need to be monitored closely by a health care professional.**

What Nutrients and Behaviors Are Important in the Third Trimester?

By the end of the third trimester, a pregnant woman should be taking in an extra 450 calories daily and be gaining about 1 pound per week (adding a banana to the English muffin, peanut butter, and carrot snack will increase this to about 450 calories). At the end of the third trimester, the baby will weigh approximately 7 pounds.

The mother is likely to have a harder time getting around due to her expanding body. As the growing baby exerts pressure on her intestines and stomach, and hormonal changes slow the movement of food through the gastrointestinal (GI) tract, she may experience heartburn. To minimize heartburn, pregnant women should eat frequent, small meals and avoid foods that may irritate the esophagus, such as spicy or highly seasoned foods. They also shouldn't lie down after meals, and they should elevate their heads during sleep.[26]

Constipation is also common near the end of pregnancy. The slower movement of food through the GI tract and a tendency for less physical activity are factors. The large amount of iron in prenatal supplements can also contribute to constipation.[27] Eating more fiber-rich foods, such as oatmeal, bran cereals, beans, whole grains, fruits, and vegetables, along with drinking plenty of fluids, can help keep things moving along.

The Take-Home Message **During the third trimester, a woman needs an additional 450 calories per day and should continue gaining about a pound per week. Heartburn and constipation commonly occur during the third trimester. Eating smaller meals and eating more fiber can help.**

Pregnancy is especially challenging for teens, who have not yet completed their own physical and emotional development.

What Special Concerns Do Teen Mothers-to-Be Face?

Pregnancy and childbirth place demands on the body of a mother-to-be no matter what her age, but teens who become pregnant face particular challenges. Because a teenage girl's body is still growing, she has higher nutrient needs than an adult woman has. In addition, teenage girls, like many adolescents, are more likely to consume inadequate amounts of whole grains, fruits, vegetables, and lean dairy products. Add this unbalanced diet to the increased needs of pregnancy, and these young girls are likely falling short of many of their nutrient requirements.

Teenage mothers are also more likely to engage in unhealthy lifestyle habits, such as smoking, drinking alcohol, and taking illicit drugs, all of which can seriously compromise a baby's health.[28]

In the United States, over 400,000 babies are born to young girls every year.[29] The National Campaign to Prevent Teen Pregnancy, a nonprofit organization, has set a goal to reduce the rate of teen pregnancy by one-third between 2006 and 2015. More information on this effort can be found at its website listed at the end of this concept under Web Resources.

The Take-Home Message **Because a teenage girl is still growing and developing, she will likely have difficulty meeting both her own nutrient needs and her baby's unless she's diligent about eating a well-balanced diet.**

What Is Breast-Feeding and Why Is It Beneficial?

A woman who has just given birth will begin a period of *lactation*; that is, her body will produce milk to nourish her new infant through breast-feeding. Milk production is stimulated by the infant's suckling at the mother's nipple. Signals sent from the nipple to the hypothalamus in the mother's brain prompt her pituitary gland to release two hormones, prolactin and oxytocin, which cause milk to be produced in the breast and then to be released, or *let down*, so that the infant can receive it through the nipple (Figure 29.4).[30]

The old adage "breast is best" when it comes to nourishing an infant is still true. Through breast-feeding, also called nursing, mothers provide food that is uniquely tailored to meet their infant's nutritional needs in an easily digestible form. Breast-feeding also provides many other advantages for both the mother and the baby.

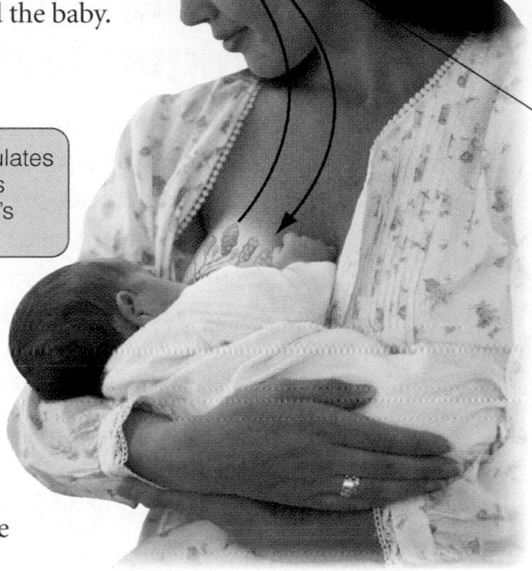

Figure 29.4 Let-Down Response

Breast-Feeding Benefits the Mother's Health

In addition to stimulating the release of breast milk, the hormone oxytocin stimulates contractions in the uterus, which helps the organ return to its prepregnancy size and shape. Breast-feeding also reduces blood loss in the mother after delivery.[31] Because breast-feeding requires significant calories, it may help some women return to their prepregnancy weight and manage their postpregnancy weight.

Breast-feeding, especially if it is done exclusively (not combining it with formula-feeding), can also help delay the return of the menstrual cycle, giving women a chance to recover from the pregnancy before becoming pregnant again. However, this does not mean that women who breast-feed their newborns should assume they won't get pregnant. They still need to take precautions if they wish to avoid pregnancy.

Women in their 20s who breast-feed for up to two years may reduce their risk for breast and ovarian cancer. Breast-feeding has also been shown to reduce the risk for hip fractures later in life, increase bone density, and reduce the risk for type 2 diabetes.[32]

Breast Milk Is Less Expensive and More Convenient Than Formula

A new mother who opts to buy formula rather than breast-feed her baby will spend an estimated $1,200 for the first year's worth of powdered formula (more if she buys the ready-to-feed variety). The costs associated with breast-feeding, in contrast, are primarily for buying the extra food a woman needs to eat to produce her infant's milk, and they average about $300 for the first year.[33]

Other costs are associated with formula-feeding beyond the price of the product. For instance, an estimated $2 million is spent yearly to produce, package, and ship formula throughout the United States. There are also environmental costs of dealing with the 550 million formula cans and 800,000 pounds of paper packaging and waste that are disposed of in landfills each year, as well as costs associated with the energy needed to properly clean the feeding bottles.[34] For the family, the environment, and society as a whole, breast-feeding is cheaper than formula-feeding.

Feeding from the breast is more convenient than bottle-feeding because the milk is always sterile and at the right temperature, and there isn't any need to prepare bottles. The mother also doesn't need to prepare the milk before feeding, and she has less cleanup to do afterwards.

Women can express breast milk using a breast pump and store the milk in the refrigerator or freezer for later use.

Breast-Feeding Promotes Bonding

The close interaction between mother and child during nursing promotes a unique bonding experience. The physical contact helps the baby feel safe, secure, and emotionally attached to the mother.[35] Breast-feeding may also play a role in reducing incidences of infants being abandoned by their mothers.[36]

Breast Milk Provides for an Infant's Unique Nutrition Needs

The nutritional composition of breast milk changes as the infant grows. During the first few days after she gives birth, a new mother produces a carotenoid-rich, yellowish fluid, called *colostrum*, that has little fat but a lot of protein, vitamin A, and minerals. Colostrum also contains antibodies that help protect the infant from infections, particularly in the digestive tract.

Four to seven days later, actual breast milk begins to flow. Breast milk is high in lactose, fat, and B vitamins, proportionally balanced to enhance their absorption.[37] Breast milk is low in protein, so as not to stress the infant's immature kidneys with excessive amounts of nitrogen waste products. The protein is also mostly in a form that is easy for the infant to digest.[38] By the time the infant has breast-fed for six months, the mother's milk will contain less protein than it did during the first month.[39]

Breast-Feeding Benefits the Infant's Health

Breast milk provides the infant with a disease-fighting boost until the baby's own immune system matures. Research supports that breast-feeding decreases the risk and severity of diarrhea and other intestinal disorders, respiratory infections, meningitis, ear infections, and urinary tract infections.[40]

Breast milk provides other beneficial compounds, such as antioxidants, hormones, enzymes, and growth factors, that play a role in the infant's development and protect the baby from pathogens, inflammation, diseases, and allergies.[41] Some research suggests that breast milk may also protect against SIDS, asthma, leukemia, heart disease, and diabetes mellitus.[42]

Breast-feeding, especially if continued beyond six months, may help reduce the risk for childhood obesity. The reason for this isn't clear, but it might be associated with the tendency of breast-fed infants to gain less weight during the first year of life than formula-fed infants. The lower weight gain may be due to breast-fed infants' having more control over when they start and stop eating than do their bottle-fed counterparts.[43]

Finally, breast milk may help infants with their intellectual development. Breast milk is rich in two unsaturated fatty acids that are important for brain development. Research suggests that breast-fed infants may have greater cognitive function, measured by IQ and academic success in school, than formula-fed babies, which may be due in part to these two fatty acids.[44]

Because of all the benefits, the American Academy of Pediatrics (AAP) and the American Dietetic Association (ADA) recommend that women exclusively breast-feed for the first six months and then use a combination of appropriate foods and breast-feeding during at least the first year. Currently, over 70 percent of American women initiate breast-feeding when their infants are born.[45] However, only 35 percent are still breast-feeding their infants at 6 months and only 17 percent continue until the baby is 1 year of age.[46]

The breast-fed infant doesn't always have to consume breast milk directly from the breast. Milk can be pumped, or expressed, with a breast pump, refrigerated, and fed to the baby in a bottle by another caregiver at another time. This allows the mother to work outside the home or enjoy a few hours "off duty."

Kathy, the young mom and part-time student you read about in the beginning of this concept, can pump her milk before she leaves for class, so that a child-care provider can feed her baby while she's away.

Breast-Feeding Mothers Have Unique Nutrient Needs

To maintain an adequate supply of breast milk, a mother needs to consume additional amounts of fluid, calories, and other nutrients:

- *Fluid.* A breast-feeding woman should drink about 13 cups of water and other beverages daily.
- *Calories.* A breast-feeding woman needs 500 extra calories daily during the first six months of lactating. However, not all of these calories have to come from the diet. Approximately 170 calories are mobilized daily from fat that was stored during pregnancy. Therefore, only 330 extra calories need to come from food. This use of fat stores allows for a potential weight loss of about 2 pounds a month. During the second six months of breast-feeding, fewer calories are available from stored body fat, so a lactating woman needs to consume about 400 extra calories daily to meet her needs.[47]
- *Other nutrients.* A breast-feeding woman's dietary requirements for carbohydrates, some vitamins, and minerals increase slightly. However, a well-balanced diet similar to the one she consumed during pregnancy will meet her needs. Lactating women who are vegans should make sure that they consume adequate amounts of vitamin B_{12} and zinc.

Breast-Feeding Mothers Must Avoid Harmful Substances

Anything that goes into a breast-feeding mother's body can pass into her breast milk, and ultimately her baby. Alcohol, recreational drugs, and even medications can be transferred to a breast-fed infant and cause harm. Caffeine should be limited to two to three cups of coffee daily because it can interfere with the baby's sleep and cause crankiness. *Methylmercury*, which a mother can overconsume if she doesn't avoid certain fish, can also be harmful, so nursing mothers should adhere to the FDA's guidelines about fish to minimize the infant's exposure (see Table 29.1). Finally, inhaling tobacco smoke is associated with a decrease in milk production and smaller weight gains in the baby, and nicotine can be passed on to the baby in breast milk, so nursing women should not smoke.[48]

Formula Can Be a Healthy Alternative to Breast Milk

For women who cannot safely breast-feed, infant formula is a healthy option. Women who are infected with the human immunodeficiency virus (HIV) or have acquired immune deficiency syndrome (AIDS), should not breast-feed, as the virus

Infant formula is available in several forms and varies in cost and ingredients. Infant formula is highly regulated by the FDA, so any formula on the market in the United States can be considered safe.

can be transmitted to the child through breast milk. Also, women who have human T-cell leukemia or active tuberculosis, are receiving chemotherapy and/or radiation, or use illegal drugs should not breast-feed. Any woman taking prescribed medications should check with her health care provider to ensure that it is safe to continue breast-feeding. Lastly, infants born with a genetic disorder called *galactosemia* can't metabolize lactose and shouldn't be breast-fed.[49]

The only alternative to breast milk is commercially made formula. Cow's milk cannot be fed to infants, as it does not meet their nutritional needs and is difficult for infants to digest.[50] Soy milk and rice milk are also unsuitable for infant feeding. Infant formula is developed to be as similar as possible to breast milk, so formula-fed infants can grow and develop quite normally. The FDA regulates all infant formulas sold in the United States and has set requirements for the nutrients that formula must contain.

Formula can be purchased as powder, as a concentrated liquid, or in ready-to-use forms. Powdered formula is the cheapest, and the ready-to-use form tends to be the most expensive. Care should be taken to mix the powdered or concentrated liquid with the correct amount of water, so that the formula will not be too diluted or too concentrated.

The Take-Home Message Breast-feeding can help mothers return to their prepregnancy weight and can reduce the risk for certain diseases. It is also the least expensive and most convenient way to nourish an infant, and it helps a mother and baby bond. Human breast milk is rich in nutrients, antibodies, and other compounds that can protect a baby against diseases and may promote a child's cognitive development. Women are advised to breast-feed exclusively for the first six months, then breast-feed to supplement solid food for at least the first year. Breast-feeding mothers need to increase their fluid, calorie, and nutrient intakes. Anything a woman consumes can be passed on to her baby in breast milk, so nursing mothers should avoid all potentially harmful substances. Commercial infant formulas are a healthy alternative to breast milk for women who cannot breast-feed.

What Are the Nutrient Needs of an Infant and Why Are They So High?

During infancy, the period starting at birth through the first year of life, children's nutritional needs are extraordinarily high for their small size. Let's find out why.

Infants Grow at an Accelerated Rate

Infants double their birth weight by about 6 months of age, and triple it by their first birthday. Length doubles around the end of the first year as well. Let's try to imagine the physical growth of an infant in adult terms. On January 1, you weigh 100 pounds. By June, you have grown to 200 pounds. By New Year's Eve, you weigh 300 pounds! You would have to eat an enormous amount of food every day to make this happen, but for an infant, this is a normal growth rate.

Newborns eat as often as twelve times a day!

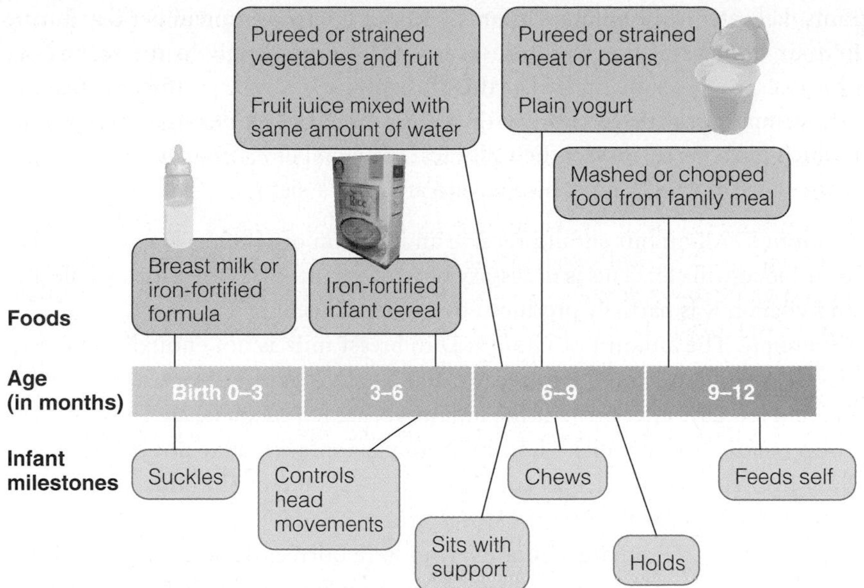

Figure 29.5 Nutrition and Milestones for Baby's First Year
During the first year after birth, an infant's diet will progress from breast milk or formula only to age-appropriate versions of family meals. Adequate nourishment at each stage helps infants achieve certain developmental milestones.

Infants are doing much more than just getting heavier and longer. Intellectual and social development is also underway. As time goes by, infant communication skills go beyond crying, and at around 3 months of age a baby usually starts to smile. The infant's preferences also become clearer: for particular people (such as the mom), for specific activities (getting kisses or being held), and for certain foods (such as mashed bananas).[51]

An infant who does not receive adequate nutrition (whether in terms of quantity or quality) may have difficulty reaching developmental *milestones* (Figure 29.5). Think of these as developmental checkpoints, which can be physical, social, or intellectual. Although most parents do not know the specific nutrient needs of their infant, it's important that the infant attains the specific milestones at the appropriate times. This assures them that they are providing the right amount and type of nourishment.

In addition to milestones, parents and health care providers can use growth charts to track physical development. Typically, measures of head circumference, length, and weight are used to assess growth. These measures are taken at each visit to the health care provider during the first year.

The information obtained from the measurements is plotted on a growth chart, placing the child into a percentile. In the United States, percentiles are the most commonly used indicators to assess the size and growth patterns of infants and children and to rank them relative to others in the same age in a reference group. For example, a 4-month-old who is in the 25th percentile for weight for age is at a lower weight than 75 percent of 4-month-olds and is at the same or a higher weight than 25 percent of 4-month-olds (Figure 29.6).[52]

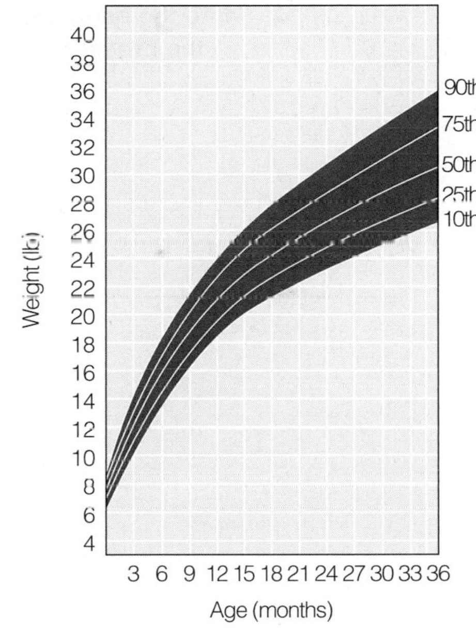

Figure 29.6 Growth Chart
Growth charts can help determine if a child is growing at a healthy rate for his or her age.

Infants Have Unique Nutrient Needs

When it comes to feeding infants, one size does not fit all, but there are certain guidelines for meeting their unique nutrient needs. For example, an average intake of 108 calories per kilogram (kg) of body weight per day is recommended for the first six months of life.[53] A similar proportion of calories at that scale for an adult who weighed 150 pounds (68 kg) would be 7,344 (68 kg × 108) calories per day. That's the equivalent of 13 large chocolate milkshakes!

Carbohydrate, protein, and fat needs all change with age. Infants age 0 to 6 months should consume 60 grams of carbohydrate per day, which increases to

95 grams daily at 7 to 12 months. Infants need 9.1 grams of protein per day during the first six months of life, which increases to 11 grams daily in the second six months. Fat should not be limited at this stage of the life cycle, as this practice can negatively impact growth. In fact, healthy babies should never be put on weight-loss diets, which can severely impact their physical or mental development.

Three micronutrients must be added to an infant's diet:

- *Vitamin K.* All infants should receive an injection of vitamin K to ensure that their blood will clot. This is necessary because infants are born with a sterile gut, and vitamin K is partially produced by intestinal bacteria.[54]
- *Vitamin D.* The amount of vitamin D in breast milk is not enough to prevent rickets, so infants should also receive 400 IU of vitamin D drops daily, starting the first few days after birth. If the infant is being fed adequate amounts of a vitamin D–fortified formula, vitamin D supplementation may not be necessary.
- *Iron.* Iron-rich foods, such as enriched cereals, should be introduced at around 6 months of age, as the infant's stores of iron are depleted at about this time. Premature infants, who were born early and thus have lower iron stores, may need iron supplementation before 6 months.[55]

Colic is an infant's chronic, inconsolable crying for long periods of time. Possible causes may be an immature digestive tract, cow's milk allergy or intolerance, food backup into the esophagus, intestinal gas, or the breast-feeding mother's diet.

Since vitamin B_{12} is naturally found only in animal foods, a supplement may be recommended if the infant is being breast-fed by a strict vegan mother. If the child's water supply is nonfluoridated or if bottled water is used for mixing formula, a fluoride supplement may also be necessary.[56]

The baby's fluid needs are generally met with breast milk or formula. Extra fluid is necessary only in hot climates or to replenish stores following episodes of diarrhea, fever, or vomiting when the body loses fluid and electrolytes.[57]

The Take-Home Message Infants grow at a dramatic rate during the first year of life. Health care providers monitor infant growth by making sure the child achieves appropriate developmental milestones and by using growth charts. The infant's nutrient needs during the first year of life are substantial, and supplements are needed in some circumstances.

When Are Solid Foods Safe?

Often, proud parents can hardly wait to show off how their baby is eating "real food." It is an exciting time because eating solid foods represents maturing skills in the baby. Typically, solid foods are introduced around 6 months of age.[58] However, parents should not suddenly decide to serve their baby steak! The infant must be nutritionally, physiologically, and physically ready to eat solid foods. Let's take a look at what that means.

Solid Foods May Be Introduced Once Certain Milestones Are Met

First, the infant needs to be nutritionally ready for solid foods. At about 6 months old, an infant has depleted his or her stored iron and will need to begin consuming it in foods. Also, common sense tells us that, as babies get bigger in size, they need more nutrients. Although technically breast milk can still provide most nutrients, introducing solid foods at 6 months of age will further meet the infant's needs and help him or her develop feeding skills.

The infant also needs to be physiologically ready; that is, the body systems must be able to process solid foods. At birth, and in early infancy, the GI tract and organs such as the kidneys cannot process solid foods. Introducing solid foods too early can also increase a child's risk for allergic reactions to common foods (see the box feature "A Taste Could Be Dangerous: Food Allergies").

These next questions are very specific to the individual child. Is the infant physically ready? Has he or she met the necessary developmental milestones? To determine this, caretakers need to answer the following questions:

- Has the *tongue-thrust reflex* faded? This is an oral reflex infants have to protect them from choking. The tongue automatically pushes outward when a substance or an item, such as a spoon, is placed on it. The reflex fades around 4 to 6 months of age.
- Can the infant control his or her head and neck? Without control, the infant is at greater risk of choking on solids and cannot turn his or her head away to indicate, "I'm full!"
- Is the infant able to sit with support?

All of these questions should be answered with "yes" before it is safe and realistic to begin offering solid foods. If not, parents and caregivers would be wise to wait until the infant develops these skills.[59]

Solid Foods Should Be Introduced Gradually

Solid foods should be introduced gradually to make sure the child isn't allergic or intolerant. The best suggestion is to introduce only one new food per week.[60] Parents and caregivers should be mindful of how the infant reacts to the new food. If he or she develops hives or a rash, or starts sneezing or vomiting, the food may be the culprit.

Iron-fortified rice cereal is a great first food because it provides iron and is one of the grains least likely to promote an allergic reaction. After a week of feeding the infant rice cereal (assuming there has been no negative reaction), a suggested next step is to proceed with other single-grain cereals, such as barley or oats. Once all of these have been fed to the infant without difficulty, then other grain cereals (such as rice, barley, and oats) can be offered.

The next step is to offer puréed or strained vegetables, one new variety each week, so that the infant will become familiar with the more bitter taste of these foods; then fruits in the same manner; then meats or beans (see Figure 29.5 on page 17). Phasing in solid foods should take place over a period of several months. Mashed or chopped food from the family meal can be introduced toward the end of the first year. Rather than deciding that the infant does not like a food because he or she spits it out on the first taste, parents and caregivers should offer a given food more than once, over several days, to give the infant an opportunity to accept the food.[61]

Some Foods Are Dangerous and Should Be Avoided

Many foods are not appropriate for a baby. For example, some foods, such as hot dogs, raw carrot slices, grapes, and raisins, present a choking hazard and should be avoided. Because infants have few teeth, foods should be soft and should "melt" in

A Taste Could Be Dangerous: Food Allergies

One-year-old Adam was playing in the sandbox at the neighborhood playground when his baby-sitter pulled a peanut butter cookie from her backpack. She broke off a small bite of the cookie and handed it to Adam, knowing that he must be hungry for his afternoon snack.

After a minute of chewing, Adam started to wheeze and have difficulty breathing. Then he vomited. The sitter quickly used her cell phone to call for emergency help. She gave the rest of the cookie to one of the paramedics, who rushed Adam to the hospital. Unbeknownst to the sitter, Adam was allergic to peanuts.

A **food allergy** is an abnormal physical reaction of the immune system in response to the consumption of a particular food allergen. Food **allergens** are proteins that are not broken down during cooking or by the gastric juices and enzymes in the body during digestion. Because they are not degraded, they enter the body intact and can cause an adverse reaction from the immune system if the allergen is perceived as a foreign invader.

A food allergy reaction occurs in two stages, the "sensitization stage" followed by the actual response, or "allergic reaction stage." In the first stage (see Figure 29.7) the food allergens don't produce a reaction but, rather, sensitize or introduce themselves to the person's immune system. In response to the initial introduction of the food allergens, the immune system creates an army of antibodies, which enter the blood. The antibodies attach to mast cells (cells in connective tissue), setting the stage for a potential future allergic reaction.

The second stage, the reaction stage, occurs when a person eats the food allergens a subsequent time. After they are consumed, the food allergens come in contact with the mast cells. The mast cells release chemicals, such as histamine, that cause inflammation in the body's tissues. The areas in the body that manifest a food allergy reaction are the areas where mast cells are prevalent. For example, wheezing can result from inflammation of the airways. In very sensitive individuals, a minute exposure of a food allergen—1/44,000 of a peanut, for example—can trigger an allergic reaction.[1]

Reactions can appear as quickly as a few minutes after eating a food. In fact, an itchiness in the mouth can occur as soon as the food touches the tongue. After the food reaches the stomach and begins to be digested, vomiting and/or diarrhea may result. When the food allergens enter the blood, they can cause the dilation of blood vessels and a drop in blood pressure. When the allergens are near the skin, hives can develop, and as the allergens make their way to the lungs, asthma can ensue.[2]

In the United States, food allergies are the cause of 2,000 hospital admissions and almost 200 deaths annually.[3] Many of these deaths result from **anaphylactic reactions** (*ana* = without, *phlyaxis* = protection). An anaphylactic reaction can cause vomiting, a life-threatening drop in blood pressure, and constriction (narrowing) of the airways in the lungs, which inhibits breathing.

Many people with allergies, or their caretakers, carry a syringe injector of epinephrine (adrenaline) to be self-administered in severe reactions to help treat the symptoms. Epinephrine constricts blood vessels, relaxes the muscles in the lungs to help with breathing, and decreases swelling and hives.

Eggs, milk, and peanuts are the most common sources of food allergens in children. In adults, shellfish, peanuts, tree nuts, fish, wheat, soy, and eggs are the most common sources. Together, these foods cause 90 percent of all allergic reactions to foods. Some children outgrow their reactions to milk, and up to 20 percent of them will outgrow a peanut allergy.[4] In contrast, adults are rarely able to rid themselves of an established food allergy.

The FDA requires that virtually all food ingredients be listed on the food label, and that the food label state whether the product contains protein from any of the major foods known to cause an allergic reaction: milk, egg, fish, shellfish, tree nuts, peanuts, soybeans, and wheat.[5]

The FDA is continually working with food manufacturers and consumer groups to improve public education on food allergies and the seriousness of anaphylactic reactions, in particular, for the most common sources of food allergies.[6]

food allergy An abnormal physical reaction of the immune system to a particular food or substance.

allergens Substances in food (often proteins) that are not broken down by cooking or digestion and enter the body intact, causing an allergic reaction by the immune system.

anaphylactic reaction A severe, life-threatening reaction causing a sudden drop in blood pressure and airway constriction. Symptoms may include a rapid or weak pulse, a pale complexion, a flush on parts of the body, difficulty breathing, and/or a blank expression. Sometimes called *anaphylactic shock.*

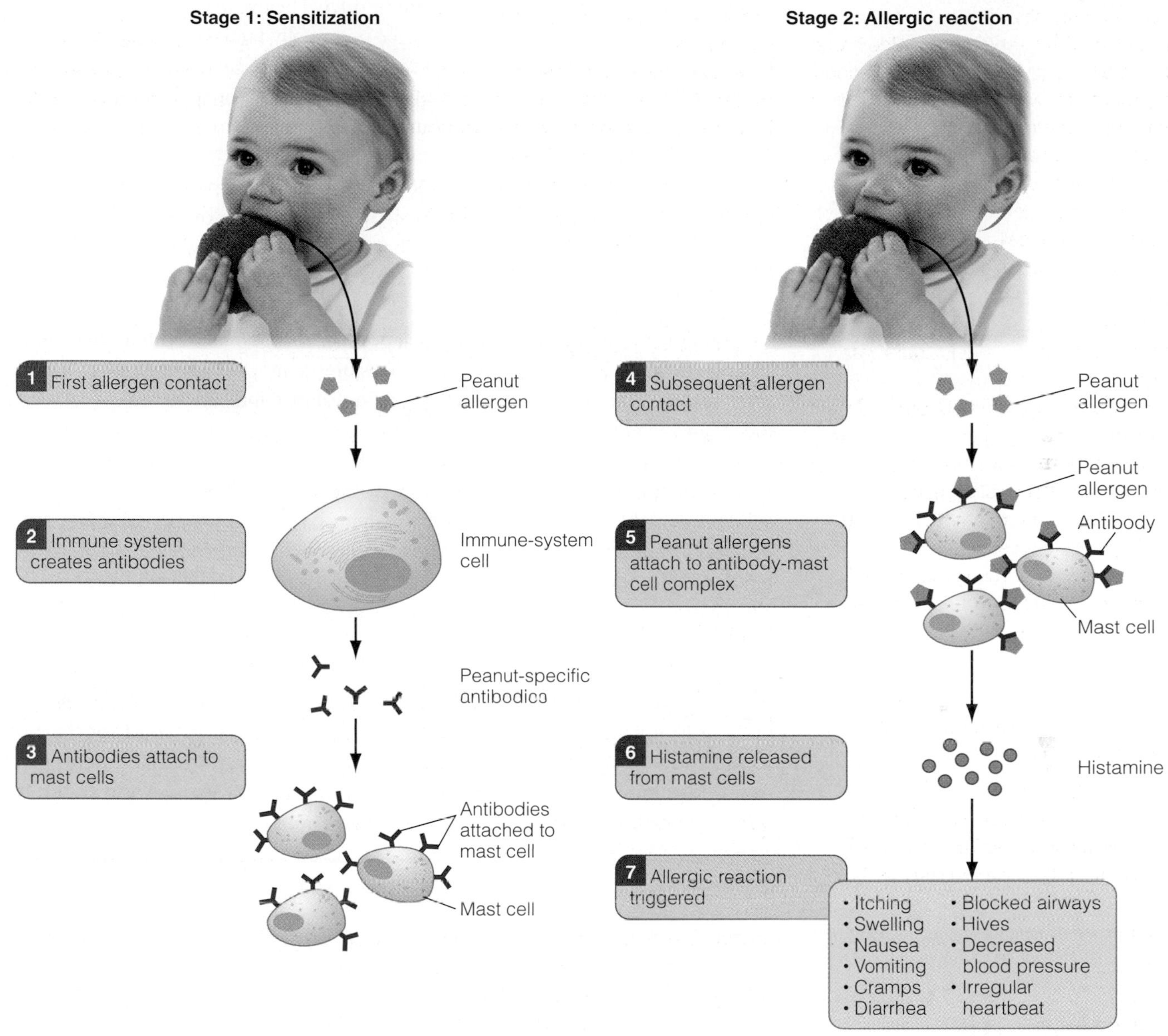

Figure 29.7 Immune Response to a Food Allergy

the mouth, as a cracker does. No matter what infants are eating, they should always be supervised.

Parents and caregivers should also avoid feeding common allergens, as discussed in the box feature. Waiting a few months until the infant's digestive system has matured is a smart way to keep the infant safe.[62] Other common allergens, such as egg whites, cow's milk, and peanut butter, should not be offered before the child is a year old.

Some foods are so dangerous as to be potentially fatal. Honey has been known to carry a bacterium that can cause a fatal illness called *botulism*, a rare but serious paralytic illness. Older children and adults can consume honey without fear of botulism because they have adequate amounts of intestinal microorganisms that compete with the bacteria and inhibit their growth in the intestines.[63]

Parents and caregivers also need to think before adding seasonings, such as salt, sugar, and butter, to their infants' foods. Our consumption of restaurant foods and processed foods has taught us to think that food only tastes "right" if it is salty, sweet, or buttery. Infants have no such experiences, and they can find the natural flavors in whole foods to be satisfying, without added sugar or salt.

Beverages, such as apple juice, are a popular component of infant diets. In fact, 100 percent juice is one of the major sources of infants' calories.[64] Although juice can provide some nutrients, it may provide so many calories and have such a sweet taste that the infant will prefer to drink rather than to eat food, displacing necessary nutrients.

An overabundance of breast milk and formula is not always suitable, either. This is important at the end of the first year, as the infant will likely be learning to use solid food to obtain calories, rather than relying on milk or formula. If infants spend too much time drinking, they may not be interested in the foods that will help expand their feeding skills. Of course, breast milk or formula will still be the primary source of calories, and some parents and caregivers prefer not to start solid foods until after the first year.

The Take-Home Message **An infant must be physically, physiologically, and nutritionally ready before being introduced to solid foods. Solid foods should be introduced gradually and cautiously. Parents and caregivers must educate themselves about foods that are appropriate and those that are not in order to keep their infant safe and healthy.**

Check out these recipes and more suggestions at **www.pearsonhighered.com/blake**

UCook

Easy Carrot Raisin Bread

Who said baby food is only for babies? This easy-to-make, delicious carrot raisin bread uses baby food carrots for a moist bread that kids of all ages will love!

UDo

Does Your Diet Have Enough Folic Acid?

Consuming enough folic acid is key for both men and women when they are planning to start a family. Go to the link on our website to determine if you are meeting your folic acid needs.

The Top Five Points to Remember

1. Both the father and the mother should make healthy diet and lifestyle changes, if needed, prior to pregnancy. For healthy sperm, men should stop smoking, abstain from alcohol or drink only in moderation, strive for a healthy body weight, and consume a well-balanced diet with adequate amounts of fruits and vegetables, whole grains, lean meats, dairy foods, and legumes. Women should maintain a healthy weight;

abstain from tobacco, alcohol, and other harmful substances; avoid fish that contain high amounts of methylmercury; and consume adequate amounts of folic acid prior to conception.

2. To alleviate the symptoms of morning sickness, pregnant women should eat small, frequent meals that are high in carbohydrates. Healthy women should gain approximately 25 to 35 pounds during pregnancy. Most of a pregnant woman's increased nutrient needs can be met through a nutrient-dense, balanced diet. An iron supplement is necessary, but care should be taken to avoid consuming too much preformed vitamin A, which can cause birth defects. An awareness of food safety is important, as bacteria, such as *Listeria monocytogenes*, can cause miscarriages and other problems, and methylmercury in certain types of fish can harm the fetus.

3. A pregnant woman should consume an additional 340 calories daily during the second trimester and an extra 450 calories daily during the third trimester. This will enable her to gain slightly less than about a pound per week until delivery. Exercise during pregnancy can help improve health and allow women to return more quickly to their prepregnancy weight after delivery. Low-impact activities, such as walking, swimming, and stationary cycling, are recommended to prevent injury to both mother and baby.

4. Breast-feeding is the gold standard for feeding an infant. It provides physical, emotional, convenience, and financial benefits for the mother and nutritional and health benefits for the infant. Breast-feeding mothers need to consume 330 to 400 extra calories daily to produce breast milk. If an infant isn't breast-fed, the only healthy option is commercial formula.

5. An infant doubles his or her birth weight around 6 months of age and triples it by 12 months. With proper nutrition, an infant should reach certain developmental milestones within a distinct time frame. Infants need approximately 108 calories per kilogram of body weight during the first six months of life. All infants should receive a vitamin K injection at birth. Breast-fed, and possibly formula-fed, infants need vitamin D supplements. Infants older than 6 months need to begin taking in iron through food sources, as their stored iron supply is depleted around this time. Infants need to be nutritionally, physiologically, and physically ready before they begin eating solid foods. Foods should be introduced gradually and one at a time to monitor possible allergies, and all foods that could promote choking should be avoided.

Test Yourself

1. To prevent neural tube birth defects, a woman should start taking 400 micrograms of folic acid
   a. at least one month prior to conception.
   b. as soon as she learns she is pregnant.
   c. during the second trimester.
   d. during the third trimester.

2. The production and functioning of sperm in males may decrease because of
   a. smoking.
   b. obesity.
   c. alcohol abuse.
   d. all of the above.

3. Diane is pregnant and going out to a seafood restaurant for dinner. She should *not* order
   a. flounder.
   b. shrimp.
   c. grilled swordfish.
   d. lobster.

4. Andy is a healthy 3-month-old who is being breast-fed by his mother. Which of the following nutrients should be added to his diet?
   a. vitamin D
   b. potassium
   c. vitamin C
   d. all of the above

5. Six-month-old Cathy is ready to take on solid foods. The first food that should be introduced in her diet is
   a. oatmeal.
   b. iron-fortified rice cereal.
   c. whole milk.
   d. none of the above.

Answers

1. (a) To reduce the risk of these birth defects, a woman should begin consuming adequate amounts of folic acid prior to conception. Waiting until pregnancy occurs will be too late. Because pregnancy increases the need for this vitamin, the mother should continue to make sure that her folate intake is adequate throughout her pregnancy.

2. (d) Smoking, alcohol abuse, and obesity have all been associated with decreased production and functioning of sperm.

3. (c) The grilled swordfish is off-limits during pregnancy because of its high methylmercury content. However, Diane can enjoy a shrimp cocktail as an appetizer and either the flounder or the lobster as an entrée.

4. (a) Although breast milk is an ideal food for baby Andy, it doesn't contain enough vitamin D, so he should receive drops in his diet daily. He doesn't need to be supplemented with vitamin C or the mineral potassium.
5. (b) Iron-fortified rice cereal is the perfect choice, as it is the least likely to cause an allergic reaction. If Cathy tolerates the rice cereal well, oatmeal can be the next grain added to her diet. Milk shouldn't be introduced into Cathy's diet until she turns 1 year old.

Web Resources

- For more information on breast-feeding, visit the La Leche League International website at: www.lalecheleague.org.
- For more food safety guidance for moms-to-be during pregnancy and after the baby is born, visit the FDA's Center for Food Safety and Applied Nutrition website at: www.cfsan.fda.gov/~pregnant/pregnant.html
- For more on infant nutrition, visit the USDA's Food and Nutrition Center website at: www.nal.usda.gov/fnic
- For more information on food allergies, visit the Food Allergy and Anaphylaxis Network at: www.foodallergy.org
- For information on the National Drug and Alcohol Treatment Referral Routing Service, phone 1-800-662-HELP (4357) or visit the website at: www.niaaa.nih.gov
- For information from The National Campaign to Prevent Teen Pregnancy, including its goal to reduce the rate of teen pregnancy by one-third between 2006 and 2015, visit its website at: www.teenpregnancy.org

30 Life Cycle Nutrition

Childhood through the Later Years

1. The rise in childhood obesity is due almost entirely to **fast food.** T/F

2. Only 25 percent of American elementary schools provide daily **physical education** for students. T/F

3. As long as teens drink **diet soda,** they don't need to worry about negative health effects. T/F

4. **Older adults** don't need as many calories daily as they did in their youth. T/F

5. Almost 7 percent of U.S. **households** with elders experience food insecurity. T/F

Three-year-old Cara has a very busy life. When she gets up each morning, her mom seats her at the kitchen table to eat a few pieces of banana and some whole-grain cereal, but she usually squirms after just a few bites. Once she's dressed, she spends at least 8 or 9 minutes playing with her dog, Murphy, before running outside to grab her shovel and dig in the sandbox. When she gets bored with shoveling, she shouts for her mom to push her on the swing or dashes over to investigate an anthill on the sidewalk. Then, she's zipping up to her room in urgent need of her toy trains. By lunchtime, her mom is saying it's time to come to the kitchen

and eat, but Cara isn't interested. There's too much to see, do, and explore before she has to lie down for her afternoon nap.

Cara's parents are worried that she may be missing some essential nutrients from her diet, but they're not sure how to get their young daughter to slow down and eat when she should. Do you have any advice for Cara's mom and dad? What do you think is the best strategy for ensuring that a child like Cara gets all the nutrients she needs, without putting her at risk for obesity? In this concept, we'll explore these questions, as well as the unique nutritional needs of children, adolescents, and older adults.

Answers

1. False. Fast food is only part of the problem. Too little exercise and too much screen time also contribute. Read more about the obesity epidemic among children on page 6.
2. False. The percentage is actually much lower: Only about 8 percent of U.S. elementary schools provide daily P.E. See page 7 for more on this issue.
3. False. Sodas are nutritionally empty beverages. Turn to page 11 to find out which beverages help adolescents achieve healthy adult bodies.
4. True. Because a person's metabolism slows naturally with age, older adults need fewer calories than their younger counterparts. Learn more about the energy and nutrient needs associated with aging on page 12.
5. True. Food insecurity increases the risks for malnutrition and poor health, to which seniors are especially vulnerable. Turn to page 15 for more.

What Are the Nutritional Needs and Issues of Young Children?

There are two distinct age categories during early childhood: toddlers (1- and 2-year-olds) and preschoolers (ages 3 to 5 years). Toddlers and preschoolers are still growing, but their growth rates have slowed significantly, especially compared with those of infants. During the second year of life, the average weight gain is only about 3 to 5 pounds, and the average height or length gain is about 3 to 5 inches a year.[1] As a result of this slowed growth, the nutritional needs and appetites of toddlers diminish, relative to the needs of infants.

Young Children Need to Eat Frequent, Small, Nutrient-Dense Meals

Using child-sized dishes at mealtimes can help monitor portion sizes.

Just watching young children maneuver from activity to activity would exhaust most adults. Because they are always on the go, they need between 1,000 and 1,400 calories per day (Table 30.1). Since young children tend to eat in small quantities, what they eat during their meals and snacks has to be nutrient dense. Meals and snacks should consist of small portions of meat and beans, fruits, vegetables, milk, and whole grains, instead of items such as chicken nuggets, french fries, sugary drinks, cookies, and crackers.[2] You can use MyPyramid for Preschoolers to determine specific numbers of servings for young children (Figure 30.1).

Parents should be mindful about portion sizes for young children and avoid pushing children to eat more than they need. One way to help ensure proper portion sizes is to use child-sized plates and cups, which are usually sized more appropriately for the amount of food that can fit into a child's stomach. A useful guideline is to serve a portion size that corresponds to the child's age. For example, a 1-year-old

Table 30.1
Calorie Needs for Children and Adolescents

Age (years)	Gender	Activity Level* Sedentary	Moderately Active	Active
2–3 (toddlers and preschoolers)	Female or male	1,000	1,000–1,400	1,000–1,400
4–8 (preschoolers and school-aged children)	Female	1,200	1,400–1,600	1,400–1,800
4–8 (preschoolers and school-aged children)	Male	1,400	1,400–1,600	1,600–2,000
9–13 (school-aged children)	Female	1,600	1,600–2,000	1,800–2,200
9–13 (school-aged children)	Male	1,800	1,800–2,200	2,000–2,600
14–18 (adolescents)	Female	1,800	2,000	2,400
14–18 (adolescents)	Male	2,200	2,400–2,800	2,800–3,200

*These levels are based on Estimated Energy Requirements (EER) from the Institute of Medicine (IOM) Dietary Reference Intakes Macronutrients Report, 2002, calculated by gender, age, and activity level for reference-sized individuals. "Reference size," as determined by the Institute of Medicine, is based on median height and weight for ages up to 18 years.

Data from: Department of Health and Human Services and U.S. Department of Agriculture *Dietary Guidelines for Americans,* 2005.

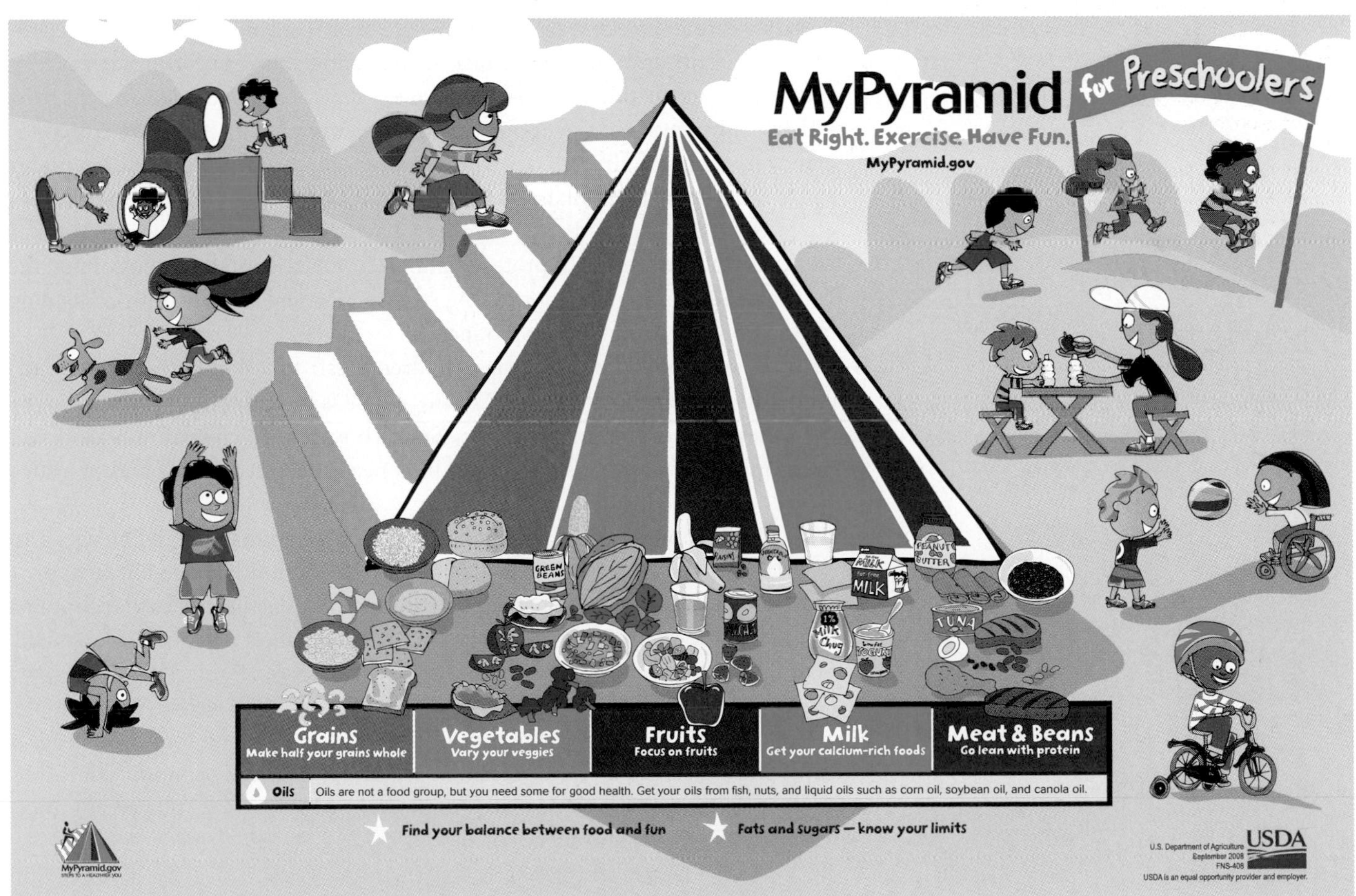

Figure 30.1 MyPyramid for Preschoolers
Good nutrition is so important for preschoolers that they have their own MyPyramid devoted to their unique needs.
Poster is available at: www.mypyramid.gov/downloads/PreschoolerMiniPoster.pdf.

TABLE TIPS

Tasty Treats for Toddlers

Fresh pear, peach, or plum peeled and cut into very small bites

Mini bagel (not toasted, cut into small bites)

Whole-grain pumpkin or bran muffin

Natural (no added sugar) applesauce

Yogurt with sliced bananas

Remember: Young children should always be supervised while eating!

would be served a 1 tablespoon portion of food, a 2 year-old would get a serving of 2 tablespoons, and so on. If the child is still hungry, another tablespoon can be offered, repeating slowly until the child is satisfied.

Children should not be given solid foods that pose a choking hazard. The American Academy of Pediatrics recommends keeping hot dogs, nuts and seeds, chunks of meat or cheese, whole grapes, hard candy, popcorn, chunks of peanut butter, raw vegetables, raisins, and chewing gum away from children younger than age 4.[3] Having the child sit when eating, rather than running around, decreases the likelihood that food will become lodged in the windpipe during a trip or fall. The Table Tips provide some ideas for healthy, toddler-friendly snacks.

Young Children Have Unique Nutrient Needs

The following nutrients are of special concern in the diets of young children:

- *Calcium.* Young children need calcium to develop healthy bones. Children between 1 and 3 years of age should consume 500 milligrams of calcium per day, and children age 4 and 5 should consume 800 milligrams.[4] They can easily meet their needs with milk, since each 8-ounce glass provides 300 milligrams of calcium.
- *Iron.* Young children are at particular risk for iron deficiency, which can lead to developmental delays, such as diminished mental, motor, and behavioral functioning.[5] In the United States, an estimated 9 percent of children aged 1 to 2 years old, and 4 percent of children aged 3 to 4 years old, experience iron deficiency.[6] Parents and caregivers must include good sources of iron, such as lean meats and iron-fortified cereals, in children's diets. The Table Tips on page 5 list kid-friendly ways to enjoy foods that have plenty of iron. Although iron deficiency is a concern, iron toxicity is a leading cause of death in children under age 6. Because so little iron is excreted from the body, it can build up to toxic levels in the tissues and organs. Children have died from ingesting as little as 200 milligrams of iron.[7] To protect children from accidental iron poisoning, the Food and Drug Administration (FDA) requires warning labels on iron-containing drugs, supplements, and other products.[8]
- *Vitamin D.* To build healthy bones, children ages 1 to 8 should consume 10 micrograms (or 400 IU) of vitamin D daily, which is the latest recommendation by the American Academy of Pediatrics. Since consuming 2 cups of milk daily will meet only half of a child's daily vitamin D needs, fortified cereals and/or a supplement is needed.[9]
- *Fiber.* The recommended daily intake for fiber is 19 grams for children ages 1 to 3 and 25 grams for 4- to 8-year olds.[10] Like adults, toddlers need fiber to promote bowel regularity and prevent constipation. A balanced diet that contains whole fruits, vegetables, and whole grains can easily meet a young person's daily fiber needs.
- *Fluids.* Daily fluid recommendations are based on a child's weight. For example, a 7-pound child needs about 2 cups of fluid per day; a 21-pound child needs 5 cups; and a 44-pound child needs 8 cups. Caregivers need to monitor a child's beverage intake and provide water, milk, and possibly some 100 percent juice, while avoiding soda and sugary drinks.

Picky Eating and "Food Jags" Are Common in Young Children

Having kids help in the kitchen is one way to get them excited about trying new foods and eating healthy meals.

As a young child grows, so should the variety of healthy food choices in his or her diet. If a child's first encounter with cooked peas results in all the peas ending up on the floor, it doesn't mean that peas should be permanently off the child's menu. Research shows that a child may need to be exposed to a food 10 times or more before accepting it.[11] Also, parents should not deprive their children of healthy foods, such as broccoli or brussels sprouts, simply because the parents don't like them. Children will often adapt to the foods made available to them.

Often, parents encourage their children to "clean their plates," even though the children may have indicated that they are finished eating. This is a risky habit that encourages overconsumption of calories, which can ultimately lead to obesity. Children should be allowed to stop eating once they are full.

Small children can sometimes seem to have very narrow food preferences. Parents may think, "My child eats only chicken nuggets and fries," or "She hates vegetables." Although it's true that toddlers often demonstrate picky eating, parents should not give up on encouraging them to try and accept new foods.

One way to help small children accept a varied diet is to eat a varied diet yourself. Research suggests that adults' vegetable consumption should serve as a "model" for younger diners.[12] That is, adults should load up their own plates with a variety of vegetables, and snack on items such as carrot sticks and apple slices between meals, so that children will be more likely to follow suit. Children often mimic adults' behaviors, including the unhealthy ones. A father who insists that his 3-year-old eat asparagus but never puts it on his own plate is sending confusing messages. Involving children in the food shopping, menu selection, and preparation of meals is another way to encourage them to enjoy a variety of foods.

When 5-year-old girls were asked, "What do people do when they are on a diet?" their responses included "Can't eat snacks; smoke instead" and "Cook for the kids but **don't eat** the food they make."

While picky eating involves not wanting to try new foods, *food jags* are a child's tendency to want to eat only a limited selection of foods. Did your parents ever mention that, when you were small, all you wanted to eat was macaroni and cheese or peanut butter? This behavior of getting "stuck" on a small selection of foods is quite common and normal in young children. Luckily, food jags are usually temporary.

If parents or caregivers sense that the food jag is not going away, they can keep a food diary of everything the child eats and drinks for a few days to help them identify any major problems. Sharing concerns (and the food diary) with the child's health care provider and asking for advice may prevent serious nutrient deficiencies in the long run.

The Take-Home Message Young children grow at a much slower rate than infants, and they have reduced appetites. Caregivers need to be sure that young children get adequate amounts of calcium, iron, vitamin D, fiber, and fluids. Adults should offer children appropriate portion sizes. Toddlers and preschoolers will stop eating when full and shouldn't be forced to clean their plates. Caregivers should be good role models when it comes to getting children to try new foods. New foods may need to be offered 10 times or more before they are accepted. Food jags are normal and usually temporary.

Food jags, such as wanting to eat only one type of food are common among toddlers.

TABLE TIPS 

Kid-Friendly, Iron-Rich Foods

Stir raisins into warm cereal, or provide a small box of raisins for a snack.

Add cooked chickpeas (garbanzo beans) to tossed salads for an iron boost.

Tote a baggy with enriched breakfast cereal on car trips and errands for an iron-rich snack.

Use iron-enriched pastas, such as macaroni or spaghetti. Toss in some lean meatballs for a double dose of iron.

Mix enriched rice with dinnertime veggies for a nutrient-dense side dish.

What Are the Nutritional Needs and Issues of School-Aged Children?

School-aged children, usually considered those between the ages of 6 and 13, still have plenty of growing to do: Most boys and girls grow an average of 2 inches per year, and between ages 6 and 13, their weight approximately doubles.[13] See Table 30.1 for the range of calorie needs for children in this age group.

School-Aged Children Are Experiencing Higher Rates of Obesity

In recent decades, overweight and obesity have increased dramatically among children in this age group (Figure 30.2). Approximately, 17 percent of U.S. children and adolescents are considered obese.[14] The reason for the increase in childhood obesity is likely a combination of several factors, including too many calories and too little physical activity.

Children Are Overeating

Children are taking in excess calories from several sources, including sodas, candy, and chips and other snack items. Food is everywhere, including in places where it was previously unavailable, such as at gas stations and bookshops. Portion sizes, both in restaurants and at home, are bigger than they used to be.[15] American children, on the whole, eat a diet higher in fat, sodium, and added sugars, and lower in whole grains, fruits, vegetables, and lean dairy products, than they should be consuming.[16]

Although excess sugar and sweets may make weight management a challenge for children, research doesn't support that it negatively affects a child's behavior. The box feature "Does Sugar Cause ADHD?" discusses this further.

Children Are Not Getting Enough Physical Activity

Children are not getting enough physical activity to balance the energy they're consuming. The following are two of the multiple factors contributing to the decreased level of physical activity in recent years:

- *Increased screen time.* Research shows that 8- to 18-year-olds spend an average of 4½ hours daily watching TV, videos, DVDs, and movies. Children in the United

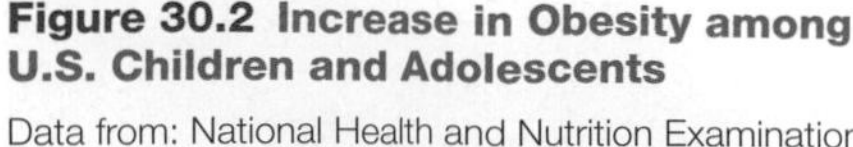

Figure 30.2 Increase in Obesity among U.S. Children and Adolescents

Data from: National Health and Nutrition Examination Surveys (NHANES) Center for Diesease Control. Accessed February 2009. Graph is available at: www.cdc.gov/nccdphp/dnpa/obesity/childhood/prevalence.htm.

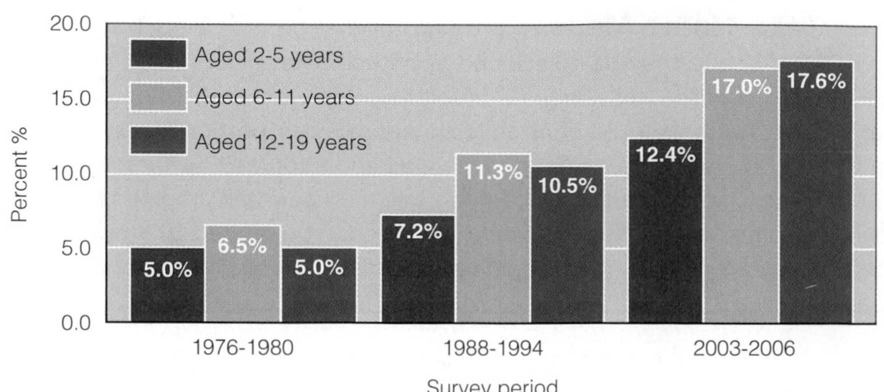

Does Sugar Cause ADHD?

An estimated 3 to 5 percent of children (about 2 million) in the United States have been diagnosed with **attention deficit hyperactivity disorder (ADHD)** (sometimes referred to as attention deficit disorder, or ADD). ADHD is a condition in which children are inattentive, hyperactive, and impulsive.[1] Children with ADHD have difficulty controlling their behavior, and their academic performance can be affected.

Parents of children with ADHD often wonder if dietary factors, such as sugar intake or food additives, are responsible for their children's behavior. Although the myth that sugar contributes to ADHD persists, there isn't any research to support this. In one study, children whose mothers felt they were sugar sensitive were given aspartame as a substitute for sugar. Half of the mothers were told their children were given sugar, half that their children were given aspartame. The mothers who thought their children had received sugar rated them as more hyperactive than the other children and were more critical of their behavior.[2]

The American Dietetic Association has concluded that sugar doesn't have an effect on behavior or learning. The American Academy of Pediatrics has also confirmed that there is no evidence that ADHD is caused by too much dietary sugar or by food additives, allergies, or immunizations.[3]

With so many children and families affected by ADHD, more theories about the cause have emerged in recent years. Some studies cite a possible connection between cigarette and alcohol use during pregnancy and the child's increased risk for ADHD. Other studies have noted a higher risk for ADHD with high levels of lead in preschoolers' bodies. Attention disorders often run in families, so genetic influences are also likely.[4]

Medication, psychotherapy, and behavioral therapies, as well as dietary restrictions, are among the treatments for ADHD. A serious nutritional side effect of some medications is growth stunting and underweight due to decreased appetite. Organizations such as the National Institute of Mental Health (www.nimh.nih.gov) and the American Academy of Child and Adolescent Psychiatry (www.aacap.org/index.ww) provide information for families with children who have ADHD.

attention deficit hyperactivity disorder (ADHD) A condition in which children, particularly, are easily distracted and have difficulty listening and following directions, focusing and sustaining attention, concentrating and staying on task, and/or inconsistent performance in school. Previously known as *attention deficit disorder* (ADD).

States also spend slightly more than 1 hour daily on the computer.[17] Screen time should be limited to no more than 2 hours daily.

- *Decreased physical activity at school.* Children are getting less physical activity while at school and during other parts of their day. Only 8 percent of U.S. elementary schools and 6.4 percent of middle schools provide daily physical education to students.[18] In addition, 20 percent of U.S. elementary schools have abolished recess, and less than 25 percent of children engage in 30 minutes of any kind of physical activity daily.[19]

To reduce their children's risk of becoming overweight or obese, parents and caregivers need to be sure that children receive adequate nutrients without overloading on calories, sugar, and fat and that they participate in plenty of physical activity. To help prevent children from becoming overweight, the American Academy of Pediatrics recommends that parents and caregivers serve as role models for healthy eating coupled with physical activity.[20]

Obesity Contributes to Diabetes

One result of increased obesity among children is an associated increase in rates of type 2 diabetes, which used to be seen solely in adulthood. For children diagnosed with type 2 diabetes, early intervention and treatment are a must. The sooner the family learns what the child needs to eat and how to manage all other aspects of the disease, the better off the child will be. In fact, the entire family should consider eating in the same fashion as the child, because managing type 2 diabetes involves moderation, variety, and balance.

Physical activity is also a major part of managing diabetes, and everyone can take part in this as well. Taking a family walk or bike ride after dinner instead of turning on the TV and enjoying weekend games of basketball or tennis are excellent ways to teach the importance of exercise. The child is more likely to feel supported and succeed with keeping his or her diabetes under control if everyone in the family is educated about what to do to help.

MyPyramid for Kids Can Help Guide Food Choices

Since parents are not nutrition experts, they can feel overwhelmed and confused by the task of trying to meet all of the nutrient needs of their children. Fortunately, a child-friendly (and therefore parent-friendly) MyPyramid for Kids is available (Figure 30.3). The slogan for both the preschoolers' and kids' versions of MyPyramid is "Eat Right. Exercise. Have Fun." These are the key messages:

- *Be physically active every day.* The child climbing the steps reminds children that physical activity should be done every day.
- *Choose healthier foods from each group.* Every food group has foods that should be eaten more often than others.
- *Eat more of some food groups than others.* As in MyPyramid for adults, the size of the color bands suggests how much food should be chosen from each group.
- *Eat foods from every food group every day.* The different colors of the pyramid represent the five food groups, plus oils.

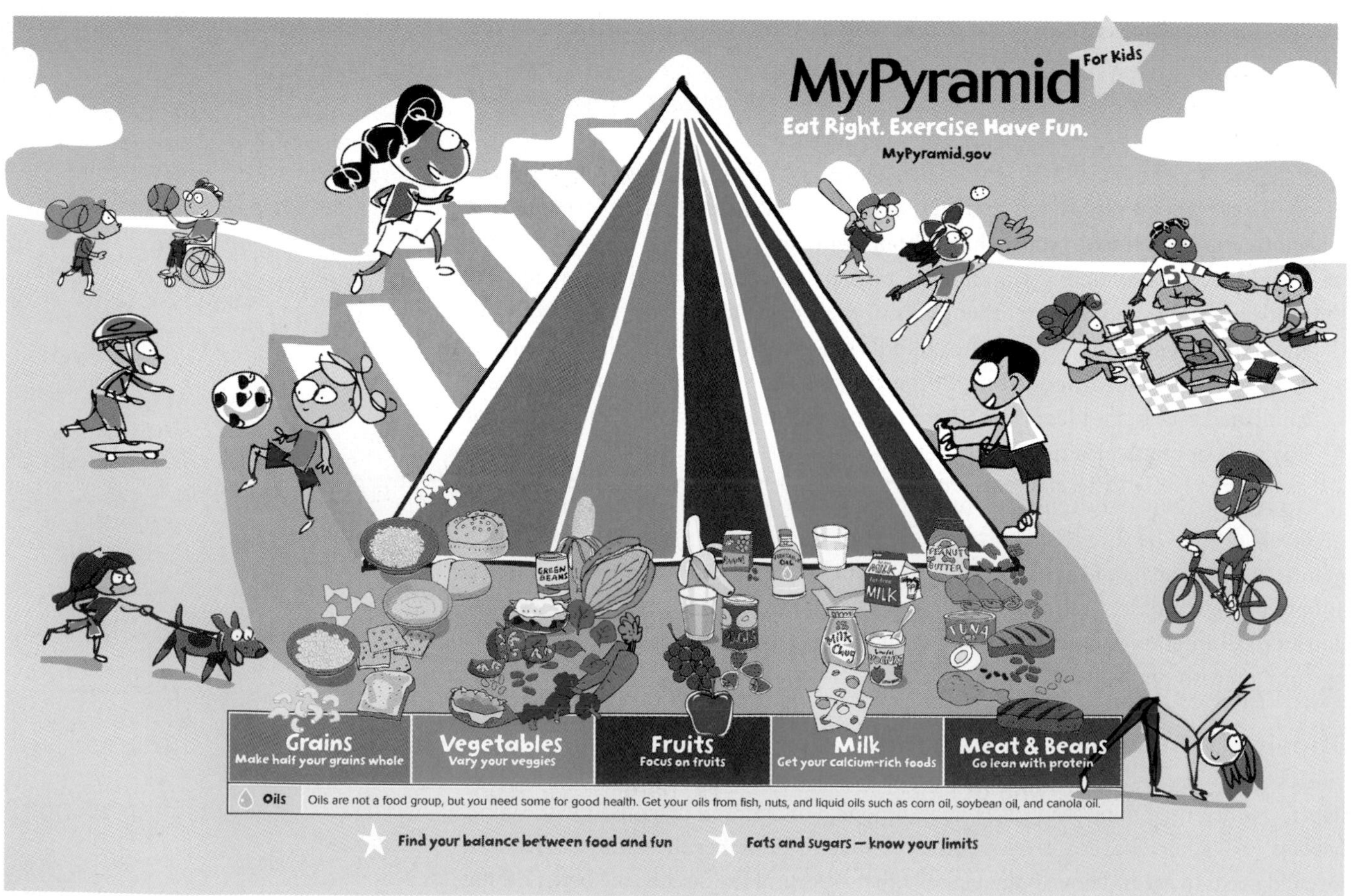

Figure 30.3 MyPyramid for Kids
MyPyramid for Kids is a tool parents and caregivers can use to help plan healthy meals for children.

- *Make the right choices for you.* MyPyramid.gov gives everyone in the family personal ideas on how to eat better and exercise more.
- *Take it one step at a time.* Start with one new, good thing a day, and continue to add another new one each day.

Children who have special health-related issues may not be able to follow MyPyramid for Kids. Overcoming health issues generally requires intervention and support from professionals who work with children with special needs, such as health care providers or registered dietitians.

The National School Lunch Program provides breakfast and noontime meals for millions of school-aged children.

School Lunches Contribute to Children's Nutritional Status

The National School Lunch Program (NSLP) provides nutritionally balanced, low-cost or free lunches to more than 28 million American children each school day.[21] The NSLP meals are designed to meet certain nutrient guidelines, including minimum levels of calories, protein, calcium, iron, vitamin A, and vitamin C as well as maximum levels for the percent of calories from fat and saturated fat. Every day, food-service directors in America's schools must meet the challenge of planning balanced meals, using a variety of food groups, in the right portions, depending on the ages of the students. For some children, the food they eat at school is the healthiest meal—perhaps the only meal—they eat all day.

Many schools are taking measures to ensure that their students eat healthfully during the day, including offering more fresh fruit in cafeterias, banning soda and snack vending machines, and monitoring students' food choices.

If children are not eating school lunches, it's up to the parents and caregivers to come up with a healthy substitute. By using MyPyramid for Kids as a guide, they can work with children to put together a mutually agreeable healthy packed lunch. A lunch that the child has helped plan has a better chance of being eaten. Without the child's input, the "healthy lunch" may end up being swapped for unhealthy foods, or worse, tossed in the trash can. The Table Tips provides some useful ideas to improve the likelihood that children will eat their packed lunch.

In addition to serving lunches, some schools also have school breakfast programs. Research has shown that eating breakfast may be associated with healthier body weight in children and adolescents. Breakfast can also improve cognitive function (especially memory), academic performance, school attendance rates, psychosocial function, and mood.[22] If children are hungry during the midmorning hours, they will have difficulty concentrating and learning during this time period.

If children don't have time to eat breakfast at home, and aren't receiving a school breakfast, caregivers can still provide quick, nutritious morning meals that can be eaten on the way to school. See the Table Tips for on-the-go breakfast ideas.

The Take-Home Message **Increasing obesity rates are contributing to rising rates of type 2 diabetes in school-aged children. Parents and caregivers need to be sure children limit their consumption of empty-calorie foods and get enough physical activity. MyPyramid for Kids addresses the nutritional needs of school-aged children. School meals provide nourishment for children. For children who don't eat school lunches, parents and caregivers need to provide a healthy alternative.**

TABLE TIPS 

Tips for Packing School Lunches

Get children excited about their lunches by having them pick out a fun lunch box or decorate a brown paper bag with stickers.

Involve kids in planning lunches and then shop for food items together.

Make a lunch calendar and review the days your child will eat a school-provided lunch and the days he or she will pack a lunch. On packing days, be sure to provide some food options.

Select new foods your child likes and ask if there are new items he or she wants to try.

Be mindful of what your child is actually eating and is being left behind or thrown away. For example, if an apple keeps coming back day after day, it's time to try an orange.

TABLE TIPS 

Breakfast on the Go

Mix some dry, unsweetened, whole-grain cereal with an individual-sized container of low-fat yogurt. Throw in some banana slices, berries, or dried fruit to make it even more nutritious.

Sprinkle reduced-fat cheese on a corn tortilla and melt it in the oven or microwave. Add some salsa and corn and roll it up into a portable tortilla tube.

Spread a thin layer of peanut butter or all-fruit preserves on a toasted whole-wheat waffle, and pair it with a travel cup of skim milk.

What Are the Nutritional Needs and Issues of Adolescents?

Adolescence is the stage of the life cycle between the start of puberty and adulthood. With adolescence come many hormonal, physical, and emotional changes, including:

- *Hormonal changes.* Under the influence of hormones, adolescents develop secondary sex characteristics, such as pubic hair and, for boys, a lower speaking voice. Girls experience breast development and their first menstrual period (called *menarche*). Adolescents of either sex can experience their first outbreak of acne.
- *Physical changes.* Among the physical changes are a rapid growth spurt, which must be supported with appropriate quantities of nutrients, and adequate calories (energy) and protein. Adolescents attain about 15 percent of their adult height during this stage, and about 50 percent of their ideal adult weight. Bones grow significantly, and lean muscle mass and body fat stores also increase. Thus, calcium, vitamin D, and iron are particularly important at this stage. As with younger age groups, the rate of obesity is increasing among adolescents, and 17.6 percent are considered obese (see Figure 30.2, on page 6).
- *Emotional changes.* Some nutrition-related issues that arise during adolescence may be indirectly caused by the emotional growth that is occurring. Adolescents experience a strong desire for independence and individuality, and most want to make their own food choices, which may be less nutritious than what is being served at home. Some defy authority by adopting more rigid dietary choices than their parents, such as insisting on organically grown foods or adopting a vegan diet. The influence of peers, the media, and other nonparental role models may prompt adolescents to adopt damaging habits, such as smoking to lose weight or drinking alcohol to gain acceptance as one of the "in crowd." Unfortunately, these habits not only are unhealthy but also can contribute to low self-esteem when the outcomes do not meet expectations.

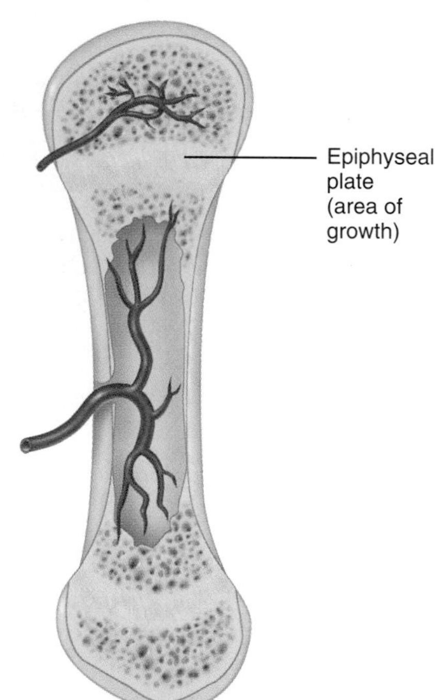

Figure 30.4 Epiphyseal Plate in Long Bone
Adolescent bone growth takes place in the epiphyseal plate. Once the plates close, lengthening of the bone stops.

Adolescents Need Calcium and Vitamin D for Bone Growth

Adolescents experience rapid bone growth. Most of the growth occurs in the *epiphyseal plate* (Figure 30.4), the area of tissue near the end of the long bones in children and adolescents. The growth plate determines the future length and shape of the mature bone. At some point during adolescence, bone growth is complete. The plates close and are replaced by solid bone.[23] In contrast, bone density increases through early adulthood, and peak bone mass may not be reached until age 30.

Inadequate intakes of calcium and vitamin D during adolescence are factors that can lead to low peak bone mass and increase the risk for osteoporosis.[24] A study followed females ages 15 to 18 for seven years and looked at their bone health. The results indicated that the subjects' hip and forearm bone density was increased in those who had been given calcium supplements or dairy products, rather than a placebo.[25] Another study instructed boys ages 13 to 17 to consume an additional three servings per day of either 1 percent milk or unfortified juice. The boys in the milk group had

adolescence The developmental period between the start of puberty and adulthood.

significantly greater increases in bone mineral density than those in the juice group.[26] As with children, the recommendation for vitamin D has recently been increased to 400 IU daily.[27]

Inadequate intakes of calcium and vitamin D among adolescents are common. One reason for this trend is teens' increased preference for soft drinks instead of milk or other beverages providing calcium and vitamin D. One study found that about 66 percent of boys and 56 percent of girls between the ages of 12 and 17 drink one or more calorie-containing soft drinks daily.[28] Sodas and other empty-calorie beverages, such as energy drinks and sports drinks, may taste good and be popular with peers, but they lack the nutrients that are so crucial for developing bones.

Adolescents experience changes in their bodies, their emotions, and their relationships with others.

Teenagers Need More Iron

Adolescents need additional iron to support muscle growth and increased blood volume. Adolescent girls also need more iron to support the onset of menstruation.

Many adolescents, especially those who are dieting, have an inadequate iron intake. In a large study, iron deficiency was found in over 14 percent of the girls ages 15 to 18 and 12 percent of the boys ages 11 to 14 in the United States.[29] Iron deficiency has been shown to exist in both male and female teens of all races and socioeconomic levels.[30] Teens who limit enriched grains, lean meats, and legumes in their diet are running the risk of failing to meet their daily iron needs.

Adolescents Are Sometimes at Risk for Disordered Eating

Teens must adjust to new bodies, new thoughts, new experiences, and new social networks. These changes, along with the typical adolescent feeling of immortality, increase the potential for an adolescent to engage in risky tactics to reach and maintain a desired weight, and can ultimately lead to disordered eating behaviors. These can include eating very little food, using a food substitute, skipping meals, smoking cigarettes, taking diet pills, engaging in self-induced vomiting, and/or using laxatives or diuretics. These behaviors typically fail. A study found that, compared with teens who did not use any weight-control methods, adolescents who engaged in unhealthful behaviors to control their weight exhibited a slightly higher body mass index and a greater risk of being overweight, binge eating, or extreme dieting five years later.[31] In essence, the teen ends up with two problems: the feeling of failure as well as the health consequences associated with the risky tactic used to try to change his or her weight.

The Take-Home Message Adolescents face hormonal, physical, and emotional changes. They typically want to have control over their food and lifestyle decisions, and peers and the media exert a tremendous amount of influence. Calcium, vitamin D, and iron intakes are particularly important during adolescence to ensure adequate bone and muscle growth. Increased consumption of soft drinks and decreased milk consumption can compromise bone health. Adolescents are sometimes at risk of developing disordered eating patterns due to poor body image, emotional issues, and peer pressure. Because many adolescents live in the "here and now," they may not realize the long-term health consequences of the poor diet and lifestyle habits they adopt during their teenage years.

What Are the Nutritional Needs of Older Adults?

People are living longer now than in earlier times.

At about age 50, a person is considered an older adult. Reaching this age wasn't always a given. If you were born in 1900, you would have been lucky to see your fiftieth birthday, as the average **life expectancy** at that time was 47 years. People born in the 1960s can expect to live to about age 70, while those born in the 1990s are expected to live past age 75.[32] Currently, the population of the United States includes over 50,000 centenarians, people who are 100 years of age or older.[33]

Adults Are Living Longer

What happened in the last 100-plus years to so dramatically increase the average life expectancy? Advances in research and health care, coupled with public health promotion programs, have all contributed to Americans' longer lives. For example, the incidence of infectious and deadly diseases of the 1900s, such as tuberculosis, pneumonia, polio, mumps, and measles, has been dramatically reduced by the development of vaccinations and antibiotics. Screening exams detect disease at earlier stages, and surgery, when needed, is safer. Public education campaigns have targeted chronic diseases to discourage smoking, increase physical activity, and adopt a healthy diet.

The number of individuals 65 years of age and older is projected to increase to over 80 million in 2050.[34] Good nutrition continues to play a key role in healthful aging. Nutrient needs, and the way the body uses some nutrients, change as you age.[35] Let's look at some of the specific changes that occur during older age.

Older Adults Need Fewer Calories, Not Less Nutrition

People need fewer overall calories in their senior years than when they were younger, but their need for certain nutrients increases.

Because a person's metabolic rate naturally declines with age, older adults need fewer calories. The decline in their metabolism is a combination of the natural loss of muscle mass (muscle mass requires more energy than fat mass to be maintained) and the tendency to engage in less daily physical activity. This decline amounts to approximately 10 calories a year for men and 7 calories yearly for women beginning at age 30.[36] In other words, a man at age 60 needs 300 fewer daily calories—about the amount in a turkey sandwich—than he needed at age 30.

Although calorie needs may be reduced, the need for many nutrients and phytochemicals isn't. In fact, the requirement for some nutrients actually increases in older adults, making nutrient-dense food selections even more important. Since phytochemicals, especially antioxidants, may help reduce the risk for certain cancers, heart disease, and age-related vision disorders, foods need to be both nutrient dense and phytochemical dense.

life expectancy The number of years that a majority of people within a population are expected to live.

Older Adults Need to Get Enough Fiber and Fluids

Older adults' requirements for dietary protein, fat, and carbohydrates don't change from their younger years, and research shows that these three nutrient needs can be met easily by a balanced diet.[37] Because they are consuming fewer calories, older adults need to eat high-fiber foods, such as whole grains, fruits, and vegetables, at each meal. Although their dietary fiber needs actually decrease slightly, over 70 percent of Americans over age 50, on average, are still not meeting their daily needs.[38]

Older adults have the same fluid recommendations as younger people. Consuming adequate amounts of fluid is important, as the kidneys' ability to concentrate urine declines with age, and an older person's thirst mechanism becomes blunted. Both factors increase the risk of older adults' becoming dehydrated. Dehydration can lead to constipation, another common condition in older adults, as the stool becomes hard and compacted in the colon.

Because of the need for nutrient-dense foods, there is little room in an older adult's diet for sugar-laden soft drinks that are high in calories and low in nutrients. Water and milk are better beverages to meet their fluid needs and to avoid dehydration. Table 30.2 summarizes these dietary changes.

Table 30.2

Dietary Changes Needed As You Age

What Older Adults Need	Why Older Adults Need It	How They Can Get It
More nutrient-dense foods	Their lower metabolic rate, which reduces their daily calorie needs	Choose foods in each food group that are low in added sugar and saturated fat.
More fiber	Their consumption of fewer daily calories, which decreases their fiber intake	Choose whole-wheat bread, whole-grain cereals, brown rice, vegetables, and whole fruit.
More water and nutrient-dense fluids; less sugary, low-nutrient soft drinks	Their kidneys' decreased ability to concentrate urine and their blunted thirst mechanism, which can both increase their risk for dehydration	Drink low-fat or skim milk and water with and between meals.
More foods high in β-carotene to meet vitamin A needs and less vitamin A supplements and heavily fortified foods	Higher excess amounts of stored preformed vitamin A in their bodies, which can be unhealthy for bones	Choose carrots, cantaloupe, sweet potatoes, broccoli, and winter squash.
More vitamin D–fortified foods	Their decreased ability to make the active form of vitamin D, which decreases their absorption of calcium and phosphorus and increases their risk for osteoporosis	Choose vitamin D–fortified milk, yogurt, and cereals. Add a supplement if needed.
More synthetic vitamin B_{12}	Fewer acidic stomach juices, which lessens their absorption of vitamin B_{12} in foods	Choose vitamin B_{12}–fortified cereals and soy milk. Add a supplement if needed.
More iron-rich foods	Higher prevalence of anemia	Choose lean meat, fish, and poultry. Enjoy enriched grains and cereals along with vitamin C–rich foods (citrus fruits) to enhance absorption.
More zinc-rich foods	Their suppressed immune system and appetite due to a zinc deficiency	Choose fortified cereals, lean meats, poultry, legumes, and nuts.
More calcium-rich foods	Higher risk for osteoporosis and dietary calcium deficiency	Consume three servings of dairy foods daily, plus a serving of a calcium-fortified food. Add a supplement if needed.

Older Adults Need to Watch Micronutrient Intake

Appropriate intakes of certain micronutrients become a concern as we age:

- *Vitamin A.* Although the recommended daily amount of vitamin A doesn't change for people over the age of 50, too much preformed vitamin A (derived from animal sources), which is stored in the body, may increase the risk for osteoporosis and fractures. Older adults should be cautious when choosing supplements and fortified foods to prevent overconsuming this form of vitamin A.[39] However, beta-carotene, a vitamin A precursor, is not of concern and is actually beneficial because of its role as an antioxidant in the body.
- *Vitamin D.* The skin's ability to make vitamin D from sunlight declines with age. Further, the intestines and kidneys lose some ability to absorb and convert vitamin D into its active form.[40] Because of these changes, the need for vitamin D in the diet doubles at age 50 and triples at age 70, compared with younger adults.
- *Vitamin B_{12}.* In up to 30 percent of people over the age of 50, the stomach secretes less hydrochloric acid. One role of hydrochloric acid is to separate the vitamin B_{12} from the proteins in foods of animal origin. Thus, low acid production means that we cannot free up and absorb enough of the vitamin B_{12} that naturally occurs in foods. The synthetic form of B_{12} found in fortified foods and supplements is not affected, so these sources should be added to an older adult's diet. Vitamin B_{12}, along with adequate amounts of folate and vitamin B_6, may also help lower homocysteine levels, decreasing the risk for heart disease.
- *Iron.* Iron deficiency is common in older adults; over 10 percent of adults 65 years or older, and over 20 percent of those 85 or older, experience iron-deficiency anemia.[41] Although iron deficiency can occur from intestinal blood loss, an estimated one-third of the anemia in older adults stems from inadequate iron consumption and/or from insufficient folate and vitamin B_{12} in the diet.[42]
- *Zinc.* Zinc affects our ability to taste things, and a deficiency can depress a person's appetite, and hence, their desire to eat nutritious foods. About 25 percent of older Americans don't meet their needs for daily dietary zinc and would benefit from adding more zinc to their diets through foods such as cereals and legumes (beans).[43]
- *Calcium.* The need for calcium increases 20 percent—to 1,200 milligrams daily—for people over the age of 50. More than 70 percent of older Americans fall short of their dietary calcium needs.[44] Older adults should eat at least three servings of dairy foods daily and should add a serving of a calcium-fortified food or a supplement, to cover their increased calcium needs.

Older Adults Need to Eat a Varied, Heart-Healthy Diet

According to the World Health Organization (WHO), the best dietary strategy for aging adults in order to maintain good health and prevent chronic diseases is to consume a varied, nutrient- and phytochemical-dense, heart-healthy diet.[45] This is the same dietary advice that is recommended in both the *Dietary Guidelines for Americans* and MyPyramid.

Most older Americans aren't heeding this advice. When the diets of Americans 65 years of age and older were assessed to see if they were following these guidelines, only 19 percent of those studied had diets that could be rated as "good." More than 65 percent of the older Americans were eating diets that needed improvement, and

13 percent were consuming diets rated as "poor."[46] Older Americans are eating too few servings of fruits, vegetables, whole grains, and dairy foods. The diets of many older adults have also been shown to be too high in saturated fat, cholesterol, and sodium, increasing their risk for heart disease, hypertension, and stroke.[47]

Regular physical activity can help older adults stay physically, mentally, and socially healthy.

Older Adults Need to Stay Physically Active

Joan skis both downhill and cross-country in the winter and has been attending aerobics class six days a week for the last decade—a rather active schedule for a 76-year-old. Robert attends weekly fitness classes and skates in a hockey league three days a week. At age 78, he skates only in nonchecking leagues but admits that collisions are part of the game.

No one is too old to exercise, and physical activity is not a luxury for older adults; it's a necessity. Routine physical activity can help lower the risk for heart disease, colon and breast cancer, diabetes, hypertension, osteoporosis, arthritis, and obesity. It can help maintain healthy bones, muscles, and joints and reduce anxiety, stress, and depression. Routine exercise improves sleep, flexibility, and range of motion and can help postpone the decline in cognitive ability that naturally occurs in aging.[48] Seniors in good physical shape are also able to live independently longer, reducing the need for assistance with everyday functions.

The number-one physical activity among older Americans is **walking.** Gardening is second, followed by bicycling.

Despite the many health benefits of being physically active, only 16 percent of those ages 64 to 74 and only 12 percent of those 75 years of age and older engage in at least 30 minutes of moderate activity five days a week. Lifestyle activities, such as working in the garden, mowing the lawn, raking leaves, and even dancing, provide health benefits. Older adults also benefit from strength training activities, such as weight lifting and calisthenics, at least twice a week to help maintain muscle strength.[49]

Economic Hardship Can Affect Nutritional Health

Between his medical and pharmaceutical costs and basic living expenses, Joe exhausts his monthly Social Security check within about three weeks. For the seven to 10 days until he gets his next check, Joe makes due with a severely limited menu of oatmeal and eggs. Although technically he's not going hungry, his restricted diet is depriving him of many basic nutrients.

Joe is not alone. Almost 7 percent of households with elders in the United States live with food insecurity (see Concept 28).[50] Research has shown that elders who consistently experience food insecurity have more than twice the risk of not meeting their daily nutritional needs, and they tend to be in only fair to poor health.[51]

There are over 4,500 Meals On Wheels programs serving **housebound** Americans.

Limited finances aren't always the cause of food insecurity. Some elders may be able to afford food but lack the physical means to obtain it, prepare it, or, because of health issues such as tooth loss, consume it.[52] In 1965, the Older Americans Act was passed to provide support and services to those age 60 and older, including nutritious meals and nutrition education, in order to help them maintain good health, an adequate quality of life, and an acceptable level of independence.[53] *Congregate meals* are one type of available service. These nutritious hot meals are served at specified sites in the community, such as

Programs such as Meals On Wheels provide hot meals to elderly adults who cannot leave their homes.

churches and synagogues. Healthy meals can also be delivered to the home.[54] The Meals On Wheels Association of America is the largest organization in the United States providing meals to the homes of older adults who need them.

Young people in the community can help make sure the elderly are aware of and take advantage of the numerous services available to them. Consider "adopting" an elder family member or neighbor and, if need be, help him or her locate these services.

Depression and Alcohol Abuse Can Affect Nutritional Health

When Laura lost her husband at the age of 78, she stopped cooking a nightly dinner and took to opening a can of soup for most of her evening meals. Her energy level dropped dramatically after his death, and on many days, she didn't even bother to get out of her pajamas. Like many elders who lose a spouse, Laura became depressed.

Up to 20 percent of older adults can suffer from depression, ranging from mild to major depressive disorders.[55] The loss of significant others and friends, as well as chronic pain and concerns about their own health, can add to feelings of grief, sadness, and isolation. Depression can interfere with an elder's motivation to eat, be physically active, and socialize—all of which can impact a person's mental and physical health.

Chronic health problems, loss of friends and loved ones, and/or financial stress can make alcohol seem like an appealing sedative to older adults without adequate social support. But consuming alcohol only makes things worse. Heavy drinking can exacerbate depression, which can lead to more drinking.[56] Alcohol is expensive, and it can quickly deplete an elder's limited resources. As discussed in Concept 19, excessive alcohol intake can lead to malnutrition. Also, because alcohol impairs one's judgment and interferes with coordination and reaction time, elders who have been drinking are at a higher risk for stumbling, falling, and fracturing bones.

Family members, friends, and neighbors need to be aware of the changes in elders' moods, eating behaviors, and lifestyle habits. Younger adults need to help elders reconnect with their communities after a loss and adjust to a new lifestyle. As mentioned, neighbors can "adopt an elder" who may be living alone and coordinate regular visits and delivery of meals. A quick visit by several supportive friends over the course of a month can go a long way to help elders stay healthy.

The Take-Home Message **Life expectancy has increased in the last century because of improved research and health care, dietary and lifestyle changes, and other factors. Older adults need fewer calories, but not less nutrition, as they age. Nutrient-dense food selections are important to meet their fiber, fluid, vitamin, mineral, and phytochemical needs. A healthy diet can help prevent many of the chronic diseases associated with aging. Older adults benefit from regular physical activity. Disease, food insecurity, depression, and alcohol abuse can challenge the abilities of older adults to maintain healthy diets and lifestyles.**

UCook

Turkey Pizza Cutlet

In the mood for healthy Italian food? Try this easy Turkey Pizza Cutlet for dinner. Leftovers are great for lunch the next day on a whole-wheat roll. Mangia!

UDo

Yes, You Can!

Want to learn more about how to help an older relative or friend stay active and healthy? Visit the link at our website for information on how to help older people in your life increase their physical activity.

The Top Five Points to Remember

1. Toddlers and preschoolers grow less rapidly than infants but need to eat small, frequent, nutrient-dense meals and snacks to fuel their busy lifestyles. Young children may be picky eaters and go on food jags, but these behaviors are normal and usually temporary. Iron deficiency is a common problem of young children, and adequate calcium, vitamin D, and fiber are important to ensure healthy bone growth and bowel regularity. Milk, water, and diluted juices are better beverage choices than sweetened, flavored drinks.
2. Obesity and type 2 diabetes are occurring at higher rates in children of all ages. Poor dietary choices and not enough exercise are two of the key culprits of this problem. Parents and caregivers must provide healthy foods and encourage physical activity to combat a child's likelihood of developing these conditions.
3. MyPyramid for Kids provides guidance for planning healthy meals and snacks for children. The National School Lunch Program must meet certain guidelines set by the USDA. Children with packed school lunches should be involved in the planning and preparation of the lunch, so that they are more likely to eat it.
4. Adolescents experience hormonal, physical, and emotional changes. They are heavily influenced by peers, the media, and other nonparental role models, which may lead them to adopt unhealthy eating and lifestyle habits, such as skipping meals, choosing unhealthy foods, dieting, or smoking. Because adolescent bones are still growing, teens need to consume enough calcium, and increased soda consumption may interfere with this if it displaces milk in the diet. Iron is also important for the growth of lean muscle and for girls' onset of menstruation. Some teens may be at risk for disordered eating patterns.
5. Metabolism slows with age, so older adults need fewer calories than their younger counterparts. Older adults need to be sure to consume enough fiber, fluid, vitamins D and B_{12}, and the minerals iron, calcium, and zinc. Too much preformed vitamin A, in contrast, should be avoided. Staying physically active is important during the older years. Older adults sometimes suffer from food insecurity, depression, or alcohol abuse. Social programs can help ensure the nourishment of homebound adults by delivering precooked meals.

Test Yourself

1. Because they are still growing but have diminished appetites (compared with infants), toddlers and preschoolers should
   a. consume large meals.
   b. consume nutrient-dense foods.
   c. consume foods high in fat.
   d. consume foods high in sugar.
2. There appears to be a relationship between the rise in childhood obesity and the increase in
   a. childhood cancers.
   b. ADHD.
   c. type 2 diabetes in children.
   d. childhood cavities.
3. Which mineral supports healthy bone development and is particularly important during adolescence?
   a. calcium
   b. iron
   c. vitamin D
   d. copper
4. Which of the following two nutrient needs increase in older adults?
   a. water and fiber
   b. calcium and vitamin D
   c. protein and lipids
   d. vitamin K and biotin
5. Which of the following can influence an older adult's ability to consume a nutritious diet?
   a. living on a fixed income
   b. depression
   c. alcohol abuse
   d. all of the above

Answers

1. (b) Toddlers need to eat nutrient-dense foods in order to obtain all the nutrients they need. Their reduced appetites mean they aren't likely to eat large meals, and foods high in fat and sugar may add significant calories without contributing many nutrients.
2. (c) Rates of type 2 diabetes among children have risen, along with rates of obesity.
3. (a) Adolescents need adequate amounts of calcium to support their growing bones. Iron is important during adolescence to support the development of lean muscle mass and offset the iron girls lose as they begin menstruating. Vitamin D is not a mineral, but it is also very important for bone growth. Copper is a trace mineral that most people consume in adequate amounts.
4. (b) The need for both calcium and vitamin D is increased in older adults. Protein, fat, and water needs don't change with aging. Fiber needs can decrease slightly. Vitamin K and biotin are necessary for health, but you don't need them in higher amounts as you age.
5. (d) Older adults who may have a limited income may not be able to purchase adequate amounts of healthy food to meet their nutrient needs. Depression can interfere with an elder's motivation to eat. An alcohol-heavy diet not only displaces nutritious foods but can also increase the risk for falls and injuries.

Web Resources

- For more information on nutrition during the younger years, visit: www.cdc.gov/HealthyYouth/nutrition/index.htm
- For more information on children's and teens' health, visit: www.kidshealth.org
- For more about ADHD, visit: www.nimh.nih.gov
- To learn about practical tools for keeping kids at a healthy weight, visit We Can! at: www.nhlbi.nih.gov/health/public/heart/obesity/wecan/index.htm
- For more about the USDA's School Lunch Program, visit: www.fns.usda.gov/cnd/lunch
- For more nutrition information for older adults, visit: www.cdc.gov/aging/info.htm

Appendices

Appendix A Organizations and Resources

Academic Journals

International Journal of Sport Nutrition and Exercise Metabolism
Human Kinetics
P.O. Box 5076
Champaign, IL 61825-5076
(800) 747-4457
www.humankinetics.com/IJSNEM

Journal of Nutrition
A. Catharine Ross, Editor
Department of Nutrition
Pennsylvania State University
126-S Henderson Building
University Park, PA 16802-6504
(814) 865-4721
www.nutrition.org

Nutrition Research
Elsevier: Journals Customer Service
6277 Sea Harbor Drive
Orlando, FL 32887
(877) 839-7126
www.journals.elsevierhealth.com/periodicals/NTR

Nutrition
Elsevier: Journals Customer Service
6277 Sea Harbor Drive
Orlando, FL 32887
(877) 839-7126
www.journals.elsevierhealth.com/periodicals/NUT

Nutrition Reviews
International Life Sciences Institute
Subscription Office
P.O. Box 830430
Birmingham, AL 35283
(800) 633-4931
www.ingentaconnect.com/content/ilsi/nure

Obesity Research
North American Association for the Study of Obesity (NAASO)
8630 Fenton Street, Suite 918
Silver Spring, MD 20910
(301) 563-6526
www.obesityresearch.org

International Journal of Obesity
Journal of the International Association for the Study of Obesity
Nature Publishing Group
The Macmillan Building
4 Crinan Street
London N1 9XW
United Kingdom
www.nature.com/ijo

Journal of the American Medical Association
American Medical Association
P.O. Box 10946
Chicago, IL 60610-0946
(800) 262-2350
http://jama.ama-assn.org

New England Journal of Medicine
10 Shattuck Street
Boston, MA 02115-6094
(617) 734-9800
http://content.nejm.org/

American Journal of Clinical Nutrition
The American Journal of Clinical Nutrition
9650 Rockville Pike
Bethesda, MD 20814-3998
(301) 634-7038
www.ajcn.org

Journal of the American Dietetic Association
Elsevier: Health Sciences Division
Subscription Customer Service
6277 Sea Harbor Drive
Orlando, FL 32887
(800) 654-2452
www.adajournal.org

Aging

Administration on Aging
U.S. Health & Human Services
200 Independence Avenue, SW
Washington, DC 20201
(877) 696-6775
www.aoa.gov

American Association of Retired Persons (AARP)
601 E. Street, NW
Washington, DC 20049
(888) 687-2277
www.aarp.org

Health and Age
Sponsored by the Novartis Foundation for Gerontology & The Web-Based Health Education Foundation
Robert Griffith, MD
Executive Director
573 Vista de la Ciudad
Santa Fe, NM 87501
www.healthandage.com

National Council on the Aging
300 D Street, SW, Suite 801
Washington, DC 20024
(202) 479-1200
www.ncoa.org

International Osteoporosis Foundation
5 Rue Perdtemps
1260 Nyon
Switzerland
41 22 994 01 00
www.osteofound.org

National Institute on Aging
Building 31, Room 5C27
31 Center Drive, MSC 2292
Bethesda, MD 20892
(301) 496-1752
www.nia.nih.gov

Osteoporosis and Related Bone Diseases National Resource Center
2 AMS Circle
Bethesda, MD 20892-3676
(800) 624-BONE
www.osteo.org

American Geriatrics Society
The Empire State Building
350 Fifth Avenue, Suite 801
New York, NY 10118
(212) 308-1414
www.americangeriatrics.org

National Osteoporosis Foundation
1232 22nd Street, NW
Washington, DC 20037-1292
(202) 223-2226
www.nof.org/

Alcohol and Drug Abuse

National Institute on Drug Abuse
6001 Executive Boulevard, Room 5213
Bethesda, MD 20892-9561
(301) 443-1124
www.nida.nih.gov

National Institute on Alcohol Abuse and Alcoholism
5635 Fishers Lane, MSC 9304
Bethesda, MD 20892-9304
www.niaaa.nih.gov

Alcoholics Anonymous
Grand Central Station
P.O. Box 459
New York, NY 10163
www.alcoholics-anonymous.org

Narcotics Anonymous
P.O. Box 9999
Van Nuys, California 91409
(818) 773-9999
www.na.org

National Council on Alcoholism and Drug Dependence
20 Exchange Place, Suite 2902
New York, NY 10005
(212) 269-7797
www.ncadd.org

National Clearinghouse for Alcohol and Drug Information
11420 Rockville Pike
Rockville, MD 20852
(800) 729-6686
http://ncadi.samhsa.gov

Canadian Government

Health Canada
A.L. 0900C2
Ottawa, ON K1A 0K9
(613) 957-2991
www.hc-sc.gc.ca/english

National Institute of Nutrition
408 Queen Street, 3rd Floor
Ottawa, ON K1R 5A7
(613) 235-3355
www.nin.ca/public_html/index.html

Agricultural and Agri-Food Canada
Public Information Request Service
Sir John Carling Building
930 Carling Avenue
Ottawa, ON K1A 0C5
(613) 759-1000
www.arg.gc.ca

Bureau of Nutritional Sciences
Sir Frederick G. Banting Research Centre
Tunney's Pasture (2203A)
Ottawa, ON K1A 0L2
(613) 957-0352
www.hc-sc.gc.ca/food-aliment/ns-sc/e_nutrition.html

Canadian Food Inspection Agency
59 Camelot Drive
Ottawa, ON K1A 0Y9
(613) 225-2342
www.inspection.gc.ca/english/toce.shtml

Canadian Institute for Health Information
CIHI Ottawa
377 Dalhousie Street, Suite 200
Ottawa, ON K1N 9N8
(613) 241-7860
www.cihi.ca

Canadian Public Health Association
1565 Carling Avenue, Suite 400
Ottawa, ON K1Z 8R1
(613) 725-3769
www.cpha.ca

Canadian Nutrition and Professional Organizations

Dietitians of Canada, Canadian Dietetic Association
480 University Avenue, Suite 604
Toronto, ON M5G 1V2
(416) 596-0857
www.dietitians.ca

Canadian Diabetes Association
National Life Building
1400-522 University Avenue
Toronto, ON M5G 2R5
(800) 226-8464
www.diabetes.ca

National Eating Disorder Information Centre
CW 1-211, 200 Elizabeth Street
Toronto, ON M5G 2C4
(866) NEDIC-20
www.nedic.ca

Canadian Pediatric Society
100-2204 Walkley Road
Ottawa, ON K1G 4G8
(613) 526-9397
www.cps.ca

Disordered Eating/ Eating Disorders

American Psychiatric Association
1000 Wilson Boulevard, Suite 1825
Arlington, VA 22209
(703) 907-7300
www.psych.org

Harvard Eating Disorders Center
WACC 725
15 Parkman Street
Boston, MA 02114
(617) 236-7766
www.hedc.org

National Institute of Mental Health
Office of Communications
6001 Executive Boulevard, Room 8184, MSC 9663
Bethesda, MD 20892
(866) 615-6464
www.nimh.nih.gov

National Association of Anorexia Nervosa and Associated Disorders (ANAD)
P.O. Box 7
Highland Park, IL 60035
(847) 831-3438
www.anad.org

National Eating Disorders Association
603 Stewart Street, Suite 803
Seattle, WA 98101
(206) 382-3587
www.nationaleatingdisorders.org

Eating Disorder Referral and Information Center
2923 Sandy Pointe, Suite 6
Del Mar, CA 92014
(858) 792-7463
www.edreferral.com

Anorexia Nervosa and Related Eating Disorders, Inc. (ANRED)
E-mail: jarinor@rio.com
www.anred.com

Overeaters Anonymous
P.O. Box 44020
Rio Rancho, NM 87174
(505) 891-2664
www.oa.org

Exercise, Physical Activity, and Sports

American College of Sports Medicine (ACSM)
P.O. Box 1440
Indianapolis, IN 46206-1440
(317) 637-9200
www.acsm.org

American Physical Therapy Association (APTA)
1111 North Fairfax Street
Alexandria, VA 22314
(800) 999-APTA
www.apta.org

Gatorade Sports Science Institute (GSSI)
617 West Main Street
Barrington, IL 60010
(800) 616-GSSI
www.gssiweb.com

National Coalition for Promoting Physical Activity (NCPPA)
1010 Massachusetts Avenue, Suite 350
Washington, DC 20001
(202) 454-7518
www.ncppa.org

Sports, Wellness, Eating Disorder and Cardiovascular Nutritionists (SCAN)
P.O. Box 60820
Colorado Springs, CO 80960
(719) 635-6005
www.scandpg.org

President's Council on Physical Fitness and Sports
Department W
200 Independence Avenue, SW
Room 738-H
Washington, DC 20201-0004
(202) 690-9000
www.fitness.gov

American Council on Exercise
4851 Paramount Drive
San Diego, CA 92123
(858) 279-8227
www.acefitness.org

The International Association for Fitness Professionals (IDEA)
10455 Pacific Center Court
San Diego, CA 92121
(800) 999-4332, ext. 7
www.ideafit.com

Food Safety

Food Marketing Institute
655 15th Street, NW
Washington, DC 20005
(202) 452-8444
www.fmi.org

Agency for Toxic Substances and Disease Registry (ATSDR)
ORO Washington Office
Ariel Rios Building
1200 Pennsylvania Avenue, NW
M/C 5204G
Washington, DC 20460
(888) 422-8737
www.atsdr.cdc.gov

Food Allergy and Anaphylaxis Network
11781 Lee Jackson Highway, Suite 160
Fairfax, VA 22033-3309
(800) 929-4040
www.foodallergy.org

Foodsafety.gov
www.foodsafety.gov

The USDA Food Safety and Inspection Service
Food Safety and Inspection Service
United States Department of Agriculture
Washington, DC 20250
www.fsis.usda.gov

Consumer Reports
Web Site Customer Relations Department
101 Truman Avenue
Yonkers, NY 10703
www.consumerreports.org

Center for Science in the Public Interest: Food Safety
1875 Connecticut Avenue, NW
Washington, DC 20009
(202) 332-9110
www.cspinet.org/foodsafety/index.html

Center for Food Safety and Applied Nutrition
5100 Paint Branch Parkway
College Park, MD 20740
(888) SAFEFOOD
www.cfsan.fda.gov

Food Safety Project
Dan Henroid, MS, RD, CFSP
HRIM Extension Specialist and Website Coordinator
Hotel, Restaurant and Institution Management
9e MacKay Hall
Iowa State University
Ames, IA 50011
(515) 294-3527
www.extension.iastate.edu/foodsafety

Organic Consumers Association
6101 Cliff Estate Road
Little Marais, MN 55614
(218) 226-4164
www.organicconsumers.org

Infancy and Childhood

Administration for Children and Families
370 L'Enfant Promenade, SW
Washington, DC 20447
www.acf.dhhs.gov

The American Academy of Pediatrics
141 Northwest Point Boulevard
Elk Grove Village, IL 60007
(847) 434-4000
www.aap.org

Kidshealth: The Nemours Foundation
1600 Rockland Road
Wilmington, DE 19803
(302) 651-4046
www.kidshealth.org

National Center for Education in Maternal and Child Health
Georgetown University
Box 571272
Washington, DC 20057
(202) 784-9770
www.ncemch.org

Birth Defects Research for Children, Inc.
930 Woodcock Road, Suite 225
Orlando, FL 32803
(407) 895-0802
www.birthdefects.org

USDA/ARS Children's Nutrition Research Center at Baylor College of Medicine
1100 Bates Street
Houston, TX 77030
www.kidsnutrition.org

Centers for Disease Control—Healthy Youth
www.cdc.gov/healthyyouth

International Agencies

UNICEF
3 United Nations Plaza
New York, NY 10017
(212) 326-7000
www.unicef.org

World Health Organization
Avenue Appia 20
1211 Geneva 27
Switzerland
41 22 791 21 11
www.who.int/en

The Stockholm Convention on Persistent Organic Pollutants
11–13 Chemin des Anémones
1219 Châtelaine
Geneva, Switzerland
41 22 917 8191
www.pops.int

Food and Agricultural Organization of the United Nations
Viale delle Terme di Caracalla
00100 Rome, Italy
39 06 57051
www.fao.org

International Food Information Council
1100 Connecticut Avenue, NW
Suite 430
Washington, DC 20036
(202) 296-6540
www.ific.org

Pregnancy and Lactation

San Diego County Breastfeeding Coalition
c/o Children's Hospital and Health Center
3020 Children's Way, MC 5073
San Diego, CA 92123
(800) 371-MILK
www.breastfeeding.org

National Alliance for Breastfeeding Advocacy
Barbara Heiser, Executive Director
9684 Oak Hill Drive
Ellicott City, MD 21042-6321
OR
Marsha Walker, Executive Director
254 Conant Road
Weston, MA 02493-1756
www.naba-breastfeeding.org

American College of Obstetricians and Gynecologists
409 12th Street, SW, P.O. Box 96920
Washington, DC 20090
www.acog.org

La Leche League
1400 N. Meacham Road
Schaumburg, IL 60173
(847) 519-7730
www.lalecheleague.org

National Organization on Fetal Alcohol Syndrome
900 17th Street, NW
Suite 910
Washington, DC 20006
(800) 66 NOFAS
www.nofas.org

March of Dimes Birth Defects Foundation
1275 Mamaroneck Avenue
White Plains, NY 10605
(888) 663-4637
http://modimes.org

Professional Nutrition Organizations

North American Association for the Study of Obesity (NAASO)
8630 Fenton Street, Suite 918
Silver Spring, MD 20910
(301) 563-6526
www.naaso.org

American Dental Association
211 East Chicago Avenue
Chicago, IL 60611-2678
(312) 440-2500
www.ada.org

American Heart Association
National Center
7272 Greenville Avenue
Dallas, TX 75231
(800) 242-8721
www.americanheart.org

American Dietetic Association (ADA)
120 South Riverside Plaza, Suite 2000
Chicago, IL 60606-6995
(800) 877-1600
www.eatright.org

The American Society for Nutrition (ASN)
9650 Rockville Pike, Suite L-4500
Bethesda, MD 20814-3998
(301) 634-7050
www.nutrition.org

The Society for Nutrition Education
7150 Winton Drive, Suite 300
Indianapolis, IN 46268
(800) 235-6690
www.sne.org

American College of Nutrition
300 S. Duncan Avenue, Suite 225
Clearwater, FL 33755
(727) 446-6086
www.amcollnutr.org

American Obesity Association
1250 24th Street, NW, Suite 300
Washington, DC 20037
(800) 98-OBESE
www.obesity.org

American Council on Science and Health
1995 Broadway
Second Floor
New York, NY 10023
(212) 362-7044
www.acsh.org

American Diabetes Association
ATTN: National Call Center
1701 North Beauregard Street
Alexandria, VA 22311
(800) 342-2383
www.diabetes.org

Institute of Food Technologies
525 W. Van Buren, Suite 1000
Chicago, IL 60607
(312) 782-8424
www.ift.org

ILSI Human Nutrition Institute
One Thomas Circle, Ninth Floor
Washington, DC 20005
(202) 659-0524
http://hni.ilsi.org

Trade Organizations

American Meat Institute
1700 North Moore Street
Suite 1600
Arlington, VA 22209
(703) 841-2400
www.meatami.com

National Dairy Council
10255 W. Higgins Road, Suite 900
Rosemont, IL 60018
(312) 240-2880
www.nationaldairycouncil.org

United Fresh Fruit and Vegetable Association
1901 Pennsylvania Ave., NW, Suite 1100
Washington, DC 20006
(202) 303-3400
www.uffva.org

U.S.A. Rice Federation
4301 North Fairfax Drive, Suite 425
Arlington, VA 22203
(703) 236-2300
www.usarice.com

U.S. Government

The USDA National Organic Program
Agricultural Marketing Service
USDA-AMS-TMP-NOP
Room 4008-South Building
1400 Independence Avenue, SW
Washington, DC 20250-0020
(202) 720-3252
www.ams.usda.gov

U.S. Department of Health and Human Services
200 Independence Avenue, SW
Washington, DC 20201
(877) 696-6775
www.hhs.gov

Food and Drug Administration (FDA)
5600 Fishers Lane
Rockville, MD 20857
(888) 463-6332
www.fda.gov

Environmental Protection Agency
Ariel Rios Building
1200 Pennsylvania Avenue, NW
Washington, DC 20460
(202) 272-0167
www.epa.gov

Federal Trade Commission
600 Pennsylvania Avenue, NW
Washington, DC 20580
(202) 326-2222
www.ftc.gov

Partnership for Healthy Weight Management
www.consumer.gov/weightloss

Office of Dietary Supplements
National Institutes of Health
6100 Executive Boulevard, Room 3B01, MSC 7517
Bethesda, MD 20892
(301) 435-2920
http://dietary-supplements.info.nih.gov

Nutrient Data Laboratory Homepage
Beltsville Human Nutrition Center
10300 Baltimore Avenue
Building 307-C, Room 117
BARC-East
Beltsville, MD 20705
(301) 504-8157
www.nal.usda.gov/fnic/foodcomp

National Digestive Disease Clearinghouse
2 Information Way
Bethesda, MD 20892-3570
(800) 891-5389
http://digestive.niddk.nih.gov

The National Cancer Institute
NCI Public Inquiries Office
Suite 3036A
6116 Executive Boulevard, MSC 8322
Bethesda, MD 20892-8322
(800) 4-CANCER
www.cancer.gov

The National Eye Institute
31 Center Drive, MSC 2510
Bethesda, MD 20892-2510
(301) 496-5248
www.nei.nih.gov

The National Heart, Lung, and Blood Institute
Building 31, Room 5A52
31 Center Drive, MSC 2486
Bethesda, MD 20892
(301) 592-8573
www.nhlbi.nih.gov/index.htm

Institute of Diabetes and Digestive and Kidney Diseases
Office of Communications and Public Liaison
NIDDK, NIH, Building 31, Room 9A04
Center Drive, MSC 2560
Bethesda, MD 20892
(301) 496-4000
www.niddk.nih.gov

National Center for Complementary and Alternative Medicine
NCCAM Clearinghouse
P.O. Box 7923
Gaithersburg, MD 20898
(888) 644-6226
http://nccam.nih.gov

U.S. Department of Agriculture (USDA)
1400 Independence Avenue, SW
Washington, DC 20250
(202) 720-2791
www.usda.gov

Centers for Disease Control and Prevention (CDC)
1600 Clifton Road
Atlanta, GA 30333
(404) 639-3311 / Public Inquiries: (800) 311-3435
www.cdc.gov

National Institutes of Health (NIH)
9000 Rockville Pike
Bethesda, MD 20892
(301) 496-4000
www.nih.gov

Food and Nutrition Information Center
Agricultural Research Service, USDA
National Agricultural Library, Room 105
10301 Baltimore Avenue
Beltsville, MD 20705-2351
(301) 504-5719
www.nal.usda.gov/fnic

National Institute of Allergy and Infectious Diseases
NIAID Office of Communications and Public Liaison
6610 Rockledge Drive, MSC 6612
Bethesda, MD 20892
(301) 496-5717
www.niaid.nih.gov

Weight and Health Management

The Vegetarian Resource Group
P.O. Box 1463, Dept. IN
Baltimore, MD 21203
(410) 366-VEGE
www.vrg.org

American Obesity Association
1250 24th Street, NW
Suite 300
Washington, DC 20037
(202) 776-7711
www.obesity.org

Anemia Lifeline
(888) 722-4407
www.anemia.com

The Arc
(301) 565-3842
E-mail: info@thearc.org
www.thearc.org

Bottled Water Web
P.O. Box 5658
Santa Barbara, CA 93150
(805) 879-1564
www.bottledwaterweb.com

The Food and Nutrition Board
Institute of Medicine
500 Fifth Street, NW
Washington, DC 20001
(202) 334-2352
www.iom.edu/board.asp?id-3788

The Calorie Control Council
www.caloriecontrol.org

TOPS (Take Off Pounds Sensibly)
4575 South Fifth Street
P.O. Box 07360
Milwaukee, WI 53207
(800) 932-8677
www.tops.org

Shape Up America!
15009 Native Dancer Road
N. Potomac, MD 20878
(240) 631-6533
www.shapeup.org

World Hunger

Center on Hunger, Poverty, and Nutrition Policy
Tufts University
Medford, MA 02155
(617) 627-3020
www.tufts.edu/nutrition

Freedom from Hunger
1644 DaVinci Court
Davis, CA 95616
(800) 708-2555
www.freefromhunger.org

Oxfam International
1112 16th Street, NW, Suite 600
Washington, DC 20036
(202) 496-1170
www.oxfam.org

WorldWatch Institute
1776 Massachusetts Avenue, NW
Washington, DC 20036
(202) 452-1999
www.worldwatch.org

The Hunger Project
15 East 26th Street
New York, NY 10010
(212) 251-9100
www.thp.org

U.S. Agency for International Development
Information Center
Ronald Reagan Building
Washington, DC 20523
(202) 712-0000
www.usaid.gov

America's Second Harvest
35 E. Wacker Drive #2000
Chicago, IL 60601
www.secondharvest.org

Appendix B Calculations and Conversions

Calculation and Conversion Aids

Commonly Used Metric Units

millimeter (mm):	one-thousandth of a meter (0.001)
centimeter (cm):	one-hundredth of a meter (0.01)
kilometer (km):	one-thousand times a meter (1000)
kilogram (kg):	one-thousand times a gram (1000)
milligram (mg):	one-thousandth of a gram (0.001)
microgram (μg):	one-millionth of a gram (0.000001)
milliliter (ml):	one-thousandth of a liter (0.001)

International Units

Some vitamin supplements may report vitamin content as International Units (IU).

To convert IU to:

- Micrograms of vitamin D (cholecalciferol), divide the IU value by 40 or multiply by 0.025.
- Milligrams of vitamin E (alpha-tocopherol), divide the IU value by 1.5 if vitamin E is from natural sources. Divide the IU value by 2.22 if vitamin E is from synthetic sources.
- Vitamin A: 1 IU = 0.3 μg retinol or 3.6 μg beta-carotene

Retinol Activity Equivalents

Retinol Activity Equivalents (RAE) are a standardized unit of measure for vitamin A. RAE account for the various differences in bioavailability from sources of vitamin A. Many supplements will report vitamin A content in IU, as shown above, or Retinol Equivalents (RE).

1 RAE = 1 μg retinol
12 μg beta-carotene
24 μg other vitamin A carotenoids

To calculate RAE from the RE value of vitamin carotenoids in foods, divide RE by 2.

For vitamin A supplements and foods fortified with vitamin A, 1 RE = 1 RAE.

Folate

Folate is measured as Dietary Folate Equivalents (DFE). DFE account for the different factors affecting bioavailability of folate sources.

1 DFE = 1 μg food folate
0.6 μg folate from fortified foods
0.5 μg folate supplement taken on an empty stomach
0.6 μg folate as a supplement consumed with a meal

To convert micrograms of synthetic folate, such as that found in supplements or fortified foods, to DFE:

μg synthetic folate × 1.7 = μg DFE

For naturally occurring food folate, such as spinach, each microgram of folate equals 1 microgram DFE:

μg folate = μg DFE

Conversion Factors

Use the following table to convert U.S. measurements to metric equivalents:

Original Unit	Multiply by	To Get
ounces avdp	28.3495	grams
ounces	0.0625	pounds
pounds	0.4536	kilograms
pounds	16	ounces
grams	0.0353	ounces
grams	0.002205	pounds
kilograms	2.2046	pounds
liters	1.8162	pints (dry)
liters	2.1134	pints (liquid)
liters	0.9081	quarts (dry)
liters	1.0567	quarts (liquid)
liters	0.2642	gallons (U.S.)
pints (dry)	0.5506	liters
pints (liquid)	0.4732	liters
quarts (dry)	1.1012	liters
quarts (liquid)	0.9463	liters
gallons (U.S.)	3.7853	liters
millimeters	0.0394	inches
centimeters	0.3937	inches
centimeters	0.03281	feet
inches	25.4000	millimeters
inches	2.5400	centimeters
inches	0.0254	meters
feet	0.3048	meters
meters	3.2808	feet
meters	1.0936	yards
cubic feet	0.0283	cubic meters
cubic meters	35.3145	cubic feet
cubic meters	1.3079	cubic yards
cubic yards	0.7646	cubic meters

Length: U.S. and Metric Equivalents

¼ inch	= 0.6 centimeters
1 inch	= 2.5 centimeters
1 foot	= 0.3048 meter
	30.48 centimeters
1 yard	= 0.91144 meter
1 millimeter	= 0.03937 inch
1 centimeter	= 0.3937 inch
1 decimeter	= 3.937 inches
1 meter	= 39.37 inches
	1.094 yards
1 micrometer	= 0.00003937 inch

Weights and Measures

Food Measurement Equivalencies from U.S. to Metric

Capacity

⅕ teaspoon = 1 milliliter
¼ teaspoon = 1.25 milliliters
½ teaspoon = 2.5 milliliters
1 teaspoon = 5 milliliters
1 tablespoon = 15 milliliters
1 fluid ounce = 28.4 milliliters
¼ cup = 60 milliliters
⅓ cup = 80 milliliters
½ cup = 120 milliliters
1 cup = 225 milliliters
1 pint (2 cups) = 473 milliliters
1 quart (4 cups) = 0.95 liter
1 liter (1.06 quarts) = 1,000 milliliters
1 gallon (4 quarts) = 3.84 liters

Weight

0.035 ounce = 1 gram
1 ounce = 28 grams
¼ pound (4 ounces) = 114 grams
1 pound (16 ounces) = 454 grams
2.2 pounds (35 ounces) = 1 kilogram

U.S. Food Measurement Equivalents

3 teaspoons = 1 tablespoon
½ tablespoon = 1½ teaspoons
2 tablespoons = ⅛ cup
4 tablespoons = ¼ cup
5 tablespoons + 1 teaspoon = ⅓ up
8 tablespoons = ½ cup
10 tablespoons + 2 teaspoons = ⅔ cup
12 tablespoons = ¾ cup
16 tablespoons = 1 cup
2 cups = 1 pint
4 cups = 1 quart
2 pints = 1 quart
4 quarts = 1 gallon

Volumes and Capacities

1 cup = 8 fluid ounces
½ liquid pint
1 milliliter = 0.061 cubic inches
1 liter = 1.057 liquid quarts
0.908 dry quart
61.024 cubic inches
1 U.S. gallon = 231 cubic inches
3.785 liters
0.833 British gallon
128 U.S. fluid ounces
1 British Imperial gallon = 277.42 cubic inches
1.201 U.S. gallons
4.546 liters
160 British fluid ounces
1 U.S. ounce, liquid or fluid = 1.805 cubic inches
29.574 milliliters
1.041 British fluid ounces
1 pint, dry = 33.600 cubic inches
0.551 liter
1 pint, liquid = 28.875 cubic inches
0.473 liter
1 U.S. quart, dry = 67.201 cubic inches
1.101 liters
1 U.S. quart, liquid = 57.75 cubic inches
0.946 liter
1 British quart = 69.354 cubic inches
1.032 U.S. quarts, dry
1.201 U.S. quarts, liquid

Energy Units

1 kilocalorie (kcal) = 4.2 kilojoules
1 millijoule (MJ) = 240 kilocalories
1 kilojoule (kJ) = 0.24 kcal
1 gram carbohydrate = 4 kcal
1 gram fat = 9 kcal
1 gram protein = 4 kcal

Temperature Standards

	°Fahrenheit	°Celsius
Body temperature	98.6°	37°
Comfortable room temperature	65–75°	18–24°
Boiling point of water	212°	100°
Freezing point of water	32°	0°

Temperature Scales

To Convert Fahrenheit to Celsius:

[(°F − 32) × 5]/9

1. Subtract 32 from °F
2. Multiply (°F − 32) by 5, then divide by 9

To Convert Celsius to Fahrenheit:

[(°C × 9)/5] + 32

1. Multiply °C by 9, then divide by 5
2. Add 32 to (°C × 9/5)

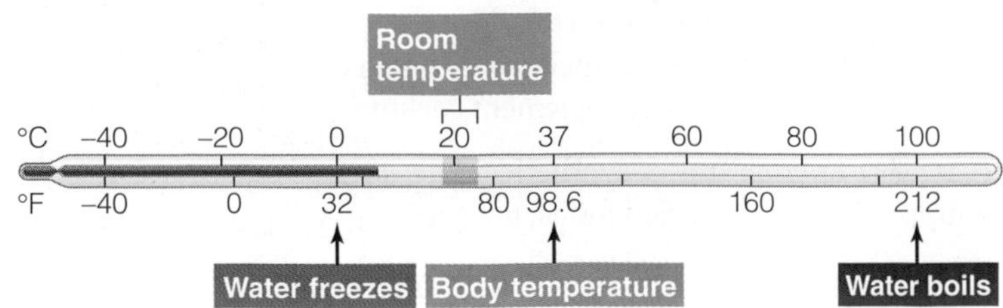

Appendix C U.S. Exchange Lists for Meal Planning

The "Exchange Lists for Meal Planning" group foods together according to their carbohydrate, protein, and fat composition. There are three main groups: the Carbohydrate Group, the Meat and Meat Substitutes Group, and the Fat Group. As you will see in the charts on the following pages, the Carbohydrate Group contains starchy foods such as bread and other grain products, as well as fruit, milk, and vegetables; the Meat and Meat Substitutes Group includes meat, fish, poultry, eggs, luncheon meats, and legumes; and the Fat Group contains oils, nuts, and other spreads. Also note that two of these main groups (specifically, the Carbohydrate Group and the Meat and Meat Substitutes Group) also contain subgroups.

Specific portion sizes are provided for each of the foods within each group. This ensures that all the foods in each subgroup contain relatively the same amount of carbohydrates, protein, and fats, and thus, will have a similar amount of calories per serving. Because any food within a food subgroup will have similar amounts of these nutrients, they can be exchanged or swapped with each other at meals and snacks. This flexible meal plan is a useful tool to help individuals, such as those with diabetes and/or those who want to lose weight, better control the amount of nutrient and calories at all meals and snacks. A diet with a set amount of nutrients, such as carbohydrates and calories, can help individuals with diabetes better control their blood glucose levels and calories throughout the day. Calorie control is important for those who are trying to improve or manage their body weight.

The following chart shows the amount of nutrients in one serving from each of the three main groups.

Group/List	Carbohydrate (grams)	Protein (grams)	Fat (grams)	Calories
Carbohydrate Group				
Starch	15	3	0–1	80
Fruit	15	—	—	60
Milk				
Fat-free, low-fat	12	8	0–3	90
Reduced-fat	12	8	5	120
Whole	12	8	8	150
Other carbohydrates	15	varies	varies	varies
Nonstarchy vegetables	5	2	—	25
Meat and Meat Substitutes Group				
Very lean	—	7	0–1	35
Lean	—	7	3	55
Medium-fat	—	7	5	75
High-fat	—	7	8	100
Fat Group				
	—	—	5	45

The charts on the following pages show the exchange lists for each of the subgroups shown above (i.e., Starch, Fruit, Milk, etc.).

Starch List

Food	Serving Size
Bread	
Bagel, 4 oz	¼ (1 oz)
Bread, white, whole-wheat, pumpernickel, rye	1 slice (1 oz)
English muffin	½
Hot dog bun or hamburger bun	½
Pancake, 4″ across, ¼″ thick	1
Pita, 6″ across	½
Roll, plain, small	1 (1 oz)
Tortilla, flour, 6″ across	1
Cereals and Grains	
Bran cereals	½ cup
Bulgur	½ cup
Cereals, cooked	½ cup
Cereals, unsweetened, ready-to-eat	¾ cup
Couscous	⅓ cup
Oats	½ cup
Pasta	⅓ cup
Puffed cereal	1½ cup
Rice, white or brown	⅓ cup
Shredded Wheat	½ cup
Sugar-frosted cereal	½ cup
Starchy Vegetables	
Baked beans	⅓ cup
Corn	½ cup
Peas, green	½ cup
Potato, mashed	½ cup
Squash, winter (acorn, butternut, pumpkin)	1 cup
Yam, sweet potato, plain	½ cup
Crackers and Snacks	
Animal crackers	8
Graham crackers, 2½″ square	3
Popcorn (popped, no fat added or low-fat microwave)	3 cups
Pretzels	¾ oz
Rice cakes, 4″ across	2
Saltine-type crackers	6
Snack chips, fat-free or baked (tortilla, potato)	15–20 (¾ oz)
Whole-wheat crackers, no fat added	2–5 (¾ oz)
Beans, Peas, and Lentils *(Count as 1 starch exchange, plus 1 very lean meat exchange)*	
Beans and peas (garbanzo, pinto, kidney, white, split, black-eyed)	½ cup
Lima beans	⅔ cup
Starchy Foods Prepared with Fat *(Count as 1 starch exchange plus 1 fat exchange)*	
Biscuit, 2½″ across	1
Crackers, round butter type	6
Croutons	1 cup
French-fried potatoes (oven-baked) (see also the fast foods list)	1 cup (2 oz)
Muffin, 5 oz	⅕ (1 oz)
Popcorn, microwaved	3 cups

Source: © American Dietetic Association. Used with permission.

Fruit List

Food	Serving Size
Apples, unpeeled, small	1 (4 oz)
Applesauce, unsweetened	½ cup
Apricots, dried	8 halves
Banana, small	1 (4 oz)
Blueberries	⅓ cup
Cantaloupe, small or 1 cup cubes	⅓ melon (11 oz)
Cherries, sweet, fresh	12 (3 oz)
Dates	3
Figs, dried	1½
Grapefruit, large	½ (11 oz)
Grapes, small	17 (3 oz)
Honeydew melon or 1 cup cubes	1 slice (10 oz)
Kiwi	1 (3½ oz)
Mango, small	½ (5½ oz) or ½ cup
Orange, small	1 (6½ oz)
Peach, medium, fresh	1 (4 oz)
Pear, large, fresh	½ (4 oz)
Pineapple, fresh	¾ cup
Plums, small	2 (5 oz)
Raisins	2 tbsp
Raspberries	1 cup
Strawberries	1¼ cup whole berries
Watermelon	1 slice (13½ oz) or 1¼ cup cubes
Fruit Juice, Unsweetened	
Apple juice/cider	½ cup
Cranberry juice cocktail	⅓ cup
Cranberry juice cocktail, reduced-calorie	1 cup
Fruit juice blends, 100% juice	⅓ cup
Grape juice	⅓ cup
Grapefruit juice	½ cup
Orange juice	½ cup
Pineapple juice	½ cup

Milk List

Food	Serving Size
Fat-Free and Low-Fat Milk	
(0–3 g fat per serving)	
Fat-free milk	1 cup
½% milk	1 cup
1% milk	1 cup
Buttermilk, low-fat or fat-free	1 cup
Soy milk, low-fat or fat-free	1 cup
Yogurt, plain, fat-free	6 oz
Yogurt, fat-free, flavored, sweetened with nonnutritive sweetener and fructose	1 cup
Reduced-Fat Milk	
(5 g fat per serving)	
2% milk	1 cup
Soy milk	1 cup
Whole Milk	
(8 g fat per serving)	
Whole milk	1 cup
Yogurt, plain (made from whole milk)	8 oz

Other Carbohydrates List

These carbohydrate-rich foods can be substituted for a starch, fruit, or milk choice.

Food	Serving Size	Exchanges per Serving
Angel food cake, unfrosted	1/12 cake (about 2 oz)	2 carbohydrates
Brownies, small, unfrosted	2″ square (about 1 oz)	1 carbohydrate, 1 fat
Cake, frosted	2″ square (about 2 oz)	2 carbohydrates, 1 fat
Cookie or sandwich cookie with creme filling	2 small (about ⅔ oz)	1 carbohydrate, 1 fat
Cranberry sauce, jellied	¼ cup	1½ carbohydrates
Doughnut, plain cake	1 medium, (1½ oz)	1½ carbohydrates, 2 fats
Energy, sport, or breakfast bar	1 bar (2 oz)	2 carbohydrates, 1 fat
Fruit juice bars, frozen, 100% juice	1 bar (3 oz)	1 carbohydrate
Granola or snack bar, regular or low-fat	1 bar (1 oz)	1½ carbohydrates
Ice cream	½ cup	1 carbohydrate, 2 fats
Ice cream, light	½ cup	1 carbohydrate, 1 fat
Milk, chocolate, whole	1 cup	2 carbohydrates, 1 fat
Pudding, regular (made with reduced-fat milk)	½ cup	2 carbohydrates
Pudding, sugar-free, or sugar-free and fat-free (made with fat-free milk)	½ cup	1 carbohydrate
Sherbet, sorbet	½ cup	2 carbohydrates
Sports drink	8 oz (1 cup)	1 carbohydrate
Yogurt, frozen, fat-free	⅓ cup	1 carbohydrate
Yogurt, frozen, fat-free, no sugar added	½ cup	1 carbohydrate, 0–1 fat

Vegetable List

Serving size — ½ c cooked vegetables or vegetable juice or 1 c raw vegetables

Asparagus
Beans (green, wax, Italian)
Broccoli
Brussels sprouts
Cabbage
Carrots
Cauliflower
Celery
Cucumber
Eggplant
Mushrooms
Okra
Onions
Pea pods
Peppers (all varieties)
Radishes
Salad greens (endive, escarole, lettuce, romaine, spinach)
Spinach
Summer squash
Tomato
Tomatoes, canned
Tomato sauce*
Tomato/vegetable juice*
Zucchini

*= 400 mg or more sodium per exchange.

Meat and Meat Substitutes List

Food	Serving Size
Very Lean Meat and Substitutes	
Poultry: Chicken or turkey (white meat, no skin)	1 oz
Fish: Fresh or frozen cod, flounder, haddock, halibut, trout, lox (smoked salmon)*; tuna, fresh or canned in water	1 oz
Shellfish: Clams, crab, lobster, scallops, shrimp, imitation shellfish	1 oz
Cheese with 1 g fat/oz:	
Fat-free or low-fat cottage cheese	¼ cup
Fat-free cheese	1 oz
Other:	
Processed sandwich meats with 1 g fat/oz (such as deli thin, shaved meats, chipped beef*, turkey ham)	1 oz
Egg whites	2
Hot dogs with 1 g fat/oz*	1 oz
Sausage with 1 g fat/oz	1 oz
Count as one very lean meat and one starch exchange:	
Beans, peas, lentils (cooked)	½ cup
Lean Meat and Substitutes	
Beef: USDA Select or Choice grades of lean beef trimmed of fat (round, sirloin); tenderloin; roast; steak; ground round	1 oz
Pork: Lean pork (fresh ham); canned, cured, or boiled ham; Canadian bacon*; tenderloin, center loin chop	1 oz
Lamb: Roast, chop, leg	1 oz
Veal: Lean chop, roast	1 oz
Poultry: Chicken, turkey (dark meat, no skin), chicken white meat (with skin)	1 oz
Fish:	
Oysters	6 medium
Salmon (fresh or canned), catfish	1 oz
Tuna (canned in oil, drained)	1 oz
Cheese:	
4.5% fat cottage cheese	¼ cup
Grated Parmesan	2 tbsp
Cheeses with 3 g fat/oz	1 oz

Food	Serving Size
Other:	
Hot dogs with 3 g fat/oz*	1½ oz
Processed sandwich meat with 3 g fat/oz (turkey, pastrami, or kielbasa)	1 oz
Medium-Fat Meat and Substitutes	
Beef: Most beef products (ground beef, meatloaf, corned beef, short ribs, Prime grades of meat trimmed of fat, such as prime rib)	1 oz
Pork: Top loin, chop, cutlet	1 oz
Lamb: Rib roast, ground	1 oz
Veal: Cutlet (ground or cubed, unbreaded)	1 oz
Poultry: Chicken dark meat (with skin), ground turkey or ground chicken, fried chicken (with skin)	1 oz
Fish: Any fried fish product	1 oz
Cheese with 5 g fat/oz:	
Feta	1 oz
Mozzarella	1 oz
Ricotta	¼ cup (2 oz)
Other:	
Egg (high in cholesterol, limit to 3/week)	1
Sausage with 5 g fat/oz	1 oz
Tempeh	¼ cup
Tofu	4 oz or ½ cup
High-Fat Meat and Substitutes	
Pork: Spareribs, ground pork, pork sausage	1 oz
Cheese: All regular cheeses (American* cheddar, Monterey Jack, Swiss)	1 oz
Other:	
Processed sandwich meats with 8 g fat/oz (bologna, salami)	1 oz
Sausage (bratwurst, Italian, knockwurst, Polish, smoked)	1 oz
Hot dog (turkey or chicken)*	1 (10/lb)
Bacon	3 slices
Peanut butter (contains unsaturated fat)	1 tbsp
Count as one high-fat meat plus one fat exchange:	
Hot dog (beef, pork, or combination)*	1 (10/lb)

**= 400 mg or more of sodium per serving.*

Fat List

Food	Serving Size
Monounsaturated Fats	
Avocado, medium	2 tbsp (1 oz)
Oil (canola, olive, peanut)	1 tsp
Olives, ripe (black)	8 large
Olives, green, stuffed*	10 large
Almonds, cashews	6 nuts
Peanuts	10 nuts
Pecans	4 halves
Peanut butter, smooth or crunchy	½ tbsp
Sesame seeds	1 tbsp
Polyunsaturated Fats	
Margarine, stick, tub, or squeeze	1 tsp
Margarine, lower-fat (30 to 50% vegetable oil)	1 tbsp
Mayonnaise, regular	1 tsp
Mayonnaise, reduced-fat	1 tbsp
Nuts, walnuts, English	4 halves
Oil (corn, safflower, soybean)	1 tsp
Salad dressing, regular*	1 tbsp
Salad dressing, reduced-fat	2 tbsp
Seeds, pumpkin, sunflower	1 tbsp
Saturated Fats	
Bacon, cooked	1 slice (20 slices/lb)
Butter, stick	1 tsp
Butter, whipped	2 tsp
Butter, reduced-fat	1 tbsp
Cream, half and half	2 tbsp
Cream cheese, regular	1 tbsp (½ oz)
Cream cheese, reduced-fat	1½ tbsp (¾ oz)
Sour cream, regular	2 tbsp
Sour cream, reduced-fat	3 tbsp

*= 400 mg or more sodium per exchange.

Free Foods List

A free food *is any food that contains less than 20 calories or less than 5 grams of carbohydrate per serving. Free foods should be limited to three servings per day.*

Food	Serving Size
Fat-Free or Reduced-Fat Foods	
Cream cheese, fat-free	1 tbsp (½ oz)
Creamers, nondairy, liquid	1 tbsp
Mayonnaise, fat-free	1 tbsp
Mayonnaise, reduced-fat	1 tsp
Margarine, spread, fat-free	4 tbsp
Nonstick cooking spray	
Salad dressing, fat-free or low-fat	1 tbsp
Sour cream, fat-free, reduced-fat	1 tbsp
Sugar-Free Foods	
Candy, hard, sugar-free	1 candy
Gelatin dessert, sugar-free	
Gum, sugar-free	
Jam or jelly, light	2 tsp
Syrup, sugar-free	2 tbsp
Drinks	
Bouillon, broth, consommé*	
Bouillon or broth, low-sodium	
Carbonated or mineral water	
Club soda	
Cocoa powder, unsweetened	1 tbsp
Coffee	
Diet soft drinks, sugar-free	
Drink mixes, sugar-free	
Tea	
Tonic water, sugar-free	
Condiments	
Catsup	1 tbsp
Horseradish	
Lemon juice	
Lime juice	
Mustard	
Salsa	¼ cup
Soy sauce, regular or light*	1 tbsp
Taco sauce	1 tbsp
Vinegar	
Yogurt	2 tbsp

*= 400 mg or more sodium per choice.

Combination Foods List

Food	Serving Size	Exchanges per Serving
Entrées		
Tuna noodle casserole, lasagna, spaghetti with meatballs, chili with beans, macaroni and cheese*	1 cup (8 oz)	2 carbohydrates, 2 medium-fat meats
Tuna or chicken salad	½ cup (3½ oz)	½ carbohydrate, 2 lean meats, 1 fat
Frozen Entrées		
Dinner-type meal*	generally 14–17 oz.	3 carbohydrates, 3 medium-fat meats, 3 fats
Meatless burger, soy based	3 oz	½ carbohydrate, 2 lean meats
Meatless burger, vegetable and starch based	3 oz	1 carbohydrate, 1 lean meat
Pizza, cheese, thin crust* (5 oz)	¼ of 12″ (6 oz)	2 carbohydrates, 2 medium-fat meats
Pizza, meat topping, thin crust* (5 oz)	¼ of 12″ (6 oz)	2 carbohydrates, 2 medium-fat meats, 1½ fats
Entrée with less than 340 calories*	about 8–11 oz	2–3 carbohydrates, 1–2 lean meats
Soups		
Bean*	1 cup	1 carbohydrate, 1 very lean meat
Cream (made with water)*	1 cup (8 oz)	1 carbohydrate, 1 fat
Split pea (made with water)*	½ cup (4 oz)	1 carbohydrate
Tomato (made with water)*	1 cup (8 oz)	1 carbohydrate
Vegetable beef, chicken noodle, or other broth-type*	1 cup (8 oz)	1 carbohydrate

**= 400 mg or more sodium per exchange.*

Fast Foods List[a]

Food	Serving Size	Exchanges per Serving
Burrito with beef*	1 (5–7 oz)	3 carbohydrates, 1 medium-fat meat, 1 fat
Chicken nuggets*	6	1 carbohydrate, 2 medium-fat meats, 1 fat
Chicken breast and wing, breaded and fried*	1 each	1 carbohydrate, 4 medium-fat meats, 2 fats
Chicken sandwich, grilled*	1	2 carbohydrates, 3 very lean meats
Chicken wings, hot*	6 (5 oz)	1 carbohydrate, 3 medium-fat meats, 4 fats
Fish sandwich/tartar sauce*	1	3 carbohydrates, 1 medium-fat meat, 3 fats
French fries, thin	20–25	2 carbohydrates, 2 fats
Hamburger, regular	1	2 carbohydrates, 2 medium-fat meats
Hamburger, large*	1	2 carbohydrates, 3 medium-fat meats, 1 fat
Hot dog with bun*	1	1 carbohydrate, 1 high-fat meat, 1 fat
Individual pan pizza*	1	5 carbohydrates, 3 medium-fat meats, 3 fats
Pizza, cheese, thin crust*	¼ of 12″ (about 6 oz)	2½ carbohydrates, 2 medium-fat meats, 1½ fats
Pizza, meat, thin crust*	¼ of 12″ (about 6 oz)	2½ carbohydrates, 2 medium-fat meats, 2 fats
Soft serve cone	1 medium	2 carbohydrates, 1 fat
Submarine sandwich*	1 (6″)	3 carbohydrates, 1 vegetable, 2 medium-fat meats, 1 fat
Taco, hard shell*	1 (6 oz)	2 carbohydrates, 2 medium-fat meats, 2 fats
Taco, soft shell*	1 (3 oz)	1 carbohydrate, 1 medium-fat meat, 1 fat

**= 400 mg or more sodium per exchange.*

[a]Ask at your fast-food restaurant for nutrition information about your favorite fast foods or check Web sites.

The following charts show a possible distribution of exchanges for an individual consuming 2,000 calories. This set amount of exchanges can help you plan meals and snacks for a day, such as shown in the "One Day Sample Meal Plan."

Daily Meal Pattern

Targets:
Total kcal = 2,000/day

	Percent of Kcal	Amount in Grams
Carbohydrate	50–55	250–275
Protein	15–20	75–100
Fat	27–30	60–67

Exchange	Number of Exchanges	Protein (g)	Fat (g)	Carbohydrate (g)
Milk, low-fat	3	24	9	36
Fruit	4	0	0	60
Vegetable	6	12	0	30
Starch/Bread/Cereal	9	27	0	135
Meat, lean	6	42	18	0
Fat	6	0	30	0
Total		105	57	261
Total kcals	1,977	420	513	1,044
% kcals		21	26	53

Distributiuon of Exchanges at Meals and Snacks

Exchanges	Total Number	Breakfast	AM Snack	Lunch	PM Snack	Dinner	Night Snack
Milk	3	1	1	0	0	1	0
Fruit	4	1	1	1	0	0	1
Vegetable	6	0	0	2	1	3	0
Starch/Bread/Cereal	9	2	1	2	2	2	0
Meat	6	0	0	3	0	3	0
Fat	6	2	0	2	1	1	0
Total	34	6	3	10	4	10	1
Total carbohydrate (g)	261	57	42	55	35	57	15
% Total Carb.		22	16	21	13	22	6

One Day Sample Meal Plan

Breakfast

1% milk (8 oz glass) . . . . . . 1 milk exchange
Honeydew melon (1 cup cubes) . . . . 1 fruit exchange
Whole-wheat English muffin (1) . . . . 2 starch exchanges
Peanut butter (1 tbsp) . . . . 2 fat exchanges

Morning Snack

Low-fat plain yogurt (6 oz) . . . . 1 milk exchange
Strawberries (1¼ cup whole berries) . . . . 1 fruit exchange
Low-fat granola (¼ cup) . . . . 1 starch exchange

Lunch

2 slices whole-wheat bread . . . . 2 starch exchanges
Canned light tuna (3 oz) . . . . 3 meat exchanges
Reduced-fat mayonnaise (1 tbsp) . . . . 1 fat exchange
Small tossed salad (1 c romain lettuce, 1 c raw veggies) . . . . 2 vegetable exchanges
Reduced-fat Italian dressing (2 tbsp) . . . . 1 fat exchange
Apple (1 small). . . . . 1 fruit exchange
Unsweetened ice tea. . . . . Free food

Afternoon Snack

Baby carrots (1 cup raw) . . . . . . 1 vegetable exchange
4 whole-wheat crackers, no fat added . . . . . 1 starch exchange
Hummus (⅓ cup) . . . 1 starch exchange
1 fat exchange

Dinner

1% milk (8 oz glass) . . . . . . 1 milk exchange
3 oz grilled chicken breast. . . . . 3 meat exchanges
⅔ c rice pilaf (prepared with reduced-fat butter). . . . . 2 starch exchanges
1 fat exchange
¾ c steamed broccoli. . . . . 1½ vegetable exchanges
1½ c baby salad greens . . . . 1½ vegetable exchanges
Low-fat salad dressing (1 tbsp) . . . . Free food

Night Snack

Reduced-calorie cranberry juice cocktail (8 oz) . . . 1 fruit exchange

Glossary

A

absorption The process by which digested nutrients move into the tissues, where they can be transported and used by the body's cells.
added sugars Sugars that are added to processed foods and sweets.
adolescence The developmental period between the start of puberty and adulthood.
aerobic With oxygen.
age-related macular degeneration (AMD) A disease that affects the macula area of the eye's retina, causing blurry vision.
alcohol poisoning A condition in which a person's BAC, (blood alcohol content) rises to such an extreme level that the central nervous system is affected and breathing and heart rate are interrupted.
alcoholism A chronic disease with genetic, psychological, and environmental components. Alcoholics crave alcohol, can't control their intake, develop a high tolerance for it, and become dependent on it. Abstaining from drinking alcohol causes withdrawal symptoms in alcoholics.
allergens Substances in food (often proteins) that are not broken down by cooking or digestion and enter the body intact, causing an allergic reaction by the immune system.
amino acids The building blocks of protein. Amino acids contain carbon, hydrogen, oxygen, and nitrogen. All amino acids include a unique side chain.
anaerobic Without oxygen.
anaphylactic reaction A severe, life-threatening physical reaction causing a sudden drop in blood pressure and airway constriction. Symptoms may include a rapid or weak pulse, pale complexion, a flush on parts of the body, difficulty breathing, and/or a blank expression. Sometimes called *anaphylactic shock*.
anorexia A serious, potentially life-threatening eating disorder characterized by self-starvation and excessive weight loss. Also known by the medical term *anorexia nervosa*.
antibiotics Drugs that kill or slow the growth of bacteria.
antibodies Bodily proteins that bind to and neutralize foreign invaders (such as harmful bacteria, fungi, and viruses) as part of the body's immune response.
antioxidants Substances that neutralize free radicals, which can cause cell damage. Vitamins A, C, and E and beta-carotene are antioxidants.
appetite The psychological desire to eat or drink.
atherosclerosis Narrowing of the coronary arteries due to a buildup of debris along the artery walls.
attention deficit hyperactivity disorder (ADHD) A condition in which children, particularly, are easily distracted and have difficulty in several areas, including listening and following directions, focusing and sustaining attention, concentrating and staying on task, and/or inconsistent performance in school. Previously known as *attention deficit disorder* (ADD).

B

baby bottle tooth decay The decay of baby teeth in children due to continual exposure to fermentable sugary liquids.
bacteria Microscopic organisms that can exist and flourish on both living and nonliving surfaces. Many bacteria are harmless, and some are beneficial. Pathogenic bacteria can cause illness.
basal metabolism The amount of energy the body expends to meet its basic physiological needs. Also referred to as *basal metabolic rate*.
behavior modification The process of changing behavior to improve health, including identifying and altering eating patterns that contribute to weight gain or impede weight loss.
binge eating A form of disordered eating marked by eating large amounts of food in a short period of time.
biotechnology The application of biological techniques to living cells, which alters their genetic makeup.
blood alcohol concentration (BAC) The amount of alcohol in your blood, measured in grams of alcohol per deciliter, usually expressed as a percentage.
bile A greenish-yellow fluid, made in the liver and concentrated and stored in the gallbladder, that helps emulsify fat and prepare it for digestion.
body composition The relative proportion of muscle, fat, water, and other tissues in the body.
body mass index (BMI) A calculation of your weight relative to your height. A BMI between 18.5 and 24.9 is considered healthy.
bone mineral density (BMD) A measure of the amount of minerals, particularly calcium, per volume in an individual's bone. The denser bones are, the stronger they are.
botanicals Products made from herbs or woody plants and used for cosmetic, culinary, or therapeutic purposes.
bran The indigestible outer shell of a grain kernel.
bulimia A serious, potentially life-threatening eating disorder characterized by binge eating followed by purging. Also known by the medical term *bulimia nervosa*.

C

cancer The name used to identify a group of diseases characterized by the uncontrolled growth and spread of abnormal cells within the body.
carbohydrate loading A diet and training strategy that maximizes glycogen stores in the body before an endurance event.
carcinogen Any substance capable of initiating cell changes that can lead to cancer.
cardiorespiratory endurance The body's ability to sustain prolonged cardiorespiratory exercise.
cataract A common eye disorder affecting the lens of the eye, in which vision becomes cloudy.
celiac disease A malabsorption disease in which consuming the protein gluten causes an immune system response that damages the lining of the small intestine.
central obesity An excess storage of visceral fat in the abdominal area, which increases the risk of heart disease, diabetes, and hypertension.
coenzymes Substances needed by enzymes to perform many chemical reactions in your body. Many vitamins act as coenzymes.
complemented proteins An incomplete protein that is combined with small amounts of animal or soy proteins, or with other plant proteins, to create a complete protein.
complete protein A protein that provides all the essential amino acids your body needs, along with some nonessential amino acids. Soy protein and protein from animal sources, in general, are complete.
complex carbohydrates Carbohydrates containing many sugar units combined. Polysaccharides are complex carbohydrates.
conception The moment when a sperm fertilizes an egg.
consensus The collective opinion of a group of experts based on a body of information.

constipation The condition of having difficulty passing stools caused by slow movement of undigested residue in the colon.
control group The group not receiving intervention in a research study. This group is given a placebo.

D

Daily Values (DVs) Established reference levels of nutrients, based on a 2,000 calorie-per-day diet, that are used on food labels.
DASH diet A diet based on the DASH (Dietary Approaches to Stop Hypertension) study, that significantly reduces blood pressure. The DASH diet is low in fat, saturated fat, cholesterol, and sweets; and high in whole grains, fruits, vegetables, and low-fat dairy products.
dehydration The state in which there is too little water in the body due to too much water being lost, too little being consumed, or a combination of both.
dental caries The decay or erosion of teeth.
deoxyribonucleic acid (DNA) The substance that contains the genetic instructions needed to develop and direct the activities of the body.
diabetes The disease in which the body is unable to process blood glucose levels normally due to lack of the hormone insulin, or insulin resistance. Also known by the medical term *diabetes mellitus*.The three types of diabetes are type 1, type 2, and gestational diabetes. Type 2 diabetes is the most common form.
diarrhea The condition of having frequent, loose, and/or watery stools.
Dietary Guidelines for Americans 2005 Guidelines published in 2005 that provide dietary and lifestyle advice to healthy individuals age 2 and older to help them maintain good health and prevent chronic diseases.
Dietary Reference Intakes (DRIs) A collection of five specific reference values for the essential nutrients needed to maintain good health, prevent chronic diseases, and avoid unhealthy excesses. The five reference values are: the estimated average requirement (EAR); the recommended dietary allowance (RDI); the adequate intake (AI); the tolerable upper intake level (UL); and the acceptable macronutrient distribution range (AMDR).
dietary supplements Products containing nutrients, botanicals, amino acids, or enzymes intended to supplement the diet, but are not intended as a substitute for food or as a stand-alone item in a meal or the diet.
digestion The body's breakdown of foods into absorbable components using mechanical and chemical means.
disaccharides Simple carbohydrates containing two sugar units combined. There are three disaccharides: sucrose, lactose, and maltose.
discretionary calorie allowance Calories left over in the diet once all nutrient needs have been met from the basic food groups.
disordered eating Abnormal and potentially harmful eating behaviors that do not meet the criteria for anorexia or bulimia.
DNA (deoxyribonucleic acid) Genetic material within cells that develops the synthesis of proteins in the body and directs bodily activities.
double-blind placebo-controlled study A study designed and conducted in such a way that neither the study participants nor the experimenters know to whom the treatment is given.

E

eating disorders The term used for psychological illnesses that involve abnormal eating behaviors, specifically anorexia (self-starvation) and bulimia (bingeing and purging).
electrolytes Minerals important to bodily fluid balance that conduct an electrical current in a solvent such as water. Sodium, potassium, and chloride are examples of electrolytes in the body.
embryo A fertilized egg during the third through the eighth week of pregnancy.
empty calories Calories with little or no nutrition value. Jelly beans are an example of a food that provides many calories from sugar but few nutrients.
endosperm The starchy part of a grain kernel.
energy balance The state in which energy (calorie) intake and energy (calorie) output in the body are equal.
enriched grains Refined grain foods to which folic acid, thiamin, niacin, riboflavin, and iron have been added.
enzymes Substances (often proteins) that speed up reactions in the body without being changed or used up in the process.
epidemiological research Research that examines populations of people, often observational in its approach.
ergogenic aid A substance, such as a dietary supplement, used to enhance athletic performance.
esophagus The tube that extends from the throat to the stomach.
essential amino acids The nine amino acids that the body cannot synthesize, and must therefore be obtained through dietary sources.
essential fatty acids Fatty acids (linoleic acid and alpha-linolenic acid) which the body needs but cannot make, and therefore must be obtained from foods.
estimated energy requirement (EER) The average calorie intake estimated to maintain energy balance, based on a person's gender, age, height, body weight, and level of physical activity.
estrogen The hormone responsible for female sex characteristics.
ethanol The type of alcohol in alcoholic beverages such as wine, beer, and liquor.
exercise Any type of structured or planned physical activity.
experimental group The group given a specific treatment in a research study.
experimental research Research involving at least two groups of subjects.
extreme obesity Having an excessive amount of body fat; specifically, a BMI greater than 40.0.

F

famine A severe shortage of food caused by crop destruction due to weather, pestilence, war, or civil unrest within a region.
fat substitutes Substances that replace added fat in foods by providing the creamy properties of fat with fewer calories and fewer total fat grams.
fats See triglycerides.
fatty acid The most basic unit of lipids, composed of triglyercides and phospholipids.
feces See stool.
fermentation The process by which yeast converts sugars in grains or fruits into ethanol and carbon dioxide, resulting in an alcoholic beverage.
fetal alcohol syndrome (FAS) A cluster of physical, mental, and behavioral abnormalities that can occur in children who are exposed to alcohol in utero.
fetus A developing baby in the womb after the eighth week of pregnancy.
fiber The portion of plant foods that is not digested in the small intestine.
flexibility The range of motion around a body joint.
food allergy An abnormal physical reaction by the immune system to a particular food or substance.
foodborne illness Sickness caused by consuming contaminated food or beverages; also known as *foodborne disease* or *food poisoning*.
food guidance systems Visual diagrams that provide a variety of food recommendations to help create a well-balanced diet.
food insecurity Circumstances in which people have uncertain access to enough food to meet their nutritional needs due to lack of financial or other resources.
fortified foods Foods with added nutrients.
free radicals Unstable oxygen-containing molecules that can damage the cells of the body and contribute to increased risk for chronic diseases.
functional fiber A nondigestable polysaccharide added to foods because of a specific desired effect on health.
functional food A food that has a positive effect on health beyond providing basic nutrients.

G

gallbladder A small, muscular organ that stores bile.
gallstones Small, hard structures formed in the gallbladder or bile duct due to abnormally thick bile.

gastric bypass surgeries Surgical procedures that reduce the functional volume of the stomach, so that less food is eaten; sometimes used in the treatment of extreme obesity.
gastrointestinal (GI) tract The organs of the digestive tract, extending from the mouth to the anus.
gene A DNA segment that identifies a specific protein.
gene expression The processing of genetic information to create a specific protein.
gestational diabetes The form of diabetes that develops in women during pregnancy.
germ In grains, the seed of a grain kernel.
glucose The most abundant sugar in foods and the main energy source for your body.
glycogen The storage form of glucose in humans and other animals.

H

health A state of complete physical, mental and social well-being; not merely the absence of disease or infirmity.
health claim A claim on a food label that describes a relationship between a food or dietary compound and a disease or health-related condition.
Healthy People 2010 A set of disease prevention and health promotion objectives for Americans to meet during the first decade of the new millennium.
healthy weight A body weight in relation to your height that doesn't increase the risk of developing any weight-related health problems or diseases.
heart disease A term encompassing several disorders affecting the heart, of which coronary heart disease is the most common.
heartburn A burning sensation originating in the esophagus, usually caused by the reflux of gastric contents from the stomach into the esophagus.
high density lipoprotein (HDL) A lipoprotein that removes cholesterol from the tissues and delivers it to the liver to be used in the production of bile or to be excreted from the body. Because of this, it is known as the "good" cholesterol carrier.
hormones Protein- or lipid-based chemical substances that act as "messengers" in the body to initiate or direct metabolic actions and processes. Insulin, glucagon, and estrogen are examples of bodily hormones.
Human Genome Project The project sponsored by the U.S. government to determine the complete set and sequencing of DNA in the body's cells, and to identify all human genes.
hunger The physical need for food.
hydrogenation Adding hydrogen to unsaturated fatty acids, making them more saturated and solid at room temperature, and resulting in *trans fat.*
hypertension High blood pressure, generally measured as a level of "140 over 90" or higher.
hypoglycemia A condition in which blood glucose levels drop to lower than 70 mg/dl. Hunger, shakiness, dizziness, perspiration, irritability, and light-headedness are common symptoms of hypoglycemia.
hypothesis An idea scientists generate as a tentative explanation for their observations prior to further study and testing.

I

immunity The body's ability to develop antibodies (blood proteins) that help protect it from potentially harmful foreign substances, such as bacteria or viruses.
incomplete protein A protein that is low in one or more of the essential amino acids. Protein from plant sources tend to be incomplete.
initiation stage The first stage in the development of cancer, in which a body cell is exposed to an agent that damages its DNA.
inorganic A characteristic of compounds that do not contain carbon and are not formed by living things. Inorganic compounds include minerals, water, and salts.
insoluble fiber A type of fiber that doesn't dissolve in water and is not fermented by intestinal bacteria.
insulin The hormone, produced in and released from the pancreas, that directs glucose from the blood into the body's cells.
insulin resistance The inability or reduced ability of the body's cells to respond to the hormone insulin.
irradiation The process in which foods are subjected to a radiant energy source that kills specific pathogens by breaking up their cells' DNA.
irritable bowel syndrome (IBS) A bowel function disorder in which the large intestine is overly sensitive to stimuli.
isoflavones Naturally occurring plant estrogens which function similarly to the estrogen hormone in the human body.

K

kilocalories The measurement of energy in foods.
kwashiorkor A serious protein-energy malnutrition (PEM) disorder caused by a severe deficiency of dietary protein.

L

lactose intolerance A significant deficiency in the enzyme lactase, resulting in symptoms such as nausea, cramps, bloating, flatulence, and diarrhea following the consumption of foods containing lactose.
lactose maldigestion The inability to digest lactose in foods because of inadequate levels of the enzyme lactase.
large intestine The final organ of the GI tract, responsible for absorbing water and eliminating food residue as feces.
lean body mass Body mass after fat mass has been subtracted, containing mostly muscle but also organs and fluids. Lean body mass is the metabolically active tissue in the body.
licensed dietitian (LD) An individual who has met specified educational and experience criteria that a state licensing board has deemed necessary to be considered an expert in the field of nutrition. A Registered Dietitian (RD) meets all the qualifications to be an LD.
life expectancy The number of years that a majority of people within a population are expected to live.
lipids A broad category of compounds that contain carbon, oxygen, and hydrogen, and which are insoluble in water.
lipoprotein A capsule-shaped fat "carrier" that enables fats and cholesterol to travel through the lymph and blood.
liposuction The surgical removal of subcutaneous fat; performed most commonly on the abdomen, hips, and/or thighs.
liver The largest abdominal organ in the body. The liver aids in digestion and is responsible for the metabolism of nutrients, the detoxification of alcohol, and the storage of some nutrients.
low density lipoprotein (LDL) A lipoprotein that deposits cholesterol in the walls of the arteries. Because this can lead to heart disease, LDL is referred to as the "bad" cholesterol carrier.

M

macronutrients The energy-containing essential nutrients that you need in higher amounts: carbohydrates, lipids (fats), and proteins.
major minerals Seven key dietary minerals the body needs in amounts greater than 100 milligrams daily. The major minerals are sodium, chloride, potassium, calcium, phosphorus, magnesium, and sulfur.
malnourished The long-term outcome of consuming a diet that doesn't meet nutrient needs.
marasmus A serious condition of protein-energy malnutrition (PEM) stemming from severe deficiency of calories that results in wasting; commonly called *starvation.*
metabolism Numerous reactions that occur within the cells of the body, including the processes in which food calories are converted into energy.
micronutrients The essential nutrients you need in smaller amounts; vitamins and minerals.
minerals Inorganic elements that are essential to human nutrition.
monosaccharides Simple carbohydrates containing one sugar unit. There are three monosaccharides: glucose, fructose, and galactose.
muscle endurance The ability of a muscle to produce prolonged effort without fatigue.

muscle strength The ability of a muscle to produce force for a brief period of time.
MyPyramid A food guidance system that illustrates the recommendations in the *Dietary Guidelines for Americans 2005* and the Dietary Reference Intakes (DRIs) nutrient goals.

N

naturally occurring sugars Sugars such as fructose (in fruit) and lactose (in dairy products) that are found naturally in foods.
negative energy balance The condition in which you expend more energy than you consume, resulting in weight loss over time.
nitrates (nitrites) Chemical food additives that act as preservatives, in addition to enhancing the color of foods.
nonessential amino acids The 11 amino acids that the body can synthesize.
nutrigenomics The study of the body's ability to respond to various dietary functions based on a person's unique genetic makeup.
nutrient content claim A claim on a food label that describes the level or amount of a nutrient in the food product.
nutrient-dense The amount of nutrients per calorie in a given food. High nutrient-dense foods provide more nutrients per calorie than lower nutrient-dense foods.
nutrients Compounds in foods that sustain your body processes. There are six classes of nutrients: carbohydrates, fats (lipids), proteins, vitamins, minerals, and water.
nutrition The science that studies how the nutrients and compounds in foods nourish and affect body functions and health.
Nutrition Facts panel The area on a food label that provides a uniform listing of specific nutrients obtained in one serving of the food.
nutritionist A generic term with no recognized legal or professional meaning. Some people may call themselves nutritionists without having any credible training in nutrition.
nutritional genomics The field of study that researches the relationship between nutrition and genomics (the study of genes and gene expression).

O

obesity Having an unhealthy amount of body fat; specifically, a BMI 30.0 or more.
observational research Research that involves looking at factors in two or more groups of subjects to see if there is a relationship to certain outcomes.
oils Lipids that are liquid at room temperature.
organic A characteristic of compounds that contain carbon.
organic foods Foods that are free of most (though not all) chemical-based pesticides, synthetic fertilizers, irradiation, and bioengineering. A USDA-accredited certifying inspector must certify organic foods.
osteoporosis A condition in which the bones lose density, increasing the risk for fractures and breaks.
overnutrition A condition of excess nutrients and calories in the diet.
overweight Weighing roughly 10 to 15 pounds above a healthy weight relative to your height; specifically, a BMI between 25 and 29.9.
oxidation A chemical reaction in the body in which oxygen combines with other molecules.

P

pancreas An accessory organ for digestion that produces enzymes and other substances, and is connected to the small intestine via the bile duct.
pasteurization The process of heating liquids or food at high temperatures to destroy foodborne pathogens.
pathogens Disease-causing micro-organisms (microbes). Viruses, bacteria, and parasites are the pathogens most likely to cause foodborne illness.
peer-reviewed journal A research journal in which fellow scientists (peers) review studies to assess their accuracy and soundness before publication.
peptic ulcer A sore, erosion, or break in the lining of the stomach.
physical activity Voluntary movements that result in energy expenditure (burning calories).
physical fitness The ability to perform physical activities requiring cardiorespiratory endurance, muscle endurance, strength, and/or flexibility. Physical fitness is acquired through a combination of physical activity and adequate nutrition.
phytochemicals Naturally-occuring substances in fruits, vegetables, beans, and whole grains that help protect against certain chronic diseases.
phytosterols Naturally occurring substances found in plants. Phytosterols lower LDL cholesterol levels by competing with cholesterol for absorption in the intestinal tract.
placebo In a research study, a substance or item with no therapeutic value, provided to members of a control group in order to test it against expectations.
plaque The hardened buildup of cholesterol, fats, and cellular materials that results in atherosclerosis.
polysaccharides Complex carbohydrates containing many combined sugar units. Starch, glycogen, and fiber are polysaccharides.
positive energy balance The condition in which you store more energy than you expend, resulting in weight gain over time.
prediabetes The condition in which a person's blood glucose levels suggest an increased risk of developing diabetes, but which are not high enough to confirm it.
probiotics Live micro-organisms (sometimes called "healthy bacteria") that may have beneficial health effects.
progression stage The third stage in the development of cancer, in which damaged cells progress to form a tumor that invades surrounding tissues.
promotion stage The second stage in the development of cancer, in which damaged body cells are exposed to agents or conditions that promote their rapid reproduction.
proportionality The relationship of one entity to another. For example, grains, fruits, and vegetables should be consumed in a higher proportion than oils and meats in the diet.
protein-energy malnutrition (PEM) A lack of sufficient dietary protein and/or calories.
proteins Compounds in your body that consist of numerous amino acids and are found in all living cells.
public health nutritionist An individual who may have an undergraduate degree in nutrition but isn't a Registered Dietitian (RD).
purging An eating disorder behavior that assists in removing eaten food in order to prevent weight gain; including self-induced vomiting, laxatives, diuretics (water pills), excessive exercise, and/or fasting.

Q

quackery The promotion and selling of health products and services of questionable validity. A quack is a person who promotes these products and services in order to make money.

R

rancidity The decomposition or spoiling of fats through oxidation.
rectum The lowest part of the large intestine.
refined grains Grain foods made with only the endosperm of the kernel; the bran and germ are not included.
registered dietitian (RD) A health professional who has completed at least a bachelor's degree in an accredited university or college in the United States, has completed a supervised practice, and has passed an exam administered by the American Dietetic Association (ADA).
remineralization The repairing of teeth by adding back the minerals lost during tooth decay, e.g., saliva can help remineralize teeth.

S

saliva Watery fluid secreted by the salivary glands in the mouth that moistens food and makes it easier to swallow.
satiety The sensation experienced when you have eaten enough. Satiety helps determine how long you may go between meals and/or snacks.

saturated fats Fats in which the fatty acid chain is saturated with hydrogen. Foods high in saturated fats with long fatty acid chains are solid at room temperature, and are unhealthy.
scientific method A process of experimental steps scientists use to generate sound research findings.
simple carbohydrates Carbohydrates containing a single sugar unit, or two sugar units combined. Monosaccharides and disaccharides are simple carbohydrates.
sugar substitutes Alternatives to table sugar that sweeten foods while using fewer calories.
small intestine The longest part of the GI tract, where most of the digestion and absorption of food occurs.
soluble fiber A type of fiber that dissolves in water and is fermented by intestinal bacteria. Many soluble fibers are viscous, with gummy or thickening properties.
starch The storage form of glucose in plants.
stomach The digestive organ that receives food from the esophagus, mixes it with digestive juices, and stores it before it is gradually released into the small intestine.
stool (feces) Waste product stored in the large intestine and excreted from the body, consisting mostly of bacteria, sloughed-off gastrointestinal cells, water, unabsorbed nutrients, undigested fibers, and remnants of digestive fluids.
structure or function claim A claim on a food label describing how a nutrient or dietary compound affects the structure or function of the human body.
subcutaneous fat Body fat located under the skin and between the muscles.

T

thirst The physical need for water.
thirst mechanism Various bodily reactions caused by dehydration, signaling you to drink fluids.
toxicity The level at which exposure to a substance becomes harmful.
trace minerals Nine dietary minerals the body needs in small amounts (less than 20 milligrams daily). The trace minerals are iron, zinc, selenium, fluoride, chromium, copper, iodine, manganese, and molybdenum.
***trans* fats** Fats primarily resulting from the hydrogenation of unsaturated fatty acids, a process used widely in commercially-made foods to add texture, longer shelf life and better resistance to rancidity. *Trans* fats are bad for heart health in numerous ways.
triglycerides The most common type of lipid found in foods and in your body; commonly known as *fats*.
trimesters The three time periods of pregnancy.

U

undernutrition A state of malnutrition in which a person's nutrient and/or calorie needs aren't met through the diet.
underweight Weighing too little for your height; clinically, a BMI below 18.5.
unsaturated fats Fats in which the fatty acid chain contains less hydrogen. Foods containing unsaturated fats are liquid at room temperature, and have health benefits.

vegetarian A person who doesn't eat meat, fish, or poultry or, in some cases, food products made from these animal sources.
viruses Microscopic organisms that must have a living "host," such as a plant or animal, to survive. Viruses can infect a host and cause illness.
visceral fat Body fat stored in the abdominal area.
vitamins Essential nutrients that your body needs in small amounts to grow, reproduce, and maintain good health.

water balance The state in which an equal amount of water is lost and replenished daily in the body.
weight management Maintaining your weight within a healthy range.
weight training Exercising with weights to build, strengthen, and tone muscle and/or to improve or maintain overall fitness; also called *resistance training*.
whole grains Grain foods made with the entire edible grain kernel; the bran, the germ, and the endosperm.
working poor The term used for people or families who are steadily employed but still experience poverty due to low wages or high dependent expenses.

zoochemicals Compounds found within animal food products that are beneficial to human health, such as omega-3 fatty acids.

References

Concept 1

1. Glanz, K., M. Basil, E. Maibach, J. Goldberg, and D. Snyder. 1998. Why Americans Eat What They Do: Taste, Nutrition, Cost, Convenience, and Weight Control Concerns as Influences on Food Consumption. *Journal of the American Dietetic Association* 98: 1118–1126.
2. National Turkey Federation. 2004. Turkey Facts and Trivia. www.eatturkey.com/consumer/history/history.html (accessed February 2006).
3. Freeland-Graves, J., and S. Nitzke. 2002. Total Diet Approach to Communicating Food and Nutrition Information. *Journal of the American Dietetic Association* 102: 100–108.
4. Coomes, S. Pizza Marketplace. Personal communication. February 2006.
5. Mintel International Group. 2005. Cinemas and Movie Theaters—United States, Mintel Reports—USA, Leisure—USA. www.reports.mintel.com (accessed March 2006).
6. Gallo, A. 1999. Food Advertising in the United States. In America's Eating Habits: Changes and Consequences. Economic Research Service. Agriculture Information Bulletin No. AIB750. www.ers.usda.gov/Publications/aib750 (accessed March 2006).
7. Story, M., and S. French. 2004. Food Advertising and Marketing Directed at Children and Adolescents in the U.S. *International Journal of Behavioral Nutrition and Physical Activity* 1: 1–17.
8. Blisard, N. 1999. Advertising and How We Eat: The Case of Dairy Products. In *America's Eating Habits: Changes and Consequences.* Economic Research Service. Agriculture Information Bulletin No. AIB750. www.ers.usda.gov/Publications/aib750.
9. U.S. Department of Agriculture (USDA). 2006. Food Security in the United States: Conditions and Trends. Economic Research Service. www.ers.usda.gov/Briefing/FoodSecurity/trends.htm.
10. Freeland-Graves and Nitzke. Total Diet Approach to Communicating Food and Nutrition Information.
11. Specialty Coffee Association. 2006. Retail in the USA 2004–2007. www.scaa.org (accessed March 2006).
12. Economic Research Service. 2005. Table 12 in *Food CPI, Prices and Expenditure Tables: Food Expenditure Table.* www.ers.usda.gov/Briefing/CPIFoodAndExpenditures/Data/table12.htm (accessed February 2006).
13. Mintel International Group. 2004. Breakfast Foods: The Consumer—US, Mintel Reports—USA, Food and Food Service—USA. www.reports.mintel.com (accessed February 2006).

Concept 2

1. World Health Organization. What Is the WHO Definition of Health? Preamble to the Constitution of the World Health Organization as Adopted by the International Health Conference, New York, 19 June–22 July 1946. www.who.int/suggestions/faq/en/index.html (accessed September 2008).
2. World Health Organization. New WHO Publication on Risk Factors for Health. May 6, 2005. www.who.int/mediacentre/news/new/2005/nw04/en/index.html (accessed September 2008).
3. Persons, Susan M. Risk Factors Cluster to Harm Health. National Institutes of Health. http://obssr.od.nih.gov/Content/Publications/Articles/RISKCLU.htm (accessed September 2008).
4. Persons. Risk Factors Cluster to Harm Health.
5. Debusk, R., C. Fogarty, J. Ordovas, and K. Kornman. 2005. Nutrition Genomics in Practice: Where Do We Begin? *Journal of the American Dietetic Association* 105: 589–598.
6. Mashfegh, A. L., J. Goldman, and L. Cleveland. 2005. What We Eat in America, NHANES 2001–2002; Usual Nutrient Intakes from Food Compared to Dietary Reference Intakes. U.S. Department of Agriculture, Agricultural Research Service.
7. Centers for Disease Control and Prevention. 2005. Overweight and Obesity: Obesity Trends. www.cdc.gov (accessed February 2006).
8. *Healthy People 2010.* 2000. Health Finder: Nutrition and Overweight. www.healthypeople.gov (accessed March 2006).

Feature Box References

1. Drewnowski, A., and S. E. Specter. 2004. Poverty and Obesity: The Role of Energy Density and Energy Costs. *American Journal of Clinical Nutrition* 79: 6–16. © 2004 American Society for Clinical Nutrition.
2. Scheier, L. M. What Is the Hunger-Obesity Paradox? *Journal of the American Dietetic Association*. Practice Applications: Beyond the Headlines. Pages 883–886. © 2005 American Dietetic Association.
3. Scheier. What Is the Hunger-Obesity Paradox?
4. Drewnowski and Specter. Poverty and Obesity: The Role of Energy Density and Energy Costs.
5. Scheier. What Is the Hunger-Obesity Paradox?

Concept 3

1. Krane, D. 2005. Number of "Cyberchondriacs"—U.S. Adults Who Go Online for Health Information—Increases to Estimated 117 Million. HarrisInteractive Healthcare Research. www.harrisinteractive.com (accessed March 2006).
2. National Center for Complementary and Alternative Medicine. Updated 2006. 10 Things to Know about Evaluating Medical Resources on the Web. www.nccam.nih.gov (accessed March 2006).

Concept 4

1. Institute of Medicine. 2003. *Dietary Reference Intakes: Applications in Dietary Planning.* Washington, D.C.: The National Academies Press.
2. Davis, C., and E. Saltos. 1999. Chapter 2: Dietary Recommendations and How They Have Changed over Time. In Frazo, E., ed., *America's Eating Habits: Changes and Consequences.* Agriculture Information Bulletin No. AIB750. www.ers.usda.gov/publications/aib750 (accessed September 2005).
3. Lee, P. R. 1978. Nutrition Policy: From Neglect and Uncertainty to Debate and Action. *Journal of the American Dietetic Association* 72: 581–588.
4. U.S. Department of Agriculture. 2005. *2005 Report of the Dietary Guidelines Advisory Committee.* www.health.gov/dietaryguidelines/dga2005/report (accessed February 2005).
5. Ibid.
6. Painter, J., J. Rah, and Y. Lee. 2002. Comparison of International Food Guide Pictorial Representations. *Journal of the American Dietetic Association* 102: 483–489.
7. U.S. Department of Agriculture. 2005. The New Look and Messages of USDA's MyPyramid: Background. www.mypyramid.gov/global_nav/media_backgrounder.html (accessed June 2005).

Concept 5

1. Center for Food Safety and Applied Nutrition. 1999. A Food Labeling Guide. www.cfsan.fda.gov/~dms/flg-toc.html (accessed March 2009).
2. U.S. Food and Drug Administration. December 20, 2005. FDA to Require Food Manufactureres to List Food Allergens. FDA News. www.fda.gov/bbs/topics/NEWS/2005/NEW01281.html (accessed September 2008).
3. Center for Food Safety and Applied Nutrition. A Food Labeling Guide.
4. Center for Food Safety and Applied Nutrition. 2004. How to Understand and Use the Nutrition Facts Label. www.cfsan.fda.gov/~acrobat/foodlab.pdf (accessed March 2009).
5. Farley, D. 1993. Look for "Legit" Health Claims on Foods. *FDA Consumer Magazine,* available at www.fda.gov. (accessed March 2009).
6. Center for Food Safety and Applied Nutrition. 2003. Claims That Can Be Made for Conventional Foods and Dietary Supplements. www.cfsan.fda.gov/~dms/hclaims.html (accessed March 2009).
7. Hasler, C. M., A. S. Bloch, C. A. Thomson, E. Enrione, and C. Manning. 2004. Position of the American Dietetic Association: Functional Foods. *Journal of the American Dietetic Association* 104: 814–826.
8. Institute of Food Technologists. 2005. Expert Report on Functional Foods: Opportunities and Challenges, Executive Summary. www.ift.org/cms/?pid=1001247 (accessed March 2009).

Feature Box References

1. Neroulias, N. 2008. Menus Listing Calories May Come to County. *New York Times,* October 12, 2008. www.nytimes.com/2008/10/12/nyregion/westchester//12caloriewe.html (accessed October 2008).
2. Ibid.; Rabin, R. C. 2007. Calorie Labels May Clarify Options, Not Actions. *New York Times,* July 17, 2007. www.nytimes.com/2007/07/17/health/nutrition/17cons.html (accessed October 2008).

Concept 6

1. Mahan, K., and S. Escott-Stump. 2004. *Krause's Food, Nutrition, and Diet Therapy.* 11th ed. Philadelphia: Saunders.
2. Ibid.
3. Ganong, W. F. 1977. *Review of Medical Physiology.* 8th ed. Los Altos, CA: Lange Medical Publications.
4. Mahan. *Krause's Food, Nutrition, and Diet Therapy.*
5. Gropper, S. S., J. L. Smith, and J. L. Groff. 2005. *Advanced Nutrition and Human Metabolism.* 4th ed. Belmont, CA: Thomson Wadsworth.
6. Hole, J. W. 1984. *Human Anatomy and Physiology.* 3rd ed. Dubuque, IA: WC Brown.
7. Guyton, A. C. 1981. *Textbook of Medical Physiology.* 6th ed. Philadelphia: Saunders.
8. Ganong. *Review of Medical Physiology.*
9. Gropper. *Advanced Nutrition and Human Metabolism.*
10. U.S. Department of Health and Human Services. Oral Health. www.4woman.gov/faq/oral_health.htm (accessed June 2006).
11. Nelson, J. K., K. E. Moxness, M. D. Jensen, and C. F. Gastineau. 1994. *Mayo Clinic Diet Manual.* 7th ed. St. Louis: Mosby.
12. Anderson, D. M. 2002. *Mosby's Medical, Nursing and Allied Health Dictionary.* 6th ed. St. Louis: Mosby.
13. Nelson. *Mayo Clinic Diet Manual.*

Feature Box References

1. National Digestive Diseases Information Clearinghouse. 2008. Celiac Disease. NIH Publication No. 08-4269. September 2008. http://digestive.niddk.nih.gov/ddisases/pubs/celiac/#other (accessed October 2008).
2. Ibid.

Concept 7

1. Painter, J., J. Rah, and Y. Lee. 2002. Comparison of International Food Guide Pictorial Respresentations. *Journal of the American Dietetic Association* 102: 483–489; Gifford, K. D. The Asian Diet Pyramid. *Oldways Preservation and Exchange Trust.* www.oldwayspt.org (accessed March 2003).
2. McBean, L., and G. Miller. 1998. Allaying Fears and Fallacies about Lactose Intolerance. *Journal of the American Dietetic Association* 98: 671–676; Suarez, M. D., D. Savaiano, and M. Levitt. 1995. A Comparison of Symptoms after the Consumption of Milk or Lactose-Hydrolyzed Milk by People with Self-Reported Severe Lactose Intolerance. *New England Journal of Medicine* 333: 1–4.
3. Suarez. A Comparison of Symptoms; Johnson, A., J. Semenya, M. Buchowski, C. Enownwu, and N. Scrimshaw. 1993. Correlation of Lactose Maldigestion, Lactose Intolerance, and Mik Intolerance. *American Journal of Clinical Nutrition* 57: 399–401.
4. Putnam, J., J. Allshouse, and L. Kantor. Winter 2002. U.S. per Capita Food Supply Trends: More Calories, Refined Carbohydrates, and Fats. *Food Review* 25: 2–15.
5. National Digestive Diseases Information Clearinghouse. May 2002. *Lactose Intolerance.* National Institutes of Health Publication No. 02-2751.
6. McBean. Allaying Fears and Fallacies.
7. Suarez, F., and M. Levitt. 1996. Abdominal Symptoms and Lactose: The Discrepancy between Patients' Claims and the Results of Blinded Trials. *American Journal of Clinical Nutrition* 64: 251–252; Suarez, F. L., D. Savaiano, P. Arbisi, and M. Levitt. 1997. Tolerance to the Daily Ingestion of Two Cups of Milk by Individuals Claiming Lactose Intolerance. *American Journal of Clinical Nutrition* 65: 1502–1506.
8. Suarez. Tolerance to the Daily Ingestion; Dehkordi, N., D. R. Rao, A. P. Warren, and C. B. Chawan. 1995. Lactose Malabsorption as Influenced by Chocolate Milk, Skim Milk, Sucrose, Whole Milk, and Lactic Cultures. *Journal of the American Dietetic Association* 95: 484–486.
9. Lee, C., and C. Hardy. 1989. Cocoa Feeding and Human Lactose Intolerance. *American Journal of Clinical Nutrition* 49: 840–844; Hertzler, S., B. Huynh, and D. Savaiano. 1996. How Much Lactose Is Low Lactose? *Journal of the American Dietetic Association* 96: 243–246.

Feature Box References

1. Putnam, J., J. Allshouse, and L. Kantor. Winter 2002. U.S. per Capita Food Supply Trends: More Calories, Refined Carbohydrates, and Fats. *Food Review* 25: 2–15.
2. Slavin, J., D. Jacobs, L. Marquart, and K. Wiemer. 2001. The Role of Whole Grains in Disease Prevention. *Journal of the American Dietetic Association* 101: 780–785.
3. Jacobs, D., K. Meyer, L. Kushi, and A. Folsom. 1999. Is Whole Grain Intake Associated with Reduced Total and Cause-Specific Death Rates in Older Women? The Iowa Women's Health Study. *American Journal of Public Health* 89: 322–329; Liu, S., J. Manson, M. Stampfer, K. Rexrode, F. Hu, E. Rimm, and W. Willett. 2000. Whole Grain Consumption and Risk of Ischemic Stroke in Women. *Journal of the American Medical Association* 284: 1534–1540.
4. Jorge, S., A. Ascherio, E. Rimm, G. Colditz, D. Spiegelman, D. Jenkins, M. Stampfer, A. Wing, and W. Willett. 1997. Dietary Fiber, Glycemic Load, and Risk of NIDDM in Men. *Diabetes Care* 20: 545–550; Salmeron, J., J. Manson, M. Stampfer, G. Colditz, A. Wing, and W. Willett. 1997. Dietary Fiber, Glycemic Load, and Risk of Non-Insulin-Dependent Diabetes Mellitus in Women. *Journal of the American Medical Association* 277: 472–477; Meyer, K., L. Kushi, D. Jacobs, J. Slavin, T. Seller, and A. Folsom. 2000. Carbohydrates, Dietary Fiber, and Incident Type 2 Diabetes in Older Women. *American Journal of Clinical Nutrition* 71: 921–930.
5. Slavin. The Role of Whole Grains.
6. U.S. Department of Health and Human Services. 2000. *Healthy People 2010. With Understanding and Improving Health and Objectives for Improving Health.* 2 vols. Washington, D.C.: U.S. Government Printing Office.

Concept 8

1. Institute of Medicine. 2002. *Dietary Reference Intakes for Energy, Carbohydrate, Fiber, Fat, Fatty Acids, Cholesterol, Protein, and Amino Acids.* Washington, D.C.: The National Academies Press.
2. Lin, B., and R. Morrison. Winter 2002. Higher Fruit Consumption Linked with Lower Body Mass Index. *Food Review* 25: 28–32.
3. Putnam, J., J. Allshouse, and L. Kantor. 2002. U.S per Capita Food Supply Trends: More Calories, Refined Carbohydrates, and Fats. Economic Research Service, *Food Review* 25: 2–15.
4. American Dietetic Association. 1998. Use of Nutritive and Nonnutritive Sweeteners. *Journal of the American Dietetic Association* 98: 580–587.
5. Howard, B., and J. Wylie-Rosett. 2002. Sugar and Cardiovascular Disease: A Statement for Healthcare Professionals from the Committee on Nutrition of the Council on Nutrition, Physical Activity, and Metabolism of the American Heart Association. *Circulation* 106: 523–527.
6. American Dietetic Association. Use of Nutritive and Nonnutritive Sweeteners.
7. Institute of Medicine. Dietary Reference Intakes for Energy.
8. World Health Organization and Food and Agricultural Organization. 2003. Report of the Joint WHO/FAO Expert Consultation on Diet, Nutrition and the Prevention of Chronic Diseases. www.who.int.
9. Putnam, J., J. Allshouse, and L. Kantor. 2002. U.S per Capita Food Supply Trends: More Calories, Refined Carbohydrates, and Fats. Economic Research Service, *Food Review* 25: 2–15.
10. American Dietetic Association. Use of Nutritive and Nonnutritive Sweeteners.
11. National Toxicology Program. 2000. *Report on Carcinogens.* 9th ed.
12. Ajinomoto USA, Inc. The History of Aspartame. www.aspartame.net/media/history.html (accessed April 2003).
13. Council on Scientific Affairs. 1985. Aspartame: Review of Safety Issues. *Journal of the American Medical Association* 254: 400–402.
14. Scientific Committee on Food. December 2002. Opinion of the Scientific Committee on Food: Update on the Safety of Aspartame. www.europa.eu.int (accessed March 2003).
15. The NutraSweet Company. Neotame: A Scientific Overview. www.neotame.com (accessed March 2003).
16. Institute of Medicine. Dietary Reference Intakes for Energy.
17. National Digestive Diseases Information Clearinghouse. May 2000. Constipation. National Institutes of Health Publication No. 95-2754. www.niddk.nih.gov (accessed April 2003).
18. National Digestive Diseases Information Clearinghouse. January 2002. Diverticulosis and Diverticulitis. National Institutes of Health Publication No. 02-1163. www.niddk.nih.gov (accessed April 2003).
19. Miller, W., M. Niederpruem, J. Wallace, and A. Lindeman. 1994. Dietary Fat, Sugar, and Fiber Predict Body Fat Content. *Journal of the American*

Dietetic Association 94: 612–615; Appley, P., M. Thorogood, J. Mann, and T. Key. 1998. Low Body Mass Index in Non-Meat Eaters: The Possible Roles of Animal Fat, Dietary Fibre and Alcohol. *International Journal of Obesity-Related Metabolic Disorders* 22: 454–460.

20. Pietinen, P., E. Rimm, P. Korhonen, A. Hartman, W. Willett, D. Albanes, and J. Virtamo. 1996. Intake of Dietary Fiber and Risk of Coronary Heart Disease in a Cohort of Finnish Men: The Alpha-Tocopherol, Beta-Carotene Cancer Prevention Study. *Circulation* 94: 2720–2727; Rimm, E., A. Ascherio, E. Giovannucci, D. Spiegelman, M. Stampfer, and W. Willett. 1996. Vegetable, Fruit, and Cereal Fiber Intake and Risk of Coronary Heart Disease among Men. *Journal of the American Medical Association* 275: 447–451.
21. Wolk, A., J. Manson, M. Stampfer, G. Colditz, F. Hu, F. Speizer, C. Hennekens, and W. Willett. 1999. Long-Term Intake of Dietary Fiber and Decreased Risk of Coronary Heart Disease among Women. *Journal of the American Medical Association* 281: 1998–2004.
22. Institute of Medicine. Dietary Reference Intakes for Energy.
23. National Cancer Institute. 2008. Colorectal Cancer Prevention (PDQ®). www.cancer.gov (accessed June 2008).
24. Bingham, S., N. Day, R. Luben, P. Ferrari, N. Slimani, T. Norat, et al. 2003. Dietary Fiber in Food and Protection against Colorectal Cancer in the European Prospective Investigation into Cancer and Nutrition (EPIC): An Observation Study. *The Lancet* 361: 1496–1501; Ferguson, L., and P. Harris. 2003. The Dietary Fiber Debate: More Food for Thought. *The Lancet* 361: 1487–1488.
25. Ibid.

Feature Box References

1. Burt, A., and P. Satishchandra. 2001. Sugar Consumption and Caries Risk: A Systematic Review. *Journal of Dental Education* 65: 1017–1023.
2. NIH Consenus Statement. 2001. Diagnosis and Management of Dental Caries throughout Life. www.concensus.nih.gov (accessed March 2003).
3. Heller, K., B. Burt, and S. Ekund. 2001. Sugared Soda Consumption and Dental Caries in the United States. *Journal of Dental Research* 80, no. 10: 1949–1953; American Dental Association. 2002. Diet and Tooth Decay. *Journal of the American Dental Association* 133: 527; Joint Report of the American Dental Association Council on Access, Prevention and Interprofessional Relations and the Council on Scientific Affairs to the House of Delegates. 2001. Response to Resolution 73H-200. www.ada.org (accessed May 2003).
4. Moynihan, P. 2002. Dietary Advice in Dental Practice. *British Dental Journal* 193: 563–568.
5. American Dental Association. 2003. Early Childhood Tooth Decay. www.ada.org (accessed May 2003).
6. Moynihan, P., S. Ferrier, and G. Jenkins. 1999. Eating Cheese: Does It Reduce Caries? *British Dental Journal* 187: 664–667; Kashket, S., and D. DePaola. 2002. Cheese Consumption and the Development and Progression of Dental Caries. *Nutrition Reviews* 60: 97–103.
7. Mandel, I. 1996. Caries Prevention: Current Strategies, New Directions. *Journal of the American Dental Association* 127: 1477–1488.

Concept 9

1. Centers for Disease Control and Prevention (CDC). June 2008. 2007 National Diabetes Fact Sheet. www.cdc.gov/diabetes (accessed July 2008).
2. American Diabetes Association. 2002. The Prevention or Delay of Type 2 Diabetes. *Diabetes Care* 25: 742–749.
3. Centers for Disease Control and Prevention (CDC). 2007 National Diabetes Fact Sheet.
4. American Diabetes Association. 2004. Type 2 Diabetes in the Young: The Evolving Epidemic. *Diabetes Care* 27: 1798–1811.
5. Centers for Disease Control and Prevention (CDC). 2007 National Diabetes Fact Sheet.
6. Ibid.
7. National Digestive Diseases Information Clearinghouse. May 2002. Diabetes Overview. National Institutes of Health Publication No. 02-3873. www.niddk.nih.gov (accessed April 2003).
8. Ibid.
9. National Center for Health Statistics (NCHS). Prevalence of Overweight and Obesity among Adults: United States, 2003–2004. www.cdc.gov/nchs/products/pubs/pubd/hestats/overweight/overwght_adult_03.htm (accessed July 2008).
10. National Center for Health Statistics (NCHS). Prevalence of Overweight and Obesity among Children and Adolescents: United States, 1999–2002. www.cdc.gov/nchs/products/pubs/pubd/hestats/overweight99.htm (accessed July 2008).
11. American Diabetes Association. 2004. Type 2 Diabetes in the Young: The Evolving Epidemic. *Diabetes Care* 27: 1798–1811.
12. National Diabetes Information Clearinghouse (NDIC). 2005. National Diabetes Statistics. National Institutes of Health (NIH) Publication No. 06-3892. http://diabetes.niddk.nih.gov/dm/pubs/statistics/index.htm#race (accessed July 2008).
13. Centers for Disease Control and Prevention (CDC). 2007 National Diabetes Fact Sheet.
14. National Digestive Diseases Information Clearinghouse. Diabetes Overview.
15. Kaiser, L., and L. Allen. 2002. Position of the American Dietetic Association: Nutrition and Lifestyle for a Healthy Pregnancy Outcome. *Journal of the American Dietetic Association* 102: 1479–1490.
16. Centers for Disease Control and Prevention (CDC). 2002. Diabetes: Disabling, Deadly, and on the Rise. www.cdc.gov (accessed March 2003).
17. American Diabetes Association. 2003. Nutrition Recommendations and Interventions for Diabetes. A Position Statement of the American Diabetes Association. *Diabetes Care* 31: S61–S78.
18. Sheard, N., N. Clark, J. Brand-Miller, M. Franz, F. Pi-Sunyer, E. Mayer-Davis, K. Kulkarni, and P. Geil. 2004. Dietary Carbohydrate (Amount and Type) in the Prevention and Management of Diabetes. *Diabetes Care* 27: 2266–2271.
19. Ludwig, D. 2002. The Glycemic Index: Physiological Mechanisms Relating to Obesity, Diabetes, and Cardiovascular Disease. *Journal of the American Medical Association* 287: 2414–2423.
20. Roberts, S. 2000. High-Glycemic Index Foods, Hunger, and Obesity: Is There a Connection? *Nutrition Reviews* 58: 163–169; Foster-Powell, K., and J. Brand-Miller. 1995. International Tables of Glycemic Index. *American Journal of Clinical Nutrition* 62: 871S–893S.
21. American Diabetes Association. Nutrition Recommendations and Interventions for Diabetes.
22. Diabetes Prevention Program Research Group. 2002. Reduction in the Incidence of Type 2 Diabetes with Lifestyle Intervention or Metformin. *New England Journal of Medicine* 346: 393–403.
23. National Digestive Diseases Information Clearinghouse. October 2008. Hypoglycemia. National Institutes of Health Publication No. 03-3926. http://diabetes.niddk.nih.gov/dm/pubs/hypoglycemia/ (accessed April 2009).

Feature Box Reference

1. Data adapted from the *U.S. Department of Health and Human Services' National Diabetes Education Program. 2008.* Your Healthy Food Guide. *Available at:* http://ndep.nih.gov/diabetes/youth/youthtips/youthtips_eat.htm. (accessed July 2008).

Concept 10

1. Institute of Medicine. 2002. *Dietary Reference Intakes for Energy, Carbohydrate, Fiber, Fat, Fatty Acids, Cholesterol, Protein, and Amino Acids.* Washington, D.C.: The National Academies Press.
2. Kris-Etherton, P. M., W. S. Harris, and L. J. Appel. 2002. Fish Consumption, Fish Oil, Omega-3 Fatty Acids, and Cardiovascular Disease. *Circulation* 106: 2747–2757.

Concept 11

1. Stephen, A. M., and N. J. Wald. 1990. Trends in Individual Consumption of Dietary Fat in the United States, 1920–1984. *American Journal of Clinical Nutrition* 52: 457–469; Agriculture Research Service. 2000. Pyramid Servings Intakes by Children and Adults: 1994–1996, 1998. ARS Community Nutrition Research Group. www.barc.usda.gov/bhnrc/cnrg (accessed August 2003).
2. Chanmugam, P., J. F. Guthrie, S. Cecilio, J. F. Morton, P. Basiotis, and R. Anand. 2003. Did Fat Intake in the United States Really Decline between 1989–1991 and 1994–1996? *Journal of the American Dietetic Association* 103: 867–872.
3. Institute of Medicine. 2002. *Dietary Reference Intakes for Energy, Carbohydrate, Fiber, Fat, Fatty Acids, Cholesterol, Protein, and Amino Acids.* Washington, D.C.: The National Academies Press.
4. Ibid.
5. Ibid.
6. U.S. Department of Agriculture. 2000. Nutrition and Your Health: Dietary Guidelines for Americans. Home and Garden Bulletin No. 232.
7. Allison, D. B., S. K. Egan, L. M. Barraj, C. Caughman, M. Infante, and J. T. Heimbach. 1999. Estimated Intakes of *Trans* Fatty and Other Fatty Acids in the U.S. Population. *Journal of the American Dietetic Association* 99: 166–174.

8. Center for Food Safety and Applied Nutrition. July 9, 2003. Questions and Answers about *Trans* Fat Nutrition Labeling. CFSAN Office of Nutritional Products, Labeling and Dietary Supplements. www.cfsan.fda.gov/~dams/qatrans2.html (accessed July 2003).
9. Ibid.
10. Calorie Control Council. Fat Replacers: Food Ingredients for Healthy Eating. www.caloriedcontrol.org/fatreprint.html (accessed August 2003).
11. Mattes, R. D. 1998. Fat Replacers. *Journal of the American Dietetic Association* 98: 463–468.
12. Ibid.
13. Mattes. Fat Replacers; Wylie-Rosett, J. 2002. Fat Substitutes and Health: An Advisory from the Nutrition Committee of the American Heart Association. *Circulation* 105: 2800–2804.
14. Ibid.
15. Mattes. Fat Replacers.
16. Ibid.
17. Sandler, R. S., N. L. Zorich, T. G. Filloon, H. B. Wiseman, D. J. Lietz, M. H. Brock, M. G. Royer, and R. K. Miday. 1999. Gastrointestinal Symptoms in 3,181 Volunteers Ingesting Snack Foods Containing Olestra or Triglycerides: A 6-Week Randomized, Placebo-Controlled Trial. *Annals of Internal Medicine* 130: 253–261; Cheskin, L. J., R. Miday, N. Zorich, and T. Filloon. 1998. Gastrointestinal Symptoms Following Consumption of Olestra or Regular Triglyceride Potato Chips: A Controlled Comparison. *Journal of the American Medical Association* 279: 150–152.

Feature Box References

1. Helsing, E. 1995. Traditional Diets and Disease Patterns of the Mediterranean, circa 1960. *American Journal of Clinical Nutrition* 61: 1329S–1337S.
2. Trichopoulou, A. N., T. Costacou, C. Bamia, and D. Trichopoulos. 2003. Adherence to a Mediterranean Diet and Survival in a Greek Population. *New England Journal of Medicine* 348: 2599–2608; de Lorgeril, M., P. Salen, J. L. Martin, I. Monjaud, J. Delaye, and N. Mamelle. 1999. Mediterranean Diet, Traditional Risk Factors, and the Rate of Cardiovascular Complications after Myocardial Infarction: Final Report of the Lyon Diet Heart Study. *Circulation* 99: 779–785; Kris-Etherton, P., R. H. Eckel, B. V. Howard, S. St. Jeor, and T. L. Bazzarre. 2001. Lyon Diet Heart Study. Benefits of a Mediterranean-Style, National Cholesterol Education Program/American Heart Association Step I Dietary Pattern on Cardiovascular Disease. *Circulation* 103: 1823–1825.
3. Willett, W. C., F. Sacks, A. N. Trichopoulou, G. Drescher, A. Ferro-Luzzi, E. Helsing, and D. Trichopoulos. 1995. Mediterranean Diet Pyramid: A Cultural Model for Healthy Eating. *American Journal of Clinical Nutrition* 61: 1402S–1406S.
4. Ibid.
5. de Lorgeril. Mediterranean Diet, Traditional Risk Factors, and the Rate of Cardiovascular Complications after Myocardial Infarction.
6. Willett. Mediterranean Diet Pyramid; Nestle, M. 1995. Mediterranean Diets: Historical and Research Overview. *American Journal of Clinical Nutrition* 61: 1313S–1320S.
7. Nestle, M. 1995. Mediterranean Diets: Historical and Research Overview. *American Journal of Clinical Nutrition* 61: 1313S–1320S.
8. Ibid.
9. Keys, A. 1995. Mediterranean Diet and Public Health: Personal Reflections. *American Journal of Clinical Nutrition* 61: 1321S–1323S.

Concept 12

1. Centers for Disease Control and Prevention. Division for Heart Disease and Stroke Prevention. Heart Disease. www.cdc.gov/HeartDisease/ (accessed August 2008).
2. The American Heart Association. Heart Disease and Stroke Statistics—2008 Update. www.aha.org (accessed August 2008).
3. Sandmaier, M. 2007. *The Healthy Heart Handbook for Women.* National Institutes of Health, National Heart, Lung and Blood Institute. NIH Publication No. 03-2720.
4. The American Heart Association. Heart Disease and Stroke Statistics—2008 Update. www.aha.org (accessed August 2008).
5. National Heart, Lung and Blood Institute. Quitting Smoking. www.nhlbi.nih.gov/hbp/prevent/q_smoke/know.htm (accessed August 2008).
6. Institute of Medicine. 2002. *Dietary Reference Intakes for Energy, Carbohydrate, Fiber, Fat, Fatty Acids, Cholesterol, Protein, and Amino Acids.* Washington, D.C.: The National Academies Press.
7. Krauss, R. M., H. B. Eckel, and committee. 2000. 2000 AHA Dietary Guidelines. Revision 2000: A Statement for Healthcare Professionals from the Nutrition Committee of the American Heart Association. *Circulation* 102: 2296–2311. Hu, F. B., M. J. Stampfer, E. B. Rimm, J. E. Manson, A. Ascherio, G. Colditz, B. Rosner, D. Spiegelman, F. E. Speizer, F. M. Sacks, C. H. Hennekens, and W. C. Willett. 1999. A Prospective Study of Egg Consumption and Risk of Cardiovascular Disease in Men and Women. *Journal of the American Medical Association* 281: 1387–1394.
8. Kramhout, D., E. B. Bosschieter, and C. Coulander. 1985. The Inverse Relation between Fish Consumption and 20-Year Mortality from Coronary Heart Disease. *New England Journal of Medicine* 312: 1205–1209.
9. Kris-Etherton, P. M., W. S. Harris, and L. J. Appel. 2002. Fish Consumption, Fish Oil, Omega-3 Fatty Acids, and Cardiovascular Disease. *Circulation* 106: 2747–2757; Center for Food Safety and Applied Nutrition. October 2000. Letter Regarding Dietary Supplement Health Claim for Omega-3 Fatty Acids and Coronary Heart Disease. Docket No. 91 N-0103. http://vm.cfsan.fda.gov/~dms/ds-ltr11.html (accessed July 2003).
10. Kris-Etherton, P. M., D. S. Taylor, S. Yu-Poth, P. Huth, K. Moriarty, V. Fishell, R. L. Hargrove, G. Zhao, and T. D. Etherton. 2000. Polyunsaturated Fatty Acids in the Food Chain in the United States. *American Journal of Clinical Nutrition* 71: 179S–188S.
11. Brown, L., B. Rosner, W. Willett, and F. Sacks. 1999. Cholesterol-Lowering Effects of Dietary Fiber: A Meta-Analysis. *American Journal of Clinical Nutrition* 69: 30–42.
12. Anderson, J., B. Johnstone, and M. Cook-Newell. 1995. Meta-Analysis of the Effects of Soy Protein Intake on Serum Lipids. *New England Journal of Medicine* 333: 276–282.
13. Miettinen, T. A., Puska, P., Gylling, H., Vanhanen, H., and Vartiainen, E. 1995. Reduction of Serum Cholesterol with Sitostanol-Ester Margarine in a Mildly Hypercholesterolemic Population. *New England Journal of Medicine* 333: 1308–1312.
14. Hu, F. B., M. J. Stampfer, J. E. Manson, E B Rimm, G. A. Colditz, B. A. Rosner, F. E. Speizer, C. H. Hennekens, and W. C. Willett. 1998. Frequent Nut Consumption and Risk of Coronary Heart Disease in Women: Prospective Cohort Study. *British Medical Journal* 317: 1341–1345.
15. Hertog, M. G. L., E. J. M. Feskens, P. C. H. Hollman, M. B. Katan, and D. Kromhout. 1993. Dietary Antioxidant Flavonoids and Risk of Coronary Heart Disease: The Zutphen Elderly Study. *The Lancet* 342: 1007–1011.
16. Thompson, P. D., D. Buchner, I. Pina, G. Balady, M. A. Williams, B. H. Marcus, K. Berra, S. N. Blair, F. Costa, B. Franklin, G. F. Fletcher, N. F. Gordon, R. R. Pate, B. J. Rodriguez, A. K. Yancey, and N. K. Wenger. 2003. Exercise and Physical Activity in the Prevention and Treatment of Atherosclerotic Cardiovascular Disease. A Statement from the Council on Clinical Cardiology (Subcommittee on Exercise, Rehabilitation, and Prevention) and the Council on Nutrition, Physical Activity, and Metabolism (Subcommittee on Physical Activity). *Circulation* 107: 3109–3116.
17. Rimm, E. G., A. Klatsky, D. Grobbee, and M. J. Stampfer. 1996. Review of Moderate Alcohol Consumption and Reduced Risk of Coronary Heart Disease: Is the Effect Due to Beer, Wine or Spirits? *British Medical Journal* 312: 731–736.

Feature Box References

1. American Heart Association. 2004. What Is High Blood Pressure? www.americanheart.org (accessed October 2005).
2. Chobanian, A. V., G. L. Bakris, H. R. Black, W. C. Cushman, L. A. Green, J. L. Izzo, D. W. Jones, B. J. Materson, S. Oparil, J. T. Wright, E. J. Roccella, and the National High Blood Pressure Education Program Coordinating Committee. 2003. The Seventh Report of the Joint National Committee on Prevention, Detection, Evaluation, and Treatment of High Blood Pressure. *Journal of the American Medical Association* 289: 2560–2572; National Heart, Lung, and Blood Institute. 2004. High Blood Pressure. www.nhlbi.nih.gov/health/dci/Diseases/Hbp/HBP_WhatIs.html (accessed September 2005).
3. American Heart Association. 2005. Am I at Risk? www.americanheart.org (accessed September 2005).
4. U.S. Department of Health and Human Services. Overweight and Obesity: Health Consequences. www.surgeongeneral.gov/topics/obesity/calltoaction/fact_consequences.htm (accessed September 2005); National Heart, Lung, and Blood Institute. 2004. The Seventh Report of the Joint National Committee on Prevention, Detection, Evaluation, and Treatment of High Blood Pressure (JNC 7). www.nhlbi.nih.gov/guidelines/hypertension/jnc7full.htm (accessed September 2005); Wharton, S. P., A. Chin, X. Xin, and J. He. 2002. Effect of Aerobic Exercise on Blood Pressure: A Meta-analysis of Randomized Controlled Trials. *Annals of Internal Medicine* 136 (7): 493–503.
5. Xin, X., J. He, M. G. Frontini, L. G. Ogden, O. I. Motsamai, and P. K. Whelton. 2001. Effects of Alcohol Reduction on Blood Pressure: A Meta-analysis of Randomized Controlled Trials. *Hypertension* 38: 1112–1117.
6. National Heart, Lung and Blood Institute. 2003. The DASH Eating Plan. www.nhlbi.nih.gov/health/public/heart/hbp/dash (accessed September 2005).

7. Food and Drug Administration. April 2003. FDA's Advisory on Methylmercury in Fish. www.fda.gov/bbs/topics/ANSWERS/2003/ANS01209.html (accessed July 2003); Food and Drug Administration. Revised May 1995. Mercury in Fish: Cause for Concern? *FDA Consumer Magazine*. www.fda.gov/fdac/reprints/mercury.html (accessed July 2003).
8. Center for Food Safety and Applied Nutrition. March 2001. An Important Message for Pregnant Women and Women of Childbearing Age Who May Become Pregnant about the Risks of Mercury in Fish. www.cfsan.fda.gov/~acrobat/hgadv1.pdf (accessed July 2003).
9. Food and Drug Administration. FDA's Advisory on Methylmercury in Fish; Food and Drug Administration. Mercury in Fish: Cause for Concern?
10. Environmental Protection Agency. Updated January 2003. Consumption Advice: EPA National Advice on Mercury in Freshwater Fish for Women Who Are or May Become Pregnant, Nursing Mothers, and Young Children. www.epa.gov/waterscience/fishadvice/advice.html (accessed July 2003).

Concept 13

1. Johnson, M. D. 2003. *Human Biology: Concepts and Current Issues.* 2nd ed. San Francisco: Benjamin Cummings.
2. Institute of Medicine. 2002. *Dietary Reference Intakes for Energy, Carbohydrate, Fiber, Fat, Fatty Acids, Cholesterol, Protein, and Amino Acids.* Washington, D.C.: The National Academies Press.
3. Bennion, M. 1980. *The Science of Food.* New York: Harper and Row.
4. Food Safety and Inspection Service. 1999. Poultry: Basting, Brining, and Marinating. www.fsis.usda.gov/OA/pubs/bastebrine.htm (accessed May 2004).
5. Institute of Medicine. *Dietary Reference Intakes for Energy.*
6. National Human Genome Research Institute. 2004. Learning about Sickle Cell Disease. www.genome.gov (accessed June 2004); National Institutes of Health. Genes and Disease, Sickle Cell Anemia. www.ncbi.nlm.nih.gov/disease/sickle.html (accessed June 2004).
7. Marieb, E. N. 2004. *Human Anatomy and Physiology.* 6th ed. San Francisco: Benjamin Cummings.
8. Murray, R. K., D. K. Granner, P. A. Mayes, and V. W. Rodwell. 2000. *Harper's Illustrated Biochemistry.* 26th ed. New York: Lange Medical Books/McGraw-Hill.

Feature Box References

1. Debusk, R. M., C. P. Fogarty, J. M. Ordovas, and K. S. Kornman. 2005. Nutritional Genomics in Practice: Where Do We Begin? *Journal of the American Dietetic Assocation* 105: 589–598.
2. German, J. B. 2005. Genetic Dietetics: Nutrigenomics and the Future of Dietetics Practice. *Journal of the American Dietetic Assocation* 105: 530–531.
3. World Cancer Research Fund/American Institute for Cancer Research. 2007. *Food, Nutrition, Physical Activity, and the Prevention of Cancer: A Global Perspective.* Washington, D.C.: American Institute for Cancer Research.

Concept 14

1. Stipanuk, M. 2000. *Biochemical and Physiological Aspects of Human Nutrition.* Philadelphia: W. B. Saunders.
2. Institute of Medicine. *Dietary Reference Intakes for Energy, Carbohydrate, Fiber, Fat, Fatty Acids, Cholesterol, Protein, and Amino Acids.* 2002. Washington, D.C.: The National Academies Press.
3. American Dietetic Association, Dietitians of Canada, and the American College of Sports Medicine. 2000. Nutrition and Athletic Performance. *Journal of the American Dietetic Association* 100: 1543–1556; Eschbach, L. C. October–December 2002. *Nutrition: Protein and Creatine: Some Basic Facts.* American College of Sports Medicine, Fit Society Page. www.acsm.org/health%2Bfitness/fit_society.htm (accessed June 2004); Gibala, M. J., K. Tipton, and M. Hargreaves. 2000. *Amino Acids, Proteins, and Exercise Performance.* Gatorade Sports Science Institute, Sports Science Exchange Roundtable 42. www.gssiweb.com (accessed June 2004); Kleiner, S. M. Summer 2002. *Nutrition: Eating for Strength and Power.* American College of Sports Medicine, Fit Society Page. www.acsm.org/health%2Bfitness/fit_society.htm (accessed June 2004).
4. Institute of Medicine. *Dietary Reference Intakes for Energy.*
5. Allen, L. H., E. A. Oddoye, and S. Margen. 1979. Protein-induced Calciuria: A Longer-term Study. *American Journal of Clinical Nutrition* 32: 741–749; Lemann, J. 1999. Relationship between Urinary Calcium and Net Acid Excretion as Determined by Dietary Protein and Potassium: A Review. *Nephron* 81: 1–25; Reddy, S. T., C. Wang, K. Sahaee, L. Brinkley, and C. Pak. 2002. Effect of Low-carbohydrate High-protein Diets on Acid-base Balance, Stone-forming Propensity, and Calcium Metabolism. *American Journal of Kidney Diseases* 40: 265–274.
6. Heaney, R. P. 1998. Excess Dietary Protein May Not Adversely Affect Bone. *Journal of Nutrition* 128: 1054–1057.
7. Key, T. J., N. E. Allen, E. A. Spencer, and R. C. Travis. 2002. The Effect of Diet on Risk of Cancer. *The Lancet* 360: 861–868.
8. Promislow, J. H. E., D. Goodman-Gruen, D. J. Slymen, and E. Barrett-Connor. 2002. Protein Consumption and Bone Mineral Density in the Elderly. The Rancho Bernardo Study. *American Journal of Epidemiology* 155: 636–644; Wengreen, H. J., R. G. Munger, N. A. West, D. R. Cutler, C. D. Corcoran, J. Zhang, and N. E. Sassano. 2004. Dietary Protein Intake and Risk of Osteoporotic Hip and Fracture in Elderly Residents of Utah. *Journal of Bone and Mineral Research* 19: 537–545.
9. Institute of Medicine. *Dietary Reference Intakes for Energy.*
10. Shils, M. E., J. A. Olson, M. Shike, and A. C. Ross. 1999. *Modern Nutrition in Health and Disease.* 9th ed. Baltimore, MD: Williams and Wilkins; World Health Organization/Programme of Nutrition. *WHO Global Database on Child Growth and Malnutrition Introduction.* www.who.intnutgrowthdb/about/introduction/en (accessed June 2004).
11. Caulfield, L. E., M. de Onis, M. Blossner, and R. E. Black. 2004. Undernutrition as an Underlying Cause of Child Deaths Associated with Diarrhea, Pneumonia, Malaria, and Meals. *American Journal of Clinical Nutrition* 80: 193–198; de Onis, M., M. Blossner, E. Borghi, E. Frongillo, and R. Morris. 2004. Estimates of Global Prevalence of Childhood Underweight in 1990 and 2015. *Journal of the American Medical Association* 291: 2600–2606.
12. Shils. *Modern Nutrition.*
13. Ibid.

Feature Box Reference

1. "Energy Bars, Unwrapped." *Consumer Reports* (June 2003): 19–21.

Concept 15

1. American Dietetic Association and Dietitians of Canada. 2003. Vegetarian Diets. *Journal of the American Dietetic Association* 103: 745–765.
2. Mintel Consumer Intelligence. 2003. Vegetarian Foods, United States. www.consumer.mintel.com (accessed June 2004); The Vegetarian Resource Group. 2003. How Many Vegetarians Are There? www.vrg.org/press/2003poll.htm (accessed June 2004).
3. Burger King Corporation Nutritional Facts. www.burgerking.com/Food/Nutrition/ingredients.aspx (accessed June 2004); Ginsberg. *Market for Vegetarian Foods.*
4. Food and Agriculture Organization of the United Nations. 2006. Livestock: A Major Threat to the Environment: Remedies Urgently Needed. www.fao.org/newsroom/en/news/2006/1000448/index.html (accessed September 2008).
5. Koneswaran, G., and D. Nierenberg. 2008. Global Farm Animal Production and Global Warming: Impacting and Mitigating Climate Change. *Environmental Health Perspectives* 116: 578–582.
6. Appleby, P. N., M. Thorogood, J. Mann, and T. J. Key. 1999. The Oxford Vegetarian Study: An Overview. *American Journal of Clinical Nutrition* 70: 525S–531S; Key, T. J., G. E. Fraser, M. Thorogood, P. N. Appleby, B. Beral, G. Reeves, M. L. Burr, J. Chang-Claude, R. Grentzel-Beyme, J. W. Kuzma, J. Mann, and K. McPherson. 1999. Mortality in Vegetarians and Nonvegetarians: Detailed Findings from a Collaborative Analysis of Five Prospective Studies. *American Journal of Clinical Nutrition* 70: 516S–524S.
7. Fraser, G. E. 1999. Associations between Diet and Cancer, Ischemic Heart Disease, and All-cause Mortality in Non-Hispanic White California Seventh-Day Adventists. *American Journal of Clinical Nutrition* 70: 532S–538S.
8. Fraser. Associations between Diet and Cancer; Jenkins, D. J., C. Kendall, A. Marchie, A. L. Jenkins, L. Augustin, D. S. Ludwig, N. D. Barnard, and J. W. Anderson. 2003. Type 2 Diabetes and the Vegetarian Diet. *American Journal of Clinical Nutrition* 78: 610S–616S.
9. Fraser. Association between Diet and Cancer.
10. American Dietetic Association. 2003. A New Food Guide for North American Vegetarians. www.eatright.org/cps/rde/xchg/ada/hs.xsl/governance_5105_ENU_HTML.htm (accessed August 2008).

Feature Box References

1. The United Soybean Board. 2008. The 15th Annual Consumer Attitudes about Nutrition Study, 2008. www.soyconnection.com/health_nutrition/pdf/ConsumerAttitudes2008.pdf (accessed August 2008).
2. Mintel Consumer Intelligence. 2007. *Soy-based Food and Drink—US.* Chicago: Mintel Group.
3. Henkel, J. 2000. Soy Health Claims for Soy Protein, Questions about Other Components, *FDA Consumer Magazine.* www.cfsan.fda.gov/~dms/fdsoypr.html (accessed August 2008).

4. Munro, I. C., M. Harwood, J. J. Hlywka, A. M. Stephen, J. Doull, W. G. Flammn, and H. Adlercrutz. 2003. Soy Isoflavoncs: A Safety Review. *Nutrition Reviews* 61: 1–33; Vegetarian Nutrition, a Practice Group of the American Dietetics Association. 1999. Isoflavones. www.vegetarian-nutrition.net.
5. Sacks, F. M., A. Lichtenstein, L. Van Horn, W. Harris, P. Krist-Etherton, M. Winston. American Heart Association Nutrition Committee. 2006. *Circulation* 113: 1034–1044.
6. Anderson, J. W., B. M. Johnstone, and M. E. Cook-Newell. 1995. Meta-analysis of the Effects of Soy Protein Intake on Serum Lipids. *New England Journal of Medicine* 333: 276–282. Henkel Soy Health Claims for Soy Protein.
7. Messina, M. 1995. Modern Uses for an Ancient Bean: Soyfoods and Disease. *Chemistry and Industry* 11: 412–415; Messina, M. J., V. Persky, K. D. R. Setchell, and S. Barnes. 1994. Soy Intake and Cancer Risk: A Review of the in Vitro and in Vivo Data. *Nutrition and Cancer* 21: 113–131; Messina, M. J., and C. L. Loprinzi. 2001. Soy for Breast Cancer Survivors: A Critical Review of the Literature. *Journal of Nutrition* 131: 3095S–3108S.
8. Shu, X. O., F. Jin, Q. Dai, W. Wen, J. D. Potter, L. H. Kushi, Z. Ruan, Y. Gao, and W. Zheng. 2001. Soyfood Intake during Adolescence and Subsequent Risk of Breast Cancer among Chinese Women. *Cancer Epidemiology, Biomarkers & Prevention* 10: 483–488.
9. American Cancer Society. 2003. Frequently Asked Questions about Nutrition and Physical Activity. www.cancer.org (accessed August 2008); McMichael-Phillips, D. F., C. Harding, M. Morton, S. A. Roberts, A. Howell, C. S. Potten, and N. J. Bundred. 1998. Effects of Soy-Protein Supplementation on Epithelial Proliferation in the Histologically Normal Human Breast. *American Journal of Clinical Nutrition* 68: 1431S–1436S.

Concept 16

1. Rosenfeld, L. 1997. Vitamine-Vitamin. The Early Years of Discovery. *Clinical Chemistry* 43: 680–685.
2. Young, I. S., and J. V. Woodside. 2001. Antioxidants in Health and Disease. *Journal of Clinical Pathology* 54: 176–186.
3. Dröge, W. 2002. Free Radicals in the Physiological Control of Cell Function. *Physiology Review* 82: 47–95; Traber, M. G., and H. Sies. 1996. Vitamin E in Humans: Demand and Delivery. *Annual Review of Nutrition* 16: 321–347; Young. Antioxidants in Health.
4. National Eye Institute. 2004. Age-Related Macular Degeneration: What You Should Know. Updated June 2004. www.nei.nih.gov/health/maculardegen/armd_facts.asp#1 (accessed September 2004).
5. Age-Related Eye Disease Study Research Group. 2001. A Randomized, Placebo-Controlled, Clinical Trial of High-Dose Supplementation with Vitamins C and E, Beta Carotene, and Zinc for Age-Related Macular Degeneration and Vision Loss: AREDS Report No. 8. *Archives of Ophthalmology* 119: 1417–1436; Brown, L., E. B. Rimm, J. M. Seddon, E. L. Giovannucci., L. Chasan-Tabar, D. Spiegelman, W. C. Willett, and S. E. Hankinson. 1999. A Prospective Study of Carotenoid Intake and Risk of Cataract Extraction in U.S. Men. *American Journal of Clinical Nutrition* 70: 517–524; Chasan-Tabar, L., W. C. Willett, J. M. Seddon, M. J. Stampfer, B. Rosner, G. A. Colditz, F. E. Speizer, and S. E. Hankinson. 1999. A Prospective Study of Carotenoid Intake and Risk of Cataract Extraction in U.S. Women. *American Journal of Clinical Nutrition* 70: 509–516; The National Eye Institute. 2004. The AREDS Formulation and Age-Related Macular Degeneration: Are These High Levels of Antioxidants and Zinc Right for You? Updated June 2004. www.nei.nih.gov/amd/summary.asp (accessed September 2004).
6. Ibid.
7. Mares, J. A., T. L. La Rowe, and B. A. Blodi. 2004. Doctor, What Vitamins Should I Take for My Eyes? *Archives of Ophthalmology* 122: 628–635; The National Eye Institute. 2004. Cataract: What You Should Know. Updated August 2004. www.nei.nih.gov/health/cataract/cataract_facts.asp (accessed September 2004).
8. Craig, W. J. 1997. Phytochemicals: Guardians of Our Health. *Journal of the American Dietetic Association* 97: S199–S204.
9. U.S. Department of Agriculture Food and Nutrition Services. 2002. Chapter 5 in Building Blocks for Fun and Healthy Meals—a Menu Planner for the Child and Adult Care Food Program. USDA Team Nutrition Resources. www.fns.usda.gov/tn/Resources/buildingblocks.html (accessed July 2005).
10. Lee, S. K., and A. A. Kader. 2000. Preharvest and Postharvest Factors Influencing Vitamin C Content of Horticultural Crops. *Postharvest Biology and Technology* 20: 207–220.
11. Pandrangi, S., and L. E. LaBorde. 2004. Retention of Folate, Carotenoid, and Other Quality Characteristics in Commercially Packaged Fresh Spinach. *Journal of Food Science* 69: C702–C707.
12. Institute of Medicine. 2001. *Dietary Reference Intakes: Vitamin A, Vitamin K, Arsenic, Boron, Chromium, Copper, Iodine, Iron, Manganese, Molybdenum, Nickel, Silicon, Vanadium, and Zinc.* Washington, D.C.: The National Academies Press; Ross, A. C. 1999. Vitamin A and Retinoids. In M. E. Shils, J. Olson, M. Shike, and A. C. Ross, eds. *Modern Nutrition in Health and Disease.* 9th ed. Baltimore, MD: Williams and Wilkins.
13. Institute of Medicine. 2001. *Dietary Reference Intakes: Vitamin A.*
14. Office of Dietary Supplements. 2003. Vitamin A and Carotenoids. http://ods.od.nih.gov/factsheets/vitamina.asp; Ross, A. C. 1993. Vitamin A as Hormone: Recent Advances in Understanding the Actions of Retinol, Retinoic Acid, and Beta Carotene. *Journal of the American Dietetic Association* 93: 1285–1290.
15. Institute of Medicine. *Dietary Reference Intakes: Vitamin A;* Ross. Vitamin A as Hormone.
16. Institute of Medicine. *Dietary Reference Intakes: Vitamin A.*
17. Institute of Medicine. 2000. *Dietary Reference Intakes: Vitamin C, Vitamin E, Selenium, and Carotenoids.* Washington, D.C.: The National Academies Press.
18. Giovannuci, E. 1999. Tomatoes, Tomato-Based Products, Lycopene, and Cancer: Review of the Epidemiologic Literature. *Journal of the National Cancer Institute* 91: 317–331.
19. Institute of Medicine. *Dietary Reference Intakes: Vitamin A;* Office of Dietary Supplements. Vitamin A.
20. Institute of Medicine. *Dietary Reference Intakes: Vitamin A.*
21. Office of Dietary Supplements. Vitamin A.
22. Brinkley, N., and D. Krueger. 2000. Hypervitaminosis A and Bone. *Nutrition Reviews* 58: 138–144; de Souza, P. G., and L. G. Martini. 2004. Vitamin A Supplementation and Risk of Skeletal Fracture. Mark, R. Berstrom, L. Holmber, H. Mallmin, A. Wolk, and S. Ljunghall. 1998. Excessive Dietary Intake of Vitamin A is Associated with Reduced Bone Mineral Density and Increased Risk for Hip Fractures. *Annals of Internal Medicine* 129: 770–778; Office of Dietary Supplements. Vitamin A.
23. Feskanich, D., V. Singh, W. Willett, and G. Colditz. 2002. Vitamin A Intake and Hip Fractures among Postmenopausal Women. *Journal of the American Medical Association* 287: 47–54; Lips, P. 2003. Hypervitaminosis A and Fractures. *New England Journal of Medicine* 348: 347–349; Michaelsson, K., H. Lithell, B. Bvessby, and H. Melhus. 2003. Serum Retinol Levels and the Risk of Fractures. *New England Journal of Medicine* 348: 287–294.
24. Institute of Medicine. *Dietary Reference Intakes: Vitamin A.*
25. The Alpha-Tocopherol, Beta Carotene Cancer Prevention Study Group. 1994. The Effects of Vitamin E and Beta Carotene on the Incidence of Lung Cancer and Other Cancers in Male Smokers. *New England Journal of Medicine* 330: 1029–1035.
26. World Health Organization. 2004. Nutrition, Micronutrient Deficiencies. www.who.int/nut/vad.htm (accessed September 2004).
27. Mertz, W. 1994. A Balanced Approach to Nutrition for Health: The Need for Biologically Essential Minerals and Vitamins. *Journal of the American Dietetic Association* 94: 1259–1262.
28. Office of Dietary Supplements. 2003. Vitamin E and Carotenoids. http://ods.od.nih.gov/factsheets/vitamine.asp (accessed November 2004).
29. Young, I. S., and J. V. Woodside. 2001. Antioxidants in Health and Disease. *Journal of Clinical Pathology* 54: 176–186.
30. Office of Dietary Supplements. Vitamin E.
31. Institute of Medicine. *Dietary Reference Intakes: Vitamin E.*
32. Miller, E. R., R. Pastor-Barriso, D. Dalal, R. A. Riemersma, L. J. Appel, and E. Guallar. 2005. Meta-Analysis: High-Dosage Vitamin E Supplementation May Increase All-Cause Mortality. *Annals of Internal Medicine* 142: 37–46.
33. Feskanich, D., P. Weber, W. C. Willet, H. Rockett, S. L. Booth, and G. A. Colditz. 1999. Vitamin K Intake and Hip Fractures in Women: A Prospective Study. *American Journal of Clinical Nutrition* 69: 74–79.
34. Brinkley, N. C., and J. W. Suttie. 1995. Vitamin K Nutrition and Osteoporosis. *Journal of Nutrition* 125: 1812–1821. Institute of Medicine. *Dietary Reference Intakes: Vitamin A.*
35. National Institutes of Health. 2003. Coumadin and Vitamin K. http://ods.od.nih.gov/factsheets/cc/coumadin1.pdf (accessed March 2005).
36. Institute of Medicine. *Dietary Reference Intakes: Vitamin K.*
37. Institute of Medicine. 1997. *Dietary Reference Intakes for Calcium, Phosphorus, Magnesium, Vitamin D, and Fluoride.* Washington, D.C.: The National Academies Press.
38. Heaney, R. P. 2003. Long-Latency Deficiency Disease: Insights from Calcium and Vitamin D. *American Journal of Clinical Nutrition* 78: 912–919; National Institutes of Health Conference. 2003. Vitamin D and Health in the 21st Century. www.nichd.nih.gov/about/od/prip/index.htm (accessed October 2004).

39. Chiu, K. C., A. Chu, V. L. W. Go, and M. F. Saad. 2004. Hypovitaminosis D Is Associated with Insulin Resistance and Cell Dysfunction. *American Journal of Clinical Nutrition* 79: 820–825.
40. Newark, H. J., R. P. Heaney, and P. A. Lachance. 2004. Should Calcium and Vitamin D Be Added to the Current Enrichment Program for Cereal-Grain Products? *American Journal of Clinical Nutrition* 80: 264–270.
41. Hollis, B.W. 2005. Circulating 25-Hydroxyvitamin D Levels Indicative of Vitamin D Sufficiency: Implications for Establishing a New Effective Dietary Intake Recommendation for Vitamin D[1]. *Journal of Nutrition* 135: 317–322; Prentice, A., G. R. Goldberg, and I. Schoenmakers, 2008. Vitamin D across the Lifecycle: Physiology and Biomarkers.[1,2,3]. *American Journal of Clinical Nutrition* 88: 500S–506S.
42. Ibid.
43. Ibid.
44. National Institutes of Health. 2004. Dietary Supplement Fact Sheet: Vitamin D. http://ods.od.nih.gov/factsheets/vitamind.asp (accessed October 2004); Wharton, B., and N. Bishop. 2003. Rickets. *The Lancet* 362: 1389–1400.
45. Centers for Disease Control and Prevention. 2001. Severe Malnutrition among Young Children—Georgia, January 1997–June 1999. *Morbidity and Mortality Weekly Report.* www.cdc.gov/mmwr/preview/mmwrhtml/mm5012a3.htm (accessed October 2004); Gordon, C. M., K. C. DePeter, H. A. Feldman, E. Grace, and S. J. Emans. 2004. Prevalence of Vitamin D Deficiency among Healthy Adolescents. *Archives of Pediatric and Adolescent Medicine* 158: 531–537; Weisberg, P., K. S. Scanlon, R. Li, and M. E. Cogswell. 2004. Nutritional Rickets among Children in the United States: Review of Cases Reported between 1986 and 2003. *American Journal of Clinical Nutrition* 80: 1697S–1705S.
46. Lin, B., and K. Ralston. 2003. Competitive Foods: Soft Drinks vs. Milk. Washington, D.C.: U.S. Department of Agriculture, Economic Research Service. www.ers.usda.gov/publications/fanrr34/fanrr34-7 (accessed October 2004).
47. Gartner, L. M., and F. R. Greer. 2003. Prevention of Rickets and Vitamin D Deficiency: New Guidelines for Vitamin D Intake. *Pediatric* 111: 908–910; Scanlon, K. S. 2001. Vitamin D Expert Panel Meeting. www.cdc.gov/nccdphp/dnpa/nutrition/pdf/Vitamin_D_Expert_Panel_Meeting.pdf (accessed October 2004).
48. Wharton. Rickets.
49. Heaney. Long-Latency Deficiency Disease; Holick, M. F. 1999. Vitamin D. In M. E. Shils, J. Olson, M. Shike, and A. C. Ross, eds. *Modern Nutrition in Health and Disease.* 9th ed. Baltimore, MD: Williams and Wilkins.
50. Rosenfeld. Vitamine-Vitamin.
51. Institute of Medicine. 1998. *Dietary Reference Intakes: Thiamin, Riboflavin, Niacin, Vitamin B_6, Folate, Vitamin B_{12}, Pantothenic Acid, Biotin, and Choline.* Washington, D.C.: The National Academies Press.
52. National Institute of Neurological Disorders and Stroke (NINDS). 2004. NINDS Wernicke-Korsakoff Syndrome Information Page. Updated 2004. www.ninds.nih.gov/disorders/wernicke_korsakoff/wernicke-korsakoff.htm (accessed December 2005).
53. Herreid, E. O., B. Ruskin, G. L. Clark, and T. B. Parks. 1952. Ascorbic Acid and Riboflavin Destruction and Flavor Development in Milk Exposed to the Sun in Amber, Clear, Paper, and Ruby Bottles. *Journal of Dairy Science* 35: 772–778.
54. Institute of Medicine. *Dietary Reference Intakes: Riboflavin.*
55. Institute of Medicine. *Dietary Reference Intakes: Niacin.*
56. Cervantes-Laurean, D., G. McElvaney, and J. Moss. Niacin. In M. E. Shils, J. Olson, M. Shike, and A. C. Ross, eds. *Modern Nutrition in Health and Disease.* 9th ed. Baltimore, MD: Williams and Wilkins.
57. Institute of Medicine. *Dietary Reference Intakes: Nicacin.*
58. Ibid.
59. National Institutes of Health. 2002. Vitamin B_6. www.nih.gov (accessed February 2005).
60. Leklem, J. M. 1999. Vitamin B_6. In M. E. Shils, J. Olson, M. Shike, and A. C. Ross, eds. *Modern Nutrition in Health and Disease.* 9th ed. Baltimore, MD: Williams and Wilkins.
61. American College of Obstetricians and Gynecologists. 2000. ACOG Practice Bulletin. Premenstrual Syndrome. No. 15; National Institute of Neurological Disorders and Stroke. 2002. Carpal Tunnel Syndrome Fact Sheet. www.ninds.nih.gov/disorders/carpal_tunnel/detail_carpal_tunnel.htm (accessed February 2005); National Women's Health Information Center. 2002. Premenstrual Syndrome. www.4woman.gov/faq/pms.htm (accessed February 2005); Schaumburg, H., J. Kaplan, A. Windebran, N. Vick, S. Rasmus, D. Pleasure, and M. J. Brown. 1983. Sensory Neuropathy from Pyridoxine Abuse. *New England Journal of Medicine* 309: 445–448.
62. Institute of Medicine. *Dietary Reference Intakes: Thiamin;* Office of Dietary Supplements. 2004. Dietary Supplement Fact Sheet: Folate. http://ods.od.nih.gov/factsheets/folate.asp (accessed February 2005).
63. Centers for Disease Control and Prevention. 2003. Folic Acid Now Fact Sheet. www.cdc.gov/doc.do/id/0900f3ec8000d615 (accessed February 2005).
64. Centers for Disease Control and Prevention. May 7, 2004. Spina Bifida and Anencephaly before and after Folic Acid Mandate—United States, 1995–1996 and 1999–2000. *Morbidity and Mortality Weekly Reports* 17: 362–365. www.cdc.gov/mmwr/preview/mmwrhtml/mm5317a3.htm (accessed February 2005); Centers for Disease Control and Prevention. 2003. Information for Health Professionals—Recommendations. www.cdc.gov/doc.do/id/0900f3ec800523d6 (accessed February 2005); Centers for Disease Control and Prevention. August 2, 1991. Effectiveness in Disease and Injury Prevention Use of Folic Acid for Prevention of Spina Bifida and Other Neural Tube Defects: 1983–1991. *Morbidity and Mortality Weekly Reports* 40: 513–516. www.cdc.gov/mmwr/preview/mmwrhtml/00014915.htm (accessed February 2005).
65. Centers for Disease Control. Folic Acid Now; Institute of Medicine. *Dietary Reference Intakes: Thiamin.*
66. Giovannucci, E., M. J. Stampfer, G. A. Colditz, D. J. Hunter, C. Fuchs, B. A. Rosner, F. E. Speizer, and W. C. Willett. 1998. Multivitamin Use, Folate, and Colon Cancer in Women in the Nurses' Health Study. *Annals of Internal Medicine* 129: 517–524.
67. Institute of Medicine. *Dietary Reference Intakes: Thiamin.*
68. Centers for Disease Control. Effectiveness in Disease; Centers for Disease Control. Information for Health Professionals.
69. Institute of Medicine. *Dietary Reference Intakes: Thiamin.*
70. Office of Dietary Supplements. 2004. Dietary Supplement Fact Sheet: Vitamin B_{12}. www.ods.od.nih.gov/factsheets/vitaminb12.asp (accessed February 2005); Shane, B. 2000. Folic Acid, Vitamin B_{12}, and Vitamin B_6. In M. H. Stipanuk, ed. *Biochemical and Physiological Aspects of Human Nutrition.* Philadelphia: W. B. Saunders.
71. Institute of Medicine. *Dietary Reference Intakes: Thiamin;* Office of Dietary Supplements. Fact Sheet: Vitamin B_{12}.
72. Ibid.
73. Ibid.
74. Institute of Medicine. *Dietary Reference Intakes: Vitamin C.*
75. Iqbal, K., A. Khan, and M. Khattak. 2004. Biological Significance of Ascorbic Acid (Vitamin C) in Human Health. *Pakistan Journal of Nutrition* 3: 5–13.
76. Ibid.
77. Institute of Medicine. *Dietary Reference Intakes: Vitamin C.*
78 Rosenfeld. Vitamine-Vitamin.
79. Ibid.
80. Glusman, M.1947. The Syndrome of "Burning Feet" (Nutritional Melagia) as a Manifestation of Nutritional Deficiency. *America Journal of Medicine* 3: 211–223.
81. Sweetmna, L. 2005. Pantothenic Acid and Biotin. In M.H. Stipanuk, ed., *Biochemical and Physiological Aspects of Human Nutrition.* Philadelphia: Saunders.
82. Mock, D. M. 1999. Biotin. In M. E. Shils, J. Olson, M. Shike, A. C. Ross, eds., *Modern Nutrition in Health and Disease.* 9th ed. Baltimore: Williams & Wilkins.
83. Institute of Medicine. *Dietary Reference Intakes: Thiamin;* Zeisel, S. H., K. H. Da Costa, P. D. Franklin, E. A. Alexander, J. T. Lamont, N. F. Sheard, and A. Beiser. 1991. Choline, an Essential Nutrient for Humans. *Federation of American Societies for Experimental Biology* 5: 2093–2098.
84. National Institutes of Health. 2004. Carnitine: The Science behind a Conditionally Essential Nutrient. http://ods.od.nih.gov/News/Carnitine_Conference_Summary.aspx (accessed September 2004).
85. Packer, L., E. H. Witt, and H. J. Tritschler. 1994. Alpha-Lipoic Acid as a Biological Antioxidant. *Free Radical Biology and Medicine* 19: 227–250.
86. U.S. Department of Agriculture. 2005. 2005 Report of the Dietary Guidelines Advisory Committee on the Dietary Guidelines for Americans. www.health.gov/dietaryguidelines/dga2005/report (accessed February 2005).
87. Packaged Facts. 2002. The U.S. Market for Fortified Foods: Expanding the Boundaries. www.marketresearch.com.
88. Kris-Etherton, P., A. H. Lichtenstein, B. V. Howard, D. Steinberg, and J. L. Witztum. 2004. Antioxidant Vitamin Supplements and Cardiovascular Disease. *Circulation* 110: 637–641; U.S. Preventive Services Task Force. 2003. Routine Vitamin Supplementation to Prevent Cancer and Cardiovascular Disease: Recommendations and Rationale. *Annals of Internal Medicine* 139: 51–55.

Feature Box References

1. Chalmers, T. C. 1975. Effects of Ascorbic Acid on the Common Cold. An Evaluation of the Evidence. *American Journal of Medicine* 58: 532–536; Hemila, H., and Z. S. Herman. 1995. Vitamin C and the Common Cold: A Retrospective Analysis of Chalmers' Review. *American College of Nutrition* 14: 116–123; Institute of Medicine. 2001. *Dietary Reference Intakes: Vitamin A, Vitamin K, Arsenic, Boron, Chromium, Copper, Iodine, Iron, Manganese, Molybdenum, Nickel, Silicon, Vanadium, and Zinc.* Washington, D.C.: The National Academies Press; Institute of Medicine. 2000. *Dietary Reference Intakes: Vitamin C, Vitamin E, Selenium, and Carotenoids.* Washington, D.C.: The National Academies Press; Mossad, S. B. 2005. Treatment of the Common Cold. *British Medical Journal* 317: 33–36; National Institute of Allergy and Infectious Diseases. 2004. The Common Cold. www.niaid.nih.gov/factsheets/cold.htm (accessed March 2005); Pauling, L. 1971. The Significance of the Evidence about Ascorbic Acid and the Common Cold. *Proceedings from the National Academy of Sciences* 68: 2678–2681.
2. Caruso, T. J., and J. M. Gwaltney. 2005. Treatment of the Common Cold with Echinacea: A Structured Review. *Clinical Infectious Diseases* 40: 807–810; Taylor, J. A., W. Weber, L. Standish, H. Quinn, J. Goesling, M. McGann, and C. Calabrese. 2003. Efficacy and Safety of Echinacea in Treating Upper Respiratory Tract Infections in Children. *Journal of the American Medical Association* 290: 2824–2830; Turner, R. B., R. Bauer, K. Woelkart, T. C. Haulsey, and D. Gangemie. 2005. An Evaluation of Echinacea Angustifolia in Experimental Rhinovirus Infections. *New England Journal of Medicine* 353: 341–348.
3. Centers for Disease Control and Prevention. 2004. Stopping Germs at Home, Work and School. www.cdc.gov/germstopper/home_work_school.htm (accessed March 2005); Food and Drug Administration Center for Foods Safety and Applied Nutrition, National Science Teachers Association. 2001. Hand Washing. www.cfsan.fda.gov/~dms/a2z-h.html (accessed March 2005).
4. Appel, L. J., E. R. Miller, S. H. Jee, R. Stolzenberg-Solomon, P. Lin, T. Erlinger, M. R. Nadeau, and J. Selhub. 2000. Effect of Dietary Patterns on Serum Homocysteine: Results of a Randomized Controlled Feeding Study. *Circulation* 102: 852–857; Finklestein, J. D. 2000. Homocysteine: A History in Progress. *Nutrition Reviews* 58: 193–204; Institute of Medicine. 1998. *Dietary Reference Intakes: Thiamin, Riboflavin, Niacin, Vitamin B_6, Folate, Vitamin B_{12}, Pantothenic Acid, Biotin, and Choline.* Washington, D.C.: The National Academies Press.
5. Jacques, P. F., J. Selhum, A. G. Bostom, P. W. F. Wilson, and I. H. Rosenberg. 1999. The Effects of Folic Acid Fortification on Plasma Folate and Total Homocysteine Concentrations. *New England Journal of Medicine* 340: 1449–1454; Malinow, M. R., A. G. Bostom, and R. M. Krauss. 1999. Homocyst(e)ine, Diet and Cardiovascular Diseases. A Statement for Health Care Professionals from the Nutrition Committee. *Circulation* 99: 178–182; Miller, J. W. 2000. Does Lowering Plasma Homocysteine Reduce Vascular Disease Risk? *Nutrition Reviews* 59: 241–244.

Concept 17

1. Anderson, J. B. 2004. Minerals. In *Krause's Food, Nutrition and Diet Therapy.* 11th ed. Philadelphia: W. B. Saunders.
2. Institute of Medicine. 2001. *Dietary Reference Intakes: Vitamin A, Vitamin K, Arsenic, Boron, Chromium, Copper, Iodine, Iron, Manganese, Molybdenum, Nickel, Silicon, Vanadium, and Zinc.* Washington, D.C.: The National Academies Press. www.nap.edu.
3. Sheng, H. 2000. Body Fluids and Water Balance. In *Biochemical and Physiological Aspects of Human Nutrition.* Philadelphia: W. B. Saunders.
4. Institute of Medicine. 2004. *Dietary Reference Intakes: Water, Potassium, Sodium, Chloride, and Sulfate.* Washington, D.C.: The National Academies Press. www.nap.edu.
5. Ibid.
6. Ibid.
7. Institute of Medicine. 1997. *Dietary Reference Intakes: Calcium, Phosphorus, Magnesium, Vitamin D, and Fluoride.* Washington, D.C.: The National Academies Press. www.nap.edu.
8. Institute of Medicine. *Dietary Reference Intakes: Calcium;* Office of Dietary Supplements. Updated 2005. Dietary Supplement Fact Sheet: Calcium. http://ods.od.nih.gov/factsheets/calcium.asp (accessed October 2005).
9. Institute of Medicine. *Dietary Reference Intakes: Calcium;* Miller, G. D., G. D. DiRienzo, M. E. Reusser, and D. A. McCarron. 2000. Benefits of Dairy Product Consumption on Blood Pressure in Humans: A Summary of the Biomedical Literature. *Journal of the American College of Nutrition* 19: 147S–164S.
10. Baron, J. A., M. Beach, J. S. Mandel, R. U. van Stolk, R. W. Haile, R. S. Sandler, R. Rothstein, R. W. Summers, D. C. Snover, G. J. Beck, J. H. Bond, and E. R. Greenberg. 1999. Calcium Supplements for the Prevention of Colorectal Adenomas. *New England Journal of Medicine* 340: 101–107; Wu, K., W. C. Willet, C. S. Fuchs, G. A. Colditz, and E. L. Giovannucci. 2002. Calcium Intake and Risk of Colon Cancer in Women and Men. *Journal of the National Cancer Institute* 94: 437–446.
11. National Kidney and Urologic Diseases Information Clearinghouse. 2004. Kidney and Urologic Diseases Statistics for the United States. http://kidney.niddk.nih.gov/kudiseases/pubs/kustats/index.htm (accessed October 2005); Reynolds, T. M. 2005. Chemical Pathology Clinical Investigation and Management of Nephrolithiasis. *Journal of Clinical Pathology* 58: 134–140.
12. Borghi, L., R. Schianchi, T. Meschi, A. Guerra, U. Maggiore, and A. Novarini. 2002. Comparison of Two Diets for the Prevention of Recurrent Stones in Idiopathic Hypercalciuria. *New England Journal of Medicine* 346: 77–84; Bushinsky, D. A. 2002. Recurrent Hypercalciuric Nephrolithiasis: Does Diet Help? *New England Journal of Medicine* 346: 124–125; Curhan, G. C., W. C. Willett, E. B. Rimm, and M. J. Stampfer. 1993. A Prospective Study of Dietary Calcium and Other Nutrients and the Risk of Symptomatic Kidney Stones. *New England Journal of Medicine* 328: 838–888.
13. Zemel, M. B., W. Thompson, K. Morris, and P. Campbell. 2004. Calcium and Dairy Acceleration of Weight and Fat Loss during Energy Restriction in Obese Adults. *Obesity Research* 12: 582–590.
14. Parikh, S. J., and J. A. Yanovski. 2003. Calcium Intake and Adiposity. *American Journal of Clinical Nutrition* 77: 281–287.
15. U.S. Department of Agriculture. Results from USDA's 1996 Continuing Survey of Food Intakes by Individuals and 1996 Diet and Health Knowledge Survey, Table Set 6. www.ars.usda.gov/SP2UserFiles/Place/12355000/pdf/Csfii96.PDF (accessed October 2005).
16. U.S. Department of Agriculture. Pyramid Servings Data: Results from the USDA's 1995 and 1996 Continuing Survey of Food Intakes by Individuals, Table Set 7. www.ars.usda.gov/SP2UserFiles/Place/12355000/pdf/3yr_py.PDF (accessed October 2005).
17. Osteoporosis and Related Bone Diseases—National Resource Center. 2005. Osteoporosis Overview. www.osteo.org/osteo.html (accessed October 2005); U.S. Department of Health and Human Services. 2004. *Bone Health and Osteoporosis: A Report of the Surgeon General.* Rockville, MD: Office of the Surgeon General.
18. National Institutes of Health (NIH). 2000. Osteoporosis Prevention, Diagnosis, and Therapy. NIH Consensus Statement Online. http://consensus.nih.gov/2000/2000Osteoporosis111html.htm (accessed October 2005).
19. Osteoporosis and Related Bone Diseases—National Resource Center. 2005. Calcium Supplements: What to Look For. www.niams.nih.gov/bone/hi/calcium_supp.pdf (accessed October 2005).
20. Institute of Medicine. *Dietary Reference Intakes: Calcium.*
21. Ibid.
22. Office of Dietary Supplements. Updated 2005. Magnesium. http://ods.od.nih.gov (accessed October 2005).
23. Appel, L. J., T. J. Moore, E. Obarzanek, W. M. Vollmer, L. P. Svetkey, F. M. Sacks, G. A. Bray, T. M. Vogt, J. A. Cutler, M. M. Windhauser, P. Lin, and N. Karanja. 1997. A Clinical Trial of the Effects of Dietary Patterns on Blood Pressure. *New England Journal of Medicine* 336: 1117–1124.
24. Harsha, D. W., P. Lin, E. Obarzanek, N. M. Karanja, T. J. Moore, and B. Caballero. 1999. Dietary Approaches to Stop Hypertension: A Summary of Study Results. *Journal of the American Dietetic Association* 99: S35–S39.
25. American Diabetes Association. 2004. Nutrition Principles and Recommendations in Diabetes. *Diabetes Care* 27: S36; Lopez-Ridaura, R., W. C. Willet, E. B. Rimm, S. Liu, M. J. Stampfer, J. E. Manson, and F. B. Hu. 2004. Magnesium Intake and Risk of Type 2 Diabetes in Men and Women. *Diabetes Care* 27: 134–140.
26. Institute of Medicine, *Dietary Reference Intakes: Calcium.*
27. Institute of Medicine. *Dietary Reference Intakes: Water.*
28. Anderson. Minerals.
29. Institute of Medicine. 2001. *Dietary Reference Intakes: Vitamin A, Vitamin K, Arsenic, Boron, Chromium, Copper, Iodine, Iron, Manganese, Molybdenum, Nickel, Silicon, Vanadium, and Zinc.* Washington, D.C.: The National Academies Press. www.nap.edu.
30. Ibid.
31. Ibid.
32. Ibid.
33. Beard, J. 2003. Iron Deficiency Alters Brain Development and Functioning. *Journal of Nutrition* 133: 1468S–1472S; Black, M. M. 2003. Micronutrient Deficiencies and Cognitive Function. *Journal of Nutrition* 133: 3972S–3931S.

34. Institute of Medicine. *Dietary Reference Intakes: Vitamin A;* Office of Dietary Supplements. Updated 2002. Zinc. http://ods.od.nih.gov/factsheets/cc/zinc.html (accessed November 2005).
35. Ibs, K., and L. Rink. 2003. Zinc-Altered Immune Function. *Journal of Nutrition* 133: 1452S–1456S; Schwartz, J. R., R. G. Marsh, and Z. D. Draelos. 2005. Zinc and Skin Health: Overview of Physiology and Pharmacology. *Dermatological Surgery* 31: 837–847; Walravens, P. A. 1979. Zinc Metabolism and Its Implications in Clinical Medicine. *Western Journal of Medicine* 130: 133–142.
36. Russell, R. M., M. E. Cox, and N. Solomons. 1983. Zinc and the Special Senses. *Annals of Internal Medicine* 99: 227–239.
37. Farr, B. M., and J. M. Gwaltney. 1987. The Problems of Taste in Placebo Matching: An Evaluation of Zinc Gluconate for the Common Cold. *Journal of Chronic Disease* 40: 875–879.
38. Desbiens, M. A. 2000. Lessons Learned from Attempts to Establish the Blind in Placebo-Controlled Trial of Zinc for the Common Cold. *Annals of Internal Medicine* 133: 302–303; Jackson, J. L., E. Lesho, and C. Peterson. 2000. Zinc and the Common Cold: A Meta-analysis Revisited. *Journal of Nutrition* 130: 1512S–1515S; King, J. C., and R. J. Cousins. 2006. Zinc. In M. Shils, M. Shike, A. C. Ross, B. Caballero, and R. J. Cousins, eds. *Modern Nutrition in Health and Disease.* 10th ed. Philadelphia: Lippincott Williams and Wilkins; Mossad, S. B., M. L. Macknin, S. V. Medendorp, and P. Mason. 1996. Zinc Gluconate Lozenges for Treating the Common Cold: A Randomized, Double-Blind, Placebo-Controlled Study. *Annals of Internal Medicine* 125: 81–88; Prasad, A. S., J. T. Fitzgerald, B. Bao, F. W. J. Beck, and P. H. Chandrasekar. 2000. Duration of Symptoms and Plasma Cytokine Levels in Patients with the Common Cold Treated with Zinc Acetate. *Annals of Internal Medicine* 133: 245–252.
39. King. Zinc; Walravens. Zinc Metabolism.
40. Combs, G. F. 2005. Current Evidence and Research Needs to Support a Health Claim for Selenium and Cancer Prevention. *Journal of Nutrition* 135: 343–347; Institute of Medicine. 2000. *Dietary Reference Intakes: Vitamin C, Vitamin E, Selenium, and Carotenoids.* Washington, D.C.: The National Academies Press. www.nap.edu.; Office of Dietary Supplements. Updated 2004. Selenium. http://ods.od.nih.gov/factsheets/Selenium_pf.asp (accessed November 2005).
41. Beck, M. A., O. A. Levander, and O. Handy. 2003. Selenium Deficiency and Viral Infection. *Journal of Nutrition* 133: 1463S–1467S; Li, H., M. J. Stampfer, E. L. Giovannucci, J. S. Morris, W. C. Willett, M. Gaziano, and J. Ma. 2004. A Prospective Study of Plasma Selenium Levels and Prostate Cancer Risk. *Journal of the National Cancer Institute* 96: 696–703; Sunde, R. A. 2000. Selenium. In M. H. Stipnauk, ed. *Biochemical and Physiological Aspects of Human Nutrition.* Philadelphia: W. B. Saunders; Center for Food Safety and Applied Nutrition. 2005. Qualified Health Claims Subject to Enforcement Discretion. www.cfsan.fda.gov/~dms/qhc-sum.html (accessed November 2005); Wei, W., C. C. Abnet, Y. Qiao, S. M. Dawsey, Z. Dong, X. Sun, J. Fan, E. Q. Gunter, P. R. Taylor, and S. D. Mark. 2004. Prospective Study of Serum Selenium Concentrations and Esophageal and Gastric Cardia Cancer, Heart Disease, Stroke, and Total Death. *American Journal of Nutrition* 79: 80–85.
42. Beck. Selenium Deficiency and Viral Infection.
43. American Dental Association. 2005. Fluoridation Facts. www.ada.org/public/topics/fluoride/facts/fluoridation_facts.pdf (accessed November 2005).
44. Centers for Disease Control and Prevention (CDC). 1999. Achievements in Public Health, 1900–1999: Fluoridation of Drinking Water to Prevent Dental Caries. *Morbidity and Mortality Weekly Report* 48(41): 933–940. www.cdc.gov/mmwr/preview/mmwrhtml/mm4841a1.htm (accessed November 2005); CDC. Updated 2005. Water Fluoridation: Benefits, Background Information. www.cdc.gov/oralhealth/waterfluoridation/benefits/background.htm (accessed November 2005). CDC. Updated 2005. Water Fluoridation: Fact Sheets, Benefits. www.cdc.gov/oralhealth/waterfluoridation/fact_sheets/benefits.htm (accessed November 2005).
45. Institute of Medicine. *Dietary Reference Intakes: Calcium.*
46. Centers for Disease Control and Prevention. Updated 2005. Water Fluoridation. Safety—Enamel Fluorosis. www.cdc.gov/oralhealth/waterfluoridation/safety/enamel_fluorosis.htm (accessed November 2005).
47. Mertz, W. 1993. Chromium in Human Nutrition: A Review. *Journal of Nutrition* 123: 626–633.
48. Hopkins, L. L., O. Ransome-Kuti, and A. S. Majaj. 1968. Improvement of Impaired Carbohydrate Metabolism by Chromium (III) in Malnourished Infants. *American Journal of Clinical Nutrition* 21: 203–211; Jeejeebhoy, K. N., R. C. Clu, E. B. Marliss, G. R. Greenberg, and A. Bruce-Robertson. 1977. Chromium Deficiency, Glucose Intolerance, and Neuropathy Reversed by Chromium Supplementation in a Patient Receiving Long-term Total Parenteral Nutrition. *American Journal of Clinical Nutrition* 30: 531–538; Mertz., W. 1998. Interaction of Chromium with Insulin: A Progress Report. *Nutrition Reviews* 56: 174–177; Office of Dietary Supplements. Updated 2005. Chromium. http://ods.od.nih.gov/factsheets/Chromium_pf.asp (accessed November 2005).
49. Cefalu, W. T., and F. B. Hu. 2004. Role of Chromium in Human Health and in Diabetes. *Diabetes Care* 27: 2741–2751; Center for Food Safety and Applied Nutrition. 2005. Qualified Health Claims Subject to Enforcement Discretion: Chromium Picolinate and Insulin Resistance. www.cfsan.fda.gov/~dms/qhccr.html (accessed November 2005).
50. National Institutes of Health. Chromium.
51. Institute of Medicine. *Dietary Reference Intakes: Vitamin A;* Turnlund, J. R. 2006. Copper. In M. E. Shils, M. Shike, A. C. Ross, B. Caballero, and R. J. Cousins, eds. *Modern Nutrition in Health and Disease.* 10th ed. Philadelphia: Lippincott Williams and Wilkins; Uaruy, R., M. Olivares, and M. Gonzalez. 1998. Essentiality of Copper in Humans. *American Journal of Clinical Nutrition* 67: 952S–959S.
52. Anderson. Minerals.
53. Freake, H. C. 2000. Iodine. In M. H. Stipnauk, ed. *Biochemical and Physiological Aspects of Human Nutrition.* Philadelphia: W. B. Saunders; Stanbury, J. B., A. E. Ermans, P. Bourdouz, C. Todd, E. Oken, R. Tonglet, T. G. Vidor, L. E. Braverman, and G. Medeiros-Neto. 1998. Iodine-induced Hyperthyroidism: Occurrence and Epidemiology. *Thyroid* 8: 83–100; Institute of Medicine. *Dietary Reference Intakes: Vitamin A.*
54. Ibid.
55. Institute of Medicine. *Dietary Reference Intakes: Vitamin A.*
56. Ibid.
57. Barceloux, D. G. 1999. Manganese. *Clinical Toxicology* 37: 293–307.

Feature Box References

1. Franklin, S. S., et al. 1997. Hemodynamic Patterns of Age-related Changes in Blood Pressure. *Circulation* 96: 308–315. www.circ.ahajournals.org/cgi/content/full/96/1/308 (accessed August 2005).
2. American Heart Association. 2004. What Is High Blood Pressure? www.americanheart.org (accessed October 2005).
3. Chobanian, A. V., G. L. Bakris, H. R. Black, W. C. Cushman, L. A. Green, J. L. Izzo, D. W. Jones, B. J. Materson, S. Oparil, J. T. Wright, E. J. Roccella, and the National High Blood Pressure Education Program Coordinating Committee. 2003. The Seventh Report of the Joint National Committee on Prevention, Detection, Evaluation, and Treatment of High Blood Pressure. *Journal of the American Medical Association* 289: 2560–2572; National Heart, Lung, and Blood Institute. 2004. High Blood Pressure. www.nhlbi.nih.gov/health/dci/Diseases/Hbp/HBP_WhatIs.html (accessed September 2005).
4. American Heart Association. 2005. Am I at Risk? www.americanheart.org (accessed September 2005).
5. U.S. Department of Health and Human Services. Overweight and Obesity: Health Consequences. www.surgeongeneral.gov/topics/obesity/calltoaction/fact_consequences.htm (accessed September 2005); National Heart, Lung, and Blood Institute. 2004. The Seventh Report of the Joint National Committee on Prevention, Detection, Evaluation, and Treatment of High Blood Pressure (JNC 7). www.nhlbi.nih.gov/guidelines/hypertension/jnc7full.htm (accessed September 2005); Wharton, S. P., A. Chin, X. Xin, and J. He. 2002. Effect of Aerobic Exercise on Blood Pressure: A Meta-analysis of Randomized Controlled Trials. *Annals of Internal Medicine* 136 (7): 493–503.
6. Xin, X., J. He, M. G. Frontini, L. G. Ogden, O. I. Motsamai, and P. K. Whelton. 2001. Effects of Alcohol Reduction on Blood Pressure: A Meta-analysis of Randomized Controlled Trials. *Hypertension* 38: 1112–1117.
7. Harsha, D. W., P. Lin, E. Obarzanek, N. M. Karanja, T. J. Moore, and B. Caballero. 1999. Dietary Approaches to Stop Hypertension: A Summary of Study Results. *Journal of the American Dietetic Association* 99: S35–S39; Kotchen, T.A., and J. M. Kotchen. 2006. Nutrition, Diet, and Hypertension. In M. Shils, M. Shike, A. C. Ross, B. Caballero, and R. J. Cousins, eds. *Modern Nutrition in Health and Disease.* 10th ed. Philadelphia: Lippincott Williams and Wilkins; National Heart, Lung, and Blood Institute. 2002. Primary Prevention of Hypertension: Clinical and Public Health Advisory from the National Blood Pressure Education Program. www.nhlbi.nih.gov/health/prof/heart/hbp/pphbp.pdf (accessed September 2005).
8. National Heart, Lung, and Blood Institute. 2003. The DASH Eating Plan. www.nhlbi.nih.gov/health/public/heart/hbp/dash (accessed September 2005).
9. Patlak, M. 2001. Bone Builders: The Discoveries behind Preventing and Treating Osteoporosis. *FASEB Journal* 15: 1677.
10. Osteoporosis and Related Bone Diseases—National Resource Center. 2005. Osteoporosis Overview. www.osteo.org/osteo.html (accessed October 2005); U.S. Department of Health and Human Services. 2004. *Bone Health and Osteoporosis: A Report of the Surgeon General.* Washington, D.C.: Office of the Surgeon General.

11. National Institutes of Health, Consensus Development Conference Statement. 2000. Osteoporosis Prevention, Diagnosis, and Therapy. www.consensus.nih.gov/2000/2000Osteoporosis111html.htm (accessed October 2005).
12. U.S. Department of Health and Human Services. *Bone Health and Osteoporosis.*
13. Office of Dietary Supplements. Updated 2005. Dietary Supplement Fact Sheet: Calcium. http://ods.od.nih.gov/factsheets/calcium.asp (accessed October 2005); U.S. Department of Health and Human Services. *Bone Health and Osteoporosis.*
14. U.S. Department of Health and Human Services. *Bone Health and Osteoporosis;* Osteoporosis in Postmenopausal Women: Diagnosis and Monitoring Evidence Report/Technology Assessment No. 28. Agency for Healthcare Research and Quality. 2001. Publication No. 01-E032.
15. Miller, K. K. 2003. Mechanisms by Which Nutritional Disorders Cause Reduced Bone Mass in Adults. *Journal of Women's Health* 12: 145–150.
16. National Institutes of Health. *Osteoporosis* Overview.
17. U.S. Department of Health and Human Services. *Bone Health and Osteoporosis.*
18. Ibid.

Concept 18

1. Grandjean, A., and S. Campbell. 2004. *Hydration: Fluids for Life.* Washington, D.C.: ILSI Press. www.ilsi.org (accessed August 2005); Institute of Medicine. 2004. *Dietary Reference Intakes: Water, Potassium, Sodium, Chloride, and Sulfate.* Washington, D.C.: The National Academies Press. www.nap.edu; Marieb, E. N. 2004. Chemistry Comes Alive. In *Human Anatomy and Physiology.* 6th ed. San Francisco: Pearson/Benjamin Cummings.
2. Sheng, H. 2000. Body Fluids and Water Balance. In *Biochemical and Physiological Aspects of Human Nutrition.* Philadelphia: W. B. Saunders.
3. Institute of Medicine. *Dietary Reference Intakes: Water.*
4. Grandjean. *Hydration; Fluids for Life;* Institute of Medicine. *Dietary Reference Intakes: Water;* Marieb, *Chemistry Comes Alive.*
5. Marieb. *Chemistry Comes Alive.*
6. Institute of Medicine. *Dietary Reference Intakes: Water.*
7. Ibid.
8. Casa, D. J., L. E. Armstrong, S. K. Hillman, S. J. Montain, R. C. Reiff, B. S. E. Rich, W. O. Roberts, and J. A. Stone. 2000. National Athletic Trainers Association Position Statement: Fluid Replacement for Athletes. *Journal of Athletic Training* 35: 212–224.
9. Institute of Medicine. *Dietary Reference Intakes: Water.*
10. Arnold, D. To the End, Marathon Was at Center of Student's Life. *Boston Globe,* April 18, 2002; Aucoin, D. Tribute to a Fallen Champion of the Needs of the Afflicted. *Boston Globe.* October 26, 2002; Noakes, T. D. 2003. Overconsumption of Fluids by Athletes. *British Medical Journal* 327: 113–114; Rosinski, J. Friends Remember Marathoner Who Died. www.remembercynthia.com (accessed August 2005); Smith, S. Marathon Runner's Death Linked to Excessive Fluid Intake. *Boston Globe,* August 13, 2002.
11. Grandjean, A. C., K. J. Reimers, and M. E. Buyckx. 2003. Hydration: Issues for the 21st Century. *Nutrition Reviews* 61: 261–271.
12. Grandjean. *Hydration; Fluids for Life;* Institute of Medicine. *Dietary Reference Intakes: Water.*
13. Institute of Medicine. *Dietary Reference Intakes: Water.*
14. Grandjean. Hydration: Issues for the 21st Century; Institute of Medicine. *Dietary Reference Intakes: Water.*

Feature Box References

1. U.S. Environmental Protection Agency. 2008. Ground Water and Drinking Water: Frequently Asked Questions. www.epa.gov/safewater/faq/faq.html (accessed October 2008).
2. Bullers, A. C. 2002. Bottled Water: Better Than the Tap? *FDA Consumer Magazine.* www.fda.gov/fdac/features/2002/402_h2o.html (accessed August 2005); U.S. Environmental Protection Agency. 2003. Water on Tap: What You Need to Know. www.epa.gov/safewater/wot/index.html (accessed August 2005).
3. Centers for Disease Control and Prevention. 2005. Oral Health: Water Fluoridation Fact Sheets and States' Statistics 2002. www.cdc.gov/oralhealth/waterfluoridation/fact_sheets/states_stats2002.html (accessed December 2005).
4. Natural Resources Defense Council. 1999. Bottled Water: Pure Drink or Pure Hype? www.nrdc.org (accessed August 2005); San Francisco Department of Public Health, Environmental Health Section, and San Francisco Public Utilities Commission. 2004. Bottled Water vs Tap Water: Making a Healthy Choice. www.dph.sf.ca.us/ehs/phes/publications/water/FactSheets/bottled_water.pdf (accessed August 2005).
5. Fluoride Recommendations Work Group. 2001. Recommendations for Using Fluoride to Prevent and Control Dental Caries in the United States 50 (RR14): 1–42. www.cdc.gov/mmwr/preview/mmwrhtml/rr5014a1.htm (accessed November 2005).

Concept 19

1. Distilled Spirits Councils in the United States. 2001. Reporters' Guide to the Distilled Spirits Industry. www.discus.org/mediaroom/guide.htm (accessed December 2005).
2. Centers for Disease Control and Prevention. 2005. Alcohol and Public Health: General Alcohol Information. www.cdc.gov/alcohol/factsheets/general_information.htm (accessed January 2006).
3. Mandelbaum, D. G. 1965. Alcohol and Culture. *Current Anthropology* 6: 281–288.
4. U.S. Department of Agriculture. 2005. 2005 Report of the Dietary Guidelines Advisory Committee. www.health.gov/dietaryguidelines/dga2005/report/ (accessed January 2006); Goldberg, I. J., L. Mosca, M. R. Piano, and E. A. Fisher. 2001. Wine and Your Heart. A Science Advisory for Healthcare Professionals from the Nutrition Committee, Council on Epidemiology and Prevention, and Council on Cardiovascular Nursing of the American Heart Association. *Circulation* 103: 472–475.
5. U.S. Department of Agriculture. 2005 Report; Goldberg. Wine and Your Heart.
6. Andreasson, S., P. Allebeck, and A. Romelsjo. 1988. Alcohol and Mortality among Young Men: Longitudinal Study of Swedish Conscripts. *British Medical Journal* 296: 1021–1025.
7. National Institute on Alcohol Abuse and Alcoholism. 1997. Alcohol Alert: Alcohol Metabolism. www.niaaa.nih.gov/Publications/AlcoholAlerts (accessed December 2005).
8. Frezza, M., C. diPadova, G. Pozzato, M. Terpin, E. Baraona, and C. S. Leiber. High Blood Alcohol Levels in Women: The Role of Decreased Gastric Alcohol Dehydrogenase Activity and First-Pass Metabolism. *New England Journal of Medicine* 332: 95–99.
9. National Institute on Alcohol Abuse and Alcoholism. 1998. Alcohol Alert: Alcohol and Sleep. www.niaaa.nih.gov/Publications/AlcoholAlerts (accessed December 2005).
10. National Institute on Alcohol Abuse and Alcoholism. Alcohol Alert: Alcohol and Sleep; Roehrs, T., D. Beare, F. Zorick, and T. Roth. 1994. Sleepiness and Ethanol Effects on Simulated Driving. *Alcoholism: Clinical and Experimental Research* 18: 154–158.
11. Swift, R. S., and D. Davidson. 1998. Alcohol Hangover, Mechanisms and Mediators. *Alcohol Health & Research World* 22: 54–60. http://pubs.niaaa.nih.gov/publications/arh22-1/54-60.pdf (accessed January 2006).
12. National Institute on Alcohol Abuse and Alcoholism. Alcohol Alert: Alcohol Metabolism; Swift. Alcohol Hangover.
13. Swift. Alcohol Hangover; National Institute on Alcohol Abuse and Alcoholism. 1994. Alcohol Alert: Alcohol and Hormones. www.niaaa.nih.gov/Publications/AlcoholAlerts (accessed December 2005).
14. National Institute on Alcohol Abuse and Alcoholism. 2003. State of the Science Report on the Effects of Moderate Drinking. http://pubs.niaaa.nih.gov/publications/ModerateDrinking-03.htm (accessed January 2003); National Institute on Alcohol Abuse and Alcoholism. Updated 2000. Alcohol Alert: Alcohol and Cancer. http://pubs.niaaa.nih.gov/publications/aa21.htm (accessed January 2005); National Institute on Alcohol Abuse and Alcoholism. Updated 2000. Alcohol Alert: Alcohol and Tobacco. http://pubs.niaaa.nih.gov/publications/aa21.htm (accessed June 2006).
15. National Institute on Alcohol Abuse and Alcoholism. Alcohol Alert: Alcohol and Cancer; National Institute on Alcohol Abuse and Alcoholism. Alcohol Alert: Alcohol and Tobacco.
16. National Institute on Alcohol Abuse and Alcoholism. 2003. Understanding Alcohol: Investigations into Biology and Behavior. http://science.education.nih.gov/supplements/nih3/alcohol/default.htm (accessed December 2007).
17. Ibid.
18. Lieber, C. S. 2000. Alcohol: Its Metabolism and Interaction with Nutrients. *Annual Review of Nutrition* 20: 394–430.
19. Centers for Disease Control and Prevention. Alcohol and Public Health.
20. Jones, K., and D. Smith. 1973. Recognition of the Fetal Alcohol Syndrome in Early Infancy. *The Lancet* 2: 999–1001; Bertrand, J., R. L. Floyd, and M. K. Weber. 2005. Guidelines for Identifying and Referring Persons with Fetal Alcohol Syndrome. *Morbidity and Mortality Weekly Report* 54 (RR11): 1–10. www.cdc.gov/mmwr/preview/mmwrhtml/rr5411a1.htm (accessed January 2006); Substance Abuse and Mental Health Services

Administrator. 2005. Fetal Alcohol Spectrum Disorders, the Basics. http://fasdcenter.samhsa.gov/misc/FASDBASICS/FASDTheBasics.pdf (accessed January 2006).
21. National Institute on Alcohol Abuse and Alcoholism. Understanding Alcohol.
22. Henao, L. A. 2005. Obituary. *Boston Globe,* July 5, 2005.
23. Centers for Disease Control and Prevention. Alcohol and Public Health.
24. National Institute on Alcohol Abuse and Alcoholism. Understanding Alcohol.
25. National Institute on Alcohol Abuse and Alcoholism. 2004. Alcohol Alert: Alcohol's Damaging Effects on the Brain. http://pubs.niaaa.nih.gov/publications/aa63/aa63.htm (accessed December 2005); White, A. M., D. W. Jamieson-Drake, and H. S. Swartzwelder. 2002. Prevalence and Correlates of Alcohol-Induced Blackouts among College Students: Results of an E-mail Survey. *Journal of American College Health* 51: 117–131.
26. National Institute on Alcohol Abuse and Alcoholism. Understanding Alcohol.
27. National Institute on Alcohol Abuse and Alcoholism. Publication No. 29 PH 357. Updated 2000. www.niaaa.nih.gov/Publications/AlcoholAlerts/default.htm (accessed January 2006).
28. National Highway Traffic Safety Administration. 2005. Traffic Safety Facts: Crash Statistics on Alcohol-Related Fatalities in 2004. www.nrd.nhtsa.dot.gov/pdf/nrd-30/NCSA/RNotes/2005/809904.pdf (accessed January 2006).
29. National Institute on Alcohol Abuse and Alcoholism. 2003. Underage Drinking: A Major Public Health Challenge. www.niaaa.nih.gov/Publications/AlcoholAlerts/default.htm (accessed January 2006).
30. Institute of Medicine. 2003. *Reducing Underage Drinking: A Collective Responsibility.* Washington, D.C.: The National Academies Press.
31. National Institute on Alcohol Abuse and Alcoholism. Underage Drinking.
32. Ibid.
33. Ibid.
34. National Institute on Alcohol Abuse and Alcoholism. College Drinking, Changing the Culture; Alcoholism: Getting the Facts. www.collegedrinkingprevention.gov (accessed January 2006).
35. Alcoholics Anonymous. 2004. Membership Survey. www.aa.org (accessed January 2006).
36. U.S. Department of Agriculture. 2005 Report.

Feature Box References

1. Austin, E., and S. Hust. 2005. Targeting Adolescents? The Content and Frequency of Alcoholic and Nonalcoholic Beverage Ads in Magazine and Video Formats November 1999–April 2000. *Journal of Health Communications* 10: 769–785.
2. Austin, E., M. Chen, and J. Grube. 2006. How Does Alcohol Advertising Influence Underage Drinking? The Role of Desirability, Identification, and Skepticism. *Journal of Adolescent Health* 38: 376–384.

Concept 20

1. Centers for Disease Control and Prevention. 2008. Healthy Weight: Introduction. www.cdc.gov/nccdphp/dnpa/healthyweight/index.htm (accessed October 2008).
2. National Institutes of Health. Clinical Guidelines on the Identification, Evaluation, and Treatment of Overweight and Obesity in Adults.
3. Ibid.
4. Ibid.
5. Ibid.
6. Institute of Medicine. 2002. *Dietary Reference Intakes for Energy, Carbohydrate, Fiber, Fat, Fatty Acids, Cholesterol, Protein, and Amino Acids.* www.iom.edu (accessed Dec. 2008).

Feature Box Reference

1. Pischon, T., et al. 2008. General and Abdominal Adiposity and Risk of Death in Europe. *New England Journal of Medicine.* 359: 2105–2120. November 13, 2008. https://content.nejm.org/cgi/content/abstract/359/20/2105?ck=nck (accessed November 2008).

Concept 21

1. National Center for Health Statistics. FastStats A to Z: Overweight. www.cdc.gov/nchs/fastats/overwt.htm (accessed November 2008).
2. IFIC Foundation. 2005. Food for Thought VI, Reporting of Diet, Nutrition, and Food Safety News. www.ific.org/research/fftres.cfm (accessed July 2006).
3. Mintel Reports: USA, Health and Medical: USA, Health and Wellness: USA. 2005. Commercial Weight Loss Programs—U.S. http://reports.mintel.com/sinatra/reports/display/id=121277/display/id=192441 (accessed June 2006).
4. Weight-control Information Network. 2004. Do You Know the Health Risks of Being Overweight? http://win.niddk.nih.gov/publications/health_risks.htm (accessed June 2006).
5. National Institutes of Health. 1998. Clinical Guidelines on the Identification, Evaluation, and Treatment of Overweight and Obesity in Adults. www.nhlbi.nih.gov/guidelines/obesity/ob_gdlns.htm (accessed June 2006).
6. Centers for Disease Control and Prevention. 2008. Obesity and Overweight: Introduction. www.cdc.gov/nccdphp/dnpa/obesity.htm (accessed November 2008).
7. National Institutes of Health. Clinical Guidelines.
8. Ibid.
9. Weight-control Information Network. Do You Know the Health Risks of Being Overweight?; National Institutes of Health. Clinical Guidelines.
10. Mattes, R., J. Hollis, D. Hayes, and A. Stunkard. 2005. Appetite: Measurement and Manipulations Misgivings. *Journal of the American Dietetic Association* 105 (supplement): S87–S97.
11. Smith, G. 2006. Controls of Food Intake. In M. Shils et al., eds., *Modern Nutrition.*
12. Mattes. Appetite.
13. Smith. G. Controls of Food Intake.
14. Center for Genomics and Public Health. 2004. Obesity and Current Topics in Genetics. www.cdc.gov/genomics/training/perspectives/obesity.htm#Perspective (accessed June 2006).
15. Hill, J., V. Catenacci, and H. Wyatt. 2006. Obesity: Etiology. In M. Shils et al., eds., *Modern Nutrition.*
16. Hill, J. Obesity: Etiology. In M. Shils et al., eds., *Modern Nutrition.*
17. Bray, G., and C. Champagne. 2005. Beyond Energy Balance: There Is More to Obesity than Kilocalories. *Journal of the American Dietetic Association* 105 (supplement): S17–S23.
18. Brodsky, I. 2006. Hormones and Growth Factors. In M. Shils et al., eds., *Modern Nutrition.*
19. Hill. Obesity.
20. Ibid.
21. Bray. Beyond Energy Balance; Loos, R., and T. Rankinen. 2005. Gene-Diet Interactions on Body Weight Changes. *Journal of the American Dietetic Association* 105 (supplement): S29–S34.
22. Gale, S., T. Van Itallie, and I. Faust. 1981. Effects of Palatable Diets on Body Weight and Adipose Tissue Cellularity in the Adult Obese Female Zucker Rat (fa/fa). *Metabolism* 30: 105–110.
23. Ravussin, E., M. Valencia, J. Esparza, P. Bennett, and L. Schulz. 1994. Effects of a Traditional Lifestyle on Obesity in Pima Indians. *Diabetes Care* 17: 1067–1074; Wang, S., and K. Brownell. 2005. Public Policy and Obesity: The Need to Marry Science with Advocacy. *Psychiatric Clinics of North America* 28: 235–252.
24. The Keystone Group. 2006. The Keystone Forums on Away-from-Home Food, Opportunities for Preventing Weight Gain and Obesity. www.keystone.org/spp/documents/Forum_Report_FINAL_5-30-06.pdf (accessed June 2006).
25. Ibid.
26. Wang. Public Policy and Obesity.
27. The Keystone Group. The Keystone Forums on Away-from-Home Food.
28. Ibid.; Clemens, L., D. Slawson, and R. Klesges. 1999. The Effect of Eating Out on Quality of Diet in Premenopausal Women. *Journal of the American Dietetic Association* 99: 442–444.
29. The Keystone Group. The Keystone Forums on Away-from-Home Food; Meyers, A., A. Stunkard, and M. Coll. 1980. Food Accessibility and Food Choice. *Archives of General Psychiatry* 37: 1133–1135.
30. The Keystone Group. The Keystone Forums on Away-from-Home Food; Rolls, B. 1986. Sensory-Specific Satiety. *Nutrition Reviews* 44: 93–101.
31. Rolls, B. 2003. The Supersizing of America. *Nutrition Today* 38: 42–53.
32. Wansink, B. 1996. Can Package Size Accelerate Usage Volume? *Journal of Marketing* 60: 1–14.
33. Rolls, B., L. Roe, and J. Meengs. 2006. Larger Portion Sizes Lead to a Sustained Increase in Energy Intake over 2 Days. *Journal of the American Dietetic Association* 106: 543–549.
34. Putnam, J., J. Allshouse, and L. Kantor. 2002. U.S. per Capita Food Supply Trends: More Calories, Refined Carbohydrates, and Fats. Economic Research Service, USDA. *FoodReview* 25: 2–15; French, S., M. Story, and R. Jeffery. 2001. Environmental Influences on Eating and Physical Activity. *Annual Reviews of Public Health* 22: 309–335.
35. French. Environmental Influences on Eating.
36. Mummery, W., G. Schofield, R. Steele, E. Eakin, and W. Brown. 2005. Occupational Sitting Time and Overweight and Obesity in Australian Workers. *American Journal of Preventative Medicine* 29: 91–97.
37. French. Environmental Influences on Eating.

38. Wang. Public Policy and Obesity.
39. Lanningham-Foster, L., L. Nysse, and J. Levine. 2003. Labor Saved, Calories Lost: The Energetic Impact of Domestic Labor-Saving Devices. *Obesity Research* 11: 1178–1181.
40. Ibid.
41. Centers for Disease Control and Prevention. 2003. Prevalence of Physical Activity, Including Lifestyle Activities among Adults—United States, 2000–2001. *Morbidity and Mortality Weekly Report* 52: 763–769. www.cdc.gov/mmwr/preview/mmwrhtml/mm5232a2.htm (accessed June 2006).
42. Centers for Disease Control and Prevention. 2005. Trends in Leisure-Time Physical Inactivity by Age, Sex, and Race/Ethnicity—United States, 1994–2004. *Morbidity and Mortality Weekly Report* 54: 991–994. www.cdc.gov/mmwr/preview/mmwrhtml/mm5439a5.htm (accessed June 2006).
43. Nielsen Media Research. 2000. Report on Television. www.nielsenmedia.com (accessed July 2006).
44. Roberts, D., U. Foehr, V. Rideout, and M. Brodie. 1999. Kids & Media @ the New Millennium. The Kaiser Family Foundation. www.kff.org/entmedia/index.cfm (accessed July 2006).
45. National Institutes of Health. Clinical Guidelines.
46. Mattes. Appetite; Lissner, L., D. Levitsky, B. Strupp, H. Kalkwarf, and D. Roe. 1987. Dietary Fat and the Regulation of Energy Intake in Human Subjects. *American Journal of Clinical Nutrition* 46: 886–892.
47. Tohill, B., J. Seymour, M. Serdula, L. Kettel-Khan, and B. Rolls. 2004. What Epidemiologic Studies Tell Us about the Relationship between Fruit and Vegetable Consumption and Body Weight. *Nutrition Reviews* 62: 365–374.
48. Rolls, B., E. Bell, and E. Thorwart. 1999. Water Incorporated into a Food but Not Served with a Food Decreases Energy Intake in Lean Women. *American Journal of Clinical Nutrition* 70: 448–455.
49. Burton-Freeman, B. 2000. Dietary Fiber and Energy Regulation. *Journal of Nutrition* 130: 272S–275S.
50. Davis, J., V. Hodges, and B. Gillham. 2006. Normal-weight Adults Consume More Fiber and Fruit Than Their Age- and Height-Matched Overweight/Obese Counterparts. *Journal of the American Dietetic Association* 106: 833–840.
51. Mattes. Appetite.
52. Saries, W., S. Blair, M. van Baak, et al. 2003. How Much Physical Activity Is Enough to Prevent Unhealthy Weight Gain? Outcome of the IASO Stock Conference and Consensus Statement. *Obesity Reviews* 4: 101–114.
53. Keim, N., C. Blanton, and M. Kretsch. 2004. America's Obesity Epidemic: Measuring Physical Activity to Promote an Active Lifestyle. *Journal of the American Dietetic Association* 104: 1398–1409.
54. Jakicic, J., and A. Otto. 2005. Physical Activity Consideration for the Treatment and Prevention of Obesity. *American Journal of Clinical Nutrition* 82: 226S–229S.
55. Shape Up America! n.d. 10,000 Steps. www.shapeup.org/shape/steps.php (accessed July 2006).
56. Edwards, J., and H. Meiselman. 2003. Changes in Dietary Habits during the First Year at University. *British Nutrition Foundation Nutrition Bulletin* 28: 21–34.
57. Graham, M., and A. Jones. 2002. Freshman 15: Valid Theory or Harmful Myth? *Journal of American College Health* 50: 171–173.
58. Poston, W., and J. Foreyt. 2000. Successful Management of the Obese Patient. *American Family Physician* 61: 3615–3622.
59. Schlundt, D., J. Hill, T. Sbrocco, J. Pope-Cordle, and T. Sharp. 1992. The Role of Breakfast in the Treatment of Obesity: A Randomized Clinical Trial. *American Journal of Clinical Nutrition* 55: 645–651.
60. Rosenbaum, M., R. Leibel, and J. Hirsch. 1997. Obesity. *New England Journal of Medicine* 337: 396–407.
61. National Institute of Diabetes and Digestive and Kidney Diseases. 2006. Weight Cycling. http://win.niddk.nih.gov/publications/cycling.htm (accessed July 2006).
62. Rosenbaum. Obesity; Klem, M. L., R. R. Wing, M. T. McGuire, H. M. Seagle, and J. O. Hill. 1997. A Descriptive Study of Individuals Successful at Long-term Maintenance of Substantial Weight Loss. *American Journal of Clinical Nutrition* 66: 239–246.
63. Klem. A Descriptive Study.
64. Hill, J., H. Wyatt, G. Reed, and J. Peters. 2003. Obesity and the Environment: Where Do We Go from Here? *Science* 299: 853–897.
65. Hill, J., H. Thompson, and H. Wyatt. 2005. Weight Maintenance: What's Missing? *Journal of the American Dietetic Association* 105: S63–S66.
66. U.S. Department of Health and Human Services. 2005. Report of the Dietary Guidelines Advisory Committee on the *Dietary Guidelines for Americans, 2005*. www.health.gov/DietaryGuidelines/dga2005/report (accessed July 2006).
67. Ibid.

Feature Box References

1. National Heart, Lung, and Blood Institute. 1998. Clinical Guidelines on the Identification, Evaluation, and Treatment of Overweight and Obesity in Adults. Available at www.nhlbi.nih.gov/guidelines/obesity/ob_gdlns.htm. Accessed June 2006.
2. Mariant, M. 2005. Oprah Regrets Her 1988 Liquid Diet. *USA Today* (November). Available at www.usatoday.com/life/people/2005-11-16-oprah-liquid-diet_x.htm. Accessed July 2006.
3. DeWald, T., L. Khaodhiar, M. Donahue, and G. Blackburn. 2006. Pharmacological and Surgical Treatments for Obesity. *American Heart Journal* 151: 604–624.
4. Meadows, M. 2003. Public Health Officials Caution Against Ephedra Use. *FDA Consumer Magazine*. Available at www.fda.gov/fdac/features/2003/303_ephedra.html. Accessed July 2006; Food and Drug Administration. 2004. FDA Issues Regulation Prohibiting Sale of Dietary Supplements Containing Ephedrine Alkaloids and Reiterates Its Advice That Consumers Stop Using These Products. Available at www.cfsan.fda.gov/~lrd/fpephed6.html. Accessed July 2006.
5. Encinosa, W., D. Bernard, C. Steiner, and C. Chen. 2005. Trends: Use and Costs of Bariatric Surgery and Prescription Weight-Loss Medications. *Health Affairs* 24: 1039–1046.
6. Crookes, P. 2006. Surgical Treatment of Morbid Obesity. *Annual Review of Medicine* 57: 243–264.
7. DeWald. Pharmacological and Surgical Treatments for Obesity; Crookes. Surgical Treatment of Morbid Obesity.

Concept 22

1. Laquatra, I. 2004. Nutrition for Weight Management. In L. Mahan and S. Escott-Stump, eds. *Krause's Food, Nutrition, and Diet Therapy.* 11th ed. Philadelphia: Saunders.
2. U.S. Department of Health and Human Services. 2002. A Century of Women's Health, 1900–2000. www.4woman.gov/TimeCapsule/century/century.pdf (accessed July 2006).
3. Hammond, K. 2004. Dietary and Clinical Assessment. In L. Mahan and S. Escott-Stump, eds. *Krause's Food, Nutrition, and Diet Therapy.* 11th ed. Philadelphia: Saunders.
4. Maconochie, N., et al. 2006. Risk Factors for First Trimester Miscarriage: Results from a UK-Population-Based Case-Control Study. *BJOG: An International Journal of Obstetrics and Gynaecology.*
5. National Eating Disorders Association. 2006. Statistics: Eating Disorders and Their Precursors. www.nationaleatingdisorders.org/p.asp?WebPage_ID=286&Profile_ID=41138 (accessed July 2006).
6. National Association of Anorexia Nervosa and Associated Eating Disorders (ANAD). 2008. Facts about Eating Disorders. www.anad.org/22385/index.html (accessed November 2008).
7. Chamorro, R., and Y. Flores-Ortiz. 2000. Acculturation and Disordered Eating Patterns among Mexican American Women. *International Journal of Eating Disorders* 28, no. 1: 125–129; Crago, M., C. M. Shisslak, and L. S. Estes. 1996. Eating Disturbances among American Minority Groups: A Review. *International Journal of Eating Disorders* 19, no. 3: 239–248; Kjelsas, E., C. Bjornstrom, and K. G. Gotestam. 2004. Prevalence of Eating Disorders in Female and Male Adolescents (14–15 Years). *Eating Behaviors* 5, no. 1: 13–25; O'Dea, J., and S. Abraham. 2002. Eating and Exercise Disorders in Young College Men. *Journal of American College Health* 50, no. 6: 273–278.
8. Strober, M., and C. M. Bulik. 2002. Genetic Epidemiology of Eating Disorders. In D. G. Fairburn and K. D. Brownell, eds. *Eating Disorders and Obesity: A Comprehensive Handbook.* 2nd ed. New York: Guilford Press, pp. 238–242.
9. Lilenfeld, L. R. R., S. Wonderlich, L. P. Riso, R. Crosby, and J. Mitchell. 2005. Eating Disorders and Personality: A Methodological and Empirical Review. *Clinical Psychology Review* 26, no. 3: 299–320.
10. Woodside, D. B., P. E. Garfinkel, E. Lin, P. Goering, A. S. Kaplan, D. S. Goldbloom, and S. H. Kennedy. 2001. Comparisons of Men with Full or Partial Eating Disorders, Men without Eating Disorders, and Women with Eating Disorders in the Community. *American Journal of Psychiatry* 158: 570–574.
11. Birketvedt, G. S., J. Florholmen, J. Sundsfjord, B. Osterud, D. Dinges, W. Bilker, and A. Stunkard. 1999. Behavioral and Neuroendocrine Characteristics of the Night Eating Syndrome. *Journal of the American Medical Association* 282, no. 7: 657–663.
12. Marshall, H. M., K. C. Allison, J. P. O'Reardon, G. Birketvedt, and A. J. Stunkard. 2004. Night Eating Syndrome among Nonobese Persons. *International Journal of Eating Disorders* 35, no. 2: 217–222.

13. Birketvedt. Behavioral and Neuroendocrine Characteristics.
14. Gluck, M., A. Geliebter, and T. Satov. 2001. Night Eating Syndrome Is Associated with Depression, Low Self-Esteem, Reduced Daytime Hunger, and Less Weight Loss in Obese Outpatients. *Obesity Research* 9: 264–267.
15. Birketvedt, G. S., J. Sundsfjord, and J. R. Florholmen. 2002. Hypothalamic-Pituitary-Adrenal Axis in the Night Eating Syndrome. *American Journal of Physiology–Endocrinology and Metabolism* 282, no. 2: E366–E369.

Feature Box References

1. Stein, K. 2000. High-Protein, Low-Carbohydrate Diets: Do They Work? *Journal of the American Dietetic Association* 100: 760–761.
2. Freedman, M., J. King, and E. Kennedy. 2001. Popular Diets: A Scientific Review. *Obesity Research* 9: 1S–40S.
3. Dansinger, M., J. Gleason, J. Griffith, H. Selker, and E. Schaefer. 2005. Comparison of the Atkins, Ornish, Weight Watchers, and Zone Diets for Weight Loss and Heart Disease Risk Reduction. *Journal of the American Medical Association* 293: 43–53.
4. Yudkin, J., and M. Carey. 1960. The Treatment of Obesity by the "Highfat" Diet: The Inevitability of Calories. *The Lancet* 2: 939–941.
5. Ornish, D. 2004. Was Dr. Atkins Right? *Journal of the American Dietetic Association* 104: 537–542.
6. Denke, M. 2001. Metabolic Effects of High-Protein, Low-Carbohydrate Diets. *American Journal of Cardiology* 88: 59–61.
7. Ibid.
8. Federal Trade Commission. 2000. Marketers of "The Enforma System" Settle FTC Charges of Deceptive Advertising for Their Weight Loss Products. www.quackwatch.org/02ConsumerProtection/FTCActions/enforma.html (accessed July 2006).
9. Dwyer, J., D. Allison, and P. Coates. 2005. Dietary Supplements in Weight Reduction. *Journal of the American Dietetic Association* 105: S80–S86; Pittler, M., and E. Ernst. 2004. Dietary Supplements for Body-Weight Reduction: A Systematic Review. *American Journal of Clinical Nutrition* 79: 529–536.
10. Pittler. Dietary Supplements for Body-Weight Reduction.
11. Dwyer. Dietary Supplements in Weight Reduction.

Concept 23

1. National Cancer Institute. 2007. Cancer Trends Progress Report—2007 Update. http://progressreport.cancer.gov/ (accessed July 2008).
2. American Cancer Society. 2008. Cancer Facts and Figures 2008. http://www.cancer.org/downloads/STT/2008CAFFfinalsecured.pdf (accessed July 2008).
3. World Cancer Research Fund/American Institute for Cancer Research (AICR). 2007. *Food, Nutrition, Physical Activity, and the Prevention of Cancer: A Global Perspective.* Washington, D.C.: AICR.
4. Ibid.
5. American Cancer Society. Cancer Facts and Figures 2008.
6. Ibid.
7. World Cancer Research Fund/American Institute for Cancer Research (AICR). Food, Nutrition, Physical Activity, and the Prevention of Cancer.
8. Food and Drug Administration. 2008. Beware of Online Cancer Fraud. www.fda.gov/consumer/updates/cancerfraud061708.html (accessed in July 2008).

Feature Box References

1. American Cancer Society. 2008. Phytochemicals. www.cancer.org (accessed July 2008).
2. Ibid.

Concept 24

1. Whelton, S. P., A. Chin, X. Xin, and J. He. 2002. Effect of Aerobic Exercise on Blood Pressure: A Meta-Analysis of Randomized, Controlled Trials. *Annals of Internal Medicine* 136: 493–503.
2. Alhassan S., K. A. Reese, J. Mahurin, E. P. Plaisance, B. D. Hilson, J. C. Garner, S. O. Wee, and P. W. Grandjean. 2006. Blood Lipid Responses to Plant Stanol Ester Supplementation and Aerobic Exercise Training. *Metabolism* 55: 541–549.
3. Janssen, I., P. T. Katzmarzyk, R. Ross, A. S. Leon, J. S. Skinner, D. C. Rao, J. H. Wilmore, T. Rankinen, and C. Bouchard. 2004. Fitness Alters the Associations of BMI and Waist Circumference with Total and Abdominal Fat. *Obesity* 12: 525–537.
4. O'Donovan, G., E. M. Kearney, A. M. Nevill, K. Woolf-May, and S. R. Bird. 2005. The Effects of 24 Weeks of Moderate- or High-Intensity Exercise on Insulin Resistance. *European Journal of Applied Physiology* 95: 522–528.
5. Kato, T., T. Terashima, T. Yamashita, Y. Hatanaka, A. Honda, and Y. Umemura. 2006. Effect of Low-Repetition Jump Training on Bone Mineral Density in Young Women. *Journal of Applied Physiology* 100: 839–843; Daly, R. M., D. W. Dunstan, N. Owen, D. Jolley, J. E. Shaw, and P. Z. Zimmet. 2005. Does High-Intensity Resistance Training Maintain Bone Mass during Moderate Weight Loss in Older Overweight Adults with Type 2 Diabetes? *Osteoporosis International* 16: 1703–1712; Yung, P. S., Y. M. Lai, P. Y. Tung, H. T. Tsui, C. K. Wong, V. W. Hung, and L. Qin. 2005. Effects of Weight Bearing and Nonweight Bearing Exercises on Bone Properties Using Calcaneal Quantitative Ultrasound. *British Journal of Sports Medicine* 39: 547–551.
6. Karacabey, K., O. Saygin, R. Ozmerdivenli, E. Zorba, A. Godekmerdan, and V. Bulut. 2005. The Effects of Exercise on the Immune System and Stress Hormones in Sportswomen. *Neuroendocrinology Letters* 26: 361–366.
7. Tworoger, S. S., Y. Yasui, M. V. Vitiello, R. S. Schwartz, C. M. Ulrich, E. J. Aiello, M. L. Irwin, D. Bowen, J. D. Potter, and A. McTiernan. 2003. Effects of a Yearlong Moderate-Intensity Exercise and a Stretching Intervention on Sleep Quality in Postmenopausal Women. *Sleep* 26: 830–836.
8. Centers for Disease Control and Prevention. 2003. Prevalence of Physical Activity, Including Lifestyle Activities among Adults—United States, 2000–2001. *Morbidity and Mortality Weekly Report* 52: 768–769.

Feature Box References

1. Centers for Disease Control and Prevention. 2008. Yoga Activity Card. *Body and Mind: Physical Activity*. www.bam.gov/sub_physicalactivity/activitycards_yoga.html (accessed December 2008).
2. National Center for Complementary and Alternative Medicine. May 2008. Yoga for Health: An Introduction. http://nccam.nih.gov/health/yoga/yoga.htm (accessed December 2008).
3. Ibid.

Concept 25

1. Coyle, E. F., A. R. Coggan, M. K. Hemmert, and J. L. Ivy. 1986. Muscle Glycogen Utilization during Prolonged Strenuous Exercise When Fed Carbohydrate. *Journal of Applied Physiology* 61: 165–172; Hargreaves, M. 2004. Muscle Glycogen and Metabolic Regulation. *Proceedings of the Nutrition Society* 63: 217–220.
2. Costill, D., R. Thomas, R. Robergs, D. Pascoe, C. Lambert, S. Barr, and W. Fink. 1991. Adaptations to Swimming Training: Influence of Training Volume. *Medicine & Science in Sports & Exercise* 23: 371–377; Sherman W., M. Peden, and D. Wright. 1991. Carbohydrate Feedings 1 Hour before Exercise Improves Cycling Performance. *American Journal of Clinical Nutrition* 54: 866–870.
3. Brooks, G. 2002. Lactate Shuttles in Nature. *Biochemical Society Transactions* 30: 258–264.
4. Romijn, J. A., E. F. Coyle, L. S. Sidossis, A. Gastaldelli, J. F. Horowitz, E. Endert, and R. R. Wolfe. 1993. Regulation of Endogenous Fat and Carbohydrate Metabolism in Relation to Exercise Intensity and Duration. *American Journal of Physiology—Endocrinology and Metabolism* 265: E380–E391.
5. Rosenbloom, C., ed. 2000. *Sports Nutrition: A Guide for the Professional Working with Active People.* 3rd ed. Chicago: The American Dietetic Association, 16.
6. Tarnopolsky, M. A., S. A. Atkinson, S. M. Phillips, and J. D. MacDougall. 1995. Carbohydrate Loading and Metabolism during Exercise in Men and Women. *Journal of Applied Physiology* 78: 1360–1368.
7. American College of Sports Medicine, American Dietetic Association, and Dietitians of Canada. 2000. Nutrition and Athletic Performance Joint Position Statement. *Medicine & Science in Sports & Exercise* 32: 2130–2145.
8. Ibid.
9. Brownell, K. D., S. N. Steen, and J. H. Wilmore. 1987. Weight Regulation Practices in Athletes: Analysis of Metabolic and Health Effects. *Medicine & Science in Sports & Exercise* 19: 546–556; Horvath, P. J., C. K. Eagen, S. D. Ryer-Calvin, and D. R. Pendergast. 2000. The Effects of Varying Dietary Fat on the Nutrient Intake in Male and Female Runners. *Journal of the American College of Nutrition* 19: 42–51.
10. American College of Sports Medicine, American Dietetic Association, and Dietitians of Canada. Nutrition and Athletic Performance Joint Position Statement.
11. Yaspelkis, B. B., J. G. Patterson, P. A. Anderla, Z. Ding, and J. L. Ivy. 1993. Carbohydrate Supplementation Spares Muscle Glycogen during Variable-Intensity Exercise. *Journal of Applied Physiology* 75: 1477–1485; Coyle, E. F., J. M. Hagberg, B. F. Hurley, W. H. Martin, A. A. Ehsani, and J. O. Holloszy. 1983. Carbohydrate Feeding during Prolonged Strenuous Exercise Can Delay Fatigue. *Journal of Applied Physiology* 55: 230–235.

12. Miller, S. L., K. D. Tipton, D. L. Chinkes, S. E. Wolf, and R. R. Wolfe. 2003. Independent and Combined Effects of Amino Acids and Glucose after Resistance Exercise. *Medicine & Science in Sports & Exercise* 35: 449–455.
13. Koopman, R., D. L. Pannemans, A. E. Jeukendrup, A. P. Gijsen, J. M. Senden, D. Halliday, W. H. Saris, L. J. van Loon, and A. J. Wagenmakers. 2004. Combined Ingestion of Protein and Carbohydrate Improves Protein Balance during Ultra-Endurance Exercise. *American Journal of Physiology—Endocrinology and Metabolism* 287: E712–E720.
14. Ivy, J. L., A. L. Katz, C. L. Cutler, W. M. Sherman, and E. F. Coyle. 1988. Muscle Glycogen Synthesis after Exercise: Effect of Time of Carbohydrate Ingestion. *Journal of Applied Physiology* 64: 1480–1485.
15. Roy, B. D., M. A. Tarnopolsky, J. D. MacDougall, J. Fowles, and K. E. Yarasheski. 1997. Effect of Glucose Supplement Timing on Protein Metabolism after Resistance Training. *Journal of Applied Physiology* 82: 1882–1888.
16. Rasmussen, B. B., K. D. Tipton, S. L. Miller, S. E. Wolf, and R. R. Wolfe. 2000. An Oral Essential Amino Acid-Carbohydrate Supplement Enhances Muscle Protein Anabolism after Resistance Exercise. *Journal of Applied Physiology* 88: 386–392; Zawadzki, K. M., B. B. Yaspelkis, and J. L. Ivy. 1992. Carbohydrate-Protein Complex Increases the Rate of Muscle Glycogen Storage after Exercise. *Journal of Applied Physiology* 72: 1854–1859.
17. Zawadzki. Carbohydrate-Protein Complex; Ivy, J. L., H. W. Goforth, B. M. Damon, T. R. McCauley, E. C. Parsons, and T. B. Price. 2002. Early Postexercise Muscle Glycogen Recovery Is Enhanced with a Carbohydrate-Protein Supplement. *Journal of Applied Physiology* 93: 1337–1344.
18. Karp, J. R., J. D. Johnston, S. Tecklenburg, T. D. Mickleborough, A. D. Fly, and J. M. Stager. 2006. Chocolate Milk as a Post-Exercise Recovery Aid. *International Journal of Sport Nutrition and Exercise Metabolism* 16: 78–91.
19. Krumbach, C. J., D. R. Ellis, and J. A. Driskell. 1999. A Report of Vitamin and Mineral Supplement Use among University Athletes in a Division I Institution. *International Journal of Sport Nutrition and Exercise Metabolism* 9: 416–425; Herbold, N. H., B. K. Visconti, S. Frates, and L. Bandini. 2004. Traditional and Nontraditional Supplement Use by Collegiate Female Varsity Athletes. *International Journal of Sport Nutrition and Exercise Metabolism* 14: 586–593.
20. Singh, A., F. M. Moses, and P. A. Deuster. 1992. Chronic Multivitamin-Mineral Supplementation Does Not Enhance Physical Performance. *Medicine & Science in Sports & Exercise* 24: 726–732.
21. Dubnov, G., and N. W. Constantini. 2004. Prevalence of Iron Depletion and Anemia in Top-Level Basketball Players. *International Journal of Sport Nutrition and Exercise Metabolism* 14: 30–37.
22. Klesges, R. C., K. D. Ward, M. L. Shelton, W. B. Applegate, E. D. Cantler, G. M. Palmieri, K. Harmon, and J. Davis. 1996. Changes in Bone Mineral Content in Male Athletes: Mechanisms of Action and Intervention Effects. *Journal of the American Medical Association* 276: 226–230.
23. Rosenbloom. *Sports Nutrition*, 102–104.
24. Wilk, B., and O. Bar-Or. 1996. Effect of Drink Flavor and NaCl on Voluntary Drinking and Hydration in Boys Exercising in the Heat. *Journal of Applied Physiology* 80: 1112–1117.
25. American College of Sports Medicine. 1996. Position Stand on Exercise and Fluid Replacement. *Medicine and Science in Sports and Exercise* 28: i–vii.
26. McGee, W. 2005. Caffeine in the Diet. National Institutes of Health Medline Plus Medical Encyclopedia. www.nlm.nih.gov/medlineplus/ency/article/002445.htm.
27. USA Track & Field. Press Release, April 19, 2003. USATF Announces Major Change in Hydration Guidelines. www.usatf.org/news/showRelease.asp?article=/news/releases/2003-04-19-2.xml.

Concept 26

1. Office of Dietary Supplements. What Dietary Supplements Are You Taking? http://ods.od.nih.gov/pubs/partnersbrochure.asp (accessed December 2008).
2. Hunt, J., and J. Dwyer. 2001. Position of the American Dietetic Association: Food Fortification and Dietary Supplements. *Journal of the American Dietetic Association* 101: 115–125.
3. Food and Drug Administration. 2004. FDA Announces Major Initiatives for Dietary Supplements. www.cfsan.fda.gov/~lrd/fpsupp.html (accessed March 2005); Center for Food Safety and Applied Nutrition. 2002. Overview of Dietary Supplements. www.cfsan.fda.gov/~dms/supplmnt.html (accessed March 2005); National Center for Complementary and Alternative Medicine. 2004. What's in the Bottle? An Introduction to Dietary Supplements. http://nccam.nih.gov/health/supplements.htm (accessed March 2005).
4. United States Pharmacopoeia. USP's Dietary Supplement Verification Program. www.uspverified.org/index.html (accessed March 2005).
5. Food and Drug Administration. 2002. Tips for the Savvy Supplement User: Making Informed Decisions. FDA Consumer Magazine. Available at www.fda.gov/fdac/features/2002/202_supp.html. (accessed December 2008.
6. Greenhaff, P. L., A. Casey, A. H. Short, R. Harris, K. Söderlund, and E. Hultman. 1993. Influence of Oral Creatine Supplementation on Muscle Torque during Repeated Bouts of Maximal Voluntary Exercise in Man. *Clinical Science* 84: 565–571.
7. Vandenberghe, K., M. Goris, P. Van Hecke, M. Van Leemputte, L. Vangerven, and P. Hespel. 1997. Long-Term Creatine Intake Is Beneficial to Muscle Performance during Resistance Training. *Journal of Applied Physiology* 83: 2055–2063; Kreider, R. B., M. Ferreira, M. Wilson, P. Grindstaff, S. Plisk, J. Reinardy, E. Cantler, and A. L. Almada. 1998. Effects of Creatine Supplementation on Body Composition, Strength, and Sprint Performance. *Medicine & Science in Sports & Exercise* 30(1): 73–82.
8. Mayhew, D. L., J. L. Mayhew, and J. S. Ware. 2002. Effects of Long-Term Creatine Supplementation on Liver and Kidney Functions in American College Football Players. *International Journal of Sport Nutrition and Exercise Metabolism* 12: 453–460; Kreider, R. B., C. Melton, C. J. Rasmussen, M. Greenwood, S. Lancaster, E. C. Cantler, P. Milnor, and A. L. Almada. 2003. Long-Term Creatine Supplementation Does Not Significantly Affect Clinical Markers of Health in Athletes. *Molecular and Cellular Biochemistry* 244: 95–104.
9. Pritchard, N. R., and P. A. Kalra. 1998. Renal Dysfunction Accompanying Oral Creatine Supplements. *The Lancet* 351: 1252–1253; Greenhaff, P. 1998. Renal Dysfunction Accompanying Oral Creatine Supplements. *The Lancet* 352: 233–234.
10. Wiles, J. D., S. R. Bird, J. Hopkins, and M. Riley. 1992. Effect of Caffeinated Coffee on Running Speed, Respiratory Factors, Blood Lactate and Perceived Exertion during 1500 M Treadmill Running. *British Journal of Sports Medicine* 26:116–120; Spriet, L. L., D. A. MacLean, D. J. Dyck, E. Hultman, G. Cederblad, and T. E. Graham. 1992. Caffeine Ingestion and Muscle Metabolism during Prolonged Exercise in Humans. *American Journal of Physiology—Endocrinology and Metabolism* 262: E891–E898.
11. Paton, C. D., W. G. Hopkins, and L. Vollebregt. 2001. Little Effect of Caffeine Ingestion on Repeated Sprints in Team-Sport Athletes. *Medicine & Science in Sports & Exercise* 33: 822–825.
12. Crist, D. M., G. T. Peake, P. A. Egan, and D. L. Waters. 1988. Body Composition Responses to Exogenous GH during Training in Highly Conditioned Adults. *Journal of Applied Physiology* 65: 579–584; Foss, M., and S. Keteyian. 1998. *Physiological Basis for Exercise and Sport.* 6th ed. New York: McGraw-Hill, 498.
13. Deyssig, R., H. Frisch, W. Blum, and T. Waldorf. 1993. Effect of Growth Hormone Treatment on Hormonal Parameters, Body Composition, and Strength in Athletes. *Acta Endocrinologica* 128: 313–318; Lange, K., J. Andersen, N. Beyer, F. Isaksson, B. Larsson, M. Rasmussen, A. Juul, J. Bülow, and M. Kjær. 2002. GH Administration Changes Myosin Heavy Chain Isoforms in Skeletal Muscle but Does Not Augment Muscle Strength or Hypertrophy, Either Alone or Combined with Resistance Exercise Training in Healthy Elderly Men. *Journal of Clinical Endocrinology & Metabolism* 87: 513–523.
14. Woodhouse, L. J., S. L. Asa, S. G. Thomas, and S. Ezzat. 1999. Measures of Submaximal Aerobic Performance Evaluate and Predict Functional Response to Growth Hormone (GH) Treatment in GH-Deficient Adults. *Journal of Clinical Endocrinology and Metabolism* 84: 4570–4577.
15. Ekblom, B., and B. Berglund. 1991. Effect of Erythropoietin Administration on Maximal Aerobic Power. *Scandinavian Journal of Medicine and Science in Sports* 1: 88–93.
16. Hasler, C. M., A. S. Bloch, C. A. Thomson, E. Enrione, and C. Manning. 2004. Position of the American Dietetic Association: Functional Foods. *Journal of the American Dietetic Association* 104: 814–826. The International Food Information Council. 2004. Background on Functional Foods. www.ific.org (accessed June 2005).
17. Palmer, S. 2008 The American Dietetic Association, Hot Topics: Functional Beverages. www.eatright.org.
18. Hasler, C. M. 2002. Functional Foods: Benefits, Concerns and Challenges: A Position Paper from the American Council on Science and Health. *Journal of Nutrition* 132: 3772–3781; International Food Information Council. 2002. The Consumer View on Functional Foods: Yesterday and Today. Food Insight. www.ific.org/foodinsight/2002/mj/funcfdsfi302.cfm?renderforprint=1 (accessed June 2005); International Food Information Council. 2002. Functional Foods: Attitudinal Research. www.ific.org/research/funcfoodsres02.cfm?renderforprint=1 (accessed June 2005).

19. Clydesdale, F. 2004. Functional Foods: Opportunities and Challenges. IFT Expert Panel Report, Executive Summary. www.ift.org/pdfs/expert/ff/Executive-Summary.pdf (accessed June 2005); Hasler, C. M. 2000. The Changing Face of Functional Foods. *Journal of the American College of Nutrition* 19: 499S–506S.
20. Douglas, L. C., and Sanders, M. E. 2008. Probiotics and Prebiotics in Dietetics Practice. *Journal of the American Dietetic Association* 108: 510–521.
21. Hasler. Position of the American Dietetic Association.
22. Institute of Food Technologists. 2005. Expert Report on Functional Foods: Opportunities and Challenges, Executive Summary. www.ift.org/cms/?pid=1001247 (accessed June 2005).

Feature Box References

1. American Cancer Society. 2007. Dietary Supplements: How to Know What Is Safe. www.cancer.org (accessed in December 2008).
2. National Center for Complementary and Alternative Medicine. December 2006. Herbal Supplements: Consider Safety, Too. http://nccam.nih.gov/health/supplement-safety/D190.pdf (accessed December 2008).
3. Ibid.

Concept 27

1. Centers for Disease Control Division of Bacterial and Mycotic Diseases. 2002. Updated 2003. Foodborne Illness: General Information. www.cdc.gov/ncidod/dbmd/diseaseinfo/foodborneinfections_g.htm (accessed October 2003).
2. Centers for Disease Control and Prevention. 1999. Safer and Healthier Foods: 1900–1999. *Journal of the American Medical Association* 48: 905–913; Young, J. H. 1981. Updated 1999. The Long Struggle for the 1906 Law. *FDA Consumer Magazine.* www.cfsan.fda.gov/~lrd/history2.html (accessed December 2006).
3. Young. The Long Struggle for the 1906 Law.
4. Food Safety and Inspection Service. 1999. Origins of the Federal Food Safety System. *Food Safety Educator* 4: 3–4. www.fsis.usda.gov/News_&_Events/food_safety_educator/index.asp (accessed December 2006).
5. Centers for Disease Control and Prevention. Safer and Healthier Foods.
6. Center for Food Safety and Applied Nutrition. Updated 2002. Food Safety A to Z Reference Guide: Virus. www.cfsan.fda.gov/~dms/a2z-uvw.html#virus (accessed December 2006).
7. Centers for Disease Control. September 9, 2003. Public Health Dispatch: Multistate Outbreak of Hepatitis A among Young Adult Concert Attendees, United States, 2003. *Morbidity and Mortality Weekly Report* 52: 844–845. www.cdc.gov/mmwr/preview/mmwrhtml/mm5235a5.htm (accessed December 2006).
8. Food Safety and Inspection Service. 2001. Parasites and Foodborne Illness. www.fsis.usda.gov/Fact_Sheets/Parasites_and_Foodborne_Illness/index.asp (accessed December 2006).
9. Gerald, B. J., and J. E. Perkin. 2003. Position of the American Dietetic Association: Food and Water Safety. *Journal of the American Dietetic Association* 103: 1203–1218.
10. Gerald. Position of the American Dietetic Association: Food and Water Safety.
11. Ibid.
12. Center for Food Safety and Applied Nutrition. Updated 2002. Food Safety A to Z Reference Guide: Handwashing. www.cfsan.fda.gov/~dms/a2z-h.html (accessed December 2006).
13. Agriculture Research Service, Food Safety and Inspection Service. 1998. Premature Browning of Cooked Ground Beef. www.fsis.usda.gov/OPHS/prebrown.htm (accessed December 2006).
14. Food Safety and Inspection Service. Updated 2006. How Temperatures Affect Food. www.fsis.usda.gov/Fact_Sheets/How_Temperatures_Affect_Food/index.asp (accessed December 2006).
15. Ibid.
16. Food and Drug Administration and U.S. Department of Agriculture. 2000. A Description of the US Food Safety System. www.fsis.usda.gov/OA/codex/system.htm (accessed December 2006).
17. Food Safety and Inspection Service. 2003. Enhancing Public Health: Strategies for the Future—2003 FSIS Food Safety Vision. www.fsis.usda.gov/oa/programs/vision071003.htm (accessed December 2006).
18. Center for Food Safety and Applied Nutrition. 1998. Updated 2001. What Consumers Need to Know about Juice Safety. www.cfsan.fda.gov/~dms/juicsafe.html (accessed December 2006).
19. Center for Food Safety and Applied Nutrition. 2001. Analysis and Evaluation of Preventive Control Measures for the Control and Reduction/Elimination of Microbial Hazards on Fresh and Fresh-Cut Produce. www.cfsan.fda.gov/~comm/ift3-toc.html (accessed November 2006).
20. Finley, J., D. Deming, and R. Smith. 2006. Food Processing: Nutrition, Safety, and Quality. In M. E. Shils, M. Shike, A. C. Ross, B. Caballero, and R. J. Cousins, eds. *Modern Nutrition in Health and Disease.* 10th ed. Philadelphia: Lippincott Williams and Wilkins.
21. Tauxe, R. B. Food Safety and Irradiation; Emmert, K., V. Duffy, and R. Earl. 2000. Position of the American Dietetic Association: Food Irradiation. Journal of the American Dietetic Association 100: 246–253.
22. Tauxe, R. B. Food Safety and Irradiation; Food and Drug Administration. 2000. Food Irradiation: A Safe Measure. www.fda.gov/opacom/catalog/irradbro.html (accessed December 2006).
23. Ibid.
24. Food and Drug Administration. Food Irradiation.
25. Tauxe, R. B. Food Safety and Irradiation; Emmert. Position of the American Dietetic Association: Food Irradiation.
26. Lewis, C. 2002. Food Freshness and "Smart" Packaging. *FDA Consumer Magazine.* www.fda.gov/fdac/features/2002/502_food.html (accessed November 2006).
27. Food Safety and Inspection Service. Updated 2006. Focus On: Food Product Dating. www.fsis.usda.gov/Fact_Sheets/Food_Product_Dating/index.asp (accessed December 2006).
28. Center for Food Safety and Applied Nutrition. 2001. Food Additives. www.cfsan.fda.gov/~lrd/foodaddi.html (accessed December 2006).
29. Ibid.
30. Rados, C. 2004. GRAS: Time-Tested and Trusted Food Ingredients. *FDA Consumer Magazine.* www.fda.gov/fdac/features/2004/204_gras.html (accessed December 2006).
31. Center for Food Safety and Applied Nutrition. Food Additives.
32. Rados. GRAS.
33. Rados. GRAS; Centers for Disease Control and Prevention. 1998. Ciguatera Fish Poisoning: Texas 1997. *Morbidity and Mortality Weekly Report.* www.cdc.gov/mmwr/preview/mmwrhtml/00054548.htm (accessed December 2006).
34. U.S. Environmental Protection Agency. Updated 2003. Polychlorinated Biphenyls (PCBs). www.epa.gov/opptintr/pcb/ (accessed December 2006).
35. U.S. Environmental Protection Agency. Polychlorinated Biphenyls (PCBs).
36. Persistent Bioaccumulative and Toxic (PBT) Chemical Program. Updated 2006. Polychlorinated Biphenyls (PCBs). www.epa.gov/pbt/pubs/pcbs.htm (accessed December 2006).
37. Ibid.
38. Center for Veterinary Medicine. 2002. The Use of Steroid Hormones for Growth Promotion in Food-Producing Animals. www.fda.gov/cvm/hormones.htm (accessed December 2006).
39. Ibid.
40. Centers for Disease Control and Prevention. 2005. Frequently Asked Questions about NARMS. www.cdc.gov/narms/faq_antiresis.htm (accessed November 2006).
41. U.S. Environmental Protection Agency. Updated 2003. About Pesticides: What Is a Pesticide? www.epa.gov/pesticides/about/index.htm#what_pesticide (accessed December 2006).
42. Ibid.
43. Ibid.
44. U.S. Environmental Protection Agency. 2006. Organophosphate Pesticides (OP) Cumulative Assessment: 2006 Update. www.epa.gov/pesticides/cumulative/2006-op/index.htm (accessed November 2006).
45. U.S. Environmental Protection Agency. About Pesticides.
46. U.S. Environmental Protection Agency. Updated 2006. Pesticides: Regulating Pesticides—Potassium Bicarbonate (073508) and Sodium Bicarbonate (073505). www.epa.gov/pesticides/biopesticides/ingredients/factsheets/factsheet_073508.htm (accessed December 2006).
47. U.S. Environmental Protection Agency. About Pesticides.
48. U.S. Environmental Protection Agency, Pesticides and Safety. Updated 2006. Health Problems Pesticides May Pose. www.epa.gov/pesticides/food/risks.htm (accessed December 2006).
49. U.S. Environmental Protection Agency, Pesticides and Safety. Updated 2006. Health Problems Pesticides May Pose. Available at www.epa.gov/pesticides/food/risks.htm. Accessed December 2006. Office of Disease Prevention and Health Promotion. 2000. *Healthy People 2010.* Available at www.healthypeople.gov/document/HTML/Volume1/08Environmental.htm. Accessed December 2006.
50. U.S. Environmental Protection Agency. Updated 2006. Pesticides: Regulating Pesticides—Laws. www.epa.gov/pesticides/regulating/laws.htm (accessed December 2006).
51. U.S. Environmental Protection Agency. Updated 2006. Pesticides and Food: How the Government Regulates Pesticides. www.epa.gov/pesticides/food/govt.htm (accessed December 2006); U.S. Environmental Protection Agency. Pesticides: Regulating Pesticides—Laws.

52. Krieger, R. I., P. Brutsche-Keiper, H. R. Crosby, and A. D. Krieger. 2003. Reduction of Pesticide Residues of Fruit Using Water Only or Plus Fit Fruit and Vegetable Wash. *Bulletin of Environmental Contamination and Toxicology* 70: 213–218.
53. American Cancer Society. 2000. The Environment and Cancer Risk. www.cancer.org/docroot/NWS/content/NWS_2_1x_The_Environment_and_Cancer_Risk.asp (accessed December 2006).
54. National Organic Program. 2002. Organic Food Standards and Labels: The Facts. www.ams.usda.gov/nop/Consumers/Consumerhome.html (accessed December 2006).
55. The Organic Industry. Organic Trade Association's 2007 Manufacturer Survey. www.ota.com (accessed January 2009); Organic Trade Association. 2005. The Past, Present and Future of the Organic Industry: A Retrospective of the First 20 Years, a Look at the Current State of the Organic Industry and Forecasting the Next 20 Years. www.ota.com/pics/documents/Forecasting2005.pdf (accessed November 2006).
56. Agricultural Marketing Service, National Organic Program. Organic Food Standards.
57. Agency for Toxic Substances and Disease Registry. ToxFAQ for Polychlorinated Biphenyls (PCBs).
58. National Organic Program. Organic Food Standards; Dangour, A. D., Dodhia, S. K., Hayter, A., Allen, E., Lock, E., and Uauy, R. 2009. Nutritional quality of organic foods: a systematic review. *American Journal of Clinical Nutrition,* doi:10.3945/ajcn.2009.28041
59. Organic Trade Association. The Past, Present and Future of the Organic Industry.
60. McCullum, C. 2000. Food Biotechnology in the New Millennium: Promises, Realities, and Challenges. *Journal of the American Dietetic Association* 100: 1311–1315; Bren, L. 2003. Genetic Engineering: The Future of Foods. *FDA Consumer Magazine.* www.fda.gov/fdac/features/2003/603_food.html (accessed March 2004).
61. McCullum. Food Biotechnology.
62. Gregar, J. L. 2000. Biotechnology; Mobilizing Dietitians to Be a Resource. *Journal of the American Dietetic Association* 100: 1306–1308.
63. Thompson. Are Bioengineered Foods Safe?
64. McCullum. Food Biotechnology.
65. Gregar. Biotechnology.
66. American Dietetic Association. 1995. Biotechnology and the Future of Food. *Journal of the American Dietetic Association* 95: 1429–1432.
67. Ibid.
68. Shoemaker, R., D. D. Johnson, and E. Golan. 2003. Consumers and the Future of Biotech Foods in the United States. Amber Waves. Available at www.ers.usda.gov/Amberwaves/November03/Features/futureofbiotech.htm. (accessed December 2006).
69. U.S. Department of Agriculture. 2007. Q&A: Bt Corn and Monarch Butterflies. www.ars.usda.gov/is/br/btcorn/index.html?pf=1 (accessed February 2007).
70. U.S. Department of Agriculture. Q&A; Jones, L. 1999. Genetically Modified Foods. *British Medical Journal* 318: 581–584.
71. Thompson. Are Bioengineered Foods Safe?; Maryanski, J. H. 1997. Bioengineered Foods: Will They Cause Allergic Reactions? www.cfsan.fda.gov/~dms/pubalrgy.html (accessed December 2006); American Medical Association. 2005. Report 10 of the Council on Scientific Affairs (I-94). Genetically Modified Crops and Foods. www.ama-assn.org/ama/pub/category/13595.html (accessed December 2006).
72. Thompson. Are Bioengineered Foods Safe?
73. Formanek, R. 2001. Proposed Rules Issued for Bioengineered Foods. *FDA Consumer Magazine.* www.cfsan.fda.gov/~dms/fdbioen2.html (accessed March 2004).
74. Thompson. Are Bioengineered Foods Safe?
75. International Food Information Council. 2006. Support for Food Biotechnology Stable Despite News on Unrelated Food Safety Issues. www.ific.org/research/biotechres03.cfm (accessed December 2006).
76. Bruemmer, B. 2003. Food Biosecurity. *Journal of the American Dietetic Association* 203: 687–691.
77. Centers for Disease Control and Prevention. 2003. Food Safety Threats. www.bt.cdc.gov/agent/food/index.asp (accessed December 2006).
78. Meadows, M. 2004. The FDA and the Fight against Terrorism. *FDA Consumer Magazine.* www.fda.gov/fdac/features/2004/104_terror.html (accessed December 2006).

Feature Box References

1. Centers for Disease Control and Prevention. 2002. Probable Variant Creutzfeldt-Jakob Disease in a U.S. Resident—Florida, 2002. *Morbidity and Mortality Weekly Report.* www.cdc.gov/mmwr/preview/mmwrhtml/mm5141a3.htm (accessed December 2006).
2. Animal and Plant Health Inspection Service. 2003. Bovine Spongiform Encephalopathy (BSE) Q & As. www.aphis.usda.gov/lpa/issues/bse/bse_trade.html (accessed December 2006).
3. Animal and Plant Health Inspection Service. Bovine Spongiform Encephalopathy; U.S. Department of Health and Human Services. 2001. Federal Agencies Take Special Precautions to Keep "Mad Cow Disease" Out of the United States. Available at www.hhs.gov/news/press/2001pres/01fsbse.html. Accessed December 2006; Centers for Disease Control and Prevention. 2003. Questions and Answers Regarding Bovine Spongiform Encephalopathy (BSE) and Creutzfeldt-Jakob Disease (CJD) www.cdc.gov/ncidod/dvrd/bse/ (accessed December 2006).
4. U.S. Department of Agriculture. 2004. Hot Issues: BSE. www.aphis.usda.gov/lpa/issues/bse/bse.html (accessed December 2006).
5. U.S. Department of Health and Human Services. 2001. HHS Launches Expanded Plan to Combat "Mad Cow Disease." www.hhs.gov/news/press/2001pres/20010823.html (accessed December 2006).
6. U.S. Department of Agriculture. Hot Issues.

Concept 28

1. Nord, M., M. Andrews, and S. Carlson. 2008. Household Food Security in the United States, 2007. United States Department of Agriculture (USDA), Economic Research Report No. (ERR-66), November 2008. www.ers.usda.gov/Publications/ERR66/ (accessed January 2009).
2. Ibid.
3. Ibid.
4. Food and Agriculture Organization of the United Nations. 2008. The State of Food Insecurity in the World 2008. www.fao.org (accessed January 2009).
5. Food and Agriculture Organization of the United Nations. 2004. Undernourished Population (2002–2004). www.fao.org.es.ess.faostat/foodsecurity/FS%20Map/map14.htm (accessed January 2009).
6. Hunger in the United States. 2007. Food Research and Action Center (ERAC). www.frac.org/html/hunger_in_the_us/poverty.html (accessed January 2009).
7. USDA Food Security in the United States: Key Statistics and Graphics. Updated 2008. http://www.ers.usda.gov/Briefing/FoodSecurity/stats_graphs.htm#food_insecurity (accessed January 2009).
8. United Nations Association of the United States of America and the Business Council for the United Nations. 2006. Millennium Development Goals—Goal 3: Gender Equity. www.unausa.org (accessed March 2006).
9. Ibid.
10. U.S. Department of Health and Human Services. 2006. 2006 HHS Poverty Guidelines. *Federal Register* 71: 3848–3849. http://aspe.hhs.gov/poverty/06poverty.shtml.
11. Smith, L. C., and L. Haddad. 2000. *Explaining Child Malnutrition in Developing Countries: A Cross-Country Analysis of International Food Policy.* Washington, D.C.: International Food Policy Research Institute.
12. United Nations Association of the United States of America and the Business Council for the United Nations. Millennium Development Goals.
13. Department of Foreign Affairs and International Trade, Canada. 2002. Protecting Children from Sanctions. www.epals.com/waraffectedchildren/chap11 (accessed March 2006).
14. United States Census. Historical Poverty Tables.
15. ADA Reports: Position of the American Dietetic Association. Addressing World Hunger.
16. Food and Agriculture Organization. 2005. *The State of Food Insecurity in the World, 2005.* Rome: Food and Agriculture Organization of the United Nations.
17. Agriculture and Agri-Food Canada. 1997. The Pros and Cons of Pesticides. www.ns.ec.gc.ca/epb/factsheets/pesticides/pro_con.html (accessed March 2006).
18. ADA Reports. Position of the American Dietetic Association.
19. Food and Agriculture Organization. *The State of Food Insecurity in the World, 2003.*
20. Bread for the World Institute. Hunger Basics; Rosegrant, M. W., and M. A. Sombilia. 1997. Critical Issues Suggested by Trends in Food, Population, and the Environment for the Year 2020. *American Journal of Agricultural Economics* 79: 1467–1471; Brown, L. R., G. Gardner, and B. Halweil. 1999. 16 Impacts of Population Growth. *Futurist* 33: 36–41.
21. World Health Organization. 2002. *The Optimal Duration of Exclusive Breast-Feeding: A Systematic Review.* Geneva, Switzerland: World Health Organization.
22. King, F. S., and A. Burgess. 1993. *Nutrition for Developing Countries.* 2nd ed. Oxford, England: Oxford Medical Publications, Oxford University Press.

23. ADA Reports. Position of the American Dietetic Association.
24. Beers, M., R. Porter, T. Jones, J. Kaplan, and M. Berkwits, eds. 2006. Starvation. In *The Merck Manual of Diagnosis and Therapy, Section 1—Nutritional Disorders, Chapter 2: Malnutrition Topics*. www.merck.com/mrkshared/mmanual/section1/chapter2/2b.jsp (accessed April 2006).
25. U.S. Department of Labor, Bureau of Labor Statistics. 2003. A Profile of the Working Poor. www.bls.gov/cps/cpswp2000.htm (accessed December 2006).
26. Beers, M., R. Porter, T. Jones, J. Kaplan, and M. Berkwits, eds. 2006. Starvation. In *The Merck Manual of Diagnosis and Therapy, Section 1—Nutritional Disorders, Chapter 2: Malnutrition Topics*. www.merck.com/mrkshared/mmanual/section1/chapter2/2b.jsp (accessed April 2006).
27. SUSTAIN. 2002. Malnutrition Overview. www.sustaintech.org/world.htm (accessed March 2006).
28. Kleinman, R. E., et al. 1998. Hunger in Children in the United States: Potential Behavioral and Emotional Correlates. *Pediatrics* 101: 3–10.
29. Martorell, R., J. Rivera, and H. Kaplowitz. 1992. Consequences of Stunting in Early Childhood for Adult Body Size in Rural Guatemala. *Annales Nestle* 48: 85–92; Martorell, R., J. Rivera, H. Kaplowitz, and E. Pollit. 1992. *Proceedings of the VIth International Congress of Auxiology. Long-Term Consequences of Growth Retardation during Early Childhood*. New York: Elsevier Science.
30. U.S. Department of Health and Human Services. 2006 HHS Poverty Guidelines; United Nations Administrative Committee on Coordination Sub-Committee on Nutrition. 2000. *Fourth Report on the World Situation*. Geneva, Switzerland: ACC/SCN in collaboration with the International Food Policy Research Institute.
31. SUSTAIN. Malnutrition Overview; King. *Nutrition for Developing Countries*; Bread for the World Institute. Hunger Report 2004.
32. U.S. Department of Health and Human Services. 2006 HHS Poverty Guidelines.
33. Black, R. E., L. H. Allen, Z. A. Bhutta, et al. 2008. Maternal and Child Undernutrition: Global and Regional Exposures and Health Consequences. *The Lancet*. 371 (January 19, 2008): 243–260.
34. UNICEF Statistics. 2006. Integrated Management of Childhood Illness (IMCI). www.childinfo.org/eddb/imci/index.htm (accessed April 2006).
35. UNESCO (United Nations Educational, Scientific and Cultural Organization) Ten Population Myths: Exposing the Myths. www.unesco.org (accessed April 2006). Adapted from Lappe, F., and J. Collins. 1998. *World Hunger: Twelve Myths*. 2nd ed. New York: Grove Press.
36. Ibid.
37. UNICEF. Water, Environment, and Sanitation. 2005 Proceedings. www.unicef.org/wes (accessed April 2006).
38. BBC News, Africa. 2006. Using the Sun to Sterilize Water. http://news.bbc.co.uk/2/hi/africa/4786216.stm (accessed April 2006).
39. Ibid.
40. UNICEF Nutrition Section. 1996. 18 Nations Fortify Foods. www.unicef.org/pon96/nufortif.htm (accessed April 2006); Global Alliance for Improved Nutrition. 1996. Why Food Fortification? www.gainhealth.org (accessed January 2007).
41. Bergeson, T. 2006. *Agriculture and Science*. Office of Washington Superintendent of Public Instruction, Career, and Technical Education Pathways. Agriculture and Science. www.k12.wa.us/CareerTechEd/pathways/Agriculture/default/aspx (accessed April 2006); Silent Killer Film. 2005. The Unfinished Campaign against Hunger. www.silentkillerfilm.org (accessed April 2006).
42. Cleland, J. G., and J. K. Van Ginneken. 1988. Maternal Education and Child Survival in Developing Countries: The Search for Pathways of Influence. *Social Science and Medicine* 27: 1357–1368.

Feature Box References

1. Food and Agriculture Organization. 2000. *The State of Food Insecurity in the World, 2000*. Rome: Food and Agriculture Organization of the United Nations.
2. Department of Foreign Affairs and International Trade, Canada. 2002. Protecting Children from Sanctions. www.epals.com/waraffectedchildren/chap11 (accessed March 2006).

Concept 29

1. Wong, W., C. Thomas, J. Merkus, G. Zielhuis, and R. Steegers-Theunissen. 2000. Male Factor Subfertility: Possible Causes and the Impact of Nutritional Factors. *Fertility and Sterility* 73: 435–442; Magnusdottir, E., T. Thorsteinsson, S. Thorsteinsdottir, M. Heimisdottir, and K. Olagsdottir. 2005. Persistent Organochlorines, Sedentary Occupation, Obesity, and Human Male Subfertility. *Human Reproduction* 20: 208–225.
2. Eskenazi, B., S. Kidd, A. Marks, E. Sloter, G. Block, and A. Wyrobek. 2005. Antioxidant Intake Is Associated with Semen Quality in Healthy Men. *Human Reproduction* 20: 1006–1012.
3. Wong. Male Factor Subfertility; Magnusdottir. Persistent Organochlorines, Sedentary Occupation, Obesity, and Human Male Subfertility; Eskenazi. Antioxidant Intake Is Associated with Semen Quality in Healthy Men.
4. Kaiser, L., and L. Allen. 2002. Position of the American Dietetic Association: Nutrition and Lifestyle for a Healthy Pregnancy Outcome. *Journal of the American Dietetic Association* 102: 1479–1490; Norman, R., and A. Clark. 1998. Obesity and Reproductive Disorders. *Reproduction Fertility and Development* 10: 55–63.
5. Bolumar, F., J. Olsen, M. Rebagliato, L. Bisanti, and the European Study Group on Infertility and Subfecundity. 1997. Caffeine Intake and Delayed Conception: A European Multicenter Study on Infertility and Subfecundity. *American Journal of Epidemiology* 145: 324–334.
6. U.S. Department of Health and Human Services. 2004. *The Health Consequences of Smoking: A Report of the Surgeon General*. Atlanta: National Center for Chronic Disease Prevention and Health Promotion, Office on Smoking and Health.
7. U.S. Department of Health and Human Services. 2005. U.S. Surgeon General Advisory on Alcohol Use in Pregnancy. www.cdc.gov/ncbddd/fas/documents/Released%20Advisory.pdf (accessed April 2005).
8. Quilan. Nausea and Vomiting of Pregnancy; Strong, T. 2001. Alternative Therapies of Morning Sickness. *Clinical Obstetrics and Gynecology* 44: 653–660.
9. Kaiser. Position of the American Dietetic Association.
10. Institute of Medicine. 1990. *Nutrition during Pregnancy*; U.S. Department of Health and Human Services. *The Health Consequences of Smoking*.
11. Picciano, M. 2003. Pregnancy and Lactation: Physiological Adjustments, Nutritional Requirements and the Role of Dietary Supplements. *Journal of Nutrition* 133: 1997S–2002S.
12. Rooney, B., and C. Schauberger. 2002. Excess Pregnancy Weight Gain and Long-Term Obesity: One Decade Later. *Obstetrics & Gynecology* 100: 245–252.
13. Institute of Medicine. *Nutrition during Pregnancy*.
14. Ibid.; Picciano. Pregnancy and Lactation.
15. Kaiser. Position of the American Dietetic Association.
16. Hornstra, G. 2000. Essential Fatty Acids in Mothers and Their Neonates. *American Journal of Clinical Nutrition* 71: 1262S–1269S.
17. Institute of Medicine. 1990. *Nutrition during Pregnancy*; U.S. Department of Health and Human Services. *The Health Consequences of Smoking*.
18. Kaiser. Position of the American Dietetic Association.
19. Substance Abuse and Mental Health Services Administration. 2005. Results from the 2004 National Survey on Drug Use and Health: National Findings. http://oas.samhsa.gov/nsduh/2k4nsduh/2k4Results/2k4Results.htm (accessed April 2004).
20. Wend, X., R. Odouli, and D. K. Li. 2008. Maternal Caffeine Consumption during Pregnancy and the Risk of Miscarriage: A Prospective Cohort Study. *American Journal of Obstetrics & Gynecology* 198: 279.e1–e8.
21. Wang, T., and B. Apgar. 1998. Exercise during Pregnancy. *American Family Physician* 57: 1846–1856; The National Women's Health Information Center. 2006. Healthy Pregnancy: Have a Fit Pregnancy. www.4woman.org/pregnancy (accessed April 2006).
22. ACOG Committee Obstetric Practice. 2002. ACOG Committee Opinion No. 267, Exercise during Pregnancy and the Postpartum Period. *Obstetrics and Gynecology* 99: 171–173.
23. Kaiser. Position of the American Dietetic Association.
24. Chobanian, A., G. Bakris, H. Black, W. Cushman, L. Green, J. Izzo, D. Jones, B. Materson, S. Oparil, J. Wright, E. Roccella, and the National High Blood Pressure Education Program Coordinating Committee. 2003. Seventh Report of the Joint National Committee on Prevention, Detection, Evaluation, and Treatment of High Blood Pressure. *Hypertension* 42: 1206–1252; Casro, L., and R. Avinoa. 2002. Maternal Obesity and Pregnancy Outcomes. *Current Opinion in Obstetrics and Gynecology* 14: 601–606; Institute of Medicine. 1990. *Nutrition During Pregnancy*. Washington, D.C.: National Academies Press.
25. Kaiser. Position of the American Dietetic Association; National Heart, Lung, and Blood Institute. High Blood Pressure in Pregnancy.
26. Kaiser. Position of the American Dietetic Association.
27. Ibid.
28. Rees, J., and B. Worthington-Roberts. 1994. Position of the American Dietetic Association: Nutrition Care for Pregnant Adolescents. *Journal of the American Dietetic Association* 94: 449–450.
29. Martin, J., B. Hamilton, P. Sutton, S. Ventura, F. Menacker, and M. Munson. 2005. Births: Final Data for 2003. *National Vital Statistics*

Reports, Centers for Disease Control and Prevention. www.cdc.gov/nchs/data/nvsr/nvsr54/nvsr54_02.pdf (accessed April 2006).

30. Shabert, J. 2000. Nutrition during Pregnancy and Lactation. In Krause, *Food, Nutrition, & Diet Therapy.* 11th ed. Philadelphia: Saunders.
31. U.S. Department of Health and Human Services (HSS). 2000. HHS Blueprint for Action on Breastfeeding. www.cdc.gov/breastfeeding/pdf/bluprntbk2.pdf (accessed April 2006).
32. Ibid.
33. U.S. Breastfeeding Committee. 2002. Economic Costs of Breastfeeding. www.usbreastfeeding.org/Issue-Papers/Economics.pdf (accessed April 2006).
34. Ibid.
35. U.S. Breastfeeding Committee. 2002. Benefits of Breastfeeding. www.usbreastfeeding.org/Issue-Papers/Benefits.pdf (accessed April 2006).
36. Klaus, M. 1998. Mother and Infant: Early Emotional Ties. *Pediatrics* 102: 1244–1246.
37. James, D., and B. Dobson. 2005. Position of the American Dietetic Association: Promoting and Supporting Breastfeeding. *Journal of the American Dietetic Association* 105: 810–818; Picciano, M., and S. McDonald. 2006. Lactation. In M. Shils, ed. *Modern Nutrition in Health and Disease.* Philadelphia: Lippincott Williams & Wilkins.
38. U.S. Department of Health and Human Services. HHS Blueprint for Action on Breastfeeding; James. Position of the American Dietetic Association.
39. Allen, J., R. Keler, P. Archer, and M. Neville. 1991. Studies in Human Lactation: Milk Composition and Daily Secretion Rates of Macronutrients in the First Year of Lactation. *American Journal of Clinical Nutrition* 54: 69–80.
40. James. Position of the American Dietetic Association.
41. Picciano. Lactation. In M. Shils, ed. *Modern Nutrition in Health and Disease.* Philadelphia. Lippincott Williams & Wilkins.
42. James. Position of the American Dietetic Association; Gartner, L., A. Eidelman, J. Morton, R. Lawrence, A. Naylor, D. O'Hare, and R. Schanler. 2005. Breastfeeding and the Use of Human Milk. *Pediatrics* 115: 496–506.
43. U.S. Department of Health and Human Services. HHS Blueprint for Action on Breastfeeding; Dewey, K. 2003. Is Breastfeeding Protective against Child Obesity? *Journal of Human Lactation* 19: 9–18.
44. Kaiser. Position of the American Dietetic Association; U.S. Department of Health and Human Services. HHS Blueprint for Action on Breastfeeding; Picciano. Lactation; Horwood, L., and D. Fergusson. 1998. Breastfeeding and Later Cognitive Academic Outcomes. *Pediatrics* 101: e1–e9.
45. Centers for Disease Control and Prevention. 2005. Breastfeeding Data and Statistics: Breastfeeding Practices—Results from the 2004 National Immunization Survey. www.cdc.gov/breastfeeding/data/NIS_data/data_2004.htm (accessed May 2006); U.S. Department of Health and Human Services. 2000. Healthy People 2010, Maternal, Infant, and Child Health. www.healthypeople.gov/document/HTML/Volume2/16MICH.htm (accessed April 2006).
46. Centers for Disease Control and Prevention. Breastfeeding Data and Statistics.
47. Institute of Medicine. *Nutrition during Lactation.*
48. Ward, R., B. Bates, W. Benitz, D. Burchfield, J. Ring, J. Walls, and P. Walson. 2001. The Transfer of Drugs and Other Chemicals into Human Milk. *Pediatrics* 108: 776–784.
49. Ibid.; Gartner, L., 2005. Breastfeeding and the Use of Human Milk. *Pediatrics* 115: 496–506.
50. Udall, J., and R. Suskind. 1999. Cow's Milk versus Formula in Older Infants: Consequences for Human Nutrition. *Acta paediatrica. Supplementum* 430: 61–70.
51. American Academy of Pediatrics. www.aap.org (accessed April 2006); Institute of Medicine. *Dietary Reference Intakes for Energy, Carbohydrate, Fiber, Fat, Fatty Acids, Cholesterol, Protein, and Amino Acids.*
52. National Center for Health Statistics. www.cdc.gov/nchs/about/nhanes/growthcharts/background.htm (accessed April 2006).
53. Institute of Medicine. 2002. *Dietary Reference Intakes for Energy, Carbohydrate, Fiber, Fat, Fatty Acids, Cholesterol, Protein, and Amino Acids.* Washington, D.C.: The National Academies Press.
54. Gartner. Breastfeeding and the Use of Human Milk.
55. Ibid.
56. Institute of Medicine. *Dietary Reference Intakes for Energy, Carbohydrate, Fiber, Fat, Fatty Acids, Cholesterol, Protein, and Amino Acids.*
57. American Academy of Pediatrics. www.aap.org (accessed April 2006); Institute of Medicine. *Dietary Reference Intakes for Energy, Carbohydrate, Fiber, Fat, Fatty Acids, Cholesterol, Protein, and Amino Acids.*
58. American Heart Association, S. Gidding, B. Dennison, L. Birch, S. Daniels, M. Gilman, A. Lichtenstein, K. Rattay, J. Steinberger, N. Stettler, and L. Horn. 2006. Dietary Recommendations for Children and Adolescents: A Guide for Practitioners. *Pediatrics* 117: 544–559.
59. Guthrie, H. A. 1966. Effect of Early Feeding of Solid Foods on Nutritive Intake of Infants. *Pediatrics* 38: 879–885; Briley, M., and C. Roberts-Gray, 2005. Position of the American Dietetic Association: Benchmarks for Nutrition Programs in Child Care Settings. *Journal of the American Dietetic Association* 105: 979–986.
60. Ibid.; Butte, N., K. Cobb, J. Dwyer, L. Graney, W. Heird, and K. Rickard. 2004. The Start Healthy Feeding Guidelines for Infants and Toddlers. *Journal of the American Dietetic Association* 104: 442–454.
61. Butte. The Start Healthy Feeding Guidelines for Infants and Toddlers.
62. The Food Allergy and Anaphylaxis Network. 2004. Common Food Allergens. www.foodallergy.org/allergens.html (accessed October 2006).
63. Centers for Disease Control and Prevention. www.cdc.gov/ncidod/dbmd/diseaseinfo/botulism_g.htm (accessed April 2006).
64. Briefel R., P. Ziegler, T. Novak, and M. Ponza. 2006. Feeding Infants and Toddlers Study: Characteristics and Usual Nutrient Intake of Hispanic and Non-Hispanic Infants and Toddlers. *Journal of the American Dietetic Association* 106 (supplement): S84–S95.

Feature Box References

1. National Institute of Allergy and Infectious Diseases. 2004. Food Allergy and Intolerances. www.niaid.nih.gov/factsheets/food.htm (accessed May 2004).
2. Ibid.
3. Long, A. 2002. The Nuts and Bolts of Peanut Allergy. *New England Journal of Medicine* 346: 1320–1322.
4. Ibid.; The Food Allergy and Anaphylaxis Network. 2004. Common Food Allergens. www.foodallergy.org/allergens.html (accessed October 2006).
5. U.S. Food and Drug Administration. 2006. Food Allergen Labeling and Consumer Protection Act of 2004 (Title II of Public Law 108–282). Report to The Committee on Health, Education, Labor, and Pensions United States Senate and the Committee on Energy and Commerce United States House of Representatives. www.cfsan.fda.gov/~acrobat/alrgrep.pdf (accessed January 2007).
6. U.S. Food and Drug Administration. 2005. Compliance Policy Guide. Section 555.250. Statement of Policy for Labeling and Preventing Cross-Contact of Common Food Allergens. www.fda.gov/ora/compliance_ref/cpg/cpgfod/cpg555-250.htm (accessed October 2006).

Concept 30

1. National Center for Health Statistics. 2000. *NCHS Growth Curves for Children 0–19 Years.* Washington, D.C.: U.S. Government Printing Office.
2. Ziegler, P., C. Hanson, M. Ponza, T. Novak, and K. Hendricks. 2006. Feeding Infants and Toddlers Study: Meal and Snack Intakes of Hispanic and Non-Hispanic Infants and Toddlers. *Journal of the American Dietetic Association* 106 (supplement): 107–123.
3. American Academy of Pediatrics. Parenting Corner Q & A: Choking Prevention. www.aap.org (accessed April 2006).
4. U.S. Department of Health and Human Services. 2004. *The 2004 Surgeon General's Report on Bone Health and Osteoporosis: What It Means to You.* Washington, D.C.: Office of the Surgeon General.
5. Kazal, L. A., Jr. 2002. Prevention of Iron Deficiency in Infants and Toddlers. *American Family Physician* 66: 1217–1224.
6. Healthy People 2010. Nutrition and Overweight. www.healthypeople.gov U.S. Dept. of Health & Human Services (accessed October 2006).
7. Corbett, J. V. 1995. Accidental Poisoning with Iron Supplements. *MCN: The American Journal of Maternal Child Nursing* 20: 234.
8. Food and Drug Administration. 1997. Preventing Iron Poisoning in Children. http://vm.cfsan.fda.gov/~dms.bgiron.html (accessed August 2009).
9. Wagner, C. L., F. R. Greer, and the Section on Breastfeeding and Committee on Nutrition. 2008. Prevention of Rickets and Vitamin D Deficiency in Infants, Children, and Adolescents. *Pediatrics* 122: 1142–1152.
10. Ibid.
11. American Academy of Pediatrics (AAP). 2003. *Pediatric Nutrition Handbook.* Elk Grove Village, IL: AAP.
12. Rolls, B. J., D. Engell, and L. L. Birch. 2000. Serving Portion Size Influences 5-Year-Old but Not 3-Year-Old Children's Food Intakes. *Journal of the American Dietetic Association* 100: 232–234.
13. National Center for Health Statistics (NCHS). 2000. CDC Growth Charts: United States. www.cdc.gov/growthcharts (accessed January 2009).
14. National Center for Health Statistics (NCHS): Overweight Prevalance. National Health and Nutrition Examination Survey Data. Hyattsville, MD: Centers for Disease Control and Prevention. www.cdc.gov/nchs/fastats/overwt.htm (accessed February 2007).

15. National Institutes of Health. Obesity Education Initiative. www.nhlbi.nih.gov/health/public/heart/obesity/wecan (accessed April 2006).
16. Batada, A., Seitz., M, Wootan, M., and Story, M. 2008 Nine out of 10 food advertisements shown during Saturday morning children's television programming are for foods high in fat, sodium, or added sugars, or low in nutrients. The Journal of the American Dietetic Association; 108: 673–678.
17. Henry J. Kaiser Family Foundation. 2005. Generation M: Media in the Lives of 8–18-Year-Olds: Report. Available at: http://www.cff.org/entmedia/entmedia030905pkg.cfm. (accessed August 2009).
18. School Health Policies and Programs Study (SHPPS). 2006. Fact Sheet: Physical Education and Activity from SHPPS 2000. www.cdc.gov/HealthyYouth/shpps.
19. Satcher, D. 2005. Healthy and Ready to Learn: Research Shows That Nutrition and Physical Activity Affect Student Academic Achievement. *Educational Leadership* 63: 26–30.
20. American Academy of Pediatrics. 2003. Prevention of Pediatric Overweight and Obesity. *Pediatrics* 112: 424–430.
21. U.S. Department of Agriculture, Food and Nutrition Service. 2005. National School Lunch Program Fact Sheet. http://www.fns.usda.gov/cnd/Lunch/AboutLunch/NSLPFactSheet.pdf (accessed August 2009).
22. Rampersaud, G. C., M. A. Pereira, B. L. Girard, J. Adams, and J. D. Metzl. 2005. Breakfast Habits, Nutritional Status, Body Weight, and Academic Performance in Children and Adolescents. *Journal of the American Dietetic Association* 105. 743–760.
23. National Institute of Arthritis and Musculoskeletal and Skin Diseases Growth Plate Injuries. 2001. www.niams.nih.gov/hi/topics/growth_plate/growth.htm (accessed April 2006).
24. U.S. Food and Drug Administration. 1993. Health Claims: Calcium and Osteoporosis. www.cfsan.fda.gov/~lrd/cf101-72.html (accessed October 2006).
25. Lanou, A. J., S. E. Berkow, and N. D. Barnard. 2005. Calcium, Dairy Products, and Bone Health in Children and Young Adults: A Reevaluation of the Evidence. *Pediatrics* 115: 736–743.
26. Volek, J. S., et al. 2003. Increasing Fluid Milk Favorably Affects Bone Mineral Density Responses to Resistance Training in Adolescent Boys. *Journal of the American Dietetic Association* 103: 1353–1356.
27. Wagner. Prevention of Rickets and Vitamin D Deficiency in Infants, Children, and Adolescents.
28. U.S. Department of Agriculture. 1998. Food and Nutrient Intakes by Children 1994–1996, Table Set 17. www.ars.usda.gov/Services/docs.htm?docid=7716 (accessed October 2006).
29. Alaimo, K. 1994. *Dietary Intake of Vitamins, Minerals and Fiber of Persons Ages 2 Months and Over in the United States*. Hyattsville, MD: National Center for Health Statistics.
30. Johnson R. K., D. G. Johnson, M. Q. Wang, H. Smiciklas-Wright, and H. Guthrie. 1994. Characterizing Nutrient Intakes of Adolescents by Sociodemographic Factors. *Journal of Adolescent Health* 15: 149–152.
31. Neumark-Sztainer, D., M. Wall, J. Guo, M. Story, J. Haines, and M. Eisenberg. 2006. Obesity, Disordered Eating, and Eating Disorders in a Longitudinal Study of Adolescents: How Do Dieters Fare Five Years Later? *Journal of the American Dietetic Association* 106. 559–68.
32. Centers for Disease Control and Prevention. 2006. Health, United States, 2005, with Chartbook on Trends in the Health of Americans with Special Feature on Adults 55–64 Years. www.cdc.gov/nchs/hus.htm (accessed May 2006).
33. He, W., M. Sengupta, V. Velkoff, and K. Debarros. 2005. *65+ in the United States, Current Population Reports*. Washington, D.C.: U.S. Government Printing Office.
34. Centers for Disease Control and Prevention. 2003. Public Health and Aging: Trends in Aging—United States and Worldwide. *Morbidity and Mortality Weekly Report* 52: 101–106.
35. Bales, C., and C. Ritchie. 2006. The Elderly. In M. E. Shils, M. Shike, A. C. Ross, B. Caballero, and R. Cousins, eds. *Modern Nutrition in Health and Disease.* 10th ed. Philadelphia: Lippincott Williams and Wilkins.
36. Institute of Medicine. 2003. *Dietary Reference Intakes for Energy, Carbohydrate Fiber, Fat, Protein, and Amino Acids.* Washington, D.C.: National Academies Press.
37. Ibid.
38. Moshfegh, A., J. Goldman, and L. Cleveland. 2005. *What We Eat in America. NHANES 2001–2002: Usual Nutrient Intakes from Food Compared to Dietary Reference Intakes.* U.S. Department of Agriculture, Agricultural Research Service.
39. Penniston, K., and S. Tanumihardjo. 2003. Vitamin A in Dietary Supplements and Fortified Foods: Too Much of a Good Thing. *Journal of the American Dietetic Association* 103: 1185–1187.
40. Bales. The Elderly.
41. Kurczmarski, M., and D. Weddle. 2005. Position Paper of the American Dietetic Association: Nutrition across the Spectrum of Aging. *Journal of the American Dietetic Association* 105: 616–633; Wakimoto, P., and G. Block. 2001. Dietary Intake, Dietary Patterns, and Changes with Age: An Epidemiological Perspective. *Journals of Gerontology Series A: Biological Sciences and Medical Sciences* 56A: 65–80.
42. Ibid.
43. Institute of Medicine. *Dietary Reference Intakes for Energy.*
44. Cooke, A., and J. Friday. 2005. Pyramid Servings Intakes in the United States 1999–2002: CNRG Table Set 3.0. Community Nutrition Research Group, Agricultural Research Service. www.ba.ars.usda.gov/cnrg (accessed May 2006).
45. World Health Organization. 2002. *Keep Fit for Life: Meeting the Nutritional Needs of Older Persons.* Geneva, Switzerland: World Health Organization. www.who.int/nutrition/publications/olderpersons/en/index.html (accessed May 2006).
46. Juan, W., M. Lino, and P. Basiotis. 2004. Quality of Diet of Older Americans. *Nutrition Insight* 29. www.cnpp.usda.gov/insights.html (accessed May 2006).
47. Juan. Quality of Diet of Older Americans; Cooke. Pyramid Servings Intakes in the United States 1999–2002.
48. World Health Organization. *Keep Fit for Life.*
49. Agency for Healthcare Research and Quality and the Centers for Disease Control and Prevention. 2002. Physical Activity and Older Americans: Benefits and Strategies. www.ahrq.gov/ppip/activity.htm (accessed May 2006).
50. Nord, M., M. Andrews, and S. Carlson. 2005. *Household Food Security in the United States, 2005.* www.ers.usda.gov/publications/err11 (accessed May 2006).
51. Lee, J., and E. Frongillo. 2001. Nutritional and Health Consequences Are Associated with Food Insecurity among U.S. Elderly Persons. *Journal of Nutrition* 131: 1503–1509.
52. Wolfe, W., E. Frongillo, and P. Valois. 2003. Understanding the Experience of Food Insecurity by Elders Suggests Ways to Improve Its Measurement. *Journal of Nutrition* 133: 2762–2769.
53. Administration on Aging. 2006. Older Americans Act. www.aoa.gov/about/legbudg/oaa/legbudg_oaa.asp (accessed May 2006).
54. Kurczmarski. Position Paper of the American Dietetic Association.
55. U.S. Department of Health and Human Services. 1999. *Mental Health: A Report of the Surgeon General—Executive Summary*. Rockville, MD: U.S. Department of Health and Human Services.
56. Administration on Aging. Older Americans Act.

Feature Box References

1. National Institute of Mental Health. Attention Deficit Hyperactivity Disorder, (ADHD) www.nimh.nih.gov/publicat/adhd.cfm (accessed April 2006).
2. Consensus Development Panel. 1982. Defined Diets and Childhood Hyperactivity. *National Institutes of Health Consensus Development Conference Summary* 4(3); National Institute of Mental Health.
3. Duffy, V. B., and M. Sigman-Grant. Position of the American Dietetic Association 2004. Use of Nutritive and Nonnutritive Sweeteners. *Journal of the American Dietetic Association.* 104: 255–275.
4. Biederman J., S. V. Faraone, K. Keenan, D. Knee, and M. F. Tsuang. 1990. Family-Genetic and Psychosocial Risk Factors in DSM-III Attention Deficit Disorder. *Journal of the American Academy of Child and Adolescent Psychiatry* 29: 526–533.

Index

C

D

E

G

H

I

T

U

V

Credits

Concept 1 **Chapter Opener:** Solus Photograph/Veer; **p.2:** Kristin Piljay, Pearson Benjamin Cummings; **p.3:** Erich Lessing/Art Resource, N.Y.; **p. 4, top:** Blend Images Photography/Veer; **p.4, left, bottom:** foodfolio/Alamy; **p.4, left, top:** Burke/Triolo Productions/Foodpix/Jupiter Images; **p.5, top:** Marc Romanelli/Workbook Stock/Getty Images; **p.5, bottom:** Philipp Hympendahl/ Alamy; **p.8:** Bruce Ayres/Getty Images

Concept 2 **Chapter Opener:** Envision/CORBIS; **p.2:** Thomas Barwick/ Getty Images; **p.3:** Juice Images Photography/Veer; **p.9:** Bruce Ayres/Getty Images; **p.11:** Graham Barclay/Bloomberg News/Landov

Concept 3 **Chapter Opener:** Brian Goodman/Alamy; **p.2:** Randy Faris/CORBIS/Jupiter Images; **p.3, bottom:** Biophoto Associates/Photo Researchers, Inc.; **p.3, top right front:** Aaron Goodman/Time Magazine/Time & Life Pictures/Getty Images; **p.7:** Liquidlibrary/Jupiter Images; **p.10:** BrandX photos

Concept 4 **Chapter Opener:** Stockbyte Photograph/Veer; **p.2:** Dave and Les Jacobs/Getty Images; **p.5:** Thomas Firak/Foodpix/Jupiter Images; **p.6:** Dorling Kindersley Media Library; **p.7:** Brian Hagiwara/Foodpix/Jupiter Images; **p.12:** Kristin Piljay, Pearson Benjamin Cummings; **p.15:** Richard Megna/Fundamental Photographs

Concept 5 **Chapter Opener:** Jonathan A.Meyers/Jupiter Images; **p.2, top:** Michael Keller/Image Stock Imagery; **p.2, bottom:** James Keyser//Time Life Pictures/Getty Images

Concept 6 **Chapter Opener:** Randy Faris/CORBIS; **p.2:** Stockbyte/Getty Images; **p.3:** Mark Thomas/FoodPix/Jupiter Images; **p.4, top:** Tom Grill/CORBIS; **p.6:** Steve Gschmeissner/SPL/Photo Researchers, Inc.; **p.11:** Darque/agefotostock; **p.12, top left:** Dr. E. Walker/SPL/Photo Researchers, Inc.; **p.12, top right:** C. James Webb/Phototake

Concept 7 **Chapter Opener:** Bryan F. Peterson/CORBIS; **p.2:** John Cumming/Getty Images; **p.3:** Jeff Oshiro/Foodpix/Jupiter Images; **p.5:** Food Image Source/Foodfolio Studios/StockFood; **p.9:** Virgo Productions/zefa/ CORBIS; **p.11:** Felicia Martinez/PhotoEdit Inc.; **p.13:** Brand X Pictures; **p.14, top:** davis & starr/Getty Images; **p.14, bottom:** Envision/CORBIS; **p.15:** Paula Hible/Foodpix/Jupiter Images; **p.16:** Brand X Pictures

Concept 8 **Chapter Opener:** liquidlibrary/Jupiter Images; **p.2:** Simon Jarratt/CORBIS; **p.3:** Masterfile; **p.4, top:** Cindy Jones/Foodpix/Jupiter Images; **p.4, bottom left:** Kristin Piljay, Pearson Benjamin Cummings; **p.4, bottom right:** Kristin Piljay, Pearson Benjamin Cummings; **p.5:** Foodcollection.com/Alamy; **p.7:** Hemera Technologies/Alamy; **p.8:** Michael Newman/PhotoEdit Inc.; **p.11, top:** Kristin Piljay, Pearson Benjamin Cummings; **p.11, bottom:** Kristin Piljay, Pearson Benjamin Cummings; **p.13:** PhotoLink/Getty Images; **p.16, top:** BSIP/Phototake; **p.16, bottom:** Coston Stock/Alamy;

Concept 9 **Chapter Opener:** Erik Isakson/Jupiter Images; **p.2:** David Caton/Alamy; **p.4:** Sports Illustrated/Getty Images; **p.5:** altrendo images/Getty Images; **p.10:** Japack/agefotostock; **p.11:** BSIP/Phototake; **p.12:** D. Hurst / Alamy

Concept 10 **Chapter Opener:** Maximilian Stock Ltd/PhotoCuisine/ CORBIS; **p.2:** Don Smetzer/Alamy; **p.3:** Ryan McVay/Getty Images; **p.6:** Colin Young-Wolff / PhotoEdit; **p.7:** Comstock Images/Jupiter Images; **p.10:** Jonelle Weaver/Getty Images

Concept 11 **Chapter Opener:** Plush Studios/Getty Images; **p.2:** Stockbyte/Getty Images; **p.4:** Dianne McFadden/shutterstock; **p.5:** Ligia Botero/ Digital Vision/Getty Images; **p.10:** Comstock/Jupiter Images; **p.12:** Kirsten Piljay/ Pearson Benjamin Cummings; **p.13:** Eric Schrader

Concept 12 **Chapter Opener:** Brian Hagiwara/Getty Images; **p.2:** Masterfile; **p.10:** Michael Rosenfeld/Getty Images; **p.11,top:** Doug Perrine/ naturepl.com; **p.11, bottom:** Kristin Piljay, Pearson Benjamin Cummings

Concept 13 **Chapter Opener:** Teubner/Stockfood Creative/Getty Images; **p. 2:** Lucianne Pashley/agefotostock; **p.5, top:** Virgo/zefa/CORBIS; **p.5, bottom:** Push/Foodpix/Jupiter Images; **p.7:** Oliver Meckes/Nicole Ottawa/ Photo Researchers, Inc.; **p.10:** Safia Fatimi/Getty Images; **p.11:** Dr. P. Marazzi/ Science Photo Library/Photo Researchers, Inc.; **p. 14, top:** Push/Foodpix/Jupiter Images; **p.14, middle right:** Envision/CORBIS; **p.14, bottom right:** Foodpix/Jupiter Images

Concept 14 **Chapter Opener:** Nick M. Do/Getty Images; **p.2, bottom:** Lisa Romerein/Foodpix/Jupiter Images; **p.2, top:** Digital Vision/Getty Images; **p.3:** Brian Hagiwara/Foodpix/Jupiter Images; **p.4:** Dorling Kindersley; **p.5, top:** Charles Gullung/Getty Images; **p.5, middle:** Jeff Boyle/Getty Images; **p.5, bottom:** Brian Yarvin Photography/Photo Researchers, Inc.; **p.7:** Royalty Free/CORBIS; **p.11:** Kristin Piljay; **p.12:** Brand X Pictures; **p.13:** Hartmut Schwarzbach/Peter Arnold, Inc.; **p.14:** John Isaac/United Nations

Concept 15 **Chapter Opener:** Frank Wieder/StockFood Munich/StockFood; **p.2:** BananaStock/age fotostock; **p.4:** Glowimages/Getty Images; **p.5:** AP Photo/Rajesh Kumar Singh; **p.10, top, left:** Luzia Ellert/ StockFood Creative/Getty Images; **p.10, top right:** White Wave Foods; **p.10, bottom left:** Mark Thomas/Foodpix/Jupiter Images; **p. 10, bottom right:** Dorling Kindersley; **p.11, top left:** Steven Mark Needham/Foodpix/Jupiter Images; **p.11, top right:** Kristin Piljay, Pearson Benjamin Cummings; **p.11, bottom left:** Dorling Kindersley; **p.11, bottom right:** Lisa Romerein/ Foodpix/Jupiter Images; **p.12:** Vasko Miokovic/iStockphoto

Concept 16 **Chapter Opener:** Lluis Real/age fotostock, **p.2:** Darren Robb/Getty Images; **p.3, top left:** James Baigrie/Foodpix/Jupiter Images; **p.3, top right:** Photodisc/Getty Images; **p.3, bottom:** CORBIS; **p.5:** National Eye Institute, National Institute of Health; **p.6:** Mary Ellen Bartley/Foodpix/Jupiter Images; **p.8, top:** Dr. P. Marazzi/Photo Researchers, Inc.; **p.8, bottom:** Digital Vision/Getty Images; **p.9:** altrendo images/Getty Images; **p.10, top:** Dorling Kindersley; **p.10, middle left:** Stewart Cohen/Index Stock Imagery; **p.10, bottom:** Rachel Epstein/ PhotoEdit Inc.; **p.11, top:** Brian Hagiwaraj/Foodpix/ Jupiter Images; **p.11, bottom:** Maurice Nimmo; Frank Lane Picture Agency/ CORBIS; **p. 12, top left:** Eye of Science/Photo Researchers, Inc.; **p.12, top right:** Hugh Turvey/Photo Researchers, Inc.; **p.12, bottom left:** Cristina Pedrassini/ Photo Researchers, Inc.; **p.12, bottom right:** CORBIS; **p. 13, middle top:** Dee Breger/Photo Researchers, Inc; **p. 13, middle bottom;** ISM/Phototake; **p. 13, bottom left:** Lisa Hubbard/Foodpix/Jupiter Images; **p.14, top:** Zephyr Photography/Photo Researchers, Inc.; **p.14, bottom:** Pearson Education/PH College; **p.15:** Biophoto Associates/ Photo Researchers, Inc.; **p.18, top right:** Isabelle Rozenbaum/AGE Fotostock; **p.18, bottom left:** Leigh Belsch/Foodpix/ Jupiter Images; **p.18, bottom right:** Brian Leatart/Foodpix/Jupiter Images; **p.19, top right:** David Prince/Foodpix/Jupiter Images; **p.19, bottom:** Leigh Belsch/ Foodpix/Jupiter Pictures; **p. 20, left:** Ralph Morse/Getty Images; **p. 20, top right:** Eisenhut & Mayer/Foodpix/Jupiter Images; **p. 20, bottom right:** Pornchai Mittongtare/Foodpix/Jupiter Images; **p.21, bottom:** Johner/Getty Images; **p. 21,**

right: Gibson & Smith/Foodpix/Jupiter Images; **p.22, top:** Michael Deuson/ Foodpix/Jupiter Images; **p.22, bottom:** Lisa Thompson/Foodpix/Jupiter Images; **p.23, right:** Dr. M.A. Ansary/Photo Researchers, Inc.; **p.23, bottom:** davies & starr/Getty Images; **p.24, top:** Anthony-Masterson/Foodpix/Jupiter Images; **p.24, bottom left:** Photodisc Green/Getty Images; **p.24, bottom right:** CORBIS; **p.25, top:** Michael Newman/PhotoEdit Inc.; **p.25, bottom:** Cristina Cassinelli/ Foodpix/Jupiter Images; **p.26, top:** Dorling Kindersley; **p.26, bottom:** NMSB/Custom Medical Stock Photo; **p. 27:** CORBIS; **p. 28, bottom left:** Dorling Kindersley; **p. 28, bottom right:** Lew Robertson/Foodpix/Jupiter Images; **p. 29, top:** Rick Souders/Foodpix/Jupiter Images; **p.29, left:** Getty Images; **p. 29, middle:** Martin Jacobs/Foodpix/Jupiter Images; **p.30, top:** CORBIS; **p.30, bottom left:** Dimitri Vervits/Getty Images; **p.30, bottom right:** SPL/Photo Researchers, Inc.; **p.31, right:** St. Mary"s Hospital Medical School/ Photo Researchers, Inc.; **p.31, bottom left:** Wally Eberhart/Botanica/ Jupiter Images; **p.31, bottom middle:** CORBIS; **p. 32, top:** Dick Clintsman/ CORBIS; **p. 32, bottom:** Richard Radstone/Getty Images; **p.33, top left:** Lew Robertson/ Foodpix/Jupiter Images; **p.33, top right:** Chris Everard/Getty Images; **p.33, bottom left:** Photodisc/Getty Images; **p.33, bottom right:** Robin MacDougall/ Foodpix/Jupiter Images; **p. 37, top:** Kristin Piljay, Pearson Benjamin Cummings; **p. 37, bottom:** Kristin Piljay, Pearson Benjamin Cummings

Concept 17 **Chapter Opener:** IPS Co., Ltd./Beateworks/CORBIS; **p. 2:** Peter Nicholson/Getty Images; **p. 6, top:** Office of the Surgeon General; **p. 6, bottom:** Office of the Surgeon General; **p. 10, top:** Kristin Piljay, Pearson Benjamin Cummings; **p. 10, bottom:** D. Hurst/Alamy; **p. 11:** Michael Klein/ Peter Arnold, Inc.; **p.12, middle:** Richard Megna/Fundamental Photographs; **p. 12, bottom left:** Kristin Piljay, Pearson Benjamin Cummings; **p. 12, bottom right:** Kristin Piljay, Pearson Benjamin Cummings; **p. 13, top:** J.Garcia/ photocuisine/Corbis; **p. 13, bottom:** Kristin Piljay, Pearson Benjamin Cummings; **p. 14, top:** John Lund/Tiffany Schoepp/Getty Images; **p. 14, bottom left:** Ingram Publishing/age fotostock; **p. 14, bottom right:** ISM/Phototake; **p. 15:** Mary Ellen Bartley/Foodpix/Jupiter Images; **p. 16, top:** Craig van der Lende/Getty Images; **p. 16, middle** John E. Kelly/Foodpix/Jupiter Images; **p. 16, bottom:** Dorling Kindersley; **p. 17, top left:** Envision/Corbis; **p. 17, right:** Thomas Firak/Foodpix/Jupiter Images; **p. 17, bottom left:** Michael Pohuski/ FoodPix/Jupiter Images; **p. 18, top:** Stockbyte Gold/Alamy; **p. 18, bottom left:** Andrea Barton-Elson/Foodpix/Jupiter Images; **p. 18, bottom right:** Nick Emm/ Alamy; **p. 19, top left:** BananaStock/Jupiter Images; **p. 19, top right:** Ingram Publishing / Alamy; **p. 19, middle:** Burke/Triolo Productions/FoodPix/Jupiter Images; **p. 20,top:** foodfolio/Alamy; **p. 20, middle:** Poisson d'Avril/ photocuisine/Corbis; **p. 20, bottom:** Christina Peters/Foodpix/Jupiter Images; **p. 21:** Brand X Pictures; **p. 22, left:** C Squared Studios/Getty Images; **p. 22, right:** Steven Mark Needham/Foodpix/Jupiter Images; **p. 23, top left:** Eric Grave /Photo Researchers, Inc.; **p. 23, bottom left:** Joaquin Carrillo Farga/Photo Researchers, Inc.; **p. 24, top:** Steve Cohen/Foodpix/Jupiter Images; **p. 24, middle:** foodfolio/Alamy; **p. 24, bottom:** Bruce James/Foodpix/Jupiter Images; **p. 25:** Leigh Beisch/Foodpix/Jupiter Images; **p. 26, top:** Corbis; **p. 26, middle:** Sang An/Foodpix/Jupiter Images; **p. 26, bottom:** Image Source/Jupiter Images; **p. 27, top left:** FoodCollection/age fotostock; **p. 27, middle:** Bill Aron/Photo Edit; **p. 27, bottom left:** Foodcollection/Getty Images; **p. 28, top:** Don Farrall/ Getty Images; **p. 28, bottom:** John A Rizzo/age fotostock; **p. 29, top:** National Institute of Dental Research; **p. 29, bottom:** foodfolio/Alamy; **p. 30, top:** Mary Ellen Bartley/Getty Images; **p. 30, bottom:** Foodcollection.com/Alamy; **p. 31, top:** FoodCollection/age fotostock; **p. 31, bottom:** Food Features/Alamy; **p. 33, middle:** Richard Megna/Fundamental Photographs, NYC; **p. 33, left:** Stockbyte/Getty Images; **p. 33, bottom left:** Corbis/Bettmann; **p. 33, bottom right:** John Paul Kay/Peter Arnold, Inc.; **p. 34, bottom middle:** Foodcollection/ Getty Images; **p. 34, bottom left:** Kristin Lee/Foodpix/Jupiter Images

Concept 18 **Chapter Opener:** Michael Pole/CORBIS; **p. 2:** Stephen Beaudet/zefa/CORBIS; **p. 4:** Warren Morgan/CORBIS; **p.5:** Claude Edelmann/ Photo Researchers, Inc.; **p.6:** Tony Anderson/Getty Images; **p .7:** Pete Saloutos/ Getty Images; **p.11:** PhotoObjects.net/Jupiter Images

Concept 19 **Chapter Opener:** Jerry Alexander/Getty Images; **p.2:** George Doyle/Getty Images; **p.3, top.:** Adam Woolfitt/CORBIS; **p.3, bottom:** David Young-Wolff/PhotoEdit Inc.; **p.4, top:** Stockdisc Classic/Alamy; **p.4, middle left:** Laszlo Selly/Foodpix/Jupiter Images; **p.4, middle right:** Foodcollection/Getty Images; **p.4, bottom left:** Kristin Piljay/Pearson Benjamin Cummings; **p.4, bottom right:** Kristin Piljay/Pearson Benjamin Cummings; **p. 5, top:** Digital Vision/Getty Images; **p.5, bottom:** A. Ramey/PhotoEdit Inc.; **p 6:** CORBIS; **p.9:** CORBIS; **p.10, top left:** Lew Robertson/Brand X Pictures/ Jupiter Pictures; **p.10, top middle right:** Penina/Foodpix/Jupiter Pictures; **p.10, top bottom left:** Simon Watson/Foodpix/Jupiter Pictures; **p.10, bottom left:** Fundamental Photos; **p.10, bottom right:** Fundamental Photos; **p.11:** Arthur Glauberman/Photo Researchers, Inc.; **p.12:** Fetal Alcohol & Drug Unit (FAS); **p.15:** At-Bristol; **p.17:** The Image Works; **p.18:** image100/Jupiter Pictures

Concept 20 **Chapter Opener:** Tetra Images/CORBIS; **p.2:** Bloomimage/CORBIS; **p.4:** Fernando Medina/NBAE via Getty Images; **p.5, top left:** Sean Aidan; Eye Ubiquitous/CORBIS; **p.5, top right:** Mauro Fermariello/ Photo Researchers, Inc.; **p.5, middle:** Mauro Fermariello/Photo Researchers, Inc.; **p.5, bottom left:** David Young-Wolff/PhotoEdit; **p.5, bottom right:** Joe Traver//Time Life Pictures/Getty Images; **p.7:** George Doyle/Getty Images; **p.8, top:** Pixland/CORBIS; **p.8, middle:** pintailpictures/Alamy; **p.8, bottom:** John Terence Turner/Getty Images

Concept 21 **Chapter Opener:** Creatas/SuperStock; **p. 2:** Bananastock/Jupiter Images; **p.2:** Brendan Howard/Shutterstock; **p.3:** Time & Life Pictures/Getty Images; **p.4:** Bruce Ayres/Getty Images; **p.7:** Vasko Miokovic/iStockphoto; **p.8:** Comstock Images/Jupiter Images; **p.10, top left:** Envision/CORBIS; **p.10, right:** Tom Kola/Stock Image/Jupiter Images; **p.10, bottom left:** Comstock Images/Jupiter Images; **p. 11, top right and left:** U.S. Department of Health and Human Services; **p.11, bottom middle:** Photolibrary/Alamy; **p.11, bottom left:** Radius Images/Jupiter Images; **p.11, bottom right:** Foodcollection/Getty Images; **p.12, bottom left and right:** Richard Megna/Fundamental Photographs, NYC; **p.16, top:** AP Photo/Charles Bennet; **p.17, top:** LIU JIN/AFP/Getty Images

Concept 22 **Chapter Opener:** Image Source/CORBIS; **p.2:** Scott Thomas/Getty Images; **p.3, top left:** Harrison G. Pope, Jr., MD; **p.3, top right:** 20th Century Fox/The Kobal Collection/Sam Shaw; **p.3, middle left:** Bettmann/CORBIS; **p.3, middle right:** AP photo/Remy de la Mauviniere; **p.3, bottom left:** AP Photo/Women's Wear Daily; **p.10:** Veit Mette/laif/Redux; **p.11:** PhotoAlto/Alamy; **p.12:** image100/Jupiter Images; **p.13:** Anthony-Masterson/FoodPix/Jupiter Images

Concept 23 **Chapter Opener:** CORBIS; **p.2:** Stockbyte Gold/Alamy; **p.4:** Lisa Thompson/Foodpix/Jupiter Images; **p.7:** Proles Productions/ agefotostock; **p.9:** Taylor S. Kennedy /Getty Images; **p.11:** Courtesy of the U.S. Department of Health and Human Services

Concept 24 **Chapter Opener:** Robert Bossi/Getty Images; **p. 2:** Image Source/Getty Images; **p. 3:** Dan Dalton/Getty Images; **p. 4, top left:** Charles Thatcher/Getty Images; **p. 4, top middle:** Tamara Lackey/Getty Images; **p. 4, top right:** Richard Price/Getty Images; **p. 4, bottom left:** Photodisc/Getty Images; **p. 4, bottom middle:** Ryan McVay/Getty Images; **p. 4, bottom right:** Stockbyte/Getty Images; **p. 5:** BananaStock/Jupiter Images; **p. 6:** Creatas Images/Jupiter Images

Concept 25 **Chapter Opener:** Blend Images/Alamy; **p. 2:** Stockbyte/Getty Images; **p. 5:** Getty Images; **p. 7:** Christophe Simon/AFP/Getty Images; **p. 9:** Michael Newman/PhotoEdit; **p. 10:** Kayte M. Deioma/PhotoEdit; **p. 11:** Kristin Piljay; **p. 13:** Image Source/Jupiter Images; **p. 14:** Ulrich Kerth/StockFood Creative/Getty Images

Concept 26 **Chapter Opener:** Solus Photography/Veer; **p. 2:** Radius Images/Alamy; **p. 3, top:** Elizabeth Simpson/Getty Images; **p. 3, bottom:** Century/Foodpix/Jupiter Images; **p. 4, top:** Brian Hagiwara/Foodpix/Jupiter Images; **p. 4, bottom:** United States Pharmacopeia; **p. 6:** Najlah Feanny/ CORBIS; **p. 7:** SPL/Photo Researchers, Inc.; **p. 8, top:** Bart's Medical Library/Phototake; **p. 8, bottom:** BananaStock/Jupiter Images; **p. 9:** altrendo images/Getty Images; **p. 10:** POMAH/Shutterstock;

Concept 27 **Chapter Opener: p. 2:** Michael Newman/PhotoEdit Inc.; **p. 3, top:** Phanie/Photo Researchers, Inc.; **p. 3, middle:** Eye of Science/Photo Researchers, Inc.; **p. 3, bottom:** Dr. Gary D. Gaugler/Phototake; **p. 7:** Foodcollection.com Alamy; **p. 8:** piga&catalano/age fotostock; **p. 9:** USDA; **p. 16:** Kristin Piljay, Pearson Benjamin Cummings; **p. 20:** Dennis MacDonald/PhotoEdit Inc.; **p. 24:** Durand Florence/SIPA; **p. 25, top:** Durand Florence/SIPA; **p. 25, bottom:** JOEL NITO/AFP/Getty Images;

Concept 28 **Chapter Opener:** Viviane Moos/CORBIS; **p. 2:** A. Inden/zefa/CORBIS; **p. 4:** Photofusion Picture Library/Alamy; **p. 6:** David Cavagnaro/Peter Arnold, Inc.; **p. 7, top:** Abid Katib/Getty Images; **p. 7, bottom:** Mike Boyatt/agefotostock; **p. 8:** Paul Almasy/CORBIS; **p. 9:** Peter Turnley/CORBIS; **p. 10:** Barbara Galati/Phototake; **p. 11:** Jeff Greenberg/PhotoEdit Inc.; **p. 12, top:** Jim West/Alamy; **p. 12, bottom:** Alan Evrard/Robert Harding World Imagery; **p. 13:** Jon Jones/Sygma/CORBIS;

Concept 29 **Chapter Opener:** Jon Feingersh/CORBIS; **p. 2:** Stock4B/Nonstock/Jupiter Images; **p. 3:** Stewart Cohen/Index Stock Imagery; **p. 4:** FoodPix/Jupiter Images; **p. 7, top:** Dorling Kindersley; **p. 7, bottom:** Pornchai Mittongtare/Foodpix/Jupiter Images; **p. 8:** Eiichi Onodera/Emi Kimata /DEX Image/Jupiter Images; **p.9, top:** Gusto/Photo Researchers, Inc.; **p. 9, bottom:** Foodcollection/Getty Images; **p. 10, top:** Richard Megna/Fundamental Photos; **p. 10, bottom:** Mango Productions/CORBIS; **p. 12:** ArtisticCaptures/Stockphoto; **p. 13:** Ariel Skelley/CORBIS; **p. 14:** Sally and Richard Greenhill/Alamy; **p. 16:** Kayte M. Deioma/PhotoEdit; **p. 21:** Digital Vision/Getty Images;

Concept 30 **Chapter Opener:** altrendo images/Getty Images; **p. 2, top:** N. Aubrier/age fotostock; **p. 2, bottom:** Dorling Kindersley; **p. 5, top** Creatas Images/Jupiter Images; **p. 5, bottom:** Jilly Wendell/Nonstock/Jupiter Images; **p. 9:** Charles Gupton/CORBIS; **p. 11:** Corbis/Jupiter Images; **p. 12, top:** Ariel Skelley/Jupiter Images; **p. 12, bottom:** Kin Images/Getty Images; **p. 13, left:** Darque/agefotostock; **p. 13, right:** Rick Souders/Foodpix/Jupiter Images; **p. 14:** Johner/Getty Images; **p. 15:** Ronnie Kaufman/CORBIS; **p. 16:** Tina Manley/Charity/Alamy